PRINCIPLES OF ECONOMICS

Eighth Edition

ROBERT H. FRANK

Cornell University

BEN S. BERNANKE

Brookings Institution [affiliated]
Former Chair, Board of Governors of the Federal Reserve System

KATE ANTONOVICS

University of California, San Diego

ORI HEFFETZ

Cornell University and the Hebrew University of Jerusalem

PRINCIPLES OF ECONOMICS: EIGHTH EDITION

Published by McGraw Hill LLC, 1325 Avenue of the Americas, New York, NY 10121. Copyright ©2022 by McGraw Hill LLC. All rights reserved. Printed in the United States of America. Previous editions ©2019, 2016, and 2013. No part of this publication may be reproduced or distributed in any form or by any means, or stored in a database or retrieval system, without the prior written consent of McGraw Hill LLC, including, but not limited to, in any network or other electronic storage or transmission, or broadcast for distance learning.

Some ancillaries, including electronic and print components, may not be available to customers outside the United States.

This book is printed on acid-free paper.

1 2 3 4 5 6 7 8 9 LWI 24 23 22 21

ISBN 978-1-260-93289-8 (bound edition)
MHID 1-260-93289-3 (bound edition)
ISBN 978-1-264-25048-6 (loose-leaf edition)
MHID 1-264-25048-7 (loose-leaf edition)

Portfolio Director: *Anke Weekes*
Senior Product Developer: *Christina Kouvelis*
Marketing Manager: *Bobby Pearson*
Lead Content Project Manager: *Christine Vaughan*
Content Project Manager: *Emily Windelborn*
Senior Buyer: *Laura Fuller*
Senior Designer: *Matt Diamond*
Senior Content Licensing Specialist: *Melissa Homer*
Cover Image: *Shutterstock/photoff*
Compositor: *Aptara®, Inc.*

Library of Congress Cataloging-in-Publication Data

Names: Frank, Robert H., author. | Bernanke, Ben, author.
Title: Principles of economics / Robert H. Frank, Cornell University, Ben
   S. Bernanke, Brookings Institution, Former Chairman, Board of Governors
   of the Federal Reserve System, Kate L. Antonovics, University of
   California, San Diego, Ori Heffetz, Cornell University and the Hebrew
   University of Jerusalem.
Description: Eighth edition. | New York, NY : McGraw Hill Education, [2022]
   | Includes bibliographical references and index.
Identifiers: LCCN 2020042543 (print) | LCCN 2020042544 (ebook) | ISBN
   9781260932898 (hardcover) | ISBN 9781266052309 (hardcover) | ISBN
   9781264250486 (spiral bound) | ISBN 9781264250509 (ebook) | ISBN
   9781264250479 (ebook other)
Subjects: LCSH: Economics.
Classification: LCC HB171.5 .F734 2022 (print) | LCC HB171.5 (ebook) |
   DDC 330–dc23
LC record available at https://lccn.loc.gov/2020042543
LC ebook record available at https://lccn.loc.gov/2020042544

DEDICATION

For Ellen
R. H. F.

For Anna
B. S. B.

For Fiona and Henry
K. A.

For Katrina, Eleanor, Daniel, and Amalia
O. H.

ROBERT H. FRANK

Courtesy of Robert H. Frank

Robert H. Frank is the H. J. Louis Professor of Management and Professor of Economics, emeritus, at Cornell's Johnson School of Management, where he taught from 1972 to 2020. After receiving his B.S. from Georgia Tech in 1966, he taught math and science for two years as a Peace Corps Volunteer in rural Nepal. He received his M.A. in statistics in 1971 and his Ph.D. in economics in 1972 from The University of California at Berkeley. He also holds honorary doctorate degrees from the University of St. Gallen and Dalhousie University. During leaves of absence from Cornell, he has served as chief economist for the Civil Aeronautics Board (1978–1980), a Fellow at the Center for Advanced Study in the Behavioral Sciences (1992–1993), Professor of American Civilization at l'Ecole des Hautes Etudes en Sciences Sociales in Paris (2000–2001), and the Peter and Charlotte Schoenfeld Visiting Faculty Fellow at the NYU Stern School of Business in 2008–2009. His papers have appeared in the *American Economic Review, Econometrica,* the *Journal of Political Economy,* and other leading professional journals, and for more than two decades, his economics columns appeared regularly in *The New York Times.*

Professor Frank is the author of a best-selling intermediate economics textbook—*Microeconomics and Behavior,* Tenth Edition (McGraw Hill, 2021). His research has focused on rivalry and cooperation in economic and social behavior. His books on these themes include *Choosing the Right Pond* (Oxford, 1985), *Passions Within Reason* (W. W. Norton, 1988), *What Price the Moral High Ground?* (Princeton, 2004), *Falling Behind* (University of California Press, 2007), *The Economic Naturalist* (Basic Books, 2007), *The Economic Naturalist's Field Guide* (Basic Books, 2009), *The Darwin Economy* (Princeton, 2011), *Success and Luck* (Princeton, 2016), and *Under the Influence* (Princeton, 2020), which have been translated into 24 languages. *The Winner-Take-All Society* (The Free Press, 1995), co-authored with Philip Cook, received a Critic's Choice Award, was named a Notable Book of the Year by *The New York Times,* and was included in *BusinessWeek's* list of the 10 best books of 1995. *Luxury Fever* (The Free Press, 1999) was named to the *Knight-Ridder* Best Books list for 1999.

Professor Frank is a co-recipient of the 2004 Leontief Prize for Advancing the Frontiers of Economic Thought. He was awarded the Johnson School's Stephen Russell Distinguished Teaching Award in 2004, 2010, 2012, and 2018, and the School's Apple Distinguished Teaching Award in 2005. His introductory microeconomics course has graduated more than 7,000 enthusiastic economic naturalists over the years.

BEN S. BERNANKE

Courtesy of Ben S. Bernanke

Professor Bernanke received his B.A. in economics from Harvard University in 1975 and his Ph.D. in economics from MIT in 1979. He taught at the Stanford Graduate School of Business from 1979 to 1985 and moved to Princeton University in 1985, where he was named the Howard Harrison and Gabrielle Snyder Beck Professor of Economics and Public Affairs and where he served as chair of the Economics Department. Professor Bernanke is currently a Distinguished Fellow in Residence with the Economic Studies Program at the Brookings Institution.

Professor Bernanke was sworn in on February 1, 2006, as chair and a member of the Board of Governors of the Federal Reserve System; his second term expired January 31, 2014. Professor Bernanke also served as chair of the Federal Open Market Committee, the Fed's principal monetary policymaking body. Professor Bernanke was also chair of the President's Council of Economic Advisers from June 2005 to January 2006.

Professor Bernanke's intermediate textbook, with Andrew Abel and Dean Croushore, *Macroeconomics,* Ninth Edition (Addison-Wesley, 2017), is a best seller in its field. He has authored numerous scholarly publications in macroeconomics, macroeconomic history, and finance. He has done significant research on the causes of the Great Depression, the role of financial markets and institutions in the business cycle, and measurement of the effects of monetary policy on the economy.

Professor Bernanke has held a Guggenheim Fellowship and a Sloan Fellowship, and he is a Fellow of the Econometric Society and of the American Academy of Arts and Sciences. He served as the director of the Monetary Economics Program of the National Bureau of Economic Research (NBER) and as a member of the NBER's Business Cycle Dating Committee. From 2001 to 2004 he served as editor of the *American Economic Review,* and as president of the American Economic Association in 2019. Professor Bernanke's work with civic and professional groups includes having served two terms as a member of the Montgomery Township (New Jersey) Board of Education.

KATE ANTONOVICS

Courtesy of Kate Antonovics

Professor Antonovics received her B.A. from Brown University in 1993 and her Ph.D. in economics from the University of Wisconsin in 2000. Shortly thereafter, she joined the faculty in the Economics Department at the University of California, San Diego. Professor

Antonovics is also currently serving as the Provost of UC San Diego's Seventh College.

Professor Antonovics is known for her excellence in teaching and her innovative use of technology in the classroom. Her popular introductory-level microeconomics courses have regularly enrolled over 900 students each fall. She also teaches labor economics at both the undergraduate and graduate level. She has received numerous teaching awards, including the UCSD Department of Economics award for Best Undergraduate Teaching, the UCSD Academic Senate Distinguished Teaching Award, and the UCSD Chancellor's Associates Faculty Excellence Award in Undergraduate Teaching.

Professor Antonovics's research has focused on racial discrimination, gender discrimination, affirmative action, intergenerational income mobility, learning, and wage dynamics. Her papers have appeared in the *American Economic Review,* the *Review of Economics and Statistics,* the *Journal of Labor Economics,* and the *Journal of Human Resources.* She is a member of both the American Economic Association and the Society of Labor Economists.

ORI HEFFETZ

Courtesy of Ori Heffetz

Professor Heffetz received his B.A. in physics and philosophy from Tel Aviv University in 1999 and his Ph.D. in economics from Princeton University in 2005. He is an Associate Professor of Economics at the Samuel Curtis Johnson Graduate School of Management at Cornell University, and at the Economics Department at the Hebrew University of Jerusalem.

Bringing the real world into the classroom, Professor Heffetz has created a unique macroeconomics course that introduces basic concepts and tools from economic theory and applies them to current news and global events. His popular classes are taken by hundreds of students every year on Cornell's Ithaca and New York City campuses and via live videoconferencing in dozens of cities across the United States, Canada, and Latin America.

Professor Heffetz's research studies the social and cultural aspects of economic behavior, focusing on the mechanisms that drive consumers' choices and on the links between economic choices, individual well-being, and policymaking. He has published scholarly work on household consumption patterns, individual economic decision making, and survey methodology and measurement. He was a visiting researcher at the Bank of Israel during 2011, is currently a Research Associate at the National Bureau of Economic Research (NBER), and serves on the editorial board of *Social Choice and Welfare.*

FOCUSED ON SEVEN CORE PRINCIPLES TO PRODUCE ECONOMIC NATURALISTS THROUGH ACTIVE LEARNING

Our eighth edition arrives in the midst of some of the most dramatic upheavals ever witnessed, both in the economy generally and in higher education in particular. The COVID-19 pandemic has produced levels of unemployment not seen since the Great Depression and has created dramatic changes in the ways we teach across educational institutions at every level.

These developments have reinforced our confidence in the instructional philosophy that motivated us to produce our first edition—the need to strip away clutter and focus more intensively on central concepts. This approach, we believe, is especially well suited for the new environment.

In earlier editions, we noted that although many millions of dollars are spent each year on introductory economics instruction in American colleges and universities, the return on this investment has been disturbingly low. Studies have shown, for example, that several months after having taken a principles of economics course, former students are no better able to answer simple economics questions than others who never even took the course. Most students, it seems, leave our introductory courses without having learned even the most important basic economic principles. Such dismal performance, never defensible, has become even more difficult to justify in the face of looming resource shortages in higher education.

The problem, in our view, has almost always been that courses try to teach students far too much. In the process, really important ideas get little more coverage than minor ones, and everything ends up going by in a blur. The human brain tends to ignore new information unless it comes up repeatedly. That's hardly surprising, since only a tiny fraction of the terabytes of information that bombard us each day is likely to be relevant for anything we care about. Only when something comes up a third or fourth time does the brain start laying down new circuits for dealing with it. Yet when planning their lectures, many instructors ask themselves, "How much can I cover today?" And because modern electronic media enable them to click through upwards of 100 PowerPoint slides in an hour, they feel they better serve their students when they put more information before them. But that's not the way learning works. Professors should instead be asking, "How much can my students absorb?"

Our approach to this text was inspired by our conviction that students will learn far more if we attempt to cover much less. Our basic premise is that a small number of basic principles do most of the heavy lifting in economics, and that if we focus narrowly and repeatedly on those principles, students can actually master them in just a single semester. The enthusiastic reactions of users of previous editions of our textbook affirm the validity of this premise. Avoiding excessive reliance on formal mathematical derivations, we present concepts intuitively through examples drawn from familiar contexts. We rely throughout on a well-articulated list of seven Core Principles, which we reinforce repeatedly by illustrating and applying each principle in numerous contexts. We ask students periodically to apply these principles themselves to answer related questions, exercises, and problems.

Another distinguishing feature of this text is its explicit recognition of the pedagogical challenge posed by the broad variance in students' quantitative backgrounds and in instructor preferences about the optimal level of mathematical detail for the course. We confront this challenge by relegating more detailed mathematical treatment of selected topics to chapter appendices. For example, Chapter 5, *Demand,* emphasizes the key intuition that underpins utility maximization, and relegates the formal presentation of indifference curves and budget constraints to the appendix, allowing instructors the freedom to choose the approach that best suits their needs. Similarly, Chapter 25, *Spending and Output in the Short Run,* uses diagrams and numerical examples to convey the main ideas behind the basic Keynesian model (the "Keynesian cross"), saving a more general algebraic analysis to Appendix A and a derivation of the multiplier formula to Appendix B—again providing flexibility to instructors. Many adopters have cited this additional flexibility as a reason for having chosen our book.

Throughout the body of the text, however, our principal focus is not on quantitative detail, but rather on students to become "economic naturalists," people who employ basic economic principles to understand and explain what they observe in the world around them. An economic naturalist understands, for example, that infant safety seats are required in cars but not in airplanes because the marginal cost of space to accommodate these seats is typically zero in cars but often hundreds of dollars in airplanes. Scores of such examples are sprinkled throughout the book. Each one, we believe, poses a question that should make any curious person eager to learn the answer. These examples stimulate interest while teaching students to see each feature of their economic landscape as the reflection of one or more of the Core Principles. Students talk about these examples with their friends and families.

Learning economics is like learning a language. In each case, there is no substitution for actually speaking. By inducing students to speak economics, The Economic Naturalist examples serve this purpose.

For those who would like to learn more about the role of examples in learning economics, Bob Frank's lecture on this topic is posted on YouTube's "Authors@Google" series (www.youtube.com/watch?v=QalNVxeIKEE), or search "Authors@Google Robert Frank".

KEY THEMES AND FEATURES

Emphasis on Seven Core Principles

Because a few Core Principles do most of the work in economics, focusing almost exclusively on these principles ensures that students leave the course with a deep mastery of them. In contrast, traditional encyclopedic texts so overwhelm students with detail that they often leave the course with little useful working knowledge at all.

1. **The Scarcity Principle:** Although we have boundless needs and wants, the resources available to us are limited. So having more of one good thing usually means having less of another.

2. **The Cost-Benefit Principle:** An individual (or a firm or a society) should take an action if, and only if, the extra benefits from taking the action are at least as great as the extra costs.

3. **The Incentive Principle:** A person (or a firm or a society) is more likely to take an action if its benefit rises, and less likely to take it if its cost rises. In short, incentives matter.

4. **The Principle of Comparative Advantage:** Everyone does best when each concentrates on the activity for which his or her opportunity cost is lowest.

5. **The Principle of Increasing Opportunity Cost:** In expanding the production of any good, first employ those resources with the lowest opportunity cost, and only afterward turn to resources with higher opportunity costs.

6. **The Efficiency Principle:** Efficiency is an important social goal because when the economic pie grows larger, everyone can have a larger slice.

7. **The Equilibrium Principle:** A market in equilibrium leaves no unexploited opportunities for individuals but may not exploit all gains achievable through collective action.

Economic Naturalism

Our ultimate goal is to produce economic naturalists—people who see each human action as the result of an implicit or explicit cost-benefit calculation. The economic naturalist sees mundane details of ordinary existence in a new light and becomes actively engaged in the attempt to understand them. Some representative examples:

In Micro:

- Why do movie theaters offer discount tickets to students?

- Why do we often see convenience stores located on adjacent street corners?

- Why do supermarket checkout lines all tend to be roughly the same length?

In Macro:

- Why does the average Argentine hold more U.S. dollars than the average U.S. citizen?

- Why does news of inflation hurt the stock market?

- Why do almost all countries provide free public education?

Economic Naturalist Video Series: We are very excited to offer an expanded video series based on Economic Naturalist examples. A series of videos covering some of our favorite micro- and macro-focused examples can be used as part of classroom presentations or assigned for homework along with accompanying questions within McGraw Hill Connect®. These fascinating, fun, and thought-provoking applications of economics in everyday life encourage students to think like an economist. Refer to the distinguishing features pages of the preface for additional information. You can view one of these dynamic videos here: http://econeveryday.com/why-do-cooked-rotisserie-chickens-cost-less-than-fresh-uncooked-chickens/.

Active Learning Stressed

The only way to learn to hit an overhead smash in tennis is through repeated practice. The same is true for learning economics. Accordingly, we consistently introduce new ideas in the context of simple examples and then follow them with applications showing how they work in familiar settings. At frequent intervals, we pose self-tests that both test and reinforce the understanding of these ideas. The end-of-chapter questions and problems are carefully crafted to help students internalize and extend basic concepts and are available within Connect as assignable content so that instructors can require students to engage with this material. Experience with earlier editions confirms that this approach really does prepare students to apply basic economic principles to solve economic puzzles drawn from the real world.

Learning Glass Lecture Videos: A collection of brief instructional videos featuring the authors Kate Antonovics and

Ori Heffetz utilize learning glass technology to provide students with an overview of important economic concepts. Perfect for an introduction to basic concepts before coming to class, or as a quick review, these videos, with accompanying questions, can be assigned within Connect or used as part of classroom discussion.

Both The Economic Naturalist and Learning Glass videos and accompanying multiple-choice questions that test students' understanding of the principles illustrated in the videos have become valued tools for instructors who incorporate elements of the flipped-classroom approach in their teaching, or those who are relying more heavily on other forms of remote learning.

Modern Microeconomics

Economic surplus is more fully developed here than in any other text. This concept underlies the argument for economic efficiency as an important social goal. Rather than speak of trade-offs between efficiency and other goals, we stress that maximizing economic surplus facilitates the achievement of *all* goals.

One of the biggest hurdles to the fruitful application of cost-benefit thinking is to recognize and measure the relevant costs and benefits. Common decision pitfalls identified by 2002 Nobel laureate Daniel Kahneman and others—such as the tendency to ignore implicit costs, the tendency not to ignore sunk costs, and the tendency to confuse average and marginal costs and benefits—are introduced in Chapter 1, *Thinking Like an Economist,* and discussed repeatedly in subsequent chapters.

There is perhaps no more exciting toolkit for the economic naturalist than a few principles of elementary game theory. In Chapter 9, *Games and Strategic Behavior,* we show how these principles enable students to answer a variety of strategic questions that arise in the marketplace and everyday life. In new Chapter 10, *An Introduction to Behavioral Economics,* we survey many of the most exciting developments in what has become the economics profession's most vibrant new field. We believe that the insights of Nobel laureate Ronald Coase are indispensable for understanding a host of familiar laws, customs, and social norms. In Chapter 11, *Externalities, Property Rights, and the Environment,* we show how such devices function to minimize misallocations that result from externalities.

Modern Macroeconomics

Both the Great Recession and the COVID-19 pandemic have renewed interest in cyclical fluctuations without challenging the importance of such long-run issues as growth, productivity, the evolution of real wages, and capital formation. Our treatment of these issues is organized as follows:

- A five-chapter treatment of *long-run issues,* followed by a modern treatment of *short-term fluctuations and stabilization policy,* emphasizes the important distinction between short- and long-run behavior of the economy.

- *Designed to allow for flexible treatment of topics,* these chapters are written so that short-run material (Chapters 24–27) can be used before long-run material (Chapters 19–23) with no loss of continuity.

- The analysis of aggregate demand and aggregate supply relates output to inflation, rather than to the price level, sidestepping the necessity of a separate derivation of the link between the output gap and inflation. The discussion of monetary policy has two parts. It starts with a standard supply and demand analysis of the market for money that is centered on the short-run interest rate. It then introduces the new tools of monetary policy, such as quantitative easing and forward guidance, that have been so important since 2008, and that again took center stage in the 2020 response to the pandemic.

- This book places a heavy emphasis on *globalization,* starting with an analysis of its effects on real wage inequality and progressing to such issues as the costs and benefits of—and the likely winners and losers from—trade, the causes and effects of protectionism, the role of capital flows in domestic capital formation, the link between exchange rates and monetary policy, and the sources of speculative attacks on currencies.

CHANGES IN THE EIGHTH EDITION

Changes Common to All Chapters

In all chapters, the narrative has been tightened. Many of the examples have been updated, with a focus on student-centered examples that connect to current topics such as the COVID-19 pandemic and the rise of the gig economy. The examples, self-tests, and end-of-chapter material from the previous edition have been redesigned to provide more clarity and ease of use. Data have been updated throughout.

Chapter-by-Chapter Changes

Chapter 1

- Updated student-centered examples, such as Netflix, wireless keyboards, dogwalking, and Jeff Bezos

- New and updated end-of-chapter problems that reinforce the chapter's learning objectives

- Updated appendix on working with equations, graphs, and tables based on electric scooter rentals

Chapter 2

- Updated student-centered examples, such as interior designer Kelly Wearstler

- Updated section on comparative advantage and outsourcing, including updates related to the United States-Mexico-Canada Agreement

- New end-of-chapter problem related to outsourcing

Chapter 3

- Updated student-centered examples, such as digital versus print ads and Marvel Studio films

- New Economic Naturalist, "Why was there a shortage of toilet paper during the COVID-19 pandemic?"

- Three new end-of-chapter questions that reinforce the chapter's learning objectives, including a question related to the drop in crude oil prices during the coronavirus pandemic

Chapter 4

- Minor updates only

Chapter 5

- Updated student-centered examples, such as LeBron James

- New Economic Naturalist, "Why would Jeff Bezos live in a smaller house in Manhattan than in Medina, Washington?"

Chapter 6

- Minor updates only

Chapter 7

- Minor updates only

Chapter 8

- Updated student-centered examples, such as Instagram, electric scooter rentals, iTunes, HBO, Netflix, and cable Internet

- Updated end-of-chapter problems

Chapter 9

- Updated student-centered examples, such as the Ford Mustang and Chevrolet Camaro

Chapter 10

- New Economic Naturalist, "Why have attempts to privatize Social Security proved so politically unpopular in the United States?"

- New Economic Naturalist, "If prosperous voters would be happier if they spent less on positional goods and lived in environments with more generously funded public sectors, why haven't they elected politicians who would deliver what they want?"

- Updated the discussion of relative position

Chapter 11

- Updated student-centered examples, such as roommate conflicts

- Updated information on carbon taxes, including mention of the Paris Agreement

- Updated end-of-chapter questions

Chapter 12

- Updated student-centered examples, such as the gig economy and apps like Uber and Lyft

- Updated discussion of the Affordable Care Act

Chapter 13

- Updated student-centered examples, such as Serena Williams and Taylor Swift

- Updated discussion of welfare benefits and in-kind transfers

- New end-of-chapter question related to income redistribution

Chapter 14

- Updated student-centered examples, such as video streaming services like Netflix

Chapter 15

- Revised Economic Naturalist that discusses the U.S.-China trade war that started in 2018, highlighting that there is more to trade than the exchange of goods and services and its supply and demand analysis in this chapter; also covers issues such as intellectual property and national security

Chapter 16

- Updated discussion of growth that reflects higher Internet and cell phone penetration

- Updated discussion of recessions and expansions that mentions the COVID-19 economic disruptions

Chapter 17

- Updated discussion of the correlation between per capita GDP and health outcomes such as life expectancy that now mentions that within high-income countries, the relationship can even reverse, with examples of data from the U.S., Canada, and Japan

Chapter 18

- Updated discussion of the development of real wages for production workers and for highly paid baseball players over time that is now linked together, in the context of a new discussion about increasing wage inequalities between the highest- and lowest-paid U.S. workers

Chapter 19

- Updated examples, data, and figures

Chapter 20

- Clarification throughout the chapter of the difference between trends in *average* incomes and trends in income inequality

- Updated discussion of globalization that now includes recent developments, including the political opposition to the Trans-Pacific Partnership trade agreement and the Trump administration's resistance to increased economic integration of the U.S. with China

- New Economic Naturalist, "Can technology hurt workers?," that includes what was previously a paragraph on workers' resistance to new technology (with anecdotes on Ned Ludd and the tale of John Henry); the new EN highlights workers' concerns about automation, robotics, and artificial intelligence (AI)

- New Economic Naturalist, "How did the COVID-19 pandemic affect the demand for U.S. jobs," that discusses the different effects the epidemic is having on different jobs in different sectors

- New discussion of European labor markets that highlights the deregulation in southern Europe following the global financial crisis and that, on some metrics, Europe's labor market does better than the U.S. labor market

Chapter 21

- Updates related to the COVID-19 economic downturn that include the discussion of U.S. household saving early in the chapter and the discussion of the U.S. government deficit later in the chapter

- New Economic Naturalist, "Why have real interest rates declined globally in recent decades?," that discusses the combination of higher global saving and lower global investment that helps explain the downward trend in real interest rates

Chapter 22

- New discussion of the Fed's role in stabilizing financial markets and as lender of last resort, which took center stage in recent episodes of financial panic; the discussion covers Section 13(3) landing during the 2008 and 2020 crises

Chapter 23

- Updates related to recent U.S.-China trade frictions, in the discussion of the saving rate and the trade deficit

- Updates related to the COVID-19 pandemic and financial markets

Chapter 24

- Updates related to the COVID-19 downturn

- Revised Economic Naturalist 24.3 that includes discussion of the gig economy in the context of the natural rate of unemployment in the U.S.

Chapter 25

- Revised Economic Naturalist 25.5 that discusses the U.S. government's response to the COVID-19 pandemic and covers details of the Coronavirus Aid, Relief, and Economic Security (CARES) Act of 2020 and their economic rationale

- Other COVID-19-related updates

Chapter 26

- Updates related to COVID-19: in the context of banks' excess reserves, in the context of the Fed's quick cuts of the federal funds rate, in the context of quantitative easing (QE) and the Fed's special landing in 2020, and in the context of the Fed's return to forward guidance in 2020; the chapter highlights the unprecedented speed and severity of the pandemic's economic hit, and therefore the unprecedented speed and size of the policy response

- Revisions throughout the chapter that reflect recent developments in thinking about QE, forward guidance, and other methods; when introduced in 2008, these methods were viewed as "unconventional" and "temporary"; the chapter now observes that such methods are increasingly recognized as a "new normal"

Chapter 27

- Updates to The Economic Naturalist 27.5, "Can inflation be too low?," to cover the Fed's unprecedented response to COVID-19

Chapter 28

- New The Economic Naturalist 28.2, "What is a safe haven currency?," (such as the U.S. dollar, the Swiss franc, and the Japanese yen), and how they tend to appreciate in periods of uncertainty; includes specific examples from the 2008 global financial crisis and the 2020 global coronavirus crisis

- Updated The Economic Naturalist 28.4 that covers the IMF's COVID-19-related landing in early 2020

A NOTE ON THE WRITING OF THIS EDITION

Ben Bernanke was sworn in on February 1, 2006, as chair and a member of the Board of Governors of the Federal Reserve System, a position to which he was reappointed in January 2010. From June 2005 until January 2006, he served as chair of the President's Council of Economic Advisers. These positions have allowed him to play an active role in making U.S. economic policy, but the rules of government service have restricted his ability to participate in the preparation of previous editions. Since his second term as chair of the Federal Reserve has completed, we are happy that Ben is actively involved in the revision of the macro portion of this edition.

ACKNOWLEDGMENTS

Our thanks first and foremost go to our portfolio director, Anke Weekes, and our product developer, Christina Kouvelis. Anke encouraged us to think deeply about how to improve the book and helped us transform our ideas into concrete changes. Christina shepherded us through the revision process with intelligence, sound advice, and good humor. We are grateful as well to the production team, whose professionalism (and patience) was outstanding: Christine Vaughan, content project manager; Keri Johnson, assessment project manager; Matt Diamond, lead designer; and all of those who worked on the production team to turn our manuscript into the text you see now. Finally, we also thank Bobby Pearson, marketing manager, for getting our message into the wider world.

Special thanks to Per Norander, University of North Carolina at Charlotte, for his energy, creativity, and help in refining the assessment material in Connect; Sukanya Kemp, University of Akron, for her detailed accuracy check of the learning glass and economic naturalist videos; Alvin Angeles and team at the University of California, San Diego, for their efforts in the production and editing of the learning glass videos; and Kevin Bertotti and the team at ITVK for their creativity in transforming Economic Naturalist examples into dynamic and engaging video vignettes.

Finally, our sincere thanks to the following teachers and colleagues, whose thorough reviews and thoughtful suggestions led to innumerable substantive improvements to *Principles of Economics*, 8/e.

Mark Abajian, *San Diego Mesa College*

Richard Agesa, *Marshall University*

Seemi Ahmad, *Dutchess Community College*

Donald L. Alexander, *Western Michigan University*

Jason Aimone, *Baylor University*

Chris Azevedo, *University of Central Missouri*

Narine Badasyan, *Murray State University*

Sigridur Benediktsdottir, *Yale University*

Robert Blewett, *St. Lawrence University*

Brian C. Brush, *Marquette University*

Christopher Burkart, *University of West Florida*

Colleen Callahan, *American University*

Giuliana Campanelli Andreopoulos, *William Paterson University*

J. Lon Carlson, *Illinois State University*

David Chaplin, *Northwest Nazarene University*

Monica Cherry, *Saint John Fisher College*

Joni Charles, *Texas State University*

Anoshua Chaudhuri, *San Francisco State University*

Nan-Ting Chou, *University of Louisville*

Maria Luisa Corton, *University of South Florida-St. Petersburg*

Manabendra Dasgupta, *University of Alabama at Birmingham*

Craig Dorsey, *College of DuPage*

Dennis Edwards, *Coastal Carolina University*

Tracie Edwards, *University of Missouri-St. Louis*

Roger Frantz, *San Diego State University*

Mark Frascatore, *Clarkson University*

Amanda Freeman, *Kansas State University*

Greg George, *Macon State College*

Seth Gershenson, *Michigan State University*

Amy D. Gibson, *Christopher Newport University*

Rajeev Goel, *Illinois State University*

Mehdi Haririan, *Bloomsburg University of Pennsylvania*

Susan He, *Washington State University*

John Hejkal, *University of Iowa*

Kuang-Chung Hsu, *Kishwaukee College*

Greg Hunter, *California State University-Pomona*

Nick Huntington-Klein, *California State University-Fullerton*

Andres Jauregui, *Columbus State University*

David W. Johnson, *University of Wisconsin-Madison*

Derek Johnson, *University of Connecticut*

Sukanya Kemp, *University of Akron*

Brian Kench, *University of Tampa*

Fredric R. Kolb, *University of Wisconsin-Eau Claire*

Daniel D. Kuester, *Kansas State University*

Valerie Lacarte, *American University*

Donald J. Liu, *University of Minnesota-Twin Cities*

Brian Lynch, *Lake Land College*

Christine Malakar, *Lorain Community College*

Ida Mirzaie, *The Ohio State University*

Thuy Lan Nguyen, *Santa Clara University*

Jelena Nikolic, *Northeastern University*

Anthony A. Noce, *State University of New York (SUNY)-Plattsburgh*

Diego Nocetti, *Clarkson University*

Stephanie Owings, *Fort Lewis College*

Dishant Pandya, *Spalding University*

Martin Pereyra, *University of Missouri*

Tony Pizelo, *Northwest University*

Ratha Ramoo, *Diablo Valley College*

Thomas Rhoads, *Towson University*

Bill Robinson, *University of Nevada-Las Vegas*

Brian Rosario, *University of California-Davis*

Elyce Rotella, *Indiana University*

Jeffrey Rubin, *Rutgers University*

Naveen Sarna, *Northern Virginia Community College*

Henry Schneider, *Queen's University*

Sumati Srinivas, *Radford University*

Thomas Stevens, *University of Massachusetts*

Carolyn Fabian Stumph, *Indiana University and Purdue University-Fort Wayne*

Albert Sumell, *Youngstown State University*

Markland Tuttle, *Sam Houston State University*

David Vera, *California State University-Fresno*

Nancy Virts, *California State University-Northridge*

Gilbert J. Werema, *Texas Woman's University*

Elizabeth Wheaton, *Southern Methodist University*

Amanda Wilsker, *Georgia Gwinnett College*

William C. Wood, *James Madison University*

DISTINGUISHING FEATURES

ECONOMIC NATURALIST EXAMPLES

Each Economic Naturalist example starts with a question to spark curiosity and interest in learning an answer. These examples fuel interest while teaching students to see economics in the world around them. Videos of select and new Economic Naturalist examples are denoted in the margin of the material to which they pertain and they are housed within Connect. A full list of Economic Naturalist examples and videos can be found in the following pages.

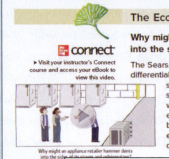

The Economic Naturalist 8.3

▶ Visit your instructor's Connect course and access your eBook to view this video.

Why might an appliance retailer instruct its clerks to hammer dents into the sides of its stoves and refrigerators?

The Sears "Scratch 'n' Dent Sale" is another example of how retailers use quality differentials to segregate buyers according to their reservation prices. Many Sears stores hold an annual sale in which they display appliances with minor scratches and blemishes in the parking lot at deep discounts. People who don't care much about price are unlikely to turn out for these events, but those with very low reservation prices often get up early to be first in line. Indeed, these sales have proven so popular that it might even be in a retailer's interest to put dents in some of its sale items deliberately.

Why might an appliance retailer hammer dents into the sides of its stoves and refrigerators?

▶ Visit your instructor's Connect course and access your eBook to view this video.

ECONOMIC NATURALISM

With the rudiments of the cost-benefit framework under your belt, you are now in a position to become an "economic naturalist," someone who uses insights from economics to help make sense of observations from everyday life. People who have studied biology are able to observe and marvel at many details of nature that would otherwise have escaped their notice. For example, on a walk in the woods in early April, the novice may see only trees. In contrast, the biology student notices many different species of trees and understands why some are already in leaf while others still lie dormant. Likewise, the novice may notice that in some animal species males are much larger than females, but the biology student knows that pattern occurs only in species in which males take several mates. Natural selection favors larger males in those species because their greater size

NUMBERED EXAMPLES

Throughout the text, numbered and titled examples are referenced and called out to further illustrate concepts. Our engaging questions and examples from everyday life highlight how each human action is the result of an implicit or explicit cost-benefit calculation.

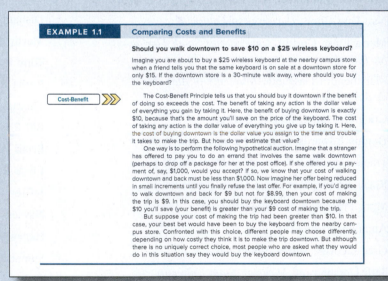

EXAMPLE 1.1 **Comparing Costs and Benefits**

Should you walk downtown to save $10 on a $25 wireless keyboard?

Imagine you are about to buy a $25 wireless keyboard at the nearby campus store when a friend tells you that the same keyboard is on sale at a downtown store for only $15. If the downtown store is a 30-minute walk away, where should you buy the keyboard?

Cost-Benefit ⟩⟩

The Cost-Benefit Principle tells us that you should buy it downtown if the benefit of doing so exceeds the cost. The benefit of taking any action is the dollar value of everything you gain by taking it. Here, the benefit of buying downtown is exactly $10, because that's the amount you'll save on the price of the keyboard. The cost of taking any action is the dollar value of everything you give up by taking it. Here, the cost of buying downtown is the dollar value you assign to the time and trouble it takes to make the trip. But how do we estimate that value?

One way is to perform the following hypothetical auction. Imagine that a stranger has offered to pay you to do an errand that involves the same walk downtown (perhaps to drop off a package for her at the post office). If she offered you a payment of, say, $1,000, would you accept? If so, we know that your cost of walking downtown and back must be less than $1,000. Now imagine her offer being reduced in small increments until you finally refuse the last offer. For example, if you'd agree to walk downtown and back for $9 but not for $8.99, then your cost of making the trip is $9. In this case, you should buy the keyboard downtown because the $10 you'll save (your benefit) is greater than your $9 cost of making the trip.

But suppose your cost of making the trip had been greater than $10. In that case, your best bet would have been to buy the keyboard from the nearby campus store. Confronted with this choice, different people may choose differently, depending on how costly they think it is to make the trip downtown. But although there is no uniquely correct choice, most people who are asked what they would do in this situation say they would buy the keyboard downtown.

Scarcity ⟩⟩

EXCHANGE AND OPPORTUNITY COST

The Scarcity Principle (see Chapter 1, *Thinking Like an Economist*) reminds us that the opportunity cost of spending more time on any one activity is having less time available to spend on others. As the following example makes clear, this principle helps explain why everyone can do better by concentrating on those activities at which he or she performs best relative to others.

CORE PRINCIPLES

There are seven Core Principles that we focus on to ensure student mastery. Throughout the text, these principles are called out and are denoted by an icon in the margin. Again, the seven Core Principles are: scarcity, cost-benefit, incentive, comparative advantage, increasing opportunity cost, efficiency, and equilibrium.

SELF-TESTS

These self-test questions in the body of the chapter enable students to determine whether the preceding material has been understood and reinforce understanding before reading further. Detailed answers to the self-test questions are found at the end of each chapter.

✓ SELF-TEST 3.1

In Figure 3.1, what is the marginal buyer's reservation price when the quantity of pizza sold is 10,000 slices per day? For the same demand curve, what will be the quantity of pizza demanded at a price of $2.50 per slice?

RECAP ↻

MARKET EQUILIBRIUM

Market equilibrium, the situation in which all buyers and sellers are satisfied with their respective quantities at the market price, occurs at the intersection of the supply and demand curves. The corresponding price and quantity are called the *equilibrium price* and the *equilibrium quantity*.

Unless prevented by regulation, prices and quantities are driven toward their equilibrium values by the actions of buyers and sellers. If the price is initially too high, so that there is excess supply, frustrated sellers will cut their price in order to sell more. If the price is initially too low, so that there is excess demand, competition among buyers drives the price upward. This process continues until equilibrium is reached.

RECAP

Sprinkled throughout each chapter are Recap boxes that underscore and summarize the importance of the preceding material and key concept takeaways.

WORKED PROBLEM VIDEOS

Brief videos work through end-of-chapter problems to aid in student understanding of core economic concepts and offer assistance with more challenging material. The videos are available as hints within Connect.

To earn extra money in the summer, you grow tomatoes and sell them at a local farmers' market for 30 cents per pound. By adding compost to your garden, you can increase your yield as shown in the table below. If compost costs 50 cents per pound and your goal is to make as much profit as possible, how many pounds of compost should you add?

Additional cost (or marginal cost)

Pounds of compost	Pounds of tomatoes	Additional pounds of tomatoes	Additional revenue (or marginal benefit)
	100		
1	120	20	$6.00 ✓
2	125	5	$1.50 ✓
3	128		
4	130		
5	131		
6	131.5		

LEARNING GLASS VIDEOS

Dozens of lecture videos featuring authors Kate Antonovics and Ori Heffetz utilize learning glass technology to provide you with an overview of important concepts. These videos can be accessed as resources within SmartBook® or as assignable content via McGraw Hill Connect®

ECONOMIC NATURALIST VIDEO SERIES

Asymmetric Information: Why do "almost new" used cars sell for so much less than brand new ones?

Behavioral Economics: Why do real estate agents often show clients two nearly identical houses, even though one is both cheaper and in better condition than the other?

Commercial Banking: Why can it be more expensive to transfer funds between banks electronically than it is to send a check through the mail?

Comparative Advantage: iPhones: Designed in California, but assembled in China

Cost Benefit 1: Why does the light come on when you open the refrigerator door but not when you open the freezer?

Cost Benefit 2: Why are child safety seats required in automobiles but not in airplanes?

Discount Pricing: Why might an appliance retailer hammer dents into the sides of its stoves and refrigerators?

Economy Strength and Currency Value: Does a strong currency imply a strong economy?

Elasticity: Why do people buy the same amount of salt as before even when the price of salt doubles?

Human Capital: Why do almost all countries provide free education?

Incentive Problems and Inefficiency: Why does the practice of check splitting cause people to spend more at restaurants?

Inflation and Cost of Living: Do official inflation figures overstate actual increases in our living costs?

Inflation: Can inflation be too low?

Marginal Product of Labor: Why do female models earn so much more than male models?

Menu Costs: Will new technologies eliminate menu costs?

Money and Its Uses: Is there such a thing as private, or communicably traded, money?

Monopolistic Competition: Why do we often see convenience stores located on adjacent street corners?

Prisoner's Dilemma: Why do people shout at parties?

Production Costs: Why are brown eggs more expensive than white ones?

Saving: Why do American households save so little while Chinese households save so much?

Sources of Increasing Inequality: Why have the salaries of top earners been growing so much faster than everyone else's?

Supply and Demand: Why are rotisserie chickens less expensive than fresh chickens?

Tariffs: Why do consumers in the United States often pay more than double the world price for sugar?

The Demand for Money: Why does the average Argentine citizen hold more U.S. dollars than the average U.S. citizen?

The Invisible Hand: Why do supermarket checkout lines all tend to be roughly the same length?

The Law of Demand: Why are smaller automobile engines more common in Europe than in the United States?

The Optimal Amount of Information: Why might a patient be more likely to receive an expensive magnetic resonance imaging (MRI) exam for a sore knee if covered under a conventional health insurance rather than a health maintenance organization (HMO) plan?

The Tragedy of the Commons and Property Rights: Why do blackberries in public parks get picked before they're completely ripe?

ECONOMIC NATURALIST EXAMPLES

1.1 Why do many hardware manufacturers include more than $1,000 worth of "free" software with a computer selling for only slightly more than that?

1.2 Why don't auto manufacturers make cars without heaters?

1.3 Why do the keypad buttons on drive-up automated teller machines have Braille dots?

2.1 Where have all the .400 hitters gone?

2.2 What happened to the U.S. lead in the television market?

2.3 If trade among nations is so beneficial, why are free-trade agreements so controversial?

2.4 Is PBS economics reporter Paul Solman's job a likely candidate for outsourcing?

3.1 When the federal government implements a large pay increase for its employees, why do rents for apartments located near Washington Metro stations go up relative to rents for apartments located far away from Metro stations?

3.2 Why do major term papers go through so many more revisions today than in the 1970s?

3.3 Why do the prices of some goods, like airline tickets to Europe, go up during the months of heaviest consumption, while others, like sweet corn, go down?

3.4 Why was there a shortage of toilet paper during the COVID-19 pandemic?

4.1 Will a higher tax on cigarettes curb teenage smoking?

4.2 Why was the luxury tax on yachts such a disaster?

4.3 Why are gasoline prices so much more volatile than car prices?

5.1 Why does California experience chronic water shortages?

5.2 Why would Jeff Bezos live in a smaller house in Manhattan than in Medina, Washington?

5.3 Why did people turn to four-cylinder cars in the 1970s, only to shift back to six- and eight-cylinder cars in the 1990s?

5.4 Why are automobile engines smaller in England than in the United States?

5.5 Why are waiting lines longer in poorer neighborhoods?

6.1 When recycling is left to private market forces, why are many more aluminum beverage containers recycled than glass ones?

7.1 Why do supermarket checkout lines all tend to be roughly the same length?

7.2 Are there "too many" smart people working as corporate earnings forecasters?

8.1 Why does Intel sell the overwhelming majority of all microprocessors used in personal computers?

8.2 Why do many movie theaters offer discount tickets to students?

8.3 Why might an appliance retailer instruct its clerks to hammer dents into the sides of its stoves and refrigerators?

9.1 Why are cartel agreements notoriously unstable?

9.2 How did Congress unwittingly solve the television advertising dilemma confronting cigarette producers?

9.3 Why do people shout at parties?

9.4 Why do we often see convenience stores located on adjacent street corners?

10.1 Why did the American Olympic swimmer Shirley Babashoff, who set one world record and six national records at the 1976 Olympics, refuse to appear on the cover of *Sports Illustrated?*

10.2 Why would people pay thousands of dollars to attend a weight-loss camp that will feed them only 1,500 calories per day?

10.3 Why was Obamacare difficult to enact and harder still to repeal?

10.4 Why have attempts to privatize Social Security proved so politically unpopular in the United States?

10.5 If prosperous voters would be happier if they spent less on positional goods and lived in environments with more generously funded public sectors, why haven't they elected politicians who would deliver what they want?

11.1 What is the purpose of free speech laws?

11.2 Why do many states have laws requiring students to be vaccinated against childhood illnesses?

11.3 Why does the government subsidize private property owners to plant trees on their hillsides?

11.4 Why do blackberries in public parks get picked too soon?

11.5 Why are shared milkshakes consumed too quickly?

11.6 Why do football players take anabolic steroids?

12.1 Why is finding a knowledgeable salesclerk often difficult?

12.2 Why did Rivergate Books, the last bookstore in Lambertville, New Jersey, go out of business?

12.3 Why do firms insert the phrase "As advertised on TV" when they advertise their products in magazines and social media?

12.4 Why do many companies care so much about elite educational credentials?

12.5 Why do many clients seem to prefer lawyers who wear expensive suits?

12.6 Why do males under 25 years of age pay more than other drivers for auto insurance?

12.7 Why do opponents of the death penalty often remain silent?

12.8 Why do proponents of legalized drugs remain silent?

13.1 If unionized firms have to pay more, how do they manage to survive in the face of competition from their nonunionized counterparts?

13.2 Why do some ad copywriters earn more than others?

13.3 Why does Taylor Swift earn many millions more than singers with only slightly less talent?

The following ancillaries are available for quick download and convenient access via the Instructor Resource material available through McGraw Hill Connect®.

Solutions Manual

Prepared by the authors with assistance from Per Norander, University of North Carolina at Charlotte, this manual provides detailed answers to the end-of-chapter review questions and problems.

Test Bank

The test bank has been carefully revised and reviewed for accuracy. Thousands of questions have been categorized by chapter learning objectives, AACSB learning categories, Bloom's Taxonomy objectives, and level of difficulty.

Test Builder in Connect

Available within Connect, Test Builder is a cloud-based tool that enables instructors to format tests that can be printed or administered within an LMS. Test Builder offers a modern, streamlined interface for easy content configuration that matches course needs, without requiring a download.

Test Builder allows you to:

- access all test bank content from a particular title.

- easily pinpoint the most relevant content through robust filtering options.

- manipulate the order of questions or scramble questions and/or answers.

- pin questions to a specific location within a test.

- determine your preferred treatment of algorithmic questions.

- choose the layout and spacing.

- add instructions and configure default settings.

Test Builder provides a secure interface for better protection of content and allows for just-in-time updates to flow directly into assessments.

PowerPoints

Presentation slides contain a detailed, chapter-by-chapter review of the important ideas presented in the textbook, accompanied by animated graphs and slide notes. You can edit, print, or rearrange the slides to fit the needs of your course.

Customizable Micro Lecture Notes

One of the biggest hurdles to an instructor considering changing textbooks is the prospect of having to prepare new lecture notes and slides. For the microeconomics chapters, this hurdle no longer exists. A full set of lecture notes for Principles of Microeconomics, prepared by Bob Frank for his award-winning introductory microeconomics course at Cornell University, is available as Microsoft Word files that instructors are welcome to customize as they see fit. The challenge for any instructor is to reinforce the lessons of the text in lectures without generating student unrest by merely repeating what's in the book. These lecture notes address that challenge by constructing examples that run parallel to those presented in the book, yet are different from them in interesting contextual ways.

Writing Assignment

Available within McGraw Hill Connect® and McGraw Hill Connect® Master, the Writing Assignment tool delivers a learning experience to help students improve their written communication skills and conceptual understanding. As an instructor you can assign, monitor, grade, and provide feedback on writing more efficiently and effectively.

Remote Proctoring & Browser-Locking Capabilities

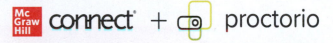

New remote proctoring and browser-locking capabilities, hosted by Proctorio within Connect, provide control of the assessment environment by enabling security options and verifying the identity of the student.

Seamlessly integrated within Connect, these services allow instructors to control students' assessment experience by restricting browser activity, recording students' activity, and verifying students are doing their own work.

Instant and detailed reporting gives instructors an at-a-glance view of potential academic integrity concerns, thereby avoiding personal bias and supporting evidence-based claims.

FOR MORE INFORMATION ABOUT CONNECT AND ITS AVAILABLE RESOURCES, REFER TO THE PAGES THAT FOLLOW.

Because learning changes everything.®

Connect Economics Asset Alignment with Bloom's Taxonomy

Principles of Economics, 8e

We Take Students Higher

As a learning science company we create content that supports higher order thinking skills. Within Connect®, we tag assessments accordingly so you can filter your search, assign it, and receive reporting on it. These content asset types can be associated with one or more levels of Bloom's Taxonomy.

The chart below shows a few of the key assignable economics assets with *McGraw Hill Connect* aligned with Bloom's Taxonomy. Take your students higher by assigning a variety of applications, moving them from simple memorization to concept application.

		SmartBook 2.0	ECON Adaptive Math Prep	Videos	Exercises	Interactive Graphs	Application-Based Activities	Econ Everyday Current Events Blog*	Writing Assignment Plus
Higher Order Thinking Skills	CREATE								✓
	EVALUATE						✓	✓	✓
	ANALYZE			✓	✓	✓	✓	✓	✓
	APPLY	✓	✓	✓	✓	✓	✓		✓
	UNDERSTAND	✓	✓	✓	✓	✓	✓	✓	✓
Lower Order Thinking Skills	REMEMBER	✓	✓	✓	✓	✓	✓	✓	✓

* Outside of Connect.

SmartBook 2.0

Adaptively aids students to study more efficiently by highlighting where in the chapter to focus, asking review questions and pointing them to passages in the text until they understand. Assignable and assessable.

ECON Adaptive Math Prep

Math preparedness assignments help students refresh important prerequisite topics necessary to be successful in economics. New Adaptive Math Prep Tool provides students just-in-time math remediation that are prerequisite to success in Principles of Economics courses and adapt to each student.

Videos

Worked examples and real-world application videos help students learn economics. **Learning Glass videos** reinforcing challenging topics featuring the authors and innovative learning glass technology. **Economic Naturalist videos** bring examples to life showing interesting applications of economic concepts. **Worked Problem videos** work through select end-of-chapter questions for extra help and guidance through challenging material.

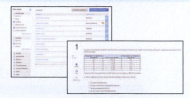

Exercises

Exercises with algorithmic variations provide ample opportunities for students to practice and hone quantitative skills. Graphing Exercises provide opportunities for students to draw, interact with, manipulate, and analyze graphs.

Interactive Graphs

Interactive Graphs provide visual displays of real data and economic concepts for students to manipulate. All graphs are accompanied by assignable assessment questions and feedback to guide students through the experience of learning to read and interpret graphs and data.

Application-Based Activities

Immersive real-life scenarios engage students and put them in the role of everyday economists. Students practice their economic thinking and problem-solving skills as they apply course concepts and see the implications of their decisions as they go. Each activity is designed as a 15-minute experience, unless students eagerly replay for a better outcome.

ECON Everyday Current Events Blog*

Our Econ Everyday blog saves instructors time bringing current, student-centered content into their course all semester long. Short articles, written for principles-level students, is tagged by topic to bring currency into your course. We also provide discussion questions to help you drive the conversation forward. Visit www.econeveryday.com and subscribe for updates. (*Outside of Connect.)

Writing Assignment Plus

Writing Assignment Plus delivers a learning experience that helps students improve their written communication skills and conceptual understanding. Faculty can assign, monitor, grade, and provide feedback on writing projects efficiently. Built-in grammar and writing review helps students improve writing quality while an originality check helps students correct central plagiarism before submission. End result? Improved workplace skills of writing in critical thinking.

For more information, please visit: **www.mheducation.com/highered/economics**

Instructors: Student Success Starts with You

Tools to enhance your unique voice

Want to build your own course? No problem. Prefer to use our turnkey, prebuilt course? Easy. Want to make changes throughout the semester? Sure. And you'll save time with Connect's auto-grading too.

65%
Less Time Grading

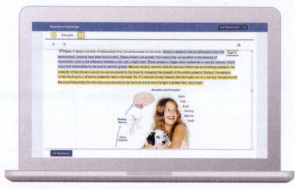

Laptop: McGraw Hill; Woman/dog: George Doyle/Getty Images

Study made personal

Incorporate adaptive study resources like SmartBook® 2.0 into your course and help your students be better prepared in less time. Learn more about the powerful personalized learning experience available in SmartBook 2.0 at **www.mheducation.com/highered/connect/smartbook**

Affordable solutions, added value

Make technology work for you with LMS integration for single sign-on access, mobile access to the digital textbook, and reports to quickly show you how each of your students is doing. And with our Inclusive Access program you can provide all these tools at a discount to your students. Ask your McGraw Hill representative for more information.

Padlock: Jobalou/Getty Images

Solutions for your challenges

A product isn't a solution. Real solutions are affordable, reliable, and come with training and ongoing support when you need it and how you want it. Visit **www. supportateverystep.com** for videos and resources both you and your students can use throughout the semester.

Checkmark: Jobalou/Getty Images

Students: Get Learning that Fits You

Effective tools for efficient studying

Connect is designed to make you more productive with simple, flexible, intuitive tools that maximize your study time and meet your individual learning needs. Get learning that works for you with Connect.

Study anytime, anywhere

Download the free ReadAnywhere app and access your online eBook or SmartBook 2.0 assignments when it's convenient, even if you're offline. And since the app automatically syncs with your eBook and SmartBook 2.0 assignments in Connect, all of your work is available every time you open it. Find out more at **www.mheducation.com/readanywhere**

> *"I really liked this app—it made it easy to study when you don't have your textbook in front of you."*
>
> - Jordan Cunningham, Eastern Washington University

Calendar: owattaphotos/Getty Images

Everything you need in one place

Your Connect course has everything you need—whether reading on your digital eBook or completing assignments for class, Connect makes it easy to get your work done.

Learning for everyone

McGraw Hill works directly with Accessibility Services Departments and faculty to meet the learning needs of all students. Please contact your Accessibility Services Office and ask them to email accessibility@mheducation.com, or visit **www.mheducation.com/about/accessibility** for more information.

Top: Jenner Images/Getty Images, Left: Hero Images/Getty Images, Right: Hero Images/Getty Images

COMPARISON GUIDE FOR FRANK, BERNANKE, ANTONOVICS, AND HEFFETZ PRODUCTS

Principles of Economics provides enhanced coverage, offers more topics, and more mathematical rigor. *Principles of Economics: A Streamlined Approach* is a stripped down version of the big book featuring core content with a less is more approach. See which product is right for you!

<table>
<tr><td colspan="10" align="center">Comparison Guide</td></tr>
<tr><td colspan="4">Principles of Economics, 8th edition</td><td colspan="6">Principles of Economics: A Streamlined Approach, 4th edition</td></tr>
<tr><td>Chapter Title</td><td>Econ 8e</td><td>Micro 8e</td><td>Macro 8e</td><td>Chapter Title</td><td>Streamlined 4e Econ</td><td>Streamlined 4e Micro</td><td>Streamlined 4e Macro</td></tr>
<tr><td>Thinking Like an Economist</td><td>1</td><td>1</td><td>1</td><td>Thinking Like An Economist</td><td>1</td><td>1</td><td>1</td></tr>
<tr><td>Comparative Advantage</td><td>2</td><td>2</td><td>2</td><td></td><td></td><td></td><td></td></tr>
<tr><td>Supply and Demand</td><td>3</td><td>3</td><td>3</td><td>Supply and Demand</td><td>2</td><td>2</td><td>2</td></tr>
<tr><td>Elasticity</td><td>4</td><td>4</td><td></td><td rowspan="2">Demand and Elasticity</td><td rowspan="2">3</td><td rowspan="2">3</td><td rowspan="2"></td></tr>
<tr><td>Demand</td><td>5</td><td>5</td><td></td></tr>
<tr><td>Perfectly Competitive Supply</td><td>6</td><td>6</td><td></td><td>Perfectly Competitive Supply</td><td>4</td><td>4</td><td></td></tr>
<tr><td>Efficiency, Exchange, and the Invisible Hand in Action</td><td>7</td><td>7</td><td></td><td>Efficiency, Exchange, and the Invisible Hand in Action</td><td>5</td><td>5</td><td></td></tr>
<tr><td>Monopoly, Oligopoly, and Monopolistic Competition</td><td>8</td><td>8</td><td></td><td>Monopoly, Oligopoly, and Monopolistic Competition</td><td>6</td><td>6</td><td></td></tr>
<tr><td>Games and Strategic Behavior</td><td>9</td><td>9</td><td></td><td>Games and Strategic Behavior</td><td>7</td><td>7</td><td></td></tr>
<tr><td>An Introduction to Behavioral Economics</td><td>10</td><td>10</td><td></td><td>An Introduction to Behavioral Economics (NEW)</td><td>8</td><td>8</td><td></td></tr>
<tr><td>Externalities, Property Rights, and the Environment</td><td>11</td><td>11</td><td></td><td>Externalities and Property Rights</td><td>9</td><td>9</td><td></td></tr>
<tr><td>The Economics of Information</td><td>12</td><td>12</td><td></td><td rowspan="3">Using Economics to Make Better Policy Decisions</td><td rowspan="3">10</td><td rowspan="3">10</td><td rowspan="3"></td></tr>
<tr><td>Labor Markets, Poverty, and Income Distribution</td><td>13</td><td>13</td><td></td></tr>
<tr><td>Public Goods and Tax Policy</td><td>14</td><td>14</td><td></td></tr>
<tr><td>International Trade and Trade Policy</td><td>15</td><td>15</td><td>16</td><td>International Trade and Trade Policy</td><td>11</td><td>11</td><td>12</td></tr>
<tr><td>Macroeconomics: The Bird's-Eye View of the Economy</td><td>16</td><td></td><td>4</td><td>Macroeconomics: The Bird's Eye View of the Economy</td><td>12</td><td></td><td>3</td></tr>
<tr><td>Measuring Economic Activity: GDP and Unemployment</td><td>17</td><td></td><td>5</td><td rowspan="2">Measuring Economic Activity: GDP, Unemployment, and Inflation</td><td rowspan="2">13</td><td rowspan="2"></td><td rowspan="2">4</td></tr>
<tr><td>Measuring the Price Level and Inflation</td><td>18</td><td></td><td>6</td></tr>
<tr><td>Economic Growth, Productivity, and Living Standards</td><td>19</td><td></td><td>7</td><td>Economic Growth, Productivity, and Living Standards</td><td>14</td><td></td><td>5</td></tr>
<tr><td>The Labor Market: Workers, Wages, and Unemployment</td><td>20</td><td></td><td>8</td><td>The Labor Market: Workers, Wages, and Unemployment</td><td>15</td><td></td><td>6</td></tr>
<tr><td>Saving and Capital Formation</td><td>21</td><td></td><td>9</td><td>Saving and Capital Formation</td><td>16</td><td></td><td>7</td></tr>
<tr><td>Money, Prices, and the Federal Reserve</td><td>22</td><td></td><td>10</td><td rowspan="2">Money, The Federal Reserve, and Global Financial Markets</td><td rowspan="2">17</td><td rowspan="2"></td><td rowspan="2">8</td></tr>
<tr><td>Financial Markets and International Capital Flows</td><td>23</td><td></td><td>11</td></tr>
<tr><td>Short-Term Economic Fluctuations: An Introduction</td><td>24</td><td></td><td>12</td><td rowspan="2">Short-Term Economic Fluctuations and Fiscal Policy</td><td rowspan="2">18</td><td rowspan="2"></td><td rowspan="2">9</td></tr>
<tr><td>Spending and Output in the Short Run</td><td>25</td><td></td><td>13</td></tr>
<tr><td>Stabilizing the Economy: The Role of the Fed</td><td>26</td><td></td><td>14</td><td>Stabilizing the Economy: The Role of the Fed</td><td>19</td><td></td><td>10</td></tr>
<tr><td>Aggregate Demand, Aggregate Supply, and Inflation</td><td>27</td><td></td><td>15</td><td>Aggregate Demand, Aggregate Supply, and Inflation</td><td>20</td><td></td><td>11</td></tr>
<tr><td>Exchange Rates and the Open Economy</td><td>28</td><td></td><td>17</td><td>Exchange Rates and the Open Economy</td><td>21</td><td></td><td>13</td></tr>
</table>

BRIEF CONTENTS

CONTENTS

Thinking Like an Economist

Nick Dolding/Cultura/Corbis

People often make bad decisions because they fail to compare the relevant costs and benefits.

LEARNING OBJECTIVES

After reading this chapter, you should be able to:

LO1 Explain and apply the *Scarcity Principle*, which says that having more of any good thing necessarily requires having less of something else.

LO2 Explain and apply the *Cost-Benefit Principle*, which says that an action should be taken if, but only if, its benefit is at least as great as its cost.

LO3 Discuss three important pitfalls that occur when applying the *Cost-Benefit Principle* inconsistently.

LO4 Explain and apply the *Incentive Principle*, which says that if you want to predict people's behavior, a good place to start is by examining their incentives.

How many students are in your introductory economics class? Some classes have just 20 or so. Others average 35, 100, or 200 students. At some schools, introductory economics classes may have as many as 2,000 students. What size is best?

If cost were no object, the best size might be a single student. Think about it: the whole course, all term long, with just you and your professor! Everything could be custom-tailored to your own background and ability. You could cover the material at just the right pace. The tutorial format also would promote close communication and personal trust between you and your professor. And your grade would depend more heavily on what you actually learned than on your luck when taking multiple-choice exams. Let's suppose, for the sake of discussion, that students have been shown to learn best in the tutorial format.

Why, then, do so many introductory classes still have hundreds of students? The simple reason is that costs *do* matter. They matter not just to the university administrators who must build classrooms and pay faculty salaries, but also to *you*. The direct cost of providing you with your own personal introductory economics course might easily top $50,000. *Someone* has to pay these costs. In private universities, a large share of the cost would be recovered directly from higher tuition payments. In state universities, the burden

Are small classes "better" than large ones?

economics the study of how people make choices under conditions of scarcity and of the results of those choices for society

would be split between higher tuition payments and higher tax payments. But, in either case, the course would be unaffordable for most students.

With larger classes, of course, the cost per student goes down. For example, an introductory economics course with 300 students might cost as little as $200 per student. But a class that large could easily compromise the quality of the learning environment. Compared to the custom tutorial format, however, it would be dramatically more affordable.

In choosing what size introductory economics course to offer, then, university administrators confront a classic economic trade-off. In making the class larger, they risk lowering the quality of instruction—a bad thing. At the same time, they reduce costs and hence the tuition students must pay—a good thing.

In this chapter, we'll introduce three simple principles that will help you understand and explain patterns of behavior you observe in the world around you. These principles also will help you avoid three pitfalls that plague decision makers in everyday life.

ECONOMICS: STUDYING CHOICE IN A WORLD OF SCARCITY

Even in rich societies like the United States, *scarcity* is a fundamental fact of life. There is never enough time, money, or energy to do everything we want to do or have everything we'd like to have. **Economics** is the study of how people make choices under conditions of scarcity and of the results of those choices for society.

In the class-size example just discussed, a motivated economics student might definitely prefer to be in a class of 20 rather than a class of 100, everything else being equal. But other things, of course, are not equal. Students can enjoy the benefits of having smaller classes, but only at the price of having less money for other activities. The student's choice inevitably will come down to the relative importance of competing activities.

That such trade-offs are widespread and important is one of the core principles of economics. We call it the *Scarcity Principle* because the simple fact of scarcity makes trade-offs necessary. Another name for the scarcity principle is the *No-Free-Lunch Principle* (which comes from the observation that even lunches that are given to you are never really free—somebody, somehow, always has to pay for them).

The Scarcity Principle (also called the No-Free-Lunch Principle): Although we have boundless needs and wants, the resources available to us are limited. So having more of one good thing usually means having less of another.

Inherent in the idea of a trade-off is the fact that choice involves compromise between competing interests. Economists resolve such trade-offs by using cost-benefit analysis, which is based on the disarmingly simple principle that an action should be taken if, and only if, its benefits exceed its costs. We call this statement the *Cost-Benefit Principle,* and it, too, is one of the core principles of economics:

The Cost-Benefit Principle: An individual (or a firm or a society) should take an action if, and only if, the extra benefits from taking the action are at least as great as the extra costs.

With the Cost-Benefit Principle in mind, let's think about our class-size question again. Imagine that classrooms come in only two sizes—100-seat lecture halls and 20-seat classrooms—and that your university currently offers introductory economics courses to classes of 100 students. Question: Should administrators reduce the class size to 20 students? Answer: Reduce if, and only if, the value of the improvement in instruction outweighs its additional cost.

This rule sounds simple. But to apply it we need some way to measure the relevant costs and benefits, a task that's often difficult in practice. If we make a few simplifying assumptions, however, we can see how the analysis might work. On the cost side, the primary expense of reducing class size from 100 to 20 is that we'll now need five professors instead of just one. We'll also need five smaller classrooms rather than a single big one, and this too may add slightly to the expense of the move. Let's suppose that classes with 20 cost $1,000 per student more than those with 100. Should administrators switch to the smaller class size? If they apply the Cost-Benefit Principle, they will realize that *doing so makes sense only if the value of attending the smaller class is at least $1,000 per student greater than the value of attending the larger class.*

Would you (or your family) be willing to pay an extra $1,000 for a smaller class? If not, and if other students feel the same way, then sticking with the larger class size makes sense. But if you and others would be willing to pay the extra tuition, then reducing the class size makes good economic sense.

Notice that the "best" class size, from an economic point of view, will generally not be the same as the "best" size from the point of view of an educational psychologist. That's because the economic definition of "best" takes into account both the benefits *and* the costs of different class sizes. The psychologist ignores costs and looks only at the learning benefits of different class sizes.

In practice, of course, different people feel differently about the value of smaller classes. People with high incomes, for example, tend to be willing to pay more for the advantage. That helps explain why average class size is smaller, and tuition higher, at private schools whose students come predominantly from high-income families.

The cost-benefit framework for thinking about the class-size problem also suggests a possible reason for the gradual increase in average class size that has been taking place in American colleges and universities. During the last 30 years, professors' salaries have risen sharply, making smaller classes more costly. During the same period, median family income—and hence the willingness to pay for smaller classes—has remained roughly constant. When the cost of offering smaller classes goes up but willingness to pay for smaller classes does not, universities shift to larger class sizes.

Scarcity and the trade-offs that result also apply to resources other than money. Jeff Bezos is one of the richest people on Earth. His wealth is estimated at more than $180 billion. That's more than the combined wealth of the poorest 54 percent of Americans. Bezos could buy more houses, cars, vacations, and other consumer goods than he could possibly use. Yet he, like the rest of us, has only 24 hours each day and a limited amount of energy. So even he confronts trade-offs. Any activity he pursues—whether it be building his business empire or redecorating his mansion—uses up time and energy that he could otherwise spend on other things. Indeed, someone once calculated that the value of Bezos's time is so great that pausing to pick up a $100 bill from the sidewalk simply wouldn't be worth his while.

If Jeff Bezos saw a $100 bill lying on the sidewalk, would it be worth his time to pick it up?

APPLYING THE COST-BENEFIT PRINCIPLE

In studying choice under scarcity, we'll usually begin with the premise that people are **rational,** which means they have well-defined goals and try to fulfill them as best they can. The Cost-Benefit Principle is a fundamental tool for the study of how rational people make choices.

rational person someone with well-defined goals who tries to fulfill those goals as best he or she can

As in the class-size example, often the only real difficulty in applying the cost-benefit rule is to come up with reasonable measures of the relevant benefits and costs. Only in rare instances will exact dollar measures be conveniently available. But the cost-benefit framework can lend structure to your thinking even when no relevant market data are available.

To illustrate how we proceed in such cases, the following example asks you to decide whether to perform an action whose cost is described only in vague, qualitative terms.

EXAMPLE 1.1

Comparing Costs and Benefits

Should you walk downtown to save $10 on a $25 wireless keyboard?

Imagine you are about to buy a $25 wireless keyboard at the nearby campus store when a friend tells you that the same keyboard is on sale at a downtown store for only $15. If the downtown store is a 30-minute walk away, where should you buy the keyboard?

The Cost-Benefit Principle tells us that you should buy it downtown if the benefit of doing so exceeds the cost. The benefit of taking any action is the dollar value of everything you gain by taking it. Here, the benefit of buying downtown is exactly $10, because that's the amount you'll save on the price of the keyboard. The cost of taking any action is the dollar value of everything you give up by taking it. Here, the cost of buying downtown is the dollar value you assign to the time and trouble it takes to make the trip. But how do we estimate that value?

One way is to perform the following hypothetical auction. Imagine that a stranger has offered to pay you to do an errand that involves the same walk downtown (perhaps to drop off a package for her at the post office). If she offered you a payment of, say, $1,000, would you accept? If so, we know that your cost of walking downtown and back must be less than $1,000. Now imagine her offer being reduced in small increments until you finally refuse the last offer. For example, if you'd agree to walk downtown and back for $9 but not for $8.99, then your cost of making the trip is $9. In this case, you should buy the keyboard downtown because the $10 you'll save (your benefit) is greater than your $9 cost of making the trip.

But suppose your cost of making the trip had been greater than $10. In that case, your best bet would have been to buy the keyboard from the nearby campus store. Confronted with this choice, different people may choose differently, depending on how costly they think it is to make the trip downtown. But although there is no uniquely correct choice, most people who are asked what they would do in this situation say they would buy the keyboard downtown.

ECONOMIC SURPLUS

economic surplus the benefit of taking an action minus its cost

Suppose that in Example 1.1 your "cost" of making the trip downtown was $9. Compared to the alternative of buying the keyboard at the campus store, buying it downtown resulted in an **economic surplus** of $1, the difference between the benefit of making the trip and its cost. In general, your goal as an economic decision maker is to choose those actions that generate the largest possible economic surplus. This means taking all actions that yield a positive total economic surplus, which is just another way of restating the Cost-Benefit Principle.

Note that the fact that your best choice was to buy the keyboard downtown doesn't imply that you *enjoy* making the trip, any more than choosing a large class means that you prefer large classes to small ones. It simply means that the trip is less unpleasant than the prospect of paying $10 extra for the keyboard. Once again, you've faced a trade-off. In this case, the choice was between a cheaper keyboard and the free time gained by avoiding the trip.

OPPORTUNITY COST

opportunity cost the value of what must be forgone to undertake an activity

Of course, your mental auction could have produced a different outcome. Suppose, for example, that the time required for the trip is the only time you have left to study for a difficult test the next day. Or suppose you are watching one of your favorite shows on Netflix, or that you are tired and would love a short nap. In such cases, we say that the **opportunity cost** of making the trip—that is, the value of what you must sacrifice to walk downtown and back—is high and you are more likely to decide against making the trip.

Strictly speaking, your opportunity cost of engaging in an activity is the value of everything you must sacrifice to engage in it. For instance, if seeing a movie requires not only that you buy a $10 ticket, but also that you give up a $20 dogwalking job that you would have been willing to do for free, then the opportunity cost of seeing the film is $30.

Under this definition, *all* costs—both implicit and explicit—are opportunity costs. Unless otherwise stated, we will adhere to this strict definition.

We must warn you, however, that some economists use the term *opportunity cost* to refer only to the implicit value of opportunities forgone. Thus, in the example just discussed, these economists wouldn't include the $10 ticket price when calculating the opportunity cost of seeing the film. But virtually all economists would agree that your opportunity cost of not doing the dogwalking job is $20.

In the previous example, if watching another hour of your favorite show on Netflix is the most valuable opportunity that conflicts with the trip downtown, the opportunity cost of making the trip is the dollar value you place on pursuing that opportunity. It is the largest amount you'd be willing to pay to avoid watching your show at another time. Note that the opportunity cost of making the trip is not the combined value of *all* possible activities you could have pursued, but only the value of your *best* alternative—the one you would have chosen had you not made the trip.

Throughout the text we'll pose self-tests like the one that follows. You'll find that pausing to answer them will help you to master key concepts in economics. Because doing these self-tests isn't very costly (indeed, many students report that they're actually fun), the Cost-Benefit Principle indicates that it's well worth your while to do them.

 SELF-TEST 1.1

You would again save $10 by buying the wireless keyboard downtown rather than at the campus store, but your cost of making the trip is now $12, not $9. By how much would your economic surplus be smaller if you bought the keyboard downtown rather than at the campus store?

THE ROLE OF ECONOMIC MODELS

Economists use the Cost-Benefit Principle as an abstract model of how an idealized rational individual would choose among competing alternatives. (By "abstract model" we mean a simplified description that captures the essential elements of a situation and allows us to analyze them in a logical way.) A computer model of a complex phenomenon like climate change, which must ignore many details and includes only the major forces at work, is an example of an abstract model.

Noneconomists are sometimes harshly critical of the economist's cost-benefit model on the grounds that people in the real world never conduct hypothetical mental auctions before deciding whether to make trips downtown. But this criticism betrays a fundamental misunderstanding of how abstract models can help explain and predict human behavior. Economists know perfectly well that people don't conduct hypothetical mental auctions when they make simple decisions. All the Cost-Benefit Principle really says is that a rational decision is one that is explicitly or implicitly based on a weighing of costs and benefits.

Most of us make sensible decisions most of the time, without being consciously aware that we are weighing costs and benefits, just as most people ride a bike without being consciously aware of what keeps them from falling. Through trial and error, we gradually learn what kinds of choices tend to work best in different contexts, just as bicycle riders internalize the relevant laws of physics, usually without being conscious of them.

Even so, learning the explicit principles of cost-benefit analysis can help us make better decisions, just as knowing about physics can help in learning to ride a bicycle. For instance, when a young economist was teaching his oldest son to ride a bike, he followed the time-honored tradition of running alongside the bike and holding onto his son, then giving him a push and hoping for the best. After several hours and painfully skinned elbows and knees, his son finally got it. A year later, someone pointed out that the trick to riding a bike is to turn slightly in whichever direction the bike is leaning. Of course! The economist passed this information along to his second son, who learned to ride almost instantly. Just as knowing a little physics can help you learn to ride a bike, knowing a little economics can help you make better decisions.

> *RECAP* ↱
>
> **COST-BENEFIT ANALYSIS**
>
> Scarcity is a basic fact of economic life. Because of it, having more of one good thing almost always means having less of another (the *scarcity principle*). The *Cost-Benefit Principle* holds that an individual (or a firm or a society) should take an action if, and only if, the extra benefit from taking the action is at least as great as the extra cost. The benefit of taking any action minus the cost of taking the action is called the *economic surplus* from that action. Hence, the Cost-Benefit Principle suggests that we take only those actions that create additional economic surplus.

THREE IMPORTANT DECISION PITFALLS[1]

Rational people will apply the Cost-Benefit Principle most of the time, although probably in an intuitive and approximate way, rather than through explicit and precise calculation. Knowing that rational people tend to compare costs and benefits enables economists to predict their likely behavior. As noted earlier, for example, we can predict that students from wealthy families are more likely than others to attend colleges that offer small classes. (Again, while the cost of small classes is the same for all families, their benefit, as measured by what people are willing to pay for them, tends to be higher for wealthier families.)

Yet researchers have identified situations in which people tend to apply the Cost-Benefit Principle inconsistently. In these situations, the Cost-Benefit Principle may not predict behavior accurately. But it proves helpful in another way, by identifying specific strategies for avoiding bad decisions.

PITFALL 1: MEASURING COSTS AND BENEFITS AS PROPORTIONS RATHER THAN ABSOLUTE DOLLAR AMOUNTS

As the next example makes clear, even people who seem to know they should weigh the pros and cons of the actions they are contemplating sometimes don't have a clear sense of how to measure the relevant costs and benefits.

EXAMPLE 1.2	**Comparing Costs and Benefits**

Should you walk downtown to save $10 on a $2,020 laptop computer?

You are about to buy a $2,020 laptop computer at the nearby campus store when a friend tells you that the same computer is on sale at a downtown store for only $2,010. If the downtown store is half an hour's walk away, where should you buy the computer?

---

[1]The examples in this section are inspired by the pioneering research of Daniel Kahneman and the late Amos Tversky. Kahneman was awarded the 2002 Nobel Prize in Economics for his efforts to integrate insights from psychology into economics. You can read more about this work in Kahneman's brilliant 2011 book, *Thinking Fast and Slow* (New York: Macmillan).

Assuming that the laptop is light enough to carry without effort, the structure of this example is exactly the same as that of Example 1.1. The only difference is that the price of the laptop is dramatically higher than the price of the wireless keyboard. As before, the benefit of buying downtown is the dollar amount you'll save, namely, $10. And because it's exactly the same trip, its cost also must be the same as before. So if you are perfectly rational, you should make the same decision in both cases. Yet when people are asked what they would do in these situations, the overwhelming majority say they'd walk downtown to buy the keyboard but would buy the laptop at the campus store. When asked to explain, most of them say something like, "The trip was worth it for the keyboard because you save 40 percent, but not worth it for the laptop because you save only $10 out of $2,020."

This is faulty reasoning. The benefit of the trip downtown is not the *proportion* you save on the original price. Rather, it is the *absolute dollar amount* you save. The benefit of walking downtown to buy the laptop is $10, exactly the same as for the wireless keyboard. And because the cost of the trip must also be the same in both cases, the economic surplus from making both trips must be exactly the same. That means that a rational decision maker would make the same decision in both cases. Yet, as noted, most people choose differently.

The pattern of faulty reasoning in the decision just discussed is one of several decision pitfalls to which people are often prone. In the discussion that follows, we will identify two additional decision pitfalls. In some cases, people ignore costs or benefits that they ought to take into account. On other occasions they are influenced by costs or benefits that are irrelevant.

 SELF-TEST 1.2

Which is more valuable: saving $100 on a $2,000 plane ticket to Tokyo or saving $90 on a $200 plane ticket to Chicago?

PITFALL 2: IGNORING IMPLICIT COSTS

Sherlock Holmes, Arthur Conan Doyle's legendary detective, was successful because he saw details that most others overlooked. In *Silver Blaze*, Holmes is called on to investigate the theft of an expensive racehorse from its stable. A Scotland Yard inspector assigned to the case asks Holmes whether some particular aspect of the crime requires further study. "Yes," Holmes replies, and describes "the curious incident of the dog in the night-time."[2] "The dog did nothing in the nighttime," responds the puzzled inspector. But, as Holmes realized, that was precisely the problem! The watchdog's failure to bark when Silver Blaze was stolen meant that the watchdog knew the thief. This clue ultimately proved the key to unraveling the mystery.

Just as we often don't notice when a dog fails to bark, many of us tend to overlook the implicit value of activities that fail to happen. As discussed earlier, however, intelligent decisions require taking the value of forgone opportunities properly into account.

The opportunity cost of an activity, once again, is the value of all that must be forgone in order to engage in that activity. If buying a wireless keyboard downtown means not watching another hour of your favorite show on Netflix, then the value to you of watching the show is an implicit cost of the trip. Many people make bad decisions because they tend to ignore the value of such forgone opportunities. To avoid overlooking implicit costs, economists often translate questions like "Should I walk downtown?" into ones like "Should I walk downtown or watch another hour of my favorite show?"

Implicit costs are like dogs that fail to bark in the night. Many of us tend to overlook activities that fail to happen.

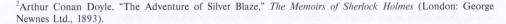

[2]Arthur Conan Doyle, "The Adventure of Silver Blaze," *The Memoirs of Sherlock Holmes* (London: George Newnes Ltd., 1893).

EXAMPLE 1.3	Implicit Cost

Should you use your frequent-flyer coupon to fly to Cancun for spring break?

With spring break only a week away, you are still undecided about whether to go to Cancun with a group of classmates at the University of Iowa. The round-trip airfare from Cedar Rapids is $500, but you have a frequent-flyer coupon you could use for the trip. All other relevant costs for the vacation week at the beach total exactly $1,000. The most you would be willing to pay for the Cancun vacation is $1,350. That amount is your benefit of taking the vacation. Your only alternative use for your frequent-flyer coupon is for a trip to Boston the weekend after spring break to attend your brother's wedding. (Your coupon expires shortly thereafter.) If the Cedar Rapids–Boston round-trip airfare is $400, should you use your frequent-flyer coupon to fly to Cancun for spring break?

 Cost-Benefit >>>

The Cost-Benefit Principle tells us that you should go to Cancun if the benefits of the trip exceed its costs. If not for the complication of the frequent-flyer coupon, solving this problem would be a straightforward matter of comparing your benefit from the week at the beach to the sum of all relevant costs. And because your airfare and other costs would add up to $1,500, or $150 more than your benefit from the trip, you would not go to Cancun.

But what about the possibility of using your frequent-flyer coupon to make the trip? Using it for that purpose might make the flight to Cancun seem free, suggesting you'd reap an economic surplus of $350 by making the trip. But doing so also would mean you'd have to fork over $400 for your airfare to Boston. So the implicit cost of using your coupon to go to Cancun is really $400. If you use it for that purpose, the trip still ends up being a loser because the cost of the vacation, $1,400, exceeds the benefit by $50. In cases like these, you're much more likely to decide sensibly if you ask yourself, "Should I use my frequent-flyer coupon for this trip or save it for an upcoming trip?"

Is your flight to Cancun "free" if you travel on a frequent-flyer coupon?

We cannot emphasize strongly enough that the key to using the Cost-Benefit Principle correctly lies in recognizing precisely what taking a given action prevents us from doing. Self-Test 1.3 illustrates this point by modifying the details of Example 1.3 slightly.

> **SELF-TEST 1.3**
>
> Refer to given information in Example 1.3, but this time your frequent-flyer coupon expires in a week, so your only chance to use it will be for the Cancun trip. Should you use your coupon?

PITFALL 3: FAILING TO THINK AT THE MARGIN

When deciding whether to take an action, the only relevant costs and benefits are those that would occur as a result of taking the action. Sometimes people are influenced by costs they ought to ignore. Other times they compare the wrong costs and benefits. *The only costs that should influence a decision about whether to take an action are those we can avoid by not taking the action. Similarly, the only benefits we should consider are those that would not occur unless the action were taken.* As a practical matter, however, many decision makers appear to be influenced by costs or benefits that would have occurred no matter what. Thus, people are often influenced by **sunk costs**—costs that are beyond recovery at the

sunk cost a cost that is beyond recovery at the moment a decision must be made

moment a decision is made. For example, money spent on a nontransferable, nonrefundable airline ticket is a sunk cost.

As the following example illustrates, sunk costs must be borne *whether or not an action is taken,* so they are irrelevant to the decision of whether to take the action.

EXAMPLE 1.4   Sunk Cost

How much should you eat at an all-you-can-eat restaurant?

Sangam, an Indian restaurant in Philadelphia, offers an all-you-can-eat lunch buffet for $10. Customers pay $10 at the door, and no matter how many times they refill their plates, there is no additional charge. One day, as a goodwill gesture, the owner of the restaurant tells 20 randomly selected guests that they can eat at the all-you-can-eat buffet for free. The remaining guests pay the usual price. If all diners are rational, will those who are able to eat at the buffet for free consume a different amount of food, on average, than those who have to pay $10 for the buffet?

Having eaten their first helping, diners in each group confront the following question: "Should I go back for another helping?" For rational diners, if the benefit of doing so exceeds the cost, the answer is yes; otherwise it is no. Note that at the moment of decision, the $10 charge for the lunch is a sunk cost. Those who paid it have no way to recover it. Thus, for both groups, the (extra) cost of another helping is exactly zero. And because the people who received the free lunch were chosen at random, there's no reason their appetites or incomes should be any different from those of other diners. The benefit of another helping thus should be the same, on average, for people in both groups. And because their respective costs and benefits are the same, the two groups should eat the same number of helpings, on average.

Psychologists and economists have experimental evidence, however, that people in such groups do *not* eat similar amounts.[3] In particular, those who have to pay for the all-you-can-eat buffet tend to eat substantially more than those for whom the buffet is free. People in the former group somehow seem determined to "get their money's worth." Their implicit goal is apparently to minimize the average cost per bite of the food they eat. Yet minimizing average cost is not a particularly sensible objective. The irony is that diners who are determined to get their money's worth usually end up eating too much.

The fact that the cost-benefit criterion failed the test of prediction in Example 1.4 does nothing to invalidate its advice about what people *should* do. If you are letting sunk costs influence your decisions, you can do better by changing your behavior.

In addition to paying attention to costs and benefits that should be ignored, people often use incorrect measures of the relevant costs and benefits. This error often occurs when we must choose the *extent* to which an activity should be pursued (as opposed to choosing whether to pursue it at all). We can apply the Cost-Benefit Principle in such situations by repeatedly asking the question, "Should I increase the level at which I am currently pursuing the activity?"

In attempting to answer this question, the focus should always be on the benefit and cost of an *additional* unit of activity. To emphasize this focus, economists refer to the cost of an additional unit of activity as its **marginal cost.** Similarly, the benefit of an additional unit of the activity is its **marginal benefit.**

marginal cost the increase in total cost that results from carrying out one additional unit of an activity

marginal benefit the increase in total benefit that results from carrying out one additional unit of an activity

---

[3]See, for example, Richard Thaler, "Toward a Positive Theory of Consumer Choice," *Journal of Economic Behavior and Organization* 1, no. 1 (1980).

When the problem is to discover the proper level for an activity, the cost-benefit rule is to keep increasing the level as long as the marginal benefit of the activity exceeds its marginal cost. As the following example illustrates, however, people often fail to apply this rule correctly.

| EXAMPLE 1.5 | Focusing on Marginal Costs and Benefits |

Should SpaceX expand its launch program from four launches per year to five?

SpaceX accountants have estimated that the gains from the company's jumbo rocket launch program are currently $24 billion a year (an average of $6 billion per launch) and that its costs are currently $20 billion a year (an average $5 billion per launch). On the basis of these estimates, they have recommended that the company should increase its number of launches. Should SpaceX CEO Elon Musk follow their advice?

To discover whether the advice makes economic sense, we must compare the marginal cost of a launch to its marginal benefit. The accountants' estimates, however, tell us only the **average cost** and **average benefit** of the program. These are, respectively, the total cost of the program divided by the number of launches and the total benefit divided by the number of launches.

Knowing the average benefit and average cost per launch for all rockets launched thus far is simply not useful for deciding whether to expand the program. Of course, the average cost of the launches undertaken so far *might* be the same as the cost of adding another launch. But it also might be either higher or lower than the marginal cost of a launch. The same holds true regarding average and marginal benefits.

Suppose, for the sake of discussion, that the benefit of an additional launch is in fact the same as the average benefit per launch thus far, $6 billion. Should SpaceX add another launch? Not if the cost of adding the fifth launch would be more than $6 billion. And the fact that the average cost per launch is only $5 billion simply does not tell us anything about the marginal cost of the fifth launch.

Suppose, for example, that the relationship between the number of rockets launched and the total cost of the program is as described in Table 1.1. The average cost per launch (third column) when there are four launches would then be $20 billion/4 = $5 billion per launch, just as the accountants reported. But note in the second column of the table that adding a fifth launch would raise costs from $20 billion to $32 billion, making the marginal cost of the fifth launch $12 billion. So if the benefit of an additional launch is $6 billion, increasing the number of launches from four to five would make absolutely no economic sense.

average cost the total cost of undertaking n units of an activity divided by n

average benefit the total benefit of undertaking n units of an activity divided by n

TABLE 1.1
How Total Cost Varies with the Number of Launches

Number of launches	Total cost ($ billions)	Average cost ($ billion/launch)
0	0	0
1	3	3
2	7	3.5
3	12	4
4	20	5
5	32	6.4

The following example illustrates how to apply the *Cost-Benefit Principle* correctly in this case.

EXAMPLE 1.6   Focusing on Marginal Costs and Benefits

How many rockets should SpaceX launch?

SpaceX must decide how many rockets to launch. The benefit of each launch is estimated to be $6 billion, and the total cost of the program again depends on the number of launches as shown in Table 1.1. How many rockets should SpaceX launch?

SpaceX should continue to launch its jumbo rockets as long as the marginal benefit of the program exceeds its marginal cost. In this example, the marginal benefit is constant at $6 billion per launch, regardless of the number of rockets launched. SpaceX should thus keep launching rockets as long as the marginal cost per launch is less than or equal to $6 billion.

Applying the definition of marginal cost to the total cost entries in the second column of Table 1.1 yields the marginal cost values in the third column of Table 1.2. (Because marginal cost is the change in total cost that results when we change the number of launches by one, we place each marginal cost entry midway between the rows showing the corresponding total cost entries.) Thus, for example, the marginal cost of increasing the number of launches from one to two is $4 billion, the difference between the $7 billion total cost of two launches and the $3 billion total cost of one launch.

TABLE 1.2
How Marginal Cost Varies with the Number of Launches

Number of launches	Total cost ($ billions)	Marginal cost ($ billion/launch)
0	0	
		3
1	3	
		4
2	7	
		5
3	12	
		8
4	20	
		12
5	32	

As we see from a comparison of the $6 billion marginal benefit per launch with the marginal cost entries in the third column of Table 1.2, the first three launches satisfy the cost-benefit test, but the fourth and fifth launches do not. SpaceX should thus launch three rockets.

 SELF-TEST 1.4

If the marginal benefit of each launch had been not $6 billion but $9 billion, how many rockets should SpaceX have launched?

The cost-benefit framework emphasizes that the only relevant costs and benefits in deciding whether to pursue an activity further are *marginal* costs and benefits—measures that correspond to the *increment* of activity under consideration. In many contexts, however, people seem more inclined to compare the *average* cost and benefit of the activity. As Example 1.5 made clear, increasing the level of an activity may not be justified, even though its average benefit at the current level is significantly greater than its average cost.

 SELF-TEST 1.5

Should a basketball team's best player take all the team's shots?

A professional basketball team has a new assistant coach. The assistant notices that one player scores on a higher percentage of her shots than other players. Based on this information, the assistant suggests to the head coach that the star player should take *all* the shots. That way, the assistant reasons, the team will score more points and win more games.

On hearing this suggestion, the head coach fires her assistant for incompetence. What was wrong with the assistant's idea?

RECAP ↑

THREE IMPORTANT DECISION PITFALLS

1. **The pitfall of measuring costs or benefits proportionally.** Many decision makers treat a change in cost or benefit as insignificant if it constitutes only a small proportion of the original amount. Absolute dollar amounts, not proportions, should be employed to measure costs and benefits.

2. **The pitfall of ignoring implicit costs.** When performing a cost-benefit analysis of an action, it is important to account for all relevant costs, including the implicit value of alternatives that must be forgone in order to carry out the action. A resource (such as a frequent-flyer coupon) may have a high implicit cost, even if you originally got it "for free," if its best alternative use has high value. The identical resource may have a low implicit cost, however, if it has no good alternative uses.

3. **The pitfall of failing to think at the margin.** When deciding whether to perform an action, the only costs and benefits that are relevant are those that would result from taking the action. It is important to ignore sunk costs—those costs that cannot be avoided even if the action isn't taken. Even though a ticket to a concert may have cost you $100, if you've already bought it and cannot sell it to anyone else, the $100 is a sunk cost and shouldn't influence your decision about whether to go to the concert. It's also important not to confuse average costs and benefits with marginal costs and benefits. Decision makers often have ready information about the total cost and benefit of an activity, and from these it's simple to compute the activity's average cost and benefit. A common mistake is to conclude that an activity should be increased if its average benefit exceeds its average cost. The Cost-Benefit Principle tells us that the level of an activity should be increased if, and only if, its *marginal* benefit exceeds its *marginal* cost.

Some costs and benefits, especially marginal costs and benefits and implicit costs, are important for decision making, while others, like sunk costs and average costs and benefits, are essentially irrelevant. This conclusion is implicit in our original statement of the Cost-Benefit Principle (an action should be taken if, and only if, the extra benefits of taking it exceed the extra costs). When we encounter additional examples of decision pitfalls, we will flag them by inserting the icon for the Cost-Benefit Principle as shown here.

 Cost-Benefit ≫

NORMATIVE ECONOMICS VERSUS POSITIVE ECONOMICS

The examples discussed in the preceding section make the point that people *sometimes* choose irrationally. We must stress that our purpose in discussing these examples was not to suggest that people *generally* make irrational choices. On the contrary, most people appear to choose sensibly most of the time, especially when their decisions are important or familiar ones. The economist's focus on rational choice thus offers not only useful advice about making better decisions, but also a basis for predicting and explaining human behavior. We used the cost-benefit approach in this way when discussing how rising faculty salaries have led to larger class sizes. And as we will see, similar reasoning helps explain human behavior in virtually every other domain.

The Cost-Benefit Principle is an example of a **normative economic principle,** one that provides guidance about how we *should* behave. For example, according to the Cost-Benefit Principle, we should ignore sunk costs when making decisions about the future. As our discussion of the various decision pitfalls makes clear, however, the Cost-Benefit Principle is not always a **positive,** or **descriptive, economic principle,** one that describes how we actually *will* behave. As we saw, the Cost-Benefit Principle can be tricky to implement, and people sometimes fail to heed its prescriptions.

That said, we stress that knowing the relevant costs and benefits surely does enable us to predict how people will behave much of the time. If the benefit of an action goes up, it is generally reasonable to predict that people will be more likely to take that action. And conversely, if the cost of an action goes up, the safest prediction will be that people will be less likely to take that action. This point is so important that we designate it as the *Incentive Principle.*

The Incentive Principle: A person (or a firm or a society) is more likely to take an action if its benefit rises, and less likely to take it if its cost rises. In short, incentives matter.

Incentive

The Incentive Principle is a positive economic principle. It stresses that the relevant costs and benefits usually help us predict behavior, but at the same time does not insist that people behave rationally in each instance. For example, if the price of heating oil were to rise sharply, we would invoke the Cost-Benefit Principle to say that people *should* turn down their thermostats, and invoke the Incentive Principle to predict that average thermostat settings *will* in fact go down.

ECONOMICS: MICRO AND MACRO

By convention, we use the term **microeconomics** to describe the study of individual choices and of group behavior in individual markets. **Macroeconomics,** by contrast, is the study of the performance of national economies and of the policies that governments use to try to improve that performance. Macroeconomics tries to understand the determinants of such things as the national unemployment rate, the overall price level, and the total value of national output.

Our focus in this chapter is on issues that confront the individual decision maker, whether that individual confronts a personal decision, a family decision, a business decision, a government policy decision, or indeed any other type of decision. Further on, we'll consider economic models of groups of individuals such as all buyers or all sellers in a specific market. Later still we'll turn to broader economic issues and measures.

No matter which of these levels is our focus, however, our thinking will be shaped by the fact that, although economic needs and wants are effectively unlimited, the material and human resources that can be used to satisfy them are finite. Clear thinking about economic problems must therefore always take into account the idea of trade-offs—the idea that having more of one good thing usually means having less of another. Our economy and our society are shaped to a substantial degree by the choices people have made when faced with trade-offs.

normative economic principle one that says how people should behave

positive (or **descriptive**) **economic principle** one that predicts how people will behave

microeconomics the study of individual choice under scarcity and its implications for the behavior of prices and quantities in individual markets

macroeconomics the study of the performance of national economies and the policies that governments use to try to improve that performance

THE APPROACH OF THIS TEXT

Choosing the number of students to register in each class is just one of many important decisions in planning an introductory economics course. Another, to which the Scarcity Principle applies just as strongly, concerns which topics to include on the course syllabus. There's a virtually inexhaustible set of issues that might be covered in an introductory course, but only limited time in which to cover them. There's no free lunch. Covering some inevitably means omitting others.

All textbook authors are forced to pick and choose. A textbook that covered *all* the issues would take up more than a whole floor of your campus library. It is our firm view that most introductory textbooks try to cover far too much. One reason that each of us was drawn to the study of economics is that a relatively short list of the discipline's core ideas can explain a great deal of the behavior and events we see in the world around us. So rather than cover a large number of ideas at a superficial level, our strategy is to focus on this short list of core ideas, returning to each entry again and again, in many different contexts. This strategy will enable you to internalize these ideas remarkably well in the brief span of a single course. And the benefit of learning a small number of important ideas well will far outweigh the cost of having to ignore a host of other, less important ones.

So far, we've already encountered three core ideas: the Scarcity Principle, the Cost-Benefit Principle, and the Incentive Principle. As these core ideas reemerge in the course of our discussions, we'll call your attention to them. And shortly after a *new* core idea appears, we'll highlight it by formally restating it.

A second important element in our philosophy is a belief in the importance of active learning. In the same way that you can learn Spanish only by speaking and writing it, or tennis only by playing the game, you can learn economics only by *doing* economics. And because we want you to learn how to do economics, rather than just to read or listen passively as the authors or your instructor does economics, we'll make every effort to encourage you to stay actively involved.

For example, instead of just telling you about an idea, we'll usually first motivate the idea by showing you how it works in the context of a specific example. Often, these examples will be followed by self-tests for you to try, as well as applications that show the relevance of the idea to real life. Try working the self-tests *before* looking up the answers (which are at the back of the corresponding chapter).

Think critically about the applications: Do you see how they illustrate the point being made? Do they give you new insight into the issue? Work the problems at the end of the chapters and take extra care with those relating to points that you don't fully understand. Apply economic principles to the world around you. (We'll say more about this when we discuss economic naturalism below.) Finally, when you come across an idea or example that you find interesting, tell a friend about it. You'll be surprised to discover how much the mere act of explaining it helps you understand and remember the underlying principle. The more actively you can become engaged in the learning process, the more effective your learning will be.

ECONOMIC NATURALISM

▶ Visit your instructor's Connect course and access your eBook to view this video.

Why does the light come on when you open the refrigerator door but not when you open the freezer?

With the rudiments of the cost-benefit framework under your belt, you are now in a position to become an "economic naturalist," someone who uses insights from economics to help make sense of observations from everyday life. People who have studied biology are able to observe and marvel at many details of nature that would otherwise have escaped their notice. For example, on a walk in the woods in early April, the novice may see only trees. In contrast, the biology student notices many different species of trees and understands why some are already in leaf while others still lie dormant. Likewise, the novice may notice that in some animal species males are much larger than females, but the biology student knows that pattern occurs only in species in which males take several mates. Natural selection favors larger males in those species because their greater size helps them prevail in the often bloody contests among males for access to females. In contrast, males tend to be roughly the same size as females in monogamous species, in which there is much less fighting for mates.

Learning a few simple economic principles broadens our vision in a similar way. It enables us to see the mundane details of ordinary human existence in a new light. Whereas the uninitiated often fail even to notice these details, the economic naturalist not only sees them, but becomes actively engaged in the attempt to understand them. Let's consider a few examples of questions economic naturalists might pose for themselves.

The Economic Naturalist 1.1

Why do many hardware manufacturers include more than $1,000 worth of "free" software with a computer selling for only slightly more than that?

The software industry is different from many others in the sense that its customers care a great deal about product compatibility. When you and your classmates are working on a project together, for example, your task will be much simpler if you all use the same word-processing program. Likewise, an executive's life will be easier at tax time if her financial software is the same as her accountant's.

The implication is that the benefit of owning and using any given software program increases with the number of other people who use that same product. This unusual relationship gives the producers of the most popular programs an enormous advantage and often makes it hard for new programs to break into the market.

Recognizing this pattern, Intuit Corp. offered computer makers free copies of *Quicken*, its personal financial-management software. Computer makers, for their part, were only too happy to include the program because it made their new computers more attractive to buyers. *Quicken* soon became the standard for personal financial-management programs. By giving away free copies of the program, Intuit "primed the pump," creating an enormous demand for upgrades of *Quicken* and for more advanced versions of related software. Thus, *TurboTax*, Intuit's personal income-tax software, has become the standard for tax-preparation programs.

Inspired by this success story, other software developers have jumped onto the bandwagon. Most hardware now comes bundled with a host of free software programs. Some software developers are even rumored to *pay* computer makers to include their programs!

▶ Visit your instructor's Connect course and access your eBook to view this video.

Why are child safety seats required in automobiles but not in airplanes?

The Economic Naturalist 1.1 illustrates a case in which the *benefit* of a product depends on the number of other people who own that product. As the next Economic Naturalist demonstrates, the *cost* of a product may also depend on the number of others who own it.

The Economic Naturalist 1.2

Why don't auto manufacturers make cars without heaters?

Virtually every new car sold in the United States today has a heater. But not every car has a satellite navigation system. Why this difference?

One might be tempted to answer that, although everyone *needs* a heater, people can get along without navigation systems. Yet heaters are of limited use in places like Hawaii and Southern California.

Although heaters cost extra money to manufacture and are not useful in all parts of the country, they do not cost *much* money and are useful on at least a few days each year in most parts of the country. As time passed and people's incomes grew, manufacturers found that people were ordering fewer and fewer cars without heaters. At some point it actually became cheaper to put heaters in *all* cars, rather than bear the administrative expense of making some cars with heaters and others without. No doubt a few buyers would still order a car without a heater if they could save some money in the process, but catering to these customers is just no longer worth it.

Similar reasoning explains why certain cars today cannot be purchased without a satellite navigation system. Buyers of the 2020 BMW 750i, for example, got one whether they wanted it or not. Most buyers of this car, which sells for more than $85,000, have high incomes, so the overwhelming majority of them would have chosen to order a navigation system had it been sold as an option. Because of the savings made possible when all cars are produced with the same equipment, it would have actually cost BMW more to supply cars for the few who would want them without navigation systems.

Buyers of the least-expensive makes of car have much lower incomes on average than BMW 750i buyers. Accordingly, most of them have more pressing alternative uses for their money than to buy navigation systems for their cars, and this explains why some inexpensive makes continue to offer navigation systems only as options. But as incomes continue to grow, new cars without navigation systems will eventually disappear.

The insights afforded by The Economic Naturalist 1.2 suggest an answer to the following strange question:

The Economic Naturalist 1.3

Why do the keypad buttons on drive-up automated teller machines have Braille dots?

Braille dots on elevator buttons and on the keypads of walk-up automated teller machines enable blind people to participate more fully in the normal flow of daily activity. But even though blind people can do many remarkable things, they cannot drive automobiles on public roads. Why, then, do the manufacturers of automated teller machines install Braille dots on the machines at drive-up locations?

Why do the keypad buttons on drive-up automated teller machines have Braille dots?

The answer to this riddle is that once the keypad molds have been manufactured, the cost of producing buttons with Braille dots is no higher than the cost of producing smooth buttons. Making both would require separate sets of molds and two different types of inventory. If the patrons of drive-up machines found buttons with Braille dots harder to use, there might be a reason to incur these extra costs. But since the dots pose no difficulty for sighted users, the best and cheapest solution is to produce only keypads with dots.

The preceding example was suggested by Cornell student Bill Tjoa, in response to the following assignment:

✅ SELF-TEST 1.6

In 500 words or less, use cost-benefit analysis to explain some pattern of events or behavior you have observed in your own environment.

There is probably no more useful step you can take in your study of economics than to perform several versions of the assignment in Self-Test 1.6. Students who do so almost invariably become lifelong economic naturalists. Their mastery of economic concepts not only does not decay with the passage of time, but it actually grows stronger. We urge you, in the strongest possible terms, to make this investment!

SUMMARY

- Economics is the study of how people make choices under conditions of scarcity and of the results of those choices for society. Economic analysis of human behavior begins with the assumption that people are rational—that they have well-defined goals and try to achieve them as best they can. In trying to achieve their goals, people normally face trade-offs: Because material and human resources are limited, having more of one good thing means making do with less of some other good thing. *(LO1)*

- Our focus in this chapter has been on how rational people make choices among alternative courses of action. Our basic tool for analyzing these decisions is cost-benefit analysis. The Cost-Benefit Principle says that a person should take an action if, and only if, the benefit of that action is at least as great as its cost. The benefit of an action is defined as the largest dollar amount the person would be willing to pay in order to take the action. The cost of an action is defined as the dollar value of everything the person must give up in order to take the action. *(LO2)*

- In using the cost-benefit framework, we need not presume that people choose rationally all the time. Indeed, we identified three common pitfalls that plague decision makers in all walks of life: a tendency to treat small proportional changes as insignificant, a tendency to ignore implicit costs, and a tendency to fail to think at the margin—for example, by failing to ignore sunk costs or by failing to compare marginal costs and benefits. *(LO3)*

- Often the question is not whether to pursue an activity but rather how many units of it to pursue. In these cases, the rational person pursues additional units as long as the marginal benefit of the activity (the benefit from pursuing an additional unit of it) exceeds its marginal cost (the cost of pursuing an additional unit of it). *(LO4)*

- Microeconomics is the study of individual choices and of group behavior in individual markets, while macroeconomics is the study of the performance of national economics and of the policies that governments use to try to improve economic performance.

CORE PRINCIPLES

 Scarcity

The Scarcity Principle (also called the No-Free-Lunch Principle)
Although we have boundless needs and wants, the resources available to us are limited. So having more of one good thing usually means having less of another.

 Cost-Benefit

The Cost-Benefit Principle
An individual (or a firm or a society) should take an action if, and only if, the extra benefits from taking the action are at least as great as the extra costs.

 Incentive

The Incentive Principle
A person (or a firm or a society) is more likely to take an action if its benefit rises, and less likely to take it if its cost rises. In short, incentives matter.

KEY TERMS

average benefit
average cost
economic surplus
economics
macroeconomics

marginal benefit
marginal cost
microeconomics
normative economic principle

opportunity cost
positive (or descriptive) economic
principle
rational person
sunk cost

REVIEW QUESTIONS

1. A friend of yours on the tennis team says, "Private tennis lessons are definitely better than group lessons." Explain what you think she means by this statement. Then use the Cost-Benefit Principle to explain why private lessons are not necessarily the best choice for everyone. *(LO2)*

2. True or false: Your willingness to drive downtown to save $30 on a new appliance should depend on what fraction of the total selling price $30 is. Explain. *(LO3)*

3. Why might someone who is trying to decide whether to see a movie be more likely to focus on the $10 ticket price than on the $20 he or she would fail to earn by not dogwalking? *(LO3)*

4. Many people think of their air travel as being free when they use frequent-flyer coupons. Explain why these people are likely to make wasteful travel decisions. *(LO3)*

5. Is the nonrefundable tuition payment you made to your university this semester a sunk cost? How would your answer differ if your university were to offer a full tuition refund to any student who dropped out of school during the first two months of the semester? *(LO3)*

PROBLEMS

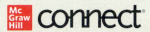

1. Suppose your school is considering whether to spend $20 million building a new state-of-the-art recreation facility. All of the students agree that the existing facility is in disrepair and that a new facility would be much nicer. Despite this, however, when students are asked to vote on whether they would like the school to build the new recreation facility, over 78 percent vote no. Why might such a large fraction of students vote no even though they all agree that a new recreation facility would be much nicer than the existing one? *(LO1)*

2. Suppose the most you would be willing to pay to have a freshly washed car before going out on a date is $6. The smallest amount for which you would be willing to wash someone else's car is $3.50. You are going out this evening and your car is dirty. How much economic surplus would you receive from washing it? *(LO2)*

3. To earn extra money in the summer, you grow tomatoes and sell them at a local farmers' market for 30 cents per pound. By adding compost to your garden, you can increase your yield as shown in the accompanying table. If compost costs 50 cents per pound and your goal is to make as much profit as possible, how many pounds of compost should you add? *(LO2)*

Pounds of compost	Pounds of tomatoes
	100
1	120
2	125
3	128
4	130
5	131
6	131.5

4.* You and your friend Jamal have identical tastes. At 2 p.m., you go to the local Ticketmaster outlet and buy a non-refundable $30 ticket to a basketball game to be played that night in Syracuse, 50 miles north of your home in Ithaca. Jamal plans to attend the same game, but because he cannot get to the Ticketmaster outlet, he plans to buy his ticket at the game. Tickets sold at the game cost only $25 because they carry no Ticketmaster surcharge. (Many people nonetheless pay the higher price at Ticketmaster, to be sure of getting good seats.) At 4 p.m., an unexpected snowstorm begins, making the prospect of the drive to Syracuse much less attractive than before (but ensuring the availability of good seats). If both you and Jamal are rational, is one of you more likely to attend the game than the other? *(LO2)*

5. Kenya is a mushroom farmer. She invests all her spare cash in additional mushrooms, which grow on otherwise useless land behind her barn. The mushrooms double in weight during their first year, after which time they are harvested and sold at a constant price per pound. Kenya's friend Fatima asks Kenya for a loan of $200, which she promises to repay after one year. How much interest will Fatima have to pay Kenya in order for Kenya to recover her opportunity cost of making the loan? Explain briefly. *(LO3)*

6. Suppose that in the last few seconds you devoted to question 1 on your physics exam you earned 4 extra points, while in the last few seconds you devoted to question 2 you earned 10 extra points. You earned a total of 48 and 12 points, respectively, on the two questions, and the total time you spent on each was the same. If you could take the exam again, how—if at all—should you reallocate your time between these questions? *(LO3)*

7. Monica and Rachel have the same preferences and incomes. Just as Monica arrived at the theater to see a

*Denotes more difficult problem.

play, she discovered that she had lost the $10 ticket she had purchased earlier. Rachel also just arrived at the theater planning to buy a ticket to see the same play when she discovered that she had lost a $10 bill from her wallet. If both Monica and Rachel are rational and both still have enough money to pay for a ticket, is one of them more likely than the other to go ahead and see the play anyway? *(LO3)*

8. Residents of your city are charged a fixed weekly fee of $6 for garbage collection. They are allowed to put out as many cans as they wish. The average household disposes of three cans of garbage per week under this plan. Now suppose that your city changes to a "tag" system. Each can of garbage to be collected must have a tag affixed to it. The tags cost $2 each and are not reusable. What effect do you think the introduction of the tag system will have on the total quantity of garbage collected in your city? Explain briefly. *(LO4)*

9. Once a week, Hector purchases a six-pack of cola and puts it in his refrigerator for his two children. He invariably discovers that all six cans are gone on the first day. Jin also purchases a six-pack of cola once a week for his two children, but unlike Hector, he tells them that each may drink no more than three cans per week. If the children use cost-benefit analysis each time they decide whether to drink a can of cola, explain why the cola lasts much longer at Jin's house than at Hector's. *(LO4)*

10.* Suppose there is only one electric scooter company in Adriana's hometown. Currently, the company charges 20 cents per minute, and there is no fee to unlock a scooter. The scooter company is considering changing its pricing plan so that it would charge $1 to unlock a scooter and 10 cents per minute. If Adriana never takes a ride that lasts less than 10 minutes, then what will happen to the average length of her rides if the scooter company switches to the new pricing plan? Explain. *(L04)*

11.* The meal plan at University A lets students eat as much as they like for a fixed fee of $500 per semester. The average student there eats 250 pounds of food per semester. University B charges $500 for a book of meal tickets that entitles the student to eat 250 pounds of food per semester. If the student eats more than 250 pounds, he or she pays $2 for each additional pound; if the student eats less, he or she gets a $2 per pound refund. If students are rational, at which university will average food consumption be higher? Explain briefly. *(LO4)*

ANSWERS TO SELF-TESTS

1.1 The benefit of buying the wireless keyboard downtown is again $10 but the cost is now $12, so your economic surplus would be $2 smaller than if you'd bought it at the campus store. *(LO2)*

1.2 Saving $100 is $10 more valuable than saving $90, even though the percentage saved is much greater in the case of the Chicago ticket. *(LO3)*

1.3 Since you now have no alternative use for your coupon, the opportunity cost of using it to pay for the Cancun trip is zero. That means your economic surplus from the trip will be $1,350 − $1,000 = $350 > 0, so you should use your coupon and go to Cancun. *(LO3)*

1.4 The marginal benefit of the fourth launch is $9 billion, which exceeds its marginal cost of $8 billion, so the fourth launch should be added. But the fifth launch should not, because its marginal cost ($12 billion) exceeds its marginal benefit ($9 billion). *(LO3)*

1.5 If the star player takes one more shot, some other player must take one less. The fact that the star player's *average* success rate is higher than the other players' does not mean that the probability of making her *next* shot (the marginal benefit of having her shoot once more) is higher than the probability of another player making her next shot. Indeed, if the best player took all her team's shots, the other team would focus its defensive effort entirely on her, in which case letting others shoot would definitely pay. *(LO3)*

1.6 Answers will vary.

*Denotes more difficult problem.

Working with Equations, Graphs, and Tables

lthough many of the examples and most of the end-of-chapter problems in this book are quantitative, none requires mathematical skills beyond rudimentary high school algebra and geometry. In this brief appendix, we review some of the skills you'll need for dealing with these examples and problems.

One important skill is to be able to read simple verbal descriptions and translate the information they provide into the relevant equations or graphs. You'll also need to be able to translate information given in tabular form into an equation or graph, and sometimes you'll need to translate graphical information into a table or equation. Finally, you'll need to be able to solve simple systems with two equations and two unknowns. The following examples illustrate all the tools you'll need.

USING A VERBAL DESCRIPTION TO CONSTRUCT AN EQUATION

We begin with an example that shows how to construct a billing equation for a ride on an electric scooter from a verbal description of the billing plan.

| EXAMPLE 1A.1 | A Verbal Description |

equation a mathematical expression that describes the relationship between two or more variables

variable a quantity that is free to take a range of different values

dependent variable a variable in an equation whose value is determined by the value taken by another variable in the equation

independent variable a variable in an equation whose value determines the value taken by another variable in the equation

constant (or **parameter**) a quantity that is fixed in value

An electric scooter company charges \$1 to unlock a scooter plus 20 cents per minute. Write an equation that describes your bill for riding this scooter.

An **equation** is a simple mathematical expression that describes the relationship between two or more **variables,** or quantities, that are free to assume different values in some range. The most common type of equation we'll work with contains two types of variables: **dependent variables** and **independent variables.** In this example, the dependent variable is the dollar amount of your scooter bill and the independent variable is the variable on which your bill depends, namely, the number of minutes you ride the scooter. Your bill also depends on the \$1 fee to unlock the scooter and the 20 cents per minute charge. But, in this example, those amounts are **constants,** not variables. A constant, also called a **parameter,** is a quantity in an equation that is fixed in value, not free to vary. As the terms suggest, the dependent variable describes an outcome that depends on the value taken by the independent variable.

Once you've identified the dependent variable and the independent variable, choose simple symbols to represent them. In algebra courses, X is typically used to represent the independent variable and Y the dependent variable. Many people find it easier to remember what the variables stand for, however, if they choose symbols that are linked in some straightforward way to the quantities that the variables represent. Thus, in this example, we might use B to represent your scooter *bill* in dollars and T to represent the total *time* in minutes of your ride.

Having identified the relevant variables and chosen symbols to represent them, you are now in a position to write the equation that links them

$$B = 1 + 0.20T, \tag{1A.1}$$

where B is your scooter bill in dollars and T is the number of minutes you spend riding the scooter. The fee to unlock the scooter (1) and the charge per minute (0.20) are parameters in this equation. Note the importance of being clear about the units of measure. Because B represents the scooter bill in dollars, we must also express the fee to unlock the scooter and the per-minute charge in dollars, which is why the latter number appears in Equation 1A.1 as 0.20 rather than 20. Equation 1A.1 follows the normal convention in which the dependent variable appears by itself on the left-hand side while the independent variable or variables and constants appear on the right-hand side.

Once we have the equation for the scooter bill, we can use it to calculate how much you'll owe as a function of the number of minutes you spend riding. For example, if you ride the scooter for 16 minutes, you can calculate your scooter bill by simply substituting 16 minutes for T in Equation 1A.1

$$B = 1 + 0.20(16) = 4.20. \tag{1A.2}$$

Your scooter bill when you ride for 16 minutes is thus equal to $4.20.

 SELF-TEST 1A.1

Under the scooter billing plan described in Example 1A.1, how much would you owe for a 22-minute ride?

GRAPHING THE EQUATION OF A STRAIGHT LINE

The next example shows how to portray the billing plan described in Example 1A.1 as a graph.

EXAMPLE 1A.2   **Graphing an Equation**

Construct a graph that portrays the scooter billing plan described in Example 1A.1, putting your total bill, in dollars, on the vertical axis and the length of your ride, in minutes, on the horizontal axis.

The first step in responding to this instruction is the one we just took, namely, to translate the verbal description of the billing plan into an equation. When graphing an equation, the normal convention is to use the vertical axis to represent the dependent variable and the horizontal axis to represent the independent variable. In Figure 1A.1, we therefore put B on the vertical axis and T on the horizontal axis. One way to construct the graph shown in the figure is to begin by plotting the bill values that correspond to several different ride lengths. For example, someone who rides for 10 minutes would have a bill of $B = 1 + 0.20(10) = \$3$. Thus, in Figure 1A.1 the value of 10 minutes on the horizontal axis corresponds to a bill of $3 on the vertical axis (point A). Someone who rides for 15 minutes

FIGURE 1A.1

The Scooter Billing Plan in Example 1A.1.

The graph of the equation $B = 1 + 0.20T$ is the straight line shown. Its vertical intercept is 1 and its slope is 0.20.

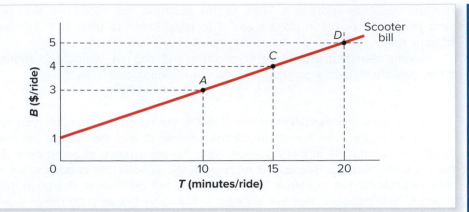

would have a bill of $B = 1 + 0.20(15) = \$4$, so the value of 15 minutes on the horizontal axis corresponds to $4 on the vertical axis (point C). Similarly, someone who rides for 20 minutes would have a bill of $B = 1 + 0.20(20) = \$5$, so the value of 20 minutes on the horizontal axis corresponds to $5 on the vertical axis (point D). The line joining these points is the graph of the billing Equation 1A.1.

As shown in Figure 1A.1, the graph of the equation $B = 1 + 0.20T$, is a straight line. The parameter 1 is the **vertical intercept** of the line—the value of B when $T = 0$, or the point at which the line intersects the vertical axis. The parameter 0.20 is the **slope** of the line, which is the ratio of the **rise** of the line to the corresponding **run**. The ratio rise/run is simply the vertical distance between any two points on the line divided by the horizontal distance between those points. For example, if we choose points A and C in Figure 1A.1, the rise is $4 - 3 = 1$ and the corresponding run is $15 - 10 = 5$, so rise/run $= 1/5 = 0.20$. More generally, for the graph of any equation $Y = a + bX$, the parameter a is the vertical intercept and the parameter b is the slope.

vertical intercept in a straight line, the value taken by the dependent variable when the independent variable equals zero

slope in a straight line, the ratio of the vertical distance the straight line travels between any two points *(rise)* to the corresponding horizontal distance *(run)*

DERIVING THE EQUATION OF A STRAIGHT LINE FROM ITS GRAPH

The next example shows how to derive the equation for a straight line from a graph of the line.

EXAMPLE 1A.3   **Deriving an Equation from a Graph**

Figure 1A.2 shows the graph of the billing plan for an electric scooter company. What is the equation for this graph? How much is the fee to unlock a scooter under this plan? How much is the charge per minute?

The slope of the line shown is the rise between any two points divided by the corresponding run. For points A and C, rise $= 3.50 - 3 = 0.50$ and run $= 15 - 10 = 5$, so the slope equals rise/run $= 0.50/5 = 0.10$. And since the horizontal intercept of the line is 2, its equation must be given by

$$B = 2 + 0.10T. \tag{1A.3}$$

Under this plan, the fee to unlock a scooter is the value of the bill when $T = 0$, which is $2. The charge per minute is the slope of the billing line, 0.10, or 10 cents per minute.

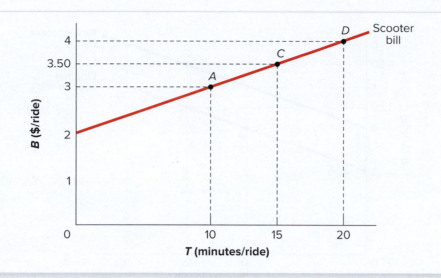

FIGURE 1A.2

Another Scooter Billing Plan.
The vertical distance between points A and C is $3.50 - 3 = 0.50$ units, and the horizontal distance between points A and C is $15 - 10 = 5$, so the slope of the line is $0.50/5 = 0.10$. The vertical intercept (the value of B when $T = 0$) is 2. So the equation for the billing plan shown is $B = 2 + 0.10T$.

✔ **SELF-TEST 1A.2**

Write the equation for the billing plan shown in the accompanying graph. How much does it cost to unlock a scooter? What is the charge per minute?

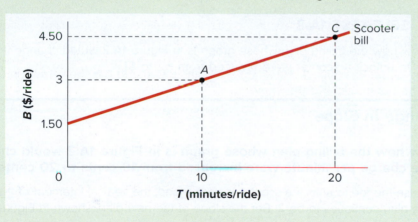

CHANGES IN THE VERTICAL INTERCEPT AND SLOPE

The next two examples and self-tests provide practice in seeing how a line shifts with a change in its vertical intercept or slope.

EXAMPLE 1A.4   **Change in Vertical Intercept**

Show how the billing plan whose graph is in Figure 1A.2 would change if the fee to unlock a scooter were increased from $2 to $3.

An increase in the fee to unlock a scooter from $2 to $3 would increase the vertical intercept of the billing plan by $1 but would leave its slope unchanged. An increase in the fee to unlock a scooter thus leads to a parallel upward shift in the billing plan by $1, as shown in Figure 1A.3. For any given number of minutes the new bill will be $1 higher than the old bill. Thus, a 10-minute ride cost $3 under the original plan (point A) but $4 under the new plan (point A'). And a 15-minute

FIGURE 1A.3

The Effect of an Increase in the Vertical Intercept.

An increase in the vertical intercept of a straight line produces an upward parallel shift in the line.

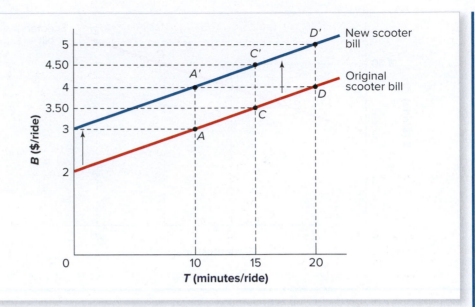

ride cost $3.50 under the original plan (point *C*), but $4.50 under the new plan (point *C'*); and a 20-minute ride cost $4 under the original plan (point *D*), but $5 under the new plan (point *D'*).

✔ SELF-TEST 1A.3

Show how the billing plan whose graph is in Figure 1A.2 would change if the fee to unlock a scooter were reduced from $2 to $1.

EXAMPLE 1A.5 | Change in Slope

Show how the billing plan whose graph is in Figure 1A.2 would change if the charge per minute were increased from 10 cents to 20 cents.

Because the fee to unlock a scooter is unchanged, the vertical intercept of the new billing plan continues to be 2. But the slope of the new plan, shown in Figure 1A.4,

FIGURE 1A.4

The Effect of an Increase in the Charge per Minute.

Because the fixed monthly fee continues to be $2, the vertical intercept of the new plan is the same as that of the original plan. With the new charge per minute of 20 cents, the slope of the billing plan rises from 0.10 to 0.20.

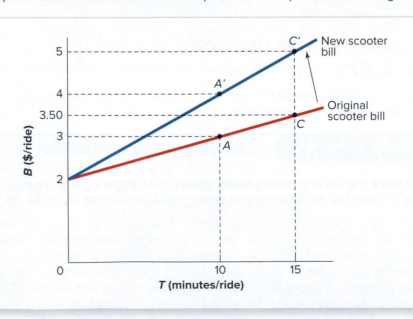

is 0.20, or twice the slope of the original plan. More generally, in the equation $Y = a + bX$, an increase in b makes the slope of the graph of the equation steeper.

 SELF-TEST 1A.4

Show how the billing plan whose graph is in Figure 1A.2 would change if the charge per minute were reduced from 10 cents to 5 cents.

Self-Test 1A.4 illustrates the general rule that in an equation $Y = a + bX$, a reduction in b makes the slope of the graph of the equation less steep.

CONSTRUCTING EQUATIONS AND GRAPHS FROM TABLES

The next example and self-test show how to transform tabular information into an equation or graph.

EXAMPLE 1A.6   Transforming a Table to a Graph

Table 1A.1 shows four points from a scooter billing equation. If all points on this billing equation lie on a straight line, find the vertical intercept of the equation and graph it. What is the fee to unlock a scooter? What is the charge per minute? Calculate the total bill for a 30-minute ride.

TABLE 1A.1
Points on a Scooter Billing Plan

Total bill ($/ride)	Length of ride (minutes/ride)
2.50	5
3.75	10
5.00	15
6.25	20

One approach to this problem is simply to plot any two points from the table on a graph. Because we are told that the billing equation is a straight line, that line must be the one that passes through any two of its points. Thus, in Figure 1A.5 we use A to denote the point from Table 1A.1 for which a bill of $3.75 corresponds to a 10-minute ride (second row) and C to denote the point for which a bill of $6.25 corresponds to a 20-minute ride (fourth row). The straight line passing through these points is the graph of the billing equation.

Unless you have a steady hand, however, or use extremely large graph paper, the method of extending a line between two points on the billing plan is unlikely to be very accurate. An alternative approach is to calculate the equation for the billing plan directly. Because the equation is a straight line, we know that it takes

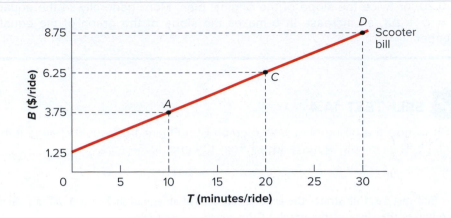

FIGURE 1A.5

Plotting the Scooter Billing Plan from a Sample of Points.

Point *A* is taken from row 2, Table 1A.1, and point *C* from row 4. The billing plan is the straight line that passes through these points.

the general form $B = f + sT$, where f is the fixed monthly fee and s is the slope. Our goal is to calculate the vertical intercept f and the slope s. From the same two points we plotted earlier, A and C, we can calculate the slope of the billing plan as $s =$ rise/run $= 2.50/10 = 0.25$.

So all that remains is to calculate f, the fee to unlock a scooter. At point C on the billing plan, the total bill is \$6.25 for 20 minutes, so we can substitute $B = 6.25$, $s = 0.25$, and $T = 20$ into the general equation $B = f + sT$ to obtain

$$6.25 = f + 0.25(20), \tag{1A.4}$$

or

$$6.25 = f + 5, \tag{1A.5}$$

which solves for $f = 1.25$. So the billing equation must be

$$B = 1.25 + 0.25T. \tag{1A.6}$$

For this billing equation, the fee to unlock a scooter is \$1.25, the charge per minute is 25 cents (\$0.25/minute), and the total bill for a 30-minute ride is $B = 1.25 + 0.25(30) = \$8.75$, just as shown in Figure 1A.5.

 SELF-TEST 1A.5

The following table shows four points from a scooter billing plan.

Total bill ($/ride)	Length of ride (minutes/ride)
2.50	5
4.25	10
6.00	15
7.75	20

If all points on this billing plan lie on a straight line, find the vertical intercept of the corresponding equation without graphing it. What is the fee to unlock a scooter? What is the charge per minute? How much would the charges be for a 30-minute ride?

SOLVING SIMULTANEOUS EQUATIONS —————————————

The next example and self-test demonstrate how to proceed when you need to solve two equations with two unknowns.

EXAMPLE 1A.7   **Solving Simultaneous Equations**

Suppose you are trying to choose between two electric scooter companies, each with a different pricing plan. If you choose Company 1, your charges will be computed according to the equation

$$B = 0.50 + 0.30T, \tag{1A.7}$$

where B is again your bill in dollars and T is the length of your ride in minutes. If you choose Company 2, your bill will be computed according to the equation

$$B = 2 + 0.15T. \tag{1A.8}$$

How many minutes long would your ride have to be to make Company 2 cheaper?

Company 1 has the attractive feature of a relatively low fee to unlock a scooter, but also the unattractive feature of a relatively high rate per minute. In contrast, Company 2 has a relatively high fee to unlock a scooter but a relatively low rate per minute. Someone who wanted to make a short ride (for example, 4 minutes) would do better under Company 1 (bill = $1.70) than under Company 2 (bill = $2.60) because the low fee to unlock a scooter for Company 1 would more than compensate for its higher rate per minute. Conversely, someone who wanted to make a long ride (say, 15 minutes) would do better under Company 2 (bill = $4.25) than under Company 1 (bill = $5.00) because Company 2's lower rate per minute would more than compensate for its higher fee to unlock a scooter.

Our task here is to find the break-even ride length, which is ride length for which the bill is the same under the two plans. One way to answer this question is to graph the two billing plans and see where they cross. At that crossing point, the two equations are satisfied simultaneously, which means that the length of the rides will be the same, as will the bills.

In Figure 1A.6, we see that the graphs of the two plans cross at A, where both yield a bill of $3.50 for a 10-minute ride. The break-even ride length for these two

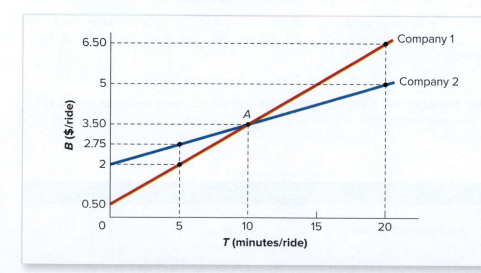

FIGURE 1A.6

The Break-Even Volume of Ride Length.

For 10-minute rides, your bill will be the same under both plans. For longer rides, Company 2 is cheaper; Company 1 is cheaper for shorter rides.

companies is thus 10 minutes. If the length of your ride is longer than that, you will save money by choosing Company 2. For example, if you take a 20-minute ride, your bill under Company 2 ($5) will be $1.50 cheaper than under Company 1 ($6.50). Conversely, if you ride for less than 10 minutes, you will do better under Company 1. For example, if you take a 5-minute ride, your bill under Company 1 ($2) will be 75 cents cheaper than under Company 2 ($2.75). For 10-minute rides, the two companies cost exactly the same ($3.50).

The question posed here also may be answered algebraically. As in the graphical approach just discussed, our goal is to find the point (T, B) that satisfies both billing equations simultaneously. As a first step, we rewrite the two billing equations, one on top of the other, as follows:

$$B = 0.50 + 0.30T \qquad \text{(Company 1).}$$
$$B = 2 + 0.15T \qquad \text{(Company 2).}$$

As you'll recall from high school algebra, if we subtract the terms from each side of one equation from the corresponding terms of the other equation, the resulting differences must be equal. So if we subtract the terms on each side of the Company 2 equation from the corresponding terms in the Company 1 equation, we get:

$$B = 0.50 + 0.30T \qquad \text{(Company 1).}$$
$$-B = -2 - 0.15T \qquad \text{(−Company 2).}$$
$$\overline{}$$
$$0 = -1.5 + 0.15T \qquad \text{(Company 1 − Company 2).}$$

Finally, we solve the last equation (Company 1 − Company 2) to get $T = 10$.

Plugging $T = 10$ into either plan's equation, we then find $B = 3.50$. For example, Company 1's equation yields $0.5 + 0.30(10) = 3.50$, as does Company 2's $2 + 0.15(10) = 3.50$.

Because the point $(T, B) = (10, 3.50)$ lies on the equations for both plans simultaneously, the algebraic approach just described is often called the *method of simultaneous equations*.

 SELF-TEST 1A.6

Suppose you are trying to choose between two electric scooter companies. If you choose Company 1, your bill will be computed according to the equation

$$B = 0.20 + 0.40T \qquad \text{(Company 1),}$$

where B is again your bill in dollars and T is the length of your ride in minutes. If you choose Company 2, your bill will be computed according to the equation

$$B = 5 + 0.10T \qquad \text{(Company 2).}$$

Use the algebraic approach described in the preceding example to find the break-even ride length for these plans.

KEY TERMS

constant or parameter	independent variable	slope
dependent variable	rise	variable
equation	run	vertical intercept

ANSWERS TO APPENDIX SELF-TESTS

1A.1 To calculate your bill for a 22-minute ride, substitute 22 minutes for T in Equation 1A.1 to get $B = 1 + 0.20(22) = \$5.40$.

1A.2 Calculating the slope using points A and C, we have rise $= 4.50 - 3 = 1.50$ and run $= 20 - 10 = 10$, so rise/run $= 1.5/10 = 0.15$. And since the horizontal intercept of the line is 1.5, its equation is $B = 1.5 + 0.15T$. Under this plan, the fee to unlock a scooter is \$1.50 and the charge per minute is the slope of the billing line, 0.15, or 15 cents per minute.

1A.3 A \$1 reduction in the fee to unlock a scooter would produce a downward parallel shift in the billing plan by \$1.

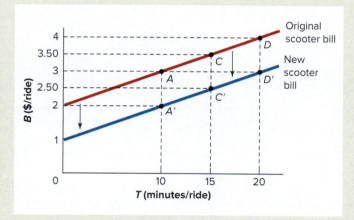

1A.4 With the fee to unlock a scooter unchanged, the vertical intercept of the new billing plan continues to be 2. The slope of the new plan is 0.05, half the slope of the original plan.

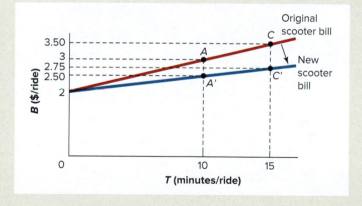

1A.5 Let the billing equation be $B = f + sT$, where f is the fee to unlock a scooter and s is the slope. From the first two points in the table, calculate the slope $s = $ rise/run $= 1.75/5 = 0.35$. To calculate f, we can use the information in row 1 of the table to write the billing equation as $2.50 = f + 0.35(5)$ and solve for $f = 0.75$. So the billing equation must be $B = 0.75 + 0.35T$. For this billing equation, the fee to unlock a scooter is 75 cents, the charge per minute is 35 cents, and the total bill for a 30-minute ride is $B = 0.75 + 0.35(30) = \$11.25$.

1A.6 Subtracting the Company 2 equation from the Company 1 equation yields the equation

$$0 = -4.8 + 0.30T \qquad (\text{Company 1} - \text{Company 2}),$$

which solves for $T = 16$. So if you ride for more than 16 minutes, you'll do better with Company 2.

CHAPTER 2

Comparative Advantage

Jason Patrick Ross/Shutterstock

Always pick the low-hanging fruit first.

LEARNING OBJECTIVES

After reading this chapter, you should be able to:

LO1 Explain and apply the *Principle of Comparative Advantage* and explain how it differs from absolute advantage.

LO2 Explain and apply the *Principle of Increasing Opportunity Cost* (also called the *Low-Hanging-Fruit Principle*). Use a production possibilities curve to illustrate opportunity cost and comparative advantage.

LO3 Identify factors that shift the menu of production possibilities.

LO4 Explain the role of comparative advantage in international trade and describe why some jobs are more vulnerable to outsourcing than others.

During a stint as a Peace Corps volunteer in rural Nepal, a young economic naturalist employed a cook named Birkhaman, who came from a remote Himalayan village in neighboring Bhutan. Although Birkhaman had virtually no formal education, he was spectacularly resourceful. His primary duties, to prepare food and maintain the kitchen, he performed extremely well. But he also had other skills. He could thatch a roof, butcher a goat, and repair shoes. An able tinsmith and a good carpenter, he could sew and fix a broken alarm clock, as well as plaster walls. And he was a local authority on home remedies.

Birkhaman's range of skills was broad even in Nepal, where the least-skilled villager could perform a wide range of services that most Americans hire others to perform. Why this difference in skills and employment?

One might be tempted to answer that the Nepalese are simply too poor to hire others to perform these services. Nepal is indeed a poor country, whose income per person is less than one one-sixtieth that of the United States. Few Nepalese have spare cash to spend on outside services. But as reasonable as this poverty explanation may seem, the reverse is actually the case. The Nepalese do not perform their own services because they are poor; rather, they are poor largely *because* they perform their own services.

The alternative to a system in which everyone is a jack-of-all-trades is one in which people *specialize* in particular goods and services and then satisfy their needs by trading among themselves. Economic systems based on specialization and the exchange of goods and services are generally far more productive than those with little specialization. Our task in this chapter is to investigate why this is so.

As this chapter will show, the reason that specialization is so productive is *comparative advantage*. Roughly, a person has a comparative advantage at producing a particular good or service (say, haircuts) if that person is *relatively* more efficient at producing haircuts than at producing other goods or services. We will see that we can all have more of *every* good and service if each of us specializes in the activities at which we have a comparative advantage.

Did this man perform most of his own services because he was poor, or was he poor because he performed most of his own services?

This chapter also will introduce the *production possibilities curve*, which is a graphical method of describing the combinations of goods and services that an economy can produce. This tool will allow us to see more clearly how specialization enhances the productive capacity of even the simplest economy.

EXCHANGE AND OPPORTUNITY COST

Scarcity ▷▷

The Scarcity Principle (see Chapter 1, *Thinking Like an Economist*) reminds us that the opportunity cost of spending more time on any one activity is having less time available to spend on others. As the following example makes clear, this principle helps explain why everyone can do better by concentrating on those activities at which he or she performs best relative to others.

EXAMPLE 2.1	Scarcity Principle

Should Kelly Wearstler design her own web page?

Kelly Wearstler is among the most famous and influential interior designers in the United States today. She has received numerous accolades for her commercial and residential design work, has completed projects for top celebrities such as Cameron Diaz, Gwen Stefani, and Ben Stiller, and boasts more than 700,000 followers on Instagram.

Although Kelly devotes most of her time and talent to interior design, she is well equipped to do a broad range of other design work. Suppose Kelly could design her own web page in 300 hours, half the time it would take any other web designer. Does that mean that Kelly should design her own web page?

Suppose that on the strength of her talents as an interior designer, Kelly earns more than $1 million a year, implying that the opportunity cost of any time she spent designing her web page would be over $500 per hour. Kelly would have little difficulty engaging a highly qualified web designer whose hourly wage is considerably less than $500 per hour. So even though Kelly's substantial skills might enable her to design her web page more quickly than most web designers, it would not be in her interest to do so.

Should Kelly Wearstler design her own web page?

In Example 2.1, economists would say that Wearstler has an **absolute advantage** at designing her web page but a **comparative advantage** at interior design. She has an absolute advantage at designing her web page because she can perform that task in less time than a web designer could. Even so, the web designer has a comparative advantage at designing web pages because his or her opportunity cost of performing that task is lower than Wearstler's.

Example 2.1 makes the implicit assumption that Wearstler would be equally happy to spend an hour designing her web page or working on an interior design project. But suppose she is tired of interior design work and feels it might be enjoyable to try her hand at web design. Designing her own web page might then make perfect sense! But unless she expects to gain extra satisfaction from performing that task, she almost certainly will do better to hire a web designer. The web designer will also benefit, or else he or she wouldn't have offered to design web pages for the stated price.

THE PRINCIPLE OF COMPARATIVE ADVANTAGE

One of the most important insights of modern economics is that when two people (or two nations) have different opportunity costs of performing various tasks, they can always increase the total value of available goods and services by trading with one another. The following example captures the logic behind this insight.

absolute advantage one person has an absolute advantage over another if he or she takes fewer hours to perform a task than the other person

comparative advantage one person has a comparative advantage over another if his or her opportunity cost of performing a task is lower than the other person's opportunity cost

---

EXAMPLE 2.2 | **Comparative Advantage**

Should Ana update her own web page?

Consider a small community in which Ana is the only professional bicycle mechanic and Xin is the only professional web designer. If the amount of time for each of them to update a web page and repair a bicycle is as shown in Table 2.1, and if each regards the two tasks as equally pleasant (or unpleasant), does the fact that Ana can update a web page faster than Xin imply that Ana should update her own web page?

TABLE 2.1
Productivity Information for Ana and Xin

	Time to update a web page	Time to complete a bicycle repair
Ana	20 minutes	10 minutes
Xin	30 minutes	30 minutes

The entries in the table show that Ana has an absolute advantage over Xin in both activities. While Ana, the mechanic, needs only 20 minutes to update a web page, Xin, the web designer, needs 30 minutes. Ana's advantage over Xin is even greater when the task is fixing bikes: She can complete a repair in only 10 minutes, compared to Xin's 30 minutes.

But the fact that Ana is a better web designer than Xin does *not* imply that Ana should update her own web page. Xin has a comparative advantage over Ana at web design: She is *relatively* more productive at updating a web page than Ana. Similarly, Ana has a comparative advantage in bicycle repair. (Remember that a person has a comparative advantage at a given task if his or her opportunity cost of performing that task is lower than another person's.)

What is Xin's opportunity cost of updating a web page? Because she takes 30 minutes to update each page—the same amount of time she takes to fix a bicycle—her opportunity cost of updating a web page is one bicycle repair. In other words, by taking the time to update a web page, Xin is effectively giving up the opportunity to do one bicycle repair. Ana, in contrast, can complete two bicycle repairs in the time she takes to update a single web page. For her, the opportunity cost of updating a web page is two bicycle repairs. Ana's opportunity cost to update a web page, measured in terms of bicycle repairs forgone, is twice as high as Xin's. Thus, Xin has a comparative advantage at web design.

The interesting and important implication of the opportunity cost comparison summarized in Table 2.2 is that the total number of bicycle repairs and web updates accomplished if Xin and Ana both spend part of their time at each activity will always be smaller than the number accomplished if each specializes in the activity in which she has a comparative advantage. Suppose, for example, that people in their community demand a total of 16 web page updates per day. If Ana spent half her time updating web pages and the other half repairing bicycles, an 8-hour workday would yield 12 web page updates and 24 bicycle repairs. To complete the remaining 4 updates, Xin would have to spend 2 hours web designing, which would leave her 6 hours to repair bicycles. And because she takes 30 minutes to do each repair, she would have time to complete 12 of them. So when the two women try to be jacks-of-all-trades, they end up completing a total of 16 web page updates and 36 bicycle repairs.

TABLE 2.2
Opportunity Costs for Ana and Xin

	Opportunity cost of updating a web page	Opportunity cost of a bicycle repair
Ana	2 bicycle repairs	0.5 web page update
Xin	1 bicycle repair	1 web page update

Consider what would have happened had each woman specialized in her activity of comparative advantage. Xin could have updated 16 web pages on her own and Ana could have performed 48 bicycle repairs. Specialization would have created an additional 12 bicycle repairs out of thin air.

When computing the opportunity cost of one good in terms of another, we must pay close attention to the form in which the productivity information is presented. In Example 2.2, we were told how many minutes each person needed to perform each task. Alternatively, we might be told how many units of each task each person can perform in an hour. Work through the following self-test to see how to proceed when information is presented in this alternative format.

 SELF-TEST 2.1

Should Miguel update his own web page?

Consider a small community in which Miguel is the only professional bicycle mechanic and Monique is the only professional web designer. If their productivity rates at the two tasks are as shown in the table, and if each regards the two tasks as equally pleasant (or unpleasant), does the fact that Miguel can update a web page faster than Monique imply that Miguel should update her own web page?

	Productivity in web design	Productivity in bicycle repair
Monique	2 web page updates per hour	1 repair per hour
Miguel	3 web page updates per hour	3 repairs per hour

The principle illustrated by the preceding examples is so important that we state it formally as one of the core principles of the course:

The Principle of Comparative Advantage: Everyone does best when each person (or each country) concentrates on the activities for which his or her opportunity cost is lowest.

Comparative Advantage

Indeed, the gains made possible from specialization based on comparative advantage constitute the rationale for market exchange. They explain why each person does not devote 10 percent of his or her time to producing cars, 5 percent to growing food, 25 percent to building housing, 0.0001 percent to performing brain surgery, and so on. By concentrating on those tasks at which we are relatively most productive, together we can produce vastly more than if we all tried to be self-sufficient.

This insight brings us back to Birkhaman the cook. Though Birkhaman's versatility was marvelous, he was neither as good a doctor as someone who has been trained in medical school, nor as good a repair person as someone who spends each day fixing things. If a number of people with Birkhaman's native talents had joined together, each of them specializing in one or two tasks, together they would have enjoyed more and better goods and services than each could possibly have produced independently. Although there is much to admire in the resourcefulness of people who have learned through necessity to rely on their own skills, that path is no route to economic prosperity.

Specialization and its effects provide ample grist for the economic naturalist. Here's an example from the world of sports.

The Economic Naturalist 2.1

Where have all the .400 hitters gone?

In baseball, a .400 hitter is a player who averages at least four hits every 10 times he comes to bat. Though never common in professional baseball, .400 hitters used to appear relatively frequently. Early in the twentieth century, for example, a player known as Wee Willie Keeler batted .432, meaning that he got a hit in over 43 percent of his times at bat. But since Ted Williams of the Boston Red Sox batted .406 in 1941, there hasn't been a single .400 hitter in the major leagues. Why not?

Why has no major league baseball player batted .400 since Ted Williams did it more than half a century ago?

Some baseball buffs argue that the disappearance of the .400 hitter means today's baseball players are not as good as yesterday's. But that claim does not withstand close examination. For example, today's players are bigger, stronger, and faster than those of Willie Keeler's day. (Wee Willie himself was just a little over 5 feet 4 inches and weighed only 140 pounds.)

Bill James, a leading analyst of baseball history, argues that the .400 hitter has disappeared because the quality of play in the major leagues has *improved*, not declined. In particular, pitching and fielding standards are higher, which makes batting .400 more difficult.

Why has the quality of play in baseball improved? Although there are many reasons, including better nutrition, training, and equipment, specialization also has played an important role.[1] At one time, pitchers were expected to pitch for the entire game. Now pitching staffs include pitchers who specialize in starting the game ("starters"), others who specialize in pitching two or three innings in the middle of the game ("middle relievers"), and still others who specialize in pitching only the last inning ("closers"). Each of these roles requires different skills and tactics. Pitchers also may specialize in facing left-handed or right-handed batters, in striking batters out, or in getting

---

[1]For an interesting discussion of specialization and the decline of the .400 hitter from the perspective of an evolutionary biologist, see Stephen Jay Gould, *Full House* (New York: Three Rivers Press, 1996), part 3.

batters to hit balls on the ground. Similarly, few fielders today play multiple defensive positions; most specialize in only one. Some players specialize in defense (to the detriment of their hitting skills); these "defensive specialists" can be brought in late in the game to protect a lead. Even in managing and coaching, specialization has increased markedly. Relief pitchers now have their own coaches, and statistical specialists use computers to discover the weaknesses of opposing hitters. The net result of these increases in specialization is that even the weakest of today's teams play highly competent defensive baseball. With no "weaklings" to pick on, hitting .400 over an entire season has become a near-impossible task.

▶ Visit your instructor's Connect course and access your eBook to view this video.

Why are many products designed in one place yet assembled in another?

SOURCES OF COMPARATIVE ADVANTAGE

At the individual level, comparative advantage often appears to be the result of inborn talent. For instance, some people seem to be naturally gifted at programming computers while others seem to have a special knack for fixing bikes. But comparative advantage is more often the result of education, training, or experience. Thus, we usually leave the design of kitchens to people with architectural training, the drafting of contracts to people who have studied law, and the teaching of physics to people with advanced degrees in that field.

At the national level, comparative advantage may derive from differences in natural resources or from differences in society or culture. The United States, which has a disproportionate share of the world's leading research universities, has a comparative advantage in the design of electronic computing hardware and software. Canada, which has one of the world's highest per-capita endowments of farm and forest land, has a comparative advantage in the production of agricultural products. Topography and climate explain why Colorado specializes in the skiing industry while Hawaii specializes as an ocean resort.

Seemingly noneconomic factors also can give rise to comparative advantage. For instance, the emergence of English as the de facto world language gives English-speaking countries a comparative advantage over non-English-speaking nations in the production of books, movies, and popular music. Even a country's institutions may affect the likelihood that it will achieve comparative advantage in a particular pursuit. For example, cultures that encourage entrepreneurship will tend to have a comparative advantage in the introduction of new products, whereas those that promote high standards of care and craftsmanship will tend to have a comparative advantage in the production of high-quality variants of established products.

The Economic Naturalist 2.2

What happened to the U.S. lead in the television market?

Why was the United States unable to remain competitive as a manufacturer of televisions and other electronic equipment?

Televisions were developed and first produced in the United States, but today this country accounts for only a minuscule share of the total world production of TVs. The early lead is explained in part by this country's comparative advantage in technological research, which in turn was supported by the country's outstanding system of higher education. Other contributing factors were high expenditures on the development of electronic components for the military and a culture that actively encourages entrepreneurship. As for the production of these products, the United States enjoyed an early advantage partly because the product designs were themselves evolving rapidly at first, which favored production facilities located in close proximity to the product designers. Early production techniques also relied intensively on skilled labor, which is abundant in the United States. In time, however, product designs stabilized and many of the more complex manufacturing operations were automated. Both of these changes gradually led to greater reliance on relatively less-skilled production workers. And at that point, factories located in high-wage countries like the United States could no longer compete with those located in low-wage areas overseas.

EXCHANGE AND OPPORTUNITY COST

Gains from exchange are possible if trading partners have comparative advantages in producing different goods and services. You have a comparative advantage in producing, say, web pages if your opportunity cost of producing a web page—measured in terms of other production opportunities forgone—is smaller than the corresponding opportunity costs of your trading partners. Maximum production is achieved if each person specializes in producing the good or service in which he or she has the lowest opportunity cost (the *Principle of Comparative Advantage*). Comparative advantage makes specialization worthwhile even if one trading partner is more productive than others, in absolute terms, in every activity.

COMPARATIVE ADVANTAGE AND PRODUCTION POSSIBILITIES

Comparative advantage and specialization allow an economy to produce more than if each person tries to produce a little of everything. In this section, we gain further insight into the advantages of specialization by introducing a graph that can be used to describe the various combinations of goods and services that an economy can produce.

THE PRODUCTION POSSIBILITIES CURVE

We begin with a hypothetical economy in which only two goods are produced: coffee and pine nuts. It's a small island economy and "production" consists either of picking coffee beans that grow on small bushes on the island's central valley floor or of gathering pine nuts that fall from trees on the steep hillsides overlooking the valley. The more time workers spend picking coffee, the less time they have available for gathering nuts. So if people want to drink more coffee, they must make do with a smaller amount of nuts.

If we know how productive workers are at each activity, we can summarize the various combinations of coffee and nuts they can produce each day. This menu of possibilities is known as the **production possibilities curve (PPC).**

To keep matters simple, we begin with an example in which the economy has only a single worker, who can divide her time between the two activities.

production possibilities curve (PPC) a graph that describes the maximum amount of one good that can be produced for every possible level of production of the other good

---

EXAMPLE 2.3	**Production Possibilities Curve**

What is the production possibilities curve for an economy in which Krisha is the only worker?

Consider a society consisting only of Krisha, who allocates her production time between coffee and nuts. She has nimble fingers, a quality that makes her more productive at picking coffee than at gathering nuts. She can gather 2 pounds of nuts or pick 4 pounds of coffee in an hour. If she works a total of 6 hours per day, describe her production possibilities curve—the graph that displays, for each level of nut production, the maximum amount of coffee that she can pick.

The vertical axis in Figure 2.1 shows Krisha's daily production of coffee and the horizontal axis shows her daily production of nuts. Let's begin by looking at two extreme allocations of her time. First, suppose she employs her entire workday (6 hours) picking coffee. In that case, since she can pick 4 pounds of coffee per hour, she would pick 24 pounds per day of coffee and gather zero pounds of nuts. That combination of coffee and nut production is represented by point *A* in Figure 2.1. It is the vertical intercept of Krisha's production possibilities curve.

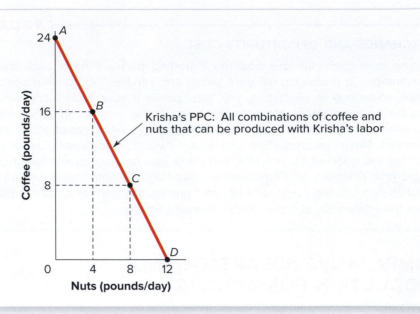

Krisha's PPC: All combinations of coffee and nuts that can be produced with Krisha's labor

Now suppose, instead, that Krisha devotes all her time to gathering nuts. Since she can gather 2 pounds of nuts per hour, her total daily production would be 12 pounds of nuts. That combination is represented by point *D* in Figure 2.1, the horizontal intercept of Krisha's PPC. Because Krisha's production of each good is exactly proportional to the amount of time she devotes to that good, the remaining points along her PPC will lie on the straight line that joins *A* and *D*.

For example, suppose that Krisha devotes 4 hours each day to picking coffee and 2 hours to gathering nuts. She will then end up with (4 hours/day) × (4 pounds/hour) = 16 pounds of coffee per day and (2 hours/day) × (2 pounds/hour) = 4 pounds of nuts. This is the point labeled *B* in Figure 2.1. Alternatively, if she devotes 2 hours to coffee and 4 hours to nuts, she will get (2 hours/day) × (4 pounds/hour) = 8 pounds of coffee per day and (4 hours/day) × (2 pounds/hour) = 8 pounds of nuts. This alternative combination is represented by point *C* in Figure 2.1.

Because Krisha's PPC is a straight line, its slope is constant. The absolute value of the slope of Krisha's PPC is the ratio of its vertical intercept to its horizontal intercept: (24 pounds of coffee/day)/(12 pounds of nuts/day) = (2 pounds of coffee)/(1 pound of nuts). (Be sure to keep track of the units of measure on each axis when computing this ratio.) *This ratio means that Krisha's opportunity cost of an additional pound of nuts is 2 pounds of coffee.*

Note that Krisha's opportunity cost (*OC*) of nuts can also be expressed as the following simple formula:

$$OC_{nuts} = \frac{\text{loss in coffee}}{\text{gain in nuts}}, \tag{2.1}$$

where "loss in coffee" means the amount of coffee given up and "gain in nuts" means the corresponding increase in nuts. Likewise, Krisha's opportunity cost of coffee is expressed by this formula:

$$OC_{coffee} = \frac{\text{loss in nuts}}{\text{gain in coffee}}. \tag{2.2}$$

To say that Krisha's opportunity cost of an additional pound of nuts is 2 pounds of coffee is thus equivalent to saying that her opportunity cost of a pound of coffee is ½ pound of nuts.

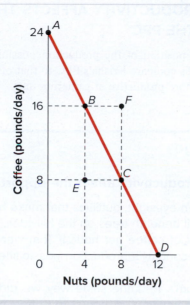

FIGURE 2.2

Attainable and Efficient Points on Krisha's Production Possibilities Curve.

Points that lie either along the production possibilities curve (for example, *A*, *B*, *C*, and *D*) or within it (for example, *E*) are said to be attainable. Points that lie outside the production possibilities curve (for example, *F*) are unattainable. Points that lie along the curve are said to be efficient, while those that lie within the curve are said to be inefficient.

The downward slope of the production possibilities curve shown in Figure 2.1 illustrates the Scarcity Principle—the idea that because our resources are limited, having more of one good thing generally means having to settle for less of another (see Chapter 1, *Thinking Like an Economist*). Krisha can have an additional pound of coffee if she wishes, but only if she is willing to give up half a pound of nuts. If Krisha is the only person in the economy, her opportunity cost of producing a good becomes, in effect, its price. Thus, the price she has to pay for an additional pound of coffee is half a pound of nuts, or the price she has to pay for an additional pound of nuts is 2 pounds of coffee.

Scarcity

Any point that lies either along the production possibilities curve or within it is said to be an **attainable point,** meaning that it can be produced with currently available resources. In Figure 2.2, for example, points *A, B, C, D,* and *E* are attainable points. Points that lie outside the production possibilities curve are said to be **unattainable,** meaning that they cannot be produced using currently available resources. In Figure 2.2, *F* is an unattainable point because Krisha cannot pick 16 pounds of coffee per day *and* gather 8 pounds of nuts. Points that lie within the curve are said to be **inefficient,** in the sense that existing resources would allow for production of more of at least one good without sacrificing the production of any other good. At *E,* for example, Krisha is picking only 8 pounds of coffee per day and gathering 4 pounds of nuts. This means that she could increase her coffee harvest by 8 pounds per day without giving up any nuts (by moving from *E* to *B*). Alternatively, Krisha could gather as many as 4 additional pounds of nuts each day without giving up any coffee (by moving from *E* to *C*). An **efficient point** is one that lies along the production possibilities curve. At any such point, more of one good can be produced only by producing less of the other.

attainable point any combination of goods that can be produced using currently available resources

unattainable point any combination of goods that cannot be produced using currently available resources

inefficient point any combination of goods for which currently available resources enable an increase in the production of one good without a reduction in the production of the other

efficient point any combination of goods for which currently available resources do not allow an increase in the production of one good without a reduction in the production of the other

✔ **SELF-TEST 2.2**

For the PPC shown in Figure 2.2, state whether the following points are attainable and/or efficient:

a.   20 pounds per day of coffee, 4 pounds per day of nuts.

b.   12 pounds per day of coffee, 6 pounds per day of nuts.

c.   4 pounds per day of coffee, 8 pounds per day of nuts.

HOW INDIVIDUAL PRODUCTIVITY AFFECTS THE SLOPE AND POSITION OF THE PPC

To see how the slope and position of the production possibilities curve depend on an individual's productivity, let's compare Krisha's PPC to that of Tom's, who is less productive at picking coffee but more productive at gathering nuts.

| EXAMPLE 2.4 | Productivity Changes |

How do changes in productivity affect the opportunity cost of nuts?

Tom is short and has keen eyesight, qualities that make him especially well suited for gathering nuts that fall beneath trees on the hillsides. He can gather 4 pounds of nuts or pick 2 pounds of coffee per hour. If Tom were the only person in the economy, describe the economy's production possibilities curve.

We can construct Tom's PPC the same way we did Krisha's. Note first that if Tom devotes an entire workday (6 hours) to coffee picking, he ends up with (6 hours/day) × (2 pounds/hour) = 12 pounds of coffee per day and zero pounds of nuts. So the vertical intercept of Tom's PPC is *A* in Figure 2.3. If instead he devotes all his time to gathering nuts, he gets (6 hours/day) × (4 pounds/hour) = 24 pounds of nuts per day and no coffee. That means the horizontal intercept of his PPC is *D* in Figure 2.3. Because Tom's production of each good is proportional to the amount of time he devotes to it, the remaining points on his PPC will lie along the straight line that joins these two extreme points.

For example, if he devotes 4 hours each day to picking coffee and 2 hours to gathering nuts, he'll end up with (4 hours/day) × (2 pounds/hour) = 8 pounds of coffee per day and (2 hours/day) × (4 pounds/hour) = 8 pounds of nuts per day. This is the point labeled *B* in Figure 2.3. Alternatively, if he devotes 2 hours to coffee and 4 hours to nuts, he'll get (2 hours/day) × (2 pounds/hour) = 4 pounds of coffee per day and (4 hours/day) × (4 pounds/hour) = 16 pounds of nuts. This alternative combination is represented by point *C* in Figure 2.3.

How does Tom's PPC compare with Krisha's? Note in Figure 2.4 that because Tom is absolutely less productive than Krisha at picking coffee, the vertical intercept of his PPC lies closer to the origin than Krisha's. By the same token, because Krisha is absolutely less productive than Tom at gathering nuts, the horizontal intercept of her PPC lies closer to the origin than Tom's. For Tom, the opportunity cost of an additional pound of nuts is ½ pound of coffee, which is one-fourth

FIGURE 2.3

Tom's Production Possibilities Curve.

Tom's opportunity cost of producing 1 pound of nuts is only ½ pound of coffee.

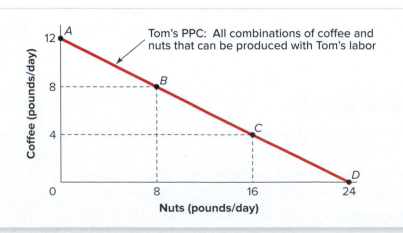

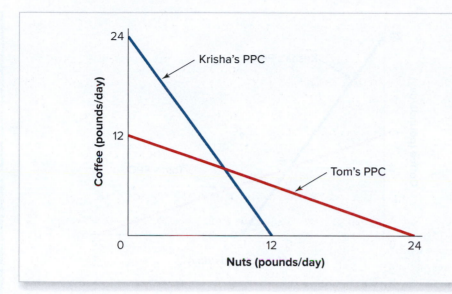

FIGURE 2.4

Individual Production Possibilities Curves Compared.
Tom is less productive in coffee than Krisha, but more productive in nuts.

Krisha's opportunity cost of nuts. This difference in opportunity costs shows up as a difference in the slopes of their PPCs: The absolute value of the slope of Tom's PPC is ½, whereas Krisha's is 2.

In this example, Tom has both an absolute advantage and a comparative advantage over Krisha in gathering nuts. Krisha, for her part, has both an absolute advantage and a comparative advantage over Tom in picking coffee.

We cannot emphasize strongly enough that the principle of comparative advantage is a relative concept—one that makes sense only when the productivities of two or more people (or countries) are being compared.

 SELF-TEST 2.3

Suppose Krisha can pick 2 pounds of coffee per hour or gather 4 pounds of nuts per hour; Tom can pick 1 pound of coffee per hour and gather 1 pound of nuts per hour. What is Krisha's opportunity cost of gathering a pound of nuts? What is Tom's opportunity cost of gathering a pound of nuts? Where does Krisha's comparative advantage now lie?

THE GAINS FROM SPECIALIZATION AND EXCHANGE

Earlier we saw that a comparative advantage arising from disparities in individual opportunity costs creates gains for everyone (see Examples 2.1 and 2.2). The following example shows how the same point can be illustrated using production possibility curves.

EXAMPLE 2.5   **Specialization**

How costly is failure to specialize?

Suppose that in Example 2.4 Krisha and Tom had divided their time so that each person's output consisted of half nuts and half coffee. How much of each good would Tom and Krisha have been able to consume? How much could they have consumed if each had specialized in the activity for which he or she enjoyed a comparative advantage?

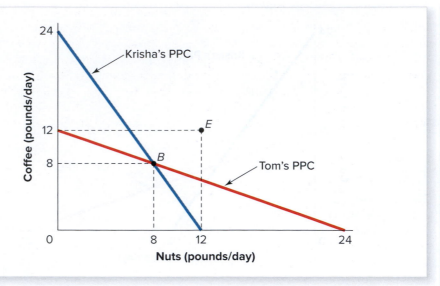

Because Tom can produce twice as many pounds of nuts in an hour as pounds of coffee, to produce equal quantities of each, he must spend 2 hours picking coffee for every hour he devotes to gathering nuts. And since he works a 6-hour day, that means spending 2 hours gathering nuts and 4 hours picking coffee. Dividing his time in this way, he'll end up with 8 pounds of coffee per day and 8 pounds of nuts. Similarly, since Krisha can produce twice as many pounds of coffee in an hour as pounds of nuts, to pick equal quantities of each, she must spend 2 hours gathering nuts for every hour she devotes to picking coffee. And because she too works a 6-hour day, that means spending 2 hours picking coffee and 4 hours gathering nuts. So, like Tom, she'll end up with 8 pounds of coffee per day and 8 pounds of nuts. (See Figure 2.5.) Their combined daily production will thus be 16 pounds of each good. By contrast, had they each specialized in their respective activities of comparative advantage, their combined daily production would have been 24 pounds of each good.

If they exchange coffee and nuts with one another, each can consume a combination of the two goods that would have been unattainable if exchange had not been possible. For example, Krisha can give Tom 12 pounds of coffee in exchange for 12 pounds of nuts, enabling each to consume 4 pounds per day more of each good than when each produced and consumed alone. Note that point E in Figure 2.5, which has 12 pounds per day of each good, lies beyond each person's PPC, yet is easily attainable with specialization and exchange.

As the following self-test illustrates, the gains from specialization grow larger as the difference in opportunity costs increases.

 SELF-TEST 2.4

How do differences in opportunity cost affect the gains from specialization?

Krisha can pick 5 pounds of coffee or gather 1 pound of nuts in an hour. Tom can pick 1 pound of coffee or gather 5 pounds of nuts in an hour. Assuming they again work 6-hour days and want to consume coffee and nuts in equal quantities, by how much will specialization increase their consumption compared to the alternative in which each produced only for his or her own consumption?

Although the gains from specialization and exchange grow with increases in the differences in opportunity costs among trading partners, these differences alone still seem insufficient to account for the enormous differences in living standards between rich and poor countries. Average income in the 20 richest countries in the year 2019, for example, was over $60,000 per person, compared to roughly $600 per person in the 20 poorest countries.[2] Although we will say more later about specialization's role in explaining these differences, we first discuss how to construct the PPC for an entire economy and examine how factors other than specialization might cause it to shift outward over time.

A PRODUCTION POSSIBILITIES CURVE FOR A MANY-PERSON ECONOMY

Although most actual economies consist of millions of workers, the process of constructing a production possibilities curve for an economy of that size is really no different from the process for a one-person economy. Consider again an economy in which the only two goods are coffee and nuts, with coffee again on the vertical axis and nuts on the horizontal axis. The vertical intercept of the economy's PPC is the total amount of coffee that could be picked if all available workers worked full time picking coffee. Thus, the maximum attainable amount of coffee production is shown for the hypothetical economy in Figure 2.6 as 100,000 pounds per day (an amount chosen arbitrarily, for illustrative purposes). The horizontal intercept of the PPC is the amount of nuts that could be gathered if all available workers worked full time gathering nuts, shown for this same economy as 80,000 pounds per day (also an amount chosen arbitrarily). But note that the PPC shown in the diagram is not a straight line—as in the earlier examples involving only a single worker—but rather a curve that is bowed out from the origin.

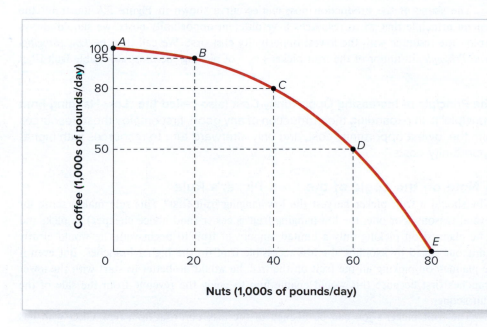

FIGURE 2.6

Production Possibilities Curve for a Large Economy.

For an economy with millions of workers, the PPC typically has a gentle outward bow shape.

[2]The 20 richest countries tracked by the International Monetary Fund: Australia, Austria, Belgium, Canada, Denmark, Finland, France, Germany, Iceland, Ireland, Luxembourg, Netherlands, Norway, Qatar, San Marino, Singapore, Sweden, Switzerland, United Kingdom, and United States. The 20 poorest countries tracked by the International Monetary Fund: Afghanistan, Burkina Faso, Burundi, Central African Republic, Comoros, Democratic Republic of the Congo, Haiti, Liberia, Madagascar, Malawi, Mozambique, Niger, Rwanda, Sierra Leone, South Sudan, Sudan, Tajikistan, The Gambia, Togo, and Uganda. (Source: IMF World Economic Outlook Database, April 2019, www.imf.org/external/pubs/ft/weo/2019/01/weodata/download.aspx.)

We'll say more in a moment about the reasons for this shape. But first note that a bow-shaped PPC means that the opportunity cost of producing nuts increases as the economy produces more of them. Notice, for example, that when the economy moves from *A,* where it is producing only coffee, to *B,* it gets 20,000 pounds of nuts per day by giving up only 5,000 pounds per day of coffee. When nut production is increased still further, however—for example, by moving from *B* to *C*—the economy again gains 20,000 pounds of nuts each day, but this time gives up 15,000 pounds of coffee. This pattern of increasing opportunity cost persists over the entire length of the PPC. For example, note that in moving from *D* to *E,* the economy again gains 20,000 pounds of nuts per days, but now gives up 50,000 pounds of coffee. Note, finally, that the same pattern of increasing opportunity cost applies to coffee. Thus, as more coffee is produced, the opportunity cost of producing additional coffee—as measured by the amount of nuts that must be sacrificed—also rises.

Why is the PPC for the multiperson economy bow-shaped? The answer lies in the fact that some resources are relatively well suited for gathering nuts while others are relatively well suited for picking coffee. If the economy is initially producing only coffee and wants to begin producing some nuts, which workers will it reassign? Recall Krisha and Tom, the two workers discussed in the preceding example, in which Tom's comparative advantage was gathering nuts and Krisha's comparative advantage was picking coffee. If both workers were currently picking coffee and you wanted to reassign one of them to gather nuts instead, whom would you send? Tom would be the clear choice because his departure would cost the economy only half as much coffee as Krisha's and would augment nut production by twice as much.

The principle is the same in any large multiperson economy, except that the range of opportunity cost differences across workers is even greater than in the earlier two-worker example. As we keep reassigning workers from coffee production to nut production, sooner or later we must withdraw even coffee specialists like Krisha from coffee production. Indeed, we must eventually reassign others whose opportunity cost of producing nuts is far higher than hers.

The shape of the production possibilities curve shown in Figure 2.6 illustrates the general principle that when resources have different opportunity costs, we should always exploit the resource with the lowest opportunity cost first. We call this the *Low-Hanging-Fruit Principle,* in honor of the fruit picker's rule of picking the most accessible fruit first:

Increasing Opportunity Cost

The Principle of Increasing Opportunity Cost (also called the "Low-Hanging-Fruit Principle"): In expanding the production of any good, first employ those resources with the lowest opportunity cost, and only afterward turn to resources with higher opportunity costs.

A Note on the Logic of the Fruit Picker's Rule

Why should a fruit picker harvest the low-hanging fruit first? This rule makes sense for several reasons. For one, the low-hanging fruit is easier (and hence cheaper) to pick, and if he planned on picking only a limited amount of fruit to begin with, he would clearly come out ahead by avoiding the less-accessible fruit on the higher branches. But even if he planned on picking all the fruit on the tree, he would do better to start with the lower branches first because this would enable him to enjoy the revenue from the sale of the fruit sooner.

The fruit picker's job can be likened to the task confronting a new CEO who has been hired to reform an inefficient, ailing company. The CEO has limited time and attention, so it makes sense to focus first on problems that are relatively easy to correct and whose elimination will provide the biggest improvements in performance—the low-hanging fruit. Later on, the CEO can worry about the many smaller improvements needed to raise the company from very good to excellent.

Again, the important message of the Low-Hanging-Fruit Principle is to be sure to take advantage of your most favorable opportunities first.

COMPARATIVE ADVANTAGE AND PRODUCTION POSSIBILITIES

For an economy that produces two goods, the production possibilities curve describes the maximum amount of one good that can be produced for every possible level of production of the other good. Attainable points are those that lie on or within the curve and efficient points are those that lie along the curve. The slope of the production possibilities curve tells us the opportunity cost of producing an additional unit of the good measured along the horizontal axis. The *Principle of Increasing Opportunity Cost*, or the *Low-Hanging-Fruit Principle*, tells us that the slope of the production possibilities curve becomes steeper as we move downward to the right. The greater the differences among individual opportunity costs, the more bow-shaped the production possibilities curve will be; and the more bow-shaped the production possibilities curve, the greater the potential gains from specialization will be.

FACTORS THAT SHIFT THE ECONOMY'S PRODUCTION POSSIBILITIES CURVE

As its name implies, the production possibilities curve provides a summary of the production options open to any society. At any given moment, the PPC confronts society with a trade-off. The only way people can produce and consume more nuts is to produce and consume less coffee. In the long run, however, it is often possible to increase production of all goods. This is what is meant when people speak of economic growth. As shown in Figure 2.7, economic growth is an outward shift in the economy's production possibilities curve. It can result from increases in the amount of productive resources available or from improvements in knowledge or technology that render existing resources more productive.

What causes the quantity of productive resources to grow in an economy? One factor is investment in new factories and equipment. When workers have more and better equipment to work with, their productivity increases, often dramatically. This is surely an important factor behind the differences in living standards between rich and poor countries. According to one study, for example, the value of capital investment per worker in the United States is about 30 times as great as in Nepal.[3]

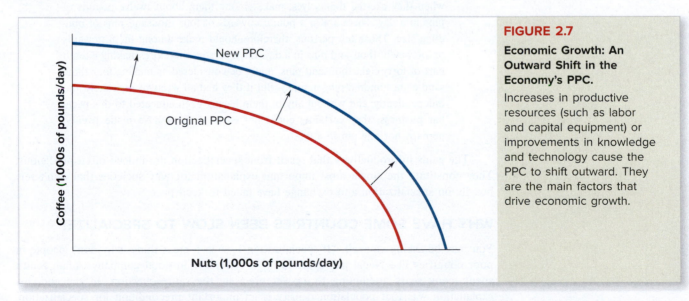

FIGURE 2.7

Economic Growth: An Outward Shift in the Economy's PPC.

Increases in productive resources (such as labor and capital equipment) or improvements in knowledge and technology cause the PPC to shift outward. They are the main factors that drive economic growth.

[3]Alan Heston and Robert Summers, "The Penn World Table (Mark 5): An Expanded Set of International Comparisons, 1950–1988," *Quarterly Journal of Economics,* May 1991, pp. 327–368.

Such large differences in capital per worker don't occur all at once. They are a consequence of decades, even centuries, of differences in rates of savings and investment. Over time, even small differences in rates of investment can translate into extremely large differences in the amount of capital equipment available to each worker. Differences of this sort are often self-reinforcing: Not only do higher rates of saving and investment cause incomes to grow, but the resulting higher income levels also make it easier to devote additional resources to savings and investment. Over time, then, even small initial productivity advantages from specialization can translate into very large income gaps.

Population growth also causes an economy's PPC curve to shift outward and thus is often listed as one of the sources of economic growth. But because population growth also generates more mouths to feed, it cannot by itself raise a country's standard of living. Indeed it may even cause a decline in the standard of living if existing population densities have already begun to put pressure on available land, water, and other resources.

Perhaps the most important sources of economic growth are improvements in knowledge and technology. As economists have long recognized, such improvements often lead to higher output through increased specialization. Improvements in technology often occur spontaneously. More frequently they are directly or indirectly the result of increases in education.

Earlier we discussed a two-person example in which individual differences in opportunity cost led to a tripling of output from specialization (Self-Test 2.4). Real-world gains from specialization often are far more spectacular than those in the example. One reason is that specialization not only capitalizes on preexisting differences in individual skills but also deepens those skills through practice and experience. Moreover, it eliminates many of the switching and start-up costs people incur when they move back and forth among numerous tasks. These gains apply not only to people but also to the tools and equipment they use. Breaking down a task into simple steps, each of which can be performed by a different machine, greatly multiplies the productivity of individual workers.

Even in simple settings, these factors can combine to increase productivity hundreds- or even thousands-fold. Adam Smith, the Scottish philosopher who is remembered today as the founder of modern economics, was the first to recognize the enormity of the gains made possible by the division and specialization of labor. Consider, for instance, his description of work in an eighteenth-century Scottish pin factory:

> One man draws out the wire, another straightens it, a third cuts it, a fourth points it, a fifth grinds it at the top for receiving the head; to make the head requires two or three distinct operations . . . I have seen a small manufactory of this kind where only ten men were employed . . . [who] could, when they exerted themselves, make among them about twelve pounds of pins in a day. There are in a pound upwards of four thousand pins of middling size. Those ten persons, therefore, could make among them upwards of forty-eight thousand pins in a day. Each person, therefore, making a tenth part of forty-eight thousand pins, might be considered as making four thousand eight hundred pins in a day. But if they had all wrought separately and independently, and without any of them having been educated to this peculiar business, they certainly could not each of them have made twenty, perhaps not one pin in a day.[4]

The gains in productivity that result from specialization are indeed often prodigious. They constitute the single most important explanation for why societies that don't rely heavily on specialization and exchange have failed to keep pace.

WHY HAVE SOME COUNTRIES BEEN SLOW TO SPECIALIZE?

You may be asking yourself, "If specialization is such a great thing, why don't people in poor countries like Nepal just specialize?" If so, you're in good company. Adam Smith spent many years attempting to answer precisely the same question. In the end, his explanation was that population density is an important precondition for specialization.

[4]Adam Smith, *The Wealth of Nations* (New York: Everyman's Library, Book 1, 1910).

Smith, ever the economic naturalist, observed that work tended to be far more specialized in the large cities of England in the eighteenth century than in the rural Highlands of Scotland:

> In the lone houses and very small villages which are scattered about in so desert a country as the Highlands of Scotland, every farmer must be butcher, baker, and brewer for his own family. . . . A country carpenter . . . is not only a carpenter, but a joiner, a cabinet maker, and even a carver in wood, as well as a wheelwright, a ploughwright, a cart and waggon maker.[5]

In contrast, each of these same tasks was performed by a different specialist in the large English and Scottish cities of Smith's day. Scottish Highlanders also would have specialized had they been able to, but the markets in which they participated were simply too small and fragmented. Of course, high population density by itself provides no guarantee that specialization will result in rapid economic growth. But especially before the arrival of modern shipping and electronic communications technology, low population density was a definite obstacle to gains from specialization.

Nepal remains one of the most remote and isolated countries on the planet. As recently as the mid-1960s, its average population density was less than 30 people per square mile (as compared, for example, to more than 1,200 people per square mile in New Jersey). Specialization was further limited by Nepal's rugged terrain. Exchanging goods and services with residents of other villages was difficult, because the nearest village in most cases could be reached only after trekking several hours, or even days, over treacherous Himalayan trails. More than any other factor, this extreme isolation accounts for Nepal's long-standing failure to benefit from widespread specialization.

Population density is by no means the only important factor that influences the degree of specialization. Specialization may be severely impeded, for example, by laws and customs that limit people's freedom to transact freely with one another. The communist governments of North Korea and the former East Germany restricted exchange severely, which helps explain why those countries achieved far less specialization than South Korea and the former West Germany, whose governments were far more supportive of exchange.

CAN WE HAVE TOO MUCH SPECIALIZATION?

Of course, the mere fact that specialization boosts productivity does not mean that more specialization is always better than less, for specialization also entails costs. For example, most people appear to enjoy variety in the work they do, yet variety tends to be one of the first casualties as workplace tasks become ever more narrowly specialized.

Indeed, one of Karl Marx's central themes was that the fragmentation of workplace tasks often exacts a heavy psychological toll on workers. Thus, he wrote,

> All means for the development of production . . . mutilate the laborer into a fragment of a man, degrade him to the level of an appendage of a machine, destroy every remnant of charm in his work and turn it into hated toil.[6]

Charlie Chaplin's 1936 film *Modern Times* paints a vivid portrait of the psychological costs of repetitive factory work. As an assembly worker, Chaplin's only task, all day every day, is to tighten the nuts on two bolts as they pass before him on the assembly line. Finally, he snaps and staggers from the factory, wrenches in hand, tightening every nutlike protuberance he encounters.

Do the extra goods made possible by specialization simply come at too high a price? We must certainly acknowledge at least the *potential* for specialization to proceed too far. Yet specialization need not entail rigidly segmented, mind-numbingly repetitive work. And it is important to recognize that *failure* to specialize entails costs as well. Those who don't specialize must accept low wages or work extremely long hours.

When all is said and done, we can expect to meet life's financial obligations in the shortest time—thereby freeing up more time to do whatever else we wish—if we concentrate at least a significant proportion of our efforts on those tasks for which we have a comparative advantage.

[5]Adam Smith, *The Wealth of Nations* (New York: Everyman's Library, Book I, 1910).
[6]Karl Marx, *Das Kapital* (New York: Modern Library, 1906), pp. 708, 709.

COMPARATIVE ADVANTAGE AND OUTSOURCING

The same logic that leads the individuals in an economy to specialize and exchange goods with one another also leads nations to specialize and trade among themselves. As with individuals, each nation can benefit from exchange, even though one may be generally more productive than the other in absolute terms.

The Economic Naturalist 2.3

If trade among nations is so beneficial, why are free-trade agreements so controversial?

One of the most heated issues in the 1996 presidential campaign was President Clinton's support for the North American Free Trade Agreement (NAFTA), a treaty to sharply reduce trade barriers between the United States and its immediate neighbors north and south. The treaty attracted fierce opposition from third-party candidate Ross Perot, who insisted that it would mean unemployment for millions of American workers. If exchange is so beneficial, why does anyone oppose it?

If free trade is so great, why do so many people oppose it?

The answer is that, while reducing barriers to international trade increases the total value of all goods and services produced in each nation, it does not guarantee that each individual citizen will do better. One specific concern regarding NAFTA was that it would help Mexico exploit a comparative advantage in the production of goods made by unskilled labor. Although U.S. consumers would benefit from reduced prices for such goods, many Americans feared that unskilled workers in the United States would lose their jobs to workers in Mexico.

In the end, NAFTA was enacted over the vociferous opposition of American labor unions. So far, however, studies have failed to detect significant overall job losses among unskilled workers in the United States, although there have been some losses in specific industries. Nonetheless, opposition to NAFTA has remained fervent, and when U.S. president Donald Trump took office, he pledged to re-negotiate NAFTA. The resulting new agreement, the United States-Mexico-Canada Agreement (or USMCA, for short), has a wide range of new provisions. Although the agreement has been signed by the leaders of all three countries, it will go into effect only if is ratified by each country's legislature.

OUTSOURCING

outsourcing a term increasingly used to connote having services performed by low-wage workers overseas

An issue very much in the news in recent years has been the **outsourcing** of U.S. service jobs. Although the term once primarily meant having services performed by subcontractors anywhere outside the confines of the firm, increasingly it connotes the act of replacing relatively expensive American service workers with much cheaper service workers in overseas locations.

A case in point is the transcription of medical records. In an effort to maintain accurate records, many physicians dictate their case notes for later transcription after examining their patients. In the past, transcription was often performed by the physician's secretary in spare moments. But secretaries also must attend to a variety of other tasks that disrupt concentration. They must answer phones, serve as receptionists, prepare correspondence, and so on. As insurance disputes and malpractice litigation became more frequent during the 1980s and 1990s, errors in medical records became much more costly to physicians. In response, many turned to independent companies that offered transcription services by full-time, dedicated specialists.

These companies typically served physicians whose practices were located in the same community. But while many of the companies that manage transcription services are still located in the United States, an increasing fraction of the actual work itself is now performed outside the United States. For example, Eight Crossings, a company headquartered in northern California, enables physicians to upload voice dictation files securely to the Internet, whereupon they are transmitted to transcribers who perform the work in India. The finished documents are then transmitted back, in electronic form, to physicians, who may edit and even sign them online. The advantage for physicians, of course, is that the fee for this service is much lower than for the same service performed domestically because wage rates in India are much lower than in the United States.

In China, Korea, Indonesia, India, and elsewhere, even highly skilled professionals still earn just a small fraction of what their counterparts in the United States are paid. Accordingly, companies face powerful competitive pressure to import not just low-cost goods from overseas suppliers, but also a growing array of professional services.

As Microsoft chair Bill Gates put it in a 1999 interview,

> As a business manager, you need to take a hard look at your core competencies. Revisit the areas of your company that aren't directly involved in those competencies, and consider whether Web technologies can enable you to spin off those tasks. Let another company take over the management responsibilities for that work, and use modern communication technology to work closely with the people—now partners instead of employees are doing the work. In the Web work style, employees can push the freedom the Web provides to its limits.[7]

In economic terms, the outsourcing of services to low-wage foreign workers is exactly analogous to the importation of goods manufactured by low-wage foreign workers. In both cases, the resulting cost savings benefit consumers in the United States. And in both cases, jobs in the United States may be put in jeopardy, at least temporarily. An American manufacturing worker's job is at risk if it is possible to import the good he produces from another country at lower cost. By the same token, an American service worker's job is at risk if a lower-paid worker can perform that same service somewhere else.

The Economic Naturalist 2.4

Is PBS economics reporter Paul Solman's job a likely candidate for outsourcing?

Paul Solman produces video segments that provide in-depth analysis of current economic issues for the PBS evening news program *PBS NewsHour*. Is it likely that his job will someday be outsourced to a low-wage reporter from Hyderabad, India?

In the book *The New Division of Labor*, economists Frank Levy and Richard Murnane attempt to identify the characteristics of a job that make it a likely candidate for outsourcing.[8] In their view, any job that is amenable to computerization is also vulnerable to outsourcing. To computerize a task means to break it down into units that can be managed with simple rules. ATMs, for example, were able to replace many of the tasks that bank tellers once performed because it was straightforward to reduce these tasks to a simple series of questions that a machine could answer. By the same token, the workers in offshore call centers

---

[7]Bill Gates, *Business @ The Speed of Thought: Using a Digital Nervous System* (New York: Warner Books, March 1999).
[8]Frank Levy and Richard Murnane, *The New Division of Labor: How Computers Are Creating the Next Job Market* (Princeton, NJ: Princeton University Press, 2004).

who increasingly book our airline and hotel reservations are basically following simple scripts much like computer programs.

So the less rules-based a job is, the less vulnerable to outsourcing it is. Safest of all are those that Levy and Murnane describe as "face-to-face" jobs. Unlike most rules-based jobs, these jobs tend to involve complex face-to-face communication with other people, precisely the kind of communication that dominates Solman's economics reporting.

In an interview for PBS *NewsHour*, Solman asked Levy what he meant, exactly, by "complex communication":

> "Suppose I say the word *bill*," Levy responded, "and you hear that. And the question is what does that mean? . . . Am I talking about a piece of currency? Am I talking about a piece of legislation, the front end of a duck? The only way you're going to answer that is to think about the whole context of the conversation. But that's very complicated work to break down into some kind of software."[9]

Levy and Murnane describe a second category of tasks that are less vulnerable to outsourcing—namely, those that for one reason or another require the worker to be physically present. For example, it is difficult to see how someone in China or India could build an addition to someone's house in a Chicago suburb or repair a blown head gasket on someone's Chevrolet Corvette in Atlanta or fill a cavity in someone's tooth in Los Angeles.

So on both counts, Paul Solman's job appears safe for the time being. Because it involves face-to-face, complex communication, and because many of his interviews can be conducted only in the United States, it is difficult to see how a reporter from Hyderabad could displace him.

Of course, the fact that a job is relatively safe does not mean that it is completely sheltered. For example, although most dentists continue to think themselves immune from outsourcing, it is now possible for someone requiring extensive dental work to have the work done in New Delhi and still save enough to cover his airfare and a two-week vacation in India.

There are more than 160 million Americans in the labor force. Each month almost 4 percent of workers leave their jobs and a roughly equal number find new ones.[10] At various points in your life, you are likely to be among this group in transition. In the long run, the greatest security available to you or any other worker is the ability to adapt quickly to new circumstances. Having a good education provides no guarantee against losing your job, but it should enable you to develop a comparative advantage at the kinds of tasks that require more than just executing a simple set of rules.

RECAP

COMPARATIVE ADVANTAGE AND OUTSOURCING

Nations, like individuals, can benefit from exchange, even though one trading partner may be more productive than the other in absolute terms. But expansions of exchange do not guarantee that each individual citizen will be better off. For example, unskilled workers in high-wage countries may be hurt in the short run by the reduction of barriers to trade with low-wage nations.

[9]www.pbs.org/newshour/bb/business-july-dec04-jobs_8-16/
[10]www.bls.gov/jlt/#data.

SUMMARY

- One person has an *absolute* advantage over another in the production of a good if she can produce more of that good than the other person. One person has a *comparative* advantage over another in the production of a good if she is relatively more efficient than the other person at producing that good, meaning that her opportunity cost of producing it is lower than her counterpart's. Specialization based on comparative advantage is the basis for economic exchange. When each person specializes in the task at which he or she is relatively most efficient, the economic pie is maximized, making possible the largest slice for everyone. *(LO1)*

- At the individual level, comparative advantage may spring from differences in talent or ability or from differences in education, training, and experience. At the national level, sources of comparative advantage include those innate and learned differences, as well as differences in language, culture, institutions, climate, natural resources, and a host of other factors. *(LO1)*

- The production possibilities curve is a simple device for summarizing the possible combinations of output that a society can produce if it employs its resources efficiently. In a simple economy that produces only coffee and nuts, the PPC shows the maximum quantity of coffee production (vertical axis) possible at each level of nut production (horizontal axis). The slope of the PPC at any point represents the opportunity cost of nuts at that point, expressed in pounds of coffee. *(LO2)*

- The gains from specialization and exchange tend to be larger the larger the differences are between trading partners' opportunity costs. *(LO2)*

- All production possibilities curves slope downward because of the *Scarcity Principle*, which states that the only way a consumer can get more of one good is to settle for less of another. In economies whose workers have different opportunity costs of producing each good, the slope of the PPC becomes steeper as consumers move downward along the curve. This change in slope illustrates the *Principle of Increasing Opportunity Cost (or the Low-Hanging-Fruit Principle)*, which states that in expanding the production of any good, a society should first employ those resources that are relatively efficient at producing that good, only afterward turning to those that are less efficient. *(LO2)*

- Factors that cause a country's PPC to shift outward over time include investment in new factories and equipment, population growth, and improvements in knowledge and technology. *(LO3)*

- The same logic that prompts individuals to specialize in their production and exchange goods with one another also leads nations to specialize and trade with one another. Just because a country as a whole benefits from trade, however, does not mean that each individual citizen will be better off. For example, trade between nations may lead some workers to lose their jobs due to outsourcing. *(LO4)*

CORE PRINCIPLES

 Comparative Advantage

The Principle of Comparative Advantage
Everyone does best when each person (or each country) concentrates on the activities for which his or her opportunity cost is lowest.

 Increasing Opportunity Cost

The Principle of Increasing Opportunity Cost (also called the "Low-Hanging-Fruit Principle")
In expanding the production of any good, first employ those resources with the lowest opportunity cost, and only afterward turn to resources with higher opportunity costs.

KEY TERMS

absolute advantage
attainable point
comparative advantage

efficient point
inefficient point
outsourcing

production possibilities curve (PPC)
unattainable point

REVIEW QUESTIONS

1. Explain what "having a comparative advantage" at producing a particular good or service means. What does "having an absolute advantage" at producing a good or service mean? *(LO1)*

2. What factors have helped the United States to become the world's leading exporter of movies, books, and popular music? *(LO1)*

3. Why does saying that people are poor because they do not specialize make more sense than saying that people perform their own services because they are poor? *(LO2, LO3)*

4. How will a reduction in the number of hours worked each day affect an economy's production possibilities curve? *(LO3)*

5. How will technological innovations that boost labor productivity affect an economy's production possibilities curve? *(LO3)*

PROBLEMS

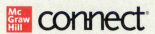

1. Ted can wax a car in 20 minutes or wash a car in 60 minutes. Ishana can wax a car in 15 minutes or wash a car in 30 minutes. What is each person's opportunity cost of washing a car? Who has a comparative advantage in washing cars? *(LO1)*

2. Ted can wax 4 cars per day or wash 12 cars. Ishana can wax 3 cars per day or wash 6 cars. What is each person's opportunity cost of washing a car? Who has a comparative advantage in washing cars? *(LO1)*

3. Isabella and Antonio are auto mechanics. Isabella takes 4 hours to replace a clutch and 2 hours to replace a set of brakes. Antonio takes 6 hours to replace a clutch and 2 hours to replace a set of brakes. State whether anyone has an absolute advantage at either task and, for each task, identify who has a comparative advantage. *(LO1)*

4. Consider a society consisting only of Helen, who allocates her time between sewing dresses and baking bread. Each hour she devotes to sewing dresses yields 4 dresses and each hour she devotes to baking bread yields 8 loaves of bread. *(LO2)*
   a. If Helen works a total of 8 hours per day, graph her production possibilities curve.
   b. Using your graph, which of the points listed below are attainable and/or efficient?
      28 dresses per day, 16 loaves per day.
      16 dresses per day, 32 loaves per day.
      18 dresses per day, 24 loaves per day.

5. Suppose that in Problem 4 a new sewing machine is introduced that enables Helen to sew 8 dresses per hour rather than only 4. *(LO3)*
   a. Show how this development shifts her production possibilities curve.
   b. Indicate if the following points are attainable and/or efficient before and after the introduction of the sewing machine.
      16 dresses per day, 48 loaves per day.
      24 dresses per day, 16 loaves per day.

c. Explain what is meant by the following statement: "An increase in productivity with respect to any one good increases our options for producing and consuming all other goods."

6. Krisha can pick 4 pounds of coffee beans in an hour or gather 2 pounds of nuts. Tom can pick 2 pounds of coffee beans in an hour or gather 4 pounds of nuts. Each works 6 hours per day. *(LO2)*
   a. Together, what is the maximum number of pounds of coffee beans the two can pick in a day? What is the maximum number of pounds of nuts the two can gather in a day?
   b. Now suppose Krisha and Tom were gathering the maximum number of pounds of nuts when they decided that they would like to begin picking 8 pounds of coffee per day. Who would pick the coffee, and how many pounds of nuts would they still be able to gather?
   c. Would it be possible for Krisha and Tom in total to gather 26 pounds of nuts and pick 20 pounds of coffee each day? If so, how much of each good should each person pick?
   d. Is the point at 30 pounds of coffee per day, 12 pounds of nuts per day an attainable point? Is it an efficient point?
   e. On a graph with pounds of coffee per day on the vertical axis and pounds of nuts per day on the horizontal axis, show all the points you identified in parts a–d.

7.* Refer to the two-person economy described in Problem 6. *(LO2)*
   a. Suppose that Krisha and Tom could buy or sell coffee and nuts in the world market at a price of $2 per pound for coffee and $2 per pound for nuts. If each person specialized completely in the good for which he or she had a comparative advantage, how much could they earn by selling all they produce?
   b. At the prices just described, what is the maximum amount of coffee Krisha and Tom could buy in the

*Denotes more difficult problem.

world market with the income they earned? What is the maximum amount of nuts? Would it be possible for them to consume 40 pounds of nuts and 8 pounds of coffee each day?

c. In light of their ability to buy and sell in world markets at the stated prices, show on the same graph all

combinations of the two goods it would be possible for them to consume.

8. Which of the following U.S. jobs is likely to be the most vulnerable to outsourcing: an in-home health care provider, a hairstylist, or a computer programmer? Explain. *(LO4)*

ANSWERS TO SELF-TESTS

2.1

	Productivity in web design	Productivity in bicycle repair
Monique	2 web page updates per hour	1 repair per hour
Miguel	3 web page updates per hour	3 repairs per hour

The entries in the table tell us that Miguel has an absolute advantage over Monique in both activities. While Miguel, the mechanic, can update 3 web pages per hour, Monique, the web designer, can update only 2. Miguel's absolute advantage over Monique is even greater in the task of fixing bikes—3 repairs per hour versus Monique's 1.

But as in the second example in this chapter, the fact that Miguel is a better web designer than Monique does not imply that Miguel should update his own web page. Miguel's opportunity cost of updating a web page is 1 bicycle repair, whereas Monique must give up only half a repair to update a web page. Monique has a comparative advantage over Miguel at web design and Miguel has a comparative advantage over Monique at bicycle repair. *(LO1)*

2.2 In the accompanying graph, *A* (20 pounds per day of coffee, 4 pounds per day of nuts) is unattainable; *B* (12 pounds per day of coffee, 6 pounds per day of nuts) is both attainable and efficient; and *C* (4 pounds per day of coffee, 8 pounds per day of nuts) is attainable and inefficient. *(LO2)*

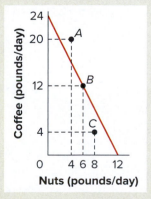

2.3 Krisha's opportunity cost of gathering a pound of nuts is now ½ pound of coffee and Tom's opportunity cost of gathering a pound of nuts is now only 1 pound of coffee. So Tom has a comparative advantage at picking coffee and Krisha has a comparative advantage at gathering nuts. *(LO2)*

2.4 Because Tom can produce five times as many pounds of nuts in an hour as pounds of coffee, to produce equal quantities of each, he must spend 5 hours picking coffee for every hour he devotes to gathering nuts. And because he works a 6-hour day, that means spending 5 hours picking coffee and 1 hour gathering nuts. Dividing his time in this way, he will end up with 5 pounds of each good. Similarly, if she is to produce equal quantities of each good, Krisha must spend 5 hours gathering nuts and 1 hour picking coffee. So she, too, produces 5 pounds of each good if she divides her 6-hour day in this way. Their combined daily production will thus be 10 pounds of each good. By working together and specializing, however, they can produce and consume a total of 30 pounds per day of each good. *(LO2)*

CHAPTER 3

Supply and Demand

When there's excess demand for a product, its price tends to rise.

Johnny Michael/Shutterstock

LEARNING OBJECTIVES

After reading this chapter, you should be able to:

LO1 Describe how the demand and supply curves summarize the behavior of buyers and sellers in the marketplace.

LO2 Discuss how the supply and demand curves interact to determine equilibrium price and quantity.

LO3 Illustrate how shifts in supply and demand curves cause prices and quantities to change.

LO4 Explain and apply the *Efficiency Principle* and the *Equilibrium Principle* (also called the *No-Cash-on-the-Table Principle*).

The stock of foodstuffs on hand at any moment in New York City's grocery stores, restaurants, and private kitchens is sufficient to feed the area's 10 million residents for at most a week or so. Since most of these residents have nutritionally adequate and highly varied diets, and since almost no food is produced within the city proper, provisioning New York requires that millions of pounds of food and drink be delivered to locations throughout the city each day.

No doubt many New Yorkers, buying groceries at their favorite local markets or eating at their favorite Italian restaurants, give little or no thought to the nearly miraculous coordination of people and resources required to feed city residents on a daily basis. But near-miraculous it is, nevertheless. Even if the supplying of New York City consisted only of transporting a fixed collection of foods to a given list of destinations each day, it would be quite an impressive operation, requiring at least a small (and well-managed) army to carry out.

Yet the entire process is astonishingly more complex than that. For example, the system must somehow ensure that not only *enough* food is delivered to satisfy New Yorkers' discriminating palates, but also the *right kinds* of food. There can't be too much pheasant and not enough smoked eel, or too much bacon and not enough eggs, or too much caviar and not enough canned tuna, and so on. Similar judgments must be made *within* each category of food and drink: there must be the right amount of Swiss cheese and the right amounts of provolone, gorgonzola, and feta.

But even this doesn't begin to describe the complexity of the decisions and actions required to provide our nation's largest city with its daily bread. Someone has to decide where each particular type of food gets produced, and how, and by whom. Someone must decide how much of each type of food gets delivered to *each* of the tens of thousands of restaurants and grocery stores in the city. Someone must determine whether the deliveries should be made in big trucks or small ones, arrange that the trucks be in the right place at the right time, and ensure that gasoline and qualified drivers be available.

Thousands of individuals must decide what role, if any, they will play in this collective effort. Some people—just the right number—must choose to drive food delivery trucks rather than trucks that deliver lumber. Others—again, just the right number—must become the mechanics who fix these trucks rather than carpenters who build houses. Others must become farmers rather than architects or bricklayers. Still others must become chefs in upscale restaurants, or flip burgers at McDonald's, instead of becoming plumbers or electricians.

Yet despite the almost incomprehensible number and complexity of the tasks involved, somehow the supplying of New York City manages to get done remarkably smoothly. Oh, a grocery store will occasionally run out of flank steak or a diner will sometimes be told that someone else has just ordered the last serving of roast duck. But if episodes like these stick in memory, it is only because they are rare. For the most part, New York's food delivery system—like that of every other city in the country—functions so seamlessly that it attracts virtually no notice.

The situation is strikingly different in New York City's rental housing market. According to one estimate, growth in the city's population has long outstripped growth in the city's supply of housing units (with the exception of a recent surge in construction of ultra-luxury condominiums).[1] As a result, America's most densely populated city has been experiencing a protracted housing shortage. Yet, paradoxically, in the midst of this shortage, apartment houses are being demolished; and in the vacant lots left behind, people from the neighborhoods are planting flower gardens!

Melissamn/Shutterstock

New York City is experiencing not only a growing shortage of rental housing, but also chronically strained relations between landlords and tenants. In one all-too-typical case, for example, a photographer living in a loft on the Lower East Side waged an eight-year court battle with his landlord that generated literally thousands of pages of legal documents. "Once we put up a doorbell for ourselves," the photographer recalled, "and [the landlord] pulled it out, so we pulled out the wires to his doorbell."[2] The landlord, for his part, accused the photographer of obstructing his efforts to renovate the apartment. According to the landlord, the tenant preferred for the apartment to remain in substandard condition since that gave him an excuse to withhold rent payments.

Thinkstock/Jupiter Images

Same city, two strikingly different patterns: In the food industry, goods and services are available in wide variety and people (at least those with adequate income) are generally satisfied with what they receive and the choices available to them. In contrast, in the rental housing industry, chronic shortages and chronic dissatisfaction are rife among both buyers and sellers. Why this difference?

Why does New York City's food distribution system work so much better than its housing market?

The brief answer is that New York City relies on a complex system of administrative rent regulations to allocate housing units but leaves the

---

[1] For additional information see www.citylab.com/equity/2017/05/is-housing-catching-up/528246/.
[2] John Tierney, "The Rentocracy: At the Intersection of Supply and Demand," *New York Times Magazine,* May 4, 1997, p. 39.

allocation of food essentially in the hands of market forces—the forces of supply and demand. Although intuition might suggest otherwise, both theory and experience suggest that the seemingly chaotic and unplanned outcomes of market forces, in most cases, can do a better job of allocating economic resources than can (for example) a government agency, even if the agency has the best of intentions.

In this chapter we'll explore how markets allocate food, housing, and other goods and services, usually with remarkable efficiency despite the complexity of the tasks. To be sure, markets are by no means perfect, and our stress on their virtues is to some extent an attempt to counteract what most economists view as an underappreciation by the general public of their remarkable strengths. But, in the course of our discussion, we'll see why markets function so smoothly most of the time and why bureaucratic rules and regulations rarely work as well in solving complex economic problems.

To convey an understanding of how markets work is a major goal of this course, and in this chapter we provide only a brief introduction and overview. As the course proceeds, we'll discuss the economic role of markets in considerably more detail, paying attention to some of the problems of markets as well as their strengths.

WHAT, HOW, AND FOR WHOM? CENTRAL PLANNING VERSUS THE MARKET

No city, state, or society—regardless of how it is organized—can escape the need to answer certain basic economic questions. For example, how much of our limited time and other resources should we devote to building housing, how much to the production of food, and how much to providing other goods and services? What techniques should we use to produce each good? Who should be assigned to each specific task? And how should the resulting goods and services be distributed among people?

In the thousands of different societies for which records are available, issues like these have been decided in essentially one of two ways. One approach is for all economic decisions to be made centrally, by an individual or small number of individuals on behalf of a larger group. For example, in many agrarian societies throughout history, families or other small groups consumed only those goods and services that they produced for themselves, and a single clan or family leader made most important production and distribution decisions. On an immensely larger scale, the economic organization of the former Soviet Union (and other communist countries) was also largely centralized. In so-called centrally planned communist nations, a central bureaucratic committee established production targets for the country's farms and factories, developed a master plan for how to achieve the targets (including detailed instructions concerning who was to produce what), and set up guidelines for the distribution and use of the goods and services produced.

Neither form of centralized economic organization is much in evidence today. When implemented on a small scale, as in a self-sufficient family enterprise, centralized decision making is certainly feasible. For the reasons discussed in the preceding chapter, however, the jack-of-all-trades approach was doomed once it became clear how dramatically people could improve their living standards by specialization—that is, by having each individual focus his or her efforts on a relatively narrow range of tasks. And with the fall of the Soviet Union and its satellite nations in the late 1980s, there are now only three communist economies left in the world: Cuba, North Korea, and China. The first two of these appear to be on their last legs, economically speaking, and China has largely abandoned any attempt to control production and distribution decisions from the center. The major remaining examples of centralized allocation and control now reside in the bureaucratic agencies that administer programs like New York City's rent controls—programs that are themselves becoming increasingly rare.

At the beginning of the twenty-first century, we are therefore left, for the most part, with the second major form of economic system, one in which production and distribution decisions are left to individuals interacting in private markets. In the so-called capitalist, or free-market, economies, people decide for themselves which careers to pursue and which products to produce or buy. In fact, there are no *pure* free-market economies today. Modern industrial countries are more properly described as "mixed economies." Their goods and services are allocated by a combination of free markets, regulation, and other forms of collective control. Still, it makes sense to refer to such systems as free-market economies because people are for the most part free to start businesses, shut them down, or sell them. And within broad limits, the distribution of goods and services is determined by individual preferences backed by individual purchasing power, which in most cases comes from the income people earn in the labor market.

In country after country, markets have replaced centralized control for the simple reason that they tend to assign production tasks and consumption benefits much more effectively. The popular press and conventional wisdom often assert that economists disagree about important issues. (As someone once quipped, "If you lay all the economists in the world end to end, they still wouldn't reach a conclusion.") The fact is, however, that there is overwhelming agreement among economists about a broad range of issues. A substantial majority believes that markets are the most effective means for allocating society's scarce resources. For example, a recent survey found that more than 90 percent of American professional economists believe that rent regulations like the ones implemented by New York City do more harm than good. That the stated aim of these regulations—to make rental housing more affordable for middle- and low-income families—is clearly benign was not enough to prevent them from wreaking havoc on New York City's housing market. To see why, we must explore how goods and services are allocated in private markets and why nonmarket means of allocating goods and services often do not produce the expected results.

BUYERS AND SELLERS IN MARKETS

market the market for any good consists of all buyers or sellers of that good

Beginning with some simple concepts and definitions, we will explore how the interactions among buyers and sellers in markets determine the prices and quantities of the various goods and services traded. We begin by defining a market: the **market** for any good consists of all the buyers and sellers of that good. So, for example, the market for pizza on a given day in a given place is just the set of people (or other economic actors such as firms) potentially able to buy or sell pizza at that time and location.

In the market for pizza, sellers comprise the individuals and companies that either do sell—or might, under the right circumstances, sell—pizza. Similarly, buyers in this market include all individuals who buy—or might buy—pizza.

In most parts of the country, a decent pizza can still be had for less than $10. Where does the market price of pizza come from? Looking beyond pizza to the vast array of other goods that are bought and sold every day, we may ask, "Why are some goods cheap and others expensive?" Aristotle had no idea. Nor did Plato, or Copernicus, or Newton. On reflection, it is astonishing that, for almost the entire span of human history, not even the most intelligent and creative minds on Earth had any real inkling of how to answer that seemingly simple question. Even Adam Smith, the Scottish moral philosopher whose *Wealth of Nations* launched the discipline of economics in 1776, suffered confusion on this issue.

Smith and other early economists (including Karl Marx) thought that the market price of a good was determined by its cost of production. But although costs surely do affect prices, they cannot explain why one of Claude Monet's paintings sells for so much more than one of Pierre-Auguste Renoir's.

Why do Claude Monet's paintings sell for so much more than Pierre-Auguste Renoir's?

The Metropolitan Museum of Art, New York, H. O. Havemeyer Collection, Bequest of Mrs. H. O. Havemeyer, 1929

Stanley Jevons and other nineteenth-century economists tried to explain price by focusing on the value people derived from consuming different goods and services. It certainly seems plausible that people will pay a lot for a good they value highly. Yet willingness to pay cannot be the whole story, either. Deprive a person in the desert of water, for example, and he will be dead in a matter of hours, and yet water sells for less than a penny a gallon. By contrast, human beings can get along perfectly well without gold, and yet gold sells for more than $1,800 an ounce.

Cost of production? Value to the user? Which is it? The answer, which seems obvious to today's economists, is that both matter. Writing in the late nineteenth century, the British economist Alfred Marshall was among the first to show clearly how costs and value interact to determine both the prevailing market price for a good and the amount of it that is bought and sold. Our task in the pages ahead will be to explore Marshall's insights and gain some practice in applying them. As a first step, we introduce the two main components of Marshall's pathbreaking analysis: the demand curve and the supply curve.

A Pierre-Auguste Renoir painting.
Source: Courtesy of National Gallery of Art, Washington

THE DEMAND CURVE

In the market for pizza, the **demand curve** for pizza is a simple schedule or graph that tells us how many slices people would be willing to buy at different prices. By convention, economists usually put price on the vertical axis of the demand curve and quantity on the horizontal axis.

A fundamental property of the demand curve is that it is downward-sloping with respect to price. For example, the demand curve for pizza tells us that as the price of pizza falls, buyers will buy more slices. Thus, the daily demand curve for pizza in Chicago on a given day might look like the curve seen in Figure 3.1. (Although economists usually refer to demand and supply "curves," we often draw them as straight lines in examples.)

The demand curve in Figure 3.1 tells us that when the price of pizza is low—say, $2 per slice—buyers will want to buy 16,000 slices per day, whereas they will want to buy only 12,000 slices at a price of $3 and only 8,000 at a price of $4. The demand curve for pizza—as for any other good—slopes downward for multiple reasons. Some have to do with the individual consumer's reactions to price changes. Thus, as pizza becomes more expensive, a consumer may switch to chicken sandwiches, hamburgers, or other foods that substitute for pizza. This is called the **substitution effect** of a price change. In addition, a price increase reduces the quantity demanded because it reduces purchasing power: a consumer simply can't afford to buy as many slices of pizza at higher prices as at lower prices. This is called the **income effect** of a price change.

demand curve a schedule or graph showing the quantity of a good that buyers wish to buy at each price

substitution effect the change in the quantity demanded of a good that results because buyers switch to or from substitutes when the price of the good changes

income effect the change in the quantity demanded of a good that results because a change in the price of a good changes the buyer's purchasing power

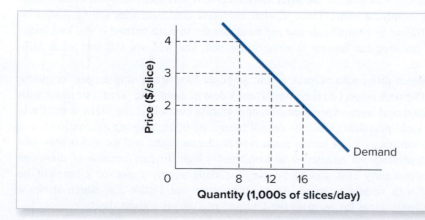

FIGURE 3.1

The Daily Demand Curve for Pizza in Chicago.

The demand curve for any good is a downward-sloping function of its price.

buyer's reservation price
the largest dollar amount the buyer would be willing to pay for a good

Another reason the demand curve slopes downward is that consumers differ in terms of how much they're willing to pay for the good. The Cost-Benefit Principle tells us that a given person will buy the good if the benefit she expects to receive from it exceeds its cost. The benefit is the **buyer's reservation price,** the highest dollar amount she'd be willing to pay for the good. The cost of the good is the actual amount that the buyer actually must pay for it, which is the market price of the good. In most markets, different buyers have different reservation prices. So, when the good sells for a high price, it will satisfy the cost-benefit test for fewer buyers than when it sells for a lower price.

To put this same point another way, the fact that the demand curve for a good is downward-sloping reflects the fact that the reservation price of the marginal buyer declines as the quantity of the good bought increases. Here the marginal buyer is the person who purchases the last unit of the good sold. If buyers are currently purchasing 12,000 slices of pizza a day in Figure 3.1, for example, the reservation price for the buyer of the 12,000th slice must be $3. (If someone had been willing to pay more than that, the quantity demanded at a price of $3 would have been more than 12,000 to begin with.) By similar reasoning, when the quantity sold is 16,000 slices per day, the marginal buyer's reservation price must be only $2.

We defined the demand curve for any good as a schedule telling how much of it consumers wish to purchase at various prices. This is called the *horizontal interpretation* of the demand curve. Using the horizontal interpretation, we start with price on the vertical axis and read the corresponding quantity demanded on the horizontal axis. Thus, at a price of $4 per slice, the demand curve in Figure 3.1 tells us that the quantity of pizza demanded will be 8,000 slices per day.

The demand curve also can be interpreted in a second way, which is to start with quantity on the horizontal axis and then read the marginal buyer's reservation price on the vertical axis. Thus, when the quantity of pizza sold is 8,000 slices per day, the demand curve in Figure 3.1 tells us that the marginal buyer's reservation price is $4 per slice. This second way of reading the demand curve is called the *vertical interpretation*.

 SELF-TEST 3.1

In Figure 3.1, what is the marginal buyer's reservation price when the quantity of pizza sold is 10,000 slices per day? For the same demand curve, what will be the quantity of pizza demanded at a price of $2.50 per slice?

THE SUPPLY CURVE

supply curve a graph or schedule showing the quantity of a good that sellers wish to sell at each price

In the market for pizza, the **supply curve** is a simple schedule or graph that tells us, for each possible price, the total number of slices that all pizza vendors would be willing to sell at that price. What does the supply curve of pizza look like? The answer to this question is based on the logical assumption that suppliers should be willing to sell additional slices as long as the price they receive is sufficient to cover their opportunity cost of supplying them. Thus, if what someone could earn by selling a slice of pizza is insufficient to compensate her for what she could have earned if she had spent her time and invested her money in some other way, she will not sell that slice. Otherwise, she will.

Just as buyers differ with respect to the amounts they are willing to pay for pizza, sellers also differ with respect to their opportunity cost of supplying pizza. For those with limited education and work experience, the opportunity cost of selling pizza is relatively low (because such individuals typically do not have a lot of high-paying alternatives). For others, the opportunity cost of selling pizza is of moderate value, and for still others—like rock stars and professional athletes—it is prohibitively high. In part because of these differences in opportunity cost among people, the daily supply curve of pizza will be *upward-sloping* with respect to price. As an illustration, see Figure 3.2, which shows a hypothetical supply curve for pizza in the Chicago market on a given day.

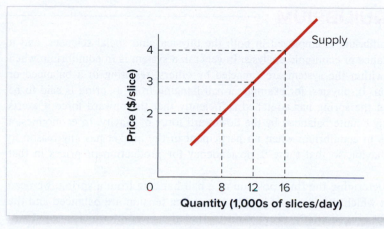

FIGURE 3.2

The Daily Supply Curve of Pizza in Chicago.

At higher prices, sellers generally offer more units for sale.

The fact that the supply curve slopes upward may be seen as a consequence of the Low-Hanging-Fruit Principle, discussed in Chapter 2, *Comparative Advantage*. This principle tells us that as we expand the production of pizza, we turn first to those whose opportunity cost of producing pizza is lowest, and only then to others with a higher opportunity cost.

Increasing Opportunity Cost

Like the demand curve, the supply curve can be interpreted either horizontally or vertically. Under the horizontal interpretation, we begin with a price and then go over to the supply curve to read the quantity that sellers wish to sell at that price on the horizontal axis. For instance, at a price of $2 per slice, sellers in Figure 3.2 wish to sell 8,000 slices per day.

Under the vertical interpretation, we begin with a quantity and then go up to the supply curve to read the corresponding marginal cost on the vertical axis. Thus, if sellers in Figure 3.2 are currently supplying 12,000 slices per day, the opportunity cost of the marginal seller is $3 per slice. In other words, the supply curve tells us that the marginal cost of producing the 12,000th slice of pizza is $3. (If someone could produce a 12,001st slice for less than $3, she would have an incentive to supply it, so the quantity of pizza supplied at $3 per slice would not have been 12,000 slices per day to begin with.) By similar reasoning, when the quantity of pizza supplied is 16,000 slices per day, the marginal cost of producing another slice must be $4. The **seller's reservation price** for selling an additional unit of a good is her marginal cost of producing that good. It is the smallest dollar amount for which she would not be worse off if she sold an additional unit.

seller's reservation price the smallest dollar amount for which a seller would be willing to sell an additional unit, generally equal to marginal cost

 SELF-TEST 3.2

In Figure 3.2, what is the marginal cost of a slice of pizza when the quantity of pizza sold is 10,000 slices per day? For the same supply curve, what will be the quantity of pizza supplied at a price of $3.50 per slice?

RECAP

DEMAND AND SUPPLY CURVES

The *market* for a good consists of the actual and potential buyers and sellers of that good. For any given price, the *demand curve* shows the quantity that demanders would be willing to buy and the *supply curve* shows the quantity that suppliers of the good would be willing to sell. Suppliers are willing to sell more at higher prices (supply curves slope upward) and demanders are willing to buy less at higher prices (demand curves slope downward).

MARKET EQUILIBRIUM

equilibrium a balanced or unchanging situation in which all forces at work within a system are canceled by others

The concept of **equilibrium** is employed in both the physical and social sciences, and it is of central importance in economic analysis. In general, a system is in equilibrium when all forces at work within the system are canceled by others, resulting in a balanced or unchanging situation. In physics, for example, a ball hanging from a spring is said to be in equilibrium when the spring has stretched sufficiently that the upward force it exerts on the ball is exactly counterbalanced by the downward force of gravity. In economics, a market is said to be in equilibrium when no participant in the market has any reason to alter his or her behavior, so that there is no tendency for production or prices in that market to change.

equilibrium price and equilibrium quantity the price and quantity at the intersection of the supply and demand curves for the good

If we want to determine the final position of a ball hanging from a spring, we need to find the point at which the forces of gravity and spring tension are balanced and the system is in equilibrium. Similarly, if we want to find the price at which a good will sell (which we will call the **equilibrium price**) and the quantity of it that will be sold (the **equilibrium quantity**), we need to find the equilibrium in the market for that good. The basic tools for finding the equilibrium in a market for a good are the supply and demand curves for that good. For reasons we will explain, the equilibrium price and equilibrium quantity of a good are the price and quantity at which the supply and demand curves for the good intersect. For the hypothetical supply and demand curves shown earlier for the pizza market in Chicago, the equilibrium price will therefore be $3 per slice, and the equilibrium quantity of pizza sold will be 12,000 slices per day, as shown in Figure 3.3.

Note that at the equilibrium price of $3 per slice, both sellers and buyers are "satisfied" in the following sense: buyers are buying exactly the quantity of pizza they wish to buy at that price (12,000 slices per day) and sellers are selling exactly the quantity of pizza they wish to sell (also 12,000 slices per day). And since they are satisfied in this sense, neither buyers nor sellers face any incentives to change their behavior.

market equilibrium occurs in a market when all buyers and sellers are satisfied with their respective quantities at the market price

Note the limited sense of the term *satisfied* in the definition of **market equilibrium.** It doesn't mean that sellers would be displeased to receive a price higher than the equilibrium price. Rather, it means only that they're able to sell all they wish to sell at that price. Similarly, to say that buyers are satisfied at the equilibrium price doesn't mean that they wouldn't be happy to pay less than that price. Rather, it means only that they're able to buy exactly as many units of the good as they wish to at the equilibrium price.

Note also that if the price of pizza in our Chicago market were anything other than $3 per slice, either buyers or sellers would be frustrated. Suppose, for example, that the price of pizza were $4 per slice, as shown in Figure 3.4. At that price, buyers wish to buy only 8,000 slices per day, but sellers wish to sell 16,000. And since no one can force someone to buy a slice of pizza against her wishes, this means that buyers will buy only the 8,000 slices they wish to buy. So when price exceeds the equilibrium price, it is sellers

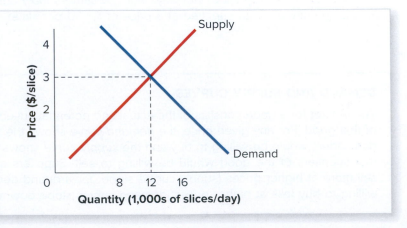

FIGURE 3.3

The Equilibrium Price and Quantity of Pizza in Chicago.

The equilibrium quantity and price of a product are the values that correspond to the intersection of the supply and demand curves for that product.

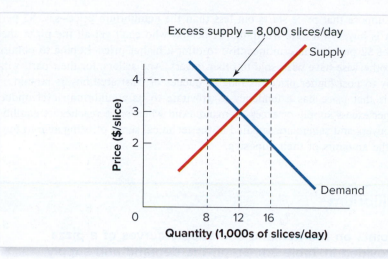

FIGURE 3.4

Excess Supply.

When price exceeds equilibrium price, there is excess supply, or surplus, the difference between quantity supplied and quantity demanded.

who end up being frustrated. At a price of $4 in this example, they are left with an **excess supply,** or **surplus,** of 8,000 slices per day.

Conversely, suppose that the price of pizza in our Chicago market were less than the equilibrium price—say, $2 per slice. As shown in Figure 3.5, buyers want to buy 16,000 slices per day at that price, whereas sellers want to sell only 8,000. And since sellers cannot be forced to sell pizza against their wishes, this time it is the buyers who end up being frustrated. At a price of $2 per slice in this example, they experience an **excess demand,** or **shortage,** of 8,000 slices per day.

An extraordinary feature of private markets for goods and services is their automatic tendency to gravitate toward their respective equilibrium prices and quantities. This tendency is a simple consequence of the Incentive Principle. The mechanisms by which the adjustment happens are implicit in our definitions of excess supply and excess demand. Suppose, for example, that the price of pizza in our hypothetical market was $4 per slice, leading to excess supply as shown in Figure 3.4. Because sellers are frustrated in the sense of wanting to sell more pizza than buyers wish to buy, sellers have an incentive to take whatever steps they can to increase their sales. The simplest strategy available to them is to cut their price slightly. Thus, if one seller reduced her price from $4 to, say, $3.95 per slice, she would attract many of the buyers who had been paying $4 per slice for pizza supplied by other sellers. Those sellers, in order to recover their lost business, would then have an incentive to match the price cut. But notice that if all sellers lowered their prices to $3.95 per slice, there would still be considerable excess supply. So sellers would face continuing incentives to cut their prices. This pressure to cut prices won't go away until prices fall all the way to $3 per slice.

excess supply (or **surplus**) the amount by which quantity supplied exceeds quantity demanded when the price of the good exceeds the equilibrium price

excess demand (or **shortage**) the amount by which quantity demanded exceeds quantity supplied when the price of a good lies below the equilibrium price

Incentive

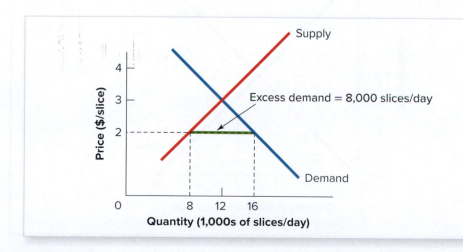

FIGURE 3.5

Excess Demand.

When price lies below equilibrium price, there is excess demand, the difference between quantity demanded and quantity supplied.

Conversely, suppose that price starts out less than the equilibrium price—say, $2 per slice. This time it is buyers who are frustrated. A person who can't get all the pizza she wants at a price of $2 per slice has an incentive to offer a higher price, hoping to obtain pizza that would otherwise have been sold to other buyers. And sellers, for their part, will be only too happy to post higher prices as long as queues of frustrated buyers remain.

The upshot is that price has a tendency to gravitate to its equilibrium level under conditions of either excess supply or excess demand. And when price reaches its equilibrium level, both buyers and sellers are satisfied in the technical sense of being able to buy or sell precisely the amounts of their choosing.

EXAMPLE 3.1   Market Equilibrium

Samples of points on the demand and supply curves of a pizza market are provided in Table 3.1. Graph the demand and supply curves for this market and find its equilibrium price and quantity.

TABLE 3.1
Points along the Demand and Supply Curves of a Pizza Market

Demand for Pizza		Supply of Pizza	
Price ($/slice)	Quantity demanded (1,000s of slices/day)	Price ($/slice)	Quantity supplied (1,000s of slices/day)
1	8	1	2
2	6	2	4
3	4	3	6
4	2	4	8

The points in the table are plotted in Figure 3.6 and then joined to indicate the supply and demand curves for this market. These curves intersect to yield an equilibrium price of $2.50 per slice and an equilibrium quantity of 5,000 slices per day.

FIGURE 3.6

Graphing Supply and Demand and Finding Equilibrium Price and Quantity.

To graph the demand and supply curves, plot the relevant points given in the table and then join them with a line. Equilibrium price and quantity occur at the intersection of these curves.

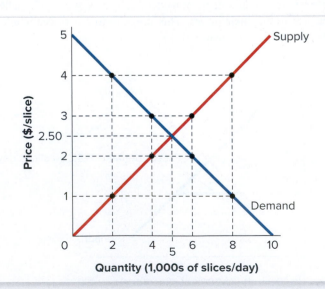

We emphasize that market equilibrium doesn't necessarily produce an ideal outcome for all market participants. Thus, in Example 3.1, market participants are satisfied with the amount of pizza they buy and sell at a price of $2.50 per slice, but for a poor buyer this may signify little more than that he *can't* buy additional pizza without sacrificing other more highly valued purchases.

Indeed, buyers with extremely low incomes often have difficulty purchasing even basic goods and services, which has prompted governments in almost every society to attempt to ease the burdens of the poor. Yet the laws of supply and demand cannot simply be repealed by an act of the legislature. In the next section, we'll see that when legislators attempt to prevent markets from reaching their equilibrium prices and quantities, they often do more harm than good. Fortunately, there are other, more effective, ways of providing assistance to families in need.

RENT CONTROLS RECONSIDERED

Consider again the market for rental housing units in New York City and suppose that the demand and supply curves for one-bedroom apartments are as shown in Figure 3.7. This market, left alone, would reach an equilibrium monthly rent of $1,600, at which 2 million one-bedroom apartments would be rented. Both landlords and tenants would be satisfied, in the sense that they would not wish to rent either more or fewer units at that price.

This wouldn't necessarily mean, of course, that all is well and good. Many potential tenants, for example, might simply be unable to afford a rent of $1,600 per month and thus be forced to remain homeless (or to move out of the city to a cheaper location). Suppose that, acting purely out of benign motives, legislators made it unlawful for landlords to charge more than $800 per month for one-bedroom apartments. Their stated aim in enacting this law was that no person should have to remain homeless because decent housing was unaffordable.

But note in Figure 3.8 that when rents for one-bedroom apartments are prevented from rising above $800 per month, landlords are willing to supply only 1 million apartments per month, 1 million fewer than at the equilibrium monthly rent of $1,600. Note also that at the controlled rent of $800 per month, tenants want to rent 3 million one-bedroom apartments per month. (For example, many people who would have decided to live in New Jersey rather than pay $1,600 a month in New York will now choose to live in the city.) So when rents are prevented from rising above $800 per month, we see an excess demand for one-bedroom apartments of 2 million units each month. Put another way, the rent controls result in a housing shortage of 2 million units each month. What is more, the number of apartments actually available *declines* by 1 million units per month.

If the housing market were completely unregulated, the immediate response to such a high level of excess demand would be for rents to rise sharply. But here the law prevents them from rising above $800. Many other ways exist, however, in which market participants

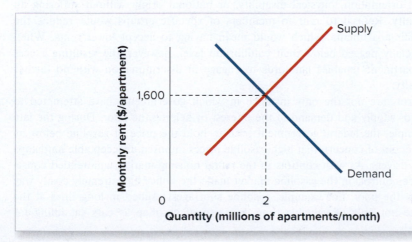

FIGURE 3.7

An Unregulated Housing Market.

For the supply and demand curves shown, the equilibrium monthly rent is $1,600 and 2 million apartments will be rented at that price.

FIGURE 3.8

Rent Controls.

When rents are prohibited from rising to the equilibrium level, the result is excess demand in the housing market.

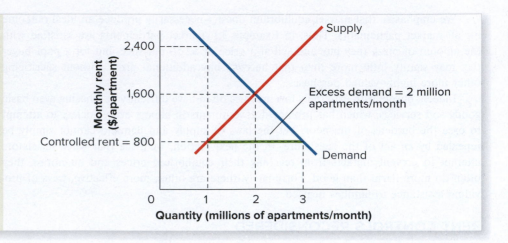

can respond to the pressures of excess demand. For instance, owners will quickly learn that they are free to spend less on maintaining their rental units. After all, if there are scores of renters knocking at the door of each vacant apartment, a landlord has considerable room to maneuver. Leaking pipes, peeling paint, broken furnaces, and other problems are less likely to receive prompt attention—or, indeed, any attention at all—when rents are set well below market-clearing levels.

Nor are reduced availability of apartments and poorer maintenance of existing apartments the only difficulties. With an offering of only 1 million apartments per month, we see in Figure 3.8 that there are renters who'd be willing to pay as much as $2,400 per month for an apartment. As the Incentive Principle suggests, this pressure will almost always find ways, legal or illegal, of expressing itself. In New York City, for example, it is not uncommon to see "finder's fees" or "key deposits" as high as several thousand dollars. Owners who cannot charge a market-clearing rent for their apartments also have the option of converting them to condominiums or co-ops, which enables them to sell their assets for prices much closer to their true economic value.

Incentive

Even when rent-controlled apartment owners don't hike their prices in these various ways, serious misallocations result. For instance, ill-suited roommates often remain together despite their constant bickering because each is reluctant to reenter the housing market. Or a widow might steadfastly remain in her seven-room apartment even after her children have left home because it is much cheaper than alternative dwellings not covered by rent control. It would be much better for all concerned if she relinquished that space to a larger family that valued it more highly. But under rent controls, she has no economic incentive to do so.

There's also another more insidious cost of rent controls. In markets without rent controls, landlords cannot discriminate against potential tenants on the basis of race, religion, sexual orientation, physical disability, or national origin without suffering an economic penalty. Refusal to rent to members of specific groups would reduce the demand for their apartments, which would mean having to accept lower rents. When rents are artificially pegged below their equilibrium level, however, the resulting excess demand for apartments enables landlords to engage in discrimination with no further economic penalty.

Rent controls are not the only instance in which governments have attempted to repeal the law of supply and demand in the interest of helping the poor. During the late 1970s, for example, the federal government tried to hold the price of gasoline below its equilibrium level out of concern that high gasoline prices imposed unacceptable hardships on low-income drivers. As with controls in the rental housing market, unintended consequences of price controls in the gasoline market made the policy an extremely costly way of trying to aid the poor. For example, gasoline shortages resulted in long lines at the pumps, a waste not only of valuable time, but also of gasoline as cars sat idling for extended periods.

In their opposition to rent controls and similar measures, are economists revealing a total lack of concern for the poor? Although this claim is sometimes made by those who don't understand the issues, or who stand to benefit in some way from government regulations, there is little justification for it. *Economists simply realize that there are much more effective ways to help poor people than to try to give them apartments and other goods at artificially low prices.*

One straightforward approach would be to give the poor additional income and let them decide for themselves how to spend it. True, there are also practical difficulties involved in transferring additional purchasing power into the hands of the poor—most importantly, the difficulty of targeting cash to the genuinely needy without weakening others' incentives to fend for themselves. But there are practical ways to overcome this difficulty. For example, for far less than the waste caused by price controls, the government could afford generous subsidies to the wages of the working poor and could sponsor public-service employment for those who are unable to find jobs in the private sector.

Regulations that peg prices below equilibrium levels have far-reaching effects on market outcomes. The following self-test asks you to consider what happens when a price control is established at a level above the equilibrium price.

✓ SELF-TEST 3.3

In the rental housing market whose demand and supply curves are shown below, what will be the effect of a law that prevents rents from rising above $1,200 per month?

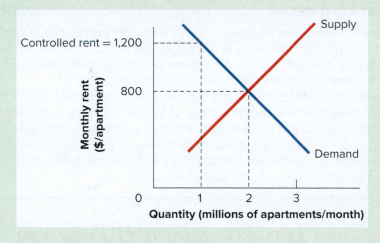

PIZZA PRICE CONTROLS?

The sources of the contrast between the rent-controlled housing market and the largely unregulated food markets in New York City can be seen more vividly by trying to imagine what would happen if concern for the poor led the city's leaders to implement price controls on pizza. Suppose, for example, that the supply and demand curves for pizza are as shown in Figure 3.9 and that the city imposes a **price ceiling** of $2 per slice, making it unlawful to charge more than that amount. At $2 per slice, buyers want to buy 16,000 slices per day, but sellers want to sell only 8,000.

At a price of $2 per slice, every pizza restaurant in the city will have long queues of buyers trying unsuccessfully to purchase pizza. Frustrated buyers will behave rudely to clerks, who will respond in kind. Friends of restaurant managers will begin to get preferential treatment. Devious pricing strategies will begin to emerge (such as the $2 slice of pizza sold in combination with a $5 cup of Coke). Pizza will be made from poorer-quality ingredients. Rumors will begin to circulate about sources of black-market pizza. And so on.

price ceiling a maximum allowable price, specified by law

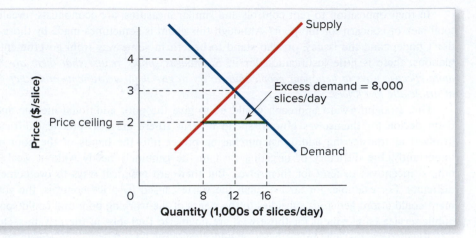

FIGURE 3.9

Price Controls in the Pizza Market.

A price ceiling below the equilibrium price of pizza would result in excess demand for pizza.

The very idea of not being able to buy a pizza seems absurd, yet precisely such things happen routinely in markets in which prices are held below the equilibrium levels. For example, prior to the collapse of communist governments, it was considered normal in those countries for people to stand in line for hours to buy bread and other basic goods, while the politically connected had first choice of those goods that were available.

> **RECAP** ↑
>
> **MARKET EQUILIBRIUM**
>
> *Market equilibrium*, the situation in which all buyers and sellers are satisfied with their respective quantities at the market price, occurs at the intersection of the supply and demand curves. The corresponding price and quantity are called the *equilibrium price* and the *equilibrium quantity*.
>
> Unless prevented by regulation, prices and quantities are driven toward their equilibrium values by the actions of buyers and sellers. If the price is initially too high, so that there is excess supply, frustrated sellers will cut their price in order to sell more. If the price is initially too low, so that there is excess demand, competition among buyers drives the price upward. This process continues until equilibrium is reached.

PREDICTING AND EXPLAINING CHANGES IN PRICES AND QUANTITIES

If we know how the factors that govern supply and demand curves are changing, we can make informed predictions about how prices and the corresponding quantities will change. But when describing changing circumstances in the marketplace, we must take care to recognize some important terminological distinctions. For example, we must distinguish between the meanings of the seemingly similar expressions **change in the quantity demanded** and **change in demand.** When we speak of a "change in the quantity demanded," this means the change in the quantity that people wish to buy that occurs in response to a change in price. For instance, Figure 3.10(a) depicts an increase in the quantity demanded that occurs in response to a reduction in the price of tuna. When the price falls from $2 to $1 per can, the quantity demanded rises from 8,000 to 10,000 cans per day. By contrast, when we speak of a "change in demand," this means a *shift in the entire demand curve.* For example, Figure 3.10(b) depicts an increase in demand, meaning that at every price the quantity demanded is higher than before. In summary, a "change in the quantity demanded" refers to a movement *along* the demand curve and a "change in demand" means a *shift* of the entire curve.

change in the quantity demanded a movement along the demand curve that occurs in response to a change in price

change in demand a shift of the entire demand curve

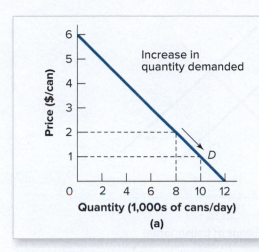

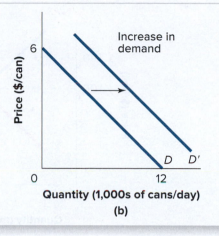

FIGURE 3.10

An Increase in the Quantity Demanded versus an Increase in Demand.

(a) An increase in quantity demanded describes a downward movement along the demand curve as price falls. (b) An increase in demand describes an outward shift of the demand curve.

A similar terminological distinction applies on the supply side of the market. A **change in supply** means a shift in the entire supply curve, whereas a **change in the quantity supplied** refers to a movement along the supply curve.

Alfred Marshall's supply and demand model is one of the most useful tools of the economic naturalist. Once we understand the forces that govern the placements of supply and demand curves, we're suddenly in a position to make sense of a host of interesting observations in the world around us.

change in supply a shift of the entire supply curve

change in the quantity supplied a movement along the supply curve that occurs in response to a change in price

SHIFTS IN DEMAND

To get a better feel for how the supply and demand model enables us to predict and explain price and quantity movements, it's helpful to begin with a few simple examples. The first one illustrates a shift in demand that results from events outside the particular market itself.

| EXAMPLE 3.2 | Complements |

What will happen to the equilibrium price and quantity of tennis balls if court-rental fees decline?

Let the initial supply and demand curves for tennis balls be as shown by the curves *S* and *D* in Figure 3.11, where the resulting equilibrium price and quantity are $1 per ball and 40 million balls per month, respectively. Tennis courts and tennis balls are what economists call **complements,** goods that are more valuable when used in combination than when used alone. Tennis balls, for example, would be of little value if there were no tennis courts on which to play. (Tennis balls would still have *some* value even without courts—for example, to the parents who pitch them to their children for batting practice.) As tennis courts become cheaper to use, people will respond by playing more tennis, and this will increase their demand for tennis balls. A decline in court-rental fees will thus shift the demand curve for tennis balls rightward to *D'*. (A "rightward shift" of a demand curve also can be described as an "upward shift." These distinctions correspond, respectively, to the horizontal and vertical interpretations of the demand curve.)

complements two goods are complements in consumption if an increase in the price of one causes a leftward shift in the demand curve for the other (or if a decrease causes a rightward shift)

Note in Figure 3.11 that, for the illustrative demand shift shown, the new equilibrium price of tennis balls, $1.40, is higher than the original price and the new equilibrium quantity, 58 million balls per month, is higher than the original quantity.

FIGURE 3.11

The Effect on the Market for Tennis Balls of a Decline in Court-Rental Fees.

When the price of a complement falls, demand shifts right, causing equilibrium price and quantity to rise.

EXAMPLE 3.3 Substitutes

What will happen to the equilibrium price and quantity of print ads as the price of digital ads falls?

substitutes two goods are substitutes in consumption if an increase in the price of one causes a rightward shift in the demand curve for the other (or if a decrease causes a leftward shift)

Most businesses purchase a mix of digital and print ads to promote their products. Suppose the initial supply and demand curves print ads are as shown by the curves S and D in Figure 3.12, and the resulting equilibrium price and quantity are denoted P and Q. Print ads and digital ads are examples of what economists call **substitutes,** meaning that, in many applications at least, the two serve similar functions. (Many noneconomists would call them substitutes, too. Economists don't *always* choose obscure terms for important concepts!) When two goods or services are substitutes, a decrease in the price of one will cause a leftward shift in the demand curve for the other. (A "leftward shift" in a demand curve can also be described as a "downward shift.") Diagrammatically, the demand curve for print ads shifts from D to D' in Figure 3.12.

FIGURE 3.12

The Effect on the Market for Print Ads of a Decline in the Price of Digital Ads.

When the price of a substitute falls, demand shifts left, causing equilibrium price and quantity to fall.

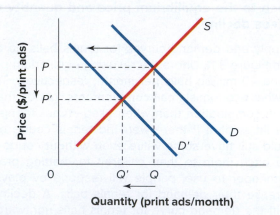

As the figure shows, both the new equilibrium price, *P'*, and the new equilibrium quantity, *Q'*, are lower than the initial values, *P* and *Q*. Cheaper digital ads probably won't put print advertising companies out of business, but it will definitely lead to a drop in sales.

To summarize, economists define goods as substitutes if an increase in the price of one causes a rightward shift in the demand curve for the other. By contrast, goods are complements if an increase in the price of one causes a leftward shift in the demand curve for the other.

The concepts of substitutes and complements enable you to answer questions like the one posed in Self-Test 3.4.

▶ Visit your instructor's Connect course and access your eBook to view this video.

✔ **SELF-TEST 3.4**

How will a decline in airfares affect intercity bus fares and the price of hotel rooms in resort communities?

Why are rotisserie chickens less expensive than fresh chickens?

Demand curves are shifted not just by changes in the prices of substitutes and complements but also by other factors that change the amounts people are willing to pay for a given good or service. One of the most important such factors is income.

The Economic Naturalist 3.1

When the federal government implements a large pay increase for its employees, why do rents for apartments located near Washington Metro stations go up relative to rents for apartments located far away from Metro stations?

For the citizens of Washington, D.C., a substantial proportion of whom are government employees, it's more convenient to live in an apartment located 1 block from the nearest subway station than to live in one that is 20 blocks away. Conveniently located apartments thus command relatively high rents. Suppose the initial demand and supply curves for such apartments are as shown in Figure 3.13. Following a federal pay raise, some government employees who live in less convenient apartments will be willing and able to use part of their extra income to bid for more conveniently located apartments, and those who already live in such apartments will be willing and able to pay more to keep them. The effect of the pay raise is thus to shift the demand curve for conveniently located apartments to the right, as indicated by the demand curve labeled D'. As a result, both the equilibrium price and quantity of such apartments, P' and Q', will be higher than before.

Who gets to live in the most conveniently located apartments?

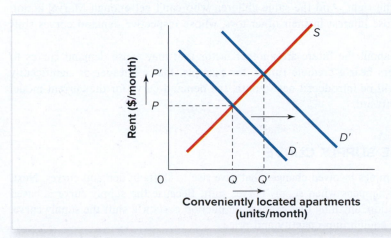

FIGURE 3.13

The Effect of a Federal Pay Raise on the Rent for Conveniently Located Apartments in Washington, D.C.

An increase in income shifts demand for a normal good to the right, causing equilibrium price and quantity to rise.

Incentive

It might seem natural to ask how there could be an increase in the number of conveniently located apartments, which might appear to be fixed by the constraints of geography. But the Incentive Principle reminds us never to underestimate the ingenuity of sellers when they confront an opportunity to make money by supplying more of something that people want. For example, if rents rose sufficiently, some landlords might respond by converting warehouse space to residential use. Or perhaps people with cars who do not place high value on living near a subway station might sell their co-op apartments to landlords, thereby freeing them for people eager to rent them. (Note that these responses constitute movements along the supply curve of conveniently located apartments, as opposed to shifts in that supply curve.)

When incomes increase, the demand curves for most goods will behave like the demand curve for conveniently located apartments, and in recognition of that fact, economists have chosen to call such goods **normal goods.**

Not all goods are normal goods, however. In fact, the demand curves for some goods actually shift leftward when income goes up. Such goods are called **inferior goods.**

When would having more money tend to make you want to buy less of something? In general, this happens with goods for which there exist attractive substitutes that sell for only slightly higher prices. Apartments in unsafe, inconveniently located neighborhoods are an example. Most residents would choose to move out of such neighborhoods as soon as they could afford to, which means that an increase in income would cause the demand for such apartments to shift leftward.

normal good a good whose demand curve shifts rightward when the incomes of buyers increase and leftward when the incomes of buyers decrease

inferior good a good whose demand curve shifts leftward when the incomes of buyers increase and rightward when the incomes of buyers decrease

✔ SELF-TEST 3.5

How will a large pay increase for federal employees affect the rents for apartments located far away from Washington Metro stations?

Ground beef with high fat content is another example of an inferior good. For health reasons, most people prefer grades of meat with low fat content, and when they do buy high-fat meats it's usually a sign of budgetary pressure. When people in this situation receive higher incomes, they usually switch quickly to leaner grades of meat.

Cost-Benefit

Preferences, or tastes, are another important factor that determines whether the purchase of a given good will satisfy the Cost-Benefit Principle. The release of each Marvel Studio film appears to kindle a powerful preference among children for Marvel action figures. When these films are released, the demand for Marvel action figures shifts sharply to the right. And the same children who can't get enough Marvel action figures suddenly lose interest in their other toys, whose respective demand curves shift to the left.

Expectations about the future are another factor that may cause demand curves to shift. If Apple users hear a credible rumor, for example, that a cheaper or significantly upgraded model will be introduced next month, the demand curve for the current model is likely to shift leftward.

SHIFTS IN THE SUPPLY CURVE

The preceding examples involved changes that gave rise to shifts in demand curves. Next, we'll look at what happens when supply curves shift. Because the supply curve is based on costs of production, anything that changes production costs will shift the supply curve, resulting in a new equilibrium quantity and price.

EXAMPLE 3.4   Increasing Opportunity Cost

What will happen to the equilibrium price and quantity of skateboards if the price of fiberglass, a substance used for making skateboards, rises?

Suppose the initial supply and demand curves for skateboards are as shown by the curves *S* and *D* in Figure 3.14, resulting in an equilibrium price and quantity

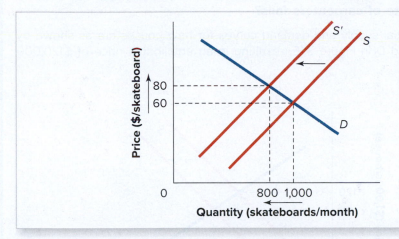

FIGURE 3.14

The Effect on the Skateboard Market of an Increase in the Price of Fiberglass.

When input prices rise, supply shifts left, causing equilibrium price to rise and equilibrium quantity to fall.

of $60 per skateboard and 1,000 skateboards per month, respectively. Since fiberglass is one of the materials used to produce skateboards, the effect of an increase in its price is to raise the marginal cost of producing skateboards. How will this affect the supply curve of skateboards?

Recall that the supply curve is upward-sloping because when the price of skateboards is low, only those potential sellers whose marginal cost of making skateboards is low can sell boards profitably, whereas at higher prices, those with higher marginal costs also can enter the market profitably (again, the Low-Hanging-Fruit Principle). So if the cost of one of the materials used to produce skateboards rises, the number of potential sellers who can profitably sell skateboards at any given price will fall. And this, in turn, implies a leftward shift in the supply curve for skateboards. Note that a "leftward shift" in a supply curve also can be viewed as an "upward shift" in the same curve. The first corresponds to the horizontal interpretation of the supply curve, while the second corresponds to the vertical interpretation. We will use these expressions to mean exactly the same thing. The new supply curve (after the price of fiberglass rises) is the curve labeled *S'* in Figure 3.14.

Does an increase in the cost of fiberglass have any effect on the demand curve for skateboards? The demand curve tells us how many skateboards buyers wish to purchase at each price. Any given buyer is willing to purchase a skateboard if her reservation price for it exceeds its market price. And since each buyer's reservation price, which is based on the benefits of owning a skateboard, does not depend on the price of fiberglass, there should be no shift in the demand curve for skateboards.

In Figure 3.14, we can now see what happens when the supply curve shifts leftward and the demand curve remains unchanged. For the illustrative supply curve shown, the new equilibrium price of skateboards, $80, is higher than the original price, and the new equilibrium quantity, 800 per month, is lower than the original quantity. (These new equilibrium values are merely illustrative. There is insufficient information provided in the example to determine their exact values.) People who don't place a value of at least $80 on owning a skateboard will choose to spend their money on something else.

Increasing
Opportunity Cost

The effects on equilibrium price and quantity run in the opposite direction whenever marginal costs of production decline, as illustrated in the next example.

EXAMPLE 3.5	**Reduction of Marginal Cost**

What will happen to the equilibrium price and quantity of new houses if the wage rate of carpenters falls?

Suppose the initial supply and demand curves for new houses are as shown by the curves S and D in Figure 3.15, resulting in an equilibrium price of $120,000

FIGURE 3.15

The Effect on the Market for New Houses of a Decline in Carpenters' Wage Rates.

When input prices fall, supply shifts right, causing equilibrium price to fall and equilibrium quantity to rise.

per house and an equilibrium quantity of 40 houses per month, respectively. A decline in the wage rate of carpenters reduces the marginal cost of making new houses, and this means that, for any given price of houses, more builders can profitably serve the market than before. Diagrammatically, this means a rightward shift in the supply curve of houses, from S to S'. (A "rightward shift" in the supply curve also can be described as a "downward shift.")

Does a decrease in the wage rate of carpenters have any effect on the demand curve for houses? The demand curve tells us how many houses buyers wish to purchase at each price. Because carpenters are now earning less than before, the maximum amount that they are willing to pay for houses may fall, which would imply a leftward shift in the demand curve for houses. But because carpenters make up only a tiny fraction of all potential home buyers, we may assume that this shift is negligible. Thus, a reduction in carpenters' wages produces a significant rightward shift in the supply curve of houses, but no appreciable shift in the demand curve.

We see from Figure 3.15 that the new equilibrium price, $90,000 per house, is lower than the original price and the new equilibrium quantity, 50 houses per month, is higher than the original quantity.

Examples 3.4 and 3.5 involved changes in the cost of a material, or input, in the production of the good in question—fiberglass in the production of skateboards and carpenters' labor in the production of houses. As the following example illustrates, supply curves also shift when technology changes.

The Economic Naturalist 3.2

Why do major term papers go through so many more revisions today than in the 1970s?

Students in the dark days before word processors were in widespread use could not make even minor revisions in their term papers without having to retype their entire manuscript from scratch. The availability of word-processing technology has, of course, radically changed the picture. Instead of having to retype the entire draft, now only the changes need be entered.

In Figure 3.16, the curves labeled S and D depict the supply and demand curves for revisions in the days before word processing, and the curve S' depicts the supply curve for revisions today. As the diagram shows, the result is not only a sharp decline in the price per revision, but also a corresponding increase in the equilibrium number of revisions.

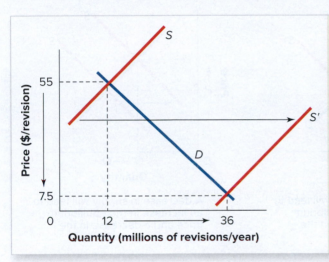

Quantity (millions of revisions/year)

FIGURE 3.16

The Effect of Technical Change on the Market for Term-Paper Revisions.

When a new technology reduces the cost of production, supply shifts right, causing equilibrium price to fall and equilibrium quantity to rise.

Why does written work go through so many more revisions now than in the 1970s?

Note that in The Economic Naturalist 3.2 we implicitly assumed that students purchased typing services in a market. In fact, however, many students type their own term papers. Does that make a difference? Even if no money actually changes hands, students pay a price when they revise their term papers—namely, the opportunity cost of the time it takes to perform that task. Because technology has radically reduced that cost, we would expect to see a large increase in the number of term-paper revisions even if most students type their own work.

Changes in input prices and technology are two of the most important factors that give rise to shifts in supply curves. In the case of agricultural commodities, weather may be another important factor, with favorable conditions shifting the supply curves of such products to the right and unfavorable conditions shifting them to the left. (Weather also may affect the supply curves of nonagricultural products through its effects on the national transportation system.) Expectations of future price changes also may shift current supply curves, as when the expectation of poor crops from a current drought causes suppliers to withhold supplies from existing stocks in the hope of selling at higher prices in the future. Changes in the number of sellers in the market also can cause supply curves to shift.

FOUR SIMPLE RULES

For supply and demand curves that have the conventional slopes (upward-sloping for supply curves, downward-sloping for demand curves), the preceding examples illustrate the four basic rules that govern how shifts in supply and demand affect equilibrium prices and quantities. These rules are summarized in Figure 3.17.

FIGURE 3.17

Four Rules Governing the Effects of Supply and Demand Shifts.

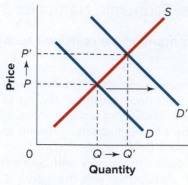

An increase in demand will lead to an increase in both the equilibrium price and quantity.

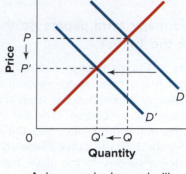

A decrease in demand will lead to a decrease in both the equilibrium price and quantity.

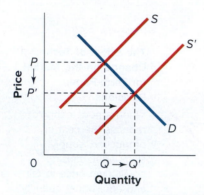

An increase in supply will lead to a decrease in the equilibrium price and an increase in the equilibrium quantity.

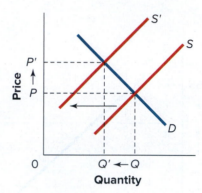

A decrease in supply will lead to an increase in the equilibrium price and a decrease in the equilibrium quantity.

RECAP

FACTORS THAT SHIFT SUPPLY AND DEMAND

Factors that cause an increase (rightward or upward shift) in demand:

1. A decrease in the price of complements to the good or service.
2. An increase in the price of substitutes for the good or service.
3. An increase in income (for a normal good).
4. An increased preference by demanders for the good or service.
5. An increase in the population of potential buyers.
6. An expectation of higher prices in the future.

When these factors move in the opposite direction, demand will shift left.

Factors that cause an increase (rightward or downward shift) in supply:

1. A decrease in the cost of materials, labor, or other inputs used in the production of the good or service.
2. An improvement in technology that reduces the cost of producing the good or service.
3. An improvement in the weather (especially for agricultural products).
4. An increase in the number of suppliers.
5. An expectation of lower prices in the future.

When these factors move in the opposite direction, supply will shift left.

The qualitative rules summarized in Figure 3.17 hold for supply or demand shifts of any magnitude, provided the curves have their conventional slopes. But as the next example demonstrates, when both supply and demand curves shift at the same time, the direction in which equilibrium price or quantity changes will depend on the relative magnitudes of the shifts.

| **EXAMPLE 3.6** | **Shifts in Supply and Demand** |

How do shifts in *both* demand and supply affect equilibrium quantities and prices?

What will happen to the equilibrium price and quantity in the corn tortilla chip market if both of the following events occur: (1) researchers prove that the oils in which tortilla chips are fried are harmful to human health and (2) the price of corn harvesting equipment falls?

The conclusion regarding the health effects of the oils will shift the demand for tortilla chips to the left because many people who once bought chips in the belief that they were healthful will now switch to other foods. The decline in the price of harvesting equipment will shift the supply of chips to the right because additional farmers will now find it profitable to enter the corn market. In Figure 3.18(a) and 3.18(b), the original supply and demand curves are denoted by *S* and *D*, while the new curves are denoted by *S'* and *D'*. Note that in both panels the shifts lead to a decline in the equilibrium price of chips.

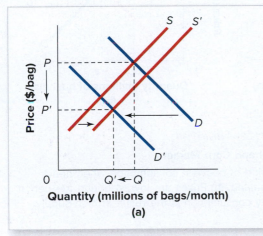
(a)

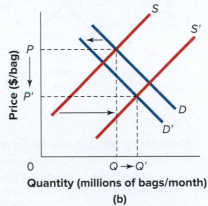
(b)

FIGURE 3.18

The Effects of Simultaneous Shifts in Supply and Demand.

When demand shifts left and supply shifts right, equilibrium price falls, but equilibrium quantity may either rise (b) or fall (a).

But note also that the effect of the shifts on equilibrium quantity cannot be determined without knowing their relative magnitudes. Taken separately, the demand shift causes a decline in equilibrium quantity, whereas the supply shift causes an increase in equilibrium quantity. The net effect of the two shifts thus depends on which of the individual effects is larger. In Figure 3.18(a), the demand shift dominates, so equilibrium quantity declines. In Figure 3.18(b), the supply shift dominates, so equilibrium quantity goes up.

The following Self-Test 3.6 asks you to consider a simple variation on the problem posed in the previous example.

✅ **SELF-TEST 3.6**

What will happen to the equilibrium price and quantity in the corn tortilla chip market if both of the following events occur: (1) researchers discover that a vitamin found in corn helps protect against cancer and heart disease and (2) a swarm of locusts destroys part of the corn crop?

The Economic Naturalist 3.3

Why do the prices of some goods, like airline tickets to Europe, go up during the months of heaviest consumption, while others, like sweet corn, go down?

Seasonal price movements for airline tickets are primarily the result of seasonal variations in demand. Thus, ticket prices to Europe are highest during the summer months because the demand for tickets is highest during those months, as shown in Figure 3.19(a), where the w and s subscripts denote winter and summer values, respectively.

Why are some goods cheapest during the months of heaviest consumption, while others are most expensive during those months?

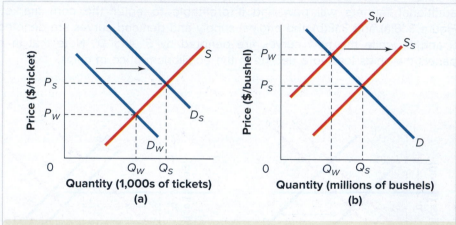

FIGURE 3.19

Seasonal Variation in the Air Travel and Corn Markets.

(a) Prices are highest during the period of heaviest consumption when heavy consumption is the result of high demand. (b) Prices are lowest during the period of heaviest consumption when heavy consumption is the result of high supply.

By contrast, seasonal price movements for sweet corn are primarily the result of seasonal variations in supply. The price of sweet corn is lowest in the summer months because its supply is highest during those months, as seen in Figure 3.19(b).

EFFICIENCY AND EQUILIBRIUM

Markets represent a highly effective system of allocating resources. When a market for a good is in equilibrium, the equilibrium price conveys important information to potential suppliers about the value that potential demanders place on that good. At the same time, the equilibrium price informs potential demanders about the opportunity cost of supplying the good. This rapid, two-way transmission of information is the reason that markets can coordinate an activity as complex as supplying New York City with food and drink, even though no one person or organization oversees the process.

But are the prices and quantities determined in market equilibrium socially optimal, in the sense of maximizing total economic surplus? That is, does equilibrium in unregulated markets always maximize the difference between the total benefits and total costs experienced by market participants? As we'll see, the answer is "it depends": a market that is out of equilibrium, such as the rent-controlled New York housing market, always creates opportunities for individuals to arrange transactions that will increase their individual economic surplus. As we'll also see, however, a market for a good that is in equilibrium makes the largest possible contribution to total economic surplus only when its supply and demand curves fully reflect all costs and benefits associated with the production and consumption of that good.

CASH ON THE TABLE

In economics we assume that all exchange is purely voluntary. This means that a transaction cannot take place unless the buyer's reservation price for the good exceeds the seller's reservation price. When that condition is met and a transaction takes place, both parties receive an economic surplus. The **buyer's surplus** from the transaction is the difference between his or her reservation price and the price he or she actually pays. The **seller's surplus** is the difference between the price he or she receives and his or her reservation price. The **total surplus** from the transaction is the sum of the buyer's surplus and the seller's surplus. It is also equal to the difference between the buyer's reservation price and the seller's reservation price.

Suppose there is a potential buyer whose reservation price for an additional slice of pizza is $4 and a potential seller whose reservation price is only $2. If this buyer purchases a slice of pizza from this seller for $3, the total surplus generated by this exchange is $4 − $2 = $2, of which $4 − $3 = $1 is the buyer's surplus and $3 − $2 = $1 is the seller's surplus.

A regulation that prevents the price of a good from reaching its equilibrium level unnecessarily prevents exchanges of this sort from taking place, and in the process reduces total economic surplus. Consider again the effect of price controls imposed in the market for pizza. The demand curve in Figure 3.20 tells us that if a price ceiling of $2 per slice were imposed, only 8,000 slices of pizza per day would be sold. At that quantity, the vertical interpretations of the supply and demand curves tell us that a buyer would be willing to pay as much as $4 for an additional slice and that a seller would be willing to sell one for as little as $2. The difference—$2 per slice—is the additional economic surplus that would result if an additional slice were produced and sold. As noted earlier, an extra slice sold at a price of $3 would result in an additional $1 of economic surplus for both buyer and seller.

When a market is out of equilibrium, it's always possible to identify mutually beneficial exchanges of this sort. When people have failed to take advantage of all mutually beneficial exchanges, we often say that there's **"cash on the table"**—the economist's metaphor for unexploited opportunities. When the price in a market is below the equilibrium price, there's cash on the table because the reservation price of sellers (marginal cost)

buyer's surplus the difference between the buyer's reservation price and the price he or she actually pays

seller's surplus the difference between the price received by the seller and his or her reservation price

total surplus the difference between the buyer's reservation price and the seller's reservation price

cash on the table an economic metaphor for unexploited gains from exchange

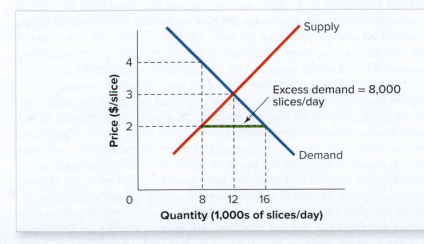

FIGURE 3.20

Price Controls in the Pizza Market.

A price ceiling below the equilibrium price of pizza would result in excess demand for pizza.

will always be lower than the reservation price of buyers. In the absence of a law preventing buyers from paying more than $2 per slice, restaurant owners would quickly raise their prices and expand their production until the equilibrium price of $3 per slice were reached. At that price, buyers would be able to get precisely the 12,000 slices of pizza they want to buy each day. All mutually beneficial opportunities for exchange would have been exploited, leaving no more cash on the table.

With the Incentive Principle in mind, it should be no surprise that buyers and sellers in the marketplace have an uncanny ability to detect the presence of cash on the table. It is almost as if unexploited opportunities give off some exotic scent triggering neuro-chemical explosions in the olfactory centers of their brains. The desire to scrape cash off the table and into their pockets is what drives sellers in each of New York City's thousands of individual food markets to work diligently to meet their customers' demands. That they succeed to a far higher degree than participants in the city's rent-controlled housing market is plainly evident. Whatever flaws it might have, the market system moves with considerably greater speed and agility than any centralized allocation mechanisms yet devised. But as we emphasize in the following section, this does not mean that markets *always* lead to the greatest good for all.

SMART FOR ONE, DUMB FOR ALL

socially optimal quantity
the quantity of a good that results in the maximum possible economic surplus from producing and consuming the good

The **socially optimal quantity** of any good is the quantity that maximizes the total economic surplus that results from producing and consuming the good. From the Cost-Benefit Principle, we know that we should keep expanding production of the good as long as its marginal benefit is at least as great as its marginal cost. This means that the socially optimal quantity is that level for which the marginal cost and marginal benefit of the good are the same.

When the quantity of a good is less than the socially optimal quantity, boosting its production will increase total economic surplus. By the same token, when the quantity of a good exceeds the socially optimal quantity, reducing its production will increase total economic surplus. **Efficiency, or economic efficiency,** occurs when all goods and services in the economy are produced and consumed at their respective socially optimal levels.

efficiency (or **economic efficiency**) a condition that occurs when all goods and services are produced and consumed at their respective socially optimal levels

Efficiency is an important social goal. Failure to achieve efficiency means that total economic surplus is smaller than it could have been. Movements toward efficiency make the total economic pie larger, making it possible for everyone to have a larger slice. The importance of efficiency will be a recurring theme as we move forward, and we state it here as one of the core principles:

The Efficiency Principle: Efficiency is an important social goal because when the economic pie grows larger, everyone can have a larger slice.

Is the market equilibrium quantity of a good efficient? That is, does it maximize the total economic surplus received by participants in the market for that good? When the private market for a given good is in equilibrium, we can say that the cost *to the seller* of producing an additional unit of the good is the same as the benefit *to the buyer* of having an additional unit. If all costs of producing the good are borne directly by sellers, and if all benefits from the good accrue directly to buyers, it follows that the market equilibrium quantity of the good will equate the marginal cost and marginal benefit of the good. And this means that the equilibrium quantity also maximizes total economic surplus.

But sometimes the production of a good entails costs that fall on people other than those who sell the good. This will be true, for instance, for goods whose production generates significant levels of environmental pollution. As extra units of these goods are produced, the extra pollution harms other people besides sellers. In the market equilibrium for such goods, the benefit *to buyers* of the last good produced is, as before, equal to the cost incurred by sellers to produce that good. But since producing that good also imposes pollution costs on others, we know that the *full* marginal cost of the last unit produced—the seller's private marginal cost plus the marginal pollution cost borne by others—must be higher than the benefit of the last unit produced. So, in this case, the market equilibrium quantity of the good will be larger than the socially optimal quantity. Total economic

The Economic Naturalist 3.4

Why was there a shortage of toilet paper during the COVID-19 pandemic?

During the COVID-19 pandemic many consumers in search of toilet paper arrived at their local grocery stores only to be faced with empty shelves. If prices are supposed to adjust to equate the quantity supplied and the quantity demanded, then why was there a shortage of toilet paper during the COVID-19 pandemic?

Faced with the public health crisis brought about the COVID-19, many, if not most, consumers in the United States stocked up on essential items such as toilet paper. Indeed, some consumers purchased excessive quantities of these items, and this type of hoarding behavior received much of the blame for the shortage of toilet paper during the pandemic.

But there is another important factor as well. The toilet paper market in the United States is divided into two distinct segments. There is a market for the lower-quality commercial-grade toilet paper, typically used in restaurants, schools, workplaces and other public venues, and a separate market for the higher-quality consumer-grade toilet paper, generally used in people's homes. Even though the overall use of toilet paper did not substantially change during the pandemic, there was a large shift away from commercial-grade toilet paper toward consumer-grade toilet paper. That is, the widespread stay-at-home orders led to a sharp decrease in the demand for commercial-grade toilet paper, and an equally abrupt increase in the demand for consumer-grade toilet paper, and toilet paper producers, who are accustomed to relatively stable demand, had difficulty adjusting to this rapid change.

Of course, in normal times, an increase in demand would not lead to a shortage. Instead we would expect prices to rise. During times of emergency, however, both social norms and price gouging laws limit retailers' ability to raise prices. Thus while the demand for consumer-grade toilet paper surged during the pandemic (both because of hoarding and the shift away from commercial-grade toilet paper), prices did not adjust, leading to empty shelves and anxious consumers.

---

surplus would be higher if output of the good were lower. Yet neither sellers nor buyers have any incentive to alter their behavior.

Another possibility is that people other than those who buy a good may receive significant benefits from it. For instance, when someone purchases a vaccination against measles from her doctor, she not only protects herself, but also makes it less likely that others will catch this disease. From the perspective of society as a whole, we should keep increasing the number of vaccinations until their marginal cost equals their marginal benefit. The marginal benefit of a vaccination is the value of the protection it provides the person vaccinated *plus* the value of the protection it provides all others. Private consumers, however, will choose to be vaccinated only if the marginal benefit *to them* exceeds the price of the vaccination. In this case, then, the market equilibrium quantity of vaccinations will be smaller than the quantity that maximizes total economic surplus. Again, however, individuals would have no incentive to alter their behavior.

Situations like the ones just discussed provide examples of behaviors that we may call "smart for one but dumb for all." In each case, the individual actors are behaving rationally. They are pursuing their goals as best they can, and yet there remain unexploited opportunities for gain from the point of view of the whole society. The difficulty is that these opportunities cannot be exploited by individuals acting alone. In subsequent chapters, we will see how people can often organize collectively to exploit such opportunities. For now, we simply summarize this discussion in the form of the following core principle:

The Equilibrium Principle (also called the No-Cash-on-the-Table Principle): A market in equilibrium leaves no unexploited opportunities for individuals but may not exploit all gains achievable through collective action.

 Equilibrium

> **RECAP** ↑
>
> **EFFICIENCY AND EQUILIBRIUM**
>
> When the supply and demand curves for a good reflect all significant costs and benefits associated with the production and consumption of that good, the market equilibrium will result in the largest possible economic surplus. But if people other than buyers benefit from the good, or if people other than sellers bear costs because of it, market equilibrium need not result in the largest possible economic surplus.

SUMMARY

- The demand curve is a downward-sloping line that tells what quantity buyers will demand at any given price. The supply curve is an upward-sloping line that tells what quantity sellers will offer at any given price. *(LO1)*

- Alfred Marshall's model of supply and demand explains why neither cost of production nor value to the purchaser (as measured by willingness to pay) is, by itself, sufficient to explain why some goods are cheap and others are expensive. To explain variations in price, we must examine the interaction of cost and willingness to pay. As we've seen in this chapter, goods differ in price because of differences in their respective supply and demand curves. *(LO2)*

- Market equilibrium occurs when the quantity buyers demand at the market price is exactly the same as the quantity that sellers offer. The equilibrium price–quantity pair is the one at which the demand and supply curves intersect. In equilibrium, market price measures both the value of the last unit sold to buyers and the cost of the resources required to produce it. *(LO2)*

- When the price of a good lies above its equilibrium value, there is an excess supply of that good. Excess supply motivates sellers to cut their prices and price continues to fall until equilibrium price is reached. When price lies below its equilibrium value, there is excess demand. With excess demand, frustrated buyers are motivated to offer higher prices and the upward pressure on prices persists until equilibrium is reached. A remarkable feature of the market system is that, relying only on the tendency of people to respond in self-interested ways to market price signals, it somehow manages to coordinate the actions of literally billions of buyers and sellers worldwide. When excess demand or excess supply occurs, it tends to be small and brief, except in markets where regulations prevent full adjustment of prices. *(LO2)*

- The basic supply and demand model is a primary tool of the economic naturalist. Changes in the equilibrium price of a good, and in the amount of it traded in the marketplace, can be predicted on the basis of shifts in its supply or demand curves. The following four rules hold for any good with a downward-sloping demand curve and an upward-sloping supply curve:
  1. An increase in demand will lead to an increase in equilibrium price and quantity.
  2. A reduction in demand will lead to a reduction in equilibrium price and quantity.
  3. An increase in supply will lead to a reduction in equilibrium price and an increase in equilibrium quantity.
  4. A decrease in supply will lead to an increase in equilibrium price and a reduction in equilibrium quantity. *(LO3)*

- Incomes, tastes, population, expectations, and the prices of substitutes and complements are among the factors that shift demand schedules. Supply schedules, in turn, are primarily governed by such factors as technology, input prices, expectations, the number of sellers, and, especially for agricultural products, the weather. *(LO3)*

- The efficiency of markets in allocating resources does not eliminate social concerns about how goods and services are distributed among different people. For example, we often lament the fact many buyers enter the market with too little income to buy even the most basic goods and services. Concern for the well-being of the poor has motivated many governments to intervene in a variety of ways to alter the outcomes of market forces. Sometimes these interventions take the form of laws that peg prices below their equilibrium levels. Such laws almost invariably generate harmful, if unintended, consequences. Programs like rent-control laws, for example, lead to severe housing shortages, black marketeering, and a rapid deterioration of the relationship between landlords and tenants. *(LO4)*

- If the difficulty is that the poor have too little money, the best solution is to discover ways of boosting their incomes directly. The law of supply and demand cannot be repealed by the legislature. But legislatures do have the capacity to alter the underlying forces that govern the shape and position of supply and demand schedules. *(LO4)*

- When the supply and demand curves for a good reflect all significant costs and benefits associated with the production and consumption of that good, the market equilibrium price will guide people to produce and consume the quantity of the good that results in the largest possible economic surplus. This conclusion, however, does not apply if others, besides buyers, benefit from the good (as when someone benefits from his neighbor's purchase of a vaccination against measles) or if others besides sellers bear costs because of the good (as when its production generates pollution). In such cases, market equilibrium does not result in the greatest gain for all. *(LO4)*

CORE PRINCIPLES

 >> **The Efficiency Principle**
Efficiency is an important social goal because when the economic pie grows larger, everyone can have a larger slice.

 >> **The Equilibrium Principle (also called the No-Cash-on-the-Table Principle)**
A market in equilibrium leaves no unexploited opportunities for individuals but may not exploit all gains achievable through collective action.

KEY TERMS

buyer's reservation price	demand curve	market equilibrium
buyer's surplus	efficiency (or economic efficiency)	normal good
cash on the table	equilibrium	price ceiling
change in demand	equilibrium price and equilibrium quantity	seller's reservation price
change in supply		seller's surplus
change in the quantity demanded	excess demand (or shortage)	socially optimal quantity
	excess supply (or surplus)	substitutes
change in the quantity supplied	income effect	substitution effect
	inferior good	supply curve
complements	market	total surplus

REVIEW QUESTIONS

1. Explain the distinction between the horizontal and vertical interpretations of the demand curve. *(LO1)*

2. Why isn't knowing the cost of producing a good sufficient to predict its market price? *(LO2)*

3. In recent years, a government official proposed that gasoline price controls be imposed to protect the poor from rising gasoline prices. What evidence could you consult to discover whether this proposal was enacted? *(LO2)*

4. Distinguish between the meaning of the expressions "change in demand" and "change in the quantity demanded." *(LO3)*

5. Give an example of behavior you have observed that could be described as "smart for one but dumb for all." *(LO4)*

PROBLEMS

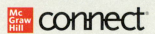

1. How would each of the following affect the U.S. market supply curve for corn? *(LO1)*
   a. A new and improved crop rotation technique is discovered.
   b. The price of fertilizer falls.
   c. The government offers new tax breaks to farmers.
   d. A tornado sweeps through Iowa.

2. Indicate how you think each of the following would shift demand in the indicated market. *(LO1)*
   a. The incomes of buyers in the market for Adirondack vacations increase.
   b. Buyers in the market for pizza read a study linking pepperoni consumption to heart disease.

c. Buyers in the market for gas-powered cars learn of an increase in the price of electric cars (a substitute for gas-powered cars).

d. Buyers in the market for electric cars learn of an increase in the price of electric cars.

3. An Arizona student claims to have spotted a UFO over the desert outside of Tucson. How will this claim affect the *supply* (not the quantity supplied) of binoculars in Tucson stores? *(LO1)*

4. Suppose that when milk sells for $4.50 per gallon, the quantity of milk demanded is 3,250 gallons per day and the quantity of milk supplied is 3,860 gallons per day. Will the equilibrium price of milk be greater than, less than, or equal to $4.50 per gallon? Explain. *(LO2)*

5. State whether the following pairs of goods are complements, or substitutes, or both. *(LO3)*
   a. Washing machines and dryers.
   b. Tennis rackets and tennis balls.
   c. Birthday cake and birthday candles.
   d. Cloth diapers and disposable diapers.

6. How will an increase in the birth rate affect the equilibrium price of land? *(LO3)*

7. What will happen to the equilibrium price and quantity of beef if the price of chickenfeed increases (assume that chicken and beef are substitutes)? *(LO3)*

8. How will a new law mandating an increase in required levels of automobile insurance affect the equilibrium price and quantity in the market for new automobiles? *(LO3)*

9. Predict what will happen to the equilibrium price and quantity of oranges if the following events take place. *(LO3)*
   a. A study finds that a daily glass of orange juice reduces the risk of heart disease.
   b. The price of grapefruit falls drastically.
   c. The wage paid to orange pickers rises.
   d. Exceptionally good weather provides a much greater than expected harvest.

10. Suppose the current issue of *The New York Times* reports an outbreak of mad cow disease in Nebraska, as well as the discovery of a new breed of chicken that gains more weight than existing breeds that consume the same amount of food. How will these developments affect the equilibrium price and quantity of chickens sold in the United States? *(LO3)*

11. Twenty-five years ago, tofu was available only from small businesses operating in predominantly Asian sections of large cities. Today tofu has become popular as a high-protein health food and is widely available in supermarkets throughout the United States. At the same time, tofu production has evolved to become factory-based using modern food-processing technologies. Draw a diagram with demand and supply curves depicting the market for tofu 25 years ago and the market for tofu today. Given the information above, what does the demand–supply model predict about changes in the volume of tofu sold in the United States between then and now? What does it predict about changes in the price of tofu? *(LO3)*

12. For each of the following statements about a market equilibrium identify whether the statement is always true, never true, or sometimes true. *(LO4)*
   a. A market equilibrium maximizes total economic surplus.
   b. A market equilibrium exploits all gains achievable through collective action.
   c. A market equilibrium leaves no unexploited opportunities for individuals.

13. In March 2020, global crude oil prices tumbled from over $50 a barrel to below $23 per barrel, bringing prices to their lowest level in nearly two decades. This precipitous drop in crude oil prices was fueled by two major shocks to the oil market. First, the COVID-19 pandemic led to a massive reduction in all forms of travel as large numbers of people around the world were advised to shelter in place. Second, Russia, Saudi Arabia, and a number of other major oil-producing nations typically reach collective agreements to limit the world supply of oil in order to keep prices high, but these negotiations broke down in March 2020, prompting a sharp increase in oil production. Using a supply and demand graph, show how each of these factors affected the market price and quantity of crude oil. *(LO3)*

ANSWERS TO SELF-TESTS

3.1 At a quantity of 10,000 slices per day, the marginal buyer's reservation price is $3.50 per slice. At a price of $2.50 per slice, the quantity demanded will be 14,000 slices per day. *(LO1)*

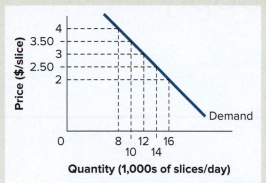

3.2 At a quantity of 10,000 slices per day, the marginal cost of pizza is $2.50 per slice. At a price of $3.50 per slice, the quantity supplied will be 14,000 slices per day. *(LO1)*

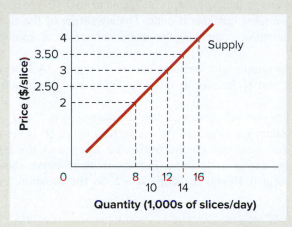

3.3 Because landlords are permitted to charge less than the maximum rent established by rent-control laws, a law that sets the maximum rent at $1,200 will have no effect on the rents actually charged in this market, which will settle at the equilibrium value of $800 per month. *(LO2)*

3.4 Travel by air and travel by intercity bus are substitutes, so a decline in airfares will shift the demand for bus travel to the left, resulting in lower bus fares and fewer bus trips taken. Travel by air and the use of resort hotels are complements, so a decline in airfares will shift the demand for resort hotel rooms to the right, resulting in higher hotel rates and an increase in the number of rooms rented. *(LO3)*

3.5 Apartments located far from Washington Metro stations are an inferior good. A pay increase for federal workers will thus shift the demand curve for such apartments downward, which will lead to a reduction in their equilibrium rent. *(LO3)*

3.6 The vitamin discovery shifts the demand for tortilla chips to the right and the crop losses shift the supply of tortilla chips to the left. Both shifts result in an increase in the equilibrium price of tortilla chips. But depending on the relative magnitude of the shifts, the equilibrium quantity of tortilla chips may either rise (top panel) or fall (bottom panel). *(LO3)*

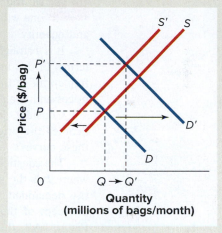

The Algebra of Supply and Demand

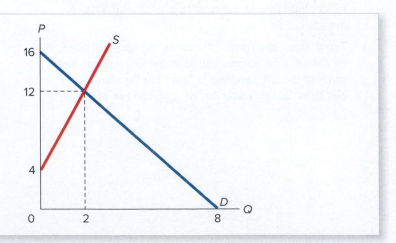

In the text of this chapter, we developed supply and demand analysis in a geometric framework. The advantage of this framework is that many find it an easier one within which to visualize how shifts in either curve affect equilibrium price and quantity.

It is a straightforward extension to translate supply and demand analysis into algebraic terms. In this brief appendix, we show how this is done. The advantage of the algebraic framework is that it greatly simplifies computing the numerical values of equilibrium prices and quantities.

Consider, for example, the supply and demand curves in Figure 3A.1, where P denotes the price of the good and Q denotes its quantity. What are the equations of these curves?

The equation of a straight-line demand curve must take the general form $P = a + bQ^d$, where P is the price of the product (as measured on the vertical axis), Q^d is the quantity demanded at that price (as measured on the horizontal axis), a is the vertical intercept of the demand curve, and b is its slope. For the demand curve shown in Figure 3A.1, the vertical intercept is 16 and the slope is -2. So the equation for this demand curve is

$$P = 16 - 2Q^d. \tag{3A.1}$$

FIGURE 3A.1

Supply and Demand Curves.

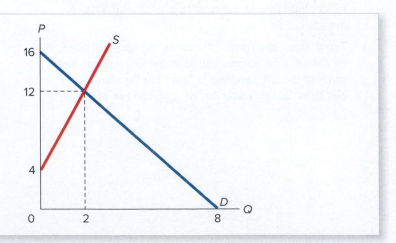

Similarly, the equation of a straight-line supply curve must take the general form $P = c + dQ^s$, where P is again the price of the product, Q^s is the quantity supplied at that price, c is the vertical intercept of the supply curve, and d is its slope. For the supply curve shown in Figure 3A.1, the vertical intercept is 4 and the slope is also 4. So the equation for this supply curve is

$$P = 4 + 4Q^s. \tag{3A.2}$$

If we know the equations for the supply and demand curves in any market, it is a simple matter to solve them for the equilibrium price and quantity using the method of simultaneous equations. The following example illustrates how to apply this method.

EXAMPLE 3A.1   **Simultaneous Equations**

If the supply and demand curves for a market are given by $P = 4 + 4Q^s$ and $P = 16 - 2Q^d$, respectively, find the equilibrium price and quantity for this market.

In equilibrium, we know that $Q^s = Q^d$. Denoting this common value as Q^*, we may then equate the right-hand sides of Equations 3A.1 and 3A.2 and solve

$$4 + 4Q^* = 16 - 2Q^*, \tag{3A.3}$$

which yields $Q^* = 2$. Substituting $Q^* = 2$ back into either the supply or demand equation gives the equilibrium price $P^* = 12$.

Of course, having already begun with the graphs of Equations 3A.1 and 3A.2 in hand, we could have identified the equilibrium price and quantity by a simple glance at Figure 3A.1. (That is why it seems natural to say that the graphical approach helps us visualize the equilibrium outcome.) As the following Self-Test 3A.1 illustrates, the advantage of the algebraic approach to finding the equilibrium price and quantity is that it is much less painstaking than having to produce accurate drawings of the supply and demand schedules.

 SELF-TEST 3A.1

Find the equilibrium price and quantity in a market whose supply and demand curves are given by $P = 2Q^s$ and $P = 8 - 2Q^d$, respectively.

ANSWER TO APPENDIX SELF-TEST

3A.1 Let Q^* denote the equilibrium quantity. Since the equilibrium price and quantity lie on both the supply and demand curves, we equate the right-hand sides of the supply and demand equations to obtain

$$2Q^* = 8 - 2Q^*,$$

which solves for $Q^* = 2$. Substituting $Q^* = 2$ back into either the supply or demand equation gives the equilibrium price $P^* = 4$.

CHAPTER 4

Elasticity

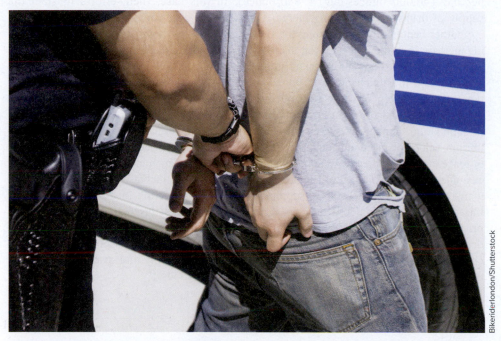

If the demand for illegal drugs is inelastic, increased arrests of illegal-drug sellers will increase total expenditures on illegal drugs.

LEARNING OBJECTIVES

After reading this chapter, you should be able to:

LO1 Define the price elasticity of demand and explain what determines whether demand is elastic or inelastic.

LO2 Calculate the price elasticity of demand using information from a demand curve.

LO3 Understand how changes in the price of a good affect total revenue and total expenditure depending on the price elasticity of demand.

LO4 Explain the cross-price elasticity of demand and the income elasticity of demand.

LO5 Discuss the price elasticity of supply, explain what determines whether supply is elastic or inelastic, and calculate the price elasticity of supply using information from a supply curve.

Many illicit-drug users commit crimes to finance their addiction. The connection between drugs and crime has led to calls for more vigorous efforts to stop the smuggling of illicit drugs. But can such efforts reduce the likelihood that your iPhone or laptop computer will be stolen? If attempts to reduce the supply of illicit drugs are successful, our basic supply and demand analysis tells us that the supply curve for drugs will shift to the left and the market price of drugs will increase. Given that demand curves are downward-sloping, drug users will respond by consuming a smaller quantity of drugs. But the amount of crime drug users commit depends not on the *quantity* of drugs they consume, but rather on their *total expenditure* on drugs. Depending on the specific characteristics of the demand curve for illicit drugs, a price increase might reduce total expenditure on drugs, but it also could raise total expenditure.

Suppose, for example, that extra border patrols shift the supply curve in the market for illicit drugs to the left, as shown in Figure 4.1. As a result, the equilibrium quantity of drugs would fall from 50,000 to 40,000 ounces per day and the price of drugs would rise from $50 to $80 per ounce. The total amount spent on drugs, which was $2,500,000 per day (50,000 ounces/day × $50/ounce), would rise to $3,200,000

FIGURE 4.1

The Effect of Extra Border Patrols on the Market for Illicit Drugs.

Extra patrols shift supply left-ward and reduce the quantity demanded, but they may actually increase the total amount spent on drugs.

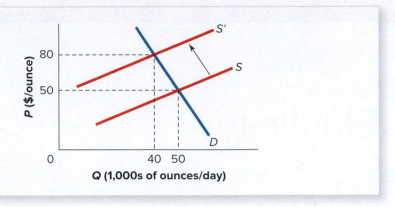

Could reducing the supply of illegal drugs cause an increase in drug-related burglaries?

per day (40,000 ounces/day × $80/ounce). In this case, then, efforts to stem the supply of drugs would actually increase the likelihood of your laptop being stolen.

Other benefits from stemming the flow of illicit drugs might still outweigh the resulting increase in crime. But knowing that the policy might increase drug-related crime would clearly be useful to law-enforcement authorities.

Our task in this chapter will be to introduce the concept of elasticity, a measure of the extent to which quantity demanded and quantity supplied respond to variations in price, income, and other factors. In Chapter 3, *Supply and Demand,* we saw how shifts in supply and demand curves enabled us to predict the direction of change in the equilibrium values of price and quantity. An understanding of price elasticity will enable us to make even more precise statements about the effects of such changes. In the illicit-drug example just considered, the decrease in supply led to an increase in total spending. In many other cases, a decrease in supply will lead to a reduction in total spending. Why this difference? The underlying phenomenon that explains this pattern, as we'll see, is price elasticity of demand. We'll explore why some goods have higher price elasticity of demand than others and the implications of that fact for how total spending responds to changes in prices. We'll also discuss price elasticity of supply and examine the factors that explain why it takes different values for different goods.

PRICE ELASTICITY OF DEMAND

When the price of a good or service rises, the quantity demanded falls. But to predict the effect of the price increase on total expenditure, we also must know by how much quantity falls. The quantity demanded of some goods such as salt is not very sensitive to changes in price. Indeed, even if the price of salt were to double, or to fall by half, most people would hardly alter their consumption of it. For other goods, however, the quantity demanded is extremely responsive to changes in price. For example, when a luxury tax was imposed on yachts in the early 1990s, purchases of yachts plummeted sharply. (Refer to The Economic Naturalist 4.2 example presented later in this chapter.)

PRICE ELASTICITY DEFINED

price elasticity of demand
the percentage change in the quantity demanded of a good or service that results from a 1 percent change in its price

The **price elasticity of demand** for a good is a measure of the responsiveness of the quantity demanded of that good to changes in its price. Formally, the price elasticity of demand for a good is defined as the percentage change in the quantity demanded that results from a 1 percent change in its price. For example, if the price of beef falls by 1 percent and the quantity demanded rises by 2 percent, then the price elasticity of demand for beef has a value of −2.

Although the definition just given refers to the response of quantity demanded to a 1 percent change in price, it also can be adapted to other variations in price, provided they're relatively small. In such cases, we calculate the price elasticity of demand as the percentage change in quantity demanded divided by the corresponding percentage change in price. Thus, if a 2 percent reduction in the price of pork led to a 6 percent increase in the quantity of pork demanded, the price elasticity of demand for pork would be

$$\frac{\text{Percentage change in quantity demanded}}{\text{Percentage change in price}} = \frac{6 \text{ percent}}{-2 \text{ percent}} = -3. \qquad (4.1)$$

Strictly speaking, the price elasticity of demand will always be negative (or zero) because price changes are always in the opposite direction from changes in quantity demanded. So for convenience, we drop the negative sign and speak of price elasticities in terms of absolute value. The demand for a good is said to be **elastic** with respect to price if the absolute value of its price elasticity is greater than 1. It is said to be **inelastic** if the absolute value of its price elasticity is less than 1. Finally, demand is said to be **unit elastic** if the absolute value of its price elasticity is equal to 1. (See Figure 4.2.)

elastic the demand for a good is elastic with respect to price if its price elasticity of demand is greater than 1

inelastic the demand for a good is inelastic with respect to price if its price elasticity of demand is less than 1

unit elastic the demand for a good is unit elastic with respect to price if its price elasticity of demand equals 1

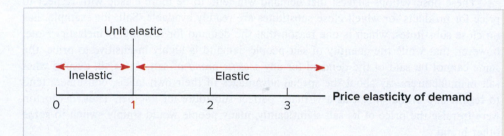

FIGURE 4.2
Elastic and Inelastic Demand.
Demand for a good is called elastic, unit elastic, or inelastic with respect to price if the price elasticity is greater than 1, equal to 1, or less than 1, respectively.

EXAMPLE 4.1   Elasticity of Demand

What is the elasticity of demand for pizza?

When the price of pizza is $1 per slice, buyers wish to purchase 400 slices per day, but when price falls to $0.97 per slice, the quantity demanded rises to 404 slices per day. At the original price, what is the price elasticity of demand for pizza? Is the demand for pizza elastic with respect to price?

The fall in price from $1 to $0.97 is a decrease of 3 percent. The rise in quantity demanded from 400 slices to 404 slices is an increase of 1 percent. The price elasticity of demand for pizza is thus (1 percent)/(3 percent) = 1/3. So when the initial price of pizza is $1, the demand for pizza is not elastic with respect to price; it is inelastic.

 SELF-TEST 4.1

What is the elasticity of demand for season ski passes?
When the price of a season ski pass is $400, buyers, whose demand curve for passes is linear, wish to purchase 10,000 passes per year, but when price falls to $380, the quantity demanded rises to 12,000 passes per year. At the original price, what is the price elasticity of demand for ski passes? Is the demand for ski passes elastic with respect to price?

DETERMINANTS OF PRICE ELASTICITY OF DEMAND

What factors determine the price elasticity of demand for a good or service? To answer this question, recall that before a rational consumer buys any product, the purchase decision must first satisfy the Cost-Benefit Principle. For instance, consider a good (such as a dorm refrigerator) that you buy only one unit of (if you buy it at all). Suppose that, at the current price, you have decided to buy it. Now imagine that the price goes up by 10 percent. Will a price increase of this magnitude be likely to make you change your mind? The answer will depend on factors like the following.

If the price of salt were to double, would you use less of it?

Substitution Possibilities

When the price of a product you want to buy goes up significantly, you're likely to ask yourself, "Is there some other good that can do roughly the same job, but for less money?" If the answer is yes, then you can escape the effect of the price increase by simply switching to the substitute product. But if the answer is no, you are more likely to stick with your current purchase.

These observations suggest that demand will tend to be more elastic with respect to price for products for which close substitutes are readily available. Salt, for example, has no close substitutes, which is one reason that the demand for it is highly inelastic. Note, however, that while the quantity of salt people demand is highly insensitive to price, the same cannot be said of the demand for any *specific brand* of salt. After all, despite what salt manufacturers say about the special advantages of their own labels, consumers tend to regard one brand of salt as a virtually perfect substitute for another. Thus, if Morton were to raise the price of its salt significantly, many people would simply switch to some other brand.

The vaccine against rabies is another product for which there are essentially no attractive substitutes. A person who is bitten by a rabid animal and does not take the vaccine faces a certain and painful death. Most people in that position would pay any price they could afford rather than do without the vaccine.

▶ Visit your instructor's Connect course and access your eBook to view this video.

Why do people buy the same amount of (table) salt—even when the price rises substantially?

Budget Share

Suppose the price of key rings suddenly were to double. How would that affect the number of key rings you buy? If you're like most people, it would have no effect at all. Think about it—a doubling of the price of a $1 item that you buy only every few years is simply nothing to worry about. By contrast, if the price of the new car you were about to buy suddenly doubled, you would definitely want to check out possible substitutes such as a used car or a smaller new model. You also might consider holding on to your current car a little longer. The larger the share of your budget an item accounts for, the greater is your incentive to look for substitutes when the price of the item rises. Big-ticket items, therefore, tend to have higher price elasticities of demand.

Time

Home appliances come in a variety of models, some more energy-efficient than others. As a general rule, the more efficient an appliance is, the higher its price. Suppose that you were about to buy a new air conditioner and electric rates suddenly rose sharply. It would probably be in your interest to buy a more efficient machine than you'd originally planned. However, what if you'd already bought a new air conditioner before you learned of the rate increase? You wouldn't think it worthwhile to discard the machine right away and replace it with a more efficient model. Rather, you'd wait until the machine wore out, or until you moved, before making the switch.

As this example illustrates, substitution of one product or service for another takes time. Some substitutions occur in the immediate aftermath of a price increase, but many others take place years or even decades later. For this reason, the price elasticity of demand for any good or service will be higher in the long run than in the short run.

FACTORS THAT INFLUENCE PRICE ELASTICITY

The price elasticity of demand for a good or service tends to be larger when substitutes for the good are more readily available, when the good's share in the consumer's budget is larger, and when consumers have more time to adjust to a change in price.

SOME REPRESENTATIVE ELASTICITY ESTIMATES

The entries in Table 4.1 show that the price elasticities of demand for different products often differ substantially—in this sample, ranging from a high of 3.5 for public transportation to a low of 0.1 for food. This variability is explained in part by the determinants of elasticity just discussed. Note, for example, that the price elasticity of demand for green peas is more than nine times that for coffee, reflecting the fact that there are many more close substitutes for green peas than for coffee.

TABLE 4.1

Historical Price Elasticity of Demand Estimates for Selected Products

Product or service	Estimated price elasticity
Food	0.1
Coffee	0.3
Magazines and newspapers	0.3
Housing	0.6
Tobacco	0.6
Clothing	0.6
Medical care	0.8
Oil	0.9
Motor vehicles	1.1
Beer	1.2
Furniture	1.3
Restaurant meals	1.6
Household electricity	1.9
Boats, pleasure aircraft	2.4
Green peas	2.8
Public transportation	3.5

Sources: K. Elzinga, "The Beer Industry," *The Structure of American Industry,* ed. Walter Adams (New York: Macmillan, 1977); R. Fisher, *State and Local Public Finance* (Chicago, IL: Irwin, 1996); H. S. Houthakker and L. Taylor, *Consumer Demand in the United States: Analyses and Projections,* 2nd ed. (Cambridge, MA: Harvard University Press, 1970); A. Mansur and J. Whalley, "Numerical Specification of Applied General Equilibrium Models: Estimation, Calibration, and Data," *Applied General Equilibrium Analysis,* ed. Herbert Scarf and John Shoven (New York: Cambridge University Press, 1984); J. Möller, "Income and Price Elasticities in Different Sectors of the Economy—An Analysis of Structural Change for Germany, the U.K., and the U.S.A." December 1998; L. Taylor, "The Demand for Electricity: A Survey," *Bell Journal of Economics,* Spring 1975; H. Theil, C. Chung, and J. Seale, "Advances in Econometrics," Supplement I, *International Evidence on Consumption Patterns* (Greenwich, CT: JAI Press, 1989).

Note also the contrast between the low price elasticity of demand for food and the high price elasticity of demand for green peas. Unlike green peas, food occupies a substantial share of most family budgets and there are few substitutes for broad spending categories like food.

USING PRICE ELASTICITY OF DEMAND

An understanding of the factors that govern price elasticity of demand is necessary not only to make sense of consumer behavior, but also to design effective public policy. Consider, for example, the debate about how taxes affect smoking among teenagers.

The Economic Naturalist 4.1

Will a higher tax on cigarettes curb teenage smoking?

Do high cigarette prices discourage teen smoking?

Consultants hired by the tobacco industry have testified in Congress against higher cigarette taxes aimed at curbing teenage smoking. The main reason teenagers smoke is that their friends smoke, these consultants testified, and they concluded that higher taxes would have little effect. Does the consultants' testimony make economic sense?

The consultants are almost certainly right that peer influence is the most important determinant of teen smoking. But that does not imply that a higher tax on cigarettes would have little impact on adolescent smoking rates. Because most teenagers have little money to spend at their own discretion, cigarettes constitute a significant share of a typical teenage smoker's budget. The price elasticity of demand is thus likely to be far from negligible. For at least some teenage smokers, a higher tax would make smoking unaffordable. And even among those who could afford the higher prices, at least some others would choose to spend their money on other things rather than pay the higher prices.

Given that the tax would affect at least *some* teenage smokers, the consultants' argument begins to unravel. If the tax deters even a small number of smokers directly through its effect on the price of cigarettes, it will also deter others indirectly, by reducing the number of peer role models who smoke. And those who refrain because of these indirect effects will in turn no longer influence others to smoke, and so on. So even if the direct effect of higher cigarette taxes on teen smoking is small, the cumulative effects may be extremely large. The mere fact that peer pressure may be the primary determinant of teen smoking therefore does not imply that higher cigarette taxes will have no significant impact on the number of teens who smoke.

The Economic Naturalist 4.2

Why was the luxury tax on yachts such a disaster?

In 1990, Congress imposed a luxury tax on yachts costing more than $100,000, along with similar taxes on a handful of other luxury goods. Before these taxes were imposed, the Joint Committee on Taxation estimated that they would yield more than $31 million in revenue in 1991. However, the tax actually generated only a bit more than half that amount, $16.6 million.[1] Several years later, the Joint Economic

---

[1]For an alternative view, see Dennis Zimmerman, "The Effect of the Luxury Excise Tax on the Sale of Luxury Boats," Congressional Research Service, February 10, 1992.

Committee estimated that the tax on yachts had led to a loss of 7,600 jobs in the U.S. boating industry. Taking account of lost income taxes and increased unemployment benefits, the U.S. government actually came out $7.6 million behind in fiscal 1991 as a result of its luxury taxes—almost $39 million worse than the initial projection. What went wrong?

The 1990 law imposed no luxury taxes on yachts built and purchased outside the United States. What Congress failed to consider was that foreign-built yachts are almost perfect substitutes for yachts built and purchased in the United States. And, no surprise, when prices on

Why did the luxury tax on yachts backfire?

domestic yachts went up because of the tax, yacht buyers switched in droves to foreign models. A tax imposed on a good with a high price elasticity of demand stimulates large rearrangements of consumption but yields little revenue. Had Congress done the economic analysis properly, it would have predicted that this particular tax would be a big loser. Facing angry protests from unemployed New England shipbuilders, Congress repealed the luxury tax on yachts in 1993.

A GRAPHICAL INTERPRETATION OF PRICE ELASTICITY

For small changes in price, price elasticity of demand is the proportion by which quantity demanded changes divided by the corresponding proportion by which price changes. This formulation enables us to construct a simple expression for the price elasticity of demand for a good using only minimal information about its demand curve.

Look at Figure 4.3. P represents the current price of a good and Q the quantity demanded at that price. ΔP represents a small change in the current price, and the resulting change in quantity demanded is given by ΔQ. The expression $\Delta P/P$ will then stand for the proportion by which price changes and $\Delta Q/Q$ will stand for the corresponding proportion by which quantity changes. These two expressions, along with our definition of the price elasticity of demand (Equation 4.1), give us the formula for price elasticity

$$\text{Price elasticity} = \in = \frac{\Delta Q/Q}{\Delta P/P}. \qquad (4.2)$$

Suppose, for example, that 20 units were sold at the original price of 100 and that when price rose to 105, quantity demanded fell to 15 units. Neglecting the negative sign of the quantity change, we would then have $\Delta Q/Q = 5/20$ and $\Delta P/P = 5/100$ which yields $\in = (5/20)/(5/100) = 5$.

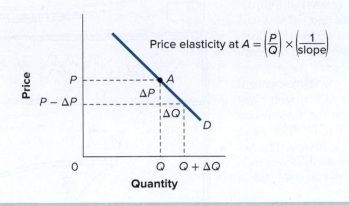

One attractive feature of this formula is that it has a straightforward graphical interpretation. Thus, if we want to calculate the price elasticity of demand at point A on the demand curve shown in Figure 4.3, we can begin by rewriting the right-hand side of Equation 4.2 as $(P/Q) \times (\Delta Q/\Delta P)$. And since the slope of the demand curve is equal to $\Delta P/\Delta Q$, $\Delta Q/\Delta P$ is the reciprocal of that slope: $\Delta Q/\Delta P = 1/\text{slope}$. The price elasticity of demand at point A, denoted $\in_A$, therefore has the following simple formula

$$\in_A = \frac{P}{Q} \times \frac{1}{\text{slope}}. \tag{4.3}$$

To demonstrate how convenient this graphical interpretation of elasticity can be, suppose we want to find the price elasticity of demand at point A on the demand curve in Figure 4.4. The slope of this demand curve is the ratio of its vertical intercept to its horizontal intercept: $20/5 = 4$. So $1/\text{slope} = 1/4$. (Actually, the slope is -4, but we again ignore the minus sign for convenience since price elasticity of demand always has the same sign.) The ratio P/Q at point A is $8/3$, so the price elasticity at point A is equal to $(P/Q) \times (1/\text{slope}) = (8/3) \times (1/4) = 2/3$. This means that when the price of the good is 8, a 3 percent reduction in price will lead to a 2 percent increase in quantity demanded.

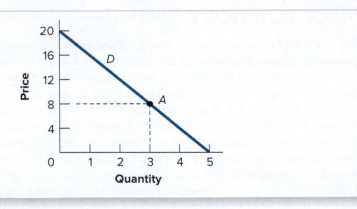

✔ **SELF-TEST 4.2**

What is the price elasticity of demand when $P = 4$ on the demand curve in Figure 4.4?

EXAMPLE 4.2   The Relationship between Elasticity and Slope

For the demand curves D_1 and D_2 shown in Figure 4.5, calculate the price elasticity of demand when $P = 4$. What is the price elasticity of demand on D_2 when $P = 1$?

These elasticities can be calculated easily using the formula $\in = (P/Q) \times (1/\text{slope})$. The slope of D_1 is the ratio of its vertical intercept to its horizontal intercept: $12/6 = 2$. So ($1/\text{slope}$) is $1/2$ for D_1. Similarly, the slope of D_2 is the ratio of its vertical intercept to its horizontal intercept: $6/12 = 1/2$. So the reciprocal of the slope of D_2 is 2. For both demand curves, $Q = 4$ when $P = 4$, so $(P/Q) = 4/4 = 1$ for each. Thus the price elasticity of demand when $P = 4$ is $(1) \times (1/2) = 1/2$ for D_1 and $(1) \times (2) = 2$ for D_2. When $P = 1$, $Q = 10$ on D_2, so $(P/Q) = 1/10$. Thus price elasticity of demand $= (1/10) \times (2) = 1/5$ when $P = 1$ on D_2.

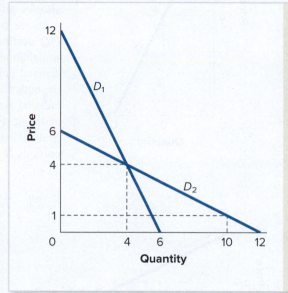

FIGURE 4.5

Price Elasticity and the Steepness of the Demand Curve.

When price and quantity are the same, price elasticity of demand is always greater for the less steep of two demand curves.

This example illustrates a general rule: If two demand curves have a point in common, the steeper curve must be the less price-elastic of the two with respect to price at that point. However, this does not mean that the steeper curve is less elastic at *every* point. Thus, we saw that at $P = 1$, price elasticity of demand on D_2 was only 1/5, or less than half the corresponding elasticity on the steeper D_1 at $P = 4$.

PRICE ELASTICITY CHANGES ALONG A STRAIGHT-LINE DEMAND CURVE

As a glance at our elasticity formula makes clear, price elasticity has a different value at every point along a straight-line demand curve. The slope of a straight-line demand curve is constant, which means that 1/slope is also constant. But the price–quantity ratio P/Q declines as we move down the demand curve. The elasticity of demand thus declines steadily as we move downward along a straight-line demand curve.

Since price elasticity is the percentage change in quantity demanded divided by the corresponding percentage change in price, this pattern makes sense. After all, a price movement of a given absolute size is small in percentage terms when it occurs near the top of the demand curve, where price is high, but large in percentage terms when it occurs near the bottom of the demand curve, where price is low. Likewise, a quantity movement of a given absolute value is large in percentage terms when it occurs near the top of the demand curve, where quantity is low, and small in percentage terms when it occurs near the bottom of the curve, where quantity is high.

The graphical interpretation of elasticity also makes it easy to see why the price elasticity of demand at the midpoint of any straight-line demand curve must always be 1. Consider, for example, the price elasticity of demand at point A on the demand curve D shown in Figure 4.6. At that point, the ratio P/Q is equal to $6/3 = 2$. The slope of this

FIGURE 4.6

Elasticity at the Midpoint of a Straight-Line Demand Curve.

The price elasticity of demand at the midpoint of any straight-line demand curve always takes the value 1.

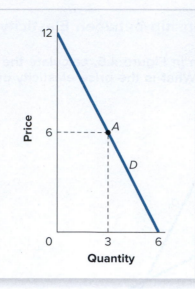

demand curve is the ratio of its vertical intercept to its horizontal intercept, $12/6 = 2$. So $(1/\text{slope}) = 1/2$ (again, we neglect the negative sign for simplicity). Inserting these values into the graphical elasticity formula yields $\in_A = (P/Q) \times (1/\text{slope}) = (2) \times (1/2) = 1$.

This result holds not just for Figure 4.6, but also for any other straight-line demand curve.[2] A glance at the formula also tells us that since P/Q declines as we move downward along a straight-line demand curve, price elasticity of demand must be less than 1 at any point below the midpoint. By the same token, price elasticity must be greater than 1 for any point above the midpoint. Figure 4.7 summarizes these findings by denoting the elastic, inelastic, and unit elastic portions of any straight-line demand curve.

FIGURE 4.7

Price Elasticity Regions along a Straight-Line Demand Curve.

Demand is elastic on the top half, unit elastic at the midpoint, and inelastic on the bottom half of a straight-line demand curve.

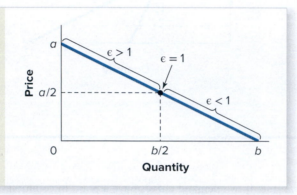

TWO SPECIAL CASES

There are two important exceptions to the general rule that elasticity declines along straight-line demand curves. First, the horizontal demand curve in Figure 4.8(a) has a slope of zero, which means that the reciprocal of its slope is infinite. Price elasticity of demand is thus infinite at every point along a horizontal demand curve. Such demand curves are said to be **perfectly elastic.**

Second, the demand curve in Figure 4.8(b) is vertical, which means that its slope is infinite. The reciprocal of its slope is thus equal to zero. Price elasticity of demand is thus exactly zero at every point along the curve. For this reason, vertical demand curves are said to be **perfectly inelastic.**

perfectly elastic demand
demand is perfectly elastic with respect to price if price elasticity of demand is infinite

perfectly inelastic demand
demand is perfectly inelastic with respect to price if price elasticity of demand is zero

---

RECAP ↑

CALCULATING PRICE ELASTICITY OF DEMAND

The price elasticity of demand for a good is the percentage change in the quantity demanded that results from a 1 percent change in its price. Mathematically, the elasticity of demand at a point along a demand curve is equal to $(P/Q) \times (1/\text{slope})$, where P and Q represent price and quantity and $(1/\text{slope})$ is the reciprocal of the slope of the demand curve at that point. Demand is elastic with respect to price if the absolute value of its price elasticity exceeds 1; inelastic if price elasticity is less than 1; and unit elastic if price elasticity is equal to 1.

---

[2]To see why, note that at the midpoint of any such curve, P is exactly half the vertical intercept of the demand curve and Q is exactly half the horizontal intercept. Since the ratio of the vertical intercept to the horizontal intercept is the slope of the demand curve, the ratio (P/Q) must also be equal to the slope of the demand curve. And this means that $(1/\text{slope})$ will always be equal to (Q/P). Thus, the product $(P/Q) \times (1/\text{slope}) = (P/Q) \times (Q/P)$ will always be exactly 1 at the midpoint of any straight-line demand curve.

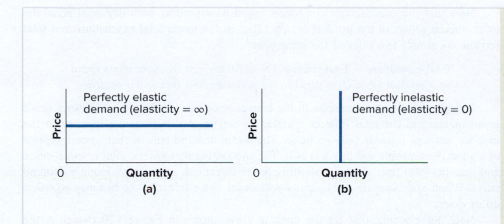

FIGURE 4.8
Perfectly Elastic and Perfectly Inelastic Demand Curves.

The horizontal demand curve (a) is perfectly elastic, or infinitely elastic, at every point. Even the slightest increase in price leads consumers to desert the product in favor of substitutes. The vertical demand curve (b) is perfectly inelastic at every point. Consumers do not, or cannot, switch to substitutes even in the face of large increases in price.

ELASTICITY AND TOTAL EXPENDITURE

Sellers of goods and services have a strong interest in being able to answer questions like "Will consumers spend more on my product if I sell more units at a lower price or fewer units at a higher price?" As it turns out, the answer to this question depends critically on the price elasticity of demand. To see why, let's first examine how the total amount spent on a good varies with the price of the good.

The total daily expenditure on a good is simply the daily number of units bought times the price for which it sells. The market demand curve for a good tells us the quantity that will be sold at each price. We can thus use the information on the demand curve to show how the total amount spent on a good will vary with its price.

To illustrate, let's calculate how much moviegoers will spend on tickets each day if the demand curve is as shown in Figure 4.9 and the price is $2 per ticket (a). The demand curve tells us that at a price of $2 per ticket, 500 tickets per day will be sold, so total expenditure at that price will be $1,000 per day. If tickets sell not for $2 but for $4 apiece, 400 tickets will be sold each day (b), so total expenditure at the higher price will be $1,600 per day.

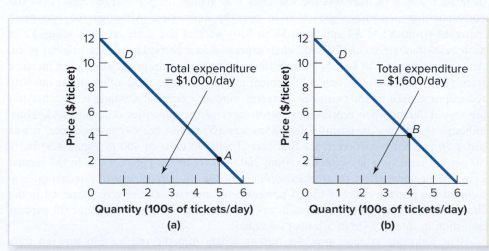

FIGURE 4.9
The Demand Curve for Movie Tickets.

An increase in price from $2 to $4 per ticket increases total expenditure on tickets.

Note that the total amount consumers spend on a product each day must equal the total amount sellers of the product receive. That is, the terms **total expenditure** and **total revenue** are simply two sides of the same coin:

total expenditure (or **total revenue**) the dollar amount that consumers spend on a product ($P \times Q$) is equal to the dollar amount that sellers receive

> **Total expenditure = Total revenue:** The dollar amount that consumers spend on a product ($P \times Q$) is equal to the dollar amount that sellers receive.

It might seem that an increase in the market price of a product should always result in an increase in the total revenue received by sellers. Although that happened in the case we just saw, it needn't always be so. The law of demand tells us that when the price of a good rises, people will buy less of it. The two factors that govern total revenue—price and quantity—will thus always move in opposite directions as we move along a demand curve. When price goes up and quantity goes down, the product of the two may go either up or down.

Note, for example, that for the demand curve shown in Figure 4.10 (which is the same as the one in Figure 4.9), a rise in price from $8 per ticket (a) to $10 per ticket (b) will cause total expenditure on tickets to go down. Thus people will spend $1,600 per day on tickets at a price of $8, but only $1,000 per day at a price of $10.

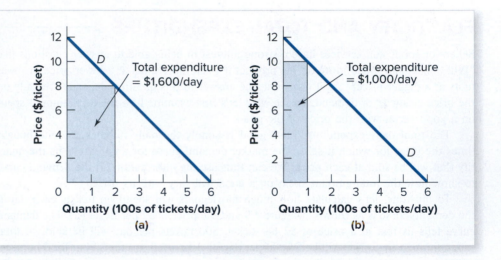

FIGURE 4.10

The Demand Curve for Movie Tickets.

An increase in price from $8 to $10 per ticket results in a fall in total expenditure on tickets.

The general rule illustrated by Figures 4.9 and 4.10 is that a price increase will produce an increase in total revenue whenever it is greater, in percentage terms, than the corresponding percentage reduction in quantity demanded. Although the two price increases (from $2 to $4 and from $8 to $10) were of the same absolute value—$2 in each case—they are much different when expressed as a percentage of the original price. An increase from $2 to $4 represents a 100 percent increase in price, whereas an increase from $8 to $10 represents only a 25 percent increase in price. And although the quantity reductions caused by the two price increases were also equal in absolute terms, they too are very different when expressed as percentages of the quantities originally sold. Thus, although the decline in quantity demanded was 100 tickets per day in each case, it was just a 20 percent reduction in the first case (from 500 units to 400 in Figure 4.9) but a 50 percent reduction in the second (from 200 units to 100 in Figure 4.10). In the second case, the negative effect on total expenditure of the 50 percent quantity reduction outweighed the positive effect of the 25 percent price increase. The reverse happened in the first case: The 100 percent increase in price (from $2 to $4) outweighed the 20 percent reduction in quantity (from 5 units to 4 units).

The following example provides further insight into the relationship between total revenue and price.

EXAMPLE 4.3   Elasticity and Total Expenditure

For the demand curve shown in Figure 4.11, draw a separate graph showing how total expenditure varies with the price of movie tickets.

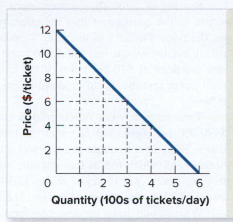

FIGURE 4.11

The Demand Curve for Movie Tickets.

The first step in constructing this graph is to calculate total expenditure for each price shown in the graph and record the results, as in Table 4.2. The next step is to plot total expenditure at each of the price points on a graph, as in Figure 4.12. Finally, sketch the curve by joining these points. (If greater accuracy is required, you can use a larger sample of points than the one shown in Table 4.2.)

TABLE 4.2

Total Expenditure as a Function of Price

Price ($/ticket)	Total expenditure ($/day)
12	0
10	1,000
8	1,600
6	1,800
4	1,600
2	1,000
0	0

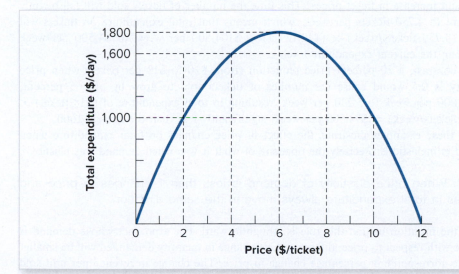

FIGURE 4.12

Total Expenditure as a Function of Price.

For a good whose demand curve is a straight line, total expenditure reaches a maximum at the price corresponding to the midpoint of the demand curve.

Note in Figure 4.12 that as the price per ticket increases from $0 to $6, total expenditure increases. But as the price rises from $6 to $12, total expenditure decreases. Total expenditure reaches a maximum of $1,800 per day at a price of $6.

The pattern observed in the preceding example holds true in general. For a straight-line demand curve, total expenditure is highest at the price that lies on the midpoint of the demand curve.

Bearing in mind these observations about how expenditure varies with price, let's return to the question of how the effect of a price change on total expenditure depends on the price elasticity of demand. Suppose, for example, that the business manager of a rock band knows she can sell 5,000 tickets to the band's weekly summer concerts if she sets the price at $20 per ticket. If the elasticity of demand for tickets is equal to 3, will total ticket revenue go up or down in response to a 10 percent increase in the price of tickets?

Total revenue from tickets sold is currently ($20/ticket) × (5,000 tickets/week) = $100,000 per week. The fact that the price elasticity of demand for tickets is 3 implies that a 10 percent increase in price will produce a 30 percent reduction in the number of tickets sold, which means that quantity will fall to 3,500 tickets per week. Total expenditure on tickets will therefore fall to (3,500 tickets/week) × ($22/ticket) = $77,000 per week, which is significantly less than the current spending total.

What would have happened to total expenditure if the band manager had *reduced* ticket prices by 10 percent, from $20 to $18? Again assuming a price elasticity of 3, the result would have been a 30 percent increase in tickets sold—from 5,000 per week to 6,500 per week. The resulting total expenditure would have been ($18/ticket) × (6,500 tickets/week) = $117,000 per week, significantly more than the current total.

These examples illustrate the following important rule about how price changes affect total expenditure for an elastically demanded good:

Rule 1: When price elasticity of demand is greater than 1, changes in price and changes in total expenditure always move in opposite directions.

Let's look at the intuition behind this rule. Total expenditure is the product of price and quantity. For an elastically demanded product, the percentage change in quantity will be larger than the corresponding percentage change in price. Thus the change in quantity will more than offset the change in revenue per unit sold.

Now let's see how total spending responds to a price increase when demand is *inelastic* with respect to price. Consider a case like the one just considered except that the elasticity of demand for tickets is not 3 but 0.5. How will total expenditure respond to a 10 percent increase in ticket prices? This time the number of tickets sold will fall by only 5 percent to 4,750 tickets per week, which means that total expenditure on tickets will rise to (4,750 tickets/week) × ($22/ticket) = $104,500 per week, or $4,500 per week more than the current expenditure level.

In contrast, a 10 percent price reduction (from $20 to $18 per ticket) when price elasticity is 0.5 would cause the number of tickets sold to grow by only 5 percent, from 5,000 per week to 5,250 per week, resulting in total expenditure of ($18/ticket) × (5,250 tickets/week) = $94,500 per week, significantly less than the current total.

As these examples illustrate, the effect of price changes on total expenditure when demand is inelastic is precisely the opposite of what it was when demand was elastic:

Rule 2: When price elasticity of demand is less than 1, changes in price and changes in total expenditure always move in the same direction.

Again, the intuition behind this rule is straightforward. For a product whose demand is inelastic with respect to price, the percentage change in quantity demanded will be smaller than the corresponding percentage change in price. The change in revenue per unit sold (price) will thus more than offset the change in the number of units sold.

The relationship between elasticity and the effect of a price change on total revenue is summarized in Figure 4.13, where the symbol ∈ is used to denote elasticity.

Recall that in the example with which we began this chapter, an increase in the price of drugs led to an increase in the total amount spent on drugs. That will happen whenever

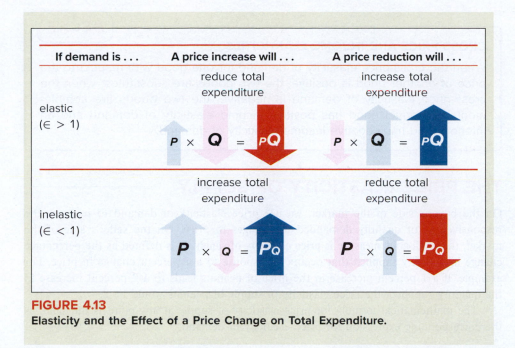

FIGURE 4.13
Elasticity and the Effect of a Price Change on Total Expenditure.

the demand for drugs is inelastic with respect to price, as it was in that example. Had the demand for drugs instead been elastic with respect to price, the drug supply interruption would have led to a reduction in total expenditure on drugs.

INCOME ELASTICITY AND CROSS-PRICE ELASTICITY OF DEMAND

The elasticity of demand for a good can be defined not only with respect to its own price but also with respect to the prices of substitutes or complements, or even to income. For example, the elasticity of demand for peanuts with respect to the price of cashews—also known as the **cross-price elasticity of demand** for peanuts with respect to cashew prices—is the percentage by which the quantity of peanuts demanded changes in response to a 1 percent change in the price of cashews. The **income elasticity of demand** for peanuts is the percentage by which the quantity demanded of peanuts changes in response to a 1 percent change in income.

Unlike the elasticity of demand for a good with respect to its own price, these other elasticities may be either positive or negative, so it is important to note their algebraic signs carefully. The income elasticity of demand for inferior goods, for example, is negative, whereas the income elasticity of demand for normal goods is positive. When the cross-price elasticity of demand for two goods is positive—as in the peanuts–cashews example—the two goods are substitutes. When it is negative, the two goods are complements. The elasticity of demand for tennis racquets with respect to court rental fees, for example, is less than zero.

cross-price elasticity of demand the percentage by which the quantity demanded of the first good changes in response to a 1 percent change in the price of the second

income elasticity of demand the percentage by which a good's quantity demanded changes in response to a 1 percent change in income

✔ **SELF-TEST 4.3**

If a 10 percent increase in income causes the number of students who choose to attend private universities to go up by 5 percent, what is the income elasticity of demand for private universities?

THE PRICE ELASTICITY OF SUPPLY

price elasticity of supply
the percentage change in quantity supplied that occurs in response to a 1 percent change in price

On the buyer's side of the market, we use price elasticity of demand to measure the responsiveness of quantity demanded to changes in price. On the seller's side of the market, the analogous measure is **price elasticity of supply.** It is defined as the percentage change in quantity supplied that occurs in response to a 1 percent change in price. For example, if a 1 percent increase in the price of peanuts leads to a 2 percent increase in the quantity supplied, the price elasticity of supply of peanuts would be 2.

The mathematical formula for price elasticity of supply at any point is the same as the corresponding expression for price elasticity of demand:

$$\text{Price elasticity of supply} = \frac{\Delta Q/Q}{\Delta P/P}, \tag{4.4}$$

where P and Q are the price and quantity at that point, ΔP is a small change in the initial price, and ΔQ the resulting change in quantity.

As with the corresponding expression for price elasticity of demand, Equation 4.4 can be rewritten as $(P/Q) \times (\Delta Q/\Delta P)$. And since $(\Delta Q/\Delta P)$ is the reciprocal of the slope of the supply curve, the right-hand side of Equation 4.4 is equal to $(P/Q) \times (1/\text{slope})$—the same expression we saw in Equation 4.3 for price elasticity of demand. Price and quantity are always positive, as is the slope of the typical supply curve, so price elasticity of supply will be a positive number at every point.

Consider the supply curve shown in Figure 4.14. The slope of this supply curve is 2, so the reciprocal of this slope is 1/2. Using the formula, this means that the price elastic-ity of supply at A is $(8/2) \times (1/2) = 2$. The corresponding expression at B is $(10/3) \times (1/2) = 5/3$, a slightly smaller value.

✅ **SELF-TEST 4.4**

For the supply curve shown in Figure 4.14, calculate the elasticity of supply when $P = 6$.

FIGURE 4.14

A Supply Curve for Which Price Elasticity Declines as Quantity Rises.

For the supply curve shown, (1/slope) is the same at every point, but the ratio P/Q declines as Q increases. So elasticity = $(P/Q) \times (1/\text{slope})$ declines as quantity increases.

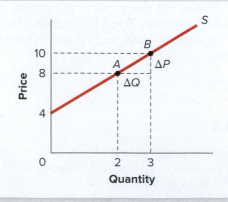

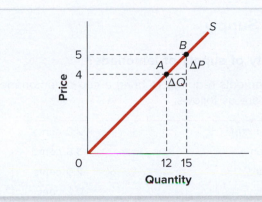

FIGURE 4.15

Calculating the Price Elasticity of Supply Graphically.

Price elasticity of supply is $(P/Q) \times (1/\text{slope})$, which at A is $(4/12) \times (12/4) = 1$, exactly the same as at B. The price elasticity of supply is equal to 1 at any point along a straight-line supply curve that passes through the origin.

Not all supply curves, however, have the property that price elasticity declines as quantity rises. Consider, for example, the supply curve shown in Figure 4.15. Because the ratio P/Q is the same at every point along this supply curve, and because the slope of the supply curve is also constant, price elasticity of supply will take exactly the same value at every point along this curve. At A, for example, price elasticity of supply = $(P/Q) \times (1/\text{slope}) = (4/12) \times (12/4) = 1$. Similarly, at B price elasticity of supply = $(5/15) \times (12/4) = 1$ again.

Indeed, the price elasticity of supply will always be equal to 1 at any point along a straight-line supply curve that passes through the origin. The reason is that for movements along any such line, both price and quantity always change in exactly the same proportion.

On the buyer's side of the market, two important polar cases are demand curves with infinite price elasticity and zero price elasticity. As the next two examples illustrate, analogous polar cases exist on the seller's side of the market.

EXAMPLE 4.4   Perfectly Inelastic Supply

What is the elasticity of supply of land within the borough limits of Manhattan?

Land in Manhattan sells in the market for a price, just like aluminum or corn or automobiles or any other product. And the demand for land in Manhattan is a downward-sloping function of its price. For all practical purposes, however, its supply is completely fixed. No matter whether its price is high or low, the same amount of it is available in the market. The supply curve of such a good is vertical, and its price elasticity is zero at every price. Supply curves like the one shown in Figure 4.16 are said to be **perfectly inelastic.**

perfectly inelastic supply
supply is perfectly inelastic with respect to price if elasticity is zero

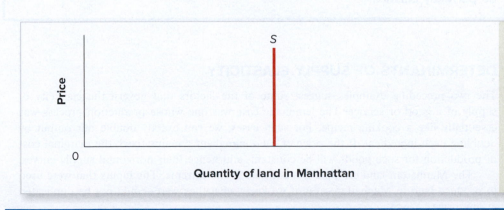

FIGURE 4.16

A Perfectly Inelastic Supply Curve.

Price elasticity of supply is zero at every point along a vertical supply curve.

EXAMPLE 4.5   Perfectly Elastic Supply

What is the elasticity of supply of lemonade?

Suppose that the ingredients required to bring a cup of lemonade to market and their respective costs are as follows:

Paper cup	2.0 cents
Lemon	3.8 cents
Sugar	2.0 cents
Water	0.2 cent
Ice	1.0 cent
Labor (30 seconds @ $6/hour)	5.0 cents

If these proportions remain the same no matter how many cups of lemonade are made, and the inputs can be purchased in any quantities at the stated prices, draw the supply curve of lemonade and compute its price elasticity.

Since each cup of lemonade costs exactly 14 cents to make, no matter how many cups are made, the marginal cost of lemonade is constant at 14 cents per cup. And since each point on a supply curve is equal to marginal cost (see Chapter 3, *Supply and Demand*), this means that the supply curve of lemonade is not upward-sloping but is instead a horizontal line at 14 cents per cup (Figure 4.17). The price elasticity of supply of lemonade is infinite.

FIGURE 4.17

A Perfectly Elastic Supply Curve.

The elasticity of supply is infinite at every point along a horizontal supply curve.

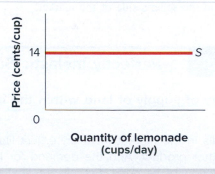

perfectly elastic supply
supply is perfectly elastic with respect to price if elasticity of supply is infinite

Whenever additional units of a good can be produced by using the same combination of inputs, purchased at the same prices, as have been used so far, the supply curve of that good will be horizontal. Such supply curves are said to be **perfectly elastic.**

DETERMINANTS OF SUPPLY ELASTICITY

The two preceding examples suggest some of the factors that govern the elasticity of supply of a good or service. The lemonade case was one whose production process was essentially like a cooking recipe. For such cases, we can exactly double our output by doubling each ingredient. If the price of each ingredient remains fixed, the marginal cost of production for such goods will be constant—and hence their horizontal supply curves.

The Manhattan land example is a contrast in the extreme. The inputs that were used to produce land in Manhattan—even if we knew what they were—could not be duplicated at any price.

The key to predicting how elastic the supply of a good will be with respect to price is to know the terms on which additional units of the inputs involved in producing that good can be acquired. In general, the more easily additional units of these inputs can be acquired, the higher price elasticity of supply will be. The following factors (among others) govern the ease with which additional inputs can be acquired by a producer.

Flexibility of Inputs

To the extent that production of a good requires inputs that are also useful for the production of other goods, it is relatively easy to lure additional inputs away from their current uses, making supply of that good relatively elastic with respect to price. Thus the fact that lemonade production requires labor with only minimal skills means that a large pool of workers could shift from other activities to lemonade production if a profitable opportunity arose. Brain surgery, by contrast, requires elaborately trained and specialized labor, which means that even a large price increase would not increase available supplies, except in the very long run.

Mobility of Inputs

If inputs can be easily transported from one site to another, an increase in the price of a product in one market will enable a producer in that market to summon inputs from other markets. For example, the supply of agricultural products is made more elastic with respect to price by the fact that thousands farmworkers are willing to migrate northward during the growing season. The supply of entertainment is similarly made more elastic by the willingness of entertainers to hit the road. Cirque performers, lounge singers, comedians, and dancers often spend a substantial fraction of their time away from home.

For most goods, the price elasticity of supply increases each time a new highway is built, or when the telecommunications network improves, or indeed when any other development makes it easier to find and transport inputs from one place to another.

Ability to Produce Substitute Inputs

The inputs required to produce finished diamond gemstones include raw diamond crystal, skilled labor, and elaborate cutting and polishing machinery. In time, the number of people with the requisite skills can be increased, as can the amount of specialized machinery. The number of raw diamond crystals buried in the earth is probably fixed in the same way that Manhattan land is fixed, but unlike Manhattan land, rising prices will encourage miners to spend the effort required to find a larger proportion of those crystals. Still, the supply of natural gemstone diamonds tends to be relatively inelastic because of the difficulty of augmenting the number of diamond crystals.

The day is close at hand, however, when gemstone makers will be able to produce synthetic diamond crystals that are indistinguishable from real ones. Indeed, there are already synthetic crystals that fool even highly experienced jewelers. The introduction of a perfect synthetic substitute for natural diamond crystals would increase the price elasticity of supply of diamonds (or, at any rate, the price elasticity of supply of gemstones that look and feel just like diamonds).

Time

Because it takes time for producers to switch from one activity to another, and because it takes time to build new machines and factories and train additional skilled workers, the price elasticity of supply will be higher for most goods in the long run than in the short run. In the short run, a manufacturer's inability to augment existing stocks of equipment and skilled labor may make it impossible to expand output beyond a certain limit. But if a shortage of managers was the bottleneck, new MBAs can be trained in only two years. Or if a shortage of legal staff is the problem, new lawyers can be trained in three years.

In the long run, firms can always buy new equipment, build new factories, and hire additional skilled workers.

The conditions that gave rise to the perfectly elastic supply curve for lemonade in the example we discussed earlier are satisfied for many other products in the long run. If a product can be copied (in the sense that any company can acquire the design and other technological information required to produce it), and if the inputs needed for its production are used in roughly fixed proportions and are available at fixed market prices, then the long-run supply curve for that product will be horizontal. But many products do not satisfy these conditions, and their supply curves remain steeply upward-sloping, even in the very long run.

The Economic Naturalist 4.3

Why are gasoline prices so much more volatile than car prices?

Automobile price changes in the United States usually occur just once a year, when manufacturers announce an increase of only a few percentage points. In contrast, gasoline prices often fluctuate wildly from day to day. As shown in Figure 4.18, for example, the highest daily gasoline prices in California's two largest cities were three times higher than the lowest daily prices in 2001 and early 2002. Why this enormous difference in volatility?

FIGURE 4.18

Gasoline Prices in Two California Cities.

Source: Oil Price Information Service, www.opisnet.com.

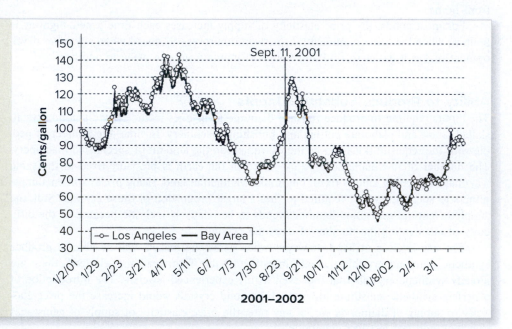

With respect to price volatility, at least two important features distinguish the gasoline market from the market for cars. One is that the short-run price elasticity of demand for gasoline is much smaller than the corresponding elasticity for cars. The other is that supply shifts are much more pronounced and frequent in the gasoline market than in the car market. (See Figure 4.19.)

Why are the two markets different in these ways? Consider first the difference in price elasticities of demand. The quantity of gasoline we demand

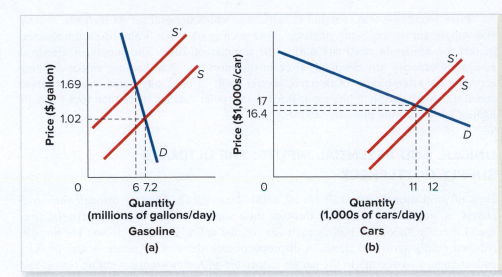

FIGURE 4.19

Greater Volatility in Gasoline Prices Than in Car Prices. Gasoline prices are more volatile prices because supply shifts are larger and more frequent in the gasoline market (a) than in the car market (b) and also because supply and demand are less elastic in the short run in the gasoline market.

depends largely on the kinds of cars we own and the amounts we drive them. In the short run, car ownership and commuting patterns are almost completely fixed, so even if the price of gasoline were to change sharply, the quantity we demand would not change by much. In contrast, if there were a sudden dramatic change in the price of cars, we could always postpone or accelerate our next car purchases.

To see why the supply curve in the gasoline market experiences larger and more frequent shifts than the supply curve in the car market, we need only examine the relative stability of the inputs employed by sellers in these two markets. Most of the inputs used in producing cars—steel, glass, rubber, plastics, electronic components, labor, and others—are reliably available to carmakers. In contrast, the key input used in making gasoline—crude oil—is subject to profound and unpredictable supply interruptions.

This is so in part because much of the world's supply of crude oil is controlled by the Organization of the Petroleum Exporting Countries (OPEC), which has sharply curtailed its oil shipments to the United States on several previous occasions. Even in the absence of formal OPEC action, however, large supply curtailments often occur in the oil market— for example, whenever producers fear that political instability might engulf the major oil-producing countries of the Middle East.

Note in Figure 4.18 the sharp spike in gasoline prices that occurred just after the terrorist attacks on the World Trade Center and Pentagon on September 11, 2001. Because many believed that the aim of these attacks was to provoke large-scale war between Muslim societies and the West, fears of an impending oil supply interruption were perfectly rational. Similar oil price spikes occurred in the early months of 2011, when political upheaval in several Middle Eastern countries threatened to disrupt oil supplies. Such fears alone can trigger a temporary supply interruption, even if war is avoided. The prospect of war creates the expectation of oil supply cutbacks that would cause higher prices in the future, which leads producers to withdraw some of their oil from current markets (in order to sell it at higher prices later). But once the fear of war recedes, the supply curve of gasoline reverts with equal speed to its earlier position. Given the low short-run price elasticity of demand for gasoline, that's all it takes to generate the considerable price volatility we see in this market.

Why are gasoline prices so much less stable than automobile prices?

Price volatility is also common in markets in which demand curves fluctuate sharply and supply curves are highly inelastic. One such market was California's unregulated market for wholesale electricity during the summer of 2000. The supply of electrical generating capacity was essentially fixed in the short run. And because air-conditioning accounts for a large share of demand, several spells of unusually warm weather caused demand to shift sharply to the right. Price at one point reached more than four times its highest level from the previous summer.

UNIQUE AND ESSENTIAL INPUTS: THE ULTIMATE SUPPLY BOTTLENECK

Fans of professional basketball are an enthusiastic bunch. Directly through their purchases of tickets and indirectly through their support of television advertisers, they spend literally billions of dollars each year on the sport. But these dollars are not distributed evenly across all teams. A disproportionate share of all revenues and product endorsement fees accrues to the people associated with consistently winning teams, and at the top of this pyramid generally stands the National Basketball Association's championship team.

Consider the task of trying to produce a championship team in the NBA. You would need inputs such as talented players, a shrewd and dedicated coach and assistants, trainers, physicians, an arena, practice facilities, means for transporting players to away games, a marketing staff, and so on. And whereas some of these inputs can be acquired at reasonable prices in the marketplace, many others cannot. Indeed, the most important input of all—highly talented players—is in extremely limited supply. This is so because the very definition of talented player is inescapably relative—simply put, such a player is one who is better than most others.

Given the huge payoff that accrues to the NBA championship team, it is no surprise that the bidding for the most talented players has become so intense. If there were a long list of players with the potential to boost a team's winning percentage substantially, the Golden State Warriors wouldn't have agreed to pay Steph Curry a salary of more than $40 million a year. But, of course, the supply of such players is extremely limited. There are many hungry organizations that would like nothing better than to claim the NBA championship each year, yet no matter how much each is willing to spend, only one can succeed. The supply of NBA championship teams is perfectly inelastic with respect to price even in the very long run.

Sports champions are by no means the only important product whose supply elasticity is constrained by the inability to reproduce unique and essential inputs. In the movie industry, for example, although the supply of movies starring Dwayne Johnson is not perfectly inelastic, there are only so many films he can make each year. Because his films consistently generate huge box office revenues, scores of film producers want to sign him for their projects. But because there isn't enough of him to go around, his salary per film typically exceeds $20 million.

In the long run, unique and essential inputs are the only truly significant supply bottleneck. If it were not for the inability to duplicate the services of such inputs, most goods and services would have extremely high price elasticities of supply in the long run.

SUMMARY

- The price elasticity of demand is a measure of how strongly buyers respond to changes in price. It is the percentage change in quantity demanded that occurs in response to a 1 percent change in price. The demand for a good is called elastic with respect to price if the absolute value of its price elasticity is more than 1, inelastic if its price elasticity is less than 1, and unit elastic if its price elasticity is equal to 1. *(LO1)*

- Goods such as salt, which occupy only a small share of the typical consumer's budget and have few or no good substitutes, tend to have low price elasticity of demand. Goods like new cars of a particular make and model, which occupy large budget shares and have many attractive substitutes, tend to have high price elasticity of demand. Price elasticity of demand is higher in the long run than in the short run because people often need time to adjust to price changes. *(LO1)*

- The price elasticity of demand at a point along a demand curve also can be expressed as the formula $\in = (\Delta Q/Q)/(\Delta P/P)$. Here, P and Q represent price and quantity at that point and ΔP and ΔQ represent small changes in price and quantity. For straight-line demand curves, this formula can also be expressed as $\in = (P/Q) \times (1/\text{slope})$. These formulations tell us that price elasticity declines in absolute terms as we move down a straight-line demand curve. *(LO2)*

- A cut in price will increase total spending on a good if demand is elastic but reduce it if demand is inelastic. An increase in price will increase total spending on a good if demand is inelastic but reduce it if demand is elastic. Total expenditure on a good reaches a maximum when price elasticity of demand is equal to 1. *(LO3)*

- Analogous formulas are used to define the elasticity of demand for a good with respect to income and the prices of other goods. In each case, elasticity is the percentage change in quantity demanded divided by the corresponding percentage change in income or price. *(LO4)*

- Price elasticity of supply is defined as the percentage change in quantity supplied that occurs in response to a 1 percent change in price. The mathematical formula for the price elasticity of supply at any point is $(\Delta Q/Q)/(\Delta P/P)$, where P and Q are the price and quantity at that point, ΔP is a small change in the initial price, and ΔQ is the resulting change in quantity. This formula also can be expressed as $(P/Q) \times (1/\text{slope})$, where $(1/\text{slope})$ is the reciprocal of the slope of the supply curve. *(LO5)*

- The price elasticity of supply of a good depends on how difficult or costly it is to acquire additional units of the inputs involved in producing that good. In general, the more easily additional units of these inputs can be acquired, the higher price elasticity of supply will be. It is easier to expand production of a product if the inputs used to produce that product are similar to inputs used to produce other products, if inputs are relatively mobile, or if an acceptable substitute for existing inputs can be developed. And like the price elasticity of demand, the price elasticity of supply is greater in the long run than in the short run. *(LO5)*

KEY TERMS

cross-price elasticity of demand
elastic
income elasticity of demand
inelastic
perfectly elastic demand

perfectly elastic supply
perfectly inelastic demand
perfectly inelastic supply
price elasticity of demand
price elasticity of supply

total expenditure (or total revenue)
unit elastic

REVIEW QUESTIONS

1. Why does a consumer's price elasticity of demand for a good depend on the fraction of the consumer's income spent on that good? *(LO1)*

2. Why does the price elasticity of demand for a good decline as we move down along a straight-line demand curve? *(LO2)*

3. Under what conditions will an increase in the price of a product lead to a reduction in total spending for that product? *(LO3)*

4. Why do economists pay little attention to the algebraic sign of the elasticity of demand for a good with respect to its own price, yet pay careful attention to the algebraic sign of the elasticity of demand for a good with respect to another good's price? *(LO4)*

5. Why is supply elasticity higher in the long run than in the short run? *(LO5)*

PROBLEMS

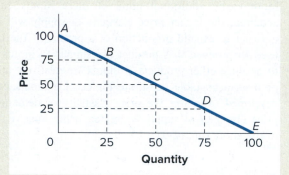

1. Is the demand for a particular brand of car, like a Chevrolet, likely to be more or less price-elastic than the demand for all cars? Explain. *(LO1)*

2. Among the following groups—senior executives, junior executives, and students—which is likely to have the most and which is likely to have the least price-elastic demand for membership in the Association of Business Professionals? *(LO1)*

3. Calculate the price elasticity of demand (in absolute value) at points *A*, *B*, *C*, *D*, and *E* on the demand curve below. *(LO2)*

4. Suppose, while rummaging through your uncle's closet, you found the original painting of *Dogs Playing Poker*, a valuable piece of art. You decide to set up a display in your uncle's garage. The demand curve to see this valuable piece of art is as shown in the diagram. What price should you charge if your goal is to maximize your revenues from tickets sold? On a graph, show the inelastic and elastic regions of the demand curve. *(LO2, LO3)*

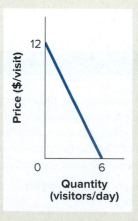

5. The schedule below shows the number of packs of bagels bought in Davis, California, each day at a variety of prices. *(LO2, LO3)*

Price of bagels ($/pack)	Number of packs purchased per day
6	0
5	3,000
4	6,000
3	9,000
2	12,000
1	15,000
0	18,000

a. Graph the daily demand curve for packs of bagels in Davis.

b. Calculate the price elasticity of demand at the point on the demand curve at which the price of bagels is $4 per pack.

c. If all bagel shops increased the price of bagels from $4 per pack to $5 per pack, what would happen to total revenues?

d. Calculate the price elasticity of demand at a point on the demand curve where the price of bagels is $1 per pack.

e. If bagel shops increased the price of bagels from $1 per pack to $2 per pack, what would happen to total revenues?

6.* At point *A* on the demand curve shown, by what percentage will a 1 percent increase in the price of the product affect total expenditure on the product? *(LO3)*

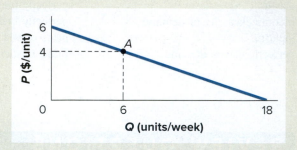

7.* Suppose that, in an attempt to induce citizens to conserve energy, the government enacted regulations requiring that all air conditioners be more efficient in their use of electricity. After this regulation was implemented, government officials were then surprised to discover that people used even more electricity than before. Using the concept of price elasticity, explain how this increase might have occurred. *(LO1)*

* Denotes more difficult problem.

8. A 2 percent increase in the price of milk causes a 4 percent reduction in the quantity demanded of chocolate syrup. What is the cross-price elasticity of demand for chocolate syrup with respect to the price of milk? Are the two goods complements or substitutes? *(LO4)*

9. What are the respective price elasticities of supply at A and B on the supply curve shown in the accompanying figure? *(LO5)*

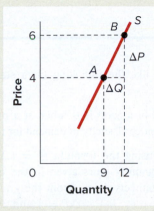

10. The price elasticity of supply for basmati rice (an aromatic strain of rice) is likely to be which of the following? *(LO5)*
   a. Higher in the long run than in the short run because farmers cannot easily change their decisions about how much basmati rice to plant once the crop has been planted.

   b. High because consumers have many other kinds of rice and other staple foods to choose from.
   c. Low in both the long run and the short run because rice farming requires only unskilled labor.
   d. High in both the long run and the short run because the inputs required to produce basmati rice can easily be duplicated.

11. Suppose that the ingredients required to bring a slice of pizza to market and their respective costs are as listed in the table:

Paper plate	2 cents
Flour	8 cents
Tomato sauce	20 cents
Cheese	30 cents
Labor (3 minutes @ $12/hour)	60 cents

If these proportions remain the same no matter how many slices are made, and the inputs can be purchased in any quantities at the stated prices, draw the supply curve of pizza slices and compute its price elasticity. *(LO5)*

ANSWERS TO SELF-TESTS

4.1 In response to a 5 percent reduction in the price of ski passes, the quantity demanded increased by 20 percent. The price elasticity of demand for ski passes is thus (20 percent)/(5 percent) = 4, and that means that at the initial price of $400, the demand for ski passes is elastic with respect to price. *(LO1)*

4.2 At point A in the accompanying diagram, $P/Q = 4/4 = 1$. The slope of this demand curve is 20/5 = 4, so $\in = 1 \times (1/\text{slope}) = 1/4$. *(LO2)*

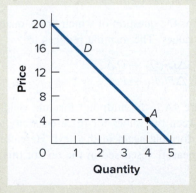

4.3 Income elasticity = Percentage change in quantity demanded/Percentage change in income = 5 percent/10 percent = 0.5. *(LO4)*

4.4 For the supply curve below, $Q = 1$ when $P = 6$, so elasticity of supply = $(P/Q) \times (1/\text{slope}) = (6) \times (1/2) = 3$. *(LO5)*

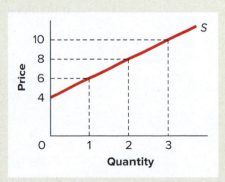

APPENDIX

The Midpoint Formula

Suppose you encounter a question like the following on a standardized test in economics:

> At a price of 3, quantity demanded of a good is 6, while at a price of 4, quantity demanded is 4. What is the price elasticity of demand for this good?

Let's attempt to answer this question by using the formula $\in = (\Delta Q/Q)/(\Delta P/P)$. In Figure 4A.1, we first plot the two price–quantity pairs given in the question and then draw the straight-line demand curve that connects them. From the graph, it is clear that $\Delta P = 1$ and $\Delta Q = 2$. But what values do we use for P and Q? If we use $P = 4$ and $Q = 4$ (point A), we get an elasticity of 2. But if we use $P = 3$ and $Q = 6$ (point B), we get an elasticity of 1. Thus, if we reckon price and quantity changes as proportions of their values at point A we get one answer, but if we compute them as proportions of their values at point B we get another. Neither of these answers is incorrect. The fact that they differ is merely a reflection of the fact that the elasticity of demand differs at every point along a straight-line demand curve.

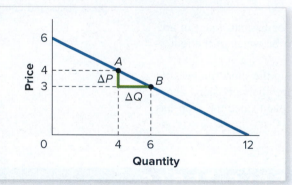

FIGURE 4A.1

Two Points on a Demand Curve.

Strictly speaking, the original question ("What is the price elasticity of demand for this good?") was not well posed. To have elicited a uniquely correct answer, it should have been "What is the price elasticity of demand at point A?" or "What is the price elasticity of demand at point B?" Economists have nonetheless developed a convention, which we call the *midpoint formula*, for answering ambiguous questions like the one originally posed. If the two points in question are (Q_A, P_A) and (Q_B, P_B), this formula is given by

$$\in = \frac{\Delta Q/[(Q_A + Q_B)/2]}{\Delta P/[(P_A + P_B)/2]}. \tag{4A.1}$$

The midpoint formula thus sidesteps the question of which price–quantity pair to use by using averages of the new and old values. The formula reduces to

$$\in = \frac{\Delta Q/(Q_A + Q_B)}{\Delta P/(P_A + P_B)}. \tag{4A.2}$$

For the two points shown in Figure 4A.1, the midpoint formula yields $\in = [2/(4 + 6)]/[1/(4 + 3)] = 1.4$, which lies between the values for price elasticity at A and B.

We will not employ the midpoint formula again in this text. Hereafter, all questions concerning elasticity will employ the measure discussed in the text of this chapter, which is called *point elasticity*.

CHAPTER 5

Demand

Because of changes in the distribution of income, demand for premium wines has surged, while demand for low-priced wines has declined.

LEARNING OBJECTIVES

After reading this chapter, you should be able to:

LO1 Relate the law of demand to the *Cost-Benefit Principle*.

LO2 Discuss how individual wants are translated into demand using utility maximization.

LO3 Explain the reasoning behind the rational spending rule and apply it to consumer decision making to show how the rule is related to substitution and income effects.

LO4 Discuss the relationship between the individual demand curve and the market demand curve.

LO5 Define and calculate consumer surplus.

O n the northern border of a large university in the East, a creek widens to form a picturesque lake, fondly remembered by generations of alumni as a popular recreation spot. Over the years, the lake had gradually silted in, and by the late 1980s, even paddling a canoe across it had become impossible. A generous alumnus then sponsored an effort to restore the lake. Heavy dredging equipment hauled out load after load of mud, and months later the lake was silt-free.

To mark the occasion, the university held a ceremony. Bands played, the president spoke, a chorus sang, and distinguished visitors applauded the donor's generosity. Hundreds of faculty and students turned out for the festivities. Spotting a good opportunity to promote their product, the proprietors of a local ice cream store set up a temporary stand at the water's edge, with a large sign: "Free Ice Cream."

Word spread. Soon scores of people were lined up waiting to try Vanilla Almond Delight, Hazelnut Cream, and Fudge Faire. The ice cream was plentiful, and because it was free, everyone could obviously afford it—or so it seemed. In fact, many people who wanted ice cream that day never got any. The reason, of course, was that they found waiting in a long line too steep a price to pay.

When a good or service is scarce, it must somehow be rationed among competing users. In most markets, monetary prices perform that task. But in the case of a stand offering free ice cream, waiting time becomes the effective rationing device. Having to stand in line is a cost, no less so than having to part with some money.

This example drives home the point that although the demand curve is usually described as a relationship between the quantity demanded of a good and its monetary price, the relationship is really a much more general one. At bottom, the demand curve is a relationship between the quantity demanded and *all* costs—monetary and nonmonetary—associated with acquiring a good.

Our task in this chapter will be to explore the demand side of the market in greater depth than was possible in Chapter 3, *Supply and Demand*. There we merely asked you to accept as an intuitively plausible claim that the quantity demanded of a good or service declines as its price rises. This relationship is known as the **law of demand,** and we'll see how it emerges as a simple consequence of the assumption that people spend their limited incomes in rational ways. In the process, we'll see more clearly the dual roles of income and substitution as factors that account for the law of demand. We'll also see how to generate market demand curves by adding the demand curves for individual buyers horizontally. Finally, we'll see how to use the demand curve to generate a measure of the total benefit that buyers reap from their participation in a market.

law of demand people do less of what they want to do as the cost of doing it rises

THE LAW OF DEMAND

With our discussion of the free ice cream offer in mind, let us restate the law of demand as follows:

Law of Demand: People do less of what they want to do as the cost of doing it rises.

By stating the law of demand this way, we can see it as a direct consequence of the Cost-Benefit Principle, which says that an activity should be pursued if (and only if) its benefits are at least as great as its costs. Recall that we measure the benefit of an activity by the highest price we'd be willing to pay to pursue it—namely, our reservation price for the activity. When the cost of an activity rises, it's more likely to exceed our reservation price, and we're therefore less likely to pursue that activity.

The law of demand applies to BMWs, cheap key rings, and "free" ice cream, not to mention manicures, medical care, and acid-free rain. It stresses that a "cost" is the sum of *all* the sacrifices—monetary and nonmonetary, implicit and explicit—we must make to engage in an activity.

THE ORIGINS OF DEMAND

How much are you willing to pay for the latest Beyoncé album? The answer will clearly depend on how you feel about her music. To her diehard fans, buying the new release might seem absolutely essential; they'd pay a steep price indeed. But those who don't like her music may be unwilling to buy it at any price.

Wants (also called "preferences" or "tastes") are clearly an important determinant of a consumer's reservation price for a good. But that raises the question of where wants come from. Many tastes—such as the taste for water on a hot day or for a comfortable place to sleep at night—are largely biological in origin. But many others are heavily shaped by culture, and even basic cravings may be socially molded. For example, people raised in southern India develop a taste for hot curry dishes, while those raised in France generally prefer milder foods.

Tastes for some items may remain stable for many years, but tastes for others may be highly volatile. Although books about the *Titanic* disaster have been continuously available since the vessel sank in spring 1912, not until the appearance of James Cameron's blockbuster film did these books begin to sell in large quantities. In spring 1998, 5 of the 15 books on *The New York Times* paperback bestseller list were about the *Titanic* itself or one of the actors in the film. Yet none of these books, or any other book about the *Titanic*, has made the bestseller list in the years since then. Still, echoes of the film continue to reverberate in the marketplace. In the years since its release, for example, demand for ocean cruises has grown sharply, and several television networks have introduced shows set on cruise ships.

Peer influence provides another example of how social forces often influence demand. Indeed, it is often the most important single determinant of demand. For instance, if our goal is to predict whether a young man will purchase an illegal recreational drug, knowing how much income he has is not very helpful. Knowing the prices of whiskey and other legal substitutes for illicit drugs also tells us little. Although these factors do influence purchase decisions, by themselves they are weak predictors. But if we know that most of the young man's best friends are heavy drug users, there's a reasonably good chance that he'll use drugs as well.

Another important way in which social forces shape demand is in the relatively common desire to consume goods and services that are recognized as the best of their kind. For instance, many people want to see LeBron James play basketball not just because of his skills on the court, but because he is widely regarded as one of the best basketball players of all time.

Consider, too, the decision of how much to spend on an interview suit. Employment counselors never tire of reminding us that making a good first impression is extremely important when you go for a job interview. At the very least, that means showing up in a suit that looks good. But looking good is a relative concept. If everyone else shows up in a $200 suit, you'll look good if you show up in a $300 suit. But you won't look as good in that same $300 suit if everyone else shows up in suits costing $1,000. The amount you'll choose to spend on an interview suit, then, clearly depends on how much others in your circle are spending.

NEEDS VERSUS WANTS

In everyday language, we distinguish between goods and services people need and those they merely want. For example, we might say that someone wants a ski vacation in Utah, but what he really needs is a few days off from his daily routine; or that someone wants a house with a view, but what she really needs is shelter from the elements. Likewise, because people need protein to survive, we might say that a severely malnourished person needs more protein. But it would strike us as odd to say that anyone—even a malnourished person—needs more prime filet of beef because health can be restored by consuming far less expensive sources of protein.

Economists like to emphasize that once we have achieved bare subsistence levels of consumption—the amount of food, shelter, and clothing required to maintain our health— we can abandon all reference to needs and speak only in terms of wants. This linguistic distinction helps us think more clearly about the true nature of our choices.

For instance, someone who says, "Californians don't have nearly as much water as they need" will tend to think differently about water shortages than someone who says, "Californians don't have nearly as much water as they want when the price of water is low." The first person is likely to focus on regulations to prevent people from watering their lawns, or on projects to capture additional runoff from the Sierra Nevada. The second person is more likely to focus on the artificially low price of water in California. Whereas remedies of the first sort are often costly and extremely difficult to implement, raising the price of water is both simple and effective.

The Economic Naturalist 5.1

Why does California experience chronic water shortages?

Some might respond that the state must serve the needs of a large population with a relatively low average annual rainfall. Yet other states, like New Mexico, have even less rainfall per person and do not experience water shortages nearly as often as California. California's problem exists because local governments sell water at extremely low prices, which encourages Californians to use water in ways

Why do farmers grow water-intensive crops like rice in an arid state like California?

that make no sense for a state with low rainfall. For instance, rice, which is well suited for conditions in high-rainfall states like South Carolina, requires extensive irrigation in California. But because California farmers can obtain water so cheaply, they plant and flood hundreds of thousands of acres of rice paddies each spring in the Central Valley. Two thousand tons of water are needed to produce one ton of rice, but many other grains can be produced with only half that amount. If the price of California water were higher, farmers would simply switch to other grains.

Likewise, cheap water encourages homeowners in Los Angeles and San Diego to plant water-intensive lawns and shrubs, like the ones common in the East and Midwest. By contrast, residents of cities like Santa Fe, New Mexico, where water prices are high, choose native plantings that require little or no watering.

TRANSLATING WANTS INTO DEMAND

It's a simple fact of life that although our resources are finite, our appetites for good things are boundless. Even if we had unlimited bank accounts, we'd quickly run out of the time and energy needed to do all the things we wanted to do. Our challenge is to use our limited resources to fulfill our desires to the greatest possible degree. That leaves us with a practical question: How should we allocate our incomes among the various goods and services that are available? To answer this question, it's helpful to begin by recognizing that the goods and services we buy are not ends in themselves, but rather means for satisfying our desires.

MEASURING WANTS: THE CONCEPT OF UTILITY

Economists use the concept of *utility* to represent the satisfaction people derive from their consumption activities. The assumption is that people try to allocate their incomes so as to maximize their satisfaction, a goal that is referred to as *utility maximization*.

Early economists imagined that the utility associated with different activities might someday be subject to precise measurement. The nineteenth-century British economist Jeremy Bentham, for example, wrote of a "utilometer," a device that could be used to measure the amount of utility provided by different consumption activities. Although no such device existed in Bentham's day, contemporary neuropsychologists now have equipment that can generate at least crude measures of satisfaction.

The accompanying photo, for example, shows a subject who is connected to an apparatus that measures the intensity of electrical waves emanating from different parts of his brain. University of Wisconsin psychologist Richard Davidson and his colleagues documented that subjects with relatively heavy brain-wave measures emanating from the left prefrontal cortex tend to be happier (as assessed by a variety of other measures) than subjects with relatively heavy brain-wave measures emanating from the right prefrontal cortex.

Jeremy Bentham would have been thrilled to learn that a device like the one pictured here might exist someday. His ideal utilometer would measure utility in utils, much as a thermometer measures temperature in degrees Fahrenheit or Celsius. It would assign a numerical utility value to every activity—watching a movie, eating a cheeseburger, and so on. Unfortunately, even sophisticated devices are far from capable of such fine-grained assessments.

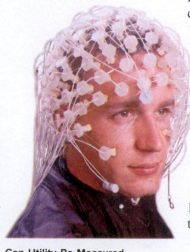

Courtesy of Waisman Brain Imaging Lab, University of Wisconsin-Madison

Can Utility Be Measured Electronically?

Scientists have shown that higher levels of electrical activity on the brain's left side are strongly associated with higher levels of satisfaction.

For Bentham's intellectual enterprise, however, the absence of a real utilometer was of no practical significance. Even without such a machine, he could continue to envision the consumer as someone whose goal was to maximize the total utility she obtained from the goods she consumed. Bentham's "utility maximization model," as we'll see, affords important insights about how a rational consumer ought to spend her income.

To explore how the model works, we begin with a very simple problem, the one facing a consumer who reaches the front of the line at a free ice cream stand. How many cones of ice cream should this person, whom we'll call Sarah, ask for? Table 5.1 shows the relationship between the total number of ice cream cones Sarah eats per hour and the total utility, measured in utils per hour, she derives from them. Note that the measurements in the table are stated in terms of cones per hour and utils per hour. Why "per hour"? Because without an explicit time dimension, we would have no idea whether a given quantity was a lot or a little. Five ice cream cones in a lifetime isn't much, but five in an hour would be more than most of us would care to eat.

TABLE 5.1
Sarah's Total Utility from Ice Cream Consumption

Cone quantity (cones/hour)	Total utility (utils/hour)
0	0
1	50
2	90
3	120
4	140
5	150
6	140

As the entries in Table 5.1 show, Sarah's total utility increases with each cone she eats, up to the fifth cone. Eating five cones per hour makes her happier than eating four, which makes her happier than eating three, and so on. But beyond five cones per hour, consuming more ice cream actually makes Sarah less happy. Thus, the sixth cone reduces her total utility from 150 utils per hour to 140 utils per hour.

We can display the utility information in Table 5.1 graphically, as in Figure 5.1. Note in the graph that the more cones per hour Sarah eats, the more utils she gets—but again only up to the fifth cone. Once she moves beyond five, her total utility begins to decline. Sarah's happiness reaches a maximum of 150 utils when she eats five cones per hour. At that point she has no incentive to eat the sixth cone, even though it's absolutely free. Eating it would actually make her worse off.

Table 5.1 and Figure 5.1 illustrate another important aspect of the relationship between utility and consumption—namely, that the additional utility from additional units of consumption declines as total consumption increases. Thus, whereas one cone per hour is a *lot* better—by 50 utils—than zero, five cones per hour is just a *little* better than four (just 10 utils' worth).

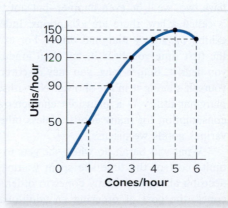

FIGURE 5.1

Sarah's Total Utility from Ice Cream Consumption.

For most goods, utility rises at a diminishing rate with additional consumption.

TABLE 5.2
Sarah's Total and Marginal Utility from Ice Cream Consumption

Cone quantity (cones/hour)	Total utility (utils/hour)	Marginal utility (utils/cone)
0	0	—
		50
1	50	
		40
2	90	
		30
3	120	
		20
4	140	
		10
5	150	
		−10
6	140	

$$\text{Marginal utility} = \frac{\text{Change in utility}}{\text{Change in consumption}}$$

$$= \frac{90 \text{ utils} - 50 \text{ utils}}{2 \text{ cones} - 1 \text{ cone}}$$

$$= 40 \text{ utils/cone}$$

marginal utility the additional utility gained from consuming an additional unit of a good

The term **marginal utility** denotes the amount by which total utility changes when consumption changes by one unit. In Table 5.2, the third column shows the marginal utility values that correspond to changes in Sarah's level of ice cream consumption. For example, the second entry in that column represents the increase in total utility (measured in utils per cone) when Sarah's consumption rises from one cone per hour to two. Note that the marginal utility entries in the third column are placed midway between the rows of the preceding columns. We do this to indicate that marginal utility corresponds to the movement from one consumption quantity to the next. Thus, we'd say that the marginal utility of moving from one to two cones per hour is 40 utils per cone.

Because marginal utility is the change in utility that occurs as we move from one quantity to another, when we graph marginal utility, we normally adopt the convention of plotting each specific marginal utility value halfway between the two quantities to which it corresponds. Thus, in Figure 5.2, we plot the marginal utility value of 40 utils per cone midway between one cone per hour and two cones per hour, and so on. (In this example, the marginal utility graph is a downward-sloping straight line for the region shown, but this need not always be the case.)

law of diminishing marginal utility the tendency for the additional utility gained from consuming an additional unit of a good to diminish as consumption increases beyond some point

The tendency for marginal utility to decline as consumption increases beyond some point is called the **law of diminishing marginal utility.** It holds not just for Sarah's consumption of ice cream in this illustration, but also for most other goods for most consumers. If we have one brownie or one Ferrari, we're happier than we are with none; if we have two, we'll be even happier—but not twice as happy—and so on. Though this pattern is called a law, there are exceptions. Indeed, some consumption activities even seem to exhibit *increasing* marginal utility. For example, an unfamiliar song may seem irritating the first time you hear it, but then gradually become more tolerable the next few times you hear it. Before long, you may discover that you *like* the song, and you may even find yourself singing it in the shower. Notwithstanding such exceptions, the law of diminishing marginal utility is a plausible characterization of the relationship between utility and consumption for many goods. Unless otherwise stated, we'll assume that it holds for the various goods we discuss.

What will Sarah do when she gets to the front of the line? At that point, the opportunity cost of the time she spent waiting is a sunk cost and is hence irrelevant to her decision about how many cones to order. And since there is no monetary charge for the cones, the cost of ordering an additional one is zero. According to the Cost-Benefit

Cost-Benefit ⟩⟩

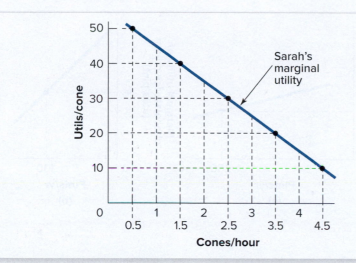

FIGURE 5.2
Diminishing Marginal Utility.
The more cones Sarah consumes each hour, the smaller her marginal utility will be. For Sarah, consumption of ice cream cones satisfies the law of diminishing marginal utility.

Principle, Sarah should therefore continue to order cones as long as the marginal benefit (here, the marginal utility she gets from an additional cone) is greater than or equal to zero. As we can see from the entries in Table 5.2, marginal utility is positive up to and including the fifth cone but becomes negative after five cones. Thus, as noted earlier, Sarah should order five cones.

ALLOCATING A FIXED INCOME BETWEEN TWO GOODS

Most of the time we face considerably more complex purchasing decisions than the one Sarah faced. For one thing, we generally must make decisions about many goods, not just a single one like ice cream. Another complication is that the cost of consuming additional units of each good will rarely be zero.

To see how to proceed in more complex cases, let's suppose Sarah must decide how to spend a fixed sum of money on two different goods, each with a positive price. Should she spend all of it on one of the goods or part of it on each? The law of diminishing marginal utility suggests that spending it all on a single good isn't a good strategy. Rather than devote more and more money to the purchase of a good we already consume in large quantities (and whose marginal utility is therefore relatively low), we generally do better to spend that money on other goods we don't have much of, whose marginal utility will likely be higher.

The simplest way to illustrate how economists think about the spending decisions of a utility-maximizing consumer is to work through a series of examples, beginning with the following.

EXAMPLE 5.1	**The Rational Spending Rule (Part 1)**

Is Sarah maximizing her utility from consuming chocolate and vanilla ice cream?

Chocolate ice cream sells for $2 per pint and vanilla sells for $1. Sarah has a budget of $400 per year to spend on ice cream, and her marginal utility from consuming each type varies with the amount consumed, as shown in Figure 5.3. If she is currently buying 200 pints of vanilla and 100 pints of chocolate each year, is she maximizing her utility?

Note first that with 200 pints per year of vanilla and 100 pints of chocolate, Sarah is spending $200 per year on each type of ice cream, for a total expenditure

FIGURE 5.3

Marginal Utility Curves for Two Flavors of Ice Cream (Part 1).

At Sarah's current consumption levels, her marginal utility of chocolate ice cream is 25 percent higher than her marginal utility of vanilla. But chocolate is twice as expensive as vanilla.

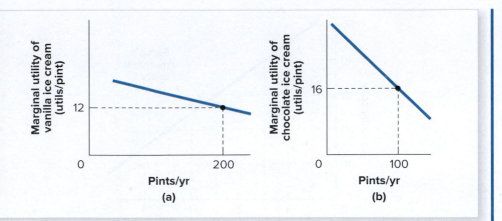

of $400 per year on ice cream, exactly the amount in her budget. By spending her money in this fashion, is she getting as much utility as possible? Note in Figure 5.3(b) that her marginal utility from chocolate ice cream is 16 utils per pint. Since chocolate costs $2 per pint, her current spending on chocolate is yielding additional utility at the rate of (16 utils/pint)/($2/pint) = 8 utils per dollar. Similarly, note in Figure 5.3(a) that Sarah's marginal utility for vanilla is 12 utils per pint. And since vanilla costs only $1 per pint, her current spending on vanilla is yielding (12 utils/pint)/($1/pint) = 12 utils per dollar. In other words, at her current rates of consumption of the two flavors, her spending yields higher marginal utility per dollar for vanilla than for chocolate. And this means that Sarah cannot possibly be maximizing her total utility.

To see why, note that if she spent $2 less on chocolate (that is, if she bought one pint less than before), she would lose about 16 utils;[1] but with the same $2, she could buy two additional pints of vanilla, which would boost her utility by about 24 utils,[2] for a net gain of about 8 utils. Under Sarah's current budget allocation, she is thus spending too little on vanilla and too much on chocolate.

In the next example, we'll see what happens if Sarah spends $100 per year less on chocolate and $100 per year more on vanilla.

EXAMPLE 5.2

The Rational Spending Rule (Part 2)

Is Sarah maximizing her utility from consuming chocolate and vanilla ice cream?

Sarah's total ice cream budget and the prices of the two flavors are the same as in the earlier example. If her marginal utility from consuming each type varies with the amount consumed, as shown in Figure 5.4, and if she's currently buying 300 pints of vanilla and 50 pints of chocolate each year, is she maximizing her utility?

---

[1]The actual reduction would be slightly larger than 16 utils because her marginal utility of chocolate rises slightly as she consumes less of it.
[2]The actual increase will be slightly smaller than 24 utils because her marginal utility of vanilla falls slightly as she buys more of it.

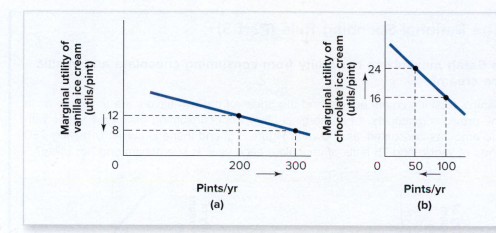

FIGURE 5.4

Marginal Utility Curves for Two Flavors of Ice Cream (Part 2).

When Sarah increases her consumption of vanilla (a), her marginal utility of vanilla falls. Conversely, when she reduces her consumption of chocolate (b), her marginal utility of chocolate rises.

Note first that the direction of Sarah's rearrangement of her spending makes sense in light of the original example, in which we saw that she was spending too much on chocolate and too little on vanilla. Spending $100 less on chocolate ice cream causes her marginal utility from that flavor to rise from 16 to 24 utils per pint [Figure 5.4(b)]. By the same token, spending $100 more on vanilla ice cream causes her marginal utility from that flavor to fall from 12 to 8 utils per pint [Figure 5.4(a)]. Both movements are a simple consequence of the law of diminishing marginal utility.

Since chocolate still costs $2 per pint, her spending on chocolate now yields additional utility at the rate of (24 utils/pint)/($2/pint) = 12 utils per dollar. Similarly, since vanilla still costs $1 per pint, her spending on vanilla now yields additional utility at the rate of only (8 utils/pint)/($1/pint) = 8 utils per dollar. So at her new rates of consumption of the two flavors, her spending yields higher marginal utility per dollar for chocolate than for vanilla—precisely the opposite of the ordering we saw in the original example.

Sarah has thus made too big an adjustment in her effort to remedy her original consumption imbalance. Starting from the new combination of flavors (300 pints per year of vanilla and 50 pints per year of chocolate), for example, if she then bought two fewer pints of vanilla (which would reduce her utility by about 16 utils) and used the $2 she saved to buy an additional pint of chocolate (which would boost her utility by about 24 utils), she would experience a net gain of about 8 utils. So, again, her current combination of the two flavors fails to maximize her total utility. This time, she is spending too little on chocolate and too much on vanilla.

 SELF-TEST 5.1

In the preceding examples, verify that the stated combination of flavors costs exactly the amount that Sarah has budgeted for ice cream.

What is Sarah's **optimal combination** of the two flavors? In other words, among all the combinations of vanilla and chocolate ice cream that Sarah can afford, which one provides the maximum possible total utility? The following example illustrates the condition that this optimal combination must satisfy.

optimal combination of goods the affordable combination that yields the highest total utility

EXAMPLE 5.3   The Rational Spending Rule (Part 3)

Is Sarah maximizing her utility from consuming chocolate and vanilla ice cream?

Sarah's total ice cream budget and the prices of the two flavors are the same as in the previous examples. If her marginal utility from consuming each type varies with the amounts consumed, as shown in Figure 5.5, and if she is currently buying 250 pints of vanilla and 75 pints of chocolate each year, is she maximizing her utility?

FIGURE 5.5

Marginal Utility Curves for Two Flavors of Ice Cream (Part 3).

At her current consumption levels, marginal utility per dollar is exactly the same for each flavor.

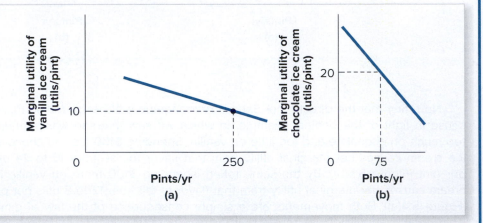

As you can easily verify, the combination of 250 pints per year of vanilla and 75 pints per year of chocolate again costs a total of $400, exactly the amount of Sarah's ice cream budget. Her marginal utility from chocolate is now 20 utils per pint [Figure 5.5(b)], and since chocolate still costs $2 per pint, her spending on chocolate now yields additional utility at the rate of (20 utils/pint)/($2/pint) = 10 utils per dollar. Sarah's marginal utility for vanilla is now 10 utils per pint [Figure 5.5(a)], and since vanilla still costs $1 per pint, her last dollar spent on vanilla now also yields (10 utils/pint)/($1/pint) = 10 utils per dollar. So at her new rates of consumption of the two flavors, her spending yields precisely the same marginal utility per dollar for each flavor. Thus, if she spent a little less on chocolate and a little more on vanilla (or vice versa), her total utility would not change at all. For example, if she bought two more pints of vanilla (which would increase her utility by 20 utils) and one fewer pint of chocolate (which would reduce her utility by 20 utils), both her total expenditure on ice cream and her total utility would remain the same as before. *When her marginal utility per dollar is the same for each flavor, it's impossible for Sarah to rearrange her spending to increase total utility.* Therefore, 250 pints of vanilla and 75 pints of chocolate per year form the optimal combination of the two flavors.

RECAP

Scarcity ⟩⟩

TRANSLATING WANTS INTO DEMAND

The Scarcity Principle challenges us to allocate our incomes among the various goods that are available so as to fulfill our desires to the greatest possible degree. The optimal combination of goods is the affordable combination that yields the highest total utility. For goods that are perfectly divisible, the rational spending rule tells us that the optimal combination is one for which the marginal utility per dollar is the same for each good. If this condition were not satisfied, the consumer could increase her utility by spending less on goods for which the marginal utility per dollar was lower and more on goods for which her marginal utility was higher.

THE RATIONAL SPENDING RULE

The examples we have worked through illustrate the **rational spending rule** for solving the problem of how to allocate a fixed budget across different goods. The optimal, or utility-maximizing, combination must satisfy this rule.

rational spending rule
spending should be allocated across goods so that the marginal utility per dollar is the same for each good

The Rational Spending Rule: Spending should be allocated across goods so that the marginal utility per dollar is the same for each good.

The rational spending rule can be expressed in the form of a simple formula. If we use MU_C to denote marginal utility from chocolate ice cream consumption (again measured in utils per pint) and P_C to denote the price of chocolate (measured in dollars per pint), then the ratio MU_C/P_C will represent the marginal utility per dollar spent on chocolate, measured in utils per dollar. Similarly, if we use MU_V to denote the marginal utility from vanilla ice cream consumption and P_V to denote the price of vanilla, then MU_V/P_V will represent the marginal utility per dollar spent on vanilla. The marginal utility per dollar will be exactly the same for the two types—and hence total utility will be maximized—when the following simple equation for the rational spending rule for two goods is satisfied

$$MU_C/P_C = MU_V/P_V.$$

The rational spending rule is easily generalized to apply to spending decisions regarding large numbers of goods. In its most general form, it says that the ratio of marginal utility to price must be the same for each good the consumer buys. If the ratio were higher for one good than for another, the consumer could always increase her total utility by buying more of the first good and less of the second.

Strictly speaking, the rational spending rule applies to goods that are perfectly divisible, such as milk or gasoline. Many other goods, such as bus rides and television sets, can be consumed only in whole-number amounts. In such cases, it may not be possible to satisfy the rational spending rule exactly. For example, when you buy one television set, your marginal utility per dollar spent on televisions may be somewhat higher than the corresponding ratio for other goods, yet if you bought a second set, the reverse might well be true. Your best alternative in such cases is to allocate each additional dollar you spend to the good for which your marginal utility per dollar is highest.

Notice that we have not chosen to classify the rational spending rule as one of the *Core Principles* of economics. We omit it from this list not because the rule is unimportant, but because it follows directly from the Cost-Benefit Principle. As we noted earlier, there is considerable advantage in keeping the list of Core Principles as small as possible.

 **Cost-Benefit**

INCOME AND SUBSTITUTION EFFECTS REVISITED

In Chapter 3, *Supply and Demand*, we saw that the quantity of a good that consumers wish to purchase depends on its own price, on the prices of substitutes and complements, and on consumer incomes. We also saw that when the price of a good changes, the quantity of it demanded changes for two reasons: the substitution effect and the income effect. The substitution effect refers to the fact that when the price of a good goes up, substitutes for that good become relatively more attractive, causing some consumers to abandon the good for its substitutes.

The income effect refers to the fact that a price change makes the consumer either poorer or richer in real terms. Consider, for instance, the effect of a change in the price of one of the ice cream flavors in the preceding examples. At the original prices ($2 per pint for chocolate, $1 per pint for vanilla), Sarah's $400 annual ice cream budget enabled her to buy at most 200 pints per year of chocolate or 400 pints per year of vanilla. If the price of vanilla rose to $2 per pint, that would reduce not only the maximum amount of vanilla she could afford (from 400 to 200 pints per year), but also the maximum amount of chocolate she could afford in combination with any given amount of vanilla. For example, at the original price of $1 per pint for vanilla, Sarah could afford to buy 150 pints of chocolate while buying 100 pints of vanilla, but when the price of vanilla rises to $2, she can buy only

100 pints of chocolate while buying 100 pints of vanilla. As noted in Chapter 3, *Supply and Demand*, a reduction in real income shifts the demand curves for normal goods to the left.

The rational spending rule helps us see more clearly why a change in the price of one good affects demands for other goods. The rule requires that the ratio of marginal utility to price be the same for all goods. This means that if the price of one good goes up, the ratio of its current marginal utility to its new price will be lower than for other goods. Consumers can then increase their total utility by devoting smaller proportions of their incomes to that good and larger proportions to others.

EXAMPLE 5.4	**Response to a Price Reduction**

How should Sarah respond to a reduction in the price of chocolate ice cream?

Suppose that Sarah's total ice cream budget is still $400 per year and the prices of the two flavors are again $2 per pint for chocolate and $1 per pint for vanilla. Her marginal utility from consuming each type varies with the amounts consumed, as shown in Figure 5.6. As we showed in the previous example, she is currently buying 250 pints of vanilla and 75 pints of chocolate each year, which is the optimal combination for her at these prices. How should she reallocate her spending among the two flavors if the price of chocolate ice cream falls to $1 per pint?

FIGURE 5.6

Marginal Utility Curves for Two Flavors of Ice Cream (Part 4).

At the current combination of flavors, marginal utility per dollar is the same for each flavor. When the price of chocolate falls, marginal utility per dollar becomes higher for chocolate than for vanilla. To redress this imbalance, Sarah should buy more chocolate and less vanilla.

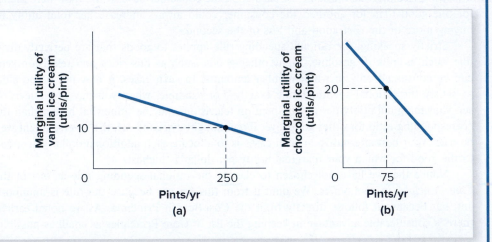

Because the quantities shown in Figure 5.6 constitute the optimal combination of the two flavors for Sarah at the original prices, they must exactly satisfy the rational spending rule:

$$MU_C/P_C = (20 \text{ utils/pint})/(\$2/\text{pint}) = 10 \text{ utils/dollar}$$
$$= MU_V/P_V = (10 \text{ utils/pint})/(\$1/\text{pint}).$$

When the price of chocolate falls to $1 per pint, the original quantities will no longer satisfy the rational spending rule because the marginal utility per dollar for chocolate will suddenly be twice what it was before:

$$MU_C/P_C = (20 \text{ utils/pint})/(\$1/\text{pint}) = 20 \text{ utils/dollar}$$
$$> MU_V/P_V = 10 \text{ utils/dollar}.$$

To redress this imbalance, Sarah must rearrange her spending on the two flavors in such a way as to increase the marginal utility per dollar for vanilla relative to the marginal utility per dollar for chocolate. And as we see in Figure 5.6, that will happen if she buys a larger quantity than before of chocolate and a smaller quantity than before of vanilla.

SELF-TEST 5.2

John spends all of his income on two goods: food and shelter. The price of food is $5 per pound and the price of shelter is $10 per square yard. At his current consumption levels, his marginal utilities for the two goods are 20 utils per pound and 30 utils per square yard, respectively. Is John maximizing his utility? If not, how should he reallocate his spending?

In Chapter 1, *Thinking Like an Economist*, we saw that people often make bad decisions because they fail to appreciate the distinction between average and marginal costs and benefits. As the following example illustrates, this pitfall also arises when people attempt to apply the economist's model of utility maximization.

EXAMPLE 5.5	Marginal vs. Average Utility

Should Juan consume more apples?

Juan gets a total of 1,000 utils per week from his consumption of apples and a total of 400 utils per week from his consumption of oranges. The price of apples is $2 each, the price of oranges is $1 each, and he consumes 50 apples and 50 oranges each week. True or false: Juan should consume more apples and fewer oranges.

Juan spends $100 per week on apples and $50 on oranges. He thus averages (1,000 utils/week)/($100/week) = 10 utils per dollar from his consumption of apples and (400 utils/week)/($50/week) = 8 utils per dollar from his consumption of oranges. Many might be tempted to respond that because Juan's average utility per dollar for apples is higher than for oranges, he should consume more apples. But knowing only his *average* utility per dollar for each good doesn't enable us to say whether his current combination is optimal. To make that determination, we need to compare Juan's *marginal* utility per dollar for each good. The information given simply doesn't permit us to make that comparison.

APPLYING THE RATIONAL SPENDING RULE

The real payoff from learning the law of demand and the rational spending rule lies in using these abstract concepts to make sense of the world around you. To encourage you in your efforts to become an economic naturalist, we turn now to a sequence of Economic Naturalist examples in this vein.

Substitution at Work

In the first of these examples, we focus on the role of substitution. When the price of a good or service goes up, rational consumers generally turn to less expensive substitutes. Can't meet the payments on a new car? Then buy a used one, or rent an apartment on a bus or subway line. French restaurants too pricey? Then go out for Chinese, or eat at home more often. National Football League tickets too high? Watch the game on television, or read a book. Can't afford a book? Check one out of the library, or download some reading matter from the Internet. Once you begin to see substitution at work, you'll be amazed by the number and richness of the examples that confront you every day.

The Economic Naturalist 5.2

Why would Jeff Bezos live in a smaller house in Manhattan than in Medina, Washington?

Among his many residences, Amazon CEO Jeff Bezos owns a 29,000-square-foot home in Medina, Washington. Bezos also owns a 17,000-square-foot apartment in Manhattan. Although both residences are enormous, Bezos's apartment in Manhattan is much smaller than his home in Medina. Bezos is one of the richest people in the world, so why would he choose to purchase a much smaller home in Manhattan than Medina?

For people trying to decide how large a home to buy, the most obvious difference between Manhattan and Medina is the huge difference in housing prices. The cost of land alone is several times higher in Manhattan than in Medina, and construction costs are also much higher. So even though Bezos could *afford* to purchase a 29,000-square-foot home in Manhattan, housing prices are so high that he simply chooses to purchase a smaller home and spend his fortune in other ways.

Here we note in passing that an additional factor in Bezos's decision may have been the link between context and evaluation: A house seems small only if it is small relative to other houses in the same local environment. Because Manhattan prices are so high, others choose to build smaller houses there, too, so a 17,000-square-foot house in Manhattan is a larger dwelling, in relative terms, than a 29,000-square-foot house in Medina. We will discuss this point more thoroughly in Chapter 10, *An Introduction to Behavioral Economics*.

An especially vivid illustration of substitution occurred during the late 1970s, when fuel shortages brought on by interruptions in the supply of oil from the Middle East led to sharp increases in the price of gasoline and other fuels. In a variety of ways—some straightforward, others remarkably ingenious—consumers changed their behavior to economize on the use of energy. They formed car pools; switched to public transportation; bought four-cylinder cars; moved closer to work; took fewer trips; turned down their thermostats; installed insulation, storm windows, and solar heaters; and bought more efficient appliances. Many people even moved farther south to escape high winter heating bills.

As the next example points out, consumers not only abandon a good in favor of substitutes when it gets more expensive, but they also return to that good when prices return to their original levels.

The Economic Naturalist 5.3

Why did people turn to four-cylinder cars in the 1970s, only to shift back to six- and eight-cylinder cars in the 1990s?

In 1973, the price of gasoline was 38 cents per gallon. The following year the price shot up to 52 cents per gallon in the wake of a major disruption of oil supplies. A second disruption in 1979 drove the 1980 price to $1.19 per gallon. These sharp increases in the price of gasoline led to big increases in the demand for cars with four-cylinder engines, which delivered much better fuel economy than the six- and eight-cylinder cars most people had owned. After 1980, however, fuel supplies stabilized, and prices rose only slowly, reaching $1.40 per gallon by 1999. Yet despite the continued rise in the price of gasoline, the switch to smaller engines did not continue. By the late 1980s, the proportion of cars sold with six- and eight-cylinder engines began rising again. Why this reversal?

real price the dollar price of a good relative to the average dollar price of all other goods

The key to explaining these patterns is to focus on changes in the **real price** of gasoline. When someone decides how big an automobile engine to choose, what matters is not the **nominal price** of gasoline, but the price of gasoline *relative* to all other goods. After all, for a consumer faced with a decision of whether to spend $1.40 for a gallon of gasoline, the important question is how much utility she could get from other things she could purchase with the same money. Even though the price of gasoline continued to rise slowly in nominal, or dollar, terms through the 1980s and 1990s, it declined sharply relative to the price of other goods. Indeed, in terms of real purchasing power, the 1999 price was actually slightly lower than the 1973 price. (That is, in 1999 $1.40 bought slightly fewer goods and services than 38 cents bought in 1973.) It is this decline in the real price of gasoline that accounts for the reversal of the trend toward smaller engines.

nominal price the absolute price of a good in dollar terms

▶ Visit your instructor's Connect course and access your eBook to view this video.

Why are smaller automobile engines more common in Europe than in the United States?

A sharp decline in the real price of gasoline also helps account for the explosive growth in sport-utility vehicles in the 1990s. Almost 4 million SUVs were sold in the United States in 2001, up from only 750,000 in 1990. Some of them—like the Ford Excursion—weigh more than 7,500 pounds (three times as much as a Honda Civic) and get less than 10 miles per gallon on city streets. Vehicles like these would have been dismal failures during the 1970s, but they were by far the hottest sellers in the cheap-energy environment of 2001.

In 2004, gasoline prices yet again began to rise sharply in real terms, and by 2012 had reached almost $5 per gallon in some parts of the country. Just as expected, the patterns of vehicle purchases began to shift almost immediately. Large SUVs, in high demand just months earlier, began selling at deep discounts. And with long waiting lists for fuel-efficient cars such as the Toyota Prius, buyers not only seldom received discounts, but they frequently paid even more than the sticker price. More recently, with the dramatic fall in gasoline prices since 2012, sales for large SUVs and other light trucks are again on the rise, while sales for more fuel-efficient passenger cars have reached their lowest point in decades.

Here's another closely related example of the influence of price on spending decisions.

The Economic Naturalist 5.4

Why are automobile engines smaller in England than in the United States?

In England, the most popular model of BMW's 5-series car is the 516i, whereas in the United States it is the 530i. The engine in the 516i is almost 50 percent smaller than the engine in the 530i. Why this difference?

In both countries, BMWs appeal to professionals with roughly similar incomes, so the difference cannot be explained by differences in purchasing power. Rather, it is the direct result of the heavy tax the British levy on gasoline. With tax, a gallon of gasoline sells for more than two times the price in the United States. This difference encourages the British to choose smaller, more fuel-efficient engines.

Does the quantity of horsepower demanded depend on gasoline prices?

The Importance of Income Differences

The most obvious difference between the rich and the poor is that the rich have higher incomes. To explain why the wealthy generally buy larger houses than the poor, we need not assume that the wealthy feel more strongly about housing than the poor. A much simpler explanation is that the total utility from housing, as with most other goods, increases with the amount that one consumes.

As the next example illustrates, income influences the demand not only for housing and other goods, but also for quality of service.

Why are lines longer in low-income neighborhoods?

The Economic Naturalist 5.5

Why are waiting lines longer in poorer neighborhoods?

As part of a recent promotional campaign, a Baskin-Robbins retailer offered free ice cream at two of its franchise stores. The first was located in a high-income neighborhood, the second in a low-income neighborhood. Why was the queue for free ice cream longer in the low-income neighborhood?

Residents of both neighborhoods must decide whether to stand in line for free ice cream or go to some other store and avoid the line by paying the usual price. If we make the plausible assumption that people with higher incomes are more willing than others to pay to avoid standing in line, we should expect to see shorter lines in the high-income neighborhood.

Similar reasoning helps explain why lines are shorter in grocery stores that cater to high-income consumers. Keeping lines short at *any* grocery store means hiring more clerks, which means charging higher prices. High-income consumers are more likely than others to be willing to pay for shorter lines.

> **RECAP**
>
> **THE RATIONAL SPENDING RULE**
>
> Application of the rational spending rule highlights the important roles of income and substitution in explaining differences in consumption patterns—among individuals, among communities, and across time. The rule also highlights the fact that real, as opposed to nominal, prices and income are what matter. The demand for a good falls when the real price of a substitute falls or the real price of a complement rises.

INDIVIDUAL AND MARKET DEMAND CURVES

If we know what each individual's demand curve for a good looks like, how can we use that information to construct the market demand curve for the good? We must add the individual demand curves together, a process that is straightforward but requires care.

HORIZONTAL ADDITION

Suppose that there are only two buyers—Raj and Zora—in the market for canned tuna and that their demand curves are as shown in Figure 5.7(a) and (b). To construct the market demand curve for canned tuna, we simply announce a sequence of prices and then add the quantity demanded by each buyer at each price. For example, at a price of 40 cents per can, Raj demands six cans per week (a) and Zora demands two cans per week (b), for a market demand of eight cans per week (c).

The process of adding individual demand curves to get the market demand curve is known as *horizontal addition*, a term used to emphasize that we are adding quantities, which are measured on the horizontal axes of individual demand curves.

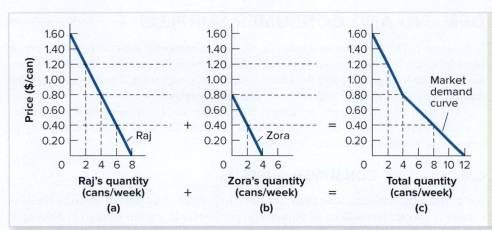

FIGURE 5.7

Individual and Market Demand Curves for Canned Tuna.

The quantity demanded at any price on the market demand curve (c) is the sum of the individual quantities demanded at that price, (a) and (b).

 SELF-TEST 5.3

The buyers' side of the market for movie tickets consists of two consumers whose demands are as shown in the diagram below. Graph the market demand curve for this market.

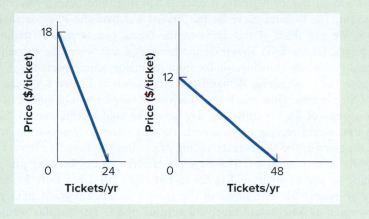

Figure 5.8 illustrates the special case in which each of 1,000 consumers in the market has the same demand curve (a). To get the market demand curve (b) in this case, we simply multiply each quantity on the representative individual demand curve by 1,000.

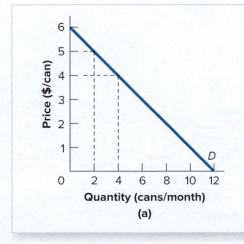

FIGURE 5.8

The Individual and Market Demand Curves When All Buyers Have Identical Demand Curves.

When individual demand curves are identical, we get the market demand curve (b) by multiplying each quantity on the individual demand curve (a) by the number of consumers in the market.

DEMAND AND CONSUMER SURPLUS

In Chapter 1, *Thinking Like an Economist*, we first encountered the concept of economic surplus, which in a buyer's case is the difference between the most she would have been willing to pay for a product and the amount she actually pays for it. The economic surplus received by buyers is often referred to as **consumer surplus.**

The term *consumer surplus* sometimes refers to the surplus received by a single buyer in a transaction. On other occasions, it's used to denote the total surplus received by all buyers in a market or collection of markets.

consumer surplus the difference between a buyer's reservation price for a product and the price actually paid

CALCULATING CONSUMER SURPLUS

For performing cost-benefit analysis, it's often important to be able to measure the total consumer surplus received by all buyers who participate in a given market. For example, a road linking a mountain village and a port city would create a new market for fresh fish in the mountain village; in deciding whether the road should be built, analysts would want to count as one of its benefits the gains that would be reaped by buyers in this new market.

To illustrate how economists actually measure consumer surplus, we'll consider a hypothetical market for a good with 11 potential buyers, each of whom can buy a maximum of one unit of the good each day. The first potential buyer's reservation price for the product is $11; the second buyer's reservation price is $10; the third buyer's reservation price is $9; and so on. The demand curve for this market will have the staircase shape shown in Figure 5.9. We can think of this curve as the digital counterpart of traditional analog demand curves. (If the units shown on the horizontal axis were fine enough, this digital curve would be visually indistinguishable from its analog counterparts.)

Suppose the good whose demand curve is shown in Figure 5.9 were available at a price of $6 per unit. How much total consumer surplus would buyers in this market reap? At a price of $6, six units per day would be sold in this market. The buyer of the sixth unit would receive no economic surplus since his reservation price for that unit was exactly $6, the same as its selling price. But the first five buyers would reap a surplus for their purchases. The buyer of the first unit, for example, would have been willing to pay as much as $11 for it, but since she'd pay only $6, she'd receive a surplus of exactly $5. The buyer of the second unit, who would have been willing to pay as much as $10, would receive a surplus of $4. The surplus would be $3 for the buyer of the third unit, $2 for the buyer of the fourth unit, and $1 for the buyer of the fifth unit.

If we add all the buyers' surpluses together, we get a total of $15 of consumer surplus each day. That surplus corresponds to the shaded area shown in Figure 5.10.

FIGURE 5.9

A Market with a "Digital" Demand Curve.

When a product can be sold only in whole-number amounts, its demand curve has the stair-step shape shown.

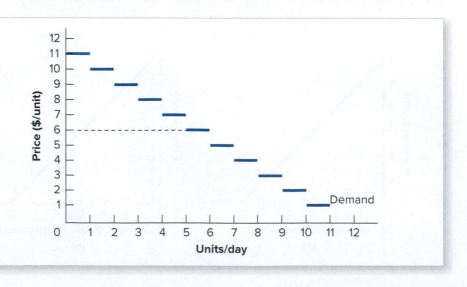

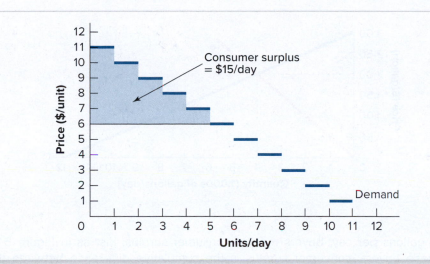

FIGURE 5.10

Consumer Surplus.

Consumer surplus (shaded region) is the cumulative difference between the most that buyers are willing to pay for each unit and the price they actually pay.

 SELF-TEST 5.4

Calculate consumer surplus for a demand curve like the one just described except that the buyers' reservation prices for each unit are $2 higher than before, as shown in the graph below.

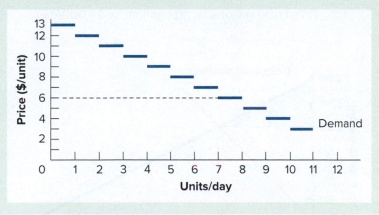

Now suppose we want to calculate consumer surplus in a market with a conventional straight-line demand curve. As the following example illustrates, this task is a simple extension of the method used for digital demand curves.

EXAMPLE 5.6   Measuring Consumer Surplus

How much do buyers benefit from their participation in the market for milk?

Consider the market for milk whose demand and supply curves are shown in Figure 5.11, which has an equilibrium price of $2 per gallon and an equilibrium quantity of 4,000 gallons per day. How much consumer surplus do the buyers in this market reap?

In Figure 5.11, note first that, as in Figure 5.10, the last unit exchanged each day generates no consumer surplus at all. Note also that for all milk sold up to

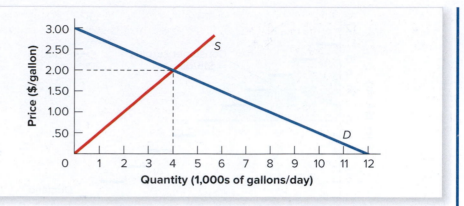

4,000 gallons per day, buyers receive consumer surplus, just as in Figure 5.10. For these buyers, consumer surplus is the cumulative difference between the most they'd be willing to pay for milk (as measured on the demand curve) and the price they actually pay.

Total consumer surplus received by buyers in the milk market is thus the shaded triangle between the demand curve and the market price in Figure 5.12. Note that this area is a right triangle whose vertical arm is $h = \$1$/gallon and whose horizontal arm is $b = 4{,}000$ gallons/day. And because the area of any triangle is equal to $(1/2)bh$, consumer surplus in this market is equal to

$$(1/2)(4{,}000 \text{ gallons/day})(\$1/\text{gallon}) = \$2{,}000/\text{day}.$$

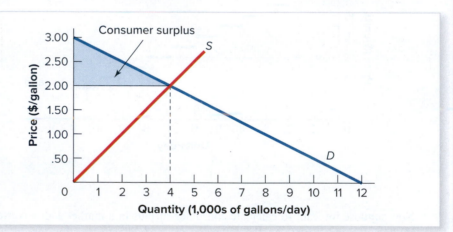

A useful way of thinking about consumer surplus is to ask what is the highest price consumers would pay, in the aggregate, for the right to continue participating in this milk market. The answer is $2,000 per day, since that's the amount by which their combined benefits exceed their combined costs.

As discussed in Chapter 3, *Supply and Demand*, the demand curve for a good can be interpreted either horizontally or vertically. The horizontal interpretation tells us, for each price, the total quantity that consumers wish to buy at that price. The vertical interpretation tells us, for each quantity, the most a buyer would be willing to pay for the good at that quantity. For the purpose of computing consumer surplus, we rely on the vertical interpretation of the demand curve. The value on the vertical axis that corresponds to each point along the demand curve corresponds to the marginal buyer's reservation price for the good. Consumer surplus is the cumulative sum of the differences between these reservation prices and the market price. It is the area bounded above by the demand curve and bounded below by the market price.

SUMMARY

- The rational consumer allocates income among different goods so that the marginal utility gained from the last dollar spent on each good is the same. This rational spending rule gives rise to the law of demand, which states that people do less of what they want to do as the cost of doing it rises. Here, "cost" refers to the sum of all monetary and nonmonetary sacrifices—explicit and implicit—that must be made in order to engage in the activity. *(LO1, LO2)*

- As the price of a good rises, people tend to choose less expensive alternatives. The ability to substitute one good for another is an important factor behind the law of demand. Because virtually every good or service has at least some substitutes, economists prefer to speak in terms of wants rather than needs. *(LO3)*

- For normal goods, the income effect is a second important reason that demand curves slope downward. When the price of such a good rises, not only does it become

less attractive relative to its substitutes, but the consumer also has less real purchasing power, and this, too, reduces the quantity demanded. *(LO3)*

- The demand curve is a schedule that shows the amounts of a good people want to buy at various prices. Demand curves can be used to summarize the price–quantity relationship for a single individual, but more commonly we employ them to summarize that relationship for an entire market. At any quantity along a demand curve, the corresponding price represents the amount by which the consumer (or consumers) would benefit from having an additional unit of the product. For this reason, the demand curve is sometimes described as a summary of the benefit side of the market. *(LO4)*

- Consumer surplus is a quantitative measure of the amount by which buyers benefit as a result of their ability to purchase goods at the market price. It is the area between the demand curve and the market price. *(LO5)*

KEY TERMS

consumer surplus
law of demand
law of diminishing marginal utility

marginal utility
nominal price
optimal combination of goods

rational spending rule
real price

REVIEW QUESTIONS

1. Why do economists prefer to speak of demands arising out of "wants" rather than "needs"? *(LO1)*

2. Explain why economists consider the concept of utility useful, even if psychologists cannot measure it precisely. *(LO2)*

3. Why does the law of diminishing marginal utility encourage people to spread their spending across many different types of goods? *(LO2)*

4. Explain why a good or service that is offered at a monetary price of zero is unlikely to be a truly "free" good from an economic perspective. *(LO3)*

5. Give an example of a good that you have consumed for which your marginal utility increased with the amount of it you consumed. *(LO3)*

PROBLEMS

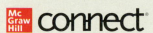

1. Any consumer trying to decide whether to buy a given good or service will base the decision on his or her reservation price and the existing market price. When making

this decision, what does the buyer's reservation price measure? What does the market price measure? *(LO1)*

2. Which of the following factors would affect a buyer's reservation price for a given good or service: social influence, the price of the good, or the cost of producing the item? *(LO1)*

3. You are having lunch at an all-you-can-eat buffet. If you are rational, what should be your marginal utility from the last morsel of food you swallow? *(LO2)*

4. Kai's current marginal utility from consuming orange juice is 75 utils per ounce and her marginal utility from consuming coffee is 50 utils per ounce. If orange juice costs 25 cents per ounce and coffee costs 20 cents per ounce, is Kai maximizing her total utility from the two beverages? If so, explain how you know. If not, how should she rearrange her spending? *(LO2)*

5. Rohan's current marginal utility from consuming peanuts is 100 utils per ounce and his marginal utility from consuming cashews is 200 utils per ounce. If peanuts cost 10 cents per ounce and cashews cost 25 cents per ounce, is Rohan maximizing his total utility from the kinds of nuts? If so, explain how you know. If not, how should he rearrange his spending? *(LO2)*

6. Sienna gets a total of 20 utils per week from her consumption of pizza and a total of 40 utils per week from her consumption of yogurt. The price of pizza is $1 per slice, the price of yogurt is $1 per cup, and she consumes 10 slices of pizza and 20 cups of yogurt each week. True or false: Sienna is consuming the optimal combination of pizza and yogurt. *(LO2)*

7. Zander has a weekly allowance of $24, all of which he spends on pizza and movie rentals, whose prices are $6 per slice and $3 per rental, respectively. We assume that pizza slices and movie rentals are available only in whole-number amounts. *(LO2)*
   a. List all possible combinations of the two goods that Zander can purchase each week with his allowance.
   b. Zander's total utility is the sum of the utility he derives from pizza and movie rentals. If these utilities vary with the amounts consumed as shown in the table, and pizza slices and movie rentals are again consumable only in whole-number amounts, how many pizza slices and how many movie rentals should Zander consume each week?

Pizza slices/ week	Utils/week from pizza	Movie rentals/ week	Utils/week from rentals
0	0	0	0
1	20	1	40
2	36	2	46
3	48	3	50
4	58	4	54
5	66	5	56
6	72	6	57
7	76	7	57
8	78	8	57

8. Ishana lives in Princeton, New Jersey, and commutes by train each day to her job in New York City (20 round-trips per month). When the price of a round-trip goes up from $10 to $20, she responds by consuming exactly the same number of trips as before, while spending $200 per month less on restaurant meals. Does the fact that her quantity of train travel is completely unresponsive to the price increase imply that Ishana is not a rational consumer? *(LO3)*

9.* The buyers' side of the market for amusement park tickets consists of two consumers whose demands are as shown in the diagram below. *(LO4, LO5)*
   a. Graph the market demand curve for this market.
   b. Calculate the total consumer surplus in the amusement park market if tickets sell for $12 each.

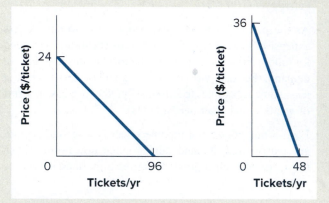

10. For the demand curve shown, find the total amount of consumer surplus that results in the gasoline market if gasoline sells for $2 per gallon. *(LO5)*

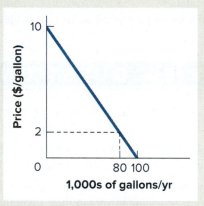

*Denotes more difficult problem.

ANSWERS TO SELF-TESTS

5.1 The combination of 300 pints per year of vanilla ($300) and 50 pints of chocolate ($100) costs a total of $400, which is exactly equal to Sarah's ice cream budget. *(LO2)*

5.2 The rational spending rule requires $MU_F/P_F = MU_S/P_S$ where MU_F and MU_S are Juan's marginal utilities from food and shelter and P_F and P_S are the prices of food and shelter, respectively. At Juan's original combination, $MU_F/P_F = 4$ utils per dollar and $MU_S/P_S = 3$ utils per dollar. Juan should thus spend more of his income on food and less on shelter. *(LO3)*

5.3 Adding the two individual demand curves, (a) and (b), horizontally yields the market demand curve (c): *(LO4)*

5.4 Consumer surplus is now the new shaded area, $28 per day. *(LO5)*

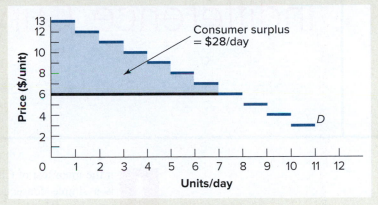

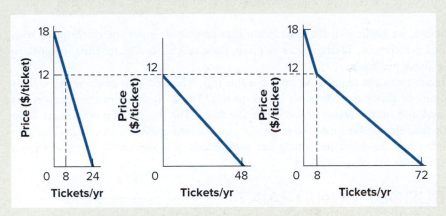

Indifference Curves

In the main text of Chapter 5, *Demand*, we showed why the rational spending rule is a simple consequence of diminishing marginal utility. In this appendix, we introduce the concept of indifference curves to develop the same rule in another way.

As before, we begin with the assumption that consumers enter the marketplace with well-defined preferences. Taking prices as given, their task is to allocate their incomes to best serve these preferences.

There are two steps required to carry out this task. The first is to describe the various combinations of goods the consumer is *able* to buy. These combinations depend on her income level and on the prices of the goods she faces. The second step is to select from among the feasible combinations the particular one that she *prefers* to all others. This step will require some means of describing her preferences. We begin with the first step, a description of the set of possibilities.

THE BUDGET CONSTRAINT

As before, we keep the discussion simple by focusing on a consumer who spends her entire income on only two goods: chocolate and vanilla ice cream. A *bundle* of goods is the term used to describe a particular combination of the two types of ice cream, measured in pints per year. Thus, in Figure 5A.1, one bundle (bundle *A*) might consist of five pints per year of chocolate and seven pints per year of vanilla, while another (bundle *B*) consists of three pints per year of chocolate and eight pints per year of vanilla. For brevity's sake, we may use the notation (5, 7) to denote bundle *A* and (3, 8) to denote bundle *B*.

FIGURE 5A.1

Two Bundles of Goods.

A bundle is a specific combination of goods. Bundle *A* has five units of chocolate and seven units of vanilla. Bundle *B* has three units of chocolate and eight units of vanilla.

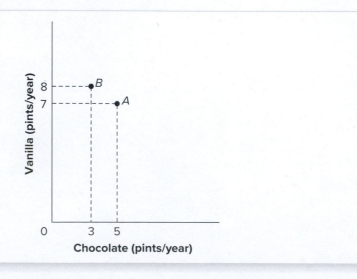

More generally, (C_0, V_0) will denote the bundle with C_0 pints per year of chocolate and V_0 pints per year of vanilla. By convention, the first number of the pair in any bundle represents the good measured along the horizontal axis.

Note that the units on both axes are *flows,* which means physical quantities per unit of time—in this case, pints per year. Consumption is always measured as a flow. It is important to keep track of the time dimension because, without it, there would be no way to evaluate whether a given quantity of consumption was large or small. (Again, suppose all you know is that your consumption of vanilla ice cream is four pints. If that's how much you eat each hour, it's a lot. But if that's all you eat in a decade, it's not very much.)

Suppose the consumer's income is $M = \$100$ per year, all of which she spends on some combination of vanilla and chocolate. (Note that income is also a flow.) Suppose further that the prices of chocolate and vanilla are $P_C = \$5$ per pint and $P_V = \$10$ per pint, respectively. If she spent her entire income on chocolate, she could buy $M/P_C =$ ($\$100$/year) $\div$ ($\$5$/pint) $= 20$ pints/year. That is, she could buy the bundle consisting of 20 pints per year of chocolate and 0 pints per year of vanilla, denoted (20, 0). Alternatively, suppose she spent her entire income on vanilla. She would then get the bundle consisting of $M/P_V =$ ($\$100$/year) $\div$ ($\$10$/pint) $= 10$ pints per year of vanilla and 0 pints per year of chocolate, denoted (0, 10).

In Figure 5A.2, these polar cases are labeled K and L, respectively. The consumer is also able to purchase any other bundle that lies along the straight line that joins points K and L. (Verify, for example, that the bundle (12, 4) lies on this same line.) This line is called the *budget constraint,* and is labeled B in the diagram.

Note that the slope of the budget constraint is its vertical intercept (the rise) divided by its horizontal intercept (the corresponding run)

$$-(10 \text{ pints/year})/(20 \text{ pints/year}) = -1/2.$$

The minus sign signifies that the budget line falls as it moves to the right—that it has a negative slope. More generally, if M denotes income and P_C and P_V denote the prices of chocolate and vanilla respectively, the horizontal and vertical intercepts will be given by (M/P_C) and (M/P_V), respectively. Thus, the general formula for the slope of the budget constraint is given by $-(M/P_V)/(M/P_C) = -P_C/P_V$, which is simply the negative of the price ratio of the two goods. Given their respective prices, it is the rate at which vanilla can be exchanged for chocolate. Thus, in Figure 5A.2, one pint of vanilla can be exchanged for two pints of chocolate. In the language of opportunity cost from Chapter 1, *Thinking Like an Economist,* we would say that the opportunity cost of an additional pint of chocolate is $P_C/P_V = 1/2$ pint of vanilla.

In addition to being able to buy any of the bundles along her budget constraint, the consumer is also able to purchase any bundle that lies within the *budget triangle* bounded by it and the two axes. D is one such bundle in Figure 5A.2. Bundle D costs $\$65$ per year,

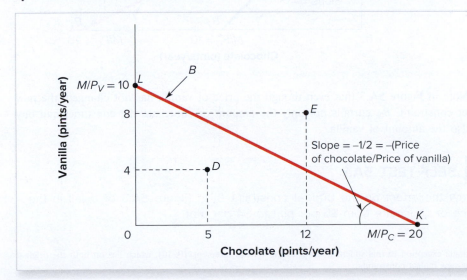

FIGURE 5A.2

The Budget Constraint.

The line B describes the set of all bundles the consumer can purchase for given values of income and prices. Its slope is the negative of the price of chocolate divided by the price of vanilla. In absolute value, this slope is the opportunity cost of an additional unit of chocolate: the number of pints of vanilla that must be sacrificed in order to purchase one additional pint of chocolate at market prices.

which is well below the consumer's ice cream budget of $100 per year. Bundles like E that lie outside the budget triangle are unaffordable. At a cost of $140 per year, E is simply beyond the consumer's reach.

If C and V denote the quantities of chocolate and vanilla, respectively, the budget constraint must satisfy the following equation

$$P_C C + P_V V = M, \tag{5A.1}$$

which says simply that the consumer's yearly expenditure on chocolate ($P_C C$) plus her yearly expenditure on vanilla ($P_V V$) must add up to her yearly income (M). To express the budget constraint in the manner conventionally used to represent the formula for a straight line, we solve Equation 5A.1 for V in terms of C, which yields

$$V = M/P_V - (P_C/P_V)C. \tag{5A.2}$$

Equation 5A.2 provides another way of seeing that the vertical intercept of the budget constraint is given by M/P_V, and its slope by $-(P_C/P_V)$. The equation for the budget constraint in Figure 5A.2 is $V = 10 - (1/2)C$.

BUDGET SHIFTS DUE TO INCOME OR PRICE CHANGES

Price Changes

The slope and position of the budget constraint are fully determined by the consumer's income and the prices of the respective goods. Change any one of these and we have a new budget constraint. Figure 5A.3 shows the effect of an increase in the price of chocolate from $P_{C1} = \$5$ per pint to $P_{C2} = \$10$ per pint. Since both her budget and the price of vanilla are unchanged, the vertical intercept of the consumer's budget constraint stays the same. The rise in the price of chocolate rotates the budget constraint inward about this intercept, as shown in the diagram.

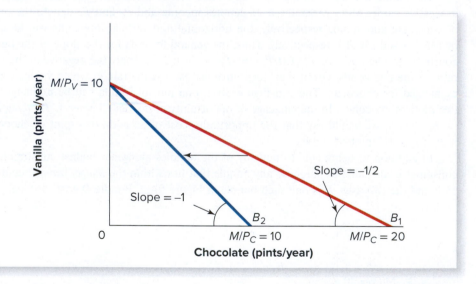

FIGURE 5A.3

The Effect of a Rise in the Price of Chocolate.

When chocolate goes up in price, the vertical intercept of the budget constraint remains the same. The original budget constraint rotates inward about this intercept.

Note in Figure 5A.3 that even though the price of vanilla has not changed, the new budget constraint, B_2, curtails not only the amount of chocolate the consumer can buy but also the amount of vanilla.[1]

 SELF-TEST 5A.1

Show the effect on the budget constraint B_1 in Figure 5A.3 of a fall in the price of chocolate from $5 per pint to $4 per pint.

---

[1] The single exception to this statement involves the vertical intercept, (0, 10), which lies on both the original and the new budget constraints.

In Self-Test 5A.1, you saw that a fall in the price of vanilla again leaves the vertical intercept of the budget constraint unchanged. This time the budget constraint rotates outward. Note also in Self-Test 5A.1 that although the price of vanilla remains unchanged, the new budget constraint enables the consumer to buy bundles that contain not only more chocolate but also more vanilla than she could afford on the original budget constraint.

 SELF-TEST 5A.2

Show the effect on the budget constraint B_1 in Figure 5A.3 of a rise in the price of vanilla from $10 per pint to $20 per pint.

Self-Test 5A.2 demonstrates that when the price of vanilla changes, the budget constraint rotates about its horizontal intercept. Note also that even though income and the price of chocolate remain the same, the new budget constraint curtails not only the amount of vanilla he can buy but also the amount of chocolate.

When we change the price of only one good, we necessarily change the slope of the budget constraint, $-P_C/P_V$. The same is true if we change both prices by different proportions. But as Self-Test 5A.3 will illustrate, changing both prices by exactly the same proportion gives rise to a new budget constraint with the same slope as before.

 SELF-TEST 5A.3

Show the effect on the budget constraint B_1 in Figure 5A.3 of a rise in the price of vanilla from $10 per pint to $20 per pint and a rise in the price of chocolate from $5 per pint to $10 per pint.

Note from Self-Test 5A.3 that the effect of doubling the prices of both vanilla and chocolate is to shift the budget constraint inward and parallel to the original budget constraint. The important lesson of this exercise is that the slope of the budget constraint tells us only about *relative prices,* nothing about how high prices are in absolute terms. When the prices of vanilla and chocolate change in the same proportion, the opportunity cost of chocolate in terms of vanilla remains the same as before.

Income Changes

The effect of a change in income is much like the effect of an equal proportional change in all prices. Suppose, for example, that our hypothetical consumer's income is cut by half, from $100 per year to $50 per year. The horizontal intercept of her budget constraint will then fall from 20 pints per year to 10 pints per year and the vertical intercept from 10 pints per year to 5 pints per year, as shown in Figure 5A.4. Thus the new budget, B_2, is parallel to the old, B_1, each with a slope of $-1/2$. In terms of its effect on what the consumer can buy, cutting income by half is thus no different from doubling each price. Precisely the same budget constraint results from both changes.

 SELF-TEST 5A.4

Show the effect on the budget constraint B_1 in Figure 5A.3 of an increase in income from $100 per year to $120 per year.

Self-Test 5A.4 illustrates that an increase in income shifts the budget constraint parallel outwards. As in the case of an income reduction, the slope of the budget constraint remains the same.

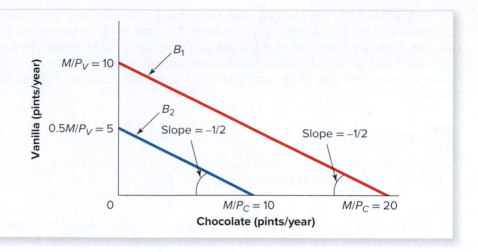

FIGURE 5A.4

The Effect of Cutting Income by Half.

Both horizontal and vertical intercepts fall by half. The new budget constraint has the same slope as the old but is closer to the origin.

BUDGETS INVOLVING MORE THAN TWO GOODS

The examples discussed so far have all been ones in which the consumer is faced with the opportunity to buy only two different goods. Needless to say, not many consumers have such narrow options. In its most general form, the consumer budgeting problem can be posed as a choice between not two but N different goods, where N can be an indefinitely large number. With only two goods ($N = 2$), the budget constraint is a straight line, as we have just seen. With three goods ($N = 3$), it is a plane. When we have more than three goods, the budget constraint becomes what mathematicians call a *hyperplane,* or multidimensional plane. The only real difficulty is in representing this multidimensional case geometrically. We are just not very good at visualizing surfaces that have more than three dimensions.

The nineteenth-century economist Alfred Marshall proposed a disarmingly simple solution to this problem. It is to view the consumer's choice as being one between a particular good—call it X—and an amalgam of other goods denoted Y. This amalgam is called the *composite good.* We may think of the composite good as the amount of income the consumer has left over after buying the good X.

To illustrate how this concept is used, suppose the consumer has an income level of $\$M$ per year, and the price of X is given by P_X. The consumer's budget constraint may then be represented as a straight line in the X,Y plane, as shown in Figure 5A.5. For simplicity, the price of a unit of the composite good is taken to be one, so that if the consumer devotes none of his income to X, he will be able to buy M units of the composite good. All this means is that he will have $\$M$ available to spend on other goods if he buys no X. Alternatively, if he spends all his income on X, he will be able to purchase

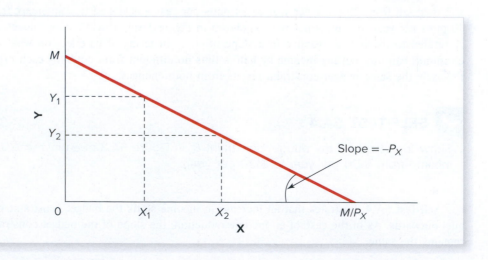

FIGURE 5A.5

The Budget Constraint with the Composite Good.

The vertical axis measures the amount of money spent each month on all goods other than X.

the bundle $(M/P_X, 0)$. Since the price of Y is assumed to be one, the slope of the budget constraint is simply $-P_X$.

As before, the budget constraint summarizes the various combinations of bundles that are affordable. For example, the consumer can have X_1 units of X and Y_1 units of the composite good in Figure 5A.5, or X_2 and Y_2, or any other combination that lies on the budget constraint.

Summing up briefly, the budget constraint or opportunity set summarizes the combinations of bundles that the consumer is able to buy. Its position is determined jointly by income and prices. From the set of feasible bundles, the consumer's task is to pick the particular one she likes best. To identify this bundle, we need some means of summarizing the consumer's preferences over all possible bundles she might consume. To this task we now turn.

CONSUMER PREFERENCES

For simplicity, we again begin by considering a world with only two goods, chocolate and vanilla ice cream, and assume that a particular consumer is able to rank different bundles of goods in terms of their desirability or order of preference. Suppose this consumer currently has bundle A in Figure 5A.6, which has six pints per year of chocolate and four pints per year of vanilla. If we then take one pint per year of chocolate away from her, she is left with bundle D, which has only five pints per year of chocolate and the same four pints per year of vanilla. Let us suppose that this consumer feels worse off than before, as most people would, because although D has just as much vanilla as A, it has less chocolate. We can undo the damage by giving her some additional vanilla. If our goal is to compensate for exactly her loss, how much extra vanilla do we need to give her?

Suppose we start by giving her an additional half pint per year, which would move her to bundle E in Figure 5A.6. For some consumers, that might be enough to make up for the lost pint of chocolate, even though the total amount of ice cream at E (9.5 pints per year) is smaller than at A (10 pints per year). Indeed, consumers who *really* like vanilla

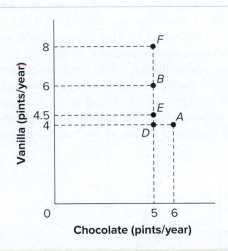

FIGURE 5A.6

Ranking Bundles.

This consumer will prefer A to D because A has more chocolate than D and just as much vanilla. She is assumed to prefer bundle A to bundle E and to prefer bundle F to bundle A. This means there must be a bundle between E and F (shown here as B) that she likes equally well as A. This consumer is said to be indifferent between A and B. If she moves from A to B, her gain of two pints per year of vanilla exactly compensates for her loss of one pint per year of chocolate. She will prefer F to B because F has more vanilla than B and just as much chocolate. For the same reason, she will prefer B to E and E to D.

FIGURE 5A.7

Equally Preferred Bundles.

This consumer is assumed to be indifferent between the bundles *A* and *C*. In moving from *A* to *C*, her gain of one pint per year of chocolate exactly compensates for her loss of one pint per year of vanilla. And since she was indifferent between *A* and *B*, she also must be indifferent between *B* and *C*.

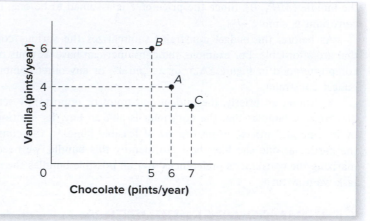

might actually prefer *E* to *A*. But we'll assume that this particular consumer would still prefer *A* to *E*. So to compensate fully for her lost pint of chocolate, we would have to give her more than an additional half pint of vanilla. Suppose we gave her a *lot* more vanilla—say, an additional four pints per year. This would move her to bundle *F* in Figure 5A.6, and we'll assume that she regards the extra four pints per year of vanilla at *F* as more than enough to compensate for the lost pint of chocolate.

The fact that this particular consumer prefers *F* to *A* but prefers *A* to *E* tells us that the amount of extra vanilla needed to *exactly* compensate for the lost pint of chocolate must be between one-half pint per year (the amount of extra vanilla at *E*) and four pints per year (the amount of extra vanilla at *F*). Suppose, for the sake of discussion, that she would feel exactly compensated if we gave her an additional two pints of vanilla. This consumer would then be said to be indifferent between bundles *A* and *B* in Figure 5A.6. Alternatively, we could say that she likes the bundles *A* and *B* equally well, or that she regards these bundles as equivalent.

Now suppose that we again start at bundle *A* and pose a different question: How many pints of vanilla would this consumer be willing to sacrifice in order to obtain an additional pint of chocolate? This time let's suppose that her answer is exactly one pint. We have thus identified another point—call it *C*—that is equally preferred to *A*. In Figure 5A.7, *C* is shown as the bundle (7, 3). *C* is also equally preferred to *B* (since *C* is equally preferred to *A,* which is equally preferred to *B*).

If we continue to generate additional bundles that the consumer likes equally well as bundle *A*, the end result is an *indifference curve*, a set of bundles all of which the consumer views as equivalent to the original bundle *A*, and hence also equivalent to one another. This set is shown as the curve labeled IC_1 in Figure 5A.8. It is called an indifference curve because the consumer is indifferent among all the bundles that lie along it.

FIGURE 5A.8

An Indifference Curve.

An indifference curve, such as IC_1, is a set of bundles that the consumer prefers equally. Any bundle, such as *K*, that lies above an indifference curve is preferred to any bundle on the indifference curve. Any bundle on the indifference curve, in turn, is preferred to any bundle, such as *L*, that lies below the indifference curve.

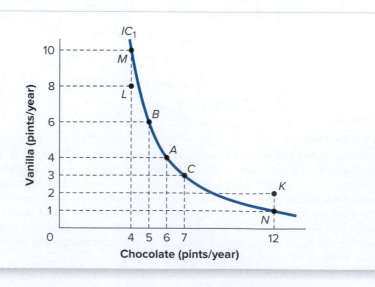

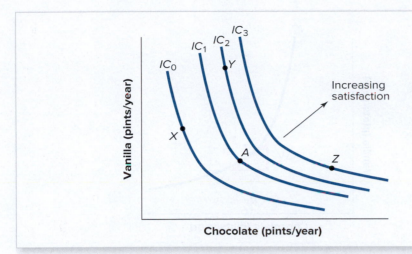

FIGURE 5A.9

Part of an Indifference Map.
The entire set of a consumer's indifference curves is called the consumer's indifference map. Bundles on any indifference curve are less preferred than bundles on a higher indifference curve and more preferred than bundles on a lower indifference curve. Thus, Z is preferred to Y, which is preferred to A, which is preferred to X.

An indifference curve also permits us to compare the satisfaction implicit in bundles that lie along it with those that lie either above or below it. It permits us, for example, to compare bundle C (7, 3) to a bundle like K (12, 2), which has less vanilla and more chocolate than C has. We know that C is equally preferred to N (12, 1) because both bundles lie along the same indifference curve. K, in turn, is preferred to N because it has just as much chocolate as N and one pint per year more vanilla. So if K is preferred to N, and N is just as attractive as C, then K must be preferred to C.

By analogous reasoning, we can say that bundle A is preferred to L. A and M are equivalent, and M is preferred to L since M has just as much chocolate as L and two pints per year more of vanilla. *In general, bundles that lie above an indifference curve are all preferred to the bundles that lie on it. Similarly, those that lie on an indifference curve are all preferred to those that lie below it.*

We can represent a useful summary of the consumer's preferences with an *indifference map,* an example of which is shown in Figure 5A.9. This indifference map shows just four of the infinitely many indifference curves that, taken together, yield a complete description of the consumer's preferences. As we move to the northeast on an indifference map, successive indifference curves represent higher levels of satisfaction. If we want to know how a consumer ranks any given pair of bundles, we simply compare the indifference curves on which they lie. The indifference map shown tells us, for example, that Z is preferred to Y because Z lies on a higher indifference curve (IC_3) than Y does (IC_2). By the same token, Y is preferred to A, and A is preferred to X.

TRADE-OFFS BETWEEN GOODS

An important property of a consumer's preferences is the rate at which she is willing to exchange, or "trade off," one good for another. This property is represented at any point on an indifference curve by the *marginal rate of substitution* (MRS), which is defined as the absolute value of the slope of the indifference curve at that point. In the left panel of Figure 5A.10, for example, the marginal rate of substitution at point T is given by the absolute value of the slope of the tangent to the indifference curve at T, which is the ratio $\Delta V_T/\Delta C_T$. (The notation ΔV_T means "small change in vanilla from the amount at point T.") If we take ΔC_T units of chocolate away from the consumer at point T, we have to give her ΔV_T additional units of vanilla to make her just as well off as before. If the marginal rate of substitution at T is 1.5, that means that the consumer must be given 1.5 pints per year of vanilla in order to make up for the loss of 1 pint per year of chocolate.

Whereas the slope of the budget constraint tells us the rate at which we can substitute vanilla for chocolate without changing total expenditure, the MRS tells us the rate at which we can substitute vanilla for chocolate without changing total satisfaction. Put another way, the slope of the budget constraint is the marginal cost of chocolate in terms of vanilla, while the MRS is the marginal benefit of chocolate in terms of vanilla.

FIGURE 5A.10

The Marginal Rate of Substitution.

The MRS at any point along an indifference curve is defined as the absolute value of the slope of the indifference curve at that point. It is the amount of vanilla the consumer is willing to give up to get another pint of chocolate.

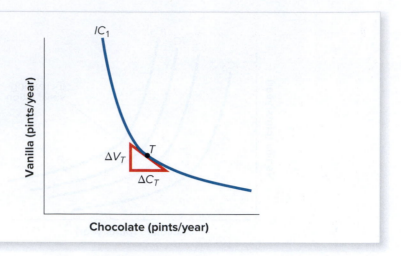

A common (but not universal) property of indifference curves is that the more a consumer has of one good, the more she must be given of that good before she will be willing to give up a unit of the other good. Stated differently, the MRS generally declines as we move downward to the right along an indifference curve. Indifference curves that exhibit diminishing marginal rates of substitution are thus convex—or bowed inward—when viewed from the origin. The indifference curves shown in Figures 5A.8, 5A.9, and 5A.10 all have this property, as does the curve shown in Figure 5A.11. This property is the indifference curve analog of the concept of diminishing marginal utility discussed in the main text of Chapter 5, *Demand*.

In Figure 5A.11, note that at bundle *A*, vanilla is relatively plentiful and the consumer would be willing to sacrifice three pints per year of it in order to obtain an additional pint of chocolate. Her MRS at *A* is 3. At *B*, the quantities of vanilla and chocolate are more balanced, and there she would be willing to give up only one pint per year to obtain an additional pint per year of chocolate. Her MRS at *B* is 1. Finally, note that vanilla is relatively scarce at *C*, where the consumer would need five additional pints per year of chocolate in return for giving up one pint per year of vanilla. Her MRS at *C* is 1/5.

Intuitively, diminishing MRS means that consumers like variety. We are usually willing to give up goods we already have a lot of in order to obtain more of those goods we now have only little of.

FIGURE 5A.11

Diminishing Marginal Rate of Substitution.

The more vanilla the consumer has, the more she is willing to give up to obtain an additional unit of chocolate. The marginal rates of substitution at bundles *A*, *B*, and *C* are 3, 1, and 1/5, respectively.

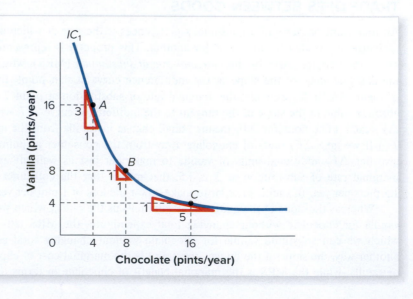

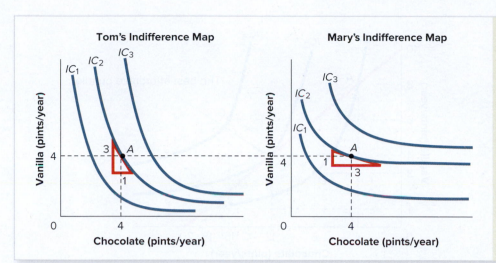

People with Different Tastes.
Relatively speaking, Tom is a chocolate lover, Mary a vanilla lover. This difference shows up in the fact that at any given bundle, Tom's marginal rate of substitution of vanilla for chocolate is greater than Mary's. At bundle A, for example, Tom would give up three pints of vanilla to get another pint of chocolate, whereas Mary would give up three pints of chocolate to get another pint of vanilla.

USING INDIFFERENCE CURVES TO DESCRIBE PREFERENCES

To get a feel for how indifference maps describe a consumer's preferences, it is helpful to work through a simple example. Suppose that Tom and Mary like both chocolate and vanilla ice cream but that Tom's favorite flavor is chocolate while Mary's favorite is vanilla. This difference in their preferences is captured by the differing slopes of their indifference curves in Figure 5A.12. Note in the left panel, which shows Tom's indifference map, that he would be willing to exchange three pints of vanilla for one pint of chocolate at the bundle A. But at the corresponding bundle in the right panel, which shows Mary's indifference map, we see that Mary would trade three pints of chocolate to get another pint of vanilla. Their difference in preferences shows up clearly in this difference in their marginal rates of substitution of vanilla for chocolate.

THE BEST AFFORDABLE BUNDLE ───────────────

We now have all the tools we need to determine how the consumer should allocate her income between two goods. The indifference map tells us how the various bundles are ranked in order of preference. The budget constraint, in turn, tells us which bundles are affordable. The consumer's task is to put the two together and choose the most preferred affordable bundle. (Recall from Chapter 1, *Thinking Like an Economist,* that we need not suppose that consumers think explicitly about budget constraints and indifference maps when deciding what to buy. It is sufficient that people make decisions *as if* they were thinking in these terms, just as experienced bicyclists ride as if they knew the relevant laws of physics.)

For the sake of concreteness, we again consider the choice between vanilla and chocolate ice cream that confronts a consumer with an income of $M = \$100$ per year facing prices of $P_V = \$10$ per pint and $P_C = \$5$ per pint. Figure 5A.13 shows this consumer's budget constraint and part of her indifference map. Of the five labeled bundles—A, D, E, F, and G—in the diagram, G is the most preferred because it lies on the highest indifference curve. G, however, is not affordable, nor is any other bundle that lies beyond the budget constraint. In general, the best affordable bundle will lie on the budget constraint, not inside it. (Any bundle inside the budget constraint would be less desirable than one just slightly to the northeast, which also would be affordable.)

Where, exactly, is the best affordable bundle located along the budget constraint? We know that it cannot be on an indifference curve that lies partly inside the budget constraint. On the indifference curve IC_1, for example, the only points that are even candidates for the best affordable bundle are the two that lie on the budget constraint, namely A and E. But A cannot be the best affordable bundle because it is equally preferred to D, which

FIGURE 5A.13

The Best Affordable Bundle.
The best the consumer can do is to choose the bundle on the budget constraint that lies on the highest attainable indifference curve. Here, that is bundle *F*, which lies at a tangency between the indifference curve and the budget constraint.

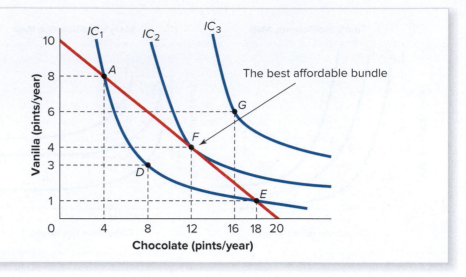

in turn is less desirable than *F*. So *A* also must be less desirable than *F*. For the same reason, *E* cannot be the best affordable bundle.

Since the best affordable bundle cannot lie on an indifference curve that lies partly inside the budget constraint, and since it must lie on the budget constraint itself, we know it has to lie on an indifference curve that intersects the budget constraint only once. In Figure 5A.13, that indifference curve is the one labeled IC_2, and the best affordable bundle is *F*, which lies at the point of tangency between IC_2 and the budget constraint. With an income of $100 per year and facing prices of $5 per pint for chocolate and $10 per pint of vanilla, the best this consumer can do is to buy 4 pints per year of vanilla and 12 pints per year of chocolate.

The choice of bundle *F* makes perfect sense on intuitive grounds. The consumer's goal, after all, is to reach the highest indifference curve she can, given her budget constraint. Her strategy is to keep moving to higher and higher indifference curves until she reaches the highest one that is still affordable. For indifference maps for which a tangency point exists, as in Figure 5A.13, the best bundle will always lie at the point of tangency. (See Problem 6 for an example in which a tangency does not exist.)

In Figure 5A.13, note that the marginal rate of substitution at *F* is exactly the same as the absolute value of the slope of the budget constraint. This will always be so when the best affordable bundle occurs at a point of tangency. The condition that must be satisfied in such cases is therefore

$$MRS = P_C/P_V. \qquad (5A.3)$$

In the indifference curve framework, Equation 5A.3 is the counterpart to the rational spending rule developed in the main text of Chapter 5, *Demand*. The right-hand side of Equation 5A.3 represents the opportunity cost of chocolate in terms of vanilla. Thus, with $P_C = \$5$ per pint and $P_V = \$10$ per pint, the opportunity cost of an additional pint of chocolate is one-half pint of vanilla. The left-hand side of Equation 5A.3 is $|\Delta V/\Delta C|$, the absolute value of the slope of the indifference curve at the point of tangency. It is the amount of additional vanilla the consumer must be given in order to compensate her fully for the loss of one pint of chocolate. In the language of cost-benefit analysis discussed in Chapter 1, *Thinking Like an Economist*, the slope of the budget constraint represents the opportunity cost of chocolate in terms of vanilla, while the slope of the indifference curve represents the benefits of consuming chocolate as compared with consuming vanilla. Since the slope of the budget constraint is $-1/2$ in this example, the tangency condition tells us that one-half pint of vanilla would be required to compensate for the benefits given up with the loss of one pint of chocolate.

If the consumer were at some bundle on the budget line for which the two slopes were not the same, then it would always be possible for her to purchase a better bundle.

To see why, suppose she were at a point where the slope of the indifference curve (in absolute value) is less than the slope of the budget constraint, as at point E in Figure 5A.13. Suppose, for instance, that the MRS at E is only 1/4. This tells us that the consumer can be compensated for the loss of one pint of chocolate by being given an additional one-quarter pint of vanilla. But the slope of the budget constraint tells us that by giving up one pint of chocolate, he can purchase an additional one-half pint of vanilla. Since this is one-quarter pint more than he needs to remain equally satisfied, he will clearly be better off if he purchases more vanilla and less chocolate than at point E. The opportunity cost of an additional pint of vanilla is less than the benefit it confers.

SELF-TEST 5A.5

Suppose that the marginal rate of substitution at point A in Figure 5A.13 is 1.0. Show that this means that the consumer will be better off if he purchases less vanilla and more chocolate than at A.

PROBLEMS

1. Suppose a consumer's income is $M = \$1,200$ per month, all of which he spends on some combination of rent and restaurant meals. If restaurant meals cost $12 each and if the monthly rent for an apartment is $3 per square foot, draw this consumer's budget constraint, with his monthly quantities of restaurant meals per month on the vertical axis and apartment size on the horizontal axis. Is the bundle (300 square feet/month, 50 meals/month) affordable?

2. Show what happens to the budget constraint in Problem 1 if the price of restaurant meals falls to $8. Is the bundle (300, 50) affordable?

3. What happens to the budget constraint in Problem 2 if the monthly rent for apartments falls to $2 per square foot? Is the bundle (300, 50) affordable?

4. When inflation happens, prices and incomes generally rise at about the same rate each year. What happens to the budget constraint from Problem 1 if the consumer's income rises by 10 percent and the prices of restaurant meals and apartment rents also rise by 10 percent? Has the consumer been harmed by inflation?

5. A consumer spends all his income on two goods, X and Y. Of the labeled points on his indifference map, indicate which ones are affordable and which ones are unaffordable. Indicate how the consumer ranks these bundles, ranging from most preferred to least preferred. Identify the best affordable bundle.

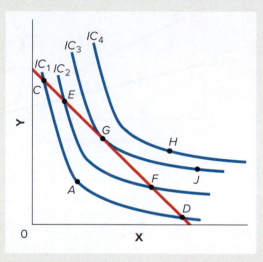

6. A consumer spends all his income on two goods, X and Y. His income and the prices of X and Y are such that his budget constraint is the line AF. Of the labeled points on his indifference map, indicate which is the best affordable bundle. (*Hint:* This problem does not have a tangency solution.)

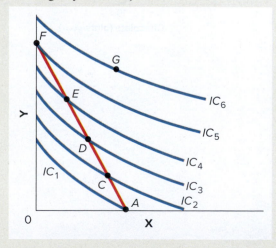

ANSWERS TO APPENDIX SELF-TESTS

5A.1

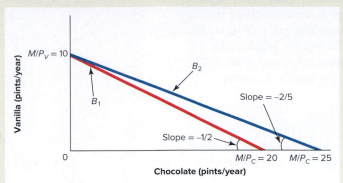

5A.4

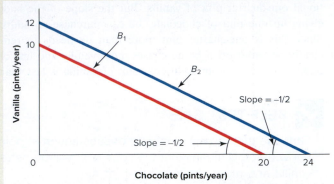

5A.2

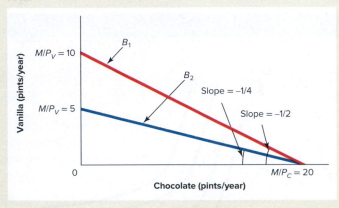

5A.3

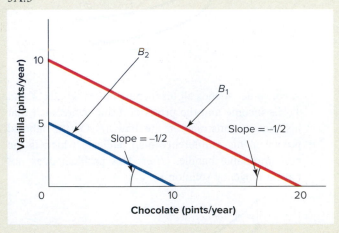

5A.5 At bundle *A*, the consumer is willing to give up one pint of vanilla in order to get an additional pint of chocolate. But at market prices it is necessary to give up only one-half pint of vanilla in order to buy an additional pint of chocolate. It follows that the consumer will be better off than at bundle *A* if he buys one pint less of vanilla and 2 pints more of chocolate.

CHAPTER 6

Perfectly Competitive Supply

Competitive markets never leave profit opportunities unexploited for long.

Emilio Ereza/Pixtal/age fotostock

LEARNING OBJECTIVES

After reading this chapter, you should be able to:

LO1 Explain how opportunity cost is related to the supply curve.

LO2 Discuss the relationship between the supply curve for an individual firm and the market supply curve for an industry.

LO3 Determine a perfectly competitive firm's profit-maximizing output level and profit in the short run and long run.

LO4 Match the determinants of supply with the factors that affect individual firms' costs and apply the theory of supply.

LO5 Define and calculate producer surplus.

Cars that took more than 50 hours to assemble in the 1970s are now built in less than 8 hours. Similar productivity growth has occurred in many other manufacturing industries. Yet in many service industries, productivity has grown only slowly, if at all. For example, the London Philharmonic Orchestra performs Beethoven's Fifth Symphony with no fewer musicians today than it did in 1850. And it still takes a barber about half an hour to cut someone's hair, just as it always has.

Given the spectacular growth in manufacturing workers' productivity, it's no surprise that their real wages have risen more than fivefold during the last century. But why have real wages for service workers risen just as much? If barbers and musicians are no more productive than they were at the turn of the century, why are they now paid five times as much?

An answer is suggested by the observation that the opportunity cost of pursuing any given occupation is the most one could have earned in some other occupation. Most people who become barbers or musicians could instead have chosen jobs in manufacturing. If workers in service industries were not paid roughly as much as they could have earned in other occupations, many of them would not have been willing to work in service industries in the first place.

Why are barbers paid five times as much now as in 1900, even though they can't cut hair any faster than they could then?

Cost-Benefit

The trajectories of wages in manufacturing and service industries illustrate the intimate link between the prices at which goods and services are offered for sale in the market and the opportunity cost of the resources required to produce them.

In Chapter 5, *Demand*, we saw that the demand curve is a schedule that tells how many units buyers wish to purchase at different prices. Our task here is to gain insight into the factors that shape the supply curve, the schedule that tells how many units suppliers wish to sell at different prices.

Although the demand side and the supply side of the market are different in several ways, many of these differences are superficial. Indeed, the behavior of both buyers and sellers is, in an important sense, fundamentally the same. After all, the two groups confront essentially similar questions—in the buyer's case, "Should I buy another unit?" and in the seller's, "Should I sell another unit?" What is more, buyers and sellers use the same criterion for answering these questions. Thus, a rational consumer will buy another unit if its benefit exceeds its cost and a rational seller will sell another unit if the cost of making it is less than the extra revenue he can get from selling it (the familiar Cost-Benefit Principle again).

THINKING ABOUT SUPPLY: THE IMPORTANCE OF OPPORTUNITY COST

Do you live in a state that requires refundable soft drink container deposits? If so, you've probably noticed that some people always redeem their own containers while other people pass up this opportunity, leaving their used containers to be recycled by others. Recycling used containers is a service and its production obeys the same logic that applies to the production of other goods and services. The following sequence of recycling examples shows how the supply curve for a good or service is rooted in the individual's choice of whether to produce it.

| EXAMPLE 6.1 | Opportunity Cost and Supply |

How much time should Ushi spend recycling soft drink containers?

Ushi is trying to decide how to divide his time between his job as a dishwasher in the dining hall, which pays $6 an hour for as many hours as he chooses to work, and gathering soft drink containers to redeem for deposit, in which case his pay depends on both the deposit per container and the number of containers he finds. Earnings aside, Ushi is indifferent between the two tasks, and the number of containers he'll find depends, as shown in the table below, on the number of hours per day he searches:

Search time (hours/day)	Total number of containers found	Additional number of containers found
0	0	
		600
1	600	
		400
2	1,000	
		300
3	1,300	
		200
4	1,500	
		100
5	1,600	

If the containers may be redeemed for 2 cents each, how many hours should Ushi spend searching for containers?

For each additional hour Ushi spends searching for soft drink containers, he loses the $6 he could have earned as a dishwasher. This is his hourly opportunity cost of searching for soft drink containers. His benefit from each hour spent searching for containers is the number of additional containers he finds (shown in column 3 of the table) times the deposit he collects per container. Since he can redeem each container for 2 cents, his first hour spent collecting containers will yield earnings of 600($0.02) = $12, or $6 more than he could have earned as a dishwasher.

By the Cost-Benefit Principle, then, Ushi should spend his first hour of work each day searching for soft drink containers rather than washing dishes. A second hour searching for containers will yield 400 additional containers, for additional earnings of $8, so it too satisfies the cost-benefit test. A third hour spent searching yields 300 additional containers, for 300($0.02) = $6 of additional earnings. Since this is exactly what Ushi could have earned washing dishes, he's indifferent between spending his third hour of work each day on one task or the other. For the sake of discussion, however, we'll assume that he resolves ties in favor of searching for containers, in which case he'll spend three hours each day searching for containers.

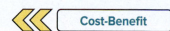

Cost-Benefit

Using the data provided in Example 6.1, what is the lowest redemption price that would induce Ushi to spend at least one hour per day recycling? Since he'll find 600 containers in his first hour of search, a 1 cent deposit on each container would enable him to match his $6 per hour opportunity cost. More generally, if the redemption price is p, and the next hour spent searching yields ΔQ additional containers, then Ushi's additional earnings from searching the additional hour will be $p(\Delta Q)$. This means that the smallest redemption price that will lead Ushi to search another hour must satisfy the equation:

$$p(\Delta Q) = \$6. \tag{6.1}$$

How high would the redemption price of containers have to be to induce Ushi to search for a second hour? Since he can find $\Delta Q = 400$ additional containers if he searches for a second hour, the smallest redemption price that will lead him to do so must satisfy $p(400) = \$6$, which solves for $p = 1.5$ cents.

 SELF-TEST 6.1

In the example above, calculate the lowest container redemption prices that will lead Ushi to search a third, fourth, and fifth hour.

By searching for soft drink containers, Ushi becomes, in effect, a supplier of container-recycling services. In Self-Test 6.1, we saw that Ushi's reservation prices for his third, fourth, and fifth hours of container search are 2, 3, and 6 cents, respectively. Having calculated these reservation prices, we can now plot his supply curve of container-recycling services. This curve, which plots the redemption price per container on the vertical axis and the number of containers recycled each day on the horizontal axis, is shown in Figure 6.1. Ushi's individual supply curve of container-recycling services tells us the number of containers he is willing to recycle at various redemption prices.

The supply curve shown in Figure 6.1 is upward-sloping, just like those we saw in Chapter 3, *Supply and Demand*. There are exceptions to this general rule, but sellers of most goods will offer higher quantities at higher prices.

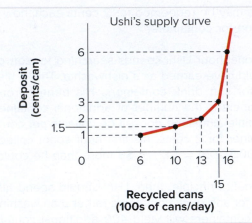

INDIVIDUAL AND MARKET SUPPLY CURVES

The relationship between the individual and market supply curves for a product is analogous to the relationship between the individual and market demand curves. The quantity that corresponds to a given price on the market demand curve is the sum of the quantities demanded at that price by all individual buyers in the market. Likewise, the quantity that corresponds to any given price on the market supply curve is the sum of the quantities supplied at that price by all individual sellers in the market.

Suppose, for example, that the supply side of the recycling-services market consists only of Ushi and his identical twin, Yoshi, whose individual supply curve is the same as Ushi's. To generate the market supply curve, we first put the individual supply curves side by side, as shown in Figure 6.2(a) and (b). We then announce a price, and for that price add the individual quantities supplied to obtain the total quantity supplied in the market. Thus, at a price of 3 cents per container, both Ushi and Yoshi wish to recycle 1,500 cans per day, so the total market supply at that price is 3,000 cans per day. Proceeding in like manner for a sequence of prices, we generate the market supply curve for recycling services shown in Figure 6.2(c). This is the same process of horizontal summation by which we generated market demand curves from individual demand curves in Chapter 5, *Demand*.

Alternatively, if there were many suppliers with individual supply curves identical to Ushi's, we could generate the market supply curve by simply multiplying each quantity value on the individual supply curve by the number of suppliers. For instance, Figure 6.3

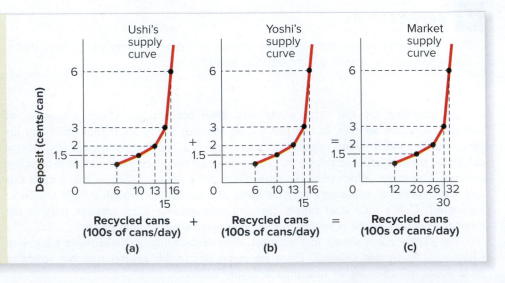

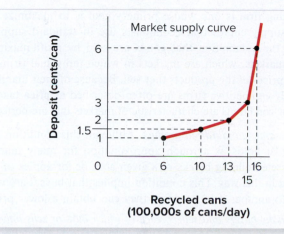

Market supply curve

FIGURE 6.3

The Market Supply Curve with 1,000 Identical Sellers.

To generate the market supply curve for a market with 1,000 identical sellers, we simply multiply each quantity value on the individual supply curve by 1,000.

shows the supply curve for a market in which there are 1,000 suppliers with individual supply curves like Ushi's.

Why do individual supply curves tend to be upward-sloping? One explanation is suggested by the Principle of Increasing Opportunity Cost, or the Low-Hanging-Fruit Principle. Container recyclers will tend to be more productive if they always look first for the containers that are easiest to find—such as those in plain view in readily accessible locations. As the redemption price rises, it will pay to incur the additional cost of searching farther from the beaten path.

If all individuals have identical upward-sloping supply curves, the market supply curve will be upward-sloping as well. But there is an important additional reason for the positive slope of market supply curves: Individual suppliers generally differ with respect to their opportunity costs of supplying the product. (The Principle of Increasing Opportunity Cost applies not only to each individual searcher, but also *across* individuals.) Thus, whereas people facing unattractive employment opportunities in other occupations may be willing to recycle soft drink containers even when the redemption price is low, those with more attractive options will recycle only if the redemption price is relatively high.

In summary, then, the upward slope of the supply curve reflects the fact that costs tend to rise at the margin when producers expand production, partly because each individual exploits her most attractive opportunities first, but also because different potential sellers face different opportunity costs.

PROFIT-MAXIMIZING FIRMS IN PERFECTLY COMPETITIVE MARKETS

To explore the nature of the supply curve of a product more fully, we must say more about the goals of the organizations that supply the product and the kind of economic environment in which they operate. In virtually every economy, goods and services are produced by a variety of organizations that pursue a host of different motives. The Red Cross supplies blood because its organizers and donors want to help people in need; the local government fixes potholes because the mayor was elected on a promise to do so; karaoke singers perform because they like public attention; and car-wash employees are driven primarily by the hope of making enough money to pay their rent.

PROFIT MAXIMIZATION

Notwithstanding this rich variety of motives, *most* goods and services that are offered for sale in a market economy are sold by private firms whose main reason for existing is to earn **profit** for their owners. A firm's profit is the difference between the total revenue it receives from the sale of its product and all costs it incurs in producing it.

profit the total revenue a firm receives from the sale of its product minus all costs—explicit and implicit—incurred in producing it

profit-maximizing firm
a firm whose primary goal is to maximize the difference between its total revenues and total costs

perfectly competitive market
a market in which no individual supplier has significant influence on the market price of the product

price taker a firm that has no influence over the price at which it sells its product

A **profit-maximizing firm** is one whose primary goal is to maximize the amount of profit it earns. The supply curves that economists use in standard supply and demand theory are based on the assumption that goods are sold by profit-maximizing firms in **perfectly competitive markets,** which are markets in which individual firms have no influence over the market prices of the products they sell. Because of their inability to influence market price, perfectly competitive firms are often described as **price takers.**

The following four conditions are characteristic of markets that are perfectly competitive:

1. *All firms sell the same standardized product.* Although this condition is almost never literally satisfied, it holds as a rough approximation for many markets. Thus, the markets for concrete building blocks of a given size, or for apples of a given variety, may be described in this way. This condition implies that buyers are willing to switch from one seller to another if by so doing they can obtain a lower price.

2. *The market has many buyers and sellers, each of which buys or sells only a small fraction of the total quantity exchanged.* This condition implies that individual buyers and sellers will be price takers, regarding the market price of the product as a fixed number beyond their control. For example, a single farmer's decision to plant fewer acres of wheat would have no appreciable impact on the market price of wheat, just as an individual consumer's decision to become a vegetarian would have no perceptible effect on the price of beef.

3. *Productive resources are mobile.* This condition implies that if a potential seller identifies a profitable business opportunity in a market, he or she will be able to obtain the labor, capital, and other productive resources necessary to enter that market. By the same token, sellers who are dissatisfied with the opportunities they confront in a given market are free to leave that market and employ their resources elsewhere.

4. *Buyers and sellers are well informed.* This condition implies that buyers and sellers are aware of the relevant opportunities available to them. If that were not so, buyers would be unable to seek out sellers who charge the lowest prices, and sellers would have no means of deploying their resources in the markets in which they would earn the most profit.

The market for wheat closely approximates a perfectly competitive market. The market for operating systems for desktop computers, however, does not. Roughly 80 percent of desktop operating systems are sold by Microsoft, giving the company enough influence in that market to have significant control over the price it charges. For example, if it were to raise the price of its latest edition of Windows by, say, 20 percent, some consumers might switch to macOS or Linux, and others might postpone their purchase; but many—perhaps even most—would continue with their plans to buy Windows.

By contrast, if an individual wheat farmer were to charge even a few cents more than the current market price for a bushel of wheat, he wouldn't be able to sell any of his wheat at all. And since he can sell as much wheat as he wishes at the market price, he has no motive to charge less.

THE DEMAND CURVE FACING A PERFECTLY COMPETITIVE FIRM

From the perspective of an individual firm in a perfectly competitive market, what does the demand curve for its product look like? Since it can sell as much or as little as it wishes at the prevailing market price, the demand curve for its product is perfectly elastic at the market price. Figure 6.4(a) shows the market demand and supply curves intersecting to determine a market price of P_0. Figure 6.4(b) shows the product demand curve, D_i, as seen by any individual firm in this market, a horizontal line at the market price level P_0.

imperfectly competitive firm (or **price setter**) a firm that has at least some control over the market price of its product

Many of the conclusions of the standard supply and demand model also hold for **imperfectly competitive firms** (or **price setters**)—those firms, like Microsoft, that have at least some ability to vary their own prices. But certain other conclusions do not, as we shall see when we examine the behavior of such firms more closely in Chapter 8, *Monopoly, Oligopoly, and Monopolistic Competition.*

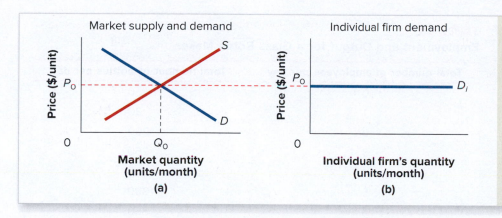

FIGURE 6.4

The Demand Curve Facing a Perfectly Competitive Firm.

The market demand and supply curves intersect to determine the market price of the product (a). The individual firm's demand curve, D_i (b), is a horizontal line at the market price.

Since a perfectly competitive firm has no control over the market price of its product, it needn't worry about choosing the level at which to set that price. As we've seen, the equilibrium market price in a competitive market comes from the intersection of the industry supply and demand curves. The challenge confronting the perfectly competitive firm is to choose its output level so that it makes as much profit as it can at that price. As we investigate how the competitive firm responds to this challenge, we'll see that some costs are more important than others.

PRODUCTION IN THE SHORT RUN

To gain a deeper understanding of the origins of the supply curve, it is helpful to consider a perfectly competitive firm confronting the decision of how much to produce. The firm in question is a small company that makes glass bottles. To keep things simple, suppose that the silica required for making bottles is available free of charge from a nearby desert and that the only costs incurred by the firm are the wages it pays its employees and the lease payment on its bottle-making machine. The employees and the machine are the firm's only two **factors of production**—inputs used to produce goods and services. In more complex examples, factors of production also might include land, structures, entrepreneurship, and possibly others, but for the moment we consider only labor and capital.

When we refer to the **short run,** we mean a period of time during which at least some of the firm's factors of production cannot be varied. For our bottle maker, we will assume that the number of employees can be varied on short notice but that the capacity of its bottle-making machine can be altered only with significant delay. For this firm, then, the short run is simply that period of time during which the firm cannot alter the capacity of its bottle-making machine. By contrast, when we speak of the **long run,** we refer to a time period of sufficient length that all the firm's factors of production are variable.

Table 6.1 shows how the company's bottle production depends on the number of hours its employees spend on the job each day. The output–employment relationship described in Table 6.1 exhibits a pattern that is common to many such relationships. Each time we add an additional unit of labor, output grows, but beyond some point the additional output that results from each additional unit of labor begins to diminish. Note in the right column, for example, that output gains begin to diminish with the third employee. Economists refer to this pattern as the **law of diminishing returns,** and it always refers to situations in which at least some factors of production are fixed.

Law of Diminishing Returns: When some factors of production are held fixed, increased production of the good eventually requires ever-larger increases in the variable factor.

Here, the **fixed factor** is the bottle-making machine, and the **variable factor** is labor. In the context of this example, the law of diminishing returns says simply that successive increases in the labor input eventually yield smaller and smaller increments in bottle output. (Strictly

factor of production an input used in the production of a good or service

short run a period of time sufficiently short that at least some of the firm's factors of production are fixed

long run a period of time of sufficient length that all the firm's factors of production are variable

law of diminishing returns a property of the relationship between the amount of a good or service produced and the amount of a variable factor required to produce it; the law says that when some factors of production are fixed, increased production of the good eventually requires ever-larger increases in the variable factor

fixed factor of production an input whose quantity cannot be altered in the short run

variable factor of production an input whose quantity can be altered in the short run

TABLE 6.1

Employment and Output for a Glass Bottle Maker

Total number of employees per day	Total number of bottles per day
0	0
1	80
2	200
3	260
4	300
5	330
6	350
7	362

speaking, the law ought to be called the law of *eventually* diminishing returns because output may initially grow at an increasing rate with additional units of the variable factor.)

Typically, returns from additional units of the variable input eventually diminish because of some form of congestion. For instance, in an office with three secretaries and only a single desktop computer, we would not expect to get three times as many letters typed per hour as in an office with only one secretary because only one person can use a computer at a time.

SOME IMPORTANT COST CONCEPTS

For the bottle-making firm described in Table 6.1, suppose the lease payment for the company's bottle-making machine is $40 per day, which must be paid whether the company makes any bottles or not. This payment is both a **fixed cost** (since it does not depend on the number of bottles per day the firm makes) and, for the duration of the lease, a sunk cost. The first two columns of Table 6.2 reproduce the employment and output entries from Table 6.1, and the firm's fixed cost appears in column 3.

The company's payment to its employees is called **variable cost** because, unlike fixed cost, it varies with the number of bottles the company produces. The variable cost of producing 200 bottles per day, for example, is shown in column 4 of Table 6.2 as $24 per day. Column 5 shows the firm's **total cost,** which is the sum of its fixed and variable costs.

fixed cost the sum of all payments made to the firm's fixed factors of production

variable cost the sum of all payments made to the firm's variable factors of production

total cost the sum of all payments made to the firm's fixed and variable factors of production

TABLE 6.2

Fixed, Variable, and Total Costs of Bottle Production

(1) Employees per day	(2) Bottles per day	(3) Fixed cost ($/day)	(4) Variable cost ($/day)	(5) Total cost ($/day)	(6) Marginal cost ($/bottle)
0	0	40	0	40	
					0.15
1	80	40	12	52	
					0.10
2	200	40	24	64	
					0.20
3	260	40	36	76	
					0.30
4	300	40	48	88	
					0.40
5	330	40	60	100	
					0.60
6	350	40	72	112	
					1.00
7	362	40	84	124	

Column 6, finally, shows the firm's **marginal cost,** a measure of how its total cost changes when its output changes. Specifically, marginal cost is defined as the change in total cost divided by the corresponding change in output. Note, for example, that when the firm expands production from 80 to 200 bottles per day, its total cost goes up by $12, which gives rise to the marginal cost entry of ($12/day)/(120 bottles/day) = $0.10 per bottle. To emphasize that marginal cost refers to the change in total cost when quantity changes, we place the marginal cost entries between the corresponding quantity rows of the table.

marginal cost the increase in total cost that results from carrying out one additional unit of an activity

CHOOSING OUTPUT TO MAXIMIZE PROFIT

In the following examples and exercises, we'll explore how the company's decision about how many bottles to produce depends on the price of bottles, the wage, and the cost of capital. Again, our starting assumption is that the firm's basic goal is to maximize the amount of profit it earns from the production and sale of bottles, where profit is the difference between its total revenue and its total cost:

$$
\begin{aligned}
\text{Profit} &= \text{Total revenue} - \text{Total cost} \\
&= \text{Total revenue} - \text{Variable cost} - \text{Fixed cost.} \quad (6.2)
\end{aligned}
$$

EXAMPLE 6.2   The Profit-Maximizing Output Level

If bottles sell for 35 cents each, how many bottles should the company described in Table 6.2 produce each day?

To answer this question, we need simply apply the Cost-Benefit Principle to the question "Should the firm expand its level of output?" If its goal is to maximize its profit, the answer to this question will be to expand as long as the marginal benefit from expanding is at least as great as the marginal cost. Since the perfectly competitive firm can sell as many bottles as it wishes at the market price of $0.35 per bottle, its marginal benefit from selling an additional bottle is $0.35. If we compare this marginal benefit with the marginal cost entries shown in column 6 of Table 6.2, we see that the firm should keep expanding until it reaches 300 bottles per day (four employees per day). To expand beyond that level, it would have to hire a fifth employee, and the resulting marginal cost ($0.40 per bottle) would exceed the marginal benefit.

Cost-Benefit

To confirm that the Cost-Benefit Principle thus applied identifies the profit-maximizing number of bottles to produce, we can calculate profit levels directly, as in Table 6.3. Column 3 of this table reports the firm's revenue from the

TABLE 6.3
Output, Revenue, Costs, and Profit

(1) Employees per day	(2) Output (bottles/day)	(3) Total revenue ($/day)	(4) Total cost ($/day)	(5) Profit ($/day)
0	0	0	40	−40
1	80	28	52	−24
2	200	70	64	6
3	260	91	76	15
4	300	105	88	17
5	330	115.50	100	15.50
6	350	122.50	112	10.50
7	362	126.70	124	2.70

sale of bottles, which is calculated as the product of the number of bottles pro-duced per day and the price of $0.35 per bottle. Note, for example, that in the third row of that column, total revenue is (200 bottles/day)($0.35/bottle) = $70 per day. Column 5 reports the firm's total daily profit, which is just the difference between its total revenue (column 3) and its total cost (column 4). Note that the largest profit entry in column 5, $17 per day, occurs at an output of 300 bottles per day, just as suggested by our earlier application of the Cost-Benefit Principle.

As the Self-Test 6.2 demonstrates, an increase in the price of the product gives rise to an increase in the profit-maximizing level of output.

 SELF-TEST 6.2

How would the profit-maximizing level of bottle production change in Example 6.2 if bottles sell for 62 cents each?

The Self-Test 6.3 illustrates that a fall in the wage rate leads to a decline in marginal cost, which also causes an increase in the profit-maximizing level of output.

 SELF-TEST 6.3

How would the profit-maximizing level of bottle production change in Example 6.2 if bottles sell for 35 cents each, but wages fall to $6 per day?

Suppose that in the example the firm's fixed cost had been not $40 per day but $45 per day. How, if at all, would that have affected the firm's profit-maximizing level of output? The answer is not at all. Each entry in the profit column of Table 6.3 would have been $5 per day smaller than before, but the maximum profit entry still would have been 300 bottles per day.

The observation that the profit-maximizing quantity does not depend on fixed costs is not an idiosyncrasy of this example. That it holds true in general is an immediate consequence of the Cost-Benefit Principle, which says that a firm should increase its output if, and only if, the *marginal* benefit exceeds the *marginal* cost. Neither the marginal benefit of expanding (which is the market price of bottles) nor the marginal cost of expanding is affected by a change in the firm's fixed cost.

Cost-Benefit ≫

When the law of diminishing returns applies (i.e., when some factors of production are fixed), marginal cost goes up as the firm expands production beyond some point. Under these circumstances, the firm's best option is to keep expanding output as long as marginal cost is less than price.

Note that if the bottle company's fixed cost had been any more than $57 per day, it would have made a loss at *every* possible level of output. As long as it still had to pay its fixed cost, however, its best bet would have been to continue producing 300 bottles per day. It's better, after all, to experience a smaller loss than a larger one. If a firm in that situation expected conditions to remain the same, though, it would want to get out of the bottle business as soon as its equipment lease expired.

A NOTE ON THE FIRM'S SHUTDOWN CONDITION

It might seem that a firm that can sell as much output as it wishes at a constant market price would *always* do best in the short run by producing and selling the output level for which price equals marginal cost. But there are exceptions to this rule. Suppose, for example, that the market price of the firm's product falls so low that its revenue from sales is smaller than its variable cost at all possible levels of output. The firm should then cease production for the time being. By shutting down, it will suffer a loss equal to its fixed costs. But by remaining open, it would suffer an even larger loss.

More formally, if P denotes the market price of the product and Q denotes the number of units produced and sold, then $P \times Q$ is the firm's total revenue from sales, and if we use VC to denote the firm's variable cost, the rule is that the firm should shut down in the short run if $P \times Q$ is less than VC for every level of Q:

Short-run shutdown condition: $P \times Q < VC$ for all levels of Q.   (6.3)

 SELF-TEST 6.4

Using the bottle company example, suppose bottles sold not for $0.35 but only $0.10. Calculate the profit corresponding to each level of output, as in Table 6.3, and verify that the firm's best option is to cease operations in the short run.

AVERAGE VARIABLE COST AND AVERAGE TOTAL COST

Suppose that the firm is unable to cover its variable cost at any level of output—that is, suppose that $P \times Q < VC$ for all levels of Q. It must then also be true that $P < VC/Q$ for all levels of Q, since we obtain the second inequality by simply dividing both sides of the first one by Q. VC/Q is the firm's **average variable cost (AVC)**—its variable cost divided by its output. The firm's short-run shutdown condition may thus be restated a second way: Discontinue operations in the short run if the product price is less than the minimum value of its average variable cost (AVC). Thus,

average variable cost variable cost divided by total output

Short-run shutdown condition (alternate version): $P <$ minimum value of AVC.   (6.4)

As we'll see in the next section, this version of the shutdown condition often enables us to tell at a glance whether the firm should continue operations.

A related cost concept that facilitates assessment of the firm's profitability is **average total cost (ATC),** which is total cost (TC) divided by output (Q): $ATC = TC/Q$. The firm's profit, again, is the difference between its total revenue ($P \times Q$) and its total cost. And since total cost is equal to average total cost times quantity, the firm's profit is also equal to $(P \times Q) - (ATC \times Q)$. A firm is said to be **profitable** if its revenue ($P \times Q$) exceeds its total cost ($ATC \times Q$). A firm can thus be profitable only if the price of its product price (P) exceeds its ATC for some level of output.

average total cost total cost divided by total output

profitable firm a firm whose total revenue exceeds its total cost

Keeping track of all these cost concepts may seem tedious. In the next section, however, we'll see that the payoff from doing so is that they enable us to recast the profit-maximization decision in a simple graphical framework.

A GRAPHICAL APPROACH TO PROFIT MAXIMIZATION

For the bottle-making firm we've been discussing, average variable cost and average total cost values are shown in columns 4 and 6 of Table 6.4. Using the entries in this table, we plot the firm's average total cost, average variable cost, and marginal cost curves in Figure 6.5. (Because marginal cost corresponds to the change in total cost as we move between two output levels, each marginal cost value in Table 6.4 is plotted at an output level midway between those in the adjacent rows.)

We call your attention to several features of the cost curves in Figure 6.5. Note, for example, that the upward-sloping portion of the marginal cost curve (MC) corresponds to the region of diminishing returns discussed earlier. Thus, as the firm moves beyond two employees per day (200 bottles per day), the increments to total output become

TABLE 6.4
Average Variable Cost and Average Total Cost of Bottle Production

(1) Employees per day	(2) Bottles per day	(3) Variable cost ($/day)	(4) Average variable cost ($/unit of output)	(5) Total cost ($/day)	(6) Average total cost ($/unit of output)	(7) Marginal cost ($/bottle)
0	0	0		40		
						0.15
1	80	12	0.15	52	0.65	
						0.10
2	200	24	0.12	64	0.32	
						0.20
3	260	36	0.138	76	0.292	
						0.30
4	300	48	0.16	88	0.293	
						0.40
5	330	60	0.182	100	0.303	
						0.60
6	350	72	0.206	112	0.32	
						1.00
7	362	84	0.232	124	0.343	

smaller with each additional employee, which means that the cost of producing additional bottles (*MC*) must be increasing in this region.

Note also that the definition of marginal cost implies that the marginal cost curve must intersect both the average variable cost curve (*AVC*) and the average total cost curve (*ATC*) at their respective minimum points. To see why, consider the logic that explains what happens to the average weight of children in a third-grade class when a new student joins the class. If the new (marginal) student is lighter than the previous average weight for the class, average weight will fall, but if the new student is heavier than the previous average, average weight will rise. By the same token, when marginal cost is below average total cost or average variable cost, the corresponding average cost must be falling, and vice versa. And this ensures that the marginal cost curve must pass through the minimum points of both average cost curves.

Seeing the bottle maker's *AVC* curve displayed graphically makes the question posed in Self-Test 6.4 much easier to answer. The question, recall, was whether the firm should shut down in the short run if the price per bottle was only $0.10. A glance at Figure 6.5 reveals that the firm should indeed shut down because this price lies below the minimum value of its *AVC* curve, making it impossible for the firm to cover its variable costs at any output level.

FIGURE 6.5

The Marginal, Average Variable, and Average Total Cost Curves for a Bottle Manufacturer.

The *MC* curve cuts both the *AVC* and *ATC* curves at their minimum points. The upward-sloping portion of the marginal cost curve corresponds to the region of diminishing returns.

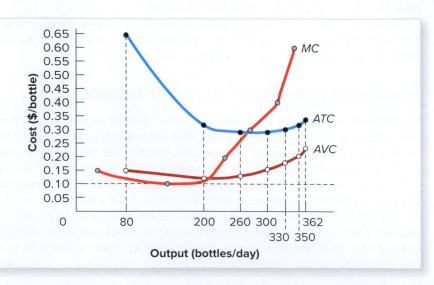

PRICE = MARGINAL COST: THE MAXIMUM-PROFIT CONDITION

So far, we've implicitly assumed that the bottle maker could employ workers only in whole-number amounts. Under these conditions, we saw that the profit-maximizing output level was one for which marginal cost was somewhat less than price (because adding yet another employee would have pushed marginal cost higher than price). In the next example, we'll see that when output and employment can be varied continuously, the maximum-profit condition is that price be equal to marginal cost.

EXAMPLE 6.3	The Graphical Approach to Profit Maximization

For the bottle maker whose cost curves are shown in Figure 6.6, find the profit-maximizing output level if bottles sell for $0.20 each. How much profit will this firm earn? What is the lowest price at which this firm would continue to operate in the short run?

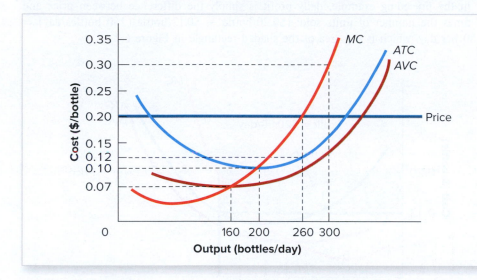

FIGURE 6.6

Price = Marginal Cost: The Perfectly Competitive Firm's Profit-Maximizing Supply Rule.

If price is greater than marginal cost, the firm can increase its profit by expanding production and sales. If price is less than marginal cost, the firm can increase its profit by producing and selling less output.

The Cost-Benefit Principle tells us that this firm should continue to expand as long as price is at least as great as marginal cost. In Figure 6.6 we see that if the firm follows this rule, it will produce 260 bottles per day, the quantity at which price and marginal cost are equal. To gain further confidence that 260 must be the profit-maximizing quantity when the price is $0.20 per bottle, first suppose that the firm had sold some amount less than that—say, only 200 bottles per day. Its benefit from expanding output by one bottle would then be the bottle's market price, here 20 cents. The cost of expanding output by one bottle is equal (by definition) to the firm's marginal cost, which at 200 bottles per day is only 10 cents (see Figure 6.6). So by selling the 201st bottle for 20 cents and producing it for an extra cost of only 10 cents, the firm will increase its profit by 20 − 10 = 10 cents per day. In a similar way, we can show that for *any* quantity less than the level at which price equals marginal cost, the seller can boost profit by expanding production.

Conversely, suppose that the firm was currently selling more than 260 bottles per day—say, 300—at a price of 20 cents each. In Figure 6.6 we see that marginal cost at an output of 300 is 30 cents per bottle. If the firm then contracted its output by one bottle per day, it would cut its costs by 30 cents while losing only 20 cents in revenue. As a result, its profit would grow by 10 cents per day. The same argument can be made regarding any quantity larger than 260, so if the firm is currently selling an output at which price is less than marginal cost, it can always do better by producing and selling fewer bottles.

We've thus established that if the firm sold fewer than 260 bottles per day, it could earn more profit by expanding; and if it sold more than 260, it could earn more by contracting. It follows that at a market price of 20 cents per bottle, the seller maximizes its profit by selling 260 units per day, the quantity for which price and marginal cost are exactly the same.

At that quantity the firm will collect total revenue of $P \times Q = (\$0.20/\text{bottle})(260 \text{ bottles/day}) = \$52$ per day. Note in Figure 6.6 that at 260 bottles per day the firm's average total cost is $ATC = \$0.12$ per bottle, which means that its total cost is $ATC \times Q = (\$0.12/\text{bottle})(260 \text{ bottles/day}) = \$31.20$ per day. The firm's profit is the difference between its total revenue and its total cost, or $\$20.80$ per day. Note, finally, that the minimum value of the firm's AVC curve is $\$0.07$. So if the price of bottles fell below 7 cents each, the firm would shut down in the short run.

Another attractive feature of the graphical method of finding the profit-maximizing output level is that it permits us to calculate the firm's profit graphically. Thus, for the firm in the preceding example, daily profit is simply the difference between price and ATC times the number of units sold: $(\$0.20/\text{bottle} - \$0.12/\text{bottle})(260 \text{ bottles/day}) = \$20.80$ per day, which is the area of the shaded rectangle in Figure 6.7.

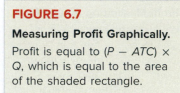

FIGURE 6.7

Measuring Profit Graphically.
Profit is equal to $(P - ATC) \times Q$, which is equal to the area of the shaded rectangle.

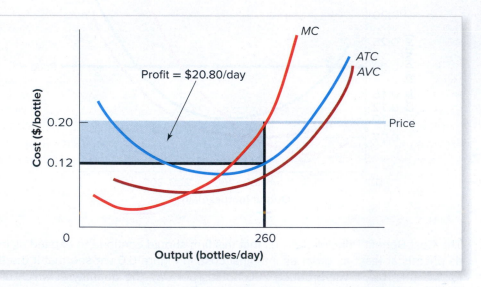

Not all firms are as fortunate as the one shown in Figure 6.7. Suppose, for example, that the price of bottles had been not 20 cents but only 8 cents. Since that price is greater than the minimum value of AVC (see Figure 6.8), the firm should continue to operate in the short run by producing the level of output for which price equals marginal cost (180 bottles per day). But because price is less than ATC at that level of output, the firm will now experience a loss, or negative profit, on its operations. This profit is calculated as $(P - ATC) \times Q = (\$0.08/\text{bottle} - \$0.10/\text{bottle}) \times (180 \text{ bottles/day}) = -\$3.60$ per day, which is equal to the area of the shaded rectangle in Figure 6.8.

In Chapter 7, *Efficiency, Exchange, and the Invisible Hand in Action*, we'll see how firms move resources from one market to another in response to the incentives implicit in profits and losses. But such movements occur in the long run, and our focus here is on production decisions in the short run.

THE "LAW" OF SUPPLY

The law of demand tells us that consumers buy less of a product when its price rises. If there were an analogous law of supply, it would say that producers offer more of a product for sale when its price rises. Is there such a law? We know that supply curves are essentially marginal cost curves and that because of the law of diminishing returns,

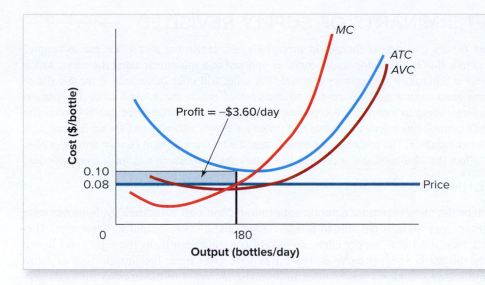

FIGURE 6.8

A Negative Profit.
When price is less than *ATC* at the profit-maximizing quantity, the firm experiences a loss, which is equal to the area of the shaded rectangle.

marginal cost curves are upward-sloping in the short run. And so there is indeed a law of supply that applies as stated in the short run.

In the long run, however, the law of diminishing returns does not apply. (Recall that it holds only if at least some factors of production are fixed.) Because firms can vary the amounts of *all* factors of production they use in the long run, they can often double their production by simply doubling the amount of each input they use. In such cases, costs would be exactly proportional to output and the firm's marginal cost curve in the long run would be horizontal, not upward-sloping. So for now we'll say only that the "law" of supply holds as stated in the short run but not necessarily in the long run. For both the long run and the short run, however, *the perfectly competitive firm's supply curve is its marginal cost curve.*[1]

Every quantity of output along the market supply curve represents the summation of all the quantities individual sellers offer at the corresponding price. So the correspondence between price and marginal cost exists for the market supply curve as well as for the individual supply curves that lie behind it. That is, *for every price–quantity pair along the market supply curve, price will be equal to each seller's marginal cost of production.*

This is why we sometimes say that the supply curve represents the cost side of the market, whereas the demand curve represents the benefit side of the market. At every point along a market demand curve, price represents what buyers would be willing to pay for an additional unit of the product—and this, in turn, is how we measure the amount by which they'd benefit by having an additional unit of the product. Likewise, at every point along a market supply curve, price measures what it would cost producers to expand production by one unit.

RECAP ↑

PROFIT-MAXIMIZING FIRMS IN PERFECTLY COMPETITIVE MARKETS

The perfectly competitive firm faces a horizontal demand curve for its product, meaning that it can sell any quantity it wishes at the market price. In the short run, the firm's goal is to choose the level of output that maximizes its profits. It will accomplish this by choosing the output level for which its marginal cost is equal to the market price of its product, provided that price exceeds average variable cost. The perfectly competitive firm's supply curve is the portion of its marginal cost curve that lies above its average variable cost curve. At the profit-maximizing quantity, the firm's profit is the product of that quantity and the difference between price and average total cost.

---

[1]Again, this rule holds subject to the provision that total revenue exceed variable production cost at the output level for which price equals marginal cost.

DETERMINANTS OF SUPPLY REVISITED

What factors give rise to changes in supply? (Again, remember that a "change in supply" refers to a shift in the entire supply curve, as opposed to a movement along the curve, which we call a "change in the quantity supplied.") A seller will offer more units if the benefit of selling extra output goes up relative to the cost of producing it. And since the benefit of selling output in a perfectly competitive market is a fixed market price that is beyond the seller's control, our search for factors that influence supply naturally focuses on the cost side of the calculation. The preceding examples suggest why the following factors, among others, will affect the likelihood that a product will satisfy the cost-benefit test for a given supplier.

TECHNOLOGY

Perhaps the most important determinant of production cost is technology. Improvements in technology make it possible to produce additional units of output at lower cost. This shifts each individual supply curve downward (or, equivalently, to the right) and hence shifts the market supply curve downward as well. Over time, the introduction of more sophisticated machinery has resulted in dramatic increases in the number of goods produced per hour of effort expended. Every such development gives rise to a rightward shift in the market supply curve.

But how do we know technological change will reduce the cost of producing goods and services? Might not new equipment be so expensive that producers who used it would have higher costs than those who relied on earlier designs? If so, then rational producers simply would not use the new equipment. The only technological changes that rational producers will adopt are those that will reduce their cost of production.

INPUT PRICES

Whereas technological change generally (although not always) leads to gradual shifts in supply, changes in the prices of important inputs can give rise to large supply shifts literally overnight. As discussed in Chapter 4, *Elasticity,* for example, the price of crude oil, which is the most important input in the production of gasoline, often fluctuates sharply, and the resulting shifts in supply cause gasoline prices to exhibit corresponding fluctuations.

Similarly, when wage rates rise, the marginal cost of any business that employs labor also rises, shifting supply curves to the left (or, equivalently, upward). When interest rates fall, the opportunity cost of capital equipment also falls, causing supply to shift to the right.

THE NUMBER OF SUPPLIERS

Just as demand curves shift to the right when population grows, supply curves also shift to the right as the number of individual suppliers grows. For example, if container recyclers die or retire at a higher rate than new recyclers enter the industry, the supply curve for recycling services will shift to the left. Conversely, if a rise in the unemployment rate leads more people to recycle soft drink containers (by reducing the opportunity cost of time spent recycling), the supply curve of recycling services will shift to the right.

EXPECTATIONS

Expectations about future price movements can affect how much sellers choose to offer in the current market. Suppose, for example, that recyclers expect the future price of aluminum to be much higher than the current price because of growing use of aluminum components in cars. The rational recycler would then have an incentive to withhold aluminum from the market at today's lower price, thereby to have more available to sell at the higher future price. Conversely, if recyclers expected next year's price of aluminum to be lower than this year's, their incentive would be to offer more aluminum for sale in today's market.

CHANGES IN PRICES OF OTHER PRODUCTS

Apart from technological change, perhaps the most important determinant of supply is variation in the prices of other goods and services that sellers might produce. Prospectors, for example, search for those precious metals for which the surplus of benefits over costs is greatest. When the price of silver rises, many stop looking for gold and start looking for silver. Conversely, when the price of platinum falls, many platinum prospectors shift their attention to gold.

> ### RECAP ↑
>
> **THE DETERMINANTS OF SUPPLY**
>
> Among the relevant factors causing supply curves to shift are new technologies, changes in input prices, changes in the number of sellers, expectations of future price changes, and changes in the prices of other products that firms might produce.

▶ Visit your instructor's Connect course and access your eBook to view this video.

APPLYING THE THEORY OF SUPPLY

Whether the activity is producing new soft drink containers or recycling used ones, or indeed any other production activity at all, the same logic governs all supply decisions in perfectly competitive markets (and in any other setting in which sellers can sell as much as they wish to at a constant price): keep expanding output until marginal cost is equal to the price of the product. This logic helps us understand why recycling efforts are more intensive for some products than others.

Why are brown eggs more expensive than white ones?

The Economic Naturalist 6.1

When recycling is left to private market forces, why are many more aluminum beverage containers recycled than glass ones?

In both cases, recyclers gather containers until their marginal costs are equal to the containers' respective redemption prices. When recycling is left to market forces, the redemption price for a container is based on what companies can sell it (or the materials in it) for. Aluminum containers can be easily processed into scrap aluminum, which commands a high price, and this leads profit-seeking companies to offer a high redemption price for aluminum cans. By contrast, the glass from which glass containers are made has only limited resale value, primarily because the raw materials required to make new glass containers are so cheap. This difference leads profit-seeking companies to offer much lower redemption prices for glass containers than for aluminum ones.

The high redemption prices for aluminum cans induce many people to track down these cans, whereas the low redemption prices for glass containers lead most people to ignore them. If recycling is left completely to market forces, then we would expect to see aluminum soft drink containers quickly recycled, whereas glass containers would increasingly litter the landscape. This is in fact the pattern we do see in states without recycling laws. (More on how these laws work in a moment.) This pattern is a simple consequence of the fact that the supply curves of container-recycling services are upward-sloping.

In states that don't have beverage container deposit laws, why are aluminum cans more likely to be recycled than glass bottles?

The acquisition of valuable raw materials is only one of two important benefits from recycling. The second is that, by removing litter, recycling makes the environment more pleasant for everyone. As the next example suggests, this second benefit might easily justify the cost of recycling substantial numbers of glass containers.

EXAMPLE 6.4

Why the Optimal Amount of Pollution Isn't Zero

What is the socially optimal amount of recycling of glass containers?

Suppose that the 60,000 citizens of Burlington, Vermont, would collectively be willing to pay 6 cents for each glass container removed from their local environment. If the local market supply curve of glass container-recycling services is as shown in Figure 6.9, what is the socially optimal level of glass container recycling?

FIGURE 6.9

The Supply Curve of Container-Recycling Services for Burlington, Vermont.

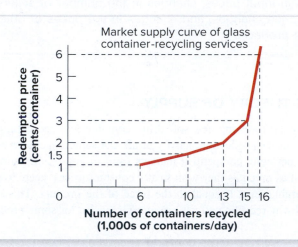

Suppose the citizens of Burlington authorize their city government to collect tax money to finance litter removal. If the benefit of each glass container removed, as measured by what residents are collectively willing to pay, is 6 cents, the government should offer to pay 6 cents for each glass container recycled. To maximize the total economic surplus from recycling, we should recycle that number of containers for which the marginal cost of recycling is equal to the 6-cent marginal benefit. Given the market supply curve shown, the optimal quantity is 16,000 containers per day, and that is how many will be redeemed when the government offers 6 cents per container.

Although 16,000 containers per day will be removed from the environment in the preceding example, others will remain. After all, some are discarded in remote locations, and a redemption price of 6 cents per container is simply not high enough to induce people to track them all down.

So why not offer an even higher price and get rid of *all* glass container litter? For the example given, the reason is that the marginal cost of removing the 16,001st glass container each day is greater than the benefit of removing it. Total economic surplus is largest when we remove litter only up to the point that the marginal benefit of litter removal is equal to its marginal cost, which occurs when 16,000 containers per day are recycled. To proceed past that point is actually wasteful.

Many people become upset when they hear economists say that the socially optimal amount of litter is greater than zero. In the minds of these people, the optimal amount of litter is *exactly* zero. But this position completely ignores the Scarcity Principle. Granted, there would be benefits from reducing litter further, but there also would be costs. Spending more on litter removal therefore means spending less on other useful things. No one would insist that the optimal amount of dirt in his own home is zero. (If someone does make this claim, ask him why he doesn't stay home all day vacuuming the dust that is accumulating in his absence.) If it doesn't pay to remove all the dust from your house, it doesn't pay to remove all the bottles from the environment. Precisely the same logic applies in each case.

 Scarcity ≫

If 16,000 containers per day is the optimal amount of litter removal, can we expect the individual spending decisions of private citizens to result in that amount of litter removal? Unfortunately we cannot. The problem is that anyone who paid for litter removal individually would bear the full cost of those services while reaping only a tiny fraction of the benefit. In Example 6.4, the 60,000 citizens of Burlington reaped a total benefit of 6 cents per container removed, which means a benefit of only (6/60,000) = 0.0001 cent per person! Someone who paid 6 cents for someone else to remove a container would thus be incurring a cost 60,000 times greater than his share of the resulting benefit.

Note that the incentive problem here is similar to the one discussed in Chapter 3, *Supply and Demand,* for the person deciding whether to be vaccinated against an illness. The problem was that the incentive to be vaccinated was too weak because, even though the patient bears the full cost of the vaccination, many of the resulting benefits accrue to others. Thus, an important part of the extra benefit from any one person being vaccinated is that others also become less likely to contract the illness.

The case of glass container litter is an example in which private market forces do not produce the best attainable outcome for society as a whole. Even people who carelessly toss containers on the ground, rather than recycle them, are often offended by the unsightly landscape to which their own actions contribute. Indeed, this is why they often support laws mandating adequate redemption prices for glass containers.

James Hardy/PhotoAlto

Is the socially optimal quantity of litter zero?

Activities that generate litter are a good illustration of the Equilibrium Principle described in Chapter 3, *Supply and Demand*. People who litter do so not because they don't care about the environment, but because their private incentives make littering misleadingly attractive. Recycling requires some effort, after all, yet no individual's recycling efforts have a noticeable effect on the quality of the environment. The soft drink container deposit laws enacted by numerous states were a simple way to bring individual interests more closely into balance with the interests of society as a whole. The vast majority of container litter disappeared almost overnight in states that enacted these laws.

Equilibrium

✓ SELF-TEST 6.5

If the supply curve of glass container-recycling services is as shown in the diagram, and each of the city's 60,000 citizens would be willing to pay 0.00005 cent for each glass container removed from the landscape, at what level should the city government set the redemption price for glass containers, and how many will be recycled each day?

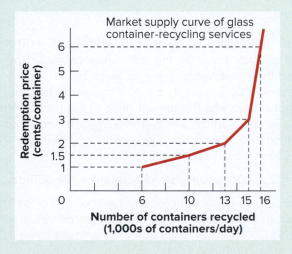

SUPPLY AND PRODUCER SURPLUS

producer surplus the amount by which price exceeds the seller's reservation price

The economic surplus received by a buyer is called *consumer surplus.* The analogous construct for a seller is **producer surplus,** the difference between the price a seller actually receives for the product and the lowest price for which she would have been willing to sell it (her reservation price, which in general will be her marginal cost).

As in the case of consumer surplus, the term *producer surplus* sometimes refers to the surplus received by a single seller in a transaction, while on other occasions it describes the total surplus received by all sellers in a market or collection of markets.

CALCULATING PRODUCER SURPLUS

In Chapter 5, *Demand*, we saw that consumer surplus in a market is the area bounded above by the demand curve and bounded below by the market price. Producer surplus in a market is calculated in an analogous way. As the following example illustrates, it is the area bounded above by the market price and bounded below by the market supply curve.

EXAMPLE 6.5	**Measuring Producer Surplus**

How much do sellers benefit from their participation in the market for milk?

Consider the market for milk, whose demand and supply curves are shown in Figure 6.10, which has an equilibrium price of $2 per gallon and an equilibrium quantity of 4,000 gallons per day. How much producer surplus do the sellers in this market reap?

FIGURE 6.10

Supply and Demand in the Market for Milk.

For the supply and demand curves shown, the equilibrium price of milk is $2 per gallon and the equilibrium quantity is 4,000 gallons per day.

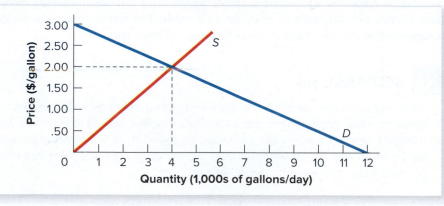

In Figure 6.10, note first that for all milk sold up to 4,000 gallons per day, sellers receive a surplus equal to the difference between the market price of $2 per gallon and their reservation price as given by the supply curve. Total producer surplus received by buyers in the milk market is thus the shaded triangle between the supply curve and the market price in Figure 6.11. Note that this area is a right triangle whose vertical arm is $h = $2/gallon and whose horizontal arm is $b = 4,000$ gallons/day. And since the area of any triangle is equal to $(1/2)bh$, producer surplus in this market is equal to

$$(1/2)(4,000 \text{ gallons/day})(\$2/\text{gallon}) = \$4,000/\text{day}.$$

Producer surplus in this example may be thought of as the highest price sellers would pay, in the aggregate, for the right to continue participating in the milk market. It is $4,000 per day since that's the amount by which their combined benefits exceed their combined costs.

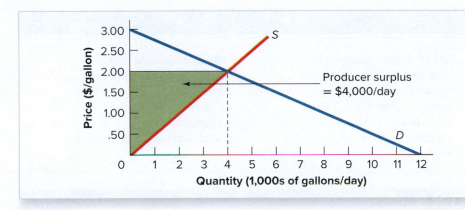

FIGURE 6.11

Producer Surplus in the Market for Milk.

Producer surplus is the area of the shaded triangle ($4,000/day).

As discussed in Chapter 3, *Supply and Demand*, the supply curve for a good can be interpreted either horizontally or vertically. The horizontal interpretation tells us, for each price, the total quantity that producers wish to sell at that price. The vertical interpretation tells us, for each quantity, the smallest amount a seller would be willing to accept for the good. For the purpose of computing producer surplus, we rely on the vertical interpretation of the supply curve. The value on the vertical axis that corresponds to each point along the supply curve corresponds to the marginal seller's reservation price for the good, which is the marginal cost of producing it. Producer surplus is the cumulative sum of the differences between the market price and these reservation prices. It is the area bounded above by market price and bounded below by the supply curve.

SUMMARY

• The supply curve for a good or service is a schedule that, for any price, tells us the quantity that sellers wish to supply at that price. The prices at which goods and services are offered for sale in the market depend, in turn, on the opportunity cost of the resources required to produce them. *(LO1)*

• The demand curve facing a perfectly competitive firm is a horizontal line at the price for which industry supply and demand intersect. *(LO2)*

• Supply curves tend to be upward-sloping, at least in the short run, in part because of the *Principle of Increasing Opportunity Cost*. In general, rational producers will always take advantage of their best opportunities first, moving on to more difficult or costly opportunities only after their best ones have been exhausted. Reinforcing this tendency is the law of diminishing returns, which says that when some factors of production are held fixed, the amount of additional variable factors required to produce successive increments in output grows larger. The industry supply curve is the horizontal summation of the supply curves of individual firms in the industry. *(LO2, LO3)*

• For perfectly competitive markets—or, more generally, for markets in which individual sellers can sell whatever quantity they wish at a constant price—the seller's best option

is to sell that quantity of output for which price equals marginal cost, provided price exceeds the minimum value of average variable cost. The supply curve for the seller thus coincides with the portion of his marginal cost curve that exceeds average variable cost. This is why we sometimes say the supply curve represents the cost side of the market (in contrast to the demand curve, which represents the benefit side of the market). *(LO3)*

• Remember a "change in supply" means a shift in the entire supply curve, whereas a "change in quantity supplied" means a movement along the supply curve, Among the relevant factors causing supply curves to shift are new technologies, changes in input prices, changes in the number of sellers, expectations of future price changes, and changes in the prices of other products that firms might produce. You are now ready to apply the theory of supply. The logic that governs all supply decisions in perfectly competitive markets is as follows: keep expanding output until marginal cost is equal to the price of the product. *(LO4)*

• Producer surplus is a measure of the economic surplus reaped by a seller or sellers in a market. It is the cumulative sum of the differences between the market price and their reservation prices, which is the area bounded above by market price and bounded below by the supply curve. *(LO5)*

KEY TERMS

average total cost (*ATC*)	law of diminishing returns	profit-maximizing firm
average variable cost (*AVC*)	long run	profitable firm
factor of production	marginal cost	short run
fixed cost	perfectly competitive market	total cost
fixed factor of production	price taker	variable cost
imperfectly competitive firm	producer surplus	variable factor of production
(or price setter)	profit	

REVIEW QUESTIONS

1. Explain why you would expect supply curves to slope upward on the basis of the Principle of Increasing Opportunity Cost. *(LO1)*

2. True or false: The perfectly competitive firm should *always* produce the output level for which price equals marginal cost. *(LO3)*

3. Economists often stress that congestion helps account for the law of diminishing returns. With this in mind, explain why it would be impossible to feed all the people on Earth with food grown in a single flowerpot, even if unlimited water, labor, seed, fertilizer, sunlight, and other inputs were available. *(LO4)*

4. Which do you think is more likely to be a fixed factor of production for an ice cream producer during the next two months: its factory building or its workers who operate the machines? Explain. *(LO4)*

5. Why do we use the vertical interpretation of the supply curve when we measure producer surplus? *(LO5)*

PROBLEMS

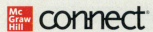

1. Zoe is trying to decide how to divide her time between her job as a wedding photographer, which pays $27 per hour for as many hours as she chooses to work, and as a fossil collector, in which her pay depends on both the price of fossils and the number of fossils she finds. Earnings aside, Zoe is indifferent between the two tasks, and the number of fossils she can find depends on the number of hours a day she searches, as shown in the table below: *(LO1)*

Hours per day	Total fossils per day
1	5
2	9
3	12
4	14
5	15

a. Using the information above, compute the lowest price that Zoe would accept per fossil in order to justify her spending more time collecting fossils and less time working as a wedding photographer.

b. Plot these points in a graph with price on the vertical axis and quantity per day on the horizontal. What is this curve called?

2. The supply curves for the only two firms in a competitive industry are given by, respectively, $P = 2Q_1$ and $P = 2 + Q_2$, where Q_1 is the output of firm 1 and Q_2 is the output of firm 2. What is the market supply curve for this industry? (*Hint:* Graph the two curves side by side; then add their respective quantities at a sample of different prices.) *(LO2)*

3. A price-taking firm makes air conditioners. The market price of one of its new air conditioners is $120. The firm's total cost information is given in the table below:

Air conditioners per day	Total cost ($ per day)
1	100
2	150
3	220
4	310
5	405
6	510
7	650
8	800

How many air conditioners should the firm produce per day if its goal is to maximize its profit? *(LO3)*

4. For the pizza seller whose marginal, average variable, and average total cost curves are shown in the

accompanying diagram, what is the profit-maximizing level of output and how much profit will this producer earn if the price of pizza is $2.50 per slice? *(LO3)*

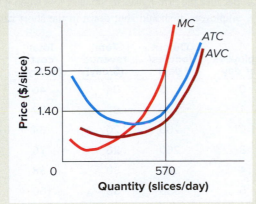

5.* For the pizza seller whose marginal, average variable, and average total cost curves are shown in the accompanying diagram, what is the profit-maximizing level of output and how much profit will this producer earn if the price of pizza is $0.50 per slice? *(LO3)*

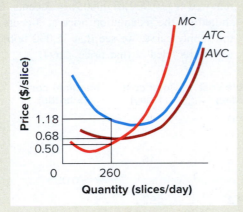

6.* For the pizza seller whose marginal, average variable, and average total cost curves are shown in the accompanying diagram (who is the same seller as in Problem 5), what is the profit-maximizing level of output and how much profit will this producer earn if the price of pizza is $1.18 per slice? *(LO3)*

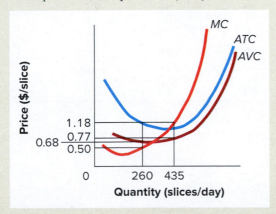

*Denotes more difficult problem.

7. Paducah Slugger Company makes baseball bats out of lumber supplied to it by Acme Sporting Goods, which pays Paducah $10 for each finished bat. Paducah's only factors of production are lathe operators and a small building with a lathe. The number of bats it produces per day depends on the number of employee-hours per day, as shown in the table below. *(LO3, LO4)*

Number of bats per day	Number of employee-hours per day
0	0
5	1
10	2
15	4
20	7
25	11
30	16
35	22

a. If the wage is $15 per hour and Paducah's daily fixed cost for the lathe and building is $60, what is the profit-maximizing quantity of bats?
b. What would be the profit-maximizing number of bats if the government imposed a tax of $10 per day on the company? (*Hint:* Think of this tax as equivalent to a $10 increase in fixed cost.)
c. What would be the profit-maximizing number of bats if the government imposed a tax of $2 per bat? (*Hint:* Think of this tax as equivalent to a $2-per-bat increase in marginal cost.)
d. Why do the taxes in parts b and c have such different effects?

8. The demand and supply curves for the pizza market are shown in the graph below. Calculate daily producer surplus. *(LO5)*

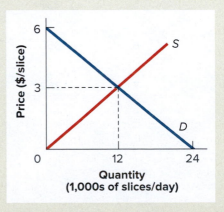

ANSWERS TO SELF-TESTS

6.1 Since Ushi will find 300 containers if he searches a third hour, we find his reservation price for searching a third hour by solving $p(300) = \$6$ for $p = 2$ cents. His reservation prices for additional hours of search are calculated in an analogous way. *(LO1)*

Fourth hour: $p(200) = \$6$, so $p = 3$ cents.

Fifth hour: $p(100) = \$6$, so $p = 6$ cents.

6.2 If bottles sell for 62 cents each, the firm should continue to expand up to and including the sixth employee (350 bottles per day). *(LO3)*

6.3 The relevant costs are shown in the table below. With each variable and marginal cost entry half what it was in the original example, the firm should now hire six employees and produce 350 bottles per day. *(LO3)*

6.4 Because the firm makes its smallest loss when it hires zero employees, it should shut down in the short run. *(LO3)*

Employees per day	Output (bottles/ day)	Total revenue ($/day)	Total cost ($/day)	Profit ($/day)
0	0	0	40	−40
1	80	8	52	−44
2	200	20	64	−44
3	260	26	76	−50
4	300	30	88	−58
5	330	33	100	−67
6	350	35	112	−77
7	362	36.20	124	−87.80

6.5 The fact that each of the city's 60,000 residents is willing to pay 0.00005 cent for each bottle removed means that the collective benefit of each bottle removed is $(60,000)(0.00005) = 3$ cents. So the city should set the redemption price at 3 cents, and from the supply curve, we see that 15,000 bottles per day will be recycled at that price. *(LO4)*

Employees per day	Bottles per day	Fixed cost ($/day)	Variable cost ($/day)	Total cost ($/day)	Marginal cost ($/bottle)
0	0	40	0	40	
					0.075
1	80	40	6	46	
					0.05
2	200	40	12	52	
					0.10
3	260	40	18	58	
					0.167
4	300	40	24	64	
					0.20
5	330	40	30	70	
					0.30
6	350	40	36	76	
					0.50
7	362	40	42	82	

Efficiency, Exchange, and the Invisible Hand in Action

Early suppliers of more fuel-efficient cars were able to charge premium prices for them, but that ability faded as other suppliers adopted similar technologies.

Robert Churchill/E+/Getty Images

LEARNING OBJECTIVES

After reading this chapter, you should be able to:

LO1 Define and explain the differences between accounting profit, economic profit, and normal profit.

LO2 Explain the invisible hand theory and show how economic profit and economic loss affect the allocation of resources across industries.

LO3 Explain why economic profit, unlike economic rent, tends toward zero in the long run.

LO4 Identify whether the market equilibrium is socially efficient and why no opportunities for gain remain open to individuals when a market is in equilibrium.

LO5 Calculate total economic surplus and explain how it is affected by policies that prevent markets from reaching equilibrium.

T he restaurant market in Ithaca, New York, offered little variety in the 1970s: The city had only one Japanese, two Greek, four Italian, and three Chinese restaurants. Today, some 40 years later and with essentially the same population, Ithaca has one Sri Lankan, three Indian, one French, one Spanish, six Thai, two Korean, two Vietnamese, four Mexican, three Greek, seven Italian, two Caribbean, two Japanese, one Ethiopian, and nine Chinese restaurants. In some of the city's other markets, however, the range of available choices has narrowed. For example, several companies provided telephone answering services in 1972, but only one does so today.

Rare indeed is the marketplace in which the identities of the buyers and sellers remain static for extended periods. New businesses enter; established ones leave. There are more body-piercing studios in Ithaca now and fewer watch-repair shops; more marketing consultants and fewer intercity bus companies; and more appliances in stainless steel or black finishes, fewer in avocado or coppertone.

Driving these changes is the business owner's quest for profit. Businesses migrate to industries and locations in which profit opportunities abound and desert those whose

Why do most American cities now have more tattoo parlors and fewer watch-repair shops than in 1972?

Incentive ⟫

prospects appear bleak. In perhaps the most widely quoted passage from his landmark treatise, *The Wealth of Nations,* Adam Smith wrote,

> It is not from the benevolence of the butcher, the brewer, or the baker that we expect our dinner, but from their regard of their own interest. We address ourselves not to their humanity, but to their self-love, and never talk to them of our necessities, but of their advantage.[1]

Smith went on to argue that although the entrepreneur "intends only his own gain," he is "led by an invisible hand to promote an end which was no part of his intention." As Smith saw it, even though self-interest is the prime mover of economic activity, the end result is an allocation of goods and services that serves society's collective interests remarkably well. If producers are offering "too much" of one product and "not enough" of another, profit opportunities stimulate entrepreneurs into action. All the while, the system exerts relentless pressure on producers to hold the price of each good close to its cost of production, and indeed to reduce that cost in any ways possible. The invisible hand, in short, is about all the good things that can happen because of the Incentive Principle.

Our task in this chapter is to gain deeper insight into the nature of the forces that guide the invisible hand. What exactly does "profit" mean? How is it measured, and how does the quest for it serve society's ends? And if competition holds price close to the cost of production, why do so many entrepreneurs become fabulously wealthy? We will also discuss cases in which misunderstanding of Smith's theory results in costly errors, both in everyday decision making and in the realm of government policy.

THE CENTRAL ROLE OF ECONOMIC PROFIT

The economic theory of business behavior is built on the assumption that the firm's goal is to maximize its profit. So we must be clear at the outset about what, exactly, profit means.

THREE TYPES OF PROFIT

explicit costs the actual payments a firm makes to its factors of production and other suppliers

accounting profit the difference between a firm's total revenue and its explicit costs

implicit costs the opportunity costs of the resources supplied by the firm's owners

economic profit (or **excess profit**) the difference between a firm's total revenue and the sum of its explicit and implicit costs

The economist's understanding of profit is different from the accountant's, and the distinction between the two is important for understanding how the invisible hand works. Accountants define the annual profit of a business as the difference between the revenue it takes in and its **explicit costs** for the year, which are the actual payments the firm makes to its factors of production and other suppliers. Profit thus defined is called **accounting profit:**

Accounting profit = Total revenue − Explicit costs.

Accounting profit is the most familiar profit concept in everyday discourse. It is the one that companies use, for example, when they provide statements about their profits in press releases or annual reports.[2]

Economists, by contrast, define profit as the difference between the firm's total revenue and not just its explicit costs, but also its **implicit costs,** which are the opportunity costs of all the resources supplied by the firm's owners. Profit thus defined is called **economic profit** (or **excess profit**):

Economic profit = Total revenue − Explicit costs − Implicit costs.

[1]Adam Smith, *The Wealth of Nations* (New York: Everyman's Library, Book 1, 1910).
[2]For simplicity, this discussion ignores any costs associated with depreciation of the firm's capital equipment. Because the buildings and machines owned by a firm tend to wear out over time, the government allows the firm to consider a fraction of their value each year as a current cost of doing business. For example, a firm that employs a $1,000 machine with a 10-year life span might be allowed to record $100 as a current cost of doing business each year.

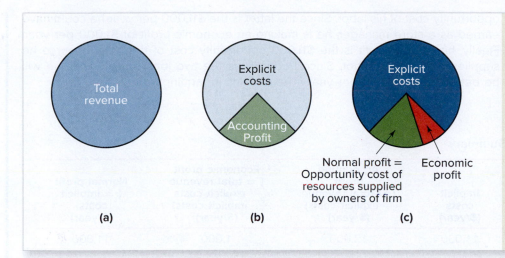

FIGURE 7.1

The Difference between Accounting Profit and Economic Profit.
Accounting profit (b) is the difference between total revenue and explicit costs. Normal profit (c) is the opportunity cost of all resources supplied by a firm's owners. Economic profit (c) is the difference between total revenue and all costs, explicit and implicit (also equal to the difference between accounting profit and normal profit).

To illustrate the difference between accounting profit and economic profit, consider a firm with $400,000 in total annual revenue whose only explicit costs are workers' salaries, totaling $250,000 per year. The owners of this firm have supplied machines and other capital equipment with a total resale value of $1 million. This firm's accounting profit then is $150,000, or the difference between its total revenue of $400,000 per year and its explicit costs of $250,000 per year.

To calculate the firm's economic profit, sometimes called its excess profit, we must first calculate the opportunity cost of the resources supplied by the firm's owners. Suppose the current annual interest rate on savings accounts is 10 percent. Had owners not invested in capital equipment, they could have earned an additional $100,000 per year interest by depositing their $1 million in a savings account. So the firm's economic profit is $400,000 per year − $250,000 per year − $100,000 per year = $50,000 per year.

Note that this economic profit is smaller than the accounting profit by exactly the amount of the firm's implicit costs—the $100,000 per year opportunity cost of the resources supplied by the firm's owners. This difference between a business's accounting profit and its economic profit is called its **normal profit.** Normal profit is simply the opportunity cost of the resources supplied to a business by its owners.

Figure 7.1 illustrates the difference between accounting and economic profit. A firm's total revenue is represented in Figure 7.1(a), while (b) and (c) show how this revenue is apportioned among the various cost and profit categories.

The following examples illustrate why the distinction between accounting and economic profit is so important.

normal profit the opportunity cost of the resources supplied by the firm's owners, equal to accounting profit minus economic profit

---

EXAMPLE 7.1   **Accounting versus Economic Profit, Part 1**

Should Pudge Buffet stay in the farming business?

Pudge Buffet is a corn farmer who lives near Lincoln, Nebraska. His payments for land and equipment rental and for other supplies come to $10,000 per year. The only input he supplies is his own labor, and he considers farming just as attractive as his only other employment opportunity, managing a retail store at a salary of $11,000 per year. Apart from the matter of pay, Pudge is indifferent between farming and being a manager. Corn sells for a constant price per bushel in an international market too large to be affected by changes in one farmer's corn production. Pudge's revenue from corn sales is $22,000 per year. What is his accounting profit? His economic profit? His normal profit? Should he remain a corn farmer?

As shown in Table 7.1, Pudge's accounting profit is $12,000 per year, the difference between his $22,000 annual revenue and his $10,000 yearly payment for land, equipment, and supplies. His economic profit is that amount less the opportunity cost of his labor. Since the latter is the $11,000 per year he could have earned as a store manager, he is making an economic profit of $1,000 per year. Finally, his normal profit is the $11,000 opportunity cost of the only resource he supplies, namely, his labor. Since Pudge likes the two jobs equally well, he will be better off by $1,000 per year if he remains in farming.

TABLE 7.1
Revenue, Cost, and Profit Summary

Total revenue ($/year)	Explicit costs ($/year)	Implicit costs ($/year)	Accounting profit (= total revenue − explicit costs) ($/year)	Economic profit (= total revenue − explicit costs − implicit costs) ($/year)	Normal profit (= implicit costs) ($/year)
22,000	10,000	11,000	12,000	1,000	11,000

 SELF-TEST 7.1

In Example 7.1, how will Pudge's economic profit change if his annual revenue from corn production is not $22,000, but $20,000? Should he continue to farm?

economic loss an economic profit that is less than zero

When revenue falls from $22,000 to $20,000, Pudge has an economic profit of −$1,000 per year. A negative economic profit is also called an **economic loss.** If Pudge expects to sustain an economic loss indefinitely, his best bet would be to abandon farming in favor of managing a retail store.

You might think that if Pudge could just save enough money to buy his own land and equipment, his best option would be to remain a farmer. But as the following example illustrates, that impression is based on a failure to perceive the difference between accounting profit and economic profit.

EXAMPLE 7.2   **Accounting versus Economic Profit, Part 2**

Does owning one's own land make a difference?

Let's build on Example 7.1 and Self-Test 7.1. Suppose Pudge's Uncle Warren, who owns the farmland Pudge has been renting, dies and leaves Pudge that parcel of land. If the land could be rented to some other farmer for $6,000 per year, should Pudge remain in farming?

As shown in Table 7.2, if Pudge continues to farm his own land, his accounting profit will be $16,000 per year, or $6,000 more than in Self-Test 7.1. But his economic profit will still be the same as before—that is, −$1,000 per year—

TABLE 7.2
Revenue, Cost, and Profit Summary

Total revenue ($/year)	Explicit costs ($/year)	Implicit costs ($/year)	Accounting profit (= total revenue − explicit costs) ($/year)	Economic profit (= total revenue − explicit costs − implicit costs) ($/year)	Normal profit (= implicit costs) ($/year)
20,000	4,000	17,000	16,000	−1,000	17,000

because Pudge must deduct the $6,000 per year opportunity cost of farming his own land, even though he no longer must make an explicit payment to his uncle for it. The normal profit from owning and operating his farm will be $17,000 per year—the opportunity cost of the land and labor he provides. But since Pudge earns an accounting profit of only $16,000, he will again do better to abandon farming for the managerial job.

Pudge obviously would be wealthier as an owner than he was as a renter. But the question of whether to remain a farmer is answered the same way whether Pudge rents his farmland or owns it. He should stay in farming only if that is the option that yields the highest economic profit.

> **RECAP ↑**
>
> ### THE CENTRAL ROLE OF ECONOMIC PROFIT
>
> A firm's accounting profit is the difference between its revenue and the sum of all explicit costs it incurs. Economic profit is the difference between the firm's revenue and *all* costs it incurs—both explicit and implicit. Normal profit is the opportunity cost of the resources supplied by the owners of the firm. When a firm's accounting profit is exactly equal to the opportunity cost of the inputs supplied by the firm's owners, the firm's economic profit is zero. For a firm to remain in business in the long run, it must earn an economic profit greater than or equal to zero.

THE INVISIBLE HAND THEORY

TWO FUNCTIONS OF PRICE

In the free enterprise system, market prices serve two important and distinct functions. The first, the **rationing function of price,** is to distribute scarce goods among potential claimants, ensuring that those who get them are the ones who value them most. Thus, if three people want the only antique clock for sale at an auction, the clock goes home with the person who bids the most for it. The second function, the **allocative function of price,** is to direct productive resources to different sectors of the economy. Resources leave markets in which price cannot cover the cost of production and enter those in which price exceeds the cost of production.

Both the allocative and rationing functions of price underlie Adam Smith's celebrated **invisible hand theory** of the market. Recall that Smith thought the market system channeled the selfish interests of individual buyers and sellers so as to promote the greatest good for society. The carrot of economic profit and the stick of economic loss, he argued, were often the only forces necessary to ensure that existing supplies in any market would be allocated efficiently and that resources would be allocated across markets to produce the most efficient possible mix of goods and services.

RESPONSES TO PROFITS AND LOSSES

To get a feel for how the invisible hand works, we begin by looking at how firms respond to economic profits and losses. If a firm is to remain in business in the long run, it must cover all its costs, both explicit and implicit. A firm's normal profit is just a cost of doing business. Thus, the owner of a firm that earns no more than a normal profit has managed only to recover the opportunity cost of the resources invested in the firm. By contrast, the owner of a firm that makes a positive economic profit earns more than the opportunity cost of the invested resources; she earns a normal profit and then some.

Naturally, everyone would be delighted to earn more than a normal profit, and no one wants to earn less. The result is that those markets in which firms are earning an

rationing function of price changes in prices distribute scarce goods to those consumers who value them most highly

allocative function of price changes in prices direct resources away from overcrowded markets and toward markets that are underserved

invisible hand theory Adam Smith's theory that the actions of independent, self-interested buyers and sellers will often result in the most efficient allocation of resources

FIGURE 7.2

Economic Profit in the Short Run in the Corn Market.

At an equilibrium price of $2 per bushel (a), the typical farm earns an economic profit of $104,000 per year (b).

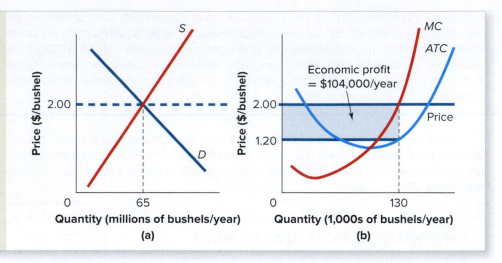

(a)

(b)

economic profit tend to attract additional resources, whereas markets in which firms are experiencing economic losses tend to lose resources.

To see how this happens, we'll examine the workings of the market for corn, whose short-run supply and demand curves are shown in Figure 7.2(a). Figure 7.2(b) depicts the marginal and average total cost curves for a representative farm. The equilibrium price of $2 per bushel is determined by the supply–demand intersection in (a). The representative farm whose *MC* and *ATC* curves are shown in (b) then maximizes its profit by producing the quantity for which price equals marginal cost, 130,000 bushels of corn per year.

Recall from Chapter 6, *Perfectly Competitive Supply,* that average total cost at any output level is the sum of all costs, explicit and implicit, divided by output. The difference between price and *ATC* is thus equal to the average amount of economic profit earned per unit sold. In Figure 7.2(b), that difference is $0.80 per unit. With 130,000 bushels per year sold, the representative farm earns an economic profit of $104,000 per year.

The existence of positive economic profit in the corn market means that producers in that market are earning more than their opportunity cost of farming. For simplicity, we assume that the inputs required to enter the corn market—land, labor, equipment, and the like—are available at constant prices and that anyone is free to enter this market if he or she chooses. The key point is that because price exceeds the opportunity cost of the resources required to enter the market, others *will* want to enter. And as they add their corn production to the amount already on offer, supply shifts to the right, causing the market equilibrium price to fall, as shown in Figure 7.3(a). At the new price of $1.50 per bushel, the representative farm now earns much less economic profit than before, only $50,400 per year [Figure 7.3(b)].

FIGURE 7.3

The Effect of Entry on Price and Economic Profit.

At the original price of $2 per bushel, existing farmers earned economic profit, prompting new farmers to enter. With entry, supply shifts right [from S to S' in (a)] and equilibrium price falls, as does economic profit (b).

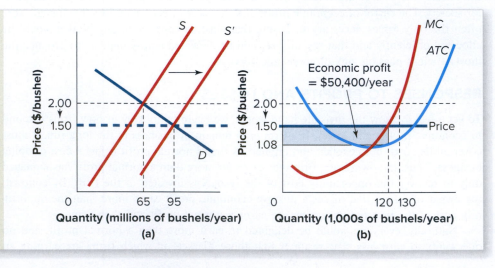

(a)

(b)

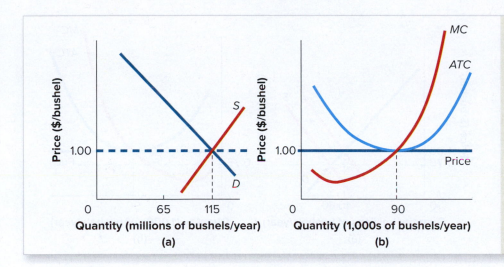

FIGURE 7.4

Equilibrium When Entry Ceases.

Further entry ceases once price falls to the minimum value of *ATC*. At that point, all firms earn a normal economic profit. Equivalently, each earns an economic profit of zero.

For simplicity, we assume that all farms employ the same standard production method, so that their *ATC* curves are identical. Entry will then continue until price falls all the way to the minimum value of *ATC*. (At any price higher than that, economic profit would still be positive, and entry would continue, driving price still lower.) Recall from Chapter 6, *Perfectly Competitive Supply,* that the short-run marginal cost curve intersects the *ATC* curve at the minimum point of the *ATC* curve. This means that once price reaches the minimum value of *ATC,* the profit-maximizing rule of setting price equal to marginal cost results in a quantity for which price and *ATC* are the same. And when that happens, economic profit for the representative farm will be exactly zero, as shown in Figure 7.4(b).

In the adjustment process just considered, the initial equilibrium price was above the minimum value of *ATC,* giving rise to positive economic profits. Suppose instead that the market demand curve for corn had intersected the short-run supply curve at a price below the minimum value of each firm's *ATC* curve, as shown in Figure 7.5(a). As long as this price is above the minimum value of average variable cost,[3] each farm will supply that quantity of corn for which price equals marginal cost, shown as 70,000 bushels per year in Figure 7.5(b). Note, however, that at that quantity, the farm's average total cost is $1.05 per bushel, or $0.30 more than the price for which it sells each bushel. As shown in (b), the farm thus sustains an economic loss of $21,000 per year.

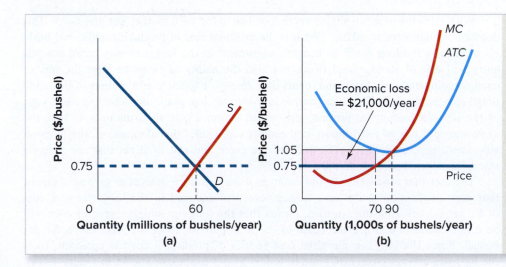

FIGURE 7.5

A Short-Run Economic Loss in the Corn Market.

When price is below the minimum value of *ATC* (a), each farm sustains an economic loss (b).

[3] This qualification refers to the firm's shutdown condition, discussed in Chapter 6, *Perfectly Competitive Supply.*

FIGURE 7.6

Equilibrium When Exit Ceases.

Further exit ceases once price rises to the minimum value of *ATC*. At that point, all firms earn a normal economic profit. Equivalently, each earns an economic profit of zero.

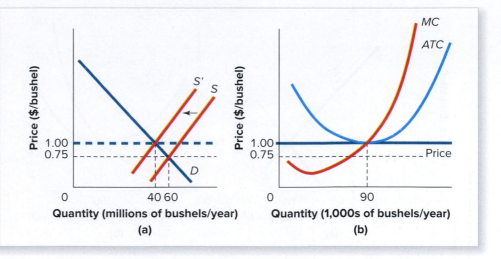

(a)   (b)

If the demand curve that led to the low price and resulting economic losses in Figure 7.5 is expected to persist, farmers will begin to abandon farming for other activities that promise better returns. This means that the supply curve for corn will shift to the left, resulting in higher prices and smaller losses. Exit from corn farming will continue, in fact, until price has again risen to $1 per bushel, at which point there will be no incentive for further exit. Once again we see a stable equilibrium in which price is $1 per bushel, as shown in Figure 7.6.

Given our simplifying assumptions that all corn farms employ a standardized production method and that inputs can be purchased in any quantities at fixed prices, the price of corn cannot remain above $1 per bushel (the minimum point on the *ATC* curve) in the long run. Any higher price would stimulate additional entry until price again fell to that level. Further, the price of corn cannot remain below $1 per bushel in the long run because any lower price would stimulate exit until the price of corn again rose to $1 per bushel.

The fact that firms are free to enter or leave an industry at any time ensures that, in the long run, all firms in the industry will tend to earn zero economic profit. Their *goal* is not to earn zero profit. Rather, the zero-profit tendency is a consequence of the price movements associated with entry and exit. As the Equilibrium Principle—also called the No-Cash-on-the-Table Principle (see Chapter 3, *Supply and Demand*)—predicts, when people confront an opportunity for gain, they are almost always quick to exploit it.

What does the long-run supply curve look like in the corn market just discussed? This question is equivalent to asking, "What is the marginal cost of producing additional bushels of corn in the long run?" In general, adjustment in the long run may entail not just entry and exit of standardized firms, but also the ability of firms to alter the mix of capital equipment and other fixed inputs they employ. Explicit consideration of this additional step would complicate the analysis considerably but would not alter the basic logic of the simpler account we present here, which assumes that all firms operate with the same standard mix of fixed inputs in the short run. Under this assumption, the long-run adjustment process consists exclusively of the entry and exit of firms that use a single standardized production method.

The fact that a new firm could enter or leave this corn market at any time means that corn production can always be augmented or reduced in the long run at a cost of $1 per bushel. And this, in turn, means that the long-run supply curve of corn will be a horizontal line at a price equal to the minimum value of the *ATC* curve, $1 per bushel. Since the long-run marginal cost (*LMC*) of producing corn is constant, so is the long-run average cost (*LAC*) and it, too, is $1 per bushel, as shown in Figure 7.7(a). Figure 7.7(b) shows the *MC* and *ATC* curves of a representative corn farm. At a price of $1 per bushel, this corn market is said to be in long-run equilibrium. The

Equilibrium

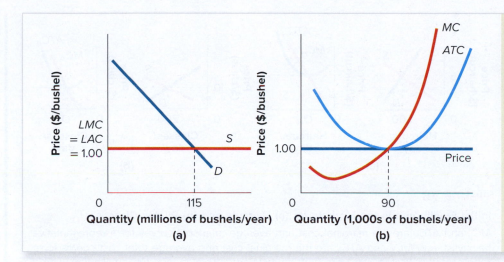

FIGURE 7.7

Long-Run Equilibrium in a Corn Market with Constant Long-Run Average Cost.
When each producer has the same *ATC* curve, the industry can supply as much or as little output as buyers wish to buy at a price equal to the minimum value of *ATC* (a). At that price, the representative producer (b) earns zero economic profit.

representative farm produces 90,000 bushels of corn each year, the quantity for which price equals its marginal cost. And since price is exactly equal to *ATC*, this farm also earns an economic profit of zero.

These observations call attention to two attractive features of the invisible hand theory. One is that the market outcome is efficient in the long run. Note, for example, that when the corn market is in long-run equilibrium, the value to buyers of the last unit of corn sold is $1 per bushel, which is exactly the same as the long-run marginal cost of producing it. Thus, there is no possible rearrangement of resources that would make some participants in this market better off without causing harm to some others. If farmers were to expand production, for example, the added costs incurred would exceed the added benefits; and if they were to contract production, the cost savings would be less than the benefits forgone.

A second attractive feature of long-run competitive equilibrium is the market outcome can be described as fair, in the sense that the price buyers must pay is no higher than the cost incurred by suppliers. That cost includes a normal profit, the opportunity cost of the resources supplied by owners of the firm.

We must emphasize that Smith's invisible hand theory does not mean that market allocation of resources is optimal in every way. It simply means that markets are efficient in the limited technical sense discussed in Chapter 6, *Perfectly Competitive Supply*. Thus, if the current allocation differs from the market equilibrium allocation, the invisible hand theory implies that we can reallocate resources in a way that makes some people better off without harming others.

The following example affords additional insight into how Smith's invisible hand works in practice.

EXAMPLE 7.3   Movement toward Equilibrium

What happens in a city with "too many" hairstylists and "too few" Pilates instructors?

At the initial equilibrium quantities and prices in the markets for haircuts and Pilates classes shown in Figure 7.8, all suppliers are currently earning zero economic profit. Now suppose that styles suddenly change in favor of longer hair and increased physical fitness. If the long-run marginal cost of altering current production levels is constant in both markets, describe how prices and quantities will change in each market, in both the short run and the long run. Are the new equilibrium quantities socially optimal?

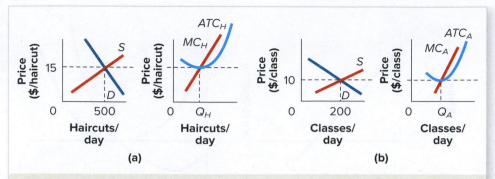

FIGURE 7.8

Initial Equilibrium in the Markets for (a) Haircuts and (b) Pilates Classes.

MC_H and ATC_H are the marginal cost and average total cost curves for a representative hairstylist, and MC_A and ATC_A are the marginal cost and average total cost curves for a representative Pilates instructor. Both markets are initially in long-run equilibrium, with sellers in each market earning zero economic profit.

The shift to longer hairstyles means a leftward shift in the demand for haircuts, while the increased emphasis on physical fitness implies a rightward shift in the demand curve for Pilates classes, as seen in Figure 7.9. As a result of these demand shifts, the new short-run equilibrium prices change. For the sake of illustration, these new prices are shown as $12 per haircut and $15 per Pilates class.

FIGURE 7.9

The Short-Run Effect of Demand Shifts in Two Markets.

(a) The decline in demand for haircuts causes the price of haircuts to fall from $15 to $12 in the short run.

(b) The increase in demand for Pilates classes causes the price of classes to rise from $10 to $15 in the short run.

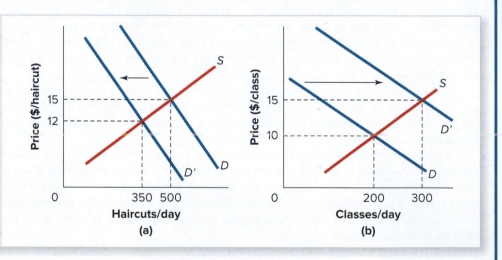

Because each producer was earning zero economic profit at the original equilibrium prices, hairstylists will experience economic losses and Pilates instructors will experience economic profits at the new prices, as seen in Figure 7.10.

Because the short-run equilibrium price of haircuts results in economic losses for hairstylists, some hairstylists will begin to leave that market in search of more favorable opportunities elsewhere. As a result, the short-run supply curve of haircuts will shift leftward, resulting in a higher equilibrium price. Exit of hairstylists will continue until the price of haircuts rises sufficiently to cover the long-run opportunity cost of providing them, which by assumption is $15.

By the same token, because the short-run equilibrium price of Pilates classes results in economic profits for instructors, outsiders will begin to enter that market, causing the short-run supply curve of classes to shift rightward. New instructors will continue to enter until the price of classes falls to the long-run opportunity cost of providing them. By assumption, that cost is $10. Once all adjustments have taken

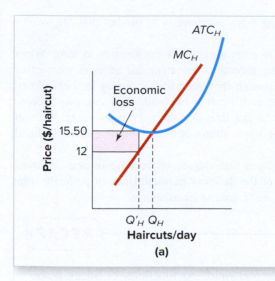
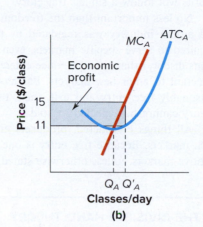

FIGURE 7.10

Economic Profit and Loss in the Short Run.

The assumed demand shifts result in an economic loss for the representative hairstylist (a) and an economic profit for the representative Pilates instructor (b).

place, there will be fewer haircuts and more Pilates classes than before. But because marginal costs in both markets were assumed constant in the long run, the prices of the two goods will again be at their original levels.

It bears mention that those stylists who leave the hair-cutting market won't necessarily be the same people who enter the Pilates teaching market. Indeed, given the sheer number of occupations a former hairstylist might choose to pursue, the likelihood of such a switch is low. Movements of resources will typically involve several indirect steps. Thus, a former hairstylist might become a secretary, and a former postal worker might become a Pilates instructor.

We also note that the invisible hand theory says nothing about how long these adjustments might take. In some markets, especially labor markets, the required movements might take months or even years. But if the supply and demand curves remain stable, the markets will eventually reach equilibrium prices and quantities. And the new prices and quantities will be socially optimal in the same sense as before. Because the value to buyers of the last unit sold will be the same as the marginal cost of producing it, no additional transactions will be possible that benefit some without harming others.

THE IMPORTANCE OF FREE ENTRY AND EXIT

The allocative function of price cannot operate unless firms can enter new markets and leave existing ones at will. If new firms could not enter a market in which existing firms were making a large economic profit, economic profit would not tend to fall to zero over time, and price would not tend to gravitate toward the marginal cost of production.

Forces that inhibit firms from entering new markets are called **barriers to entry.** In the book publishing market, for example, the publisher of a book enjoys copyright protection granted by the government. Copyright law forbids other publishers from producing and selling their own editions of protected works. This barrier allows the price of a popular book to remain significantly above its cost of production for an extended period, all the while generating an economic profit for its publisher. (A copyright provides no *guarantee* of a profit, and indeed most new books actually generate an economic loss for their publishers.)

Barriers to entry may result from practical as well as legal constraints. Some economists, for example, have argued that the compelling advantages of product compatibility have created barriers to entry in the computer software market. Since roughly 80 percent of new desktop computers come with Microsoft's Windows operating system already installed, rival companies have difficulty selling other operating systems that may limit users' ability to exchange files with friends and colleagues. This fact, more than any other, explains Microsoft's spectacular profit history. But the share of computers equipped with

barrier to entry any force that prevents firms from entering a new market

Windows has been steadily falling, leading many economists to predict that Microsoft's profits will follow a similar trajectory.

No less important than the freedom to enter a market is the freedom to leave. When the airline industry was regulated by the federal government, air carriers were often required to serve specific markets, even though they were losing money in them. When firms discover that a market, once entered, is difficult or impossible to leave, they become reluctant to enter new markets. Barriers to exit thus become barriers to entry. Without reasonably free entry and exit, then, the implications of Adam Smith's invisible hand theory cannot be expected to hold.

All things considered, producers enjoy a high degree of freedom of entry in most U.S. markets. Because free entry is one of the defining characteristics of perfectly competitive markets, unless otherwise stated, we'll assume its existence.

RECAP↑

THE INVISIBLE HAND THEORY

In market economies, the allocative and rationing functions of prices guide resources to their most highly valued uses. Prices influence how much of each type of good gets produced (the allocative function). Firms enter industries in which prices are sufficiently high to sustain an economic profit and leave those in which low prices result in an economic loss. Prices also direct existing supplies of goods to the buyers who value them most (the rationing function).

Industries in which firms earn a positive economic profit tend to attract new firms, shifting industry supply to the right. Firms tend to leave industries in which they sustain an economic loss, shifting supply curves to the left. In each case, the supply movements continue until economic profit reaches zero. In long-run equilibrium, the value of the last unit produced to buyers is equal to its marginal cost of production, leaving no possibility for additional mutually beneficial transactions.

ECONOMIC RENT VERSUS ECONOMIC PROFIT

Microsoft cofounder Bill Gates is one of the wealthiest people on the planet, largely because the problem of compatibility prevents rival suppliers from competing effectively in the many software markets dominated by his company. Yet numerous people have become fabulously rich even in markets with no conspicuous barriers to entry. If market forces push economic profit toward zero, how can that happen?

The answer to this question hinges on the distinction between economic profit and **economic rent.** Most people think of rent as the payment they make to a landlord or the supplier of a dorm refrigerator, but the term *economic rent* has a different meaning. Economic rent is that portion of the payment for an input that is above the supplier's reservation price for that input. Suppose, for example, that a landowner's reservation price for an acre of land is $100 per year. That is, suppose he would be willing to lease it to a farmer as long as he received an annual payment of at least $100, but for less than that amount he would rather leave it fallow. If a farmer gives him an annual payment not of $100 but of $1,000, the landowner's economic rent from that payment will be $900 per year.

Economic profit is like economic rent in that it, too, may be seen as the difference between what someone is paid (the business owner's total revenue) and her reservation price for remaining in business (the sum of all her costs, explicit and implicit). But whereas competition pushes economic profit toward zero, it has no such effect on the economic rent for inputs that cannot be replicated easily. For example, although the lease payments for land may remain substantially above the landowner's reservation price, year in and year out, new land cannot come onto the market to reduce or eliminate the economic rent through competition. There is, after all, only so much land to be had.

As the following example illustrates, economic rent can accrue to people as well as land.

economic rent that part of the payment for a factor of production that exceeds the owner's reservation price, the price below which the owner would not supply the factor

EXAMPLE 7.4	**Economic Rent**

How much economic rent will a talented chef get?

A community has 100 restaurants, 99 of which employ chefs of normal ability at a salary of $30,000 per year, the same as the amount they could earn in other occupations that are equally attractive to them. But the 100th restaurant has an unusually talented chef. Because of her reputation, diners are willing to pay 50 percent more for the meals she cooks than for those prepared by ordinary chefs. Owners of the 99 restaurants with ordinary chefs each collect $300,000 per year in revenue, which is just enough to ensure that each earns exactly a normal profit. If the talented chef's opportunities outside the restaurant industry are the same as those of ordinary chefs, how much will she be paid by her employer at equilibrium? How much of her pay will be economic rent? How much economic profit will her employer earn?

Because diners are willing to pay 50 percent more for meals cooked by the talented chef, the owner who hires her will take in total receipts not of $300,000 per year but of $450,000. In the long run, competition should ensure that the talented chef's total pay each year will be $180,000 per year, the sum of the $30,000 that ordinary chefs get and the $150,000 in extra revenues for which she is solely responsible. Since the talented chef's reservation price is the amount she could earn outside the restaurant industry—by assumption, $30,000 per year, the same as for ordinary chefs—her economic rent is $150,000 per year. The economic profit of the owner who hires her will be exactly zero.

Since the talented chef's opportunities outside the restaurant industry are no better than an ordinary chef's, why is it necessary to pay the talented chef so much? Suppose her employer were to pay her only $60,000, which they both would consider a generous salary since it is twice what ordinary chefs earn. The employer would then earn an economic profit of $120,000 per year since his annual revenue would be $150,000 more than that of ordinary restaurants, but his costs would be only $30,000 more.

But this economic profit would create an opportunity for the owner of some other restaurant to bid the talented chef away. For example, if the owner of a competing restaurant were to hire the talented chef at a salary of $70,000, the chef would be $10,000 per year better off and the rival owner would earn an economic profit of $110,000 per year, rather than his current economic profit of zero. Furthermore, if the talented chef is the sole reason that a restaurant earns a positive economic profit, the bidding for that chef should continue as long as any economic profit remains. Some other owner will pay her $80,000, still another $90,000, and so on. Equilibrium will be reached only when the talented chef's salary has been bid up to the point that no further economic profit remains—in our example, at an annual paycheck of $180,000.

This bidding process assumes, of course, that the reason for the chef's superior performance is that she possesses some personal talent that cannot be copied. If instead it were the result of, say, training at a culinary institute in France, then her privileged position would erode over time, as other chefs sought similar training.

RECAP ↑

ECONOMIC RENT VERSUS ECONOMIC PROFIT

Economic rent is the amount by which the payment to a factor of production exceeds the supplier's reservation price. Unlike economic profit, which is driven toward zero by competition, economic rent may persist for extended periods, especially in the case of factors with special talents that cannot easily be duplicated.

THE INVISIBLE HAND IN ACTION

To help develop your intuition about how the invisible hand works, we will examine how it helps us gain insight into patterns we observe in a wide variety of different contexts. In each case, the key idea we want you to focus on is that opportunities for private gain seldom remain unexploited for very long. Perhaps more than any other, this idea encapsulates the essence of that distinctive mindset known as "thinking like an economist."

The Invisible Hand at the Supermarket and on the Freeway

As the following example illustrates, the No-Cash-on-the-Table Principle refers not just to opportunities to earn economic profits in cash, but also any other opportunity to achieve a more desirable outcome.

The Economic Naturalist 7.1

Why do supermarket checkout lines all tend to be roughly the same length?

Pay careful attention the next few times you go grocery shopping and you'll notice that the lines at all the checkout stations tend to be roughly the same length. Suppose you saw one line that was significantly shorter than the others as you wheeled your cart toward the checkout area. Which line would you choose? The shorter one, of course; because most shoppers would do the same, the short line seldom remains shorter for long.

Why do supermarket checkout lines all tend to be roughly the same length?

✅ SELF-TEST 7.2

Use the No-Cash-on-the-Table Principle to explain why all lanes on a crowded, multilane freeway move at about the same speed.

The Invisible Hand and Cost-Saving Innovations

When economists speak of perfectly competitive firms, they have in mind businesses whose contribution to total market output is too small to have a perceptible impact on market price. As explained in Chapter 6, *Perfectly Competitive Supply*, such firms are often called price takers: they take the market price of their product as given and then produce that quantity of output for which marginal cost equals that price.

This characterization of the competitive firm gives the impression that the firm is essentially a passive actor in the marketplace. Yet for most firms, that is anything but the case. As the next example illustrates, even those firms that cannot hope to influence the market prices of their products have very powerful incentives to develop and introduce cost-saving innovations.

EXAMPLE 7.5 **The Impact of Cost-Saving Innovations on Economic Profit**

How do cost-saving innovations affect economic profit in the short run? In the long run?

Forty merchant marine companies operate supertankers that carry oil from the Middle East to the United States. The cost per trip, including a normal profit, is

$500,000. An engineer at one of these companies develops a more efficient propeller design that results in fuel savings of $20,000 per trip. How will this innovation affect the company's accounting and economic profits? Will these changes persist in the long run?

In the short run, the reduction in a single firm's costs will have no impact on the market price of transoceanic shipping services. The firm with the more efficient propeller will thus earn an economic profit of $20,000 per trip (since its total revenue will be the same as before, while its total cost will now be $20,000 per trip lower). As other firms learn about the new design, however, they will begin to adopt it, causing their individual supply curves to shift downward (since the marginal cost per trip at these firms will drop by $20,000). The shift in these individual supply curves will cause the market supply curve to shift, which in turn will result in a lower market price for shipping and a decline in economic profit at the firm where the innovation originated. When all firms have adopted the new, efficient design, the long-run supply curve for the industry will have shifted downward by $20,000 per trip and each company will again be earning only a normal profit. At that point, any firm that did *not* adopt the new propeller design would suffer an economic loss of $20,000 per trip.

The incentive to come up with cost-saving innovations in order to reap economic profit is one of the most powerful forces on the economic landscape. Its beauty, in terms of the invisible hand theory, is that competition among firms ensures that the resulting cost savings will be passed along to consumers in the long run.

THE DISTINCTION BETWEEN AN EQUILIBRIUM AND A SOCIAL OPTIMUM

The Equilibrium, or No-Cash-on-the-Table, Principle tells us that when a market reaches equilibrium, no further opportunities for gain are available to individuals. This principle implies that the market prices of resources that people own will typically reflect their economic value. (As we will see in later chapters, the same cannot be said of resources that are not owned by anyone, such as fish in international waters.)

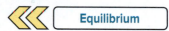

The No-Cash-on-the-Table Principle is sometimes misunderstood to mean that there are *never* any valuable opportunities to exploit. For example, the story is told of two economists on their way to lunch when they spot what appears to be a $100 bill lying on the sidewalk. When the younger economist stoops to pick up the bill, his older colleague restrains him, saying, "That can't be a $100 bill." "Why not?" asks the younger colleague. "If it were, someone would have picked it up by now," the older economist replies.

The No-Cash-on-the-Table Principle means not that there *never* are any unexploited opportunities, but that there are none when the market is *in equilibrium*. Occasionally a $100 bill does lie on the sidewalk, and the person who first spots it and picks it up gains a windfall. Likewise, when a company's earnings prospects improve, *somebody* must be the first to recognize the opportunity, and that person can make a lot of money by purchasing the stock quickly.

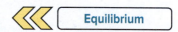

Still, the No-Cash-on-the-Table Principle is important. It tells us, in effect, that there are only three ways to earn a big payoff: to work especially hard; to have some unusual skill, talent, or training; or simply to be lucky. The person who finds a big bill on the sidewalk is lucky, as are many of the investors whose stocks perform better than average. Other investors whose stocks do well achieve their gains through hard work or special talent. For example, the legendary investor Warren Buffett, whose portfolio has grown in value at almost three times the stock market average for the last 60 years, spends long hours studying annual financial reports and has a remarkably keen eye for the telling detail. Thousands of others work just as hard yet fail to beat the market averages.

It is important to stress, however, that a market being in equilibrium implies only that no additional opportunities are available *to individuals*. It does not imply that the resulting allocation is necessarily best from the point of view of society as a whole.

SMART FOR ONE, DUMB FOR ALL

Adam Smith's profound insight was that the individual pursuit of self-interest often promotes the broader interests of society. But unlike some of his modern disciples, Smith was under no illusion that this is *always* the case. Note, for example, Smith's elaboration on his description of the entrepreneur led by the invisible hand "to promote an end which was no part of his intention":

> Nor is it *always* the worse for society that it was no part of it. By pursuing his own interest he *frequently* promotes that of society more effectually than when he really intends to promote it. [Emphasis added.][4]

Smith was well aware that the individual pursuit of self-interest often does not coincide with society's interest. In Chapter 3, *Supply and Demand*, we cited activities that generate environmental pollution as an example of conflicting economic interests, noting that behavior in those circumstances may be described as smart for one but dumb for all. As the following example suggests, extremely high levels of investment in earnings forecasts also can be smart for one, dumb for all.

The Economic Naturalist 7.2

Are there "too many" smart people working as corporate earnings forecasters?

Stock analysts use complex mathematical models to forecast corporate earnings. The more analysts invest in the development of these models, the more accurate the models become. Thus, the analyst whose model produces a reliable forecast sooner than others can reap a windfall by buying stocks whose prices are about to rise. Given the speed with which stock prices respond to new information, however, the results of even the second-fastest forecasting model may come too late to be of much use. Individual stock analysts thus face a powerful incentive to invest more and more money in their models, in the hope of generating the fastest forecast. Does this incentive result in the socially optimal level of investment in forecast models?

Beyond some point, increased speed of forecasting is of little benefit to society as a whole, whose interests suffer little when the price of a stock moves to its proper level a few hours more slowly. If *all* stock analysts spent less money on their forecasting models, *someone's* model would still produce the winning forecast, and the resources that might otherwise be devoted to fine-tuning the models could be put to more valued uses. Yet if any one individual spends less, he can be sure the winning forecast will not be his.

[4]Adam Smith, *The Wealth of Nations* (New York: Everyman's Library, Book 1, 1910).

The invisible hand went awry in the situation just described because the benefit of an investment to the individual who made it was larger than the benefit of that investment to society as a whole. In later chapters we will discuss a broad class of investments with this property. In general, the efficacy of the invisible hand depends on the extent to which the individual costs and benefits of actions taken in the marketplace coincide with the respective costs and benefits of those actions to society. These exceptions notwithstanding, some of the most powerful forces at work in competitive markets clearly promote society's interests.

MARKET EQUILIBRIUM AND EFFICIENCY

Private markets cannot by themselves guarantee an income distribution that most people regard as fair. Nor can they ensure clean air, uncongested highways, or safe neighborhoods for all.

In virtually all successful societies, markets are supplemented by active political coordination in at least some instances. We will almost always achieve our goals more effectively if we know what tasks private markets can do well, and then allow them to perform those tasks. Unfortunately, the discovery that markets cannot solve *every* problem seems to have led some critics to conclude that markets cannot solve *any* problems. This misperception is a dangerous one because it has prompted attempts to prevent markets from doing even those tasks for which they are ideally suited.

We will explore why many tasks are best left to the market and the conditions under which unregulated markets generate the largest possible economic surplus. We also will discuss why attempts to interfere with market outcomes often lead to unintended and undesired consequences.

As noted in Chapter 3, *Supply and Demand*, the mere fact that markets coordinate the production of a large and complex list of goods and services is reason enough to marvel at them. But in the absence of pollution and other externalities like the ones discussed in the preceding section, economists make an even stronger claim—namely, that markets not only produce these goods, but also produce them as efficiently as possible.

The term **efficient,** as economists use it, has a narrow technical meaning. When we say that market equilibrium is efficient, we mean simply this: *If price and quantity take anything other than their equilibrium values, a transaction that will make at least some people better off without harming others can always be found.* This conception of efficiency is also known as **Pareto efficiency,** after Vilfredo Pareto, the nineteenth-century Italian economist who introduced it.

Why is market equilibrium efficient in this sense? The answer is that it is always possible to construct an exchange that helps some without harming others whenever a market is out of equilibrium. Suppose, for example, that the supply and demand curves for milk are as shown in Figure 7.11 and that the current price of milk is $1 per gallon. At that price, sellers offer only 2,000 gallons of milk a day. At that quantity, the marginal buyer values an extra gallon of milk at $2. This is the price that corresponds to 2,000 gallons a day on the

efficient (or **Pareto efficient**) a situation is efficient if no change is possible that will help some people without harming others

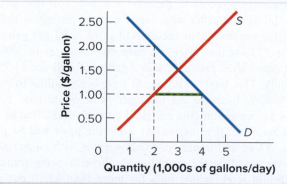

FIGURE 7.11

A Market in Which Price Is Below the Equilibrium Level.

In this market, milk is currently selling for $1 per gallon, $0.50 below the equilibrium price of $1.50 per gallon.

FIGURE 7.12

How Excess Demand Creates an Opportunity for a Surplus-Enhancing Transaction.

At a market price of $1 per gallon, the most intensely dissatisfied buyer is willing to pay $2 for an additional gallon, which a seller can produce at a cost of only $1. If this buyer pays the seller $1.25 for the extra gallon, the buyer gains an economic surplus of $0.75 and the seller gains an economic surplus of $0.25.

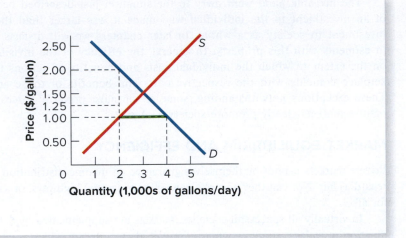

demand curve, which represents what the marginal buyer is willing to pay for an additional gallon (another application of the vertical interpretation of the demand curve). We also know that the cost of producing an extra gallon of milk is only $1. This is the price that corresponds to 2,000 gallons a day on the supply curve, which equals marginal cost (another application of the vertical interpretation of the supply curve).

Furthermore, a price of $1 per gallon leads to excess demand of 2,000 gallons per day, which means that many frustrated buyers cannot buy as much milk as they want at the going price. Now suppose a supplier sells an extra gallon of milk to the most eager of these buyers for $1.25, as in Figure 7.12. Since the extra gallon cost only $1 to produce, the seller is $0.25 better off than before. And since the most eager buyer values the extra gallon at $2, that buyer is $0.75 better off than before. In sum, the transaction creates an extra $1 of economic surplus out of thin air!

Note that none of the other buyers or sellers is harmed by this transaction. Thus, milk selling for only $1 per gallon cannot be efficient. As the following Self-Test 7.3 illustrates, there was nothing special about the price of $1 per gallon. Indeed, if milk sells for *any* price below $1.50 per gallon (the market equilibrium price), we can design a similar transaction, which means that selling milk for any price less than $1.50 per gallon cannot be efficient.

 SELF-TEST 7.3

In Figure 7.11, suppose that milk initially sells for 50 cents per gallon. Describe a transaction that will create additional economic surplus for both buyer and seller without causing harm to anyone else.

Furthermore, it is always possible to describe a transaction that will create additional surplus for both buyer and seller whenever the price lies *above* the market equilibrium level. Suppose, for example, that the current price is $2 per gallon in the milk market shown in Figure 7.13. At that price, we have excess supply of 2,000 gallons per day. Suppose the most dissatisfied producer sells a gallon of milk for $1.75 to the buyer who values it most highly. This buyer, who would have been willing to pay $2, will be $0.25 better off than before. Likewise the producer, who would have been willing to sell milk for as little as $1 per gallon (the marginal cost of production at 2,000 gallons per day), will be $0.75 better off than before. As when the price was $1 per gallon, the new transaction creates $1 of additional economic surplus without harming any other buyer or seller. Since we could design a similar surplus-enhancing transaction at any price above the equilibrium level, selling milk for more than $1.50 per gallon cannot be efficient.

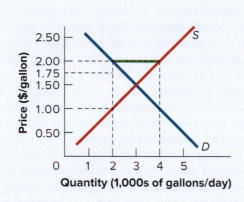

FIGURE 7.13

How Excess Supply Creates an Opportunity for a Surplus-Enhancing Transaction.
At a market price of $2 per gallon, dissatisfied sellers can produce an additional gallon of milk at a cost of only $1, which is $1 less than a buyer would be willing to pay for it. If the buyer pays the seller $1.75 for an extra gallon, the buyer gains an economic surplus of $0.25 and the seller gains an economic surplus of $0.75.

The vertical interpretations of the supply and demand curves thus make it clear why only the equilibrium price in a market can be efficient. When the price is either higher or lower than the equilibrium price, the quantity exchanged in the market will always be lower than the equilibrium quantity. If the price is below equilibrium, the quantity sold will be the amount that sellers offer. If the price is above equilibrium, the quantity sold will be the amount that buyers wish to buy. In either case, the vertical value on the demand curve at the quantity exchanged, which is the value of an extra unit to buyers, must be larger than the vertical value on the supply curve, which is the marginal cost of producing that unit.

So the market equilibrium price is the *only* price at which buyers and sellers cannot design a surplus-enhancing transaction. The market equilibrium price leads, in other words, to the largest possible total economic surplus. In this specific, limited sense, free markets are said to produce and distribute goods and services efficiently.

Actually, to claim that market equilibrium is always efficient even in this limited sense is an overstatement. The claim holds only if markets are perfectly competitive and if the demand and supply curves satisfy certain other restrictions. For example, market equilibrium will not be efficient if the individual marginal cost curves that add up to the market supply curve fail to include all relevant costs of producing the product. Thus, as we saw in Chapter 3, *Supply and Demand*, the true cost of expanding output will be higher than indicated by the market supply curve if production generates pollution that harms others. The equilibrium output will then be inefficiently large and the equilibrium price inefficiently low.

Likewise, market equilibrium will not be efficient if the individual demand curves that make up the market demand curve do not capture all the relevant benefits of buying additional units of the product. For instance, if a homeowner's willingness to pay for ornamental shrubs is based only on the enjoyment she herself gains from them, and not on any benefits that may accrue to her neighbors, the market demand curve for shrubs will understate their value to the neighborhood. The equilibrium quantity of ornamental shrubs will be inefficiently small and the market price for shrubs will be inefficiently low.

We will take up such market imperfections in greater detail in later chapters. For now, we will confine our attention to perfectly competitive markets whose demand curves capture all relevant benefits and whose supply curves capture all relevant costs. For such goods, market equilibrium will always be efficient in the limited sense described earlier.

Efficiency Is Not the Only Goal

The fact that market equilibrium maximizes economic surplus is an attractive feature, to be sure. Bear in mind, however, that "efficient" does not mean the same thing as "good." For example, the market for milk may be in equilibrium at a price of $1.50 per gallon, yet many poor families may be unable to afford milk for their children at that price. Still others may not even have a place for their children to sleep.

Efficiency is a concept that is based on predetermined attributes of buyers and sellers—their incomes, tastes, abilities, knowledge, and so on. Through the combined effects of individual cost-benefit decisions, these attributes give rise to the supply and demand curves for each good produced in an economy. If we are concerned about inequality in the distribution of attributes like income, we should not be surprised to discover that markets do not always yield outcomes we like.

Most of us could agree, for example, that the world would be a better one if all people had enough income to feed their families adequately. The claim that equilibrium in the market for milk is efficient means simply that *taking people's incomes as given*, the resulting allocation of milk cannot be altered so as to help some people without at the same time harming others.

To this a critic of the market system might respond: So what? As such critics rightly point out, imposing costs on others may be justified if doing so will help those with sufficiently important unmet demands. For example, most people would prefer to fund homeless shelters with their tax dollars rather than let homeless people freeze to death. Arguing in these terms, American policymakers responded to rapid increases in the price of oil in the late 1970s by imposing price controls on home heating oil. Many of us might agree that if the alternative had been to take no action at all, price controls might have been justified in the name of social justice.

The economist's concept of market efficiency makes clear that there *must* be a better alternative policy. Price controls on oil prevent the market from reaching equilibrium, and as we've seen, that means forgoing transactions that would benefit some people without harming others.

Why Efficiency Should Be the First Goal

Efficiency is important not because it is a desirable end in itself, but because it enables us to achieve all our other goals to the fullest possible extent. It is always possible to generate additional economic surplus when a market is out of equilibrium. To gain additional economic surplus is to gain more of the resources we need to do the things we want to do.

RECAP

EQUILIBRIUM, SOCIAL OPTIMUM, AND EFFICIENCY

- A market in equilibrium is one in which no additional opportunities for gain remain available to individual buyers or sellers. The No-Cash-on-the-Table Principle describes powerful forces that help push markets toward equilibrium. But even if all markets are in equilibrium, the resulting allocation of resources need not be socially optimal. Equilibrium will be socially optimal only if markets are perfectly competitive and if the costs and benefits to individual participants in the market are the same as those experienced by society as a whole.

- A market in equilibrium is said to be efficient, or Pareto efficient, meaning that no reallocation is possible that will benefit some people without harming others.

- When a market is not in equilibrium—because price is either above the equilibrium level or below it—the quantity exchanged is always less than the equilibrium level. At such a quantity, a transaction can always be made in which both buyer and seller benefit from the exchange of an additional unit of output.

- Total economic surplus in a market is maximized when exchange occurs at the equilibrium price. But the fact that equilibrium is "efficient" in this sense does not mean that it is "good." All markets can be in equilibrium, yet many people may lack sufficient income to buy even basic goods and services. Still, permitting markets to reach equilibrium is important because, when economic surplus is maximized, it is possible to pursue every goal more fully.

THE COST OF PREVENTING PRICE ADJUSTMENTS

PRICE CEILINGS

During 1979, an interruption in oil supplies from the Middle East caused the price of home heating oil to rise by more than 100 percent. Concern about the hardship this sudden price increase would impose on poor families in northern states led the government to impose a price ceiling in the market for home heating oil. This price ceiling prohibited sellers from charging more than a specified amount for heating oil.

The following example illustrates why imposing a price ceiling on heating oil, though well intended, was a bad idea.

EXAMPLE 7.6 A Price Ceiling on Heating Oil

How much waste does a price ceiling on heating oil cause?

Suppose the demand and supply curves for home heating oil are as shown in Figure 7.14, in which the equilibrium price is $1.40 per gallon. Suppose that, at that price, many poor families cannot heat their homes adequately. Out of concern for the poor, legislators pass a law setting the maximum price at $1 per gallon. How much lost economic surplus does this policy cost society?

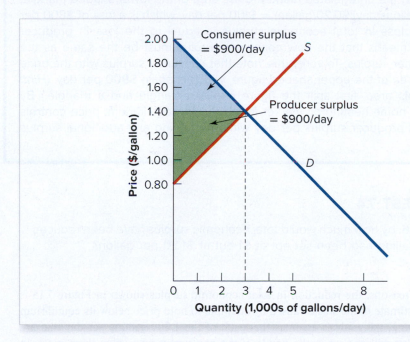

FIGURE 7.14

Economic Surplus in an Unregulated Market for Home Heating Oil.

For the supply and demand curves shown, the equilibrium price of home heating oil is $1.40 per gallon and the equilibrium quantity is 3,000 gallons per day. Consumer surplus is the area of the upper shaded triangle ($900 per day). Producer surplus is the area of the lower shaded triangle (also $900 per day).

First, let's calculate total economic surplus without price controls. If this market is not regulated, 3,000 gallons per day will be sold at a price of $1.40 per gallon. In Figure 7.14, the economic surplus received by buyers is the area of the upper shaded triangle. Since the height of this triangle is $0.60 per gallon and its base is 3,000 gallons per day, its area is equal to (1/2)(3,000 gallons/day)($0.60/gallon) = $900 per day. The economic surplus received by producers is the area of the lower shaded triangle. This triangle also has an area of $900 per day, so total economic surplus in this market will be $1,800 per day.

If the price of heating oil is prevented from rising above $1 per gallon, only 1,000 gallons per day will be sold and the total economic surplus will be reduced by the area of the lined triangle shown in Figure 7.15. Since the height of this

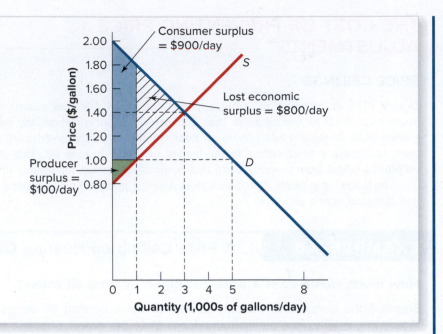

FIGURE 7.15

The Waste Caused by Price Controls.

By limiting output in the home heating oil market to 1,000 gallons per day, price controls cause a loss in economic surplus of $800 per day (area of the lined triangle).

triangle is $0.80 per gallon and its base is 2,000 gallons per day, its area is (1/2)(2,000 gallons/day)($0.80/gallon) = $800 per day. Producer surplus falls from $900 per day in the unregulated market to the area of the lower shaded triangle, or (1/2)(1,000 gallons/day)($0.20/gallon) = $100 per day, which is a loss of $800 per day. Thus, the loss in total economic surplus is equal to the loss in producer surplus, which means that the new consumer surplus must be the same as the original consumer surplus. To verify this, note that consumer surplus with the price ceiling is the area of the upper shaded figure, which is again $900 per day. (*Hint:* To compute this area, first split the figure into a rectangle and a triangle.) By preventing the home heating oil market from reaching equilibrium, price controls waste $800 of producer surplus per day without creating any additional surplus for consumers!

✅ **SELF-TEST 7.4**

In Example 7.6, by how much would total economic surplus have been reduced if the price ceiling had been set not at $1 but at $1.20 per gallon?

For several reasons, the reduction in total economic surplus shown in Figure 7.15 is a conservative estimate of the waste caused by attempts to hold price below its equilibrium level. For one thing, the analysis assumes that each of the 1,000 gallons per day that are sold in this market will end up in the hands of the consumers who value them most—in the diagram, those whose reservation prices are above $1.80 per gallon. But since any buyer whose reservation price is above $1 per gallon will want to buy at the ceiling price, much of the oil actually sold is likely to go to buyers whose reservation prices are below $1.80. Suppose, for example, that a buyer whose reservation price was $1.50 per gallon made it into the line outside a heating oil supplier just ahead of a buyer whose reservation price was $1.90 per gallon. If each buyer had a 20-gallon tank to fill, and if the first buyer got the last of the day's available oil, then total surplus would be smaller by $8 that day than if the oil had gone to the second buyer.

A second reason that the reduction in surplus shown in Figure 7.15 is likely to be an underestimate is that shortages typically prompt buyers to take costly actions to enhance their chances of being served. For example, if the heating oil distributor begins selling its

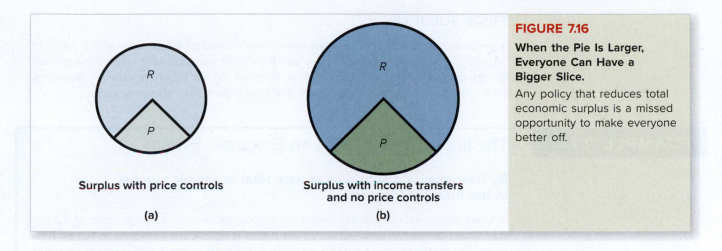

FIGURE 7.16

When the Pie Is Larger, Everyone Can Have a Bigger Slice.
Any policy that reduces total economic surplus is a missed opportunity to make everyone better off.

Surplus with price controls

(a)

Surplus with income transfers and no price controls

(b)

available supplies at 6:00 a.m., many buyers may arrive several hours early to ensure a place near the front of the line. Yet when all buyers incur the cost of arriving earlier, no one gets any more oil than before.

Notwithstanding the fact that price ceilings reduce total economic surplus, their defenders might argue that controls are justified because they enable at least some low-income families to buy heating oil at affordable prices. Yes, but the same objective could have been accomplished in a much less costly way—namely, by giving the poor more income with which to buy heating oil.

It may seem natural to wonder whether the poor, who have limited political power, can really hope to receive income transfers that would enable them to heat their homes. On reflection, the answer to this question would seem to be yes, *if the alternative is to impose price controls that would be even more costly than the income transfers.* After all, the price ceiling as implemented ends up costing heating oil sellers $800 per day in lost economic surplus. So they ought to be willing to pay some amount less than $800 a day in additional taxes in order to escape the burden of controls. The additional tax revenue could finance income transfers that would be far more beneficial to the poor than price controls.

This point is so important, and so often misunderstood by voters and policymakers, that we will emphasize it by putting it another way. Think of the economic surplus from a market as a pie to be divided among the various market participants. Figure 7.16(a) represents the $1,000 per day of total economic surplus available to participants in the home heating oil market when the government limits the price of oil to $1 per gallon. We divided this pie into two slices, labeled R and P, to denote the surpluses received by rich and poor participants. Figure 7.16(b) represents the $1,800 per day of total economic surplus available when the price of home heating oil is free to reach its equilibrium level. This pie is divided among rich and poor participants in the same proportion as the pie in the left panel.

The important point to notice is this: *Because the pie on the right side is larger, both rich and poor participants in the home heating oil market can get a bigger slice of the pie than they would have had under price controls.* Rather than tinker with the market price of oil, it is in everyone's interest to simply transfer additional income to the poor.

With the Incentive Principle in mind, supporters of price controls may object that income transfers to the poor might weaken people's incentive to work, and thus might prove extremely costly in the long run. Difficult issues do indeed arise in the design of programs for transferring income to the poor—issues we will consider in some detail in later chapters. But for now, suffice it to say that ways exist to transfer income without undermining work incentives significantly. One such method is the Earned Income Tax Credit, a program that supplements the wages of low-income workers. Given such programs, transferring income to the poor will always be more efficient than trying to boost their living standard through price controls.

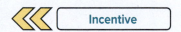

Incentive

PRICE SUBSIDIES

Sometimes governments try to assist low-income consumers by subsidizing the prices of "essential" goods and services. France and Russia, for example, have taken this approach at various points by subsidizing the price of bread. As the following example illustrates, such subsidies are like price ceilings in that they reduce total economic surplus.

EXAMPLE 7.7　　**The Impact of Subsidies on Economic Surplus**

By how much do subsidies reduce total economic surplus in the market for bread?

A small island nation imports bread for its population at the world price of $2 per loaf. If the domestic demand curve for bread is as shown in Figure 7.17, by how much will total economic surplus decline in this market if the government provides a $1-per-loaf subsidy?

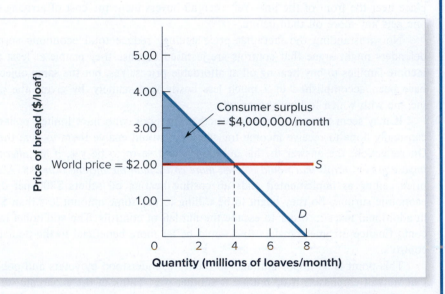

FIGURE 7.17

Economic Surplus in a Bread Market without Subsidy.

For the demand curve shown, consumer surplus (area of the shaded triangle) is $4,000,000 per month. This amount is equal to total economic surplus in the domestic bread market since no bread is produced domestically.

　　With no subsidy, the equilibrium price of bread in this market would be the world price of $2 per loaf and the equilibrium quantity would be 4,000,000 loaves per month. The shaded triangle in Figure 7.17 represents consumer economic surplus for buyers in the domestic bread market. The height of this triangle is $2 per loaf, and its base is 4,000,000 loaves per month, so its area is equal to (1/2)(4,000,000 loaves/month)($2/loaf) = $4,000,000 per month. Because the country can import as much bread as it wishes at the world price of $2 per loaf, supply is perfectly elastic in this market. Because the marginal cost of each loaf of bread to sellers is exactly the same as the price buyers pay, producer surplus in this market is zero. So total economic surplus is exactly equal to consumer surplus, which, again, is $4,000,000 per month.

　　Now suppose that the government administers its $1 per loaf subsidy program by purchasing bread in the world market at $2 per loaf and reselling it in the domestic market for only $1 per loaf. At the new lower price, buyers will now consume not 4,000,000 loaves per month but 6,000,000. Consumer surplus for buyers in the bread market is now the area of the larger shaded triangle in Figure 7.18: (1/2)($3/loaf)(6,000,000 loaves/month) = $9,000,000 per month, or $5,000,000 per month more than before. The catch is that the subsidy wasn't free. Its cost, which must be borne by taxpayers, is ($1/loaf)(6,000,000 loaves/month) = $6,000,000 per month. So even though consumer surplus in the bread

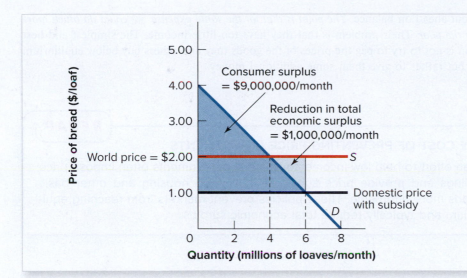

FIGURE 7.18

The Reduction in Economic Surplus from a Subsidy.
Since the marginal cost of bread is $2 per loaf, total economic surplus is maximized at 4,000,000 loaves per month, the quantity for which the marginal buyer's reservation price is equal to marginal cost. The reduction in economic surplus from consuming an additional 2,000,000 loaves per month is $1,000,000 per month, the area of the smaller shaded triangle.

market is larger than before, the net effect of the subsidy program is actually to reduce total economic surplus by $1,000,000 per month.

Another way to see why the subsidy reduces total economic surplus by that amount is to note that total economic surplus is maximized at 4,000,000 loaves per month, the quantity for which the marginal buyer's reservation price is equal to marginal cost, and that the subsidy induces additional consumption of 2,000,000 loaves per month. Each additional loaf has a marginal cost of $2 but is worth less than that to the buyer (as indicated by the fact that the vertical coordinate of the demand curve lies below $2 for consumption beyond 4,000,000). As consumption expands from 4,000,000 to 6,000,000 loaves per month, the cumulative difference between the marginal cost of bread and its value to buyers is the area of the smaller shaded triangle in Figure 7.18, which is $1,000,000 per month.

This reduction in economic surplus constitutes pure waste—no different, from the perspective of participants in this market, than if they had siphoned that much cash out of their bank accounts each month and thrown it into a bonfire.

 SELF-TEST 7.5

How much total economic surplus would have been lost if the bread subsidy, as illustrated in Example 7.7, had been set at $0.50 per loaf instead of $1?

Compared to a bread subsidy, a much better policy would be to give low-income people some additional income and then let them buy bread on the open market. Subsidy advocates who complain that taxpayers would be unwilling to give low-income people income transfers must be asked to explain why people would be willing to tolerate subsidies, which are *more* costly than income transfers. Logically, if voters are willing to support subsidies, they should be even more eager to support income transfers to low-income persons.

This is not to say that the poor reap no benefit at all from bread subsidies. Because they get to buy bread at lower prices and because the subsidy program is financed by taxes collected primarily from middle- and upper-income families, poor families probably come out ahead on balance. *The point is that for the same expense, we could do much more to help the poor.* Their problem is that they have too little income. The simplest and best solution is not to try to peg the prices of the goods they and others buy below equilibrium levels, but rather to give them some additional money.

RECAP

THE COST OF PREVENTING PRICE ADJUSTMENTS

In an effort to help low-income consumers, governments often impose price ceilings and provide price subsidies that make housing and other basic goods more affordable. These policies prevent markets from reaching equilibrium and typically reduce total economic surplus.

SUMMARY

- Accounting profit is the difference between a firm's revenue and its explicit expenses. It differs from economic profit, which is the difference between revenue and the sum of the firm's explicit and implicit costs. Normal profit is the difference between accounting profit and economic profit. It is the opportunity cost of the resources supplied to a business by its owners. *(LO1)*

- The quest for economic profit is the invisible hand that drives resource allocation in market economies. Markets in which businesses earn an economic profit tend to attract additional resources, whereas markets in which businesses experience an economic loss tend to lose resources. If new firms enter a market with economic profits, that market's supply curve shifts to the right, causing a reduction in the price of the product. Prices will continue to fall until economic profits are eliminated. By contrast, the departure of firms from markets with economic losses causes the supply curve in such markets to shift left, increasing the price of the product. Prices will continue to rise until economic losses are eliminated. In the long run, market forces drive economic profits and losses toward zero. *(LO2, LO3)*

- Economic rent is the portion of the payment for an input that exceeds the reservation price for that input. If a professional basketball player who is willing to play for as little as $100,000 per year is paid $15 million, he earns an economic rent of $14,900,000 per year. Whereas the invisible hand drives economic profit toward zero over the long run, economic rent can persist indefinitely because replicating the services of players like Steph Curry is impossible. Talented individuals who are responsible for the superior performance of a business will tend to capture the resulting financial gains as economic rents. *(LO3)*

- The benefit of an investment to an individual sometimes differs from its benefit to society as a whole. Such conflicting incentives may give rise to behavior that is smart for one but dumb for all. Despite such exceptions, the invisible hand of the market works remarkably well much of the time. One of the market system's most important contributions to social well-being is the pressure it creates to adopt cost-saving innovations. Competition among firms ensures that the resulting cost savings get passed along to consumers in the long run. *(LO4)*

- When the supply and demand curves for a product capture all the relevant costs and benefits of producing that product, then market equilibrium for that product will be efficient. In such a market, if price and quantity do not equal their equilibrium values, a transaction can be found that will make at least some people better off without harming others. *(LO4)*

- When market supply and demand curves reflect the underlying costs and benefits to society of the production of a good or service, the quest for economic profit ensures not only that existing supplies are allocated efficiently among individual buyers, but also that resources are allocated across markets in the most efficient way possible. In any allocation other than the one generated by the market, resources could be rearranged to benefit some people without harming others. *(LO4)*

- The No-Cash-on-the-Table Principle implies that if someone owns a valuable resource, the market price of that resource will typically reflect its economic value. The implication of this principle is not that lucrative opportunities never exist, but rather that such opportunities cannot exist when markets are in equilibrium. *(LO4)*

- Total economic surplus is a measure of the amount by which participants in a market benefit by participating in it. It is the sum of total consumer surplus and total producer surplus in the market. One of the attractive properties of market equilibrium is that it maximizes the value of total economic surplus. *(LO5)*

- Efficiency should not be equated with social justice. If we believe that the distribution of income among people is unjust, we won't like the results produced by the intersection of the supply and demand curves based on that income distribution, even though those results are efficient. *(LO5)*

- Even so, we should always strive for efficiency because it enables us to achieve all our other goals to the fullest possible extent. Whenever a market is out of equilibrium, the economic pie can be made larger. And with a larger pie, everyone can have a larger slice. *(LO5)*

- Regulations or policies that prevent markets from reaching equilibrium—such as price ceilings and price subsidies—are often defended on the grounds that they help the poor. But such schemes reduce economic surplus, meaning that we can find alternatives under which both rich and poor would be better off. The main difficulty of the poor is that they have too little income. Rather than trying to control the prices of the goods they buy, we could do better by enacting policies that raise the incomes of the poor and then letting prices seek their equilibrium levels. Those who complain that the poor lack the political power to obtain such income transfers must explain why the poor have the power to impose regulations that are far more costly than income transfers. *(LO5)*

KEY TERMS

accounting profit
allocative function of price
barrier to entry
economic loss
economic profit (or excess profit)
economic rent
efficient (or Pareto efficient)
explicit costs
implicit costs
invisible hand theory
normal profit
rationing function of price

REVIEW QUESTIONS

1. How can a business owner who earns $10 million per year from his business credibly claim to earn zero economic profit? *(LO1)*

2. Why do most cities in the United States now have more radios but fewer radio-repair shops than they did in 1960? *(LO2)*

3. Why do market forces drive economic profit but not economic rent toward zero? *(LO3)*

4. Why do economists emphasize efficiency as an important goal of public policy? *(LO4)*

5. You are a senator considering how to vote on a policy that would increase the economic surplus of workers by $100 million per year but reduce the economic surplus of retirees by $1 million per year. What additional measure might you combine with the policy to ensure that the overall result is a better outcome for everyone? *(LO5)*

PROBLEMS

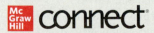

1. Explain why the following statements are true or false. *(LO1, LO2, LO3, LO4)*
   a. The economic maxim "There's no cash on the table" means that there are never any unexploited economic opportunities.
   b. Firms in competitive environments make no accounting profit when the market is in long-run equilibrium.
   c. Firms that can introduce cost-saving innovations can make an economic profit in the short run.

2. Jaime owns and manages a café in Collegetown whose annual revenue is $5,000. Annual expenses are as follows: *(LO1, LO2)*

Labor	$2,000
Food and drink	500
Electricity	100
Vehicle lease	150
Rent	500
Interest on loan for equipment	1,000

a. Calculate Jaime's annual accounting profit.

b. Jaime could earn $1,000 per year as a recycler of aluminum cans. However, she prefers to run the café. In fact, she would be willing to pay up to $275 per year to run the café rather than to recycle. Is the café making an economic profit? Should Jaime stay in the café business? Explain.

c. Suppose the café's revenues and expenses remain the same, but recyclers' earnings rise to $1,100 per year. Is the café still making an economic profit? Explain.

d. Suppose Jaime had not gotten a $10,000 loan at an annual interest rate of 10 percent to buy equipment, but instead had invested $10,000 of her own money in equipment. How would your answer to parts a and b change?

e. If Jaime can earn $1,000 a year as a recycler, and she likes recycling just as well as running the café, how much additional revenue would the café have to collect each year to earn a normal profit?

3. The city of New Orleans has 200 advertising companies, 199 of which employ designers of normal ability at a salary of $100,000 a year. The companies that employ normal designers each collect $500,000 in revenue a year, which is just enough to ensure that each earns exactly a normal profit. The 200th company, however, employs Janus, an unusually talented designer. Because of Janus's talent, this company collects $1,000,000 in revenue a year. *(LO3)*

a. How much will Janus earn? What proportion of her annual salary will be economic rent?

b. Why won't the advertising company for which Janus works be able to earn an economic profit?

4. Unskilled workers in a poor cotton-growing region must choose between working in a factory for $6,000 a year and being a tenant cotton farmer. One farmer can work a 120-acre farm, which rents for $10,000 a year. Such farms yield $20,000 worth of cotton each year. The total nonlabor cost of producing and marketing the cotton is $4,000 a year. A local politician whose motto is "Working people come first" has promised that if she is elected, her administration will fund a fertilizer, irrigation, and marketing scheme that will triple cotton yields on tenant farms at no charge to tenant farmers. *(LO3)*

a. If the market price of cotton would be unaffected by this policy and no new jobs would be created in the cotton-growing industry, how would the project affect the incomes of tenant farmers in the short run? In the long run?

b. Who would reap the benefit of the scheme in the long run? How much would they gain each year?

5. Suppose the weekly demand and supply curves for used DVDs in Lincoln, Nebraska, are as shown in the diagram. Calculate the following: *(LO5)*

a. The weekly consumer surplus.

b. The weekly producer surplus.

c. The maximum weekly amount that producers and consumers in Lincoln would be willing to pay to be able to buy and sell used DVDs in any given week (total economic surplus).

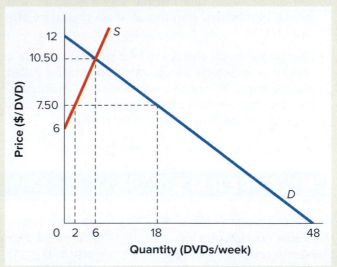

6. Refer to Problem 5. Suppose a coalition of students from Lincoln High School succeeds in persuading the local government to impose a price ceiling of $7.50 on used DVDs, on the grounds that local suppliers are taking advantage of teenagers by charging exorbitant prices. *(LO5)*

a. Calculate the weekly shortage of used DVDs that will result from this policy.

b. Calculate the total economic surplus lost every week as a result of the price ceiling.

7.* The government of Islandia, a small island nation, imports heating oil at a price of $2 per gallon and makes it available to citizens at a price of $1 per gallon. If Islandians' demand curve for heating oil is given by $P = 6 - Q$, where P is the price per gallon in dollars and Q is the quantity in millions of gallons per year, how much economic surplus is lost as a result of the government's policy? *(LO5)*

8.* Refer to Problem 7. Suppose each of the 1 million Islandian households has the same demand curve for heating oil. *(LO5)*

a. What is the household demand curve?

b. How much consumer surplus would each household lose if it had to pay $2 per gallon instead of $1 per gallon for heating oil, assuming there were no other changes in the household budget?

c. With the money saved by not subsidizing oil, by how much could the Islandian government afford to cut each family's annual taxes?

d. If the government abandoned its oil subsidy and implemented the tax cut, by how much would each family be better off?

*Denotes more difficult problem.

ANSWERS TO SELF-TESTS

7.1 As shown in the table below, Pudge's accounting profit is now $10,000, the difference between his $20,000 annual revenue and his $10,000-per-year payment for land, equipment, and supplies. His economic profit is that amount minus the opportunity cost of his labor—again, the $11,000 per year he could have earned as a store manager. So Pudge is now earning a negative economic profit, −$1,000 per year. As before, his normal profit is the $11,000-per-year opportunity cost of his labor. Although an accountant would say Pudge is making an annual profit of $10,000, that amount is less than a normal profit for his activity. An economist would therefore say that he is making an economic loss of $1,000 per year. Since Pudge likes the two jobs equally well, he will be better off by $1,000 per year if he leaves farming to become a manager. *(LO1)*

Total revenue ($/year)	Explicit costs ($/year)	Implicit costs ($/year)	Accounting profit (= total revenue − explicit costs) ($/year)	Economic profit (= total revenue − explicit costs − implicit costs) ($/year)	Normal profit (= implicit costs) ($/year)
20,000	10,000	11,000	10,000	−1,000	11,000

7.2 If each lane did not move at about the same pace, any driver in a slower lane could reduce his travel time by simply switching to a faster one. People will exploit these opportunities until each lane moves at about the same pace. *(LO3)*

7.3 At a price of 50 cents per gallon, there is excess demand of 4,000 gallons per day. Suppose a seller produces an extra gallon of milk (marginal cost = 50 cents) and sells it to the buyer who values it most (reservation price = $2.50) for $1.50. Both buyer and seller will gain additional economic surplus of $1, and no other buyers or sellers will be hurt by the transaction. *(LO4)*

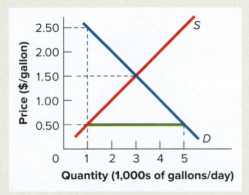

7.4 As shown in the accompanying diagram, the new loss in total economic surplus is $200 per day. *(LO5)*

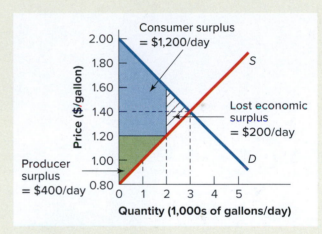

7.5 With a $0.50-per-loaf subsidy, the new domestic price becomes $1.50 per loaf. The new lost surplus is the area of the small shaded triangle in the diagram: (1/2)($0.50/loaf)(1,000,000 loaves/month) = $250,000 per month. *(LO5)*

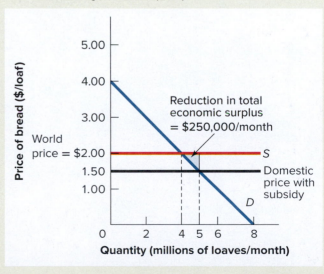

CHAPTER 8

Monopoly, Oligopoly, and Monopolistic Competition

Monopoly sellers almost always offer discount prices to buyers who are willing to mail in a rebate coupon or endure some other type of inconvenience.

icosha/Shutterstock

LEARNING OBJECTIVES

After reading this chapter, you should be able to:

LO1 Distinguish among three types of imperfectly competitive industries and describe how imperfect competition differs from perfect competition.

LO2 Identify the five sources of market power.

LO3 Describe how economies of scale are affected by how large fixed costs are in relation to marginal cost.

LO4 Apply the concepts of marginal cost and marginal revenue to find the output level and price that maximize a monopolist's profit.

LO5 Explain why the profit-maximizing output level for a monopolist is too small from society's perspective.

LO6 Discuss why firms often offer discounts to buyers who are willing to jump some form of hurdle.

LO7 Discuss public policies that are often applied to natural monopolies.

Some years ago, fantasy game enthusiasts around the country became obsessed with the game of Magic: The Gathering. To play, you need a deck of Magic cards, available only from the creators of the game. But unlike ordinary playing cards, which can be bought in most stores for only a dollar or two, a deck of Magic cards sells for many times that. And because Magic cards cost no more to manufacture than ordinary playing cards, their producer earns an enormous economic profit.

In a perfectly competitive market, entrepreneurs would see this economic profit as cash on the table. It would entice them to offer Magic cards at slightly lower prices so that, eventually, the cards would sell for roughly their cost of production, just as ordinary playing cards do. But Magic cards have been on the market for years now, and that hasn't happened. The reason is that the cards are copyrighted, which means the government has granted the creators of the game an exclusive license to sell them.

bigjom/Getty Images

Why do Magic cards sell for 10 times as much as ordinary playing cards, even though they cost no more to produce?

The holder of a copyright is an example of an **imperfectly competitive firm,** or **price setter**—that is, a firm with at least some latitude to set its own price. The competitive firm, by contrast, is a price taker, a firm with no influence over the price of its product.

Our focus in this chapter will be on the ways in which markets served by imperfectly competitive firms differ from those served by perfectly competitive firms. One salient difference is the imperfectly competitive firm's ability, under certain circumstances, to charge more than its cost of production. But if the producer of Magic cards could charge any price it wished, why does it charge only $10? Why not $100, or even $1,000? We'll see that even though such a company may be the only seller of its product, its pricing freedom is far from absolute. We'll also see how some imperfectly competitive firms manage to earn an economic profit, even in the long run, and even without government protections like copyright. And we'll explore why Adam Smith's invisible hand is less evident in a world served by imperfectly competitive firms.

PERFECT AND IMPERFECT COMPETITION

The perfectly competitive market is an ideal; the actual markets we encounter in everyday life differ from the ideal in varying degrees. Economics texts usually distinguish among three types of imperfectly competitive market structures. The classifications are somewhat arbitrary, but they are quite useful in analyzing real-world markets.

DIFFERENT FORMS OF IMPERFECT COMPETITION

imperfectly competitive firm (or **price setter**) a firm that has at least some control over the market price of its product

pure monopoly the only supplier of a unique product with no close substitutes

Farthest from the perfectly competitive ideal is the **pure monopoly,** a market in which a single firm is the lone seller of a unique product. The producer of Magic cards is a pure monopolist, as are many providers of electric power. If the residents of Miami don't buy their electricity from Florida Power and Light Company, they simply do without. In between these two extremes are many different types of imperfect competition. We focus on two of them here: monopolistic competition and oligopoly.

Monopolistic Competition

monopolistic competition an industry structure in which a large number of firms produce slightly differentiated products that are reasonably close substitutes for one another

Recall from Chapter 6, *Perfectly Competitive Supply,* that in a perfectly competitive industry, a large number of firms typically sell products that are essentially perfect substitutes for one another. In contrast, **monopolistic competition** is an industry structure in which a large number of rival firms sell products that are close, but not quite perfect, substitutes. Rival products may be highly similar in many respects, but there are always at least some features that differentiate one product from another in the eyes of some consumers. Monopolistic competition has in common with perfect competition the feature that there are no significant barriers preventing firms from entering or leaving the market.

Local gasoline retailing is an example of a monopolistically competitive industry. The gas sold by different stations may be nearly identical in chemical terms, but a station's particular location is a feature that matters for many consumers. Convenience stores are another example. Although most of the products found on any given store's shelves are also carried by most other stores, the product lists of different stores are not identical. Some offer sim cards and lottery tickets, for example, while others offer foam coolers and flashlights. And even more so than in the case of gasoline retailing, location is an important differentiating feature of convenience stores.

Recall that if a perfectly competitive firm were to charge even just slightly more than the prevailing market price for its product, it would not sell any output at all. Things are different for the monopolistically competitive firm. The fact that its offering is not a perfect substitute for those of its rivals means that it can charge a slightly higher price than they do and not lose all its customers.

But that does not mean that monopolistically competitive firms can expect to earn positive economic profits in the long run. On the contrary, because new firms are able to enter freely, a monopolistically competitive industry is essentially the same as a perfectly competitive industry in this respect. If existing monopolistically competitive firms were earning positive economic profits at prevailing prices, new firms would have an incentive to enter the industry. Downward pressure on prices would then result as the larger number of firms competed for a limited pool of potential customers.[1] As long as positive economic profits remained, entry would continue and prices would be driven ever lower. Conversely, if firms in a monopolistically competitive industry were initially suffering economic losses, some firms would begin leaving the industry. As long as economic losses remained, exit and the resulting upward pressure on prices would continue. So in long-run equilibrium, monopolistically competitive firms are in this respect essentially like perfectly competitive firms: All expect to earn zero economic profit.

Although monopolistically competitive firms have some latitude to vary the prices of their product in the short run, pricing is not the most important strategic decision they confront. A far more important issue is how to differentiate their products from those of existing rivals. Should a product be made to resemble a rival's product as closely as possible? Or should the aim be to make it as different as possible? Or should the firm strive for something in between? We'll consider these questions in Chapter 9, *Games and Strategic Behavior,* where we'll focus on this type of strategic decision making.

Oligopoly

Further along the continuum between perfect competition and pure monopoly lies **oligopoly,** a structure in which the entire market is supplied by a small number of large firms. Cost advantages associated with large size are one of the primary reasons for pure monopoly, as we will discuss presently. Oligopoly is also typically a consequence of cost advantages that prevent small firms from being able to compete effectively.

In some cases, oligopolists sell undifferentiated products. In the market for wireless phone service, for example, the offerings of AT&T, Verizon, and T-Mobile are very similar. The cement industry is another example of an oligopoly selling an essentially undifferentiated product. The most important strategic decisions facing firms in such cases are more likely to involve pricing and advertising than specific features of their product. Here, too, we leave a more detailed discussion of such decisions to Chapter 9, *Games and Strategic Behavior.*

In other cases, such as the automobile and tobacco industries, oligopolists are more like monopolistic competitors than pure monopolists, in the sense that differences in their product features have significant effects on consumer demand. Many long-time Ford buyers, for example, would not even consider buying a Chevrolet, and very few smokers ever switch from Camels to Marlboros. As with oligopolists who produce undifferentiated products, pricing and advertising are important strategic decisions for firms in these industries, but so, too, are those related to specific product features.

Because cost advantages associated with large size are usually so important in oligopolies, there is no presumption that entry and exit will push economic profit to zero. Consider, for example, an oligopoly served by two firms, each of which currently earns an economic profit. Should a new firm enter this market? Possibly, but it also might be that a third firm large enough to achieve the cost advantages of the two incumbents would

oligopoly an industry structure in which a small number of large firms produce products that are either close or perfect substitutes

[1]See Edward Chamberlin, *The Theory of Monopolistic Competition* (Cambridge, MA: Harvard University Press, 1st ed. 1933, 8th ed. 1962); and Joan Robinson, *The Economics of Imperfect Competition* (London: Macmillan, 1st ed. 1933, 2nd ed. 1969).

effectively flood the market, driving price so low that all three firms would suffer economic losses. There is no guarantee, however, that an oligopolist will earn a positive economic profit.

As we'll see in the next section, the essential characteristic that differentiates imperfectly competitive firms from perfectly competitive firms is the same in each of the three cases. So for the duration of this chapter, we'll use the term *monopolist* to refer to any of the three types of imperfectly competitive firms. In the next chapter, we'll consider the strategic decisions confronting oligopolists and monopolistically competitive firms in greater detail.

THE ESSENTIAL DIFFERENCE BETWEEN PERFECTLY AND IMPERFECTLY COMPETITIVE FIRMS

In advanced economics courses, professors generally devote much attention to the analysis of subtle differences in the behavior of different types of imperfectly competitive firms. Far more important for our purposes, however, will be to focus on the single, common feature that differentiates all imperfectly competitive firms from their perfectly competitive counterparts—namely, that *whereas the perfectly competitive firm faces a perfectly elastic demand curve for its product, the imperfectly competitive firm faces a downward-sloping demand curve.*

In the perfectly competitive industry, the supply and demand curves intersect to determine an equilibrium market price. At that price, the perfectly competitive firm can sell as many units as it wishes. It has no incentive to charge more than the market price because it won't sell anything if it does so. Nor does it have any incentive to charge less than the market price because it can sell as many units as it wants to at the market price. The perfectly competitive firm's demand curve is thus a horizontal line at the market price, as we saw in previous chapters.

By contrast, if a local gasoline retailer—an imperfect competitor—charges a few pennies more than its rivals for a gallon of gas, some of its customers may desert it. But others will remain, perhaps because they are willing to pay a little extra to continue stopping at their most convenient location. An imperfectly competitive firm thus faces a negatively sloped demand curve. Figure 8.1 summarizes this contrast between the demand curves facing perfectly competitive and imperfectly competitive firms.

If the BP station at State and Meadow Streets raised its gasoline prices by 3 cents per gallon, would all its customers shop elsewhere?

FIGURE 8.1

The Demand Curves Facing Perfectly and Imperfectly Competitive Firms.

(a) The demand curve confronting a perfectly competitive firm is perfectly elastic at the market price. (b) The demand curve confronting an imperfectly competitive firm is downward-sloping.

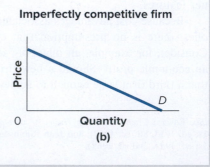

PERFECT AND IMPERFECT COMPETITION

Monopolistic competition is the industry structure in which a large number of small firms offer products that are similar in many respects, yet not perfect substitutes in the eyes of at least some consumers. Monopolistically competitive industries resemble perfectly competitive industries, in that entry and exit cause economic profits to tend toward zero in the long run.

Oligopoly is the industry structure in which a small number of large firms supply the entire market. Cost advantages associated with large-scale operations tend to be important. Oligopolists may produce either standardized products or differentiated products.

In contrast to each form of imperfect competition, in which all firms face downward-sloping demand curves, perfectly competitive firms face demand curves that are horizontal at the prevailing market price.

FIVE SOURCES OF MARKET POWER

Firms that confront downward-sloping demand curves are said to enjoy **market power,** a term that refers to their ability to set the prices of their products. A common misconception is that a firm with market power can sell any quantity at any price it wishes. It cannot. All it can do is pick a price–quantity combination on its demand curve. If the firm chooses to raise its price, it must settle for reduced sales.

Why do some firms have market power while others don't? Market power often carries with it the ability to charge a price above the cost of production, so such power tends to arise from factors that limit competition. In practice, the following five factors often confer such power: exclusive control over inputs, patents and copyrights, government licenses or franchises, economies of scale, and network economies.

market power a firm's ability to raise the price of a good without losing all its sales

EXCLUSIVE CONTROL OVER IMPORTANT INPUTS

If a single firm controls an input essential to the production of a given product, that firm will have market power. For example, to the extent that some U.S. tenants are willing to pay a premium for office space in the country's tallest building, One World Trade Center, the owner of that building has market power.

PATENTS AND COPYRIGHTS

Patents give the inventors or developers of new products the exclusive right to sell those products for a specified period of time. By insulating sellers from competition for an interval, patents enable innovators to charge higher prices to recoup their product's development costs. Pharmaceutical companies, for example, spend millions of dollars on research in the hope of discovering new drug therapies for serious illnesses. The drugs they discover are insulated from competition for an interval—currently 20 years in the United States—by government patents. For the life of the patent, only the patent holder may legally sell the drug. This protection enables the patent holder to set a price above the marginal cost of production to recoup the cost of the research on the drug. In the same way, copyrights protect the authors of movies, software, music, books, and other published works.

GOVERNMENT LICENSES OR FRANCHISES

Yosemite Hospitality, LLC has an exclusive license from the U.S. government to run the lodging and concession operations at Yosemite National Park. One of the government's goals in granting this monopoly was to preserve the wilderness character of the area to the greatest degree possible. And indeed, the inns and cabins offered by Yosemite Hospitality, LLC blend nicely with the valley's scenery. No garish neon signs mar the national park as they do in places where rivals compete for the tourist's dollars.

ECONOMIES OF SCALE AND NATURAL MONOPOLIES

constant returns to scale a production process is said to have constant returns to scale if, when all inputs are changed by a given proportion, output changes by the same proportion

increasing returns to scale (or **economies of scale**) a production process is said to have increasing returns to scale if, when all inputs are changed by a given proportion, output changes by more than that proportion

natural monopoly a monopoly that results from economies of scale (increasing returns to scale)

When a firm doubles all its factors of production, what happens to its output? If output exactly doubles, the firm's production process is said to exhibit **constant returns to scale.** If output more than doubles, the production process is said to exhibit **increasing returns to scale,** or **economies of scale.** When production is subject to economies of scale, the average cost of production declines as the number of units produced increases. For example, in the generation of electricity, the use of larger generators lowers the unit cost of production. The markets for such products tend to be served by a single seller, or perhaps only a few sellers, because having a large number of sellers would result in significantly higher costs. A monopoly that results from economies of scale is called a **natural monopoly.**

NETWORK ECONOMIES

Although most of us don't care what brand of a product like dental floss others use, many other products become more valuable to us as more people use them. In the case of social media, for instance, the more people use a particular social media platform, the more valuable it becomes. After all, the goal of social media is to connect with others. With over 1 billion active monthly users, posts on Instagram, for example, have the potential to be seen by large numbers of people. If, instead, Instagram had only a handful of users, none of whom you knew, the value of posting would be much smaller. Indeed, if many of your friends stopped using Instagram, you might follow suit.

A similar network economy helps account for the dominant position of Microsoft's Windows operating system, which, as noted earlier, is currently installed in roughly 80 percent of all desktop computers. Because Microsoft's initial sales advantage gave software developers a strong incentive to write for the Windows format, the inventory of available software in the Windows format is now vastly larger than that for any competing operating system. And although general-purpose software such as word processors and spreadsheets continues to be available for multiple operating systems, specialized professional software and games usually appear first—and often only—in the Windows format. This software gap and the desire to achieve compatibility for file sharing gave people a good reason for choosing Windows, even if, as in the case of many Apple users, they believed a competing system was otherwise superior. But, again, network dominance need not be permanent, as witnessed by Apple's dramatic resurgence in recent years.

By far the most important and enduring of these sources of market power are economies of scale and network economies. Lured by economic profit, firms almost always find substitutes for exclusive inputs. If there's enough profit to be had by renting out space in this country's tallest building, some real estate developer will eventually build one taller than One World Trade Center in New York. Likewise, firms can often evade patent laws by making slight changes in the design of products. Patent protection is only temporary, in any case. Finally, governments grant very few franchises each year. But economies of scale are both widespread and enduring, even if not completely insurmountable.

Firmly entrenched network economies can be as persistent a source of natural monopoly as economies of scale. Indeed, network economies are essentially similar to economies of scale. When network economies are of value to the consumer, a product's quality increases as the number of users increases, so we can say that any given quality level can be produced at lower cost as sales volume increases. Thus network economies may be viewed as just another form of economies of scale in production, and that's how we'll treat them here.

ECONOMIES OF SCALE AND THE IMPORTANCE OF START-UP COSTS

As we saw in Chapter 6, *Perfectly Competitive Supply*, variable costs are those that vary with the level of output produced, while fixed costs are independent of output. Suppose, for example, that a firm produces output by employing one fixed input, capital, and one variable input, labor. Its payment to capital would then be a fixed cost, and its payment to labor a variable cost. Strictly speaking, there are no fixed costs in the long run because all inputs can be varied. But as a practical matter, start-up costs often loom large for the duration of a product's useful life. Most of the costs involved in the production of computer software, for example, are start-up costs of this sort, one-time costs incurred in writing and testing the software. Once those tasks are done, additional copies of the software can be produced at a very low marginal cost. A good such as software, whose production entails large fixed start-up costs and low variable costs, will be subject to significant economies of scale. Because, by definition, fixed costs don't increase as output increases, the average total cost of production for such goods will decline sharply as output increases.

To illustrate, consider a production process for which total cost is given by the equation $TC = F + M \times Q$, where F is fixed cost, M is marginal cost (assumed constant in this illustration), and Q is the level of output produced. For the production process with this simple total cost function, variable cost is simply $M \times Q$, the product of marginal cost and quantity. Average total cost (ATC), TC/Q, is equal to $F/Q + M$. As Q increases, average cost declines steadily because the fixed costs are spread out over more and more units of output.

Figure 8.2 shows the total production cost (a) and average total cost (b) for a firm with the total cost curve $TC = F + M \times Q$ and the corresponding average total cost curve $ATC = F/Q + M$. The average total cost curve (b) shows the decline in per-unit cost as output grows. Though average total cost is always higher than marginal cost for this firm, the difference between the two diminishes as output grows. At extremely high levels of output, average total cost becomes very close to marginal cost (M). Because the firm is spreading out its fixed cost over an extremely large volume of output, fixed cost per unit becomes almost insignificant.

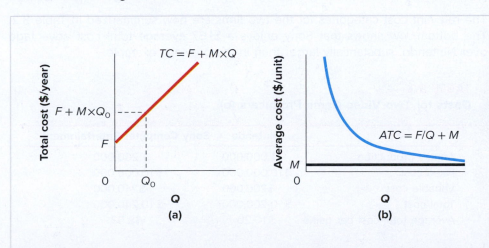

(a)   (b)

FIGURE 8.2

Total and Average Total Costs for a Production Process with Economies of Scale.

For a firm whose total cost curve of producing Q units of output per year is $TC = F + M \times Q$, total cost (a) rises at a constant rate as output grows, while average total cost (b) declines. Average total cost is always higher than marginal cost for this firm, but the difference becomes less significant at high output levels.

As the following examples illustrate, the importance of economies of scale depends on how large fixed cost is in relation to marginal cost.

EXAMPLE 8.1 — Economies of Scale—Small Fixed Cost

Two video game producers, Nintendo and Sony Computer Entertainment, each have fixed costs of $200,000 and marginal costs of $0.80 per game. If Nintendo produces 1 million units per year and Sony produces 1.2 million, how much lower will Sony's average total production cost be?

Table 8.1 summarizes the relevant cost categories for the two firms. Note in the bottom row that Sony enjoys only a 3-cent average cost advantage over Nintendo. Even though Nintendo produces 20 percent fewer copies of its video game than Sony, it does not suffer a significant cost disadvantage because fixed cost is a relatively small part of total production cost.

TABLE 8.1

Costs for Two Video Game Producers (a)

	Nintendo	Sony Computer Entertainment
Annual production	1,000,000	1,200,000
Fixed cost	$200,000	$200,000
Variable cost	$800,000	$960,000
Total cost	$1,000,000	$1,160,000
Average total cost per game	$1.00	$0.97

In the next example, note how the picture changes when fixed cost looms large relative to marginal cost.

EXAMPLE 8.2 — Economies of Scale—Large Fixed Cost

Two video game producers, Nintendo and Sony Computer Entertainment, each have fixed costs of $10,000,000 and marginal costs of $0.20 per video game. If Nintendo produces 1 million units per year and Sony produces 1.2 million, how much lower will Sony's average total cost be?

The relevant cost categories for the two firms are now summarized in Table 8.2. The bottom row shows that Sony enjoys a $1.67 average total cost advantage over Nintendo, substantially larger than in the previous example.

TABLE 8.2

Costs for Two Video Game Producers (b)

	Nintendo	Sony Computer Entertainment
Annual production	1,000,000	1,200,000
Fixed cost	$10,000,000	$10,000,000
Variable cost	$200,000	$240,000
Total cost	$10,200,000	$10,240,000
Average total cost per game	$10.20	$8.53

If the video games the two firms produce are essentially similar, the fact that Sony can charge significantly lower prices and still cover its costs should enable it to attract customers away from Nintendo. As more and more of the market goes to Sony, its cost advantage will become self-reinforcing. Table 8.3 shows how a shift of 500,000 units from Nintendo to Sony would cause Nintendo's average total cost to rise to $20.20 per unit, while Sony's average total cost would fall to $6.08 per unit. The fact that a firm cannot long survive at such a severe disadvantage explains why the video game market is served now by only a small number of firms.

TABLE 8.3
Costs for Two Video Game Producers (c)

	Nintendo	Sony Computer Entertainment
Annual production	500,000	1,700,000
Fixed cost	$10,000,000	$10,000,000
Variable cost	$100,000	$340,000
Total cost	$10,100,000	$10,340,000
Average total cost per game	$20.20	$6.08

 SELF-TEST 8.1

How big will Sony's unit cost advantage be if it sells 2,000,000 units per year, while Nintendo sells only 200,000?

An important worldwide economic trend during recent decades is that an increasing share of the value embodied in the goods and services we buy stems from fixed investment in research and development. For example, in 1984 some 80 percent of the cost of a computer was in its hardware (which has relatively high marginal cost); the remaining 20 percent was in its software. But by 1990 those proportions were reversed. Fixed cost now accounts for about 85 percent of total costs in the computer software industry, whose products are included in a growing share of ordinary manufactured goods.

The Economic Naturalist 8.1

Why does Intel sell the overwhelming majority of all microprocessors used in personal computers?

The fixed investment required to produce a new leading-edge microprocessor such as the Intel Core i9-9900KS microprocessor runs upward of several billion dollars. But once the chip has been designed and the manufacturing facility built, the marginal cost of producing each chip is only pennies. This cost pattern explains why Intel currently sells almost 80 percent of all microprocessors.

As fixed cost becomes more and more important, the perfectly competitive pattern of many small firms, each producing only a small share of its industry's total output, becomes less common. For this reason, we must develop a clear sense of how the behavior of firms with market power differs from that of the perfectly competitive firm.

> **RECAP** ↑
>
> **ECONOMIES OF SCALE AND THE IMPORTANCE OF START-UP COSTS**
>
> Research, design, engineering, and other fixed costs account for an increasingly large share of all costs required to bring products successfully to market. For products with large fixed costs, marginal cost is lower, often substantially, than average total cost, and average total cost declines, often sharply, as output grows. This cost pattern explains why many industries are dominated by either a single firm or a small number of firms.

PROFIT MAXIMIZATION FOR THE MONOPOLIST

Cost-Benefit ⟫

Regardless of whether a firm is a price taker or a price setter, economists assume that its basic goal is to maximize its profit. In both cases, the firm expands output as long as the benefit of doing so exceeds the cost. Further, the calculation of marginal cost is also the same for the monopolist as for the perfectly competitive firm.

The profit-maximizing decision for a monopolist differs from that of a perfectly competitive firm when we look at the benefits of expanding output. For both the perfectly competitive firm and the monopolist, the marginal benefit of expanding output is the additional revenue the firm will receive if it sells one additional unit of output. In both cases, this marginal benefit is called the firm's **marginal revenue.** For the perfectly competitive firm, marginal revenue is exactly equal to the market price of the product. If that price is $6, for example, then the marginal benefit of selling an extra unit is exactly $6.

marginal revenue the change in a firm's total revenue that results from a one-unit change in output

MARGINAL REVENUE FOR THE MONOPOLIST

The situation is different for a monopolist. *To a monopolist, the marginal benefit of selling an additional unit is strictly less than the market price.* As the following discussion will make clear, the reason is that while the perfectly competitive firm can sell as many units as it wishes at the market price, the monopolist can sell an additional unit only if it cuts the price—and it must do so not just for the additional unit but for the units it is currently selling.

Suppose, for example, that a monopolist with the demand curve shown in Figure 8.3 is currently selling 2 units of output at a price of $6 per unit. What would be its marginal revenue from selling an additional unit?

FIGURE 8.3

The Monopolist's Benefit from Selling an Additional Unit.

The monopolist shown receives $12 per week in total revenue by selling 2 units per week at a price of $6 each. This monopolist could earn $15 per week by selling 3 units per week at a price of $5 each. In that case, the benefit from selling the third unit would be $15 − $12 = $3, less than its selling price of $5.

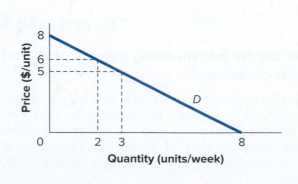

This monopolist's total revenue from the sale of 2 units per week is ($6 per unit) (2 units per week) = $12 per week. Its total revenue from the sale of 3 units per week would be $15 per week. The difference—$3 per week—is the marginal revenue from the sale of the third unit each week. Note that this amount is not only smaller than the original price ($6) but smaller than the new price ($5) as well.

 SELF-TEST 8.2

Calculate marginal revenue for the monopolist in Figure 8.3 as it expands output from 3 to 4 units per week, and then from 4 to 5 units per week.

For the monopolist whose demand curve is shown in Figure 8.3, a sequence of increases in output—from 2 to 3, from 3 to 4, and from 4 to 5—will yield marginal revenue of $3, $1, and −$1, respectively. We display these results in tabular form in Table 8.4.

TABLE 8.4
Marginal Revenue for a Monopolist ($ per unit)

Quantity	Marginal revenue
2	
	3
3	
	1
4	
	−1
5	

Note in the table that the marginal revenue values are displayed between the two quantity figures to which they correspond. For example, when the firm expanded its output from 2 units per week to 3, its marginal revenue was $3 per unit. Strictly speaking, this marginal revenue corresponds to neither quantity but to the movement between those quantities, hence its placement in the table. Likewise, in moving from 3 to 4 units per week, the firm earned marginal revenue of $1 per unit, so that figure is placed midway between the quantities of 3 and 4, and so on.

To graph marginal revenue as a function of quantity, we would plot the marginal revenue for the movement from 2 to 3 units of output per week ($3) at a quantity value of 2.5, because 2.5 lies midway between 2 and 3. Similarly, we would plot the marginal revenue for the movement from 3 to 4 units per week ($1) at a quantity of 3.5 units per week, and the marginal revenue for the movement from 4 to 5 units per week (−$1) at a quantity of 4.5. The resulting marginal revenue curve, *MR*, is shown in Figure 8.4.

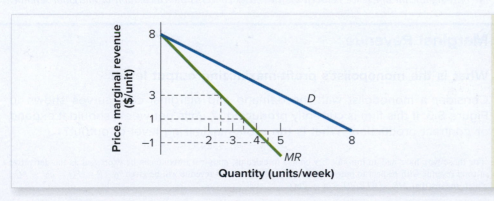

FIGURE 8.4

Marginal Revenue in Graphical Form.

Because a monopolist must cut price to sell an extra unit, not only for the extra unit sold but also for all existing units, marginal revenue from the sale of the extra unit is less than its selling price.

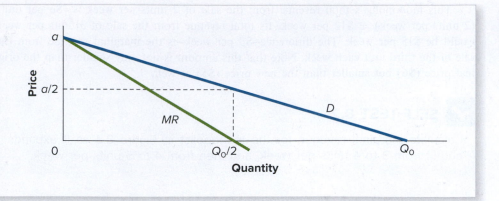

FIGURE 8.5

The Marginal Revenue Curve for a Monopolist with a Straight-Line Demand Curve.

For a monopolist with the demand curve shown, the corresponding marginal revenue curve has the same vertical intercept as the demand curve, and a horizontal intercept only half as large as that of the demand curve.

More generally, consider a monopolist with a straight-line demand curve whose vertical intercept is a and whose horizontal intercept is Q_0, as shown in Figure 8.5. This monopolist's marginal revenue curve also will have a vertical intercept of a, and it will be twice as steep as the demand curve. Thus, its horizontal intercept will be not Q_0, but $Q_0/2$, as shown in Figure 8.5.

Marginal revenue curves also can be expressed algebraically. If the formula for the monopolist's demand curve is $P = a - bQ$, then the formula for its marginal revenue curve will be $MR = a - 2bQ$. If you have had calculus, this relationship is easy to derive,[2] but even without calculus you can verify it by working through a few numerical examples. First, translate the formula for the demand curve into a diagram, and then construct the corresponding marginal revenue curve graphically. Reading from the graph, write the formula for that marginal revenue curve.

THE MONOPOLIST'S PROFIT-MAXIMIZING DECISION RULE

Having derived the monopolist's marginal revenue curve, we're now in a position to describe how the monopolist chooses the output level that maximizes profit. As in the case of the perfectly competitive firm, the Cost-Benefit Principle says that the monopolist should continue to expand output as long as the gain from doing so exceeds the cost. At the current level of output, the benefit from expanding output is the marginal revenue value that corresponds to that output level. The cost of expanding output is the marginal cost at that level of output. Whenever marginal revenue exceeds marginal cost, the firm should expand. Conversely, whenever marginal revenue falls short of marginal cost, the firm should reduce its output. *Profit is maximized at the level of output for which marginal revenue precisely equals marginal cost.*

When the monopolist's profit-maximizing rule is stated in this way, we can see that the perfectly competitive firm's rule is actually a special case of the monopolist's rule. When the perfectly competitive firm expands output by one unit, its marginal revenue exactly equals the product's market price (because the perfectly competitive firm can expand sales by a unit without having to cut the price of existing units). So when the perfectly competitive firm equates price with marginal cost, it is also equating marginal revenue with marginal cost. *Thus, the only significant difference between the two cases concerns the calculation of marginal revenue.*

EXAMPLE 8.3   **Marginal Revenue**

What is the monopolist's profit-maximizing output level?

Consider a monopolist with the demand and marginal cost curves shown in Figure 8.6. If this firm is currently producing 12 units per week, should it expand or contract production? What is the profit-maximizing level of output?

---

[2]For those who have had an introductory course in calculus, marginal revenue can be expressed as the derivative of total revenue with respect to output. If $P = a - bQ$, then total revenue will be given by $TR = PQ = aQ - bQ^2$, which means that $MR = dTR/dQ = a - 2bQ$.

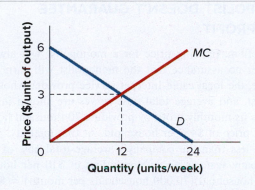

FIGURE 8.6

The Demand and Marginal Cost Curves for a Monopolist.

At the current output level of 12 units per week, price equals marginal cost. Because the monopolist's price is always greater than marginal revenue, marginal revenue must be less than marginal cost, which means this monopolist should produce less.

In Figure 8.7, we begin by constructing the marginal revenue curve that corresponds to the monopolist's demand curve. It has the same vertical intercept as the demand curve, and its horizontal intercept is half as large. Note that the monopolist's marginal revenue at 12 units per week is zero, which is clearly less than its marginal cost of $3 per unit. This monopolist will therefore earn a higher profit by contracting production until marginal revenue equals marginal cost, which occurs at an output level of 8 units per week. At this profit-maximizing output level, the firm will charge $4 per unit, the price that corresponds to 8 units per week on the demand curve.

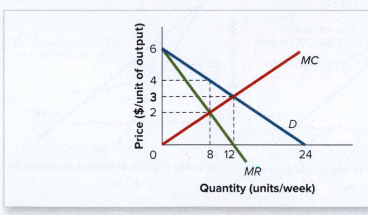

FIGURE 8.7

The Monopolist's Profit-Maximizing Output Level.

This monopolist maximizes profit by selling 8 units per week, the output level at which marginal revenue equals marginal cost. The profit-maximizing price is $4 per unit, the price that corresponds to the profit-maximizing quantity on the demand curve.

 SELF-TEST 8.3

For the monopolist with the demand and marginal cost curves shown, find the profit-maximizing price and level of output.

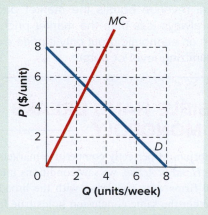

BEING A MONOPOLIST DOESN'T GUARANTEE AN ECONOMIC PROFIT

The fact that the profit-maximizing price for a monopolist will always be greater than marginal cost provides no assurance that the monopolist will earn an economic profit. Consider, for example, the local cable Internet service provider whose demand, marginal revenue, marginal cost, and average total cost curves are shown in Figure 8.8(a). This monopolist maximizes its monthly profit by providing 70 thousand households per month with cable Internet at price of $45 per household. At that quantity, $MR = MC$, yet price is $10 per household less than the company's average total cost of $55 per household. As a result, the company sustains an economic loss of $10 per household served, or a total loss of ($10 per household)(70,000 households per month) = $700,000 per month.

The monopolist in Figure 8.8(a) suffered a loss because its profit-maximizing price was lower than its *ATC*. If the monopolist's profit-maximizing price exceeds its average total cost, however, the company will, of course, earn an economic profit. Consider, for example, the local cable Internet provider shown in Figure 8.8(b). This firm has the same demand, marginal revenue, and marginal cost curves as the firm shown in Figure 8.8(a). But because the firm in (b) has lower fixed costs, its *ATC* curve is lower at every level of output than the *ATC* curve in (a). At the profit-maximizing price of $45 per household, the firm in Figure 8.8(b) earns an economic profit of $10 per household, for a total economic profit of $700,000 per month.

FIGURE 8.8

Even a Monopolist May Suffer an Economic Loss.

The monopolist in (a) maximizes its profit by providing cable Internet service to 70,000 households per month but suffers an economic loss of $700,000 per month in the process. Because the profit-maximizing price of the monopolist in (b) exceeds *ATC*, this monopolist earns an economic profit.

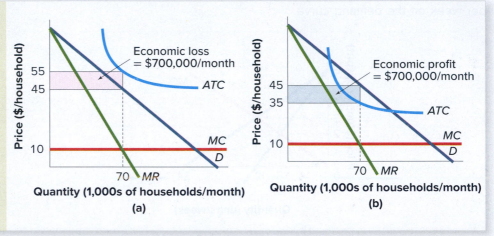

RECAP

PROFIT MAXIMIZATION FOR THE MONOPOLIST

Both the perfectly competitive firm and the monopolist maximize profit by choosing the output level at which marginal revenue equals marginal cost. But whereas marginal revenue equals the market price for the perfectly competitive firm, it is always less than the market price for the monopolist. A monopolist will earn an economic profit only if price exceeds average total cost at the profit-maximizing level of output.

WHY THE INVISIBLE HAND BREAKS DOWN UNDER MONOPOLY

In our discussion of equilibrium in perfectly competitive markets in Chapter 7, *Efficiency, Exchange, and the Invisible Hand in Action,* we saw conditions under which the self-serving pursuits of consumers and firms were consistent with the broader interests of society as a whole. Let's explore whether the same conclusion holds true for the case of imperfectly competitive firms.

Consider the monopolist in Figures 8.6 and 8.7. Is this firm's profit-maximizing output level efficient from society's point of view? For any given level of output, the corresponding price on the demand curve indicates the amount buyers would be willing to pay for an additional unit of output. When the monopolist is producing 8 units per week, the marginal benefit to society of an additional unit of output is thus $4 (see Figure 8.7). And since the marginal cost of an additional unit at that output level is only $2 (again, see Figure 8.7), society would gain a net benefit of $2 per unit if the monopolist were to expand production by 1 unit above the profit-maximizing level. Because this economic surplus is not realized, the profit-maximizing monopolist is socially inefficient.

Recall that the existence of inefficiency means that the economic pie is smaller than it might be. If that is so, why doesn't the monopolist simply expand production? The answer is that the monopolist would gladly do so, if only there were some way to maintain the price of existing units and cut the price of only the extra units. As a practical matter, however, that is not always possible.

Now, let's look at this situation from a different angle. For the market served by this monopolist, what *is* the socially efficient level of output?

At any output level, the cost to society of an additional unit of output is the same as the cost to the monopolist, namely, the amount shown on the monopolist's marginal cost curve. The marginal benefit *to society* (not to the monopolist) of an extra unit of output is simply the amount people are willing to pay for it, which is the amount shown on the monopolist's demand curve. To achieve social efficiency, the monopolist should expand production until the marginal benefit to society equals the marginal cost, which in this case occurs at a level of 12 units per week. Social efficiency is thus achieved at the output level at which the market demand curve intersects the monopolist's marginal cost curve.

The fact that marginal revenue is less than price for the monopolist results in a **deadweight loss.** For the monopolist just discussed, the size of this deadweight loss is equal to the area of the pale blue triangle in Figure 8.9, which is (1/2)($2 per unit) (4 units per week) = $4 per week. That is the amount by which total economic surplus is reduced because the monopolist produces too little.

For a monopolist, profit maximization occurs when marginal cost equals marginal revenue. Since the monopolist's marginal revenue is always less than price, the monopolist's profit-maximizing output level is always below the socially efficient level. Under perfect competition, by contrast, profit maximization occurs when marginal cost equals the market price—the same criterion that must be satisfied for social efficiency. This difference explains why the invisible hand of the market is less evident in monopoly markets than in perfectly competitive markets.

If perfect competition is socially efficient and monopoly is not, why isn't monopoly against the law? Congress has, in fact, tried to limit the extent of monopoly through antitrust laws. But even the most enthusiastic proponents of those laws recognize the limited usefulness of the legislative approach since the alternatives to monopoly often entail problems of their own.

deadweight loss the loss of consumer and producer surplus caused by disparity between price and marginal cost

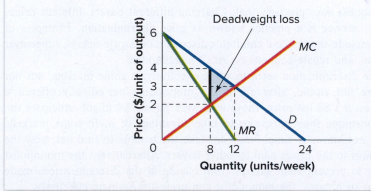

FIGURE 8.9

The Deadweight Loss from Monopoly.

A loss in economic surplus results because the profit-maximizing level of output (8 units per week) is less than the socially optimal level of output (12 units per week). This deadweight loss is the area of the pale blue triangle, $4 per week.

Suppose, for example, that a monopoly results from a patent that prevents all but one firm from manufacturing some highly valued product. Would society be better off without patents? Probably not because eliminating such protection would discourage innovation. Virtually all successful industrial nations grant some form of patent protection, which gives firms a chance to recover the research and development costs without which new products would seldom reach the market.

Or suppose that the market in question is a natural monopoly—one that, because of economies of scale, is most cheaply served by a single firm. Would society do better to require this market to be served by many small firms, each with significantly higher average costs of production? Such a requirement would merely replace one form of inefficiency with another.

In short, we live in an imperfect world. Monopoly is socially inefficient, and that, needless to say, is bad. But the alternatives to monopoly aren't perfect either.

> **RECAP**
>
> **WHY THE INVISIBLE HAND BREAKS DOWN UNDER MONOPOLY**
>
> The monopolist maximizes profit at the output level for which marginal revenue equals marginal cost. Because its profit-maximizing price exceeds marginal revenue, and hence also marginal cost, the benefit to society of the last unit produced (the market price) must be greater than the cost of the last unit produced (the marginal cost). So the output level for an industry served by a profit-maximizing monopolist is smaller than the socially optimal level of output.

USING DISCOUNTS TO EXPAND THE MARKET

The source of inefficiency in monopoly markets is the fact that the benefit to the monopolist of expanding output is less than the corresponding benefit to society. From the monopolist's point of view, the price reduction the firm must grant existing buyers to expand output is a loss. But from the point of view of those buyers, each dollar of price reduction is a gain—one dollar more in their pockets.

Efficiency

Note the tension in this situation, which is similar to the tension that exists in all other situations in which the economic pie is smaller than it might otherwise be. As the Efficiency Principle reminds us, when the economic pie grows larger, everyone can have a larger slice. To say that monopoly is inefficient means that steps could be taken to make some people better off without harming others. If people have a healthy regard for their own self-interest, why doesn't someone take those steps? Why, for example, doesn't the monopolist from the earlier examples sell 8 units of output at a price of $4, and then once those buyers are out the door, cut the price for more price-sensitive buyers?

PRICE DISCRIMINATION DEFINED

price discrimination the practice of charging different buyers different prices for essentially the same good or service

Sometimes the monopolist does precisely that. Charging different buyers different prices for the same good or service is a practice known as **price discrimination.** Examples of price discrimination include seniors' and children's discounts on movie tickets, supersaver discounts on air travel, and rebate coupons on retail merchandise.

Attempts at price discrimination seem to work effectively in some markets, but not in others. Buyers are not stupid, after all; if the monopolist periodically offered a 50 percent discount on the $8 list price, those who were paying $8 might anticipate the next price cut and postpone their purchases to take advantage of it. In some markets, however, buyers may not know, or simply may not take the trouble to find out, how the price they pay compares to the prices paid by other buyers. Alternatively, the monopolist may be in a position to prevent some groups from buying at the discount prices made available to others. In such cases, the monopolist can price-discriminate effectively.

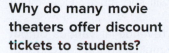

The Economic Naturalist 8.2

Why do many movie theaters offer discount tickets to students?

Whenever a firm offers a discount, the goal is to target that discount to buyers who would not purchase the product without it. People with low incomes generally have lower reservation prices for movie tickets than people with high incomes. Because students generally have lower disposable incomes than working adults, theater owners can expand their audiences by charging lower prices to students than to adults. Student discounts are one practical way of doing so. Offering student discounts also entails no risk of some people buying the product at a low price and then reselling it to others at a higher price.

Why do students pay lower ticket prices at many movie theaters?

HOW PRICE DISCRIMINATION AFFECTS OUTPUT

In the following examples, we'll see how the ability to price-discriminate affects the monopolist's profit-maximizing level of output. First we'll consider a baseline case in which the monopolist must charge the same price to every buyer.

EXAMPLE 8.4   Profit Maximization and Opportunity Cost

How many manuscripts should Preeti edit?

Preeti supplements her income as a teaching assistant by editing term papers for undergraduates. There are eight students per week for whom she might edit, each with a reservation price as given in the following table.

Student	Reservation price
A	$40
B	38
C	36
D	34
E	32
F	30
G	28
H	26

Preeti is a profit maximizer. If the opportunity cost of her time to edit each paper is $29 and she must charge the same price to each student, how many papers should she edit? How much economic profit will she make? How much accounting profit?

Table 8.5 summarizes Preeti's total and marginal revenue at various output levels. To generate the amounts in column 3, we simply multiplied the corresponding reservation price by the number of students whose reservation prices were at least that high. For example, to edit 4 papers per week (for students A, B, C, and D), Preeti must charge a price no higher than D's reservation price ($34). So her total revenue when she edits 4 papers per week is (4)($34) = $136 per week. Preeti should keep expanding the number of students she serves as long as her marginal revenue exceeds the opportunity cost of her time. Marginal revenue, or the difference in total revenue that results from adding another student, is shown in column 4 of Table 8.5.

TABLE 8.5
Total and Marginal Revenue from Editing

(1) Student	(2) Reservation price ($ per paper)	(3) Total revenue ($ per week)	(4) Marginal revenue ($ per paper)
			40
A	40	40	
			36
B	38	76	
			32
C	36	108	
			28
D	34	136	
			24
E	32	160	
			20
F	30	180	
			16
G	28	196	
			12
H	26	208	

Note that if Preeti were editing 2 papers per week, her marginal revenue from editing a third paper would be $32. Since that amount exceeds her $29 opportunity cost, she should take on the third paper. But since the marginal revenue of taking on a fourth paper would be only $28, Preeti should stop at 3 papers per week. The total opportunity cost of the time required to edit the 3 papers is (3)($29) = $87, so Preeti's economic profit is $108 − $87 = $21 per week. Since Preeti incurs no explicit costs, her accounting profit will be $108 per week.

EXAMPLE 8.5   **Social Efficiency**

What is the socially efficient number of papers for Preeti to edit?

Again, suppose that Preeti's opportunity cost of editing is $29 per paper and that she could edit as many as 8 papers per week for students whose reservation prices are again as listed in the following table.

Student	Reservation price
A	$40
B	38
C	36
D	34
E	32
F	30
G	28
H	26

What is the socially efficient number of papers for Preeti to edit? If she must charge the same price to each student, what will her economic and accounting profits be if she edits the socially efficient number of papers?

Students *A* to *F* are willing to pay more than Preeti's opportunity cost, so serving these students is socially efficient. But students *G* and *H* are unwilling to pay at least $29 for Preeti's services. The socially efficient outcome, therefore, is for Preeti to edit 6 papers per week. To attract that number, she must charge a price no higher than $30 per paper. Her total revenue will be (6)($30) = $180 per week, slightly more than her total opportunity cost of (6)($29) = $174 per week. Her economic profit will thus be only $6 per week. Again, because Preeti incurs no explicit costs, her accounting profit will be the same as her total revenue, $180 per week.

EXAMPLE 8.6	Price Discrimination

If Preeti can price-discriminate, how many papers should she edit?

Suppose Preeti is a shrewd judge of human nature. After a moment's conversation with a student, she can discern that student's reservation price. The reservation prices of her potential customers are again as given in the following table. If Preeti confronts the same market as before, but can charge students their respective reservation prices, how many papers should she edit, and how much economic and accounting profit will she make?

Student	Reservation price
A	$40
B	38
C	36
D	34
E	32
F	30
G	28
H	26

Preeti will edit papers for students *A* to *F* and charge each exactly his or her reservation price. Because students *G* and *H* have reservation prices below $29, Preeti will not edit their papers. Preeti's total revenue will be $40 + $38 + $36 +

$34 + $32 + $30 = $210 per week, which is also her accounting profit. Her total opportunity cost of editing 6 papers is (6)($29) = $174 per week, so her economic profit will be $210 − $174 = $36 per week, $30 per week more than when she edited 6 papers but was constrained to charge each customer the same price.

A monopolist who can charge each buyer exactly his or her reservation price is called a **perfectly discriminating monopolist.** Notice that, when Preeti was discriminating among customers in this way, her profit-maximizing level of output was exactly the same as the socially efficient level of output: 6 papers per week. With a perfectly discriminating monopoly, there is no loss of efficiency. All buyers who are willing to pay a price high enough to cover marginal cost will be served.

Note that although total economic surplus is maximized by a perfectly discriminating monopolist, consumers would have little reason to celebrate if they found themselves dealing with such a firm. After all, consumer surplus is exactly zero for the perfectly discriminating monopolist. In this instance, total economic surplus and producer surplus are one and the same.

In practice, of course, perfect price discrimination can never occur because no seller knows each and every buyer's precise reservation price. But even if some sellers did know, practical difficulties would stand in the way of their charging a separate price to each buyer. For example, in many markets the seller could not prevent buyers who bought at low prices from reselling to other buyers at higher prices, capturing some of the seller's business in the process. Despite these difficulties, price discrimination is widespread. But it is generally *imperfect price discrimination*—that is, price discrimination in which at least some buyers are charged less than their reservation prices.

THE HURDLE METHOD OF PRICE DISCRIMINATION

The profit-maximizing seller's goal is to charge each buyer the highest price that buyer is willing to pay. Two primary obstacles prevent sellers from achieving this goal. First, sellers don't know exactly how much each buyer is willing to pay. And second, they need some means of excluding those who are willing to pay a high price from buying at a low price. These are formidable problems, which no seller can hope to solve completely.

One common method by which sellers achieve a crude solution to both problems is to require buyers to overcome some obstacle to be eligible for a discount price. This method is called the **hurdle method of price discrimination.** For example, the seller might sell a product at a standard list price and offer a rebate to any buyer who takes the trouble to mail in a rebate coupon.

The hurdle method solves both of the seller's problems, provided that buyers with low reservation prices are more willing than others to jump the hurdle. Because a decision to jump the hurdle must satisfy the Cost-Benefit Principle, such a link seems to exist. As noted earlier, buyers with low incomes are more likely than others to have low reservation prices (at least in the case of normal goods). Because of the low opportunity cost of their time, they are more likely than others to take the trouble to send in rebate coupons. Rebate coupons thus target a discount toward those buyers whose reservation prices are low and who therefore might not buy the product otherwise.

A **perfect hurdle** is one that separates buyers precisely according to their reservation prices, and in the process imposes no cost on those who jump the hurdle. With a perfect hurdle, the highest reservation price among buyers who jump the hurdle will be lower than the lowest reservation price among buyers who choose not to jump the hurdle. In practice, perfect hurdles do not exist. Some buyers will always jump the hurdle, even though their reservation prices are high. And hurdles will always exclude at least some buyers with low reservation prices. Even so, many commonly used hurdles do a remarkably good job of targeting discounts to buyers with low reservation prices. In the example that follows, we will assume for convenience that the seller is using a perfect hurdle.

EXAMPLE 8.7	Perfect Hurdle

How much should Preeti charge for editing if she uses a perfect hurdle?

Suppose Preeti again has the opportunity to edit as many as 8 papers per week for the students whose reservation prices are as given in the following table. This time she can offer a rebate coupon that gives a discount to any student who takes the trouble to mail it back to her. Suppose further that students whose reservation prices are at least $36 never mail in the rebate coupons, while those whose reservation prices are below $36 always do so.

Student	Reservation price
A	$40
B	38
C	36
D	34
E	32
F	30
G	28
H	26

If Preeti's opportunity cost of editing each paper is again $29, what should her list price be, and what amount should she offer as a rebate? Will her economic profit be larger or smaller than when she lacked the discount option?

The rebate coupon allows Preeti to divide her original market into two submarkets in which she can charge two different prices. The first submarket consists of students *A, B,* and *C,* whose reservation prices are at least $36 and who therefore will not bother to mail in a rebate coupon. The second submarket consists of students *D* through *H,* whose lower reservation prices indicate a willingness to use rebate coupons.

In each submarket, Preeti must charge the same price to every buyer, just like an ordinary monopolist. She should therefore keep expanding output in each submarket as long as marginal revenue in that market exceeds her marginal cost. The relevant data for the two submarkets are displayed in Table 8.6.

On the basis of the entries in column 4 for the list price submarket, we see that Preeti should serve all three students *(A, B,* and *C)* since marginal revenue for each exceeds $29. Her profit-maximizing price in the list price submarket is $36, the highest price she can charge in that market and still sell her services to students *A, B,* and *C.* For the discount price submarket, marginal revenue exceeds $29 only for the first two students *(D* and *E).* So the profit-maximizing price in this submarket is $32, the highest price Preeti can charge and still sell her services to *D* and *E.* (A discount price of $32 means that students who mail in the coupon will receive a rebate of $4 on the $36 list price.)

Note that the rebate offer enables Preeti to serve a total of five students per week, compared to only three without the offer. Preeti's combined total revenue for the two markets is (3)($36) + 2($32) = $172 per week. Since her opportunity cost is $29 per paper, or a total of (5)($29) = $145 per week, her economic profit is $172 per week − $145 per week = $27 per week, $6 more than when she edited 3 papers and did not offer the rebate.

TABLE 8.6
Price Discrimination with a Perfect Hurdle

(1) Student	(2) Reservation price ($ per paper)	(3) Total revenue ($ per week)	(4) Marginal revenue ($ per paper)
List Price Submarket			
			40
A	40	40	
			36
B	38	76	
			32
C	36	108	
Discount Price Submarket			
			34
D	34	34	
			30
E	32	64	
			26
F	30	90	
			22
G	28	112	
			18
H	26	130	

SELF-TEST 8.4

In Example 8.7, how much should Preeti charge in each submarket if she knows that only those students whose reservation prices are below $34 will use rebate coupons?

IS PRICE DISCRIMINATION A BAD THING?

We are so conditioned to think of discrimination as bad that we may be tempted to conclude that price discrimination must run counter to the public interest. In Example 8.7, however, both consumer surplus and producer surplus were actually enhanced by the monopolist's use of the hurdle method of price discrimination. To show this, let's compare consumer and producer surplus when Preeti employs the hurdle method to the corresponding values when she charges the same price to all buyers.

When Preeti had to charge the same price to every customer, she edited only the papers of students *A, B,* and *C,* each of whom paid a price of $36. We can tell at a glance that the total surplus must be larger under the hurdle method because not only are students *A, B,* and *C* served at the same price ($36), but also students *D* and *E* are now served at a price of $32.

To confirm this intuition, we can calculate the exact amount of the surplus. For any student who hires Preeti to edit her paper, consumer surplus is the difference between her reservation price and the price actually paid. In both the single price and discount price examples, student *A*'s consumer surplus is thus $40 − $36 = $4; student *B*'s consumer surplus is $38 − $36 = $2; and student *C*'s consumer surplus is $36 − $36 = 0. Total consumer surplus in the list price submarket is thus $4 + $2 = $6 per week, which is the same as total consumer surplus in the original situation. But now the discount price submarket generates additional consumer surplus. Specifically, student D receives $2 per week of consumer surplus since this student's reservation price of $34 is $2 more than the discount price of $32. So total consumer surplus is now $6 + $2 = $8 per week, or $2 per week more than before.

Preeti's producer surplus also increases under the hurdle method. For each paper she edits, her producer surplus is the price she charges minus her reservation price ($29). In the single-price case, Preeti's surplus was (3)($36 − $29) = $21 per week. When she offers a rebate coupon, she earns the same producer surplus as before from students A, B, and C and an additional (2)($32 − $29) = $6 per week from students D and E. Total producer surplus with the discount is thus $21 + $6 = $27 per week. Adding that amount to the total consumer surplus of $8 per week, we get a total economic surplus of $35 per week with the rebate coupons, $8 per week more than without the rebate.

Note, however, that even with the rebate, the final outcome is not socially efficient because Preeti does not serve student F, even though this student's reservation price of $30 exceeds her opportunity cost of $29. Although the hurdle method is not perfectly efficient, it's still more efficient than charging a single price to all buyers.

EXAMPLES OF PRICE DISCRIMINATION

Once you grasp the principle behind the hurdle method of price discrimination, you'll begin to see examples of it all around you. Next time you visit a grocery, hardware, or appliance store, for instance, notice how many different product promotions include cash rebates. Temporary sales are another illustration of the hurdle method. Most of the time, retailers sell most of their merchandise at the "regular" price but periodically offer special sales at a significant discount. The hurdle in this instance is taking the trouble to find out when and where the sales occur and then making a purchase during that period. This technique works because buyers who care most about price (mainly, those with low reservation prices) are more likely to monitor advertisements carefully and buy only during sale periods.

To give another example, book publishers typically launch a new book in hardcover at a price from $20 to $30, and a year later they bring out a paperback edition priced between $5 and $15. In this instance, the hurdle involves having to wait the extra year and accepting a slight reduction in the quality of the finished product. People who are strongly concerned about price end up waiting for the paperback edition, while those with high reservation prices usually spring for the hardback.

Or take the example of automobile producers, who typically offer several different models with different trim and accessories. Although GM's actual cost of producing a Cadillac may be only $2,000 more than its cost of producing a Chevrolet, the Cadillac's selling price may be $10,000 to $15,000 higher than the Chevrolet's. Buyers with low reservation prices purchase the Chevrolet, while those with high reservation prices are more likely to choose the Cadillac.

Commercial air carriers have perfected the hurdle method to an extent matched by almost no other seller. Their supersaver fares are often less than half their regular coach fares. To be eligible for these discounts, travelers must purchase their tickets 7 to 21 days in advance and their journey must include a Saturday night stayover. Vacation travelers can more easily satisfy these restrictions than business travelers, whose schedules often change at the last moment and whose trips seldom involve Saturday stayovers. And—no surprise—the business traveler's reservation price tends to be much higher than the vacation traveler's.

Many sellers employ not just one hurdle but several by offering deeper discounts to buyers who jump successively more difficult hurdles. For example, movie studios initially release their major films to first-run theaters at premium prices and then, several months later, on DVD and video-on-demand platforms like iTunes. Still later they make the films available through subscription television providers like HBO and Netflix, and finally permit them to be shown on network television. Each successive hurdle involves waiting a little longer and, in the case of the televised versions, accepting lower quality. These hurdles are remarkably effective in segregating moviegoers according to their reservation prices.

Recall that the efficiency loss from single-price monopoly occurs because, to the monopolist, the benefit of expanding output is smaller than the benefit to society as a whole. The hurdle method of price discrimination reduces this loss by giving the monopolist a practical means of cutting prices for price-sensitive buyers only. In general, the more finely the monopolist can partition a market using the hurdle method, the smaller the efficiency loss. Hurdles are not perfect, however, and some degree of efficiency will inevitably be lost.

The Economic Naturalist 8.3

▶ Visit your instructor's Connect course and access your eBook to view this video.

Why might an appliance retailer hammer dents into the sides of its stoves and refrigerators?

Why might an appliance retailer instruct its clerks to hammer dents into the sides of its stoves and refrigerators?

The Sears "Scratch 'n' Dent Sale" is another example of how retailers use quality differentials to segregate buyers according to their reservation prices. Many Sears stores hold an annual sale in which they display appliances with minor scratches and blemishes in the parking lot at deep discounts. People who don't care much about price are unlikely to turn out for these events, but those with very low reservation prices often get up early to be first in line. Indeed, these sales have proven so popular that it might even be in a retailer's interest to put dents in some of its sale items deliberately.

RECAP ↑

USING DISCOUNTS TO EXPAND THE MARKET

A price-discriminating monopolist is one who charges different prices to different buyers for essentially the same good or service. A common method of price discrimination is the hurdle method, which involves granting a discount to buyers who jump over a hurdle such as mailing in a rebate coupon. An effective hurdle is one that is more easily cleared by buyers with low reservation prices than by buyers with high reservation prices. Such a hurdle enables the monopolist to expand output and thereby reduce the deadweight loss from monopoly pricing.

PUBLIC POLICY TOWARD NATURAL MONOPOLY ——

Monopoly is problematic not only because of the loss in efficiency associated with restricted output, but also because the monopolist earns an economic profit at the buyer's expense. Many people are understandably uncomfortable about having to purchase from the sole provider of any good or service. For this reason, voters in many societies have empowered government to adopt policies aimed at controlling natural monopolists.

There are several ways to achieve this aim. A government may assume ownership and control of a natural monopoly, or it may merely attempt to regulate the prices it charges. In some cases, government solicits competitive bids from private firms to produce natural monopoly services. In still other cases, governments attempt to dissolve natural monopolies into smaller entities that compete with one another. But many of these policies create economic problems of their own. In each case, the practical challenge is to come up with the solution that yields the greatest surplus of benefits over costs. Natural monopoly may be inefficient and unfair, but, as noted earlier, the alternatives to natural monopoly are far from perfect.

STATE OWNERSHIP AND MANAGEMENT

Natural monopoly is inefficient because the monopolist's profit-maximizing price is greater than its marginal cost. But even if the natural monopolist *wanted* to set price equal to marginal cost, it could not do so and hope to remain in business. After all, the defining feature of a natural monopoly is economies of scale in production, which means that marginal cost will always be less than average total cost. Setting price equal to marginal cost would fail to cover average total cost, which implies an economic loss.

Consider the case of a local cable Internet provider. Once an area has been wired for cable Internet, the marginal cost of adding an additional subscriber is very low. For the sake of efficiency, all subscribers should pay a price equal to that marginal cost. Yet a cable company that priced in this manner would never be able to recover the fixed cost of setting up the network. This same problem applies not just to Internet providers but to all other natural monopolies. Even if such firms wanted to set price equal to marginal cost (which, of course, they do not since they will earn more by setting marginal revenue equal to marginal cost), they cannot do so without suffering an economic loss.

One way to attack the efficiency and fairness problems is for the government to take over the industry, set price equal to marginal cost, and then absorb the resulting losses out of general tax revenues. This approach has been followed with good results in the state-owned electric utility industry in France, whose efficient pricing methods have set the standard for electricity pricing worldwide.

But state ownership and efficient management do not always go hand in hand. Granted, the state-owned natural monopoly is free to charge marginal cost, while the private natural monopoly is not. Yet the Incentive Principle directs our attention to the fact that private natural monopolies often face a much stronger incentive to cut costs than their government-owned counterparts. When the private monopolist figures out a way to cut $1 from the cost of production, its profit goes up by $1. But when the government manager of a state-owned monopoly cuts $1 from the cost of production, the government typically cuts the monopoly's budget by $1. Think back to your last visit to the Department of Motor Vehicles. Did it strike you as an efficiently managed organization?

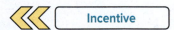

Incentive

Whether the efficiency that is gained by being able to set price equal to marginal cost outweighs the inefficiency that results from a weakened incentive to cut costs is an empirical question.

STATE REGULATION OF PRIVATE MONOPOLIES

In the United States, the most common method of curbing monopoly profits is for government to regulate the natural monopoly rather than own it. Most states, for example, take this approach with electric utilities, natural gas providers, local telephone companies, and cable Internet providers. The standard procedure in these cases is called **cost-plus regulation:** Government regulators gather data on the monopolist's explicit costs of production and then permit the monopolist to set prices that cover those costs, plus a markup to ensure a normal return on the firm's investment.

cost-plus regulation a method of regulation under which the regulated firm is permitted to charge prices that cover explicit costs of production plus a markup to cover the opportunity cost of resources provided by the firm's owners

While it may sound reasonable, cost-plus regulation has several pitfalls. First, it generates costly administrative proceedings in which regulators and firms quarrel over which of the firm's expenditures can properly be included in the costs it is allowed to recover. This question is difficult to answer even in theory. Consider a firm like AT&T, whose local telephone service is subject to cost-plus regulation but whose other products and services are unregulated. Many AT&T employees, from the president on down, are involved in both regulated and unregulated activities. How should their salaries be allocated between the two? The company has a strong incentive to argue for greater allocation to the regulated activities, which allows it to capture more revenue from captive customers in the local telephone market.

A second problem with cost-plus regulation is that it blunts the firm's incentive to adopt cost-saving innovations for when it does, regulators require the firm to cut its rates. The firm gets to keep its cost savings in the current period, which is a stronger incentive to cut costs than the one facing a government-owned monopoly. But the incentive to cut costs would be stronger still if the firm could retain its cost savings indefinitely. Furthermore, in cases in which regulators set rates by allowing the monopolist to add a fixed markup to costs incurred, the regulated monopolist may actually have an incentive to *increase* costs rather than reduce them. Outrageous though the thought may be, the monopolist may earn a higher profit by installing gold-plated faucets in the company restrooms.

Finally, cost-plus regulation does not solve the natural monopolist's basic problem: the inability to set price equal to marginal cost without losing money. Although these are all serious problems, governments seem to be in no hurry to abandon cost-plus regulation.

EXCLUSIVE CONTRACTING FOR NATURAL MONOPOLY

One of the most promising methods for dealing with natural monopoly is for the government to invite private firms to bid for the natural monopolist's market. The government specifies in detail the service it wants—cable Internet, fire protection, garbage collection—and firms submit bids describing how much they will charge for the service. The low bidder wins the contract.

The incentive to cut costs under such an arrangement is every bit as powerful as that facing ordinary competitive firms. Competition among bidders should also eliminate any concerns about the fairness of monopoly profits. And if the government is willing to provide a cash subsidy to the winning bidder, exclusive contracting even allows the monopolist to set price equal to marginal cost.

Contracting has been employed with good results in municipal fire protection and garbage collection. Communities that employ private companies to provide these services often spend only half as much as adjacent communities served by municipal fire and sanitation departments.

Despite these attractive features, however, exclusive contracting is not without problems, especially when the service to be provided is complex or requires a large fixed investment in capital equipment. In such cases, contract specifications may be so detailed and complicated that they become tantamount to regulating the firm directly. And in cases involving a large fixed investment—electric power generation and distribution, for example—officials face the question of how to transfer the assets if a new firm wins the contract. The winning firm naturally wants to acquire the assets as cheaply as possible, but the retiring firm is entitled to a fair price for them. What, in such cases, is a fair price?

Fire protection and garbage collection are simple enough that the costs of contracting out these functions are not prohibitive. But in other cases, such costs might easily outweigh any savings made possible by exclusive contracting.

VIGOROUS ENFORCEMENT OF ANTITRUST LAWS

The nineteenth century witnessed the accumulation of massive private fortunes, the likes of which had never been seen in the industrialized world. Public sentiment ran high against the so-called robber barons of the period—the Carnegies, Rockefellers, Mellons, and others. In 1890, Congress passed the Sherman Act, which declared illegal any conspiracy "to monopolize, or attempt to monopolize . . . any part of the trade or commerce among the several States." And in 1914, Congress passed the Clayton Act, whose aim was to prevent corporations from acquiring shares in a competitor if the transaction would "substantially lessen competition or create a monopoly."

Antitrust laws have helped prevent the formation of cartels, or coalitions of firms that collude to raise prices above competitive levels. But they also have caused some harm. For example, federal antitrust officials spent more than a decade trying to break up IBM Corporation in the belief that it had achieved an unhealthy dominance in the computer industry. That view was proved comically wrong by IBM's subsequent failure to foresee and profit from the rise of the personal computer. By breaking up large companies and discouraging mergers between companies in the same industry, antitrust laws may help promote competition, but they also may prevent companies from achieving economies of scale.

A final possibility is simply to ignore the problem of natural monopoly: to let the monopolist choose the quantity to produce and sell it at whatever price the market will bear. The obvious objections to this policy are the two we began with, namely, that a natural monopoly is not only inefficient but also unfair. But just as the hurdle method of price discrimination mitigates efficiency losses, it also lessens the concern about taking unfair advantage of buyers.

Consider first the source of the natural monopolist's economic profit. This firm, recall, is one with economies of scale, which means that its average production cost declines as output increases. Efficiency requires that price be set at marginal cost, but because the natural monopolist's marginal cost is lower than its average cost, it cannot charge all buyers the marginal cost without suffering an economic loss.

The depth and prevalence of discount pricing suggest that whatever economic profit a natural monopolist earns generally will not come out of the discount buyer's pocket. Although discount prices are higher than the monopolist's marginal cost of production, in most cases they are lower than the average cost. Thus, the monopolist's economic profit, if any, must come from buyers who pay list price. And since those buyers have the option, in most cases, of jumping a hurdle and paying a discount price, their contribution, if not completely voluntary, is at least not strongly coerced.

So much for the source of the monopolist's economic profit. What about its disposition? Who gets it? A large chunk—some 35 percent, in many cases—goes to the federal government via the corporate income tax. The remainder is paid out to shareholders, some of whom are wealthy and some of whom are not. These shareholder profits are also taxed by state and even local governments. In the end, two-thirds or more of a monopolist's economic profit may fund services provided by governments of various levels.

Both the source of the monopolist's economic profit (the list-price buyer) and the disposition of that profit (largely, to fund public services) cast doubt on the claim that monopoly profit constitutes a social injustice on any grand scale. Nevertheless, the hurdle method of differential pricing cannot completely eliminate the fairness and efficiency problems that result from monopoly pricing. In the end, then, we are left with a choice among imperfect alternatives. As the Cost-Benefit Principle emphasizes, the best choice is the one for which the balance of benefits over costs is largest. But which choice that is will depend on the circumstances at hand.

Cost-Benefit

RECAP ↑

PUBLIC POLICY TOWARD NATURAL MONOPOLY

The natural monopolist sets price above marginal cost, resulting in too little output from society's point of view (the efficiency problem). The natural monopolist also may earn an economic profit at buyers' expense (the fairness problem). Policies for dealing with the efficiency and fairness problems include state ownership and management, state regulation, exclusive contracting, and vigorous enforcement of antitrust laws. Each of these remedies entails problems of its own.

SUMMARY

- Our concern in this chapter was the conduct and performance of the imperfectly competitive firm, a firm that has at least some latitude to set its own price. Economists often distinguish among three different types of imperfectly competitive firms: the pure monopolist, the lone seller of a product in a given market; the oligopolist, one of only a few sellers of a given product; and the monopolistic competitor, one of a relatively large number of firms that sell similar though slightly differentiated products. *(LO1)*

- Although advanced courses in economics devote much attention to differences in behavior among these three types of firms, our focus was on the common feature that differentiates them from perfectly competitive firms. Whereas the perfectly competitive firm faces an infinitely elastic demand curve for its product, the imperfectly competitive firm faces a downward-sloping demand curve. For convenience, we use the term *monopolist* to refer to any of the three types of imperfectly competitive firms. *(LO1)*

- Monopolists are sometimes said to enjoy market power, a term that refers to their power to set the price of their product. Market power stems from exclusive control over important inputs, from economies of scale, from patents and government licenses or franchises, and from network economies. The most important and enduring of these five sources of market power are economies of scale and network economies. *(LO2)*

- Research, design, engineering, and other fixed costs account for an increasingly large share of all costs required to bring products successfully to market. For products with large fixed costs, marginal cost is lower, often substantially, than average total cost, and average total cost declines, often sharply, as output grows. This cost pattern explains why many industries are dominated by either a single firm or a small number of firms. *(LO3)*

- Unlike the perfectly competitive firm, for which marginal revenue exactly equals market price, the monopolist realizes a marginal revenue that is always less than its price.

This shortfall reflects the fact that to sell more output, the monopolist must cut the price not only to additional buyers but to existing buyers as well. For the monopolist with a straight-line demand curve, the marginal revenue curve has the same vertical intercept and a horizontal intercept that is half as large as the intercept for the demand curve. *(LO4)*

- Whereas the perfectly competitive firm maximizes profit by producing at the level at which marginal cost equals the market price, the monopolist maximizes profit by equating marginal cost with marginal revenue, which is significantly lower than the market price. The result is an output level that is best for the monopolist but smaller than the level that would be best for society as a whole. At the profit-maximizing level of output, the benefit of an extra unit of output (the market price) is greater than its cost (the marginal cost). At the socially efficient level of output, where the monopolist's marginal cost curve intersects the demand curve, the benefit and cost of an extra unit are the same. *(LO4, LO5)*

- Both the monopolist and its potential customers can do better if the monopolist can grant discounts to price-sensitive buyers. The extreme example is the perfectly discriminating monopolist, who charges each buyer exactly his or her reservation price. Such producers are socially efficient because they sell to every buyer whose reservation price is at least as high as the marginal cost. *(LO6)*

- The various policies that governments employ to mitigate concerns about fairness and efficiency losses arising from natural monopoly include state ownership and management of natural monopolies, state regulation, private contracting, and vigorous enforcement of antitrust laws. Each of these remedies entails costs as well as benefits. In some cases, a combination of policies will produce a better outcome than simply allowing natural monopolists to do as they please. But in other cases, a hands-off policy may be the best available option. *(LO7)*

KEY TERMS

constant returns to scale
cost-plus regulation
deadweight loss
hurdle method of price
  discrimination
imperfectly competitive firm
  (or price setter)

increasing returns to scale
  (or economies of scale)
marginal revenue
market power
monopolistic competition
natural monopoly
oligopoly

perfect hurdle
perfectly discriminating
  monopolist
price discrimination
pure monopoly

REVIEW QUESTIONS

1. What important characteristic do all three types of imperfectly competitive firms share? *(LO1)*

2. True or false: A firm with market power can sell whatever quantity it wishes at whatever price it chooses. *(LO2)*

3. Why do most successful industrial societies offer patents and copyright protection, even though these protections enable sellers to charge higher prices? *(LO2)*

4. Why is marginal revenue always less than price for a monopolist but equal to price for a perfectly competitive firm? *(LO4)*

5. True or false: Because a natural monopolist charges a price greater than marginal cost, it necessarily earns a positive economic profit. *(LO4)*

PROBLEMS

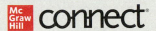

1. State whether the following statements are true or false, and explain why. *(LO1, LO2)*
   a. In a perfectly competitive industry, the industry demand curve is horizontal, whereas for a monopoly it is downward-sloping.
   b. Perfectly competitive firms have no control over the price they charge for their product.
   c. For a natural monopoly, average cost declines as the number of units produced increases over the relevant output range.

2. Two car manufacturers, Nissan and Honda, have fixed costs of $1 billion and marginal costs of $10,000 per car. If Nissan produces 50,000 cars per year and Honda produces 200,000, calculate the average production cost for each company. On the basis of these costs, which company's market share do you think will grow in relative terms? *(LO3)*

3. A single-price, profit-maximizing monopolist *(LO4)*
   a. causes excess demand, or shortages, by selling too few units of a good or service.
   b. chooses the output level at which marginal revenue begins to increase.
   c. always charges a price above the marginal cost of production.
   d. also maximizes marginal revenue.
   e. none of the above statements is true.

4. If a monopolist could perfectly price-discriminate *(LO4, LO5)*
   a. the marginal revenue curve and the demand curve would coincide.
   b. the marginal revenue curve and the marginal cost curve would coincide.
   c. every consumer would pay a different price.
   d. marginal revenue would become negative at some output level.
   e. the resulting pattern of exchange would still be socially inefficient.

5. What is the socially desirable price for a natural monopoly to charge? Why will a natural monopoly that attempts to charge the socially desirable price invariably suffer an economic loss? *(LO5, LO7)*

6. Explain why price discrimination and the existence of slightly different variants of the same product tend to go hand in hand. Give an example from your own experience. *(LO6)*

7. TotsPoses Inc., a profit-maximizing business, is the only photography business in town that specializes in portraits of small children. George, who owns and runs TotsPoses, expects to encounter an average of eight customers per day, each with a reservation price shown in the following table. Assume George has no fixed costs, and his cost of producing each portrait is $12. *(LO4, LO5, LO6)*

Customer	Reservation price ($ per photo)
1	50
2	46
3	42
4	38
5	34
6	30
7	26
8	22

   a. How much should charge if he must charge a single price to all customers? At this price, how many portraits will George produce each day? What will be his economic profit?
   b. How much consumer surplus is generated each day at this price?
   c. What is the socially efficient number of portraits?
   d. George is very experienced in the business and knows the reservation price of each of his customers. If he is allowed to charge any price he likes to

any consumer, how many portraits will he produce each day and how much economic profit will he earn?

e. In this case, how much consumer surplus is generated each day?

8. Refer back to Problem 7 and answer the following questions. *(LO5, LO6)*

a. Suppose George is permitted to charge two prices. He knows that customers with a reservation price above $30 never bother with coupons, whereas those with a reservation price of $30 or less always use them. At what level should George set the list price of a portrait? At what level should he set the discount price? How many photo portraits will he sell at each price?

b. In this case, what is George's economic profit and how much consumer surplus is generated each day?

9. Serena is a single-price, profit-maximizing monopolist in the sale of her own patented perfume, whose demand and marginal cost curves are as shown. *(LO4, LO5, LO6)*

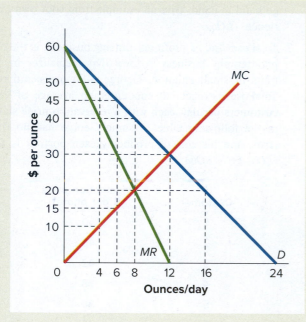

a. Relative to the consumer surplus that would result at the socially optimal quantity and price, how much consumer surplus is lost from her selling at the monopolist's profit-maximizing quantity and price?

b. How much total surplus would result if Serena could act as a perfectly price-discriminating monopolist?

10. Jada is a second-grader who sells lemonade on a street corner in your neighborhood. Each cup of lemonade costs Jada 20 cents to produce; she has no fixed costs. The reservation prices for the 10 people who walk by Jada's lemonade stand each day are listed in the following table.

Person	Reservation price
A	$1.00
B	$0.90
C	$0.80
D	$0.70
E	$0.60
F	$0.50
G	$0.40
H	$0.30
I	$0.20
J	$0.10

Jada knows the distribution of reservation prices (that is, she knows that one person is willing to pay $1, another $0.90, and so on), but she does not know any specific individual's reservation price. *(LO4, LO5, LO6)*

a. Calculate the marginal revenue of selling an additional cup of lemonade. (Start by figuring out the price Jada would charge if she produced only one cup of lemonade, and calculate the total revenue; then find the price Jada would charge if she sold two cups of lemonade; and so on.)

b. What is Jada's profit-maximizing price?

c. At that price, what are Jada's economic profit and total consumer surplus?

d. What price should Jada charge if she wants to maximize total economic surplus?

e. Now suppose Jada can tell the reservation price of each person. What price would she charge each person if she wanted to maximize profit? Compare her profit to the total surplus calculated in part d.

ANSWERS TO SELF-TESTS

8.1 The relevant cost figures are shown in the following table, which shows that Sony's unit-cost advantage is now $50.20 − $5.20 = $45.00. *(LO3)*

	Nintendo	Sony Computer Entertainment
Annual production	200,000	2,000,000
Fixed cost	$10,000,000	$10,000,000
Variable cost	$40,000	$400,000
Total cost	$10,040,000	$10,400,000
Average total cost per game	$50.20	$5.20

8.2 When the monopolist expands from 3 to 4 units per week, total revenue rises from $15 to $16 per week, which means that the marginal revenue from the sale of the fourth unit is only $1 per week. When the monopolist expands from 4 to 5 units per week, total revenue drops from $16 to $15 per week, which means that the marginal revenue from the sale of the fifth unit is actually negative, or −$1 per week. *(LO4)*

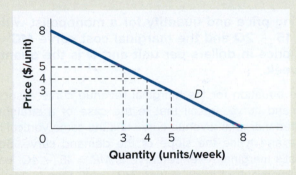

8.3 The profit-maximizing price and quantity are $P^* = $ 6/unit and $Q^* = 2$ units/week. *(LO4)*

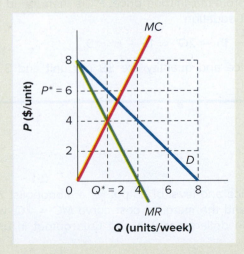

8.4 As column 4 in the following table shows, Preeti should again serve students *A, B,* and *C* in the list price submarket (at a price of $36) and only student *E* in the discount submarket (at a price of $32). *(LO6)*

(1) Student	(2) Reservation price ($ per paper)	(3) Total revenue ($ per week)	(4) Marginal revenue ($ per paper)
List Price Submarket			
			40
A	40	40	
			36
B	38	76	
			32
C	36	108	
			28
D	34	136	
Discount Price Submarket			
			32
E	32	32	
			28
F	30	60	
			24
G	28	84	
			20
H	26	104	

The Algebra of Monopoly Profit Maximization

In the text of this chapter, we developed the profit-maximization analysis for monopoly in a geometric framework. In this brief appendix, we show how this analysis can be done in an algebraic framework. The advantage of the algebraic framework is that it greatly simplifies computing the numerical values of the profit-maximizing prices and quantities.

EXAMPLE 8A.1   **Profit-Maximizing Price and Quantity**

Find the profit-maximizing price and quantity for a monopolist with the demand curve $P = 15 - 2Q$ and the marginal cost curve $MC = Q$, where P is the product price in dollars per unit and Q is the quantity in units of output per week.

The first step is to find the equation for the marginal revenue curve associated with the monopolist's demand curve. Recall that in the case of a straight-line demand curve, the associated marginal revenue curve has the same vertical intercept as the demand curve and twice the slope of the demand curve. So the equation for this monopolist's marginal revenue curve is $MR = 15 - 4Q$. Letting Q^* denote the profit-maximizing output level, setting $MR = MC$ then yields:

$$15 - 4Q^* = Q^*,$$

which solves for $Q^* = 3$. The profit-maximizing price, P^*, is then found by substituting $Q^* = 3$ into the demand equation:

$$P^* = 15 - 2Q^* = 15 - 6 = 9.$$

Thus, the profit-maximizing price and quantity are $9 per unit and 3 units per week, respectively.

✔ **SELF-TEST 8A.1**

Find the profit-maximizing price and level of output for a monopolist with the demand curve $P = 12 - Q$ and the marginal cost curve $MC = 2Q$, where P is the price of the product in dollars per unit and Q is output in units per week.

PROBLEMS

Mc Graw Hill **connect**

1. Suppose that the University of Michigan Cinema is a local monopoly whose demand curve for adult tickets on Saturday night is $P = 12 - 2Q$, where P is the price of a ticket in dollars and Q is the number of tickets sold in hundreds. The demand for children's tickets on Sunday afternoon is $P = 8 - 3Q$, and for adult tickets on Sunday afternoon, $P = 10 - 4Q$. On both Saturday night and Sunday afternoon, the marginal cost of an additional patron, child or adult, is \$2. *(LO4)*
   a. What is the marginal revenue curve in each of the three submarkets?
   b. What price should the cinema charge in each of the three markets if its goal is to maximize profit?

2. Suppose you are a monopolist in the market for a specific video game. Your demand curve is given by $P = 80 - Q/2$; your marginal cost curve is $MC = Q$. Your fixed costs equal \$400. *(LO4, LO5)*
   a. Graph the demand and marginal cost curves.
   b. Derive and graph the marginal revenue curve.
   c. Calculate and indicate on the graph the equilibrium price and quantity.
   d. What is your profit?
   e. What is the level of consumer surplus?

ANSWER TO APPENDIX SELF-TEST

8A.1 For the demand curve $P = 12 - Q$, the corresponding marginal revenue curve is $MR = 12 - 2Q$. Equating MR and MC, we solve the equation $12 - 2Q = 2Q$ for $Q = 3$. Substituting $Q = 3$ into the demand equation, we solve for the profit-maximizing price, $P = 12 - 3 = 9$. *(LO4)*

CHAPTER 9

Games and Strategic Behavior

Visual blight often results from the fact that the ability of a merchant's sign to attract attention depends on the size and brightness of other merchants' signs.

aluxum/Getty Images

LEARNING OBJECTIVES

After reading this chapter, you should be able to:

LO1 Describe the three basic elements of a game, how the possible payoffs are summarized, and the effect of dominant and dominated strategy choices.

LO2 Identify and explain the prisoner's dilemma and how it applies to real-world situations.

LO3 Explain games in which the timing of players' choices matters.

LO4 Discuss strategies that enable players to solve commitment problems through material or psychological incentives.

At a Christmas Eve dinner party in 1997, actor Robert DeNiro pulled aside singer Tony Bennett for a moment. "Hey, Tony—there's a film I want you in," DeNiro said. He was referring to the project that became the 1999 Warner Brothers hit comedy *Analyze This*, in which the troubled head of a crime family, played by DeNiro, seeks the counsel of a psychotherapist, played by Billy Crystal. In the script, both the mob boss and his therapist are big fans of Bennett's music.

Bennett heard nothing further about the project for almost a year. Then his son and financial manager, Danny Bennett, got a phone call from Warner Brothers, in which the studio offered Tony $15,000 to sing "Got the World on a String" in the movie's final scene. As Danny described the conversation, "They made a fatal mistake. They told me they had already shot the film. So I'm like: 'Hey, they shot the whole film around Tony being the end gag and they're offering me $15,000?'"[1]

---

[1]As quoted by Geraldine Fabrikant, "Talking Money with Tony Bennett," *The New York Times,* May 2, 1999, Money & Business, p. 1.

Warner Brothers wound up paying $200,000 for Bennett's performance.

In business negotiations, as in life, timing can be everything. If executives at Warner Brothers had thought the problem through carefully, they would have negotiated with Bennett *before* shooting the movie. At that point, Bennett would have realized that the script could be rewritten if he asked too high a fee. By waiting, studio executives left themselves with no attractive option other than to pay Bennett's price.

The payoff to many actions depends not only on the actions themselves, but also on when they're taken and how they relate to actions taken by others. In previous chapters, economic decision makers confronted an environment that was essentially fixed. This chapter will focus on cases in which people must consider the effect of their behavior on others. For example, an imperfectly competitive firm will want to weigh the likely responses of rivals when deciding whether to cut prices or to increase its advertising budget. Interdependencies of this sort are the rule rather than the exception in economic and social life. To make sense of the world we live in, then, we must take these interdependencies into account.

Our focus in Chapter 8, *Monopoly, Oligopoly, and Monopolistic Competition*, was on the pure monopolist. In this chapter, we'll explore how a few simple principles from the theory of games can help us better understand the behavior of oligopolists and monopolistic competitors—the two types of imperfectly competitive firms for which strategic interdependencies are most important. Along the way, we'll also see how the same principles enable us to answer a variety of interesting questions drawn from everyday social interaction.

USING GAME THEORY TO ANALYZE STRATEGIC DECISIONS

In chess, tennis, or any other game, the payoff to a given move depends on what your opponent does in response. In choosing your move, therefore, you must anticipate your opponent's responses, how you might respond, and what further moves your own response might elicit. Economists and other behavioral scientists have devised the theory of games to analyze situations in which the payoffs to different actors depend on the actions their opponents take.

THE THREE ELEMENTS OF A GAME

basic elements of a game
the players, the strategies available to each player, and the payoffs each player receives for each possible combination of strategies

A game has three **basic elements:** the players, the list of possible actions (or strategies) available to each player, and the payoffs the players receive for each possible combination of strategies. We'll use a series of examples to illustrate how these elements combine to form the basis of a theory of behavior.

The first example focuses on an important strategic decision confronting two oligopolists who produce an undifferentiated product and must decide how much to spend on advertising.

| EXAMPLE 9.1 | The Cost of Advertising |

Should United Airlines spend more money on advertising?

Suppose that United Airlines and American Airlines are the only air carriers that serve the Chicago–St. Louis market. Each currently earns an economic profit of $6,000 per flight on this route. If United increases its advertising spending in this market by $1,000 per flight, and American spends no more on advertising than it does now, United's profit will rise to $8,000 per flight and American's will fall to $2,000. If both spend $1,000 more on advertising, each will earn an economic profit of $5,500 per flight. These payoffs are symmetric so that if United spends the same amount on advertising while American increases its spending by $1,000, United's economic profit will fall to $2,000 per flight and American's will rise to $8,000. The payoff structure is also common knowledge—that is, each company knows what the relevant payoffs will be for both parties under each of the possible combinations of choices. If each must decide independently whether to increase spending on advertising, what should United do?

TABLE 9.1
The Payoff Matrix for an Advertising Game

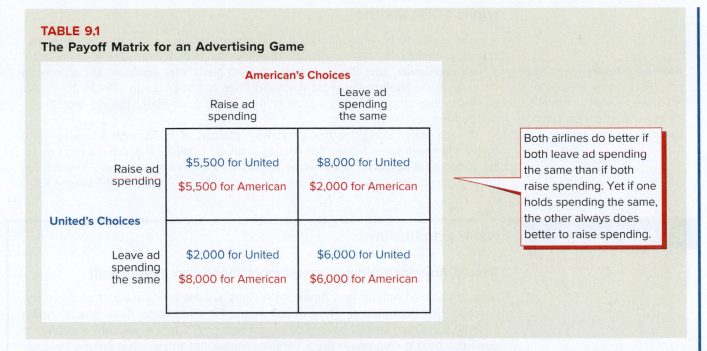

	American's Choices	
	Raise ad spending	Leave ad spending the same
Raise ad spending	$5,500 for United / $5,500 for American	$8,000 for United / $2,000 for American
Leave ad spending the same	$2,000 for United / $8,000 for American	$6,000 for United / $6,000 for American

United's Choices

> Both airlines do better if both leave ad spending the same than if both raise spending. Yet if one holds spending the same, the other always does better to raise spending.

   Think of this situation as a game. What are its three elements? The players are the two airlines. Each airline must choose one of two strategies: to raise ad spending by $1,000 or leave it the same. The payoffs are the economic profits that correspond to the four possible scenarios resulting from their choices. One way to summarize the relevant information about this game is to display the players, strategies, and payoffs in the form of a simple table called a **payoff matrix** (see Table 9.1).

   Confronted with the payoff matrix in Table 9.1, what should United Airlines do? The essence of strategic thinking is to begin by looking at the situation from the other party's point of view. Suppose United assumes that American will raise its spending on advertising (the left column in Table 9.1). In that case, United's best bet would be to follow suit (the top row in Table 9.1). Why is the top row United's best response when American chooses the left column? United's economic profits, given in the upper-left cell of Table 9.1, will be $5,500, compared to only $2,000 if it keeps spending the same (see the lower-left cell).

   Alternatively, suppose United assumes that American will keep ad spending the same (that is, that American will choose the right column in Table 9.1). In that case, United would still do better to increase spending because it would earn $8,000 (the upper-right cell), compared to only $6,000 if it keeps spending the same (the lower-right cell). In this particular game, no matter which strategy American chooses, United will earn a higher economic profit by increasing its spending on advertising. And since this game is perfectly symmetric, a similar conclusion holds for American: No matter which strategy United chooses, American will do better by increasing its spending on ads.

   When one player has a strategy that yields a higher payoff no matter which choice the other player makes, that player is said to have a **dominant strategy.** Not all games involve dominant strategies, but both players in this game have one, and that is to increase spending on ads. For both players, to leave ad spending the same is a **dominated strategy**—one that leads to a lower payoff than an alternative choice, regardless of the other player's choice.

   Notice, however, that when each player chooses the dominant strategy, the resulting payoffs are smaller than if each had left spending unchanged. When United and American increase their spending on ads, each earns only $5,500 in economic profits, compared to the $6,000 each would have earned without the increase.

payoff matrix a table that describes the payoffs in a game for each possible combination of strategies

dominant strategy one that yields a higher payoff no matter what the other players in a game choose

dominated strategy any other strategy available to a player who has a dominant strategy

NASH EQUILIBRIUM

Nash equilibrium any combination of strategy choices in which each player's choice is his or her best choice, given the other players' choices

A game is said to be in equilibrium if each player's strategy is the best he or she can choose, given the other players' choices. This definition of equilibrium is sometimes called a **Nash equilibrium,** after the mathematician John Nash, who developed the concept in the early 1950s. Nash was awarded the Nobel Prize in Economics in 1994 for his contributions to game theory.[2] When a game is in equilibrium, no player has any incentive to deviate from his current strategy.

If each player in a game has a dominant strategy, as in Example 9.1, equilibrium occurs when each player follows that strategy. But even in games in which not every player has a dominant strategy, we can often identify an equilibrium outcome. Consider, for instance, the following variation on the advertising game as illustrated in Example 9.2.

EXAMPLE 9.2	**Nash Equilibrium**

Should American Airlines spend more money on advertising?

Suppose United Airlines and American Airlines are the only carriers that serve the Chicago–St. Louis market. Their payoff matrix for advertising decisions is shown in Table 9.2. Does United have a dominant strategy? Does American? If each firm does the best it can, given the incentives facing the other, what will be the outcome of this game?

In this game, no matter what United does, American will do better to raise its ad spending, so raising the advertising budget is a dominant strategy for American. United, however, does not have a dominant strategy. If American raises its spending, United will do better to leave its spending unchanged; but if American does not raise spending, United will do better to spend more. Even though United doesn't have a dominant strategy, we can employ the Incentive Principle to predict

---

TABLE 9.2
Equilibrium When One Player Lacks a Dominant Strategy

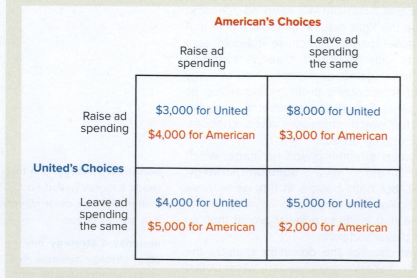

	American's Choices	
	Raise ad spending	Leave ad spending the same
Raise ad spending	$3,000 for United / $4,000 for American	$8,000 for United / $3,000 for American
United's Choices		
Leave ad spending the same	$4,000 for United / $5,000 for American	$5,000 for United / $2,000 for American

In this game, United lacks a dominant strategy, but American's dominant strategy is to raise its ad spending. Because United can predict that American will choose the left column, United will do best to leave its ad spending the same. Equilibrium occurs in the lower-left cell.

---

[2]Nash was awarded the Nobel Prize in Economics in 1994 for his contributions to game theory. His life was also the subject of the Academy Award–winning film *A Beautiful Mind*.

what is likely to happen in this game. United's managers are assumed to know what the payoff matrix is, so they can predict that American will spend more on ads since that is American's dominant strategy. Thus the best strategy for United, given the prediction that American will spend more on ads, is to keep its own spending unchanged. If both players do the best they can, taking account of the incentives each faces, this game will end in the lower-left cell of the payoff matrix: American will raise its spending on ads and United will not.

Incentive

Note that the choices corresponding to the lower-left cell in Table 9.2 satisfy the definition of a Nash equilibrium. If United found itself in that cell, its alternative would be to raise its ad spending, a move that would reduce its payoff from $4,000 to $3,000. So United has no incentive to abandon the lower-left cell. Similarly, if American found itself in the lower-left cell of Table 9.2, its alternative would be to leave ad spending the same, a move that would reduce its payoff from $5,000 to $2,000. So American also has no incentive to abandon the lower-left cell. The lower-left cell of Table 9.2 is a Nash equilibrium—a combination of strategies for which each player's choice is the best available option, given the choice made by the other player.

 SELF-TEST 9.1

What should United and American do if their payoff matrix is modified as follows?

		American	
		Raise ad spending	Leave spending the same
United	Raise ad spending	$3,000 for United $8,000 for American	$4,000 for United $5,000 for American
	Leave spending the same	$8,000 for United $4,000 for American	$5,000 for United $2,000 for American

RECAP

USING GAME THEORY TO ANALYZE STRATEGIC DECISIONS

The three elements of any game are the players, the list of strategies from which they can choose, and the payoffs to each combination of strategies. This information can be summarized in a payoff matrix.

Equilibrium in a game occurs when each player's strategy choice yields the highest payoff available, given the strategies chosen by other players. Such a combination of strategies is called a Nash equilibrium.

THE PRISONER'S DILEMMA

prisoner's dilemma a game in which each player has a dominant strategy, and when each plays it, the resulting payoffs are smaller than if each had played a dominated strategy

The first advertising example we discussed above belongs to an important class of games called the **prisoner's dilemma.** In the prisoner's dilemma, when each player chooses a dominant strategy, the result is unattractive to the group of players as a whole.

THE ORIGINAL PRISONER'S DILEMMA

The next example recounts the original scenario from which the prisoner's dilemma drew its name.

EXAMPLE 9.3   Prisoner's Dilemma

Should the prisoners confess?

Two prisoners, Horace and Jasper, are being held in separate cells for a serious crime that they did in fact commit. The prosecutor, however, has enough hard evidence to convict them of only a minor offense, for which the penalty is a year in jail. Each prisoner is told that if one confesses while the other remains silent, the confessor will be cleared of the crime, and the other will spend 20 years in prison. If both confess, they will get an intermediate sentence of 5 years. These payoffs are summarized in Table 9.3. The two prisoners are not allowed to communicate with one another. Do they have a dominant strategy? If so, what is it?

In this game, the dominant strategy for each prisoner is to confess. No matter what Jasper does, Horace will get a lighter sentence by speaking out. If Jasper confesses, Horace will get 5 years (upper-left cell) instead of 20 (lower-left cell). If Jasper remains silent, Horace will go free (upper-right cell) instead of spending a year in jail (lower-right cell). Because the payoffs are perfectly symmetric, Jasper will also do better to confess, no matter what Horace does. The difficulty is that when each follows his dominant strategy and confesses, both will do worse than if each had shown restraint. When both confess, they each get 5 years (upper-left cell), instead of the 1 year they would have gotten by remaining silent (lower-right cell). Hence the name of this game, the prisoner's dilemma.

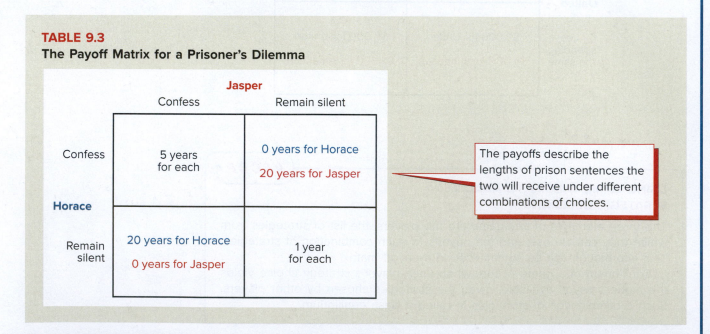

TABLE 9.3
The Payoff Matrix for a Prisoner's Dilemma

	Jasper	
	Confess	Remain silent
Horace Confess	5 years for each	0 years for Horace 20 years for Jasper
Horace Remain silent	20 years for Horace 0 years for Jasper	1 year for each

The payoffs describe the lengths of prison sentences the two will receive under different combinations of choices.

✔ SELF-TEST 9.2

GM and Chrysler must both decide whether to invest in a new process. Games 1 and 2 below show how their profits (in millions of dollars) depend on the decisions they might make. Which of these games is a prisoner's dilemma?

Game 1

Chrysler

	Don't invest	Invest
Don't invest	10 for each	4 for GM 12 for Chrysler
Invest	12 for GM 4 for Chrysler	5 for each

(GM labels the rows)

Game 2

Chrysler

	Don't invest	Invest
Don't invest	4 for GM 12 for Chrysler	5 for each
Invest	10 for each	12 for GM 4 for Chrysler

(GM labels the rows)

The prisoner's dilemma is one of the most powerful metaphors in all of human behavioral science. Countless social and economic interactions have payoff structures analogous to the one confronted by the two prisoners. Some of those interactions occur between only two players, as in the examples just discussed; many others involve larger groups. Games of the latter sort are called *multiplayer prisoner's dilemmas*. But regardless of the number of players involved, the common thread is one of conflict between the narrow self-interest of individuals and the broader interests of larger communities.

THE ECONOMICS OF CARTELS

A **cartel** is any coalition of firms that conspires to restrict production for the purpose of earning an economic profit. As we will see in the next example, the problem confronting oligopolists who are trying to form a cartel is a classic illustration of the prisoner's dilemma.

cartel a coalition of firms that agree to restrict output for the purpose of earning an economic profit

The Economic Naturalist 9.1

Why are cartel agreements notoriously unstable?

Consider a market for bottled water served by two oligopolists, Aquapure and Mountain Spring. Each firm can draw water free of charge from a mineral spring located on its own land. Customers supply their own bottles. Rather than compete with one another, the two firms decide to join together by selling water at the price a profit-maximizing pure monopolist would charge. Under their agreement (which constitutes a cartel), each firm would produce and sell half the quantity of water demanded by the market at the monopoly price (see Figure 9.1). The agreement isn't legally enforceable, however, which means that each firm has the option of charging less than the agreed price. If one firm sells water for less than the other firm, it will capture the entire quantity demanded by the market at the lower price.

Why is this agreement likely to collapse?

Since the marginal cost of mineral water is zero, the profit-maximizing quantity for a monopolist with the demand curve shown in Figure 9.1 is

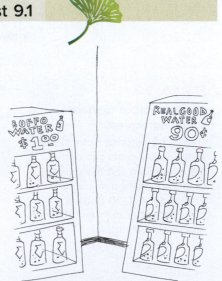

Why is it so difficult for companies to enforce agreements against price cutting?

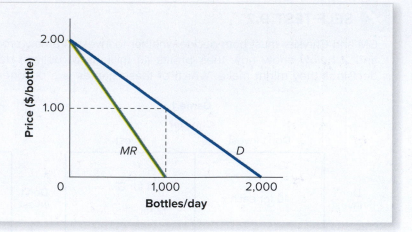

1,000 bottles per day, the quantity for which marginal revenue equals marginal cost. At that quantity, the monopoly price is $1 per bottle. If the firms abide by their agreement, each will sell half the market total, or 500 bottles per day, at a price of $1 per bottle, for an economic profit of $500 per day.

But suppose Aquapure reduced its price to 90 cents per bottle. By underselling Mountain Spring, it would capture the entire quantity demanded by the market, which, as shown in Figure 9.2, is 1,100 bottles per day. Aquapure's economic profit would rise from $500 per day to ($0.90 per bottle)(1,100 bottles per day) = $990 per day—almost twice as much as before. In the process, Mountain Spring's economic profit would fall from $500 per day to zero. Rather than see its economic profit disappear, Mountain Spring would match Aquapure's price cut, recapturing its original 50 percent share of the market. But when each firm charges $0.90 per bottle and sells 550 bottles per day, each earns an economic profit of ($0.90 per bottle)(550 bottles per day) = $495 per day, or $5 less per day than before.

Suppose we view the cartel agreement as an economic game in which the two available strategies are to sell for $1 per bottle or to sell for $0.90 per bottle. The payoffs are the economic profits that result from these strategies. Table 9.4 shows the payoff matrix for this game. Each firm's dominant strategy is to sell at the lower price, yet in following that strategy, each earns a lower profit than if each had sold at the higher price.

The game does not end with both firms charging $0.90 per bottle. Each firm knows that if it cuts the price a little further, it can recapture the entire market

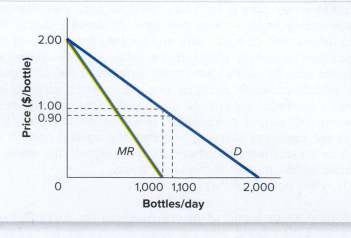

TABLE 9.4
The Payoff Matrix for a Cartel Agreement

	Mountain Spring	
	Charge $1/bottle	Charge $0.90/bottle
Aquapure Charge $1/bottle	$500/day for each	$0 for Aquapure $990/day for Mt. Spring
Charge $0.90/bottle	$990/day Aquapure $0 for Mt. Spring	$495/day for each

The dominant strategy for each firm is to charge $0.90 per bottle, or 10 cents per bottle less than called for by the cartel agreement. Hence the notorious instability of cartel agreements.

and, in the process, earn a substantially higher economic profit. At every step, the rival firm will match any price cut, until the price falls all the way to the marginal cost—in this example, zero.

Cartel agreements confront participants with the economic incentives inherent in the prisoner's dilemma, which explains why such agreements have historically been so unstable. Usually a cartel involves not just two firms, but several; an arrangement that can make retaliation against price cutters extremely difficult. In many cases, discovering which parties have broken the agreement is difficult. For example, the Organization of the Petroleum Exporting Countries (OPEC), a cartel of oil producers formed in the 1970s to restrict oil production, has no practical way to prevent member countries from secretly pumping oil offshore in the dead of night.

TIT-FOR-TAT AND THE REPEATED PRISONER'S DILEMMA

When all players cooperate in a prisoner's dilemma, each gets a higher payoff than when all defect. So people who confront prisoner's dilemmas will be on the lookout for ways to create incentives for mutual cooperation. What they need is some way to penalize players who defect. When players interact with one another only once, this turns out to be difficult. But when they expect to interact repeatedly, new possibilities emerge.

A **repeated prisoner's dilemma** is a standard prisoner's dilemma that confronts the same players not just once but many times. Experimental research on repeated prisoner's dilemmas in the 1960s identified a simple strategy that proves remarkably effective at limiting defection. The strategy is called **tit-for-tat,** and here's how it works: The first time you interact with someone, you cooperate. In each subsequent interaction, you simply do what that person did in the previous interaction. Thus, if your partner defected on your first interaction, you'd then defect on your next interaction with her. If she then cooperates, your move next time will be to cooperate as well.

On the basis of elaborate computer simulations, University of Michigan political scientist Robert Axelrod showed that tit-for-tat was a remarkably effective strategy, even when pitted against a host of ingenious counterstrategies that had been designed for the explicit purpose of trying to exploit it. The success of tit-for-tat requires a reasonably stable set of players, each of whom can remember what other players have done in

repeated prisoner's dilemma a standard prisoner's dilemma that confronts the same players repeatedly

tit-for-tat a strategy for the repeated prisoner's dilemma in which players cooperate on the first move and then mimic their partner's last move on each successive move

previous interactions. It also requires that players have a significant stake in what happens in the future, for it is the fear of retaliation that deters people from defecting.

Because rival firms in the same industry interact with one another repeatedly, it might seem that the tit-for-tat strategy would ensure widespread collusion to raise prices. And yet, as noted earlier, cartel agreements are notoriously unsuccessful. One difficulty is that tit-for-tat's effectiveness depends on there being only two players in the game. In competitive and monopolistically competitive industries, there are generally many firms, and even in oligopolies there are often several. When there are more than two firms and one defects now, how do the cooperators selectively punish the defector later? By cutting price? That will penalize everyone, not just the defector. Even if there are only two firms in an industry, these firms realize that other firms may enter their industry. So the would-be cartel members have to worry not only about each other, but also about the entire list of firms that might decide to compete with them. Each firm may see this as a hopeless task and decide to defect now, hoping to reap at least some economic profit in the short run. What seems clear, in any event, is that the practical problems involved in implementing tit-for-tat have made it difficult to hold cartel agreements together for long.

The Economic Naturalist 9.2

How did Congress unwittingly solve the television advertising dilemma confronting cigarette producers?

In 1970, Congress enacted a law making cigarette advertising on television illegal after January 1, 1971. As evidenced by the steadily declining proportion of Americans who smoke, this law seems to have achieved its stated purpose of protecting citizens against a proven health hazard. But the law also had an unintended effect, which was to increase the economic profit of cigarette makers, at least in the short run. In the year before the law's passage, manufacturers spent more than $300 million on advertising—about $60 million more than they spent during the year after the law was enacted. Much of the saving in advertising expenditures in 1971 was reflected in higher cigarette profits at year-end. But if eliminating television advertising made companies more profitable, why didn't the manufacturers eliminate the ads on their own?

When an imperfectly competitive firm advertises its product, its demand curve shifts rightward, for two reasons. First, people who have never used that type of product learn about it, and some buy it. Second, people who consume a different brand of the product may switch brands. The first effect boosts sales industrywide; the second merely redistributes existing sales among brands.

Although advertising produces both effects in the cigarette industry, its primary effect is brand switching. Thus, the decision of whether to advertise confronts the individual firm with a prisoner's dilemma. Table 9.5 shows the payoffs facing a pair of cigarette producers trying to decide whether to advertise. If both firms advertise on TV (upper-left cell), each earns a profit of only $10 million per year, compared to a profit of $20 million per year for each if neither advertises (lower-right cell). Clearly, both will benefit if neither advertises.

Yet note the powerful incentive that confronts each firm. RJR (the R.J. Reynolds Tobacco Company) sees that if Philip Morris doesn't advertise, RJR can earn higher profits by advertising ($35 million per year) than by not advertising ($20 million per year). RJR also sees that if Philip Morris does advertise, RJR will again earn more by advertising

Why were cigarette manufacturers happy when Congress made it illegal for them to advertise on television?

TABLE 9.5
Profits from Cigarette Advertising as a Prisoner's Dilemma

		Philip Morris	
		Advertise on TV	Don't advertise on TV
RJR	Advertise on TV	$10 million/yr for each	$35 million/yr for RJR $5 million/yr for Philip Morris
	Don't advertise on TV	$5 million/yr for RJR $35 million/yr for Philip Morris	$20 million/yr for each

In many industries, the primary effect of advertising is to encourage consumers to switch brands. In such industries, the dominant strategy is to advertise heavily (upper-left cell), even though firms as a group would do better by not advertising (lower-right cell).

($10 million per year) than by not advertising ($5 million per year). Thus, RJR's dominant strategy is to advertise. And because the payoffs are symmetric, Philip Morris's dominant strategy is also to advertise. So when each firm behaves rationally from its own point of view, the two together do worse than if they had both shown restraint. The congressional ad ban forced cigarette manufacturers to do what they could not have accomplished on their own.

As the following Economic Naturalist 9.3 example makes clear, understanding the prisoner's dilemma can help the economic naturalist make sense of human behavior not only in the world of business, but also in other domains of life as well.

The Economic Naturalist 9.3

Why do people shout at parties?

Whenever large numbers of people gather for conversation in a closed space, the ambient noise level rises sharply. After attending such gatherings, people often complain of sore throats and hoarse voices. If everyone spoke at a normal volume at parties, the overall noise level would be lower, and people would hear just as well. So why do people shout?

The problem involves the difference between individual incentives and group incentives. Suppose everyone starts by speaking at a normal level. But because of the crowded conditions, conversation partners have difficulty hearing one another, even when no one is shouting. The natural solution, from the point of the individual, is to simply raise one's voice a bit. But that is also the natural solution for everyone else. And when everyone speaks more loudly, the ambient noise level rises so that no one hears any better than before.

No matter what others do, the individual will do better by speaking more loudly. Doing so is a dominant strategy for everyone, in fact. Yet when everyone follows

▶ Visit your instructor's Connect course and access your eBook to view this video.

Why do people shout at parties?

the dominant strategy, the result is worse (no one can hear well) than if everyone had continued to speak normally. While shouting is wasteful, individuals acting alone have no better option. If anyone were to speak softly while others shout, that person wouldn't be heard. No one wants to go home with raw vocal cords, but people apparently prefer that cost to the alternative of not being heard at all.

> **RECAP** ↑
>
> **THE PRISONER'S DILEMMA**
>
> The prisoner's dilemma is a game in which each player has a dominant strategy, and in which the payoff to each player when each chooses that strategy is smaller than if each had chosen a dominated strategy. Incentives analogous to those found in the prisoner's dilemma help explain a broad range of behavior in business and everyday life—among them excessive spending on advertising and cartel instability. The tit-for-tat strategy can help sustain cooperation in two-player repeated prisoner's dilemmas but tends to be ineffective in multiplayer repeated prisoner's dilemmas.

GAMES IN WHICH TIMING MATTERS

In the games discussed so far, players were assumed to choose their strategies simultaneously, and which player moved first didn't matter. For example, in the prisoner's dilemma, self-interested players would follow their dominant strategies even if they knew in advance what strategies their opponents had chosen. But in other situations, such as the negotiations between Warner Brothers and Tony Bennett described at the beginning of this chapter, timing is of the essence.

We begin with an example of a game whose outcome cannot be predicted if both players move simultaneously, but whose outcome is clear if one player has the opportunity to move before the other.

EXAMPLE 9.4   **The Importance of Timing**

Should Ford build a hybrid Mustang?

The Ford Mustang and the Chevrolet Camaro compete for a limited pool of domestic sports car enthusiasts. Each company knows that the other is considering whether to bring out a hybrid version of its car. If both companies bring out hybrids, each will earn $60 million in profit. If neither brings out a hybrid, each company will earn $50 million. If Chevrolet introduces a hybrid and Ford does not, Chevrolet will earn $80 million and Ford will earn $70 million. If Ford brings out a hybrid and Chevrolet does not, Ford will earn $80 million and Chevrolet will earn $70 million. Does either firm have a dominant strategy in this situation? What will happen in this game if Ford gets to choose first, with Chevrolet choosing after having seen Ford's choice?

When both companies must make their decisions simultaneously, the payoff matrix for the example looks like Table 9.6.

The logic of the profit figures in Table 9.6 is that although consumers generally like the idea of a hybrid sports car (hence the higher profits when both companies bring out hybrids than when neither does), the companies will have to compete more heavily with one another if both offer the same type of car (and

TABLE 9.6
The Advantage of Being Different

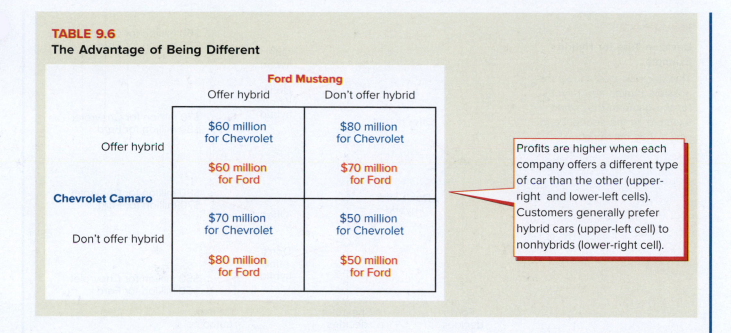

		Ford Mustang	
		Offer hybrid	Don't offer hybrid
Chevrolet Camaro	Offer hybrid	$60 million for Chevrolet $60 million for Ford	$80 million for Chevrolet $70 million for Ford
	Don't offer hybrid	$70 million for Chevrolet $80 million for Ford	$50 million for Chevrolet $50 million for Ford

> Profits are higher when each company offers a different type of car than the other (upper-right and lower-left cells). Customers generally prefer hybrid cars (upper-left cell) to nonhybrids (lower-right cell).

hence the lower profits when both offer the same type of car than when each offers a different type).

In the payoff matrix in Table 9.6, neither company has a dominant strategy. The best outcome for Ford is to offer a hybrid Mustang while Chevrolet does not offer a hybrid Camaro (lower-left cell). The best outcome for Chevrolet is to offer a hybrid Camaro while Ford does not offer a hybrid Mustang (upper-right cell). Both the lower-left and upper-right cells are Nash equilibria of this game because if the companies found themselves in either of these cells, neither would unilaterally want to change its position. Thus, in the upper-right cell, Chevrolet wouldn't want to change (that cell is, after all, the best possible outcome for Chevrolet), and neither would Ford (since switching to a hybrid would reduce its profit from $70 million to $60 million). But without being told more, we simply cannot predict where the two companies will end up.

If one side can move before the other, however, the incentives for action become instantly clearer. For games in which timing matters, a **decision tree,** or **game tree,** is a more useful way of representing the payoffs than a traditional payoff matrix. This type of diagram describes the possible moves in the sequence in which they may occur, and lists the final payoffs for each possible combination of moves.

If Ford has the first move, the decision tree for the game is shown in Figure 9.3. At *A,* Ford begins the game by deciding whether to offer a hybrid. If it chooses to offer one, Chevrolet must then make its own choice at *B.* If Ford does not offer a hybrid, Chevrolet will make its choice at *C.* In either case, once Chevrolet makes its choice, the game is over.

In thinking strategically about this game, the key for Ford is to put itself in Chevrolet's shoes and imagine how Chevrolet would react to the various choices it might confront. In general, it will make sense for Ford to assume that Chevrolet will respond in a self-interested way—that is, by choosing the available option that offers the highest profit for Chevrolet. Ford knows that if it chooses to offer a hybrid, Chevy's best option at *B* will be not to offer a hybrid (since Chevy's profit is $10 million higher at *E* than at *D*). Ford also knows that if it chooses not to offer a hybrid, Chevy's best option at *C* will be to offer one (since Chevy's profit is $30 million higher at *F* than at *G*). Ford thus knows that if it offers a hybrid, it will end up at *E,* where it will earn $80 million, whereas if it does not offer a hybrid, it will

decision tree (or **game tree**) a diagram that describes the possible moves in a game in sequence and lists the payoffs that correspond to each possible combination of moves

FIGURE 9.3

Decision Tree for Hybrid Example.

This decision tree shows the possible moves and payoffs for the game in the hybrid example, in the sequence in which they may occur.

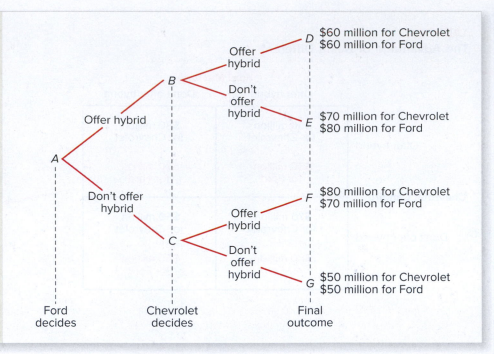

end up at *F*, where it will earn only $70 million. So when Ford has the first move in this game, its best strategy is to offer a hybrid. And Chevrolet then follows by choosing not to offer one.

Note that, in this game, the company that moves first has a considerable advantage. By moving first, Ford is able to earn $80 million compared to Chevrolet's $70 million. In general, being the first company to introduce a desirable product innovation is highly profitable. This undoubtedly explains the real-world battle between Ford and Chevrolet to introduce the first hybrid versions of their cars.

CREDIBLE THREATS AND PROMISES

credible threat a threat to take an action that is in the threatener's interest to carry out

Could Chevrolet have deterred Ford from offering a hybrid by threatening to offer a hybrid of its own, no matter what Ford did? The problem with this strategy is such a threat would not have been credible. In the language of game theory, a **credible threat** is one that will be in the threatener's interest to carry out when the time comes to act. As the Incentive Principle suggests, people are likely to be skeptical of any threat if they know there will be no incentive to follow through when the time comes. The problem here is that Ford knows that it would not be in Chevrolet's interest to carry out its threat in the event that Ford offered a hybrid. After all, once Ford has already offered the hybrid, Chevy's best option is to offer a nonhybrid.

The concept of a credible threat figured prominently in the negotiations between Warner Brothers' managers and Tony Bennett over the matter of Mr. Bennett's fee for performing in *Analyze This*. Once most of the film had been shot, managers knew they couldn't threaten credibly to refuse Mr. Bennett's salary demand because at that point adapting the film to another singer would have been extremely costly. In contrast, a similar threat made before production of the movie had begun would have been credible.

credible promise a promise to take an action that is in the promiser's interest to keep

Just as in some games credible threats are impossible to make, in others **credible promises** are impossible. A credible promise is one that is in the interests of the promiser to keep when the time comes to act. In the following example, both players suffer because of the inability to make a credible promise.

EXAMPLE 9.5   A Credible Promise

Should the business owner open a remote office?

The owner of a thriving business wants to start up an office in a distant city. If she hires someone to manage the new office, she can afford to pay a weekly salary of $1,000—a premium of $500 over what the manager would otherwise be able to earn—and still earn a weekly economic profit of $1,000 for herself. The owner's concern is that she won't be able to monitor the manager's behavior. The owner knows that by managing the remote office dishonestly, the manager can boost his take-home pay to $1,500 while causing the owner an economic loss of $500 per week. If the owner believes that all managers are selfish income-maximizers, will she open the new office?

The decision tree for the remote-office game is shown in Figure 9.4. At *A*, the managerial candidate promises to manage honestly, which brings the owner to *B*, where she must decide whether to open the new office. If she opens it, they reach *C*, where the manager must decide whether to manage honestly. If the manager's only goal is to make as much money as he can, he will manage dishonestly (bottom branch at *C*) because, that way, he will earn $500 more than by managing honestly (top branch at *C*).

So if the owner opens the new office, she will end up with an economic loss of $500. If she had not opened the office (bottom branch at *B*), she would have realized an economic profit of zero. Because zero is better than −$500, the owner will choose not to open the remote office. In the end, the opportunity cost of the manager's inability to make a credible promise is $1,500: the manager's forgone $500 salary premium and the owner's forgone $1,000 return.

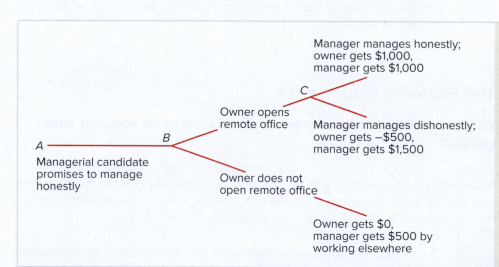

Manager manages honestly; owner gets $1,000, manager gets $1,000

C

Owner opens remote office

Manager manages dishonestly; owner gets −$500, manager gets $1,500

A

Managerial candidate promises to manage honestly

B

Owner does not open remote office

Owner gets $0, manager gets $500 by working elsewhere

FIGURE 9.4

Decision Tree for the Remote-Office Game.

The best outcome is for the owner to open the office at *B* and for the manager to manage the office honestly at *C*. But if the manager is purely self-interested and the owner knows it, this path will not be an equilibrium outcome.

✔ **SELF-TEST 9.3**

Smith and Jones are playing a game in which Smith has the first move at *A* in the decision tree shown below. Once Smith has chosen either the top or bottom branch at *A*, Jones, who can see what Smith has chosen, must choose the top or bottom branch at *B* or *C*. If the payoffs at the end of each branch are as shown, what is the equilibrium outcome of this game? If before Smith chose, Jones could make a credible commitment to choose either the top or bottom branch when his turn came, what would he do?

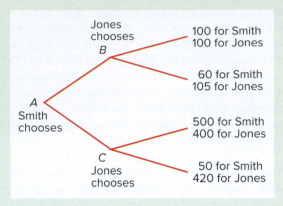

Jones chooses
B
100 for Smith
100 for Jones

60 for Smith
105 for Jones

A
Smith chooses

500 for Smith
400 for Jones

C
Jones chooses
50 for Smith
420 for Jones

MONOPOLISTIC COMPETITION WHEN LOCATION MATTERS

In many sequential games, the player who gets to move first enjoys a strategic advantage. That was the case, for instance, in the decision of whether to produce a hybrid sports car in Example 9.4. In that example, the first mover did better because he was able to exploit the knowledge that both firms do better if each one's product is different from the other's rather than similar to it. But that won't always be true. When the feature that differentiates one seller's product from another's is temporal or spatial location, the firm with the last move in a game sometimes enjoys the upper hand, as The Economic Naturalist 9.4 illustrates.

The Economic Naturalist 9.4

Why do we often see convenience stores located on adjacent street corners?

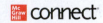

▶ Visit your instructor's Connect course and access your eBook to view this video.

Why do we often see convenience stores located on adjacent street corners?

In many cities, it's common to see convenience stores located in clusters, followed by long stretches with no stores at all. If the stores were more spread out, almost all consumers would enjoy a shorter walk to the nearest convenience store. Why do stores tend to cluster in this fashion?

In Figure 9.5, suppose that when the convenience store located at A first opened, it was the closest store for the 1,200 shoppers who live in identical apartment houses evenly distributed along the road between A and the freeway one mile to the east.[3] Those who live to the east of the freeway shop elsewhere because they cannot cross the freeway. Those who live to the west of the store at A shop either at A or at some other store still further to the west, whichever is closer. In this setting, why might a profit-maximizing entrepreneur planning

[3]"Evenly distributed" means that the number of shoppers who live on any segment of the road between A and the freeway is exactly proportional to the length of that segment. For example, the number who live along a segment one-tenth of a mile in length would be $1/10 \times 1,200 = 120$.

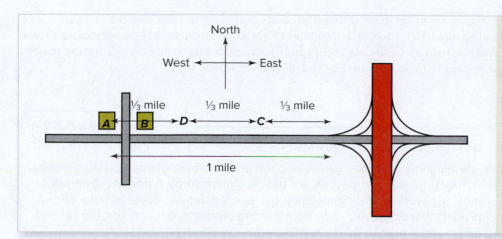

FIGURE 9.5
The Curious Tendency of Monopolistic Competitors to Cluster.

As a group, consumers would enjoy a shorter walk if the store at *B* were instead located at *C*, or even at *D*. But a second store will attract more customers by locating at *B*.

to open a new store between *A* and the freeway choose to locate at *B* rather than at some intermediate location such as *C*?

It turns out that a store located at *C* would, in fact, minimize the distance that shoppers living between *A* and the freeway would have to walk to reach the nearest store. If there were a store at *C*, no shopper on this stretch of road would have to walk more than 1/3 of a mile to reach the nearest store. The 800 people who live between point *D* (which is halfway between *A* and *C*) and the freeway would shop at *C*, while the 400 who live between *D* and *A* would shop at *A*.

Despite the fact that *C* is the most attractive location for a new store from the perspective of consumers, it is not the most advantageous for the store's owner. The reason is that the owner's profit depends on how many people choose to shop at his store, not on how far they have to walk to get there. Given that consumers shop at the store closest to where they live, the best option from the entrepreneur's perspective is to locate his store at *B*, on the street corner just east of *A*. That way, his store will be closer to all 1,200 people who live between *A* and the freeway. It is this logic that often helps explain the clustering of convenience stores, gas stations, and other monopolistically competitive firms whose most important differentiating feature is geographic location.

The insight that helped answer the question posed in The Economic Naturalist 9.4 comes from economist Harold Hotelling.[4] Hotelling employed this insight to explain why two hot dog vendors on a stretch of beach almost invariably locate next to one another midway between the endpoints of the beach.

For many oligopolistic or monopolistically competitive firms, an important dimension of product differentiation is location in time rather than in physical space. The timing of flight departures for different airlines in the New York–Los Angeles market is one example. The timing of film showings by different local movie theaters is another. In these cases, too, we often see product clustering. Thus, in the New York–Los Angeles market, both United and American have flights throughout the afternoon departing exactly on the hour. And in many local movie markets, the first evening showing starts at 7:15 p.m. in dozens of different theaters.

In other examples, the differentiating features that matter most might be said to describe the product's location in a more abstract "product space." With soft drinks, for

[4]Harold Hotelling, "Stability and Competition," *Economic Journal* 39, no. 1 (1929), pp. 41–57.

example, we might array different products according to their degrees of sweetness or carbonation. Here, too, it is common to see rival products that lie very close to one another, such as Coca-Cola and Pepsi. Clustering occurs in these cases for the reasons analogous to those discussed by Hotelling in his classic paper.

RECAP ↑

GAMES IN WHICH TIMING MATTERS

The outcomes in many games depend on the timing of each player's move. For such games, the payoffs are best summarized by a decision tree rather than a payoff matrix. Sometimes the second mover does best to offer a product that differs markedly from existing products. Other times, the second mover does best to mimic existing products closely.

COMMITMENT PROBLEMS

commitment problem a situation in which people cannot achieve their goals because of an inability to make credible threats or promises

Games like the one in Self-Test 9.3, as well as the prisoner's dilemma, the cartel game, and the remote-office game, confront players with a **commitment problem**—a situation in which they have difficulty achieving the desired outcome because they cannot make credible threats or promises. If both players in the original prisoner's dilemma could make a binding promise to remain silent, both would be assured of a shorter sentence, hence the logic of the underworld code of *Omerta*, under which the family of anyone who provides evidence against a fellow mob member is killed. A similar logic explains the adoption of military-arms-control agreements, in which opponents sign an enforceable pledge to curtail weapons spending.

The commitment problem in the remote-office game could be solved if the managerial candidate could find some way of committing himself to manage honestly if hired. The candidate needs a **commitment device**—something that provides the candidate with an incentive to keep his promise.

commitment device a way of changing incentives so as to make otherwise empty threats or promises credible

Business owners are well aware of commitment problems in the workplace and have adopted a variety of commitment devices to solve them. Consider, for example, the problem confronting the owner of a restaurant. She wants her table staff to provide good service so that customers will enjoy their meals and come back in the future. Because good service is valuable to her, she would be willing to pay servers extra for it. For their part, servers would be willing to provide good service in return for the extra pay. The problem is that the owner cannot always monitor whether the servers do provide good service. Her concern is that having been paid extra for it, the servers may slack off when she isn't looking. Unless the owner can find some way to solve this problem, she will not pay extra; the servers will not provide good service; and she, they, and the diners will suffer. A better outcome for all concerned would be for the servers to find some way to commit themselves to good service.

Restaurateurs in many countries have tried to solve this commitment problem by encouraging diners to leave tips at the end of their meals. The attraction of this solution is that the diner is *always* in a good position to monitor service quality. The diner should be happy to reward good service with a generous tip because doing so will help ensure good service in the future. And the server has a strong incentive to provide good service because he knows that the size of his tip may depend on it.

The various commitment devices just discussed—the underworld code of *Omerta*, military-arms-control agreements, the tip for the server—all work because they change the incentives facing the decision makers. But as the next example illustrates, changing incentives in precisely the desired way is not always practical.

EXAMPLE 9.6   Changing Incentives

Will Sylvester leave a tip when dining on the road?

Sylvester has just finished a $100 steak dinner at a restaurant that is 500 miles from where he lives. The server provided good service. If Sylvester cares only about himself, will he leave a tip?

Once the server has provided good service, there is no way for her to take it back if the diner fails to leave a tip. In restaurants patronized by local diners, failure to tip is not a problem because the server can simply provide poor service the next time a nontipper comes in. But the server lacks that leverage with out-of-town diners. Having already received good service, Sylvester must choose between paying $100 and paying $120 for his meal. If he is an essentially selfish person, the former choice may be a compelling one.

Will leaving a tip at an out-of-town restaurant affect the quality of service you receive?

✔ SELF-TEST 9.4

A traveler dines at a restaurant far from home. Both he and the server are rational and self-interested in the narrow sense. The server must first choose between providing good service and bad service, whereupon the diner must choose whether or not to leave a tip. The payoffs for their interaction are as summarized on the accompanying game tree. What is the most the diner would be willing to pay for the right to make a binding commitment (visible to the server) to leave a tip at the end of the meal in the event of having received good service?

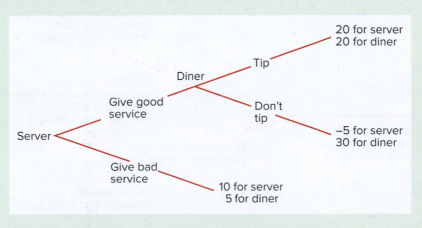

SOLVING COMMITMENT PROBLEMS WITH PSYCHOLOGICAL INCENTIVES

In all the games we have discussed so far, players were assumed to care only about obtaining the best possible outcome for themselves. Thus, each player's goal was to get the highest monetary payoff, the shortest jail sentence, the best chance to be heard, and so on. The irony, in most of these games, is that players do not attain the best outcomes. Better outcomes can sometimes be achieved by altering the material incentives selfish players face, but not always.

If altering the relevant material incentives is not possible, commitment problems can sometimes be solved by altering people's psychological incentives. As the next example illustrates, in a society in which people are strongly conditioned to develop moral sentiments—feelings of guilt when they harm others, feelings of sympathy for their trading partners, feelings of outrage when they are treated unjustly—commitment problems arise less often than in more narrowly self-interested societies.

| **EXAMPLE 9.7** | **The Impact of Moral Sentiments** |

In a moral society, will the business owner open a remote office?

Consider again the owner of the thriving business who is trying to decide whether to open an office in a distant city. Suppose the society in which she lives is one in which all citizens have been strongly conditioned to behave honestly. Will she open the remote office?

Suppose, for instance, that the managerial candidate would suffer guilt pangs if he embezzled money from the owner. Most people would be reluctant to assign a monetary value to guilty feelings. But for the sake of discussion, let's suppose that those feelings are so unpleasant that the manager would be willing to pay at least $10,000 to avoid them. On this assumption, the manager's payoff if he manages dishonestly will be not $1,500, but $1,500 − $10,000 = −$8,500. The new decision tree is shown in Figure 9.6.

In this case, the best choice for the owner at *B* will be to open the remote office because she knows that at *C* the manager's best choice will be to manage honestly. The irony, of course, is that the honest manager in this example ends up richer than the selfish manager in the previous example, who earned only a normal salary.

FIGURE 9.6
The Remote-Office Game with an Honest Manager.

If the owner can identify a managerial candidate who would choose to manage honestly at *C*, she will hire that candidate at *B* and open the remote office.

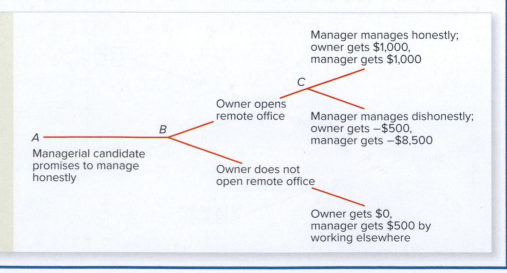

Manager manages honestly; owner gets $1,000, manager gets $1,000

Owner opens remote office

Manager manages dishonestly; owner gets −$500, manager gets −$8,500

Managerial candidate promises to manage honestly

Owner does not open remote office

Owner gets $0, manager gets $500 by working elsewhere

Are People Fundamentally Selfish?

As Example 9.7 suggests, the assumption that people are self-interested in the narrow sense of the term does not always capture the full range of motives that govern choice in strategic settings. Think, for example, about the last time you had a meal at an out-of-town restaurant. Did you leave a tip? If so, your behavior was quite normal. Researchers have found that tipping rates in restaurants patronized mostly by out-of-town diners are essentially the same as in restaurants patronized mostly by local diners.

Indeed, there are many exceptions to the outcomes predicted on the basis of the assumption that people are self-interested in the narrowest sense of the term. People who have been treated unjustly often seek revenge even at ruinous cost to themselves. Every day, people walk away from profitable transactions whose terms they believe to be "unfair." In these and countless other ways, people do not seem to be pursuing self-interest narrowly defined. And if motives beyond narrow self-interest are significant, we must take them into account in attempting to predict and explain human behavior.

Preferences as Solutions to Commitment Problems

Economists tend to view preferences as ends in themselves. Taking them as given, they calculate what actions will best serve those preferences. This approach to the study of behavior is widely used by other social scientists, and by game theorists, military strategists, philosophers, and others. In its standard form, it assumes purely self-interested preferences for present and future consumption goods of various sorts, leisure pursuits, and so on. Concerns about fairness, guilt, honor, sympathy, and the like typically play no role.

Yet such concerns clearly affect the choices people make in strategic interactions. Sympathy for one's trading partner can make a businessperson trustworthy even when material incentives favor cheating. A sense of justice can prompt a person to incur the costs of retaliation, even when incurring those costs will not undo the original injury.

Preferences can clearly shape behavior in these ways; however, this alone does not solve commitment problems. The solution to such problems requires not only that a person *have* certain preferences, but also that others have some way of *discerning* them. Unless the business owner can identify the trustworthy employee, that employee cannot land a job whose pay is predicated on trust. And unless the predator can identify a potential victim whose character will motivate retaliation, that person is likely to become a victim.

From among those with whom we might engage in ventures requiring trust, can we identify reliable partners? If people could make *perfectly* accurate character judgments, they could always steer clear of dishonest persons. That people continue to be victimized at least occasionally by dishonest persons suggests that perfectly reliable character judgments are either impossible to make or prohibitively expensive.

Vigilance in the choice of trading partners is an essential element in solving (or avoiding) commitment problems, for if there is an advantage in being honest and being perceived as such, there is an even greater advantage in only *appearing* to be honest. After all, a liar who appears trustworthy will have better opportunities than one who glances about furtively, sweats profusely, and has difficulty making eye contact. Indeed, he will have the same opportunities as an honest person but will get higher payoffs because he will exploit them to the fullest.

In the end, the question of whether people can make reasonably accurate character judgments is an empirical one. Experimental studies have shown that even on the basis of brief encounters involving strangers, subjects are adept at predicting who will cooperate and who will defect in prisoner's dilemma games. For example, in one experiment in which only 26 percent of subjects defected, the accuracy rate of predicted defections was more than 56 percent. One might expect that predictions regarding those we know well would be even more accurate.

Do you know someone who would return an envelope containing $1,000 in cash to you if you lost it at a crowded concert? If so, then you accept the claim that personal character can help people solve commitment problems. As long as honest individuals can identify at least some others who are honest, and can interact selectively with them, honest individuals can prosper in a competitive environment.

RECAP ↑

COMMITMENT PROBLEMS AND THE EFFECTS OF PSYCHOLOGICAL INCENTIVES

- Commitment problems arise when the inability to make credible threats and promises prevents people from achieving desired outcomes. Such problems can sometimes be solved by employing commitment devices—ways of changing incentives to facilitate making credible threats or promises.
- Most applications of the theory of games assume that players are self-interested in the narrow sense of the term. In practice, however, many choices—such as leaving tips in out-of-town restaurants—appear inconsistent with this assumption.
- The fact that people seem driven by a more complex range of motives makes behavior more difficult to predict, but also creates new ways of solving commitment problems. Psychological incentives often can serve as commitment devices when changing players' material incentives is impractical. For example, people who are able to identify honest trading partners, and interact selectively with them, are able to solve commitment problems that arise from lack of trust.

SUMMARY

- Economists use the theory of games to analyze situations in which the payoffs of one's actions depend on the actions taken by others. Games have three basic elements: the players; the list of possible actions, or strategies, from which each player can choose; and the payoffs the players receive for those strategies. The payoff matrix is the most useful way to summarize this information in games in which the timing of the players' moves is not decisive. In games in which timing matters, a decision tree provides a much more useful summary of the information. *(LO1, LO3)*

- Equilibrium in a game occurs when each player's strategy choice yields the highest payoff available, given the strategies chosen by the other. *(LO1)*

- A dominant strategy is one that yields a higher payoff regardless of the strategy chosen by the other player. In some games such as the prisoner's dilemma, each player has a dominant strategy. Equilibrium occurs in such games when each player chooses his or her dominant strategy. In other games, not all players have a dominant strategy. *(LO1, LO2)*

- Equilibrium outcomes are often unattractive from the perspective of players as a group. The prisoner's dilemma has this feature because it is each prisoner's dominant strategy to confess, yet each spends more time in jail if both confess than if both remain silent. The incentive structure of this game helps explain such disparate social dilemmas as excessive advertising, cartels, and failure to reap the potential benefits of interactions requiring trust. *(LO2)*

- Individuals often can resolve these dilemmas if they can make binding commitments to behave in certain ways. Some commitments—such as those involved in military-arms-control agreements—are achieved by altering the material incentives confronting the players. Other commitments can be achieved by relying on psychological incentives to counteract material payoffs. Moral sentiments such as guilt, sympathy, and a sense of justice often foster better outcomes than can be achieved by narrowly self-interested players. For this type of commitment to work, the relevant moral sentiments must be discernible by one's potential trading partners. *(LO4)*

KEY TERMS

basic elements of a game	credible threat	payoff matrix
cartel	decision tree (or game tree)	prisoner's dilemma
commitment device	dominant strategy	repeated prisoner's dilemma
commitment problem	dominated strategy	tit-for-tat
credible promise	Nash equilibrium	

REVIEW QUESTIONS

1. Identify the three basic elements of a game. *(LO1)*

2. How is your incentive to defect in a prisoner's dilemma altered if you learn that you will play the game not just once but rather indefinitely many times with the same partner? *(LO2)*

3. Explain why a cartel is an example of a prisoner's dilemma. *(LO2)*

4. Why did Warner Brothers make a mistake by waiting until the filming of *Analyze This* was almost finished before negotiating with Tony Bennett to perform in the final scene? *(LO3)*

5. Suppose General Motors is trying to hire a small firm to manufacture the door handles for Buick sedans. The task requires an investment in expensive capital equipment that cannot be used for any other purpose. Why might the president of the small firm refuse to undertake this venture without a long-term contract fixing the price of the door handles? *(LO3)*

6. Describe the commitment problem that narrowly self-interested diners and servers would confront at restaurants located on interstate highways. Given that in such restaurants tipping does seem to ensure reasonably good service, do you think people are always selfish in the narrowest sense? *(LO4)*

PROBLEMS

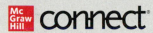

1. Consider the following game, called matching pennies, which you are playing with a friend. Each of you has a penny hidden in your hand, facing either heads up or tails up (you know which way the one in your hand is facing). On the count of "three," you simultaneously show your pennies to each other. If the face-up side of your coin matches the face-up side of your friend's coin, you get to keep the two pennies. If the faces do not match, your friend gets to keep the pennies. *(LO1)*

   a. Who are the players in this game? What are each player's strategies? Construct a payoff matrix for the game.

   b. Does either player have a dominant strategy? If so, what?

   c. Is there an equilibrium? If so, what?

2. Consider the following game. Harry has four quarters. He can offer Sally from one to four of them. If she accepts his offer, she keeps the quarters Harry offered her and Harry keeps the others. If Sally declines Harry's offer, they both get nothing ($0). They play the game only once, and each cares only about the amount of money he or she ends up with. *(LO1, LO3)*

   a. Who are the players? What are each player's strategies? Construct a decision tree for this game.

   b. Given their goal, what is the optimal choice for each player?

3. Blackadder and Baldrick are rational, self-interested criminals imprisoned in separate cells in a dark medieval dungeon. They face the prisoner's dilemma displayed in the matrix.

   Assume that Blackadder is willing to pay $1,000 for each year by which he can reduce his sentence below 20 years. A corrupt jailer tells Blackadder that before he decides whether to confess or deny the crime, she can tell him Baldrick's decision. How much is this information worth to Blackadder? *(LO2)*

		Blackadder	
		Confess	Deny
Baldrick	Confess	5 years for each	0 for Baldrick 20 years for Blackadder
	Deny	20 years for Baldrick 0 for Blackadder	1 year for each

4. In studying for your economics final, you are concerned about only two things: your grade and the amount of time you spend studying. A good grade will give you a benefit of 20; an average grade, a benefit of 5; and a poor grade, a benefit of 0. By studying a lot, you will incur a cost of 10; by studying a little, a cost of 6. Moreover, if you study a lot and all other students study a little, you will get a good grade and they will get poor ones. But if they study a lot and you study a little, they will get good grades and you will get a poor one. Finally, if you and all other students study the same amount of time, everyone will get average grades. Other students share your preferences regarding grades and study time. *(LO2)*

   a. Model this situation as a two-person prisoner's dilemma in which the strategies are to study a little and to study a lot, and the players are you and all other students. Construct a payoff matrix in which the payoffs account for both the cost and benefit of studying.

   b. What is the equilibrium outcome in this game? Which outcome would everyone (both the other students and you) prefer?

5. Newfoundland's fishing industry has recently declined sharply due to overfishing, even though fishing companies were supposedly bound by a quota agreement. If all companies had abided by the agreement, yields could have been maintained at high levels. *(LO2)*

   a. Model this situation as a prisoner's dilemma in which the players are Company A and Company B, and the strategies are to keep the quota and break the quota. Suppose that if both companies keep the quota, then each receives a payoff of $100, and if both break the quota, then each receives a payoff of $0. On the other hand, if one company breaks the quota and the other keeps the quota, then the company that breaks the quota receives a payoff of $150 and the company that keeps the quota receives a payoff of −$50. Construct the corresponding payoff matrix, and explain why overfishing is inevitable in the absence of effective enforcement of the quota agreement.

   b. Provide another environmental example of a prisoner's dilemma.

   c. In many potential prisoner's dilemmas, a way out of the dilemma for a would-be cooperator is to make reliable character judgments about the trustworthiness of potential partners. Explain why this solution is not available in many situations involving degradation of the environment.

6. Two airplane manufacturers are considering the production of a new product, a 150-passenger jet. Both are deciding whether to enter the market and produce the new planes. The payoff matrix is as follows (payoff values are in millions of dollars).

	Airbus	
	Produce	Don't produce
Boeing Produce	−5 for each	100 for Boeing 0 for Airbus
Don't produce	0 for Boeing 100 for Airbus	0 for each

The implication of these payoffs is that the market demand is large enough to support only one manufacturer. If both firms enter, both will sustain a loss. *(LO2)*

   a. Identify two possible equilibrium outcomes in this game.

   b. Consider the effect of a subsidy. Suppose the European Union decides to subsidize the European producer, Airbus, with a check for $25 million if it enters the market. Revise the payoff matrix to account for this subsidy. What is the new equilibrium outcome?

   c. Compare the two outcomes (pre- and post-subsidy). What qualitative effect does the subsidy have?

7. Jill and Jack both have two pails that can be used to carry water down a hill. Each makes only one trip down the hill, and each pail of water can be sold for $5. Carrying the pails of water down requires considerable effort. Both Jill and Jack would be willing to pay $2 each to avoid carrying one pail down the hill and an additional $3 to avoid carrying a second pail down the hill. *(LO2)*

   a. Given market prices, how many pails of water will each child fetch from the top of the hill?

   b. Jill and Jack's parents are worried that the two children don't cooperate enough with one another. Suppose they make Jill and Jack share equally their revenues from selling the water. Given that both are self-interested, construct the payoff matrix for the decisions Jill and Jack face regarding the number of pails of water each should carry. What is the equilibrium outcome?

8. The owner of a thriving business wants to open a new office in a distant city. If he can hire someone who will manage the new office honestly, he can afford to pay

that person a weekly salary of $2,000 ($1,000 more than the manager would be able to earn elsewhere) and still earn an economic profit of $800. The owner's concern is that he will not be able to monitor the manager's behavior and that the manager would therefore be in a position to embezzle money from the business. The owner knows that if the remote office is managed dishonestly, the manager can earn $3,100, which results in an economic loss of $600 per week. *(LO3)*

a. If the owner believes that all managers are narrowly self-interested income maximizers, will he open the new office?

b. Suppose the owner knows that a managerial candidate is a genuinely honest person who condemns dishonest behavior and who would be willing to pay up to $15,000 to avoid the guilt she would feel if she were dishonest. Will the owner open the remote office?

9. Consider the following "dating game," which has two players, A and B, and two strategies, to buy a movie ticket or a baseball ticket. The payoffs, given in points, are as shown in the matrix below. Note that the highest payoffs occur when both A and B attend the same event.

		B	
		Buy movie ticket	Buy baseball ticket
A	Buy movie ticket	2 for A 3 for B	0 for A 0 for B
	Buy baseball ticket	1 for A 1 for B	3 for A 2 for B

Assume that players A and B buy their tickets separately and simultaneously. Each must decide what to do

knowing the available choices and payoffs but not what the other has actually chosen. Each player believes the other to be rational and self-interested. *(LO1, LO2, LO3)*

a. Does either player have a dominant strategy?

b. How many potential equilibria are there? (*Hint:* To see whether a given combination of strategies is an equilibrium, ask whether either player could get a higher payoff by changing his or her strategy.)

c. Is this game a prisoner's dilemma? Explain.

d. Suppose player A gets to buy his or her ticket first. Player B does not observe A's choice but knows that A chose first. Player A knows that player B knows he or she chose first. What is the equilibrium outcome?

e. Suppose the situation is similar to part d, except that player B chooses first. What is the equilibrium outcome?

10. Imagine yourself sitting in your car in a campus parking lot that is currently full, waiting for someone to pull out so that you can park your car. Somebody pulls out, but at the same moment a driver who has just arrived overtakes you in an obvious attempt to park in the vacated spot before you can. Suppose this driver would be willing to pay up to $10 to park in that spot and up to $30 to avoid getting into an argument with you. (That is, the benefit of parking is $10 and the cost of an argument is $30.) At the same time he guesses, accurately, that you too would be willing to pay up to $30 to avoid a confrontation and up to $10 to park in the vacant spot. *(LO3, LO4)*

a. Model this situation as a two-stage decision tree in which his bid to take the space is the opening move and your strategies are (1) to protest and (2) not to protest. If you protest (initiate an argument), the rules of the game specify that he has to let you take the space. Show the payoffs at the end of each branch of the tree.

b. What is the equilibrium outcome?

c. What would be the advantage of being able to communicate credibly to the other driver that your *failure* to protest would be a significant psychological cost to you (for example, maybe a cost of $25)?

ANSWERS TO SELF-TESTS

9.1 No matter what American does, United will do better to leave ad spending the same. No matter what United does, American will do better to raise ad spending. So each player will play its dominant strategy: American will raise its ad spending and United will leave its ad spending the same. *(LO1)*

	American's Choice	
	Raise ad spending	Leave ad spending the same
United's Choice — Raise ad spending	United gets $3,000 American gets $8,000	United gets $4,000 American gets $5,000
Leave ad spending the same	United gets $8,000 American gets $4,000	United gets $5,000 American gets $2,000

9.2 In game 1, no matter what Chrysler does, GM will do better to invest, and no matter what GM does, Chrysler will do better to invest. Each has a dominant strategy, but in following it, each does worse than if it had not invested. So game 1 is a prisoner's dilemma. In game 2, no matter what Chrysler does, GM again will do better to invest; but no matter what GM does, Chrysler will do better *not* to invest. Each has a dominant strategy, and in following it, each gets a payoff of 10—which is 5 more than if each had played its dominated strategy. So game 2 is not a prisoner's dilemma. *(LO2)*

9.3 Smith assumes that Jones will choose the branch that maximizes his payoff, which is the bottom branch at either *B* or *C*. So Jones will choose the bottom branch when his turn comes, no matter what Smith chooses. Since Smith will do better (60) on the bottom branch at *B* than on the bottom branch at *C* (50), Smith will

choose the top branch at *A*. So equilibrium in this game is for Smith to choose the top branch at *A* and Jones to choose the bottom branch at *B*. Smith gets 60 and Jones gets 105.

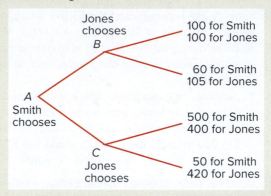

If Jones could make a credible commitment to choose the top branch no matter what, both would do better. Smith would choose the bottom branch at *A* and Jones would choose the top branch at *C*, giving Smith 500 and Jones 400. *(LO3)*

9.4 The equilibrium of this game in the absence of a commitment to tip is that the server will give bad service because if she provides good service, she knows that the diner's best option will be not to tip, which leaves the server worse off than if she had provided good service. Since the diner gets an outcome of 20 if he can commit to leaving a tip (15 more than he would get in the absence of such a commitment), he would be willing to pay up to 15 for the right to commit. *(LO4)*

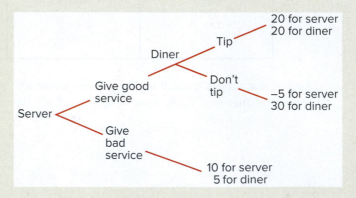

CHAPTER 10

An Introduction to Behavioral Economics

Behavioral economics introduces more realistic assumptions about human motivation and cognition.

U ntil the 1980s, traditional economic models almost invariably assumed a decision maker who was narrowly self-interested, well informed, highly disciplined, and possessed of sufficient cognitive capacity to solve relatively simple optimization problems. This mythical individual was often called **homo economicus** for short.

During the intervening years, theoretical and empirical developments in economics and psychology have challenged each of these core assumptions. The challenges fall into three broad categories: (1) we often make systematic cognitive errors that prevent us from discovering which choices will best promote our interests; (2) even when we can discern

LEARNING OBJECTIVES

After reading this chapter, you should be able to:

LO1 Describe and illustrate numerous rules of thumb people employ when making decisions using incomplete information and explain how reliance on these rules sometimes leads to poor choices.

LO2 Explain how misinterpretation of contextual clues can lead to poor choices.

LO3 Describe situations in which impulse-control problems prevent people from executing rationally conceived economic plans.

LO4 Describe the phenomenon of loss aversion and explain how it often creates a powerful bias in favor of the status quo.

LO5 Explain how relaxing the assumption that people are narrowly self-interested alters the predictions of traditional economic models.

LO6 Describe how concerns about relative position often create conflicts between the interests of individuals and those of the broader community.

LO7 List examples of laws and regulations that appear motivated by the behavioral tendencies described in this chapter.

265

homo economicus the narrowly self-interested, well-informed, highly disciplined, and cognitively formidable actor often assumed in traditional economic models

satisficing a decision-making strategy that aims for adequate results because optimal results may necessitate excessive expenditure of resources

Cost-Benefit

fungibility the property of an entity whose individual units are interchangeable, as money in separate accounts

Richard Thaler, who was awarded the Nobel Prize in Economics in 2017 for his pioneering work in behavioral economics.

which choices would be best, we often have difficulty summoning the willpower to execute them; and (3) we often pursue goals that appear inconsistent with self-interest, narrowly understood. In this chapter, we will consider each of these challenges in turn.

The late Nobel laureate Herbert Simon (1984) was the first to impress upon economists that human beings are incapable of behaving like the rational beings portrayed in standard rational choice models. Simon, a pioneer in the field of artificial intelligence, stumbled upon this realization in the process of trying to instruct a computer to "reason" about a problem. He discovered that when we ourselves confront a puzzle, we rarely reach a solution in a neat, linear fashion. Rather, we search in a haphazard way for potentially relevant facts and information and usually quit once our understanding reaches a certain threshold. Our conclusions are often inconsistent, sometimes even flatly incorrect. But much of the time, we come up with serviceable, if imperfect, solutions. In Simon's terms, we are "**satisficers**," not maximizers. We move on once we feel we've got a solution that is "good enough."

Subsequent economists have taken Simon's lead and developed a very sophisticated literature on decision making under incomplete information. We now realize that when information is costly to gather and cognitive processing ability is limited, it is not even rational to make fully informed choices of the sort portrayed in traditional models. Paradoxically, it is irrational to be completely well informed! When information is costly, the benefit from gathering more of it—from being able to make a very good decision rather than just a good one—may simply not justify the added cost. Thus, the literature on decision making under incomplete information, far from being a challenge to the traditional model, has actually bolstered our confidence in it. (More on these issues in Chapter 12, *The Economics of Information*.)

But there is another offshoot of Simon's work, one that is less friendly to traditional models. This research, which has been strongly influenced by the economist Richard Thaler and the cognitive psychologists Daniel Kahneman and the late Amos Tversky, demonstrates that even with transparently simple problems, people often violate the most fundamental axioms of rational choice. One of the most cherished tenets of the rational choice model, for example, is that wealth is fungible, or freely movable across categories. **Fungibility** implies, among other things, that our total wealth, not the amount we have in any particular account, determines what we buy. But Tversky and Kahneman provided a vivid experimental demonstration to the contrary.[1] They asked one group of people to imagine that, having earlier purchased tickets for $10, they arrive at the theater to discover they have lost them. Members of a second group were asked to picture themselves arriving just before the performance to buy their tickets when they find that they have each lost $10 from their wallets. People in both groups were then asked whether they would continue with their plans to attend the performance. In the rational choice model, the forces governing this decision are exactly the same for both groups. Losing a $10 ticket should have precisely the same effect as losing a $10 bill. And yet, in repeated trials, most people in the lost-ticket group said they would not attend the performance, while an overwhelming majority—88 percent—in the lost-bill group say they would.

Richard Thaler developed a theory of mental accounting to explain this anomaly.[2] He began by noting that people apparently organize their spending into separate "mental accounts" for food, housing, entertainment, general expenses, and so on. People who lose their tickets act as if they debit $10 from their mental entertainment accounts, while those who lose a $10 bill debit that amount from their general expense account. For people in the former group, the loss makes the apparent cost of seeing the show rise from $10 to $20, whereas for those in the second it remains $10. The rational choice model makes clear that the second group's assessment is the correct one. And on reflection, most people do, in fact, agree that losing a ticket is no better reason not to see the performance than losing a $10 bill.

Working with numerous collaborators, Thaler, Kahneman, and Tversky identified a large catalog of systematic departures from rational choice, many of which stem from the

[1] Amos Tversky and Daniel Kahneman, "Judgment under Uncertainty: Heuristics and Biases," *Science* 185 (1974), pp. 1124–1131.
[2] Richard Thaler, "Mental Accounting and Consumer Choice," *Marketing Science* 4, no. 3 (Summer 1985), pp. 199–214.

application of **judgmental and decision heuristics,** or rules of thumb. Next, we describe some of the heuristics they identified.

judgmental and decision heuristics rules of thumb that reduce computation costs

JUDGMENTAL HEURISTICS OR RULES OF THUMB

AVAILABILITY

We often estimate the frequency of an event, or class of events, by the ease with which we can summon relevant examples from memory.[3] The more easily we can recall examples, the more likely we judge an event to be. This rule of thumb is called the **availability heuristic.** On balance, it is an effective strategy since it is generally easier to recall examples of things that happen frequently. The problem is that frequency is not the only factor that influences ease of recall. If people are asked, for example, whether there are more murders than suicides in New York State each year, most answer confidently in the affirmative, yet there are always more suicides than murders. Murders are easier to recall not because they are more frequent, but because they are more salient.

availability heuristic a rule of thumb that estimates the frequency of an event by the ease with which it is possible to summon examples from memory

---

EXAMPLE 10.1	**Availability Heuristic**

Which category of words is more common in the English language: those that begin with "r" or those that have "r" as their third letter?

Using the availability heuristic, most people react by trying to summon examples in each category. And since most people find it easier to think of examples of words starting with "r," the availability heuristic leads them to answer that such words occur more frequently. Yet English words with "r" in the third slot are actually far more numerous. The availability heuristic fails here because frequency isn't the only thing that governs ease of recall. We store words in memory in multiple ways—by their meanings, by the sounds they make, by the images they evoke, by their first letters, and by numerous other features. But virtually no one stores words in memory by the identity of their third letter, which is why words with "r" in that slot are harder to recall.

REPRESENTATIVENESS

Another common rule of thumb is to assume that the likelihood of something belonging to a given category is directly related to the degree to which it shares characteristics thought to be representative of membership in that category.[4] For example, because librarians are stereotypically viewed as introverted while salespersons are viewed as gregarious, the **representativeness heuristic** suggests that a given shy person is more likely to be a librarian than a salesperson. But this reasoning leads us astray when we fail to account for other factors that influence the relevant probabilities. Suppose the popular stereotypes are accurate—that, say, 90 percent of all librarians are shy, as compared with only 20 percent of salespeople. Would it then be safe to conclude that a given shy person is more likely to be a librarian than a salesperson? Not necessarily. Suppose, conservatively, that there are 90 salespeople in the population for every 10 librarians (the true ratio is more than 1,000 to 1). Under the assumed proportions of shy persons in each group, there would then be 9 shy librarians in the population for every 18 shy salespeople. And in that case, any given shy person would actually be twice as likely to be a salesperson than to be a librarian!

representativeness heuristic a rule of thumb according to which the likelihood of something belonging to a given category increases with the extent to which it shares characteristics with stereotypical members of that category

---

[3]Amos Tversky and Daniel Kahneman, "The Framing of Decisions and the Psychology of Choice," *Science* 211 (1981), pp. 453–458.
[4]Daniel Kahneman and Amos Tversky, "Subjective Probability: A Judgment of Representativeness," *Cognitive Psychology* 3, no. 3 (1972), pp. 430–454.

EXAMPLE 10.2   Representativeness Heuristic

Only two moving companies, United and North American, provide local delivery service in a small western city. United operates 80 percent of the vans, North American the remaining 20 percent. On a dark and rainy night, a pedestrian is run over and killed by a moving van. The lone witness to the incident testifies that the van was owned by North American. The law states that a company shall be held liable for damages only if it can be shown that the probability that the company was the guilty party is at least half. An independent laboratory hired by the court finds that under dark and rainy conditions, the witness is able to identify the owner of a moving van with 60 percent accuracy. What is the probability that a North American van ran over the pedestrian?

Out of every 100 moving vans in the area, 80 are United's and 20 are North American's. Of the 80 United vans, the witness incorrectly identifies 32 (or 40 percent of them) as belonging to North American. Of the 20 North American trucks, the witness correctly identifies 12 as belonging to North American. Thus the probability that a van identified as North American's actually is North American's is 12/(32 + 12) = 3/11. So North American will not be held liable.

 SELF-TEST 10.1

A witness testifies that the taxicab that struck and injured Smith in a dark alley was green. On investigation, the attorney for Green Taxi Company discovers that the witness identifies the correct color of a taxi in a dark alley 80 percent of the time. There are two taxi companies in town, Green and Blue. Green operates 15 percent of all local taxis. The law says that Green Taxi Company is liable for Smith's injuries if and only if the probability that it caused them is greater than 0.5. Is Green liable?

REGRESSION TO THE MEAN

regression to the mean
the phenomenon that unusual events are likely to be followed by more nearly normal ones

Another common judgment error is to ignore a phenomenon known to statisticians as **regression to the mean.** The idea is that if our first measurement of something is far from its average value, a second measurement will tend to be closer to its average value. Suppose, for example, that you draw a ball from an urn containing balls numbered from 1 to 100 and get a ball numbered 85. Would you then be surprised that if you drew a second ball from that same urn, the number on it would be smaller than 85? Since the urn contains 84 balls with smaller numbers and only 15 with higher ones, it is in fact very likely that your second ball will have a smaller number. Errors often occur when people fail to take this phenomenon into account.

Suppose, for example, that you are a manager choosing whether to adopt a supportive stance toward your employees—by praising them when they perform well—or a critical stance—by criticizing them when they perform poorly. To help you decide, you do an experiment in which you adopt a critical stance toward employees who have performed unusually poorly and a supportive stance toward those who have performed unusually well. On the basis of this experiment, you decide that the critical stance works better. Why might this inference have been misleading?

When you praise an employee, it will often be after that employee has turned in an unusually good performance. Similarly, when you are critical of an employee, it will often be after that employ has performed unusually poorly. Quite apart from any direct effects of praise or blame, subsequent performances in both cases are likely to be more nearly normal. This could lead you to conclude that praise caused worse performance and that criticism caused better performance. Independent experimental work suggests that this conclusion would be erroneous. Supportive management styles, it appears, are more likely than critical styles to bring out the best in employees.

The Economic Naturalist 10.1

Why did the American Olympic swimmer Shirley Babashoff, who set one world record and six national records at the 1976 Olympics, refuse to appear on the cover of *Sports Illustrated*?

Invitations to appear on the cover of the magazine typically come, as in Babashoff's case, in the wake of outstanding athletic performances. Many athletes believed that appearing on the cover of *Sports Illustrated* made them subject to the *Sports Illustrated* jinx, which doomed them to subpar performance during the ensuing months. But this perception was a statistical illusion. As the psychologist Tom Gilovich explained, "It does not take much statistical sophistication to see how regression effects may be responsible for the belief in the *Sports Illustrated* jinx. Athletes' performances at different times are imperfectly correlated. Thus, due to regression alone, we can expect an extraordinary good performance to be followed, on the average, by a somewhat less extraordinary performance. Athletes appear on the cover of *Sports Illustrated* when they are newsworthy—i.e., when their performance is extraordinary. Thus, an athlete's superior performance in the weeks preceding a cover story is very likely to be followed by somewhat poorer performance in the weeks after. Those who believe in the jinx . . . are mistaken, not in what they observe, but in how they interpret what they see. Many athletes do suffer deterioration in their performance after being pictured on the cover of *Sports Illustrated*, and the mistake lies in citing a jinx, rather than citing regression as the proper interpretation of this phenomenon."[5]

AP Images

✔ SELF-TEST 10.2

Following an unusual increase in burglaries in a New York City neighborhood, the chief of police assigned additional officers to patrol the neighborhood. In the following month, the number of burglaries declined significantly. Does this mean the increased patrols were effective?

ANCHORING AND ADJUSTMENT

Another common judgmental heuristic is called **anchoring and adjustment.** It holds that when we try to estimate something, we often begin with a tentative initial estimate, called the anchor, which we then adjust in the light of whatever additional information is available. A common bias pattern observed in anchoring and adjustment is that the anchors are sometimes of questionable relevance, and the adjustments people make are often insufficient.

Suppose, for example, that a professor who stands 6′4″ asks his students to estimate his height. They may often anchor on the average height for men—about 5′10″ in the United States—and then adjust that value upward because their visual assessment indicates

anchoring and adjustment
an estimation technique that begins with an initial approximation (the anchor), which is then modified in accordance with additional available information (the adjustment)

[5]Thomas Gilovich, *How We Know What Isn't So: The Fallibility of Human Reason in Everyday Life* (New York: Free Press, 1991).

that their professor is significantly taller than average. Typically, however, their adjustments will fall short. In most cases, the average of their estimates of the professor's height in this example will be two or three inches shorter than his actual height.

A particularly vivid example of this potential bias comes from an experiment in which American students were asked to estimate the percentage of African countries belonging to the United Nations. Most had no idea what the true percentage was. Before even hearing the question, subjects in two groups were asked to perform the ostensibly unrelated task of spinning a wheel that could stop on any number from 1 to 100. In the first group, the wheel was rigged to stop on 65, while in the second it was rigged to stop on 10. Students in both groups surely knew that the number on which the spinning wheel stopped bore no relation to the true percentage of African nations in the UN. Yet the average estimate of the group whose wheel stopped on 65 was 45 percent, while the average estimate of the group whose wheel stopped on 10 was only 25.[6]

> **RECAP** ↑
>
> **JUDGMENTAL HEURISTICS AND RULES OF THUMB**
>
> According to the *availability heuristic*, we often estimate the frequency of an event by the ease with which we can recall relevant examples. Errors often result because frequency is only imperfectly correlated with ease of recall.
>
> The *representative heuristic* holds that the likelihood of something belonging to a given category is directly related to the degree to which it resembles stereotypical members of that category. Here, too, errors often result because other factors also influence the relevant probabilities.
>
> The tendency to ignore *regression to the mean*—the idea that extreme events are likely to be followed by more nearly normal ones—is yet another source of judgmental errors.
>
> *Anchoring and adjustment* holds that when we try to estimate something, we often begin with a tentative anchor, which we then adjust in the light of additional information. The anchors that people employ are often of questionable relevance, and the corresponding adjustments are often insufficient.

MISINTERPRETATION OF CONTEXTUAL CLUES

Another important class of judgment errors stems from misinterpretation of common contextual cues.

THE PSYCHOPHYSICS OF PERCEPTION

As psychologists have long understood, our assessments are almost always heavily shaped by the local environmental context. Consider a couple driving with their 10-year-old daughter to visit her grandparents. They are 10 miles from their destination when she asks, "Are we almost there yet?" If those 10 miles remain on a 120-mile journey, her parents will reassure her that they're nearly there. But if the same 10 miles remain on a 12-mile journey they will answer differently: "No, honey, we've still got quite a way to go." Similarly, in the year 1920, if your car could reach a speed of 60 miles per hour eventually, it would have seemed blazingly fast. But unless a car could reach 60 mph in under 6 seconds today, many motorists would think it sluggish.

Every assessment of this sort rests on an explicit or implicit frame of reference. According to a relationship known as the **Weber-Fechner law** of psychophysics, our

Weber-Fechner law the relationship according to which the perceived change in any stimulus varies according to the size of the change measured as a proportion of the original stimulus

---

[6]Amos Tversky and Daniel Kahneman, "Judgment under Uncertainty: Heuristics and Biases," *Science* 185 (1974), pp. 1124–1131.

perception of the change in any stimulus varies according to the size of the change measured as a proportion of the original stimulus. In some contexts, there is nothing problematic about reckoning importance in proportional terms. But in other contexts, it can lead us astray. Real estate developers, for example, often exploit people's tendency to think in percentage terms by bundling additional features into the prices of their houses for sale. Buyers might be reluctant to spend $5,000 for a jacuzzi for a house they already owned, but might see the same expense as far less daunting if it meant paying $250,000 for a new house instead of $245,000.[7]

THE DIFFICULTY OF ACTUALLY DECIDING

In the tale of Buridan's ass, a starving donkey stands equidistant from two identical bales of hay. But because his attraction to each bale is exactly equal, he is unable to decide which bale to approach and therefore dies of hunger. Although it is difficult to imagine such indecision causing a human to die of hunger, the fact remains that many people experience significant anxiety when forced to decide between two options that are roughly equally attractive. If the options were, in fact, equally attractive, it would of course not matter which one was chosen. But the anxiety some people experience in such situations leads them to violate basic predictions of traditional economic models.

Suppose you were faced with a choice between the two apartments labeled *A* and *B* in Figure 10.1. The attraction of *A* is that it's close to campus, but the downside is that its rent is fairly high. In contrast, *B*'s rent is much more reasonable, but unfortunately it happens to be much farther from campus. By suitable manipulation of the rent/distance values, it should be possible to describe pairs of apartments like *A* and *B* such that a given individual would be essentially indifferent between them. The interesting thing, however, is that this doesn't mean that she would find it easy to choose. On the contrary, many people experience significant anxiety when confronted with such choices.

Now suppose we gather a large group of subjects and manipulate the distance/rent values of *A* and *B* so that when forced to choose, half the subjects choose *A* and the remaining half choose *B*. What do you think would have happened if we had asked that same group of subjects to choose among three apartments—the same *A* and *B* as before plus a new option at *C*, as shown in Figure 10.2. According to traditional rational choice theory, the apartment at *C* is an irrelevant option, since it is worse along both dimensions than *B*. And, in fact, when *C* is added to the set of options, no one chooses it.

Yet the presence of the option at *C* has a profound effect on the observed pattern of choices between *A* and *B*. This time many more subjects choose *B*, and many fewer choose *A*.[8] The apparent explanation of the shift is that subjects find it easy to choose *B* over *C*, and that invests option *B* with a halo that leads subjects to favor it when confronted with the anxiety-inducing choice between *A* and *B*.

Experienced salespersons may exploit this pattern when dealing with people who have difficulty choosing among hard-to-compare alternatives. To close the deal, it may be enough to expose the client to a new option that is worse along every dimension than one of the original options.

As the preceding examples illustrate, cognitive errors often lead to departures from the predictions of standard rational choice models. We call such examples "departures from rational choice with regret," the idea being that once people are made aware of the cognitive errors they have made, they seem motivated to avoid those errors in the future.

Many proponents of traditional economic models appear reluctant to amend those models to take account of systematic cognitive errors. Some argue, for example, that in competitive environments, the penalties associated with such errors will reduce their frequency, enabling us to safely neglect them. Yet the mere fact that people make

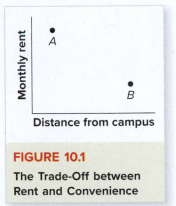

FIGURE 10.1

The Trade-Off between Rent and Convenience

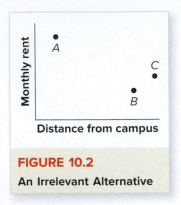

FIGURE 10.2

An Irrelevant Alternative

Mc Graw Hill **connect**

▶ Visit your instructor's Connect course and access your eBook to view this video.

Why do real estate agents often show clients two nearly identical houses, even though one is both cheaper and in better condition than the other?

---

[7]For more examples along similar lines, see Richard Thaler, "Toward a Positive Theory of Consumer Choice," *Journal of Economic Behavior and Organization* 1 (1980), pp. 39–60.

[8]Amos Tversky and Itamar Simonson, "Context-Dependent Preferences," *Management Science* 39, no. 10 (October 1993), pp. 1179–1189.

systematic cognitive errors does not imply that that reliance on heuristics is maladaptive in any global sense. The important question is whether following some alternative strategy would lead to better results on average. Rules like the availability heuristic are extremely easy to apply and work well much of the time. The costs of an occasional wrong decision must be weighed against the obvious advantages of reliance on simple decision and judgment rules.

In any event, there is clear evidence that systematic cognitive errors exist and are widespread. Absent clear evidence that reliance on heuristics is a losing strategy on balance, there is a strong methodological case for taking explicit account of cognitive errors in descriptive models of individual behavior. A plausible case can also be made that by becoming more aware of the circumstances that are likely to elicit cognitive errors, we can learn to commit those errors less frequently.

> *RECAP*
>
> **MISINTERPRETATION OF CONTEXTUAL CLUES**
>
> Almost every human judgment requires an explicit or implicit frame of reference. The *Weber-Fechner law* holds that perceptions of the change in any stimulus vary according to the size of the change as a proportion of the original stimulus. This reckoning leads many to say, for example, that they would drive across town to save $10 on a $20 radio but not to save $10 on a $1,000 computer. Yet if the benefit of driving across town exceeds the cost of driving across town for the radio, the same must be true for the computer (since the benefit is $10 in both cases and the cost of driving is the same in both cases).
>
> Other choice anomalies arise because people often have difficulty choosing between two alternatives whose characteristics are difficult to compare. When confronted by such choices, the addition of a third alternative that is worse than the first of the original alternatives on every dimension often has the effect of tilting choice heavily in favor of the first alternative. According to traditional models, the addition of such an alternative should have no effect on the choice between the other two.

IMPULSE-CONTROL PROBLEMS

Another troubling feature of traditional economic models is that they appear to rule out the possibility that people might regret having chosen behaviors whose consequences were perfectly predictable at the outset. Yet such expressions of regret are common. Many people wake up wishing they had drunk less the night before, but few wake up wishing they had drunk more.

It is likewise a puzzle within traditional economic models that people often incur great expense and inconvenience to prevent behaviors they would otherwise freely choose. For example, the model has difficulty explaining why some people would pay thousands of dollars to attend weight-loss camps that will feed them only 1,500 calories per day.

Welfare analysis based on the traditional models assigns considerable importance, as it should, to people's own judgments about what makes them better off. In this framework, it is not clear how one could ever conclude that a risk freely chosen by a well-informed person was a wrong choice. By itself, the fact that the choice led to a bad outcome is clearly not decisive. If someone is unlucky enough to be killed crossing the street, for example, we would not conclude that crossing streets is a generally bad idea.

Compelling evidence from psychology suggests, however, that expressions of regret may often be genuine, that people might sensibly impose constraints on their own behavior, and that risks freely chosen by well-informed people may not be optimal from their own point of view. Much of this evidence concerns behavior in the realm of intertemporal choice.

The rational choice model says that people will discount future costs and benefits in such a way that the choice between two rewards that are separated by a fixed time interval will be the same no matter when the choice is made.[9] Consider, for example, the pair of choices A and B:

A: $100 tomorrow vs. $110 a week from tomorrow.
B: $100 after 52 weeks vs. $110 after 53 weeks.

Both pairs of rewards are separated by exactly one week. If future receipts are discounted as assumed in traditional models, people will always make the same choice under alternative A as they do under alternative B. Since the larger payoff comes a week later in each case, the cost of choosing the smaller, but earlier, payoff is the same in each case—namely, the $10 forgone by doing so. When people confront such choices in practice, however, there is a pronounced tendency to choose differently under the two scenarios: Most pick the $100 option in A, whereas most choose the $110 option in B.

Researchers who have studied intertemporal choices experimentally have amassed substantial evidence that perceived future costs and benefits fall much more sharply with delay than assumed in traditional models.[10] One consequence is that preference reversals of the kind just observed occur frequently. The classic reversal involves choosing the larger, later reward when both alternatives occur with substantial delay, then switching to the smaller, earlier reward when its availability becomes imminent. This reversal shows up in The Economic Naturalist 10.2.

The Economic Naturalist 10.2

Why would people pay thousands of dollars to attend a weight-loss camp that will feed them only 1,500 calories per day?

Viewed within the framework of conventional rational choice models, it would be puzzling indeed that people would spend large sums to be prevented from eating food that they were free to refrain from eating on their own. But if people tend to discount future costs and benefits sharply, the answer is clear: They really want to eat less, but they know that if tempting foods are readily available, they will lack the willpower to do so. The weight-loss camp solves this problem by making tempting foods less available.

The tendency to discount future costs and benefits excessively gives rise to a variety of familiar impulse-control problems and, in turn, to a variety of strategies for solving them. Anticipating their temptation to overeat, people often try to limit the quantities of sweets, salted nuts, and other delicacies they keep on hand. Anticipating their temptation to spend cash in their checking accounts, people enroll in payroll-deduction savings plans. Foreseeing the difficulty of putting down a good mystery novel in midstream, many people know better than to start one on the evening before an important meeting. Reformed

[9]This is known as "exponential discounting."

[10]According to psychologists, people tend to discount future costs and benefits hyperbolically, not exponentially. Two of the most important earlier papers on this issue are Shin-Ho Chung and Richard Herrnstein, "Choice and Delay of Reinforcement," *Journal of the Experimental Analysis of Behavior* 10 (1967), pp. 67–74; George Ainslie, "Specious Reward: A Behavioral Theory of Impulsiveness and Impulse Control," *Psychological Bulletin* 82 (July 1975), pp. 463–496. See also Jon Elster, "Don't Burn Your Bridge before You Come to It: Seven Types of Ambiguity in Precommitment," Texas Law Review Symposium on Precommitment Theory, Bioethics, and Constitutional Law, September 2002; Thomas Schelling, "The Intimate Contest for Self-Command," *The Public Interest,* Summer 1980, pp. 94–118; R. Thaler and H. Shefrin, "An Economic Theory of Self-Control," *Journal of Political Economy* 89 (1981), pp. 392–405; Gordon Winston, "Addiction and Backsliding: A Theory of Compulsive Consumption," *Journal of Economic Behavior and Organization* 1 (1980), pp. 295–394. For a comprehensive review of work discussing the economic applications of the hyperbolic discounting model, see Shane Frederick, George Loewenstein, and Ted O'Donoghue, "Time Discounting and Time Preference: A Critical Review," *Journal of Economic Literature* 40, no. 2 (June 2002), pp. 351–401.

smokers seek the company of nonsmokers when they first try to kick the habit and are more likely than others to favor laws that limit smoking in public places. The recovering alcoholic avoids cocktail lounges.

Effective as these bootstrap methods of self-control may often be, they are far from perfect. Many people continue to express regret about having overeaten, having drunk and smoked too much, having saved too little, having stayed up too late, having watched too much television, and so on. Traditional economic models urge us to dismiss these expressions as sour grapes. But behavioral evidence suggests that these same expressions are often coherent. In each case, the actor chose an inferior option when a better one was available and later feels genuinely sorry about it. As with behaviors that stem from systematic cognitive errors, those that stem from impulse-control problems may be described as "departures from rational choice with regret."

In view of the obvious difficulties to which excessive discounting gives rise, it might seem puzzling that this particular feature of human motivation is so widespread. As with cognitive errors that stem from reliance on judgmental heuristics, however, here too it is important to stress that a behavioral tendency leading to bad outcomes some of the time does not imply that it is maladaptive in a global sense. Heavy discounting of future events forcefully directs our attention to immediate costs and benefits. If forced to choose between a motivational structure that gave heavy weight to current payoffs and an alternative that gave relatively greater weight to future payoffs, it is easy to imagine why evolutionary forces might have favored the former. After all, in highly competitive and uncertain environments, immediate threats to survival were numerous, and there must always have been compelling advantages in directing most of our energies toward meeting them.

In any case, there is clear evidence here, too, that excessive discounting exists and is widespread. Whether or not this motivational structure is disadvantageous on balance, there is a persuasive case for taking explicit account of it if our aim is to predict how people will behave under real-world conditions.

We also note that societies around the world have adopted a variety of policies that are most easily understood as attempts to mitigate the consequences of impulse-control problems. These include the treatment of so-called crimes of passion; prohibitions against gambling, addictive drugs, and prostitution; entrapment laws; and sanctions against adultery. Programs that aim to stimulate savings can also be viewed as a response to impulse-control problems that make it difficult to execute rational savings plans.

RECAP ↑

IMPULSE-CONTROL PROBLEMS

Although many traditional economic models rule out the possibility that people might regret having chosen behaviors whose consequences were perfectly predictable, such regrets are common.

Compelling evidence from psychology suggests that expressions of regret may often be genuine, that people often have difficulty waiting for a larger, better reward when an inferior reward is available immediately. Traditional models also have difficulty explaining why people might pay large sums to attend a weight-loss camp that will dramatically constrain their daily caloric intake. But if people tend to discount future costs and benefits excessively, they know that if tempting foods are readily available, they may lack the willpower to avoid them. Without taking explicit account of self-control problems, it is difficult to predict how people will behave under real-world conditions.

Some of the most important developments in economics in recent decades have entailed revisions to traditional assumptions about the nature of people's preferences. We focus next on three major changes—the introduction of asymmetries in the way people evaluate alternatives involving gains and losses, the relaxation of the assumption that people are self-interested in the narrow sense, and the introduction of concerns about relative position.

LOSS AVERSION AND STATUS QUO BIAS ———————

Traditional economic models hold that the extra satisfaction from gaining a dollar should be roughly equal to the reduction in satisfaction from losing a dollar. In practice, however, people's behavior suggests that losses often weigh much more heavily than gains.

An illustration of this tendency comes in the form of experiments designed to probe the difference in the value people assign to an object they already own versus the value they assign to one they have an opportunity to buy. In one experiment involving 44 subjects, half of participants were chosen at random to receive a coffee mug that they were free to keep or sell as they chose. The other half of the participants did not receive a mug. Participants were then given an opportunity to examine the mugs carefully—their own if they'd been given one, a neighboring subject's if they hadn't.

Subjects were then told to submit bids reflecting how much they'd be willing to pay for a mug if they didn't already have one or how much they'd be willing to accept for selling the mug they already had. In repeated rounds of this experiment, researchers used these bids to determine the prices at which the number of mugs offered would be equal to the number of mugs demanded. Those equilibrium prices varied between $4.25 and $4.75.

The researchers used the term *mug lovers* to describe the half of all subjects who happened to like the mugs most among all participants and *mug haters* to describe those who liked the mugs least. The fact that the mugs had been distributed at random implied that half of them, on average, would have ended up in the hands of mug lovers and the other half in the hands of mug haters. Thus, the apparent prediction of traditional economic models was that approximately half of the mugs—which is to say, 11 mugs on average—should be exchanged at the market-clearing prices. But the actual number of observed trades was dramatically smaller—only slightly more than two mugs changed hands, on average.

The apparent explanation was that the mere fact of owning a mug caused people to assign much greater value to it. The median price at which mug owners were willing to sell their mugs was $5.25, for example, more than twice the amount the median non-owner was willing to pay.[11]

This asymmetry in valuations is often called **loss aversion.** Similar experiments involving the exchange of modestly priced objects suggest that someone who possesses an object values it about twice as high, on average, as someone who does not possess it.

loss aversion the tendency to experience losses as more painful than the pleasures that result from gains of the same magnitude

But there is evidence that when the things at stake are significantly more important, loss aversion becomes even more pronounced. In another experiment by Richard Thaler, subjects were asked to imagine that there was a 1 in 1,000 chance they had been exposed to an invariably fatal disease.[12] How much would they be willing to pay for the only available dose of an antidote that would save their lives? Their median response to this question was $2,000. A second group of subjects was asked how much they would have to be paid to be willing to volunteer to be exposed to that same disease if there was no available antidote. This time the median response was close to $500,000—more than 250 times higher than in the first case.

Note that in both cases, subjects are being asked how much they value a one-in-a-thousand reduction in their probability of dying. If people treated gains and losses symmetrically, their answers to the two questions would be roughly the same. But in the first case, they were being asked to buy an increase in their survival prospects (a gain), and in the second case, they were asked to sell a health benefit they already owned (a loss). People do not treat gains and losses symmetrically, and it appears that loss aversion becomes much more pronounced when the objects in question are more important.

Because every change in policy generates winners and losers, loss aversion has important implications for public policy. When the total benefits from a change in policy exceed the total cost, it will sometimes be practical for the winners to compensate the losers so that everyone comes out ahead. But when large numbers of people are involved, compensation often becomes impractical. And in such cases, resistance from those who stand to lose from the policy change often overwhelms the support of those who stand to gain,

[11]Daniel Kahneman, Jack L. Knetsch, and Richard H. Thaler, "Anomalies: The Endowment Effect, Loss Aversion, and Status Quo Bias," *The Journal of Economic Perspectives* 5, no. 1 (Winter 1991), pp. 193–206.
[12]Michael Lewis, "The Economist Who Realized How Crazy We Are," *Bloomberg View,* May 29, 2015.

status quo bias the general resistance to change, often stemming from *loss aversion*

Cost-Benefit

even when the total benefits substantially exceed the total costs. Loss aversion is thus an important source of what has been called **status quo bias** in the domain of public policy. The difficulty of enacting policy changes is encapsulated in the fabled *iron law of politics*: The losers always cry louder than the winners sing.

Is status quo bias a bad thing? It might seem reasonable to wonder whether the best posture for cost-benefit analysts might be to simply accept at face value the inflated weights that people assign to losses. In other words, perhaps the widespread resistance to change that we observe in practice should be interpreted to mean that change often does more harm than good.

Weighing against this interpretation, however, is evidence that people's initial estimates of how painful losses will be often fail to take into account the remarkable human tendency to adapt to altered circumstances. Many people say, for example, that they would prefer to be killed in an accident than to survive as a paraplegic. And most people who have become paralyzed have indeed experienced the transition as devastating. But what psychologists were surprised to discover was that paraplegics adapt more quickly and completely than they ever would have thought possible. According to one study, the post-accident happiness levels of paralyzed accident victims were significantly lower than they had been before their accidents, but not statistically different from those of a control group.[13] Parting with a possession, similarly, is likely to be far more aversive at first than it is after a period of adaptation to living without it.

There are thus reasonable grounds for believing that steps to counteract status quo bias will often serve community interests. Behavioral economists have begun to explore such steps. One effective way to mitigate status quo bias is to focus more carefully on how different alternatives are presented to people. Suppose, for example, that policymakers want to encourage citizens to save a larger proportion of their incomes. Researchers have discovered that an effective and relatively painless way to accomplish that goal is to make participation in employer payroll-deduction savings the default option. Historically, most employers required their employees to take an active step in setting up a payroll-deduction savings plan. But researchers persuaded a sample of firms to make enrollment in the plan automatic, allowing those who didn't want to participate to take the active step of opting out. An influential study by Brigitte Madrian and Dennis Shea found that when participation became the status quo, savings plan enrollments shot up dramatically—in one case, a jump from less than 50 percent participation to 86 percent of all first-year employees.[14] Similar experiments have demonstrated the power of default options to alter behavior in other domains, ranging from the kinds of insurance people buy to their willingness to be organ donors.

The Economic Naturalist 10.3

Why was Obamacare difficult to enact and harder still to repeal?

The Obama administration's strategy for reforming the American health care system was heavily shaped by its understanding of status quo bias. Most other developed countries guarantee universal health care coverage either by having the government hire health care providers directly (as in the UK) or by having the government reimburse private health care providers for their services (as in France and Canada). But in the United States, most people received health insurance provided by their employers. Although there are sound policy reasons to favor the approach used elsewhere (where health systems deliver care at about half the cost as in the United States), government officials realized that many citizens had grown accustomed to employer-sponsored insurance and would

[13]Philip Brinkman, Dan Coates, and Ronnie Janoff-Bulman, "Lottery Winners and Accident Victims: Is Happiness Relative?," *Journal of Personality and Social Psychology* 36, no. 8 (1978), pp. 917–927.
[14]Brigitte C. Madrian and Dennis F. Shea, "The Power of Suggestion: Inertia in 401(k) Participation and Savings Behavior," *Quarterly Journal of Economics* 116, no. 4 (2001), pp. 1149–1187.

resist attempts to require them to abandon it for a different approach. So the Affordable Care Act as passed in 2010 left the employer-provided insurance system intact, supplementing it with private market exchanges through which people without employer-provided insurance could purchase health insurance at affordable rates. Despite this compromise, the legislative effort to enact the Affordable Care Act was extremely contentious, and it passed by the slimmest of margins.

Once the act was implemented, it came under relentless attack from Republicans in the House of Representatives, who voted scores of times to repeal it. But to the surprise of no one familiar with loss aversion and status quo bias, these efforts also met stiff resistance. Obamacare had boosted the number of Americans with health insurance by more than 20 million, and estimates by the nonpartisan Congressional Budget Office suggested that repeal would reduce that number by a similar amount.

In short, once the Affordable Care Act was enacted into law, the conditions it brought about became the new status quo. So even as loss aversion helps explain why passage of the Affordable Care Act was so difficult in the first place, it also explains why it was so difficult to repeal once it became law.

RECAP ↑

LOSS AVERSION AND STATUS QUO BIAS

Widespread behavioral evidence suggests that people tend to weigh losses much more heavily than gains. The minimum price for which people would be willing to sell objects they already own is substantially higher than the price they would be willing to pay to acquire those same objects if they do not already own them.

This asymmetry is often called *loss aversion*. In experiments involving low-priced items, the difference between willingness to accept and willingness to pay is often on the order of two to one. But the ratio can be dramatically higher for high-valued items, such as conditions related to health and safety.

Because every change in policy generates winners and losers, loss aversion implies a large bias in favor of the status quo in public policy decisions. Evidence suggests that this bias often has harmful consequences since people's initial estimates of how painful losses will be often fail to take into account their ability to adapt to altered circumstances.

The strategic use of default options has proven to be an effective way to mitigate *status quo bias*. For example, making participation in employer payroll-deduction savings plans the default option has been shown to significantly reduce the tendency to save too little.

BEYOND NARROW SELF-INTEREST ———————

Most traditional economic models exclude other-regarding motives. They concede, for example, that homo economicus might volunteer in a United Way campaign in order to reap the benefits of an expanded network of business or social contacts, but insist that he would never make anonymous donations to charity. Yet charitable donations, many of them completely anonymous, totaled more than $425 billion a year in the U.S. in 2018.[15] Traditional models acknowledge that homo economicus might tip in a local restaurant to ensure good service

---

[15] https://givingusa.org/giving-usa-2019-americans-gave-427-71-billion-to-charity-in-2018-amid-complex-year-for-charitable-giving/.

on his next visit, but predict that he would not tip when dining alone in a restaurant far from home. Yet tipping rates are essentially the same in these two situations.[16] Traditional models also concede that homo economicus might go to the polls in a local ward election, in which a single vote might be decisive, but predict universal abstention in presidential elections. Yet tens of millions of people regularly vote in presidential elections. In short, traditional self-interest models are simple and elegant, but they also predict incorrectly much of the time.

THE PRESENT-AIM STANDARD OF RATIONALITY

The most widely employed alternative to the self-interest model is the present-aim model, which holds that people are efficient in the pursuit of whatever objectives they happen to hold at the moment of action.[17] The obvious appeal of the present-aim model is that it enables us to accommodate the plurality of goals that many people actually seem to hold, thus permitting us to account for behaviors that are anomalous within the self-interest framework. Someone donates anonymously to charity not because she hopes to receive indirect material benefits, but because she gets a warm glow from helping others in need. Someone tips in restaurant away from home not to ensure good service on his next visit, but because he feels sympathy for the server's interests. Someone votes in a presidential election not because his vote might tip the balance, but because he feels it his civic duty to do so. And so on.

But the present-aim model's flexibility also turns out to be a significant liability. The problem is that virtually any bizarre behavior can be "explained" after the fact simply by assuming a sufficiently strong taste for it. We call this the "crankcase-oil problem": If someone drinks a gallon of used crankcase oil from his car, then writhes in agony and dies, a present-aim theorist has a ready explanation—the man must have *really* liked crankcase oil. Proponents of traditional models thus have sound reasons for their methodological skepticism about the present-aim model. As they correctly point out, a model that can explain virtually everything is not really a scientific model at all.

We are confronted, then, with a choice between two flawed alternatives. The self-interest standard of rationality generates testable predictions about behavior, but these predictions often turn out to be flatly incorrect. The **present-aim standard of rationality** accommodates a much broader range of observed behavior, but remains vulnerable to the charge of excessive flexibility. In addition to these two, we consider a third standard, one that is significantly more flexible than the self-interest standard, but also one whose flexibility sidesteps the most serious objections to the present-aim standard.

THE ADAPTIVE RATIONALITY STANDARD[18]

Like both the self-interest and present-aim standards, the **adaptive rationality standard** assumes that people choose efficient means to achieve their ends. But unlike the other conceptions, which take goals as given, adaptive rationality regards goals as objects of choice themselves and, as such, subject to a similar efficiency requirement.

By what criterion might we evaluate the efficiency of an individual's choice of goals? Since the problem that plagues the present-aim standard is excessive flexibility, the efficiency standard we employ for evaluating alternatives to this model should be both objective and strict. On both counts, Charles Darwin's theory of natural selection, enriched to allow for the influence of cultural and other environmental forces during development, is an attractive candidate. In this framework, the design criterion for a goal or taste is the same as for an arm or a leg or an eye—namely, the extent to which it assists the individual in the struggle to acquire the resources required for survival and reproduction. If it works better than the available alternatives, selection pressure will favor it. Otherwise,

present-aim standard of rationality a variant of the rational choice model that permits greater flexibility in assumptions about preferences

adaptive rationality standard a variant of the rational choice model that permits additional preferences to be added if they can be shown not to handicap resource acquisition in competitive environments

[16]O. Bodvarsson and W. Gibson, "Gratuities and Customer Appraisal of Service: Evidence from Minnesota Restaurants," *Journal of Socio-Economics* 23, no. 3 (1994), pp. 287–302.
[17]Derek Parfit, *Reasons and Persons* (Oxford: Clarendon Press, 1984).
[18]The discussion that follows draws heavily on Robert H. Frank, "If *Homo Economicus* Could Choose His Own Utility Function, Would He Want One with a Conscience?," *American Economic Review* 77 (September 1987), pp. 593–604; Robert H. Frank, *Passions within Reason* (New York: Norton, 1988).

selection pressure will work against it. Our proposal, in brief, is that analysts be free to add a preference to the individual's list of concerns, but only upon showing that an individual motivated by that preference need not be handicapped in the competition to acquire the resources needed for survival and reproduction.

This standard passes the simple test of ruling out a taste for drinking crankcase oil. Indeed, it might seem such a stringent standard as to rule out any conception of rationality other than narrow self-interest. After all, if natural selection favors the traits and behaviors that maximize individual reproductive fitness, and if we *define* behaviors that enhance personal fitness as selfish, then self-interest becomes the only viable human motive by definition. This tautology was a central message of much of the sociobiological literature of the 1970s and 1980s.

On a closer look, however, the issues are less simple. For there are many situations in which individuals whose only goal is self-interest are likely to fare worse than others who pursue a richer mix of goals. Such is the case, for example, when individuals confront commitment problems, of which the one-shot prisoner's dilemma, discussed in Chapter 9, *Games and Strategic Behavior*, provides a clear illustration. If both players in this game cooperate, each does better than if both defect, and yet each gets a higher payoff by defecting no matter which strategy the other player chooses. If both players could commit themselves to a strategy of mutual cooperation, they would have a clear incentive to do so. Yet mere promises issued by narrowly self-interested persons would not seem to suffice, for each person would have no incentive to keep such a promise.

Suppose, however, that some people have a (perhaps context-specific) taste for cooperating in one-shot prisoner's dilemmas. If two players knew one another to have this taste, they could interact selectively, thereby reaping the gains of mutual cooperation. It is important to stress that merely having the taste is by itself insufficient to solve the problem. One must also be able to communicate its presence credibly to others and be able to identify its presence in them.

Can the presence of a taste for cooperation be reliably discerned by outsiders? Some experiments suggest that subjects are surprisingly accurate at predicting who would cooperate and who would defect in one-shot prisoner's dilemmas played with near strangers.[19] In these experiments, the base rate of cooperation was 73.7 percent and the base rate of defection only 26.3 percent. If subjects randomly guessed that a player would cooperate, they would thus have been accurate 73.7 percent of the time and a random prediction of defection accurate only 26.3 percent of the time. The actual accuracy rates for these two kinds of prediction were 80.7 percent and 56.8 percent, respectively. The likelihood of such high accuracy rates occurring by chance is less than 1 in 1,000.

Subjects in this experiment were strangers at the outset and were able to interact with one another for only 30 minutes before making their predictions. It is plausible to suppose that predictions would be considerably more accurate for people we have known for a long time.

For example, consider a thought experiment based on the following scenario:

> An individual has a gallon jug of unwanted pesticide. To protect the environment, the law requires that unused pesticide be turned in to a government disposal facility located 30 minutes' drive from her home. She knows, however, that she could simply pour the pesticide down her basement drain with no chance of being caught and punished. She also knows that her one gallon of pesticide, by itself, will cause only negligible harm to her if disposed of in this fashion. (But the harm would of course be far from negligible if everyone disposed of unwanted pesticide in this way.)

Can you think of anyone who you feel certain would dispose of the pesticide properly? Most people say they can. Usually they have in mind friends they have known for a long

---

[19]Robert H. Frank, Thomas Gilovich, and Dennis Regan, "The Evolution of One-Shot Cooperation," *Ethology and Sociobiology* 14 (July 1993), pp. 247–256.

time. If you feel you can identify such a person, then you, too, accept the central premise of the adaptive rationality account—namely, that it is possible to identify unselfish motives in at least some other people.

The presence of such motives, coupled with the ability of outsiders to discern them, makes it possible to solve a broad range of important commitment problems. Knowing this, even a rational, self-interested individual would have every reason to choose preferences that were not narrowly self-interested. Of course, people do not choose their preferences in any literal sense. The point is that if moral sentiments can be reliably discerned by others, then the complex interaction of genes and culture that yields human preferences can sustain preferences that lead people to subordinate narrow self-interest to the pursuit of other goals.

For example, although homo economicus might want to deter a potential aggressor by threatening to retaliate, his threat would not be credible if the cost of retaliation exceeded the value of what he stood to recover. By contrast, someone known to care strongly about honor for its own sake could credibly threaten to retaliate even in such cases. Such a person would thus be much less vulnerable to aggression than someone believed to be narrowly self-interested.

Similarly, although homo economicus might want to deter a one-sided offer from a potential trading partner by threatening to reject it, his threat would not be credible if his incentives clearly favored accepting the offer. By contrast, someone known to care strongly about equity for its own sake could credibly threaten to refuse such offers. Such a person would thus be a more effective bargainer than someone believed to be narrowly self-interested.

A second potential pathway whereby moral sentiments might be adaptive at the individual level is by helping people solve a variety of impulse control problems.[20] Consider, for example, the repeated prisoner's dilemma. As Rapoport, Axelrod, and others have shown, the tit-for-tat strategy fares well against alternative strategies in the repeated prisoner's dilemma.[21] Self-interested persons thus have good reasons to play tit-for-tat, yet to do so they must first solve an impulse-control problem. Playing tit-for-tat means cooperating on the first interaction, which in turn implies a lower payoff on that move than could have been had by defecting. The reward for playing tit-for-tat lies in the prospect of a string of mutually beneficial interactions in the future. The rational choice model holds that if the benefits of future cooperation, suitably discounted, outweigh the current costs, people will cooperate. But because the gain from defecting comes now, whereas its cost comes in the future, the decision maker confronts a classic impulse-control problem. (For more information on game theory, see Chapter 9, *Games and Strategic Behavior.*)

The moral sentiment of sympathy, which figured so prominently in Adam Smith's early writings, helps to solve this problem. Someone who feels sympathy for the interests of her trading partner faces an additional cost of defecting, one that occurs at the same time as the gain from defecting. Because of this cost, the person who sympathizes with her trading partners is less likely to defect and is thus more likely to reap the long-run gains of cooperation.

Moral sentiments and other non-self-interested motives figure prominently in economic and social life. Traditional economic models often ignore such motives, implicitly viewing the behaviors they provoke as irrational. But it is more descriptive to call them "departures from traditional rational choice models without regret" because, when people are told that they are behaving irrationally under the self-interest standard, they typically do not seem to want to alter their behavior. The attraction of the adaptive rationality standard is that it provides a methodologically rigorous framework within which to expand the narrow range of motives considered in traditional models. In the same fashion, it provides a coherent framework within which to take explicit account of systematic cognitive errors and impulse-control problems.

[20]Robert H. Frank, *Passions within Reason* (New York: Norton, 1988).
[21]In tit-for-tat, each player cooperates on the first move, and on each successive move does whatever her partner did on the previous move. See Anatol Rapoport and A. Chammah, *Prisoner's Dilemma* (Ann Arbor: University of Michigan Press, 1965); Robert Axelrod, *The Evolution of Cooperation* (New York: Basic Books, 1984).

CONCERNS ABOUT FAIRNESS

Additional evidence for the claim that narrow self-interest is not the only important human motive comes from an elegant experiment known as the **ultimatum bargaining game**.[22] The game is played by two players, "Proposer" and "Responder." It begins with Proposer being given a sum of money (say, $100) that he must then propose how to divide between himself and Responder. Responder then has two options: (1) he can accept, in which case each party gets the amount proposed, or (2) he can refuse, in which each party gets zero and the $100 goes back to the experimenter.

ultimatum bargaining game
a game in which the first player has the power to confront the second player with a take-it-or-leave-it offer

If both players cared only about their own absolute incomes, as assumed by economic orthodoxy, Proposer should propose $99 for himself and $1 for Responder (only whole-dollar amounts are allowed). And Responder will then accept this one-sided offer because he will reason that getting $1 is better than nothing.

Yet in scores of experiments performed in many different countries, this is almost never what happens. Thus, in one typical study in which the total amount to be divided was $10, the average amount offered by Proposer was $4.71, and in more than 80 percent of all cases Proposer offered exactly $5, a 50-50 split.[23] When Responders in this same study were asked to report the minimum amounts they would accept, their average response was $2.59. These experiments suggest clearly that laboratory subjects care not only about how much money they get, but also about how it is apportioned in relative terms.[24] Most people seem predisposed to reject offers whose terms they find sufficiently "unfair."

A large literature has emerged in recent years, much of it based on laboratory experiments, showing that concerns about fairness influence numerous similar economic choices. As in the laboratory, so in life. Believing their current contracts to be unfair, workers are often willing to go on strike, even when they know it may cost them their jobs. Customers often refuse to patronize merchants whose terms they believe to be inequitable, even when it will be more costly or less convenient to buy from alternative suppliers.[25]

Material incentives clearly matter. Ultimately, however, the law can do only so much to constrain individual behavior. To achieve a well-ordered society, we must rely at least in part on people's willingness to subordinate personal interests for the common good. Although the adaptive rationality standard embraces the possibility of voluntary self-restraint in such cases, the self-interest standard all but denies that possibility.

It is troubling, therefore, that at least some evidence suggests that exposure to self-interest models tends to inhibit self-restraint. For example, one study found that economics majors were more than twice as likely as non-majors to defect when playing one-shot prisoner's dilemmas with strangers, a difference that was not merely a reflection of the fact that people who chose to major in economics were more opportunistic to begin with.[26] The same study also found that academic economists were more than twice as likely as the members of other disciplines to report giving no money at all to any private charity.[27]

---

[22]Werner Guth, Rolf Schmittberger, and Bernd Schwarze, "An Experimental Analysis of Ultimatum Bargaining," *Journal of Economic Behavior and Organization* 3 (1982), pp. 367–388.

[23]See Table 1 in Daniel Kahneman, Jack Knetsch, and Richard Thaler, "Perceptions of Unfairness: Constraints on Wealthseeking," *American Economic Review* 76 (September 1986), pp. 728–741.

[24]For evidence in favor of this interpretation, see especially Lawrence M. Kahn and J. Keith Murnighan, "A General Experiment on Bargaining in Demand Games with Outside Options," *American Economic Review* 83 (December 1993), pp. 1260–1280.

[25]For an engaging survey of relevant evidence, see Chapters 14 and 15 of Richard Thaler, *Misbehaving* (New York: Norton, 2015).

[26]Robert H. Frank, Thomas Gilovich, and Dennis Regan, "Does Studying Economics Inhibit Cooperation?," *Journal of Economic Perspectives* 7 (Spring 1993), pp. 159–171. We found, for example, that the difference in defection rates grew larger the longer a student had studied economics. Questionnaire responses also indicated that first-year college students in their first microeconomics course were more likely at the end of the term to expect opportunistic behavior from others than they were at the beginning.

[27]For more information on the issue of whether exposure to the self-interest model inhibits cooperation, see Gerald Marwell and Ruth Ames, "Economists Free Ride, Does Anyone Else?," *Journal of Public Economics* 15 (1981), pp. 295–310; John Carter and Michael Irons, "Are Economists Different, and If So, Why?," *Journal of Economic Perspectives* 5 (Spring 1991); Antony Yezer, Robert Goldfarb, and Paul Poppen, "Does Studying Economics Discourage Cooperation? Watch What We Do, Not What We Say," *Journal of Economic Perspectives*, Spring 1996; Robert H. Frank, Thomas Gilovich, and Dennis Regan, "Do Economists Make Bad Citizens?," *Journal of Economic Perspectives*, Spring 1996.

These findings suggest that our choice among standards of rationality may be important not just for our attempts to predict and explain behavior, but also because of its potential impact on our willingness to engage in self-restraint. If so, we have even greater reason to reconsider the welfare implications of traditional economic models.

RECAP ↑

BEYOND NARROW SELF-INTEREST

Self-interest is without doubt an important human motive. But predictions based on the assumption that it is the only important motive fall short. Most people vote in presidential elections, despite the negligible possibility that their votes will tip the balance. Most people leave tips even in restaurants they never expect to visit again. And people donate billions of dollars to charity each year, much of it anonymously.

The *present-aim model of rational choice* asserts that people often behave unselfishly because they get a warm glow from doing so. That enables the present-aim model to accommodate many behaviors that the narrow self-interest model cannot. But that flexibility also turns out to be a significant liability since virtually any bizarre behavior can be "explained" after the fact simply by assuming a sufficiently strong taste for it. For this reason, critics object that the present-aim model doesn't make any testable predictions.

Like both the self-interest and present-aim standards, the *adaptive rationality standard* assumes that people choose efficient means to achieve their ends. But unlike the other conceptions, which take goals as given, adaptive rationality regards goals as objects of choice themselves and, as such, subject to a similar efficiency requirement. Analysts are free to add a preference to the individual's list, but only upon showing that the preference not compromise efforts to acquire the resources needed for survival in competitive environments. Certain unselfish motives qualify under this standard because they help people solve important commitment problems, such as the one-shot prisoner's dilemma. If two players had reason to believe one another to be trustworthy, they could interact selectively, thereby reaping the gains of mutual cooperation. But merely being trustworthy is not enough. One must also be able to communicate one's trustworthiness to others credibly and be able to identify its presence in them. Experimental evidence suggests that these conditions are often met.

Additional evidence for the claim that narrow self-interest is not the only important human motive comes from experiments showing that people reject transactions that would have benefited them if they believe the terms of those transactions to be unfair.

CONCERNS ABOUT RELATIVE POSITION

Many traditional economic models assume that well-being depends on current and future levels of absolute consumption. Considerable evidence suggests, however, that well-being depends as much or more on current and future levels of relative consumption.[28] The adaptive rationality standard holds that a taste for relative consumption can be introduced into the utility function if being thus motivated need not compromise resource acquisition in competitive environments. If people known to care about relative consumption are indeed better bargainers than those thought to care only about absolute consumption, this test is met.

---

[28]The points developed in this section are developed in greater detail in Robert H. Frank, "The Demand for Unobservable and Other Nonpositional Goods," *American Economic Review 75* (March 1985), pp. 101–116; Robert H. Frank, *Choosing the Right Pond* (New York: Oxford University Press, 1985).

The following thought experiment provides an intuitive test of whether relative consumption matters:

Which world would you choose?

World A: You and your family live in a neighborhood with 4,000-square-foot houses, and all other neighborhoods have 6,000-square-foot houses.

World B: You and your family live in a neighborhood with 3,000-square-foot houses, and all other neighborhoods have 2,000-square-foot houses.

If the satisfaction provided by a house depended only on its absolute features, World A would be the unambiguously better choice. Yet significantly more than half of respondents faced with this question choose World B. Some of the minority who choose World A seem to do so out of concern that they *shouldn't* care about others' houses. Even so, few among them seem puzzled that others might choose differently. The point is not that World B is the uniquely correct choice here. But if our goal is to predict people's actual choices, the traditional assumption that only absolute consumption matters is often misleading.

In some domains, however, the traditional assumption serves reasonably well. Consider a second thought experiment, one with exactly the same structure as the one for house size:

Which world would you choose?

World A: You have a 2 in 100,000 chance of dying on the job this year, and others have a 1 in 100,000 chance.

World B: You have a 4 in 100,000 chance of dying, and others have a 6 in 100,000 chance.

As before, this choice is between absolute advantage (World A) and relative advantage (World B). When people face that choice in the domain of housing, most choose relative advantage. But when their choice involves safety, almost everyone opts for absolute advantage.

The late British economist Fred Hirsch coined the term **positional good** to describe things that derive their value primarily from their relative scarcity rather than from their absolute characteristics. "The value of my education," he wrote, "depends on how much the man ahead of me in the job line has."[29] In what follows, we use Hirsch's term to mean a good whose value depends relatively heavily on how it compares with other goods in the same category. For people who chose relative over absolute advantage in the first thought experiment, housing would thus be a positional good.

Similarly, we use the term **nonpositional good** to describe one whose value depends relatively little on how it compares with other goods in the same category. For people who chose absolute advantage in the second thought experiment, workplace safety would be a nonpositional good.

To call housing positional is not to say that only the relative attributes of a house matter. Someone who chose World B in the first thought experiment, for example, might well have preferred to live in a world in which her neighborhood had 3,500-square-foot houses and others had houses of 3,000 square feet.

Similarly, choosing a world with high absolute safety doesn't mean that relative safety levels are of no concern. Most people choosing World A would almost certainly notice that their jobs were much more dangerous than others'. But if their only recourse were to move to World B, where their own absolute risk of death would double, they would decline.

Caring more about relative consumption in some domains than in others distorts people's spending decisions. It leads to what we call *positional arms races*—patterns of escalating expenditure focused on positional goods. The resulting dynamic is exactly analogous to the one that drives military arms races. In both cases, wasteful spending occurs only because some categories of expenditure are more context-sensitive than others.

Military arms races occur only because relative differences in spending on weapons have more important consequences than relative differences in nonmilitary spending. If,

positional good a good whose value depends relatively heavily on how it compares with other goods in the same category

nonpositional good a good whose value does not depend heavily on how it compares with other goods in the same category

[29] Fred Hirsch, *Social Limits to Growth* (Cambridge, MA: Harvard University Press, 1976).

to the contrary, spending less than a rival nation spent on toasters and television sets had more serious consequences than spending less on bombs, we would expect expenditure imbalances of precisely the opposite sort: Countries would spend ever less on armaments in a quest to gain relative advantage in the domain of nonmilitary spending. That is of course not what we see. Military arms races are a consequence, pure and simple, of relative spending on armaments being more important—because it contributes so heavily to the outcome of military conflict.

Similar distortions appear to occur in domestic consumption patterns. Because relative spending matters more, by definition, for positional goods than for nonpositional goods, people often end up spending too much on the former and too little on the latter. To see how the dynamic unfolds, consider a worker's choice between two jobs that offer different levels of risk to safety. Both because safety devices are costly and because workers prefer safe jobs to risky ones, employers who want to attract workers to riskier jobs can and must pay higher wages. Choosing additional safety on the job therefore comes at the expense of having less income to spend on other things. Choosing a riskier job would enable a worker to buy a nicer house. If she has children, that option might look doubly attractive since she knows that in almost every jurisdiction, better schools are those located in more expensive neighborhoods.

So let's imagine that she chooses the higher-paying but riskier job. The same logic would also lead similarly situated workers to make the same choice. And if they too chose riskier jobs to be able to afford houses in better school districts, their increased bidding would serve only to bid up the prices of those houses. Half of all children would still attend bottom-half schools, the same as if no one had sacrificed safety for higher wages. All will have sold their safety in pursuit of a goal that none achieves.

Since Adam Smith's day, classical economic theory has held that well-informed workers in competitive markets will sensibly navigate this trade-off between income and safety. They will accept additional risk in return for higher pay only if the satisfaction from having what they can buy with the extra income is greater than the corresponding loss in satisfaction from reduced safety. According to proponents of this view, regulations that mandate higher safety levels harm workers by forcing them to buy safety they value at less than its cost.

But why, then, does virtually every country in the world regulate workplace safety?[30] (Even the poorest countries have at least rudimentary safety requirements.) Classical economic theory doesn't have a good answer. It portrays such regulations as either anomalous, or else needed because workers are uninformed, or because markets aren't competitive enough. Yet we regulate many safety risks that workers clearly understand. Most coal miners, for example, know their work entails risk of black lung disease since their fathers and grandfathers died of it.

Nor is imperfect competition the problem. Most safety regulations, after all, have their greatest impact in precisely those markets that most closely approximate the competitive ideal. They have little effect on engineers in Silicon Valley or on investment bankers on Wall Street, whose conditions of employment are substantially safer than required by the Occupational Safety and Health Administration. It's the employers who compete most fiercely with one another to attract the workers they need, such as fast-food restaurants and manufacturing firms that employ unskilled labor, that seldom go long without a visit from a safety inspector.

Analogous reasoning suggests that individual incentives are misleadingly high for many other things we might sell for money—our leisure time, future job security, and a host of other environmental amenities. The problem is not that we exchange these items for money, but that our incentives lead us to sell them too cheaply. In the case of workplace safety, the solution is not to ban risk, but to make it less attractive to individuals. As concerns the length of the workweek, the best solution is not strict limits on hours worked, but rather a change in incentives (such as overtime laws) that make long hours less attractive.

[30]Scott Coulter, "Advancing Safety around the World," *Occupational Health and Safety,* February 1, 2009.

One rationale for policy measures to stimulate additional savings is that impulse-control problems often prevent people from adhering to rationally chosen savings plans. But savings shortfalls also stem from a second source, one that is difficult to address by unilateral action. The following thought experiment illustrates the basic problem:

> If you were society's median earner, which of these two worlds would you prefer?
>
> World A. You save enough to support a comfortable standard of living in retirement, but your children attend a school whose students score in bottom 20 percent on standardized tests in reading and math.
>
> World B. You save too little to support a comfortable standard of living in retirement, but your children attend a school whose students score in the 50th percentile on those tests.

Because the concept of a "good" school is inescapably relative, this thought experiment captures an essential element of the savings decision confronting most middle-income families. If others bid for houses in better school districts, failure to do likewise will often consign one's children to inferior schools. But as noted earlier, no matter how much each family spends, half of all children must attend schools in the bottom half. The choice posed by the thought experiment is one that most parents would prefer to avoid. But when forced to choose, most say they would pick the second option.

Like workplace safety decisions, savings decisions are thus also examples of the collective action problem inherent in a military arms race. Each nation knows that it would be better if all spent less on arms. Yet if others keep spending, it is simply too dangerous not to follow suit. Curtailing an arms race thus requires an enforceable agreement. Similarly, unless all families can bind themselves to save more, those who do so unilaterally will pay the price of having to send their children to inferior schools. In these observations lie the seeds of a possible answer to the question posed in The Economic Naturalist 10.4.

The Economic Naturalist 10.4

Why have attempts to privatize Social Security proved so politically unpopular in the United States?

Since its inception during the Great Depression, the Social Security system has required universal participation. People's labor earnings are subject to the payroll tax, which is then used to finance pension payments for older Americans in retirement. Early in his second term in office, President George W. Bush promoted a proposal to privatize Social Security. Under this proposal, people would be free to decide for themselves how much to save each month and how much to spend. To the president's surprise, however, this proposal proved deeply unpopular. Why didn't most people welcome the additional freedom that privatization would have offered?

As discussed, if parents had complete access to their retirement savings accounts, some would undoubtedly withdraw money from those accounts in order to bid for houses in better school districts. Rather than see their own children fall behind, many other parents would feel compelled to follow suit. But the increased bidding would serve only to drive up the prices of the houses in better school districts, even as many parents would end up with inadequate savings to support themselves in retirement. Mandatory participation in the Social Security system solves this dilemma. The money paid in payroll taxes, which is unavailable to bid for houses in better school districts, remains available to finance pension payments to retirees.

Positional concerns also appear to alter the distribution between public and private spending. Public goods are fundamentally different from private goods: When some people spend more on houses or wedding celebrations, for example, others may feel pressure to follow suit, but the same dynamic does not occur for public goods, which are available on essentially equal terms to all citizens. Because public goods do not lend themselves to interpersonal comparisons, they are nonpositional almost by definition.

In any event, there is little question that levels of public investment have not kept pace in recent decades. For example, engineers report record maintenance backlogs not only in the nation's roads and bridges, but also in airports, schools, drinking water, and sewage systems.[31] And in the face of these backlogs, proposals to launch significant new infrastructure initiatives, such as high-speed rail service or a smart electric grid, have consistently failed in Congress. More troubling, we have not yet launched the investments required to confront the climate crisis, by far the biggest challenge facing the planet.

In short, substantial evidence suggests that most people would be happier if a larger share of national income were spent on nonpositional goods, including long-neglected public investment. Such misallocations tend to be stubborn, however, because they stem largely from the kinds of collective-action problems we earlier described as "departures from rational choice without regret." Just as the practice of standing at concerts persists because it is rational for each individual to continue standing when others are doing so, spending imbalances that arise from collective-action problems cannot be remedied by individual action. People must turn to the political system in search of effective ways to act collectively.

In contrast, welfare losses that arise from cognitive errors can be attacked at the individual level. Once people realize that it's irrational to take sunk costs into account, for example, they may become both motivated to—and able to—alter their choices unilaterally. That's why we earlier described choices that are driven by cognitive errors as "departures from rational choice with regret."

As noted, many of the tax and regulatory policies already in effect, such as workplace safety laws and pollution taxes, can be interpreted as positional arms control agreements. But if, as suggested above, additional implementation of such policies could in fact promote changes in spending patterns that would increase welfare substantially, we're left with the challenging question posed in The Economic Naturalist 10.5.

The Economic Naturalist 10.5

If prosperous voters would be happier if they spent less on positional goods and lived in environments with more generously funded public sectors, why haven't they elected politicians who would deliver what they want?

A partial answer to this question might begin with the observation that voters are extremely reluctant to pay the higher taxes necessary to refurbish decaying infrastructure and underwrite massive investment in green energy. But that begs the question. If the gains from the additional investment would indeed be much larger than the corresponding losses from reduced positional consumption, why would voters be opposed?

Here we consider the possibility that opposition is itself rooted in a powerful cognitive illusion. But first, we offer a few general observations about the nature of cognitive illusions: Life is complicated. Because we are bombarded by terabytes of information each day, our nervous systems employ shortcuts, or rules of thumb, for evaluating it. As noted earlier, these heuristics work reasonably well most of the time—but not always.

[31] *2017 Infrastructure Report Card: D+*, www.infrastructurereportcard.org.

In the diagram below, which square is darker, A or B? If you think A looks darker, your eyes and brain are functioning normally. But in this instance, your judgment is incorrect. In what's called the checker-shadow illusion, Square A is exactly the same shade of gray as Square B. Look at the figure carefully. If your reaction is typical, you might be thinking, "That can't be true!" And yet it is.

The psychologist Richard Wiseman offers this explanation:

> Your eyes and brain see that the two squares are the same shade of gray, but then think, "Hold on—if a square in a shadow reflects the same amount of light as a square outside of the shadow, then in reality [Square B] must be a much lighter shade of gray." As a result, your brain alters your perception of the image so that you see what it thinks is out there in the real world.[32]

This is of course an adaptive response, something we'd want our brains to do. Yet Wiseman's explanation, plausible though it sounds, is insufficient to convince most people.

Now study the amended image below, and note the complete lack of contrast between Squares A and B and the added strip that joins them. Only upon seeing this second image are many people even able to consider the possibility that A and B might actually be the same shade of gray.

As the checker-shadow illusion dramatically illustrates, a statement that seems incontrovertibly true ("Square A is darker than Square B") may in fact be false. This example should affirm at least the possibility that self-evidently true beliefs about the effect of higher taxes may be false as well.

[32]Richard Wiseman, "Ten of the Greatest Optical Illusions," *Daily Mail,* September 25, 2010.

When someone asks, "How will an event affect me?," the natural first step is to try to recall the effects of similar events in the past. When parents are trying to decide whether to take their children to Disney World, for example, they might try to summon memories of how well they had enjoyed past visits to similar theme parks. In like fashion, when high-income people try to imagine the impact of higher taxes, Plan A is to summon memories of how they felt in the wake of past tax increases.

But that strategy doesn't work in the current era, since most high-income people alive today have experienced steadily declining tax rates. In WWII, the top marginal tax rate in the United States was 92 percent. In 1966, it was 70 percent, and in 1982, just 50 percent. Currently it is 37 percent. Apart from brief and isolated increases almost too small to notice, top marginal tax rates have fallen steadily throughout the lifetimes of voters born after WWII.

When Plan A fails, we go to Plan B. Because paying higher taxes means having less money to spend on other things, a plausible alternative cognitive strategy is to estimate the effect of tax hikes by recalling earlier events that resulted in lower disposable income—an occasional business reverse, for example, or a losing lawsuit, or a divorce, or a house fire, maybe even a health crisis. Rare is the life history that is completely devoid of events like these, which share a common attribute: They make people feel miserable.

More important, such events share a second feature, one that is absent from an increase in taxes: They reduce our own incomes while leaving others' incomes unaffected. Higher taxes, in contrast, reduce all incomes in tandem. This difference holds the key to understanding why people think higher taxes would be so painful.

As most prosperous people would themselves be quick to concede, they have everything anybody might reasonably be said to need. If higher taxes pose any threat, it would be to make it more difficult for them to buy life's special extras. But as we have seen, "special" is an inescapably relative concept. To be special means to stand out in some way from what is expected. And almost without exception, special things are in limited supply. There are only so many penthouse apartments with sweeping views of Central Park, for instance. To get one, a wealthy person must outbid peers who also want it. The outcomes of such bidding contests depend almost exclusively on relative purchasing power. And since relative purchasing power is completely unaffected when the wealthy all pay higher taxes, the same penthouses end up in the same hands as before.

A plausible objection is that higher tax rates on prosperous Americans would put them at a disadvantage relative to oligarchs from other countries in the bidding wars for trophy properties in the United States. But that disadvantage could be eliminated easily by the imposition of a purchase levy on nonresident buyers.

In short, the answer to the question of why voters haven't supported the taxes necessary to finance desperately needed public investment may be that many suffer from the illusionary belief that higher taxes would make it harder for them to buy what they want. Measured by its consequences for public welfare, it would be no exaggeration to call this false belief *the mother of all cognitive illusions*.

RECAP ↑

CONCERNS ABOUT RELATIVE POSITION

Evidence suggests that well-being depends not only on absolute levels of current and future consumption, but also on the corresponding levels of relative consumption.

Adding a taste for relative consumption alters many of the predictions and prescriptions of traditional economic models. Traditional models hold, for example, that the optimal amount of workplace safety will be provided in competitive labor markets. Critics respond that because labor markets are not effectively competitive, safety regulation is needed to prevent employers from exploiting workers. The puzzle for both camps is why safety regulations are most binding in those labor markets that, on traditional measures, are the most highly competitive.

Models that incorporate concerns about relative position address this puzzle by noting that by accepting riskier jobs, parents can use their higher pay to bid for housing in better school districts. But because school quality is an inherently relative concept, when other parents follow suit, the collective effect of their efforts is merely to bid up the prices of houses in better school districts. As before, half of all children end up attending bottom-half schools.

Workers confronting these incentives might well prefer an alternative state of the world in which all enjoyed greater safety, even at the expense of all having lower wages. Analogous reasoning suggests that individual incentives are misleadingly high for many other things we might sell for money—our leisure time, future job security, and a host of other environmental amenities. The problem is not that we exchange these items for money, but rather that we tend to sell them too cheaply.

SUMMARY

- Because it is costly to gather and analyze information, it often makes sense to employ rules of thumb when making complex assessments and decisions. Although the rules that most of us use appear to work reasonably well under a broad range of circumstance, they sometimes lead to error. (LO1)

- Behavioral economists have identified numerous systematic errors that are associated with the availability and representativeness heuristics. Anchoring and adjustment can also lead to biased assessments, as can failure to take account of regression to the mean or the tendency for extreme events to be followed by more nearly normal ones. It is also common for people to misinterpret contextual cues in their assessments and choices, as, for example, by reckoning the importance of a price reduction not by its absolute magnitude, but by its fraction of the original price. (LO1, LO2)

- Traditional economic models typically rule out the possibility that people might regret having chosen behaviors whose consequences were perfectly predictable, yet such expressions of regret appear genuine. Evidence suggests that people tend to discount future costs and benefits excessively leading them to choose imminent, though inferior, rewards instead of substantially larger rewards that require waiting. (LO3)

- Although traditional models assume that the reduction in happiness from a very small decline in wealth should be approximately the same as the gain in happiness from a similar gain in wealth, evidence suggests that losses weigh much more heavily than gains. Called loss aversion, this asymmetry in valuations is approximately two to one for

minor changes, but can be substantially larger when important changes are at stake. Because every change in policy generates winners and losers, loss aversion implies a large bias in favor of the status quo in public policy decisions. Evidence suggests that this bias often has harmful consequences since people's initial estimates of how painful losses will be often fail to take into account their ability to adapt to altered circumstances. (LO4)

- Self-interest is not the only important human motive, as evidenced by the fact that most people vote in presidential elections whose outcomes their votes won't influence. The present-aim model of rational choice broadens the narrow self-interest model by asserting that people often behave unselfishly because they get a warm glow from doing so. Methodologists object that the present-aim approach is not really a testable theory since it can "explain" virtually any bizarre behavior simply by assuming a suitably strong taste for it. (LO5)

- The *adaptive rationality approach* also permits a broader conception of human motivation, but unlike the present-aim approach, permits new motives to be added only if they can be plausibly shown not to handicap people in their quest to survive in competitive environments. Certain unselfish motives qualify under this standard because they help people solve important commitment problems, such as the one-shot prisoner's dilemmas. (LO5)

- Additional evidence for the claim that narrow self-interest is not the only important human motive comes from experiments showing that when people believe the terms of a transaction to be unfair, they often reject it, even if the transaction would have increased their wealth in absolute terms. *(LO5)*

- Many traditional models assume that well-being depends only on absolute levels of current and future consumption. But evidence suggests that it also depends heavily on the corresponding levels of relative consumption. Adding concerns about relative position alters many of the predictions and prescriptions of traditional economic models. When well-being depends only on absolute levels of consumption and certain other conditions are met, traditional models hold that individual incentives produce socially optimal patterns of spending. But when reward depends on relative position, individual incentives often result in mutually offsetting, and hence partially wasteful spending patterns. *(LO6)*

- The findings of behavioral economists in recent decades have contributed to our understanding of laws and other institutions. Societies around the world, for example, have adopted a variety of policies that are most easily understood as attempts to mitigate the consequences of impulse-control problems. These include special treatment of so-called crimes of passion; prohibitions against gambling, addictive drugs, and prostitution; entrapment laws; sanctions against adultery; and programs to stimulate savings. *(LO7)*

- Many other widely adopted laws, norms, and regulations are parsimoniously interpreted as attempts to mitigate collective action problems caused by concerns about relative position. These include workplace safety regulation, limitations on work hours, and programs to stimulate savings, all of which reduce individual incentives to engage in mutually offsetting patterns of spending. *(LO7)*

KEY TERMS

adaptive rationality standard
anchoring and adjustment
availability heuristic
fungibility
homo economicus
judgmental and decision
  heuristics

loss aversion
nonpositional good
positional good
present-aim standard of
  rationality
regression to the mean

representativeness
  heuristic
satisficing
status quo bias
ultimatum bargaining game
Weber-Fechner law

REVIEW QUESTIONS

1. How does the representativeness heuristic explain why people might think, mistakenly, that a randomly chosen shy person is more likely to be a librarian than a salesperson? *(LO1)*

2. Explain why thinking of costs or benefits in proportional terms might lead to suboptimal choices. *(LO2)*

3. Explain why traditional economic models find it difficult to explain why people would pay to attend weight-loss camps that restrict their daily calorie intake. *(LO3)*

4. How does loss aversion help explain why attempts to repeal the Affordable Care Act have met such strong resistance? *(LO4)*

5. Cite two examples of behavior that appear to contradict the assumption that people are narrowly self-interested. *(LO5)*

PROBLEMS

1. Only two moving companies, United and North American, provide local delivery service in a small western city. United operates 20 percent of the trucks, North American the remaining 80 percent. On a dark and rainy night, a pedestrian is run over and killed by a moving van. The lone witness to the incident testifies that the van was owned by United. An independent laboratory hired by the court finds that under dark and rainy conditions, the witness is able to identify the owner of a moving van with 90 percent accuracy. What is the probability that the van that struck the witness was owned by United? *(LO1)*

2. Kaela, a tennis player, has been struggling to develop a more consistent serve. She made the following remark to her partner during the second set of a recent match: "I feel like I'm making progress. I haven't double-faulted once today." She then served two double faults, which caused her to say, "Every time I say I haven't double-faulted, I immediately start to." Kaela's perception may have been influenced by *(LO1)*
   a. the sunk cost effect.
   b. regression to the mean.
   c. the availability heuristic.

d. More than one of the above are correct.

e. None of the above.

3. Studies have shown that in the New York City subways crime rates fall in the years following increased police patrols. Does this pattern suggest that the increased patrols are the cause of the crime reductions? *(LO1)*

4. Dalgliesh the detective fancies himself a shrewd judge of human nature. In careful tests, it has been discovered that he is right 80 percent of the time when he says that a suspect is lying. Dalgliesh says that Jones is lying. The polygraph expert, who is right 100 percent of the time, says that 40 percent of the subjects interviewed by Dalgliesh are telling the truth. What is the probability that Jones is lying? *(LO1)*

5. Shobhana is a gourmet. She makes it a point never to visit a restaurant a second time unless she has been served a superb meal on her first visit. She is puzzled at how seldom the quality of her second meal is as high as the first. Should she be? *(LO1)*

6. Maria will drive across town to take advantage of a 40 percent off sale on a $40 blouse but will not do so to take advantage of a 10 percent off sale on a $1,000 stereo. Assuming that her alternative is to pay list price for both products at the department store next to her home, is her behavior rational? *(LO2)*

7. Tom has said he would be willing to drive across town in order to save $10 on the purchase price of a $20 clock radio. If Tom is rational, this implies that he *(LO2)*

   a. believes that the opportunity cost of the trip is not more than $10.

   b. should also drive across town to save $10 on a $500 television set.

   c. should not drive across town to save $10 on a $500 television set.

   d. should drive across town only if the savings on a $500 television set is at least $250.

   e. More than one of the above are correct.

8. Marco is having difficulty choosing between two tennis racquets, A and B. As shown in the diagram, A has more power than B, but less control. According to the rational choice model, how will the availability of a third alternative—racquet C—influence Marco's final decision? If Marco behaves like most ordinary decision makers in this situation, how will the addition of C to his choice set matter? *(LO2)*

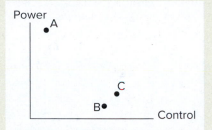

9. In the fall, Crusoe puts 50 coconuts from his harvest into a cave just before a family of bears goes in to hibernate. As a result, he is unable to get the coconuts out before the bears emerge the following spring. Coconuts spoil at the same rate no matter where he stores them, and yet he continues this practice each year. Why might he do this? *(LO3, LO5)*

10. When students in a large class were surveyed about how much they would be willing to pay for a coffee mug with their university's logo on it, their median willingness to pay was $5. At random, half of the students in this class were then given such a coffee mug, and each of the remaining students were given $5 in cash. Students who got mugs were then offered an opportunity to sell them to students who had not gotten one. According to standard economic models, how many mugs would be expected to change hands? How, if at all, would a behavioral economist's prediction differ? *(LO4)*

11. Describe the advantages and disadvantages of electing a political leader who is known to favor harsh military reprisals against foreign aggression, even when such reprisals are highly injurious to our own national interests. *(LO5)*

12. Explain why rational voters whose happiness depends on relative consumption might favor laws that require them to save a certain portion of each year's earnings for retirement. *(LO6, LO7)*

ANSWERS TO SELF-TESTS

10.1 For every 100 taxis in a dark alley, 15 will be green, 85 blue. The witness will identify $0.8(15) = 12$ of the green taxis as green, the remaining 3 green taxis as blue; he will identify $0.8(85) = 68$ of the blue taxis as blue, the remaining 17 blue taxis as green. The probability that the cab in question was green, given that the witness said it was, is thus equal to $12/(12 + 17) = 0.413$ and as this is less than half, the Green Taxi Company should not be held liable. *(LO1)*

10.2 Regression to the mean suggests that a month with an unusually high number of burglaries is likely to be followed by a month in which the number of burglaries is more nearly normal. So the increased patrols were not necessarily the cause of the observed reduction in burglaries. *(LO1)*

CHAPTER 11

Externalities, Property Rights, and the Environment

Ginosphotos/Getty Images

When costs or benefits accrue to people not directly involved in transactions, market allocations are often inefficient.

LEARNING OBJECTIVES

After reading this chapter, you should be able to:

LO1 Define negative and positive externalities and analyze their effect on resource allocation.

LO2 Explain and discuss the Coase theorem.

LO3 Explain how the effects of externalities can be remedied and discuss why the optimal amount of an externality is almost never zero.

LO4 Illustrate the tragedy of the commons and show how private ownership is a way of preventing it.

LO5 Define positional externalities and their effects and show how they can be remedied.

LO6 Compare and contrast the ways in which taxes and tradable permits reduce pollution.

A droll television ad for a British brand of pipe tobacco opens with a distinguished-looking gentleman sitting quietly on a park bench, smoking his pipe and reading a book of poetry. Before him lies a pond, unrippled except for a mother duck swimming peacefully with her ducklings. Suddenly a raucous group of teenage boys bursts onto the scene with a remote-controlled toy warship. Yelling and laughing, they launch their boat and maneuver it in aggressive pursuit of the terrified ducks.

Interrupted from his reverie, the gentleman looks up from his book and draws calmly on his pipe as he surveys the scene before him. He then reaches into his bag, pulls out a remote control of his own, and begins manipulating the joystick. The scene shifts underwater, where a miniature submarine rises from the depths of the pond. Once the boys' boat is in the sub's sights, the gentleman pushes a button on his remote control. Seconds later, the boat is blown to smithereens by a torpedo. The scene fades to a close-up of the tobacco company's label.

EXTERNAL COSTS AND BENEFITS

external cost (or **negative externality**) a cost of an activity that falls on people other than those who pursue the activity

external benefit (or **positive externality**) a benefit of an activity received by people other than those who pursue the activity

externality an external cost or benefit of an activity

External costs (or **negative externality**) and **external benefits** (or **positive externality**)—**externalities,** for short—are activities that generate costs or benefits that accrue to people not directly involved in those activities. These effects are generally unintended. From the pipe smoker's point of view, the noise generated by the marauding boys was an external cost. Had others been disturbed by the boys' rowdiness, they may well have regarded the pipe smoker's retaliatory gesture as an external benefit.

This chapter focuses on how externalities affect the allocation of resources. Adam Smith's theory of the invisible hand applies to an ideal marketplace in which externalities do not exist. In such situations, Smith argued, the self-interested actions of individuals would lead to socially efficient outcomes. We will see that when the parties affected by externalities can easily negotiate with one another, the invisible hand will still produce an efficient outcome.

But in many cases, such as the scene depicted in the tobacco ad, negotiation is impractical. In those cases, the self-serving actions of individuals won't lead to efficient outcomes. The need to deal with externalities and other collective-action problems is one of the most important rationales for the existence of government along with a variety of other forms of collective action.

HOW EXTERNALITIES AFFECT RESOURCE ALLOCATION

The following examples illustrate the ways in which externalities distort the allocation of resources.

EXAMPLE 11.1	Positive Externalities

Does the honeybee keeper face the right incentives? (Part I)

Phoebe earns her living as a keeper of honeybees. Her neighbors on all sides grow apples. Because bees pollinate apple trees as they forage for nectar, the more hives Phoebe keeps, the larger the harvests will be in the surrounding orchards. If Phoebe takes only her own costs and benefits into account in deciding how many hives to keep, will she keep the socially optimal number of hives?

Phoebe's hives constitute an external benefit, or a positive externality, for the orchard owners. If she takes only her own personal costs and benefits into account, she will add hives only until the added revenue she gets from the last hive just equals the cost of adding it. But because the orchard owners also benefit from additional hives, the total benefit of adding another hive at that point will be greater than its cost. Phoebe, then, will keep too few hives.

As we will discuss later in the chapter, problems like the one in Example 11.1 have several possible solutions. One is for orchard owners to pay beekeepers for keeping additional hives. But such solutions often require complex negotiations between the affected parties. For the moment, we assume that such negotiations are not practical.

EXAMPLE 11.2	Negative Externalities

Does the honeybee keeper face the right incentives? (Part 2)

As in Example 11.1, Phoebe earns her living as a keeper of honeybees. Now her neighbors are not apple growers but an elementary school and a nursing home. The more hives Phoebe keeps, the more students and nursing home residents will be stung by bees. If Phoebe takes only her own costs and benefits into account in deciding how many hives to keep, will she keep the socially optimal number of hives?

For the students and nursing home residents, Phoebe's hives constitute an external cost, or a negative externality. If she considers only her own costs and benefits in deciding how many hives to keep, she will continue to add hives until the added revenue from the last hive is just enough to cover its cost. But since Phoebe's neighbors also incur costs when she adds a hive, the benefit of the last hive at that point will be smaller than its cost. Phoebe, in other words, will keep too many hives.

Every activity involves costs and benefits. When all the relevant costs and benefits of an activity accrue directly to the person who carries it out—that is, when the activity generates no externalities—the level of the activity that is best for the individual will be best for society as a whole. But when an activity generates externalities, be they positive or negative, individual self-interest does not produce the best allocation of resources. Individuals who consider only their own costs and benefits will tend to engage too much in activities that generate negative externalities and too little in activities that generate positive externalities. When an activity generates both positive and negative externalities, private and social interests will coincide only in the unlikely event that the opposing effects offset one another exactly.

HOW DO EXTERNALITIES AFFECT SUPPLY AND DEMAND?

The effects of externalities on resource allocation can be shown in a supply and demand diagram. Consider first the case of negative externalities. Figure 11.1(a) depicts the supply (Private MC) and demand curves for a product whose production involves no external costs or benefits. Imagine, say, that the energy that powers the factories in this market comes from nonpolluting hydroelectric generators. The resulting equilibrium price and quantity in the market for this product will then be socially optimal: the value to buyers of the last unit of the product consumed (as measured on the demand curve) will be exactly equal to the marginal cost of producing it (as measured on the supply curve), leaving no further possible gains from exchange (see Chapter 3, *Supply and Demand*, and Chapter 7, *Efficiency, Exchange, and the Invisible Hand in Action*).

But now suppose that a protracted drought has eliminated hydroelectric power generation, forcing factories to rely instead on electric power produced by coal-burning

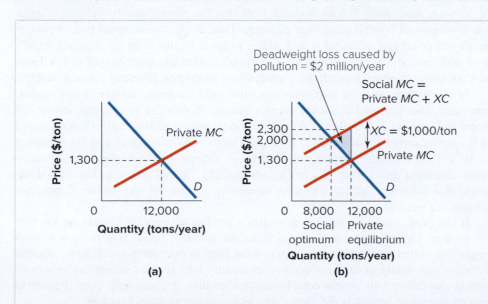

FIGURE 11.1

How External Costs Affect Resource Allocation.

(a) When a market has no external costs or benefits, the resulting equilibrium quantity and price are socially optimal. (b) By contrast, when production of a good is accompanied by an external cost, the market equilibrium price ($1,300 per ton) is too low and the market equilibrium quantity (12,000 tons per year) is too high. The deadweight loss from the negative externality is the area of the blue-shaded triangle, $2 million per year.

generators. Now each unit of output produced is accompanied by an external pollution cost of *XC,* as shown in Figure 11.1(b). Since the external pollution cost falls not on firm owners but on others who live downwind from their factories, Private *MC* is still the supply curve for this product, and its demand curve is again as before, so the equilibrium price and quantity will be exactly the same as in Figure 11.1(a). But this time the private market equilibrium is not socially optimal. As before, the market equilibrium level of output is 12,000 tons per year, the output level at which the demand curve (*D*) intersects Private *MC.* Note, however, that at that output level, the value to consumers of the last unit of output produced is only $1,300 per ton, while the true cost of producing that last unit (including the external cost) is $2,300 per ton.

This means that society could gain additional economic surplus by producing fewer units of the product. Indeed, the same conclusion will continue to hold whenever the current output exceeds 8,000 tons per year, the output level at which the demand curve intersects Social *MC.* Social *MC,* which includes all relevant marginal costs of producing the product, is constructed by adding the external pollution cost, *XC,* to every value along Private *MC.* The socially optimal level of output of the good occurs where Social *MC* intersects the demand curve. As shown in Figure 11.1(b), it is 8,000 tons per year. This is the level of output that exhausts all possibilities from exchange. At that quantity, the marginal benefit of the product, as measured by what buyers are willing to pay for it, is exactly equal to the marginal cost of producing it, which is the private marginal cost *MC* plus the marginal pollution cost *XC.* The market equilibrium quantity thus will be higher than the socially optimal quantity for a good whose production generates external costs.

By how much does the presence of pollution reduce total economic surplus from its maximum value, which occurs at an output level of 8,000 tons per year in Figure 11.1(b)? Note in the diagram that as output expands past 8,000, the marginal cost of each successive unit (as measured on the Social *MC* curve) is greater than the marginal benefit of that unit (as measured on the demand curve). Expanding output from 8,000 tons per year to the private equilibrium level, 12,000 tons per year, thus entails a cumulative reduction in total economic surplus equal to the area of the blue-shaded triangle in Figure 11.1(b), or $2 million per year. The deadweight loss from pollution is $2 million per year in this market.

What about a good whose production generates external benefits? In Figure 11.2, Private demand is the demand curve for a product whose production generates an external benefit of *XB* per unit. The market equilibrium quantity of this good, Q_{pvt}, is the output level at which Private demand intersects the supply curve of the product (*MC*). This time, market equilibrium quantity is smaller than the socially optimal level of output, denoted Q_{soc}. Q_{soc} is the output level at which *MC* intersects the socially optimal demand curve (the curve labeled Social demand in Figure 11.2), which is constructed by adding the external benefit, *XB,* to every value along Private demand. Note that the private market equilibrium again fails to exhaust all possible gains from exchange. Thus, at Q_{pvt}, the marginal cost of producing an additional unit of output is only MB_{pvt}, which is smaller than the marginal benefit of an additional unit by the amount *XB.* The market equilibrium quantity thus will be lower than the socially optimal quantity for a good whose production generates external benefits.

In comparison with the maximum attainable total economic surplus in this market, how much does the total economic surplus associated with the private equilibrium fall short? In Figure 11.2, note that at Q_{pvt}, the marginal benefit of the product (as measured on the curve labeled Social demand) is *XB* units larger than its marginal cost (as measured on *MC*). Total economic surplus will continue to increase by successively smaller increments as output grows from Q_{pvt} to Q_{soc}, the socially optimal quantity. The total deadweight loss associated with the positive externality is thus the area of the blue-shaded triangle in Figure 11.2.

If the production of a product generates a positive externality, why do we say that this product causes a reduction in total economic surplus? To say that there is a deadweight loss in this market does not mean that the positive externality causes harm. Rather, it means that failure to take the positive externality into account makes the economic surplus associated with private equilibrium smaller than it could have been. Failure to reap an economic benefit is the same thing as sustaining an economic loss.

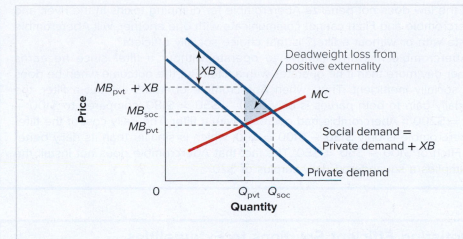

FIGURE 11.2

A Good Whose Production Generates a Positive Externality for Consumers.
For such goods, the market equilibrium quantity, Q_{pvt}, is smaller than the socially optimal quantity, Q_{soc}, because individual buyers are willing to pay only for the benefits they reap from directly consuming the product. The deadweight loss from the positive externality is the area of the blue-shaded triangle.

To summarize, whether externalities are positive or negative, they distort the allocation of resources in otherwise efficient markets. When externalities are present, the individual pursuit of self-interest will not result in the largest possible economic surplus. This outcome is thus inefficient by definition.

THE COASE THEOREM

To say that a situation is inefficient means that it can be rearranged in a way that would make at least some people better off without harming others. Such situations, we have seen, are a source of creative tension. The existence of inefficiency, after all, means that there is cash on the table, which usually triggers a race to see who can capture it. For example, we saw that because monopoly pricing results in an inefficiently low output level, the potential for gain gave monopolists an incentive to make discounts available to price-sensitive buyers. As the next examples illustrate, the inefficiencies that result from externalities create similar incentives for remedial action.

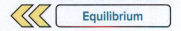

EXAMPLE 11.3   Inefficiencies That Result from Externalities

Will Abercrombie dump toxins in the river? (Part I)

Abercrombie's factory produces a toxic waste by-product. If Abercrombie dumps it in the river, he causes damage to Fitch, a fisherman located downstream. The toxins are short-lived and cause no damage to anyone other than Fitch. At a cost, Abercrombie can filter out the toxins, in which case Fitch will suffer no damage at all. The relevant gains and losses for the two individuals are listed in Table 11.1.

TABLE 11.1
Costs and Benefits of Eliminating Toxic Waste (Part I)

	With filter	Without filter
Gains to Abercrombie	$100/day	$130/day
Gains to Fitch	$100/day	$ 50/day

If the law does not penalize Abercrombie for dumping toxins in the river, and if Abercrombie and Fitch cannot communicate with one another, will Abercrombie operate with or without a filter? Is that choice socially efficient?

Abercrombie has an incentive to operate without a filter since he earns $30 per day more than if he operates with a filter. But the outcome when he does so is socially inefficient. Thus, when Abercrombie operates without a filter, the total daily gain to both parties is only $130 + $50 = $180, compared to $100 + $100 = $200 if Abercrombie had operated with a filter. The daily cost of the filter to Abercrombie is only $130 − $100 = $30, which is smaller than its daily benefit to Fitch of $100 − $50 = $50. The fact that Abercrombie does not install the filter implies a squandered daily surplus of $20.

EXAMPLE 11.4	**Negotiating Efficient Solutions to Externalities**

Will Abercrombie dump toxins in the river? (Part 2)

Suppose the costs and benefits of using the filter are as in the previous example except that Abercrombie and Fitch can now communicate with one another at no cost. Even though the law does not require him to do so, will Abercrombie use a filter?

 Efficiency ⟫

This time, Abercrombie will use a filter. Recall from Chapter 7, *Efficiency, Exchange, and the Invisible Hand*, the observation that when the economic pie grows larger, everyone can have a larger slice (the *Efficiency Principle*). Because use of a filter would result in the largest possible economic surplus, it would enable both Abercrombie and Fitch to have a larger net gain than before. Fitch thus has an incentive to *pay* Abercrombie to use a filter. Suppose, for instance, that Fitch offers Abercrombie $40 per day to compensate him for operating with a filter. Both Abercrombie and Fitch will then be exactly $10 per day better off than before, for a total daily net gain of $20.

✔ **SELF-TEST 11.1**

In Example 11.4, what is the largest whole-dollar amount by which Fitch could compensate Abercrombie for operating with a filter and still be better off than before?

Coase theorem if, at no cost, people can negotiate the purchase and sale of the right to perform activities that cause externalities, they can always arrive at efficient solutions to the problems caused by externalities

Ronald Coase, a professor at the University of Chicago Law School, was the first to see clearly that if people can negotiate with one another at no cost over the right to perform activities that cause externalities, they will always arrive at an efficient solution. This insight, which is often called the **Coase theorem,** is a profoundly important idea, for which Coase (rhymes with "rose") was awarded the 1991 Nobel Prize in Economics.

Why, you might ask, should Fitch pay Abercrombie to filter out toxins that would not be there in the first place if not for Abercrombie's factory? The rhetorical force of this question is undeniable. Yet Coase points out that externalities are reciprocal in nature. The toxins do harm Fitch, to be sure, but preventing Abercrombie from emitting them would penalize Abercrombie, by exactly $30 per day. Why should Fitch necessarily have the right to harm Abercrombie? Indeed, as the next example illustrates, even if Fitch had that right, he would exercise it only if filtering the toxins proved the most efficient outcome.

EXAMPLE 11.5   Social Efficiency

Will Abercrombie dump toxins in the river? (Part 3)

Suppose the law says that Abercrombie may *not* dump toxins in the river unless he has Fitch's permission. If the relevant costs and benefits of filtering the toxins are as shown in Table 11.2, and if Abercrombie and Fitch can negotiate with one another at no cost, will Abercrombie filter out the toxins?

TABLE 11.2
Costs and Benefits of Eliminating Toxic Waste (Part 3)

	With filter	Without filter
Gains to Abercrombie	$100/day	$150/day
Gains to Fitch	$100/day	$ 70/day

Note that this time, the most efficient outcome is for Abercrombie to operate without a filter because the total daily surplus in that case will be $220 as compared to only $200 with a filter. Under the law, however, Fitch has the right to insist that Abercrombie use a filter. We might expect him to exercise that right since his own gain would rise from $70 to $100 per day if he did so. But because this outcome would be socially inefficient, we know that each party can do better.

Suppose, for example, that Abercrombie gives Fitch $40 per day in return for Fitch's permission to operate without a filter. Each would then have a net daily gain of $110, which is $10 better for each of them than if Fitch had insisted that Abercrombie use a filter. Abercrombie's pollution harms Fitch, sure enough. But failure to allow the pollution would have caused even greater harm to Abercrombie.

The Coase theorem tells us that regardless of whether the law holds polluters liable for damages, the affected parties will achieve efficient solutions to externalities if they can negotiate costlessly with one another. Note carefully that this does not imply that affected parties will be indifferent about whether the law holds polluters responsible for damages. If polluters are liable, they will end up with lower incomes and those who are injured by pollutants will end up with higher incomes than if the law does not hold polluters liable—even though the same efficient production methods would be adopted in each case. When polluters are held liable, they must remove the pollution at their own expense. When they are not held liable, those who are injured by pollution must pay polluters to cut back.

Externalities are hardly rare and isolated occurrences. On the contrary, finding examples of actions that are altogether free of them is difficult. And because externalities can distort the allocation of resources, it is important to recognize them and deal intelligently with them. Consider the following example of an externality that arises because of shared living arrangements.

EXAMPLE 11.6   Cost-Benefit Principle—Shared Living Expenses

Will Adriana and Sofia share an apartment?

Adriana and Sofia can live together in a two-bedroom apartment for $1,000 per month, or separately in 2 one-bedroom apartments, each for $600 per month. If the rent paid were the same for both alternatives, the two women would be indifferent between living together or separately, except for one problem: Adriana often has friends over late at night when Sofia is trying to sleep. Adriana would pay up to $250 per month for this privilege. Sofia, for her part, would pay up to $150 per month to consistently get a good night's sleep. Should they live together or separately?

Adriana and Sofia should live together only if the benefit of doing so exceeds the cost. The benefit of living together is the reduction in their rent. Since 2 one-bedroom apartments would cost a total of $1,200 per month, compared to $1,000 for a two-bedroom unit, their benefit from living together is $200 per month. Their cost of living together is the least costly accommodation they can make to Adriana's objectionable habits. Adriana would be willing to pay up to $250 per month to avoid changing her behavior, so the $200 rent saving is too small to persuade her to change. But Sofia is willing to put up with Adriana's behavior for a compensation payment of only $150 per month. Since that amount is smaller than the total saving in rent, the least costly solution to the problem is for Sofia to live with Adriana and simply put up with her behavior.

 Cost-Benefit

Table 11.3 summarizes the relevant costs and benefits of this shared living arrangement. The Cost-Benefit Principle tells us that Adriana and Sofia should live together if and only if the benefit of living together exceeds the cost. The cost of the shared living arrangement is not the sum of all possible costs but the least

---

TABLE 11.3

The Gain in Surplus from Shared Living Arrangements

Benefits of Shared Living		
Total cost of separate apartments	Total cost of shared apartment	Rent savings from sharing
2 × $600/month $1,200/month	$1,000/month	$200/month

Costs of Shared Living			
Problem	Adriana's cost of solving problem	Sofia's cost of solving problem	Least costly solution to the problem
Adriana inviting friends over late at night	Limiting when her friends come over: $250/month	Tolerating the noise at night: $150/month	Sofia tolerates the noise made by Adriana's friends: $150/month

Gain in Surplus from Shared Living		
Rent savings ($200/month) —	Least costly accommodation to shared living problems ($150/month) =	Gain in surplus: ($50/month)

costly accommodation to the problem (or problems) of shared living. Since the $200 per month saving in rent exceeds the least costly accommodation to the phone problem, Adriana and Sofia can reap a total gain in economic surplus of $50 per month by sharing their living quarters.

Some people might conclude that Adriana and Sofia should not live together because if the two share the rent equally, Sofia would end up paying $500 per month—which when added to the $150 cost of putting up with Adriana's behavior comes to $50 more than the cost of living alone. As persuasive as that argument may sound, however, it is mistaken. The source of the error, as the following example illustrates, is the assumption that the two must share the rent equally.

EXAMPLE 11.7   Cost-Benefit Principle—Paying Unequal Rent Amounts

What is the highest rent Sofia would be willing to pay for the two-bedroom apartment?

In Example 11.6, Sofia's alternative is to live alone, which would mean paying $600 per month, her reservation price for a living arrangement in which she is not woken up by Adriana's friends. Since the most she would be willing to pay to avoid this problem is $150 per month, the highest monthly rent she would be willing to pay for the shared apartment is $600 − $150 = $450. If she pays that amount, Adriana will have to pay the difference, namely, $550 per month, which is clearly a better alternative for Adriana than paying $600 to live alone.

EXAMPLE 11.8   Cost-Benefit Principle—Splitting Economic Surplus

How much should Adriana and Sofia pay if they agree to split their economic surplus equally?

As we saw in Table 11.3, the total rent saving from the shared apartment is $200, and since the least costly solution to the problem is $150, the monthly gain in economic surplus is $50. We know from Example 11.7 that Adriana's reservation price for living together is $600 per month and Sofia's is $450. So if the two women want to split the $50 monthly surplus equally, each should pay $25 less than her reservation price. Adriana's monthly rent will thus be $575 and Sofia's, $425. The result is that each is $25 per month better off than if she had lived alone.

 SELF-TEST 11.2

As in Examples 11.6 and 11.7, Adriana and Sofia can live together in a two-bedroom apartment for $1,000 per month or separately in 2 one-bedroom apartments, each for $600 per month. Adriana would pay up to $250 per month rather than moderate her social habits, and Sofia would pay up to $150 per month to consistently get a good night's sleep. Now, suppose Sofia would also be willing to pay up to $60 per month to avoid the loss of privacy that comes with shared living space. Should the two women live together?

REMEDIES FOR EXTERNALITIES

LAWS AND REGULATIONS

We have seen that efficient solutions to externalities can be found whenever the affected parties can negotiate with one another at no cost. But negotiation is not always practical. A motorist with a noisy muffler imposes costs on others, yet they cannot flag him down and offer him a compensation payment to fix his muffler. In recognition of this difficulty, most governments simply require that cars have working mufflers. Indeed, the explicit or implicit purpose of a large share—perhaps the lion's share—of laws is to solve problems caused by externalities. The goal of such laws is to help people achieve the solutions they might have reached had they been able to negotiate with one another.

When negotiation is costless, the task of adjustment generally falls on the party who can accomplish it at the lowest cost. For instance, in our examples, Sofia put up with Adriana's annoying habits because doing so was less costly than asking Adriana to change her habits. Many municipal noise ordinances also place the burden of adjustment on those who can accomplish it at the lowest cost. Consider, for example, the restrictions on loud party music, which often take effect at a later hour on weekends than on weekdays. This pattern reflects both the fact that the gains from loud music tend to be larger on weekends and the fact that such music is more likely to disturb people on weekdays. By setting the noise curfew at different hours on different days of the week, the law places the burden on partygoers during the week and on sleepers during the weekend. Similar logic explains why noise ordinances allow motorists to honk their horns in most neighborhoods, but not in the immediate vicinity of a hospital.

The list of laws and regulations that may be fruitfully viewed as solutions to externalities is a long one. When a motorist drives his car at high speed, he endangers not just his own life and property, but also the lives and property of others. Speed limits, no-passing zones, right-of-way rules, and a host of other traffic laws may be seen as reasoned attempts to limit the harm one party inflicts on another. Many jurisdictions even have laws requiring that motorists install snow tires on their cars by the first of November. These laws promote not just safety, but also the smooth flow of traffic: If one motorist can't get up a snow-covered hill, he delays not only himself, but also the motorists behind him.

Similar reasoning helps us understand the logic of zoning laws that restrict the kinds of activities that take place in various parts of cities. Because many residents place a high value on living in an uncongested neighborhood, some cities have enacted zoning laws specifying minimum lot sizes. In places like Manhattan, where a shortage of land encourages developers to build very large and tall buildings, zoning laws limit both a building's height and the proportion of a lot it may occupy. Such restrictions recognize that the taller a building is, and the greater the proportion of its lot that it occupies, the more it blocks sunlight from reaching surrounding properties. The desire to control external costs also helps to explain why many cities establish separate zones for business and residential activity. Even within business districts, many cities limit certain kinds of commercial activity. For example, in an effort to revitalize the Times Square neighborhood, New York City enacted a zoning law banning adult bookstores and pornographic movie theaters from the area.

Limitations on the discharge of pollutants into the environment are perhaps the clearest examples of laws aimed at solving problems caused by externalities. The details of these laws reflect the principle of placing the burden of adjustment on those who can accomplish it at least cost. The discharge of toxic wastes into rivers, for example, tends to be most strictly regulated on those waterways whose commercial fishing or recreational uses are most highly valued. On other waterways, the burden of adjustment is likely to fall more heavily on fishermen, recreational boaters, and swimmers. Similarly, air-quality regulations tend to be strictest in the most heavily populated regions of the country, where the marginal benefit of pollution reduction is the greatest.

The following examples suggest additional ways in which Coase's insights about how societies deal with externalities provide rich fodder for the economic naturalist.

The Economic Naturalist 11.1

What is the purpose of free speech laws?

The First Amendment's protection of free speech and the pattern of exceptions to that protection are another illustration of how legal remedies are used to solve the problems caused by externalities. The First Amendment acknowledges the decisive value of open communication, as well as the practical difficulty of identifying and regulating acts of speech that cause more harm than good. Yet there are some important exceptions. The Supreme Court has ruled, for instance, that the First Amendment does not allow someone to yell "fire" in a crowded theater if there is no fire, nor does it allow someone to advocate the violent overthrow of the government. In those instances, the external benefits of free speech are far too small to justify the external costs.

Why does the U.S. Constitution protect the right of free speech?

The Economic Naturalist 11.2

Why do many states have laws requiring students to be vaccinated against childhood illnesses?

Proof of immunization against chickenpox, diphtheria, measles, mumps, pertussis, polio, rubella and tetanus is now universally required for entry into American public schools. Most states also require immunization against hepatitis B (43 states). Why these requirements?

Vaccinating children against childhood illnesses can entail a small but potentially serious risk (though the supposed link between vaccinations and autism has been thoroughly debunked). On the other hand, it can protect children against dangerous diseases. For an individual family, the decision to vaccinate involves weighing the benefits of vaccination against its potential risks and cost. The problem is that this calculation ignores the fact that a family's decision to become vaccinated benefits not just the family, but also everyone else in the community because the family would be far less likely to contract the illness and pass it on to others.

Relegating the vaccination decision to individuals would result in a suboptimally low vaccination rate because many families would fail to take adequate account of the benefit that becoming vaccinated would have on others. It is for this reason that most states require vaccinations against specific childhood illnesses.

Even these laws, however, allow parents to apply for exemptions on religious or philosophical grounds. Communities vary in the extent to which parents avail themselves of these

Why are vaccinations against many childhood illnesses required by law?

exemptions. In Colorado, for example, Boulder County heads the list of parents who opt to exempt their children from taking the pertussis vaccine, where only 84.1 percent of public school children have an up-to-date pertussis vaccination compared to 89.9 percent statewide. Not surprisingly, the incidence of whooping cough is much higher in Boulder (37.4 cases per year per 100,000 people) than in the state as a whole (22.4 cases per year per 100,000 people).[1]

THE OPTIMAL AMOUNT OF NEGATIVE EXTERNALITIES IS NOT ZERO

Curbing pollution and other negative externalities entails both costs and benefits. As we saw in Chapter 6, *Perfectly Competitive Supply*, when we analyzed how many cans should be recycled, the best policy is to curtail pollution until the cost of further abatement just equals the marginal benefit. In general, the marginal cost of abatement rises with the amount of pollution eliminated. (Following the Low-Hanging-Fruit Principle, polluters use the cheapest cleanup methods first and then turn to more expensive ones.) And the law of diminishing marginal utility suggests that beyond some point, the marginal benefit of pollution reduction tends to fall as more pollution is removed. As a result, the marginal cost and marginal benefit curves almost always intersect at less than the maximum amount of pollution reduction.

The intersection of the two curves marks the socially optimal level of pollution reduction. If pollution is curtailed by any less than that amount, society will gain more than it will lose by pushing the cleanup effort a little further. But if regulators push beyond the point at which the marginal cost and benefit curves intersect, society will incur costs that exceed the benefits. The existence of a socially optimal level of pollution reduction implies the existence of a socially optimal level of pollution, and that level will almost always be greater than zero.

Because people have been conditioned to think of pollution as bad, many cringe when they hear the phrase "socially optimal level of pollution." How can any positive level of pollution be socially optimal? *But to speak of a socially optimal level of pollution is not the same as saying that pollution is good.* It is merely to recognize that society has an interest in cleaning up the environment, but only up to a certain point. The underlying idea is no different from the idea of an optimal level of dirt in an apartment. After all, even if you spent the whole day, every day, vacuuming your apartment, there would be *some* dirt left in it. And because you have better things to do than vacuum all day, you probably tolerate substantially more than the minimal amount of dirt. A dirty apartment is not good, nor is pollution in the air you breathe. But in both cases, the cleanup effort should be expanded only until the marginal benefit equals the marginal cost.

COMPENSATORY TAXES AND SUBSIDIES

As noted, when transaction costs prohibit negotiation among affected parties, negative externalities lead to excessive output levels because activities that produce negative externalities are misleadingly attractive to those who engage in them. One solution to this problem, proposed by the British economist A. C. Pigou, is to make such activities less attractive by taxing them. Figure 11.3(a) reproduces Figure 11.1's portrayal of a market in which each unit of output generates an external cost of *XC* equal to $1,000 per ton. Because producers fail to take this external cost into account, the private equilibrium is 12,000 tons per year, or 4,000 tons per year more than the socially optimal level of 8,000 tons per year.

Figure 11.3(b) portrays that same market after the imposition of a tax of $1,000 per unit of output. This tax has the effect of raising each producer's marginal cost curve by $1,000, so the industry supply curve shifts upward by $1,000 at every quantity. Note that the resulting private equilibrium output, 8,000 tons per year, is now exactly equal to the socially optimal output. Although many critics insist that taxes always reduce economic efficiency, here we have an example of a tax that actually makes the economy *more*

[1]From the Colorado School and Childcare Immunization Data 2016–2017 (www.cohealthdata.dphe.state.co.us/ Data/Details/1) and the Colorado Department of Public Health and Environment (www.colorado.gov/pacific/ cdphe/colorado-health-indicators).

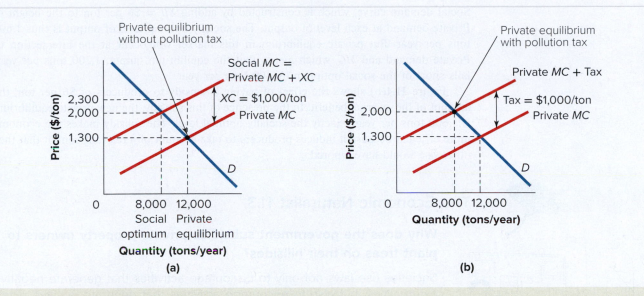

FIGURE 11.3

Taxing a Negative Externality.

(a) Negative externalities lead to an equilibrium with more than the socially optimal level of output.
(b) Imposing a tax equal to the external cost leads to an equilibrium in which the output level is
socially optimal. The tax makes the economy more efficient because it leads producers to take
account of a relevant cost that they would otherwise ignore.

efficient. The tax has that effect because it forces producers to take explicit account of
the fact that each additional unit of output they produce imposes an external cost of
$1,000 on the rest of society.

Similar reasoning suggests that a subsidy to producers can serve to counteract misallocations that result from positive externalities. Figure 11.4(a) portrays a market in which
each unit of output generates an external benefit $XB = \$6$ per ton. In this market, the
socially optimal output level occurs at the intersection of the supply curve (MC) and the

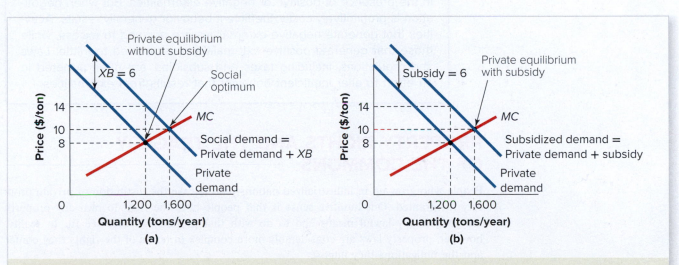

FIGURE 11.4

Subsidizing a Positive Externality.

(a) Positive externalities lead to an equilibrium with less than the socially optimal level of output. (b) Paying
producers a subsidy equal to the external benefit of the activity leads to an equilibrium in which the output level
is socially optimal. The subsidy makes the economy more efficient because it leads producers to take account
of a relevant benefit that they would otherwise ignore.

Social demand curve, which is constructed by adding $XB = \$6$ per ton to the height of Private demand at each level of output. The socially optimal level of output is thus 1,600 tons per year. But private equilibrium in this market will occur at the intersection of Private demand and MC, which means that the equilibrium output, 1,200 tons per year, falls short of the social optimum by 400 tons per year.

Figure 11.4(b) shows the effect of paying a subsidy to producers of $6 per ton, the amount of the external benefit. In the presence of this subsidy, the new private equilibrium is 1,600 tons per year, exactly the socially optimal level. The subsidy makes the economy more efficient because it induces producers to take account of a relevant benefit that they otherwise would have ignored.

The Economic Naturalist 11.3

Why does the government subsidize scientific research?

Why does the government subsidize private property owners to plant trees on their hillsides?

Societies use laws not only to discourage activities that generate negative externalities, but also to encourage activities that generate positive externalities. The planting of trees on hillsides, for example, benefits not just the landowner, but also his neighbors by limiting the danger of flooding. In recognition of this fact, many jurisdictions subsidize the planting of trees. Similarly, Congress budgets millions of dollars each year in support of basic research—an implicit acknowledgment of the positive externalities associated with the generation of new knowledge.

> **RECAP**
>
> **EXTERNAL COSTS AND BENEFITS**
>
> Externalities occur when the costs or benefits of an activity accrue to people other than those directly involved in the activity. The Coase theorem says that when affected parties can negotiate with one another without cost, activities will be pursued at efficient levels, even in the presence of positive or negative externalities. But when negotiation is prohibitively costly, inefficient behavior generally results. Activities that generate negative externalities are pursued to excess, while those that generate positive externalities are pursued too little. Laws and regulations, including taxes and subsidies, are often adopted in an effort to alter inefficient behavior that results from externalities.

PROPERTY RIGHTS AND THE TRAGEDY OF THE COMMONS

People who grow up in industrialized nations tend to take the institution of private property for granted. Our intuitive sense is that people have the right to own any property they acquire by lawful means and to do with that property as they see fit. In reality, however, property laws are considerably more complex in terms of the rights they confer and the obligations they impose.

THE PROBLEM OF UNPRICED RESOURCES

To understand the laws that govern the use of property, let's begin by asking why societies created the institution of private property in the first place. The following examples, which show what happens to property that nobody owns, suggest an answer.

| EXAMPLE 11.9 | Individual Income |

How many steers will villagers send onto the commons?

A village has five residents, each of whom has accumulated savings of $100. Each villager can use the money to buy a government bond that pays 13 percent interest per year or to buy a year-old steer, send it onto the commons to graze, and sell it after 1 year. The price the villager will get for the 2-year-old steer depends on the amount of weight it gains while grazing on the commons, which in turn depends on the number of steers sent onto the commons, as shown in Table 11.4.

TABLE 11.4
The Relationship between Herd Size and Steer Price

Number of steers on the commons	Price per 2-year-old steer ($)	Income per steer ($/year)
1	126	26
2	119	19
3	116	16
4	113	13
5	111	11

The price of a 2-year-old steer declines with the number of steers grazing on the commons because the more steers, the less grass available to each. The villagers make their investment decisions one at a time, and the results are public. If each villager decides how to invest individually, how many steers will be sent onto the commons, and what will be the village's total income?

If a villager buys a $100 government bond, he'll earn $13 of interest income at the end of 1 year. Thus, he should send a steer onto the commons if and only if that steer will command a price of at least $113 as a 2-year-old. When each villager chooses in this self-interested way, we can expect four villagers to send a steer onto the commons. (Actually, the fourth villager would be indifferent between investing in a steer or buying a bond since he would earn $13 either way. For the sake of discussion, we'll assume that in the case of a tie, people choose to be cattle owners.) The fifth villager, seeing that he would earn only $11 by sending a fifth steer onto the commons, will choose instead to buy a government bond. As a result of these decisions, the total village income will be $65 per year—$13 for the one bondholder and 4($13) = $52 for the four cattle owners.

Has Adam Smith's invisible hand produced the most efficient allocation of these villagers' resources? We can tell at a glance that it has not, since their total village income is only $65—precisely the same as it would have been had the possibility of cattle raising not existed. The source of the difficulty will become evident in the following example.

| EXAMPLE 11.10 | Maximizing Total Group Income |

What is the socially optimal number of steers to send onto the commons?

Suppose the five villagers in the previous example confront the same investment opportunities as before, except that this time they are free to make their decisions as a group rather than individually. How many steers will they send onto the commons, and what will be their total village income?

This time the villagers' goal is to maximize the income received by the group as a whole. When decisions are made from this perspective, the criterion is to send a steer onto the commons only if its marginal contribution to village income is at least $13, the amount that could be earned from a government bond. As the entries in column 5 indicate, the first steer clearly meets this criterion since it contributes $26 to total village income. But the second steer does not. Sending that steer onto the commons raises the village's income from cattle raising from $26 to $38, a gain of just $12. The $100 required to buy the second steer would thus have been better invested in a government bond. Worse, the collective return from sending a third steer is only $10; from a fourth, only $4; and from a fifth, only $3.

TABLE 11.5
Marginal Income and the Socially Optimal Herd Size

(1) Number of steers on the commons	(2) Price per 2-year-old steer ($)	(3) Income per steer ($/year)	(4) Total village income ($/year)	(5) Marginal income ($/year)
				26
1	126	26	26	
				12
2	119	19	38	
				10
3	116	16	48	
				4
4	113	13	52	
				3
5	111	11	55	

In sum, when investment decisions are made with the goal of maximizing total village income, the best choice is to buy four government bonds and send only a single steer onto the commons. The resulting village income will be $78: $26 from sending the single steer and $52 from the four government bonds. That amount is $13 more than the total income that resulted when villagers made their investment decisions individually. Once again, the reward from moving from an inefficient allocation to an efficient one is that the economic pie grows larger. And when the pie grows larger, everyone can get a larger slice. For instance, if the villagers agree to pool their income and share it equally, each will get $15.60, or $2.60 more than before.

 SELF-TEST 11.3

How would your answers to Examples 11.9 and 11.10 change if the interest rate were 11 percent per year rather than 13 percent?

Why do the villagers in Examples 11.9 and 11.10 do better when they make their investment decisions collectively? The answer is that when individuals decide alone, they ignore the fact that sending another steer onto the commons will cause existing steers to gain less weight. Their failure to consider this effect makes the return from sending another steer seem misleadingly high to them.

The grazing land on the commons is a valuable economic resource. When no one owns it, no one has any incentive to take the opportunity cost of using it into account. And when that happens, people will tend to use it until its marginal benefit is zero. This problem, and others similar to it, are known as the **tragedy of the commons.** The essential cause of the tragedy of the commons is the fact that one person's use of commonly held property imposes an external cost on others by making the property less valuable. The

tragedy of the commons the tendency for a resource that has no price to be used until its marginal benefit falls to zero

tragedy of the commons also provides a vivid illustration of the Equilibrium Principle. Each individual villager behaves rationally by sending an additional steer onto the commons, yet the overall outcome falls far short of the attainable ideal.

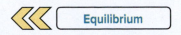

Equilibrium

THE EFFECT OF PRIVATE OWNERSHIP

As the following example illustrates, one solution to the tragedy of the commons is to place the village grazing land under private ownership.

EXAMPLE 11.11   **Private Ownership**

How much will the right to control the village commons sell for?

Suppose the five villagers face the same investment opportunities as before, except that this time they decide to auction off the right to use the commons to the highest bidder. Assuming that villagers can borrow as well as lend at an annual interest rate of 13 percent, what price will the right to use the commons fetch? How will the owner of that property right use it, and what will be the resulting village income?

To answer these questions, simply ask yourself what you would do if you had complete control over how the grazing land were used. As we saw earlier, the most profitable way to use this land is to send only a single steer to graze on it. If you do so, you will earn a total of $26 per year. Since the opportunity cost of the $100 you spent on the single yearling steer is the $13 in interest you could have earned from a bond, your economic profit from sending a single steer onto the commons will be $13 per year, provided you can use the land for free. But you cannot; to finance your purchase of the property right, you must borrow money (since you used your $100 savings to buy a year-old steer).

What is the most you would be willing to pay for the right to use the commons? Its use generates an income of $26 per year—or $13 more than the opportunity cost of your investment in the steer—so the most you would pay is $100 (since that amount used to purchase a bond that pays 13 percent interest would also generate income of $13 per year). If the land were sold at auction, $100 is precisely the amount you would have to pay. Your annual earnings from the land would be exactly enough to pay the $13 interest on your loan and cover the opportunity cost of not having put your savings into a bond.

Note that when the right to use the land is auctioned to the highest bidder, the village achieves a more efficient allocation of its resources because the owner has a strong incentive to take the opportunity cost of more intensive grazing fully into account. Total village income in this case will again be $78. If the annual interest on the $100 proceeds from selling the land rights is shared equally among the five villagers, each will again have an annual investment income of $15.60.

The logic of economic surplus maximization helps explain why the most economically successful nations have all been ones with well-developed private property laws. Property that belongs to everyone belongs, in effect, to no one. Not only is its potential economic value never fully realized; it usually ends up being of no value at all.

Bear in mind, however, that in most countries the owners of private property are not free to do *precisely* as they wish with it. For example, local zoning laws may give the owner of a residential building lot the right to build a three-story house but not a taller one. Here, too, the logic of economic surplus maximization applies, for a fully informed and rational legislature would define property rights so as to create the largest possible total economic surplus. In practice, of course, such ideal legislatures never really exist. Yet the essence of politics is the cutting of deals that make people better off. If a legislator could propose a change in the property laws that would enlarge the total economic surplus, she could also propose a scheme that would give each of her constituents a larger slice, thus enhancing her chances for reelection.

As an economic naturalist, challenge yourself to use this framework when thinking about the various restrictions you encounter in private property laws: zoning laws that constrain what you can build and what types of activities you can conduct on your land; traffic laws that constrain what you can do with your car; employment and environmental laws that constrain how you can operate your business. Your understanding of these and countless other laws will be enhanced by the insight that everyone can gain when the private property laws are defined so as to create the largest total economic surplus.

WHEN PRIVATE OWNERSHIP IS IMPRACTICAL

Don't be misled into thinking that the law provides an *ideal* resolution of all problems associated with externalities and the tragedy of the commons. Defining and enforcing efficient property rights entail costs, after all, and sometimes, as in the following examples, the costs outweigh the gains.

The Economic Naturalist 11.4

Why do blackberries in public parks get picked too soon?

Wild blackberries grow profusely at the edge of a wooded area in a crowded city park. The blackberries will taste best if left to ripen fully, but they still taste reasonably good if picked and eaten a few days early. Will the blackberries be left to ripen fully?

▶ Visit your instructor's Connect course and access your eBook to view this video.

Why do blackberries in public parks get picked before they're completely ripe?

Obviously, the costs of defining and enforcing the property rights to blackberries growing in a public park are larger than the potential gains, so the blackberries will remain common property. That means that whoever picks them first gets them. Even though everyone would benefit if people waited until the berries were fully ripe, everyone knows that those who wait are likely to end up with no berries at all. And that means that the berries will be eaten too soon.

The Economic Naturalist 11.5

Why are shared milkshakes consumed too quickly?

Sara and Susan are identical twins who have been given a chocolate milkshake to share. If each has a straw and each knows that the other is self-interested, will the twins consume the milkshake at an optimal rate?

Why are shared milkshakes drunk too quickly?

Because drinking a milkshake too quickly chills the taste buds, the twins will enjoy their shake more if they drink it slowly. Yet each knows that the other will drink any part of the milkshake she doesn't finish herself. The result is that each will consume the shake at a faster rate than she would if she had half a shake all to herself.

Here are some further examples in which the tragedy of the commons is not easily solved by defining private ownership rights.

Harvesting Timber on Remote Public Land

On remote public lands, enforcing restrictions against cutting down trees may be impractical. Each tree cutter knows that a tree that is not harvested this year will be bigger, and hence more valuable, next year. But he also knows that if he doesn't cut the tree down this year, someone else might do so. In contrast, private companies that grow trees on their own land have no incentive to harvest timber prematurely and a strong incentive to prevent outsiders from doing so.

Harvesting Whales in International Waters

Each individual whaler knows that harvesting an extra whale reduces the breeding population, and hence the size of the future whale population. But the whaler also knows that any whale that is not harvested today may be taken by some other whaler. The solution would be to define and enforce property rights to whales. But the oceans are vast, and the behavior of whalers is hard to monitor. And even if their behavior could be monitored, the concept of national sovereignty would make the international enforcement of property rights problematic.

More generally, the animal species that are most severely threatened with extinction tend to be those that are economically valuable to humans but that are not privately owned by anyone. This is the situation confronting whales as well as elephants. Contrast this with the situation confronting chickens, which are also economically valuable to humans but which, unlike whales, are governed by traditional laws of private property. This difference explains why no one worries that Colonel Sanders might threaten the extinction of chickens.

Controlling Multinational Environmental Pollution

Each individual polluter may know that if he and all others pollute, the damage to the environment will be greater than the cost of not polluting. But if the environment is common property into which all are free to dump, each has a powerful incentive to pollute. Enforcing laws and regulations that limit the discharge of pollution may be practical if all polluters live under the jurisdiction of a single government. But if polluters come from many different countries, solutions are much more difficult to implement. Thus, the Mediterranean Sea has long suffered serious pollution since none of the many nations that border it has an economic incentive to consider the effects of its discharges on other countries.

As the world's population continues to grow, the absence of an effective system of international property rights will become an economic problem of increasing significance.

> **RECAP ↑**
>
> **PROPERTY RIGHTS AND THE TRAGEDY OF THE COMMONS**
>
> When a valuable resource has a price of zero, people will continue to exploit it as long as its marginal benefit remains positive. The tragedy of the commons describes situations in which valuable resources are squandered because users are not charged for them. In many cases, an efficient remedy is to define and enforce rights to the use of valuable property. But this solution is difficult to implement for resources such as the oceans and the atmosphere because no single government has the authority to enforce property rights for these resources.

POSITIONAL EXTERNALITIES

Former tennis champion Steffi Graf received more than $1.6 million in tournament winnings in 1992; her endorsement and exhibition earnings totaled several times that amount. By any reasonable measure, the quality of her play was outstanding, yet she consistently lost to archrival Monica Seles. But in April 1993, Seles was stabbed in the back by a deranged fan and forced to withdraw from the tour. In the ensuing months, Graf's tournament winnings accumulated at almost double her 1992 pace, despite little change in the quality of her play.

PAYOFFS THAT DEPEND ON RELATIVE PERFORMANCE

In professional tennis and a host of other competitive situations, the rewards people receive typically depend not only on how they perform in absolute terms but also on how they perform relative to their closest rivals. In these situations, competitors have an incentive to take actions that will increase their odds of winning. For example, tennis players can increase their chances of winning by hiring personal fitness trainers and sports psychologists to travel with them on the tour. Yet the simple mathematics of competition tells us that the sum of all individual payoffs from such investments will be larger than the collective payoff. In any tennis match, for example, each contestant will get a sizable payoff from money spent on fitness trainers and sports psychologists, yet each match will have exactly one winner and one loser, no matter how much players spend. The overall gain to tennis spectators is likely to be small, and the overall gain to players as a group must be zero. To the extent that each contestant's payoff depends on his or her relative performance, then, the incentive to undertake such investments will be excessive, from a collective point of view.

Consider the following example.

The Economic Naturalist 11.6

Why do football players take anabolic steroids?

The offensive linemen of many National Football League teams currently average more than 330 pounds. In the 1970s, by contrast, offensive linemen in the league averaged barely 280 pounds, and the all-decade linemen of the 1940s averaged only 229 pounds. One reason that today's players are so much heavier is that players' salaries have escalated sharply over the last several decades, which has intensified competition for the positions. Size and strength are the two cardinal virtues of an offensive lineman, and other things being equal, the job will go to the larger and stronger of two rivals.

Why do so many football players take steroids?

Size and strength, in turn, can be enhanced by the consumption of anabolic steroids. But if all players consume these substances, the rank ordering of players by size and strength—and hence the question of who lands the jobs—will be largely unaffected. And because the consumption of anabolic steroids entails potentially serious long-term health consequences, football players as a group are clearly worse off if they consume these drugs. So why do football players take steroids?

The problem here is that contestants for starting berths on the offensive line confront a prisoner's dilemma, like the ones analyzed in Chapter 9, *Games and Strategic Behavior*. Consider two closely matched rivals—Smith and Jones—who are competing for a single position. If neither takes steroids, each has a 50 percent chance of winning the job and a starting salary of $1 million per year. If both take steroids, each again has a 50 percent chance of winning the job. But if one takes steroids and the other doesn't, the first is sure to win the job. The loser ends up selling insurance for $60,000 per year. Neither likes the fact that the drugs may have adverse health consequences, but each would be willing to take that risk in return for a shot at the big salary. Given these choices, the two competitors face a payoff matrix like the one shown in Table 11.6.

TABLE 11.6
Payoff Matrix for Steroid Consumption

		Jones	
		Don't take steroids	Take steroids
Smith	Don't take steroids	Second best for each	Best for Jones Worst for Smith
	Take steroids	Best for Smith Worst for Jones	Third best for each

Clearly, the dominant strategy for both Smith and Jones is to take steroids. Yet when they do, each gets only the third-best outcome, whereas they could have gotten the second-best outcome by not taking the drugs—hence the attraction of rules that forbid the consumption of anabolic steroids.

POSITIONAL ARMS RACES AND POSITIONAL ARMS CONTROL AGREEMENTS

The steroid problem is an example of a **positional externality.** Whenever the payoffs to one contestant depend at least in part on how he or she performs relative to a rival, any step that improves one side's relative position must necessarily worsen the other's. The shouting-at-parties example discussed in Chapter 9, *Games and Strategic Behavior*, is another instance of a positional externality. Just as the invisible hand of the market is weakened by the presence of standard externalities, it is also weakened by positional externalities.

We have seen that positional externalities often lead contestants to engage in an escalating series of mutually offsetting investments in performance enhancement. We call such spending patterns **positional arms races.**

Because positional arms races produce inefficient outcomes, people have an incentive to curtail them. Steps taken to reduce positional arms races, such as blue laws and rules against anabolic steroids, may therefore be thought of as **positional arms control agreements.**

Once you become aware of positional arms races, you will begin to see them almost everywhere. You can hone your skills as an economic naturalist by asking these questions about every competitive situation you observe: What form do the investments in performance enhancement take? What steps have contestants taken to limit these investments? Sometimes positional arms control agreements are achieved by the imposition of formal rules or by the signing of legal contracts. Some examples of this type of agreement follow.

Campaign Spending Limits

In the United States, presidential candidates routinely spend hundreds of millions of dollars on advertising. Yet if both candidates double their spending on ads, each one's odds of winning will remain essentially the same. Recognition of this pattern led Congress to adopt strict spending limits for presidential candidates. (That those regulations have proved difficult to enforce does not call into question the logic behind the legislation.)

positional externality this occurs when an increase in one person's performance reduces the expected reward of another's in situations in which reward depends on relative performance

positional arms race a series of mutually offsetting investments in performance enhancement that is stimulated by a positional externality

positional arms control agreement an agreement in which contestants attempt to limit mutually offsetting investments in performance enhancement

Roster Limits

Major League Baseball permits franchises to have only 25 players on the roster during the regular season. The National Football League sets its roster limit at 53; the National Basketball Association at 12. Why these limits? In their absence, any team could increase its chance of winning by simply adding players. Inevitably, other teams would follow suit. On the plausible assumption that, beyond some point, larger rosters do not add much to the entertainment value for fans, roster limits are a sensible way to deliver sports entertainment at a more reasonable cost.

Arbitration Agreements

In the business world, contracting parties often sign a binding agreement that commits them to arbitration in the event of a dispute. By doing so, they sacrifice the option of pursuing their interests as fully as they might wish to later, but they also insulate themselves from costly legal battles. Other parties in the legal system may sometimes take steps to limit spending on litigation. For example, a federal judge in South Dakota announced—presumably to the approval of litigants—that he would read only the first 15 pages of any brief submitted to his court.

Mandatory Starting Dates for Kindergarten

A child who is a year or so older than most of her kindergarten classmates is likely to perform better, in relative terms, than if she had entered school with children her own age. And since most parents are aware that admission to prestigious universities and eligibility for top jobs upon graduation depend largely on *relative* academic performance, many are tempted to keep their children out of kindergarten a year longer than necessary. Yet there is no social advantage in holding *all* children back an extra year since their relative performance would essentially be unaffected. In most jurisdictions, therefore, the law requires children who reach their fifth birthday before December 1 of a given year to start kindergarten the same year.

SOCIAL NORMS AS POSITIONAL ARMS CONTROL AGREEMENTS

In some cases, social norms may take the place of formal agreements to curtail positional arms races. Some familiar examples follow.

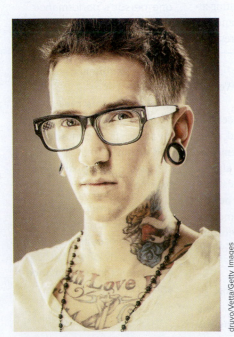

Is being on fashion's cutting edge more valuable now than in the 1950s?

Nerd Norms

Some students care more—in the short run, at least—about the grades they get than how much they actually learn. When such students are graded on the curve—that is, on the basis of their performance relative to other students—a positional arms race ensues because if all students were to double the amount of time they studied, the distribution of grades would remain essentially the same. Students who find themselves in this situation are often quick to embrace "nerd norms," which brand as social misfits those who "study too hard."

Fashion Norms

Social norms regarding dress and fashion often change quickly because of positional competition. Consider, for instance, the person who wishes to be on the cutting edge of fashion. In some American social circles during the 1950s, that goal could be accomplished by having pierced ears. But as more and more people adopted the practice, it ceased to communicate avant-garde status. At the same time, those who wanted to make a conservative fashion statement gradually became freer to have their ears pierced.

For a period during the 1960s and 1970s, one could be on fashion's cutting edge by wearing two earrings in one earlobe. But by the 1990s multiple ear piercings had lost much of their social significance, the threshold of cutting-edge status having been raised to upward of a dozen piercings of each ear or a smaller number of piercings of the nose, eyebrows, or other body parts. A similar escalation has taken place in the number, size, and placement of tattoos.

The increase in the required number of tattoos or body piercings has not changed the value of avant-garde fashion status to those who desire it. Being on the outer limits of fashion has much the same meaning now as it once did. To the extent that there are costs associated with body piercings, tattoos, and other steps required to achieve avant-garde status, the current fashions are wasteful compared to earlier ones. In this sense, the erosion of social norms against tattoos and body piercings has produced a social loss. Of course, the costs associated with this loss are small in most cases. Yet since each body piercing entails a small risk of infection, the costs will continue to rise with the number of piercings. And once those costs reach a certain threshold, support may mobilize on behalf of social norms that discourage these activities.

Norms of Taste

Similar cycles occur with respect to behaviors considered to be in bad taste. In the 1950s, for example, prevailing norms prevented major national magazines from accepting ads that featured nude photographs. Naturally, advertisers had a powerful incentive to chip away at such norms in an effort to capture the reader's limited attention. And indeed, taboos against nude photographs have eroded in the same way as with those against body piercings and tattoos.

Consider, for instance, the evolution of perfume ads. First came the nude silhouette; then, increasingly well-lit and detailed nude photographs; and more recently, photographs of what appear to be group sex acts. Each innovation achieved just the desired effect: capturing the reader's instant and rapt attention. Inevitably, however, other advertisers followed suit, causing a shift in our sense of what is considered attention-grabbing. Photographs that once would have shocked readers now often draw little more than a bored glance.

Opinions differ, of course, about whether this change is an improvement. Many believe that the earlier, stricter norms were ill-advised, the legacy of a more prudish and repressive era. Yet even people who take that view are likely to believe that *some* kinds of photographic material ought not to be used in magazine advertisements. Obviously, what is acceptable will differ from person to person, and each person's threshold of discomfort will depend in part on current standards. But as advertisers continue to break new ground in their struggle to capture attention, the point may come when people begin to mobilize in favor of stricter standards of "public decency." Such a campaign would provide yet another case of a positional arms control agreement.

Norms against Vanity

Cosmetic and reconstructive surgery has produced dramatic benefits for many people, enabling badly disfigured accident victims to recover a normal appearance. It also has eliminated the extreme self-consciousness felt by people born with strikingly unusual features. Such surgery, however, is by no means confined to the conspicuously disfigured. Increasingly, "normal" people are seeking surgical improvements to their appearance. For example, in the United States, over 18 million cosmetic procedures were performed in 2019, and demand has continued to grow. Once a carefully guarded secret, these procedures are now offered as prizes in Southern California charity raffles.

In individual cases, cosmetic surgery may be just as beneficial as reconstructive surgery is for accident victims. Buoyed by the confidence of having a straight nose or a wrinkle-free complexion, patients sometimes go on to achieve much more than they ever thought possible. But the growing use of cosmetic surgery also has had an unintended side effect: It has altered the standards of normal appearance. A nose that once would have seemed only slightly larger than average may now seem jarringly big. The same person who once would have looked like an average 55-year-old may now look nearly 70. And someone who once would have tolerated slightly thinning hair or an average amount of cellulite may now feel compelled to undergo hair transplantation or liposuction. Because such procedures shift people's frame of reference, their payoffs to individuals are misleadingly large. From a social perspective, therefore, reliance on them is likely to be excessive.

Legal sanctions against cosmetic surgery are difficult to imagine. But some communities have embraced powerful social norms against cosmetic surgery, heaping scorn and ridicule on the consumers of face-lifts and tummy tucks. In individual cases, such norms may seem cruel. Yet without them, many more people might feel compelled to bear the risk and expense of cosmetic surgery.

RECAP ↑

POSITIONAL EXTERNALITIES

Positional externalities occur when an increase in one person's performance reduces the expected reward of another person in situations in which reward depends on relative performance. Positional arms races are a series of mutually offsetting investments in performance enhancement that are stimulated by a positional externality. Positional arms control agreements are sometimes enacted in an attempt to limit positional arms races. In some cases, social norms can act as positional arms control agreements.

USING PRICE INCENTIVES IN ENVIRONMENTAL REGULATION

As we have seen, goods whose production generates negative externalities, such as atmospheric pollution, tend to be overproduced whenever negotiation among private parties is costly. Suppose we decide, as a society, that the best attainable outcome would be to have half as much pollution as would occur under completely unregulated conditions. In that case, how should the cleanup effort be distributed among those firms that currently discharge pollution into the environment?

The most efficient—and hence best—distribution of effort is the one for which each polluter's marginal cost of abatement is exactly the same. To see why, imagine that under current arrangements, the cost to one firm of removing a ton of pollution from the air is larger than the cost to another firm. Society could then achieve the same total reduction in pollution at lower cost by having the first firm discharge one ton more into the air and the second firm one ton less.

Unfortunately, government regulators seldom have detailed information on how the cost of reducing pollution varies from one firm to another. Many pollution laws therefore require all polluters simply to cut back their emissions by the same proportion or to meet the same absolute emissions standards. If different polluters have different marginal costs of pollution abatement, however, these approaches will not be efficient.

TAXING POLLUTION

Fortunately, alternative policies can distribute the cleanup more efficiently, even if the government lacks detailed information about how much it costs different firms to curtail pollution. One method is to tax pollution and allow firms to decide for themselves how much pollution to emit. The following example illustrates the logic of this approach.

| **EXAMPLE 11.12** | **Taxing Pollution** |

What is the least costly way to cut pollution by half?

Two firms, Sludge Oil and Northwest Lumber, each have access to five production processes, each of which has a different cost and produces a different amount of pollution. The daily costs of the processes and the number of tons of smoke emitted are as shown in Table 11.7. Pollution is currently unregulated, and negotiation between the firms and those who are harmed by pollution is impossible, which means that each firm uses process A, the least costly of the five. Each firm emits 4 tons of pollution per day, for a total of 8 tons of pollution per day.

TABLE 11.7
Costs and Emissions for Different Production Processes

Process (smoke)	A (4 tons/day)	B (3 tons/day)	C (2 tons/day)	D (1 ton/day)	E (0 tons/day)
Cost to Sludge Oil ($/day)	100	200	600	1,300	2,300
Cost to Northwest Lumber ($/day)	300	320	380	480	700

The government is considering two options for reducing total emissions by half. One is to require each firm to curtail its emissions by half. The other is to set a tax of T per ton of smoke emitted each day. How large must T be to curtail emissions by half? What would be the total cost to society under each alternative?

If each firm is required to cut pollution by half, each must switch from process A to process C. The result will be 2 tons per day of pollution for each firm. The cost of the switch for Sludge Oil will be $600 per day − $100 per day = $500 per day. The cost to Northwest Lumber will be $380 per day − $300 per day = $80 per day, for a total cost of $580 per day.

Consider now how each firm would react to a tax of T per ton of pollution. If a firm can cut pollution by 1 ton per day, it will save T per day in tax payments. Whenever the cost of cutting a ton of pollution is less than T, then each firm has an incentive to switch to a cleaner process. For example, if the tax were set at $40 per ton, Sludge Oil would stick with process A because switching to process B would cost $100 per day extra but would save only $40 per day in taxes. Northwest Lumber, however, would switch to process B because the $40 saving in taxes would be more than enough to cover the $20 cost of switching.

The problem is that a $40 per day tax on each ton of pollution results in a reduction of only 1 ton per day, 3 short of the 4-ton target. Suppose instead that the government imposed a tax of $101 per ton. Sludge Oil would then adopt process B because the $100 extra daily cost of doing so would be less than the $101 saved in taxes. Northwest Lumber would adopt process D because, for every process up to and including D, the cost of switching to the next process would be less than the resulting tax saving.

Overall, then, a tax of $101 per ton would result in the desired pollution reduction of 4 tons per day. The total cost of the reduction would be only $280 per day ($100 per day for Sludge Oil and $180 per day for Northwest Lumber), or $300 per day less than when each firm was required to cut its pollution by half. (The taxes paid by the firms do not constitute a cost of pollution reduction because the money can be used to reduce whatever taxes would otherwise need to be levied on citizens.)

 SELF-TEST 11.4

In Example 11.12, if the tax were $61 per ton of pollution emitted each day, which production processes would the two firms adopt?

The advantage of the tax approach is that it concentrates pollution reduction in the hands of the firms that can accomplish it at least cost. Requiring each firm to cut emissions by the same proportion ignores the fact that some firms can reduce pollution much more cheaply than others. Note that under the tax approach, the cost of the last ton of smoke removed is the same for each firm, so the efficiency condition is satisfied.

One problem with the tax approach is that unless the government has detailed knowledge about each firm's cost of reducing pollution, it cannot know how high to set the pollution tax. A tax that is too low will result in too much pollution, while a tax that is too high will result in too little. Of course, the government could start by setting a low tax rate and gradually increase the rate until pollution is reduced to the target level. But because firms often incur substantial sunk costs when they switch from one process to another, that approach might be even more wasteful than requiring all firms to cut their emissions by the same proportion.

AUCTIONING POLLUTION PERMITS

Another alternative is to establish a target level for pollution and then auction off permits to emit that level. The virtues of this approach are illustrated in the following example.

EXAMPLE 11.13	Pollution Permits

How much will pollution permits sell for?

Two firms, Sludge Oil and Northwest Lumber, again have access to the production processes described earlier (which are reproduced in Table 11.8). The government's goal is to cut the current level of pollution, 8 tons per day, by half. To do so, the government auctions off four permits, each of which entitles the bearer to emit 1 ton of smoke per day. No smoke may be emitted without a permit. What price will the pollution permits fetch at auction, how many permits will each firm buy, and what will be the total cost of the resulting pollution reduction?

TABLE 11.8
Costs and Emissions for Different Production Processes

Process (smoke)	A (4 tons/day)	B (3 tons/day)	C (2 tons/day)	D (1 ton/day)	E (0 tons/day)
Cost to Sludge Oil ($/day)	100	200	600	1,300	2,300
Cost to Northwest Lumber ($/day)	300	320	380	480	700

If Sludge Oil has no permits, it must use process E, which costs $2,300 per day to operate. If it had one permit, it could use process D, which would save it $1,000 per day. Thus, the most Sludge Oil would be willing to pay for a single 1-ton pollution permit is $1,000 per day. With a second permit, Sludge Oil could switch to process C and save another $700 per day; with a third permit, it could switch to process B and save another $400; and with a fourth permit, it could switch to process A and save another $100. Using similar reasoning, we can see that Northwest Lumber would pay up to $220 for one permit, up to $100 for a second, up to $60 for a third, and up to $20 for a fourth.

Suppose the government starts the auction at a price of $90. Sludge Oil will then demand four permits and Northwest Lumber will demand two, for a total demand of six permits. Since the government wishes to sell only four permits, it will keep raising the price until the two firms together demand a total of only four permits. Once the price reaches $101, Sludge Oil will demand three permits and Northwest Lumber will demand only one, for a total quantity demanded of four permits. Compared to the unregulated alternative, in which each firm used process A, the daily cost of the auction solution is $280: Sludge Oil spends $100 switching from process A to process B, and Northwest Lumber spends $180 switching from *A* to *D*. This total is $300 less than the cost of requiring each firm to reduce its emissions by half. (Again, the permit fees paid by the firms do not constitute a cost of cleanup because the money can be used to reduce taxes that would otherwise have to be collected.)

The auction method has the same virtue as the tax method: It concentrates pollution reduction in the hands of those firms that can accomplish it at the lowest cost. But the auction method has other attractive features that the tax approach does not. First, it does not induce firms to commit themselves to costly investments that they will have to abandon if the cleanup falls short of the target level. And second, it allows private citizens a direct voice in determining where the emission level will be set. For example, any group that believes the pollution target is too lenient could raise money to buy permits at auction. By keeping those permits locked away in a safe, the group could ensure that they will not be used to emit pollution.

Several decades ago, when economists first proposed the auctioning of pollution permits, reactions of outrage were widely reported in the press. Most of those reactions amounted to the charge that the proposal would "permit rich firms to pollute to their hearts' content." Such an assertion betrays a total misunderstanding of the forces that generate pollution. Firms pollute not because they *want* to pollute but because dirty production processes are cheaper than clean ones. Society's only real interest is in keeping the total amount of pollution from becoming excessive, not in *who* actually does the polluting. And in any event, the firms that do most of the polluting under an auction system will not be rich firms, but those for whom pollution reduction is most costly.

Economists have argued patiently against these misinformed objections to the auction system, and their efforts have finally borne fruit. The sale of pollution permits is now common in several parts of the United States, and there is growing interest in the approach in other countries.

The problem of acid rain is an instructive case in point. Electric power plants in the Midwest had long burned high-sulfur coal, in the process discharging large quantities of sulfur dioxide (SO_2) from their smokestacks. Prevailing winds carried these emissions eastward, where they precipitated out over New York State and New England as acid rain, killing large quantities of trees and fish.

Beginning in the 1960s, economists advocated addressing this problem by requiring firms to acquire marketable permits for each ton of SO_2 they emitted. But as discussed earlier, economists' proposals, despite their compelling logic, languished in Congress for more than three decades. Only with the passage of amendments to the Clean Air Act in 1995 did Congress require the establishment of a market for permits for discharging SO_2.

As economists had predicted, the permit system worked spectacularly well. Acid rain caused by SO_2 emissions quickly plummeted, and at about one-sixth the cost that more complex regulatory approaches would have entailed.[2] Once people have to pay for their emissions, they quickly find ingenious ways of reducing them.

CLIMATE CHANGE AND CARBON TAXES

Growing concentrations of carbon dioxide (CO_2) in the atmosphere are widely recognized as a principal contributor to global warming. Concerns about the consequences of climate change have led to proposals to tax (CO_2) emissions or require marketable permits for them. Critics of these proposals emphasize that forecasts involving climate change are highly uncertain, a fact they view as arguing against taking action. But uncertainty is a two-edged sword. Climate researchers themselves readily concede that estimates based on their models are extremely uncertain. But that means that although the actual outcome might be much better than their median forecast, it might also be significantly worse.

The Paris Agreement, which was adopted by representatives from nearly every nation on December 12, 2015, seeks to limit global warming to 3.6°F by the end of the twenty-first century. But even an increase that small would cause deadly harm, and the most respected

---

[2]See the United States Environmental Protection Agency, www.epa.gov/airmarkets.

climate change models estimate that there is essentially no chance that average temperature will rise by less than that amount if we take no action.

According to estimates published in 2013 by the Intergovernmental Panel on Climate Change (IPCC), the median forecast is for an average global temperature climb of 6.7°F by century's end, in the absence of effective countermeasures.[3] The IPCC also estimated that we face a 5 percent chance of temperatures rising by more than 8.6°F by 2100. Temperature increases of that magnitude would be accompanied by sea level rises that would make much of the world's most densely populated coastal regions uninhabitable. Climate scientists also believe that severe storms and droughts caused by climate change are already causing enormous damage.[4]

Again, long-term forecasts from climate models are highly uncertain. Things might not be as bad as predicted. But they could also be much worse. In other domains, uncertainty doesn't counsel against taking action. Few would recommend, for example, that we disband the military simply because adversaries might not invade. In the climate arena, the only remaining uncertainty is how much worse things will get. Should we take action? To respond to that question, we must ask, how much would it cost? The answer, as it turns out, is astonishingly little.

Early estimates by the IPCC suggest that a tax of between $20 and $80 per ton on carbon emissions would be needed by 2030 to achieve climate stability by 2100. The organization also noted, however, that technical advances might reduce the required levy to as little as $5 per ton.[5] Under a carbon tax, the prices of goods would rise in proportion to their carbon footprints. A tax of $80 per ton, for example, would raise the price of gasoline by about 70 cents a gallon, while a tax of $5 per ton would raise prices by less than 5 cents a gallon. Even a dramatically higher tax on carbon—say, $300 a ton—would raise the price of gasoline by less than $3 a gallon.

As American motorists saw in 2008, a sudden price increase of that magnitude could indeed be painful. But if phased in gradually, it would cause much less harm. Facing steadily increasing fuel prices, for example, manufacturers would scramble to develop more fuel-efficient vehicles. Many Europeans now pay $4 a gallon more for gas than Americans do. But precisely because of that fact, European automakers have pioneered development of many of the world's most fuel-efficient cars. Europeans actually spend less on gas than Americans do, yet seem no less happy with their rides.

If a family traded in its aging Ford Explorer (15 mpg) for a Ford Focus wagon (32 mpg), it would spend less on gas than before, even if it drove just as much. The tax could be phased in slowly, to give people time to adjust. People would also move closer to work, form car pools, choose less distant vacation destinations, and so on. Some of the revenue from the tax could be used to send checks to low-income families to ease the burden of higher gas prices. Portions of it could help pay down debt and rebuild crumbling infrastructure, or reduce other taxes.

In 2009 the U.S. House of Representatives actually passed an energy bill that included a comprehensive carbon cap and trade system, the functional equivalent of a carbon tax. But the bill couldn't win Senate approval, and seasoned congressional observers now see little chance that meaningful climate legislation could win passage in Congress anytime soon.

Some argue that taxing carbon emissions would be a waste of time unless other countries did likewise. It's a fair point. But World Trade Organization officials have indicated that countries could tax imported goods in proportion to their carbon dioxide emissions if exporting countries failed to enact carbon taxes at home. Access to the American market is a potent bargaining chip. Countries that sell in the U.S. would be quick to enact carbon taxes of their own rather than allow the U.S. to reap the revenue from a carbon tax levied on goods imported into the U.S. Moreover, four out of five of America's top trading partners (Canada, Germany, Japan, and Mexico) already have carbon taxes.

In short, the economist's cost-benefit framework suggests that our failure to enact carbon taxes constitutes a mystery of the highest order and is a stark example of how

Cost-Benefit ≫

---

[3]See Intergovernmental Panel on Climate Change, *Fifth Assessment Report—Climate Change 2013: The Physical Science Basis,* www.ipcc.ch/report/ar5/wg1.

[4]The Environmental Defense Fund, "How Climate Change Plunders the Planet," www.edf.org/climate/how-climate-change-plunders-planet.

[5]See Intergovernmental Panel on Climate Change, *Climate Change 2007—Synthesis Report,* pp. 59–61, www.ipcc.ch/pdf/assessment-report/ar4/syr/ar4_syr.pdf.

status quo bias and our tendency to discount future events excessively (see Chapter 10, *An Introduction to Behavioral Economics*) can lead to suboptimal policy choices.

> **RECAP ↑**
>
> **USING PRICE INCENTIVES IN ENVIRONMENTAL REGULATION**
>
> An efficient program for reducing pollution is one for which the marginal cost of abatement is the same for all polluters. Taxing pollution has this desirable property, as does the auction of pollution permits. The auction method has the advantage that regulators can achieve a desired abatement target without having detailed knowledge of the abatement technologies available to polluters.
>
> Climate scientists warn that increasing atmospheric concentrations of greenhouse gases threatens to cause catastrophic global warming. That risk could be averted by imposition of a carbon tax or equivalent carbon permit system.

SUMMARY

- Externalities are the costs and benefits of activities that accrue to people who are not directly involved in those activities. When all parties affected by externalities can negotiate with one another at no cost, the invisible hand of the market will produce an efficient allocation of resources. *(LO1)*

- According to the Coase theorem, the allocation of resources is efficient in such cases because the parties affected by externalities can compensate others for taking remedial action. *(LO2)*

- Negotiation over externalities is often impractical, however. In these cases, the self-serving actions of individuals typically will not lead to an efficient outcome. The attempt to forge solutions to the problems caused by externalities is one of the most important rationales for collective action. Sometimes collective action takes the form of laws and government regulations that alter the incentives facing those who generate, or are affected by, externalities. Such remedies work best when they place the burden of accommodation on the parties who can accomplish it at the lowest cost. Traffic laws, zoning laws, environmental protection laws, and free speech laws are examples. *(LO3)*

- Curbing pollution and other negative externalities entails costs as well as benefits. The optimal amount of pollution reduction is the amount for which the marginal benefit of further reduction just equals the marginal cost. In general, this formula implies that the socially optimal level of pollution, or of any other negative externality, is greater than zero. *(LO3)*

- When grazing land and other valuable resources are owned in common, no one has an incentive to take into account the opportunity cost of using those resources. This problem is known as the tragedy of the commons. Defining and enforcing private rights governing the use of valuable resources is often an effective solution to the tragedy of the commons. Not surprisingly, most economically successful nations have well-developed institutions of private property. Property that belongs to everyone belongs, in effect, to no one. Not only is its potential economic value never fully realized; it usually ends up having no value at all. *(LO4)*

- The difficulty of enforcing property rights in certain situations explains a variety of inefficient outcomes such as the excessive harvest of whales in international waters and the premature harvest of timber on remote public lands. The excessive pollution of seas that are bordered by many countries also results from a lack of enforceable property rights. *(LO4)*

- Situations in which people's rewards depend on how well they perform in relation to their rivals give rise to positional externalities. In these situations, any step that improves one side's relative position necessarily worsens the other's. Positional externalities tend to spawn positional arms races—escalating patterns of mutually offsetting investments in performance enhancement. Collective measures to curb positional arms races are known as positional arms control agreements. These collective actions may take the form of formal regulations or rules such as rules against anabolic steroids in sports, campaign spending limits, and binding arbitration agreements. Informal social norms can also curtail positional arms races. *(LO5)*

- An understanding of the forces that give rise to environmental pollution can help identify those policy measures that will achieve a desired reduction in pollution at the lowest possible cost. Both the taxing of pollution and the sale of transferable permits promote this goal. Each distributes the cost of the environmental cleanup effort so that the marginal cost of pollution abatement is the same for all polluters. *(LO6)*

KEY TERMS

Coase theorem
external benefit
  (or positive externality)
external cost (or negative externality)

externality
positional arms control
  agreement
positional arms race

positional externality
tragedy of the commons

REVIEW QUESTIONS

1. If Congress could declare illegal any activity that imposes external costs on others, would such legislation be advisable? *(LO2)*

2. What incentive problem explains why the freeways in cities like Los Angeles suffer from excessive congestion? *(LO3)*

3. How would you explain to a friend why the optimal amount of freeway congestion is not zero? *(LO3)*

4. Why might it be easier to reduce pollution levels in the Great Salt Lake, which is located solely in the state of

Utah, than in Lake Erie, which is bordered by several states and Canada? *(LO4)*

5. Explain why the wearing of high-heeled shoes might be viewed as the result of a positional externality. *(LO5)*

6. Why do economists believe that pollution taxes and tradable pollution permits are a more efficient way to curb pollution than laws mandating across-the-board cutbacks? *(LO6)*

PROBLEMS

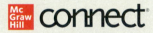

1. For each of the goods listed below, discuss whether the good is likely to entail an external cost or an external benefit. In addition, discuss whether the market is likely to provide more or less than the socially optimal quantity of the good. *(LO1)*
   a. Vaccinations.
   b. Cigarettes.
   c. Antibiotics.

2. Suppose the law says that Jones may *not* emit smoke from his factory unless he gets permission from Smith, who lives downwind. The relevant costs and benefits of filtering the smoke from Jones's production process are as shown in the following table. If Jones and Smith can negotiate with one another at no cost, will Jones emit smoke? *(LO2)*

	Jones emits smoke	Jones does not emit smoke
Surplus for Jones	$200	$160
Surplus for Smith	$400	$420

3. John and Karl can live together in a two-bedroom apartment for $900 per month, or each can rent a single-bedroom apartment for $550 per month. Aside from the rent, the two would be indifferent between living together and living separately, except for one problem: John

leaves dirty dishes in the sink every night. Karl would be willing to pay up to $175 per month to avoid John's dirty dishes. John, for his part, would be willing to pay up to $225 to be able to continue his sloppiness. *(LO2)*
   a. Should John and Karl live together? If they do, will there be dirty dishes in the sink? Explain.
   b. What if John would be willing to pay up to $30 per month to avoid giving up his privacy by sharing quarters with Karl? Should John and Karl live together?

4. Khatia and Gwendolyn are neighbors in an apartment complex. Khatia is a concert pianist, and Gwendolyn is a poet working on an epic poem. Khatia rehearses her concert pieces on the baby grand piano in her front room, which is directly above Gwendolyn's study. The following matrix shows the monthly payoffs to Khatia and Gwendolyn when Khatia's front room is and is not soundproofed. The soundproofing will be effective only if it is installed in Khatia's apartment. *(LO2)*

	Soundproofed	Not soundproofed
Gains to Khatia	$100/month	$150/month
Gains to Gwendolyn	$120/month	$80/month

   a. If Khatia has the legal right to make any amount of noise she wants and she and Gwendolyn can negotiate with one another at no cost, will Khatia install and maintain soundproofing? Explain. Is her choice socially efficient?

b. If Gwendolyn has the legal right to peace and quiet and can negotiate with Khatia at no cost, will Khatia install and maintain soundproofing? Explain. Is her choice socially efficient?

c. Does the attainment of an efficient outcome depend on whether Khatia has the legal right to make noise, or Gwendolyn the legal right to peace and quiet?

5. Refer to Problem 4. Khatia decides to buy a full-size grand piano. The new payoff matrix is as follows: *(LO2)*

	Soundproofed	Not soundproofed
Gains to Khatia	$100/month	$150/month
Gains to Gwendolyn	$120/month	$ 60/month

a. If Gwendolyn has the legal right to peace and quiet and Khatia and Gwendolyn can negotiate at no cost, will Khatia install and maintain soundproofing? Explain. Is this outcome socially efficient?

b. Suppose that Khatia has the legal right to make as much noise as she likes and that negotiating an agreement with Khatia costs $15 per month. Will Khatia install and maintain soundproofing? Explain. Is this outcome socially efficient?

c. Suppose Gwendolyn has the legal right to peace and quiet, and it costs $15 per month for Gwendolyn and Khatia to negotiate any agreement. (Compensation for noise damage can be paid without incurring negotiation cost.) Will Khatia install and maintain soundproofing? Is this outcome socially efficient?

d. Why does the attainment of a socially efficient outcome now depend on whether Khatia has the legal right to make noise?

6. Phoebe keeps a bee farm next door to an apple orchard. She chooses her optimal number of beehives by selecting the honey output level at which her private marginal benefit from beekeeping equals her private marginal cost. *(LO3)*

a. Assume that Phoebe's private marginal benefit and marginal cost curves from beekeeping are normally shaped. Draw a diagram of them.

b. Phoebe's bees help pollinate the blossoms in the apple orchard, increasing the fruit yield. Show the social marginal benefit from Phoebe's beekeeping in your diagram.

c. Phoebe's bees are Africanized killer bees that aggressively sting anyone who steps into their flight path. Phoebe, fortunately, is naturally immune to the bees' venom. Show the social marginal cost curve from Phoebe's beekeeping in your diagram.

d. Indicate the socially optimal quantity of beehives in your diagram. Is it higher or lower than the privately optimal quantity? Explain.

7. Suppose the supply curve of motorized scooter rentals in Golden Gate Park is given by $P = 5 + 0.1Q$, where

P is the daily rent per unit in dollars and Q is the volume of units rented in hundreds per day. The demand curve for motorized scooters is $20 - 0.2Q$. *(LO3)*

a. If each motorized scooter imposes $3 per day in traffic costs on others, by how much will the equilibrium number of motorized scooters rented exceed the socially optimal number?

b. How would the imposition of a tax of $3 per unit on each daily motorized scooter rental affect efficiency in this market?

8.* A village has six residents, each of whom has accumulated savings of $100. Each villager can use this money either to buy a government bond that pays 15 percent interest per year or to buy a year-old llama, send it onto the commons to graze, and sell it after 1 year. The price the villager gets for the 2-year-old llama depends on the quality of the fleece it grows while grazing on the commons. That in turn depends on the animal's access to grazing, which depends on the number of llamas sent to the commons, as shown in the following table:

Number of llamas on the commons	Price per 2-year-old llama ($)
1	122
2	118
3	116
4	114
5	112
6	109

The villagers make their investment decisions one after another, and their decisions are public. *(LO4)*

a. If each villager decides individually how to invest, how many llamas will be sent onto the commons, and what will be the resulting village income?

b. What is the socially optimal number of llamas for this village? Why is that different from the actual number? What would village income be if the socially optimal number of llamas were sent onto the commons?

c. The village committee votes to auction the right to graze llamas on the commons to the highest bidder. Assuming villagers can both borrow and lend at 15 percent annual interest, how much will the right sell for at auction? How will the new owner use the right, and what will be the resulting village income?

9. Two firms, Sludge Oil and Northwest Lumber, have access to five production processes, each one of which has a different cost and gives off a different amount of pollution. The daily costs of the processes and the corresponding number of tons of smoke emitted are as shown in the following table: *(LO6)*

*Denotes more difficult problem.

Process (smoke)	A (4 tons/day)	B (3 tons/day)	C (2 tons/day)	D (1 ton/day)	E (0 tons/day)
Cost to Sludge Oil ($/day)	50	70	120	200	500
Cost to Northwest Lumber ($/day)	100	180	500	1,000	2,000

a. If pollution is unregulated, which process will each firm use, and what will be the total daily smoke emission?

b. The City Council wants to curb smoke emissions by 50 percent. To accomplish this, it requires each firm to curb its emissions by 50 percent. What will be the total cost to society of this policy?

c. The City Council again wants to curb emissions by half. This time, it sets a tax of $T per day on each ton of smoke emitted. How large will T have to be to effect the desired reduction? What is the total cost to society of this policy?

10. Refer to Problem 9. Instead of taxing pollution, the City Council decides to auction off four permits, each of which entitles the bearer to emit 1 ton of smoke per day. No smoke may be emitted without a permit. Suppose the government conducts the auction by starting at $1 and asking how many permits each firm wants to buy at that price. If the total is more than four, it then raises the price by $1 and asks again, and so on, until the total quantity of demanded permits falls to four. How much will each permit sell for in this auction? How many permits will each firm buy? What will be the total cost to society of this reduction in pollution? *(LO6)*

ANSWERS TO SELF-TESTS

11.1 Since Fitch gains $50 per day when Abercrombie operates with a filter, he could pay Abercrombie as much as $49 per day and still come out ahead. *(LO2)*

11.2 If the two were to live together, the most efficient way to resolve the problem would be as before, for Sofia to tolerate sometimes being woken up by Adriana's friends. But on top of that cost, which is $150, Sofia would also bear a $60 cost from the loss of her privacy. The total cost of their living together would thus be $210 per month. Since that amount is greater than the $200 saving in rent, the two should live separately. *(LO2)*

11.3 The income figures from the different levels of investment in cattle would remain as before, as shown in the table. What is different is the opportunity cost of investing in each steer, which is now $11 per year instead of $13. Column 5 of the table shows that the socially optimal number of steers is now 2 instead of 1. And if individuals still favor holding cattle, all other

things being equal, they will now send 5 steers onto the commons instead of 4, as shown in the column 3. *(LO4)*

(1) Number of steers on the commons	(2) Price per 2-year-old steer ($)	(3) Income per steer ($/year)	(4) Total village income ($/year)	(5) Marginal income ($/year)
				26
1	126	26	26	
				12
2	119	19	38	
				10
3	116	16	48	
				4
4	113	13	52	
				3
5	111	11	55	

11.4 With a tax of $61 per ton each day, Sludge Oil would adopt process A and Northwest Lumber would adopt process C. *(LO6)*

Process (smoke)	A (4 tons/day)	B (3 tons/day)	C (2 tons/day)	D (1 ton/day)	E (0 tons/day)
Cost to Sludge Oil ($/day)	100	200	600	1,300	2,300
Cost to Northwest Lumber ($/day)	300	320	380	480	700

CHAPTER 12

The Economics of Information

Matching the right buyers with the right sellers creates economic value that is just as real as the value created by the actual production of goods and services.

ZikG/Shutterstock

Years ago, a naive young economist spent a week in Kashmir on a houseboat on scenic Dal Lake, outside the capital city of Srinagar. Kashmir is renowned for its woodcarvings, and one afternoon a man in a gondola stopped by to show the economist some of his wooden bowls. When the economist expressed interest in one of them, the woodcarver quoted a price of 200 rupees. The economist had lived in that part of Asia long enough to realize that the price was more than the woodcarver expected to get, so he made a counteroffer of 100 rupees.

The woodcarver appeared to take offense, saying that he couldn't possibly part with the bowl for less than 175 rupees. Suspecting that the woodcarver was merely feigning anger, the young economist held firm. The woodcarver appeared to become even angrier, but quickly retreated to 150 rupees. The economist politely restated his unwillingness to pay more than 100 rupees. The woodcarver then tried 125 rupees, and again the economist replied that 100 was his final offer. Finally, they struck a deal at 100 rupees, and with cash in hand, the woodcarver left in a huff.

Pleased with his purchase, the economist showed it to the houseboat's owner later that evening. "It's a lovely bowl," he agreed, and asked how much the economist had paid for it. The economist told him, expecting praise for his negotiating prowess. The host's failed attempt at suppressing a laugh was the economist's first clue that he had paid too much. When asked how much such a bowl would normally sell for, the houseboat owner was reluctant to respond. But the economist pressed him, and the host speculated that the seller had probably hoped for 30 rupees at most.

Adam Smith's invisible hand theory presumes that buyers are fully informed about the myriad ways in which they might spend their money—what goods and services are available, what prices they sell for, how long they last, how frequently they break down, and so on. But, of course, no one is ever really *fully* informed about anything. And sometimes, as in the transaction with the woodcarver, people are completely ignorant of even the most basic information. Still, life goes on, and most people muddle through somehow.

Consumers employ a variety of strategies for gathering information, some of which are better than others. They read *Consumer Reports*, talk to family and friends, visit stores, kick the tires on used cars, and so on. But one of the most important aspects of choosing intelligently without having complete information is having at least some idea of the extent of one's ignorance. Someone once said that there are two kinds of consumers in the world: those who don't know what they're doing and those who don't know that they don't know what they're doing. As in the case of the wooden bowl, the people in the second category are the ones who are most likely to choose foolishly.

Basic economic principles can help you identify those situations in which additional information is most likely to prove helpful. In this chapter, we will explore what those principles tell us about how much information to acquire and how to make the best use of limited information.

HOW THE MIDDLEMAN ADDS VALUE

One of the most common problems consumers confront is the need to choose among different versions of a product whose many complex features they don't fully understand. As the following example illustrates, in such cases consumers can sometimes rely on the knowledge of others.

EXAMPLE 12.1   **Consumer Choice**

How should a consumer decide which pair of skis to buy?

You need a new pair of skis, but the technology has changed considerably since you bought your last pair and you don't know which of the current brands and models would be best for you. Skis R Us has the largest selection, so you go there and ask for advice. The salesperson appears to be well informed; after asking about your experience level and how aggressively you ski, she recommends the Rossignol Experience 77. You buy a pair for $600 and then head back to your apartment and show them to your roommate, who says that you could have bought them on the Internet for only $400. How do you feel about your purchase? Are the different prices charged by the two suppliers related to the services they offer? Were the extra services you got by shopping at Skis R Us worth the extra $200?

Internet retailers can sell for less because their costs are much lower than those of full-service retail stores. Those stores, after all, must hire knowledgeable salespeople, put their merchandise on display, rent space in expensive shopping malls, and so on. Internet retailers and mail-order houses, by contrast, typically employ unskilled telephone clerks, and they store their merchandise in cheap warehouses. If you're a consumer who doesn't know which is the right product for you, the extra expense of shopping at a specialty retailer is likely to be a good investment. Spending $600 on the right skis is smarter than spending $400 on the wrong ones.

Many people believe that wholesalers, retailers, and other agents who assist manufacturers in the sale of their products play a far less important role than the one played by those who actually make the products. In this view, the production worker is the ultimate source of economic value added. Sales agents are often disparaged as mere middlemen, parasites on the efforts of others who do the real work.

On a superficial level, this view might seem to be supported by the fact that many people go to great lengths to avoid paying for the services of sales agents. Many manufacturers cater to them by offering consumers a chance to "buy direct" and sidestep the middleman's commission. But on closer examination, we can see that the economic role of sales agents is essentially the same as that of production workers. Consider this example.

EXAMPLE 12.2   The Economic Role of Sales Agents

How does better information affect economic surplus?

Ellis has just inherited a rare Babe Ruth baseball card issued during the great slugger's rookie year. He'd like to keep the card but has reluctantly decided to sell it to pay some overdue bills. His reservation price for the card is $300, but he is hoping to get significantly more for it. He has two ways of selling it: He can place a classified ad in the local newspaper for $5 or he can list the card on eBay. If he sells the card on eBay, the fee will be 5 percent of the winning bid.

Because Ellis lives in a small town with few potential buyers of rare baseball cards, the local buyer with the highest reservation price is willing to pay $400 at most. If Ellis lists the card on eBay, however, a much larger number of potential buyers will see it. If the two eBay shoppers who are willing to pay the most for Ellis's card have reservation prices of $900 and $800, respectively, by how much will the total economic surplus be larger if Ellis sells his card on eBay? (For the sake of simplicity, assume that the eBay commission and the classified ad fee equal the respective costs of providing those services.)

In an eBay auction, each bidder reports his or her reservation price for an item. When the auction closes, the bidder with the highest reservation price wins, and the price he or she pays is the reservation price of the second-highest bidder. So in this example, the Babe Ruth baseball card will sell for $800 if Ellis lists it on eBay. Net of the $40 eBay commission, Ellis will receive a payment of $760, or $460 more than his reservation price for the card. Ellis's economic surplus will thus be $460. The winning bidder's surplus will be $900 − $800 = $100, so the total surplus from selling the card on eBay will be $560.

If Ellis instead advertises the card in the local newspaper and sells it to the local buyer whose reservation price is $400, then Ellis's surplus (net of the newspaper's $5 fee) will be only $95 and the buyer's surplus will be $0. Thus, total economic surplus will be $560 − $95 = $465 larger if Ellis sells the card on eBay than if he lists it in the local newspaper.

eBay provides a service by making information available to people who can make good use of it. A real increase in economic surplus results when an item ends up in the hands of someone who values it more highly than the person who otherwise would have bought it. That increase is just as valuable as the increase in surplus that results from manufacturing cars, growing corn, or any other productive activity.

In recent years, another important type of middleman has emerged: apps and online marketplaces that connect buyers and sellers who might not otherwise be able to find one another. Consider ride-share services like Uber and Lyft. These companies provide real-time information that enables drivers and riders to find one another. These companies also provide information through ratings systems so that both drivers and riders can feel confident they will have a positive interaction. As evidenced by their massive popularity, these and other digital middlemen like Craigslist, Etsy, and eBay have been tremendously beneficial to both buyers and sellers and have helped spur the growth of the gig economy.

RECAP ↑

HOW THE MIDDLEMAN ADDS VALUE

In a world of incomplete information, sales agents and other middlemen add genuine economic value by increasing the extent to which goods and services find their way to the consumers who value them most. For example, when a sales agent causes a good to be purchased by a person who values it by $20,000 more than the person who would have bought it in the absence of a sales agent, that agent augments total economic surplus by $20,000, an achievement on a par with the production of a $20,000 car. Many apps and digital marketplaces now serve a similar function.

THE OPTIMAL AMOUNT OF INFORMATION

Increasing Opportunity Cost »

Without a doubt, having more information is better than having less. But information is generally costly to acquire. In most situations, the value of additional information will decline beyond some point. And because of the Low-Hanging-Fruit Principle, people tend to gather information from the cheapest sources first before turning to more costly ones. Typically, then, the marginal benefit of information will decline, and its marginal cost will rise, as the amount of information gathered increases.

THE COST-BENEFIT TEST

Cost-Benefit »

Information gathering is an activity like any other. The Cost-Benefit Principle tells us that a rational consumer will continue to gather information as long as its marginal benefit exceeds its marginal cost. Suppose, for the sake of discussion, that analysts had devised a scale that permits us to measure units of information, as on the horizontal axis of Figure 12.1. If the relevant marginal cost and marginal benefit curves are as shown in the diagram, a rational consumer will acquire $I*$ units of information, the amount for which the marginal benefit of information equals its marginal cost.

Another way to think about Figure 12.1 is that it shows the optimal level of ignorance. When the cost of acquiring information exceeds its benefits, acquiring additional information simply doesn't pay. If information could be acquired at no cost, decision makers would, of course, be glad to have it. But when the cost of acquiring the information exceeds the gain in value from the decision it will facilitate, people are better off to remain ignorant.

free-rider problem an incentive problem in which too little of a good or service is produced because nonpayers cannot be excluded from using it

THE FREE-RIDER PROBLEM

Does the invisible hand ensure that the optimal amount of advice will be made available to consumers in the marketplace? The next example suggests one reason why it might not.

FIGURE 12.1

The Optimal Amount of Information.

For the marginal cost and benefit curves shown, the optimal amount of information is $I*$. Beyond that point, information costs more to acquire than it is worth.

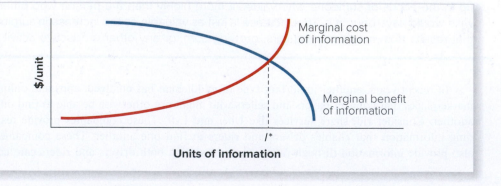

The Economic Naturalist 12.1

Why is finding a knowledgeable salesclerk often difficult?

People can choose for themselves whether to bear the extra cost of retail shopping. Those who value advice and convenience can pay slightly higher prices, while those who know what they want can buy for less from a mail-order house. True or false: It follows that private incentives lead to the optimal amount of retail service.

The market would provide the optimal level of retail service except for one practical problem, namely, that consumers can make use of the services offered by retail stores without paying for them. After benefiting from the advice of informed salespersons and after inspecting the merchandise, the consumer can return home and buy the same item from an Internet retailer or mail-order house. Not all consumers do so, of course. But the fact that customers can benefit from the information provided by retail stores without paying for it is an example of the **free-rider problem,** an incentive problem that results in too little of a good or service being produced. Because retail stores have difficulty recovering the cost of providing information, private incentives are likely to yield less than the socially optimal level of retail service. So the statement above is false.

Why are there so few knowledgeable salesclerks?

The Economic Naturalist 12.2

Why did Rivergate Books, the last bookstore in Lambertville, New Jersey, go out of business?

Small independent bookstores often manage to survive competition from large chains like Barnes & Noble by offering more personalized service. Janet Holbrooke, the proprietor of Rivergate Books, followed this strategy successfully for more than a decade before closing her doors in 1999. What finally led her to quit?

Holbrooke, a retired English teacher, said that many of her customers had experimented with Barnes & Noble when the large chain opened an outlet nearby, but that most had remained loyal because they valued the more personal service her clerks were able to provide. Customers also were drawn in by special events such as readings and book signings by authors. But during one of these events, Holbrooke saw that her store's days were numbered. She had invited Gerald Stern, a National Book Award–winning poet, to do a reading, but despite a good turnout for the event, few attendees purchased books. When she overheard a woman in the book-signing line say that she'd brought her book to the event after having purchased it from Amazon.com, Holbrooke realized it was a losing battle.

Why are so many independent booksellers going out of business?

 SELF-TEST 12.1

Apart from its possible contribution to free-rider problems, how is increased access to the Internet likely to affect total economic surplus?

TWO GUIDELINES FOR RATIONAL SEARCH

In practice, of course, the exact value of additional information is difficult to know, so the amount of time and effort one should invest in acquiring it is not always obvious. But as the following examples suggest, the Cost-Benefit Principle provides a strong conceptual framework for thinking about this problem.

EXAMPLE 12.3   Searching for an Apartment

Should a person living in Paris, Texas, spend more or less time searching for an apartment than someone living in Paris, France?

Suppose that rents for one-bedroom apartments in Paris, Texas, vary between $500 and $700 per month, with an average rent of $600 per month. Rents for similar one-bedroom apartments in Paris, France, vary between $2,000 and $3,000 per month, with an average rent of $2,500. In which city should a rational person expect to spend a longer time searching for an apartment?

In both cities, visiting additional apartments entails a cost, largely the opportunity cost of one's time. In both cities, the more apartments someone visits, the more likely it is that he or she will find one near the lower end of the rent distribution. But because rents are higher and are spread over a broader range in Paris, France, the expected saving from further time spent searching will be greater there than in Paris, Texas. A rational person will expect to spend more time searching for an apartment in France.

This example illustrates the principle that spending additional search time is more likely to be worthwhile for expensive items than for cheap ones. For example, one should spend more time searching for a good price on a diamond engagement ring than for a good price on a stone made of cubic zirconium; more time searching for a low fare to Sydney, Australia, than for a low fare to Sidney, New York; and more time searching for a car than for a bicycle. By extension, hiring an agent—someone who can assist with a search—is more likely to be a good investment in searching for something expensive than for something cheap. For example, people typically engage real estate agents to help them find a house, but they seldom hire agents to help them buy a gallon of milk.

EXAMPLE 12.4   The Cost of Searching

Who should expect to search longer for a good price on a used piano?

Both Mateo and Samuel are shopping for a used upright piano. To examine a piano listed in the classified ads, they must travel to the home of the piano's current owner. If Mateo has a car and Samuel does not and both are rational, which one should expect to examine fewer pianos before making his purchase?

The benefits of examining an additional piano are the same in both cases, namely, a better chance of finding a good instrument for a low price. But because it is more costly for Samuel to examine pianos, he should expect to examine fewer of them than Mateo.

The preceding example makes the point that when searching becomes more costly, we should expect to do less of it. And as a result, the prices we expect to pay will be higher when the cost of a search is higher.

THE GAMBLE INHERENT IN SEARCH

Suppose you are in the market for a one-bedroom apartment and have found one that rents for $900 per month. Should you rent it or search further in hopes of finding a cheaper apartment? Even in a large market with many vacant apartments, there is no guarantee that searching further will turn up a cheaper or better apartment. Searching further entails a cost, which might outweigh the gain. In general, someone who engages in further search must accept certain costs in return for unknown benefits. Thus, further search invariably carries an element of risk.

In thinking about whether to take any gamble, a helpful first step is to compute its expected value—the average amount you would win (or lose) if you played that gamble an infinite number of times. To calculate the **expected value of a gamble** with more than one outcome, we first multiply each outcome by its corresponding probability of occurring, and then add. For example, suppose you win $1 if a coin flip comes up heads and lose $1 if it comes up tails. Since 1/2 is the probability of heads (and also the probability of tails), the expected value of this gamble is $(1/2)(\$1) + (1/2)(-\$1) = 0$. A gamble with an expected value of zero is called a **fair gamble.** If you played this gamble a large number of times, you wouldn't expect to make money, but you also wouldn't expect to lose money.

A **better-than-fair gamble** is one with a positive expected value. (For instance, a coin flip in which you win $2 for heads and lose $1 for tails is a better-than-fair gamble.) A **risk-neutral person** is someone who would accept any gamble that is fair or better. A **risk-averse person** is someone who would refuse to take any fair gamble.

> ✅ **SELF-TEST 12.2**
>
> Consider a gamble in which you win $4 if you flip a fair coin and it comes up heads and lose $2 if it comes up tails. What is the expected value of this gamble? Would a risk-neutral person accept it?

In the next example, we apply these concepts to the decision of whether to search further for an apartment.

expected value of a gamble the sum of the possible outcomes of the gamble multiplied by their respective probabilities

fair gamble a gamble whose expected value is zero

better-than-fair gamble a gamble whose expected value is positive

risk-neutral person someone who would accept any gamble that is fair or better

risk-averse person someone who would refuse any fair gamble

EXAMPLE 12.5   The Gamble in the Search

Should you search further for an apartment?

You have arrived in San Francisco for a one-month summer visit and are searching for a one-bedroom sublet for the month. There are only two kinds of one-bedroom apartments in the neighborhood in which you wish to live, identical in every respect except that one rents for $2,400 and the other for $2,300. Of the vacant apartments in this neighborhood, 80 percent are of the first type and 20 percent are of the second type. The only way you can discover the rent for a vacant apartment is to visit it in person. The first apartment you visit is one that rents for $2,400. If you are risk-neutral and your opportunity cost of visiting an additional apartment is $15, should you visit another apartment or rent the one you've found?

If you visit one more apartment, you have a 20 percent chance of it being one that rents for $2,300 and an 80 percent chance of it being one that rents for $2,400. If the former, you'll save $100 in rent, but if the latter, you'll face the same rent as before. Since the cost of a visit is $15, visiting another apartment is a gamble with a 20 percent chance to win $100 − $15 = $85 and an 80 percent chance of losing $15 (which means "winning" −$15). The expected value of this gamble is thus $(0.20)(\$85) + (0.80)(-\$15) = \$5$. Visiting another apartment is a better-than-fair gamble, and since you are risk-neutral, you should take it.

✅ **SELF-TEST 12.3**

Refer to Example 12.5. Suppose you visit another apartment and discover it, too, is one that rents for $2,400. If you are risk-neutral, should you visit a third apartment?

THE COMMITMENT PROBLEM WHEN SEARCH IS COSTLY

When most people search for an apartment, they want a place to live not for just a month, but for a year or more. Most landlords, for their part, are also looking for long-term tenants. Similarly, few people accept a full-time job in their chosen field unless they expect to hold the job for several years. Firms, too, generally prefer employees who will stay for extended periods. Finally, when most people search for mates, they are looking for someone with whom to settle down.

Because in all these cases search is costly, examining every possible option will never make sense. Apartment hunters don't visit every vacant apartment, nor do landlords interview every possible tenant. Job seekers don't visit every employer, nor do employers interview every job seeker. And not even the most determined searcher can manage to date every eligible mate. In these and other cases, people are rational to end their searches, even though they know a more attractive option surely exists out there somewhere.

But herein lies a difficulty. What happens when, by chance, a more attractive option comes along after the search has ceased? Few people would rent an apartment if they thought the landlord would kick them out the moment another tenant came along who was willing to pay higher rent. Few landlords would be willing to rent to a tenant if they expected her to move out the moment she discovers a cheaper apartment. Employers, job seekers, and people who are looking for mates would have similar reservations about entering relationships that could be terminated once a better option happened to come along.

This potential difficulty in maintaining stable matches between partners in ongoing relationships would not arise in a world of perfect information. In such a world, everyone would end up in the best possible relationship, so no one would be tempted to renege. But when information is costly and the search must be limited, there will always be the potential for existing relationships to dissolve.

In most contexts, people solve this problem not by conducting an exhaustive search (which is usually impossible, in any event) but by committing themselves to remain in a relationship once a mutual agreement has been reached to terminate the search. Thus, landlords and tenants sign a lease that binds them to one another for a specified period, usually one year. Employees and firms enter into employment contracts, either formal or informal, under which each promises to honor his obligations to the other, except under extreme circumstances. And in most countries a marriage contract penalizes those who abandon their spouses. Entering into such commitments limits the freedom to pursue one's own interests. Yet most people freely accept such restrictions because they know the alternative is failure to solve the search problem.

RECAP ↑

THE OPTIMAL AMOUNT OF INFORMATION

Additional information creates value, but it's also costly to acquire. A rational consumer will continue to acquire information until its marginal benefit equals its marginal cost. Beyond that point, it's rational to remain uninformed.

Markets for information do not always function perfectly. Free-rider problems often hinder retailers' efforts to provide information to consumers.

Search inevitably entails an element of risk because costs must be incurred without any assurance that search will prove fruitful. A rational consumer can minimize this risk by concentrating search efforts on goods for which the variation in price or quality is relatively high and on those for which the cost of search is relatively low.

ASYMMETRIC INFORMATION

One of the most common information problems occurs when the participants in a potential exchange are not equally well informed about the product or service that's offered for sale. For instance, the owner of a used car may know that the car is in excellent mechanical condition, but potential buyers cannot know that merely by inspecting it or taking it for a test drive. Economists use the term **asymmetric information** to describe situations in which buyers and sellers are not equally well informed about the characteristics of products or services. In these situations, sellers are typically much better informed than buyers, but sometimes the reverse will be true.

The problem of asymmetric information can easily prevent exchanges that would benefit both parties. Here is a classic example.

asymmetric information situations in which buyers and sellers are not equally well informed about the characteristics of goods and services for sale in the marketplace

---

EXAMPLE 12.6 | Asymmetric Information

Will Katie sell her car to Samir?

Katie's 2014 Mazda Miata has 70,000 miles on the odometer, but most of these are highway miles driven during weekend trips to see her boyfriend in Toronto. (Highway driving causes less wear and tear on a car than city driving.) Moreover, Katie has maintained the car precisely according to the manufacturer's specifications. In short, she knows her car to be in excellent condition. Because she is about to start graduate school in Boston, however, Katie wants to sell the car. On average, 2014 Miatas sell for a price of $12,000, but because Katie knows her car to be in excellent condition, her reservation price for it is $14,000.

Samir wants to buy a used Miata. He would be willing to pay $16,000 for one that is in excellent condition but only $13,000 for one that is not in excellent condition. Samir has no way of telling whether Katie's Miata is in excellent condition. (He could hire a mechanic to examine the car, but doing so is expensive, and many problems cannot be detected even by a mechanic.) Will Samir buy Katie's car? Is this outcome efficient?

Because Katie's car looks no different from other 2014 Miatas, Samir will not pay $14,000 for it. After all, for only $12,000, he can buy some other 2014 Miata that's in just as good condition, *as far as he can tell*. Samir therefore will buy someone else's Miata, and Katie's will go unsold. This outcome is not efficient. If Samir had bought Katie's Miata for, say, $14,500, his surplus would have been $1,500 and Katie's another $500. Instead, Samir ends up buying a Miata that is in average condition (or worse), and his surplus is only $1,000. Katie gets no economic surplus at all.

THE LEMONS MODEL

We can't be sure, of course, that the Miata Samir ends up buying will be in worse condition than Katie's—since *someone* might have a car in perfect condition that must be sold even if the owner cannot get what it is really worth. Even so, the economic incentives created by asymmetric information suggest that most used cars that are put up for sale will be of lower-than-average quality. One reason is that people who mistreat their cars, or whose cars were never very good to begin with, are more likely than others to want to sell them. Buyers know from experience that cars for sale on the used car market are more likely to be "lemons" than cars that are not for sale. This realization causes them to lower their reservation prices for a used car.

But that's not the end of the story. Once used car prices have fallen, the owners of cars that are in good condition have an even stronger incentive to hold onto them. That

lemons model George Akerlof's explanation of how asymmetric information tends to reduce the average quality of goods offered for sale

causes the average quality of the cars offered for sale on the used car market to decline still further. Berkeley economist George Akerlof, a Nobel laureate, was the first to explain the logic behind this downward spiral.[1] Economists use the term **lemons model** to describe Akerlof's explanation of how asymmetric information affects the average quality of the used goods offered for sale.

The next example suggests that the lemons model has important practical implications for consumer choice.

EXAMPLE 12.7 **The Lemons Model in Action**

Should you buy your aunt's car?

You want to buy a used Honda Accord. Your Aunt Germaine buys a new car every four years, and she has a four-year-old Accord that she's about to trade in. You believe her report that the car is in good condition, and she's willing to sell it to you for $16,000, which is the current blue book value for four-year-old Accords. (The blue book value of a car is the average price for which cars of that age and model sell in the used car market.) Should you buy your aunt's Honda?

Akerlof's lemons model tells us that cars for sale in the used car market will be of lower average quality than cars of the same vintage that are not for sale. If you believe your aunt's claim that her car is in good condition, then being able to buy it for its blue book value is definitely a good deal for you, since the blue book price is the equilibrium price for a car that is of lower quality than your aunt's.

The following two examples illustrate the conditions under which asymmetric information about product quality results in a market in which *only* lemons are offered for sale.

EXAMPLE 12.8 **The Naive Buyer (Part 1)**

How much will a naive buyer pay for a used car?

Consider a world with only two kinds of cars: good ones and lemons. An owner knows with certainty which type of car she has, but potential buyers cannot distinguish between the two types. Ten percent of all new cars produced are lemons. Good used cars are worth $16,000 to their owners, but lemons are worth only $12,000. Consider a naive consumer who believes that the used cars currently for sale have the same quality distribution as new cars (i.e., 90 percent good, 10 percent lemons). If this consumer is risk-neutral, how much would he be willing to pay for a used car?

Buying a car of unknown quality is a gamble, but a risk-neutral buyer would be willing to take the gamble provided it is fair. If the buyer can't tell the difference between a good car and a lemon, the probability that he will end up with a lemon is simply the proportion of lemons among the cars from which he chooses. The buyer believes he has a 90 percent chance of getting a good car and a 10 percent chance of getting a lemon. Given the prices he is willing to pay for the two types of car, his expected value of the car he buys will thus be 0.90($16,000) + 0.10($12,000) = $15,600. And since he is risk-neutral, that is his reservation price for a used car.

---

[1]George Akerlof, "The Market for Lemons," *Quarterly Journal of Economics* 84 (1970), pp. 488–500.

SELF-TEST 12.4

How would your answer to the question posed in Example 12.8 differ if the proportion of new cars that are lemons had been 20 percent?

EXAMPLE 12.9	The Naive Buyer (Part 2)

Who will sell a used car for what the naive buyer is willing to pay?

Continuing with the previous example: If you were the owner of a good used car, what would it be worth to you? Would you sell it to a naive buyer? What if you owned a lemon?

Since you know your car is good, it is worth $16,000 to you, by assumption. But a naive buyer would be willing to pay only $15,600, so neither you nor any other owner of a good car would be willing to sell to that buyer. If you had a lemon, of course, you'd be happy to sell it to a naive buyer, since the $15,600 the buyer is willing to pay is $3,600 more than the lemon would be worth to you. So the only used cars for sale will be lemons. In time, buyers will revise their naively optimistic beliefs about the quality of the cars for sale on the used car market. In the end, all used cars will sell for a price of $12,000, and all will be lemons.

In practice, of course, the mere fact that a car is for sale does not guarantee that it is a lemon because the owner of a good car will sometimes be forced to sell it, even at a price that does not reflect its condition. The logic of the lemons model explains this owner's frustration. The first thing sellers in this situation want a prospective buyer to know is the reason they are selling their cars. For example, classified ads often announce, "Just had a baby, must sell my 2015 Corvette" or "Transferred to Germany, must sell my 2016 Toyota Camry." Anytime you pay the blue book price for a used car that is for sale for some reason unrelated to its condition, you are beating the market.

▶ Visit your instructor's Connect course and access your eBook to view this video.

Why do "almost new" used cars sell for so much less than brand-new ones?

THE CREDIBILITY PROBLEM IN TRADING

Why can't someone with a high-quality used car simply *tell* the buyer about the car's condition? The difficulty is that buyers' and sellers' interests tend to conflict. Sellers of used cars, for example, have an economic incentive to overstate the quality of their products. Buyers, for their part, have an incentive to understate the amount they are willing to pay for used cars and other products (in the hope of bargaining for a lower price). Potential employees may be tempted to overstate their qualifications for a job. And people searching for mates have been known to engage in deception.

That isn't to say that most people *consciously* misrepresent the truth in communicating with their potential trading partners. But people do tend to interpret ambiguous information in ways that promote their own interests. Thus, 92 percent of factory employees surveyed in one study rated themselves as more productive than the average factory worker. Psychologists call this phenomenon the "Lake Wobegon effect," after Garrison Keillor's mythical Minnesota homestead, where "all the children are above average."

Notwithstanding the natural tendency to exaggerate, the parties to a potential exchange can often gain if they can find some means to communicate their knowledge truthfully. In general, however, mere statements of relevant information will not suffice. People have long since learned to discount the used car salesman's inflated claims about the cars he's trying to unload. But as the next example illustrates, though communication between potential adversaries may be difficult, it's not impossible.

EXAMPLE 12.10	**Credible Signals**

How can a used car seller signal high-quality credibly?

Katie knows her Miata to be in excellent condition, and Samir would be willing to pay considerably more than her reservation price if he could be confident of getting such a car. What kind of signal about the car's quality would Samir find credible?

Again, the potential conflict between Samir's and Katie's interests suggests that mere statements about the car's quality may not be persuasive. But suppose Katie offers a warranty, under which she agrees to remedy any defects the car develops over the next six months. Katie can afford to extend such an offer because she knows her car is unlikely to need expensive repairs. In contrast, the person who knows his car has a cracked engine block would never extend such an offer. The warranty is a credible signal that the car is in good condition. It enables Samir to buy the car with confidence, to both his and Katie's benefit.

The Costly-to-Fake Principle

costly-to-fake principle
to communicate information credibly to a potential rival, a signal must be costly or difficult to fake

The preceding examples illustrate the **costly-to-fake principle,** which holds that if parties whose interests potentially conflict are to communicate credibly with one another, the signals they send must be costly or difficult to fake. If the seller of a defective car could offer an extensive warranty just as easily as the seller of a good car, a warranty offer would communicate nothing about the car's quality. But warranties entail costs that are significantly higher for defective cars than for good cars—hence their credibility as a signal of product quality.

To the extent that sellers have an incentive to portray a product in the most flattering light possible, their interests conflict with those of buyers, who want the most accurate assessment of product quality possible. Note that in the following example, the costly-to-fake principle applies to a producer's statement about the quality of a product.

The Economic Naturalist 12.3

Why do firms insert the phrase "As advertised on TV" when they advertise their products in magazines and social media?

Company *A* sponsors an expensive national television advertising campaign on behalf of its surround sound speakers, claiming it has the clearest sound and the best repair record of any surround sound speakers in the market. Company *B* makes similar claims in a sales brochure but does not advertise its product on television. If you had no additional information to go on, which company's claim would you find more credible? Why do you suppose Company *A* mentions its TV ads when it advertises its surround sound speakers in print and social media?

Accustomed as we are to discounting advertisers' inflated claims, the information given might seem to provide no real basis for a choice between the two products. On closer examination, however, we see that a company's decision to advertise its product on national television constitutes a credible signal about the product's quality. The cost of a national television campaign can run well into the millions of dollars, a sum a company would be foolish to spend on an inferior product.

For example, the going rate for 30-second ad slots for the 2020 Superbowl was $5.6 million. National TV ads can attract potential buyers'

Why should buyers care whether a product is advertised on TV?

attention and persuade a small fraction of them to try a product. But these huge investments pay off only if the resulting initial sales generate other new business—either repeat sales to people who tried the product and liked it or sales to others who heard about the product from a friend.

Because ads cannot persuade buyers that a bad product is a good one, a company that spends millions of dollars advertising a bad product is wasting its money. An expensive national advertising campaign is therefore a credible signal that the producer *thinks* its product is a good one. Of course, the ads don't guarantee that a product *is* a winner, but in an uncertain world, they provide one more piece of information. Note, however, that the relevant information lies in the expenditure on the advertising campaign, not in what the ads themselves say.

These observations may explain why some companies mention their television ads in their print ads. Advertisers understand the costly-to-fake principle and hope that consumers will understand it as well.

As The Economic Naturalist 12.4 illustrates, the costly-to-fake principle is also well known to many employers.

The Economic Naturalist 12.4

Why do many companies care so much about elite educational credentials?

Microsoft is looking for a hardworking, smart person for an entry-level managerial position in a new technical products division. Two candidates, Eva and Donna, seem alike in every respect but one: Eva, graduated with the highest honors from MIT, while Donna graduated with a C+ average from Somerville College. Whom should Microsoft hire?

If you want to persuade prospective employers that you are both hardworking and intelligent, there is perhaps no more credible signal than to have graduated with distinction from a highly selective educational institution. Most people would like potential employers to think of them as hardworking and intelligent. But unless you actually have both those qualities, graduating with the highest honors from a school like MIT will be extremely difficult. The fact that Donna graduated from a much less selective institution and earned only a C+ average is not proof positive that she is not diligent and talented, but companies are forced to play the percentages. In this case, the odds strongly favor Eva.

Conspicuous Consumption as a Signal of Ability

Some individuals of high ability are not highly paid. (Remember the best elementary school teacher you ever had.) And some people—such as the multibillionaire investor Warren Buffett—earn a lot, yet spend very little. But such cases run counter to general tendencies. In competitive markets, the people with the most ability tend to receive the highest salaries. And as suggested by the Cost-Benefit Principle, the more someone earns, the more he or she is likely to spend on high-quality goods and services. As the following example suggests, these tendencies often lead us to infer a person's ability from the amount and quality of the goods he or she consumes.

Cost-Benefit

The Economic Naturalist 12.5

Why do many clients seem to prefer lawyers who wear expensive suits?

If you were on trial for a serious crime, which lawyer would you hire?

You've been unjustly accused of a serious crime and are looking for an attorney. Your choice is between two lawyers who appear identical in all respects except for the things they buy. One of them wears a cheap polyester suit and arrives at the courthouse in a 10-year-old rust-eaten Dodge Caliber. The other wears an impeccably tailored suit and drives a new BMW 750i. If this were the *only* information available to you at the time you chose, which lawyer would you hire?

The correlation between salary and the abilities buyers value most is particularly strong in the legal profession. A lawyer whose clients usually prevail in court will be much more in demand than one whose clients generally lose, and their fees will reflect the difference. The fact that one of the lawyers consumes much more than the other doesn't *prove* that he is the better lawyer, but if that is the only information you have, you can ill afford to ignore it.

If the less able lawyer loses business because of the suits he wears and the car he drives, why doesn't he simply buy better suits and a more expensive car? His choice is between saving for retirement or spending more on his car and clothing. In one sense, he cannot afford to buy a more expensive car, but in another sense, he cannot afford *not* to. If his current car is discouraging potential clients from hiring him, buying a better one may simply be a prudent investment. But because *all* lawyers have an incentive to make such investments, their effects tend to be mutually offsetting.

When all is said and done, the things people consume will continue to convey relevant information about their respective ability levels. The costly-to-fake principle tells us that the BMW 750i is an effective signal precisely because the lawyer of low ability cannot afford one, no matter how little he saves for retirement. Yet from a social perspective, the resulting spending pattern is inefficient, for the same reason that other positional arms races are inefficient. (We discussed positional arms races in Chapter 11, *Externalities, Property Rights, and the Environment.*) Society would be better off if everyone spent less and saved more for retirement.

The problem of conspicuous consumption as an ability signal doesn't arise with equal force in every environment. In small towns, where people tend to know one another well, a lawyer who tries to impress people by spending beyond her means is likely to succeed only in demonstrating how foolish she is. Thus, the wardrobe a professional person "needs" in towns like Dubuque, Iowa, or Athens, Ohio, costs less than half as much as the wardrobe the same person would need in Manhattan or Los Angeles.

> **RECAP** ↑
>
> **ASYMMETRIC INFORMATION**
>
> - Asymmetric information describes situations in which not all parties to a potential exchange are equally well informed. In the typical case, the seller of a product will know more about its quality than the potential buyers. Such asymmetries often stand in the way of mutually beneficial exchange in the markets for high-quality goods because buyers' inability to identify high quality makes them unwilling to pay a commensurate price.
> - Information asymmetries and other communication problems between potential exchange partners can often be solved through the use of signals that are costly or difficult to fake. Product warranties are such a signal because the seller of a low-quality product would find them too costly to offer.

STATISTICAL DISCRIMINATION

In a competitive market with perfect information, the buyer of a service would pay the seller's cost of providing the service. In many markets, however, the seller does not know the exact cost of serving each individual buyer.

In such cases, the missing information has an economic value. If the seller can come up with even a rough estimate of the missing information, she can improve her position. As The Economic Naturalist 12.6 illustrates, firms often do so by imputing characteristics to individuals on the basis of the groups to which they belong.

The Economic Naturalist 12.6

Why do males under 25 years of age pay more than other drivers for auto insurance?

Gerald is 23 years old and is an extremely careful and competent driver. He has never had an accident, or even a moving traffic violation. His twin sister Geraldine has had two accidents, one of them serious, in the last three years and has accumulated three speeding tickets during that same period. Why does Gerald pay $1,600 per year for auto insurance, while Geraldine pays only $1,400?

Why do male teens pay so much more for auto insurance?

The expected cost to an insurance company of insuring any given driver depends on the probability that the driver will be involved in an accident. No one knows what that probability is for any given driver, but insurance companies can estimate rather precisely the proportion of drivers in specific groups who will be involved in an accident in any given year. Males under 25 are much more likely than older males and females of any age to become involved in auto accidents. Gerald pays more than his sister because even those males under 25 who have never had an accident are more likely to have one than females the same age who have had several accidents.

Of course, females who have had two accidents and accumulated several tickets in the last three years are more likely to have an accident than a female with a spotless driving record. The insurance company knows that and has increased Geraldine's premium accordingly. Yet it is still less than her brother's premium. That doesn't mean that Gerald is in fact more likely to have an accident than Geraldine. Indeed, given the twins' respective driving skills, Geraldine clearly poses the higher risk. But because insurance companies lack such detailed information, they are forced to set rates according to the information they possess.

To remain in business, an insurance company must collect enough money from premiums to cover the cost of the claims it pays out, plus whatever administrative expenses it incurs. Consider an insurance company that charges lower rates for young males with clean driving records than for females with blemished ones. Given that the former group is more likely to have accidents than the latter, the company cannot break even unless it charges females more, and males less, than the respective costs of insuring them. But if it does so, rival insurance companies will see cash on the table: They can offer females slightly lower rates and lure them away from the first company. The first company will end up with only young male policyholders and thus will suffer an economic loss at the low rates it charges. That is why, in equilibrium, young males with clean driving records pay higher insurance rates than young females with blemished records.

statistical discrimination
the practice of making judgments about the quality of people, goods, or services based on the characteristics of the groups to which they belong

The insurance industry's policy of charging high rates to young male drivers is an example of **statistical discrimination.** Other examples include the common practice of paying higher salaries to people with college degrees than to people without them and the policy of favoring college applicants with high SAT scores. Statistical discrimination occurs whenever people or products are judged on the basis of the groups to which they belong.

Competition promotes statistical discrimination, even though everyone knows that the characteristics of specific individuals can differ markedly from those of the group to which they belong. For example, insurance companies know perfectly well that *some* young males are careful and competent drivers. But unless they can identify *which* males are the better drivers, competitive pressure forces them to act on their knowledge that, as a group, young males are more likely than others to generate insurance claims.

Similarly, employers know that many people with only a high school diploma are more productive than the average college graduate. But because employers usually cannot tell in advance who those people are, competitive pressure leads them to offer higher wages to college graduates, who are more productive, on average, than high school graduates. Universities, too, realize that many applicants with low SAT scores will earn higher grades than applicants with high scores. But if two applicants look equally promising except for their SAT scores, competition forces universities to favor the applicant with higher scores since, on average, that applicant will perform better than the other.

Statistical discrimination is the *result* of observable differences in group characteristics, not the cause of those differences. Young males, for example, do not generate more insurance claims because of statistical discrimination. Rather, statistical discrimination occurs because insurance companies know that young males generate more claims. Nor does statistical discrimination cause young males to pay insurance rates that are high in relation to the claims they generate. Among any group of young male drivers, some are careful and competent, and others are not. Statistical discrimination means the more able males will pay high rates relative to the volume of claims they generate, but it also means the less able male drivers will pay low rates relative to the claims they generate. On average, the group's rates will be appropriate to the claims its members generate.

Still, these observations do little to ease the frustration of the young male who knows himself to be a careful and competent driver, or the high school graduate who knows herself to be a highly productive employee. Competitive forces provide firms an incentive to identify such individuals and treat them more favorably whenever practical. When firms succeed in this effort, however, they have often discovered some other relevant information on group differences. For example, many insurance companies offer lower rates to young males who belong to the National Honor Society or make the dean's list at school. Members of those groups generate fewer claims, on average, than other young males. But even these groups include risky drivers, and the fact that companies offer discounts to their members means that all other young males must pay higher rates.

DISAPPEARING POLITICAL DISCOURSE

An intriguing illustration of statistical discrimination arises when a politician decides what to say about controversial public issues. Politicians have an interest in supporting the positions they genuinely believe in, but they also have an interest in winning reelection. As The Economic Naturalist 12.7 and 12.8 illustrate, the two motives often conflict, especially when a politician's statements about one subject convey information about her beliefs on other subjects.

The Economic Naturalist 12.7

Why do opponents of the death penalty often remain silent?

Quite apart from the question of whether execution of convicted criminals is morally legitimate, there are important practical arguments against capital punishment. For one thing, it is extremely expensive relative to the alternative of life without parole. Execution is costly because of judicial safeguards against execution of innocent persons. In each capital case prosecuted in the United States, these safeguards consume thousands of person-hours from attorneys and other officers of the court, at a cost that runs well into the millions of dollars.[2] Such efforts notwithstanding, the record is replete with examples of executed persons who are later shown to be innocent. Another argument against capital punishment is that many statistical studies find that it does not deter people from committing capital crimes. Though many political leaders in both parties find these and other arguments against capital punishment compelling, few politicians voice their opposition to capital punishment publicly. Why not?

A possible answer to this puzzle is suggested by the theory of statistical discrimination. Voters in both parties are concerned about crime and want to elect politicians who take the problem seriously. Suppose there are two kinds of politicians: some who in their heart of hearts take the crime issue seriously and others who merely pay lip service to it. Suppose also that voters classify politicians in a second way: those who publicly favor the death penalty or remain silent and those who publicly oppose it. Some politicians will oppose the death penalty for the reasons just discussed, but others will oppose it because they are simply reluctant to punish criminals—perhaps because they believe that crime is ultimately more society's fault than the criminal's. (Politicians in the latter category are the ones voters think of as being "not serious about crime"; they are the ones many voters want to get rid of.) These two possible motives for opposing the death penalty suggest that the proportion of death penalty opponents who take the crime issue seriously, in the public's view, will be somewhat smaller than the corresponding proportion among proponents of the death penalty. For the sake of discussion, imagine that 95 percent of politicians who favor the death penalty and only 80 percent of politicians who oppose the death penalty are "serious about crime."

If you are a voter who cares about crime, how will your views about a politician be affected by hearing that he opposes the death penalty? If you knew nothing about that politician to begin with, your best guess on hearing his opposition to the death penalty would be that there is an 80 percent chance that he is serious about crime. Had he instead voiced support for the death penalty, your best guess would be that there is a 95 percent chance that he is serious about crime. And since voters are looking for politicians who are serious about crime, the mere act of speaking out against the death penalty will entail a small loss of political support even for those politicians who are extremely serious about crime.

Knowing this tendency on the part of voters, some politicians who are only marginally opposed to the death penalty may prefer to keep their views to themselves. As a result, the composition of the group that speaks out publicly against the death penalty will change slightly so that it is more heavily weighted with people reluctant to punish criminals in any way. Suppose, for example, that the proportion of death penalty opponents who are serious about crime falls from 80 to 60 percent. Now the political cost of speaking out against the death penalty rises, leading still more opponents to remain silent. Once the dust settles, very few opponents of capital punishment will risk stating their views publicly. In their desire to convince voters that they are tough on crime, some may even become outspoken proponents of the death penalty. In the end, public discourse will strongly favor capital punishment. But that is no reason to conclude that most leaders—or even most voters—genuinely favor it.

---

[2]See Philip J. Cook and Donna B. Slawson, "The Costs of Processing Murder Cases in North Carolina," The Sanford Institute of Public Policy, Duke University, Durham, NC, 1993.

disappearing political discourse the theory that people who support a position may remain silent because speaking out would create a risk of being misunderstood

The economist Glenn Loury was the first to call attention to the phenomenon described in the preceding example. We call it the problem of **disappearing political discourse**. Once you understand it, you will begin to notice examples not just in the political sphere but in everyday discourse as well.

The Economic Naturalist 12.8

Why do proponents of legalized drugs remain silent?

That addictive drugs like heroin, cocaine, and methamphetamines cause enormous harm is not a matter of dispute. The clear intent of laws that ban commerce in these drugs is to prevent that harm. But the laws also entail costs. By making the drugs illegal, they substantially increase their price, leading many addicts to commit crimes to pay for drugs. The high incomes of many illicit-drug dealers also divert people from legitimate careers and result in turf battles that often have devastating consequences for both participants and bystanders. If these drugs were legal, drug-related crime would vanish completely. Drug use would also rise, how significantly we do not know. In short, it's at least *conceivable* that legalizing addictive drugs might be sound public policy. Why, then, do virtually no politicians publicly favor such a policy?

Many politicians may simply believe that legalizing drugs is a bad idea. Theoretically, legalization could lead to such a steep rise in drug consumption that the cost of the policy might far outweigh its benefits. This concern, however, is not supported by experience in countries such as England and the Netherlands, which have tried limited forms of legalization. A second explanation is that politicians who favor legalization are reluctant to speak out for fear that others will misinterpret them. Suppose that some people favor legalization based on careful analysis of the costs and benefits, while other proponents are merely crazy. If the proportion of crazies is higher among supporters than among opponents of legalization, someone who speaks out in favor of legalization may cause those who do not know her to increase their estimate of the likelihood she is crazy. This possibility deters some proponents from speaking out, which raises the proportion of crazies among the remaining public supporters of legalization—and so on in a downward spiral, until most of the remaining public supporters really are crazy.

The disappearing political discourse problem helps explain why the United States had difficulty reestablishing normal diplomatic relations with China, which were severed in the wake of the communist revolution. One could oppose communist expansionism and yet still favor normalized relations with China on the grounds that war is less likely when antagonists communicate openly. In the Cold War environment, however, American politicians were under enormous pressure to demonstrate their steadfast opposition to communism at every opportunity. Fearing that support for the normalization of relations with China would be misinterpreted as a sign of softness toward communism, many supporters of the policy remained silent. Not until Richard Nixon—whose anticommunist credentials no one could question—was elected president were diplomatic relations with China finally reopened.

The problem of disappearing discourse also helps explain the impoverished state of public debate on issues such as the reform of Social Security, Medicare, and other entitlement programs.

RECAP ↑

STATISTICAL DISCRIMINATION

- Buyers and sellers respond to incomplete information by attempting to judge the qualities of products and people on the basis of the groups to which they belong. For example, auto insurance companies charge young male drivers higher rates because they know young men are frequently involved in accidents.
- Because people's beliefs about different things tend to be correlated, knowing what someone believes about one issue provides at least some clue to his or her beliefs about others. The problem of disappearing political discourse arises because politicians are often reluctant to speak out about some issues publicly for fear that doing so may suggest that they hold unpopular beliefs about related issues.

INSURANCE

Hurricanes, fires, car accidents, and illnesses are largely unforeseeable events. Since most people are risk-averse, they often purchase insurance to help guard against the possibility of facing the enormous expenses associated with such events.

To see how this works, consider David. Most of the time, he is healthy, but he knows there's a chance he could face a serious illness. In particular, suppose there's a 75 percent chance David won't have any health care expenses all year, but there's a 25 percent chance he'll face a serious illness and will have to pay $16,000 in medical bills. David's annual health care expenses are thus a gamble with an expected value of $(0.75)(\$0) + (0.25)$ $(\$16,000) = \$4,000$. This means that if David is risk-averse, he'd rather pay $4,000 each year than face a 25 percent chance of paying $16,000. In fact, David might be willing to pay substantially more than $4,000 to avoid this risk.

▶ Visit your instructor's Connect course and access your eBook to view this video.

This is exactly where insurance steps in. Suppose David is willing to pay $4,500 a year to avoid the risk of having to pay $16,000 in medical bills. An insurance company can charge David $4,500 a year in exchange for the promise of paying his medical expenses should he face a serious illness. This arrangement makes David better off because he no longer faces a 25 percent chance of having to pay $16,000 in medical bills should he fall ill, and it's beneficial for the insurance company, since it gets $4,500 a year from David, but expects to pay out only $4,000. This extra $500 paid to the insurance company can go toward the cost of administering the insurance plan. And, unlike David, the insurance company doesn't mind the risk associated with David's health care costs because the company has lots of other customers just like him, some of whom will have good years and others of whom will have bad years, so that, on average, the company pays only $4,000 a year for each customer.

Why might a patient be more likely to receive an expensive magnetic resonance imaging (MRI) exam for a sore knee if covered under a conventional health insurance plan rather than a Health Maintenance Organization (HMO) plan?

Despite these obvious benefits, insurance markets often do not function as well as we would like. As we discuss next, the problem of incomplete information again plays a role.

ADVERSE SELECTION

One of the most pernicious problems in insurance markets relates to asymmetric information. To remain in business, an insurance company must set premiums that are high enough to pay for the expenses it has promised to cover. Thus, for example, health insurance companies determine premiums based on the expected medical expenses of the average person. The problem is that individuals often have more information about the likelihood that they will need insurance than do the companies providing the insurance. For example, David's health insurance company might not know that he has a family history of diabetes. This means that the premiums set by insurance companies are a better deal for high-risk individuals than for low-risk individuals, and as a result, high-risk individuals are more likely to buy insurance than low-risk individuals. This pattern is

adverse selection the pattern in which insurance tends to be purchased disproportionately by those who are most costly for companies to insure

moral hazard the tendency of people to expend less effort protecting those goods that are insured against theft or damage

known as **adverse selection.** Because of it, insurance companies raise their premiums, which makes buying insurance even less attractive to low-risk individuals, which raises still further the average risk level of those who remain insured. In some cases, only those individuals faced with extreme risks may continue to find insurance an attractive purchase.

MORAL HAZARD

Moral hazard is another problem that makes buying insurance less attractive for the average person. This problem refers to the fact that some people take fewer precautions when they know they are insured. Someone whose car is insured, for example, may take less care to prevent it from being damaged or stolen. Driving cautiously and searching for safe parking spaces require effort, after all, and if the losses from failing to engage in these precautions are covered by insurance, some people will become less vigilant.

Insurance companies help many of their potential clients soften the consequences of problems like moral hazard and adverse selection by offering policies with deductible provisions. Under the terms of an automobile collision insurance policy with, say, a $1,000 deductible provision, the insurance company covers only those collision repair costs in excess of $1,000. For example, if you have an accident in which $3,000 in damage occurs, the insurance company covers only $2,000, and you pay the remaining $1,000.

How does the availability of such policies mitigate the negative effects of adverse selection and moral hazard? Because policies with high deductibles are cheaper for insurance companies to provide, they sell for lower prices. The lower prices represent a much better bargain, however, for those drivers who are least likely to file insurance claims since those drivers are least likely to incur any uncovered repair costs. Policies with deductible provisions also confront careless drivers with more of the extra costs for which they are responsible, giving them additional incentives to take precautions.

These policies benefit insurance buyers in another way. Because the holder of a policy with a deductible provision will not file a claim at all if the damage to his car in an accident is less than the deductible threshold, insurance companies require fewer resources to process and investigate claims, savings that get passed along in the form of lower premiums.

THE PROBLEM WITH HEALTH CARE PROVISION THROUGH PRIVATE INSURANCE

It is troubling, but perhaps not surprising, that access to medical care is extremely limited in many of the world's poorest nations. After all, citizens of those nations lack enough income to buy adequate food, shelter, and many other basic goods and services. What *is* surprising, however, is that almost 50 million Americans had no health coverage of any kind when President Barack Obama took office in 2009. In a country as wealthy as the United States, why was this the case?

The answer to that question is rooted in the fact that the United States was almost alone among the world's nations in its reliance on unregulated private insurance markets to orchestrate the delivery of health care to its citizens. Unregulated private insurance markets are a deeply flawed mechanism for providing access to health care because of the adverse-selection problem. As discussed above, if insurance companies set their rates based on the expected medical expenses of the average person, its policy will seem like a bargain to potential customers who know themselves to be in bad health. At the same time, its policies will seem overpriced to those who know themselves to be in excellent health. The upshot is that a disproportionate share of the customers it attracts will have below-average health status, which means its initial premiums will be too low to cover its costs. To stay in business, it will have to raise its rates. But then potential customers in good health will find its policies even less attractive. A downward spiral often ensues, with the end result that insurance becomes unaffordable for most people.

Reliance upon unregulated private health insurance markets in the United States was essentially a historical accident, a consequence of the fact that many labor unions managed to negotiate employer-provided health insurance as part of their compensation packages during the rapidly growing economy of the immediate post–WWII years. Under government policy, employer expenditures for health insurance were nontaxable.

Employer-provided insurance was thus much cheaper for employees than private insurance purchased individually with income on which they had already been taxed. That incentive induced nonunion employers to join their union counterparts in offering employer-provided health insurance. And as long as health care spending was a fairly small share of total income, coverage was broad and the system functioned reasonably well.

An important policy detail was that eligibility for the tax exemption was conditional on insurance being made available to all employees irrespective of preexisting medical conditions. Given the high cost of treating individuals with chronic medical problems, private insurance companies are generally reluctant to issue policies to people with serious health problems. But by covering large groups of employees, only a small percentage of whom would be likely to have serious health problems during any year, insurance companies could issue these policies without taking unacceptable risks. Indeed, the large new employer-provided insurance market was sufficiently lucrative that most insurance companies were eager to participate in it.

Although the employer-provided group insurance approach helped keep the adverse-selection problem at bay for many years, this approach began to unravel as medical costs continued to rise relative to all other goods and services. With health insurance premiums taking a bigger and bigger bite out of workers' paychecks and heightened competition forcing companies to look for new ways to cut costs, some began offering higher wages in lieu of employer-provided health coverage. Younger, healthier workers—for whom medical expenses are normally small—found these offers increasingly tempting.

Parents who didn't buy health insurance for their families were once viewed as irresponsible, but this stigma lost some of its sting as the number of uninsured grew. As more and more people took jobs without health coverage, going without insurance became more socially acceptable. Making matters worse was the changing composition of the pool of the insured. As more healthy families took jobs without coverage, those left tended to be sicker and more costly to treat, forcing premiums to rise still more rapidly. In short, because of adverse selection, our health insurance system was caught in a long-term death spiral.

THE AFFORDABLE CARE ACT OF 2010

Passed by Congress and signed into law by President Obama in March 2010, the Affordable Care Act (ACA) was the government's first serious attempt to halt that death spiral. It contained three main provisions, each one of which was essential for reform to succeed. First, it required insurance companies to offer coverage to everyone on roughly equal terms, irrespective of preexisting medical conditions. Without this provision, the economic imperative of every private insurance company would have been to take every step possible to deny coverage to anyone expected to incur significant medical expenses. Any insurance system that couldn't cover those who most need care would clearly be unacceptable.

Because insurance companies cannot cover their costs if they insure only the least healthy people, it was also necessary for the ACA to include a mandate requiring everyone to buy health insurance. Without a mandate, healthy individuals would face strong incentives to go without health insurance until they got sick, since they would then be able to buy affordable insurance from companies that were forbidden to charge high rates based on preexisting conditions.

The third major feature of the ACA was to provide for subsidies to low-income families. You can't require people to buy insurance if they can't afford it. With health care costs already high and rapidly rising, it was essential to include some provision to ease the burden on those who are unable to pay.

The act contained numerous other provisions, many of which were designed to slow the rate of health care costs by requiring more streamlined medical record keeping and supporting research on the questions of which treatments were most effective. But the essence of the act lies in its three main provisions—nondiscrimination on the basis of preexisting conditions, the mandate, and subsidies for low-income families. Without any one of these provisions, the decline in the percentage of Americans with health coverage would have surely continued.

In tax legislation enacted in late 2017, Congress included a measure repealing the ACA's mandate requiring that everyone purchase health insurance. Perhaps not surprisingly, between 2017 and 2018, the share of Americans without health insurance increased from 7.9 percent to 8.5 percent, suggesting that without further legislative action, the health care industry's long-term death spiral may be poised to resume.

RECAP

INSURANCE

Risk-averse people will purchase insurance to guard themselves against the risk of unanticipated and costly events like hurricanes, car accidents, and illness. Adverse selection drives up the cost of insurance because individuals who are the most expensive for companies to insure have the greatest incentive to purchase insurance. Moral hazard also drives up insurance premiums because people have less incentive to protect items that have been insured against theft or damage. In the United States, the problem of adverse selection has left large numbers of Americans without health care coverage and has led to ongoing efforts to reform our health care system.

Mounting insurance premiums have caused many people in good health to do without health coverage, resulting in higher premiums for those who remain insured. The Affordable Care Act of 2010 was enacted in an attempt to remedy market failures that exist in attempts to provide health care access through unregulated private insurance contracts. In the wake of congressional repeal of the ACA's mandate provision in late 2017, the proportion of Americans without health insurance is on the rise again.

SUMMARY

- Retailers and other sales agents are important sources of information. To the extent that they enable consumers to find the right products and services, they add economic value. In that sense they are no less productive than the workers who manufacture goods or perform services directly. Unfortunately, the free-rider problem often prevents firms from offering useful product information. *(LO1)*

- Virtually every market exchange takes place on the basis of less-than-complete information. More information is beneficial both to buyers and to sellers, but information is costly to acquire. The rational individual therefore acquires information only up to the point at which its marginal benefit equals its marginal cost. Beyond that point, one is rational to remain ignorant. *(LO2)*

- Several principles govern the rational search for information. Searching more intensively makes sense when the cost of a search is low, when quality is highly variable, or when prices vary widely. Further search is always a gamble. A risk-neutral person will search whenever the expected gains outweigh the expected costs. A rational search will always terminate before all possible options have been investigated. Thus, in a search for a partner in an ongoing bilateral relationship, there is always the possibility that a better partner will turn up after the search is over. In most contexts, people deal with this problem by entering into contracts that commit them to their partners once they have mutually agreed to terminate the search. *(LO2)*

- Many potentially beneficial transactions are prevented from taking place by asymmetric information—the fact that one party lacks information that the other has. For example, the owner of a used car knows whether it is in good condition, but potential buyers do not. Even though a buyer may be willing to pay more for a good car than the owner of such a car would require, the fact that the buyer cannot be sure she is getting a good car often discourages the sale. More generally, asymmetric information often prevents sellers from supplying the same quality level that consumers would be willing to pay for. *(LO3)*

- Both buyers and sellers often can gain by finding ways of communicating what they know to one another. But because of the potential conflict between the interests of buyers and sellers, mere statements about the relevant information may not be credible. For a signal between potential trading partners to be credible, it must be costly to fake. For instance, the owner of a high-quality used car can credibly signal the car's quality by offering a warranty—an offer that the seller of a low-quality car could not afford to make. *(LO3)*

- Firms and consumers often try to estimate missing information by making use of what they know about the groups to which people or things belong. For example, insurance firms estimate the risk of insuring individual young male drivers on the basis of the accident rates for young males as a group. This practice is known as statistical discrimination. Statistical discrimination helps explain the phenomenon of disappearing political discourse, which occurs when opponents of a practice such as the death penalty remain silent when the issue is discussed publicly. *(LO4)*

- Risk-averse people will purchase insurance to guard themselves against the risk of unanticipated and costly events like hurricanes, car accidents and illness. Adverse selection drives up the cost of insurance because individuals who are the most expensive for companies to insure have the great-

est incentive to purchase insurance. In some cases, adverse selection can lead insurance to become so costly that few choose to purchase it. Moral hazard also drives up insurance premiums because people have less incentive to protect items that have been insured against theft or damage. In the United States, the problem of adverse selection has left large numbers of Americans without health care coverage and has led to ongoing efforts to reform our health care system. *(LO5)*

KEY TERMS

adverse selection	expected value of a gamble	risk-averse person
asymmetric information	fair gamble	risk-neutral person
better-than-fair gamble	free-rider problem	statistical discrimination
costly-to-fake principle	lemons model	
disappearing political discourse	moral hazard	

REVIEW QUESTIONS

1. Explain why a gallery owner who sells a painting might actually create more economic surplus than the artist who painted it. *(LO1)*

2. Can it be rational for a consumer to buy a Chevrolet without having first taken test drives in competing models built by Ford, Chrysler, Honda, Toyota, and others? *(LO2)*

3. Explain why used cars offered for sale are different, on average, from used cars not offered for sale. *(LO3)*

4. Explain why the used car market would be likely to function more efficiently in a community in which

moral norms of honesty are strong than in a community in which such norms are weak. *(LO3)*

5. Explain why banks are generally more willing to lend money to someone who is employed than to someone who is unemployed. *(LO4)*

6. Disability insurance pays a portion of an individual's wages should a nonwork–related injury or illness prevent that person from being able to work. Explain why disability insurance premiums might be lower if everyone were required to purchase disability insurance. *(LO5)*

PROBLEMS

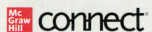

1. Carlos is risk-neutral and has an ancient farmhouse with great character for sale in Slaterville Springs. His reservation price for the house is $130,000. The only possible local buyer is Whitney, whose reservation price for the house is $150,000. The only other houses on the market are modern ranch houses that sell for $125,000, which is exactly equal to each potential buyer's reservation price for such a house. Suppose that if Carlos does not hire a realtor, Whitney will learn from her neighbor that Carlos's house is for sale and will buy it for $140,000. However, if Carlos hires a realtor, he knows that the realtor will put him in touch with an enthusiast for old farmhouses who is willing to pay up to $300,000 for the house. Carlos also knows that if he and this person negotiate, they will agree on a price of $250,000. If realtors charge a commission of 5 percent of the selling price and all realtors have opportunity costs of $2,000 for negotiating a sale, will Carlos hire a realtor? If so, how will total economic surplus be affected? *(LO1)*

2. Makenna and Sienna are computer programmers in Nashville who are planning to move to Seattle. Each owns a house that has just been appraised for $300,000. But whereas Makenna's house is one of hundreds of highly similar houses in a large, well-known suburban development, Sienna's is the only one that was built from her architect's design. Who will benefit more by hiring a realtor to assist in selling her house, Makenna or Sienna? *(LO1)*

3. Brokers who sell stocks over the Internet can serve many more customers than those who transact business by mail or over the phone. How will the expansion of Internet access affect the average incomes of stockbrokers who continue to do business in the traditional way? *(LO2)*

4. Whose income do you predict will be more affected by the expansion of Internet access: *(LO2)*
   a. Stockbrokers or lawyers?
   b. Doctors or pharmacists?
   c. Bookstore owners or the owners of galleries that sell original oil paintings?

5. Kendall, a retired accountant, and Kadence, a government manager, are 63-year-old identical twins who collect

antique pottery. Each has an annual income of $100,000 (Kendall's from a pension, Kadence's from salary). One buys most of her pottery at local auctions, and the other buys most of hers from a local dealer. Which sister is more likely to buy at an auction, and does she pay more or less than her sister who buys from the local dealer? *(LO2)*

6. How will growing Internet access affect the number of film actors and musicians who have active fan clubs? *(LO2)*

7. Consumers know that some fraction x of all new cars produced and sold in the market are defective. The defective ones cannot be identified except by those who own them. Cars do not depreciate with use. Consumers are risk-neutral and value nondefective cars at $30,000 each. New cars sell for $15,000 and used ones for $7,500. What is the fraction x? *(LO3)*

8. State whether the following are true or false, and briefly explain why: *(LO3)*
   a. Companies spend billions of dollars advertising their products on network TV primarily because the texts of their advertisements persuade consumers that the advertised products are of high quality.
   b. You may not get the optimal level of advice from a retail shop when you go in to buy a lamp for your bike because of the free-rider problem.
   c. If you need a lawyer, and all your legal expenses are covered by insurance, you should *always* choose the best-dressed lawyer with the most expensive car and the most ostentatiously furnished office.
   d. The benefit of searching for a spouse is affected by the size of the community you live in.

9. For each pair of occupations listed, identify the one for which the kind of car a person drives is more likely to be a good indication of how good she is at her job. *(LO3)*
   a. Elementary school teacher, real estate agent.
   b. Dentist, municipal government administrator.
   c. Engineer in the private sector, engineer in the military.

10. Female heads of state (e.g., Israel's Golda Meir, India's Indira Gandhi, Britain's Margaret Thatcher) have often been described as more bellicose in foreign policy matters than the average male head of state. Using Loury's theory of disappearing political discourse, suggest an explanation for this pattern. *(LO4)*

11. Anika knows there's a 2 percent chance that her house will be destroyed by fire next year, which would require $250,000 to rebuild (and if her house is not destroyed, she won't have to pay anything). If Anika is risk-averse, will she pay $5,000 a year for an insurance policy that covers the full cost of rebuilding her house should it be destroyed by fire? Might she pay $5,200? What about $5,400? *(LO5)*

12. Suppose people cannot tell for sure whether they will fall ill in any given year. High-risk people correctly perceive that their chance of falling ill in a year is 30 percent, and low-risk people correctly perceive that their chance of falling ill is 10 percent. Both high-risk people and low-risk people have to pay $10,000 in medical expenses if they fall ill, and nothing if they remain healthy. *(LO5)*
   a. What are the expected annual medical expenses of a high-risk person?
   b. What are the expected annual medical expenses of a low-risk person?
   c. Suppose insurance companies cannot tell whether someone is high-risk or low-risk. They only know that half of all people are high-risk, and half of all people are low-risk. So, they offer a health insurance policy that costs $2,000 per year in exchange for covering all of a person's medical expenses should they fall ill. If high risk-people and low-risk people are risk-neutral, then who will purchase this insurance policy? Will the insurance company be able to stay in business if it continues to charge $2,000 per year? Briefly explain.

ANSWERS TO SELF-TESTS

12.1 An Internet search is a cheap way to acquire information about many goods and services, so the effect of increased Internet access will be a downward shift in the supply curve of information. In equilibrium, people will acquire more information, and the goods and services they buy will more closely resemble those they would have chosen in an ideal world with perfect information. These effects will cause total economic surplus to grow. Some of these gains, however, might be offset if the Internet makes the free-rider problem more serious. *(LO2)*

12.2 The probability of getting heads is 0.5, the same as the probability of getting tails. Thus, the expected value of this gamble is $(0.5)(\$4) + (0.5)(-\$2) = \$1$.

Since the gamble is better than fair, a risk-neutral person would accept it. *(LO2)*

12.3 Since you still have a 20 percent chance of finding a cheaper apartment if you make another visit, the expected outcome of the gamble is again $5, and you should search again. The bad outcome of any previous search is a sunk cost and should not influence your decision about whether to search again. *(LO2)*

12.4 The expected value of a new car will now be $(0.8) \times (\$16,000) + (0.2)(\$12,000) = \$15,200$. Any risk-neutral consumer who believed that the quality distribution of used cars for sale was the same as the quality distribution of new cars off the assembly line would be willing to pay $15,200 for a used car. *(LO3)*

CHAPTER 13

Labor Markets, Poverty, and Income Distribution

Franck Boston/franckito/123RF

The growing concentration of income among top earners has led to dramatic changes in consumption patterns.

LEARNING OBJECTIVES

After reading this chapter, you should be able to:

LO1 Explain the relationship between wages and the marginal productivity of workers.

LO2 Analyze how wages and employment are determined in competitive labor markets.

LO3 Compare and contrast the various hypotheses economists have proposed to explain earnings differences.

LO4 Recall recent trends in U.S. income inequality and philosophical justifications for income redistribution.

LO5 Describe and analyze some of the methods used to reduce poverty in the United States.

By only the slimmest of margins, Serena Williams won her first professional singles title at the Open Gaz de France in 1999. Since then, Williams has gone on to become one of the most highly decorated and highly paid female tennis players of all time, having earned more than $92 million in prize money alone. In contrast, few have ever heard of the runner-up from that tournament, French player Amélie Mauresmo, one of the most talented female tennis players of her era. Although she came within a hairbreadth of beating Williams, she has received nowhere near the same level of recognition or pay.

Many physicians in France are likewise every bit as talented and hardworking as physicians in the United States. But while American physicians earn an average annual income of over $300,000, the average annual income of French physicians is only slightly more than $100,000.

Why do some people earn so much more than others? No other single question in economics has stimulated nearly as much interest and discussion. American citizenship,

Why do small differences in performance sometimes translate into enormous differences in pay?

of course, is neither necessary nor sufficient for receiving high income. Many of the wealthiest people in the world come from extremely poor countries, and many Americans are homeless and malnourished.

Our aim in this chapter will be to employ simple economic principles in an attempt to explain why different people earn different salaries. We'll first discuss the human capital model, which emphasizes the importance of differences in personal characteristics. Next, we'll focus on why people with similar personal characteristics often earn sharply different incomes. Among the factors we'll consider are labor unions, discrimination, the effect of non-wage conditions of employment, and winner-take-all markets. Finally, we'll explore whether income inequality is something society should be concerned about, and if so, whether practical remedies for it exist. As we'll see, government programs to redistribute income have costs as well as benefits. As always, policymakers must compare an imperfect status quo with the practical consequences of imperfect government remedies.

THE ECONOMIC VALUE OF WORK

In some respects, the sale of human labor is profoundly different from the sale of other goods and services. For example, although someone may legally relinquish all future rights to the use of her television set by selling it, the law does not permit people to sell themselves into slavery. The law does, however, permit employers to "rent" our services. And in many ways the rental market for labor services functions much like the market for most other goods and services. Each specific category of labor has a demand curve and a supply curve. These curves intersect to determine both the equilibrium wage and the equilibrium quantity of employment for each category of labor.

What is more, shifts in the relevant demand and supply curves produce changes analogous to those produced by shifts in the demand and supply curves for other goods and services. For instance, an increase in the demand for a specific category of labor will generally increase both the equilibrium wage and the equilibrium quantity of employment in that category. By the same token, an increase in the supply of labor to a given occupation will tend to increase the level of employment and lower the wage rate in that occupation.

As in our discussions of other markets, our strategy for investigating how the labor market works will be to go through a series of examples that shed light on different parts of the picture. In the first example, we focus on how the Equilibrium Principle helps us understand how wages will differ among workers with different levels of productive ability.

Equilibrium ⟫

| EXAMPLE 13.1 | Productive Ability and the Equilibrium Principle |

How much will the potters earn?

Mackintosh Pottery Works is one of numerous identical companies that hire potters who mold clay into pots. These companies sell the pots for $1.10 each to a finishing company that glazes and fires them and then sells them in the retail marketplace. Clay, which is available free of charge in unlimited quantities, is the only input used by the potters. Rennie and Laura are currently the only two potters who work for Mackintosh, whose only cost other than potters' salaries is a 10-cent handling cost for each pot it delivers to the finisher. Rennie delivers 100 pots per week and Laura delivers 120. If the labor market for potters is perfectly competitive, how much will each be paid?

We begin with the assumption that Rennie and Laura have decided to work full-time as potters, so our focus is not on how much they'll work but on how much they'll be paid. After taking handling costs into account, the value of the pots that Rennie delivers is $100 per week, and that is the amount Mackintosh will pay him. To pay him less would risk having him bid away by a competitor. For example, if Mackintosh paid Rennie only $90 per week, the company would then enjoy an economic profit of $10 per week as a result of hiring him. Seeing this cash on the table, a rival firm could then offer Rennie $91, thus earning an additional economic profit of $9 per week by bidding him away from Mackintosh. So under the bidding pressure from rival employers, Mackintosh will have difficulty keeping Rennie if it pays him less than $100 per week. And the company would suffer an economic loss if it paid him more than $100 per week. Similarly, the value of the pots delivered each week by Laura is $120, and this will be her competitive equilibrium wage.

In Example 13.1, the number of pots each potter delivered each week was that potter's **marginal product of labor,** or *MPL*. More generally, a worker's marginal product is the extra output the firm gets as a result of hiring that worker. When we multiply a worker's marginal product by the net price for which each unit of the product sells, we get the **value of the marginal product of labor,** or *VMPL*. (In Example 13.1, the "net price" of each pot was $1.00—the difference between the $1.10 sale price and the $0.10 handling charge.) The general rule in competitive labor markets is that *a worker's pay in long-run equilibrium will be equal to his or her* VMPL—*the net contribution he or she makes to the employer's revenue.* Employers would be delighted to pay workers less than their respective *VMPL*s, to be sure. But if labor markets are truly competitive, they cannot get away with doing so for long.

In the pottery example, each worker's *VMPL* was independent of the number of other workers employed by the firm. In such cases, we cannot predict how many workers a firm will hire. Mackintosh could break even with 2 potters, with 10, or even with 1,000 or more. In many other situations, however, we can predict exactly how many workers a firm will hire. Consider the following example.

marginal product of labor (*MPL*) the additional output a firm gets by employing one additional unit of labor

value of the marginal product of labor (*VMPL*) the dollar value of the additional output a firm gets by employing one additional unit of labor

EXAMPLE 13.2	Hiring

How many workers should Adirondack hire?

Adirondack Woodworking Company hires workers in a competitive labor market at a wage of $350 per week to make kitchen cutting boards from scrap wood that is available free of charge. If the boards sell for $20 each and the company's weekly output varies with the number of workers hired as shown in Table 13.1, how many workers should Adirondack hire?

In the pottery example, our focus was on wage differences for employees whose productive abilities differed. In contrast, we assume here that all workers are equally productive and the firm faces a fixed market wage for each. The fact that the marginal product of labor declines with the number of workers hired is a consequence of the law of diminishing returns. (As discussed in Chapter 6, *Perfectly Competitive Supply,* this law says that when a firm's capital or other productive inputs are held fixed in the short run, adding workers beyond some point results in ever smaller increases in output.) Column 3 of the table reports

TABLE 13.1

Employment and Productivity in a Woodworking Company (when cutting boards sell for $20 each)

(1) Number of workers	(2) Total number of cutting boards/week	(3) MPL (extra cutting boards/week)	(4) VMPL ($/week)
0	0		
		30	600
1	30		
		25	500
2	55		
		21	420
3	76		
		18	360
4	94		
		14	280
5	108		

the marginal product for each additional worker, and column 4 reports the value of each successive worker's marginal product—the number of cutting boards he or she adds times the selling price of $20. Adirondack should keep hiring as long as the next worker's *VMPL* is at least $350 per week (the market wage). The first four workers have *VMPL*s larger than $350, so Adirondack should hire them. But since hiring the fifth worker would add only $280 to weekly revenue, Adirondack should not hire that worker.

Note the similarity between the perfectly competitive firm's decision about how many workers to hire and the perfectly competitive firm's output decision we considered in Chapter 6, *Perfectly Competitive Supply*. When labor is the only variable factor of production, the two decisions are essentially the same. Because of the unique correspondence between the firm's total output and the total number of workers it hires, deciding how many workers to hire is the same as deciding how much output to supply.

The worker's attractiveness to the employer depends not only on how many cutting boards he or she produces, but also on the price of cutting boards and on the wage rate. For example, because *VMPL* rises when product price rises, an increase in product price will lead employers to hire more workers. Employers also will increase hiring when the wage rate falls.

 SELF-TEST 13.1

In the woodworking example, how many workers should Adirondack hire if the price of cutting boards rises to $26?

 SELF-TEST 13.2

In the woodworking example, how many workers should Adirondack hire if the wage rate falls to $275 per week?

THE EQUILIBRIUM WAGE AND EMPLOYMENT LEVELS

As we saw in Chapter 3, *Supply and Demand,* the equilibrium price and quantity in any competitive market occur at the intersection of the relevant supply and demand curves. The same is true in competitive markets for labor.

THE DEMAND CURVE FOR LABOR

An employer's reservation price for a worker is the most the employer could pay without suffering a decline in profit. As discussed, this reservation price for the employer in a perfectly competitive labor market is simply the value of the worker's marginal product (*VMPL*). Because of the law of diminishing returns, we know that the marginal product of labor, and hence *VMPL*, declines in the short run as the quantity of labor rises. The individual employer's demand curve for labor in any particular occupation—say, computer programmers—may thus be shown, as in Figure 13.1, as a downward-sloping function of the wage rate. Suppose firm 1 [Figure 13.1(a)] and firm 2 [Figure 13.1(b)] are the only two firms that employ programmers in a given community. The demand for programmers in that community will then be the horizontal sum of the individual firm demands [Figure 13.1(c)].

THE SUPPLY CURVE OF LABOR

What does the supply curve of labor for a specific occupation look like? Will more labor be offered at high wage rates than at low wage rates? An equivalent way to pose the same question is to ask whether consumers will wish to consume less leisure at high wage rates than at low wage rates? By themselves, the principles of economic theory do not provide an answer to this question because a change in the wage rate exerts two opposing effects on the quantity of leisure demanded. One is the substitution effect, which says that at a higher wage, leisure is more expensive, leading consumers to consume less of it. The second is the income effect, which says that at a higher wage, consumers have more purchasing power, leading them to consume more leisure. Which of these two opposing effects dominates is an empirical question.

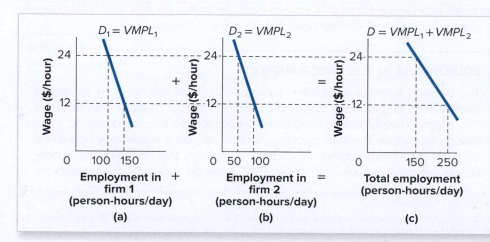

FIGURE 13.1

The Occupational Demand for Labor.

If firm 1 and firm 2 are the only firms that employ labor in a given occupation, we generate the demand curve for labor in that occupation by adding the individual demand curves horizontally.

FIGURE 13.2

The Effect of an Increase in the Demand for Computer Programmers.

An increase in the demand for programmers from D_1 to D_2 results in an increase in the equilibrium level of employment (from L_1 to L_2) and an increase in the equilibrium wage (from W_1 to W_2).

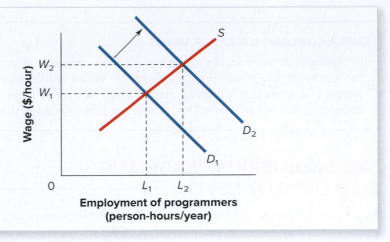

For the economy as a whole during the past several centuries, the workweek has been declining and real wages have been rising. This pattern might seem to suggest that the supply curve of labor is downward-sloping, and for the economy as a whole it may be. There is also evidence that individual workers may sometimes work fewer hours when wage rates are high than when they are low. A study of taxicab drivers in New York City, for example, found that drivers quit earlier on rainy days (when the effective wage is high because of high demand for cab rides) than on sunny days (when the effective wage is lower).[1]

These observations notwithstanding, the supply of labor *to any particular occupation* is almost surely upward-sloping because wage differences among occupations influence occupational choice. It is no accident, for example, that many more people are choosing jobs as computer programmers now than in 1970. Wages of programmers have risen sharply during the past several decades, which has led many people to forsake other career paths in favor of programming. Curve S in Figure 13.2 represents the supply curve of computer programmers. Its positive slope is typical of the supply curves for most individual occupations.

MARKET SHIFTS

As more tasks have become computerized in recent decades, the demand for programmers has grown, as shown by the shift from D_1 to D_2 in Figure 13.2. Equilibrium in the market for computer programmers occurs at the intersection of the relevant supply and demand curves. The increase in demand has led to an increase in the equilibrium level of programmers from L_1 to L_2 and a rise in the equilibrium wage from W_1 to W_2.

As discussed in Chapter 7, *Efficiency, Exchange, and the Invisible Hand in Action*, the market for stocks and other financial assets reaches equilibrium very quickly in the wake of shifts in the underlying supply and demand curves. Labor markets, by contrast, are often much slower to adjust. When the demand for workers in a given profession increases, shortages may remain for months or even years, depending on how long it takes people to acquire the skills and training needed to enter the profession.

RECAP

EQUILIBRIUM IN THE LABOR MARKET

The demand for labor in a perfectly competitive labor market is the horizontal sum of each employer's value of the marginal product of labor (*VMPL*) curve. The supply curve of labor for any particular occupation is upward-sloping, even though the supply curve of labor for the economy as a whole may be vertical or even downward-sloping. In each labor market, the demand and supply curves intersect to determine the equilibrium wage and level of employment.

[1]L. Babcock, C. Camerer, G. Loewenstein, and R. Thaler, "Labor Supply of New York City Cab Drivers: One Day at a Time," *Quarterly Journal of Economics* 111 (1997), pp. 408–41.

EXPLAINING DIFFERENCES IN EARNINGS

The theory of competitive labor markets tells us that differences in pay reflect differences in the corresponding *VMPL*s. Recall that in Example 13.1, Laura earned 20 percent more than Rennie because she made 20 percent more pots each week than he did. This difference in productivity may have resulted from an underlying difference in talent or training, or perhaps Laura simply worked harder than Rennie.

Yet often we see large salary differences even among people who appear equally talented and hardworking. Why, for instance, do lawyers earn so much more than those plumbers who are just as smart as they are and work just as hard? And why do surgeons earn so much more than general practitioners? These wage differences might seem to violate the No-Cash-on-the-Table Principle, which says that only differences in talent, luck, or hard work can account for long-run differences in earnings. For example, if plumbers could earn more by becoming lawyers, why don't they just switch occupations? Similarly, if general practitioners could boost their incomes by becoming surgeons, why didn't they become surgeons in the first place?

▶ Visit your instructor's Connect course and access your eBook to view this video.

Why do female models earn so much more than male models?

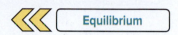
Equilibrium

HUMAN CAPITAL THEORY

Answers to these questions are suggested by **human capital theory**, which holds that an individual's *VMPL* is proportional to his or her stock of **human capital**—an amalgam of factors such as education, experience, training, intelligence, energy, work habits, trustworthiness, and initiative. According to this theory, some occupations pay better than others because they require larger stocks of human capital. For example, a general practitioner could become a surgeon, but only by extending her formal education by several more years. An even larger investment in additional education is required for a plumber to become a lawyer.

Differences in demand can result in some kinds of human capital being more valuable than others. Consider again the increase in demand for computer programmers that has been occurring for the past several decades. During that same time period, the demand for the services of tax accountants has fallen as more and more taxpayers have used tax-preparation software in lieu of hiring accountants to help them with their taxes. Both occupations require demanding technical training, but the training received by computer programmers now yields a higher return in the labor market.

human capital theory a theory of pay determination that says a worker's wage will be proportional to his or her stock of human capital

human capital an amalgam of factors such as education, training, experience, intelligence, energy, work habits, trustworthiness, and initiative that affect the value of a worker's marginal product

LABOR UNIONS

Two workers with the same amount of human capital may earn different wages if one of them belongs to a **labor union** and the other does not. A labor union is an organization through which workers bargain collectively with employers for better wages and working conditions.

Many economists believe that unions affect labor markets in much the same way that cartels affect product markets. To illustrate, consider a simple economy with two labor markets, neither of which is unionized initially. Suppose the total supply of labor to the two markets is fixed at $S_0 = 200$ workers per day, and that the demand curves are as shown by $VMPL_1$ and $VMPL_2$ in Figure 13.3(a) and (b). The sum of the two demand curves, $VMPL_1 + VMPL_2$ [Figure 13.3(c)], intersects the supply curve to determine an equilibrium wage of $18 per hour. At that wage, firms in market 1 hire 125 workers per day [Figure 13.3(a)] and firms in market 2 hire 75 [Figure 13.3(b)].

Now suppose workers in market 1 form a union and refuse to work for less than $24 per hour. Because demand curves for labor are downward-sloping, employers of unionized workers reduce employment from 125 workers per day to 100 [Figure 13.4(a)]. The 25 displaced workers in the unionized market would, of course, be delighted to find other jobs in that market at $24 per hour. But they cannot, and so they are forced to seek employment in the nonunionized market. The result is an excess supply of 25 workers in the nonunion market at the original wage of $18 per hour. In time, wages in that market

labor union a group of workers who bargain collectively with employers for better wages and working conditions

FIGURE 13.3

An Economy with Two Nonunionized Labor Markets.

Supply and demand intersect to determine a market wage of $18 per hour (c). At that wage, employers in market 1 hire 125 workers per day and employers in market 2 hire 75 workers per day. The *VMPL* is $18 in each market.

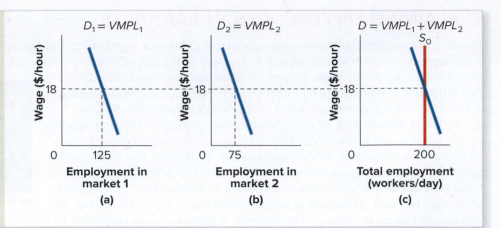

Employment in market 1

(a)

Employment in market 2

(b)

Total employment (workers/day)

(c)

decline to $W_N = \$12$ per hour, the level at which 100 workers can find jobs in the nonunionized market [Figure 13.4(b)].

It might seem that the gains of the unionized workers are exactly offset by the losses of nonunionized workers. On closer inspection, however, we see that pegging the union wage above the equilibrium level actually reduces the value of total output. If labor were allocated efficiently between the two markets, the value of the marginal product of labor would have to be the same in each. Otherwise, the total value of output could be increased by moving workers from the low-*VMPL* market to the high-*VMPL* market. With the wage set initially at $18 per hour in both markets, the condition for efficient allocation was met because the *VMPL* was $18 per hour in both markets. But because the collective bargaining process drives wages (and hence *VMPLs*) in the two markets apart, the value of total output is no longer maximized. To verify this claim, note that if a worker is taken out of the nonunionized market, the reduction in the value of output there will be only $12 per hour, which is less than the $24-per-hour gain in the value of output when that same worker is added to the unionized market.

FIGURE 13.4

The Effect of a Union Wage above the Equilibrium Wage.

When the unionized wage is pegged at $W_U = \$24$/hour (a), 25 workers are discharged. When these workers seek employment in the nonunionized market, the wage in that market falls to $W_N = \$12$/hour (b).

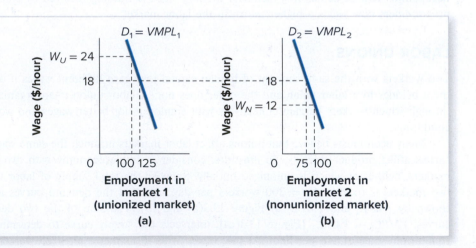

Employment in market 1 (unionized market)

(a)

Employment in market 2 (nonunionized market)

(b)

✓ **SELF-TEST 13.3**

In Figure 13.4, by how much would the value of total output be increased if the wage rate were $18 per hour in each market?

Wages paid to workers in a unionized firm are sometimes 50 percent or more above the wages paid to their nonunionized counterparts. To the alert economic naturalist, this difference prompts the following question:

The Economic Naturalist 13.1

If unionized firms have to pay more, how do they manage to survive in the face of competition from their nonunionized counterparts?

In fact, nonunionized firms sometimes do drive unionized firms out of business, as when the American textile industry moved to the South in the late nineteenth and early twentieth centuries to escape the burden of high union wages in New England. Even so, unionized and nonunionized firms often manage to compete head-to-head for extended periods. If their costs are significantly higher, how do the unionized firms manage to survive?

The observed pay differential actually overstates the difference between the labor costs of the two types of firm. Because the higher union wage attracts an excess supply of workers, unionized employers can adopt more stringent hiring requirements than their nonunionized counterparts. As a result, unionized workers tend to be more experienced and skilled than nonunionized workers. Studies estimate that the union wage premium for workers with the same amount of human capital is only about 10 percent.

Another factor is that unions may actually boost the productivity of workers with any given amount of human capital, perhaps by improving communication between management and workers. Similarly, the implementation of formal grievance procedures, in combination with higher pay, may boost morale among unionized workers, leading to higher productivity. Labor turnover is also significantly lower in unionized firms, which reduces hiring and training costs. Studies suggest that union productivity may be sufficiently high to compensate for the premium in union wages. So even though wages are higher in unionized firms, these firms may not have significantly higher labor costs per unit of output than their nonunionized counterparts.

How do firms that employ higher-paid union labor remain competitive?

In 2019, 10.3 percent of American workers belonged to a labor union, less than one-third of the union membership rate during the 1950s. Because the union wage premium is small and applies to only a small fraction of the labor force, union membership in the United States is probably not an important explanation for why workers with similar qualifications often earn sharply different incomes.

COMPENSATING WAGE DIFFERENTIALS

If people are paid the value of what they produce, why do garbage collectors earn more than lifeguards? Picking up the trash is important, to be sure, but is it more valuable than saving the life of a drowning child? Similarly, we need not question the value of a timely plumbing repair to wonder why plumbers get paid more than fourth-grade teachers. Is replacing faucet washers really more valuable than educating children? As the next example illustrates, the wage for a particular job depends not only on the value of what workers produce, but also on how attractive they find its working conditions.

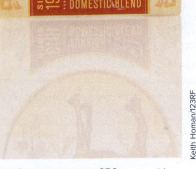

The Economic Naturalist 13.2

Why do some ad copywriters earn more than others?

You plan to pursue a career in advertising and have two job offers: one to write ad copy for the American Cancer Society, the other to write copy for Camel cigarette ads aimed at the youth market. Except for the subject matter of the ads, working conditions are identical in the two jobs. If each job paid $30,000 per year and offered the same prospects for advancement, which would you choose?

When this question was recently posed to a sample of graduating seniors at Cornell University, almost 90 percent of them chose the American Cancer Society job. When asked how much more they would have to be paid to induce them to switch to the Camel cigarettes job, their median response was a premium of $15,000 per year. As this sample suggests, employers who offer jobs with less attractive working conditions cannot hope to fill them unless they also offer higher salaries.

Keith Homan/123RF

Do tobacco company CEOs get paid extra for testifying that cigarette smoking does not cause cancer?

compensating wage differential a difference in the wage rate—negative or positive—that reflects the attractiveness of a job's working conditions

employer discrimination an arbitrary preference by an employer for one group of workers over another

Other things being equal, jobs with attractive working conditions will pay less than jobs with less attractive conditions. Wage differences associated with differences in working conditions are known as **compensating wage differentials.** Economists have identified compensating differentials for a host of specific working conditions. Studies have found, for example, that safe jobs tend to pay less than otherwise similar jobs that entail greater risks to health and safety. Studies also have found that wages vary in accord with the attractiveness of the work schedule. For instance, working night shifts commands a wage premium, and teachers must accept lower wages in part because many of those with children value having hours that coincide with the school calendar.

DISCRIMINATION IN THE LABOR MARKET

Women and minorities continue to receive lower wage rates, on average, than white males with similar measures of human capital. This pattern poses a profound challenge to standard theories of competitive labor markets, which hold that competitive pressures will eliminate wage differentials not based on differences in productivity. Defenders of standard theories attribute the wage gap to unmeasured differences in human capital. Many critics of these theories reject the idea that labor markets are effectively competitive, and instead attribute the gap to various forms of discrimination.

Discrimination by Employers

Employer discrimination is the term used to describe wage differentials that arise from an arbitrary preference by an employer for one group of workers over another. An example occurs if two labor force groups, such as males and females, are equally productive, on average, yet some employers ("discriminators") prefer hiring males and are willing to pay higher wages to do so.

Most consumers are not willing to pay more for a product produced by males than for an identical one produced by females (if indeed they even *know* which type of worker produced the product). If product price is unaffected by the composition of the workforce that produces the product, a firm's profit will be smaller the more males it employs because males cost more yet are no more productive (on the assumption that discrimination is the cause of the wage gap). Thus, the most profitable firms will be ones that employ only females.

Arbitrary wage gaps are an apparent violation of the No-Cash-on-the-Table Principle. The initial wage differential provides an opportunity for employers who hire mostly females to grow at the expense of their rivals. Because such firms make an economic profit on the

Equilibrium

sale of each unit of output, their incentive is to expand as rapidly as they possibly can. And to do that, they would naturally want to continue hiring only the cheaper females.

But as profit-seeking firms continue to pursue this strategy, the supply of females at the lower wage rate will run out. The short-run solution is to offer females a slightly higher wage. But this strategy works only if other firms do not pursue it. Once they too start offering a higher wage, females will again be in short supply. The only stable outcome occurs when the wage of females reaches parity with the wage of males. The wage for both males and females will thus settle at the common value of their *VMPL*.

Any employer who wants to voice a preference for hiring males must now do so by paying males a wage in excess of *VMPL*. Employers can discriminate against females if they wish, but only if they are willing to pay premium wages to males out of their own profits. Not even the harshest critics of the competitive model seem willing to impute such behavior to the owners of capitalist enterprises.

For this reason, if employer discrimination arises in an imperfectly competitive market, we would expect it to disappear if the market suddenly becomes more competitive. Consistent with this prediction, there is evidence that increased competition in the banking industry resulting from deregulation in the mid-1970s to the mid-1980s reduced both the male–female wage gap and the Black–white wage gap for workers in this industry.[2]

Discrimination by Others

If employer discrimination is not the primary explanation of the wage gap, what is? In some instances, **customer discrimination** may provide a plausible explanation. For example, if people believe that juries and clients are less likely to take female or minority attorneys seriously, members of these groups will face a reduced incentive to attend law school, and law firms will face a reduced incentive to hire those who do.

> **customer discrimination** the willingness of consumers to pay more for a product produced by members of a favored group, even if the quality of the product is unaffected

Another possible source of persistent wage gaps is discrimination and socialization within the family. For example, families may provide less education for their female children, or they may socialize them to believe that lofty career ambitions are not appropriate.

Other Sources of the Wage Gap

Part of the wage gap may be explained by compensating wage differentials that spring from differences in preferences for other nonwage elements of the compensation package. Jobs that involve exposure to physical risk, for example, command higher wages, and if men are relatively more willing to accept such risks, they will earn more than females with otherwise identical stocks of human capital. (The same difference would result if employers felt constrained by social norms not to assign female employees to risky jobs.)

Elements of human capital that are difficult to measure also may help explain earnings differentials. For example, productivity is influenced not only by the quantity of education an individual has, which is easy to measure, but also by its quality, which is much harder to measure. Part of the Black–white differential in wages may thus be due to the fact that schools in Black neighborhoods have not been as good, on average, as those in white neighborhoods.

Differences in the courses people take in college appear to have similar implications for differences in productivity. For instance, students in math, engineering, or business— male or female—tend to earn significantly higher salaries than those who concentrate in the humanities. The fact that males are disproportionately represented in the former group gives rise to a male wage premium that is unrelated to employer discrimination.

As economists have grown more sophisticated in their efforts to measure human capital and other factors that influence individual wage rates, unexplained wage differentials by sex and race have grown steadily smaller, and have even disappeared altogether. Many studies, however, continue to find significant unexplained differentials by race and sex. Debate about discrimination in the workplace will continue until the causes of these differentials are more fully understood.

[2]R. Levine, A. Levkov, and Y. Rubinstein, "Bank Deregulation and Racial Inequality in America," *Critical Finance Review* 3, no. 1 (2014), pp. 1–48; S. Black and P. Strahan, "The Division of Spoils: Rent Sharing and Discrimination in a Regulated Industry," *American Economic Review* 91 (2001), pp. 814–31.

WINNER-TAKE-ALL MARKETS

Differences in human capital do much to explain observed differences in earnings. Yet earnings differentials have also grown sharply in many occupations within which the distribution of human capital among workers seems essentially unchanged. Consider the following example.

The Economic Naturalist 13.3

Why does Taylor Swift earn many millions more than singers with only slightly less talent?

Why does Taylor Swift earn so much more than singers with only slightly less talent?

Kevin Mazur/Getty Images

According to *Forbes*, Taylor Swift earned an impressive $185 million in 2019, far more than any other woman in the music industry, including Beyoncé, who occupied the number two spot with a mere $88 million. And both women earned many times more than the vast majority of women in the music industry. Although the best entertainers have always earned more than those with lesser talent, the earnings gap is sharply larger now than it was in the nineteenth century. Given that the difference in talent between many singers is extremely small, why is the earnings differential so large?

The answer lies in a fundamental change in the way we consume most of our music. In the nineteenth century, virtually all professional musicians delivered their services in concert halls in front of live audiences. (In 1900, the state of Iowa alone had more than 1,300 concert halls!) Audiences of that day would have been delighted to listen to the world's best performer, but no one singer could hope to perform in more than a tiny fraction of the world's concert halls. Today, in contrast, most of the music we hear comes in recorded form, which enables the most popular singers to be literally everywhere at once. As soon as the master recording has been made, the latest Taylor Swift song can be saved as an MP3 or other audio file format at the same low cost as that of a slightly less-talented singer.

Tens of millions of buyers worldwide are willing to pay a few cents extra to hear the most popular performers. Thus, small differences in talent are amplified into massive earnings differentials, leading top singers to earn millions of dollars each year (most of which constitute economic rents, as discussed in Chapter 7, *Efficiency, Exchange, and the Invisible Hand in Action*), while slightly less-talented singers earn far less.

winner-take-all labor market one in which small differences in human capital translate into large differences in pay

The market for singers is an example of a **winner-take-all market,** one in which small differences in ability or other dimensions of human capital translate into large differences in pay. Such markets have long been familiar in entertainment and professional sports. But as technology has enabled the most talented individuals to serve broader markets, the winner-take-all reward structure has become an increasingly important feature of modern economic life, permeating such diverse fields as law, journalism, consulting, medicine, investment banking, corporate management, publishing, design, fashion, and even the hallowed halls of academe.

Contrary to what the name seems to imply, a winner-take-all market does not mean a market with literally only one winner. Indeed, hundreds of professional musicians earn multimillion-dollar annual salaries. Yet tens of thousands of others, many of them nearly as good, struggle to pay their bills.

The fact that small differences in human capital often give rise to extremely large differences in pay might seem to contradict human capital theory. Note, however, that the winner-take-all reward pattern is completely consistent with the competitive labor market theory's claim that individuals are paid in accordance with the contributions they make to the employer's net revenue. The leverage of technology often amplifies small performance differentials into very large ones.

> **RECAP**
>
> ## EXPLAINING DIFFERENCES IN EARNINGS AMONG PEOPLE
>
> Earnings differ among people in part because of differences in their human capital, an amalgam of personal characteristics that affect productivity. But pay often differs substantially between two people with the same amount of human capital. This can happen for many reasons: One may belong to a labor union while the other does not, one may work in a job with less pleasant conditions, one may be the victim of discrimination, or one may work in an arena in which technology or other factors provide greater leverage to human capital.

RECENT TRENDS IN INEQUALITY

In the United States, as in most other market economies, a majority of citizens receive most of their income from the sale of their own labor. An attractive feature of the free-market system is that it rewards initiative, effort, and risk taking. The harder, longer, and more effectively a person works, the more she will be paid.

Yet relying on the marketplace to distribute income also entails an important drawback: Those who do well often end up with vastly more money than they can spend, while those who fail often cannot afford even basic goods and services. Hundreds of thousands of American families are homeless, and still larger numbers go to bed hungry each night. Many distinguished philosophers have argued that such poverty in the midst of plenty is impossible to justify on moral grounds. It is thus troubling that income inequality has been growing rapidly in recent decades.

The period from the end of World War II until the early 1970s was one of balanced income growth in the United States. During that period, incomes grew at almost 3 percent a year for rich, middle-class, and poor Americans alike. In the ensuing years, however, the pattern of income growth has been dramatically different.

In the first row of Table 13.2, for example, notice that families in the bottom 20 percent of the income distribution saw their real incomes increase by only 9.2 percent over the entire 38-year period between 1980 and 2018 (a growth rate of less than three-tenths of 1 percent per year). The third row of the table indicates that the real incomes of families in the middle quintile grew by about 28.7 percent over that time period (a growth rate of slightly more than one-half of 1 percent per year). In contrast, for families

TABLE 13.2

Mean Income Received by Families in Each Income Quintile and by the Top 5 Percent of Families, All Races, 1980–2018 (2018 dollars)

	1980	1990	2000	2010	2018
Lowest quintile	18,653	18,374	20,650	17,224	20,378
Second quintile	40,605	42,857	47,214	42,602	49,214
Middle quintile	61,341	66,003	74,204	69,437	78,966
Fourth quintile	85,104	94,920	109,362	105,938	119,904
Highest quintile	143,288	176,405	229,453	215,971	261,762
Top 5 percent	203,696	276,788	406,594	361,116	457,189

https://www.census.gov/data/tables/time-series/demo/income-poverty/historical-income-families.html

in the highest quintile, real incomes grew by more than 82 percent between 1980 and 2018, while for families in the top 5 percent, real incomes jumped by nearly 125 percent. Even for these families, however, income growth rates were low relative to those of the immediate post–World War II decades.

The only people whose incomes have grown substantially faster than in that earlier period are those at the very pinnacle of the income ladder. Real earnings of the top 1 percent of U.S. earners, for example, have more than doubled since 1980, and those even higher up have taken home paychecks that might have seemed unimaginable just a few decades ago. The CEOs of America's largest companies, who earned roughly 30 times as much as the average worker in 1980, now earn more than 200 times as much.

It's important to emphasize that being near the bottom of the income distribution in one year does not necessarily mean being stranded there forever. On the contrary, people in the United States have always experienced a high degree of economic mobility by international standards. Many CEOs now earning multimillion-dollar paychecks, for example, were struggling young graduate students in 1980, and were hence among those classified in the bottom 20 percent of the income distribution for that year in Table 13.2. We must bear in mind, too, that not all economic mobility is upward. Many blue-collar workers, for instance, had higher real incomes in 1980 than they do today.

On balance, then, the entries in Table 13.2 tell an important story. In contrast to the economy 40 years ago, those near the top of the income ladder today are prospering as never before, while those further down have seen their living standards grow much more slowly.

IS INCOME INEQUALITY A MORAL PROBLEM?

The late John Rawls, a moral philosopher at Harvard University, constructed a cogent ethical critique of the marginal productivity system, one based heavily on the economic theory of choice itself.[3] In thinking about what constitutes a just distribution of income, Rawls asked us to imagine ourselves meeting to choose the rules for distributing income. The meeting takes place behind a "veil of ignorance," which conceals from participants any knowledge of what talents and abilities each has. Because no individual knows whether he is smart or dull, strong or weak, fast or slow, no one knows which rules of distribution would work to his own advantage.

Rawls argued that the rules people would choose in such a state of ignorance would necessarily be fair; and if the rules are fair, the income distribution to which they give rise will also be fair.

What sort of rules would people choose from behind a veil of ignorance? If the national income were a fixed amount, most people would probably give everyone an equal share. That scenario is likely, Rawls argued, because most people are strongly risk-averse. Since an unequal income distribution would involve not only a chance of doing well, but a chance of doing poorly, most people would prefer to eliminate the risk by choosing an equal distribution. Imagine, for example, that you and two friends have been told that an anonymous benefactor donated $300,000 to divide among you. How would you split it? If you are like most people, you would propose an equal division, or $100,000 for each of you.

Yet the attraction of equality is far from absolute. Indeed, the goal of absolute equality is quickly trumped by other concerns when we make the rules for distributing wealth in modern market economies. Wealth, after all, generally doesn't come from anonymous benefactors; we must produce it. In a large economy, if each person were guaranteed an equal amount of income, few would invest in education or the development of special talents; and as the next example illustrates, the incentive to work would be sharply reduced.

---

[3]John Rawls, *A Theory of Justice* (Cambridge, MA: Harvard University Press, 1971).

EXAMPLE 13.3   **Income Sharing**

Does income sharing affect labor supply?

Sue is offered a job reshelving books in the University of Montana library from noon until 1 p.m. each Friday. Her reservation wage for this task is $10 per hour. If the library director offers Sue $100 per hour, how much economic surplus will she enjoy as a result of accepting the job? Now suppose the library director announces that the earnings from the job will be divided equally among the 400 students who live in Sue's dormitory. Will Sue still accept?

When the $100 per hour is paid directly to Sue, she accepts the job and enjoys an economic surplus of $100 − $10 = $90. If the $100 were divided equally among the 400 residents of Sue's dorm, however, each resident's share would be only 25 cents. Accepting the job would thus mean a negative surplus for Sue of $0.25 − $10 = −$9.75, so she will not accept the job.

 SELF-TEST 13.4

What is the largest dorm population for which Sue would accept the job on a pay-sharing basis?

In a country without rewards for hard work and risk taking, national income would be dramatically smaller than in a country with such rewards. Of course, material rewards for effort and risk taking necessarily lead to inequality. Rawls argued, however, that people would be willing to accept a certain degree of inequality as long as these rewards produced a sufficiently large increase in the total amount of output available for distribution.

But how much inequality would people accept? Much less than the amount produced by purely competitive markets, Rawls argued. The idea is that behind the veil of ignorance, each person would fear ending up in a disadvantaged position, so each would choose rules that would produce a more equal distribution of income than exists under the marginal productivity system. And since such choices *define* the just distribution of income, he argued, fairness requires at least some attempt to reduce the inequality produced by the market system.

> **RECAP↑**
>
> **TRENDS IN INEQUALITY AND IS INCOME INEQUALITY A MORAL PROBLEM?**
>
> - From 1945 until the mid-1970s, incomes grew at almost 3 percent a year for rich, middle-class, and poor families alike. In contrast, most of the income growth since the mid-1970s has been concentrated among top earners.
> - John Rawls argued that the degree of inequality typical of unregulated market systems is unfair because people would favor substantially less inequality if they chose distributional rules from behind a veil of ignorance.

METHODS OF INCOME REDISTRIBUTION

Although we as a society have an interest in limiting income inequality, programs for reducing it are often fraught with practical difficulties. The challenge is to find ways to raise the incomes of those who cannot fend for themselves, without at the same time undermining their incentive to work, and without using scarce resources to subsidize those who are not poor. Of course, some people simply cannot work, or cannot find work that pays enough to live on. In a world of perfect information, the government could make generous cash payments to those people, and withhold support from those who can fend for themselves. In practice, however, the two groups are often hard to distinguish from each other. And so we must choose among imperfect alternative measures.

WELFARE PAYMENTS AND IN-KIND TRANSFERS

in-kind transfer a payment made not in the form of cash, but in the form of a good or service

Cash transfers and in-kind transfers are at the forefront of antipoverty efforts around the globe. **In-kind transfers** are direct transfers of goods or services to low-income individuals or families, such as the Supplemental Nutrition Assistance Program (also known as SNAP or food stamps), public housing, subsidized school lunches, and Medicaid.

From the mid-1960s until 1996, the most important federal program of cash transfers was Aid to Families with Dependent Children (AFDC), which provided cash payments to poor single-parent households. A sharp rise in AFDC caseloads in the early 1990s raised concerns among many lawmakers that AFDC recipients had become dependent on welfare and were trapped in a "cycle of poverty." Critics of the program also argued that AFDC undermined family stability because in many states a poor mother became ineligible for benefits if her husband or other able-bodied adult male lived with her and her children. This provision confronted many long-term unemployed fathers with an agonizing choice: They could leave their families, making them eligible for public assistance, or they could remain, making them ineligible. Even fathers who deeply loved their families understandably chose to leave.

Personal Responsibility and Work Opportunity Reconciliation Act

the 1996 federal law that transferred responsibility for welfare programs from the federal level to the state level and placed a five-year lifetime limit on payment of TANF benefits to any given recipient

Concern about work incentives led Congress to pass the **Personal Responsibility and Work Opportunity Reconciliation Act** in 1996, which abolished the AFDC program and replaced it with Temporary Assistance for Needy Families (TANF). Under the new law, the federal government makes lump-sum cash grants to the states, which then have broad discretion in determining TANF benefit levels and eligibility requirements. In addition, the new law set a five-year lifetime limit on the receipt of TANF benefits.

Supporters of the Personal Responsibility and Work Reconciliation Act argue that it has already reduced the nation's welfare rolls considerably and that it will encourage greater self-reliance over the long run. Skeptics fear that the five-year lifetime limit on benefits may eventually impose severe hardships on the poor, especially poor children, if overall economic conditions deteriorate. Indeed, debate continues about the extent to which the observed increases in poverty rates during the economic downturns of 2001 and 2008–2009 were attributable to the Personal Responsibility and Work Opportunity Reconciliation Act. What is clear, however, is that the new law has not eliminated the need to discover efficient ways of providing assistance to low-income families.

MEANS-TESTED BENEFIT PROGRAMS

means-tested a benefit program whose benefit level declines as the recipient earns additional income

Many welfare programs, including TANF, are **means-tested,** which means that the more income a family has, the smaller are the benefits it receives under these programs. The purpose of means testing is to avoid paying benefits to those who don't really need them. But because of the way welfare programs are administered, means testing often has a pernicious effect on work incentives.

Consider, for example, an unemployed participant in four welfare programs: food stamps, rent stamps, energy stamps, and day care stamps. Each program gives him $100 worth of stamps per month, which he is then free to spend on food, rent, energy, and day care. If he gets a job, his benefits in each program are reduced by 50 cents for each dollar he earns. Thus, if he accepts a job that pays $50 weekly, he'll lose $25 in weekly benefits from each of the four welfare programs, for a total benefit reduction of $100 per week. Taking the job thus leaves him $50 per week worse off than before. Low-income persons need no formal training in economics to realize that seeking gainful employment does not pay under these circumstances.

What is more, means-tested programs of cash and in-kind transfers are extremely costly to administer. If the government were to eliminate all existing welfare and social service agencies that are involved in these programs, the resulting savings would be enough to lift every poor person out of poverty. One proposal to do precisely this is the negative income tax.

THE NEGATIVE INCOME TAX

Under the **negative income tax (NIT),** every man, woman, and child—rich or poor—would receive a substantial income tax credit, say $5,000 per year. A person who earns no income would receive this credit in cash. People who earn income would receive the same initial credit, and their income would continue to be taxed at some rate less than 100 percent.

The negative income tax would do much less than current programs to weaken work incentives because, unlike current programs, it would ensure that someone who earned an extra dollar would keep at least a portion of it. And because the program would be administered by the existing Internal Revenue Service, administrative costs would be far lower than under the current welfare system.

Despite these advantages, however, the negative income tax is by no means a perfect solution to the income-transfer problem. Although the incentive problem under the program would be less severe than under current welfare programs, it would remain a serious difficulty. To see why, note that if the negative income tax were the *sole* means of insulating people against poverty, the payment to people with no earned income would need to be at least as large as the government's official **poverty threshold.**

The poverty threshold is the annual income level below which a family is officially classified as "poor" by the government. The threshold is based on government estimates of the cost of the so-called economy food plan, the least costly of four nutritionally adequate food plans designed by the Department of Agriculture. The department's 1955 Household Food Consumption Survey found that families of three or more people spent approximately one-third of their after-tax income on food, so the government pegs the poverty threshold at three times the cost of the economy food plan. In 2020, that threshold was approximately $26,200 for a family of four.

For a family of four living in a city, $26,200 a year is scarcely enough to make ends meet. But suppose a group of, say, eight families were to pool their negative tax payments and move to the mountains of northern New Mexico. With a total of $209,600 per year to spend, plus the fruits of their efforts at gardening and animal husbandry, such a group could live very nicely indeed.

Once a small number of experimental groups demonstrated the feasibility of quitting their jobs and living well on the negative income tax, others would surely follow suit. But two practical difficulties would ensue. First, as more and more people left their jobs to live at government expense, the program would eventually become prohibitively costly. And second, the political cost of the program would almost surely force supporters to abandon it long before that point. Reports of people living lives of leisure at taxpayers' expense would be sure to appear on the nightly news. People who work hard at their jobs all day long would wonder why their tax dollars were being used to support those who are capable of holding paying jobs, yet choose not to work. If the resulting political backlash did not completely eliminate the negative income tax program, it would force policymakers to cut back the payment so that members of rural communes could no longer afford to live comfortably. And that would mean the payment would no longer support an urban family. This difficulty has led policymakers to focus on other ways to increase the incomes of the working poor.

MINIMUM WAGES

The United States and many other industrialized countries have sought to ease the burden of low-wage workers by enacting minimum wage legislation—laws that prohibit employers from paying workers less than a specified hourly wage. The federal minimum wage in the United States is currently set at $7.25 per hour, and several states have set minimum wage

negative income tax (NIT) a system under which the government would grant every citizen a cash payment each year, financed by an additional tax on earned income

poverty threshold the level of income below which the federal government classifies a family as poor

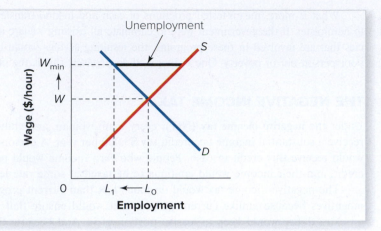

FIGURE 13.5

The Effect of Minimum Wage Legislation on Employment.

If minimum wage legislation requires employers to pay more than the equilibrium wage, the result will be a decline in employment for low-wage workers.

levels significantly higher. For example, the minimum wage in the state of Washington was $13.50 per hour for 2020.

How does a minimum wage affect the market for low-wage labor? In Figure 13.5, note that when the law prevents employers from paying less than W_{min}, employers hire fewer workers (a decline from L_0 to L_1). Unemployment results: The L_1 workers who keep their jobs earn more than before, but the $L_0 - L_1$ workers who lose their jobs earn nothing. Whether workers together earn more or less than before depends on the elasticity of demand for labor. If elasticity of demand is less than 1, workers as a group will earn more than before. If it is more than 1, workers as a group will earn less.

At one point, economists were almost unanimous in their opposition to minimum wage laws, arguing that those laws reduce total economic surplus, as do other regulations that prevent markets from reaching equilibrium. Some economists, however, have softened their opposition to minimum wage laws, citing studies that have failed to show significant reductions in employment following increases in minimum wage levels. But as we saw in Chapter 7, *Efficiency, Exchange, and the Invisible Hand in Action,* any policy that prevents a market from reaching equilibrium causes a reduction in total economic surplus—which means society ought to be able to find a more effective policy for helping low-wage workers.

THE EARNED-INCOME TAX CREDIT

earned-income tax credit (EITC) a policy under which low-income workers receive credits on their federal income tax

One such policy is the **earned-income tax credit (EITC),** which gives low-wage workers a credit on their federal income tax each year. The EITC was enacted into law in 1975, and in the years since has drawn praise from both liberals and conservatives. The program is essentially a wage subsidy in the form of a credit against the amount a family owes in federal income taxes. For example, in 2019, a married couple with two children under the age of 18 and a total annual earnings of $24,000 could have received an annual tax credit of approximately $5,800 under this program. That is, the program would have reduced the annual federal income tax payment of this family by roughly that amount. Families who earned more would have received smaller tax credit, with no credit at all for families of four earning more than $56,000. Families whose tax credit exceeds the amount of tax owed actually receive a check from the government for the difference. The EITC is thus essentially the same as a negative income tax, except that eligibility for the program is confined to people who work.

Like both the negative income tax and the minimum wage, the EITC puts extra income into the hands of workers who are employed at low wage levels. But unlike the minimum wage, the earned-income tax credit creates no incentive for employers to lay off low-wage workers.

The following examples illustrate how switching from a minimum wage to an earned-income tax credit can produce gains for both employers and workers.

EXAMPLE 13.4   Surplus in an Unregulated Labor Market

By how much will a minimum wage reduce total economic surplus?

Suppose the demand and supply curves for unskilled labor in the Tallahassee labor market are as shown in Figure 13.6. By how much will the imposition of a minimum wage at $7 per hour reduce total economic surplus? By how much do worker surplus and employer surplus change as a result of adopting the minimum wage?

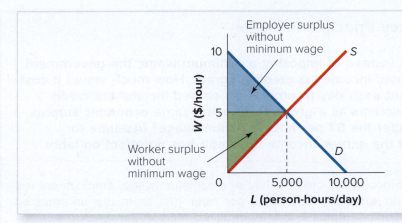

FIGURE 13.6

Worker and Employer Surplus in an Unregulated Labor Market.

For the demand and supply curves shown, worker surplus is the area of the lower shaded triangle, $12,500 per day, the same as employer surplus (upper shaded triangle).

In the absence of a minimum wage, the equilibrium wage for Tallahassee would be $5 per hour, and employment would be 5,000 person-hours per day. Both employers and workers would enjoy economic surplus equal to the area of the shaded triangles in Figure 13.6, $12,500 per day.

With a minimum wage set at $7 per hour, employer surplus is the area of the crosshatched triangle in Figure 13.7, $4,500 per day, and worker surplus is the area of the green-shaded figure, $16,500 per day. The minimum wage thus reduces employer surplus by $8,000 per day and increases worker surplus by $4,000 per day. The net reduction in surplus is the area of the blue-shaded triangle shown in Figure 13.7, $4,000 per day.

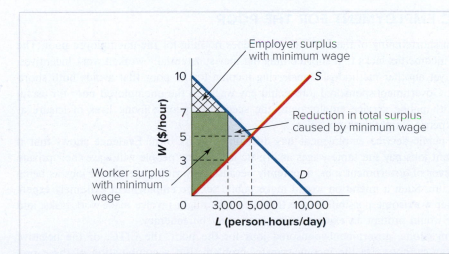

FIGURE 13.7

The Effect of a Minimum Wage on Economic Surplus.

A minimum wage of $7 per hour reduces employment in this market by 2,000 person-hours per day, for a reduction in total economic surplus of $4,000 per day (area of the blue-shaded triangle). Employer surplus falls to $4,500 per day (area of crosshatched triangle), while worker surplus rises to $16,500 per day (green-shaded area).

> ✔ **SELF-TEST 13.5**
>
> In the minimum wage example above, by how much would total economic surplus have been reduced by the $7 minimum wage if labor demand in Tallahassee had been perfectly inelastic at 5,000 person-hours per day?

Efficiency ›››

The following example illustrates the central message of the Efficiency Principle, which is that if the economic pie can be made larger, everyone can have a larger slice.

EXAMPLE 13.5   **The Efficiency Principle in Action**

Suppose that, instead of imposing a minimum wage, the government enacts an earned-income tax credit program. How much would it cost the government each day to provide an earned-income tax credit under which workers as a group receive the same economic surplus as they do under the $7 per hour minimum wage? (Assume for simplicity that the earned-income tax credit has no effect on labor supply.)

With an earned-income tax credit in lieu of a minimum wage, employment will be 5,000 person-hours per day at $5 per hour, just as in the unregulated market. Since worker surplus in the unregulated market was $4,000 per day less than under the minimum wage, the government would have to offer a tax credit worth $0.80 per hour for each of the 5,000 person-hours of employment to restore worker surplus to the level obtained under the $7 minimum wage. With an EITC of that amount in effect, worker surplus would be the same as under the $7 minimum wage. If the EITC were financed by a $4,000 tax on employers, employer surplus would be $4,000 greater than under the $7 minimum wage.

We stress that our point is not that the minimum wage produces no gains for low-income workers, but rather that it is possible to provide even larger gains for these workers if we avoid policies that try to prevent labor markets from reaching equilibrium.

PUBLIC EMPLOYMENT FOR THE POOR

The main shortcoming of the EITC is that it does nothing for the unemployed poor. The negative income tax lacks that shortcoming but may substantially weaken work incentives. There is yet another method of transferring income to the poor that avoids both shortcomings. Government-sponsored jobs could pay wages to the unemployed poor for useful work. With public service employment, the specter of people living lives of leisure at public expense simply does not arise.

But public service employment has difficulties of its own. Evidence shows that if government jobs pay the same wages as private jobs, many people will leave their private jobs in favor of government jobs, apparently because they view government jobs as being more secure. Such a migration would make public service employment extremely expensive. Other worrisome possibilities are that such jobs might involve make-work tasks, and that they would prompt an expansion in government bureaucracy.

Acting alone, government-sponsored jobs for the poor, the EITC, or the negative income tax cannot solve the income-transfer problem. But a combination of these programs might do so.

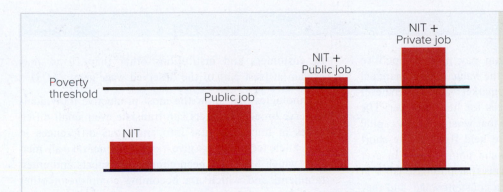

FIGURE 13.8

Income by Source in a Combination NIT–Jobs Program.

Together, a small negative income tax and a public job at below minimum wage would provide a family enough income to escape poverty, without weakening work incentives significantly.

A COMBINATION OF METHODS

Consider a negative income tax whose cash grant is far too small for anyone to live on, but that is supplemented if necessary by a public service job at below minimum wage. Keeping the wage in public service jobs well below the minimum wage would eliminate the risk of a large-scale exodus from private jobs. And while living well on either the negative income tax or the public service wage would be impossible, the two programs together could lift people out of poverty (see Figure 13.8).

To prevent an expansion of the bureaucracy, the government could solicit bids from private management companies to oversee the public service employment program. The fear that this program would inevitably become a make-work project is allayed by evidence that unskilled workers can, with proper supervision, perform many valuable tasks that would not otherwise be performed in the private sector. They can, for example, do landscaping and maintenance in public parks, provide transportation for older adults and people with disabilities, fill potholes in city streets and replace burned-out street lamps, transplant seedlings in erosion control projects, remove graffiti from public places and paint government buildings, recycle newspapers and containers, staff day care centers, and so on.

Can unskilled workers perform useful public service jobs?

This combination of a small negative income tax payment and public service employment at a subminimum wage would not be cheap. But the direct costs of existing welfare programs are also large, and the indirect costs, in the form of perverse work incentives and misguided attempts to control prices, are even larger. In economic terms, dealing intelligently with the income-transfer problem may in fact prove relatively inexpensive, once society recognizes the enormous opportunity cost of failing to deal intelligently with it.

RECAP ↑

METHODS OF INCOME REDISTRIBUTION

Minimum wage laws reduce total economic surplus by contracting employment. The earned-income tax credit boosts the incomes of the working poor without that drawback, but neither policy provides benefits for those who are not employed.

Other instruments in the battle against poverty include in-kind transfers such as food stamps, subsidized school lunches, Medicaid, and public housing as well as cash transfers such as Temporary Assistance for Needy Families. Because benefits under most of these programs are means-tested, beneficiaries often experience a net decline in income when they accept paid employment.

The negative income tax is an expanded version of the earned-income tax credit that includes those who are not employed. Combining this program with access to public service jobs would enable government to ensure adequate living standards for the poor without significantly undermining work incentives.

SUMMARY

- A worker's long-run equilibrium pay in a competitive labor market will be equal to the value of her marginal product of labor (*VMPL*)—the market value of whatever goods and services she produces for her employer. The law of diminishing returns says that when a firm's capital and other productive inputs are held fixed in the short run, adding workers beyond some point results in ever smaller increases in output. Firms that purchase labor in competitive labor markets face a constant wage, and they will hire labor up to the point at which *VMPL* equals the market wage. *(LO1, LO2)*

- Human capital theory says that an individual's *VMPL* is proportional to his stock of human capital—an amalgam of education, experience, training, intelligence, and other factors that influence productivity. According to this theory, some occupations pay better than others simply because they require larger stocks of human capital. *(LO3)*

- Wages often differ between individuals whose stocks of human capital appear nearly the same, as when one belongs to a labor union and the other does not. Compensating wage differentials—wage differences associated with differences in working conditions—are another important explanation for why individuals with similar human capital might earn different salaries. They help explain why garbage collectors earn more than lifeguards and, more generally, why individuals with a given stock of human capital tend to earn more in jobs that have less-attractive working conditions. *(LO3)*

- Many firms pay members of certain groups—notably Blacks and females—less than they pay white males who seem to have similar personal characteristics. If such wage gaps are the result of employer discrimination, their existence implies profit opportunities for firms that do not discriminate. Several other factors, including discrimination

by customers and institutions other than firms, may explain at least part of the observed wage gaps. *(LO3)*

- Technologies that allow the most productive individuals to serve broader markets can translate even small differences in human capital into enormous differences in pay. Such technologies give rise to winner-take-all markets, which have long been common in sports and entertainment, and which are becoming common in other professions. *(LO3)*

- Although incomes grew at almost 3 percent a year for all income classes during the three decades following World War II, the lion's share of income growth in the years since has been concentrated among top earners. *(LO4)*

- Philosophers have argued that at least some income redistribution is justified in the name of fairness, because if people chose society's distributional rules without knowing their own personal circumstances, most would favor less inequality than would be produced by market outcomes. *(LO4)*

- Policies and programs for reducing poverty include minimum wage laws, the earned-income tax credit, food stamps, subsidized school lunches, Medicaid, public housing, and Temporary Assistance for Needy Families. Of these, all but the earned-income tax credit fail to maximize total economic surplus, either by interfering with work incentives or by preventing markets from reaching equilibrium. *(LO5)*

- The negative income tax works much like the earned-income tax credit, except that it includes those who are not employed. A combination of a small negative income tax and access to public service jobs at subminimum wages could ensure adequate living standards for the poor without significantly undermining work incentives. *(LO5)*

KEY TERMS

compensating wage differential
customer discrimination
earned-income tax credit (EITC)
employer discrimination
human capital
human capital theory

in-kind transfer
labor union
marginal product of labor (*MPL*)
means-tested
negative income tax (NIT)

Personal Responsibility and Work
  Reconciliation Act
poverty threshold
value of the marginal product of
  labor (*VMPL*)
winner-take-all labor market

REVIEW QUESTIONS

1. Why is the supply curve of labor for any specific occupation likely to be upward-sloping, even if, for the economy as a whole, people work fewer hours when wage rates increase? *(LO2)*

2. True or false: If the human capital possessed by two workers is nearly the same, their wage rates will be nearly the same. Explain. *(LO3)*

3. How might recent changes in income inequality be related to the proliferation of technologies that enable the most productive individuals to serve broader markets? *(LO3, LO4)*

4. Mention two self-interested reasons that a top earner might favor policies to redistribute income. *(LO4)*

5. Why is exclusive reliance on the negative income tax unlikely to constitute a long-term solution to the poverty problem? *(LO5)*

PROBLEMS

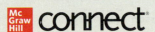

1. Mountain Breeze supplies air filters to the retail market and hires workers to assemble the components. An air filter sells for $26, and Mountain Breeze can buy the components for each filter for $1. Sandra and Bobby are two workers for Mountain Breeze. Sandra can assemble 60 air filters per month and Bobby can assemble 70. If the labor market is perfectly competitive, how much will Sandra and Bobby be paid? *(LO1)*

2. Acme Inc. supplies rocket ships to the retail market and hires workers to assemble the components. A rocket ship sells for $30,000, and Acme can buy the components for each rocket ship for $25,000. Wiley and Sam are two workers for Acme. Sam can assemble 1/5 of a rocket ship per month and Wiley can assemble 1/10. If the labor market is perfectly competitive and rocket components are Acme's only other cost, how much will Sam and Wiley be paid? *(LO1)*

3. Stone Inc. owns a clothing factory and hires workers in a competitive labor market to stitch cut denim fabric into jeans. The fabric required to make each pair of jeans costs $5. The company's weekly output of finished jeans varies with the number of workers hired, as shown in the following table: *(LO2, LO3)*

Number of workers	Jeans (pairs/week)
0	0
1	25
2	45
3	60
4	72
5	80
6	85

a. If the jeans sell for $35 a pair and the competitive market wage is $250 per week, how many workers should Stone hire? How many pairs of jeans will the company produce each week?

b. Suppose the Clothing Workers Union now sets a weekly minimum acceptable wage of $230 per week. All the workers Stone hires belong to the union. How does the minimum wage affect Stone's decision about how many workers to hire?

c. If the minimum wage set by the union had been $400 per week, how would the minimum wage affect Stone's decision about how many workers to hire?

d. If Stone again faces a market wage of $250 per week but the price of jeans rises to $45, how many workers will the company now hire?

4. Carolyn owns a soda factory and hires workers in a competitive labor market to bottle the soda. Her company's weekly output of bottled soda varies with the number of workers hired, as shown in the following table: *(LO2, LO3)*

Number of workers	Cases/week
0	0
1	200
2	360
3	480
4	560
5	600

a. If each case sells for $10 more than the cost of the materials used in producing it and the competitive market wage is $1,000 per week, how many workers should Carolyn hire? How many cases will be produced per week?

b. Suppose the Soda Bottlers Union now sets a weekly minimum acceptable wage of $1,500 per week. All the workers Carolyn hires belong to the union. How does the minimum wage affect Carolyn's decision about how many workers to hire?

c. If the wage is again $1,000 per week but the price of soda rises to $15 per case, how many workers will Carolyn now hire?

5. Malik, a high school senior, is offered a job walking his neighbor's dog for an hour each Friday afternoon. His reservation wage for this task is $6. *(LO4)*

a. If Malik's neighbor offers him $15 per hour, how much economic surplus will Malik enjoy each week as a result of accepting this job?

b. Now suppose that Malik's parents announce that he will have to split his earnings evenly with his two younger siblings. Will Malik still accept the job?

c. Explain how your answers to parts a and b illustrate one of the incentive problems inherent in income redistribution programs.

6. Jones, who is currently unemployed, is a participant in three means-tested welfare programs: food stamps, rent stamps, and day care stamps. Each program grants him $150 per month in stamps, which can be used like cash to purchase the good or service they cover. *(LO5)*

a. If benefits in each program are reduced by 40 cents for each additional dollar Jones earns in the labor market, how will Jones's economic position change if he accepts a job paying $120 per week?

b. In light of your answer to part a, explain why means testing for welfare recipients has undesirable effects on work incentives.

7. Suppose the equilibrium wage for unskilled workers in New Jersey is $16 per hour. How will the wages and employment of unskilled workers in New Jersey change if the state legislature raises the minimum wage from $8.85 per hour to $15 per hour? *(LO5)*

8.* Suppose the demand and supply curves for unskilled labor in the Corvallis labor market are as shown in the accompanying figure. *(LO5)*

a. By how much will the imposition of a minimum wage at $12 per hour reduce total economic surplus? Calculate the amounts by which employer surplus and worker surplus change as a result of the minimum wage.

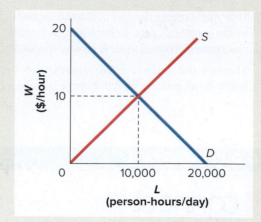

b. How much would it cost the government each day to provide an earned-income tax credit under which workers as a group receive the same economic surplus as they do under the $12-per-hour minimum wage? (Assume for simplicity that the earned-income tax credit has no effect on labor supply.)

9.* Suppose employers and workers are risk-neutral, and Congress is about to enact the $12-per-hour minimum wage described in Problem 8. Congressional staff economists have urged legislators to consider adopting an earned-income tax credit instead. Suppose neither workers nor employers would support that proposal unless the expected value of each party's economic surplus would be at least as great as under the minimum wage. Describe an earned-income tax credit (and a tax that would raise enough money to pay for it) that would receive unanimous support from both workers and employers. *(LO5)*

ANSWERS TO SELF-TESTS

13.1 At a price of $26 per cutting board, the fifth worker has a *VMPL* of $364 per week, so Adirondack should hire five workers. *(LO1)*

13.2 Since the *VMPL* of each worker exceeds $275, Adirondack should hire five workers. *(LO1)*

13.3 When the wage rate is $18 per hour in each market, 25 fewer workers will be employed in the nonunionized market and 25 more in the unionized market. The loss in output from removing 25 workers from the nonunionized market is the sum of the *VMPLs* of those workers, which is the shaded area in the right panel of the figure below. This area is $375 per hour. (*Hint:* To calculate this area, first break the figure into a rectangle and a triangle.) The gain in output from adding 25 workers to the unionized market is the shaded area in the left panel, which is $525 per hour. The net increase in output is thus $525 − $375 = $150 per hour. *(LO3)*

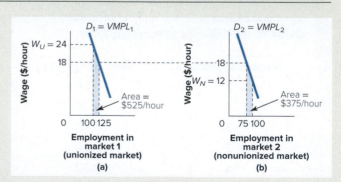

13.4 Since Sue's reservation wage is $10 per hour, she must be paid at least that amount before she will accept the job. The largest dorm population for which she will accept is thus 10 residents since her share in that case would be exactly $10 per hour. *(LO4)*

13.5 With perfectly inelastic demand, employment would remain at 5,000 person-hours per day, so the minimum wage would cause no reduction in economic surplus. *(LO5)*

*Denotes more difficult problem.

CHAPTER 14

Public Goods and Tax Policy

Government is imperfect. But markets are also imperfect, and all successful societies rely on a mix of government and private production to meet their economic demands.

Government has the power to tax. Unlike a private business, which can get our money only if we voluntarily buy its product, the government can take our money even if we don't want the particular mix of goods and services provided.

Government also has a monopoly on the legitimate use of force. If people break the law, government has the power to restrain them, using force if necessary. It also has the power to deprive lawbreakers of their liberty for extended periods, and, in some places, even to execute them. Government can draft law-abiding citizens into the armed forces and send them into situations in which they must kill others and risk being killed themselves.

These are awesome powers. And although they are often used in the pursuit of noble ends, the historical record abounds with illustrations of their abuse. Voters and politicians of both parties are keenly aware of these abuses. Indeed, contemporary political rhetoric almost invariably entails criticism of bloated, out-of-control government bureaucracy. Even mainstream Democrats—ostensibly the party of activist government in the United States—have conceded the need to curb government's role. For example, former president Clinton remarked in his 1996 State of the Union message, "the era of big government is over."

LEARNING OBJECTIVES

After reading this chapter, you should be able to:

LO1 Use the concepts of rivalry and excludability to distinguish among private goods, public goods, collective goods, and commons goods.

LO2 Show how economic concepts can be used to find the optimal quantity of a public good and describe the ways in which private firms can supply public goods.

LO3 Analyze the types of efficiencies and inefficiencies that are associated with the provision of public goods.

LO4 Identify criteria that should be applied to taxation in order to promote efficiency.

Others advocate even more radical retrenchment. For instance, Harry Browne, the 1996 Libertarian Party presidential candidate, called for abolition of the Internal Revenue Service, the agency responsible for collecting the federal income tax. This step would be tantamount to abolishing the federal government itself, for without tax revenues, there would be no way to pay for public goods and services.

Browne is right, of course, that a sure way to prevent government abuse of power is simply to have no government. But since virtually no society on earth lacks a government, we may suspect that governments, on balance, do more good than harm.

But how big, exactly, should government be? What goods and services should it provide? How should it raise the revenue to pay for them? What other powers should it have to constrain the behavior of its citizens? And how should the various powers we assign to government be apportioned among local, state, and federal levels? Our goal in this chapter will be to employ the principles of microeconomics in an attempt to answer these pragmatic questions.

GOVERNMENT PROVISION OF PUBLIC GOODS ——

public good a good or service that, to at least some degree, is both nonrival and nonexcludable

One of the primary tasks of government is to provide what economists call **public goods** such as national defense and the criminal justice system.

PUBLIC GOODS VERSUS PRIVATE GOODS

nonrival good a good whose consumption by one person does not diminish its availability for others

Public goods are those goods or services that are, in varying degrees, **nonrival** and **nonexcludable.** A nonrival good is one whose consumption by one person does not diminish its availability for others. For example, if the military prevents a hostile nation from invading your city, your enjoyment of that protection does not diminish its value to your neighbors. A good is nonexcludable if it is difficult to exclude nonpayers from consuming it. For instance, even if your neighbors don't pay their share of the cost of maintaining an army, they will still enjoy its protection.

nonexcludable good a good that is difficult, or costly, to exclude nonpayers from consuming

Another example of a nonrival and nonexcludable good is an over-the-air broadcast of *The Late Show with Stephen Colbert*. The fact that you tune in one evening does not make the program any less available to others, and once the broadcast has been beamed out over the airwaves, it is difficult to prevent anyone from tuning in. Similarly, if the City of New York puts on a fireworks display in New York harbor to celebrate a special occasion, it cannot charge admission because the harbor may be viewed from many different locations in the city. And the fact that additional persons view the display does not in any way diminish its value to other potential viewers.

In contrast, the typical private good is diminished one-for-one by any individual's consumption of it. For instance, when you eat a cheeseburger, it is no longer available for anyone else. Moreover, people can be easily prevented from consuming cheeseburgers they don't pay for.

> ✓ **SELF-TEST 14.1**
>
> Which of the following, if any, is nonrival?
>
> a. The website of the Bureau of Labor Statistics at 3 a.m.
>
> b. The World Cup soccer championship game watched in person.
>
> c. The World Cup soccer championship game watched on television.

pure public good a good or service that, to a high degree, is both nonrival and nonexcludable

Goods that are both highly nonexcludable and nonrival are often called **pure public goods.** Two reasons favor government provision of such goods. First, for-profit private companies would have obvious difficulty recovering their cost of production. Many people might be willing to pay enough to cover the cost of producing the good, but if it is nonexcludable, the company cannot easily charge for it (an example of the free-rider problem discussed in

Chapter 12, *The Economics of Information*). And second, if the marginal cost of serving additional users is zero once the good has been produced, then charging for the good would be inefficient, even if there were some practical way to do so. This inefficiency often characterizes the provision of **collective goods**—nonrival goods for which it is possible to exclude nonpayers. Subscription video streaming services like Netflix are an example. People who don't pay to get Netflix don't get to watch programs shown only on Netflix, a restriction that excludes many viewers who would have benefited from watching. Because the marginal cost to society of their tuning in is essentially zero, excluding these viewers is wasteful.

A **pure private good** is one from which nonpayers can easily be excluded and for which one person's consumption creates a one-for-one reduction in the good's availability for others. The theory of perfectly competitive supply developed in the chapter on perfectly competitive supply applies to pure private goods, of which basic agricultural products are perhaps the best examples. A **pure commons good** is a rival good that is also nonexcludable, so-called because goods with this combination of properties almost always result in a tragedy of the commons (see Chapter 11, *Externalities, Property Rights, and the Environment*). Fish in ocean waters are an example.

The classification scheme defined by the nonrival and nonexcludable properties is summarized in Table 14.1. The columns of the table indicate the extent to which one person's consumption of a good fails to diminish its availability for others. Goods in the right column are nonrival and those in the left column are not. The rows of the table indicate the difficulty of excluding nonpayers from consuming the good. Goods in the top row are nonexcludable; those in the bottom row, excludable. Private goods (lower-left cell) are rival and excludable. Public goods (upper-right cell) are nonrival and nonexcludable. The two hybrid categories are commons goods (upper-left cell), which are rival but nonexcludable, and collective goods (lower-right cell), which are excludable but nonrival.

collective good a good or service that, to at least some degree, is nonrival but excludable

pure private good one for which nonpayers can easily be excluded and for which each unit consumed by one person means one less unit available for others

pure commons good one for which nonpayers cannot easily be excluded and for which each unit consumed by one person means one less unit available for others

TABLE 14.1
Private, Public, and Hybrid Goods

		Nonrival	
		Low	High
Nonexcludable	High	Commons good (fish in the ocean)	Public good (national defense)
	Low	Private good (wheat)	Collective good (video streaming services)

Collective goods are provided sometimes by government, sometimes by private companies. Most pure public goods are provided by government, but even private companies can sometimes find profitable ways of producing goods that are both nonrival *and* nonexcludable. An example is broadcast radio and television, which covers its costs by selling airtime to advertisers.

The mere fact that a good is a pure public good does not necessarily mean that government ought to provide it. On the contrary, the only public goods the government should even *consider* providing are those whose benefits exceed their costs. The cost of a public good is simply the sum of all explicit and implicit costs incurred to provide it. The benefit of a public good is measured by asking how much people would be willing to pay for it. Although that sounds similar to the way we measure the benefit of a private good, an important distinction exists. The benefit of an additional unit of a private good such as a cheeseburger is the highest sum that any individual buyer would be willing to pay for it. In contrast, the benefit of an additional unit of a public good such as an additional broadcast episode of *The Late Show with Stephen Colbert* is the sum of the reservation prices of all people who will watch that episode.

 Cost-Benefit

Even if the amount that all beneficiaries of a public good would be willing to pay exceeds its cost, government provision of that good makes sense only if there is no other less costly way of providing it. For example, whereas city governments often pay for fireworks displays, they almost invariably hire private companies to put on these events. Finally, if the benefit of a public good does not exceed its cost, we are better off without it.

PAYING FOR PUBLIC GOODS

Not everyone benefits equally from the provision of a given public good. For example, some people find fireworks displays highly entertaining, but others simply don't care about them, and still others actively dislike them. Ideally, it might seem that the most equitable method of financing a given public good would be to tax people in proportion to their willingness to pay for the good. To illustrate this approach, suppose Jones values a public good at $100, Smith values the same good at $200, and the cost of the good is $240. Jones would then be taxed $80 and Smith would be taxed $160. The good would be provided, and each taxpayer in this example would reap a surplus equal to 25 percent of his tax payment: $20 for Jones, $40 for Smith.

In practice, however, government officials usually lack the information they would need to tax people in proportion to their willingness to pay for specific public goods. (Think about it: If an IRS agent asked you how much you would be willing to pay to have a new freeway and you knew you would be taxed in proportion to the amount you responded, what would you say?) The following three examples illustrate some of the problems that arise in financing public goods and suggest possible solutions to these problems.

| EXAMPLE 14.1 | Joint Purchase |

Will Prentice and Wilson buy a water filter?

Prentice and Wilson own adjacent summer cottages along an isolated stretch of shoreline on Cayuga Lake. Because of a recent invasion of zebra mussels, each must add chlorine to his water intake valve each week to prevent it from becoming clogged by the tiny mollusks. A manufacturer has introduced a new filtration device that eliminates the nuisance of weekly chlorination. The cost of the device, which has the capacity to serve both houses, is $1,000. Both owners feel equally strongly about having the filter. But because Wilson earns twice as much as Prentice, Wilson is willing to pay up to $800 to have the filter, whereas its value to Prentice, a retired schoolteacher, is only $400. Would either person be willing to purchase the device individually? Is it efficient for them to share its purchase?

Neither will purchase the filter individually because each has a reservation price that is below its selling price. But because the two together value the filter at $1,200, sharing its use would be socially efficient. If they were to do so, total economic surplus would be $200 higher than if they did not buy the filter.

Since sharing the filter is the efficient outcome, we might expect that Prentice and Wilson would quickly reach agreement to purchase it. Unfortunately, however, the joint purchase and sharing of facilities is often easier proposed than accomplished. One hurdle is that people must incur costs merely to get together to discuss joint purchases. With only two people involved, those costs might not be significant. But if hundreds or thousands of people were involved, communication costs could be prohibitive.

With large numbers of people, the free-rider problem also emerges (see Chapter 12, *The Economics of Information*). After all, everyone knows that the project will either succeed or fail independently of any one person's contribution to it. Everyone thus has an incentive to withhold contributions—or get a free ride—in the hope that others will give.

Finally, even when only a few people are involved, reaching agreement on a fair sharing of the total expense may be difficult. For example, Prentice and Wilson might be reluctant to disclose their true reservation prices to one another for the same reason that you might be reluctant to disclose your reservation price for a public good to an IRS agent.

These practical concerns may lead us to empower government to buy public goods on our behalf. But as the next example makes clear, this approach does not eliminate the need to reach political agreement on how public purchases are to be financed.

EXAMPLE 14.2   Head Taxes

Will government buy the water filter if there is an "equal tax" rule?

Suppose Prentice and Wilson could ask the government to help broker the water filter purchase. And suppose that the government's tax policy must follow a "nondiscrimination" rule that prohibits charging any citizen more for a public good than it charges his or her neighbor. Another rule is that public goods can be provided only if a majority of citizens approve of them. Will a government bound by these rules provide the filter that Prentice and Wilson want?

A tax that collects the same amount from every citizen is called a **head tax.** If the government must rely on a head tax, it must raise $500 from Prentice and $500 from Wilson. But because the device is worth only $400 to Prentice, he will vote against the project, thus denying it a majority. So a democratic government cannot provide the water filter if it must rely on a head tax.

head tax a tax that collects the same amount from every taxpayer

A head tax is a **regressive tax,** one for which the proportion of a taxpayer's income that is paid in taxes declines as the taxpayer's income rises.

The point illustrated by this example is not confined to the specific public good considered. It applies whenever taxpayers place significantly different valuations on public goods, as will almost always happen whenever people earn significantly different incomes. An equal-tax rule under these circumstances will almost invariably rule out the provision of many worthwhile public goods.

As our third example suggests, one solution to this problem is to allow taxes to vary by income.

regressive tax a tax under which the proportion of income paid in taxes declines as income rises

EXAMPLE 14.3   Proportional Income Tax

Will the government buy the filter if there is a proportional tax on income?

Suppose that Prentice proposes that the government raise revenue by imposing a proportional tax on income to finance the provision of the water filter. Will Wilson, who earns twice as much as Prentice, support this proposal?

A **proportional income tax** is one under which all taxpayers pay the same proportion of their incomes in taxes. Under such a tax, Wilson would support Prentice's proposal because if he didn't, each would fail to enjoy a public good whose benefit exceeds his share of its cost. Under the proportional tax on income, Prentice would contribute $333 toward the $1,000 purchase price of the filter and Wilson would contribute $667. The government would buy the filter, resulting in additional surpluses of $67 for Prentice and $133 for Wilson.

proportional income tax one under which all taxpayers pay the same proportion of their incomes in taxes

The Economic Naturalist 14.1 example makes the point that just as equal contributions are often a poor way to pay for public goods, they are also often a poor way to share expenses within the household.

The Economic Naturalist 14.1

Why don't most married couples contribute equally to joint purchases?

Why do married couples usually pool their incomes?

Suppose Hillary earns $2,000,000 per year while her husband Bill earns only $20,000. Given her income, Hillary as an individual would want to spend much more than Bill would on housing, travel, entertainment, education for their children, and the many other items they consume jointly. What will happen if the couple adopts a rule that each must contribute an equal amount toward the purchase of such items?

This rule would constrain the couple to live in a small house, take only inexpensive vacations, and skimp on entertainment, dining out, and their children's education. It is therefore easy to see why Hillary might find it attractive to pay considerably more than 50 percent for jointly consumed goods because doing so would enable *both* of them to consume in the manner their combined income permits.

Public goods and jointly consumed private goods are different from individually consumed private goods in the following important way: *Different individuals are free to consume whatever quantity and quality of most private goods they choose to buy, but jointly consumed goods must be provided in the same quantity and quality for all persons.*

As in the case of private goods, people's willingness to pay for public goods is generally an increasing function of income. Wealthy individuals tend to assign greater value to public goods than low-income people do, not because the wealthy have different tastes but because they have more money. A head tax would result in high-income persons getting smaller amounts of public goods than they want. By increasing the total economic surplus available for all to share, a tax system that assigns a larger share of the tax burden to people with higher incomes makes possible a better outcome for both rich and poor alike. Indeed, virtually all industrialized nations have tax systems that are at least mildly **progressive,** which means that the proportion of income paid in taxes actually rises with a family's income.

progressive tax
one in which the proportion of income paid in taxes rises as income rises

Progressive taxation and even proportional taxation often have been criticized as being unfair to the wealthy, who are forced to pay more than others for public goods that all consume in common. The irony in this charge, however, is that exclusive reliance on head taxes, or even proportional taxes, would curtail the provision of public goods and services that are of greatest value to high-income families. Studies have shown, for instance, that the income elasticity of demand for public goods such as parks and recreation facilities, clean air and water, public safety, uncongested roads, and aesthetically pleasing public spaces is substantially greater than 1. Failure to rely on progressive taxation would result in gross underprovision of such public goods and services.

RECAP

PUBLIC GOODS

A public good is both nonrival and nonexcludable. Private firms typically cannot recover the costs of producing such goods because they cannot exclude nonpayers from consuming them. Nor would charging for a public good promote efficiency, since one person's consumption of the good does not diminish its availability for others.

Both obstacles can be overcome by creating a government with the power to levy taxes. Even high-income citizens often favor progressive taxes because proportional or regressive taxes may generate insufficient revenue to pay for the public goods those taxpayers favor.

THE OPTIMAL QUANTITY OF A PUBLIC GOOD ──

In the examples considered thus far, the question was whether to provide a particular public good and, if so, how to pay for it. In practice, we often confront additional questions about what level and quality of a public good to provide.

Standard cost-benefit logic also applies to these questions. For example, New York City should add another rocket to a fireworks display if and only if the amount that citizens would collectively be willing to pay to see the rocket is at least as great as its cost.

Cost-Benefit

THE DEMAND CURVE FOR A PUBLIC GOOD

To calculate the socially optimal quantity of a public good, we must first construct the demand curve for that public good. The process for doing so differs in an important way from the one we use to generate the market demand curve for a private good.

For a private good, all buyers face the same price and each chooses the quantity he or she wishes to purchase at that price. Recall from Chapter 5, *Demand,* that to construct the demand curve for a private good from the demand curves for individual consumers, we place the individual demand curves side by side and add them horizontally. That is, for each of a series of fixed prices, we add the resulting quantities demanded on the individual demand curves. In Figure 14.1, for example, we add the individual demand curves for a private good, D_1 and D_2 [Figure 14.1(a) and (b)] horizontally to obtain the market demand curve for the good D [Figure 14.1(c)].

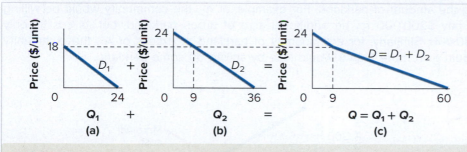

FIGURE 14.1

Generating the Market Demand Curve for a Private Good.

To construct the market demand curve for a private good (c), we add the individual demand curves (a) and (b) horizontally.

For a public good, all buyers necessarily consume the same quantity, although each may differ in terms of willingness to pay for additional units of the good. Constructing the demand curve for a public good thus entails not horizontal summation of the individual demand curves but vertical summation. That is, for each of a series of quantity values, we must add the prices that individuals are willing to pay for an additional unit of the good. The curves D_1 and D_2 in Figure 14.2(b) and (c) show individual demand curves for a public good by two different people. At each quantity, these curves tell how much the individual would be willing to pay for an additional unit of the public good. If we add D_1 and D_2 vertically, we obtain the total demand curve D for the public good [Figure 14.2(a)].

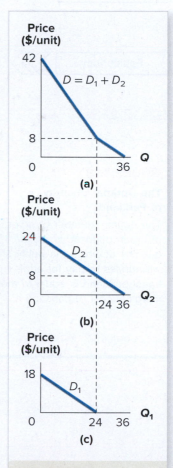

FIGURE 14.2

Generating the Demand Curve for a Public Good.

To construct the demand curve for a public good (a), we add the individual demand curves (b) and (c) vertically.

 SELF-TEST 14.2

Bill and Tom are the only demanders of a public good. If Bill's demand curve is $P_B = 6 - 0.5Q$ and Tom's is $P_T = 12 - Q$, construct the demand curve for this public good.

In the following example, we see how the demand curve for a public good might be used in conjunction with information about costs to determine the optimal level of parkland in a city.

| **EXAMPLE 14.4** | **Using the Demand Curve to Determine Optimal Levels** |

What is the optimal quantity of urban parkland?

The city government of a new planned community must decide how much parkland to provide. The marginal cost curve and the public demand curve for urban parkland are as shown in Figure 14.3. Why is the marginal cost curve upward-sloping and the demand curve downward-sloping? Given these curves, what is the optimal quantity of parkland?

The marginal cost schedule for urban parkland is upward-sloping because of the Low-Hanging-Fruit Principle: The city acquires the cheapest parcels of land first and only then turns to more expensive parcels. Likewise, the marginal willingness-to-pay curve is downward-sloping because of the law of diminishing marginal utility. Just as people are generally willing to pay less for their fifth hot dog than for their first, they are also willing to pay less for the 101st acre of parkland than for the 100th acre. Given these curves, A^* is the optimal quantity of parkland. For any quantity less than A^*, the benefit of additional parkland exceeds its cost, which means that total economic surplus can be made larger by expanding the amount of parkland. For example, at A_0, the community would be willing to pay $200,000 for an additional acre of urban parkland, but its cost is only $80,000. Similarly, for any quantity of parkland in excess of A^*, the community would gain more than it would lose by selling off some parkland.

FIGURE 14.3

The Optimal Quantity of Parkland.

The optimal number of acres of urban parkland is A^*, the quantity at which the public's willingness to pay for additional parkland is equal to the marginal cost of parkland.

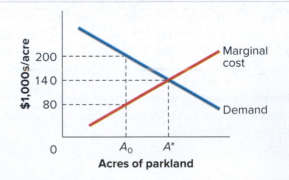

PRIVATE PROVISION OF PUBLIC GOODS

One advantage of using the government to provide public goods is that once a tax collection agency has been established to finance a single public good, it can be expanded at relatively low cost to generate revenue for additional public goods. Another advantage is that because government has the power to tax, it can summarily assign responsibility for the cost of a public good without endless haggling over who bears what share of the burden. And in the case of goods for which nonpayers cannot be excluded, the government may be the only feasible provider.

But exclusive reliance on government also entails disadvantages. Most fundamentally, the government's one-size-fits-all approach invariably requires many people to pay for public goods they don't want, while others end up having to do without public goods they want desperately. For example, many people vehemently oppose the provision of *any* sex education in the public schools, while others fervently believe that far more such instruction should be provided than is currently offered in most current public school curriculums. Mandatory taxation strikes many people as coercive, even if they approve of the particular public goods being provided.

It is no surprise, then, that governments are not the exclusive providers of public goods in any society. Indeed, many public goods are routinely provided through private channels. The challenge, in each case, is to devise a scheme for raising the required revenues. Here are some methods that seem to work.

Funding by Donation

In 2018, Americans gave more than $427 billion to private charities, many of which provide public goods to their communities. People also volunteer their time on behalf of organizations that provide public goods. When you paint your house, mow your lawn, or plant a flower garden, you are enhancing the quality of life in your neighborhood, and in that sense you are voluntarily providing a public good to your neighbors.

Development of New Means to Exclude Nonpayers

New electronic technology makes it possible to exclude nonpayers from many goods that in the past could not be thus restricted. For instance, broadcast television stations now have the ability to scramble their signals, making them available only to those consumers who purchase descrambling devices.

Private Contracting

More than 11 million Americans now live in gated private communities—private homeowners' associations that wall off contiguous properties and provide various services to residents. Many of these associations provide security services, schools, and fire protection and in other ways function much like ordinary local governments. Recognizing that individual incentives may not be strong enough to ensure socially optimal levels of maintenance and landscaping, these associations often bill homeowners for those services directly. Many of the rules imposed by these associations are even more restrictive than those imposed by local governments, a distinction that is defended on the grounds that people are always free to choose some other neighborhood if they don't like the rules of any particular homeowners' association. Many people would be reluctant to tolerate a municipal ordinance that prevents people from painting their houses purple, yet such restrictions are common in the bylaws of homeowners' associations.

Sale of By-Products

Many public goods are financed by the sale of rights or services that are generated as by-products of the public goods. For instance, as noted earlier, radio and television programming is a public good that is paid for in many cases by the sale of advertising messages. Internet services are also underwritten in part by commercial messages that pop up or appear in the headers or margins of web pages.

Given the quintessentially voluntary nature of privately provided public goods, it might seem that reliance on private provision might be preferred whenever it proved feasible. But as The Economic Naturalist 14.2 example makes clear, private provision often entails problems of its own.

The Economic Naturalist 14.2

Why do television networks favor *NFL Sunday Night Football* over *Masterpiece*?

In a given time slot, a television network faces the alternative of broadcasting either *NFL Sunday Night Football* or *Masterpiece* (formerly *Masterpiece Theatre*). If it chooses *NFL Sunday Night Football,* it will win 20 percent of the viewing audience, but only 18 percent if it chooses *Masterpiece.* Suppose those who would choose *NFL Sunday Night Football* would collectively be willing to pay $10 million for the right to see that program, while those who choose *Masterpiece* would be willing to pay $30 million. And suppose, finally, that the time slot is to be financed by a detergent company. Which program will the network choose? Which program would be socially optimal?

A detergent maker cares primarily about the number of people who will see its advertisements and will thus choose the program that will attract the largest audience—here, *NFL Sunday Night Football.* The fact that those who prefer *Masterpiece* would be willing to pay a lot more to see it is of little concern to the sponsor. But to identify the optimal result from society's point of view, we must take this difference into account. Because the people who prefer *Masterpiece* could pay *NFL Sunday Night Football* viewers more than enough to compensate them for relinquishing the time slot, *Masterpiece* is the efficient outcome. But unless its supporters happen to buy more soap in total than *NFL Sunday Night Football* viewers, the latter will prevail. In short, reliance on advertising and other indirect mechanisms for financing public goods provides no assurance that the goods chosen will maximize economic surplus.

Why do detergent companies care more about audience size than about how much people would be willing to pay to see the programs they sponsor?

Of course, the fact that the programs that best suit advertisers' needs may not be socially optimal does not mean that government decisions would necessarily be better. One can imagine, for example, a cultural affairs ministry that would choose television programming that would be "good for us" but that few of us would want to watch.

One way to avoid the inefficiency that arises when advertisers choose programming is to rely on subscription video streaming services to provide television programming. These methods allow viewers to register not just which programs they prefer but also the strength of their preferences, as measured by how much they are willing to pay.

But although a video streaming service is more likely to select the programs the public most values, it is also less efficient than broadcast TV in one important respect. As noted earlier, charging each household a fee for a subscription discourages some households from tuning in. And since the marginal social cost of serving an additional household is essentially zero, limiting the audience in this way is inefficient. Which of the two inefficiencies is more important—broadcast TV's inefficiency in choosing among programs or a video streaming service's inefficiency in excluding potential beneficiaries—is an empirical question.

In any event, the mix between private and public provision of public goods and services differs substantially from society to society and from arena to arena within any given society. These differences depend on the nature of available technologies for delivering and paying for public goods, and also on people's preferences.

EXAMPLE 14.5   **The Impact of Subscription Video Streaming Services on Economic Surplus**

By how much is total economic surplus reduced by Netflix's monthly fee for subscribers?

Suppose the demand curve for a month's access to the library of videos offered by Netflix is given in Figure 14.4. If the monthly subscription fee is $12, then by how much would economic surplus rise if the same library of videos were offered to consumers free of charge?

According to Figure 14.4, at a monthly fee of $12, 60 million consumers will subscribe to Netflix each month. But if the same library of videos were offered free of charge, 100 million consumers would want access. The additional economic surplus reaped by the extra 40 million consumers each month is the area of the blue triangle, which is $240 million. Since the marginal cost of giving these additional consumers access to Netflix is essentially zero, the total increase in surplus each month also would be $240 million.

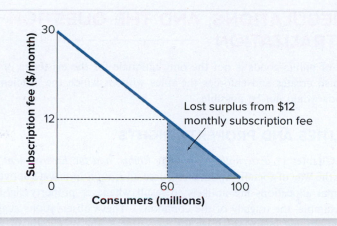

FIGURE 14.4

The Loss in Surplus from a Monthly Subscription Fee.

An additional 40 million consumers would want access to the library of videos offered by Netflix if the price were zero instead of $12 per month. The additional economic surplus is the area of the blue triangle, or $240 million per month.

In general, charging a positive price for a good whose marginal cost is zero will result in a loss in surplus. The size of the loss that results when price is set above marginal cost depends on the price elasticity of demand. When demand is more elastic, the loss in surplus is greater. Self-Test 14.3 provides an opportunity to see that principle at work.

✅ SELF-TEST 14.3

How would your answer to Example 14.5 have been different if the demand curve had instead been as shown below?

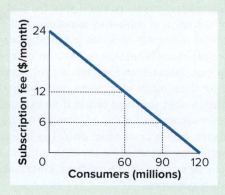

RECAP ↑

THE OPTIMAL QUANTITY OF A PUBLIC GOOD

Because the quantity of a public good must be the same for every consumer, the total demand curve for a public good is constructed by adding individual demand curves vertically. Optimal production of a public good occurs at the quantity for which the demand curve intersects the marginal cost curve for the public good.

Government need not always be the best way to provide public goods. Such goods can be provided by private organizations that rely on charitable contributions or the sale of by-products. Private for-profit companies also can become providers when new technologies such as subscription video streaming services convert public goods into collective goods.

LAWS, REGULATIONS, AND THE QUESTION OF CENTRALIZATION

The provision of public goods is not the only rationale for the existence of government. Government also creates and enforces the rules without which the efficient production of private goods would not be possible.

EXTERNALITIES AND PROPERTY RIGHTS

As we saw in Chapter 11, *Externalities, Property Rights, and the Environment,* externalities often stand in the way of socially optimal resource allocation in private activities. We saw, too, that optimal allocations are unlikely to result whenever property rights are poorly defined (for example, the tragedy of the commons). These observations suggest the existence of two additional important roles for government: the regulation of activities that generate externalities and the definition and enforcement of property rights.

These rationales for government action explain why most governments regulate activities that generate pollution, subsidize education (on the grounds that an educated public creates positive externalities), control access to fishing waters and public timberland, and enforce zoning laws. Most laws, in fact, represent attempts to define property rights or to control externalities. The law requiring motorists to drive on the right, for example, is an attempt to prevent the activities of one motorist from causing harm to others.

Proponents of minimalist government often object that the government unjustly curtails our freedom when it uses zoning laws to limit the size of the houses we build or imposes fines on motorists who violate highway speed limits. Yet the justification for such regulations is precisely the same as for the laws that prohibit your fist from occupying the same physical space as your neighbor's nose. You are free to swing your fists as you please, provided you cause no harm to others. But if your fist strikes your neighbor's nose, you become a violator of the law and subject to punishment. If the proponents of minimalist government approve of restricting behavior in this way, why do they disapprove of other attempts to discourage behaviors that cause harm to others?

Perhaps their fear is that, because externalities are so pervasive, governments that were empowered to regulate them might quickly get out of control. This is by no means an idle fear, and we emphasize that the mere fact that an externality exists does not necessarily mean that the best outcome is for the government to regulate it. As we will see in the next section, regulation entails costs of its own. The ultimate question is therefore a practical one: Will government regulation of the externality in question do more good than harm? Slogans about being free to live without government interference provide little help in answering such questions.

LOCAL, STATE, OR FEDERAL?

Framers of the U.S. Constitution were deeply skeptical of centralized government power. In drafting the Constitution, therefore, they explicitly tried to limit the powers of the federal government as much as possible, delegating most important powers to the states, which in turn delegated many of their powers to governments at the local level.

It is no surprise that the dangers of remote, centralized government ranked high among the founding fathers' concerns. After all, fresh in their memories was the autocratic treatment received by the American colonies at the hands of the monarchy in England. The founding fathers recognized that government will be more responsive the shorter the distance between officeholders and the voters who elect them.

Another obvious advantage of giving as much authority to local governments as possible is that different communities often have markedly different preferences about how much to spend on public goods, and even on what kinds of public goods to provide. When such decisions are made at the local level, people can shop for a community whose voters' preferences largely coincide with their own. Those who like high levels of public goods and services can band together and authorize high taxes to pay for them. Others who place less value on public services can choose communities in which both services and taxes are lower.

Why, given the many attractions of decisions made at the local level, did the founding fathers create federal and state governments at all? One reason is economies of scale in defense. For a country to survive politically, it must be able to deter aggression by hostile governments. A country consisting only of, say, Concord, New Hampshire, would be ill-equipped to do that. Large, well-equipped armies and navies cost a lot of money, and countries without sufficient population simply cannot afford them.

Defense, however, is not the only reason to empower governments beyond the local or state level. The problem of pollution, for example, is difficult to solve when the various sources of pollution are not subject to regulatory control by a single government. Much of the acid rain experienced in Canada, for instance, is the result of sulfur dioxide emissions from industrial sources in the upper Midwest of the United States. These emissions are beyond the reach of Canadian environmental regulations. In many instances, as with the discharge of greenhouse gases, not even a coalition of all the governments in North, Central, and South America would have power to take effective action. Carbon dioxide emitted anywhere on the planet disperses to uniform concentrations around the globe in a matter of months.

The choice between different levels of government, then, often confronts us with difficult trade-offs. Ceding the power of taxation to a federal government often entails painful compromises for voters in individual states. But the loss of political autonomy is an even less attractive option. Similarly, nations are understandably reluctant to cede any of their sovereign powers to a higher authority, but failure to take such steps may entail unacceptable environmental costs in the long run.

RECAP

LAWS, REGULATIONS, AND THE QUESTION OF CENTRALIZATION

Government creates economic surplus not only by providing public goods but also by regulating activities that generate externalities and by defining and enforcing property rights. These rationales explain why most governments regulate pollution, subsidize education, control access to fishing waters and public timberland, and enforce zoning laws.

Although the framers of the Constitution disliked centralized government power, they recognized that some government functions are not best performed at the local or even state level. Economies of scale argue for provision of defense at the national level. Externalities that transcend local boundaries provide an additional rationale for national or even international government.

SOURCES OF INEFFICIENCY IN THE POLITICAL PROCESS

In most countries, expenditures on public goods, tax policy, and laws regulating behavior are determined in large part by the votes of democratically elected representatives. This process is far from perfect. (Winston Churchill called democracy "the worst form of government, except for any other.") Inefficiencies often arise in the public sphere not because of incompetent or ignorant legislators but because of structural incentive problems.

Pork Barrel Legislation

The following example, drawn not from the public sector but from everyday private life, illustrates one of the important incentive gaps.

The Economic Naturalist 14.3

Why does the practice of check splitting cause people to spend more at restaurants?

Why does check-splitting make the total restaurant bill higher?

Sven Torvaldsen and nine friends are having dinner at La Maison de La Casa House, a four-star restaurant in Minneapolis. To simplify the task of paying for their meal, they have agreed in advance to split the cost of their meal equally, with each paying one-tenth of the total check. Having cleared the entree dishes, the server arrives with the dessert menu, on which Sven's two favorite items are pumpkin bread pudding ($10) and chocolate mousse ($6). Sven's reservation prices for these items are $4 and $3, respectively. Will he order dessert, and, if so, which one? Would he order dessert if he were dining by himself?

When Sven and his friends split the total check equally, Sven's payment goes up by one-tenth of the menu price of any dessert he orders. Thus, the prices—to him—of the bread pudding and chocolate mousse are $1 and 60 cents, respectively. Because he gets $4 − $1 = $3 of consumer surplus from the bread pudding and only $3 − $0.60 = $2.40 from the chocolate mousse, he will order the bread pudding. If Sven were dining alone, however, his bill would increase dollar for dollar with the menu price of any dessert he ordered. And since the menu prices exceed his corresponding reservation prices, he would not order dessert at all.

The irony, of course, is that if Sven's nine friends have the same preferences regarding dessert, each will order bread pudding and each person's share of the total bill will rise not by $1 but by the full $10. Compared to the alternative of no one having dessert, each diner suffers a $6 loss in consumer surplus. Still, it made sense for each to order bread pudding since failure to do so would have reduced each diner's bill by only $1.

✓ SELF-TEST 14.4

In The Economic Naturalist 14.3 example, would Sven have ordered dessert if there had been only 5 people splitting the check instead of 10?

pork barrel spending a public expenditure that is larger than the total benefit it creates but that is favored by a legislator because his or her constituents benefit from the expenditure by more than their share of the resulting extra taxes

Alert readers will have noticed the similarity between the problem posed in the preceding example and the one posed in Chapter 11, *Externalities, Property Rights, and the Environment* (The Economic Naturalist 11.5), in which identical twins had a single milkshake to share with two straws. The same incentive problem leads to the inefficient outcome in both cases.

The Economic Naturalist 14.4 example illustrates how the very same incentive problem rears its head in the legislative process.

The Economic Naturalist 14.4

Why do legislators often support one another's pork barrel spending programs?

Pork barrel programs are government programs that benefit local areas but are of questionable value from a national perspective. Why do voters seem to support legislators who initiate such projects even when the total effect of all such projects on local tax bills far exceeds the local benefits?

Consider a voter in a congressional district that contains one one-hundredth of the country's taxpayers. Suppose that voter's representative is able to deliver a public project that generates benefits of $100 million for the district but that costs the federal government $150 million. Since the district's share of the tax bill for the project will be only $150 million/100 = $1.5 million, residents of the district are $98.5 million better off with the project than without it. And that explains why so many voters favor legislators with a successful record of "bringing home the bacon."

But why would legislator A support such a project in legislator B's home district? After all, B's project will cause A's constituents' taxes to rise—albeit by a small amount—yet they will get no direct benefit from the project. The answer is that if A does not support B's project, then B will not support A's. The practice whereby legislators support one another's pet projects is known as **logrolling.** This practice creates a bias toward excessive spending, much like the bias created when a dinner check is split equally.

logrolling the practice whereby legislators support one another's legislative proposals

Rent-Seeking

A related source of inefficiency in the public sphere occurs because the gains from government projects are often concentrated in the hands of a few beneficiaries, while the costs are spread among many. This means that beneficiaries often have a powerful incentive to organize and lobby in favor of public projects. Individual taxpayers, by contrast, have little at stake in any public project and therefore have little incentive to incur the cost of mobilizing themselves in opposition.

Suppose, for example, that a price support bill for sugar will raise the price of sugar by 10 cents per pound and that the average American family currently consumes 100 pounds of sugar per year. How will this legislation affect the average family's consumption of sugar? Recall from Chapter 5, *Demand,* that a good such as salt or sugar whose share in most family budgets is small is likely to have a low price elasticity of demand. Hence, each family's sugar consumption will decline only slightly as a result of the 10-cent price hike. The resulting increase in each family's annual expenditures on sugar—roughly $10—is scarcely a noticeable burden, and surely not enough to induce many people to complain to their representatives. The same legislation, however, will raise sugar industry revenues by nearly $1 billion annually. With a sum that large at stake, it is certain that the industry will lobby vigorously in its favor.

Why don't citizens vote against those legislators who support such bills? One reason is the problem of rational ignorance, discussed in Chapter 12, *The Economics of Information.* Most voters have no idea that a price support bill for sugar and other special-interest bills even exist, much less how individual legislators vote on them. If all voters became well-informed about such bills, the resulting increase in the quality of legislation might well be sufficient to compensate each voter for the cost of becoming informed. But because of the free-rider problem, each voter knows that the outcome of votes in Congress will not be much affected by whether he or she becomes well-informed.

Still other sources of inefficiency arise even in the case of projects whose benefits exceed their costs. In the 1980s, for example, the federal government announced its decision to build a $25 billion high-energy physics research facility (the "superconducting supercollider"), which ignited an intense competition among more than 20 states vying to be chosen as the site for this facility. Hundreds of millions of dollars were spent on proposal preparation, consultants' fees, and various other lobbying activities. Such investments are known as **rent-seeking,** and they tend to be inefficient for the same reason that investments by contestants in other positional arms races are inefficient (see Chapter 11, *Externalities, Property Rights, and the Environment*).

rent-seeking the socially unproductive efforts of people or firms to win a prize

Efforts devoted to rent-seeking are socially unproductive because of the simple incentive problem illustrated in the following example.

EXAMPLE 14.6   Incentives

Why would anyone pay $50 for a $20 bill?

Suppose a $20 bill is to be auctioned off to the highest bidder. The rules of this particular auction require an initial bid of at least 50 cents, and succeeding bids must exceed the previous high bid by at least 50 cents. When the bidding ceases, both the highest bidder and the second-highest bidder must give the amounts they bid to the auctioneer. The highest bidder then receives the $20, and the second-highest bidder gets nothing. For example, if the highest bid is $11 and the second-highest bid is $10.50, the winner earns a net payment of $20 − $11 = $9, and the runner-up loses $10.50. How high will the winning bid be, on average?

Auctions like this one have been extensively studied in the laboratory. And although subjects in these experiments have ranged from business executives to college undergraduates, the pattern of bidding is almost always the same. Following the opening bid, offers proceed quickly to $10, or half the amount being auctioned. A pause then occurs as the subjects appear to digest the fact that with the next bid the sum of the two highest bids will exceed $20, thus taking the auctioneer off the hook. At this point, the second-highest bidder, whose bid stands at $9.50, invariably offers $10.50, apparently preferring a shot at winning $9.50 to a sure loss of $9.50.

In most cases, all but the top two bidders drop out at this point, and the top two quickly escalate their bids. As the bidding approaches $20, a second pause occurs, this time as the bidders appear to recognize that even the highest bidder is likely to come out behind. The second-highest bidder, at $19.50, is understandably reluctant to offer $20.50. But consider the alternative. If he drops out, he will lose $19.50 for sure. But if he offers $20.50 and wins, he will lose only 50 cents. So as long as he thinks there is even a small chance that the other bidder will drop out, it makes sense to continue. Once the $20 threshold has been crossed, the pace of the bidding quickens again, and from then on it is a war of nerves between the two remaining bidders. It is common for the bidding to reach $50 before someone finally yields in frustration.

One might be tempted to think that any intelligent, well-informed person would know better than to become involved in an auction whose incentives so strongly favor costly escalation. But many of the subjects in these auctions have been experienced business professionals; many others have had formal training in the theory of games and strategic interaction. For example, psychologist Max Bazerman reports that during one 10-year period, he earned more than $17,000 by auctioning $20 bills to his MBA students at Northwestern University's Kellogg Graduate School of Management, which is consistently among the top-rated MBA programs in the world. In the course of almost 200 of his auctions, the top two bids never totaled less than $39, and in one instance they totaled $407.

The incentives that confront participants in the $20 bill auction are strikingly similar to those that confront companies that are vying for lucrative government contracts. Consider the following example.

EXAMPLE 14.7   Bidding for an Exclusive License

How much will cable companies bid for an exclusive license?

The State of Wyoming has announced its intention to grant an exclusive license to provide cable TV and Internet services within its borders. Two firms have met the deadline for applying for this license. The franchise lasts for exactly one year, during which time the franchisee can expect to make an economic profit of $20 million. The state legislature will choose the applicant that spends the most money lobbying legislators. If the applicants cannot collude, how much will each spend on lobbying?

If both spend the same, each will have a 50-50 chance at the $20 million prize, which means an expected profit of $10 million minus the amount spent lobbying. If the lobbyists could collude, each would agree to spend the same small, token amount on lobbying. But in the absence of a binding agreement, each will be strongly tempted to try to outspend the other. Once each firm's spending reaches $10 million, each will have an expected profit of zero (a 50-50 chance to earn $20 million, minus the $10 million spent on lobbying).

Further bidding would guarantee an expected loss. And yet, if one firm spent $10,000,001 while the other stayed at $10 million, the first firm would get the franchise for sure and earn an economic profit of $9,999,999. The other firm would have an economic loss of $10 million. Rather than face a sure loss of $10 million, it may be tempted to bid $10,000,002. But then, of course, its rival would face a similar incentive to respond to that bid. No matter where the escalation stops, it is sure to dissipate much of the gains that could have been had from the project. And perhaps, as in the $20 bill auction, the total amount dissipated will be even more than the value of the franchise itself.

From the individual perspective, it's easy to see why firms might lobby in this fashion for a chance to win government benefits. From society's perspective, however, this activity is almost purely wasteful. Lobbyists are typically intelligent, well-educated, and socially skilled. The opportunity cost of their time is high. If they were not lobbying government officials on behalf of their clients, they could be producing other goods or services of value. Governments can discourage such waste by selecting contractors not according to the amount they spend lobbying but on the basis of the price they promise to charge for their services. Society will be more successful the more its institutions encourage citizens to pursue activities that create wealth rather than activities that merely transfer existing wealth from one person or company to another.

Starve the Government?

Nobel laureate Milton Friedman said that no bureaucrat spends taxpayers' money as carefully as those taxpayers themselves would have. And indeed, there can be little doubt that many government expenditures are wasteful. Beyond the fact that logrolling often results in pork barrel programs that would not satisfy the cost-benefit test, we must worry that government employees may not always face strong incentives to get the most for what they spend. The Pentagon, for example, once purchased a coffeemaker for $7,600 and on another occasion paid $600 for a toilet seat. Such expenditures may have been aberrations, but there seems little doubt that private contractors often deliver comparable services at substantially lower costs than their public counterparts.

In their understandable outrage over government waste, many critics have urged major cutbacks in the volume of public goods and services. These critics reason that if we let the government spend more money, there will be more waste. This is true, of course, but only in the trivial sense that there would be more of *everything* the government does—good and bad—if public spending were higher.

One of our most extensive experiences with the consequences of major reductions in government spending comes from the Proposition 13 movement in California. This movement began with the passage of State Proposition 13 in 1978, which mandated large reductions in property taxes. As Californians have belatedly recognized, this remedy for government waste is like trying to starve a tapeworm by not eating. Fasting does harm the tapeworm, sure enough, but it harms the host even more. Residents of the Golden State, who once proudly sent their children to the nation's best schools, are now sending them to some of its worst.

The physician treats an infected patient by prescribing drugs that are toxic to the parasite but not to the host. A similar strategy should guide our attack on government waste. For example, we might consider the adoption of campaign-finance reform laws that would prevent legislators from accepting campaign contributions from the tobacco industry and other special interests whose government subsidies they support.

The question, then, isn't whether bureaucrats know best how to spend our money. Rather, it's "How much of our money do *we* want to spend on public services?" Although we must remain vigilant against government waste, we also must remember that many public services deliver good value for our money.

RECAP ↑

SOURCES OF INEFFICIENCY IN THE POLITICAL PROCESS

Government does much to help the economy function more efficiently, but it also can be a source of waste. For example, legislators may support pork barrel projects, which do not satisfy the cost-benefit criterion but which benefit constituents by more than their share of the extra taxes required to pay for the projects.

Rent-seeking, a second important source of inefficiency, occurs when individuals or firms use real resources in an effort to win favors from the government. Voters often fail to discipline legislators who abet rent-seeking because the free-rider problem gives rise to rational ignorance on the part of many voters.

Concern about government waste has led many to conclude that the best government is necessarily the smallest one. The solution favored by these critics is to starve government by reducing the amount of money it can collect in taxes. Yet starving the government reduces one kind of waste only to increase another by curtailing public services whose benefit exceeds their cost.

WHAT SHOULD WE TAX?

Although the primary purpose of the tax system is to generate the revenue needed to fund public goods and other government expenditures, taxes also have many other consequences, some intended, others not. For example, taxes alter the relative costs and benefits of engaging in different activities. They also affect the distribution of real purchasing power in the economy. The best tax system is one that raises the needed revenues while at the same time having the most beneficial, or least deleterious, side effects.

On the first criterion, the federal tax system has not performed particularly well. Although the federal budget began to show a modest surplus in the late 1990s, until then it had been in continuous deficit since 1969, during which time the federal government had to borrow trillions of dollars to pay its bills. And now, in the early decades of the twenty-first century, the federal budget is again in deficit.

crowding out the tendency of increased government deficits to reduce investment spending

The fact that governments and private corporations borrow money in the same capital market explains the phenomenon economists call **crowding out.** When government increases its demand in the market for borrowed funds, interest rates rise, causing firms to cancel some of their planned investment projects. When the government fails to raise enough revenue from taxes to cover the amount it spends on public goods and services, it thus diverts funds from investments that would have helped the economy grow.

What about the effect of taxes on incentives? Taxes will hold production and consumption below socially optimal levels in markets in which the private costs and benefits coincide exactly with all relevant social costs and benefits. Suppose, for example, that the long-run private marginal cost of producing cars is $20,000 per unit and that the demand curve for cars is as shown in Figure 14.5. The equilibrium quantity and price will be 6 million per year and $20,000, respectively. If no externalities accompany the production or consumption of cars, these will be the socially optimal levels for quantity and price.

But if we now add a tax of $2,000 per car, the new equilibrium price and quantity will be $22,000 and 4 million, respectively. The loss in economic surplus will be equal to the area of the blue triangle ($2 billion per year), which is the cumulative sum of the differences between what excluded buyers would have been willing to pay for extra cars and the marginal cost of producing those cars.

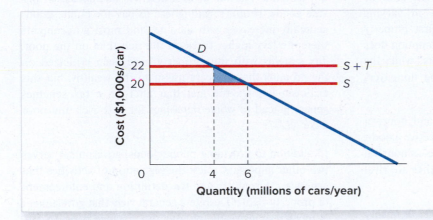

FIGURE 14.5

The Loss in Surplus from a Tax on Cars.

If the supply and demand curves for cars embody all relevant cost benefits of producing and consuming cars, then placing a tax on cars will lead to underproduction of them and a corresponding reduction in economic surplus.

Economists who write for the popular press have long focused on the loss in surplus caused by taxes like the one shown in Figure 14.5. These economists argue that the economy would perform better if taxes were lower and total government expenditures were smaller.

But arguments for that claim are far from compelling. For example, even if a tax in a market like the one shown in Figure 14.5 did produce a loss in surplus for participants in that market, it might nonetheless be justified if it led to an even larger gain in surplus from the public expenditures it financed. The deadweight loss from taxing that good (or activity) will be greater for goods whose supply and demand curves are more elastic. This principle suggests that deadweight losses could be minimized by concentrating taxes on goods with highly inelastic supply or demand curves.

Another difficulty with the argument that taxes harm the economy is more fundamental—namely, that taxes need not cause any loss in surplus at all, even in the markets in which they are directly applied. Suppose, for example, that in the market for cars considered earlier, private marginal cost is again $20,000 but that the production and use of cars now generates air pollution and congestion, negative externalities that sum to $2,000 per car each year. The socially optimal quantity of cars would then be not 6 million per year but only 4 million (see Figure 14.5). Without a tax on cars, the market would reach equilibrium at a price of $20,000 and a quantity of 6 million per year. But with a tax of $2,000 per car, the equilibrium quantity would shrink to 4 million per year, precisely the socially optimal number. Here, the direct effect of the tax is not only *not* to reduce total economic surplus but actually to augment it by $2 billion per year.

Could we raise enough tax revenue to run the government if we limited ourselves to taxing only those activities that generate negative externalities? No one knows for sure, but it might be possible, for the list of such activities is a long one.

For instance, when someone enters a congested freeway, he creates additional delays for the motorists already there. Existing technology would enable us to levy road-use taxes that reflect these congestion externalities. Each time fossil fuels are burned, they emit greenhouse gases into the atmosphere, which will accelerate the trend toward global warming. A tax on carbon would increase economic surplus by causing decision makers to take this external cost into account. Taxes on other forms of air and water pollution would have similarly benign effects on resource allocation. Recent experience with refundable taxes on food and beverage containers demonstrates that taxes like these can raise needed revenue while at the same time contributing to a cleaner environment.

SUMMARY

- Our aim in this chapter was to apply principles of microeconomics to the study of the government's role in modern society. One of government's principal tasks is to provide public goods such as national defense and the criminal justice system. Such goods are, in varying degrees, nonrival and nonexcludable. The first property describes goods for which one person's consumption does not diminish the amount available for others, while the second refers to the difficulty of preventing nonpayers from consuming certain goods. *(LO1)*

- Goods that are both highly nonexcludable and nonrival are often called pure public goods. A collective good—such as a subscription video streaming service—is nonrival but excludable. Commons goods are goods that are rival but nonexcludable. *(LO1)*

- The criterion for providing the optimal quantity or quality of a public good is to keep increasing quantity or quality as long as the marginal benefit of doing so exceeds the marginal cost. One advantage of using the government to provide public goods is that once a tax collection agency has been established to finance a single public good, it can be expanded at relatively low cost to generate revenue to finance additional public goods. A second advantage is that because government has the power to tax, it can easily assign responsibility for the cost of a public good. And in the case of goods for which nonpayers simply cannot be excluded, the government may be the only feasible provider. *(LO2)*

- One disadvantage to exclusive reliance on government for public goods provision is the element of coercion inherent in the tax system, which makes some people pay for public goods they don't want, while others do without public goods they do want. Many public goods are provided through private channels, with the necessary funding provided by donations, by sale of by-products, by development of new means to exclude nonpayers, and in many cases by private contract. A loss in surplus results, however, whenever monetary charges are levied for the consumption of a nonrival good. *(LO2)*

- Because not everyone benefits equally from the provision of any given public good, charging all taxpayers equal amounts for the provision of public goods will generally not be either feasible or desirable. As in the case of private goods, people's willingness to pay for public goods generally increases with income, and most governments therefore levy higher taxes on the rich than on the poor. Tax systems with this property have been criticized on the grounds that they are unfair to the wealthy, but this criticism ignores the fact that alternative tax schemes generally lead to worse outcomes for both rich and poor alike. *(LO2)*

- In addition to providing public goods, government serves two other important roles: the regulation of activities that generate externalities and the definition and enforcement of property rights. Despite a general view that government is more responsive the shorter the distance between citizens and their elected representatives, factors such as economies of scale in the provision of public goods and externalities with broad reach often dictate the assignment of important functions to state or national governments. *(LO3)*

- Although history has shown that democracy is the best form of government, it is far from perfect. For example, practices such as logrolling and rent-seeking, common in most democracies, often result in the adoption of laws and public projects whose costs exceed their benefits. *(LO3)*

- To finance public goods and services, governments at all levels must tax. But a tax on any activity not only generates revenue; it also creates an incentive to reduce the activity. If the activity would have been pursued at the optimal level in the absence of a tax, taxing it will result in too little of the activity. This observation has led many critics to denounce all taxes as harmful to the economy. Yet the negative effects of taxes on incentives must be weighed against the benefits of the public goods and services financed by tax revenue. *(LO4)*

KEY TERMS

collective good	nonrival good	pure commons good
crowding out	pork barrel spending	pure private good
head tax	progressive tax	pure public good
logrolling	proportional income tax	regressive tax
nonexcludable good	public good	rent-seeking

REVIEW QUESTIONS

1. Answer the following questions related to these goods: apples, Stephen King novels, street lighting on campus, and NPR radio broadcasts. *(LO1)*
   a. Which of these goods are nonrival?
   b. Which of these goods are nonexcludable?

2. Give examples of goods that are, for the most part: *(LO1)*
   a. Rival but nonexcludable.
   b. Nonrival but excludable.
   c. Both nonrival and nonexcludable.

3. Why might even a wealthy person prefer a proportional income tax to a head tax? *(LO1)*

4. True or false: A tax on an activity that generates negative externalities will improve resource allocation in the private sector and also generate revenue that could be used to pay for useful public goods. Explain. *(LO3)*

5. Consider a good that would be provided efficiently by private market forces. Why is the direct loss in surplus that would result from a tax on this good an overstatement of the loss in surplus caused by the tax? *(LO2, LO4)*

PROBLEMS

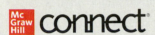

1. Two consumers, Smith and Jones, have the following demand curves for Podunk Public Radio broadcasts of recorded opera on Saturdays:

   $$\text{Smith: } P_S = 12 - Q$$
   $$\text{Jones: } P_J = 12 - 2Q,$$

   where P_S and P_J represent marginal willingness-to-pay values for Smith and Jones, respectively, and Q represents the number of hours of opera broadcast each Saturday. *(LO2)*
   a. If Smith and Jones are the only public radio listeners in Podunk, construct the demand curve for opera broadcasts.
   b. If the marginal cost of opera broadcasts is $15 per hour, what is the socially optimal number of hours of broadcast opera?

2. Suppose the demand curves for *NFL Sunday Night Football* and *Masterpiece* are as shown in the following diagram. A television network is considering whether to add one or both programs to its upcoming fall lineup. The only two time slots remaining are sponsored by Colgate, which is under contract to pay the network 10 cents for each viewer who watches the program, out of which the network would have to cover its production costs of $400,000 per episode. (Viewership can be estimated accurately with telephone surveys.) Any time slot the network does not fill with the *NFL Sunday Night Football* or *Masterpiece* will be filled by infomercials for a weight-loss program, for which the network incurs no production costs and for which it receives a fee of $500,000. Viewers will receive $5 million in economic surplus from watching each installment of the infomercial. *(LO2)*
   a. How will the network fill the two remaining slots in its fall lineup?
   b. Is this outcome socially efficient?
   c. By how much would total economic surplus be higher if each episode of *Masterpiece* were shown on PBS free of charge than if it were shown by a profit-maximizing video streaming service that charged consumers a fixed fee to watch each episode?

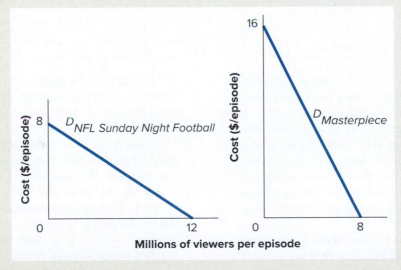

3. When a video streaming company chooses a subscription scheme to pay for programming, which of the following statements is true? Explain. *(LO2)*

   a. The outcome is socially efficient.

   b. The programs selected will maximize advertising revenue.

   c. The marginal cost to an additional viewer of watching the programs is lower than when advertising is used to finance programming.

   d. The outcome is always more socially efficient than when advertising is used to finance programming.

   e. The variety of programs provided is likely to rise.

4. When a group of people must decide whether to buy a shared public good or service, the free-rider problem frequently occurs because: *(LO2)*

   a. People have an incentive to understate how much the facility is really worth to them if they have to pay taxes to finance it.

   b. Each individual's needed contribution is an insignificant amount of the total required.

   c. People have an incentive to overstate how much the facility is worth to them if they don't have to pay taxes to finance it.

   d. People hope that others will value the facility enough to pay for it entirely.

   e. Only one of the above statements is not a reason for the existence of the free-rider problem.

5. The town of Smallsville is considering building a museum. The interest on the money Smallsville will have to borrow to build the museum will be $1,000 per year. Each citizen's marginal benefit from the museum is shown in the following table, and this marginal benefit schedule is public information. *(LO2, LO3)*

Citizen	Marginal benefit from museum ($/year)
Anita	340
Brandon	290
Carlena	240
Dallas	190
Eloise	140

   a. Assuming each citizen voted his or her private interests, would a referendum to build the museum and raise each citizen's annual taxes by $200 pass?

   b. A citizen proposes that the city let a private company build the museum and charge the citizens a lump-sum fee each year to view it as much as they like. Only citizens who paid the fee would be allowed to view the museum. If the private company were allowed to set a single fee, would any company offer to build the museum?

   c. A second citizen proposes allowing the private company to charge different prices to different citizens

and auctioning the right to build the museum to the highest-bidding company. Again, only the citizens who pay the fee may view the museum. What is the highest bid a private company would make to supply the museum to Smallsville?

6. Jack and Jill are the only two residents in a neighborhood, and they would like to hire a security guard. The value of a security guard is $50 per month to Jack and $150 per month to Jill. Irrespective of who pays the guard, the guard will protect the entire neighborhood. *(LO2)*

   a. What is the most a guard can charge per month and still be assured of being hired by at least one of them?

   b. Suppose the competitive wage for a security guard is $120 per month. The local government proposes a plan whereby Jack and Jill each pay 50 percent of this monthly fee and asks them to vote on this plan. Will the plan be voted in? Would economic surplus be higher if the neighborhood had a guard?

7. Refer to Problem 6. Suppose Jack earns $1,000 per month and Jill earns $11,000 per month. *(LO1, LO2)*

   a. Suggest a proportional tax on income that would be accepted by majority vote and would pay for the security guard.

   b. Suppose instead that Jack proposes a tax scheme under which Jack and Jill would each receive the same net benefit from hiring the guard. How much would Jack and Jill pay now? Would Jill agree to this scheme?

   c. What is the practical problem that prevents ideas like the one in part b from working in real-life situations?

8. The following table shows all the marginal benefits for each voter in a small town whose town council is considering a new swimming pool with capacity for at least three citizens. The cost of the pool would be $18 per week and would not depend on the number of people who actually used it. *(LO2, LO3)*

Voter	Marginal benefit ($/week)
A	12
B	5
C	2

   a. If the pool must be financed by a weekly head tax levied on all voters, will the pool be approved by majority vote? Is this outcome socially efficient? Explain.

   b. The town council instead decides to auction a franchise off to a private monopoly to build and maintain the pool. If it cannot find such a firm willing to operate the pool, then the pool project will be scrapped. If all such monopolies are constrained by law to charge a single price to users, will the franchise be sold, and if so, how much will it sell for? Is this outcome socially efficient? Explain.

c. Suppose now that all such monopolies can perfectly price-discriminate. Will the franchise be sold, and if so, how much will it sell for? Is this outcome socially efficient? Explain.

d. The town council decides that, rather than auction off the franchise, it will give it away to the firm that spends the most money lobbying council members. If there are four identical firms in the bidding and they cannot collude, what will happen?

ANSWERS TO SELF-TESTS

14.1 a. The BLS website at 3 in the morning has the capacity to serve far more users than it attracts, so an additional user calling up the site does not prevent some other user from doing so. Other websites, however, do not show the nonrival property, at least during certain hours, because they attract more users than their servers can accommodate. *(LO1)*

b. The stadium at the championship game is always full, so anyone who watches the game in person prevents someone else from doing so.

c. Additional people can watch the game on television without diminishing the availability of the telecast for others.

14.2 To construct the demand curve (a), we first graph Bill's demand curve (c) and Tom's demand curve (b) and then add the two individual demand curves vertically. The equation for the demand curve is $P = 18 - 1.5 Q$. *(LO2)*

14.3 The \$12 monthly fee now excludes 60 million viewers, and the resulting loss in surplus (again the area of the blue triangle) is now \$360 million. *(LO2)*

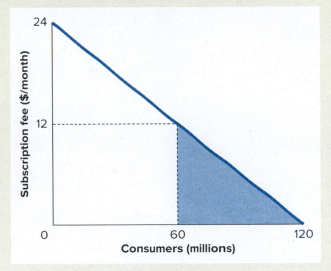

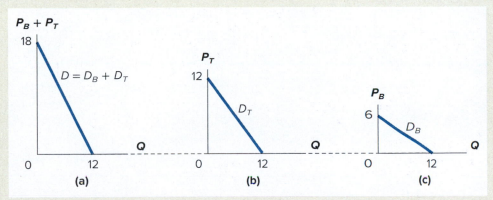

14.4 If Sven orders bread pudding, his share of the bill would now go up by \$2 instead of \$1. If he orders chocolate mousse, his share of the bill would go up by \$1.20 instead of \$0.60. So he would still order the bread pudding (surplus = \$4 − \$2 = \$2) rather than the chocolate mousse (surplus = \$3 − \$1.20 − \$1.80). *(LO3)*

CHAPTER 15

International Trade and Trade Policy

Will Austin/Spaces Images/Blend Images

Who gains and who loses when an economy opens up to trade?

LEARNING OBJECTIVES

After reading this chapter, you should be able to:

LO1 Explain and apply the concept of comparative advantage as a basis for trade.

LO2 Contrast the production and consumption opportunities in a closed economy with that of an open economy using a production possibilities curve.

LO3 Explain how the price of a tradable good is set in a closed versus an open economy, how the quantities of imports or exports are determined, and discuss who are the winners and losers from trade.

LO4 Illustrate why trade is often politically controversial, even though it promises to increase total income.

O n April 13, 1861, Southern troops fired on Fort Sumter in Charleston harbor, initiating the American Civil War. Less than a week later, on April 19, President Lincoln proclaimed a naval blockade of the South. Code-named the Anaconda Plan (after the snake that squeezes its prey to death), the blockade required the Union navy to patrol the Southern coastline, stopping and boarding ships that were attempting to land or depart. The object of the blockade was to prevent the Confederacy from shipping cotton to Europe, where it could be traded for military equipment, clothing, foodstuffs, and other supplies.

Historians are divided on the effectiveness of the Union blockade in choking off Confederate trade. In the early years of the war, the North had too few ships to cover the 3,600-mile Southern coastline, so "running" the blockade was not difficult. But in the latter part of the war the number of Union ships enforcing the blockade increased from about 90 to more than 600, and sailing ships were replaced with faster, more lethal iron-clad vessels. Still, private blockade runners attempted to elude the Union navy in small, fast ships. Because the price of raw cotton in Great Britain was between 10 and 20 times what it was in the Confederacy (a differential that indicated disruption in the normal flow of trade), blockade runners enjoyed huge profits when they were successful. But despite their efforts, by 1864 the Southern war effort was seriously hampered by a lack of military equipment and supplies, at least in part as a result of the blockade.

The use of a naval blockade as a weapon of war highlights a paradox in contemporary attitudes toward trade between nations. Presumably, an attempt by a foreign power to blockade U.S. ports would today be considered a hostile act that would elicit a strong response from the U.S. government. Yet one often hears politicians and others arguing that trade with other nations is harmful to the United States and should be restricted—in effect, that the United States should blockade its own ports! In the U.S. presidential elections of 2016, for example, both presidential candidates opposed the Trans-Pacific Partnership (TPP)—an agreement intended to increase trade between Australia, Canada, Japan, Mexico, the United States and seven other, smaller economies—on the grounds that it would cost American jobs. As another example, politicians from both the Republican and Democratic Parties occasionally complain about China's exports to the United States. Some of them propose taking action against the Chinese government because, they say, it engages in unfair policies that cause Chinese products to sell in the U.S. for prices that are too *cheap*. So is trade a good thing or not? And if it is, why does it sometimes face determined opposition?

This chapter addresses international trade and its effects on the broader economy. We will begin by reviewing the idea of *comparative advantage*, which was introduced in Chapter 2, *Comparative Advantage*. We will show that everyone can enjoy more goods and services if nations specialize in those products in which they have a comparative advantage, and then trade freely among themselves. Furthermore, if trade is unrestricted, market forces will ensure that countries produce those goods in which they have a comparative advantage.

Having shown the potential benefits of trade, we will turn next to the reasons for opposition to trade. Although opening the economy to trade *can,* in our model, increase economic welfare overall, some groups—such as workers in industries that face competition from foreign producers—may in reality be made worse off. The fact that open trade may hurt some groups creates political pressure to enact measures restricting trade, such as taxes on imported goods (called tariffs) and limits on imports (called quotas). We will analyze the effects of these trade restrictions, along with other ways of responding to concerns about affected industries and workers through direct assistance programs.

Economists understand the frustrations with trade expressed by some groups. Indeed, economists recognize that for a displaced worker who does not expect effective direct government assistance to materialize—for example, because the worker does not expect the government to pass, implement, and sustain the relevant measures—opposing trade may appear a reasonable course of action. However, from an economic point of view that takes into account both the overall size of the economic pie and how it is distributed, providing direct assistance to those who are hurt by increased trade is preferable to blocking or restricting trade.

COMPARATIVE ADVANTAGE AS A BASIS FOR TRADE

Chapter 2, *Comparative Advantage,* began with the story of the Nepalese cook Birkhaman, a remarkable jack-of-all-trades who could do everything, from butchering a goat to fixing an alarm clock. Yet despite his range of skills, Birkhaman, like most Nepalese, was quite poor. The reason for Birkhaman's poverty, as we saw in Chapter 2, was precisely his versatility. Because he did so many different things, he could not hope to become as productive in each separate activity as someone who specialized entirely in that activity.

The alternative to a nation of Birkhamans is a country in which each person specializes in the activity at which he or she is relatively most efficient, or has a *comparative advantage*. This specialization, combined with trade between producers of different goods and services, allows a society to achieve a higher level of productivity and standard of living than one in which each person is essentially self-sufficient.

This insight, that specialization and trade among individuals can yield impressive gains in productivity, applies equally well to nations. Factors such as climate, natural resources, technology, workers' skills and education, and culture provide countries with comparative advantages in the production of different goods and services. For example, as we saw in Chapter 2, the large number of leading research universities in the United States gives that nation a comparative advantage in the design of technologically sophisticated computer and mobile hardware and software. Likewise, the wide international use of the English language endows the United States with a comparative advantage in producing popular films and TV shows. Similarly, France's climate and topography, together with the accumulated knowledge of generations of vintners, provides that country a comparative advantage in producing fine wines, while Australia's huge expanses of arable land give that country a comparative advantage in producing grain.

The Principle of Comparative Advantage tells us that we can all enjoy more goods and services when each country produces according to its comparative advantage, and then trades with other countries. In the next section we explore this fundamental idea in greater detail.

Climate and long experience give France a comparative advantage in producing fine wines.

PRODUCTION AND CONSUMPTION POSSIBILITIES AND THE BENEFITS OF TRADE

In this section we will consider how international trade benefits an individual country. To do so, we will contrast the production and consumption opportunities in a **closed economy**—one that does not trade with the rest of the world—with the opportunities in an **open economy**—one that does trade with other economies. Because we will make use of the production possibilities curve, which was introduced in Chapter 2, *Comparative Advantage,* we will begin by briefly reviewing that concept. We will look first at the PPC for a two-person economy and then at the PPC for a many-person economy. After reviewing the PPC, we will see how a country's production possibilities are related to its citizens' ability to consume in a closed economy versus an open economy.

closed economy an economy that does not trade with the rest of the world

open economy an economy that trades with other countries

THE TWO-WORKER PRODUCTION POSSIBILITIES CURVE

Recall that (for a two-good economy) the production possibilities curve (PPC) is a graph that shows the maximum amount of each good that can be produced, at every possible level of production of the other good.[1] To see how the PPC is constructed, let's consider a hypothetical economy, which we'll call Costa Rica, which has only two workers, Carlos and Maria. Each of these two workers can produce two goods, coffee and computers.

---

[1]For a many-good economy, the PPC shows the maximum amount of each good that can be produced at any level of production of all the other goods. Focusing on the two-good case allows us to draw the figures on the two-dimensional page. Our conclusions apply to the many-good case, however.

| EXAMPLE 15.1 | The PPC for a Two-Worker Economy |

What is the PPC for a two-worker economy?

Two Costa Rican workers, Carlos and Maria, can each produce coffee and computers. Carlos can produce either 100 pounds of coffee or 1 computer per week. Maria can produce either 100 pounds of coffee or 2 computers per week. Both Carlos and Maria work 50 weeks per year. Find the production possibilities curve for Costa Rica.

To construct the PPC for this two-person economy, we ask first how much coffee Costa Rica could produce if both Carlos and Maria worked full time producing coffee. Between them they can produce 200 pounds of coffee per week, so in 50 weeks they could produce 10,000 pounds of coffee. Thus if we plot coffee production on the vertical axis of the graph of Costa Rica's PPC, the vertical intercept of the PPC will be 10,000 pounds of coffee per year (point A in Figure 15.1). Likewise, if Carlos and Maria produced only computers, between them they could produce 3 computers per week, or 150 computers per year. So the horizontal intercept of Costa Rica's PPC is 150 computers per year (point B in Figure 15.1).

FIGURE 15.1

Production Possibilities Curve for a Two-Worker Economy.

In the portion of the PPC between points A and C, only Maria is producing computers, so the slope of the PPC in that range reflects Maria's opportunity cost of computers in terms of coffee production forgone. At point C, Maria spends all her time on computers and Carlos spends all his time on coffee. Between points C and B, any additional computers must be produced by Carlos. Thus between points C and B the slope of the PPC reflects Carlos's opportunity cost of producing computers, in terms of coffee production forgone.

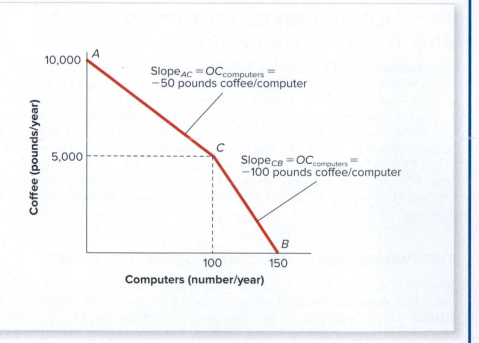

$$\text{Slope}_{AC} = OC_{computers} = -50 \text{ pounds coffee/computer}$$

$$\text{Slope}_{CB} = OC_{computers} = -100 \text{ pounds coffee/computer}$$

We have found where the Costa Rican PPC intersects the two axes of the graph. To find the rest of the PPC, imagine that Carlos and Maria are producing only coffee (point A in Figure 15.1), when they decide that they would like to have some computers as well. In this situation, which worker should switch from producing coffee to producing computers?

To answer this question, we need to find the one with a *comparative advantage* in producing computers. To do this we must calculate opportunity costs. Carlos can produce either 100 pounds of coffee or 1 computer per week. Because producing a computer leaves him one week less to devote to coffee production, which reduces his coffee output by 100 pounds, Carlos's opportunity cost of producing 1 computer is 100 pounds of coffee. Maria can produce either 100 pounds of coffee or 2 computers per week, so her opportunity cost of producing a computer is 100/2, or 50 pounds of coffee. Because Maria's opportunity cost of producing a computer is lower than Carlos's, she has a comparative advantage in producing computers. By the principle of comparative advantage, Maria should be the one to specialize in computer production. For his part, Carlos has a comparative advantage in producing coffee (see Self-Test 15.1), so he should specialize in coffee.

Starting from point A in Figure 15.1, where only coffee is produced, we can imagine that Maria begins to produce increasing numbers of computers. The slope of the line emanating from point A equals Maria's opportunity cost of producing a computer, $OC_{computers}$, where cost is measured as a negative quantity:

$$\text{Slope} = \text{Maria's } OC_{computers} = \frac{\text{loss in coffee}}{\text{gain in computers}}$$

$$= \frac{-100 \text{ pounds of coffee/week}}{2 \text{ computers/week}} = -50 \text{ pounds of coffee/computer.}$$

As Maria increases the share of her time devoted to computer production, we move down along the straight line from point A in Figure 15.1. The slope of the PPC is constant in this region at −50 pounds of coffee per computer, Maria's opportunity cost of computers.

Maria's time is limited to 50 weeks per year, however, so if she keeps increasing her computer production, she will eventually reach a point at which she produces only computers and no coffee. At that point annual production by the two workers taken together will be 100 computers (produced by Maria) and 5,000 pounds of coffee (produced by Carlos, who spends all his time producing coffee). This combination of production is shown at point C on the production possibilities curve.

Once Maria's time is fully devoted to making computers, Costa Rica can increase its computer production only if Carlos begins to build some computers, too. However, Carlos's opportunity cost, measured as pounds of coffee forgone per computer produced, is greater than Maria's. Hence at point C the slope of the PPC changes, creating a "kink" in the graph. The slope of the PPC to the right of point C is given by:

$$\text{Slope} = \text{Carlos's } OC_{computers} = \frac{\text{loss in coffee}}{\text{gain in computers}}$$

$$= \frac{-100 \text{ pounds of coffee/week}}{1 \text{ computer/week}} = -100 \text{ pounds of coffee/computer.}$$

Note that the slope of the PPC to the right of point C is more negative than the slope to the left of point C, so that the PPC declines more sharply to the right of that point. The fact that the opportunity cost of a computer increases as more computers are produced (the Principle of Increasing Opportunity Cost) implies the outwardly bowed shape that is characteristic of a production possibilities curve, as shown in Figure 15.1.

Increasing Opportunity Cost

 SELF-TEST 15.1

Example 15.1 showed that Maria has a comparative advantage in producing computers. Show by comparison of opportunity costs that Carlos has a comparative advantage in producing coffee.

THE MANY-WORKER PRODUCTION POSSIBILITIES CURVE

Although the economy considered in Example 15.1 included only two workers, the main ideas apply to economies with more workers. Suppose, for example, that we added a third Costa Rican worker, Pedro, whose opportunity cost of producing computers is higher than Maria's but lower than Carlos's. The production possibilities curve for this three-person economy would look something like Figure 15.2. Between points *A* and *C* on the PPC shown in Figure 15.2, all computers are produced by Maria, who has the greatest comparative advantage in computer production. Thus the slope of the PPC between points *A* and *C* is determined by Maria's opportunity cost, measured as the amount of coffee production forgone for each additional computer produced.

> **Increasing Opportunity Cost** »

At point *C* Maria is dedicating all her time to computer production, so someone else must produce any additional computers. Pedro has the next lowest opportunity cost of producing computers, so (following the Principle of Increasing Opportunity Cost) he begins to produce computers at point *C*. The slope of the PPC between points *C* and *D* is determined by Pedro's opportunity cost, which is greater (more negative) than Maria's opportunity cost. At point *D* in Figure 15.2, Pedro is producing all the computers he can, so finally Carlos begins to produce computers as well. Thus the slope of the PPC between points *D* and *B* reflects Carlos's opportunity cost. Because opportunity cost increases as we move from left to right in the figure, the slope of the PPC becomes more and more negative, leading once again to the outwardly bowed shape.

By similar logic, we can construct a case in which there are many workers, perhaps millions. With many workers, the part of the nation's PPC that is associated with each individual worker becomes very small. As a result, the PPC for an economy with many

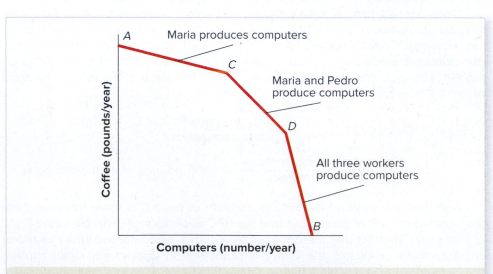

FIGURE 15.2

Production Possibilities Curve for a Three-Worker Economy.

The PPC for a three-person economy has two "kinks," at points *C* and *D*. Between points *A* and *C* only Maria produces computers, and the slope of the PPC represents her opportunity cost of producing computers. At point *C* Maria is spending all her time making computers, so any additional computers will be produced by Pedro, whose comparative advantage is the next greatest. Between points *C* and *D* the slope of the PPC is determined by Pedro's opportunity cost. At point *D* Pedro is also fully occupied producing computers, so that Carlos must begin producing them if computer production is to increase further. Between points *D* and *B* the slope of the PPC reflects Carlos's opportunity cost.

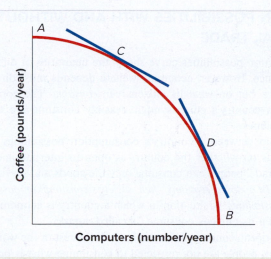

FIGURE 15.3

Production Possibilities Curve for a Many-Worker Economy.

The PPC for a many-worker economy has a smooth, outwardly bowed shape. At each point on the PPC the slope of the curve reflects the opportunity cost, in terms of coffee forgone, of producing an additional computer. For example, the opportunity cost of a computer at point *C* equals the slope of the line that just touches the PPC at that point, and the opportunity cost of a computer at point *D* equals the slope of the line that just touches the PPC there. Because the opportunity cost of producing another computer increases as more computers are produced, the slope of the PPC becomes more and more negative as we read from left to right on the graph.

workers has a smoothly bowed shape, as shown in Figure 15.3. With a smoothly curved PPC, the slope at each point still reflects the opportunity cost of producing an additional computer, as illustrated in Figure 15.3. For example, at point *C* in Figure 15.3, the opportunity cost of producing an extra computer is given by the slope of the line that just touches the PPC at that point. Because computers will be produced first by workers with the greatest comparative advantage (the lowest opportunity cost), the slope of the PPC becomes more and more sharply negative as we read from left to right in the figure.

> **RECAP**↑
>
> **PRODUCTION POSSIBILITIES CURVES**
>
> - The production possibilities curve (PPC) for a two-good economy is a graph that shows the maximum amount of one good that can be produced at every possible level of production of the other good.
> - The slope of a PPC at any point indicates the opportunity cost, in terms of forgone production of the good on the vertical axis, of increasing production of the good on the horizontal axis by one unit.
> - The more of a good that is already being produced, the greater the opportunity cost of increasing production still further. Thus the slope of the PPC becomes more and more negative as we read from left to right, imparting the characteristic outwardly bowed shape of the curve.

CONSUMPTION POSSIBILITIES WITH AND WITHOUT INTERNATIONAL TRADE

A country's production possibilities curve shows the quantities of different goods that its economy can produce. However, economic welfare depends most directly not on what a country can *produce,* but on what its citizens can *consume.* The combinations of goods and services that a country's citizens might feasibly consume are called the country's **consumption possibilities.**

consumption possibilities
the combinations of goods and services that a country's citizens might feasibly consume

The relationship between a country's consumption possibilities and its production possibilities depends on whether the country is open to international trade. In a closed economy with no trade, people can consume only the goods and services produced within their own country. *In a closed economy, then, society's consumption possibilities are identical to its production possibilities.* A situation in which a country is economically self-sufficient, producing everything its citizens consume, is called **autarky.**

autarky a situation in which a country is economically self-sufficient

The case of an open economy, which trades with the rest of the world, is quite different. In an open economy, people are not restricted to consuming what is produced in their own country, because part of what they produce can be sent abroad in exchange for other goods and services. Indeed, we will see in this section that opening an economy to trade may allow citizens to consume more of everything. Thus *in an open economy, a society's consumption possibilities are typically greater than (and will never be less than) its production possibilities.* We will illustrate this critical point with reference to the two-worker economy studied earlier in the chapter, then briefly consider the more general case of a many-worker economy.

EXAMPLE 15.2	**Costa Rica's Consumption Possibilities with Trade**

How does opening to trade affect an economy's consumption possibilities?

Two Costa Rican workers, Carlos and Maria, can produce coffee and computers as described in Example 15.1. Initially the country is closed to trade, and Maria produces only computers, while Carlos produces only coffee. Then the country opens up to trade. World prices are such that 80 pounds of coffee can be traded for 1 computer on the international market and vice versa. How does the opening of Costa Rica to trade affect Maria's and Carlos's opportunity to consume coffee and computers?

If Maria is producing only computers and Carlos is producing only coffee, then Costa Rica is at point *C* on the PPC shown in Figure 15.4 (which is the same as the PPC shown in Figure 15.1). At that point Maria is spending all her time producing 100 computers a year, and Carlos is spending all his time producing 5,000 pounds of coffee a year. If Costa Rica were closed to trade, Maria and Carlos could obtain more coffee only by producing fewer computers. Specifically, starting at point *C* on the PPC, they could obtain 50 additional pounds of coffee by giving up 1 computer—by having Maria work 1/2 week less on computers and 1/2 week more producing coffee.

If Costa Rica opens up to trade, however, then Maria and Carlos can get 80 pounds of coffee in exchange for 1 computer simply by trading computers for coffee on the international market. In other words, they can get an extra 80 pounds of coffee for each computer they give up. To illustrate the degree to which the opportunity to trade benefits Costa Rica, recall from Example 15.1 that with no trade, Maria's and Carlos's maximum coffee consumption is 10,000 pounds per year (the vertical intercept of the Costa Rican PPC). With the opportunity to trade, however, Maria can trade the 100 computers produced at point *C* for 8,000 pounds of coffee (80 pounds of coffee per computer × 100 computers). Together with the 5,000 pounds of coffee Carlos produces, the coffee obtained through trade raises Costa Rica's maximum annual coffee consumption from 10,000 to 13,000 pounds per year, as indicated by point *F* in Figure 15.4. Because trade creates the possibility for Costa Rica to consume as much as 13,000 pounds of coffee per year, point *F*

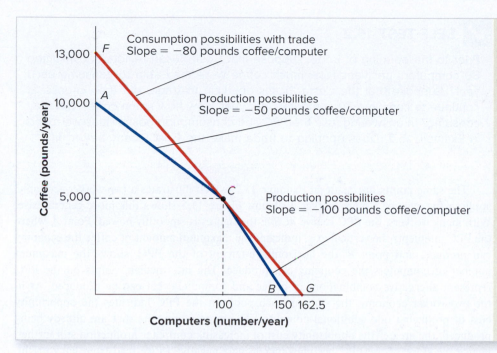

FIGURE 15.4

Costa Rica's Consumption Possibilities with Trade.

Without the opportunity to trade, Costa Rica's consumption possibilities are the same as the Costa Rican PPC, represented by line *ACB*. With the opportunity to trade, however, Costa Ricans can consume at any point along line *FG*.

is included in Costa Rica's consumption possibilities, though it would have been unattainable to the Costa Ricans before the opening up of trade.

Furthermore, with the opportunity to trade, Maria and Carlos can consume any combination of coffee and computers represented on the straight line between points *F* and *C* in Figure 15.4. This straight line has a slope of −80 pounds of coffee per 1 computer, which is the rate at which the two goods can be exchanged on the international market. So, simply by trading computers for coffee, Maria and Carlos can improve their consumption possibilities at any point except *C*, where their production and consumption possibilities are the same.

Suppose instead that, starting from point *C* on Costa Rica's PPC, Maria and Carlos decide they want to consume more computers rather than more coffee. With no ability to trade, the opportunity cost of obtaining 1 more computer at point *C* would be 100 pounds of coffee—that is, the amount of coffee that would be lost by having Carlos work 1 more week at producing an extra computer, and hence 1 week fewer at producing coffee. With trade, however, Costa Ricans can obtain an extra computer at the cost of only 80 pounds of coffee (the price of computers on the international market). In the extreme, if they wanted to consume only computers, the Costa Ricans could trade the 5,000 pounds of coffee Carlos produces at point *C* for 5,000/80 = 62.5 computers, for a total consumption (with the 100 computers Maria produces) of 162.5 computers. This maximum consumption amount is indicated by point *G* in Figure 15.4. Comparing point *G* with point *B*, we can see that the opportunity to trade increased Costa Rica's maximum consumption of computers from 150 to 162.5. (Consuming 162.5 computers a year means consuming 325 computers every two years.)

Furthermore, by trading various amounts of coffee for computers, Costa Ricans can consume any combination of computers and coffee on the straight line between points *C* and *G* in Figure 15.4. Like the segment *FC*, segment *CG* has a slope equal to −80 pounds of coffee per 1 computer, reflecting the rate at which coffee can be traded for computers on the international market. Note that since segments *FC* and *CG* have the same slopes, the line *FG* is a straight line. The line *FG* represents Costa Rica's consumption possibilities—the combinations of coffee and computers that Carlos and Maria might feasibly consume—when the Costa Rican economy is open to trade. By comparing Costa Rica's consumption possibilities without trade (line *ACB*) and with trade (line *FG*), we can see that Maria and Carlos have a wider range of consumption opportunities when their economy is open.

✓ **SELF-TEST 15.2**

Prior to the opening of trade, suppose that Costa Rican residents consumed 80 computers per year. How much coffee were they able to consume each year? Suppose that the Costa Ricans open up to trade, but they choose to continue to consume 80 computers per year. Now how much coffee can they consume? In answering, use the PPC and consumption possibilities we found in Example 15.2. Does opening to trade make the Cost Ricans better off?

The same points just made in Example 15.2, which illustrates a two-worker economy, apply in the case of a many-worker economy. Figure 15.5 shows this more general case. With many workers, the PPC (curve *ACB* in the figure) is smoothly bowed. Point *A*, where the PPC intercepts the vertical axis, indicates the maximum amount of coffee the economy can produce, and point *B*, the horizontal intercept of the PPC, shows the maximum number of computers the economy can produce. The intermediate points on the PPC represent alternative combinations of coffee and computers that can be produced. As in the two-worker economy, the slope at each point on the PPC indicates the opportunity cost of producing one additional computer. The more computers that are already being produced, the greater the opportunity cost of increasing computer production still further. Hence the slope of the PPC becomes increasingly negative as we read from left to right.

Line *FG* shows the consumption possibilities for this economy if it is open to trade. This line has two key features. First, it is drawn so that it just touches the PPC, at point *C* in Figure 15.5. Second, the slope of line *FG* is determined by the relative prices of coffee and computers on the world market. Specifically, as in the two-worker case (Figure 15.4), the slope of line *FG* tells us how much coffee must be exchanged on world markets to obtain an additional computer.

With access to international trade, Costa Rica can consume the greatest amount of both coffee and computers by producing at point *C* on the PPC and trading on the international market to obtain the desired combination of coffee and computers on line *FG*. (The exact combination of coffee and computers Cost Ricans will choose depends on the needs and wants of the population.)

Why should the Costa Ricans produce at point *C*? At point *C*, and only at that point, the slope of the PPC equals the slope of the consumption possibilities line, *FG*. Hence only

FIGURE 15.5

Consumption Possibilities in a Many-Worker Economy.

The PPC for a many-worker economy is the smooth, outwardly bowed line *ACB*. If the country is open to trade, its consumption possibilities lie on the line *FG*, which just touches the PPC at point *C*. The slope of this line equals the rate at which coffee can be traded for computers at world prices. The country maximizes its consumption possibilities by producing at point *C* and then trading so as to reach its most desired point on line *FG*.

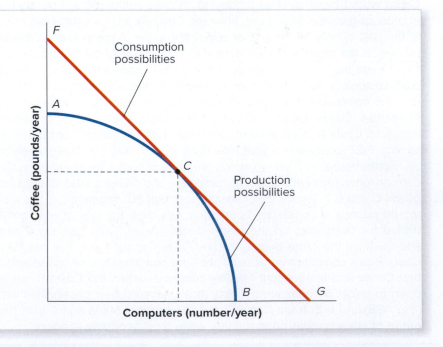

at point *C* is the opportunity cost of increasing domestic computer production equal to the opportunity cost of purchasing an extra computer on the world market. If the opportunity cost of producing a computer domestically exceeded the opportunity cost of purchasing a computer on the world market, Costa Rica would gain by reducing its computer production and importing more computers. Likewise, if the opportunity cost of producing a computer domestically were less than the opportunity cost of purchasing a computer abroad, Costa Rica would gain by increasing computer production and reducing computer imports. Costa Rica's best production combination, therefore, is at point *C,* where the domestic and international opportunity costs of acquiring an extra computer, measured in terms of coffee forgone, are equal.

We have already stated the general conclusion that can be drawn from this analysis. Once again, by opening itself up to trade, a country can consume more of *every* good than if it relied solely on its own production (a situation of *autarky*). Graphically, the consumption possibilities line in Figure 15.5 lies above the production possibilities curve, showing that through trade, Cost Rica can consume combinations of computers and coffee that would not be attainable if its economy were closed to trade.[2]

RECAP ↑

CONSUMPTION POSSIBILITIES AND PRODUCTION POSSIBILITIES

- A country's consumption possibilities are the combinations of goods and services that its citizens might feasibly consume.
- In an economy that is closed to trade, residents can consume only what is produced domestically (a situation of autarky). Hence, in a closed economy, consumption possibilities equal production possibilities.
- The residents of an open economy can trade part of what they produce on international markets. According to the principle of comparative advantage, trade allows everyone to do better than they could otherwise. Thus, in an open economy, consumption possibilities are typically greater than, and will never be less than, production possibilities.
- Graphically, consumption possibilities in an open economy are described by a downward-sloping line that just touches the production possibilities curve (PPC). The slope of this line equals the amount of the good on the vertical axis that must be traded on the international market to obtain one unit of the good on the horizontal axis. A country maximizes its consumption possibilities by producing at the point where the consumption possibilities line just touches the PPC, and then trading so as to reach its most preferred point on the consumption possibilities line.

A SUPPLY AND DEMAND PERSPECTIVE ON TRADE

To this point we have shown that a country can improve its overall consumption possibilities by trading with other countries. In this section we will look more carefully at how international trade affects supply and demand in the markets for specific goods. We will see that when it is costly for workers and firms to change industries, opening up trade with other countries may create groups of winners and losers among producers, workers, and consumers.

Let's see how trade affects the markets for computers and coffee in Costa Rica. Figure 15.6 shows the supply and demand for computers in that country. As usual, the

---

[2]The single point at which consumption possibilities do *not* lie above production possibilities in Figure 15.5 is at point *C,* where production possibilities and consumption possibilities are the same. If Costa Rican residents happen to prefer the combination of computers and coffee at point *C* to any other point on *FG,* then they realize no benefit from trade.

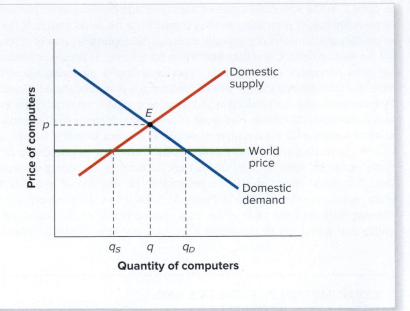

price is shown on the vertical axis and the quantity on the horizontal axis. For now, think of the price of computers as being measured in terms of coffee rather than in terms of dollars (in other words, we measure the price of computers *relative* to the price of the other good in the economy). As usual, the upward-sloping curve in Figure 15.6 is the supply curve of computers, in this case for computers produced in Costa Rica; and the downward-sloping curve is the demand curve for computers by Costa Rican residents. The supply curve for computers in Costa Rica reflects the opportunity cost of supplying computers (see Chapter 3, *Supply and Demand*). Specifically, at any level of computer production, the relative price at which Costa Rican firms are willing to supply an additional computer equals their opportunity cost of doing so. The demand curve, which tells us the number of computers Costa Ricans will purchase at each relative price, reflects the preferences and buying power of Costa Rican consumers.

If the Costa Rican economy is closed to international trade, then market equilibrium occurs where the domestic supply and demand curves intersect, at point E in Figure 15.6. The equilibrium price will be p and the equilibrium quantity, q.

If Costa Rica opens its market to trade, however, the relevant price for computers becomes the **world price** of computers, the price at which computers are traded internationally. The world price for computers is determined by the worldwide supply and demand for computers. If we assume that Costa Rica's computer market is too small to affect the world price for computers very much, the world price can be treated as fixed, and represented by a horizontal line in the figure. Figure 15.6 shows the world price for computers as being lower than Costa Rica's closed-economy price.

If Costa Ricans are free to buy and sell computers on the international market, then the price of computers in Costa Rica must be the same as the world price. (No one in Costa Rica will buy a computer at a price above the world price, and no one will sell one at a price below the world price.) Figure 15.6 shows that at the world price, Costa Rican consumers and firms demand q_D computers, but Costa Rican computer producers will supply only q_S computers. The difference between the two quantities, $q_D - q_S$, is the number of computers that Costa Rica must import from abroad. Figure 15.6 illustrates a general conclusion: *If the price of a good or service in a closed economy is greater than the world price, and that economy opens itself to trade, the economy will tend to become a net importer of that good or service.*

A different outcome occurs in Costa Rica's coffee market, shown in Figure 15.7. The price of coffee (measured relative to the price of computers) is shown on the vertical axis, and the quantity of coffee on the horizontal axis. The downward-sloping demand curve in

world price the price at which a good or service is traded on international markets

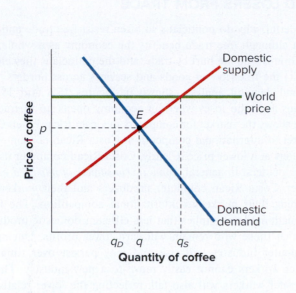

FIGURE 15.7

The Market for Coffee in Costa Rica.

With no international trade, the equilibrium price and quantity of coffee in Costa Rica are determined by the intersection of the domestic supply and demand curves (point E). But if the country opens to trade, the domestic price of coffee must equal the world price. At the higher world price, Costa Ricans will demand the quantity of coffee q_D, less than the amount supplied by Costa Rican producers, q_S. The excess coffee supplied by Costa Rican producers, $q_S - q_D$, is exported.

the figure shows how much coffee Costa Rican consumers want to buy at each relative price, and the upward-sloping supply curve how much coffee Costa Rican producers are willing to supply at each relative price. If Costa Rica's economy is closed to trade with the rest of the world, then equilibrium in the market for coffee will occur at point E, where the domestic demand and supply curves intersect. The quantity produced will be q and the price p.

Now imagine that Costa Rica opens its coffee market to international trade. As in the case of computers, if free trade in coffee is permitted, then the prevailing price for coffee in Costa Rica must be the same as the world price. Unlike the case of computers, however, the world price of coffee as shown in Figure 15.7 is *higher* than the domestic equilibrium price. How do we know that the world price of coffee will be higher than the domestic price? Recall that the price of coffee is measured relative to the price of computers, and vice versa. If the price of computers relative to the price of coffee is higher in Costa Rica than in the world market, then the price of coffee relative to the price of computers must be lower, as each price is the reciprocal of the other. More generally, as we saw in Chapter 2, *Comparative Advantage,* when two people or two countries trade with each other, neither can have a comparative advantage in *every* good and service. Thus, in an example with only two goods, if non–Costa Rican producers have a comparative advantage in computers, reflected in the lower cost of computers relative to coffee in the world market, then Costa Rican producers must have a comparative advantage in coffee. By definition, this comparative advantage implies that the opportunity cost of coffee in terms of computers must be lower in Costa Rica than in the rest of the world.

Figure 15.7 shows that at the world price for coffee, Costa Rican producers are willing to supply q_S coffee, while Costa Rican consumers want to purchase a smaller amount, q_D. The difference between domestic production and domestic consumption, $q_S - q_D$, is exported to the world market. The general conclusion of Figure 15.7 is this: *If the price of a good or service in a closed economy is lower than the world price, and that economy opens itself to trade, the economy will tend to become a net exporter of that good or service.*

These examples illustrate how the market translates comparative advantage into mutually beneficial gains from trade. If trade is unrestricted, then countries with a comparative advantage in a particular good will profit by supplying that good to the world market and using the revenue earned to import goods in which they do not have a comparative advantage. Thus the workings of the free market automatically ensure that goods will be produced where the opportunity cost is lowest, leading to the highest possible consumption possibilities for the world as a whole.

WINNERS AND LOSERS FROM TRADE

If trade is so wonderful, why do politicians so often resist free trade and "globalization"? The reason is that although free trade benefits the economy as a whole, specific groups may not benefit. Groups who are hurt by trade, and the politicians they elect, may support policies that restrict the free flow of goods and services across borders.

The supply and demand analyses shown in Figures 15.6 and 15.7 are useful in clarifying who gains and who loses when an economy opens up to trade. Look first at Figure 15.6, which shows the market for computers in Costa Rica. When Costa Rica opens its computer market to international competition, Costa Rican consumers enjoy a larger quantity of computers at a lower price. Clearly, Costa Rican computer users benefit from the free trade in computers. In general, *domestic consumers of imported goods benefit from free trade.* However, Costa Rican computer producers and their workers will not be so happy about opening their market to international competition. The fall in computer prices to the international level implies that less efficient domestic producers will go out of business, and that those who remain will earn lower profits. Unemployment in the Costa Rican computer industry will rise and may persist over time, particularly if displaced computer workers cannot easily move to a new industry. The wages paid to Costa Rican computer workers will also fall, reflecting the lower relative price of computers. We see that, in general, *domestic producers of imported goods, and workers in imported-good sectors, are hurt by free trade.*

Consumers are helped, while producers and workers are hurt, when imports increase. The opposite conclusions apply for an increase in exports (see Figure 15.7). In the example of Costa Rica, an opening of the coffee market raises the domestic price of coffee to the world price and creates the opportunity for Costa Rica to export coffee. Domestic producers of coffee benefit from the increased market (they can now sell coffee abroad as well as at home) and from the higher price of their product. Domestic workers in the coffee sector benefit too, as they are more in demand. In short, *domestic producers of exported goods, and workers in exported-good sectors, benefit from free trade.* Costa Rican coffee drinkers will be less enthusiastic, however, since they must now have to pay the higher world price of coffee, and can therefore consume less. *Thus domestic consumers of exported goods are hurt by free trade.*

> **Equilibrium** ≫

Free trade is *efficient* in the sense that it increases the size of the pie available to the economy. Indeed, the efficiency of free trade is an application of the Equilibrium Principle: Markets in equilibrium leave no unexploited opportunities for individuals. Despite the efficiency of free trade, however, some groups may lose from trade, which generates political pressures to block or restrict trade. In the next section we will discuss the major types of policy used to restrict trade.

The Economic Naturalist 15.1

What is the China trade shock?

The China trade shock, a term most commonly associated with economists David Autor, David Dorn, and Gordon Hanson, is used to describe the dramatic change in international trade patterns that resulted from China's rise as a major player in the global economy over the past few decades.

In a series of influential studies, these economists and their collaborators investigated the costs of the shock to U.S. workers. They found that employment has fallen in U.S. industries and regions most exposed to import competition from China—something that our theory in this chapter helps explain. However, they did not find strong evidence of simultaneous offsetting employment increases in other sectors in the same regions, suggesting that the transition of workers into sectors in which the U.S. has comparative advantage has been neither quick nor easy—something that the theory does not emphasize.

Overall, these economists conclude that workers' adjustment to trade shocks is often a slow and difficult process, and that local labor force participation rates and unemployment rates in affected regions may take a decade or more to recover. Moreover, the slow adjustment means that trade shocks could lead to prolonged economic and social problems in affected communities.

While the research underlying these conclusions is still new and is still being examined, it serves as a reminder that for many workers, the short-term costs of trade may outweigh the short-term benefits. While opposition to trade among such workers is understandable, we should not conclude that the overall costs of trade outweigh the overall benefits. Rather, as these economists conclude in one of their studies:

> "Better understanding when and where trade is costly, and how and why it may be beneficial, is a key item on the research agenda for trade and labor economists. Developing effective tools for managing and mitigating the costs of trade adjustment should be high on the agenda for policy-makers and applied economists."[3]

RECAP

A SUPPLY AND DEMAND PERSPECTIVE ON TRADE

- For a closed economy, the domestic supply and demand for a good or service determine the equilibrium price and quantity of that good or service.
- In an open economy, the price of a good or service traded on international markets equals the world price. If the domestic quantity supplied at the world price exceeds the domestic quantity demanded, the difference will be exported to the world market. If the domestic quantity demanded at the world price exceeds the domestic quantity supplied, the difference will be imported.
- Generally, if the price of a good or service in a closed economy is lower than the world price and the economy opens to trade, the country will become a net exporter of that good or service. If the closed-economy price is higher than the world price and the economy opens to trade, the country will tend to become a net importer of the good or service.
- Consumers of imported goods, producers of exported goods, and workers in exported-good sectors benefit from trade, whereas consumers of exported goods, producers of imported goods, and workers in imported-good sectors are hurt by trade. Those groups that are hurt, and the politicians they elect, may support enacting barriers to trade.

TRADE WINNERS AND LOSERS

Winners

- Consumers of imported goods
- Producers of exported goods
- Workers in exported-good sectors

Losers

- Consumers of exported goods
- Producers of imported goods
- Workers in imported-good sectors

---

[3]David Autor, David Dorn, and Gordon Hanson, "The China Shock: Learning from Labor Market Adjustment to Large Changes in Trade," *Annual Review of Economics* 8 (October 2016), pp. 205–240.

PROTECTIONIST POLICIES: TARIFFS AND QUOTAS

protectionism the view that free trade is injurious and should be restricted

tariff a tax imposed on an imported good

quota a legal limit on the quantity of a good that may be imported

▶ Visit your instructor's Connect course and access your eBook to view this video.

WORLD SUGAR MARKET

Why do consumers in the United States often pay more than double the world price for sugar?

The view that free trade is injurious and should be restricted is known as **protectionism.** Supporters of this view believe the government should attempt to "protect" domestic markets by raising legal barriers to imports. (Interestingly, protectionists rarely attempt to restrict exports, even though they hurt consumers of the exported good.) Two of the most common types of such barriers are tariffs and quotas. A **tariff** is a tax imposed on an imported good. A **quota** is a legal limit on the quantity of a good that may be imported.

TARIFFS

The effects of tariffs and quotas can be explained using supply and demand diagrams. Suppose that Costa Rican computer makers, dismayed by the penetration of "their" market by imported computers, persuade their government to impose a tariff—that is, a tax—on every computer imported into the country. Computers produced in Costa Rica will be exempt from the tax. Figure 15.8 shows the likely effects of this tariff on the domestic Costa Rican computer market. The lower of the two horizontal lines in the figure indicates the world price of computers, not including the tariff. The higher of the two lines indicates the price Costa Rican consumers will actually pay for imported computers, including the tariff. We refer to the price of computers including the tariff as p_T. The vertical distance between the two lines equals the amount of the tariff that is imposed on each imported computer.

From the point of view of domestic Costa Rican producers and consumers, the imposition of the tariff has the same effects as an equivalent increase in the world price of computers. Because the price (including the tariff) of imported computers has risen, Costa Rican computer producers will be able to raise the price they charge for their computers to the world price plus tariff, p_T. Thus the price Costa Rican consumers must pay—whether their computers are imported or not—equals p_T, represented by the upper horizontal line in Figure 15.8.

The rise in the price of computers created by the tariff affects the quantities of computers supplied and the quantities demanded by Costa Ricans. Domestic computer producers, facing a higher price for computers, increase their production from q_S to q'_S (see Figure 15.8).

FIGURE 15.8

The Market for Computers after the Imposition of an Import Tariff.

The imposition of a tariff on imported computers raises the price of computers in Costa Rica to the world price plus tariff, p_T, represented by the upper horizontal line. Domestic production of computers rises from q_S to q'_S, domestic purchases of computers fall from q_D to q'_D, and computer imports fall from $q_D - q_S$ to $q'_D - q'_S$. Costa Rican consumers are worse off and Costa Rican computer producers are better off. The Costa Rican government collects revenue from the tariff equal to the area of the pale blue rectangle.

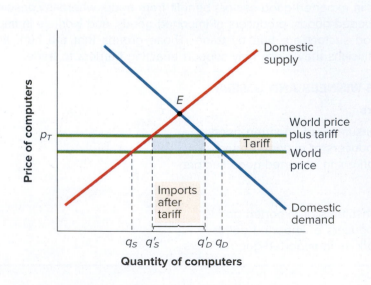

Costa Rican consumers, also reacting to the higher price, reduce their computer purchases from q_D to q'_D. As a result, the number of imported computers–the difference between domestic purchases and domestic production–falls from $q_D - q_S$ to $q'_D - q'_S$.

Who are the winners and the losers from the tariff, then? Relative to an environment with free trade and no tariff, the winners are the domestic computer producers, who sell more computers and receive a higher price for them. The clearest losers are Costa Rican consumers, who must now pay more for their computers. Another winner is the government, which collects revenue from the tariff. The blue area in Figure 15.8 shows the amount of revenue the government collects, equal to the quantity of computer imports after the imposition of the tariff, $q'_D - q'_S$, times the amount of the tariff.

EXAMPLE 15.3   A Tariff on Imported Computers

What are the effects of a tariff on trade?

Suppose that the Costa Rican market for computers is represented by Figure 15.9. Thus, if the Costa Rican economy is closed to trade, the equilibrium price for computers would be $2,000, and 2,000 computers would be bought and sold in the Costa Rican computer market every year (point E). Assuming that the world price of computers is $1,400, how would this market be affected by opening to trade, and how would it be affected by the imposition of a tariff of $400 per computer?

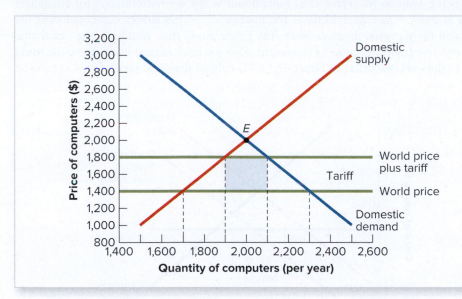

FIGURE 15.9

The Market for Computers in Costa Rica after the Imposition of an Import Tariff.

A tariff of $400 per computer raises the price of computers by $400 and reduces imports by 400 computers per year.

If the economy opens to trade, the domestic price of computers must equal the world price of $1,400. At this price, the domestic quantity demanded is 2,300 computers per year and the domestic quantity supplied is 1,700 computers per year. Imports equal the difference between the domestic quantities demanded and supplied, or $2,300 - 1,700 = 600$ computers per year.

The imposition of a tariff of $400 per computer raises the price from $1,400 to $1,800. This price rise causes Costa Rican computer producers to increase their production from 1,700 to 1,900 computers per year, and it causes Costa Rican consumers to reduce their computer purchases from 2,300 to 2,100. As a result, the number of imported computers—the difference between domestic purchases and domestic production—falls from 600 to 200 ($2,100 - 1,900$).

Thus the tariff has raised the price of computers by $400 and reduced imports by 400 computers per year. The tariff revenue collected by the government is $400 per imported computer times 200 computers per year = $80,000 per year.

QUOTAS

An alternative to a tariff is a quota, or legal limit, on the number or value of foreign goods that can be imported. One means of enforcing a quota is to require importers to obtain a license or permit for each good they bring into the country. The government then distributes exactly the same number of permits as the number of goods that may be imported under the quota.

How does the imposition of a quota on, say, computers affect the domestic market for computers? Figure 15.10, which is similar to Figure 15.8, illustrates the effect of a quota on imported computers. As before, assume that at first there are no restrictions on trade. Consumers pay the world price for computers, and $q_D - q_S$ computers are imported. Now suppose once more that domestic computer producers complain to the government about competition from foreign computer makers, and the government agrees to act. However, this time, instead of a tariff, the government imposes a quota on the number of computers that can be imported. For comparability with the tariff analyzed in Figure 15.8, let's assume that the quota permits the same level of imports as entered the country under the tariff: specifically, $q'_D - q'_S$ computers. What effect does this ruling have on the domestic market for computers?

After the imposition of the quota, the quantity of computers supplied to the Costa Rican market is the production of domestic firms plus the $q'_D - q'_S$ imported computers allowed under the quota. Figure 15.10 shows the quantity of computers supplied inclusive of the quota. The total supply curve, labeled "Domestic supply plus quota," is the same as the domestic supply curve shifted $q'_D - q'_S$ units to the right. The domestic demand curve is the same as in Figure 15.8. Equilibrium in the domestic market for computers occurs at point F in Figure 15.10, at the intersection of the supply curve including the quota and the domestic demand curve. The figure shows that, relative to the initial situation with free trade, the quota (1) raises the domestic price of computers above the world price, to the level marked p_T in Figure 15.10; (2) reduces domestic purchases of computers

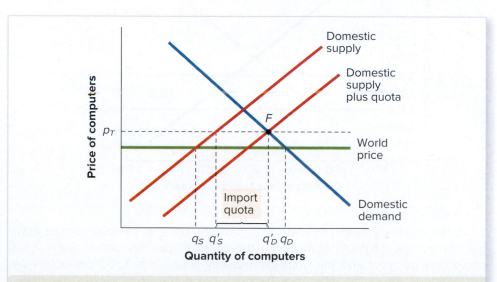

FIGURE 15.10

The Market for Computers after the Imposition of an Import Quota.

The figure shows the effects of the imposition of a quota that permits only $q'_D - q'_S$ computers to be imported. The total supply of computers to the domestic economy equals the domestic economy equals the domestic supply curve shifted to the right by $q'_D - q'_S$ units (the fixed amount of imports). Market equilibrium occurs at point F. The effects of the quota on the domestic market are identical to those of the tariff analyzed in Figure 15.8. The domestic price rises to p_T, domestic production of computers rises from q_S to q'_S, domestic purchases of computers fall from q_D to q'_D, and computer imports fall from $q_D - q_S$ to $q'_D - q'_S$. The quota differs from the tariff in that under a quota system the government collects no revenue.

from q_D to q'_D; (3) increases domestic production of computers from q_S to q'_S; and (4) reduces imports to $q'_D - q'_S$, consistent with a quota. Like a tariff, the quota helps domestic producers by increasing their sales and the price they receive for their output, while hurting domestic consumers by forcing them to pay a higher price.

Interestingly, under our assumption that the quota is set to permit the same level of imports as the tariff, the effects on the domestic market of the tariff (Figure 15.8) and the quota (Figure 15.10) are not only similar, they are *equivalent*. Comparing Figures 15.8 and 15.10, you can see that the two policies have identical effects on the domestic price, domestic purchases, domestic production, and imports.

Although the market effects of a tariff and a quota are the same, there is one important difference between the two policies, which is that a tariff generates revenue for the government, whereas a quota does not. With a quota, the revenue that would have gone to the government goes instead to those firms that hold the import licenses. A holder of an import license can purchase a computer at the world price and resell it in the domestic market at price p_T, pocketing the difference. Thus with a tariff the government collects the difference between the world price and the domestic market price of the good; with a quota, private firms or individuals collect that difference. Why then would the government ever impose a quota rather than a tariff? One possibility is that the distribution of import licenses is a means of rewarding the government's political supporters. Sometimes, international political concerns may also play a role (see The Economic Naturalist 15.2 for a possible example).

EXAMPLE 15.4   Effects of an Import Quota

What are the effects of an import quota on trade?

Suppose the supply of and demand for computers in Costa Rica, as well as the world price of computers, are as given in Figure 15.11. Suppose that the government imposes a quota of 200 on the number of computers that can be imported. What effect would this have on the domestic market for computers (relative to the free-trade alternative)?

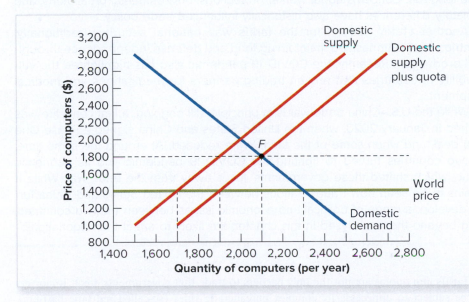

FIGURE 15.11

The Market for Computers in Costa Rica after the Imposition of an Import Quota.

A quota of 200 computers per year raises the price of computers by $400 and reduces imports by 400 computers per year.

After the quota is imposed, the equilibrium in the domestic market occurs at point *F* in the figure. As the figure shows, relative to free trade, the domestic price increases to $1,800 per computer, domestic purchases of computers decrease to 2,100, domestic production of computers increases to 1,900, and imports decrease to 200 (the difference between the 2,100 computers demanded and the 1,900 computers domestically produced).

Note that the domestic price, domestic production, and domestic demand are the same in Examples 15.3 and 15.4. Thus, under the assumptions we made, the tariff and the quota have the same effects on the domestic market for computers. The only difference between the two policies is that with a quota, the government does not get the tariff revenue it got in Example 15.3. That revenue goes instead to the holders of import licenses, who can buy computers on the world market at $1,400 and sell them in the domestic market at $1,800.

The Economic Naturalist 15.2

Why did the U.S. start a trade war with China?

Starting in 2018 and continuing during 2019, the U.S. imposed several rounds of tariffs on commodities and products imported from China. The tariffs, ranging from 10 to 25 percent, were applied to imports worth hundreds of billions of dollars in total. In retaliation, China imposed tariffs of 5 to 25 percent on more than a hundred billion dollars' worth of goods imported from the United States.

As our analysis in this chapter predicts, studies show that the U.S. tariffs were largely reflected in higher prices for American consumers and for American producers who buy the affected goods.[4] The price of these goods increased not only when they were imported, but also, through reduced competition, when they were produced in the United States. The Chinese tariffs also hurt American producers who export to China. The overall costs of the trade war to Americans were thus substantial. Why did the United States start it?

One stated reason for imposing the tariffs was that U.S. trade negotiators were concerned that China was violating U.S. intellectual property rights, for example, by not enforcing patent laws or by requiring U.S. firms to share technology if they want to do business in China. Loss of intellectual property disadvantages U.S. producers in the long run. Concerns about worker protections, environmental protections, and regulatory differences have also historically influenced trade policy.

Another stated reason for the tariffs was national security. Traditionally, countries have emphasized maintaining food and defense independence through local production. Recently, the COVID-19 pandemic also has highlighted the vulnerability of countries that rely on trading partners for medications and medical equipment.

While the U.S.–China trade war is in principle still ongoing, a first ceasefire was reached in January 2020, when the United States and China signed a Phase One trade deal, and when some of the tariffs were reduced. At around the same time, the two countries turned to fighting the COVID-19 pandemic and its economic fallout—which shifted these governments' focus away from the trade war. While it remains to be seen how trade relations between the United States and China further develop, a range of political and economic issues between the two countries, going beyond those analyzed in this chapter, are likely to affect the negotiations.

Tariffs and quotas are not the only barriers to trade that governments erect. Importers may be subject to unnecessarily complex bureaucratic rules (so-called red tape barriers), and regulations of goods that are nominally intended to promote health and safety sometimes have the side effect, whether intentionally or unintentionally, of restricting trade. One

---

[4]See, for example: Mary Amiti, Stephen J. Redding, and David Weinstein, "The Impact of the 2018 Trade War on U.S. Prices and Welfare," NBER Working Paper No. 25672 (March 2019); and Pablo D. Fajgelbaum, Pinelopi K. Goldberg, Patrick J. Kennedy, Amit K. Khandelwal, "The Return to Protectionism," NBER Working Paper No. 25638 (October 2019).

example is European restrictions on imports of genetically modified foods. Although these regulations were motivated in part by concerns about the safety of such foods, they also help protect Europe's politically powerful farmers from foreign competition.

THE INEFFICIENCY OF PROTECTIONISM

Free trade is efficient because it allows countries to specialize in the production of goods and services in which they have the greatest comparative advantage. Conversely, protectionist policies that limit trade are inefficient—they reduce the total economic pie. (Recall the Efficiency Principle introduced in Chapter 3, *Supply and Demand,* that efficiency is an important social goal.) Why, then, do governments adopt such policies? The reason is similar to why some city governments impose rent controls (see Chapter 3). Although rent controls reduce economic welfare overall, some people benefit from them—namely, the tenants whose rents are held artificially below market level. Similarly, as we have seen in this section, tariffs and quotas benefit certain groups. Those who benefit from these restrictions (such as firms facing import competition, and the workers in such firms) may support politicians who promise to enact the restrictions.

Why did the U.S. start a trade war with China?

 Efficiency

The fact that free trade is efficient suggests an alternative to trade restrictions, however. Because eliminating restrictions on trade increases the overall economic pie, in general the winners from free trade will be able to compensate the losers in such a way that everyone becomes better off. Government programs that assist workers displaced by import competition are an example of such compensation. They include programs to expand job training and retraining opportunities, especially for the less-educated, who are more likely to be hurt by competition from abroad; to provide transition assistance for displaced workers, including support for internal migration within the U.S. from regions with declining industries to regions with expanding industries; to mitigate residential and educational segregation and increase the access of those left behind to employment and educational opportunities; and to promote community redevelopment in regions with declining industries.

While by no means an easy task, developing and improving such programs, and making them widely available, could do a lot to help those who lose from trade. Spreading the benefits of free trade—or at least reducing its adverse effects on certain groups—reduces the incentives of those groups to oppose free trade.

Although we have focused on the winners and losers from trade, not all opposition to free trade is motivated by economic interest. For example, many who oppose further opening to trade cite environmental concerns. Protecting the environment is an important and laudable goal, but once again the Efficiency Principle suggests that restricting trade may not be the most effective means of achieving that goal. Restricting trade lowers world income, reducing the resources available to deal with environmental problems. Furthermore, much of the income loss arising from barriers to trade is absorbed by poor nations trying to develop their economies. For this reason, leaders of developing countries are among the strongest advocates of free trade.

The Economic Naturalist 15.3

What is fast track authority?

In practice, trade agreements among countries are very complex. For example, agreements usually spell out in great detail the goods and services for which tariffs are being reduced or quotas are being expanded. Trade negotiators must also take into account barriers to trade other than explicit tariffs or quotas, such as rules that require a country's government to buy only from domestic suppliers. Because trade negotiations can be so complex, having each country's legislature vote on each item in a proposed trade agreement is not practical.

In the United States, the solution to this problem has been for Congress to vote to give the president *fast track authority*. Under this authority, the executive branch is given discretion to negotiate the terms of a proposed trade agreement. Congress then has the opportunity to vote the agreement up or down, but it cannot amend the proposal or accept only certain parts of it.

Fast track authority has been successfully used by presidents of both parties to negotiate trade agreements. However, the granting of fast track authority itself can be contentious, reflecting political concerns about trade and globalization. In 2015, for example, Democrats strongly resisted President Obama's request for fast track authority to negotiate a trade agreement with a number of countries, and in 2018 some Congress members resisted a similar request by President Trump.

RECAP ↑

PROTECTIONIST POLICIES: TARIFFS AND QUOTAS

- The view that free trade is injurious and should be restricted is called protectionism.
- The two most common types of trade barriers are tariffs, or taxes on imported goods, and quotas, legal limits on the quantity that can be imported. A tariff raises the domestic price to the world price plus the tariff. The result is increased domestic production, reduced domestic consumption, and fewer imports. A quota has effects on the domestic market that are similar to those of a tariff. The main difference is that under a quota, the government does not collect tariff revenue.
- Trade barriers are inefficient; they reduce the overall size of the economic pie. Thus, in general, the winners from free trade should be able to compensate the losers in such a way that everyone becomes better off. Government programs to help workers displaced by import competition are an example of such compensation. They are not easy to develop and implement. Without effective compensation, however, opposition to trade by those who are hurt by it may lead to the inefficiency brought by protectionism.

SUMMARY

- According to the *Principle of Comparative Advantage,* the best economic outcomes occur when each nation specializes in the goods and services at which it is relatively most productive and then trades with other nations to obtain the goods and services its citizens desire. *(LO1)*

- The production possibilities curve (PPC) of a country is a graph that describes the maximum amount of one good that can be produced at every possible level of production of the other good. At any point the slope of a PPC indicates the opportunity cost, in terms of forgone production of the good on the vertical axis, of increasing production of the good on the horizontal axis by one unit. The more of

a good that is already being produced, the greater the opportunity cost of increasing production still further. Thus the slope of a PPC becomes more and more negative as we read from left to right. When an economy has many workers, the PPC has a smooth, outwardly bowed shape. *(LO2)*

- A country's *consumption possibilities* are the combinations of goods and services that might feasibly be consumed by its citizens. In a *closed economy*—one that does not trade with other countries—the citizens' consumption possibilities are identical to their production possibilities. But in an *open economy*—one that does trade with other countries—consumption possibilities are typically greater than, and never less than, the economy's production possibilities. Graphically, an open economy's consumption possibilities are described by a downward-sloping line that just touches the PPC, whose slope equals the amount of the good on the vertical axis that must be traded to obtain one unit of the good on the horizontal axis. A country achieves its highest consumption possibilities by producing at the point where the consumption possibilities line just touches the PPC and then trading to obtain the most preferred point on the consumption possibilities line. *(LO2)*

- In a closed economy, the relative price of a good or service is determined at the intersection of the supply curve of domestic producers and the demand curve of domestic consumers. In an open economy, the relative price of a good or service equals the *world price*—the price determined by supply and demand in the world economy. If the price of a good or service in a closed economy is greater than the world price and the country opens its market to trade, it will become a net importer of that good or service. But if the closed-economy price is below the world price and the country opens itself to trade, it will become a net exporter of that good or service. *(LO3)*

- Although free trade is beneficial to the economy as a whole, some groups—such as domestic producers of imported goods, and workers in imported-good sectors—are hurt by free trade. Groups that are hurt by trade may support political candidates who promise to impose *protectionist* measures, such as tariffs or quotas. A *tariff* is a tax on an imported good that has the effect of raising the domestic price of the good. A higher domestic price increases domestic supply, reduces domestic demand, and reduces imports of the good. A *quota*, which is a legal limit on the amount of a good that may be imported, has the same effects as a tariff, except that the government collects no tax revenue. (The equivalent amount of revenue goes instead to those firms with the legal authority to import goods.) Because free trade is efficient, the winners from free trade should be able to compensate the losers so that everyone becomes better off. Thus policies to assist those who are harmed by trade, such as assistance and retraining for workers idled by imports, are usually preferable to trade restrictions. *(LO4)*

KEY TERMS

autarky	open economy	tariff
closed economy	protectionism	world price
consumption possibilities	quota	

REVIEW QUESTIONS

1. Imagine that, all else equal, it takes U.S. workers a quarter of the time it takes Chinese workers to design a new mobile phone model. Also, imagine that it takes U.S. workers half the time it takes Chinese workers to produce a million pieces of the new model. Which of the two countries has absolute advantage, and which has comparative advantage, in designing a new model? In producing it? *(LO1)*

2. Sketch a PPC for a four-worker economy that produces two goods, hot dogs and hamburgers. Give an economic interpretation of the vertical intercept, the horizontal intercept, and the slope of the graph. *(LO2)*

3. What is meant by the "consumption possibilities" of a country? How are consumption possibilities related to production possibilities in a closed economy? In an open economy? *(LO2)*

4. A small, open economy is equally productive in producing coffee and tea. What will this economy produce if the world price of coffee is twice that of tea? Half that of tea? What will the country produce if the world price of coffee happens to equal the world price of tea? *(LO3)*

5. True or false: If a country is more productive in every sector than a neighboring country, then there is no benefit in trading with the neighboring country. Explain. *(LO3)*

6. Show graphically the effects of a tariff on imported automobiles on the domestic market for automobiles. Who is hurt by the tariff and why? Who benefits and why? *(LO4)*

7. Show graphically the effects of a quota on imported automobiles on the domestic market for automobiles. Who does the quota hurt and who benefits? Explain. *(LO4)*

PROBLEMS

Mc Graw Hill **connect**

1. An economy has two workers, Bella and Edward. Per day of work, Bella can pick 100 apples or 25 bananas, and Edward can pick 50 apples or 50 bananas. Bella and Edward each work 200 days per year. *(LO1, LO2)*
   a. Which worker has an absolute advantage in apples? Which has a comparative advantage? Calculate each worker's opportunity cost of picking an additional apple.
   b. Find the maximum number of each type of fruit that can be picked annually in this economy, assuming that none of the other type of fruit is picked. What is the most of each type that can be picked if each worker fully specializes according to his or her comparative advantage?
   c. Draw the PPC for annual production in this economy. Show numerical values for the vertical intercept, the horizontal intercept, and the slopes of each segment of the PPC.

2. A developing economy requires 1,000 hours of work to produce a television set and 10 hours of work to produce a bushel of corn. This economy has available a total of 1,000,000 hours of work per day. *(LO2)*
   a. Draw the PPC for daily output of the developing economy. Give numerical values for the PPC's vertical intercept, horizontal intercept, and slope. Relate the slope to the developing country's opportunity cost of producing each good. If this economy does not trade, what are its consumption possibilities?
   b. The developing economy is considering opening trade with a much larger, industrialized economy. The industrialized economy requires 10 hours of work to produce a television set and 1 hour of work to produce a bushel of corn. Show graphically how trading with the industrialized economy affects the developing economy's consumption possibilities. Is opening trade desirable for the developing economy? (*Hint:* When it opens to trade, the developing economy will be fully specialized in one product.)

3. Suppose that Costa Rican worker Carlos can produce either 100 pounds of coffee or 1 computer per week, and a second worker, Maria, can produce either 150 pounds of coffee or 1 computer per week. Both Carlos and Maria work 50 weeks per year. *(LO2)*
   a. Find the PPC for Costa Rica. Give numerical values for the graph's intercepts and slopes. How much of each good is produced if each worker fully specializes according to comparative advantage?
   b. World prices are such that 1 computer trades for 125 pounds of coffee on international markets. If Costa Rica is open to trade, show Costa Rica's consumption possibilities graphically. What is the most

of each good that Costa Ricans can consume when the economy is open? Compare to the situation when the economy is closed.
   c. Repeat part b under the assumption that 1 computer trades for 80 pounds of coffee on world markets.

4. Suppose that Carlos and Maria can produce coffee and computers as described in Problem 3. A third worker, Pedro, joins the Costa Rican economy. Pedro can produce either 140 pounds of coffee or 1 computer per week. Like the other two workers, Pedro works 50 weeks per year. *(LO2)*
   a. Find the PPC for Costa Rica. Give numerical values of the PPC's intercepts and slopes.
   b. Find Costa Rica's consumption possibilities if the country is open and 1 computer trades for 125 pounds of coffee on world markets. What is the most of each good that Costa Ricans can consume when the economy is open? Compare to the situation when the economy is closed.
   c. Repeat part b assuming that 1 computer trades for 200 pounds of coffee on world markets.

5. Suppose that a U.S. worker can produce 1,000 pairs of shoes or 10 industrial robots per year. For simplicity, assume there are no costs other than labor costs and firms earn zero profits. Initially, the U.S. economy is closed. The domestic price of shoes is $30 a pair, so that a U.S. worker can earn $30,000 annually by working in the shoe industry. The domestic price of a robot is $3,000, so that a U.S. worker can also earn $30,000 annually working in the robot industry.

   Now suppose that the U.S. opens trade with the rest of the world. Foreign workers can produce 500 pairs of shoes or 1 robot per year. The world price of shoes after the U.S. opens its markets is $10 a pair, and the world price of robots is $5,000. *(LO3, LO4)*
   a. What do foreign workers earn annually, in dollars?
   b. When it opens to trade, which good will the United States import and which will it export?
   c. Find the real income of U.S. workers after the opening to trade, measured in (1) the number of pairs of shoes annual worker income will buy and (2) the number of robots annual worker income will buy. Compare to the situation before the opening of trade. Does trading in goods produced by "cheap foreign labor" hurt U.S. workers?
   d. How might your conclusion in part c be modified in the short term, if it is costly for workers to change industries? What policy response might help with this problem?

6. The demand and supply for automobiles in a certain country is given in the following graph. *(LO3, LO4)*
   a. Assuming that the economy is closed, find the equilibrium price and production of automobiles.

b. The economy opens to trade. The world price of automobiles is $8,000. Find the domestic quantities demanded and supplied and the quantity of imports or exports. Who will favor the opening of the automobile market to trade, and who will oppose it?

c. The government imposes a tariff of $2,000 per car. Find the effects on domestic quantities demanded and supplied.

d. As a result of the tariff, what will happen to the quantity of imports or exports, and what is the revenue raised by the tariff? Who will favor the imposition of the tariff, and who will oppose it?

7. Suppose the domestic demand and supply for automobiles is as given in Problem 6. *(LO3, LO4)*

a. The economy opens to trade. The world price of automobiles is $10,000. Find the domestic quantities demanded and supplied and the quantity of imports or exports.

b. Now assume that the government imposes a quota on automobile imports of 2,000 cars. What will happen to the quantity of imports or exports?

c. Who will favor the imposition of the quota, and who will oppose it?

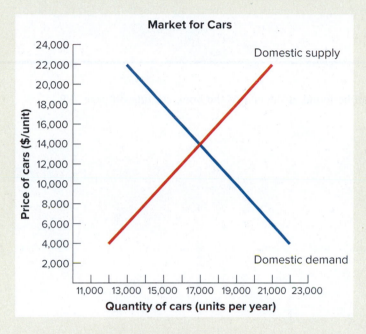

Market for Cars

ANSWERS TO SELF-TESTS

15.1 The opportunity cost of producing coffee equals the number of computers given up for each extra pound of coffee produced. Carlos can produce either 100 pounds of coffee or 1 computer per week, so his opportunity cost is given by:

$$\frac{\text{Loss in computers}}{\text{Gain in coffee}} = \frac{-1 \text{ computer/week}}{100 \text{ pounds of coffee/week}}$$
$$= -1/100 \text{ computer/pound of coffee.}$$

Maria can produce either 100 pounds of coffee or 2 computers per week, so her opportunity cost is:

$$\frac{\text{Loss in computers}}{\text{Gain in coffee}} = \frac{-2 \text{ computer/week}}{100 \text{ pounds of coffee/week}}$$
$$= -1/50 \text{ computer/pound of coffee.}$$

Since each pound of coffee Carlos produces requires the sacrifice of 1/100 of a computer, while each pound of coffee produced by Maria sacrifices 1/50 of a computer, Carlos has the smaller opportunity cost of producing coffee. Thus he has a comparative advantage in producing coffee. *(LO2)*

15.2 When the economy is closed, the Costa Ricans can obtain 80 computers by having Maria work 40 weeks making computers. If Maria works the remaining 10 weeks producing coffee and Carlos works 50 weeks producing coffee, the Costa Ricans will be able to consume $(10 + 50) \times 100 = 6,000$ pounds of coffee per year.

The world price of computers is 80 pounds of coffee, which is greater than Maria's opportunity cost of producing computers but less than Carlos's opportunity cost. Thus if the economy opens to trade, Maria will specialize in computers and Carlos will specialize in coffee. If Maria produces 100 computers, 80 of which are consumed domestically, 20 computers are available for export. Because a computer is worth 80 pounds of coffee on the world market, the 20 exported computers can be traded for 1,600 pounds of coffee. Carlos still produces 5,000 pounds of coffee. Total coffee consumption in Costa Rica is thus $1,600 + 5,000 = 6,600$ pounds. Opening to trade has allowed the Costa Ricans to consume 10 percent more coffee at no sacrifice in computers. *(LO2)*

An Algebraic Approach to Trade Analysis

his appendix can be found at the end of the book starting on page 799.

CHAPTER 16

Macroeconomics: The Bird's-Eye View of the Economy

Source: National Archives

Could better economic policies have prevented the Great Depression?

In 1929, the economy of the United States slowed dramatically. Between August of 1929 and the end of 1930, the nation's factories and mines, facing sharp declines in sales, cut their production rates by a remarkable 31 percent. These cutbacks led in turn to mass layoffs: Between 1929 and 1930, the number of people without jobs almost tripled, from about 3 percent of the workforce to nearly 9 percent.[1] Financial markets were equally shaky. The stock market crashed in October 1929, and stocks lost nearly a third of their value in just three weeks.

At first, policymakers and the general public (except for those people who had put their life savings into the stock market) were concerned but not panic stricken. Americans

[1] The source for these and most other pre-1960 statistics cited in this chapter is the U.S. Bureau of the Census, *Historical Statistics of the United States: Colonial Times to 1970* (Washington, D.C., 1975).

remembered that the nation had experienced a similar slowdown only eight years earlier, in 1921–1922. That episode had ended quickly, apparently on its own, and the decade that followed (popularly known as the Roaring Twenties) had been one of unparalleled prosperity. But the fall in production and the rise in unemployment that began in 1929 continued into 1931. In the spring of 1931, the economy seemed to stabilize briefly, and President Herbert Hoover optimistically proclaimed that "prosperity is just around the corner." But in mid-1931, the economy went into an even steeper dive. What historians now call the Great Depression had begun in earnest.

Labor statistics tell the story of the Great Depression from the worker's point of view. Unemployment was extremely high throughout the 1930s, despite government attempts to reduce it through large-scale public employment programs. At the worst point of the Depression, in 1933, one out of every four American workers was unemployed. Jobless-ness declined gradually to 17 percent of the workforce by 1936 but remained stuck at that level through 1939. Of those lucky enough to have jobs, many were able to work only part-time, while others worked for near-starvation wages.

In some other countries, conditions were even worse. In Germany, which had never fully recovered from its defeat in World War I, nearly a third of all workers were without jobs, and many families lost their savings as major banks collapsed. Indeed, the desperate economic situation was a major reason for Adolf Hitler's election as chancellor of Germany in 1933. Introducing extensive government control over the economy, Hitler rearmed the country and ultimately launched what became the most destructive war in history, World War II.

How could such an economic catastrophe have happened? One often-heard hypothesis is that the Great Depression was caused by wild speculation on Wall Street, which provoked the stock market crash. But though stock prices may have been unrealistically high in 1929, there is little evidence to suggest that the fall in stock prices was a major cause of the Depression. A similar crash in October 1987, when stock prices fell a record 23 percent in one day—an event comparable in severity to the crash of October 1929—did not slow the economy significantly. Another reason to doubt that the 1929 stock market crash caused the Great Depression is that, far from being confined to the United States, the Depression was a worldwide event, affecting countries that did not have well-developed stock markets at the time.

What *did* cause the Great Depression, then? Today most economists who have studied the period blame *poor economic policymaking* both in the United States and in other major industrialized countries. Of course, policymakers did not set out to create an economic catastrophe. Rather, they fell prey to misconceptions of the time about how the economy worked. In other words, the Great Depression, far from being inevitable, *might have been avoided*—if only the state of economic knowledge had been better. From today's perspective, the Great Depression was to economic policymaking what the voyage of the *Titanic* was to ocean navigation.

One of the few benefits of the Great Depression was that it forced economists and policymakers of the 1930s to recognize that there were major gaps in their understanding of how the economy works. This recognition led to the development of a new subfield within economics, called macroeconomics. *Macroeconomics* is the study of the performance of national economies and the policies governments use to try to improve that performance.

This chapter will introduce the subject matter and some of the tools of macroeconomics. Although understanding episodes like the Great Depression and, more recently, the Great Recession remains an important concern of macroeconomists, the field has expanded to include the analysis of many other aspects of national economies. Among the issues macroeconomists study are the sources of long-run economic growth and development, the causes of high unemployment, and the factors that determine the rate of inflation. Appropriately enough in a world in which economic "globalization" preoccupies businesspeople and policymakers, macroeconomists also study how national economies interact. Since the performance of the national economy has an important bearing on the availability of jobs, the wages workers earn, the prices they pay, and the rates of return they receive on their saving, it's clear that macroeconomics addresses bread-and-butter issues that affect virtually everyone.

In light of the nation's experience during the Great Depression, macroeconomists are particularly concerned with understanding how *macroeconomic policies* work and how they should be applied. **Macroeconomic policies** are government actions designed to affect the performance of the economy as a whole (as opposed to policies intended to affect the performance of the market for a particular good or service, such as sugar or haircuts). The hope is that by understanding more fully how government policies affect the economy, economists can help policymakers do a better job—and avoid serious mistakes, such as those that were made during the Great Depression. On an individual level, educating people about macroeconomic policies and their effects will make for a better-informed citizenry, capable of making well-reasoned decisions in the voting booth.

macroeconomic policies government actions designed to affect the performance of the economy as a whole

THE MAJOR MACROECONOMIC ISSUES

We defined macroeconomics as the study of the performance of the national economy as well as the policies used to improve that performance. Let's now take a closer look at some of the major economic issues that macroeconomists study.

ECONOMIC GROWTH AND LIVING STANDARDS

Although the wealthy industrialized countries (such as the United States, Canada, Japan, and the countries of western Europe) are certainly not free from poverty, hunger, and homelessness, the typical person in those countries enjoys a *standard of living* better than at any previous time or place in history. By **standard of living,** we mean the degree to which people have access to goods and services that make their lives easier, healthier, safer, and more enjoyable. People with a high living standard enjoy more and better consumer goods: technologically advanced cars, laptop and tablet computers, smartphones, and the like. But they also benefit from a longer life expectancy and better general health (the result of high-quality medical care, good nutrition, and good sanitation), from higher literacy rates (the result of greater access to education), from more time and opportunity for cultural enrichment and recreation, from more interesting and fulfilling career options, and from better working conditions. Of course, the *Scarcity Principle* will always apply—even for the citizen of a rich country: Having more of one good thing means having less of another. But higher incomes make these choices much less painful than they would be otherwise. Choosing between a larger apartment and a nicer car is much easier than choosing between feeding your children adequately and sending them to school, the kind of hard choice people in the poorest nations face.

standard of living the degree to which people have access to goods and services that make their lives easier, healthier, safer, and more enjoyable

Scarcity

Americans sometimes take their standard of living for granted, or even as a "right." But we should realize that the way we live today is radically different from the way people have lived throughout most of history. The current standard of living in the United States is the result of several centuries of sustained *economic growth,* a process of steady increase in the quantity and quality of the goods and services the economy can produce. The basic equation is simple: The more we can produce, the more we can consume. Of course, not everyone in a society shares equally in the fruits of economic growth and economists are rightly concerned by the increase in economic inequality that has sometimes accompanied economic growth. That said, in most cases growth brings an improvement in the average person's standard of living.

To get a sense of the extent of economic growth over time, examine Figure 16.1, which shows how the output of the U.S. economy has increased since 1929. (We discuss the measure of output used here, real gross domestic product, in the next chapter.) Although output fluctuates at times, the overall trend has been unmistakably upward. Indeed, in 2019 the output of the U.S. economy was more than 16 times what it was in 1929 and more than 4 times its level in 1965. What caused this remarkable economic growth? Can it continue? Should it? These are some of the questions macroeconomists try to answer.

One reason for the growth in U.S. output over the last century has been the rapid growth of the U.S. population, and hence the number of workers available. Because of population growth, increases in *total* output cannot be equated with improvements in the

FIGURE 16.1

Output of the U.S. Economy, 1929–2019.

The output of the U.S. economy has increased by more than 16 times since 1929 and by more than 4 times since 1965.

Source: https://fred.stlouisfed.org/series/GDPCA.

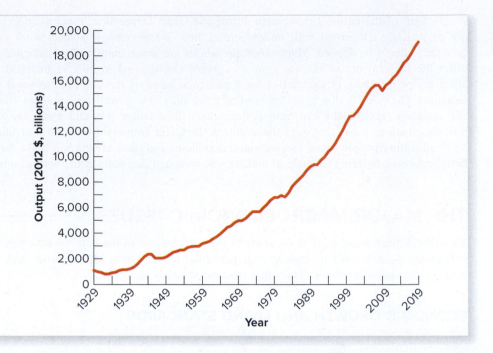

general standard of living. Although increased output means that more goods and services are available, increased population implies that more people are sharing those goods and services. Because the population changes over time, output *per person* is a better indicator of the average living standard than total output.

Figure 16.2 shows output per person in the United States since 1929 (the blue line). Note that the long-term increase in output per person is smaller than the increase in total output shown in Figure 16.1 because of population growth. Nevertheless, the gains made over this long period are still impressive: In 2019, a typical U.S. resident consumed more than six times the quantity of goods and services available to a typical resident at the onset of the Great Depression. To put this increase into perspective, according to the U.S. Census Bureau, in 2016, 87 percent of U.S. households reported that they owned a computer (desktop, laptop, notebook, tablet) or a smartphone, and 77 percent reported Internet access (home subscription or mobile

FIGURE 16.2

Output per Person and per Worker in the U.S. Economy, 1929–2019.

The red line shows the output per worker in the U.S. economy since 1929, and the blue line shows output per person. Both have risen substantially. Relative to 1929, output per person today is more than six times greater, and output per worker is more than five times greater.

Sources: U.S. Bureau of Economic Analysis, Bureau of Labor Statistics, U.S. Census Bureau.

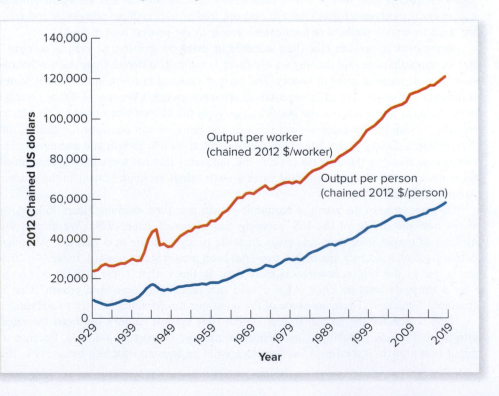

broadband plan). And in 2019, 96 percent of Americans owned a cell phone. These goods and services, now available to so many people, could hardly be imagined a few decades ago.

Nor has the rise in output been reflected entirely in increased availability of consumer goods. For example, as late as 1960, only 41 percent of U.S. adults over age 25 had completed high school, and less than 8 percent had completed four years of college. Today, about 89 percent of the adult population have at least a high school diploma, and about 32 percent have a college degree. More than two-thirds of the students currently leaving high school will go on to college. Higher incomes, which allow young people to continue their schooling rather than work to support themselves and their families, are a major reason for these increases in educational levels.

PRODUCTIVITY

While growth in output per person is closely linked to changes in what the typical person can *consume*, macroeconomists are also interested in changes in what the average worker can *produce*. Figure 16.2 shows how output per employed worker (that is, total output divided by the number of people working) has changed since 1929 (red line). The figure shows that in 2019 a U.S. worker could produce more than five times the quantity of goods and services produced by a worker at the beginning of the Great Depression, despite the fact that the workweek is now much shorter than it was 90 years ago.

Economists refer to output per employed worker as **average labor productivity.** As Figure 16.2 shows, average labor productivity and output per person are closely related. This relationship makes sense—as we noted earlier, the more we can produce, the more we can consume. Because of this close link to the average living standard, average labor productivity and the factors that cause it to increase over time are of major concern to macroeconomists.

average labor productivity
output per employed worker

Although the long-term improvement in output per worker is impressive, the *rate* of improvement has slowed somewhat since the 1970s. Between 1950 and 1973 in the United States, output per employed worker increased by more than 2 percent per year. But from 1974 to 1995, the average rate of increase in output per worker was close to 1 percent per year. From 1996 to 2007, the pace of productivity growth picked up again, to nearly 2 percent per year before slowing down again to around 1 percent per year since 2008. Slowing productivity growth leads to less rapid improvement in living standards because the supply of goods and services cannot grow as quickly as it does during periods of rapid growth in productivity. Identifying the causes of productivity slowdowns and speedups is thus an important challenge for macroeconomists.

The current standard of living in the United States is not only much higher than in the past but also much higher than in many other nations today. Why have many of the world's countries, including both the developing nations of Asia, Africa, and Latin America and some formerly communist countries of eastern Europe, for many decades not enjoyed the same rates of economic growth as the industrialized countries? How can a country's rate of economic growth be improved? Once again, these are questions of keen interest to macroeconomists.

EXAMPLE 16.1   Productivity and Living Standards

How do China's productivity and output per person compare with those of the United States?

According to data from the World Bank (http://data.worldbank.org), in 2018 the value of the output of the U.S. economy was about $20,494 billion. In the same year, the estimated value of the output of the People's Republic of China was $13,608 billion (U.S.). The populations of the United States and China in 2018 were about 327 million and 1,393 million, respectively, while the numbers of employed workers in the two countries were, respectively, approximately 159 million and 756 million.

Find output per person and average labor productivity for the United States and China in 2018. What do the results suggest about comparative living standards in the two countries?

Output per person is simply total output divided by the number of people in an economy, and average labor productivity is output divided by the number of employed workers. Doing the math we get the following results for 2018:

	United States	China
Output per person	$ 62,673	$ 9,769
Average labor productivity	$128,893	$18,000

Note that, although the total output of the Chinese economy is more than 65 percent that of the U.S. output, output per person and average labor productivity in China are each less than 16 and 14 percent, respectively, of what they are in the United States. Thus, though the Chinese economy is predicted in the next 10 or 15 years to catch up with or surpass the U.S. economy in total output, for the time being there remains a large gap in productivity. This gap translates into striking differences in the average person's living standard between the two countries—in access to consumer goods, health care, transportation, education, and other benefits of affluence.

RECESSIONS AND EXPANSIONS

Economies do not always grow steadily; sometimes they go through periods of unusual strength or weakness. A look back at Figure 16.1 shows that although output generally grows over time, it does not always grow smoothly. Particularly striking is the decline in output during the Great Depression of the 1930s, followed by the sharp increase in output during World War II (1941–1945). But the figure shows many more moderate fluctuations in output as well.

Slowdowns in economic growth are called *recessions*; particularly severe economic slowdowns, like the one that began in 1929, are called *depressions*. In the United States, major recessions occurred in 1973–1975, 1981–1982, and 2007–2009 (find those recessions in Figure 16.1). More modest downturns occurred in 1990–1991 and 2001. Time will tell how the latest recession, that started in 2020 due to the COVID-19 pandemic, will compare with the depression and these recessions.

During recessions economic opportunities decline: Jobs are harder to find, people with jobs are less likely to get wage increases, profits are lower, and more companies go out of business. Recessions are particularly hard on economically disadvantaged people, who are most likely to be thrown out of work and have the hardest time finding new jobs.

Sometimes the economy grows unusually quickly. These periods of rapid economic growth are called *expansions*, and particularly strong expansions are called *booms*. During an expansion, jobs are easier to find, more people get raises and promotions, and most businesses thrive.

The alternating cycle of recessions and expansions raises some questions that are central to macroeconomics. What causes these short-term fluctuations in the rate of economic growth? Can government policymakers do anything about them? Should they try? These questions are discussed further in Chapter 24, *Short-Term Economic Fluctuations: An Introduction*.

UNEMPLOYMENT

The *unemployment rate*, the fraction of people who would like to be employed but can't find work, is a key indicator of the state of the labor market. When the unemployment rate is high, work is hard to find, and people who do have jobs typically find it harder to get promotions or wage increases.

Figure 16.3 shows the unemployment rate in the United States since 1929. Unemployment rises during recessions—note the dramatic spike in unemployment during the Great Depression, as well as the increases in unemployment during the 1973–1975, 1981–1982, and 2007–2009 recessions. But even in the so-called good times, such as the late 1990s and the late 2010s, some people are unemployed. Why does unemployment rise so sharply during periods of recession? And why are there always unemployed people, even when the economy is booming?

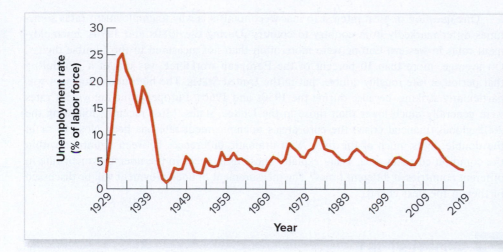

FIGURE 16.3

The U.S. Unemployment Rate, 1929–2019.

The unemployment rate is the percentage of the labor force that is out of work. Unemployment spikes upward during recessions and depressions, but the unemployment rate is always above zero, even in good times.

Source: Bureau of Labor Statistics, http://data.bls.gov.

EXAMPLE 16.2   Unemployment and Recessions

By how much did unemployment increase during five recent U.S. recessions?

Using monthly data on the national civilian unemployment rate, find the increase in the unemployment rate between the onset of recession in November 1973, January 1980, July 1990, January 2001, and December 2007 and the peak unemployment rate in the following years. Compare these increases in unemployment to the increase during the Great Depression.

Unemployment data are collected by the U.S. Bureau of Labor Statistics (BLS) and can be obtained from the BLS website (www.bls.gov/bls/unemployment.htm). Periodic publications include the *Survey of Current Business*, the *Federal Reserve Bulletin*, and *Economic Indicators*. Monthly data from the BLS website yield the following comparisons:

Unemployment rate at beginning of recession (%)	Peak unemployment rate (%)	Increase in unemployment rate (%)
4.8 (Nov. 1973)	9.0 (May 1975)	+4.2
6.3 (Jan. 1980)	10.8 (Nov./Dec. 1982)	+4.5
5.5 (July 1990)	7.8 (June 1992)	+2.3
4.1 (Jan. 2001)	6.3 (June 2003)	+2.2
5.0 (Dec. 2007)	10.0 (Oct. 2009)	+5.0

Unemployment increased significantly following the onset of each recession, although the impact of the 1990 and 2001 recessions on the labor market was clearly less serious than that of the 1973, 1980, and 2007 recessions. (Actually, the 1980 recession was a "double dip"—a short recession in 1980, followed by a longer one in 1981–1982.) In comparison, during the Great Depression the unemployment rate rose from about 3 percent in 1929 to about 25 percent in 1933, as we mentioned in the introduction to this chapter. Clearly, the 22 percentage point change in the unemployment rate that Americans experienced in the Great Depression dwarfs the effects of more recent postwar recessions.

One question of great interest to macroeconomists is why unemployment rates sometimes differ markedly from country to country. During the 1980s and 1990s, unemployment rates in western Europe were more often than not measured in the "double digits." On average, more than 10 percent of the European workforce was out of a job during that period, a rate roughly double that in the United States. The high unemployment was particularly striking, because during the 1950s and 1960s, European unemployment rates were generally much lower than those in the United States. Most recently, following the 2008 global financial crisis, the euro area's unemployment rate has been close to or in the double digits much of the time, with dramatic differences between countries within the common currency area. What explains these differences in the unemployment rate in different countries at different times? The measurement of unemployment will be discussed further in the next chapter.

 SELF-TEST 16.1

Find the most recent unemployment rates for France, Germany, Spain, and the United Kingdom, and compare them to the most recent unemployment rate for the United States. A useful source is the home page of the Organization for Economic Cooperation and Development (OECD), an organization of industrialized countries (www.oecd.org). See also the OECD's publication *Main Economic Indicators*. Is unemployment still lower in the United States than in Western Europe?

INFLATION

Another important economic statistic is the rate of *inflation*, which is the rate at which prices in general are increasing over time. As we will discuss in Chapter 18, *Measuring the Price Level and Inflation,* inflation imposes a variety of costs on the economy. And when the inflation rate is high, people on fixed incomes, such as pensioners who receive a fixed dollar payment each month, can't keep up with the rising cost of living.

In recent years, inflation has been relatively low in the United States, but that has not always been the case (see Figure 16.4 for data on U.S. inflation since 1929). During the 1970s, inflation was a major problem; in fact, many people told poll takers that inflation was "public enemy number one." Why was inflation high in the 1970s, and why is it relatively low today? What difference does it make to the average person?

FIGURE 16.4

The U.S. Inflation Rate, 1929–2019.

The U.S. inflation rate has fluctuated over time. Inflation was high in the 1970s but has been quite low recently.

Source: Bureau of Labor Statistics, http://data.bls.gov.

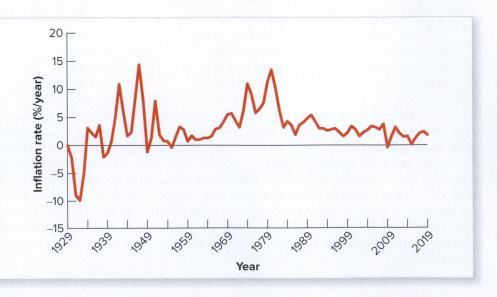

As with unemployment rates, the rate of inflation can differ markedly from country to country. For example, during the 1990s, the inflation rate averaged 3 percent per year in the United States, but the nation of Ukraine averaged over 400 percent annual inflation for the whole decade. And in 2008, when annual inflation in the United States was less than 4 percent, inflation in Zimbabwe was estimated in the hundreds of millions, and then billions, of percent, and quickly rising! What accounts for such large differences in inflation rates between countries?

Inflation and unemployment are often linked in policy discussions. One reason for this linkage is the oft-heard argument that unemployment can be reduced only at the cost of higher inflation and that inflation can be reduced only at the cost of higher unemployment. Must the government accept a higher rate of inflation to bring down unemployment, and vice versa?

ECONOMIC INTERDEPENDENCE AMONG NATIONS

National economies do not exist in isolation but are increasingly interdependent. The United States, because of its size and the wide variety of goods and services it produces, is one of the most self-sufficient economies on the planet. Even so, in 2019 the United States exported about 12 percent of all the goods and services it produced and imported from abroad 15 percent of the goods and services that Americans used. Merely 50 years earlier, in 1969, neither figure was above 5 percent.

Sometimes international flows of goods and services become a matter of political and economic concern. For example, some politicians maintain that low-priced imports threaten the farming and manufacturing jobs of their constituents. Are free-trade agreements, in which countries agree not to tax or otherwise block the international flow of goods and services, a good or bad thing?

A related issue is the phenomenon of *trade imbalances,* which occur when the quantity of goods and services that a country sells abroad (its *exports*) differs significantly from the quantity of goods and services its citizens buy from abroad (its *imports*). Figure 16.5 shows U.S. exports and imports since 1929, measured as a percentage of the economy's total output. Prior to the 1970s, the United States generally exported more than it imported. (Notice the major export boom that occurred after World War II, when the United States was helping to reconstruct Europe.) Since the 1970s, however, imports to the United States have outstripped exports, creating a situation called a *trade deficit.* Other countries—China, for example—export much more than they import. A country such as China is said to have a *trade surplus.* What causes trade deficits and surpluses? Are they harmful or helpful?

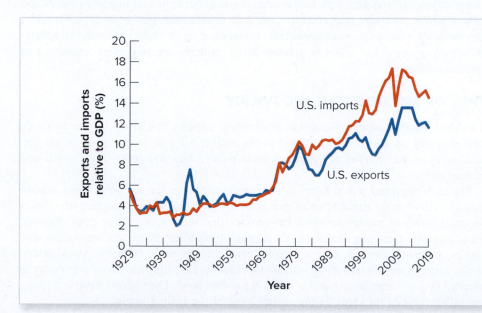

FIGURE 16.5

Exports and Imports as a Share of U.S. Output, 1929–2019.

The blue line shows U.S. exports of goods as a percentage of U.S. output. The red line shows U.S. imports of goods relative to U.S. output. For much of its history, the United States has exported more than it imported, but over the past decades, imports have greatly outstripped exports.

Sources: Import data: https://fred.stlouisfed.org/series/IMPGSA; export data: https://fred.stlouisfed.org/series/EXPGSA.

THE MAJOR MACROECONOMIC ISSUES

- *Economic growth and living standards.* Over the last century, the industrialized nations have experienced remarkable economic growth and improvements in living standards. Macroeconomists study the reasons for this extraordinary growth and try to understand why growth rates vary markedly among nations.
- *Productivity.* Average labor productivity, or output per employed worker, is a crucial determinant of living standards. Macroeconomists ask: What causes slowdowns and speedups in the rate of productivity growth?
- *Recessions and expansions.* Economies experience periods of slower growth (recessions) and more rapid growth (expansions). Macroeconomists examine the sources of these fluctuations and the government policies that attempt to moderate them.
- *Unemployment.* The unemployment rate is the fraction of people who would like to be employed but can't find work. Unemployment rises during recessions, but there are always unemployed people even during good times. Macroeconomists study the causes of unemployment, including the reasons why it sometimes differs markedly across countries.
- *Inflation.* The inflation rate is the rate at which prices in general are increasing over time. Questions macroeconomists ask about inflation include: Why does inflation vary over time and across countries? Must a reduction in inflation be accompanied by an increase in unemployment, or vice versa?
- *Economic interdependence among nations.* Modern economies are highly interdependent. Related issues studied by macroeconomists include the desirability of free-trade agreements and the causes and effects of trade imbalances.

MACROECONOMIC POLICY

We have seen that macroeconomists are interested in why different countries' economies perform differently and why a particular economy may perform well in some periods and poorly in others. Although many factors contribute to economic performance, government policy is surely among the most important. Understanding the effects of various policies and helping government officials develop better policies are important objectives of macroeconomists.

TYPES OF MACROECONOMIC POLICY

We defined macroeconomic policies as government policies that affect the performance of the economy as a whole, as opposed to the market for a particular good or service. There are three major types of macroeconomic policy: *monetary policy, fiscal policy,* and *structural policy*.

monetary policy
determination of the nation's money supply

The term **monetary policy** refers to the determination of the nation's money supply. (Cash and coin are the basic forms of money, although as we will see, modern economies have other forms of money as well.) For reasons that we will discuss in later chapters, most economists agree that changes in the money supply affect important macroeconomic variables, including national output, employment, interest rates, inflation, stock prices, and the international value of the dollar. In virtually all countries, monetary policy is controlled by a government institution called the *central bank*. The Federal Reserve System, often called the Fed for short, is the central bank of the United States.

Fiscal policy refers to decisions that determine the government's budget, including the amount and composition of government expenditures and government revenues. The balance between government spending and taxes is a particularly important aspect of fiscal policy. When government officials spend more than they collect in taxes, the government runs a *deficit*, and when they spend less, the government's budget is in *surplus*. As with monetary policy, economists generally agree that fiscal policy can have important effects on the overall performance of the economy. For example, many economists believe that the large deficits run by the federal government during the 1980s were harmful to the nation's economy. Likewise, many would say that the balancing of the federal budget that occurred during the 1990s contributed to the nation's strong economic performance during that decade. Since the early 2000s, the federal budget has moved once again into deficit. The deficit increased dramatically during and after the 2007–2009 recession.

Finally, the term **structural policy** includes government policies aimed at changing the underlying structure, or institutions, of the nation's economy. Structural policies come in many forms, from minor tinkering to ambitious overhauls of the entire economic system. The move away from government control of the economy and toward a more market-oriented approach in many formerly communist countries, such as Poland, the Czech Republic, and Hungary, is a large-scale example of structural policy. Many developing countries have tried similar structural reforms. Supporters of structural policy hope that, by changing the basic characteristics of the economy or by remaking its institutions, they can stimulate economic growth and improve living standards.

> **fiscal policy** decisions that determine the government's budget, including the amount and composition of government expenditures and government revenues

> **structural policy** government policies aimed at changing the underlying structure, or institutions, of the nation's economy

 SELF-TEST 16.2

The Congressional Budget Office (CBO) is the government agency that is charged with projecting the federal government's surpluses or deficits. From the CBO's home page (www.cbo.gov), find the most recent value of the federal government's surplus or deficit and the CBO's projected values for the next five years. How do you think these projections are likely to affect congressional deliberations on taxation and government spending?

POSITIVE VERSUS NORMATIVE ANALYSES OF MACROECONOMIC POLICY

Macroeconomists are frequently called upon to analyze the effects of a proposed policy. For example, if Congress is debating a tax cut, economists in the Congressional Budget Office or the Treasury may be asked to prepare an analysis of the likely effects of the tax cut on the overall economy, as well as on specific industries, regions, or income groups. An objective analysis aimed at determining only the economic consequences of a particular policy—not whether those consequences are desirable—is called a **positive analysis.** In contrast, a **normative analysis** includes recommendations on whether a particular policy *should* be implemented. While a positive analysis is supposed to be objective and scientific, a normative analysis involves the *values* of the person or organization doing the analysis—conservative, liberal, or middle-of-the-road.

While pundits often joke that economists cannot agree among themselves, the tendency for economists to disagree is exaggerated. When economists do disagree, the controversy often centers on normative judgments (which relate to economists' personal values) rather than on positive analysis (which reflects objective knowledge of the economy). For example, liberal and conservative economists might agree that a particular tax cut would increase the incomes of the relatively wealthy (positive analysis). But they might vehemently disagree on whether the policy *should* be enacted, reflecting their personal views about whether wealthy people deserve a tax break (normative analysis).

The next time you hear or read about a debate over economic issues, try to determine whether the differences between the two positions are primarily *positive* or *normative*. If

> **positive analysis** addresses the economic consequences of a particular event or policy, not whether those consequences are desirable

> **normative analysis** addresses the question of whether a policy *should* be used; normative analysis inevitably involves the values of the person doing the analysis

the debate focuses on the actual effects of the event or policy under discussion, then the disagreement is over positive issues. But if the main question has to do with conflicting personal opinions about the *desirability* of those effects, the debate is normative. The distinction between positive and normative analyses is important, because objective economic research can help to resolve differences over positive issues. When people differ for normative reasons, however, economic analysis is of less use.

> ✅ **SELF-TEST 16.3**
>
> Which of the following statements are positive and which are normative? How can you tell?
>
> a. A tax increase is likely to lead to lower interest rates.
>
> b. Congress should increase taxes to reduce the inappropriately high level of interest rates.
>
> c. A tax increase would be acceptable if most of the burden fell on those with incomes over $250,000.
>
> d. Higher tariffs (taxes on imports) are needed to protect American jobs.
>
> e. An increase in the tariff on imported steel would increase employment of American steelworkers.

> **RECAP ↑**
>
> **MACROECONOMIC POLICY**
>
> Macroeconomic policies affect the performance of the economy as a whole. The three types of macroeconomic policy are monetary policy, fiscal policy, and structural policy. *Monetary policy*, which in the United States is under the control of the Federal Reserve System, refers to the determination of the nation's money supply. *Fiscal policy* involves decisions about the government budget, including its expenditures and tax collections. *Structural policy* refers to government actions to change the underlying structure or institutions of the economy. Structural policy can range from minor tinkering to a major overhaul of the economic system, as with the formerly communist countries that converted to market-oriented systems.
>
> The analysis of a proposed policy can be positive or normative. A *positive analysis* addresses the policy's likely economic consequences but not whether those consequences are desirable. A *normative analysis* addresses the question of whether a proposed policy *should* be used. Debates about normative conclusions inevitably involve personal values and thus generally cannot be resolved by objective economic analysis alone.

AGGREGATION

In Chapter 1, *Thinking Like an Economist,* we discussed the difference between *macroeconomics,* the study of national economies, and *microeconomics,* the study of individual economic entities, such as households and firms, and the markets for specific goods and services. The main difference between the fields is one of perspective: Macroeconomists take a "bird's-eye view" of the economy, ignoring the fine details to understand how the system works as a whole. Microeconomists work instead at "ground level," studying the economic behavior of individual households, firms, and markets. Both perspectives are useful—indeed essential—to understanding what makes an economy work.

Although macroeconomics and microeconomics take different perspectives on the economy, the basic tools of analysis are much the same. In the chapters to come you will see that macroeconomists apply the same principles as microeconomists in their efforts to understand and predict economic behavior. Even though a national economy is a much bigger entity than a household or even a large firm, the choices and actions of individual decision makers ultimately determine the performance of the economy as a whole. So, for example, to understand saving behavior at the national level, the macroeconomist must first consider what motivates an individual family or household to save.

✔ SELF-TEST 16.4

Which of the following questions would be studied primarily by macroeconomists? By microeconomists? Explain.

a. Does increased government spending lower the unemployment rate?

b. Does Google's dominance of Internet searches harm consumers?

c. Would a school voucher program improve the quality of education in the United States? (Under a voucher program, parents are given a fixed amount of government aid, which they may use to send their children to any school, public or private.)

d. Should government policymakers aim to reduce inflation still further?

e. Why is the average rate of household saving low in the United States?

f. Does the increase in the number of consumer products being sold over the Internet threaten the profits of conventional retailers?

While macroeconomists use the core principles of economics to understand and predict individual economic decisions, they need a way to relate millions of individual decisions to the behavior of the economy as a whole. One important tool they use to link individual behavior to national economic performance is **aggregation,** the adding up of individual economic variables to obtain economywide totals.

aggregation the adding up of individual economic variables to obtain economywide totals

For example, macroeconomists don't care whether consumers drink Pepsi or Coke, go to the movie theater or stream videos, or drive a convertible or a sport-utility vehicle. These individual economic decisions are the province of microeconomics. Instead, macroeconomists add up consumer expenditures on all goods and services during a given period to obtain *aggregate,* or total, consumer expenditure. Similarly, a macroeconomist would not focus on plumbers' wages versus electricians' but would concentrate instead on the average wage of all workers. By focusing on aggregate variables, like total consumer expenditures or the average wage, macroeconomists suppress the mind-boggling details of a complex modern economy to see broad economic trends.

EXAMPLE 16.3   Aggregation (Part 1): A National Crime Index

Is crime in the United States getting better or worse?

To illustrate not only why aggregation is needed, but also some of the problems associated with it, consider an issue that is only partly economic: crime. Suppose policymakers want to know whether *in general* the problem of crime in the United States is getting better or worse. How could an analyst obtain a statistical answer to that question?

Police keep detailed records of the crimes reported in their jurisdictions, so in principle a researcher could determine precisely how many purse snatchings occurred last year on New York City subways. But data on the number of crimes of each type in each jurisdiction would produce stacks of computer output. Is there a way to add up, or aggregate, all the crime data to get some sense of the national trend?

Law enforcement agencies such as the FBI use aggregation to obtain national *crime rates*, which are typically expressed as the number of "serious" crimes committed per 100,000 population. For example, the FBI reported that in 2015, some 9.2 million serious crimes (both violent crimes and property crimes) occurred in the United States (www.fbi.gov). Dividing the number of crimes by the U.S. population in 2015, which was about 321 million, and multiplying by 100,000 yields the crime rate for 2015, equal to about 2,860 crimes per 100,000 people. This rate represented a substantial drop from the crime rate in 2000, which was about 4,100 crimes per 100,000 people. So aggregation (the adding up of many different crimes into a national index) indicates that, in general, serious crime decreased in the United States between 2000 and 2015.

Although aggregation of crime statistics reveals the "big picture," it may obscure important details. The FBI crime index lumps together relatively minor crimes such as petty theft with very serious crimes such as murder and rape. Most people would agree that murder and rape do far more damage than a typical theft, so adding together these two very different types of crimes might give a false picture of crime in the United States. For example, although the U.S. crime rate fell 30 percent between 2000 and 2015, the murder rate fell by less than 12 percent. Because murder is the most serious of crimes, the reduction in crime between 2000 and 2015 was probably less significant than the change in the overall crime rate indicates. The aggregate crime rate glosses over other important details, such as the fact that the most dramatic reductions in crime occurred in urban areas. This loss of detail is a cost of aggregation, the price analysts pay for the ability to look at broad economic or social trends.

EXAMPLE 16.4   Aggregation (Part 2): U.S. Exports

How can we add together Kansas grain with Hollywood movies?

The United States exports a wide variety of products and services to many different countries. Kansas farmers sell grain to Russia, Silicon Valley programmers sell software to France, and Hollywood movie studios sell entertainment the world over. Suppose macroeconomists want to compare the total quantities of American-made goods sold to various regions of the world. How could such a comparison be made?

Economists can't add bushels of grain, lines of code, and movie tickets—the units aren't comparable. But they can add the *dollar values* of each—the revenue farmers earned from foreign grain sales, the royalties programmers received for their exported software, and the revenues studios reaped from films shown abroad. By comparing the dollar values of U.S. exports to Europe, Asia, Africa, and other regions in a particular year, economists are able to determine which regions are the biggest customers for American-made goods.

> **RECAP** ↑
>
> ### AGGREGATION
>
> Macroeconomics, the study of national economies, differs from micro-economics, the study of individual economic entities (such as households and firms) and the markets for specific goods and services. Macroecono-mists take a "bird's-eye view" of the economy. To study the economy as a whole, macroeconomists make frequent use of aggregation, the adding up of individual economic variables to obtain economywide totals. For example, a macroeconomist is more interested in the determinants of total U.S. exports, as measured by total dollar value, than in the factors that determine the exports of specific goods. A cost of aggregation is that the fine details of the economic situation are often obscured.

STUDYING MACROECONOMICS: A PREVIEW

This chapter introduced many of the key issues of macroeconomics. In the chapters to come we will look at each of these issues in more detail. We will start with the *measurement* of economic performance, including key variables like the level of economic activity, the extent of unemployment, and the rate of inflation. Obtaining quantitative measurements of the economy, against which theories can be tested, is the crucial first step in answering basic macroeconomic questions like those raised in this chapter.

Next, we will study economic behavior over relatively long periods of time. We will examine economic growth and productivity improvement, the fundamental determinants of the average standard of living in the long run. We will then discuss the long-run determination of employment, unemployment, and wages; and study saving and its link to the creation of new capital goods, such as factories and machines. The role played in the economy by money, and its relation to the rate of inflation and to the central bank, will then be discussed, as will both domestic and international financial markets and their role in allocating saving to productive uses, in particular their role in promoting international capital flows.

John Maynard Keynes, a celebrated British economist, once wrote, "In the long run, we are all dead." Keynes's statement was intended as an ironic comment on the tendency of economists to downplay short-run economic problems on the grounds that "in the long run," the operation of the free market will always restore economic stability. Keynes, who was particularly active and influential during the Great Depression, correctly viewed the problem of massive unemployment, whether "short run" or not, as the most pressing economic issue of the time.

So why start our study of macroeconomics with the long run? Keynes's comment notwithstanding, long-run economic performance is extremely important, accounting for most of the substantial differences in living standards and economic well-being the world over. Furthermore, studying long-run economic behavior provides important background for understanding short-term fluctuations in the economy.

We turn to those short-term fluctuations by first providing background on what happens during recessions and expansions, as well as some historical perspective, before discussing one important source of short-term economic fluctuations, variations in aggregate spending. We will also show how, by influencing aggregate spending, fiscal policy may be able to moderate economic fluctuations. The second major policy tool for stabilizing the economy, monetary policy, will then be discussed, along with the circumstances under which macroeconomic policymakers may face a short-term trade-off between inflation and unemployment.

The international dimension of macroeconomics will be highlighted throughout the discussion. We will introduce topics such as exchange rates between national currencies and discuss how they are determined and how they affect the workings of the economy and macroeconomic policy.

SUMMARY

- Macroeconomics is the study of the performance of national economies and of the policies governments use to try to improve that performance. Some of the broad issues macroeconomists study are: *(LO1)*
  - Sources of economic growth and improved *living standards.*
  - Trends in *average labor productivity,* or output per employed worker.
  - Short-term fluctuations in the pace of economic growth (recessions and expansions).
  - Causes and cures of unemployment and inflation.
  - Economic interdependence among nations.

- To help explain differences in economic performance among countries, or in economic performance in the same country at different times, macroeconomists study the implementation and effects of macroeconomic policies. *Macroeconomic policies* are government actions designed to affect the performance of the economy as a whole. Macroeconomic policies include *monetary policy* (the determination of the nation's money supply), *fiscal policy* (relating to decisions about the government's budget), and *structural policy* (aimed at affecting the basic structure and institutions of the economy). *(LO2)*

- In studying economic policies, economists apply both *positive analysis* (an objective attempt to determine the consequences of a proposed policy) and *normative analysis* (which addresses whether a particular policy *should* be adopted). Normative analysis involves the values of the person doing the analysis. *(LO2)*

- Macroeconomics is distinct from microeconomics, which focuses on the behavior of individual economic entities and specific markets. Macroeconomists make heavy use of *aggregation,* which is the adding up of individual economic variables into economywide totals. Aggregation allows macroeconomists to study the "big picture" of the economy, while ignoring fine details about individual households, firms, and markets. *(LO3)*

KEY TERMS

aggregation	macroeconomic policies	positive analysis
average labor productivity	monetary policy	standard of living
fiscal policy	normative analysis	structural policy

REVIEW QUESTIONS

1. How did the experience of the Great Depression motivate the development of the field of macroeconomics? *(LO1)*

2. Generally, how does the standard of living in the United States today compare to the standard of living in other countries? To the standard of living in the United States a century ago? *(LO1)*

3. Why is average labor productivity a particularly important economic variable? *(LO1)*

4. True or false: Economic growth within a particular country generally proceeds at a constant rate. Explain. *(LO1)*

5. True or false: Differences of opinion about economic policy recommendations can always be resolved by objective analysis of the issues. Explain. *(LO2)*

6. What type of macroeconomic policy (monetary, fiscal, structural) might include each of the following actions? *(LO2)*

   a. A broad government initiative to reduce the country's reliance on agriculture and promote high-technology industries.
   b. A reduction in income tax rates.
   c. Provision of additional cash to the banking system.
   d. An attempt to reduce the government budget deficit by reducing spending.
   e. A decision by a developing country to reduce government control of the economy and to become more market-oriented.

7. Baseball statistics, such as batting averages, are calculated and reported for each individual player, for each team, and for the league as a whole. What purposes are served by doing this? Relate to the idea of aggregation in macroeconomics. *(LO3)*

PROBLEMS

McGraw Hill connect

1. Over the next 50 years the Japanese population is expected to decline, while the fraction of the population that is retired is expected to increase sharply. What are the implications of these population changes for total output and average living standards in Japan, assuming that average labor productivity continues to grow? What if average labor productivity stagnates? *(LO1)*

2. Is it possible for average living standards to rise during a period in which average labor productivity is falling? Discuss, using a numerical example for illustration. *(LO1)*

3. The Bureau of Economic Analysis, or BEA, is a government agency that collects a wide variety of statistics about the U.S. economy. From the BEA's website (www.bea.gov), find data for the most recent year available on U.S. exports and imports of goods and services. Is the United States running a trade surplus or deficit? Calculate the ratio of the surplus or deficit to U.S. exports. *(LO1)*

4. Which of the following statements are positive and which are normative? *(LO2)*
   a. If the Federal Reserve raises interest rates, demand for housing is likely to fall.
   b. The Federal Reserve should raise interest rates to keep inflation at an acceptably low level.
   c. Stock prices are likely to fall over the next year as the economy slows.
   d. A reduction in the capital gains tax (the tax on profits made in the stock market) would lead to a 10 to 20 percent increase in stock prices.
   e. Congress should not reduce capital gains taxes without also providing tax breaks for lower-income people.

5. Which of the following would be studied by a macroeconomist? By a microeconomist? *(LO3)*
   a. The worldwide operations of General Motors.
   b. The effect of government subsidies on sugar prices.
   c. Factors affecting average wages in the U.S. economy.
   d. Inflation in developing countries.
   e. The effects of tax cuts on consumer spending.

ANSWERS TO SELF-TESTS

16.1 Your answer will depend upon the current unemployment rate available at the OECD website. *(LO1)*

16.2 Your answer will depend upon the current CBO budget data. *(LO2)*

16.3 a. Positive. This is a prediction of the effect of a policy, not a value judgment on whether the policy should be used.
   b. Normative. Words like *should* and *inappropriately* express value judgments about the policy.
   c. Normative. The statement is about the desirability of certain types of policies, not their likely effects.
   d. Normative. The statement is about desirability of a policy.
   e. Positive. The statement is a prediction of the likely effects of a policy, not a recommendation on whether the policy should be used. *(LO2)*

16.4 a. Macroeconomists. Government spending and unemployment are aggregate concepts pertaining to the national economy.
   b. Microeconomists. Google, though large, is an individual firm.
   c. Microeconomists. The issue relates to the supply and demand for a specific service, education.
   d. Macroeconomists. Inflation is an aggregate, economywide concept.
   e. Macroeconomists. Average saving is an aggregate concept.
   f. Microeconomists. The focus is on a relatively narrow set of markets and products rather than on the economy as a whole. *(LO3)*

CHAPTER 17

Measuring Economic Activity: GDP and Unemployment

How do economists measure the economy's overall health?

LEARNING OBJECTIVES

After reading this chapter, you should be able to:

LO1 Explain how economists define an economy's output.

LO2 Apply the production, expenditure, and income methods for measuring GDP to analyze economic activity.

LO3 Define and compute nominal GDP and real GDP.

LO4 Discuss the relationship between real GDP and economic well-being.

LO5 Calculate the unemployment rate and the participation rate and discuss the costs of unemployment.

"Real GDP increased 2.2 percent in the fourth quarter, according to the U.S. Bureau of Economic Analysis . . ."

"Total nonfarm payroll employment increased by 209,000 in July, and the unemployment rate was little changed at 4.3 percent, the U.S. Bureau of Labor Statistics reported today . . ."

"Inflation appears subdued as the consumer price index registered an increase of only 0.1 percent last month . . ."

News reports like these fill the airwaves and the web—some TV and radio stations and some websites carry nothing else. In fact, all kinds of people are interested in economic data. The average person hopes to learn something that will be useful in a business decision, a financial investment, or a career move. The professional economist depends on economic data in much the same way that a doctor depends on a patient's vital signs—pulse, blood pressure, and temperature—to make an accurate diagnosis. To understand economic developments and to be able to give useful advice to policymakers, businesspeople, and financial investors, an economist simply must have up-to-date, accurate data. Political leaders and policymakers also need economic data to help them in their decisions and planning.

Interest in measuring the economy, and attempts to do so, date back as far as the mid-seventeenth century, when Sir William Petty (1623–1687) conducted a detailed survey of the land and wealth of Ireland. The British government's purpose in commissioning the survey was to determine the capacity of the Irish people to pay taxes to the Crown. But Petty used the opportunity to measure a variety of social and economic variables and went on to conduct pioneering studies of wealth, production, and population in several other countries. He was a firm believer in the idea that scientific progress depends first and foremost on accurate measurement, an idea that today's economists endorse.

Not until the twentieth century, though, did economic measurement come into its own. World War II was an important catalyst for the development of accurate economic statistics because its very outcome was thought to depend on the mobilization of economic resources. Two economists, Simon Kuznets in the United States and Richard Stone in the United Kingdom, developed comprehensive systems for measuring a nation's output of goods and services, which were of great help to Allied leaders in their wartime planning. Kuznets and Stone each received a Nobel Prize in Economics for their work, which became the basis for the economic accounts used today by almost all the world's countries. The governments of the United States and many other countries now collect and publish a wealth of statistics covering all aspects of their economies.

In this chapter and the next, we will discuss how economists measure three basic macroeconomic variables that arise frequently in analyses of the state of the economy: the *gross domestic product* (or *GDP*), the *rate of unemployment,* and the *rate of inflation*. The focus of this chapter is on the first two of these statistics, GDP and the unemployment rate, which both measure the overall level of economic activity in a country. The third statistic, the inflation rate covered in the next chapter, measures how fast prices change in a country.

Measuring economic activity might sound like a straightforward and uncontroversial task, but that is not the case. Indeed, the basic measure of a nation's output of goods and services—the gross domestic product, or GDP—has been criticized on many grounds. Some critics have complained that GDP does not adequately reflect factors such as the effect of economic growth on the environment or the rate of resource depletion. Because of problems like these, they charge, policies based on GDP statistics are likely to be flawed. Unemployment statistics have also been the subject of some controversy. By the end of this chapter, you will understand how official measures of output and unemployment are constructed and used and will have gained some insight into these debates over their accuracy. In particular, you will understand how these statistics are defined and measured, and you will be able to discuss the strengths and limitations of the definitions as well as the measurement difficulties that governments face when turning the definitions into actual, published estimates. You will see, for example, what goes into the calculation of a nation's GDP and, importantly, what is left out. So next time you hear or read about the most recent economic statistics, you will avoid misinterpreting them.

Understanding the strengths and limitations of economic data is the first critical step toward becoming an intelligent user of economic statistics, as well as a necessary background for careful economic analysis in the chapters to come.

GROSS DOMESTIC PRODUCT: MEASURING THE NATION'S OUTPUT

Chapter 16, *Macroeconomics: The Bird's-Eye View of the Economy,* emphasized the link between an economy's output of goods and services and its living standard. We noted that high levels of output per person, and per worker, are typically associated with a high standard of living. But what, exactly, does "output" mean? To study economic growth and productivity scientifically, we need to be more precise about how economists define and measure an economy's output.

The most frequently used measure of an economy's output is called the *gross domestic product,* or *GDP*. **Gross domestic product (GDP)** is intended to measure how much an economy produces in a given period, such as a quarter (three months) or a year. More precisely, GDP is the market value of the final goods and services produced in a country during a given period. To understand this definition, let's take it apart and examine each of its parts separately. The first key phrase in the definition is "market value."

gross domestic product (GDP) the market value of the final goods and services produced in a country during a given period

MARKET VALUE

A modern economy produces many different goods and services, from dental floss (a good) to acupuncture (a service). Macroeconomists are not interested in this kind of detail, however; rather, their goal is to understand the behavior of the economy as a whole. For example, a macroeconomist might ask: "Has the overall capacity of the economy to produce goods and services increased over time? If so, by how much?"

To be able to talk about concepts like the "total output" or "total production"—as opposed to the production of specific items like dental floss—economists need to *aggregate* the quantities of the many different goods and services into a single number. They do so by adding up the *market values* of the different goods and services the economy produces. **Market value** is the selling prices of goods and services in the open market. We use these prices because they are the prices at which buyers and sellers agree to make their transactions. Examples 17.1 and 17.2 will illustrate the process.

market value the selling prices of goods and services in the open market

EXAMPLE 17.1	Orchardia's GDP (Part 1)

What is Orchardia's GDP?

In the imaginary economy of Orchardia, total production is 4 apples and 6 bananas. To find the total output of Orchardia, we could add the number of apples to the number of bananas and conclude that total output is 10 pieces of fruit. But what if this economy also produced 3 pairs of shoes? There really is no sensible way to add apples and bananas to shoes.

Suppose though that we know that apples sell for $0.25 each, bananas for $0.50 each, and shoes for $20.00 a pair. Then the market value of this economy's production, or its GDP, is equal to

$$(4 \text{ apples} \times \$0.25/\text{apple}) + (6 \text{ bananas} \times \$0.50/\text{banana}) + (3 \text{ pairs of shoes} \times \$20.00/\text{pair}) = \$64.00.$$

Notice that when we calculate total output this way, the more expensive items (the shoes) receive a higher weighting than the cheaper items (the apples and bananas). Since, in general, the amount people are willing to pay for an item is an indication of the economic benefit they expect to receive from it, market values provide a convenient way for aggregating output into one number.

EXAMPLE 17.2	Orchardia's GDP (Part 2)

What is Orchardia's new GDP?

Now suppose instead that Orchardia were to produce 3 apples, 3 bananas, and 4 pairs of shoes at the same prices as in the preceding example. What is its GDP now?

Now the Orchardian GDP is equal to

$$(3 \text{ apples} \times \$0.25/\text{apple}) + (3 \text{ bananas} \times \$0.50/\text{banana}) + (4 \text{ pairs of shoes} \times \$20.00/\text{pair}) = \$82.25.$$

Notice that Orchardian GDP is higher in Example 17.2 than in Example 17.1, even though two of the three goods (apples and bananas) are being produced in smaller quantities than before. The reason is that the good whose production has increased (shoes) has a much higher market value than the goods whose production has decreased (apples and bananas).

SELF-TEST 17.1

Suppose Orchardia produces the same quantities of the three goods at the same prices as in Example 17.1. In addition, it produces five oranges at $0.30 each. What is the GDP of Orchardia now?

Market values provide a convenient way to add together, or aggregate, the many different goods and services produced in a modern economy. A drawback of using market values, however, is that not all economically valuable goods and services are bought and sold in markets. For example, the unpaid work of a homemaker, although it is of economic value, is not sold in markets and so isn't counted in GDP. But paid housekeeping and child-care services, which are sold in markets, do count. As a result, new moms or dads who decide to take an extended unpaid leave from work and dedicate all their time and energy to providing for their newborn's physical, cognitive, and emotional development in the first months of the child's life may be making a priceless contribution to the health and well-being (including economic) of a society in the present and future; yet their decision is likely to make present GDP smaller because it withdraws activity from markets. Example 17.3 illustrates some of the pitfalls that the distinction between market and nonmarket value creates.

EXAMPLE 17.3   Women's Labor Force Participation and GDP Measurement

How has GDP been affected by women joining the labor force?

The percentage of adult American women working, or seeking work, outside the home increased dramatically in the second half of the twentieth century, from less than 35 percent in 1950 to about 60 percent in 2019 (see Figure 17.1). This trend has led to a substantial increase in the demand for paid day care and housekeeping services as working wives and mothers require more help at home. How have these changes affected measured GDP?

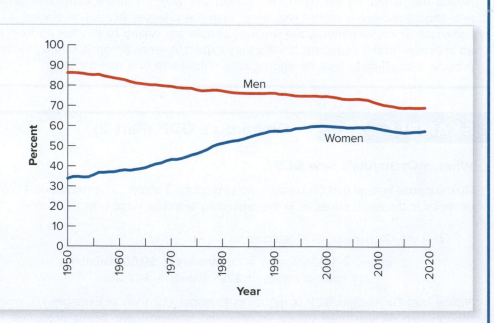

FIGURE 17.1

Percentages of American Men and Women over Age 16 Working or Seeking Work outside the Home, 1950–2019.

The fraction of American women working outside the home rose by about 25 percentage points between 1950 and 2019, while the fraction of men working outside the home declined.
Source: Bureau of Labor Statistics, www.bls.gov/cps.

The entry of many women into the labor market has raised measured GDP in two ways. First, the goods and services that women produce in their new jobs have contributed directly to increasing GDP. Second, the fact that paid workers took over previously unpaid housework and child-care duties has increased measured GDP by the amount paid to those workers. The first of these two changes represents a genuine increase in economic activity, but the second reflects a transfer of existing economic activities from the unpaid sector to the market sector (moreover, it is possible that this transfer lowered the quality of these activities). Overall, then, the increase in measured GDP associated with increased participation in the labor force by women probably overstates the actual increase in economic activity.

Although homemaking activities are excluded from measured GDP, in a few cases, goods and services that are not sold in markets are included in GDP. By far the most important are the goods and services provided by federal, state, and local governments. The protection provided by the army and navy, the transportation convenience of the interstate highway system, and the education provided by the public school system are examples of publicly provided goods and services that are not sold in markets.

Because market prices for publicly provided goods and services do not exist, economic statisticians add to the GDP the *costs* of providing those goods and services as rough measures of their economic value. For example, to include public education in the GDP, the statisticians add to GDP the salaries of teachers and administrators, the costs of textbooks and supplies, and the like. Similarly, the economic value of the national defense establishment is approximated, for the purposes of measuring GDP, by the *costs* of defense: the pay earned by soldiers and sailors, the costs of acquiring and maintaining weapons, and so on.

While approximating value by looking at costs is much better than ignoring nonmarket goods and services altogether, it is far from perfect: A more efficient government could deliver *more value* at a *lower cost*. For example, as a report by the Organization for Economic Cooperation and Development (OECD)[1] suggests, the children in countries whose governments spend *less* (per child) than other governments do not always show worse outcomes on indicators such as health and safety, educational well-being, and quality of school life. In fact, using cost as a substitute for market value means that every dollar a government spends adds a dollar to GDP regardless of how efficiently or wastefully it is spent!

With a few exceptions, like publicly provided goods and services, GDP is calculated by adding up market values. However, not all goods and services that have a market value are counted in GDP. As we will see next, GDP includes only those goods and services that are the end products of the production process, called *final goods and services*. Goods and services that are used up in the production process are not counted in GDP.

Why was the female labor force participation rate in 2019 more than 70 percent greater than in 1950?

FINAL GOODS AND SERVICES

Many goods are used in the production process. For instance, before a baker can produce a loaf of bread, grain must be grown and harvested and then ground into flour. The flour is then used along with other ingredients to make bread. Of the three major goods that are produced during this process—the grain, the flour, and the bread—only the bread is used by consumers. Because producing the bread is the ultimate purpose of the process, the bread is called a *final good*. In general, a **final good or service** is the end product of a process, the product or service that consumers actually use. The goods or services produced on the way toward making the final product—here, the grain and the flour—are called **intermediate goods or services.**

Since we are interested in measuring only those items that are of direct economic value, *only final goods and services are included in GDP*. Intermediate goods and services are *not* included. To illustrate, suppose that the grain from the previous example has a market value of $0.50 (the price the milling company paid for the grain). The grain is then ground into flour, which has a market value of $1.20 (the price the baker paid for the flour). Finally, the flour is made into a loaf of fine French bread, worth $2.00 at the local store.

final goods or services goods or services consumed by the ultimate user; because they are the end products of the production process, they are counted as part of GDP

intermediate goods or services goods or services used up in the production of final goods and services and therefore not counted as part of GDP

[1]OECD, *Doing Better for Children,* 2009. See also coverage in *The Economist,* "The Nanny State," September 3, 2009.

In calculating the contribution of these activities to GDP, would we want to add together the values of the grain, the flour, and the bread? No, because the grain and flour are intermediate goods, valuable only because they can be used to make bread. So in this example, the total contribution to GDP is $2.00, the value of the loaf of bread, the final product.

Example 17.4 illustrates the same distinction but this time with a focus on services.

EXAMPLE 17.4 | **GDP for the Barber and His Assistant**

How do we count a haircut in GDP?

Your barber charges $10 for a haircut. In turn, the barber pays his assistant $2 per haircut in return for sharpening the scissors, sweeping the floor, and other chores. For each haircut given, what is the total contribution of the barber and his assistant, taken together, to GDP?

The answer to this problem is $10, the price, or market value, of the haircut. The haircut is counted in GDP because it is the final service, the one that actually has value to the final user. The services provided by the assistant have value only because they contribute to the production of the haircut; thus they are not counted in GDP.

Example 17.5 illustrates that the same good can be either intermediate or final, depending on how it is used.

EXAMPLE 17.5 | **A Good That Can Be Either Intermediate or Final**

What is an intermediate good?

Farmer Brown produces $100 worth of milk. He sells $40 worth of milk to his neighbors and uses the rest to feed his pigs, which he sells to his neighbors for $120. What is Farmer Brown's contribution to the GDP?

The final goods in this example are the $40 worth of milk and the $120 worth of pigs sold to the neighbors. Adding $40 and $120, we get $160, which is Farmer Brown's contribution to the GDP. Note that part of the milk Farmer Brown produced serves as an intermediate good and part as a final good. The $60 worth of milk that is fed to the pigs is an intermediate good, and so it is not counted in GDP. The $40 worth of milk sold to the neighbors is a final good, and so it is counted.

---

capital good a long-lived good that is used in the production of other goods and services

A special type of good that is difficult to classify as intermediate or final is a *capital good*. A **capital good** is a long-lived good, which is itself produced and used to produce other goods and services. Factories and machines are examples of capital goods. Houses and apartment buildings, which produce dwelling services, are also a form of capital goods. Capital goods do not fit the definition of final goods since their purpose is to produce other goods. On the other hand, they are not used up during the production process, except over a very long period, so they are not exactly intermediate goods either. For purposes of measuring GDP, economists have agreed to classify newly produced capital goods as final goods. Otherwise, a country that invested in its future by building modern factories and buying new machines would be counted as having a lower GDP than a country that devoted all its resources to producing consumer goods.

We have established the rule that only final goods and services (including newly produced capital goods) are counted in GDP. Intermediate goods and services, which are used up in the production of final goods and services, are not counted. In practice, however, this rule is not easy to apply because the production process often stretches over several periods. To illustrate, recall the earlier example of the grain that was milled into flour, which in turn was baked into a loaf of French bread. The contribution of the whole process to GDP is $2, the value of the bread (the final product). Suppose, though, that the grain and the flour were produced near the end of the year 2019 and the bread was baked early the next year in 2020. In this case, should we attribute the $2 value of the bread to the GDP for the year 2019 or to the GDP for the year 2020?

Neither choice seems quite right because part of the bread's production process occurred in each year. Part of the value of the bread should probably be counted in the year 2019 GDP and part in the year 2020 GDP. But how should we make the split? To deal with this problem, economists determine the market value of final goods and services indirectly, by adding up the *value added* by each firm in the production process. The **value added** by any firm equals the market value of its product or service minus the cost of inputs purchased from other firms. As we'll see, summing the value added by all firms (including producers of both intermediate and final goods and services) gives the same answer as simply adding together the value of final goods and services. The value-added method thus eliminates the problem of dividing the value of a final good or service between two periods.

To illustrate this method, let's revisit the example of the French bread, which is the result of multiple stages of production. We have already determined that the total contribution of this production process to GDP is $2, the value of the bread. Let's show now that we can get the same answer by summing value added. Suppose that the bread is the ultimate product of three corporations: ABC Grain Company Inc. produces grain, General Flour produces flour, and Hot'n'Fresh Baking produces the bread. If we make the same assumptions as before about the market value of the grain, the flour, and the bread, what is the value added by each of these three companies?

ABC Grain Company produces $0.50 worth of grain, with no inputs from other companies, so ABC's value added is $0.50. General Flour uses $0.50 worth of grain from ABC to produce $1.20 worth of flour. The value added by General Flour is thus the value of its product ($1.20) less the cost of purchased inputs ($0.50), or $0.70. Finally, Hot'n'Fresh Baking buys $1.20 worth of flour from General Flour and uses it to produce $2.00 worth of bread. So the value added by Hot'n'Fresh is $0.80. These calculations are summarized in Table 17.1.

value added for any firm, the market value of its product or service minus the cost of inputs purchased from other firms

TABLE 17.1
Value Added in Bread Production

Company	Revenues	− Cost of purchased inputs	= Value added
ABC Grain	$0.50	$0.00	$0.50
General Flour	$1.20	$0.50	$0.70
Hot'n'Fresh	$2.00	$1.20	$0.80
Total			$2.00

You can see that summing the value added by each company gives the same contribution to GDP, $2.00, as the method based on counting final goods and services only. Basically, the value added by each firm represents the portion of the value of the final good or service that the firm creates in its stage of production. Summing the value added by all firms in the economy yields the total value of final goods and services, or GDP.

This example also illustrates how the value-added method solves the problem of production processes that bridge two or more periods. Suppose that the grain and flour are produced during the year 2019 but the bread is not baked until 2020. Using the value-added method, the contribution of this production process to the year 2019 GDP is the value added by the grain company plus the value added by the flour company, or $1.20. The contribution of the production process to the year 2020 GDP is the value added by the baker, which is $0.80. Thus part of the value of the final product, the bread, is counted in the GDP for each year, reflecting the fact that part of the production of the bread took place in each year.

Amy's card shop receives a shipment of Valentine's Day cards in December 2019. Amy pays the wholesale distributor of the cards a total of $500. In February 2020 she sells the cards for a total of $700. What are the contributions of these transactions to GDP in the years 2019 and 2020?

We have now established that GDP is equal to the market value of final goods and services. Let's look at the last part of the definition, "produced in a country during a given period."

PRODUCED IN A COUNTRY DURING A GIVEN PERIOD

The word *domestic* in the term *gross domestic product* tells us that GDP is a measure of economic activity within a given country. Thus, only production that takes place within the country's borders is counted. For example, the GDP of the United States includes the market value of *all* cars produced within U.S. borders, even if they are made in foreign-owned plants. However, cars produced in Mexico by a U.S.-based company like General Motors are *not* counted.

What about cars that are produced in the United States from parts that are produced in Mexico? The *value-added* method introduced earlier could again be used to suggest an answer. Recall that we used this method to divide the market value of a product that was produced over two years into its contribution to the GDP of each of the years. Similarly, we can use this method to divide the value of a product that was produced in part in two different countries into its contribution to each country's GDP. Revisiting our French bread example, suppose now that ABC Grain Company produces the grain in Mexico. General Flour buys $0.50 worth of grain from ABC in Mexico, imports it to the United States, and uses it to produce $1.20 worth of flour (in the U.S.). Finally, Hot'n'Fresh Baking buys $1.20 worth of flour from General Flour and uses it to produce $2.00 worth of bread (in the U.S.). Using the value-added method, Table 17.1 suggests that the total value of the bread, $2.00, is divided across the two countries' national accounts: $0.50 is included in Mexico's GDP (the value of the grain produced in Mexico), and $1.50 is included in the United States' GDP (the value added in the U.S.).

We have seen that GDP is intended to measure the amount of production that occurs during a given period, such as the calendar year. For this reason, only goods and services that are actually produced during a particular year are included in the GDP for that year. Example 17.6 and Self-Test 17.3 demonstrate this point.

EXAMPLE 17.6	The Sale of a House and GDP

Does the sale of an existing home count in GDP?

A 20-year-old house is sold to a young family for $200,000. The seller pays the real estate agent a 6 percent commission, or $12,000. What is the contribution of this transaction to GDP?

Because the house was not produced during the current year, its value is *not* counted in this year's GDP. (The value of the house was included in the GDP 20 years earlier, the year the house was built.) In general, purchases and sales of existing assets, such as old houses or used cars, do not contribute to the current year's GDP. However, the $12,000 fee paid to the real estate agent represents the market value of the agent's services in helping to sell the house and helping the family make the purchase. Since those services were provided during the current year, the agent's fee *is* counted in current-year GDP.

SELF-TEST 17.3

Lotta Doe sells 100 shares of stock in Benson Buggywhip for $50 per share. She pays her broker a 2 percent commission for executing the sale. How does Lotta's transaction affect the current-year GDP?

RECAP ↑

MEASURING GDP

Gross domestic product (GDP) equals the market value
- GDP is an aggregate of the market values of the many goods and services produced in the economy.
- Goods and services that are not sold in markets, such as unpaid housework, are not counted in GDP. An important exception is goods and services provided by the government, which are included in GDP at the government's cost of providing them.

of final goods and services
- Final goods and services (which include capital goods, such as factories and machines) are counted in GDP. Intermediate goods and services, which are used up in the production of final goods and services, are not counted.
- In practice, the value of final goods and services is determined by the value-added method. The value added by any firm equals the firm's revenue from selling its product minus the cost of inputs purchased from other firms. Summing the value added by all firms in the production process yields the value of the final good or service.

produced in a country during a given period.
- Only goods and services produced within a nation's borders are included in GDP.
- Only goods and services produced during the current year (or the portion of the value produced during the current year) are counted as part of the current-year GDP.

METHODS FOR MEASURING GDP

GDP is a measure of the quantity of goods and services *produced* by an economy. But any good or service that is produced will also be *purchased* and used by some economic agent—a consumer buying Christmas gifts or a firm investing in new machinery, for example. For many purposes, knowing not only how much is produced, but who uses it and how, is important. Furthermore, when an economic agent purchases a good or a service, that agent's spending is some other economic agent's *income*. For some purposes, it is also important to track this income from the production of goods and services.

THE EXPENDITURE METHOD FOR MEASURING GDP

Economic statisticians divide the users of the final goods and services that make up the GDP for any given year into four categories: *households, firms, governments,* and the *foreign sector* (that is, foreign purchasers of domestic products). They assume that all the final goods and services that are produced in a country in a given year will be purchased and used by members of one or more of these four groups. Furthermore, the amounts that purchasers spend on various goods and services should be equal to the market values of those goods and services. As a result, GDP can be measured with equal accuracy by either of two methods: (1) adding up the market values of all the final goods and services that are produced domestically or (2) adding up the total amount spent by each of the four groups on final goods and services and subtracting spending on imported goods and services. The values obtained by the two methods will be the same.

Corresponding to the four groups of final users are four components of expenditure: consumption, investment, government purchases, and net exports. That is, households consume, firms invest, governments make government purchases, and the foreign sector buys the nation's exports. Table 17.2 gives the dollar values for each of these components for the U.S. economy in 2019. As the table shows, GDP for the United States in 2019 was about $21.4 trillion, roughly $65,200 per person. Detailed definitions of the components of expenditure, and their principal subcomponents, follow. As you read through them, refer to Table 17.2 to get a sense of the relative importance of each type of spending.

TABLE 17.2
Expenditure Components of U.S. GDP, 2019 ($ billions)

			Percentage
Consumption		**14,562.7**	68%
Durable goods	1,526.8		
Nondurable goods	2,978.1		
Services	10,057.7		
Investment		**3,743.9**	17%
Business fixed investment	2,878.1		
Residential investment	797.5		
Inventory investment	68.3		
Government purchases		**3,753.0**	18%
Net exports		**−631.9**	−3%
Exports	2,504.3		
Imports	3,136.1		
Total: Gross domestic product		**21,427.7**	100%

Source: U.S. Bureau of Economic Analysis (www.bea.gov).

consumption expenditure (or **consumption**) spending by households on goods and services such as food, clothing, and entertainment

Consumption expenditure, or simply **consumption,** is spending by households on goods and services such as food, clothing, and entertainment. Consumption expenditure is subdivided into three subcategories:

- *Consumer durables* are long-lived consumer goods such as cars and furniture. Note that new houses are not treated as consumer durables but as part of investment.
- *Consumer nondurables* are shorter-lived goods like food and clothing.
- *Services,* a large component of consumer spending, include everything from haircuts and taxi rides to legal, financial, and educational services.

investment spending by firms on final goods and services, primarily capital goods and housing

Investment is spending by firms on final goods and services, primarily capital goods and housing. Investment is divided into three subcategories:

- *Business fixed investment* is the purchase by firms of new capital goods such as machinery, factories, and office buildings. (Remember that for the purposes of calculating GDP, long-lived capital goods are treated as final goods rather than as intermediate goods.) Firms buy capital goods to increase their capacity to produce.
- *Residential investment* is construction of new homes and apartment buildings. For GDP accounting purposes, residential investment is treated as an investment by the business sector, which then sells the homes to households.

- *Inventory investment* is the addition of unsold goods to company inventories. In other words, the goods that a firm produces but doesn't sell during the current period are treated, for accounting purposes, as if the firm had bought those goods from itself. (This convention guarantees that production equals expenditure.) Inventory investment can be positive or negative, depending on whether the value of inventories on hand rises or falls over the course of the year. In 2009, for example, inventories fell, and the *inventory investment* component contributed a negative value to GDP.

People often refer to purchases of financial assets, such as stocks or bonds, as "investments." That use of the term is different from the definition we give here. A person who buys a share of a company's stock acquires partial ownership of the *existing* physical and financial assets controlled by the company. A stock purchase does not usually correspond to the creation of *new* physical capital, however, and so is not investment in the sense we are using the term in this chapter. We will generally refer to purchases of financial assets, such as stocks and bonds, as "financial investments," to distinguish them from a firm's investment in new capital goods, such as factories and machines.

Government purchases are purchases by federal, state, and local governments of final goods, such as fighter planes, and services, such as teaching in public schools. Government purchases do *not* include *transfer payments,* which are payments made by the government in return for which no current goods or services are received. Examples of transfer payments (which, again, are *not* included in government purchases) are Social Security benefits, unemployment benefits, pensions paid to government workers, and welfare payments. Interest paid on the government debt is also excluded from government purchases.

Net exports equal exports minus imports.

- *Exports* are domestically produced final goods and services that are sold abroad.

- *Imports* are purchases by domestic buyers of goods and services that were produced abroad. Since imports are included in consumption, investment, and government purchases but do not represent spending on domestic production, they must be subtracted. Imports are subtracted from exports to find the net amount of spending on domestically produced goods and services. A shorthand way of adding exports and subtracting imports is to add net exports, which equals exports minus imports.

A country's net exports reflect the net demand by the rest of the world for its goods and services. Net exports can be negative since imports can exceed exports in any given year. As Table 17.2 shows, the United States had significantly greater imports than exports in 2019.

The relationship between GDP and expenditures on goods and services can be summarized by an equation. Let

$$Y = \text{gross domestic product, or output}$$
$$C = \text{consumption expenditure}$$
$$I = \text{investment}$$
$$G = \text{government purchases}$$
$$NX = \text{net exports.}$$

Using these symbols, we can write that GDP equals the sum of the four types of expenditure algebraically as

$$Y = C + I + G + NX.$$

government purchases purchases by federal, state, and local governments of final goods and services; government purchases do not include transfer payments, which are payments made by the government in return for which no current goods or services are received, nor do they include interest paid on the government debt

net exports exports minus imports

EXAMPLE 17.7   Measuring GDP by Production and by Expenditure

Do we get the same GDP using two different methods?

An economy produces 1,000,000 automobiles valued at $15,000 each. Of these, 700,000 are sold to consumers, 200,000 are sold to businesses, 50,000 are sold to the government, and 25,000 are sold abroad. No automobiles are imported.

The automobiles left unsold at the end of the year are held in inventory by the auto producers. Find GDP in terms of (a) the market value of production and (b) the components of expenditure. You should get the same answer both ways.

The market value of the production of final goods and services in this economy is 1,000,000 autos times $15,000 per auto, or $15 billion.

To measure GDP in terms of expenditure, we must add spending on consumption, investment, government purchases, and net exports. Consumption is 700,000 autos times $15,000, or $10.5 billion. Government purchases are 50,000 autos times $15,000, or $0.75 billion. Net exports are equal to exports (25,000 autos at $15,000, or $0.375 billion) minus imports (zero), so net exports are $0.375 billion.

But what about investment? Here we must be careful. The 200,000 autos that are sold to businesses, worth $3 billion, count as investment. But notice too that the auto companies produced 1,000,000 automobiles but sold only 975,000 (700,000 + 200,000 + 50,000 + 25,000). Hence 25,000 autos were unsold at the end of the year and were added to the automobile producers' inventories. This addition to producer inventories (25,000 autos at $15,000, or $0.375 billion) counts as inventory investment, which is part of total investment. Thus total investment spending equals the $3 billion worth of autos sold to businesses plus the $0.375 billion in inventory investment, or $3.375 billion.

Recapitulating, in this economy consumption is $10.5 billion, investment (including inventory investment) is $3.375 billion, government purchases equal $0.75 billion, and net exports are $0.375 billion. Summing these four components of expenditure yields $15 billion—the same value for GDP that we got by calculating the market value of production.

 SELF-TEST 17.4

Extending Example 17.7, suppose that 25,000 of the automobiles purchased by households are imported rather than domestically produced. Domestic production remains at 1,000,000 autos valued at $15,000 each. Once again, find GDP in terms of (a) the market value of production and (b) the components of expenditure.

GDP AND THE INCOMES OF CAPITAL AND LABOR

The GDP can be thought of equally well as a measure of total production or as a measure of total expenditure—either method of calculating the GDP gives the same final answer. There is yet a third way to think of the GDP, which is as the *incomes of capital and labor*.

Whenever a good or service is produced or sold, the revenue from the sale is distributed to the workers and the owners of the capital involved in the production of the good or service. Thus, except for some technical adjustments that we will ignore, GDP also equals labor income plus capital income.

- *Labor income* comprises wages, salaries, and the incomes of the self-employed.

- *Capital income* is made up of payments to owners of physical capital (such as factories, machines, and office buildings) and intangible capital (such as copyrights and patents). The components of capital income include items such as profits earned by business owners, the rents paid to owners of land or buildings, interest received by bondholders, and the royalties received by the holders of copyrights or patents.

How much of GDP is labor income versus capital income? Answering this question is not a simple task. Consider, for example, the income of a self-employed person (who owns his or her work equipment) or the income of a small-business owner: How much of their incomes should we count as labor income, and how much should we count as capital income? Economists do not always agree on the answers, and different estimation methods result in somewhat different numbers. For our purposes, as a rough approximation, we will think of labor income as being equal to about 75 percent of GDP and of capital income as equal to about 25 percent of GDP.

Both labor income and capital income are to be understood as measured prior to payment of taxes; ultimately, of course, a portion of both types of income is captured by the government in the form of tax collections.

Figure 17.2 may help you visualize the three equivalent ways of thinking about GDP: the market value of production, the total value of expenditure, and the sum of labor income and capital income. The figure also roughly captures the relative importance of the expenditure and income components. In 2019, about 68 percent of expenditure was consumption spending, about 18 percent was government purchases, and the rest was investment spending and net exports. (Actually, as Table 17.2 shows, net exports have been negative in recent years, reflecting the U.S. trade deficit.) As we mentioned, we think of labor income as being about 75 percent of total income, with capital income making up the rest.

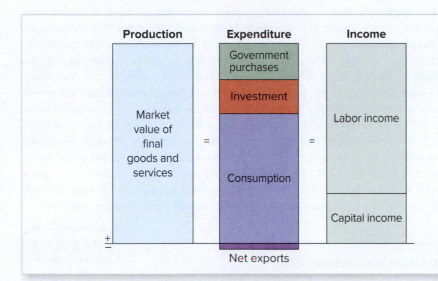

FIGURE 17.2

The Three Faces of GDP.

The GDP can be expressed equally well as (1) the market value of production, (2) total expenditure (consumption, investment, government purchases, net exports), or (3) total income (labor income and capital income).

Figure 17.2 can be also viewed in the context of what is called a *circular flow diagram* of the economy. Such a diagram is drawn in Figure 17.3. It depicts a simplified economy where consumption, *C*, is the only component of GDP—not a bad simplified model of the U.S. economy, where *C* accounts for more than two-thirds of GDP (as discussed, it was roughly 68 percent in 2019). The left panel of Figure 17.3 conveys the economy as a flow of resources from households to firms, accompanied by a flow of final goods and services from firms to households. The *production* approach to measuring GDP would amount to counting that flow of goods and services (the blue arrow on the left in Figure 17.3) produced in a country in a given time period.

The right panel of Figure 17.3 conveys the economy as a flow of spending, paid by households to firms, in return for goods and services, and a flow of income, paid by firms to households, in return for resources such as labor and capital. The *expenditure* approach to measuring GDP would amount to counting the former (the blue arrow on the right), and the *income* approach would amount to counting the latter (the red arrow on the right) in a country in a given time period. As the diagram suggests, all three methods should yield the same GDP figures because, in principle, everything that is produced (and is therefore counted with the production method) is bought by some buyer (and is therefore counted with the expenditure method), and that buyer's spending is, in turn, someone else's income (counted with the income method).

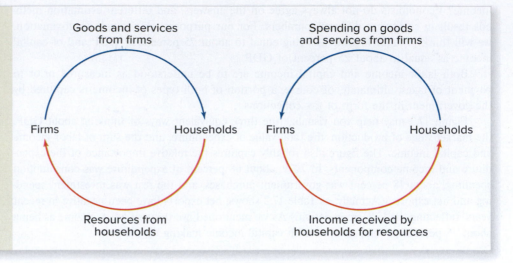

Two Circular Flow Diagrams.
The left panel shows that households supply labor and capital to firms, which use those resources to produce goods and services for households. The right panel shows that households receive income from firms for the resources they supply, which they then spend on goods and services from firms.

Figure 17.3 suggests a simple story that captures much—though far from all—of what is going on in the more complex U.S. economy. In this story, there are two main players in the economy—households and firms—and there are two main markets where these players trade: the market for production inputs and the market for goods and services. In the mornings, households meet firms in the market for production inputs (or for resources), sell labor and capital to those firms, and get paid labor and capital income. The red arrows in the figure show these transactions. In the evenings (and weekends), the same households meet the same firms in the goods and services market, and now households buy from firms the goods and services produced in the mornings, and pay for them (through household expenditures) with the same income earned in the mornings. The blue arrows in the figure show these transactions. The total value of these goods and services produced in a given time period—GDP—can thus be measured by counting total production, or total expenditures, or total income. In principle, the three methods would yield the same outcome.

RECAP

METHODS FOR MEASURING GDP

Expenditure Components of GDP
- GDP can be expressed as the sum of expenditures on domestically produced final goods and services. The four types of expenditure that are counted in the GDP, and the economic groups that make each type of expenditure, are as follows:

Type of expenditure	Who makes the expenditure?	Examples
Consumption	Households	Food, clothes, haircuts, new cars
Investment	Business firms	New factories and equipment, new houses, increases in inventory stocks
Government purchases	Governments	New school buildings, new military hardware, salaries of soldiers and government officials
Net exports, or exports minus imports	Foreign sector	Exported manufactured goods, legal or financial services provided by domestic residents to foreigners

Incomes of Capital and Labor
- GDP also equals labor income plus capital income.

NOMINAL GDP VERSUS REAL GDP

As a measure of the total production of an economy over a given period, such as a particular year, GDP is useful in comparisons of economic activity in different places. For example, GDP data for the year 2019, broken down state by state, could be used to compare aggregate production in New York and California during that year. However, economists are interested in comparing levels of economic activity not only in different *locations* but *over time* as well. For example, a president who is running for reelection on the basis of successful economic policies might want to know by how much output in the U.S. economy had increased during his or her term.

Using GDP to compare economic activity at two different points in time may give misleading answers, however, as the following example shows. Suppose, for the sake of illustration, that the economy produces only pizzas and calzones. The prices and quantities of the two goods in the years 2016 and 2020, the beginning and end of the president's term, are shown in Table 17.3. If we calculate GDP in each year as the market value of production, we find that the GDP for 2016 is (10 pizzas × $10/pizza) + (15 calzones × $5/calzone) = $175. The GDP for 2020 is (20 pizzas × $12/pizza) + (30 calzones × $6/calzone) = $420. Comparing the GDP for the year 2016 to the GDP for the year 2020, we might conclude that it is 2.4 times greater ($420/$175).

Can you see what is wrong with this conclusion? The quantities of both pizzas and calzones produced in the year 2020 are exactly twice the quantities produced in the year 2016. If economic activity, as measured by actual production of both goods, exactly doubled over the four years, why do the calculated values of GDP show a greater increase?

The answer, as you also can see from the table, is that prices as well as quantities rose between 2016 and 2020. Because of the increase in prices, the *market value* of production grew more over those four years than the *physical volume* of production. So in this case, GDP is a misleading gauge of economic growth during the president's term because the physical quantities of the goods and services produced in any given year, not the dollar values, are what determine people's economic well-being. Indeed, if the prices of pizzas and calzones had risen 2.4 times between 2016 and 2020 with no changes in the quantities of pizzas and calzones produced, GDP would have risen 2.4 times as well, with no increase in physical production! In that case, the claim that the economy's (physical) output had more than doubled during the president's term would obviously be wrong.

As this example shows, if we want to use GDP to compare economic activity at different points in time, we need some method of excluding the effects of price changes. In other words, we need to adjust for inflation. To do so, economists use a common set of prices to value quantities produced in different years. The standard approach is to pick a particular year, called the *base year,* and use the prices from that year to calculate the market value of output. When GDP is calculated using the prices from a base year, rather than the current year's prices, it is called *real GDP,* to indicate that it is a measure of real physical production. **Real GDP** is GDP adjusted for inflation. To distinguish real GDP, in which quantities produced are valued at base-year prices, from GDP valued at current-year prices, economists refer to the latter measure as **nominal GDP.**

real GDP a measure of GDP in which the quantities produced are valued at the prices in a base year rather than at current prices; real GDP measures the actual *physical volume* of production

nominal GDP a measure of GDP in which the quantities produced are valued at current-year prices; nominal GDP measures the *current dollar value* of production

TABLE 17.3
Prices and Quantities in 2016 and 2020

	Quantity of pizzas	Price of pizzas	Quantity of calzones	Price of calzones
2016	10	$10	15	$5
2020	20	$12	30	$6

EXAMPLE 17.8   **Calculating the Change in Real GDP over a Four-Year Span**

How much did real GDP grow over a four-year span?

Using data from Table 17.3 and assuming that 2016 is the base year, find real GDP for the years 2020 and 2016. By how much did real output grow between 2016 and 2020?

To find real GDP for the year 2020, we must value the quantities produced that year using the prices in the base year, 2016. Using the data in Table 17.3,

Year 2020 real GDP = (Year 2020 quantity of pizzas × Year 2016 price
of pizzas) + (Year 2020 quantity of calzones ×
Year 2016 price of calzones)

= (20 × $10) + (30 × $5)

= $350.

The real GDP of this economy in the year 2020 is $350.

What is the real GDP for 2016? By definition, the real GDP for 2016 equals 2016 quantities valued at base-year prices. The base year in this example happens to be 2016, so real GDP for 2016 equals 2016 quantities valued at 2016 prices, which is the same as nominal GDP for 2016. In general, in the base year, real GDP and nominal GDP are the same. We already found nominal GDP for 2016, $175, so that is also the real GDP for 2016.

We can now determine how much real production has actually grown over the four-year period. Since real GDP was $175 in 2016 and $350 in 2020, the physical volume of production doubled between 2016 and 2020. This conclusion makes sense—Table 17.3 shows that the production of both pizzas and calzones exactly doubled over the period. By using real GDP, we have eliminated the effects of price changes and obtained a reasonable measure of the actual change in physical production over the four-year span.

Of course, the production of all goods will not necessarily grow in equal proportion, as in the previous example. Self-Test 17.5 asks you to find real GDP when pizza and calzone production grow at different rates.

 SELF-TEST 17.5

Suppose production and prices of pizzas and calzones in 2016 and 2020 are as follows:

	Quantity of pizzas	Price of pizzas	Quantity of calzones	Price of calzones
2016	10	$10	15	$5
2020	30	$12	30	$6

These data are the same as those in Table 17.3, except that pizza production has tripled rather than doubled between 2016 and 2020. Find real GDP in 2020 and 2016, and calculate the growth in real output over the four-year period. (Continue to assume that 2016 is the base year.)

After you complete Self-Test 17.5, you will find that the growth in real GDP between 2016 and 2020 reflects a sort of average of the growth in physical production of pizzas and calzones. Real GDP therefore remains a useful measure of overall physical production, even when the production of different goods and services grows at different rates.

The Economic Naturalist 17.1

Can nominal and real GDP ever move in different directions?

In most countries, both nominal and real GDP increase in almost every year. It is possible, however, for them to move in opposite directions. The last time this happened in the United States was 2007–2008. Using 2009 as a base year, real GDP fell by 0.3 percent, from $14.87 trillion in 2007 to $14.83 trillion in 2008. This reflected an overall reduction in the physical quantities of goods and services produced. Nominal GDP, however, rose by 1.7 percent, from $14.48 trillion to $14.72 trillion, over the same period because prices rose by more than quantities fell.

The preceding example also illustrates the fact that nominal GDP will be *less* than real GDP if prices during the current year are less than prices during the base year. This will generally be the case when the current year is earlier than the base year.

Could real GDP ever rise during a year in which nominal GDP fell? Once again, the answer is yes. For example, this could happen when a country experiences economic growth and falling prices (deflation) at the same time. This actually happened in Japan during several years in the 1990s.

The method of calculating real GDP just described was followed for many decades by the Bureau of Economic Analysis (BEA), the U.S. government agency responsible for GDP statistics. However, in recent decades, the BEA has adopted a more complicated procedure of determining real GDP, called *chain weighting*. The new procedure makes the official real GDP data less sensitive to the particular base year chosen. However, the chain-weighting and traditional approaches share the basic idea of valuing output in terms of base-year prices, and the results obtained by the two methods are generally similar.

> **RECAP ↑**
>
> **NOMINAL GDP VERSUS REAL GDP**
>
> Real GDP is calculated using the prices of goods and services that prevailed in a base year rather than in the current year. Nominal GDP is calculated using current-year prices. Real GDP is GDP adjusted for inflation; it may be thought of as measuring the physical volume of production. Comparisons of economic activity at different times should always be done using real GDP, not nominal GDP.

REAL GDP AND ECONOMIC WELL-BEING

Government policymakers pay close attention to real GDP, often behaving as if the greater the real GDP, the better. However, real GDP is *not* the same as economic well-being. At best, it is an imperfect measure of economic well-being because, for the most part, it captures only those goods and services that are priced and sold in markets. Many factors that contribute to people's economic well-being are not priced and sold in markets and thus are largely or even entirely omitted from GDP. Maximizing real GDP is not, therefore, the right goal for government policymakers. Whether or not policies that increase GDP will also make people better off has to be determined on a case-by-case basis.

WHY REAL GDP ISN'T THE SAME AS ECONOMIC WELL-BEING

To understand why an increase in real GDP does not always promote economic well-being, let's look at some factors that are not included in GDP but do affect whether people are better off.

Leisure Time

Most Americans (and most people in other industrialized countries as well) work many fewer hours than their great-grandparents did 100 years ago. Early in the twentieth century, some industrial workers—steelworkers, for example—worked as many as 12 hours a day, 7 days a week. Today, the 40-hour workweek is typical. Also, Americans tend to start working later in life (after college or graduate school), and, in many cases, they are able to retire earlier. The increased leisure time available to workers in the United States and other industrialized countries—which allows them to pursue many worthwhile activities, including being with family and friends, participating in sports and hobbies, and pursuing cultural and educational activities—is a major benefit of living in a wealthy society. These extra hours of leisure are not priced in markets, however, and therefore are not reflected in GDP.

The Economic Naturalist 17.2

Why do people work fewer hours today than their great-grandparents did?

Americans start work later in life; retire earlier; and, in many cases, work fewer hours per week than people of 50 or 100 years ago. The *opportunity cost* of working less—retiring earlier, for example, or working fewer hours per week—is the earnings you forgo by not working. If you can, say, make $400 per week at a summer job in a department store, then leaving the job two weeks early to take a trip with some friends has an opportunity cost of $800. The fact that people are working fewer hours today suggests that their opportunity cost of forgone earnings is lower than their grandparents' and great-grandparents' opportunity cost. Why this difference?

Cost-Benefit

We can use the Cost-Benefit Principle to help us understand this phenomenon. Over the past century, rapid economic growth in the United States and other industrialized countries has greatly increased the purchasing power of the average worker's wages. In other words, the typical worker today can buy more goods and services with his or her hourly earnings than ever before. This fact would seem to suggest that the opportunity cost of forgone earnings (measured in terms of what those earnings can buy) is greater, not smaller, today than in earlier times. But because the buying power of wages is so much higher today than in the past, Americans can achieve a reasonable standard of living by working fewer hours than they did in the past. Thus, while your grandparents may have had to work long hours to pay the rent or put food on the table, today the extra income from working long hours is more likely to buy relative luxuries, like nicer clothes or a fancier car. Because such discretionary purchases are easier to give up than basic food and shelter, the true opportunity cost of forgone earnings is lower today than it was 50 years ago. As the opportunity cost of leisure has fallen, Americans have chosen to enjoy more of it.

Nonmarket Economic Activities

Not all economically important activities are bought and sold in markets; with a few exceptions, such as government services, nonmarket economic activities are omitted from GDP. We mentioned earlier the examples of parenting and child-care services and unpaid housekeeping services. Another example is volunteer services, such as the volunteer fire and rescue squads that serve many small towns. The fact that these unpaid services are left out of GDP does *not* mean that they are unimportant. The problem is that because there are no market prices and quantities for unpaid services, estimating their market values is very difficult.

How far do economists go wrong by leaving nonmarket economic activities out of GDP? The answer depends on the type of economy being studied. Although nonmarket economic activities exist in all economies, they are particularly important in poor economies. For example, in rural villages of developing countries, people commonly trade services with each other or cooperate on various tasks without exchanging any money. Families in these communities also tend to be relatively self-sufficient, growing their own food and providing many of their own basic services. Because such nonmarket economic activities are not counted in official statistics, GDP data may substantially understate the true amount of economic activity in the poorest countries.

Closely related to nonmarket activities is the *underground economy,* which includes transactions that are never reported to government officials and data collectors. The underground economy encompasses both legal and illegal activities, from informal babysitting jobs to organized crime. For instance, some people pay temporary or part-time workers like housecleaners and painters in cash, which allows these workers to avoid paying taxes on their income. Economists who have tried to estimate the value of such services by studying how much cash the public holds have concluded that these sorts of transactions make up an important share of overall economic activity, even in advanced industrial economies.

Environmental Quality and Resource Depletion

China has experienced tremendous growth in real GDP. But in expanding its manufacturing base, it also has suffered a severe decline in air and water quality. Increased pollution certainly detracts from the quality of life, but because air and water quality are not bought and sold in markets, the Chinese GDP does not reflect this downside of its economic growth.

The exploitation of finite natural resources also tends to be overlooked in GDP. When an oil company pumps and sells a barrel of oil, GDP increases by the value of the oil. But the fact that there is one less barrel of oil in the ground, waiting to be pumped sometime in the future, is not reflected in GDP.

A number of efforts have been made to incorporate factors like air quality and resource depletion into a comprehensive measure of GDP. Doing so is difficult since it often involves placing a dollar value on intangibles, like having a clean river to swim in instead of a dirty one. But the fact that the benefits of environmental quality and resource conservation are hard to measure in dollars and cents does not mean that they are unimportant.

Quality of Life

What makes a particular town or city an attractive place to live? Some desirable features you might think of are reflected in GDP: spacious, well-constructed homes, good restaurants and stores; a variety of entertainment; and high-quality medical services. However, other indicators of the good life are not sold in markets and so may be omitted from GDP. Examples include a low crime rate, minimal traffic congestion, active civic organizations, and open space. Thus, citizens of a rural community may oppose the construction of a new shopping center because they believe it may have a negative effect on the quality of life—even though the new shopping center may increase local GDP.

Poverty and Economic Inequality

GDP measures the *total* quantity of goods and services produced and sold in an economy, but it conveys no information about who gets to enjoy those goods and services. Two countries may have identical GDPs but differ radically in the distribution of economic welfare across the population. Suppose, for example, that in one country—call it Equalia—most people have a comfortable middle-class existence; both extreme poverty and extreme wealth are rare. But in another country, Inequalia—which has the same real GDP as Equalia—a few wealthy families control the economy, and the majority of the population lives in poverty. While most people would say that Equalia has a better economic situation overall, that judgment would not be reflected in the GDPs of the two countries, which are the same.

In the United States, absolute poverty has been declining. Today, many families whose income is below today's official "poverty line" (in 2019, $25,750 for a family of four) own a television, a car, and in some cases their own home. Some economists have argued that people who are considered poor today live as well as many middle-class people did in the 1950s.

But, though absolute poverty seems to be decreasing in the United States, inequality of income has generally been rising. The chief executive officer of a large U.S. corporation may earn hundreds of times what the typical worker in the same firm receives. Psychologists tell us that people's economic satisfaction depends not only on their absolute economic position—the quantity and quality of food, clothing, and shelter they have—but also on what they have compared to what others have. If you own an old, beat-up car but are the only person in your neighborhood to have a car, you may feel privileged. But if everyone else in the neighborhood owns a luxury car, you are likely to be less satisfied. To the extent that such comparisons affect people's well-being, inequality matters as well as absolute poverty. Again, because GDP focuses on total production rather than on the distribution of output, it does not capture the effects of inequality.

BUT GDP IS RELATED TO ECONOMIC WELL-BEING

You might conclude from the list of important factors omitted from the official figures that GDP is useless as a measure of economic welfare. Indeed, numerous critics have made that claim. Clearly, in evaluating the effects of a proposed economic policy, considering only the likely effects on GDP is not sufficient. Planners must also ask whether the policy will affect aspects of economic well-being that are not captured in GDP. Environmental regulations may reduce production of steel, for example, which reduces the GDP. But that fact is not a sufficient basis on which to decide whether such regulations are good or bad. The right way to decide such questions is to apply the Cost-Benefit Principle: Are the benefits of cleaner air worth more to people than the costs the regulations impose in terms of lost output and lost jobs? If so, then the regulations should be adopted; otherwise, they should not.

Although looking at the effects of a proposed policy on real GDP is not the only basis on which to evaluate a policy, real GDP per person *does* tend to be positively associated with many things people value, including a high material standard of living, better health and life expectancies, and better education. We discuss next some of the ways in which a higher real GDP is associated with greater economic well-being.

Availability of Goods and Services

Obviously, citizens of a country with a high GDP are likely to possess more and better goods and services (after all, that is what GDP measures). On average, people in high-GDP countries enjoy larger, better-constructed, and more comfortable homes; higher-quality food and clothing; a greater variety of entertainment and cultural opportunities; better access to transportation and travel; better communications and sanitation; and other advantages. While social commentators may question the value of material consumption—and we agree that riches do not necessarily bring happiness or peace of mind—the majority of people in the world place great importance on achieving material prosperity. Throughout history people have made tremendous sacrifices and taken great risks to secure a higher standard of living for themselves and their families. In fact, to a great extent the United States was built by people who were willing to leave their native lands, often at great personal hardship, in hopes of bettering their economic condition.

Health and Education

While some people question the value of an abundance of consumer goods and services, few question the value of literacy and education, and no one questions the value of having longer and healthier lives. Table 17.4 shows the differences between rich and poor countries with regard to some important indicators of well-being. The data are drawn from the United Nations *Human Development Report*, which measures economic development using a variety of education and health indicators in addition to GDP. The first row of Table 17.4 shows four groups of countries with radically different levels of GDP per person. Most noticeably, GDP per person in the countries with very high human development is more than 14 times that of the countries with low human development.[2]

How do these large differences in GDP relate to other measures of well-being? Table 17.4 shows that on some of the most basic measures of human welfare, the low human development countries fare much worse than the high human development countries. A child born in one of the countries with low human development has almost an 8 percent chance of dying before his or her fifth birthday. Compare this with a 0.6 percent chance of dying before the fifth birthday in the countries with very high human development. A child born in a country with very high human development has a life expectancy of more than 79 years, compared to about 61 years in the low human development countries.

Table 17.4 shows that citizens of very high human development countries attend school for almost twice as many years as those in the low human development countries. Furthermore, data on years of schooling do not capture important differences in the quality of education available in rich and poor countries, as measured by indicators such as the educational backgrounds of teachers and student–teacher ratios.

Bettmann/Getty Images

A child born in one of the low human development countries has almost an 8 percent chance of dying before his or her fifth birthday.

TABLE 17.4
GDP and Basic Indicators of Well-Being

Indicator and year	Very high human development	High human development	Medium human development	Low human development
GDP per person (U.S. dollars), 2018	40,019	14,669	6,279	2,704
Total population in group of countries (millions), 2018	1,532.1	2,857.7	2,245.3	923.2
Life expectancy at birth (years), 2018	79.5	75.1	69.3	61.3
Under-5 mortality rate (per 1,000 live births), 2017	6.2	16.1	44.5	76.6
Expected years of schooling (of children), 2018	16.4	13.8	11.7	9.3

Source: United Nations, *Human Development Report 2019*, http://hdr.undp.org/en/2019-report.

[2]GDP data in Table 17.4 use U.S. prices to value goods and services in low human development nations. Because basic goods and services tend to be cheaper in poor countries, this adjustment significantly increases measured GDP in those countries.

The Economic Naturalist 17.3

Why do far fewer children complete high school in poor countries than in rich countries?

One possible explanation is that people in poor countries place a lower priority on getting an education than people in rich countries. This seems unlikely since immigrants from poor countries often put a heavy emphasis on education—though it may be that people who emigrate from poor countries are unrepresentative of the population as a whole.

An economic naturalist's explanation for the lower schooling rates in poor countries would rely not on cultural differences, but on differences in opportunity costs. In poor societies, most of which are heavily agricultural, children are an important source of labor. Sending children to school beyond a certain age imposes a high opportunity cost on the family. Children who are in school are not available to help with planting, harvesting, and other tasks that must be done if the family is to survive. In addition, the cost of books and school supplies imposes a major hardship on poor families. The Cost-Benefit Principle thus implies that children will stay at home rather than go to school. In rich, nonagricultural countries, school-age children have few work opportunities, and their potential earnings are small relative to other sources of family income. The low opportunity cost of sending children to school in rich countries is an important reason for the higher enrollment rates in those countries. It is probably also true that the benefits or returns from receiving an education are higher in rich countries, as there are more employment opportunities for people with education than in poor countries.

We close this discussion by noting that Table 17.4 compares fairly large groups of countries that are at very different stages of economic development. Looking in the *Human Development Report* at specific countries within each group, the relationship between GDP and health outcomes is often much weaker, and is sometimes strongly reversed. For example, within the group of countries with very high human development, GDP per person in the United States is $56,140—more than 28 percent higher than Canada's $43,602, and more than 37 percent higher than Japan's $40,799. But life expectancy at birth in the United States is 78.9 years—more than three years shorter than Canada's 82.3, and more than five and a half years shorter than Japan's 84.5![3]

In Chapter 19, *Economic Growth, Productivity, and Living Standards,* we will discuss the costs and benefits of economic growth—which in practice means growth in real GDP per person—in greater depth. In that context we will return to the question of whether a growing real GDP is necessarily equated with greater economic well-being.

> **RECAP**
>
> **REAL GDP AND ECONOMIC WELL-BEING**
>
> - Real GDP is an imperfect measure of economic well-being. Among the factors affecting well-being omitted from real GDP are the availability of leisure time, nonmarket services such as unpaid homemaking and volunteer services, environmental quality and resource conservation, and quality-of-life indicators such as a low crime rate. The GDP also does not

[3]For a discussion of the recent drop in life expectancy in the United States in a broad economic and social context, see Anne Case and Angus Deaton, *Deaths of Despair and the Future of Capitalism* (Princeton, NJ: Princeton University Press, 2020).

reflect the degree of economic inequality in a country. Because real GDP is not the same as economic well-being, proposed policies should not be evaluated strictly in terms of whether or not they increase the GDP.

- Although GDP is not the same as economic well-being, it is positively associated with many things that people value, including a higher material standard of living, better health, longer life expectancies, and higher rates of literacy and educational attainment. This relationship between real GDP and economic well-being has led many people to emigrate from poor nations in search of a better life and has motivated policymakers to try to increase their nations' rates of economic growth.

UNEMPLOYMENT AND THE UNEMPLOYMENT RATE

In assessing the level of economic activity in a country, economists look at a variety of statistics. Besides real GDP, one statistic that receives a great deal of attention, both from economists and from the general public, is the rate of unemployment. The unemployment rate is a sensitive indicator of conditions in the labor market. When the unemployment rate is low, jobs are secure and relatively easier to find. Low unemployment is often associated with improving wages and working conditions as well, as employers compete to attract and retain workers.

We will discuss labor markets and unemployment in detail in Chapter 20, *The Labor Market: Workers, Wages, and Unemployment*. This section will explain how the unemployment rate and some related statistics are defined and measured. It will close with a discussion of the costs of unemployment, both to the unemployed and to the economy as a whole.

MEASURING UNEMPLOYMENT

In the United States, defining and measuring unemployment is the responsibility of the Bureau of Labor Statistics, or BLS. Each month the BLS surveys about 60,000 randomly selected households. Each person in those households who is 16 years or older is placed in one of three categories:

1. *Employed.* A person is employed if he or she worked full-time or part-time (even for a few hours) during the past week or is on vacation or sick leave from a regular job.

2. *Unemployed.* A person is unemployed if he or she did not work during the preceding week but made some effort to find work (for example, by going to a job interview) in the past four weeks.

3. *Out of the labor force.* A person is considered to be out of the labor force if he or she did not work in the past week and did not look for work in the past four weeks. In other words, people who are neither employed nor unemployed (in the sense of looking for work but not being able to find it) are "out of the labor force." Full-time students, unpaid homemakers, retirees, and people unable to work because of disabilities are examples of people who are out of the labor force.

Based on the results of the survey, the BLS estimates how many people in the whole country fit into each of the three categories. The working age population is the sum of these three categories, and consists of the population age 16 and over.[4]

To find the unemployment rate, the BLS must first calculate the size of the *labor force*. The **labor force** is defined as the total number of employed and unemployed people in the

labor force the total number of employed and unemployed people in the economy

---

[4]See www.bls.gov/cps/cps_htgm.htm for complete details on how the government collects and categorizes these data.

TABLE 17.5
U.S. Employment Data, November 2019 (in millions)

Employed	158.59
Plus:	
Unemployed	5.81
Equals: Labor force	164.40
Plus:	
Not in labor force	95.62
Equals:	
Working-age (over 16) population	260.02
Unemployment rate = Unemployed/Labor force = 5.81/164.40 = 3.5%	
Participation rate = Labor force/Working-age population = 164.40/260.02 = 63.2%	

Source: Bureau of Labor Statistics, www.bls.gov.

unemployment rate the number of unemployed people divided by the labor force

participation rate the percentage of the working-age population in the labor force (that is, the percentage that is either employed or looking for work)

economy (the first two categories of respondents to the BLS survey). The **unemployment rate** is then defined as the number of unemployed people divided by the labor force. Notice that people who are out of the labor force (because they are in school, have retired, or are disabled, for example) are not counted as unemployed and thus do not affect the unemployment rate. In general, a high rate of unemployment indicates that the economy is performing poorly.

Another useful statistic is the **participation rate,** or the percentage of the working-age population in the labor force (that is, the percentage that is either employed or looking for work). Figure 17.1 showed participation rates for American women and men since 1950. The participation rate is calculated by dividing the labor force by the working-age (16 years and older) population.[5]

Table 17.5 illustrates the calculation of key labor market statistics, using data based on the BLS survey for November 2019. In that month unemployment was 3.5 percent of the labor force. The participation rate was 63.2 percent; that is, almost two out of every three adults had a job or were looking for work.

Figure 17.4 shows the U.S. unemployment rate since 1965. Unemployment rates were exceptionally low—just below and just above 4 percent—in the late 1960s, the late 1990s, and the late 2010s. By this measure, the latter part of the 1990s was an exceptionally good time for American workers. However, unemployment rose in 2001–2002 as the nation fell into recession, then declined to a low of 4.6 percent, and then more than doubled during the 2007–2009 recession. From 2010 to 2019, unemployment declined, reflecting the economic recovery. In the last few months of 2019, the unemployment rate was the lowest it has been since May 1969—over 50 years earlier. Figure 17.4 stops at 2019—the last year for which we have full-year unemployment data right now—but as you already know, in early 2020 the COVID-19 pandemic hit the U.S. economy; by mid 2020, the monthly unemployment rate jumped to levels not seen since the Great Depression. We will discuss these economic upswings (or expansions) and downswings (recessions) and their relationship with unemployment in greater detail in Chapter 24, *Short-Term Economic Fluctuations: An Introduction.*

[5]We note that different governmental agencies use slightly different definitions of the participation rate. In particular, the numbers underlying the figures, tables, and discussion in this chapter (including Figure 17.1, Figure 17.4, Table 17.5, etc.) are published by the U.S. Bureau of Labor Statistics (BLS), which defines participation rate as "the labor force as a percent of the civilian noninstitutional population." The civilian noninstitutional population includes only those working-age (16+) people "who are not inmates of institutions (for example, penal and mental facilities, homes for the aged), and who are not on active duty in the Armed Forces."

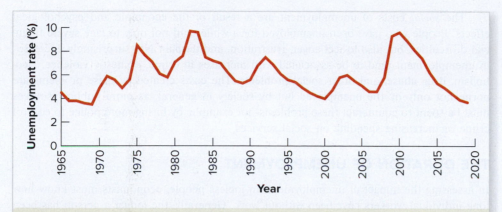

FIGURE 17.4

The U.S. Unemployment Rate, 1965–2019.

The unemployment rate—the fraction of the U.S. labor force that is unemployed—was just above 4 percent in the late 1990s. Unemployment rose to 6 percent in 2003 due to a recession and then decreased to just above 4.5 percent in 2007. During the 2007–2009 recession unemployment increased dramatically. From 2010 to 2019 it declined from its 2010 peak of 9.6 percent to a trough of 3.7 percent—the lowest recorded rate in 50 years.

Source: Bureau of Labor Statistics, www.bls.gov.

 SELF-TEST 17.6

Following are November 2019 BLS U.S. employment data for African Americans.

Employed	19.527 million
Unemployed	1.135 million
Not in the labor force	12.523 million

Find the labor force, the working-age population, the unemployment rate, and the participation rate for African Americans and compare your results to those in Table 17.5.

THE COSTS OF UNEMPLOYMENT

Unemployment imposes *economic, psychological,* and *social* costs on a nation. From an economic perspective, the main cost of unemployment is the output that is lost because the workforce is not fully utilized. Much of the burden of the reduced output is borne by the unemployed themselves, whose incomes fall when they are not working and whose skills may deteriorate from lack of use. However, society at large also bears part of the economic cost of unemployment. For example, workers who become unemployed are liable to stop paying taxes and start receiving government support payments, such as unemployment benefits. This net drain on the government's budget is a cost to all taxpayers.

The *psychological* costs of unemployment are felt primarily by unemployed workers and their families. Studies show that lengthy periods of unemployment can lead to a loss of self-esteem, feelings of loss of control over one's life, depression, and even suicidal behavior.[6] The unemployed worker's family is likely to feel increased psychological stress, compounded by the economic difficulties created by the loss of income.

[6]For a survey of the literature on the psychological effects of unemployment, see William Darity Jr. and Arthur H. Goldsmith, "Social Psychology, Unemployment and Macroeconomics," *Journal of Economic Perspectives* 10 (Winter 1996), pp. 121–140.

The *social* costs of unemployment are a result of the economic and psychological effects. People who have been unemployed for a while tend not only to face severe financial difficulties, but also to feel anger, frustration, and despair. Not surprisingly, increases in unemployment tend to be associated with increases in crime, domestic violence, alcoholism, drug abuse, and other social problems. The costs created by these problems are borne not only by the unemployed but by society in general, as more public resources must be spent to counteract these problems—for example, by hiring more police to control crime or increasing spending on social services.

THE DURATION OF UNEMPLOYMENT

In assessing the impact of unemployment on jobless people, economists must know how long individual workers have been without work. Generally, the longer a person has been out of work, the more severe are the economic and psychological costs that person will face. People who are unemployed for only a few weeks, for example, are not likely to suffer a serious reduction in their standard of living, experience psychological problems such as depression or loss of self-esteem, and have their skills deteriorate (in turn reducing future earnings)—at least not to the same extent as someone who has been out of work for months or years.

In its surveys, therefore, the BLS asks respondents how long they have been unemployed. A period during which an individual is continuously unemployed is called an **unemployment spell;** it begins when the worker becomes unemployed and ends when the worker either finds a job or leaves the labor force. (Remember, people outside the labor force are not counted as unemployed.) The length of an unemployment spell is called its **duration.** The duration of unemployment rises during recessions, reflecting the greater difficulty of finding work during those periods.

At any given time, a substantial fraction of unemployed workers have been unemployed for six months or more; we will refer to this group as the *long-term unemployed.* Long-term unemployment creates the highest economic, psychological, and social costs, both for the unemployed themselves and for society as a whole.

When the economy is not in a recession, most unemployment spells are relatively short. For example, in November 2019, 34 percent of the unemployed had been out of work for just 5 weeks or less, another 30 percent had been unemployed for 5 to 14 weeks, and about 36 percent of the unemployed had been without a job for more than 14 weeks (about three months). However, during the latest recession, unemployment spells grew longer. For example, in August 2020, 17 percent of the unemployed had been out of work for 5 weeks or less, 23 percent had been unemployed for 5 to 14 weeks, and 60 percent of the unemployed had been searching for work without any success for more than 14 weeks.

Even these statistics are a bit deceptive, however, because short unemployment spells can arise from two very different patterns of labor market experience. Some people have short unemployment spells that end in their finding a stable long-term job. For the most part, these workers, whom we will refer to as the *short-term unemployed,* do not typically bear a high cost of unemployment. But other workers have short unemployment spells that typically end either in their withdrawal from the labor force or in a short-term or temporary job that soon leaves the worker unemployed again. Workers whose unemployment spells are broken up by brief periods of employment or withdrawals from the labor force are referred to as the *chronically unemployed.* In terms of the costs of unemployment, the experience of these workers is similar to that of the long-term unemployed.

THE UNEMPLOYMENT RATE VERSUS "TRUE" UNEMPLOYMENT

Like GDP measurement, unemployment measurement has its critics. Most of them argue that the official unemployment rate understates the true extent of unemployment. They point in particular to two groups of people who are not counted among the unemployed: so-called *discouraged workers* and *involuntary part-time workers.*

unemployment spell a period during which an individual is continuously unemployed

duration the length of an unemployment spell

Discouraged workers are people who say they would like to have a job but have not made an effort to find one in the past four weeks. Often, discouraged workers tell the survey takers that they have not searched for work because they have tried without success in the past or because they are convinced that labor market conditions are such that they will not be able to find a job. Because they have not sought work in the past four weeks, discouraged workers are counted as being out of the labor force rather than unemployed. Some observers have suggested that treating discouraged workers as unemployed would provide a more accurate picture of the labor market.

Involuntary part-time workers are people who say they would like to work full-time but are able to find only part-time work. Because they do have jobs, involuntary part-time workers are counted as employed rather than unemployed. These workers are sometimes referred to as *underemployed* or part-time workers for economic reasons. Some economists have suggested that these workers should be counted as partially unemployed.

In response to these criticisms, since the 1990s, the BLS has been releasing special unemployment rates that include estimates of the number of discouraged workers and involuntary part-time workers. In November 2019, when the official unemployment rate was 3.5 percent (see Table 17.5), the BLS calculated that if both discouraged workers and involuntary part-time workers were counted as unemployed, the unemployment rate would have been 6.9 percent. So the problem of discouraged and underemployed workers appears to be fairly significant.

Whether in an official or adjusted version, the unemployment rate is a good overall indicator of labor market conditions. A high unemployment rate tends to be bad news even for those people who are employed, since raises and promotions are hard to come by in a "slack" labor market. We will discuss the causes and cures of unemployment at some length in Chapter 20, *The Labor Market: Workers, Wages, and Unemployment,* and subsequent chapters.

> **discouraged workers** people who say they would like to have a job but have not made an effort to find one in the past four weeks

> **involuntary part-time workers** people who say they would like to work full-time but are able to find only part-time work

SUMMARY

- The basic measure of an economy's output is *gross domestic product (GDP)*, the market value of the final goods and services produced in a country during a given period. Expressing output in terms of market values allows economists to aggregate the millions of goods and services produced in a modern economy. *(LO1)*

- Only *final goods and services* (which include *capital goods*) are counted in GDP since they are the only goods and services that directly benefit final users. *Intermediate goods and services,* which are used up in the production of final goods and services, are not counted in GDP, nor are sales of existing assets, such as a 20-year-old house. Summing the value added by each firm in the production process is a useful method of determining the value of final goods and services. *(LO1)*

- GDP can also be expressed as the sum of four types of expenditure: *consumption, investment, government purchases,* and *net exports*. These four types of expenditure correspond to the spending of households, firms, the government, and the foreign sector, respectively. *(LO2)*

- To compare levels of GDP over time, economists must eliminate the effects of inflation. They do so by measuring the market value of goods and services in terms of the prices in a base year. GDP measured in this way is called *real GDP*, while GDP measured in terms of current-year prices is called *nominal GDP*. Real GDP should always be used in making comparisons of economic activity over time. *(LO3)*

- Real GDP per person is an imperfect measure of economic well-being. With a few exceptions, notably government purchases of goods and services (which are included in GDP at their cost of production), GDP includes only those goods and services sold in markets. It excludes important factors that affect people's well-being, such as the amount of leisure time available to them, the value of unpaid or volunteer services, the quality of the environment, quality of life indicators such as the crime rate, and the degree of economic inequality. *(LO4)*

- Real GDP is still a useful indicator of economic well-being, however. Countries with a high real GDP per person not only enjoy high average standards of living; they also tend to have higher life expectancies, low rates of infant and child mortality, and high rates of school enrollment and literacy. *(LO4)*

- The unemployment rate, perhaps the best-known indicator of the state of the labor market, is based on surveys conducted by the Bureau of Labor Statistics. The surveys classify all respondents over age 16 as employed, unemployed, or not in the labor force. The *labor force* is the sum of employed and unemployed workers—that is, people who have a job or are looking for one. The *unemployment rate* is calculated as the number of unemployed workers divided by the labor force. The *participation rate* is the percentage of the working-age population that is in the labor force. *(LO5)*

- The costs of unemployment include the economic cost of lost output, the psychological costs borne by unemployed workers and their families, and the social costs associated with problems like increased crime and violence. The greatest costs are imposed by long *unemployment spells* (periods of unemployment). Critics of the official unemployment rate argue that it understates "true" unemployment by excluding *discouraged workers* and *involuntary part-time workers*. *(LO5)*

KEY TERMS

capital good	gross domestic product (GDP)	nominal GDP
consumption expenditure (or consumption)	intermediate goods or services	participation rate
	investment	real GDP
discouraged workers	involuntary part-time workers	unemployment rate
duration (of an unemployment spell)	labor force	unemployment spell
final goods or services	market value	value added
government purchases	net exports	

REVIEW QUESTIONS

1. Why do economists use market values when calculating GDP? What is the economic rationale for giving high-value items more weight in GDP than low-value items? *(LO1)*

2. A large part of the agricultural sector in developing countries is subsistence farming, in which much of the food that is produced is consumed by the farmer and the farmer's family. Discuss the implications of this fact for the measurement of GDP in poor countries. *(LO1)*

3. Give examples of each of the four types of aggregate expenditure. Which of the four represents the largest share of GDP in the United States? Can an expenditure component be negative? Explain. *(LO2)*

4. Sara's Rock Painting Stand painted 1,000 rocks last year and 1,200 rocks this year. She charged $4 per rock last year and $5 this year. If last year is taken as the base year, find Sara's contribution to both nominal GDP and real GDP in both years. Which measure would be better to use if you were trying to measure the change in Sara's productivity over the past year? Why? *(LO3)*

5. Would you say that real GDP per person is a useful measure of economic well-being? Defend your answer. *(LO4)*

6. True or false: A high participation rate in an economy implies a low unemployment rate. *(LO5)*

7. What are the costs of a high unemployment rate? Do you think providing more generous government benefits to the unemployed would increase these costs, reduce these costs, or leave them unchanged? Discuss. *(LO5)*

PROBLEMS

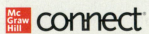

1. George and John, stranded on an island, use clamshells for money. Last year George caught 300 fish and 5 wild boars. John grew 100 bunches of bananas. In the two-person economy that George and John set up, fish sell for 3 clamshells each, boars sell for 10 clamshells each, and bananas go for 10 clamshells a bunch. George paid John a total of 30 clamshells for helping him dig bait for fishing, and he also purchased five of John's mature banana trees for 30 clamshells each. What is the GDP of George and John's island in terms of clamshells? *(LO1)*

2. How would each of the following transactions affect the GDP of the United States? *(LO1)*
   a. The U.S. government pays $1 billion in salaries for government workers.
   b. The U.S. government pays $1 billion to Social Security recipients.
   c. The U.S. government pays a U.S. firm $1 billion for newly produced airplane parts.
   d. The U.S. government pays $1 billion in interest to holders of U.S. government bonds.
   e. The U.S. government pays $1 billion to Saudi Arabia for crude oil to add to U.S. official oil reserves.

3. Intelligence Incorporated produces 300 computer chips and sells them for $200 each to Bell Computers. Using the chips and other labor and materials, Bell produces 300 personal computers. Bell sells the computers, bundled with software that Bell licenses from Macrosoft at $50 per computer, to PC Charlie's for $800 each. PC Charlie's sells the computers to the public for $1,000 each. Calculate the total contribution to GDP using the value-added method. Do you get the same answer by summing up the market values of the final goods and services? *(LO1)*

4. MNLogs harvested logs (with no inputs from other companies) from its property in northern Minnesota. It sold these logs to MNLumber for $1,500, and MNLumber cut and planed the logs into lumber. MNLumber then sold the lumber for $4,000 to MNFurniture. MNFurniture used the lumber to produce 100 tables that it sold to customers for $70 each. *(LO1)*
   a. Complete the following table to calculate the value added by each firm.

Company	Revenues	Cost of purchased inputs	Value added
MNLogs			
MNLumber			
MNFurniture			

   b. Suppose that all of these transactions took place in 2019. By how much did GDP increase because of these transactions?
   c. Suppose that MNLogs harvested the logs in October 2019 and sold them to MNLumber in December 2019. MNLumber then sold the finished lumber to MNFurniture in April 2020 and MNFurniture sold all 100 tables during the rest of 2020. By how much did GDP increase in 2019 and 2020 because of these transactions?

5. For each of the following transactions, state the effect both on U.S. GDP and on the four components of aggregate expenditure. *(LO2)*
   a. Your mother-in-law buys a new car from a U.S. producer.
   b. Your mother-in-law buys a new car imported from Sweden.
   c. Your mother-in-law's car rental business buys a new car from a U.S. producer.
   d. Your mother-in-law's car rental business buys a new car imported from Sweden.
   e. The U.S. government buys a new, domestically produced car for the use of your mother-in-law, who has been appointed the ambassador to Sweden.

6. Calculate the four components of expenditure and GDP for the following economy using data from the following table. *(LO2)*

Consumption expenditures	$550
Exports	75
Government purchases of goods and services	200
Construction of new homes and apartments	100
Sales of existing homes and apartments	200
Imports	50
Beginning-of-year inventory stocks	100
End-of-year inventory stocks	125
Business fixed investment	100
Government payments to retirees	100
Household purchases of durable goods	150

7. The nation of Potchatoonie produces hockey pucks, cases of root beer, and sandals. The following table lists prices and quantities of the three goods in the years 2017 and 2020. *(LO3)*

	Pucks		Root Beer		Sandals	
Year	Quantity	Price	Quantity	Price	Quantity	Price
2017	100	$5	300	$20	75	$20
2020	125	$9	325	$20	110	$25

Assume that 2017 is the base year. Find nominal GDP and real GDP for both years.

8. The government is considering a policy to reduce air pollution by restricting the use of "dirty" fuels by factories. In deciding whether to implement the policy, how, if at all, should the likely effects of the policy on real GDP be taken into account? *(LO4)*

9. We discussed how the opportunity cost of sending children to school affects the level of school enrollment across countries. The United Nations *Human Development Report 2019* reports the following data for per capita income in 2018 (in the equivalent of 2011 U.S. dollars): *(LO4)*

Canada	$43,602
Denmark	$48,836
Greece	$24,909
Lesotho	$ 3,244
Ethiopia	$ 1,782

Source: http://hdr.undp.org/en/countries

   a. Which country would you expect to have the highest school enrollment rate? The lowest rate?
   b. Discuss what other factors besides GDP per capita a family might consider when applying the cost-benefit principle to the decision of whether or not to send a child to school.

10. The following is a report from a BLS survey taker: "There were 65 people in the houses I visited, 10 of them children under 16; 25 people had full-time jobs,

and 5 had part-time jobs. There were 10 retirees, 5 full-time homemakers, 5 full-time students over age 16, and 2 people who were disabled and cannot work. The remaining people did not have jobs but all said they would like one. One of these people had not looked actively for work for 3 months, however." Find the labor force, the unemployment rate, and the participation rate implied by the survey taker's report. *(LO5)*

11. Skyler is downloading labor market data for the most recent month, but her connection is slow and so far this is all she has been able to get:

Unemployment rate	5.9%
Participation rate	62.5%
Not in the labor force	63 million

Find the labor force, the working-age population, the number of employed workers, and the number of unemployed workers. *(LO5)*

12. The towns of Sawyer and Thatcher each have a labor force of 1,200 people. In Sawyer, 100 people were unemployed for the entire year, while the rest of the labor force worked continuously. In Thatcher, every member of the labor force was unemployed for 1 month and employed for 11 months. *(LO5)*
    a. What is the average unemployment rate over the year in each of the towns?
    b. What is the average duration of unemployment spells in each of the towns?
    c. In which town do you think the costs of unemployment are higher?

ANSWERS TO SELF-TESTS

17.1 In the text, GDP was calculated to be $64.00. If in addition Orchardia produces 5 oranges at $0.30 each, GDP is increased by $1.50 to $65.50. *(LO1)*

17.2 The value added of the wholesale distributor together with the ultimate producers of the cards is $500. Amy's value added—her revenue less her payments to other firms—is $200. Since the cards were produced and purchased by Amy during the year 2019 (we assume), the $500 counts toward year 2019 GDP. The $200 in value added originating in Amy's card shop counts in year 2020 GDP since Amy actually sold the cards in that year. *(LO1)*

17.3 The sale of stock represents a transfer of ownership of part of the assets of Benson Buggywhip, not the production of new goods or services. Hence, the stock sale itself does not contribute to GDP. However, the broker's commission of $100 (2 percent of the stock sale proceeds) represents payment for a current service and is counted in GDP. *(LO1)*

17.4 As in Example 17.7, the market value of domestic production is 1,000,000 autos times $15,000 per auto, or $15 billion.

Also as in Example 17.7, consumption is $10.5 billion and government purchases are $0.75 billion. However, because 25,000 of the autos that are purchased are imported rather than domestic, the domestic producers have unsold inventories at the end of the year of 50,000 (rather than 25,000 as in Example 17.7). Thus inventory investment is 50,000 autos times $15,000, or $0.75 billion, and total investment (autos purchased by businesses plus inventory investment) is $3.75 billion. Because exports and imports are equal (both are 25,000 autos), net exports (equal to exports minus imports) are zero. Notice that because we subtract imports to get net exports, it is unnecessary also to subtract imports from consumption. Consumption

is defined as total purchases by households, not just purchases of domestically produced goods.

Total expenditure is $C + I + G + NX =$ $10.5 billion + $3.75 billion + $0.75 billion + 0 = $15 billion, the same as the market value of production. *(LO2)*

17.5 Real GDP in the year 2020 equals the quantities of pizzas and calzones produced in the year 2020, valued at the market prices that prevailed in the base year 2016. So real GDP in 2020 = (30 pizzas × $10/pizza) + (30 calzones × $5/calzone) = $450.

Real GDP in 2016 equals the quantities of pizzas and calzones produced in 2016, valued at 2016 prices, which is $175. Notice that because 2016 is the base year, real GDP and nominal GDP are the same for that year.

The real GDP in the year 2020 is $450/$175, or about 2.6 times what it was in 2016. Hence the expansion of real GDP lies between the threefold increase in pizza production and the doubling in calzone production that occurred between 2016 and 2020. *(LO3)*

17.6 Labor force = Employed + Unemployed = 19.527 million + 1.135 million = 20.662 million.

Working-age population = Labor force + Not in labor force = 20.662 million + 12.523 million = 33.185 million.

Unemployment rate = Unemployed/Labor force = 1.135 million/20.662 million = 5.5%.

Participation rate = Labor force/Working-age population = 20.662 million/33.185 million = 62.3%.

In November 2019, African Americans represented approximately 13 percent of the U.S. labor force and the working-age population. Note that while the participation rate for African Americans is similar to that of the overall population, the unemployment rate for African Americans is substantially higher. *(LO5)*

CHAPTER 18

Measuring the Price Level and Inflation

How do we measure inflation?

LEARNING OBJECTIVES

After reading this chapter, you should be able to:

LO1 Explain how the consumer price index (CPI) is constructed and use it to calculate the inflation rate.

LO2 Show how the CPI is used to adjust dollar amounts to eliminate the effects of inflation.

LO3 Discuss the two most important biases in the CPI.

LO4 Distinguish between inflation and relative price changes in order to find the true costs of inflation.

LO5 Summarize the connections among inflation, nominal interest rates, and real interest rates.

W ould you be able to retire comfortably in 40 years if by then you managed to save $100 million?

If you did not immediately answer "Of course!" you may have very expensive taste; alternatively, you may hesitate because you do not know what $100 million will buy for you in 40 years. What if in 40 years one loaf of bread cost $5 million?

This $100 million question illustrates a simple but very important point, which is that the value of money depends entirely on the prices of the goods and services one wants to buy. A $100 million nest egg is a substantial fortune at the prices prevailing in the United States today, but it is only a pittance if a loaf of bread costs $5 million. Likewise, high and sustained inflation—a rapid and ongoing increase in the prices of most goods and services—can radically reduce the buying power of a given amount of money. History provides some extreme examples: Many people who retired in 1923 in Germany or in 2008 in Zimbabwe found that their hard-earned lifetime savings could not buy for them even a single loaf of bread.

Over long periods of time, even much lower inflation rates—such as those in the U.S. over the past century—dramatically change the buying power of money, as Example 18.3 will illustrate. More generally, inflation can make a comparison of economic conditions at different points in time quite difficult. Your grandparents remember being able to buy both a comic book and a chocolate sundae for a quarter. Today, the same two items might cost $4 or $5. You might conclude from this fact that kids were much better off in "the good old days," but were they really? Without more information, we can't tell, for though the prices of comic books and sundaes have gone up, so have allowances. The real question is whether young people's spending money has increased as much as or more than the prices of the things they want to buy. If so, then they are no worse off today than their grandparents were when they were young and candy bars cost a nickel.

Inflation also creates uncertainty when we try to look into the future, to ask questions such as: "How much *should* I plan to save for retirement?" The answer to this question depends on how much inflation is likely to occur before one retires (and thus how much heating oil, food, and clothing will cost). Inflation can pose similar problems for policymakers. For example, to plan long-term government spending programs they must estimate how much the government's purchases will cost several years in the future.

An important benefit of studying macroeconomics is learning how to avoid the confusion inflation interjects into comparisons of economic conditions over time or projections for the future. In this chapter, a continuation of our study of the construction and interpretation of economic data, we will see how both prices and inflation are measured and how dollar amounts, such as the price of a sundae, can be "adjusted" to eliminate the effects of inflation. Quantities that are measured in dollars (or other currency units) and then adjusted for inflation are called real quantities (recall, for example, the concept of real GDP in Chapter 17, *Measuring Economic Activity: GDP and Unemployment*). By working with real quantities, economists can compare economic conditions across different years.

More important than the complications inflation creates for economic measurement are the costs that it imposes on the economy. In this chapter, we will see why high inflation can significantly impair an economy's performance, to the extent that economic policymakers claim a low and stable rate of inflation as one of their chief objectives. We will conclude the chapter by showing how inflation is linked to another key economic variable, the rate of interest on financial assets.

THE CONSUMER PRICE INDEX AND INFLATION

The basic tool economists use to measure the price level in the U.S. economy is the *consumer price index,* or CPI for short. The CPI is a measure of the "cost of living" during a particular period. Specifically, the **consumer price index (CPI)** for any period measures the cost in that period of a standard set, or basket, of goods and services *relative* to the cost of the same basket of goods and services in a fixed year, called the *base year.*

To illustrate how the CPI is constructed, suppose the government has designated 2015 as the base year. Assume for the sake of simplicity that in 2015 a typical American family's monthly household budget consisted of spending on just three items: rent on a two-bedroom apartment, hamburgers, and movie tickets. In reality, of course, families purchase hundreds of different items each month, but the basic principles of constructing the CPI are the same no matter how many items are included. Suppose too that the family's average monthly expenditures in 2015, the base year, were as shown in Table 18.1.

consumer price index (CPI) for any period, a measure of the cost in that period of a standard basket of goods and services relative to the cost of the same basket of goods and services in a fixed year, called the *base year*

TABLE 18.1
Monthly Household Budget of the Typical Family in 2015 (Base Year)

Item	Cost (in 2015)
Rent, two-bedroom apartment	$750
Hamburgers (60 at $2.00 each)	120
Movie tickets (10 at $7.00 each)	70
Total expenditure	$940

Now let's fast-forward to the year 2020. Over that period, the prices of various goods and services are likely to have changed; some will have risen and some fallen. Let's suppose that by the year 2020 the rent that our family pays for their two-bedroom apartment has risen to $945. Hamburgers now cost $2.50 each, and the price of movie tickets has risen to $8.00 each. So, in general, prices have been rising.

By how much did the family's cost of living increase between 2015 and 2020? Table 18.2 shows that if the typical family wanted to consume the *same basket of goods and services* in the year 2020 as they did in the year 2015, they would have to spend $1,175 per month, or $235 more than the $940 per month they spent in 2015. In other words, to live the same way in the year 2020 as they did in the year 2015, the family would have to spend 25 percent more ($235/$940) each month. So, in this example, the cost of living for the typical family rose 25 percent between 2015 and 2020.

TABLE 18.2

Cost of Reproducing the 2015 (Base-Year) Basket of Goods and Services in Year 2020

Item	Cost (in 2020)	Cost (in 2015)
Rent, two-bedroom apartment	$ 945	$750
Hamburgers (60 at $2.50 each)	150	120
Movie tickets (10 at $8.00 each)	80	70
Total expenditure	$1,175	$940

The government—actually, the Bureau of Labor Statistics (BLS), the same agency that is responsible for determining the unemployment rate—calculates the official consumer price index (CPI) using essentially the same method. The first step in deriving the CPI is to pick a base year and determine the basket of goods and services that were consumed by the typical family during that year. In practice, the government learns how consumers allocate their spending through a detailed survey, called the Consumer Expenditure Survey, in which randomly selected families record every purchase they make and the price they paid over a given month. (Quite a task!) Let's call the basket of goods and services that results the *base-year basket*. Then, each month BLS employees visit thousands of stores and conduct numerous interviews to determine the current prices of the goods and services in the base-year basket.[1]

The CPI in any given year is computed using this formula:

$$\text{CPI} = \frac{\text{Cost of base-year basket of goods and services in current year}}{\text{Cost of base-year basket of goods and services in base year}}.$$

Returning to the example of the typical family that consumes three goods, we can calculate the CPI in the year 2020 as

$$\text{CPI in year 2020} = \frac{\$1,175}{\$940} = 1.25.$$

In other words, in this example, the cost of living in the year 2020 is 25 percent higher than it was in 2015, the base year. Notice that the base-year CPI is always equal to 1.00 since in that year the numerator and the denominator of the CPI formula are the same. The CPI for a given period (such as a month or year) measures the cost of living in that period *relative* to what it was in the base year.

---

[1]More details on how the Bureau of Labor Statistics constructs the CPI are available at www.bls.gov/cpi/questions-and-answers.htm.

The BLS multiplies the CPI by 100 to get rid of the decimal point. If we were to do that here, the year 2020 CPI would be expressed as 125 rather than 1.25, and the base-year CPI would be expressed as 100 rather than 1.00. However, many calculations are simplified if the CPI is stated in decimal form, so we will not adopt the convention of multiplying it by 100.

EXAMPLE 18.1	Calculating the CPI

How do we measure the typical family's cost of living?

Suppose that in addition to the three goods and services the typical family consumed in 2015, they also bought four sweaters at $30 each. In the year 2020, the same sweaters cost $50 each. The prices of the other goods and services in 2015 and 2020 were the same as in Table 18.2. With this additional item, what was the change in the family's cost of living between 2015 and 2020?

In the example in the text, the cost of the base-year (2015) basket was $940. Adding four sweaters at $30 each raises the cost of the base-year basket to $1,060. What does this same basket (including the four sweaters) cost in 2020? The cost of the apartment, the hamburgers, and the movie tickets is $1,175, as before. Adding the cost of the four sweaters at $50 each raises the total cost of the basket to $1,375. The CPI equals the cost of the basket in 2020 divided by the cost of the basket in 2015 (the base year), or $1,375/$1,060 = 1.30. We conclude that the family's cost of living rose 30 percent between 2015 and 2020.

 SELF-TEST 18.1

Returning to the three-good example in Tables 18.1 and 18.2, find the year 2020 CPI if the rent on the apartment falls from $750 in 2015 to $600 in 2020. The prices for hamburgers and movie tickets in the two years remain the same as in the two tables.

The CPI does not measure the price of a specific good or service. Indeed, it has no units of measurement at all since the dollars in the numerator of the fraction cancel with the dollars in the denominator. Rather, the CPI is an *index*. The *value* of an index in a particular year has meaning only in comparison with the value of that index in another year. Thus, a **price index** measures the average price of a class of goods or services relative to the price of those same goods or services in a base year. The CPI is an especially well-known price index, one of many economists use to assess economic trends. For example, because manufacturers tend to pass on increases in the prices of raw materials to their customers, economists use indexes of raw materials' prices to forecast changes in the prices of manufactured goods. Other indexes are used to study the rate of price change in energy, food, health care, and other major sectors.

price index a measure of the average price of a given class of goods or services relative to the price of the same goods or services in a base year

---

 SELF-TEST 18.2

The consumer price index captures the cost of living for the "typical" or average family. Suppose you were to construct a personal price index to measure changes in your own cost of living over time. In general, how would you go about constructing such an index? Why might changes in your personal price index differ from changes in the CPI?

INFLATION

The CPI provides a measure of the average *level* of prices relative to prices in the base year. *Inflation,* in contrast, is a measure of how fast the average price level is *changing* over time. The **rate of inflation** is defined as the annual percentage rate of change in the price level, as measured, for example, by the CPI. Suppose, for example, that the CPI has a value of 1.25 in the year 2019 and a value of 1.27 in the year 2020. The rate of inflation between 2019 and 2020 is the percentage increase in the price level, or the increase in the price level (0.02) divided by the initial price level (1.25), which is equal to 1.6 percent.

rate of inflation the annual percentage rate of change in the price level, as measured, for example, by the CPI

| EXAMPLE 18.2 | Calculating Inflation Rates: 1972–1976 |

How do we calculate the inflation rate using the CPI?

CPI values for the years 1972 through 1976 are shown in the following table. Find the rates of inflation between 1972 and 1973, 1973 and 1974, 1974 and 1975, and 1975 and 1976.

Year	CPI
1972	0.418
1973	0.444
1974	0.493
1975	0.538
1976	0.569

The inflation rate between 1972 and 1973 is the percentage increase in the price level between those years, or (0.444 − 0.418)/0.418 = 0.026/0.418 = 0.062 = 6.2 percent. Do the calculations on your own to confirm that inflation during each of the next three years was 11.0, 9.1, and 5.8 percent, respectively. During the 1970s, inflation rates were much higher than the 1.5 to 3 percent inflation rates that have prevailed in most years during the past quarter century.

 SELF-TEST 18.3

Following are CPI values for the years 1929 through 1933. Find the rates of inflation between 1929 and 1930, 1930 and 1931, 1931 and 1932, and 1932 and 1933.

Year	CPI
1929	0.171
1930	0.167
1931	0.152
1932	0.137
1933	0.130

How did inflation rates in the 1930s differ from those of the 1970s?

> ✅ **SELF-TEST 18.4**
>
> CPI values for the years 2015 to 2019 are shown here. Calculate the inflation rate for each year.
>
> | Year | CPI |
> |------|-----|
> | 2015 | 2.37 |
> | 2016 | 2.40 |
> | 2017 | 2.45 |
> | 2018 | 2.51 |
> | 2019 | 2.56 |

The results of the calculations for Self-Test 18.3 include some examples of *negative* inflation rates. A situation in which the prices of most goods and services are falling over time so that inflation is negative is called **deflation.** The early 1930s was the last time the United States experienced significant deflation. Japan experienced relatively mild deflation during the past two decades. As Self-Test 18.4 demonstrates, most recently in the U.S. inflation rates have been low but not negative.

deflation a situation in which the prices of most goods and services are falling over time so that inflation is negative

ADJUSTING FOR INFLATION

The CPI is an extremely useful tool. Not only does it allow us to measure changes in the cost of living; it also can be used to adjust economic data to eliminate the effects of inflation. In this section, we will see how the CPI can be used to convert quantities measured at current dollar values into real terms, a process called *deflating*. We also will see that the CPI can be used to convert real quantities into current-dollar terms, a procedure called *indexing*. Both procedures are useful not only to economists but to anyone who needs to adjust payments, accounting measures, or other economic quantities for the effects of inflation.

DEFLATING A NOMINAL QUANTITY

nominal quantity a quantity that is measured in terms of its current dollar value

An important use of the CPI is to adjust **nominal quantities**—quantities measured at their current dollar values—for the effects of inflation. To illustrate, suppose we know that the typical family in a certain metropolitan area had a total income of $40,000 in 2015 and $44,000 in 2020. Was this family economically better off in the year 2020 than in 2015?

Without any more information than this, we might be tempted to say yes. After all, their income rose by 10 percent over the five-year period. But prices also might have been rising, as fast as or faster than the family's income. Suppose the prices of the goods and services the family consumes rose 25 percent over the same period. Since the family's income rose only 10 percent, we would have to conclude that the family is worse off, in terms of the goods and services they can afford to buy, despite the increase in their *nominal,* or current-dollar, income.

real quantity a quantity that is measured in physical terms—for example, in terms of quantities of goods and services

We can make a more precise comparison of the family's purchasing power in 2015 and 2020 by calculating their incomes in those years in *real* terms. In general, a **real quantity** is one that is measured in physical terms—for example, in terms of quantities of goods and services. To convert a nominal quantity into a real quantity, we must divide the nominal quantity by a price index for the period, as shown in Table 18.3. The calculations in the table show that in *real* or purchasing power terms, the family's income actually *decreased* by $4,800, or 12 percent of their initial real income of $40,000, between 2015 and 2020.

TABLE 18.3
Comparing the Real Values of a Family's Income in 2015 and 2020

Year	Nominal family income	CPI	Real family income = Nominal family income/CPI
2015	$40,000	1.00	$40,000/1.00 = $40,000
2020	$44,000	1.25	$44,000/1.25 = $35,200

The problem for this family is that though their income has been rising in nominal (dollar) terms, it has not kept up with inflation. Dividing a nominal quantity by a price index to express the quantity in real terms is called **deflating the nominal quantity.** (Be careful not to confuse the idea of deflating a nominal quantity with deflation, or negative inflation. The two concepts are different.)

Dividing a nominal quantity by the current value of a price index to measure it in real or purchasing power terms is a very useful tool. It can be used to eliminate the effects of inflation from comparisons of any nominal quantity—workers' wages, health care expenditures, the components of the federal budget—over time. Why does this method work? In general, if you know both how many dollars you have spent on a given item and the item's price, you can figure out how many of the item you bought (by dividing your expenditures by the price). For example, if you spent $100 on hamburgers last month and hamburgers cost $2.50 each, you can determine that you purchased 40 hamburgers. Similarly, if you divide a family's dollar income or expenditures by a price index, which is a measure of the average price of the goods and services they buy, you will obtain a measure of the real quantity of goods and services they purchased. Such real quantities are sometimes referred to as *inflation-adjusted* quantities.

deflating (a nominal quantity) the process of dividing a nominal quantity by a price index (such as the CPI) to express the quantity in real terms

EXAMPLE 18.3   Babe Ruth versus Stephen Strasburg

Who earned more, Babe Ruth or Stephen Strasburg?

In 1930, the great baseball player Babe Ruth earned a salary of $80,000. When it was pointed out to him that he had earned more than President Hoover, Ruth replied, with some justification, "I had a better year than he did." In 2019, the highest-paid baseball player was Stephen Strasburg, a star pitcher for the Washington Nationals. His salary was $38.3 million. Adjusting for inflation, whose salary was higher, Ruth's or Strasburg's?

To answer this question, we need to know that the CPI (using the average of 1982–1984 as the base year) was 0.167 in 1930 and as of November 2019, it was 2.57 (for simplicity, we will treat this figure as if it were the annual 2019 figure). Dividing Babe Ruth's salary by 0.167, we obtain approximately $479,000, which is Ruth's salary "in 1982–1984 dollars." In other words, to enjoy the same purchasing power during the 1982–1984 period as in 1930, the Babe would have needed a salary of $479,000. Dividing Stephen Strasburg's 2019 salary by the November 2019 CPI, 2.57, yields a salary of $14.9 million in 1982–1984 dollars. We can now compare the salaries of the two players. Although adjusting for inflation brings the two figures closer together (since part of Strasburg's higher salary compensates for the increase in prices between 1930 and 2019), in real terms Strasburg's salary was still more than 31 times Ruth's salary. Incidentally, Strasburg's salary was also more than 95 times the U.S. president's salary.

real wage the wage paid to workers measured in terms of purchasing power; the real wage for any given period is calculated by dividing the nominal (dollar) wage by the CPI for that period

Clearly, in comparing wages or earnings at two different points in time, we must adjust for changes in the price level. Doing so yields the **real wage**—the wage measured in terms of real purchasing power. The real wage for any given period is calculated by dividing the nominal (dollar) wage by the CPI for that period.

 SELF-TEST 18.5

In 2001, Barry Bonds of the San Francisco Giants hit 73 home runs, breaking the previous single-season home run record and becoming the current record holder. Bonds earned $10.3 million in 2001. In that year the CPI was 1.77. How did Bonds's real earnings compare to Ruth's and Strasburg's real salaries?

EXAMPLE 18.4 — Real Wages of U.S. Production Workers

How do you compare workers' real wages?

Production workers are nonsupervisory workers, such as those who work on factory assembly lines. According to the Bureau of Labor Statistics, the average U.S. production worker earned $3.40 per hour in 1970 and $23.51 in 2019. Compare the real wages for this group of workers in these years.

To find the real wage in 1970 and 2019, we need to know the CPI in both years and then divide the wage in each year by the CPI for that year. For 1970, the nominal wage was $3.40 and the CPI was 0.388 (using the 1982–1984 average as the base period), so the real wage in 1970 was $8.76. Similarly, in 2019 the nominal wage was $23.51 and the CPI was 2.56, so the real wage in 2019 was $9.18. Thus, we find that in real terms, production workers' wages stayed almost the same between 1970 and 2019, despite the fact that the nominal wage in 2019 was almost seven times the nominal wage in 1970.

Figure 18.1 shows nominal wages and real wages for U.S. production workers for the period 1970–2019. Notice the dramatic difference between the two trends. Looking only at nominal wages, one might conclude that production-line workers

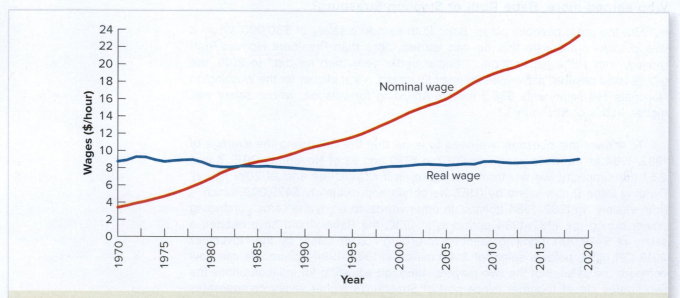

FIGURE 18.1

Nominal and Real Wages for Production Workers, 1970–2019.

Though nominal wages of production workers have risen dramatically since 1970, real wages have stagnated.

Source: FRED, Federal Reserve Economic Data, from the Federal Reserve Bank of St. Louis, http://fred.stlouisfed.org.

were much better paid in 2019 than in 1970. But once wages are adjusted for inflation, we see that, in terms of buying power, production-line workers' wages have stagnated since the early 1970s. This example illustrates the crucial importance of adjusting for inflation when comparing dollar values over time.

 SELF-TEST 18.6

In 1950, the minimum wage prescribed by federal law was $0.75 per hour. In 2019, it was $7.25 per hour. The CPI was 0.24 in 1950 and 2.56 in 2019. How does the real minimum wage in 2019 compare to that of 1950?

Example 18.3 concludes that the real salary of Stephen Strasburg in 2019 was more than 31 times Babe Ruth's salary in 1930. If you solved Self-Test 18.5, you also learned that more recently, star baseball players' real salaries increased dramatically: In real dollars, Strasburg made in 2019 more than 2.5 times what Barry Bonds made in 2001. In stark contrast, we saw in Example 18.4 that the real wages of production workers have remained essentially the same since 1970. And if you solved Self-Test 18.6, you discovered that the real minimum wage has, in fact, *decreased* since 1950.

These examples reflect a broader trend of increasing wage inequalities between the highest- and lowest-paid U.S. workers. In particular, the relative pay of the most highly paid athletes, entertainers, business leaders, and other professionals has increased significantly in recent years. We return to this and other trends in the U.S. labor market in Chapter 20, *The Labor Market: Workers, Wages, and Unemployment.*

INDEXING TO MAINTAIN BUYING POWER

The consumer price index also can be used to convert real quantities to nominal quantities. Suppose, for example, that in the year 2020 the government paid certain Social Security recipients $1,000 per month in benefits. Let's assume that Congress would like the buying power of these benefits to remain constant over time so that the recipients' standard of living is unaffected by inflation. To achieve that goal, at what level should Congress set the monthly Social Security benefit in the year 2025?

The nominal, or dollar, benefit Congress should pay in the year 2025 to maintain the purchasing power of retired people depends on how much inflation has taken place between 2020 and 2025. Suppose that the CPI has risen 20 percent between 2020 and 2025. That is, on average the prices of the goods and services consumers buy have risen 20 percent over that period. For Social Security recipients to "keep up" with inflation, their benefit in the year 2025 must be $1,000 + 0.20($1,000) = $1,200 per month, or 20 percent more than it was in 2020. In general, to keep purchasing power constant, the dollar benefit must be increased each year by the percentage increase in the CPI.

The practice of increasing a nominal quantity according to changes in a price index to prevent inflation from eroding purchasing power is called **indexing.** In the case of Social Security, federal law provides for the automatic indexing of benefits. Each year, without any action by Congress, benefits increase by an amount equal to the percentage increase in the CPI. Some labor contracts are indexed as well so that wages are adjusted fully or partially for changes in inflation (see Example 18.5).

indexing the practice of increasing a nominal quantity each period by an amount equal to the percentage increase in a specified price index; indexing prevents the purchasing power of the nominal quantity from being eroded by inflation

---

EXAMPLE 18.5   **An Indexed Labor Contract**

How much do workers get paid when they have an indexed contract?

A labor contract provides for a first-year wage of $12.00 per hour and specifies that the real wage will rise by 2 percent in the second year of the contract and by another 2 percent in the third year. The CPI is 1.00 in the first year, 1.05 in the second year, and 1.10 in the third year. Find the dollar wage that must be paid in the second and third years of the contract.

Because the CPI is 1.00 in the first year, both the nominal wage and the real wage are $12.00. Let W_2 stand for the nominal wage in the second year. Deflating by the CPI in the second year, we can express the real wage in the second year as $W_2/1.05$. The contract says that the second-year real wage must be 2 percent higher than the real wage in the first year, so $W_2/1.05 = \$12.00 \times 1.02 = \$12.24$. Multiplying through by 1.05 to solve for W_2, we get $W_2 = \$12.85$, the nominal wage required by the contract in the second year. In the third year, the nominal wage W_3 must satisfy the equation $W_3/1.10 = \$12.24 \times 1.02 = \$12.48$. (Why?) Solving this equation for W_3 yields $13.73 as the nominal wage that must be paid in the third year.

SELF-TEST 18.7

The minimum wage is not indexed to inflation, but suppose it had been starting in 1950. What would the nominal minimum wage have been in 2019? See Self-Test 18.6 for the data necessary to answer this question.

The Economic Naturalist 18.1

Every few years, there is a well-publicized battle in Congress over whether the minimum wage should be raised. Why do these heated legislative debates recur so regularly?

Because the minimum wage is not indexed to inflation, its purchasing power falls as prices rise. Congress must therefore raise the nominal minimum wage periodically to keep the real value of the minimum wage from eroding. Ironically, despite the public's impression that Congress has raised the nominal minimum wage steeply over the years, the real minimum wage has fallen almost 30 percent since 1970.

Why doesn't Congress index the minimum wage to the CPI and eliminate the need to reconsider it so often? Evidently, some members of Congress prefer to hold a highly publicized debate on the issue every few years—perhaps because it mobilizes both advocates and opponents of the minimum wage to make campaign donations to those members who represent their views.

RECAP↑

METHODS TO ADJUST FOR INFLATION

Deflating. To correct a nominal quantity, such as a family's dollar income, for changes in the price level, divide it by a price index such as the CPI. This process expresses the nominal quantity in terms of real purchasing power. If nominal quantities from two different years are deflated by a price index with the same base year, the purchasing power of the two deflated quantities can be compared.

Indexing. To ensure that a nominal payment, such as a Social Security benefit, represents a constant level of real purchasing power, increase the nominal quantity each year by a percentage equal to the rate of inflation for that year.

DOES THE CPI MEASURE "TRUE" INFLATION?

You may have concluded that measuring inflation is straightforward, but as with GDP and the unemployment rate, the issue is not free from controversy. Indeed the question of whether U.S. inflation is properly measured has been the subject of serious debate. Because the CPI is one of the most important U.S. economic statistics, the issue is far from academic. Policymakers pay close attention to the latest inflation numbers when deciding what actions to take. Furthermore, because of the widespread use of indexing, changes in the CPI directly impact the government's budget. For example, if the CPI rises by 3 percent during a given year, by law Social Security benefits—which are a significant part of the federal budget—increase automatically by 3 percent. Many other government payments and private contracts, such as union labor contracts, are indexed to the CPI as well.

One of the difficulties in measuring inflation is that in practice, government statisticians cannot always adjust adequately for changes in the *quality* of goods and services. Suppose a new laptop computer has 20 percent more memory, computational speed, and data storage capacity than last year's model. Suppose too for the sake of illustration that its price is 20 percent higher. Has there been inflation in computer prices? Economists would say no; although consumers are paying 20 percent more for a computer, they are getting a 20 percent better machine. The situation is really no different from paying 20 percent more for a pizza that is 20 percent bigger. However, because quality change is difficult to measure precisely and because they have many thousands of goods and services to consider, government statisticians often miss or understate changes in quality. In general, whenever statisticians fail to adjust adequately for improvements in the quality of goods or services, they will tend to overstate inflation. This type of overstatement is called *quality adjustment bias*.

One important consequence of quality adjustment bias, and of an overstated rate of inflation in general, is an *under*estimation of the true improvement in living standards over time. If the typical family's nominal income increases by 3 percent per year, and inflation is reported to be 3 percent per year, economists would conclude that American families are experiencing no increase in their real income. But if the "true" inflation rate, adjusting for quality improvements, is really 2 percent per year, then the family's real income is actually rising by 1 percent per year (the 3 percent increase in nominal income minus 2 percent inflation).

The Bureau of Labor Statistics (the agency responsible for calculating the CPI) makes significant efforts to adjust for quality and avoid overstating inflation. In spite of these efforts, in recent years some economists have argued that the problem of quality adjustment bias has in fact been getting *worse*. For example, some argue that as the U.S. economy shifts from producing computer hardware to producing software and digital content, accurately measuring quality change becomes increasingly harder.

An extreme example of quality adjustment bias can occur whenever a totally new good becomes available. For instance, the introduction of the first effective AIDS drugs significantly increased the quality of medical care received by AIDS patients. In practice, however, quality improvements that arise from totally new products are likely to be poorly captured by the CPI, if at all. The problem is that because the new good was not produced in the base year, there is no base-year price with which to compare the current price of the good. Government statisticians use various approaches to correct for this problem, such as comparing the cost of the new drug to the cost of the next-best therapies. But such methods are necessarily imprecise and open to criticism.

Another problem in measuring inflation arises from the fact that the CPI is calculated for a fixed basket of goods and services. This procedure does not allow for the possibility that consumers can switch from products whose prices are rising to those whose prices are stable or falling. Ignoring the fact that consumers can switch from more expensive to less expensive goods leads statisticians to overestimate the true increase in the cost of living and, again, underestimate the true improvement in living standards over time.

Suppose, for instance, that people like coffee and tea equally well and in the base year consumed equal amounts of each. But then a frost hits a major coffee-producing

▶ Visit your instructor's Connect course and access your eBook to view this video.

Do official inflation figures overstate actual increases in our living costs?

nation, causing the price of coffee to double. The increase in coffee prices encourages consumers to forgo coffee and drink tea instead–a switch that doesn't make them worse off since they like coffee and tea equally well. However, the CPI, which measures the cost of buying the base-year basket of goods and services, will rise significantly when the price of coffee doubles. This rise in the CPI, which ignores the fact that people can substitute tea for coffee without being made worse off, exaggerates the true increase in the cost of living. This type of overstatement of inflation is called *substitution bias*.

EXAMPLE 18.6	Substitution Bias

Why does substitution bias matter?

Suppose the CPI basket for 2015, the base year, is as follows:

Item	Expenditure
Coffee (50 cups at $1/cup)	$ 50.00
Tea (50 cups at $1/cup)	50.00
Scones (100 at $1 each)	100.00
Total	$200.00

Assume that consumers are equally happy to drink coffee or tea with their scones. In 2015, coffee and tea cost the same, and the average person drinks equal amounts of coffee and tea.

In the year 2020, coffee has doubled in price to $2 per cup. Tea remains at $1 per cup, and scones are $1.50 each. What has happened to the cost of living as measured by the CPI? How does this result compare to the true cost of living?

To calculate the value of the CPI for the year 2020, we must first find the cost of consuming the 2015 basket of goods in that year. At year 2020 prices, 50 cups each of coffee and tea and 100 scones cost $(50 \times \$2) + (50 \times \$1) + (100 \times \$1.50) = \$300$. Since consuming the same basket of goods cost $200 in 2015, the base year, the CPI in 2020 is $300/$200, or 1.50. This calculation leads us to conclude that the cost of living has increased 50 percent between 2015 and 2020.

However, we have overlooked the possibility that consumers can substitute a cheaper good (tea) for the more expensive one (coffee). Indeed, since consumers like coffee and tea equally well, when the price of coffee doubles, they will shift entirely to tea. Their new consumption basket—100 cups of tea and 100 scones—is just as enjoyable to them as their original basket. If we allow for the substitution of less expensive goods, how much has the cost of living really increased? The cost of 100 cups of tea and 100 scones in the year 2020 is only $250, not $300. From the consumer's point of view, the true cost of living has risen by only $50, or 25 percent. The 50 percent increase in the CPI therefore overstates the increase in the cost of living as the result of substitution bias.

While quality adjustment bias and substitution bias undoubtedly distort the measurement of inflation, estimating precisely how much of an overstatement they create is difficult. (If economists knew exactly how big these biases were, they could simply correct the data.) Nonetheless, the Bureau of Labor Statistics has in the past two decades made significant efforts to improve the quality of its data.

THE COSTS OF INFLATION: NOT WHAT YOU THINK

In the late 1970s, when inflation was considerably higher than it is now, the public told poll takers that they viewed it as "public enemy number one"—that is, as the nation's most serious problem.

Although U.S. inflation rates have not been very high in recent years, today many Americans remain concerned about inflation or the threat of inflation. Why do people worry so much about inflation? Detailed opinion surveys often find that many people are confused about the meaning of inflation and its economic effects. When people complain about inflation, they are often concerned primarily about relative price changes.

Before describing the true economic costs of inflation, which are real and serious, let's examine this confusion people experience about inflation and its costs.

We need first to distinguish between the *price level* and the *relative price* of a good or service. The **price level** is a measure of the overall level of prices at a particular point in time as measured by a price index such as the CPI. Recall that the inflation rate is the percentage change in the price level from year to year. In contrast, a **relative price** is the price of a specific good or service *in comparison to* the prices of other goods and services. For example, if the price of oil were to rise by 10 percent while the prices of other goods and services were rising on average by 3 percent, the relative price of oil would increase. But if oil prices rise by 3 percent while other prices rise by 10 percent, the relative price of oil would decrease. That is, oil would become cheaper relative to other goods and services, even though it has not become cheaper in absolute terms.

Public opinion surveys suggest that many people are confused about the distinction between inflation, which is an increase in the overall *price level*, and an increase in a specific *relative price*. Suppose that supply disruptions in the Middle East were to double the price of gas at the pump, leaving other prices unaffected. Appalled by the increase in gasoline prices, people might demand that the government do something about "this inflation." But while the increase in gas prices hurts consumers, is it an example of inflation? Gasoline is only one item in a consumer's budget, one of the thousands of goods and services that people buy every day. Thus, the increase in the price of gasoline might affect the overall price level, and hence the inflation rate, only slightly. In this example, inflation is not the real problem. What upsets consumers is the change in the *relative price* of gasoline, particularly compared to the price of labor (wages). By increasing the cost of using a car, the increase in the relative price of gasoline reduces the income people have left over to spend on other things.

Again, changes in relative prices do *not* necessarily imply a significant amount of inflation. For example, increases in the prices of some goods could well be counterbalanced by decreases in the prices of other goods, in which case the price level and the inflation rate would be largely unaffected. Conversely, inflation can be high without affecting relative prices. Imagine, for instance, that all prices in the economy, including wages and salaries, go up exactly 10 percent each year. The inflation rate is 10 percent, but relative prices are not changing. Indeed, because wages (the price of labor) are increasing by 10 percent per year, people's ability to buy goods and services is unaffected by the inflation.

These examples show that changes in the price level (inflation) and changes in the relative prices of specific goods are two quite different issues. The public's tendency to confuse the two is important because the remedies for the two problems are different. To counteract changes in relative prices, the government would need to implement policies that affect the supply and demand for specific goods. In the case of an increase in oil prices, for example, the government could try to restore supplies by mediating the peace process in the Middle East, or it could try to encourage the development of alternative sources of energy. To counteract inflation, however, the government must resort (as we will see) to changes in macroeconomic policies such as monetary or fiscal policies. If, in confusion, the public forces the government to adopt anti-inflationary policies when the real problem is a relative price change, the economy could actually be hurt by the effort. This is an important example of why economic literacy is important—to both policymakers and the general public.

price level a measure of the overall level of prices at a particular point in time as measured by a price index such as the CPI

relative price the price of a specific good or service *in comparison to* the prices of other goods and services

---

EXAMPLE 18.7   **The Price Level, Relative Prices, and Inflation**

Has the price of oil risen faster or slower than the price level?

Suppose the value of the CPI is 1.20 in the year 2018, 1.32 in 2019, and 1.40 in 2020. Assume also that the price of oil increases 8 percent between 2018 and 2019 and another 8 percent between 2019 and 2020. What is happening to the price level, the inflation rate, and the relative price of oil?

The price level can be measured by the CPI. Since the CPI is higher in 2019 than in 2018 and higher still in 2020 than in 2019, the price level is rising throughout the period. Since the CPI increases by 10 percent between 2018 and 2019, the inflation rate between those years is 10 percent. However, the CPI increases only about 6 percent between 2019 and 2020 (1.40/1.32 ≈ 1.06), so the inflation rate decreases to about 6 percent between those years. The decline in the inflation rate implies that although the price level is still rising, it is doing so at a slower pace than the year before.

The price of oil rises 8 percent between 2018 and 2019. But because the general inflation over that period is 10 percent, the relative price of oil—that is, its price *relative to all other goods and services*—falls by about 2 percent (8% − 10% = −2%). Between 2019 and 2020, the price of oil rises by another 8 percent, while the general inflation rate is about 6 percent. Hence, the relative price of oil rises between 2019 and 2020 by about 2 percent (8% − 6%).

THE TRUE COSTS OF INFLATION

Having dispelled the common confusion between inflation and relative price changes, we are now free to address the true economic costs of inflation. There are a variety of such costs, each of which tends to reduce the efficiency of the economy. Five of the most important are discussed here.

"Noise" in the Price System

In Chapter 3, *Supply and Demand,* we described the remarkable economic coordination that is necessary to provide the right amount and the right kinds of food to New Yorkers every day. This feat is not orchestrated by some food distribution ministry staffed by bureaucrats. It is done much better by the workings of free markets, operating without central guidance, than a ministry ever could.

How do free markets transmit the enormous amounts of information necessary to accomplish complex tasks like the provisioning of New York City? The answer is through the price system. When the owners of French restaurants in Manhattan cannot find sufficient quantities of chanterelles, a particularly rare and desirable mushroom, they bid up its market price. Specialty food suppliers notice the higher price for chanterelles and realize that they can make a profit by supplying more chanterelles to the market. At the same time, price-conscious diners will shift to cheaper, more available mushrooms. The market for chanterelles will reach equilibrium only when there are no more unexploited opportunities for profit and both suppliers and demanders are satisfied at the market price (the Equilibrium Principle). Multiply this example a million times, and you will gain a sense of how the price system achieves a truly remarkable degree of economic coordination.

 Equilibrium

When inflation is high, however, the subtle signals that are transmitted through the price system become more difficult to interpret, much in the way that static, or "noise," makes a radio message harder to interpret. In an economy with little or no inflation, the supplier of specialty foodstuffs will immediately recognize the increase in chanterelle prices as a signal to bring more to market. If inflation is high, however, the supplier must ask whether a price increase represents a true increase in the demand for chanterelles or is just a result of the general inflation, which causes all food prices to rise. If the price rise reflects only inflation, the price of chanterelles *relative to other goods and services* has not really changed. The supplier therefore should not change the quantity of mushrooms he brings to market.

In an inflationary environment, to discern whether the increase in chanterelle prices is a true signal of increased demand, the supplier needs to know not only the price of chanterelles, but also what is happening to the prices of other goods and services. Because this information takes time and effort to collect, the supplier's response to the change in chanterelle prices is likely to be slower and more tentative.

In summary, price changes are the market's way of communicating information to suppliers and demanders. An increase in the price of a good or service, for example, tells demanders to economize on their use of the good or service and suppliers to bring more of it to market. But in the presence of inflation, prices are affected not only by changes in the supply and demand for a product but by changes in the general price level. Inflation creates static, or "noise," in the price system, obscuring the information transmitted by prices and reducing the efficiency of the market system. This reduction in efficiency imposes real economic costs.

Distortions of the Tax System

Just as some government expenditures, such as Social Security benefits, are indexed to inflation, many taxes are also indexed. In the United States, people with higher incomes pay a higher *percentage* of their income in taxes. Without indexing, an inflation that raises people's nominal incomes would force them to pay an increasing percentage of their income in taxes, even though their *real* incomes may not have increased. To avoid this phenomenon, which is known as *bracket creep,* Congress has indexed income tax brackets to the CPI. The effect of this indexation is that a family whose nominal income is rising at the same rate as inflation does not have to pay a higher percentage of income in taxes.

Although indexing has solved the problem of bracket creep, many provisions of the tax code have not been indexed, either because of lack of political support or because of the complexity of the task. As a result, inflation can produce unintended changes in the taxes people pay, which in turn may cause them to change their behavior in economically undesirable ways.

To illustrate, an important provision in the business tax code for which inflation poses problems is the *capital depreciation allowance,* which works as follows. Suppose a firm buys a machine for $1,000, expecting it to last for 10 years. Under U.S. tax law, the firm can take one-tenth of the purchase price, or $100, as a deduction from its taxable profits in each of the 10 years. By deducting a fraction of the purchase price from its taxable profits, the firm reduces its taxes. The exact amount of the yearly tax reduction is the tax rate on corporate profits times $100.

The idea behind this provision of the tax code is that the wearing out of the machine is a cost of doing business that should be deducted from the firm's profit. Also, in giving firms a tax break for investing in new machinery, Congress intended to encourage firms to modernize their plants. Yet capital depreciation allowances are not indexed to inflation. Suppose that, at a time when the inflation rate is high, a firm is considering purchasing a $1,000 machine. The managers know that the purchase will allow them to deduct $100 per year from taxable profits for the next 10 years. But that $100 is a fixed amount that is not indexed to inflation. Looking forward, managers will recognize that 5, 6, or 10 years into the future, the real value of the $100 tax deduction will be much lower than at present because of inflation. They will have less incentive to buy the machine and may decide not to make the investment at all. Indeed, many studies have found that a high rate of inflation can significantly reduce the rate at which firms invest in new factories and equipment.

Because the U.S. tax code contains hundreds of provisions and tax rates that are not indexed, inflation can seriously distort the incentives provided by the tax system for people to work, save, and invest. The resulting effects on economic efficiency and economic growth represent a real cost of inflation.

"Shoe-Leather" Costs

As all shoppers know, cash is convenient. Unlike checks, which are not accepted everywhere, and credit cards, for which a minimum purchase is sometimes required, cash can be used in almost any routine transaction. Businesses, too, find cash convenient to hold. Having plenty of cash on hand facilitates transactions with customers and reduces the need for frequent deposits and withdrawals from the bank.

Inflation raises the cost of holding cash to consumers and businesses. Consider a miser with $10,000 in $20 bills under his mattress. What happens to the buying power of his hoard over time? If inflation is zero so that, on average, the prices of goods and services are not changing, the buying power of the $10,000 does not change over time. At the end of a year, the miser's purchasing power is the same as it was at the beginning of the year. But suppose the inflation rate is 10 percent. In that case, the purchasing power of the miser's hoard will fall by 10 percent each year. After a year, he will have only $9,000 in purchasing power. In general, the higher the rate of inflation, the less people will want to hold cash because of the loss of purchasing power that they will suffer.

Technically, currency is a debt owed by the government to the currency holder. So when currency loses value, the losses to holders of cash are offset by gains to the government, which now owes less in real terms to currency holders. Thus, from the point of view of society as a whole, the loss of purchasing power is not in itself a cost of inflation because it does not involve wasted resources. (Indeed, no real goods or services were used up when the miser's currency hoard lost part of its value.)

However, when faced with inflation, people are not likely to accept a loss in purchasing power but, instead, will take actions to try to "economize" on their cash holdings. For example, instead of drawing out enough cash for a month the next time they visit the bank, they will draw out only enough to last a week. The inconvenience of visiting the bank more often to minimize one's cash holdings is a real cost of inflation. Similarly, businesses will reduce their cash holdings by sending employees to the bank more frequently, or by installing computerized systems to monitor cash usage. To deal with the increase in bank transactions required by consumers and businesses trying to use less cash, banks will need to hire more employees and expand their operations.

The costs of more frequent trips to the bank, new cash management systems, and expanded employment in banks are real costs. They use up resources, including time and effort, that could be used for other purposes. Traditionally, the costs of economizing on cash have been called *shoe-leather costs*—the idea being that shoe leather is worn out during extra trips to the bank. Shoe-leather costs probably are not a significant problem in the United States today, where inflation is only 2 to 3 percent per year. But in economies with high rates of inflation, they can become quite significant.

Unexpected Redistributions of Wealth

When inflation is unexpected, it may arbitrarily redistribute wealth from one group to another. Consider a group of union workers who signed a contract setting their wages for the next three years. If those wages are not indexed to inflation, then the workers will be vulnerable to upsurges in the price level. Suppose, for example, that inflation is much higher than expected over the three years of the contract. In that case, the buying power of the workers' wages—their real wages—will be less than anticipated when they signed the contract.

From society's point of view, is the buying power that workers lose to inflation really "lost"? The answer is no; the loss in their buying power is exactly matched by an unanticipated gain in the employer's buying power because the real cost of paying the workers is less than anticipated. In other words, the effect of the inflation is not to *destroy* purchasing power but to *redistribute* it, in this case from the workers to the employer. If inflation had been *lower* than expected, the workers would have enjoyed greater purchasing power than they anticipated and the employer would have been the loser.

Another example of the redistribution caused by inflation takes place between borrowers (debtors) and lenders (creditors). Suppose one of the authors of this book wants to buy a house on a lake and borrows $300,000 from the bank to pay for it. Shortly after signing the mortgage agreement, he learns that inflation is likely to be much higher than expected. How should he react to the news? Perhaps as a public-spirited macroeconomist, the author should be saddened to hear that inflation is rising, but as a consumer he should be pleased. In real terms, the dollars with which he will repay his loan in the future will be worth much less than expected. The loan officer should be distraught because the dollars the bank will receive from the author will be worth less, in purchasing power terms, than expected at contract signing. Once again, no real wealth is "lost" to the inflation; rather, the borrower's gain is just offset by the lender's loss. *In general, unexpectedly high inflation rates help borrowers at the expense of lenders* because borrowers are able to repay their loans in less-valuable dollars. Unexpectedly low inflation rates, in contrast, help lenders and hurt borrowers by forcing borrowers to repay in dollars that are worth more than expected when the loan was made.

Although redistributions caused by inflation do not directly destroy wealth, but only transfer it from one group to another, they are still bad for the economy. Our economic system is based on incentives. For it to work well, people must know that if they work hard, save some of their income, and make wise financial investments, they will be rewarded in the long run with greater real wealth and a better standard of living. Some observers have compared a high-inflation economy to a casino, in which wealth is distributed largely by luck—that is, by random fluctuations in the inflation rate. In the long run, a "casino economy" is likely to perform poorly, as its unpredictability discourages people from working and saving. A high-inflation economy encourages people to use up resources in trying to anticipate inflation and protect themselves against it.

Interference with Long-Term Planning

The fifth and final cost of inflation we will examine is its tendency to interfere with the long-term planning of households and firms. Many economic decisions take place within a long time horizon. Planning for retirement, for example, may begin when workers are in their twenties or thirties. And firms develop long-term investment and business strategies that look decades into the future.

Clearly, high and erratic inflation can make long-term planning difficult. Recall, for example, the question we asked in the beginning of this chapter: Would you be able to retire comfortably in 40 years if by then you managed to save $100 million? Let's try to answer this question. Suppose that you want to enjoy a certain standard of living when you retire. How much of your income do you need to save to make your dreams a reality? That depends on what the goods and services you plan to buy will cost 40 years from now (would $100 million be enough to buy them during your retirement years?). With high and erratic inflation, even guessing what your chosen lifestyle will cost by the time you retire is extremely difficult. You may end up saving too little and having to compromise on your retirement plans; or you may save too much, sacrificing more than you need to during your working years. Either way, inflation will have proved costly.

In summary, inflation damages the economy in a variety of ways. Some of its effects are difficult to quantify and affect different segments of the population in different ways. But most economists agree that a low and stable inflation rate is instrumental in maintaining a healthy economy.

HYPERINFLATION

Although there is some disagreement about whether an inflation rate of, say, 5 percent per year imposes important costs on an economy, few economists would question the fact that an inflation rate of 500 percent or 1,000 percent per year disrupts economic performance. A situation in which the inflation rate is extremely high is called **hyperinflation.** Although there is no official threshold above which inflation becomes hyperinflation, inflation rates in the range of 500 to 1,000 percent per year would surely qualify.

hyperinflation a situation in which the inflation rate is extremely high

In the past few decades, episodes of hyperinflation have occurred in Israel (400 percent inflation in 1985); Nicaragua (33,000 percent inflation in 1988); several South American countries, including Bolivia, Argentina, Brazil, and most recently Venezuela (forecast to have 10,000,000 percent inflation in 2019); and several countries attempting to make the transition from communism to capitalism, including Russia. Zimbabwe has recently experienced a severe episode of hyperinflation, and in early 2009, the Zimbabwean government issued a Z$100 trillion bill—that's 100,000,000,000,000 Zimbabwean dollars! Perhaps the most well-known episode occurred in Germany in 1923 when inflation was 102,000,000 percent. In the German hyperinflation, prices rose so rapidly that for a time, workers were paid twice each day so their families could buy food before the afternoon price increases, and many people's life savings became worthless. But the most extreme hyperinflation ever recorded was in Hungary in 1945, at the end of the Second World War, when inflation peaked at 3.8×10^{27} percent. The United States has never experienced hyperinflation, although the short-lived Confederate States of America suffered severe inflation during the Civil War. Between 1861 and 1865, prices in the Confederacy rose to 92 times their prewar levels.

A consequence of hyperinflation.

Hyperinflation greatly magnifies the costs of inflation. For example, shoe-leather costs—a relatively minor consideration in times of low inflation—become quite important during hyperinflation. In this type of environment, people may visit the bank two or three times per day to hold money for as short a time as possible. With prices changing daily or even hourly, markets work quite poorly, slowing economic growth. Massive redistributions of wealth take place, impoverishing many and enriching only a few. Not surprisingly, episodes of hyperinflation rarely last more than a few years; they are so disruptive that they quickly lead to public outcry for relief.

> **RECAP**
>
> ### THE TRUE COSTS OF INFLATION
>
> The public sometimes confuses changes in relative prices (such as the price of oil) with inflation, which is a change in the overall level of prices. This confusion can cause problems because the remedies for undesired changes in relative prices and for inflation are different.
>
> There are a number of true costs of inflation, which together tend to reduce economic growth and efficiency. Hyperinflation—a situation in which the inflation rate is extremely high—greatly magnifies these costs. They include:
>
> - "Noise" in the price system, which occurs when general inflation makes it difficult for market participants to interpret the information conveyed by prices.
> - Distortions of the tax system (for example, when provisions of the tax code are not indexed).
> - "Shoe-leather" costs, or the costs of economizing on cash (for example, by making more frequent trips to the bank or installing a computerized cash management system).
> - Unexpected redistributions of wealth, as when higher-than-expected inflation hurts wage earners to the benefit of employers or hurts creditors to the benefit of debtors.
> - Interference with long-term planning, arising because people find it difficult to forecast prices over long periods.

INFLATION AND INTEREST RATES

So far, we have focused on the measurement and economic costs of inflation. Another important aspect of inflation is its close relationship to other key macroeconomic variables. For example, economists have long realized that during periods of high inflation, interest rates tend to be high as well. We will close this chapter with a look at the relationship between inflation and interest rates, which will provide a useful background in the chapters to come.

INFLATION AND THE REAL INTEREST RATE

Earlier in our discussion of the ways in which inflation redistributes wealth, we saw that inflation tends to hurt creditors and help debtors by reducing the value of the dollars with which debts are repaid. The effect of inflation on debtors and creditors can be explained more precisely using an economic concept called the *real interest rate*. An example will illustrate.

Suppose that there are two neighboring countries, Alpha and Beta. In Alpha, whose currency is called the alphan, the inflation rate is zero and is expected to remain at zero. In Beta, where the currency is the betan, the inflation rate is 10 percent and is expected to remain at that level. Bank deposits pay 2 percent annual interest in Alpha and 10 percent annual interest in Beta. In which countries are bank depositors getting a better deal?

You may answer Beta because interest rates on deposits are higher in that country. But if you think about the effects of inflation, you will recognize that Alpha, not Beta, offers the better deal to depositors. To see why, think about the change over a year in the real purchasing power of deposits in the two countries. In Alpha, someone who deposits 100 alphans in the bank on January 1 will have 102 alphans on December 31. Because there is no inflation in Alpha, on average, prices are the same at the end of the year as they were at the beginning. Thus, the 102 alphans the depositor can withdraw represent a 2 percent increase in buying power.

In Beta, the depositor who deposits 100 betans on January 1 will have 110 betans by the end of the year—10 percent more than she started with. But the prices of goods and services in Beta, we have assumed, also will rise by 10 percent. Thus, the Beta depositor can afford to buy precisely the same amount of goods and services at the end of the year as she could at the beginning; she gets no increase in buying power. So the Alpha depositor has the better deal, after all.

Economists refer to the annual percentage increase in the *real* purchasing power of a financial asset as the **real interest rate,** or the *real rate of return*, on that asset. In our example, the real purchasing power of deposits rises by 2 percent per year in Alpha and by 0 percent per year in Beta. So the real interest rate on deposits is 2 percent in Alpha and 0 percent in Beta. The real interest rate should be distinguished from the more familiar **nominal interest rate,** also called **market interest rate,** which is the annual percentage increase in the nominal, or dollar, value of an asset.

As the example of Alpha and Beta illustrates, we can calculate the real interest rate for any financial asset, from a checking account to a government bond, by subtracting the rate of inflation from the market or nominal interest rate on that asset. So in Alpha, the real interest rate on deposits equals the nominal interest rate (2 percent) minus the inflation rate (0 percent), or 2 percent. Likewise in Beta, the real interest rate equals the nominal interest rate (10 percent) minus the inflation rate (10 percent), or 0 percent.

We can write this definition of the real interest rate in mathematical terms

$$r = i - \pi,$$

where

r = the real interest rate,

i = the nominal, or market, interest rate,

π = the current inflation rate.

real interest rate the annual percentage increase in the purchasing power of a financial asset; the real interest rate on any asset equals the nominal interest rate on that asset minus the inflation rate

nominal interest rate (or **market interest rate**) the annual percentage increase in the nominal value of a financial asset

Notice that at the time of purchasing an asset, the inflation rate that will prevail over the life of the asset is not yet known. Economists therefore distinguish between the *expected* real interest rate, measured by the nominal interest rate minus the inflation rate that is expected at the time of purchase, and the *actual* real interest rate, measured by the nominal interest rate minus the inflation rate that actually prevailed. The expected real interest rate reflects what people who bought an asset anticipated their real rate of return to be, while the actual real interest rate reflects what their real rate of return ended up being. In order to keep things simple, our preceding discussion assumes that the two are equal, by assuming that the current inflation rate will not change. We discuss unanticipated inflation-rate changes below.

EXAMPLE 18.8	Real Interest Rates Since the 1970s

Why is the real interest rate important?

Following are interest rates on three-month government bonds for selected years since the 1970s. In which of these years did the financial investors who bought government bonds get the best deal? The worst deal?

Year	Interest rate (%)	Inflation rate (%)	Real interest rate (%)
1970	6.5	5.7	−0.8
1975	5.8	9.1	−3.3
1980	11.5	13.5	−2.0
1985	7.5	3.6	3.9
1990	7.5	5.4	2.1
1995	5.5	2.8	2.7
2000	5.8	3.4	2.4
2005	3.2	3.4	−0.2
2010	0.1	1.6	−1.5
2015	0.05	0.12	−0.07

Financial investors and lenders do best when the real (not the nominal) interest rate is high because the real interest rate measures the increase in their purchasing power. We can calculate the real interest rate for each year by subtracting the inflation rate from the nominal interest rate. The results are shown in the third column of the accompanying table. For purchasers of government bonds, the best of these years was 1985, when they enjoyed a real return of 3.9 percent. The worst year was 1975, when their real return was actually negative 3.3 percent. In other words, despite receiving 5.8 percent nominal interest, financial investors ended up losing buying power in 1975, as the inflation rate exceeded the interest rate earned by their investments.

Figure 18.2 shows the real interest rate in the United States since 1970 as measured by the nominal interest rate paid on the federal government's debt minus the inflation rate. Note that the real interest rate was negative in the 1970s, reached historically high levels in the mid-1980s, and has been negative again in many of the past 20 years.

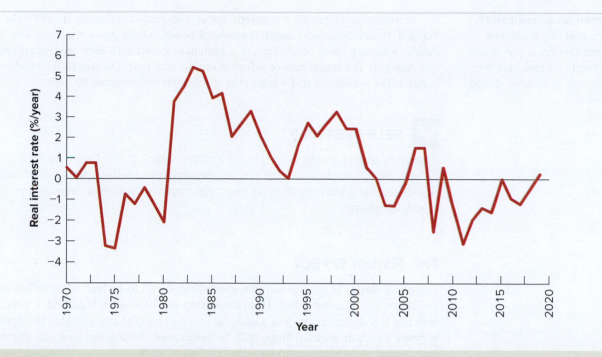

FIGURE 18.2

The Real Interest Rate in the United States, 1970–2019.

The real interest rate is the nominal interest rate—here the interest rate on funds borrowed by the federal government for a term of three months—minus the rate of inflation. In the United States, the real interest rate was negative in the 1970s, reached historically high levels in the mid-1980s, and has often been negative in many of the past 20 years.

Sources: Federal Reserve Economic Data, http://fred.stlouisfed.org; authors' calculations.

✅ **SELF-TEST 18.8**

You have some funds to invest but are unimpressed with the low interest rates your bank offers. You consult a broker, who suggests a bond issued by the government of a small island nation. The broker points out that these bonds pay 25 percent interest—much more than your bank—and that the island's government has never failed to repay its debts. What should be your next question?

The concept of the real interest rate helps explain more precisely why an unexpected surge in inflation is bad for lenders and good for borrowers. For any given nominal interest rate that the lender charges the borrower, the higher the inflation rate, the lower the real interest rate the lender actually receives. So, unexpectedly high inflation leaves the lender worse off. Borrowers, on the other hand, are better off when inflation is unexpectedly high because their real interest rate is lower than anticipated.

Although unexpectedly high inflation hurts lenders and helps borrowers, a high rate of inflation that is *expected* may not redistribute wealth at all because expected inflation can be built into the nominal interest rate. Suppose, for example, that the lender requires a real interest rate of 2 percent on new loans. If the inflation rate is confidently expected to be zero, the lender can get a 2 percent real interest rate by charging a nominal interest rate of 2 percent. But if the inflation rate is expected to be 10 percent, the lender can still ensure a real interest rate of 2 percent by charging a nominal interest rate of 12 percent. Thus, high inflation, if it is *expected*, need not hurt lenders—as long as the lenders can adjust the nominal interest they charge to reflect the expected inflation rate.

inflation-protected bonds
bonds that pay a nominal interest rate each year equal to a fixed real rate plus the actual rate of inflation during that year

In response to people's concerns about unexpected inflation, in 1997 the United States Treasury introduced **inflation-protected bonds,** which pay a fixed real interest rate. People who buy these bonds receive a nominal interest rate each year equal to a fixed real rate plus the actual rate of inflation during that year. Owners of inflation-protected bonds suffer no loss in real wealth even if inflation is unexpectedly high.

 SELF-TEST 18.9

What is the real rate of return to holding cash? (*Hint:* Does cash pay interest?) Does this real rate of return depend on whether the rate of inflation is correctly anticipated? How does your answer relate to the idea of shoe-leather costs?

THE FISHER EFFECT

Earlier we made the observation that interest rates tend to be high when inflation is high and low when inflation is low. This relationship can be seen in Figure 18.3, which shows both the U.S. inflation rate and a nominal interest rate (the rate at which the government borrows for short periods) from 1970 to the present. Notice that nominal interest rates have tended to be high in periods of high inflation, such as the late 1970s, and have been declining since then, along with inflation.

Why do interest rates tend to be high when inflation is high? Our discussion of real interest rates provides the answer. Suppose inflation has recently been high, so borrowers and lenders anticipate that it will be high in the near future. We would expect lenders to raise their nominal interest rate so that their real rate of return will be unaffected. For their part, borrowers are willing to pay higher nominal interest rates when inflation is high because they understand that the higher nominal interest rate only serves to compensate the lender for the fact that the loan will be repaid in dollars of reduced real

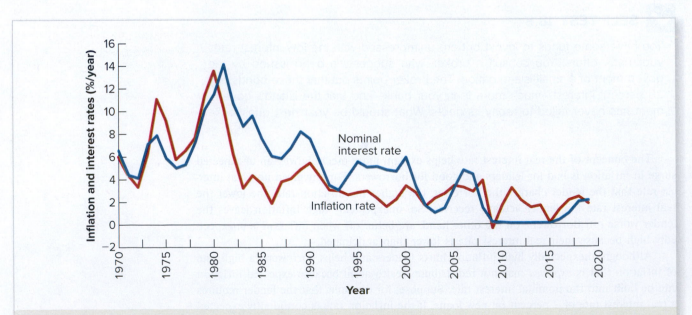

FIGURE 18.3

Inflation and Interest Rates in the United States, 1970–2019.

Nominal interest rates tend to be high when inflation is high and low when inflation is low, a phenomenon called the Fisher effect.

Source: Federal Reserve Economic Data, http://fred.stlouisfed.org.

value—in real terms, their cost of borrowing is unaffected by an equal increase in the nominal interest rate and the inflation rate. Conversely, when inflation is low, lenders do not need to charge so high a nominal interest rate to ensure a given real return. Thus, nominal interest rates will be high when inflation is high and low when inflation is low.

This tendency for nominal interest rates to follow inflation rates is called the **Fisher effect,** after the early twentieth-century American economist Irving Fisher, who first pointed out the relationship.

Fisher effect the tendency for nominal interest rates to be high when inflation is high and low when inflation is low

SUMMARY

- The basic tool for measuring inflation is the *consumer price index (CPI)*. The CPI measures the cost of purchasing a fixed basket of goods and services in any period relative to the cost of the same basket of goods and services in a base year. The *inflation rate* is the annual percentage rate of change in the price level as measured by a *price index* such as the CPI. *(LO1)*

- A *nominal quantity* is a quantity that is measured in terms of its current dollar value. Dividing a nominal quantity such as a family's income or a worker's wage in dollars by a price index such as the CPI expresses that quantity in terms of real purchasing power. This procedure is called *deflating* the nominal quantity. If nominal quantities from two different years are deflated by a common price index, the purchasing power of the two quantities can be compared. To ensure that a nominal payment such as a Social Security benefit represents a constant level of real purchasing power, the nominal payment should be increased each year by a percentage equal to the inflation rate. This method of adjusting nominal payments to maintain their purchasing power is called *indexing. (LO2)*

- The official U.S. inflation rate, based on the CPI, may overstate the true inflation rate for two reasons: First, it may not adequately reflect improvements in the quality of goods and services. Second, the method of calculating the CPI ignores the fact that consumers can substitute cheaper goods and services for more expensive ones. *(LO3)*

- The public sometimes confuses increases in the *relative prices* for specific goods or services with inflation, which is an increase in the general price level. Because the remedies for a change in relative prices are different from the remedies for inflation, this confusion can cause problems. *(LO4)*

- Inflation imposes a number of true costs on the economy, including "noise" in the price system; distortions of the tax system; "shoe-leather" costs, which are the real resources that are wasted as people try to economize on cash holdings; unexpected redistributions of wealth; and interference with long-term planning. Because of these costs, most economists agree that sustained economic growth is more likely if inflation is low and stable. *Hyperinflation*, a situation in which the inflation rate is extremely high, greatly magnifies the costs of inflation and is highly disruptive to the economy. *(LO4)*

- The *real interest rate* is the annual percentage increase in the purchasing power of a financial asset. It is equal to the *nominal*, or market, *interest rate* minus the inflation rate. When inflation is unexpectedly high, the real interest rate is lower than anticipated, which hurts lenders but benefits borrowers. When inflation is unexpectedly low, lenders benefit and borrowers are hurt. To obtain a given real rate of return, lenders must charge a high nominal interest rate when inflation is high and a low nominal interest rate when inflation is low. The tendency for nominal interest rates to be high when inflation is high and low when inflation is low is called the *Fisher effect. (LO5)*

KEY TERMS

consumer price index (CPI)	inflation-protected bonds	rate of inflation
deflating (a nominal quantity)	nominal interest rate (or market	real interest rate
deflation	interest rate)	real quantity
Fisher effect	nominal quantity	real wage
hyperinflation	price index	relative price
indexing	price level	

REVIEW QUESTIONS

1. Explain why changes in the cost of living for any particular individual or family may differ from changes in the official cost-of-living index, the CPI. *(LO1)*

2. What is the difference between the *price level* and the *rate of inflation* in an economy? *(LO1)*

3. Why is it important to adjust for inflation when comparing nominal quantities (for example, workers' average wages) at different points in time? What is the basic method for adjusting for inflation? *(LO2)*

4. Describe how indexation might be used to guarantee that the purchasing power of the wage agreed to in a multiyear labor contract will not be eroded by inflation. *(LO2)*

5. Give two reasons the official inflation rate may understate the "true" rate of inflation. Illustrate by examples. *(LO3)*

6. "It's true that unexpected inflation redistributes wealth, from creditors to debtors, for example. But what one side of the bargain loses, the other side gains. So from the perspective of the society as a whole, there is no real cost." Do you agree? Discuss. *(LO4)*

7. How does inflation affect the real return on holding cash? *(LO5)*

8. True or false: If both the potential lender and the potential borrower correctly anticipate the rate of inflation, inflation will not redistribute wealth from the creditor to the debtor. Explain. *(LO5)*

PROBLEMS

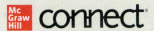

1. Government survey takers determine that typical family expenditures each month in the year designated as the base year are as follows:

>   25 pizzas at $10 each
>   Rent of apartment, $600 per month
>   Gasoline and car maintenance, $100
>   Cell phone service, $50

In the year following the base year, the survey takers determine that pizzas have risen to $11 each, apartment rent is $700, gasoline and maintenance have risen to $120, and phone service has dropped in price to $40. *(LO1)*
   a. Find the CPI in the subsequent year and the rate of inflation between the base year and the subsequent year.
   b. The family's nominal income rose by 5 percent between the base year and the subsequent year. Are they worse off or better off in terms of what their income is able to buy?

2. Here are values of the CPI (multiplied by 100) for each year from 2000 to 2010. For each year beginning with 2001, calculate the rate of inflation from the previous year. What happened to inflation rates over the 2000s? *(LO1)*

2000	122.7
2001	128.2
2002	132.3
2003	136.5
2004	140.2
2005	144.4
2006	148.9
2007	152.5
2008	155.0
2009	158.6
2010	164.2

3. Refer to the CPI data given in Problem 2. A report found that the real entry-level wage for college graduates declined by 5 percent between 2003 and 2010. The nominal entry-level wage in 2010 was $14.35 per hour. *(LO2)*
   a. What was the real entry-level wage in 2010?
   b. What was the real entry-level wage in 2003?
   c. What was the nominal entry-level wage in 2003?

4. Consider the following table. It shows a hypothetical income tax schedule, expressed in nominal terms, for the year 2014.

Family income	Taxes due (percent of income)
≤$20,000	10
$20,001–$30,000	12
$30,001–$50,000	15
$50,001–$80,000	20
>$80,000	25

The legislature wants to ensure that families with a given real income are not pushed up into higher tax brackets by inflation. The CPI (times 100) is 175 in 2014 and 185 in 2016. How should the income tax schedule above be adjusted for the year 2016 to meet the legislature's goal? *(LO2)*

5. According to the U.S. Census Bureau (www.census.gov), nominal income for the typical family of four in the United States (median income) was $23,618 in 1985, $34,076 in 1995, $46,326 in 2005, and $49,276 in 2010. In purchasing power terms, how did family income compare in each of those four years? You will need to know that the CPI (multiplied by 100, 1982–1984 = 100) was 107.6 in 1985, 152.4 in 1995, 195.3 in 2005, and 218.1 in 2010. *(LO2)*

6. The typical consumer's food basket in the base year 2015 is as follows:

> 30 chickens at $2.00 each
> 10 hams at $6.00 each
> 10 steaks at $8.00 each

A chicken feed shortage causes the price of chickens to rise to $5.00 each in the year 2016. Hams rise to $7.00 each, and the price of steaks is unchanged. *(LO1, LO3)*
a. Calculate the change in the "cost-of-eating" index between 2015 and 2016.
b. Suppose that consumers are completely indifferent between two chickens and one ham. For this example, how large is the substitution bias in the official "cost-of-eating" index?

7. The following table lists the actual per-gallon prices for unleaded regular gasoline for June of each year between 1978 and 1986, together with the values of the CPIs for those years. For each year from 1979 to 1986, find the CPI inflation rate and the change in the real price of gasoline, both from the previous year. Would it be fair to say that most of the changes in gas prices during this period were due to general inflation, or were factors specific to the oil market playing a role as well? *(LO1, LO4)*

Year	Gasoline price ($/gallon)	CPI (1982–1984 = 1.00)
1978	0.663	0.652
1979	0.901	0.726
1980	1.269	0.824
1981	1.391	0.909
1982	1.309	0.965
1983	1.277	0.996
1984	1.229	1.039
1985	1.241	1.076
1986	0.955	1.136

8. On January 1, 2012, Albert invested $1,000 at 6 percent interest per year for three years. The CPI on January 1, 2012, stood at 100. On January 1, 2013, the CPI (times 100) was 105; on January 1, 2014, it was 110; and on January 1, 2015, the day Albert's investment matured, the CPI was 118. Find the real rate of interest earned by Albert in each of the three years and his total real return over the three-year period. Assume that interest earnings are reinvested each year and themselves earn interest. *(LO5)*

9. Frank is lending $1,000 to Sarah for two years. Frank and Sarah agree that Frank should earn a 2 percent real return per year.
a. The CPI (times 100) is 100 at the time that Frank makes the loan. It is expected to be 110 in one year and 121 in two years. What nominal rate of interest should Frank charge Sarah?
b. Suppose Frank and Sarah are unsure about what the CPI will be in two years. Show how Frank and Sarah could index Sarah's annual repayments to ensure that Frank gets an annual 2 percent real rate of return.

10.* The Bureau of Labor Statistics has found that the base-year expenditures of the typical consumer break down as follows:

Food and beverages	17.8%
Housing	42.8%
Apparel and upkeep	6.3%
Transportation	17.2%
Medical care	5.7%
Entertainment	4.4%
Other goods, services	5.8%
Total	100.0%

Suppose that since the base year, the prices of food and beverages have increased by 10 percent, the price of housing has increased by 5 percent, and the price of medical care has increased by 10 percent. Other prices are unchanged. Find the CPI for the current year. *(LO5)*

*Denotes more difficult problem.

ANSWERS TO SELF-TESTS

18.1 The cost of the family's basket in 2015 remains at $940, as in Table 18.1. If the rent on their apartment falls to $600 in 2020, the cost of reproducing the 2015 basket of goods and services in 2020 is $830 ($600 for rent + $150 for hamburgers + $80 for movie tickets). The CPI for 2020 is accordingly $830/$940, or 0.883. So in this example, the cost of living fell nearly 12 percent between 2015 and 2020. *(LO1)*

18.2 To construct your own personal price index, you would need to determine the basket of goods and services that you personally purchased in the base year. Your personal price index in each period would then be defined as the cost of your personal basket in that period relative to its cost in the base year. To the extent that your mix of purchases differs from that of the typical American consumer, your cost-of-living index will differ from the official CPI. For example, if in the base year, you spent a higher share of your budget than the typical American on goods and services that have risen relatively rapidly in price, your personal inflation rate will be higher than the CPI inflation rate. *(LO1)*

18.3 The percentage changes in the CPI in each year from the previous year are as follows:

1930	−2.3% = (0.167 − 0.171)/0.171
1931	−9.0%
1932	−9.9%
1933	−5.1%

Negative inflation is called deflation. The experience of the 1930s, when prices were falling, contrasts sharply with the 1970s, during which prices rose rapidly. *(LO1)*

18.4 The percent changes in inflation rates in each year from the previous year are as follows:

2016	1.3% = (2.40 − 2.37)/2.37
2017	2.1%
2018	2.4%
2019	2.0%

In the past few years, inflation has been non-negative but low, in the 0–3 percent range. (Due to rounding, the inflation rates calculated above are slightly different from those published by the BLS.) *(LO1)*

18.5 Barry Bonds's real earnings, in 1982–1984 dollars, were $10.3 million/1.77, or $5.8 million. That is more than 12 times Babe Ruth's salary in 1930, but less than half of Stephen Strasburg's salary in 2019.

18.6 The real minimum wage in 1950 is $0.75/0.24, or $3.12 in 1982–1984 dollars. The real minimum wage in 2019 is $7.25/2.56, or $2.83 in 1982–1984 dollars. So the real minimum wage in 2019 was slightly lower than what it was in 1950. *(LO2)*

18.7 The increase in the cost of living between 1950 and 2019 is reflected in the ratio of the 2019 CPI to the 1950 CPI, or 2.56/0.24 = 10.66. That is, the cost of living in 2019 was over 10 times what it was in 1950. If the minimum wage were indexed to preserve its purchasing power, it would have been over 10 times higher in 2019 than in 1950, or 10.66 × $0.75 = $8.0. *(LO2)*

18.8 You should be concerned about the real return on your investment, not your nominal return. To calculate your likely real return, you need to know not only the nominal interest paid on the bonds of the island nation, but also the prevailing inflation rate in that country. So your next question should be, "What is the rate of inflation in this country likely to be over the period that I am holding these bonds?" *(LO5)*

18.9 The real rate of return to cash, as with any asset, is the nominal interest rate less the inflation rate. But cash pays no interest; that is, the nominal interest rate on cash is zero. Therefore, the real rate of return on cash is just minus the inflation rate. In other words, cash loses buying power at a rate equal to the rate of inflation. This rate of return depends on the actual rate of inflation and does not depend on whether the rate of inflation is correctly anticipated.

If inflation is high so that the real rate of return on cash is very negative, people will take actions to try to reduce their holdings of cash, such as going to the bank more often. The costs associated with trying to reduce holdings of cash are what economists call shoe-leather costs. *(LO5)*

CHAPTER 19

Economic Growth, Productivity, and Living Standards

How do economies grow and flourish?

Martin Ruegner/Digital Vision/Getty Images

LEARNING OBJECTIVES

After reading this chapter, you should be able to:

LO1 Show how small differences in growth rates can lead to large differences in living standards.

LO2 Explain why GDP per capita is the product of average labor productivity and the proportion of the population that is employed and use this decomposition to discuss the sources of economic growth.

LO3 List the determinants of average labor productivity within a particular country and use these concepts to analyze per capita GDP differences across countries.

LO4 Identify the costs of increasing economic growth.

LO5 Evaluate government policies that promote economic growth.

LO6 Analyze whether having finite resources implies that there are limits to growth.

One of us once attended a conference on the effects of economic growth and development on society. A speaker at the conference posed the following question: "Which would you rather be? An ordinary, middle-class American living today, or the richest person in America at the time of George Washington?"

A member of the audience spoke out immediately: "I can answer that question in one word. Dentistry."

The answer drew a laugh, perhaps because it reminded people of George Washington's famous wooden teeth. But it was a good answer. Dentistry in early America—whether the patient was rich or poor—was a primitive affair. Most dentists simply pulled a patient's rotten teeth, with a shot of whiskey for anesthetic.

Other types of medical care were not much better than dentistry. Eighteenth-century doctors had no effective weapons against tuberculosis, typhoid fever, diphtheria, influenza, pneumonia, and other communicable diseases. Such illnesses, now quite treatable, were major killers in Washington's time. Infants and children were particularly susceptible to deadly infectious diseases, especially whooping cough and measles. Even a well-to-do family often lost two or three children to these illnesses. Washington, an unusually large and vigorous man, lived to the age of 67, but the average life expectancy during his era was probably not much more than 40 years.

Medical care is not the only aspect of ordinary life that has changed drastically over the past two centuries. Author Stephen Ambrose, in his account of the Lewis and Clark expedition, described the limitations of transportation and communication in early America:

> A critical fact in the world of 1801 was that nothing moved faster than the speed of a horse. No human being, no manufactured item, no bushel of wheat, no side of beef (or any beef on the hoof for that matter), no letter, no information, no idea, order, or instruction of any kind moved faster, and, as far as Jefferson's contemporaries were able to tell, nothing ever would.
>
> And except on a racetrack, no horse moved very fast. Road conditions in the United States ranged from bad to abominable, and there weren't very many of them. The best highway in the country ran from Boston to New York; it took a light stagecoach . . . three full days to make the 175-mile journey. The hundred miles from New York to Philadelphia took two full days.[1]

Today, New Yorkers can go to Philadelphia by train in slightly more than an hour. What would George Washington have thought of that? And how would nineteenth-century pioneers, who crossed the continent by wagon train, have reacted to the idea that their great-grandchildren would be able to have breakfast in New York and lunch the same day in San Francisco?

Would you rather be a rich person living in the eighteenth century or a middle-class person living in the twenty-first century?

No doubt you can think of other enormous changes in the way average people live, even over the past few decades. The Internet, mobile and cloud computing, tablets and smartphones have changed the ways people work and study in just a few years, for example. Though these changes are due in large part to scientific advances, scientific discoveries *by themselves* usually have little effect on most people's lives. New scientific knowledge leads to widespread improvements in living standards only when it is commercially applied. Better understanding of the human immune system, for example, has little impact unless it leads to new therapies or drugs. And a new drug will do little to help unless it is affordable to those who need it.

An illustration of this point—with both tragic and more optimistic aspects—is the AIDS epidemic in Africa. Although some new drugs that moderate the effects of the virus that causes AIDS were developed in the late 1990s, they were so expensive that they were of little practical value in poverty-stricken African nations grappling with the disease. And even if affordable, the drugs would have limited benefit without modern hospitals, trained health professionals, and adequate nutrition and sanitation. Nowadays, more than 20 years after the first effective treatments were developed, around a million people a year still die from AIDS. But this number is finally declining. The reversal resulted from a combination of the scientific discovery of new potential treatments *and* their effective implementation through international aid programs funded by industrialized countries.[2] In short, most improvements in a nation's living standard are the result not just of scientific and technological advances, but of an economic system that makes the benefits of those advances available to the average person.

In this chapter, we will explore the sources of economic growth and rising living standards in the modern world. We will begin by reviewing the remarkable economic growth in the industrialized countries, as measured by real GDP per person. Since the mid-nineteenth century (and earlier in some countries), a radical transformation in living standards has occurred in these countries. What explains this transformation? The key to rising living standards is a *continuing increase in average labor productivity,* which depends on several factors, from the skills and motivation workers bring to their jobs to the legal and social environment in which they work. We will analyze each of these factors and discuss its implications for government policies to promote growth. We will then discuss the costs of rapid economic growth and consider whether there may be limits to the amount of economic growth a society can achieve.

[1]Stephen E. Ambrose, *Undaunted Courage: Meriwether Lewis, Thomas Jefferson, and the Opening of the American West* [New York: Touchstone (Simon & Schuster), 1996], p. 52.
[2]For an interesting point of view, see "How Was the AIDS Epidemic Reversed?," *The Economist,* September 26, 2013.

THE REMARKABLE RISE IN LIVING STANDARDS: THE RECORD

For millennia, the great majority of the world's inhabitants eked out a meager existence by tilling the soil. Only a small proportion of the population lived above the level of subsistence, learned to read and write, or traveled more than a few miles from their birthplaces. Large cities grew up, serving as imperial capitals and centers of trade, but the great majority of urban populations lived in dire poverty, subject to malnutrition and disease.

Then, about three centuries ago, a fundamental change occurred. Spurred by technological advances and entrepreneurial innovations, a process of economic growth began. Sustained over many years, this growth in the economy's productive capacity has transformed almost every aspect of how we live—from what we eat and wear to how we work and play.

The advances in health care and transportation mentioned in the beginning of this chapter illustrate only a few of the impressive changes that have taken place in people's material well-being over the past two centuries, particularly in industrialized countries like the United States. To study the factors that affect living standards systematically, however, we must go beyond anecdotes and adopt a specific measure of economic well-being in a particular country and time.

In Chapter 17, *Measuring Economic Activity: GDP and Unemployment,* we introduced the concept of real GDP as a basic measure of the level of economic activity in a country. Recall that, in essence, real GDP measures the physical volume of goods and services produced within a country's borders during a specific period, such as a quarter or a year. Consequently, real GDP *per person* provides a measure of the quantity of goods and services available to the typical resident of a country at a particular time. Although real GDP per person is certainly not a perfect indicator of economic well-being, as we will see later in this chapter, it is positively related to a number of pertinent variables, such as life expectancy, infant health, and literacy. Lacking a better alternative, economists have focused on real GDP per person as a key measure of a country's living standard and stage of economic development.

Figure 19.1, which reproduces the blue line from Figure 16.2, shows the remarkable growth in real GDP per person that occurred in the United States between 1929 and 2019. For comparison, Table 19.1 and Figure 19.2 show real GDP per person in eight countries in selected years from 1870 to 2010.

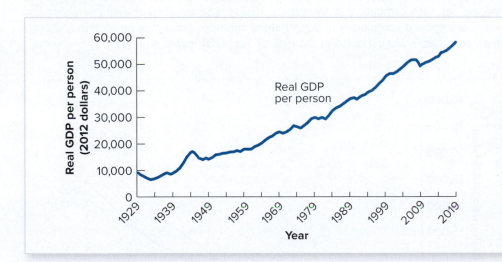

FIGURE 19.1

Real GDP per Person in the United States, 1929–2019.

The blue line shows the real GDP per person in the U.S. economy since 1929. Real GDP per person today is more than six times what it was in 1929.

Source: Bureau of Economic Analysis, www.bea.gov.

The data in Table 19.1 and Figure 19.2 tell a dramatic story. For example, in the United States (which was already a relatively wealthy industrialized country in 1870), real GDP per person grew more than 12-fold between 1870 and 2010. In Japan, real GDP per person grew almost 30 times over the same period. Underlying these statistics is an amazingly rapid process of economic growth and transformation, through which, in just a few

TABLE 19.1

Real GDP per Person in Selected Countries, 1870–2010

Country	1870	1913	1950	1980	1990	2010	Annual % change 1870–2010	Annual % change 1950–2010	Annual % change 1980–2010
United States	2,445	5,301	9,561	18,577	23,201	30,491	1.8	2.0	1.7
United Kingdom	3,190	4,921	6,939	12,931	16,430	23,777	1.4	2.1	2.1
Germany	1,839	3,648	3,881	14,114	15,929	20,661	1.7	2.8	1.3
Japan	737	1,387	1,921	13,428	18,789	21,935	2.5	4.1	1.6
China	530	552	448	1,061	1,871	8,032	2.0	4.9	7.0
Brazil	713	811	1,672	5,195	4,920	6,879	1.6	2.4	0.9
India	533	673	619	938	1,309	3,372	1.3	2.9	4.4
Ghana	439	781	1,122	1,157	1,062	1,922	1.1	0.9	1.7

Source: Angus Maddison, *The Maddison Project,* www.ggdc.net/maddison. Real GDP per person is measured in 1990 international dollars. "Germany" refers to West Germany in 1950 and 1980.

generations, relatively poor agrarian societies became highly industrialized economies—with average standards of living that could scarcely have been imagined in 1870. As Figure 19.2 shows, a significant part of this growth has occurred since 1950, particularly in Japan and China. Further, both China and India have grown significantly faster since 1990 than they did in earlier periods.

A note of caution is in order. The farther back in time we go, the less precise are historical estimates of real GDP. Most governments did not keep official GDP statistics until after World War II; production records from earlier periods are often incomplete or of questionable accuracy. Comparing economic output over a century or more is also problematic because many goods and services that are produced today were unavailable—indeed, inconceivable—in 1870. How many nineteenth-century horse-drawn wagons, for example, would be the economic equivalent of a BMW i8 plug-in hybrid sports car or a Boeing 787 Dreamliner jet? Despite the difficulty of making precise comparisons, however, we can say with certainty that the variety, quality, and quantity of available goods and services increased enormously in industrialized countries during the nineteenth and twentieth centuries, a fact reflected in the data on real GDP per capita.

FIGURE 19.2

Real GDP per Person in a Sample of Countries, 1870–2010.

The United States, the United Kingdom, and Germany began with high levels of GDP per person in 1870 and remained high-income countries throughout the period. Economic growth has been especially rapid between the 1950s and the 1980s in Japan and since 1980 in China and India. Ghana and the rest of sub-Saharan Africa experienced very low growth rates.

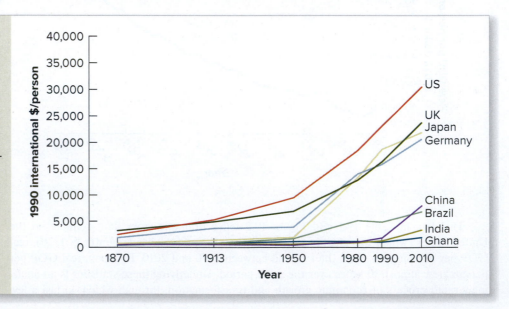

WHY "SMALL" DIFFERENCES IN GROWTH RATES MATTER

The last three columns of Table 19.1 show annual growth rates of real GDP per person for both the entire 1870–2010 period and two more recent periods. At first glance, these growth rates don't seem to differ much from country to country. For example, for the period 1870–2010, the highest growth rate is 2.5 percent (Japan) and the lowest is 1.1 percent (Ghana).

But consider the long-run effect of this seemingly "small" difference in annual growth rates. For example, in 1870 China's output per person was roughly 120 percent that of Ghana, yet by 2010 China had more than four times the output per person of Ghana. This widening of the gap between these two countries is the result of the difference between China's 2.0 percent annual growth rate and Ghana's 1.1 percent annual growth rate, maintained for almost 140 years. The fact that what seem to be small differences in growth rates can have large long-run effects results from what is called the *power of compound interest*. A good illustration of this power is the effect of compound interest on a bank deposit.

EXAMPLE 19.1   Compound Interest (Part 1)

What is compound interest?

In 1820, one of your ancestors deposited $10.00 in a checking account at 4 percent interest. Interest is compounded annually (so that interest paid at the end of each year receives interest itself in later years). Your ancestor's will specified that the account be turned over to his most direct descendant (you) in the year 2020. When you withdrew the funds in that year, how much was the account worth?

The account was worth $10.00 in 1820; $10.00 × 1.04 = $10.40 in 1821; $10.00 × 1.04 × 1.04 = $10.00 × $(1.04)^2$ = $10.82 in 1822; and so on. Since 200 years elapsed between 1820, when the deposit was made, and the year 2020, when the account was closed, the value of the account in the year 2020 was $10.00 × $(1.04)^{200}$, or $10.00 × 1.04 to the 200th power. Using a calculator, you will find that $10.00 times 1.04 to the 200th power is $25,507.50—a good return for a $10.00 deposit!

Compound interest—an arrangement in which interest is paid not only on the original deposit but on all previously accumulated interest—is distinguished from *simple interest,* in which interest is paid only on the original deposit. If your ancestor's account had been deposited at 4 percent simple interest, it would have accumulated only 40 cents each year (4 percent of the original $10.00 deposit), for a total value of $10.00 + 200 × $0.40 = $90.00 after 200 years. The tremendous growth in the value of his account came from the compounding of the interest—hence the phrase "the power of compound interest."

compound interest the payment of interest not only on the original deposit, but on all previously accumulated interest

---

EXAMPLE 19.2   Compound Interest (Part 2)

What is the difference between 2 percent interest and 6 percent interest, compounded annually?

Refer to Example 19.1. What would your ancestor's $10.00 deposit have been worth after 200 years if the annual interest rate had been 2 percent? 6 percent?

At 2 percent interest the account would be worth $10.00 in 1820; $10.00 × 1.02 = $10.20 in 1821; $10.00 × (1.02)^2 = $10.40 in 1822; and so on. In the year 2020, the value of the account would be $10.00 × (1.02)^{200}, or $524.85. If the interest rate were 6 percent, after 200 years the account would be worth $10.00 × (1.06)^{200}, or $1,151,259.04. Let's summarize the results of Examples 19.1 and 19.2.

Interest rate (%)	Value of $10 after 200 years
2	$524.85
4	$25,507.50
6	$1,151,259.04

The power of compound interest is that even at relatively low rates of interest, a small sum, compounded over a long enough period, can greatly increase in value. A more subtle point, illustrated by this example, is that small differences in interest rates matter a lot. The difference between a 2 percent and a 4 percent interest rate doesn't seem tremendous, but over a long period of time it implies large differences in the amount of interest accumulated on an account. Likewise, the effect of switching from a 4 percent to a 6 percent interest rate is enormous, as our calculations show.

Economic growth rates are similar to compound interest rates. Just as the value of a bank deposit grows each year at a rate equal to the interest rate, so the size of a nation's economy expands each year at the rate of economic growth. This analogy suggests that even a relatively modest rate of growth in output per person—say, 1 to 2 percent per year—will produce tremendous increases in average living standard over a long period. And relatively small *differences* in growth rates, as in the case of Ghana and China, will ultimately produce very different living standards.

Economists employ a useful formula for approximating the number of years it will take for an initial amount to double at various growth or interest rates. The formula is 72 divided by the growth or interest rate. Thus, if the interest rate is 2 percent per year, it will take roughly 72/2 = 36 years for the initial sum to double. If the interest rate is 4 percent, it will take roughly 72/4 = 18 years. This formula is a good approximation only for small and moderate interest rates. Over the long run, then, the rate of economic growth is an extremely important variable. Hence, government policy changes or other factors that affect the long-term growth rate even by a small amount will have a major economic impact.

 SELF-TEST 19.1

Suppose that real GDP per capita in the United States had grown at 2.5 percent per year, as Japan's did, instead of the actual 1.8 percent per year, from 1870 to 2010. How much larger would real GDP per person have been in the United States in 2010?

RECAP ↑

THE REMARKABLE RISE IN LIVING STANDARDS

Real GDP per person, a basic indicator of living standards, has grown dramatically in the industrialized countries. This growth reflects the *power of compound interest:* Even a modest growth rate, if sustained over a long period of time, can lead to large increases in the size of the economy.

WHY NATIONS BECOME RICH: THE CRUCIAL ROLE OF AVERAGE LABOR PRODUCTIVITY

What determines a nation's economic growth rate? To get some insight into this vital question, we will find it useful to express real GDP per person as the product of two terms: average labor productivity and the share of the population that is working.

To do this, let Y equal total real output (as measured by real GDP, for example), N equal the number of employed workers, and POP equal the total population. Then real GDP per person can be written as Y/POP; **average labor productivity,** or output per employed worker, equals Y/N; and the share of the population that is working is N/POP. The relationship between these three variables is

$$\frac{Y}{POP} = \frac{Y}{N} \times \frac{N}{POP},$$

which, as you can see by canceling out N on the right-hand side of the equation, always holds exactly. In words, this basic relationship is

Real GDP per person $=$ Average labor productivity
$\times$ Share of population employed.

This expression for real GDP per person tells us something very basic and intuitive: The quantity of goods and services that each person can consume depends on (1) how much each worker can produce and (2) how many people (as a fraction of the total population) are working. Furthermore, because real GDP per person equals average labor productivity times the share of the population that is employed, real GDP per person can *grow* only to the extent that there is *growth* in worker productivity and/or the fraction of the population that is employed.

Figures 19.3 and 19.4 show the U.S. figures for the three key variables in the relationship above and for a fourth variable that was mentioned in Chapter 17, *Measuring Economic Activity: GDP and Unemployment* (the labor force participation rate), for the period 1960–2019. Figure 19.3, which reproduces part of Figure 16.2, shows both real GDP per person and real GDP per worker (average labor productivity). Figure 19.4 shows the portion of the entire U.S. population (not just the working-age population) that was employed, and the portion of the (civilian, noninstitutional) adult population (16+) that participated in the labor force during that period. Once again, we see that the expansion in output per person in the United States has been impressive. Between 1960 and 2019, real GDP per person in the United States more than tripled, growing by 222 percent. Thus in 2019, the average American enjoyed more than three times as many goods and

average labor productivity
output per employed worker

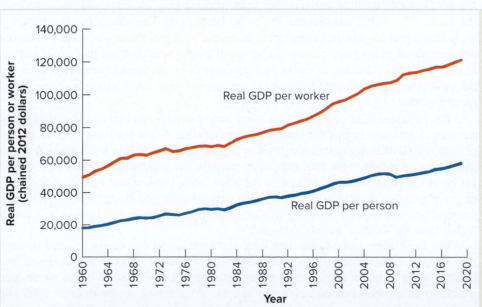

FIGURE 19.3

Real GDP per Person and Average Labor Productivity in the United States, 1960–2019.

Real GDP per person in the United States grew 222 percent between 1960 and 2019, and real GDP per worker (average labor productivity) grew by 144 percent.

Source: Federal Reserve Bank of St. Louis Economic Research, https://fred.stlouisfed.org.

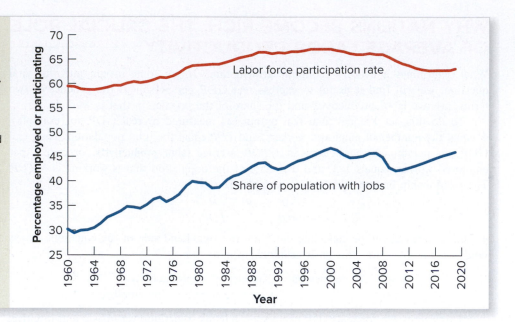

FIGURE 19.4

Share of the U.S. Population Employed and Labor Force Participation Rate, 1960–2019.

The share of the U.S. population holding a job increased from 30 percent in 1960 to almost 47 percent in 2000 and was 46 percent in 2019. The labor force participation rate increased from 59 percent in 1960 to 67 percent in the late 1990s; since 2000, it has generally declined, falling below 63 percent in recent years.

Sources: BLS (CIVPART, PAYEMS), Census (POP), retrieved from FRED, Federal Reserve Bank of St. Louis; https://fred.stlouisfed.org.

services as in 1960. Figures 19.3 and 19.4 show that until the year 2000 or so, increases in both labor productivity and the share of the population holding a job contributed to this rise in living standard. But as Figure 19.4 shows, more recently things have changed.

Let's look a bit more closely at these two contributing factors, beginning with the share of the population that is employed. As Figure 19.4 shows, between 1960 and 2000, the number of people employed in the United States rose from 30 to almost 47 percent of the entire population, a remarkable increase. The growing tendency of women to work outside the home was the most important reason for this rise in employment. Another factor leading to higher rates of employment was an increase in the share of the general population that is of working age (ages 16 to 65). The coming of age of the "baby boom" generation, born in the years after World War II, and to a lesser extent the immigration of young workers from other countries helped cause this growth in the workforce.

Although the rising share of the U.S. population with jobs contributed significantly to the increase in real GDP per person during the last four decades of the twentieth century, that trend has started to reverse. The reversal is more apparent when looking at the labor force participation rate, which differs from the share of the population with jobs in two ways. First, rather than counting only people with jobs, it counts also people *looking* for a job. In other words, rather than counting only the employed, it counts both the employed and the unemployed—the entire labor force. The size of the labor force is more stable year to year than the number of people with jobs (because during expansions and recessions, many people move in and out of employment without moving in and out of the labor force). Indeed, in Figure 19.4 the labor force participation rate fluctuates less than the other curve, making the reversal (around the year 2000) of the long-term trend more apparent.

The second difference between the labor force participation rate and the share of the population with jobs is that the labor force participation rate is the labor force as a share of only the (civilian noninstitutional) adult population. Economists are interested in this share because it tells them what portion of those in the population who could in principle be in the labor force are, in fact, in the labor force. (Notice that relative to the share of the population with jobs, the labor force participation rate counts more people, and reports their number as a share of a smaller population. For these two reasons, it is always higher than the share of people employed.)

The labor force participation rate increased from below 60 percent in 1960 to more than 67 percent in the late 1990s, and then leveled off. Since 2000, it has decreased, and in 2014, it fell to below 63 percent—for the first time since 1977. Some of the factors that we discussed earlier when explaining the increase in employed people prior to 2000 also explain the decline after 2000. The baby boomers have been aging and have recently started retiring. The participation rate of women could not increase forever, and it eventually leveled off. But the aging population and women cannot be the whole explanation because participation has been on a long-term decline also among younger men. Economists are still trying to understand all the reasons. Potential explanations include young people staying longer in school—and spending more time on schoolwork while in school—and a decline in the demand for workers with certain skills and education. We will return to these issues in the next chapter, where we use supply and demand analysis to understand long-term trends in the labor market. For now, we note that the recent downward trends in Figure 19.4 are expected to continue in the future. In the long run, then, the improvement in living standards brought about by the rising share of Americans with jobs was transitory.

What about the other factor that determines output per person, average labor productivity? As Figure 19.3 shows, between 1960 and 2019, average labor productivity in the United States increased by 144 percent, accounting for a sizable share of the overall increase in GDP per person. In other periods, the link between average labor productivity and output per person in the United States has often been even stronger because, in most earlier periods, the share of the population holding jobs was more stable than it has been recently. (See Figure 16.2 for the behavior of real GDP per person and average labor productivity in the United States over the period 1929–2019.)

This quick look at recent data supports a more general conclusion. *In the long run, increases in output per person arise primarily from increases in average labor productivity.* In simple terms, the more people can produce, the more they can consume. To understand why economies grow, then, we must understand the reasons for increased labor productivity.

> ***RECAP***
>
> ### THE CRUCIAL ROLE OF AVERAGE LABOR PRODUCTIVITY
>
> Output per person equals average labor productivity times the share of the population that is employed. Since 1960, the share of the U.S. population with jobs has risen significantly, but it has declined since 2000. In the long run, increases in output per person and hence living standards arise primarily from increases in average labor productivity.

THE DETERMINANTS OF AVERAGE LABOR PRODUCTIVITY

What determines the productivity of the average worker in a particular country at a particular time? Popular discussions of this issue often equate worker productivity with the willingness of workers of a given nationality to work hard. Everything else being equal, a culture that promotes hard work certainly tends to increase worker productivity. But intensity of effort alone cannot explain the huge differences in average labor productivity that we observe around the world. For example, according to 2018 estimates from the International Labor Organization, average labor productivity in the United States is about 12 times what it is in Indonesia and 39 times what it is in Bangladesh, though there is little doubt that Indonesians and Bangladeshis work very hard.

In this section, we will examine six factors that appear to account for the major differences in average labor productivity, both between countries and between generations. Later in the chapter we will discuss how economic policies can influence these factors to spur productivity and growth.

HUMAN CAPITAL

To illustrate the factors that determine average labor productivity, we introduce two prototypical assembly-line workers, Lucy and Ethel.

EXAMPLE 19.3   Assembly-Line Productivity

CBS/Getty Images

How productive are these workers?

Are Lucy and Ethel more productive as a team or by themselves?

Lucy and Ethel have jobs wrapping chocolate candies and placing them into boxes. Lucy, a novice wrapper, can wrap only 100 candies per hour. Ethel, who has had on-the-job training, can wrap 300 candies per hour. Lucy and Ethel each work 40 hours per week. Find average labor productivity, in terms of candies wrapped per week and candies wrapped per hour, (a) for Lucy, (b) for Ethel, and (c) for Lucy and Ethel as a team.

We have defined average labor productivity in general terms as output per worker. Note, though, that the measurement of average labor productivity depends on the time period that is specified. For example, the data presented in Figure 19.3 tell us how much the average worker produces *in a year*. In this example we are concerned with how much Lucy and Ethel can produce *per hour* of work or *per week* of work. Any one of these ways of measuring labor productivity is equally valid, as long as we are clear about the time unit we are using.

Lucy's and Ethel's hourly productivities are given in the problem: Lucy can wrap 100 candies per hour and Ethel can wrap 300. Lucy's weekly productivity is (40 hours/week) × (100 candies wrapped/hour) = 4,000 wrapped candies per week. Ethel's weekly productivity is (40 hours/week) × (300 candies wrapped/hour), or 12,000 candies per week.

Together Lucy and Ethel can wrap 16,000 candies per week. As a team, their average weekly productivity is (16,000 candies wrapped)/(2 weeks of work), or 8,000 candies per week. Their average hourly productivity as a team is (16,000 candies wrapped)/(80 hours of work) = 200 candies per hour. Notice that, taken as a team, the two women's productivity lies midway between their individual productivities.

Ethel is more productive than Lucy because she has had on-the-job training, which has allowed her to develop her candy-wrapping skills to a higher level than Lucy's. Because of her training, Ethel can produce more than Lucy can in a given number of hours.

 SELF-TEST 19.2

Suppose Ethel attends additional classes in candy wrapping and learns how to wrap 500 candies per hour. Find the output per week and output per hour for Lucy and Ethel, both individually and as a team.

human capital an amalgam of factors such as education, training, experience, intelligence, energy, work habits, trustworthiness, and initiative that affects the value of a worker's marginal product

Economists would explain the difference in the two women's performance by saying that Ethel has more *human capital* than Lucy. **Human capital** comprises the talents, education, training, and skills of workers. Workers with a large stock of human capital are more productive than workers with less training. For example, an auto mechanic who is familiar with computerized diagnostic equipment will be able to fix engine problems that less well-trained mechanics could not.

The Economic Naturalist 19.1

Why did West Germany and Japan recover so successfully from the devastation of World War II?

Germany and Japan sustained extensive destruction of their cities and industries during World War II and entered the postwar period impoverished. Yet within 30 years, both countries not only had been rebuilt, but had become worldwide industrial and economic leaders. What accounts for these "economic miracles"?

Many factors contributed to the economic recovery of West Germany and Japan from World War II, including the substantial aid provided by the United States to Europe under the Marshall Plan and to Japan during the U.S. occupation. Most economists agree, however, that high levels of human capital played a crucial role in both countries.

At the end of the war, Germany's population was exceptionally well educated, with a large number of highly qualified scientists and engineers. The country also had (and still does today) an extensive apprentice system that provided on-the-job training to young workers. As a result, Germany had a skilled industrial workforce. In addition, the area that became West Germany benefited substantially from an influx of skilled workers from East Germany and the rest of Soviet-controlled Europe, including 20,000 trained engineers and technicians. Beginning as early as 1949, this concentration of human capital contributed to a major expansion of Germany's technologically sophisticated, highly productive manufacturing sector. By 1960, West Germany was a leading exporter of high-quality manufactured goods, and its citizens enjoyed one of the highest standards of living in Europe.

Japan, which probably sustained greater physical destruction in the war than Germany, also began the postwar period with a skilled and educated labor force. In addition, occupying American forces restructured the Japanese school system and encouraged all Japanese to obtain a good education. Even more so than the Germans, however, the Japanese emphasized on-the-job training. As part of a lifetime employment system, under which workers were expected to stay with the same company their entire career, Japanese firms invested extensively in worker training. The payoff to these investments in human capital was a steady increase in average labor productivity, particularly in manufacturing. By the 1980s, Japanese manufactured goods were among the most advanced in the world and Japan's workers among the most skilled.

Although high levels of human capital were instrumental in the rapid economic growth of West Germany and Japan, human capital alone cannot create a high living standard. A case in point is Soviet-dominated East Germany, which had a level of human capital similar to West Germany's after the war but did not enjoy the same economic growth. For reasons we will discuss later in the chapter, the communist system imposed by the Soviets utilized East Germany's human capital far less effectively than the economic systems of Japan and West Germany.

Human capital is analogous to *physical capital* (such as machines and factories) in that it is acquired primarily through the investment of time, energy, and money. For example, to learn how to use computerized diagnostic equipment, a mechanic might need to attend a technical school at night. The cost of going to school includes not only the tuition paid but also the *opportunity cost* of the mechanic's time spent attending class and studying. The benefit of the schooling is the increase in wages the mechanic will earn when the course has been completed. We know by the Cost-Benefit Principle that the mechanic should learn how to use computerized diagnostic equipment only if the benefits exceed the costs, including the opportunity costs. In general, then, we would expect to see people acquire additional education and skills when the difference in the wages paid to skilled and unskilled workers is significant.

PHYSICAL CAPITAL

Workers' productivity depends not only on their skills and effort, but on the tools they have to work with. Even the most skilled surgeon cannot perform open-heart surgery without sophisticated equipment, and an expert software developer is of limited value without a computer. These examples illustrate the importance of **physical capital,** such as factories and machines. More and better capital allows workers to produce more efficiently, as Example 19.4 shows.

physical capital equipment and tools (such as machines and factories) needed to complete one's work

| EXAMPLE 19.4 | **Physical Capital and Efficiency** |

Will the introduction of a candy-wrapping machine make Lucy and Ethel more productive?

Continuing with Example 19.3, suppose that Lucy and Ethel's boss acquires an electric candy-wrapping machine, which is designed to be operated by one worker. Using this machine, an untrained worker can wrap 500 candies per hour. What are Lucy's and Ethel's hourly and weekly outputs now? Will the answer change if the boss gets a second machine? A third?

Suppose for the sake of simplicity that a candy-wrapping machine must be assigned to one worker only. (This assumption rules out sharing arrangements, in which one worker uses the machine on the day shift and another on the night shift.) If the boss buys just one machine, she will assign it to Lucy. (Why? Solve Self-Test 19.3.) Now Lucy will be able to wrap 500 candies per hour, while Ethel can wrap only 300 per hour. Lucy's weekly output will be 20,000 wrapped candies (40 hours × 500 candies wrapped per hour). Ethel's weekly output is still 12,000 wrapped candies (40 hours × 300 candies wrapped per hour). Together they can now wrap 32,000 candies per week, or 16,000 candies per week each. On an hourly basis, average labor productivity for the two women taken together is 32,000 candies wrapped per 80 hours of work, or 400 candies wrapped per hour—twice their average labor productivity before the boss bought the machine.

With two candy-wrapping machines available, both Lucy and Ethel could use a machine. Each could wrap 500 candies per hour, for a total of 40,000 wrapped candies per week. Average labor productivity for both women taken together would be 20,000 wrapped candies per week, or 500 wrapped candies per hour.

What would happen if the boss purchased a third machine? With only two workers, a third machine would be useless: It would add nothing to either total output or average labor productivity.

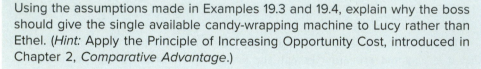

✓ SELF-TEST 19.3

Using the assumptions made in Examples 19.3 and 19.4, explain why the boss should give the single available candy-wrapping machine to Lucy rather than Ethel. (*Hint:* Apply the Principle of Increasing Opportunity Cost, introduced in Chapter 2, *Comparative Advantage.*)

Increasing
Opportunity Cost

The candy-wrapping machine is an example of a *capital good,* which was defined in Chapter 17, *Measuring Economic Activity: GDP and Unemployment,* as a long-lived good, which is itself produced and used to produce other goods and services. Capital goods include machines and equipment (such as computers, earthmovers, or assembly lines) as well as buildings (such as factories or office buildings).

Capital goods like the candy-wrapping machine enhance workers' productivity. Table 19.2 summarizes the results from Examples 19.3 and 19.4. For each number of machines the boss might acquire (column 1), Table 19.2 gives the total weekly output of Lucy and Ethel taken together (column 2), the total number of hours worked by the two women (column 3), and average output per hour (column 4), equal to total weekly output divided by total weekly hours.

Table 19.2 demonstrates two important points about the effect of additional capital on output. First, for a given number of workers, adding more capital generally increases both total output and average labor productivity. For example, adding the first candy-wrapping

TABLE 19.2

Capital, Output, and Productivity in the Candy-Wrapping Factory

(1) Number of machines (capital)	(2) Total number of candies wrapped each week (output)	(3) Total hours worked per week	(4) Candies wrapped per hour worked (productivity)
0	16,000	80	200
1	32,000	80	400
2	40,000	80	500
3	40,000	80	500

machine increases weekly output (column 2) by 16,000 candies and average labor productivity (column 4) by 200 candies wrapped per hour.

The second point illustrated by Table 19.2 is that the more capital is already in place, the smaller the benefits of adding extra capital. Notice that the first machine adds 16,000 candies to total output, but the second machine adds only 8,000. The third machine, which cannot be used since there are only two workers, does not increase output or productivity at all. This result illustrates a general principle of economics, called *diminishing returns to capital.* According to the principle of **diminishing returns to capital,** if the amount of labor and other inputs employed is held constant, then the greater the amount of capital already in use, the less an additional unit of capital adds to production. In the case of the candy-wrapping factory, diminishing returns to capital imply that the first candy-wrapping machine acquired adds more output than the second, which in turn adds more output than the third.

Diminishing returns to capital are a natural consequence of firms' incentive to use each piece of capital as productively as possible. To maximize output, managers will assign the first machine that a firm acquires to the most productive use available, the next machine to the next most productive use, and so on—an illustration of the Principle of Increasing Opportunity Cost. When many machines are available, all the highly productive ways of using them already have been exploited. Thus adding yet another machine will not raise output or productivity by very much. If Lucy and Ethel are already operating two candy-wrapping machines, there is little point to buying a third machine, except perhaps as a replacement or spare.

The implications of Table 19.2 can be applied to the question of how to stimulate economic growth. First, increasing the amount of capital available to the workforce will tend to increase output and average labor productivity. The more adequately equipped workers are, the more productive they will be. Second, the degree to which productivity can be increased by an expanding stock of capital is limited. Because of diminishing returns to capital, an economy in which the quantity of capital available to each worker is already very high will not benefit much from further expansion of the capital stock.

diminishing returns to capital if the amount of labor and other inputs employed is held constant, then the greater the amount of capital already in use, the less an additional unit of capital adds to production

Increasing Opportunity Cost

LAND AND OTHER NATURAL RESOURCES

Besides capital goods, other inputs to production help make workers more productive, among them land, energy, and raw materials. Fertile land is essential to agriculture, and modern manufacturing processes make intensive use of energy and raw materials.

In general, an abundance of natural resources increases the productivity of the workers who use them. For example, a farmer can produce a much larger crop in a land-rich country like the United States or Australia than in a country where the soil is poor or arable land is limited in supply. With the aid of modern farm machinery and great expanses of land, today's American farmers are so productive that even though they constitute less than 1 percent of the workforce, they provide enough food not only to feed the country but to export to the rest of the world.

Although there are limits to a country's supply of arable land, many other natural resources, such as petroleum and metals, can be obtained through international markets. Because resources can be obtained through trade, countries need not possess large quantities of natural resources within their own borders to achieve economic growth. Indeed, a number of countries have become rich without substantial natural resources of their own, including Japan, Hong Kong, Singapore, and Switzerland. Just as important as possessing natural resources is the ability to use them productively—for example, by means of advanced technologies.

TECHNOLOGY

Besides human capital, physical capital, and natural resources, a country's ability to develop and apply new, more productive technologies will help determine its productivity. Consider just one industry, transportation. Two centuries ago, as suggested by the quote from Stephen Ambrose in the beginning of the chapter, the horse and wagon were the primary means of transportation—a slow and costly method indeed. But in the nineteenth century, technological advances such as the steam engine supported the expansion of riverborne transportation and the development of a national rail network. In the twentieth century, the invention of the internal combustion engine and the development of aviation, supported by the construction of an extensive infrastructure of roads and airports, have produced increasingly rapid, cheap, and reliable transport. Technological change has clearly been a driving force in the transportation revolution.

New technologies can improve productivity in industries other than the one in which they are introduced. Once farmers could sell their produce only in their local communities, for example. Now the availability of rapid shipping and refrigerated transport allows farmers to sell their products virtually anywhere in the world. With a broader market in which to sell, farmers can specialize in those products best suited to local land and weather conditions. Similarly, factories can obtain their raw materials wherever they are cheapest and most abundant, produce the goods they are most efficient at manufacturing, and sell their products wherever they will fetch the best price. Both these examples illustrate the Principle of Comparative Advantage, that overall productivity increases when producers concentrate on those activities at which they are relatively most efficient.

Comparative Advantage

Numerous other technological developments led to increased productivity, including advances in communication and medicine, the introduction of computer technology, and most recently the emergence of global networks that connect mobile computing, communication, and even health devices around the world. In fact, *most economists would probably agree that new technologies are the single most important source of productivity improvement* and, hence, of economic growth in general.

However, economic growth does not automatically follow from breakthroughs in basic science. To make the best use of new knowledge, an economy needs entrepreneurs who can exploit scientific advances commercially, as well as a legal and political environment that encourages the practical application of new knowledge.

✔ **SELF-TEST 19.4**

A new kind of wrapping paper has been invented that makes candy wrapping quicker and easier. The use of this paper *increases* the number of candies a person can wrap by hand by 200 per hour, and the number of candies a person can wrap by machine by 300 per hour. Using the data from Examples 19.3 and 19.4, construct a table like Table 19.2 that shows how this technological advance affects average labor productivity. Do diminishing returns to capital still hold?

The Economic Naturalist 19.2

Why did U.S. labor productivity grow so rapidly in the late 1990s?

During the 1950s and 1960s, most industrialized countries experienced rapid growth in real GDP and average labor productivity. Between 1948 and 1973, for example, U.S. labor productivity grew by 2.5 percent per year.[3] Between 1973 and 1995, however, labor productivity growth in the United States fell by more than half to 1.1 percent per year. Other countries experienced similar productivity slowdowns, and many articles and books were written trying to uncover the reasons. Between 1995 and 2000, however, there was a rebound in productivity growth, particularly in the United States, where productivity grew 2.4 percent per year. What caused this resurgence in productivity growth? Can it be sustained?

Economists agree that the pickup in productivity growth between 1995 and 2000 was the product of rapid technological progress and increased investment in new information and communications technology (ICT). Research indicates that productivity grew rapidly in both those industries that *produced* ICT, such as silicon chips and fiber optics, and those industries that most intensively *used* ICT. The application of these advances had ripple effects in areas ranging from automobile production to retail inventory management. The rapid growth of the Internet, for example, made it possible for consumers to shop and find information online. But it also helped companies improve their efficiency by improving coordination between manufacturers and their suppliers. On the other hand, there was no acceleration in labor productivity growth in those industries that neither produced nor used much ICT.[4]

Although technological progress continued after 2000, productivity growth slowed to 1.5 percent per year from 2000 to 2007, and to 1.0 percent per year from 2007 to 2019. Why? While economists are still trying to understand all the reasons, it appears that the gains in productivity in the 1990s, which came from both improved production of ICT equipment and its use in ICT-intensive industries, were followed by smaller gains coming from broader application of ICT to other industries. It is also possible that the implosion of the NASDAQ (the "dot-com collapse") in 2000 and the mild recession of 2001 and, on a much larger scale, the global financial crisis and the recession of 2007–2009, contributed to slowing productivity growth. Indicators such as the number of new companies starting up and the amount invested in new technologies decreased somewhat during and following the 2001 recession and decreased dramatically during and following the 2007–2009 recession, impeding the introduction of new products and production techniques. In addition, the global financial crisis brought tighter credit conditions, making it difficult for companies to maintain or upgrade their equipment, and the high unemployment rates during and following the 2007–2009 recession may have caused the skills of some workers to deteriorate. If these factors are indeed the reason for the lower rates of productivity growth in recent years, then the higher rates of the late 1990s may return as the recovery from the crisis and the recession continues.

Optimists argue that advances in mobile computing, communications, biotechnology, and other ICT fields will allow productivity growth to return to the elevated rate of the late 1990s. Others are more cautious, arguing that the increases in productivity growth from these developments may be temporary rather than permanent. A great deal is riding on which view will turn out to be correct.

[3]Data refers to labor productivity growth in the nonfarm business sector and can be found at www.bls.gov.
[4]Kevin J. Stiroh, "Information Technology and the U.S. Productivity Revival: What Do the Industry Data Say?," *American Economic Review* 92 (December 2002), pp. 1559–1576.

ENTREPRENEURSHIP AND MANAGEMENT

entrepreneurs people who create new economic enterprises

The productivity of workers depends in part on the people who help decide what to produce and how to produce it: entrepreneurs and managers. **Entrepreneurs** are people who create new economic enterprises. Because of the new products, services, technological processes, and production methods they introduce, entrepreneurs are critical to a dynamic, healthy economy. In the late nineteenth and early twentieth centuries, individuals like Henry Ford and Alfred Sloan (automobiles), Andrew Carnegie (steel), John D. Rockefeller (oil), and J. P. Morgan (finance) played central roles in the development of American industry—and, not incidentally, amassed huge personal fortunes in the process. These people and others like them (including contemporary entrepreneurs like Bill Gates and Mark Zuckerberg) have been criticized for some of their business practices, in some cases with justification. Clearly, though, they and dozens of other prominent business leaders of the past century have contributed significantly to the growth of the U.S. economy. Henry Ford, for example, developed the idea of mass production, which lowered costs sufficiently to bring automobiles within reach of the average American family. Ford began his business in his garage, a tradition that has been maintained by thousands of innovators ever since. Larry Page and Sergey Brin, the cofounders of Google, revolutionized the way people conduct research by developing a method to prioritize the list of websites obtained in a search of the Internet.

Entrepreneurship, like any form of creativity, is difficult to teach, although some of the supporting skills, like financial analysis and marketing, can be learned in college or business school. How, then, does a society encourage entrepreneurship? History suggests that the entrepreneurial spirit will always exist; the challenge to society is to channel entrepreneurial energies in economically productive ways. For example, economic policymakers need to ensure that taxation is not so heavy, and regulation not so inflexible, that small businesses—some of which will eventually become big businesses—cannot get off the ground. Sociological factors may play a role as well. Societies in which business and commerce are considered to be beneath the dignity of refined, educated people are less likely to produce successful entrepreneurs. In the United States, for the most part, business has been viewed as a respectable activity. Overall, a social and economic milieu that allows entrepreneurship to flourish appears to promote economic growth and rising productivity, perhaps especially so in high-technology eras like our own.

EXAMPLE 19.5 | **Inventing the Personal Computer**

Does entrepreneurship pay?

In 1975, Steve Jobs and Steve Wozniak were two 20-year-olds who designed computer games for Atari. They had an idea to make a computer that was smaller and cheaper than the closet-sized mainframes that were then in use. To set up shop in Steve Jobs's parents' garage and buy their supplies, they sold their two most valuable possessions, Jobs's used Volkswagen van and Wozniak's Hewlett-Packard scientific calculator, for a total of $1,300. The result was the first personal computer, which they named after their new company (and Jobs's favorite fruit): Apple. The rest is history. Clearly, Jobs's and Wozniak's average labor productivity as the inventors of the personal computer eventually became many times what it was when they designed computer games. Creative entrepreneurship can increase productivity just like additional capital or land.

The Economic Naturalist 19.3

Why did medieval China stagnate economically?

The Sung period in China (A.D. 960–1270) was one of considerable technological sophistication; its inventions included paper, waterwheels, water clocks, gunpowder, and possibly the compass. Yet no significant industrialization occurred, and in subsequent centuries, Europe saw more economic growth and technological innovation than China. Why did medieval China stagnate economically?

According to research by economist William Baumol,[5] the main impediment to industrialization during the Sung period was a social system that inhibited entrepreneurship. Commerce and industry were considered low-status activities, not fit for an educated person. In addition, the emperor had the right to seize his subjects' property and to take control of their business enterprises—a right that greatly reduced his subjects' incentives to undertake business ventures. The most direct path to status and riches in medieval China was to go through a system of demanding civil service examinations given by the government every three years. The highest scorers on these national examinations were granted lifetime positions in the imperial bureaucracy, where they wielded much power and often became wealthy, in part through corruption. Not surprisingly, medieval China did not develop a dynamic entrepreneurial class, and consequently, its scientific and technological advantages did not translate into sustained economic growth. China's experience shows why scientific advances alone cannot guarantee economic growth; to have economic benefits, scientific knowledge must be commercially applied through new products and new, more efficient means of producing goods and services.

Although entrepreneurship may be more glamorous, managers—the people who run businesses on a daily basis—also play an important role in determining average labor productivity. Managerial jobs span a wide range of positions, from the supervisor of the loading dock to the CEO (chief executive officer) at the helm of a *Fortune* 500 company. Managers work to satisfy customers, deal with suppliers, organize production, obtain financing, assign workers to jobs, and motivate them to work hard and effectively. Such activities enhance labor productivity. For example, in the 1970s and 1980s, Japanese managers introduced new production methods that greatly increased the efficiency of Japanese manufacturing plants. Among them was the *just-in-time* inventory system, in which suppliers deliver production components to the factory just when they are needed, eliminating the need for factories to stockpile components. Japanese managers also pioneered the idea of organizing workers into semi-independent production teams, which allowed workers more flexibility and responsibility than the traditional assembly line. Managers in the United States and other countries studied the Japanese managerial techniques closely and adopted many of them.

THE POLITICAL AND LEGAL ENVIRONMENT

So far we have emphasized the role of the private sector in increasing average labor productivity. But government too has a role to play in fostering improved productivity. One of the key contributions government can make is to provide a *political and legal environment* that encourages people to behave in economically productive ways—to work hard, save and invest wisely, acquire useful information and skills, and provide the goods and services that the public demands.

[5]W. Baumol, "Entrepreneurship: Productive, Unproductive, and Destructive," *Journal of Political Economy,* October 1990, pp. 893–921.

One specific function of government that appears to be crucial to economic success is the establishment of *well-defined property rights*. Property rights are well defined when the law provides clear rules for determining who owns what resources (through a system of deeds and titles, for example) and how those resources can be used. Imagine living in a society in which a dictator, backed by the military and the police, could take whatever he wanted, and regularly did so. In such a country, what incentive would you have to raise a large crop or to produce other valuable goods and services? Very little, since much of what you produced would likely be taken away from you. Unfortunately, in many countries of the world today, this situation is far from hypothetical.

Political and legal conditions affect the growth of productivity in other ways, as well. Political scientists and economists have documented the fact that *political instability* can be detrimental to economic growth. This finding is reasonable, since entrepreneurs and savers are unlikely to invest their resources in a country whose government is unstable, particularly if the struggle for power involves civil unrest, terrorism, or guerrilla warfare. On the other hand, a political system that promotes the *free and open exchange of ideas* will speed the development of new technologies and products. For example, some economic historians have suggested that the decline of Spain as an economic power was due in part to the advent of the Spanish Inquisition, which permitted no dissent from religious orthodoxy. Because of the Inquisition's persecution of those whose theories about the natural world contradicted Church doctrine, Spanish science and technology languished, and Spain fell behind more tolerant nations like the Netherlands.

 SELF-TEST 19.5

A Bangladeshi worker who immigrates to America is likely to find that his average labor productivity is much higher in the United States than it was at home. The worker is, of course, the same person he was when he lived in Bangladesh. How can the simple act of moving to the United States increase the worker's productivity? What does your answer say about the incentive to immigrate?

RECAP ↑

DETERMINANTS OF AVERAGE LABOR PRODUCTIVITY

Key factors determining average labor productivity in a country include:

- The skills and training of workers, called *human capital*.
- The quantity and quality of *physical capital*—machines, equipment, and buildings.
- The availability of land and other *natural resources*.
- The sophistication of the *technologies* applied in production.
- The effectiveness of *management* and *entrepreneurship*.
- The broad *social and legal environment*.

Labor productivity growth slowed throughout the industrialized world in the early 1970s and remained slow for more than two decades. Between 1995 and 2000, labor productivity rebounded (especially in the United States), largely because of advances in information and communication technology. Since then, labor productivity in the United States has again slowed. It remains to be seen if this recent slowdown is temporary (for example, due to factors that include the last financial crisis and recession) or the beginning of a new period of slower productivity growth.

THE COSTS OF ECONOMIC GROWTH

Both this chapter and Chapter 17, *Measuring Economic Activity: GDP and Unemployment,* emphasized the positive effects of economic growth on the average person's living standard. But should societies always strive for the highest possible rate of economic growth? The answer is no. Even if we accept for the moment that increased output per person is always desirable, attaining a higher rate of economic growth does impose costs on society.

What are the costs of increasing economic growth? The most straightforward is the cost of creating new capital. We know that by expanding the capital stock we can increase future productivity and output. But, to increase the capital stock, we must divert resources that could otherwise be used to increase the supply of consumer goods. For example, to add more robot-operated assembly lines, a society must employ more of its skilled technicians in building industrial robots and fewer in developing medical assistance robots. To build new factories, more carpenters and lumber must be assigned to factory construction and less to finishing basements or renovating family rooms. In short, high rates of investment in new capital require people to tighten their belts, consume less, and save more—a real economic cost.

Should a country undertake a high rate of investment in capital goods at the sacrifice of consumer goods? The answer depends on the extent that people are willing and able to sacrifice consumption today to have a bigger economic pie tomorrow. In a country that is very poor, or is experiencing an economic crisis, people may prefer to keep consumption relatively high and savings and investment relatively low. The midst of a thunderstorm is not the time to be putting something aside for a rainy day! But in a society that is relatively well off, people may be more willing to make sacrifices to achieve higher economic growth in the future.

Consumption sacrificed to capital formation is not the only cost of achieving higher growth. In the United States in the nineteenth and early twentieth centuries, periods of rapid economic growth were often times in which many people worked extremely long hours at dangerous and unpleasant jobs. While those workers helped build the economy that Americans enjoy today, the costs were great in terms of reduced leisure time and, in some cases, workers' health and safety.

Other costs of growth include the cost of the research and development that is required to improve technology and the costs of acquiring training and skill (human capital). The fact that a higher living standard tomorrow must be purchased at the cost of current sacrifices is an example of the Scarcity Principle. Because achieving higher economic growth imposes real economic costs, we know from the Cost-Benefit Principle that higher growth should be pursued only if the benefits outweigh the costs.

> **RECAP**
>
> **THE COSTS OF ECONOMIC GROWTH**
>
> Economic growth has substantial costs, notably the sacrifice of current consumption that is required to free resources for creating new capital and new technologies. Higher rates of growth should be pursued only if the benefits outweigh the costs.

PROMOTING ECONOMIC GROWTH

If a society decides to try to raise its rate of economic growth, what are some of the measures that policymakers might take to achieve this objective? Here is a short list of suggestions, based on our discussion of the factors that contribute to growth in average labor productivity and, hence, output per person.

POLICIES TO INCREASE HUMAN CAPITAL

Because skilled and well-educated workers are more productive than unskilled labor, governments in most countries try to increase the human capital of their citizens by supporting education and training programs. In the United States, government provides public education through high school and grants extensive support to postsecondary schools, including technical schools, colleges, and universities. Publicly funded early intervention programs like Head Start also attempt to build human capital by helping disadvantaged children prepare for school. To a lesser degree than some other countries, the U.S. government also funds job training for unskilled youths and retraining for workers whose skills have become obsolete.

The Economic Naturalist 19.4

Why do almost all countries provide free public education?

▶ Visit your instructor's Connect course and access your eBook to view this video.

Why do almost all countries provide free public education?

All industrial countries provide their citizens free public education through high school, and most subsidize college and other postsecondary schools. Why?

Americans are so used to the idea of free public education that this question may seem odd. But why should the government provide free education when it does not provide even more essential goods and services, such as food or medical care, for free, except to the most needy? Furthermore, educational services can be, and indeed commonly are, supplied and demanded on the private market, without the aid of the government.

An important argument for free or at least subsidized education is that the private demand curve for educational services does not include all the social benefits of education. (Recall the Equilibrium Principle, which states in part that a market in equilibrium may not exploit all gains achievable from collective action.) For example, the democratic political system relies on an educated citizenry to operate effectively—a factor that an individual demander of educational services has little reason to consider. From a narrower economic perspective, we might argue that individuals do not capture the full economic returns from their schooling. For example, people with high human capital, and thus high earnings, pay more taxes—funds that can be used to finance government services and aid the less fortunate. Because of income taxation, the private benefit to acquiring human capital is less than the social benefit, and the demand for education on the private market may be less than optimal from society's viewpoint. Similarly, educated people are more likely than others to contribute to technological development, and hence to general productivity growth, which may benefit many other people besides themselves. Finally, another argument for public support of education is that poor people who would like to invest in human capital may not be able to do so because of insufficient income.

The late Nobel laureate Milton Friedman, among many economists, suggested that these arguments may justify government grants, called educational *vouchers*, to help citizens purchase educational services in the private sector, but they do *not* justify the government providing education directly, as through the public school system. Defenders of public education, on the other hand, argue that the government should have some direct control over education in order to set standards and monitor quality. What do you think?

POLICIES THAT PROMOTE SAVING AND INVESTMENT

Average labor productivity increases when workers can utilize a sizable and modern capital stock. To support the creation of new capital, government can encourage high rates of saving and investment in the private sector. Many provisions in the U.S. tax code are designed expressly to stimulate households to save and firms to invest. For example, a household that opens an Individual Retirement Account (IRA) is able to save for retirement without paying taxes on either the funds deposited in the IRA or the interest earned on the account. (However, taxes are due when the funds are withdrawn at retirement.) The intent of IRA legislation is to make saving more financially attractive to American households. Similarly, at various times Congress has instituted an investment tax credit, which reduces the tax bills of firms that invest in new capital. Private-sector saving and investment are discussed in greater detail in Chapter 21, *Saving and Capital Formation.*

Government can contribute directly to capital formation through *public investment,* or the creation of government-owned capital. Public investment includes the building of roads, bridges, airports, dams, and, in some countries, energy and communications networks. The construction of the U.S. interstate highway system, begun during the administration of President Eisenhower, is often cited as an example of successful public investment. The interstate system substantially reduced long-haul transportation costs in the United States, improving productivity throughout the economy. Today, the web of computers and communications links we call the Internet is having a similar effect. This project, too, received crucial government funding in its early stages. Many research studies have confirmed that government investment in the *infrastructure*, the public capital that supports private-sector economic activities, can be a significant source of growth.

POLICIES THAT SUPPORT RESEARCH AND DEVELOPMENT

Productivity is enhanced by technological progress, which in turn requires investment in research and development (R&D). In many industries private firms have adequate incentive to conduct research and development activities. There is no need, for example, for the government to finance research for developing a better underarm deodorant.

But some types of knowledge, particularly basic scientific knowledge, may have widespread economic benefits that cannot be captured by a single private firm. The developers of the silicon computer chip, for example, were instrumental in creating huge new industries, yet they received only a small portion of the profits flowing from their inventions.

Because society in general, rather than the individual inventors, may receive much of the benefit from basic research, government may need to support basic research, as it does through agencies such as the National Science Foundation. The federal government also sponsors a great deal of applied research, particularly in military and space applications. To the extent that national security allows, the government can increase growth by sharing the fruits of such research with the private sector. For example, the Global Positioning System (GPS), which was developed originally for military purposes, is now available in most cell phones, helping people find their way almost anywhere.

THE LEGAL AND POLITICAL FRAMEWORK

Although economic growth comes primarily from activities in the private sector, the government plays an essential role in providing the framework within which the private sector can operate productively. We have discussed the importance of secure property rights and a well-functioning legal system, of an economic environment that encourages entrepreneurship, and of political stability and the free and open exchange of ideas. Government policymakers should also consider the potential effects of tax and regulatory policies on activities that increase productivity, such as investment, innovation, and risk taking. Policies that affect the legal and political framework are examples of *structural macroeconomic policies.*

THE POOREST COUNTRIES: A SPECIAL CASE?

Radical disparities in living standards exist between the richest and poorest countries of the world. Achieving economic growth in the poorest countries is thus particularly urgent. Are the policy prescriptions of this section relevant to those countries, or are very different types of measures necessary to spur growth in the poorest nations?

To a significant extent, the same factors and policies that promote growth in richer countries apply to the poorest countries as well. Increasing human capital by supporting education and training, increasing rates of saving and investment, investing in public capital and infrastructure, supporting research and development, and encouraging entrepreneurship are all measures that will enhance economic growth in poor countries.

However, to a much greater degree than in richer countries, most poor countries need to improve the legal and political environment that underpins their economies. For example, many developing countries have poorly developed or corrupt legal systems, which discourage entrepreneurship and investment by creating uncertainty about property rights. Taxation and regulation in developing countries are often heavy-handed and administered by inefficient bureaucracies, to the extent that it may take months or years to obtain the approvals needed to start a small business or expand a factory. Regulation is also used to suppress market forces in poor countries; for example, the government, rather than the market, may determine the allocation of bank credit or the prices for agricultural products. Structural policies that aim to ameliorate these problems are important preconditions for generating growth in the poorest countries. But probably most important—and most difficult, for some countries—is establishing political stability and the rule of law. Without political stability, domestic and foreign savers will be reluctant to invest in the country, and economic growth will be difficult if not impossible to achieve.

Can rich countries help poor countries to develop? Historically, richer nations have tried to help by providing financial aid through loans or grants from individual countries (foreign aid) or by loans made by international agencies, such as the World Bank. Experience has shown, however, that financial aid to countries that do not undertake structural reforms, such as reducing excessive regulation or improving the legal system, is of limited value. To make their foreign aid most effective, rich countries should help poor countries achieve political stability and undertake the necessary reforms to the structure of their economies.

> **RECAP** ↑
>
> **PROMOTING ECONOMIC GROWTH**
>
> Policies for promoting economic growth include policies to increase human capital (education and training); policies that promote saving and capital formation; policies that support research and development; and the provision of a legal and political framework within which the private sector can operate productively. Deficiencies in the legal and political framework (for example, official corruption or poorly defined property rights) are a special problem for many developing countries.

ARE THERE LIMITS TO GROWTH?

Earlier in this chapter, we saw that even relatively low rates of economic growth, if sustained for a long period, will produce huge increases in the size of the economy. This fact raises the question of whether economic growth can continue indefinitely without depleting natural resources and causing massive damage to the global environment. Does the basic truth that we live in a finite world of finite resources imply that, ultimately, economic growth must come to an end?

The concern that economic growth may not be sustainable is not a new one. An influential 1972 book, *The Limits to Growth*,[6] reported the results of computer simulations that suggested that unless population growth and economic expansion were halted, the world would soon be running out of natural resources, drinkable water, and breathable air. This book, and later works in the same vein, raise some fundamental questions that cannot be done full justice here. However, in some ways its conclusions are misleading.

---

[6]Donella H. Meadows, Dennis L. Meadows, Jørgen Randers, and William W. Behrens III, *The Limits to Growth* (New York: New American Library, 1972).

One problem with the "limits to growth" thesis lies in its underlying concept of economic growth. Those who emphasize the environmental limits on growth assume implicitly that economic growth will always take the form of more of what we have now—more smoky factories, more polluting cars, more fast-food restaurants. If that were indeed the case, then surely there would be limits to the growth the planet can sustain.

But growth in real GDP does not necessarily take such a form. Increases in real GDP can also arise from new or higher-quality products. For example, not too long ago, tennis rackets were relatively simple items made primarily of wood. Today they are made of newly invented synthetic materials and designed for optimum performance using sophisticated computer simulations. Because these new high-tech tennis rackets are more valued by consumers than the old wooden ones, they increase the real GDP. Likewise, the introduction of new pharmaceuticals has contributed to economic growth, as have the expanded number of web-based services and apps. As people switch, for example, from frequent visits to the bank or the mall to frequent visits to the bank's or store's website (or mobile app), GDP may increase while the number of cars and of brick-and-mortar stores decreases. Thus, economic growth need not take the form of more and more of the same old stuff; it can mean newer, better, and perhaps cleaner and more efficient goods and services.

A second problem with the "limits to growth" conclusion is that it overlooks the fact that increased wealth and productivity expand society's capacity to take measures to safeguard the environment. In fact, the most polluted countries in the world are not the richest but those that are in a relatively early stage of industrialization. At this stage countries must devote the bulk of their resources to basic needs—food, shelter, health care—and continued industrial expansion. In these countries, clean air and water may be viewed as a luxury rather than a basic need. In more economically developed countries, where the most basic needs are more easily met, extra resources are available to keep the environment clean. Thus continuing economic growth may lead to less, not more, pollution.

A third problem with the pessimistic view of economic growth is that it ignores the power of the market and other social mechanisms to deal with scarcity. During the oil-supply disruptions of the 1970s, newspapers were filled with headlines about the energy crisis and the imminent depletion of world oil supplies. Yet 40 years later, the world's known oil reserves are actually *greater* than they were in the 1970s.

Today's energy situation is so much better than was expected 40 years ago because the market went to work. Reduced oil supplies led to an increase in prices that changed the behavior of both demanders and suppliers. Consumers insulated their homes, purchased more energy-efficient cars and appliances, and switched to alternative sources of energy. Suppliers engaged in a massive hunt for new reserves, opening up major new sources in Latin America, China, the North Sea, and more recently North America's large shale oil deposits. In short, market forces solved the energy crisis, at least for now.

In general, shortages in any resource will trigger price changes that induce suppliers and demanders to deal with the problem. Simply extrapolating current economic trends into the future ignores the power of the market system to recognize shortages and make the necessary corrections. Government actions spurred by political pressures, such as the allocation of public funds to preserve open space or reduce air pollution, can be expected to supplement market adjustments.

Despite the shortcomings of the "limits to growth" perspective, most economists would agree that not all the problems created by economic growth can be dealt with effectively through the market or the political process. Probably most important, global environmental problems, such as the possibility of global warming or the ongoing destruction of rain forests, are a particular challenge for existing economic and political institutions. Many environmental-quality goods—living in a healthy environment with clean air and water, avoiding global warming, and avoiding deforestation—are desired by many people, but they are not bought and sold in markets and thus will not automatically reach their optimal levels through market processes. Nor can local or national governments effectively address problems that are global in scope. Unless international mechanisms are established for dealing with global environmental problems, these problems may become worse as economic growth continues.

> **RECAP** ↑
>
> **ECONOMIC GROWTH: ARE THERE LIMITS?**
>
> Some have argued that finite resources imply ultimate limits to economic growth. This view overlooks the facts that growth can take the form of better, rather than more, goods and services; that increased wealth frees resources to safeguard the environment; and that political and economic mechanisms exist to address many of the problems associated with growth. However, these mechanisms may not work well when environmental or other problems arising from economic growth are global in scope.

SUMMARY

- Over the past two centuries, the industrialized nations saw enormous improvements in living standards, as reflected in large increases in real GDP per person. Because of the power of *compound interest,* relatively small differences in growth rates, if continued over long periods, can produce large differences in real GDP per person and average living standards. Thus, the rate of long-term economic growth is an economic variable of critical importance. *(LO1)*

- Real GDP per person is the product of average labor productivity (real GDP per employed worker) and the share of the population that is employed. Growth in real GDP per person can occur only through growth in *average labor productivity*, in the share of the population that is working, or both. In the period from 1960 to 2000, increases in the share of the U.S. population holding a job contributed significantly to rising real GDP per person. But, as in most periods, the main source of the increase in real GDP per person was rising average labor productivity. *(LO2)*

- Among the factors that determine labor productivity are the talents, education, training, and skills of workers, or *human capital*; the quantity and quality of the *physical capital* that workers use; the availability of land and other natural resources; the application of technology to the production and distribution of goods and services; the effectiveness of *entrepreneurs* and managers; and the broad social and legal environment. Because of *diminishing returns to capital,* beyond a certain point expansion of the capital stock is not the most effective way to increase average labor productivity. Economists generally agree that new technologies are the most important single source of improvements in productivity. *(LO3)*

- Since the 1970s, the industrial world has experienced a slowdown in productivity growth. Productivity growth rebounded between 1995 and 2000, largely as a result of advances in information and communication technology, before slowing down again. *(LO3)*

- Economic growth has costs as well as benefits. Prominent among them is the need to sacrifice current consumption to achieve a high rate of investment in new capital goods; other costs of growing more quickly include extra work effort and the costs of research and development. Thus, more economic growth is not necessarily better; whether increased economic growth is desirable depends on whether the benefits of growth outweigh the costs. *(LO4)*

- Among the ways in which government can stimulate economic growth are by adopting policies that encourage the creation of human capital; that promote saving and investment, including public investment in infrastructure; that support research and development, particularly in the basic sciences; and that provide a legal and political framework that supports private-sector activities. The poorest countries, with poorly developed legal, tax, and regulatory systems, are often in the greatest need of an improved legal and political framework and increased political stability. *(LO5)*

- Are there limits to growth? Arguments that economic growth must be constrained by environmental problems and the limits of natural resources ignore the fact that economic growth can take the form of increasing quality as well as increasing quantity. Indeed, increases in output can provide additional resources for cleaning up the environment. Finally, the market system, together with political processes, can solve many of the problems associated with economic growth. On the other hand, global environmental problems, which can be handled neither by the market nor by individual national governments, have the potential to constrain economic growth. *(LO6)*

KEY TERMS

average labor productivity
compound interest

diminishing returns to capital
entrepreneurs

human capital
physical capital

REVIEW QUESTIONS

1. What has happened to real GDP per person in the industrialized countries over the past century? What implications does this have for the average person? Are there implications for different countries in different regions (e.g., Japan versus Ghana)? *(LO1)*

2. Why do economists consider growth in average labor productivity to be the key factor in determining long-run living standards? *(LO2)*

3. What is *human capital*? Why is it economically important? How is new human capital created? *(LO3)*

4. You have employed five workers of varying physical strength to dig a ditch. Workers without shovels have zero productivity in ditchdigging. How should you assign shovels to workers if you don't have enough

shovels to go around? How should you assign any additional shovels that you obtain? Using this example, discuss (a) the relationship between the availability of physical capital and average labor productivity and (b) the concept of diminishing returns to capital. *(LO3)*

5. Discuss how talented entrepreneurs and effective managers can enhance average labor productivity. *(LO3)*

6. What are the costs of increasing economic growth? *(LO4)*

7. What major contributions can the government make to the goal of increasing average labor productivity? *(LO5)*

8. Discuss the following statement: "Because the environment is fragile and natural resources are finite, ultimately economic growth must come to an end." *(LO6)*

PROBLEMS

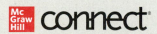

1. Richland's real GDP per person is $40,000, and Poorland's real GDP per person is $20,000. However, Richland's real GDP per person is growing at 1 percent per year and Poorland's is growing at 3 percent per year. Compare real GDP per person in the two countries after 10 years and after 20 years. Approximately how many years will it take Poorland to catch up to Richland? *(LO1)*

2. Suppose labor productivity in the United States was $100,000 per worker in 2015. Calculate the value of labor productivity in the year 2035 (20 years later) if *(LO1)*
   a. productivity continues to grow by 3.1 percent per year.
   b. productivity growth falls to 1.4 percent per year.
   (*Note:* You do not need to know the actual values of average labor productivity in any year to solve this problem.)
   How much larger would labor productivity per worker be in 2035 with the higher growth rate as compared to the lower growth rate?

3. The "graying of America" will substantially increase the fraction of the population that is retired in the decades to come. To illustrate the implications for U.S. living standards, suppose that over the 56 years following

2016, the share of the population that is working returns to its 1960 level, while average labor productivity increases by as much as it did during 1960–2016. Under this scenario, what would be the net change in real GDP per person between 2016 and 2072? The following data will be useful: *(LO2)*

	Average labor productivity	Share of population employed
1960	$ 47,263	36.4%
2016	$110,384	46.8%

4. Consider the following table containing data for Germany and Japan on the ratio of employment to population in 1980 and 2010:

	1980	2010
Germany	0.33	0.52
Japan	0.48	0.49

Using data from Table 19.1, find average labor productivity for each country in 1980 and 2010. How much of the increase in output per person in each country over the 1980 to 2010 period is due to increased labor productivity? To increased employment relative to population? *(LO2)*

5. Joanne has just completed high school and is trying to determine whether to go to community college for two years or go directly to work. Her objective is to maximize the savings she will have in the bank five years from now. If she goes directly to work she will earn $20,000 per year for each of the next five years. If she goes to community college, for each of the next two years she will earn nothing—indeed, she will have to borrow $6,000 each year to cover tuition and books. This loan must be repaid in full three years after graduation. If she graduates from community college, in each of the subsequent three years, her wages will be $38,000 per year. Joanne's total living expenses and taxes, excluding tuition and books, equal $15,000 per year. *(LO3)*
   a. Suppose for simplicity that Joanne can borrow and lend at 0 percent interest. On purely economic grounds, should she go to community college or work?
   b. Does your answer to part a change if she can earn $23,000 per year with only a high school degree?
   c. Does your answer to part a change if Joanne's tuition and books cost $8,000 per year?
   d.* Suppose that the interest rate at which Joanne can borrow and lend is 10 percent per year, but other data are as in part a. Savings are deposited at the end of the year they are earned and receive (compound) interest at the end of each subsequent year. Similarly, the loans are taken out at the end of the year in which they are needed, and interest does not accrue until the end of the subsequent year. Now that the interest rate has risen, should Joanne go to college or go to work?

6. The Good'n'Fresh Grocery Store has two checkout lanes and four employees. Employees are equally skilled, and all are able either to operate a register (checkers) or bag groceries (baggers). The store owner assigns one checker and one bagger to each lane. A lane with a checker and a bagger can check out 42 customers per hour. A lane with a checker can check out only 25 customers per hour. *(LO3)*
   a. In terms of customers checked out per hour, what is total output and average labor productivity for the Good'n'Fresh Grocery Store?
   b. The owner adds a third checkout lane and register. Assuming that no employees are added, what is the best way to reallocate the workers to tasks? What is total output and average labor productivity (in terms of customers checked out per hour) now?
   c. Repeat part b for the addition of a fourth checkout lane, and a fifth. Do you observe diminishing returns to capital in this example?

7. Harrison, Carla, and Fred are housepainters. Harrison and Carla can paint 100 square feet per hour using a standard paintbrush, and Fred can paint 80 square feet per hour. Any of the three can paint 200 square feet per hour using a roller. *(LO3)*
   a. Assume Harrison, Carla, and Fred have only paintbrushes at their disposal. What is the average labor productivity, in terms of square feet per painter-hour, for the three painters taken as a team? Assume that the three painters always work the same number of hours.
   b. Repeat part a for the cases in which the team has one, two, three, or four rollers available. Are there diminishing returns to capital?
   c. An improvement in paint quality increases the area that can be covered per hour (by either brushes or rollers) by 20 percent. How does this technological improvement affect your answers to part b? Are there diminishing returns to capital? Does the technological improvement increase or reduce the economic value of an additional roller?

8. Hester's Hatchery raises fish. At the end of the current season, Hester has 1,000 fish in the hatchery. She can harvest any number of fish that she wishes, selling them to restaurants for $5 apiece. Because big fish make little fish, for every fish that she leaves in the hatchery this year she will have two fish at the end of next year. The price of fish is expected to be $5 each next year as well. Hester relies entirely on income from current fish sales to support herself. *(LO3)*
   a. How many fish should Hester harvest if she wants to maximize the growth of her stock of fish from this season to next season?
   b. Do you think maximizing the growth of her fish stock is an economically sound strategy for Hester? Why or why not? Relate to the text discussion on the costs of economic growth.
   c. How many fish should Hester harvest if she wants to maximize her current income? Do you think this is a good strategy?
   d. Explain why Hester is unlikely to harvest either all or none of her fish, but instead will harvest some and leave the rest to reproduce.

9. Discuss the following statement, using concrete examples where possible to illustrate your arguments: For advances in basic science to translate into improvements in standards of living, they must be supported by favorable economic conditions. *(LO3, LO4, LO5)*

10. Write a short essay evaluating the U.S. economy in terms of each of the six determinants of average labor productivity discussed in the text. Are there any areas in which the United States is exceptionally strong, relative to other countries? Areas where the United States is less strong than some other countries? Illustrate your arguments with numbers from the *Statistical Abstract of the United States* (available online at www.census.gov/library/publications/time-series/statistical_abstracts.html) and other sources, as appropriate. *(LO3, LO4, LO5)*

*Denotes more difficult problem.

ANSWERS TO SELF-TESTS

19.1 If the United States had grown at the Japanese rate for the period 1870–2010, real GDP per person in 2010 would have been $(\$2,445) \times (1.025)^{140} = \$77,556.82$. Actual GDP per person in the United States in 2010 was $30,491, so at the higher rate of growth output per person would have been $\$77,556.82/\$30,491 = 2.54$ times higher. *(LO1)*

19.2 As before, Lucy can wrap 4,000 candies per week, or 100 candies per hour. Ethel can wrap 500 candies per hour, and working 40 hours weekly, she can wrap 20,000 candies per week. Together Lucy and Ethel can wrap 24,000 candies per week. Since they work a total of 80 hours between them, their output per hour as a team is 24,000 candies wrapped per 80 hours = 300 candies wrapped per hour, midway between their hourly productivities as individuals. *(LO3)*

19.3 Because Ethel can wrap 300 candies per hour by hand, the benefit of giving Ethel the machine is $500 - 300 = 200$ additional candies wrapped per hour. Because Lucy wraps only 100 candies per hour by hand, the benefit of giving Lucy the machine is 400 additional candies wrapped per hour. So the benefit of giving the machine to Lucy is greater than of giving it to Ethel. Equivalently, if the machine goes to Ethel, then Lucy and Ethel between them can wrap $500 + 100 = 600$ candies per hour, but if Lucy uses the machine the team can wrap $300 + 500 = 800$ candies per hour. So output is increased by letting Lucy use the machine. *(LO3)*

19.4 Now, working by hand, Lucy can wrap 300 candies per hour and Ethel can wrap 500 candies per hour. With a machine, either Lucy or Ethel can wrap 800 candies per hour. As in Self-Test 19.3, the benefit of giving a machine to Lucy (500 candies per hour) exceeds the benefit of giving a machine to Ethel (300 candies per hour), so if only one machine is available, Lucy should use it.

The table analogous to Table 19.2 now looks like this:

Relationship of Capital, Output, and Productivity in the Candy-Wrapping Factory

Number of machines (K)	Candies wrapped per week (Y)	Total hours worked (N)	Average hourly labor productivity (Y/N)
0	32,000	80	400
1	52,000	80	650
2	64,000	80	800
3	64,000	80	800

Comparing this table with Table 19.2, you can see that technological advance has increased labor productivity for any value of K, the number of machines available.

Adding one machine increases output by 20,000 candies wrapped per week, adding the second machine increases output by 12,000 candies wrapped per week, and adding the third machine does not increase output at all (because there is no worker available to use it). So diminishing returns to capital still hold after the technological improvement. *(LO3)*

19.5 Although the individual worker is the same person he was in Bangladesh, by coming to the United States, he gains the benefit of factors that enhance average labor productivity in this country, relative to his homeland. These include more and better capital to work with, more natural resources per person, more advanced technologies, sophisticated entrepreneurs and managers, and a political-legal environment that is conducive to high productivity. It is not guaranteed that the value of the immigrant's human capital will rise (it may not, for example, if he speaks no English and has no skills applicable to the U.S. economy), but normally it will.

Since increased productivity leads to higher wages and living standards, on economic grounds, the Bangladeshi worker has a strong incentive to immigrate to the United States if he is able to do so. *(LO3)*

The Labor Market: Workers, Wages, and Unemployment

How do globalization and technological change affect wages and employment?

Andresr/Getty Images

Why are you reading this book?

Some readers, thinking about this question in broad terms, may answer: "To better understand the economy" or even "To better understand the world around me." Others, focusing more on the here and now, may answer: "Because it is required reading for my economics class," or even just "To pass the final exam!" Still other readers would offer other answers, or more than one answer.

For an economist, by reading this book (and, more generally, by taking a course or studying for a degree) you are increasing your *human capital*. The concept of human capital was introduced in Chapter 19, *Economic Growth, Productivity, and Living Standards*. We described it as comprising one's talents, education, training, and skills, and said that it is acquired primarily through the investment of time, energy, and money. We also said that workers with more human capital are more productive than those with less human capital. How have these productivity gaps changed over time? To what extent have they translated to income gaps between workers who managed to "keep up" with a modern labor market by acquiring the right skills and those unwilling or unable to do so?

We also examined the remarkable economic growth and increased productivity that have occurred in the industrialized world over the past two centuries. These developments have greatly increased the quantity of goods and services that the economy can produce. But we have not yet discussed how the fruits of economic growth are distributed. Has everyone benefited equally from economic growth and increased productivity? Or, as some writers suggest, is the population divided between those who have caught the "train" of economic modernization, enriching themselves in the process, and those who have been left at the station?[1]

To understand how economic growth and change affect different groups, we must turn to the labor market. Except for retirees and others receiving government support, most people rely almost entirely on wages and salaries to pay their bills and put something away for the future. Hence, it is in the labor market that most people will see the benefits of the economic growth and increasing productivity. This chapter describes and explains some important trends in the labor markets of industrial countries. Using a supply and demand model of the labor market, we focus first on several important trends in real wages and employment. In the second part of the chapter, we turn to the problem of unemployment, especially long-term unemployment. We will see that two key factors contributing to recent trends in wages, employment, and unemployment are the *globalization* of the economy, as reflected in the increasing importance of international trade, and ongoing *technological change*. By the end of the chapter, you will better understand the connection between these macroeconomic developments and the economic fortunes of workers and their families.

FIVE IMPORTANT LABOR MARKET TRENDS

In recent decades, at least five trends have characterized the labor markets of the industrialized world. We divide these trends into two groups: those affecting real wages and those affecting employment and unemployment.

TRENDS IN REAL WAGES

1. Over the twentieth century, all industrial countries have enjoyed substantial growth in average real wages.

In the United States in 2018, on average, workers' yearly earnings could command more than twice as many goods and services as in 1960 and more than five times as much as in 1929, just prior to the Great Depression. Similar trends have prevailed in other industrialized countries.

2. Since the early 1970s, however, the rate of average real wage growth has slowed.

Though the post–World War II period has seen impressive increases in average real wages, the fastest rates of increase occurred during the 1960s and early 1970s. In the 13 years between 1960 and 1973, the buying power of workers' incomes rose at a rate of about 2.5 percent per year, a strong rate of increase. But from 1973 to 1995, real yearly earnings grew at only 0.9 percent per year. The good news is that from 1995 to 2007, the eve of the 2007–2009 recession, real earnings grew at 1.9 percent per year, despite a recession in 2001. However, since then earnings growth slowed again: from 2007 to 2018, real earnings grew at only 0.8 percent per year, and for the whole 1973–2018 period, earnings grew at 1.1 percent a year. It remains to be seen whether a steeper upward trend in average earnings resumes in the next few years.

3. Furthermore, recent decades have brought a pronounced increase in wage inequality in the United States.

A growing gap in real wages between skilled and unskilled workers has been of particular concern. Indeed, the real wages of the least-skilled, least-educated workers have actually *declined* since the early 1970s, according to some studies. At the same time, the best-educated, highest-skilled workers have enjoyed continuing gains in real wages. Data from the *Bureau of Labor Statistics* for a recent year showed that, in the United States, the typical worker with a master's degree earned almost twice the income of a high school graduate and three times the income of a worker with less than a high school degree. Many observers worry that the United States is developing a "two-tier" labor market: plenty of good jobs at good wages for the well-educated and highly skilled, but less and less opportunity for those without schooling or skills.

[1]See, for example, Thomas L. Friedman, *The Lexus and the Olive Tree* (New York: Farrar, Straus & Giroux, 1999).

Outside the United States, particularly in western Europe, the trend toward wage inequality has been much less pronounced. But, as we will see, employment trends in Europe have not been as encouraging as in the United States. Let's turn now to the trends in employment and unemployment.

TRENDS IN EMPLOYMENT AND UNEMPLOYMENT

4. In the United States, the number of people with jobs has grown substantially in the past 50 years. The rate of job growth has slowed recently.

In 1970, about 57 percent of the over-16 population in the United States had jobs. By 2000, total U.S. employment exceeded 136 million people, more than 64 percent of the over-16 population. Between 1980 and 2000, the U.S. economy created more than 37 million new jobs—an increase in total employment of 38 percent—while the over-16 population grew only 27 percent. The pace of new job creation has slowed since, dropping below the growth rate of the over-16 population: by late 2019, about 159 million people in the U.S. had jobs, about 61 percent of the over-16 population.

Similar job growth has been a more recent phenomenon in many other industrialized countries.

5. Compared with the U.S., western European countries have, in general, been suffering higher rates of unemployment during much of the past four decades.

In France, Italy, and Spain, for example, an average of 9.9, 9.6, and 16.6 percent of the workforce was unemployed over the period 1990–2018, compared to just 5.9 percent in the United States. In that entire period, the unemployment rate was always lower in the United States than in Spain, and it was always lower in the U.S. than in France and Italy except for one relatively short period of time, in the aftermath of the 2008 global financial crisis. Since then, the unemployment gap between the U.S. and Europe increased again. By late 2019, when the unemployment rate in the U.S. was back down to around 3.5 percent—the lowest rate in 50 years—it was around 8.5 percent in France, more than 9.5 percent in Italy, and more than 14 percent in Spain. Figure 20.8, presented later in this chapter, shows recent unemployment rates in five western European countries. As we note there, in recent years, ongoing structural reforms have been improving the unemployment situation in Europe. We also note that by some labor market metrics, such as female participation, Europe does better than the United States.

Given the trend toward increasing wage inequality in the United States and the persistence of high unemployment in Europe, we may conclude that a significant fraction of the industrial world's labor force has not been sharing in the recent economic growth and prosperity.

What explains these trends in employment and wages? In the remainder of the chapter, we will show that a supply and demand analysis of the labor market can help explain these important developments.

RECAP

FIVE IMPORTANT LABOR MARKET TRENDS

1. Over a long period, average real wages have risen substantially both in the United States and in other industrialized countries.
2. Despite the long-term upward trend in real wages, real wage growth has slowed significantly in the United States since the early 1970s.
3. In the United States, wage inequality has increased dramatically in recent decades. The real wages of some unskilled workers have actually declined, while the real wages of skilled and educated workers have continued to rise.
4. Employment has grown substantially in the United States in recent decades. However, the rate of growth has slowed since 2000.
5. Since about 1980, western European nations have experienced very high rates of unemployment and low rates of job creation.

SUPPLY AND DEMAND IN THE LABOR MARKET ⎯

We have seen how supply and demand analysis can be used to determine equilibrium prices and quantities for individual goods and services. The same approach is equally useful for studying labor market conditions. In the market for labor, the "price" is the wage paid to workers in exchange for their services. The wage is expressed per unit of time—for example, per hour or per year. The "quantity" is the amount of labor firms use, which in this book we will generally measure by number of workers employed. Alternatively, we could state the quantity of labor in terms of the number of hours worked; the choice of units is a matter of convenience.

Who are the demanders and suppliers in the labor market? Firms and other employers demand labor in order to produce goods and services. Virtually all of us supply labor during some phase of our lives. Whenever people work for pay, they are supplying labor services at a price equal to the wage they receive. In this chapter, we will discuss both the supply of and demand for labor, with an emphasis on the demand side of the labor market. Changes in the demand for labor turn out to be key in explaining the aggregate trends in wages and employment described in the preceding section.

The labor market is studied by microeconomists as well as macroeconomists, and both use the tools of supply and demand. However, microeconomists focus on issues such as the determination of wages for specific types of jobs or workers. In this chapter, we take the macroeconomic approach and examine factors that affect aggregate, or economywide, trends in employment and wages.

WAGES AND THE DEMAND FOR LABOR

Let's start by thinking about what determines the number of workers employers want to hire at any given wage—that is, the demand for labor. As we will see, the demand for labor depends both on the productivity of labor and the price that the market sets on workers' output. The more productive workers are, or the more valuable the goods and services they produce, the greater the number of workers an employer will want to hire at any given wage.

Table 20.1 shows the relationship between output and the number of workers employed at the Banana Computer Company (BCC), which builds and sells computers. Column 1 of the table shows some different possibilities for the number of technicians BCC could employ in its plant. Column 2 shows how many computers the company can produce each year, depending on the number of workers employed. The more workers, the greater the number of computers BCC can produce. For the sake of simplicity, we assume that the plant, equipment, and materials the workers use to build computers are fixed quantities.

Column 3 of Table 20.1 shows the *marginal product* of each worker, the extra production that is gained by adding one more worker. Note that each additional worker adds less to total production than the previous worker did. The tendency for marginal product to decline as more and more workers are added is called *diminishing returns to labor*. The principle of **diminishing returns to labor** states that if the amount of capital and other inputs in use is held constant, then the greater the quantity of labor already employed, the less each additional worker adds to production.

diminishing returns to labor
if the amount of capital and other inputs in use is held constant, then the greater the quantity of labor already employed, the less each additional worker adds to production

Increasing Opportunity Cost

The principle of diminishing returns to labor is analogous to the principle of diminishing returns to capital discussed in Chapter 19, *Economic Growth, Productivity, and Living Standards.* The economic basis for diminishing returns to labor is the Principle of Increasing Opportunity Cost, also known as the Low-Hanging Fruit Principle. A firm's managers want to use their available inputs in the most productive way possible. Hence, an employer who has one worker will assign that worker to the most productive job. If she hires a second worker, she will assign that worker to the second most productive job. The third worker will be given the third most productive job available, and so on. The greater the number of workers already employed, the lower the marginal product of adding another worker, as shown in Table 20.1.

If BCC computers sell for $3,000 each, then column 4 of Table 20.1 shows the *value of the marginal product* of each worker. The value of a worker's marginal product is the amount of extra revenue that the worker generates for the firm. Specifically, the value of the marginal product of each BCC worker is that worker's marginal product, stated in terms of the number of additional computers produced, multiplied by the price of output (here, $3,000 per computer). We now have all the information necessary to find BCC's demand for workers.

TABLE 20.1
Production and Marginal Product for Banana Computers

(1) Number of workers	(2) Computers produced per year	(3) Marginal product	(4) Value of marginal product (at $3,000/computer)
0	0		
		25	$ 75,000
1	25		
		23	69,000
2	48		
		21	63,000
3	69		
		19	57,000
4	88		
		17	51,000
5	105		
		15	45,000
6	120		
		13	39,000
7	133		
		11	33,000
8	144		

EXAMPLE 20.1   BCC's Demand for Labor

How many workers should BCC hire?

Suppose that the going wage for computer technicians is $60,000 per year. BCC managers know that this is the wage being offered by all their competitors, so they cannot hire qualified workers for less. How many technicians will BCC hire? What would the answer be if the wage were $50,000 per year?

BCC will hire an extra worker if and only if the value of that worker's marginal product (which equals the extra revenue the worker creates for the firm) exceeds the wage BCC must pay. The going wage for computer technicians, which BCC takes as given, is $60,000 per year. Table 20.1 shows that the value of the marginal product of the first, second, and third workers each exceeds $60,000. Hiring these workers will be profitable for BCC because the extra revenue each generates exceeds the wage that BCC must pay. However, the fourth worker's marginal product is worth only $57,000. If BCC's managers hired a fourth worker, they would be paying $60,000 in extra wages for additional output that is worth only $57,000. Since hiring the fourth worker is a money-losing proposition, BCC will hire only three workers. Thus the quantity of labor BCC demands when the going wage is $60,000 per year is three technicians.

If the market wage for computer technicians were $50,000 per year instead of $60,000, the fourth technician would be worth hiring since the value of the fourth technician's marginal product, $57,000, would be $7,000 more than the fourth technician's wages. The fifth technician would also be worth hiring since the fifth worker's marginal product is worth $51,000—$1,000 more than the going wage. The value of the marginal product of a sixth technician, however, is only $45,000, so hiring a sixth worker would not be profitable. When wages are $50,000 per year then, BCC's labor demand is five technicians.

✔ SELF-TEST 20.1

Continuing with Example 20.1, how many workers will BCC hire if the going wage for technicians is $35,000 per year?

The lower the wage a firm must pay, the more workers it will hire. Thus the demand for labor is like the demand for other goods or services in that the quantity demanded rises as the price (in this case, the wage) falls. Figure 20.1 shows a hypothetical labor demand curve for a firm or industry, with the wage on the vertical axis and employment on the horizontal axis. All else being equal, the higher the wage, the fewer workers a firm or industry will demand.

FIGURE 20.1

The Demand Curve for Labor.
The demand curve for labor is downward-sloping. The higher the wage, the fewer workers employers will hire.

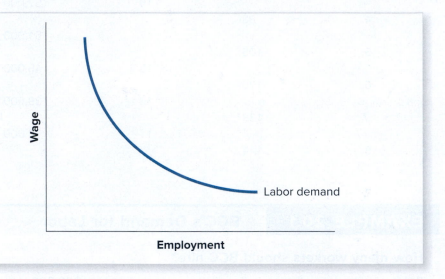

In our example thus far, we have discussed how labor demand depends on the *nominal,* or dollar, wage and the *nominal* price of workers' output. Equivalently, we could have expressed the wage and the price of output in *real* terms—that is, measured relative to the average price of goods and services. The wage measured relative to the general price level is the *real wage;* as we saw in Chapter 18, *Measuring the Price Level and Inflation,* the real wage expresses the wage in terms of its purchasing power. The price of a specific good or service measured relative to the general price level is called the *relative price* of that good or service. Because our main interest is in real rather than nominal wages, from this point on we will analyze the demand for labor in terms of the real wage and the relative price of workers' output, rather than in terms of nominal variables.

SHIFTS IN THE DEMAND FOR LABOR

The number of workers that BCC will employ at any given real wage depends on the value of their marginal product, as shown in column 4 of Table 20.1. Changes in the economy that increase the value of workers' marginal product will increase the value of extra workers to BCC, and thus BCC's demand for labor at any given real wage. In other words, any factor that raises the value of the marginal product of BCC's workers will shift BCC's labor demand curve to the right.

Two main factors could increase BCC's labor demand:

1. An increase in the relative price of the company's output (computers).
2. An increase in the productivity of BCC's workers.

The next two examples illustrate both of these possibilities.

EXAMPLE 20.2   Relative Price and an Increase in Demand

Will BCC hire more workers if the price of computers rises?

Suppose an increase in the demand for BCC's computers raises the relative price of its computers to $5,000 each. How many technicians will BCC hire now, if the real wage is $60,000 per year? If the real wage is $50,000?

The effect of the increase in computer prices is shown in Table 20.2. Columns 1 to 3 of the table are the same as in Table 20.1. The number of computers a given number of technicians can build (column 2) has not changed; hence, the marginal product of particular technicians (column 3) is the same. But because computers can now be sold for $5,000 each instead of $3,000, the *value* of each worker's marginal product has increased by two-thirds (compare column 4 of Table 20.2 with column 4 of Table 20.1).

How does the increase in the relative price of computers affect BCC's demand for labor? Recall from Example 20.1 that when the price of computers was $3,000 and the going wage for technicians was $60,000, BCC's demand for labor was three workers. But now, with computers selling for $5,000 each, the value of the marginal product of each of the first seven workers exceeds $60,000 (Table 20.2). So if the real wage of computer technicians is still $60,000, BCC would increase its demand from three workers to seven.

Suppose instead that the going real wage for technicians is $50,000. In the previous example, when the price of computers was $3,000 and the wage was $50,000, BCC demanded five workers. But if computers sell for $5,000, we can see from column 4 of Table 20.2 that the value of the marginal product of even the eighth worker exceeds the wage of $50,000. So if the real wage is $50,000, the increase in computer prices raises BCC's demand for labor from five workers to eight.

TABLE 20.2
Production and Marginal Product for Banana Computers after an Increase in Computer Prices

(1) Number of workers	(2) Computers produced per year	(3) Marginal product	(4) Value of marginal product ($5,000/computer)
0	0		
		25	$125,000
1	25		
		23	115,000
2	48		
		21	105,000
3	69		
		19	95,000
4	88		
		17	85,000
5	105		
		15	75,000
6	120		
		13	65,000
7	133		
		11	55,000
8	144		

SELF-TEST 20.2

Refer to Example 20.2. How many workers will BCC hire if the going real wage for technicians is $100,000 per year and the relative price of computers is $5,000? Compare your answer to the demand for technicians at a wage of $100,000 when the price of computers is $3,000.

The general conclusion to be drawn from Example 20.2 is that *an increase in the relative price of workers' output increases the demand for labor,* shifting the labor demand curve to the right, as shown in Figure 20.2. A higher relative price for workers' output makes workers more valuable, leading employers to demand more workers at any given real wage.

FIGURE 20.2

A Higher Relative Price of Output Increases the Demand for Labor.

An increase in the relative price of workers' output increases the value of their marginal product, shifting the labor demand curve to the right.

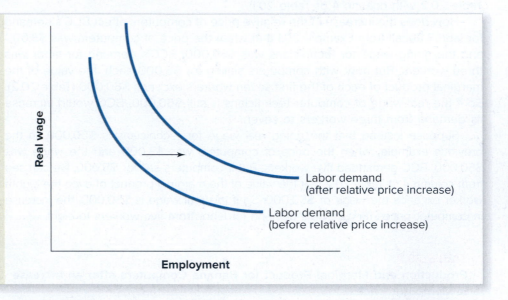

The second factor that affects the demand for labor is worker productivity. Since an increase in productivity increases the value of a worker's marginal product, it also increases the demand for labor, as Example 20.3 shows.

| **EXAMPLE 20.3** | **Worker Productivity and Demand for Labor** |

Will BCC hire more workers if their productivity rises?

Suppose BCC adopts a new technology that reduces the number of components to be assembled, permitting each technician to build 50 percent more machines per year. Assume that the relative price of computers is $3,000 per machine. How many technicians will BCC hire if the real wage is $60,000 per year?

Table 20.3 shows workers' marginal products and the value of their marginal products after the 50 percent increase in productivity, assuming that computers sell for $3,000 each.

Before the productivity increase, BCC would have demanded three workers at a wage of $60,000 (Table 20.1). After the productivity increase, however, the value of the marginal product of the first six workers exceeds $60,000 (see Table 20.3, column 4). So at a wage of $60,000, BCC's demand for labor increases from three workers to six.

TABLE 20.3

Production and Marginal Product for Banana Computers after an Increase in Worker Productivity

(1) Number of workers	(2) Computers produced per year	(3) Marginal product	(4) Value of marginal product (at $3,000/computer)
0	0		
		37.5	$112,500
1	37.5		
		34.5	103,500
2	72		
		31.5	94,500
3	103.5		
		28.5	85,500
4	132		
		25.5	76,500
5	157.5		
		22.5	67,500
6	180		
		19.5	58,500
7	199.5		
		16.5	49,500
8	216		

 SELF-TEST 20.3

Refer to Example 20.3. How many workers will BCC hire after the 50 percent increase in productivity if the going real wage for technicians is $50,000 per year? Compare this figure to the demand for workers at a $50,000 wage before the increase in productivity.

In general, *an increase in worker productivity increases the demand for labor,* shifting the labor demand curve to the right, as in Figure 20.3.

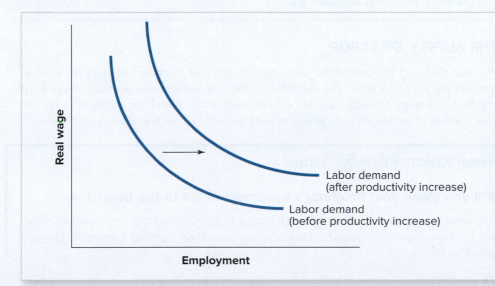

Labor demand
(after productivity increase)

Labor demand
(before productivity increase)

Employment

FIGURE 20.3

Higher Productivity Increases the Demand for Labor.

An increase in productivity raises workers' marginal product and—assuming no change in the price of output—the value of their marginal product. Since a productivity increase raises the value of marginal product, employers will hire more workers at any given real wage, shifting the labor demand curve to the right.

In Example 20.3, the increase in worker productivity that increases the demand for labor is due to the adoption of new technology. But sometimes, new technology can *reduce* the demand for certain workers, as we discuss in The Economic Naturalist 20.1.

The Economic Naturalist 20.1

Can new technology hurt workers?

Technological progress typically makes workers more productive. Examples are abundant. Electric hair dryers and hair clippers, invented more than a hundred years ago by individuals seeking to improve barber tools, make hairstylists more productive. The Global Positioning System (GPS), a satellite-based navigation system developed by the U.S. government a few decades ago, makes drivers more productive. Larger-scale examples include momentous breakthroughs like electricity, the engine, aviation, computing, mobile communication, modern medicine—and the list is still long.

But sometimes, automation and technical innovation can substitute certain types of workers, reducing the demand for such workers. From these workers' point of view, opposing new technology could be rational.

History is replete with examples of workers who opposed new technologies out of fear that their skills would become less valuable. In England in the early nineteenth century, rioting workers destroyed newly introduced labor-saving machinery. The name of the workers' reputed leader, Ned Ludd, has been preserved in the term *Luddite,* meaning a person who is opposed to the introduction of new technologies. The same theme appears in American folk history in the tale of John Henry, the mighty pile-driving man who died in an attempt to show that a human could tunnel into a rock face more quickly than a steam-powered machine.

More recently, some production and service workers have expressed concerns that automation, robotics, and artificial intelligence (AI) may "steal" their jobs. For example, some commercial drivers worry that autonomous cars may eliminate demand for their services. While many technologies unambiguously help drivers— GPS navigation and ride-sharing apps on smartphones, advanced driving-assistance systems in cars, and, of course, cars themselves—some technologies can hurt them.

Historically, the loss of jobs to new technologies has, on average, been compensated by new jobs created by technology. The overall demand for labor has not decreased, unemployment has remained low, and average real wages have risen. But while the average worker is typically much better off with new technology, not all workers are. Later in this chapter, we discuss the role of technology in increasing economic inequalities.

THE SUPPLY OF LABOR

We have discussed the demand for labor by employers; to complete the story we need to consider the supply of labor. The suppliers of labor are workers and potential workers. At any given real wage, potential suppliers of labor must decide if they are willing to work. The total number of people who are willing to work at each real wage is the supply of labor.[2]

EXAMPLE 20.4 | **Reservation Price for Labor**

Will you clean your neighbor's basement or go to the beach?

You were planning to go to the beach today, but your neighbor asks you to clean out his basement. You like the beach a lot more than fighting cobwebs. Do you take the job?

---

[2]We are still holding the general price level constant, so any increase in the nominal wage also represents an increase in the real wage.

Unless you are motivated primarily by neighborliness, your answer to this job offer would probably be "It depends on how much my neighbor will pay." You probably would not be willing to take the job for $10 or $20 unless you have a severe and immediate need for cash. But if your neighbor were wealthy and eccentric enough to offer you $500 (to take an extreme example), you would very likely say yes. Somewhere between $20 and the unrealistic figure of $500 is the minimum payment you would be willing to accept to tackle the dirty basement. This minimum payment, the *reservation price* you set for your labor, is the compensation level that leaves you just indifferent between working and not working.

In economic terms, deciding whether to work at any given wage is a straightforward application of the Cost-Benefit Principle. The cost to you of cleaning out the basement is the opportunity cost of your time (you would rather be surfing) plus the cost you place on having to work in unpleasant conditions. You can measure this total cost in dollars simply by asking yourself, "What is the minimum amount of money I would take to clean out the basement instead of going to the beach?" The minimum payment that you would accept is the same as your reservation price. The benefit of taking the job is measured by the pay you receive, which will go toward that new smartphone you want. You should take the job only if the promised pay (the benefit of working) exceeds your reservation price (the cost of working).

Cost-Benefit

In this example, your willingness to supply labor is greater the higher the wage. In general, the same is true for the population as a whole. Certainly people work for many reasons, including personal satisfaction, the opportunity to develop skills and talents, and the chance to socialize with coworkers. Still, for most people, income is one of the principal benefits of working, so the higher the real wage, the more willing they are to sacrifice other possible uses of their time. The fact that people are more willing to work when the wage they are offered is higher is captured in the upward slope of the supply curve of labor (see Figure 20.4).

Might accepting a job that pays no salary ever be a good career move?

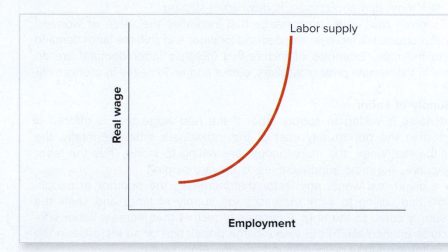

FIGURE 20.4

The Supply of Labor.

The labor supply curve is upward-sloping because, in general, the higher the real wage, the more people are willing to work.

✔ **SELF-TEST 20.4**

You want to make a career in broadcasting. The local radio station is offering an unpaid summer internship that would give you valuable experience. Your alternative to the internship is to earn $3,000 working in a car wash. How would you decide which job to take? Would a decision to take the internship contradict the conclusion that the labor supply curve is upward-sloping?

SHIFTS IN THE SUPPLY OF LABOR

Any factor that affects the quantity of labor offered at a given real wage will shift the labor supply curve. At the macroeconomic level, the most important factor affecting the supply of labor is the size of the working-age population, which is influenced by factors such as the domestic birthrate, immigration and emigration rates, and the ages at which people normally first enter the workforce and retire. All else being equal, an increase in the working-age population raises the quantity of labor supplied at each real wage, shifting the labor supply curve to the right. Changes in the percentage of people of working age who seek employment—for example, as a result of social changes that encourage women to work outside the home—can also affect the supply of labor.

Now that we have discussed both the demand for and supply of labor, we are ready to apply supply and demand analysis to real-world labor markets. But first, try your hand at using supply and demand analysis to answer the following question.

 SELF-TEST 20.5

Labor unions typically favor tough restrictions on immigration, while employers tend to favor more liberal rules. Why? (*Hint:* How is an influx of potential workers likely to affect real wages?)

RECAP ↑

SUPPLY AND DEMAND IN THE LABOR MARKET

The Demand for Labor

The extra production gained by adding one more worker is the *marginal product* of that worker. The *value of the marginal product* of a worker is that worker's marginal product times the relative price of the firm's output. A firm will employ a worker only if the worker's value of marginal product, which is the same as the extra revenue the worker generates for the firm, exceeds the real wage that the firm must pay. The lower the real wage, the more workers the firm will find it profitable to employ. Thus the labor demand curve, like most demand curves, is downward-sloping.

For a given real wage, any change that increases the value of workers' marginal products will increase the demand for labor and shift the labor demand curve to the right. Examples of factors that increase labor demand are an increase in the relative price of workers' output and an increase in productivity.

The Supply of Labor

An individual is willing to supply labor if the real wage that is offered is greater than the opportunity cost of the individual's time. Generally, the higher the real wage, the more people are willing to work. Thus the labor supply curve, like most supply curves, is upward-sloping.

For a given real wage, any factor that increases the number of people available and willing to work increases the supply of labor and shifts the labor supply curve to the right. Examples of factors that increase labor supply include an increase in the working-age population or an increase in the share of the working-age population seeking employment.

EXPLAINING THE TRENDS IN REAL WAGES AND EMPLOYMENT

We are now ready to analyze the important trends in real wages and employment discussed earlier in the chapter.

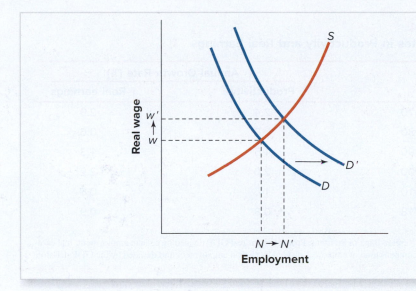

FIGURE 20.5

An Increase in Productivity Raises the Real Wage.

An increase in productivity raises the demand for labor, shifting the labor demand curve from *D* to *D'*. The real wage rises from *w* to *w'*, and employment rises from *N* to *N'*.

LARGE INCREASES IN REAL WAGES IN INDUSTRIALIZED COUNTRIES

As we discussed, real annual earnings in the United States have increased more than fivefold since 1929, and other industrialized countries have experienced similar gains. These increases have greatly improved the standard of living of workers in these countries. Why have real wages increased by so much in the United States and other industrialized countries?

The large increase in real wages results from the sustained growth in productivity experienced by the industrialized countries during the twentieth century. (We mentioned this growth in productivity in Chapter 16, *Macroeconomics: The Bird's-Eye View of the Economy*, and discussed its determinants and consequences in Chapter 19, *Economic Growth, Productivity, and Living Standards*.) As illustrated by Figure 20.5, increased productivity raises the demand for labor, increasing employment and the real wage.

Of the factors contributing to productivity growth in the industrialized countries, two of the most important were (1) the dramatic technological progress that occurred during the twentieth century and (2) large increases in capital stocks, which provided workers with more and better tools with which to work. Labor supply increased during the century as well, of course (not shown in the diagram). However, the increases in labor demand, driven by rapidly expanding productivity, have been so great as to overwhelm the depressing effect on real wages of increased labor supply.

REAL WAGE GROWTH IN THE UNITED STATES HAS STAGNATED SINCE THE EARLY 1970S, WHILE EMPLOYMENT GROWTH HAS BEEN RAPID

With the exception of the late 1990s, rates of real wage growth after 1973 in the United States have been significantly lower than in previous decades. But over much of the period, the economy has created new jobs at a record rate. What accounts for these trends?

Let's begin with the slowdown in real wage growth since the early 1970s. Supply and demand analysis tells us that a slowdown in real wage growth must result from slower growth in the demand for labor, more rapid growth in the supply of labor, or both. On the demand side, since the early 1970s the United States and other industrialized nations have experienced a slowdown in productivity growth. Thus, one possible explanation for the slowdown in the growth of real wages since the early 1970s is the decline in the pace of productivity gains.

Some evidence for a relationship between productivity and real wages is given in Table 20.4, which shows the average annual growth rates in labor productivity and real annual earnings for each decade since 1960. You can see that the growth in productivity

TABLE 20.4
Growth Rates in Productivity and Real Earnings

	Annual Growth Rate (%)	
	Productivity	Real earnings
1960–1970	2.4	2.9
1970–1980	0.8	0.6
1980–1990	1.5	1.3
1990–2000	2.0	2.2
2000–2010	1.6	0.8
2010–2018	0.8	0.9

Source: Federal Reserve Bank of St. Louis. Productivity is real GDP divided by civilian employment; real earnings equal total compensation of employees divided by civilian employment and deflated by the GDP deflator.

decade by decade corresponds closely to the growth in real earnings. Particularly striking is the rapid growth of both productivity and wages during the 1960s. Since the 1970s, growth in both productivity and real wages has been significantly slower, although some improvement was apparent in the 1990s.

While the effects of the slowdown in productivity on the demand for labor are an important reason for declining real wage growth, they can't be the whole story. We know this because, with labor supply held constant, slower growth in labor demand would lead to reduced rates of employment growth, as well as reduced growth in real wages. But job growth in the United States has been rapid in recent decades. Large increases in employment in the face of slow growth of labor demand can be explained only by simultaneous increases in the supply of labor (see Self-Test 20.6).

Labor supply in the United States does appear to have grown rapidly until recently. In particular, increased participation in the labor market by women increased the U.S. supply of labor from the mid-1970s to the late 1990s. Other factors, including the coming of age of the baby boomers and high rates of immigration, also help explain the increase in the supply of labor during those years. The combination of slower growth in labor demand (the result of the productivity slowdown) and accelerated growth in labor supply (the result of increased participation by women in the workforce, together with other factors) helps explain why real wage growth was sluggish for many years in the United States, even as employment grew rapidly.

What about the 2000s? Here the story is different. On the supply side, the participation rate of women in the workforce leveled off and then started slowly declining in the 2000s. This trend reversal, together with the aging population and other factors, slowed down the growth of labor supply. With tightening supply, why was earnings growth so disappointing? Part of the answer is slowing productivity gains. But again, productivity alone cannot be the whole story: As Table 20.4 shows, while increasing more slowly than in the 1990s, on average productivity still grew during the 2000s about twice as fast as real earnings, before slowing further in the 2010s. So another part of the answer must be that the demand for labor slowed more than the supply of labor for reasons other than productivity. One reason could be weak demand for the products of labor—namely, for goods and services. Consistent with this explanation, the 2000s started with a mild recession and ended with a severe one. (Recessions are periods of particularly weak demand, as we will see in later chapters.)

What about the 2010s and the future? As we have seen, labor supply growth is likely to continue slowing as the baby boomers retire. Productivity gains in the 2010s have so far been disappointing, in spite of the 2010s seeing the longest expansion on record. (Expansions, in contrast with recessions, are the periods of growth in demand.) If productivity starts accelerating again, perhaps reflecting the benefits of new technologies, among other factors, there seems a good chance that the more rapid increases in real wages that began around 1996 will return in years to come.

✓ **SELF-TEST 20.6**

As we have just discussed, relatively weak growth in productivity and relatively strong growth in labor supply after about 1973 can explain (1) the slowdown in real wage growth and (2) the more rapid expansion in employment after about 1973. Show this point graphically by drawing two supply and demand diagrams of the labor market, one corresponding to the period 1960–1973 and the other to 1973–1995. Assuming that productivity growth was strong but labor supply growth was modest during 1960–1973, show that we would expect to see rapid real wage growth but only moderate growth in employment in that period. Now apply the same analysis to 1973–1995, assuming that productivity growth is weaker but labor supply growth stronger than in 1960–1973. What do you predict for growth in the real wage and employment in 1973–1995 relative to the earlier period? What could account for increased real wage growth in the late 1990s?

INCREASING WAGE INEQUALITY: THE EFFECTS OF GLOBALIZATION AND TECHNOLOGICAL CHANGE

Another important trend in U.S. labor markets is increasing inequality in wages, especially the tendency for the wages of the less-skilled and less-educated to fall further and further behind those of better-trained workers. We next discuss two reasons for this increasing inequality: (1) globalization and (2) technological change.

Globalization

Many commentators have blamed the increasing divergence between the wages of skilled and unskilled workers on the phenomenon of "globalization." This term, which became popular in the late 1990s, refers to the fact that to an increasing extent, the markets for many goods and services are becoming international, rather than national or local, in scope. While Americans have long been able to buy products from all over the world, the ease with which goods and services can cross borders in recent decades has been increasing rapidly. In part, this trend is the result of international trade agreements, which reduced taxes on goods and services traded across countries. However, technological advances such as the Internet (which emerged in the 1990s) have also promoted globalization.

The main economic benefit of globalization is increased specialization and the efficiency that it brings. Instead of each country trying to produce everything its citizens consume, each can concentrate on producing those goods and services at which it is relatively most efficient. As implied by the Principle of Comparative Advantage, the result is that consumers of all countries enjoy a greater variety of goods and services, of better quality and at lower prices, than they would without international trade.

Comparative Advantage

The effects of globalization on the *labor* market are mixed, however, which explains why many politicians oppose free-trade agreements. Expanded trade means that consumers stop buying certain goods and services from domestic producers and switch to foreign-made products. Consumers would not make this switch unless the foreign products were better, cheaper, or both, so expanded trade clearly makes them better off. But the workers and firm owners in the domestic industries that lose business may well suffer from the increase in foreign competition.

The effects of increasing trade on the labor market can be analyzed using Figure 20.6. The figure contrasts the supply and demand for labor in two different industries, (a) textiles and (b) computer software. Imagine that, initially, there is little or no international trade in these two goods. Without trade, the demand for workers in each industry is indicated by the curves marked $D_{textiles}$ and $D_{software}$, respectively. Wages and employment in each industry are determined by the intersection of the demand curves and the labor supply curves in each industry. As we have drawn the figure, initially, the real wage is the same in both industries, equal to w. Employment is $N_{textiles}$ in textiles and $N_{software}$ in software.

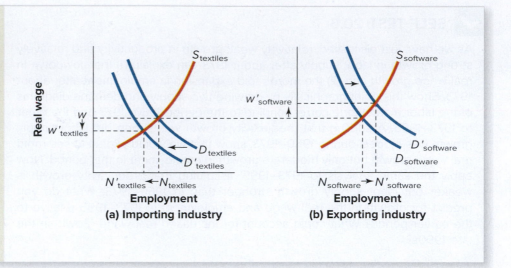

(a) Importing industry

(b) Exporting industry

What will happen when this economy is opened up to trade, perhaps because of a free-trade agreement? Under the agreement, countries will begin to produce for export those goods or services at which they are relatively more efficient and to import goods or services that they are relatively less efficient at producing. Suppose the country in this example is relatively more efficient at producing software than manufacturing textiles. With the opening of trade, the country gains new foreign markets for its software and begins to produce for export as well as for domestic use. Meanwhile, because the country is relatively less efficient at producing textiles, consumers begin to purchase foreign-made textiles, which are cheaper or of higher quality, instead of the domestic product. In short, software becomes an exporting industry and textiles an importing industry.

These changes in the demand for domestic products are translated into changes in the demand for labor. The opening of export markets increases the demand for domestic software, raising its relative price. The higher price for domestic software, in turn, raises the value of the marginal products of software workers, shifting the labor demand curve in the software industry to the right, from $D_{software}$ to $D'_{software}$ in Figure 20.6(b). Wages in the software industry rise, from w to $w'_{software}$, and employment in the industry rises as well. In the textile industry the opposite happens. Demand for domestic textiles falls as consumers switch to imports. The relative price of domestic textiles falls with demand, reducing the value of the marginal product of textile workers and hence the demand for their labor, to $D'_{textiles}$ in Figure 20.6(a). Employment in the textile industry falls, and the real wage falls as well, from w to $w'_{textiles}$.

In sum, Figure 20.6 shows how globalization can contribute to increasing wage inequality. Initially, we assumed that software workers and textile workers received the same wage. However, the opening up of trade raised the wages of workers in the "winning" industry (software) and lowered the wages of workers in the "losing" industry (textiles), increasing inequality.

In practice, the tendency of trade to increase wage inequality may be even worse than depicted in the example, because the great majority of the world's workers, particularly those in developing countries, have relatively low skill levels. Thus, when industrialized countries like the United States open up trade with developing countries, the domestic industries that are likely to face the toughest international competition are those that use mostly low-skilled labor. Conversely, the domestic industries that are likely to do the best in international competition are those that employ mostly skilled workers. Thus increased trade may lower the wages of those workers in the industrialized country who are already poorly paid and increase the wages of those who are well paid.

The fact that increasing trade may exacerbate wage inequality explains some of the political resistance to globalization. Such resistance is seen in recent years in the U.S., Europe, and other countries around the world, where voters show strong support for political candidates who promise to reverse the trend. Perhaps most consequential, in the "Brexit" (short for British exit) referendum of 2016, voters in the United Kingdom voted for withdrawal from the European Union. While the vote had many different reasons that are still being studied, it clearly expressed an anti-globalization sentiment—for example, in the form of anti-immigration positions, often in the context of labor market concerns. In the United States, in the 2016 election, presidential candidates of both parties opposed ratification of a comprehensive Asian trade agreement, the Trans-Pacific Partnership (TPP). And since his election, President Trump has shown a willingness to impose tariffs on imports for economic and political purposes and to resist increased economic integration of the U.S. with China and other trading partners.

But attempts to reverse the trend of globalization, if they succeed, would come with their own costs to society because increasing trade and specialization is a major source of improvement in living standards in the United States, Europe, the United Kingdom, and other countries. Indeed, the economic forces behind globalization—primarily, the desire of consumers for better and cheaper products and of producers for new markets—are so powerful that the process would be hard to stop even if government officials were determined to do so.

Rather than trying to stop globalization, helping the labor market adjust to the effects of globalization may be a better course. Indeed, our analysis of supply and demand in the labor market suggests that to a certain extent, *at least in theory,* the economy will adjust on its own. Figure 20.6 showed that, following the opening to trade, real wages and employment fall in (a) textiles and rise in (b) software. At that point, wages and job opportunities are much more attractive in the software industry than in textiles. Will this situation persist? Clearly, there is a strong incentive for workers who are able to do so to leave the textile industry and seek employment in the software industry.

The movement of workers between jobs, firms, and industries is called **worker mobility.** In our example, worker mobility will tend to reduce labor supply in textiles and increase it in software, as workers move from the contracting industry to the growing one. This process will reverse some of the increase in wage inequality by raising wages in textiles and lowering them in software. It will also shift workers from a less competitive sector to a more competitive sector. To some extent, then, *in theory,* the labor market can adjust on its own to the effects of globalization.

Of course, *in practice,* the adjustment process is never quick, easy, or painless. While left outside our simple supply and demand model, in reality there are many barriers to a textile worker becoming a software engineer. Indeed, as reported in The Economic Naturalist 15.1, empirical evidence suggests that the reallocation of U.S. workers from less competitive sectors to more competitive ones can be painfully slow. In the case of opening up to trade with an economy like China, which has a large supply of low-skill workers, the adjustment of many U.S. workers could be difficult and could take many years.

As we discussed in Chapter 15, *International Trade and Trade Policy,* then, there may also be a need for *transition aid* to workers in the affected sectors. Ideally, such aid helps workers train for and find new jobs. If that is not possible or desirable—say, because a worker is nearing retirement—transition aid can take the form of government payments to help the worker maintain his or her standard of living. In addition, redevelopment aid may be needed in affected communities, as the slow adjustment process of affected workers may come with both economic and social problems. The Efficiency Principle reminds us that transition aid and similar programs are useful because trade and specialization increase the total economic pie. The "winners" from globalization can afford the taxes necessary to finance aid and still enjoy a net benefit from increased trade. Developing effective aid programs is thus a priority.

worker mobility the movement of workers between jobs, firms, and industries

Efficiency

Technological Change

A second source of increasing wage inequality is ongoing technological change that favors more highly skilled or educated workers. As we have seen, new scientific knowledge and the technological advances associated with it are a major source of improved productivity and economic growth. Increases in worker productivity are in turn a driving force behind wage increases and higher average living standards. In the long run and on average, technological progress is undoubtedly the worker's friend.

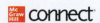

▶ Visit your instructor's Connect
course and access your eBook to
view this video.

Why have the salaries of top earners'
been growing so much faster than everyone else's?

**skill-biased technological
change** technological change
that affects the marginal
products of higher-skilled
workers differently from those
of lower-skilled workers

This sweeping statement is not true at all times and in all places, however. Whether a particular technological development is good for a particular worker depends on the effect of that innovation on the worker's value of marginal product and, hence, on his or her wage. For example, at one time the ability to add numbers rapidly and accurately was a valuable skill; a clerk with that skill could expect advancement and higher wages. However, the invention and mass production of the electronic calculator has rendered human calculating skills less valuable, to the detriment of those who have that skill. The Economic Naturalist 20.1 (on page 534) discussed more examples, from history and present.

How do these observations bear on wage inequality? According to some economists, many recent technological advances have taken the form of **skill-biased technological change**—that is, technological change that affects the marginal product of higher-skilled workers differently from that of lower-skilled workers. Specifically, technological developments in recent decades appear to have favored more-skilled and educated workers.

Developments in automobile production are a case in point. The advent of mass production techniques in the 1920s provided highly paid work for several generations of relatively low-skilled autoworkers. But in recent years automobile production, like the automobiles themselves, has become considerably more sophisticated. The simplest production jobs have been taken over by robots and computer-controlled machinery, which require skilled operatives and engineers who know how to use and maintain the new equipment. Consumer demand for luxury features and customized options has also raised the automakers' demand for highly skilled workers. Thus, in general, the skill requirements for jobs in automobile production have risen.

Figure 20.7 illustrates the effects of technological change that favors skilled workers. Figure 20.7(a) shows the market for unskilled workers; Figure 20.7(b) shows the market for skilled workers. The demand curves labeled $D_{unskilled}$ and $D_{skilled}$ show the demand for each type of worker before a skill-biased technological change. Wages and employment for each type of worker are determined by the intersection of the demand and supply curves in each market. Figure 20.7 shows that, even before the technological change, unskilled workers received lower real wages than skilled workers ($w_{unskilled} < w_{skilled}$), reflecting the lower marginal products of the unskilled.

Now suppose that a new technology—computer-controlled machinery, for example—is introduced. This technological change is biased toward skilled workers, which means that it raises their marginal productivity relative to unskilled workers. We will assume in this example that the new technology also lowers the marginal productivity of unskilled workers, perhaps because they are unable to use the new technology, but all

FIGURE 20.7

The Effect of Skill-Biased Technological Change on Wage Inequality.

The figure shows the effects of a skill-biased technological change that increases the marginal product of skilled workers and reduces the marginal product of unskilled workers. The resulting increase in the demand for skilled workers raises their wages (b), while the decline in demand for unskilled workers reduces their wages (a). Wage inequality increases.

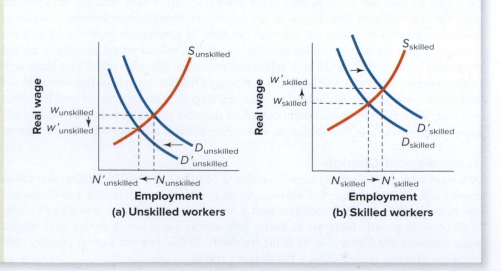

that is necessary for our conclusions is that they benefit less than skilled workers. Figure 20.7 shows the effect of this change in marginal products. In part (b) the increase in the marginal productivity of skilled workers raises the demand for those workers; the demand curve shifts rightward to $D'_{skilled}$. Accordingly, the real wages and employment of skilled workers also rise. In contrast, because they have been made less productive by the technological change, the demand for unskilled workers shifts leftward to $D'_{unskilled}$ [Figure 20.7(a)]. Lower demand for unskilled workers reduces their real wages and employment.

In summary, this analysis supports the conclusion that technological change that is biased in favor of skilled workers will tend to increase the wage gap between the skilled and unskilled. Empirical studies have confirmed the role of skill-biased technological change in recent increases in wage inequality.

Because new technologies that favor skilled workers increase wage inequality, should government regulators act to block them? As in the case of globalization, most economists would argue against trying to block new technologies since technological advances are necessary for economic growth and improved living standards. If the Luddites had somehow succeeded in preventing the introduction of labor-saving machinery in Great Britain, economic growth and development over the past few centuries might have been greatly reduced.

The remedies for the problem of wage inequalities caused by technological change are similar to those for wage inequalities caused by globalization. First among them is worker mobility. As the pay differential between skilled and unskilled work increases, unskilled workers will have a stronger incentive to acquire education and skills, to everyone's benefit. A second remedy is transition aid. Government policymakers should consider programs that will help workers retrain if they are able, or provide income support if they are not.

The Economic Naturalist 20.2

How did the COVID-19 pandemic affect the demand for U.S. jobs?

In the 10 years from February 2010 to February 2020, the U.S. economy created on average 190,000 new jobs each month, or almost 2.3 million new jobs each year. But the streak of good employment news ended in March 2020, when the U.S. was hit by the COVID-19 pandemic. In the course of a single month, almost 1.4 million jobs were eliminated, making it the worst month for job growth since September 1945—when World War II ended and almost two million jobs were eliminated.

The pandemic didn't reduce demand for these workers.

This 1.4-million figure reflects an extraordinarily large *net* reduction in jobs. It suggests that the COVID-19 pandemic as well as people's and governments' reactions to it, had disastrous effects on the *overall* demand for workers. But different jobs fared differently.

As people stayed home to keep the social distancing requirements that stop the virus from spreading, almost two-thirds of the jobs eliminated were in the leisure and hospitality sector. Jobs in restaurants, bars, and other places providing food and drink services were hit especially hard, accounting for more than 90 percent of the lost jobs in that sector. Many of these jobs are low-skilled jobs.

At the same time, the economy created tens of thousands of jobs in other sectors. It is no surprise that new jobs were created in hospitals and outpatient care centers. In addition, as the economy was transitioning to dealing with the pandemic new jobs were added in finance and insurance, management, accounting, computer systems, technical consulting, scientific research and development, data processing, and other information services. Many of these added jobs require education, training, and experience, and some of them can be done from home. But thousands of new jobs were also added that require less skill, including in retail, warehousing, storage, and supermarkets.

These different trends in different parts of the economy continued later on. For example, as tourism plummeted, jobs in airlines and hotels were eliminated with unprecedented speed. At the same time, online shopping increased so dramatically that Amazon announced in mid-March that it was going to hire 100,000 new warehouse and delivery workers. Overall, though, the pandemic's *net* effect on the demand for jobs was unambiguously large and negative. Indeed, the destruction of 1.4 million jobs in March was dwarfed by the destruction of almost 21 million jobs in April. That's almost one in seven U.S. jobs, eliminated in a single month!

These shifts in the demand for labor could have important long-run effects even after the crisis is over. For example, there might be more teleworking and online shopping in the future at the expense of transportation and brick-and-mortar stores. In addition, small businesses that do not survive might result in some industries being more dominated by larger firms. All this remains to be seen.

> **RECAP ↑**
>
> **EXPLAINING THE TRENDS IN REAL WAGES AND EMPLOYMENT**
>
> - The long-term increase in real wages enjoyed by workers in industrial countries results primarily from large productivity gains, which have raised the demand for labor. Technological progress and an expanded and modernized capital stock are two important reasons for these long-term increases in productivity.
> - The slowdown in real wage growth that began in the 1970s resulted in part from the slowdown in productivity growth (and, hence, the slower growth in labor demand) that occurred at about the same time. Increased labor supply, arising from such factors as the increased participation of women and the coming of age of the baby boom generation, depressed real wages further while also expanding employment. In the latter part of the 1990s, resurgence in productivity growth was accompanied by an increase in real wage growth. If such productivity growth returns in years to come, real wages are expected to resume their faster growth. The slower growth in labor supply since around 2000, resulting from a reversal in the earlier participation trends, is expected to further strengthen real wage growth.
> - Both globalization and skill-biased technological change contribute to wage inequality. Globalization raises the wages of workers in exporting industries by raising the demand for those workers, while reducing the wages of workers in importing industries. Technological change that favors more-skilled workers increases the demand for such workers, and hence their wages, relative to the wages of less-skilled workers.
> - Attempting to block either globalization or technological change is not the best response to the problem of wage inequality. To some extent, worker mobility (movement of workers from low-wage to high-wage industries) will offset the inequality created by these forces. Where mobility is not practical, or, as is often the case, is slow, transition aid—government assistance to workers whose employment prospects have worsened—may be the best solution. Developing effective assistance programs is thus a priority.

UNEMPLOYMENT

The concept of the unemployment rate was introduced in Chapter 17, *Measuring Economic Activity: GDP and Unemployment.* To review, government survey takers classify adults as employed (holding a job), unemployed (not holding a job, but looking for one), or not in the labor force (not holding a job and not looking for one—retirees, for example). The labor force consists of the employed and the unemployed. The unemployment rate is the percentage of the labor force that is unemployed.

Unemployment rates differ markedly from country to country. (Different countries measure their unemployment rates in slightly different ways; one should be careful to compare only unemployment rates that are either measured similarly or adjusted to be comparable.) Unemployment rates also vary with time. In the United States, unemployment rates reached historic lows in 2000—4 percent of the labor force—but were almost 2.5 times higher a decade later—reaching 9.6 percent in 2010—before gradually declining to become the lowest in 50 years—3.5 percent in late 2019. In many western European countries, unemployment rates for many years have been two to three times the U.S. rate (the years following the 2007–2009 recession were an exception). In Europe, unemployment is exceptionally high among young people.

A high unemployment rate has serious economic, psychological, and social costs. Understanding the causes of unemployment and finding ways to reduce it are therefore major concerns of macroeconomists. In the remainder of this chapter we discuss the causes and costs of three types of unemployment, and we will also consider some features of labor markets that may exacerbate the problem.

TYPES OF UNEMPLOYMENT AND THEIR COSTS

Economists have found it useful to think of unemployment as being of three broad types: *frictional* unemployment, *structural* unemployment, and *cyclical* unemployment. Each type of unemployment has different causes and imposes different economic and social costs.

Frictional Unemployment

The function of the labor market is to match available jobs with available workers. If all jobs and workers were the same, or if the set of jobs and workers were static and unchanging, this matching process would be quick and easy. But the real world is more complicated. In practice, both jobs and workers are highly *heterogeneous*. Jobs differ in their location, in the skills they require, in their working conditions and hours, and in many other ways. Workers differ in their career aspirations, their skills and experience, their preferred working hours, their willingness to travel, and so on.

The real labor market is also *dynamic*, or constantly changing and evolving. On the demand side of the labor market, technological advances, globalization, and changing consumer tastes spur the creation of new products, new firms, and even new industries, while outmoded products, firms, and industries disappear. Thus CD players replaced record players and then were replaced by media-playing apps and streaming services. As a result of this upheaval, new jobs are constantly being created, while some old jobs cease to be viable. The workforce in a modern economy is equally dynamic. People move, gain new skills, leave the labor force for a time to rear children or go back to school, and even change careers.

Because the labor market is heterogeneous and dynamic, the process of matching jobs with workers often takes time. For example, a software engineer who loses or quits her job in Silicon Valley may take weeks or even months to find an appropriate new job. In her search, she will probably consider alternative areas of software development or even totally new challenges. She may also want to think about different regions of the country in which software companies are located, such as North Carolina's Research Triangle or New York City's Silicon Alley. During the period in which she is searching for a new job, she is counted as unemployed.

Short-term unemployment that is associated with the process of matching workers with jobs is called **frictional unemployment.** The *costs* of frictional unemployment are low and may even be negative; that is, frictional unemployment may be economically beneficial. First, frictional unemployment is short term, so its psychological effects and direct economic losses are minimal. Second, to the extent that the search process leads to a better match between worker and job, a period of frictional unemployment is actually productive, in the sense that it leads to higher output over the long run. Indeed, a certain amount of frictional unemployment seems essential to the smooth functioning of a rapidly changing, dynamic economy.

frictional unemployment
the short-term unemployment associated with the process of matching workers with jobs

Structural Unemployment

structural unemployment
the long-term and chronic unemployment that exists even when the economy is producing at a normal rate

A second major type of unemployment is **structural unemployment,** or the long-term and chronic unemployment that exists even when the economy is producing at a normal rate. Several factors contribute to structural unemployment. First, a *lack of skills, language barriers,* or *discrimination* keeps some workers from finding stable, long-term jobs. Migrant farmworkers and unskilled construction workers who find short-term or temporary jobs from time to time, but never stay in one job for very long, fit the definition of chronically unemployed.

Second, economic changes sometimes create a *long-term mismatch* between the skills some workers have and the available jobs. The U.S. steel industry, for example, has declined over the years, while the computer software industry has grown rapidly. Ideally, steelworkers who lose their jobs would be able to find new jobs in software firms (worker mobility), so their unemployment would be only frictional in nature. In practice, of course, many ex-steelworkers lack the education, ability, or interest necessary to work in the software industry. Since their skills are no longer in demand, these workers may drift into chronic or long-term unemployment.

Finally, structural unemployment can result from *structural features of the labor market* that act as barriers to employment. Examples of such barriers include laws that limit certain types of government help to people without jobs, thus discouraging people from taking a job (and losing their benefits as a result).

The *costs* of structural unemployment are much higher than those of frictional unemployment. Because structurally unemployed workers do little productive work over long periods, their idleness causes substantial economic losses both to the unemployed workers and to society. Structurally unemployed workers also lose out on the opportunity to develop new skills on the job, and their existing skills wither from disuse. Long spells of unemployment are also much more difficult for workers to handle psychologically than the relatively brief spells associated with frictional unemployment.

Cyclical Unemployment

cyclical unemployment
the extra unemployment that occurs during periods of recession

The third type of unemployment occurs during periods of recession (that is, periods of unusually low production) and is called **cyclical unemployment.** Sharp peaks in unemployment reflect the cyclical unemployment that occurs during recessions. Increases in cyclical unemployment, although they are relatively short-lived, are associated with significant declines in real GDP and are therefore quite costly economically. We will study cyclical unemployment in more detail later in the chapters dealing with booms and recessions.

In principle, frictional, structural, and cyclical unemployment add up to the total unemployment rate. In practice, sharp distinctions often cannot be made between the different categories, so any breakdown of the total unemployment rate into the three types of unemployment is necessarily subjective and approximate.

IMPEDIMENTS TO FULL EMPLOYMENT

In discussing structural unemployment, we mentioned that structural features of the labor market may contribute to long-term and chronic unemployment. One such structural feature is the availability of *unemployment insurance,* or government transfer payments to unemployed workers. Unemployment insurance provides an important social benefit in that it helps the unemployed to maintain a decent standard of living while they are looking for a job. But because its availability allows the unemployed to search longer or less intensively for a job, it may lengthen the average amount of time the typical unemployed worker is without a job.

Most economists would argue that unemployment insurance should be generous enough to provide basic support to the unemployed but not so generous as to remove the incentive to actively seek work. Thus, unemployment insurance should last for only a limited time, and its benefits should not be as high as the income a worker receives when working.

Many other government regulations bear on the labor market. They include *health and safety regulations,* which establish the safety standards employers must follow, and rules that prohibit racial or gender-based discrimination in hiring. Many of these regulations are beneficial. In some cases, however, the costs of complying with regulations may exceed the benefits they provide. Further, to the extent that regulations increase employer costs and reduce productivity, they depress the demand for labor, lowering real wages and contributing to unemployment. For maximum economic efficiency, legislators should use cost-benefit criterion when deciding what regulations to impose on the labor market.

≪≪   **Cost-Benefit**

The points raised in this section can help us understand one of the important labor market trends discussed earlier in the chapter, namely, the persistence of high unemployment in western Europe. For several decades, unemployment has been exceptionally high in the major countries of western Europe, as Figure 20.8 shows. The figure shows "harmonized unemployment rates"—unemployment rates that are calculated by applying a uniform definition to data from different countries, facilitating comparisons. From 1995 to 2005, for example, the harmonized unemployment rate was roughly in the range 8–11 percent in Germany, 9–12 percent in France, 8–11 percent in Italy, and 9–21 percent in Spain, compared with 5–6 percent in the U.S. In the 1950s, 1960s, and 1970s, western Europe consistently enjoyed very low unemployment rates. Why has European unemployment been so stubbornly high for the past decades?

One explanation for the high unemployment in major western European countries is the existence of structural "rigidities" in their labor markets. Relative to the United States, European labor markets have historically been highly regulated. European governments set rules in matters ranging from the number of weeks of vacation workers must receive to the reasons for which a worker can be dismissed. Minimum wages in Europe are historically high, and unemployment benefits are much more generous than in the United States. European unions are also more powerful than those in the United States; their wage agreements are often extended by law to all firms in the industry, whether or not they are unionized. This lack of flexibility in labor markets has caused higher frictional and structural unemployment.

If European labor markets are historically so dysfunctional, why has serious European unemployment emerged only in the past few decades? One explanation turns on the increasing pace of *globalization* and *skill-biased technological change.* As we saw, these two factors decrease the demand for less-skilled labor relative to the demand for skilled labor. In the United States, falling demand has depressed the wages of the less skilled, increasing wage inequality. But in western Europe, high minimum wages, union contracts, generous unemployment insurance, and other factors may have created a floor for the wage

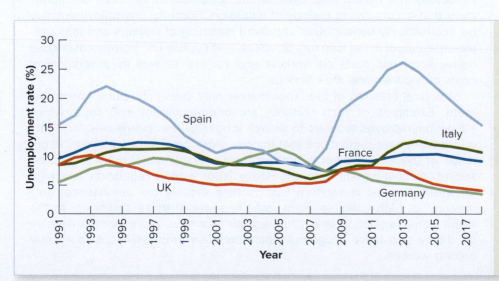

FIGURE 20.8

Unemployment Rates in Western Europe, 1991–2018.

In the largest economies in continental western Europe, unemployment rates have been high in recent decades.

Source: Harmonized unemployment rates, Federal Reserve of St. Louis Economic Data, https://fred.stlouisfed.org.

that firms could pay or that workers would accept. As the marginal productivity of the less skilled dropped below that floor, firms no longer found it profitable to employ those workers, swelling the ranks of the unemployed. Thus the combination of labor market rigidity and the declining marginal productivity of low-skilled workers may be responsible for the European unemployment problem.

Evidence for the idea that inflexible labor markets have contributed to European unemployment comes from the United Kingdom, where the government of Prime Minister Margaret Thatcher instituted a series of reforms beginning in the early 1980s. Britain has since largely deregulated its labor market so that it functions much more like that in the United States. Figure 20.8 shows that unemployment in Britain has gradually declined and is now lower than in other western European countries.

More recently, during 2003–2005, Germany enacted a series of labor market reforms (the "Hartz reforms") under the government of Chancellor Gerhard Schröder. Aimed at increasing the flexibility of Germany's labor markets, the reforms attempted, among other things, to make it easier for employers to hire for short periods and to make it harder for the unemployed to receive generous benefits for long periods. The reforms were controversial, and it is too early for a comprehensive assessment of their long-term impact. That said, as Figure 20.8 shows, the unemployment rate in Germany dropped sharply in the years since the reforms—from above 11 percent in 2005 to below 3.5 percent in 2018—setting Germany apart from the rest of continental Europe's large economies. Most recently, in the past decade (in the aftermath of the global recession following the 2008 financial crisis), countries in southern Europe have been implementing substantial labor market deregulation, including France, Spain, Italy, Greece, and Portugal. The effects of these reforms will be closely studied by economists in the next few years. Labor market reforms like those in Europe are examples of *structural policies*.

Finally, we note that on some metrics, Europe's labor market does better than the U.S. labor market. One example is female participation, where policies like greater support for child-care services make it easier for women in Europe to work in the formal labor market. Such policies, too, are examples of structural policies.

RECAP

UNEMPLOYMENT

Economists distinguish among three broad types of unemployment. *Frictional unemployment* is the short-term unemployment that is associated with the process of matching workers with jobs. *Structural unemployment* is the long-term or chronic unemployment that occurs even when the economy is producing at a normal rate. *Cyclical unemployment* is the extra unemployment that occurs during periods of recession. Frictional unemployment may be economically beneficial, as improved matching of workers and jobs may increase output in the long run. Structural and cyclical unemployment impose heavy economic costs on workers and society, as well as psychological costs on workers and their families.

Structural features of the labor market may cause structural unemployment. Examples of such features are unemployment insurance, which allows unemployed workers to search longer or less intensively for a job, and government regulations that impose extra costs on employers. Regulation of the labor market is not necessarily undesirable, but it should be subject to cost-benefit analysis. Heavy labor market regulation and high unionization rates in western Europe help explain the persistence, until recently, of high unemployment rates in some of those countries. At the same time, regulation that requires, for example, more comprehensive child-care and leave programs, could increase employment, in particular among women.

SUMMARY

- For the average person, the most tangible result of economic growth and increasing productivity is the availability of "good jobs at good wages." Over the long run, the U.S. economy has, for the most part, delivered on this promise as both real wages and employment have grown strongly. But while growth in employment has generally been rapid, two worrisome trends dog the U.S. labor market: a slowdown since the early 1970s in the growth of real wages and increasing wage inequality. Western Europe has experienced less wage inequality but significantly higher rates of unemployment than the United States. *(LO1)*

- Trends in real wages and employment can be studied using a supply and demand model of the labor market. The productivity of labor and the relative price of workers' output determine the demand for labor. Employers will hire workers only as long as the value of the marginal product of the last worker hired equals or exceeds the wage the firm must pay. Because of *diminishing returns to labor,* the more workers a firm employs, the less additional product will be obtained by adding yet another worker. The lower the going wage, the more workers will be hired; that is, the demand for labor curve slopes downward. Economic changes that increase the value of labor's marginal product, such as an increase in the relative price of workers' output or an increase in productivity, shift the labor demand curve to the right. Conversely, changes that reduce the value of labor's marginal product shift the labor demand curve to the left. *(LO2)*

- The supply curve for labor shows the number of people willing to work at any given real wage. Since more people will work at a higher real wage, the supply curve is upward-sloping. An increase in the working-age population, or a social change that promotes labor market participation (like increased acceptance of women in the labor force), will raise labor supply and shift the labor supply curve to the right. *(LO2)*

- Improvements in productivity, which raise the demand for labor, account for the bulk of the increase in U.S. real wages over the last century. The slowdown in real wage growth that has occurred in recent decades is the result of slower growth in labor demand, which was caused in turn by a slowdown in the rate of productivity improvement, and of more rapid growth in labor supply. Rapid growth in labor supply, caused by such factors as immigration and increased labor force participation by women, has until recently also contributed to the continued expansion of employment. Recently, however, overall labor force participation has been decreasing. *(LO3)*

- Two reasons for the increasing wage inequality in the United States are economic globalization and *skill-biased technological change.* Both have increased the demand for, and hence the real wages of, relatively skilled and educated workers. Attempting to block globalization and technological change is counterproductive, however, since both factors are essential to economic growth and increased productivity. To some extent, the movement of workers from lower-paying to higher-paying jobs or industries (*worker mobility*) will counteract the trend toward wage inequality. A policy of providing transition aid and training for workers with obsolete skills is a more useful response to the problem. *(LO3)*

- There are three broad types of unemployment: frictional, structural, and cyclical. *Frictional unemployment* is the short-term unemployment associated with the process of matching workers with jobs in a dynamic, heterogeneous labor market. *Structural unemployment* is the long-term and chronic unemployment that exists even when the economy is producing at a normal rate. It arises from a variety of factors, including language barriers, discrimination, structural features of the labor market, lack of skills, or long-term mismatches between the skills workers have and the available jobs. *Cyclical unemployment* is the extra unemployment that occurs during periods of recession. The costs of frictional unemployment are low, as it tends to be brief and to create more productive matches between workers and jobs. But structural unemployment, which is often long term, and cyclical unemployment, which is associated with significant reductions in real GDP, are relatively more costly. *(LO4)*

- Structural features of the labor market that may contribute to unemployment include unemployment insurance, which reduces the incentives of the unemployed to find work quickly, and other government regulations, which—although possibly conferring benefits—increase the costs of employing workers. The labor market "rigidity" created by government regulations and union contracts has historically been more of a problem in western Europe than in the United States, which may account for Europe's high unemployment rates. *(LO4)*

KEY TERMS

cyclical unemployment
diminishing returns to labor

frictional unemployment
skill-biased technological change

structural unemployment
worker mobility

REVIEW QUESTIONS

1. List and discuss the five important labor market trends given in the first section of the chapter. How do these trends either support or qualify the proposition that increasing labor productivity leads to higher standards of living? *(LO1)*

2. Acme Corporation is considering hiring Marisa Fabrizio. Based on her other opportunities in the job market, Marisa has told Acme that she will work for them for $40,000 per year. How should Acme determine whether to employ her? *(LO2)*

3. Why have real wages risen by so much in the United States in the past century? Why did real wage growth slow for 25 years beginning in the early 1970s? What has been happening to real wages recently? *(LO3)*

4. What are two major factors contributing to increased inequality in wages? Briefly, why do these factors raise wage inequality? Contrast possible policy responses to increasing inequality in terms of their effects on economic efficiency. *(LO3)*

5. List three types of unemployment and their causes. Which of these types is economically and socially the least costly? Explain. *(LO4)*

PROBLEMS

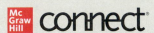

1. Data on the average earnings of people of different education levels are available from the Bureau of the Census (try online at www.census.gov/population/socdemo/education/tableA-3.txt). Using these data, prepare a table showing the earnings of college graduates relative to high school graduates and of college graduates relative to those with less than a high school degree. Show the data for the latest year available and for every fifth year going back to the earliest data available. What are the trends in relative earnings? *(LO1)*

2. Production data for Bob's Bicycle Factory are as follows:

Number of workers	Bikes assembled/day
1	10
2	18
3	24
4	28
5	30

Other than wages, Bob has costs of $100 (for parts and so on) for each bike assembled. *(LO2)*
   a. Bikes sell for $130 each. Find the marginal product and the value of the marginal product for each worker (don't forget about Bob's cost of parts).
   b. Make a table showing Bob's demand curve for labor.
   c. Repeat part b for the case in which bikes sell for $140 each.
   d. Repeat part b for the case in which worker productivity increases by 50 percent. Bikes sell for $130 each.

3. The following table lists labor marginal product per hour of workers in a lightbulb factory. Lightbulbs sell for $2 each, and there are no costs to producing them other than labor costs. *(LO2)*

Number of workers	Marginal product: lightbulbs/hr
1	24
2	22
3	20
4	18
5	16
6	14
7	12
8	10
9	8
10	6

   a. The going hourly wage for factory workers is $24 per hour. How many workers should the factory manager hire? What if the wage is $36 per hour?
   b. Graph the factory's demand for labor.
   c. Repeat part b for the case in which lightbulbs sell for $3 each.
   d. Suppose the supply of factory workers in the town in which the lightbulb factory is located is 8 workers (in other words, the labor supply curve is vertical at 8 workers). What will be the equilibrium real wage for factory workers in the town if lightbulbs sell for $2 each? If they sell for $3 each?

4. How would each of the following factors be likely to affect the economywide supply of labor? *(LO2)*
   a. The age at which people are eligible for Medicare is increased.

b. Increased productivity causes real wages to rise.

c. War preparations lead to the institution of a national draft, and many young people are called up.

d. More people decide to have children (consider both short-run and long-run effects).

e. Social Security benefits are made more generous.

5. How would each of the following likely affect the real wage and employment of unskilled workers on an automobile plant assembly line? *(LO3)*

a. Demand for the type of car made by the plant increases.

b. A sharp increase in the price of gas causes many commuters to switch to mass transit.

c. Robots are introduced to do most basic assembly-line tasks.

6. Skilled or unskilled workers can be used to produce a small toy. Initially, assume that the wages paid to both types of workers are equal. *(LO3)*

a. Suppose that electronic equipment is introduced that increases the marginal product of skilled workers (who can use the equipment to produce more toys per hours worked). The marginal products of unskilled workers are unaffected. Explain, using words and graphs, what happens to the

equilibrium wages are the equilibrium wages for the two groups?

b. Suppose that unskilled workers find it worthwhile to acquire skills when the wage differential between skilled and unskilled workers reaches a certain point. Explain what will happen to the supply of unskilled workers, the supply of skilled workers, and the equilibrium wage for the two groups. In particular, what are the equilibrium wages for skilled workers relative to unskilled workers after some unskilled workers acquire training?

7. For each of the following scenarios, state whether the unemployment is frictional, structural, or cyclical. Justify your answer. *(LO4)*

a. Ted lost his job when the steel mill closed down. He lacks the skills to work in another industry and so has been unemployed over a year.

b. Alice was laid off from her job at the auto plant because the recession reduced the demand for cars. She expects to get her job back when the economy picks up.

c. Tao looked for a job for six weeks after finishing college. He turned down a couple of offers because they didn't let him use the skills he had acquired in college, but is now about to accept a job in the area that he trained for.

ANSWERS TO SELF-TESTS

20.1 The value of the marginal product of the seventh worker is $39,000, and the value of the marginal product of the eighth worker is $33,000. So the seventh but not the eighth worker is profitable to hire at a wage of $35,000. *(LO2)*

20.2 With the computer price at $5,000, it is profitable to hire three workers at a wage of $100,000 since the third worker's value of marginal product ($105,000) exceeds $100,000 but the fourth worker's value of marginal product ($95,000) is less than $100,000. At a computer price of $3,000, we can refer to Table 20.1 to find that not even the first worker has a value of marginal product as high as $100,000, so at that computer price BCC will hire no workers. In short, at a wage of $100,000, the increase in the computer price raises the demand for technicians from zero to three. *(LO2)*

20.3 The seventh but not the eighth worker's value of marginal product exceeds $50,000 (Table 20.3), so it is profitable to hire seven workers if the going wage is $50,000. From Table 20.1, before the increase in productivity, the first five workers have values of marginal product greater than $50,000, so the demand for labor at a given wage of $50,000 is five workers. Thus the increase in productivity raises the quantity of labor

demanded at a wage of $50,000 from five workers to seven workers. *(LO2)*

20.4 Even though you are receiving no pay, the valuable experience you gain as an intern is likely to raise the pay you will be able to earn in the future, so it is an investment in human capital. You also find working in the radio station more enjoyable than working in a car wash, presumably. To decide which job to take, you should ask yourself, "Taking into account both the likely increase in my future earnings and my greater enjoyment from working in the radio station, would I be willing to pay $3,000 to work in the radio station rather than earn $3,000 working in the car wash?" If the answer is yes, then you should work in the radio station; otherwise you should go to the car wash.

A decision to work in the radio station does not contradict the idea of an upward-sloping labor supply curve, if we are willing to think of the total compensation for that job as including not just cash wages but such factors as the value of the training that you receive. Your labor supply curve is still upward-sloping in the sense that the greater the value you place on the internship experience, the more likely you are to accept the job. *(LO2)*

20.5 Immigration to a country raises labor supply—indeed, the search for work is one of the most powerful factors drawing immigrants in the first place. As shown in the accompanying figure, an increase in labor supply will tend to lower the wages that employers have to pay (from w to w'), while raising overall employment (from N to N'). Because of its tendency to reduce real wages, labor unions generally oppose large-scale immigration, while employers support it.

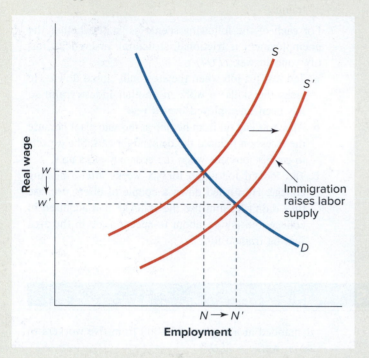

Employment

Although the figure shows the overall, or aggregate, supply of labor in the economy, the specific effects of immigration on wages depend on the skills and occupations of the immigrants. Current U.S. immigration policy makes the reunification of families the main reason for admitting immigrants, and for the most part immigrants are not screened for their education or skills. The U.S. also has a good deal of illegal immigration, made up largely of people looking for economic opportunity. These two factors create a tendency for new immigrants to the United States to be relatively low-skilled. Since immigration tends to increase the supply of unskilled labor by relatively more, it depresses wages of domestic low-skilled workers more than it does the wages of domestic high-skilled workers. Some economists, such as George Borjas of Harvard University, have argued that low-skilled immigration is another important factor reducing the wages of less-skilled workers relative to workers with greater skills and education. Borjas argues that the United States should adopt the approach used by Canada and give preference to potential immigrants with relatively higher levels of skills and education. *(LO2)*

20.6 Part (a) of the accompanying figure shows the labor market in 1960–1973; part (b) shows the labor market in 1973–1995. For comparability, we set the initial labor supply (S) and demand (D) curves the same in both parts, implying the same initial values of the real wage (w) and employment (N). In part (a), we show the effects of a large increase in labor demand (from D to D'), the result of rapid productivity growth, and a relatively small increase in labor supply (from S to S'). The real wage rises to w' and employment rises to N'. In part (b), we observe the effects of a somewhat smaller increase in labor demand (from D to D'') and a larger increase in labor supply (from S to S''). Part (b), corresponding to the 1973–1995 period, shows a smaller increase in the real wage and a larger increase in employment than part (a), corresponding to 1960–1973. These results are consistent with actual developments in the U.S. labor market over these two periods. Since 1995, more rapid productivity growth, which raises labor demand more quickly, accounts for faster growth in real wages. *(LO3)*

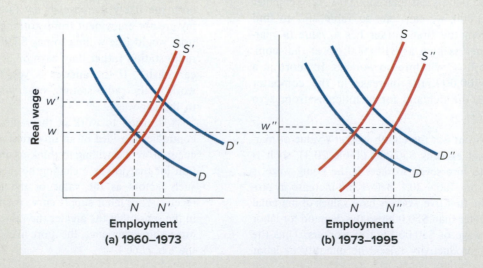

(a) 1960–1973

(b) 1973–1995

CHAPTER 21

Saving and Capital Formation

What is saving and why does it matter?

D. Hurst/Alamy Stock Photo

LEARNING OBJECTIVES

After reading this chapter, you should be able to:

LO1 Explain the relationship between saving and wealth.

LO2 Discuss the reasons people save and how psychological factors influence saving.

LO3 Identify and apply the components of national saving.

LO4 Discuss the reasons firms choose to invest in capital.

LO5 Analyze financial markets using the tools of supply and demand.

You've probably heard Aesop's fable of the ant and the grasshopper. All summer the ant worked hard laying up food for the winter. The grasshopper mocked the ant's efforts and contented himself with basking in the sunshine, ignoring the ant's earnest warnings. When winter came the ant was well-fed, while the grasshopper starved. Moral: When times are good, the wise put aside something for the future.

Of course, there is also the modern ending to the fable, in which the grasshopper breaks his leg by tripping over the anthill, sues the ant for negligence, and ends up living comfortably on the ant's savings. (Nobody knows what happened to the ant.) Moral: Saving is risky; live for today.

The pitfalls of modern life notwithstanding, saving is important, both to individuals and to nations. People need to save to provide for their retirement and for other future needs, such as their children's education or a new home. An individual's or a family's savings can also provide a crucial buffer in the event of an economic emergency, such as the loss of a job or unexpected medical bills. At the national level, the production of new capital goods—factories, equipment, office buildings, and housing—is an important factor promoting economic growth and higher living standards. As we will see in this chapter, the resources necessary to produce new capital come primarily from a nation's collective saving.

Because adequate saving is so important to both ensuring families' financial security and creating new capital goods, many people have expressed concern about the low saving rate of American households. Never very high by international standards, the U.S. household saving rate—the percentage of after-tax household income that is saved—declined from around 13 percent of household disposable income in the early 1970s to around 7 to 8 percent in the past few years. (The household saving rate had reached a low of 3.2 percent in 2005, and then increased during and following the 2007–2009 recession to its current level.)

What is the significance of such a low and declining saving rate? Some see the data as evidence of "grasshopperish" behavior and a threat to Americans' future prosperity. The reality, as we will see, is more complex. Many American families do save very little, a fact that is likely to exact a toll on their economic well-being in the long run. Economists and policymakers are particularly concerned about the low rates among lower-income people (many of whom save little, or none at all). Low saving rates may mean that people fail to build wealth, have reserves for emergencies, or be adequately prepared for retirement. On the other hand, at the aggregate level, household saving is only one part of the total saving of the U.S. economy, as businesses and governments also save. In fact, the total saving of the U.S. economy, called *national saving,* is higher and has declined less dramatically than household saving during these years. Thus, if the United States is suffering a "savings shortfall," it is less severe than might be suggested by the figures on household saving only.

In this chapter, we will look at saving and its links to the formation of new capital. We begin by defining the concepts of saving and wealth and exploring the connection between them. We will consider why people choose to save, rather than spending all their income. We then turn to national saving—the collective saving of households, businesses, and government. Because national saving determines the capacity of an economy to create new capital, it is the more important measure of saving from a macroeconomic perspective.

We next discuss capital formation. Most decisions to invest in new capital are made by firms. As we will see, a firm's decision to invest is in many respects analogous to its decision about whether to increase employment; firms will choose to expand their capital stocks when the benefits of doing so exceed the costs. We end the chapter by showing how national saving and capital formation are related, using a supply and demand approach.

SAVING AND WEALTH

saving current income minus spending on current needs

saving rate saving divided by income

wealth the value of assets minus liabilities

assets anything of value that one *owns*

liabilities the debts one *owes*

balance sheet a list of an economic unit's assets and liabilities on a specific date

net worth an economic unit's wealth determined by subtracting liabilities from assets

In general, the **saving** of an economic unit—whether a household, a business, a university, or a nation—may be defined as its *current income* minus its *spending on current needs*. For example, if Consuelo earns $300 per week; spends $280 weekly on living expenses such as rent, food, clothes, and entertainment; and deposits the remaining $20 in the bank, her saving is $20 per week. The **saving rate** of any economic unit is its saving divided by its income. Since Consuelo saves $20 of her weekly income of $300, her saving rate is $20/$300, or 6.7 percent.

The saving of an economic unit is closely related to its **wealth,** or the value of its assets minus its liabilities. **Assets** are anything of value that one *owns,* either *financial* or *real.* Examples of financial assets that you or your family might own include cash, a checking account, stocks, and bonds. Examples of real assets include a home or other real estate, jewelry, consumer durables like cars, and valuable collectibles. **Liabilities,** on the other hand, are the debts one *owes.* Examples of liabilities are credit card balances, student loans, and mortgages.

Accountants list the assets and liabilities of a family, a firm, a university, or any other economic unit on a **balance sheet.** Comparing the values of the assets and liabilities helps them determine the economic unit's wealth, also called its **net worth.**

EXAMPLE 21.1   Constructing a Balance Sheet

What is Consuelo's wealth?

To take stock of her financial position, Consuelo lists her assets and liabilities on a balance sheet. The result is shown in Table 21.1. What is Consuelo's wealth?

TABLE 21.1
Consuelo's Balance Sheet

Assets		Liabilities	
Cash	$ 80	Student loan	$ 3,000
Checking account	1,200	Credit card balance	250
Shares of stock	1,000		
Car (market value)	3,500		
Furniture (market value)	500		
Total	**$6,280**		**$3,250**
		Net worth	**$3,030**

Consuelo's financial assets are the cash in her wallet, the balance in her checking account, and the current value of some shares of stock her parents gave her. Together her financial assets are worth $2,280. She also lists $4,000 in real assets, the sum of the market values of her car and her furniture. Consuelo's total assets, both financial and real, come to $6,280. Her liabilities are the student loan she owes the bank and the balance due on her credit card, which total $3,250. Consuelo's wealth, or net worth, then, is the value of her assets ($6,280) minus the value of her liabilities ($3,250), or $3,030.

 SELF-TEST 21.1

What would Consuelo's net worth be if her student loan were for $6,500 rather than $3,000? Construct a new balance sheet for her.

flow a measure that is defined *per unit of time*

stock a measure that is defined *at a point in time*

Saving and wealth are related, because saving contributes to wealth. To understand this relationship better, we must distinguish between *stocks* and *flows*.

STOCKS AND FLOWS

Saving is an example of a **flow,** a measure that is defined *per unit of time*. For example, Consuelo's saving is $20 *per week*. Wealth, in contrast, is a **stock,** a measure that is defined *at a point in time*. Consuelo's wealth of $3,030, for example, is her wealth on a particular date—say, January 1, 2020.

To visualize the difference between stocks and flows, think of water running into a bathtub. The amount of water in the bathtub at any specific moment—for example, 40 gallons at 7:15 p.m.—is a stock because it is measured at a specific point in time. The rate at which the water flows into the tub—for example, 2 gallons per minute—is a flow because it is measured per unit of time. In many cases, a flow is the *rate of change* in a stock: If we know that there are 40 gallons of water in the tub at 7:15 p.m., for example, and that water is flowing in at 2 gallons per minute, we can easily determine that the

The flow of saving increases the stock of wealth in the same way that the flow of water through the faucet increases the amount of water in the tub.

stock of water will be changing at the rate of 2 gallons per minute and will equal 42 gallons at 7:16 p.m., 44 gallons at 7:17 p.m., and so on, until the bathtub overflows.

 SELF-TEST 21.2

Continuing the example of the bathtub: If there are 40 gallons of water in the tub at 7:15 p.m. and water is being *drained* at the rate of 3 gallons per minute, what will be the stock and flow at 7:16 p.m.? At 7:17 p.m.? Does the flow still equal the rate of change in the stock?

The relationship between saving (a flow) and wealth (a stock) is similar to the relationship between the flow of water into a bathtub and the stock of water in the tub in that the *flow* of saving causes the *stock* of wealth to change at the same rate. Indeed, as Example 21.2 illustrates, every dollar that a person saves adds a dollar to his or her wealth.

EXAMPLE 21.2   The Link between Saving and Wealth

What is the relationship between Consuelo's saving and her wealth?

Consuelo saves $20 per week. How does this saving affect her wealth? Does the change in her wealth depend on whether Consuelo uses her saving to accumulate assets or to pay down her liabilities?

Consuelo could use the $20 she saved this week to increase her assets—for example, by adding the $20 to her checking account—or to reduce her liabilities—for example, by paying down her credit card balance. Suppose she adds the $20 to her checking account, increasing her assets by $20. Since her liabilities are unchanged, her wealth also increases by $20, to $3,050 (see Table 21.1).

If Consuelo decides to use the $20 she saved this week to pay down her credit card balance, she reduces it from $250 to $230. That action would reduce her liabilities by $20, leaving her assets unchanged. Since wealth equals assets minus liabilities, reducing her liabilities by $20 increases her wealth by $20, to $3,050. Thus, saving $20 per week raises Consuelo's stock of wealth by $20 a week, regardless of whether she uses her saving to increase her assets or reduce her liabilities.

The close relationship between saving and wealth explains why saving is so important to an economy. Higher rates of saving today lead to faster accumulation of wealth, and the wealthier a nation is, the higher its standard of living. Thus a high rate of saving today contributes to an improved standard of living in the future.

CAPITAL GAINS AND LOSSES

Though saving increases wealth, it is not the only factor that determines wealth. Wealth can also change because of changes in the values of the real or financial assets one owns. Suppose Consuelo's shares of stock rise in value, from $1,000 to $1,500. This increase in the value of Consuelo's stock raises her total assets by $500 without affecting her liabilities. As a result, Consuelo's wealth rises by $500, from $3,030 to $3,530 (see Table 21.2).

capital gains increases in the value of existing assets

capital losses decreases in the value of existing assets

Changes in the value of existing assets are called **capital gains** when an asset's value increases and **capital losses** when an asset's value decreases. Just as capital gains increase

TABLE 21.2
Consuelo's Balance Sheet after an Increase in the Value of Her Stocks

Assets		Liabilities	
Cash	$ 80	Student loan	$3,000
Checking account	1,200	Credit card balance	250
Shares of stock	1,500		
Car (market value)	3,500		
Furniture (market value)	500		
Total	**$6,780**		**$3,250**
		Net worth	**$3,530**

wealth, capital losses decrease wealth. Capital gains and losses are not counted as part of saving, however. Instead, the change in a person's wealth during any period equals the saving done during the period plus capital gains or minus capital losses during that period. In terms of an equation,

$$\text{Change in wealth} = \text{Saving} + \text{Capital gains} - \text{Capital losses}.$$

 SELF-TEST 21.3

How would each of the following actions or events affect Consuelo's *saving* and her *wealth*?

a. Consuelo deposits $20 in the bank at the end of the week as usual. She also charges $50 on her credit card, raising her credit card balance to $300.

b. Consuelo uses $300 from her checking account to pay off her credit card bill.

c. Consuelo's old car is recognized as a classic. Its market value rises from $3,500 to $4,000.

d. Consuelo's furniture is damaged and as a result falls in value from $500 to $200.

Capital gains and losses can have a major effect on one's overall wealth, as The Economic Naturalist 21.1 illustrates.

The Economic Naturalist 21.1

How did many American households increase their wealth in the 1990s and 2000s while saving very little?

On the whole, Americans felt prosperous during the 1990s and, with a short pause around the relatively minor 2001 recession, the feeling of prosperity continued until the eve of the 2007–2009 recession. Measures of household wealth during this period showed enormous gains. Yet saving by U.S. households was quite low (and declining) throughout those years. How did many American households increase their wealth in the 1990s and early 2000s while saving very little?

During the 1990s, an increasing number of Americans acquired stocks, either directly through purchases or indirectly through their pension and retirement funds. At the same time, stock prices rose at record rates (see the blue line in Figure 21.1). The strongly rising "bull market," which increased the prices of most stocks, enabled many Americans to enjoy significant capital gains and increased wealth without saving much, if anything. Indeed, some economists argued that the low household saving rate of the 1990s is partially *explained* by the bull market; because capital gains increased household wealth by so much, many people saw no need to save. (Other proposed explanations include the increase in *government* saving during the 1990s, discussed below.)

FIGURE 21.1

Household Saving versus Real Stock and Home Prices, 1975–2019.

Changes in household saving often accompany changes in the opposite direction in measures of household wealth such as stocks and homes. As both stock markets and home values started declining in the later part of the 2000s, the household saving rate reversed its trend and, for a few years, started increasing.

Sources: S&P CoreLogic Case-Shiller Home Price Indices, Federal Reserve Bank of St. Louis.

The stock market peaked in early 2000 and stock prices fell quite sharply over the following two years. It is interesting that U.S. households did not choose to save more in 2000 and the following years (see the green line in Figure 21.1), despite the decline in their stock market wealth. One explanation is that an even larger component of household wealth—the value of privately owned homes—rose significantly in 2000–2006, partly offsetting the effect of the decline in stock values on household wealth (see the red line in Figure 21.1).

More generally, as Figure 21.1 shows, changes in household saving often accompany changes in the opposite direction in measures of household wealth such as stocks and homes (for example, household saving and home prices during the 1970s and 1980s often moved in opposite directions). Indeed, the figure shows that as both stock markets and home values started declining in the later part of the 2000s, the household saving rate reversed its trend and started increasing.

Household saving then peaked in 2012 when the housing market bottomed, and has since declined only slightly, in spite of steep increases in both stock and home prices in recent years. With the steep declines of the global financial crisis still fresh in their memories, American households may not feel confident that these recent capital gains are here to last. Indeed, sharp stock market declines related to the COVID-19 pandemic in early 2020 provided a still fresher reminder of the instability of capital gains.

We have seen how saving is related to the accumulation of wealth. To understand why people choose to save, however, we need to examine their motives for saving.

WHY DO PEOPLE SAVE?

Why do people save part of their income instead of spending everything they earn? Economists have identified at least three broad reasons for saving. First, people save to meet certain long-term objectives, such as a comfortable retirement. By putting away part of their income during their working years, they can live better after retirement than they would if they had to rely solely on Social Security and their company pensions, if they have one. Other long-term objectives might include college tuition for one's children and the purchase of a new home or car. Since many of these needs occur at fairly predictable stages in one's life, economists call this type of saving **life-cycle saving.**

A second reason to save is to protect oneself and family against unexpected setbacks—the loss of a job, for example, or a costly health problem. Personal financial advisors typically suggest that families maintain an emergency reserve (a "rainy-day fund") equal to three to six months' worth of income. Saving for protection against potential emergencies is called **precautionary saving.**

A third reason to save is to accumulate an estate to leave to one's heirs, usually one's children but possibly a favorite charity or other worthy cause. Saving for the purpose of leaving an inheritance, or bequest, is called **bequest saving.** Bequest saving is done primarily by people at the higher end of the income ladder. But because these people control a large share of the nation's wealth, bequest saving is an important part of overall saving.

To be sure, people usually do not mentally separate their saving into these three categories; rather, all three reasons for saving motivate most savers to varying degrees. The Economic Naturalist 21.2 shows how the three reasons for saving can explain the high rate of household saving in China.

life-cycle saving saving to meet long-term objectives such as retirement, college attendance, or the purchase of a home

precautionary saving saving for protection against unexpected setbacks such as the loss of a job or a medical emergency

bequest saving saving done for the purpose of leaving an inheritance

▶ Visit your instructor's Connect course and access your eBook to view this video.

The Economic Naturalist 21.2

Why do Chinese households save so much?

A few years ago, economists estimated that Chinese households save more than 25 percent of their disposable income, an unusually high rate.[1] Although some suggested that the Chinese "are known to be thrifty," it is unlikely that cultural factors are a main reason for their propensity to save

Why do American households save so little while Chinese households save so much?

---

[1]For these estimates, and for detail on some of the explanations and evidence we discuss here, see, for example, Dennis Tao Yang, Junsen Zhang, and Shaojie Zhou, "Why Are Saving Rates So High in China?," in *Capitalizing China,* Joseph P. H. Fan and Randall Morck, eds. (Chicago: University of Chicago Press, 2013).

because the high saving rate is a relatively recent phenomenon. Chinese households saved well below 10 percent of their income until the late 1980s, and below 5 percent from the 1950s to the 1970s. Why do the Chinese save so much, then?

Among the reasons for saving we discussed, *life-cycle* and *precautionary saving* seem important in China. As we mentioned in Chapter 19, *Economic Growth, Productivity, and Living Standards,* the Chinese economy grew very quickly over the past several decades (Table 19.1 and Figure 19.2 in that chapter show the dramatic increase in China's real GDP per person from 1990 to 2010). In a very rapidly growing economy, younger people in their working years are richer on average than people in their retirement years, as the young's incomes are much higher than the incomes the retired had during their own working years. As a result, the saving of the young outweighs the dissaving of the retired. Moreover, China's limited "social safety net"—its version of Social Security, Medicare, and other social insurance schemes (discussed in The Economic Naturalist 21.3)—provides most people little in the way of retirement income or protection against health problems. That means that young households have to save both for their own retirement—life-cycle saving—and for unexpected expenses such as health-related ones—precautionary saving.

Another explanation for the high saving rates has to do with China's financial system, which is closely controlled by the government and does not afford the average consumer much opportunity to borrow. This again translates both to higher life-cycle saving—because, for example, paying for a house or for education requires saving much of the cost in advance—and to higher precautionary saving—because households know that their ability to borrow in the case of an unexpected need would be limited.

If these explanations are correct, why is the high saving rate a relatively recent phenomenon? Starting in the late 1970s, China has undergone extensive economic reforms (recall our discussion of structural macroeconomics policies in previous chapters). These reforms have gradually turned China from a centrally planned economy to a more market-oriented economy. Before the reforms, households had less ability as well as less perceived need to engage in life-cycle and precautionary saving, because the central government controlled many aspects of their economic behavior and was considered responsible for providing for their needs. As institutions changed, households' incentives changed, and they changed their saving behavior.

Note that the many uncertainties associated with changing economic institutions (indeed, with any big societal changes) could themselves provide another reason for relatively high precautionary saving. In particular, a transition to a more market-oriented economy could imply an increase in earnings uncertainty and unemployment risk. China's transition also meant that the prices of housing, education, and other life-cycle expenditures increased, increasing the need for life-cycle saving.

Although most people are usually motivated to save for at least one of the three reasons we have discussed, the amount they choose to save may depend on the economic environment. One economic variable that is quite significant in saving decisions is the real interest rate.

SAVING AND THE REAL INTEREST RATE

Most people don't save by putting cash in a mattress. Instead, they make financial investments that they hope will provide a good return on their saving. For example, a checking account may pay interest on the account balance. More sophisticated financial investments, such as government bonds or shares of stock in a corporation (see Chapter 23,

Financial Markets and International Capital Flows), also pay returns in the form of interest payments, dividends, or capital gains. High returns are desirable, of course, because the higher the return, the faster one's savings will grow.

The rate of return that is most relevant to saving decisions is the *real interest rate,* denoted *r*. Recall from Chapter 18, *Measuring the Price Level and Inflation,* that the real interest rate is the rate at which the real purchasing power of a financial asset increases over time. The real interest rate equals the market, or *nominal,* interest rate (i) minus the inflation rate (π).

The real interest rate is relevant to savers because it is the "reward" for saving. Suppose you are thinking of increasing your saving by $1,000 this year, which you can do if you give up your habit of eating out once a week. If the real interest rate is 5 percent, then in a year your extra saving will give you extra purchasing power of $1,050, measured in today's dollars. But if the real interest rate were 10 percent, your sacrifice of $1,000 this year would be rewarded by $1,100 in purchasing power next year. All else being equal, you would probably be more willing to save today if you knew the reward next year would be greater. In either case the *cost* of the extra saving—giving up your weekly night out—is the same. But the *benefit* of the extra saving, in terms of increased purchasing power next year, is higher if the real interest rate is 10 percent rather than 5 percent.

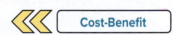 Cost-Benefit

---

EXAMPLE 21.3   Saving versus Consumption

By how much does a high saving rate enhance a family's future living standard?

The Spends and the Thrifts are similar families, except that the Spends save 5 percent of their income each year and the Thrifts save 20 percent. The two families began to save in 1995 and plan to continue to save until their respective breadwinners retire in the year 2030. Both families earn $40,000 a year in real terms in the labor market, and both put their savings in a mutual fund that has yielded a real return of 8 percent per year, a return they expect to continue into the future. Compare the amount that the two families consume in each year from 1995 to 2030, and compare the families' wealth at retirement.

In the first year, 1995, the Spends saved $2,000 (5 percent of their $40,000 income) and consumed $38,000 (95 percent of $40,000). The Thrifts saved $8,000 in 1995 (20 percent of $40,000) and hence consumed only $32,000 in that year, $6,000 less than the Spends. In 1996, the Thrifts' income was $40,640, the extra $640 representing the 8 percent return on their $8,000 savings. The Spends saw their income grow by only $160 (8 percent of their savings of $2,000) in 1996. With an income of $40,640, the Thrifts consumed $32,512 in 1996 (80 percent of $40,640) compared to $38,152 (95 percent of $40,160) for the Spends. The consumption gap between the two families, which started out at $6,000, thus fell to $5,640 after one year.

Because of the more rapid increase in the Thrifts' wealth and hence interest income, each year the Thrifts' income grew faster than the Spends'; each year the Thrifts continued to save 20 percent of their higher incomes compared to only 5 percent for the Spends. Figure 21.2 shows the paths followed by the consumption spending of the two families. You can see that the Thrifts' consumption, though starting at a lower level, grows relatively more quickly. By 2010 the Thrifts had overtaken the Spends, and from that point onward, the amount by which the Thrifts outspent the Spends grew with each passing year. Even though the Spends continued to consume 95 percent of their income each year, their income grew so slowly that by 2015, they were consuming nearly $3,000 a year less than the Thrifts ($41,158 a year versus $43,957). And by the time the two families retire, in

FIGURE 21.2

Consumption Trajectories of the Thrifts and the Spends.

The figure shows consumption spending in each year by two families, the Thrifts and the Spends. Because the Thrifts save more than the Spends, their annual consumption spending rises relatively more quickly. By the time of retirement in the year 2030, the Thrifts are both consuming significantly more each year than the Spends and also have a retirement nest egg that is five times larger.

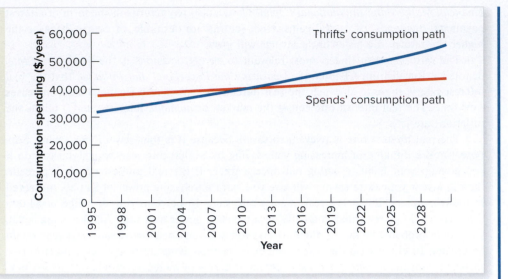

2030, the Thrifts will be consuming more than $12,000 per year more than the Spends ($55,774 versus $43,698). Even more striking is the difference between the retirement nest eggs of the two families. Whereas the Spends will enter retirement with total accumulated savings of just over $77,000, the Thrifts will have more than $385,000, five times as much.

These dramatic differences illustrated in Example 21.3 depend in part on the assumption that the real rate of return is 8 percent—around 1 percent higher than the actual real return to mutual funds tracking the S&P 500 (with dividends reinvested) since its inception in 1926. On the other hand, the Spend family in our example actually saves more than typical U.S. households, many of which carry $5,000 or more in credit card debt at high rates of interest and have no significant savings at all. The point of the example, which remains valid under alternative assumptions about the real interest rate and saving rates, is that, because of the power of compound interest, a high rate of saving pays off handsomely in the long run.

While a higher real interest rate increases the reward for saving, which tends to strengthen people's willingness to save, another force counteracts that extra incentive. Recall that a major reason for saving is to attain specific goals: a comfortable retirement, a college education, or a first home. If the goal is a specific amount—say, $25,000 for a down payment on a home—then a higher rate of return means that households can save *less* and still reach their goal, because funds that are put aside will grow more quickly. For example, to accumulate $25,000 at the end of five years, at a 5 percent interest rate a person would have to save about $4,309 per year. At a 10 percent interest rate, reaching the $25,000 goal would require saving only about $3,723 per year. To the extent that people are *target savers* who save to reach a specific goal, higher interest rates actually decrease the amount they need to save.

In sum, a higher real interest rate has both positive and negative effects on saving—a positive effect because it increases the reward for saving and a negative effect because it reduces the amount people need to save each year to reach a given target. Empirical evidence suggests that, in practice, higher real interest rates lead to modest increases in saving.

SAVING, SELF-CONTROL, AND DEMONSTRATION EFFECTS

The reasons for saving we just discussed are based on the notion that people are rational decision makers who will choose their saving rates to maximize their welfare over the long run. Yet many psychologists, and some economists, have argued instead that people's saving behavior is based as much on psychological as on economic factors. For example, psychologists stress that many people lack the *self-control* to do what they know is in their own best interest. People smoke or eat greasy food, despite the known long-term health risks. Similarly, they may have good intentions about saving but lack the self-control to put aside as much as they ought to each month.

One way to strengthen self-control is to remove temptations from the immediate environment. A person who is trying to quit smoking will make a point of not having cigarettes in the house, and a person with a weight problem will avoid going to a bakery. Similarly, a person who is not saving enough might arrange to use a payroll savings plan, through which a predetermined amount is deducted from each paycheck and set aside in a special account from which withdrawals are not permitted until retirement. Making saving automatic and withdrawals difficult eliminates the temptation to spend all of current earnings or squander accumulated savings. Payroll savings plans have helped many people increase the amount that they save for retirement or other purposes.

An implication of the self-control hypothesis is that consumer credit arrangements that make borrowing and spending easier may reduce the amount that people save. For example, in recent years banks sometimes encouraged people to borrow against the *equity* in their homes—that is, the value of the home less the value of the outstanding mortgage. Such financial innovations, by increasing the temptation to spend, may have reduced the household saving rate. The increased availability of credit cards with high borrowing limits is another temptation.

Downward pressure on the saving rate may also occur when additional spending by some consumers stimulates additional spending by others. Such *demonstration effects* arise when people use the spending of others as a yardstick by which to measure the adequacy of their own living standards. For example, a family in an upper-middle-class American suburb in which the average house has 3,000 square feet of living space might regard a 1,500-square-foot house as being uncomfortably small—too cramped, for example, to entertain friends in the manner to which community members have become accustomed. In contrast, a similar family living in a low-income neighborhood might find the very same house luxuriously large.

The implication of demonstration effects for saving is that families who live among others who consume more than they do may be strongly motivated to increase their own consumption spending. When satisfaction or social status depends in part on *relative* living standards, an upward spiral may result in which household spending is higher, and saving lower, than would be best for either the individual families involved or for the economy as a whole.

The Economic Naturalist 21.3

Why do U.S. households save so little?

Household saving in the United States, which has always been comparatively low, has fallen even further in the past decades. (Figure 21.1 shows a long-term fall from 13.1 percent in 1975 to 7.9 percent in 2019.) Surveys show that a significant fraction of American households live from paycheck to paycheck with very little saving. Why do U.S. households save so little?

Economists do not agree on the reasons for low household saving in the United States, although many hypotheses have been suggested.

One possible reason for low saving is the availability of generous government assistance to older adults. From a *life-cycle* perspective, an important motivation for saving is to provide for retirement. In general, the U.S. government provides a less comprehensive "social safety net" than other industrialized countries; that is, it offers relatively fewer programs to assist people in need. To the extent that the U.S. government does provide income support, however, it is heavily concentrated on the older segment of the population. Together the Social Security and Medicare programs, both of which are designed primarily to assist retired people, constitute a major share of the federal government's expenditures. These programs have been very successful; indeed they have virtually wiped out poverty among older adults. To the extent that Americans believe that the government will ensure them an adequate living standard in retirement, however, their incentive to save for the future is reduced.

Another important life-cycle objective is buying a home. We have seen that the Chinese must save a great deal to purchase a home because of high house prices and down payment requirements. The same is true in many other countries. But in the United States, with its highly developed financial system, people can buy homes with down payments of 15 percent or less of the purchase price. The ready availability of mortgages with low down payments reduces the need to save for the purchase of a home.

What about *precautionary saving*? Unlike Japan and Europe, which had to rebuild after World War II, and unlike China, which continued to suffer from major economic crises in the decades following the war, the United States has not known sustained economic hardship since the Great Depression of the 1930s (which fewer and fewer Americans are alive to remember). Perhaps the nation's prosperous past has led Americans to be more confident about the future and hence less inclined to save for economic emergencies than other people, even though the United States does not offer the level of employment security found in Japan or in Europe.

U.S. household saving is not only low by international standards; it has generally declined in recent decades. The good performance of the stock market in the 1990s along with continuing increases in the prices of family homes until the mid-2000s probably help explain this savings decline (see The Economic Naturalist 21.1). As long as Americans enjoy capital gains, they see their wealth increase almost without effort, and their incentive to save is reduced. Consistent with this explanation, U.S. household saving increased during and after the last recession as the value of stocks and homes declined, but stopped increasing in the last few years, as stocks and housing have been rising again.

Psychological factors may also explain Americans' saving behavior. For example, unlike in most countries, U.S. homeowners can easily borrow against their home equity. This ability, made possible by the highly developed U.S. financial markets, may exacerbate *self-control* problems by increasing the temptation to spend. Finally, *demonstration effects* may have depressed saving in recent decades. Chapter 20, *The Labor Market: Workers, Wages, and Unemployment,* discussed the phenomenon of increasing wage inequality, which has improved the relative position of more skilled and educated workers. Increased spending by households at the top of the earnings scale on houses, cars, and other consumption goods may have led those just below them to spend more as well, and so on. Middle-class families that were once content with medium-priced cars may now feel they need Volvos and BMWs to keep up with community standards. To the extent that demonstration effects lead families to spend beyond their means, they reduce their saving rate.

> **RECAP**
>
> **WHY DO PEOPLE SAVE?**
>
> Motivations for saving include saving to meet long-term objectives, such as retirement (*life-cycle saving*), saving for emergencies (*precautionary saving*), and saving to leave an inheritance or bequest (*bequest saving*). The amount that people save also depends on macroeconomic factors, such as the real

interest rate. A higher real interest rate stimulates saving by increasing the reward for saving, but it can also depress saving by making it easier for savers to reach a specific savings target. On net, a higher real interest rate appears to lead to modest increases in saving.

Psychological factors may also affect saving rates. If people have *self-control* problems, then financial arrangements (such as automatic payroll deductions) that make it more difficult to spend will increase their saving. People's saving decisions may also be influenced by *demonstration effects,* as when people feel compelled to spend at the same rate as their neighbors, even though they may not be able to afford to do so.

NATIONAL SAVING AND ITS COMPONENTS

Thus far, we have been examining the concepts of saving and wealth from the individual's perspective. But macroeconomists are interested primarily in saving and wealth for the country as a whole. In this section, we will study *national saving,* or the aggregate saving of the economy. National saving includes the saving of business firms and the government as well as that of households. Later in the chapter, we will examine the close link between national saving and the rate of capital formation in an economy.

THE MEASUREMENT OF NATIONAL SAVING

To define the saving rate of a country as a whole, we will start with a basic accounting identity that was introduced in Chapter 17, *Measuring Economic Activity: GDP and Unemployment.* According to this identity, for the economy as a whole, production (or income) must equal total expenditure. In symbols, the identity is

$$Y = C + I + G + NX,$$

where Y stands for either production or aggregate income (which must be equal), C equals consumption expenditure, I equals investment spending, G equals government purchases of goods and services, and NX equals net exports.

For now, let's assume that net exports *(NX)* is equal to zero, which would be the case if a country did not trade at all with other countries or if its exports and imports were always balanced. (We discuss the case with NX being different from zero in Chapter 23, *Financial Markets and International Capital Flows.*) With net exports set at zero, the condition that output equals expenditure becomes

$$Y = C + I + G.$$

To determine how much saving is done by the nation as a whole, we can apply the general definition of saving. As for any other economic unit, a nation's saving equals its *current income* less its *spending on current needs.* The current income of the country as a whole is its GDP, or Y—that is, the value of the final goods and services produced within the country's borders during the year.

Identifying the part of total expenditure that corresponds to the nation's spending on current needs is more difficult than identifying the nation's income. The component of aggregate spending that is easiest to classify is investment spending I. We know that investment spending—the acquisition of new factories, equipment, and other capital goods, as well as residential construction—is done to expand the economy's future productive capacity or provide more housing for the future, not to satisfy current needs. So investment spending clearly is *not* part of spending on current needs.

Deciding how much of consumption spending by households, C, and government purchases of goods and services, G, should be counted as spending on current needs is less straightforward. Certainly most consumption spending by households—on food, clothing, utilities, entertainment, and so on—is for current needs. But consumption spending also includes purchases of long-lived *consumer durables,* such as cars, furniture, and appliances. Consumer durables are only partially used up during the current year; they may continue to provide service, in fact, for years after their purchase. So household spending on consumer durables is a combination of spending on current needs and spending on future needs.

As with consumption spending, most government purchases of goods and services are intended to provide for current needs. However, like household purchases, a portion of government purchases is devoted to the acquisition or construction of long-lived capital goods, such as roads, bridges, schools, government buildings, and military hardware. And like consumer durables, these forms of *public capital* are only partially used up during the current year; most will provide useful services far into the future. So, like consumption spending, government purchases are in fact a mixture of spending on current needs and spending on future needs.

Although in reality not all spending by households and the government is for current needs, in practice, determining precisely how much of such spending is for current needs and how much is for future needs is extremely difficult. For this reason, for a long time U.S. government statistics treated *all* of both consumption expenditures (*C*) and government purchases (*G*) as spending on current needs.[2] For simplicity's sake, in this book we will follow the same practice. But keep in mind that because consumption spending and government purchases do in fact include some spending for future rather than current needs, treating all of *C* and *G* as spending on current needs will understate the true amount of national saving.

If we treat all consumption spending and government purchases as spending on current needs, then the nation's saving is its income *Y* less its spending on current needs, *C* + *G*. So we can define **national saving** *S* as

national saving the saving of the entire economy, equal to GDP less consumption expenditures and government purchases of goods and services, or $Y - C - G$

$$S = Y - C - G. \tag{21.1}$$

Figure 21.3 shows the U.S. national saving rate (national saving as a percentage of GDP) for the years 1960 through 2019. The U.S. national saving rate fell from 18 to 20 percent in the 1960s to around 13 to 15 percent in recent years. Like household saving, national saving declined over time, though by comparing Figures 21.1 and 21.3, you can see that the decline in national saving has been more modest. Furthermore, unlike household saving, national saving recovered in the latter 1990s—indeed, in 1998 the national saving rate was above 16 percent, slightly higher than the rate in 1970. As we will see next, the reason for these differences between the behavior of national saving and household saving is that saving done by business firms and, in the late 1990s, by the government has been substantial.

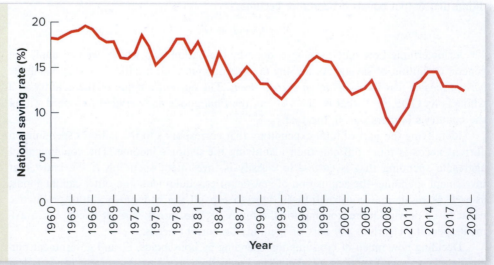

FIGURE 21.3

U.S. National Saving Rate, 1960–2019.

U.S. national saving fell from 18 to 20 percent of GDP in the 1960s to 13 to 15 percent in recent years.

Source: Bureau of Economic Analysis, www.bea.gov.

---

[2]Nowadays, the official data distinguish investment in public capital from the rest of government purchases.

PRIVATE AND PUBLIC COMPONENTS OF NATIONAL SAVING

To understand national saving better, we will divide it into two major components: private saving, which is saving done by households and businesses, and public saving, which is saving done by the government.

To see how national saving breaks down into public and private saving, we work with the definition of national saving, $S = Y - C - G$. To distinguish private-sector income from public-sector income, we must expand this equation to incorporate taxes as well as payments made by the government to the private sector. Government payments to the private sector include both *transfer payments* and *interest* paid to individuals and institutions that hold government bonds. **Transfer payments** are payments the government makes to the public for which it receives no current goods or services in return. Social Security benefits, welfare payments, farm support payments, and pensions to government workers are transfer payments.

Let T stand for taxes paid by the private sector to the government *less* transfer payments and interest payments made by the government to the private sector:

$T =$ Total taxes $-$ Transfer payments $-$ Government interest payments.

Since T equals private-sector tax payments minus the various benefits and interest payments the private sector receives from the government, we can think of T as *net taxes*. If we add and then subtract T from the definition of national saving, $S = Y - C - G$, we get

$$S = Y - C - G + T - T.$$

Rearranging this equation and grouping terms, we obtain

$$S = (Y - T - C) + (T - G). \tag{21.2}$$

This equation splits national saving S into two parts, *private saving,* or $Y - T - C$, and *public saving,* $T - G$.

Private saving, $Y - T - C$, is the saving of the private sector of the economy. Why is $Y - T - C$ a reasonable definition of private saving? Remember that saving equals current income minus spending on current needs. The income of the private (nongovernmental) sector of the economy is the economy's total income Y less net taxes paid to the government, T. The private sector's spending on current needs is its consumption expenditures C. So private-sector saving, equal to private-sector income less spending on current needs, is $Y - T - C$. Letting S_{private} stand for private saving, we can write the definition of private saving as

$$S_{\text{Private}} = Y - T - C.$$

Private saving can be further broken down into saving done by households and business firms. *Household saving,* also called personal saving, is saving done by families and individuals. Household saving corresponds to the familiar image of families putting aside part of their incomes each month, and it is the focus of much attention in the news media. But businesses are important savers as well—indeed business saving makes up the bulk of private saving in the United States. Businesses use the revenues from their sales to pay workers' salaries and other operating costs, to pay taxes, and to provide dividends to their shareholders. The funds remaining after these payments have been made are equal to *business saving.* A business firm's savings are available for the purchase of new capital equipment or the expansion of its operations. Alternatively, a business can put its savings in the bank for future use.

Public saving, $T - G$, is the saving of the government sector, including state and local governments as well as the federal government. Net taxes T are the income of the government. Government purchases G represent the government's spending on current needs (remember that, for the sake of simplicity, we are ignoring the investment portion of government purchases). Thus $T - G$ fits our definition of saving, in this case by the public sector. Letting S_{public} stand for public saving, we can write out the definition of public saving as

$$S_{\text{public}} = T - G.$$

transfer payments payments the government makes to the public for which it receives no current goods or services in return

private saving the saving of the private sector of the economy is equal to the after-tax income of the private sector minus consumption expenditures $(Y - T - C)$; private saving can be further broken down into household saving and business saving

public saving the saving of the government sector is equal to net tax payments minus government purchases $(T - G)$

Using Equation 21.2 and the definitions of private and public saving, we can rewrite national saving as

$$S = S_{\text{private}} + S_{\text{public}}. \tag{21.3}$$

This equation confirms that national saving is the sum of private saving and public saving. Since private saving in turn can be broken down into household and business saving, we see that national saving is made up of the saving of three groups: households, businesses, and the government.

PUBLIC SAVING AND THE GOVERNMENT BUDGET

government budget deficit
the excess of government spending over tax collections $(G - T)$

government budget surplus
the excess of government tax collections over government spending $(T - G)$; the government budget surplus equals public saving

Although the idea that households and businesses can save is familiar to most people, the fact that the government can also save is less widely understood. Public saving is closely linked to the government's decisions about spending and taxing. Governments finance the bulk of their spending by taxing the private sector. If taxes and spending in a given year are equal, the government is said to have a *balanced budget*. If, in any given year, the government's spending exceeds its tax collections, the difference is called the **government budget deficit.** If the government runs a deficit, it must make up the difference by borrowing from the public through issuance of government bonds. Algebraically, the government budget deficit can be written as $G - T$, or government purchases minus net tax collections.

In some years, the government may spend less than it collects in taxes. The excess of tax collections over government spending is called the **government budget surplus.** When a government has a surplus, it uses the extra funds to pay down its outstanding debt to the public. Algebraically, the government budget surplus may be written as $T - G$, or net tax collections less government purchases.

If the algebraic expression for the government budget surplus, $T - G$, looks familiar, that is because it is also the definition of public saving, as we saw earlier. Thus, *public saving is identical to the government budget surplus*. In other words, when the government collects more in taxes than it spends, public saving will be positive. When the government spends more than it collects in taxes so that it runs a deficit, public saving will be negative.

Example 21.4 illustrates the relationships among public saving, the government budget surplus, and national saving.

EXAMPLE 21.4	**Government Saving**

How do we calculate government saving?

Following are data on U.S. government revenues and expenditures for 2000, in billions of dollars. Find (a) the federal government's budget surplus or deficit, (b) the budget surplus or deficit of state and local governments, and (c) the contribution of the government sector to national saving.

Federal government:	
Receipts	2,068.4
Expenditures	1,912.9
State and local governments:	
Receipts	1,304.1
Expenditures	1,344.8

Source: Bureau of Economic Analysis, NIPA Tables 3.2 and 3.3.

The federal government's receipts minus its expenditures were 2,068.4 − 1,912.9 = 155.5, so the federal government ran a budget surplus of $155.5 billion in 2000. State and local government receipts minus expenditures were

1,304.1 − 1,344.8 = −40.7, so state and local governments ran a collective budget deficit of $40.7 billion. The budget surplus of the entire government sector—that is, the federal surplus minus the state and local deficit—was 155.5 − 40.7 = 114.8, or $114.8 billion. So the contribution of the government sector to U.S. national saving in 2000 was $114.8 billion.

 SELF-TEST 21.4

Continuing Example 21.4, here are the analogous data on government revenues and expenditures for 2018, in billions of dollars. Again, find (a) the federal government's budget surplus or deficit, (b) the budget surplus or deficit of state and local governments, and (c) the contribution of the government sector to national saving.

Federal government:	
Receipts	3,497.7
Expenditures	4,507.4
State and local governments:	
Receipts	2,623.0
Expenditures	2,862.1

If you did Self-Test 21.4 correctly, you found that the government sector's contribution to national saving in 2018 was *negative*. The reason is that the federal, state, and local governments taken together ran a budget deficit in that year, reducing national saving by the amount of the budget deficit.

Figure 21.3 showed the U.S. national saving rate since 1960. Figure 21.4 shows the behavior since 1960 of the three components of national saving: household saving, business saving, and public saving, each measured as a percentage of GDP. Note that business saving played a major role in national saving during these years, while the role of household saving was relatively modest. As we saw in Figure 21.1, household saving declined since the mid-1970s.

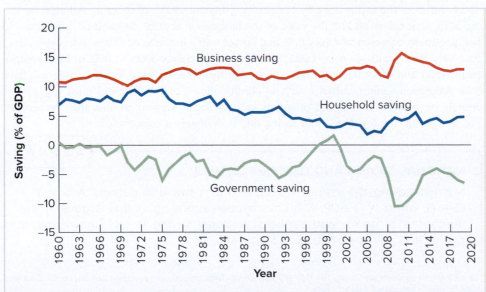

FIGURE 21.4

The Three Components of National Saving, 1960–2019.

Of the three components of national saving, business saving is the most important.

Source: Bureau of Economic Analysis, www.bea.gov.

The contribution of public saving has varied considerably over time. Until about 1970, the federal, state, and local governments typically ran a roughly balanced combined budget, making little contribution to national saving. But by the 1970s, public saving had turned negative, reflecting large budget deficits, particularly at the federal level. For the next two decades, the government was a net drain on national saving. During the late 1990s, government budgets moved closer to balance and, by the end of the decade, reached surplus, making a positive contribution to national saving. Government budgets dove again into deficits around the 2001 recession, and around the 2007–2009 recession, they reached deficits of historic scale. The relationship between government deficits and recessions was mentioned earlier in the text, and we will discuss it in more detail in future chapters.

In the years after the 2007–2009 recession, the government deficit returned more or less back to where it was from the mid-1970s to the mid-1990s. However, in the second half of the 2010s it started increasing again, and then it ballooned in 2020 due to the COVID-19 pandemic and the fight against it.

IS LOW HOUSEHOLD SAVING A PROBLEM?

In the opening to this chapter, and again in The Economic Naturalist 21.1 and 21.3, we mentioned that saving by U.S. households, never high by international standards, fell further during the past few decades. How big of a problem is the low (and declining) household saving rate in the United States? We will answer this question from both a macroeconomic and a microeconomic perspective.

From a macroeconomic perspective, the problem posed by low household saving may not be as big as it may first seem. The key point to remember is that national saving, not household saving, determines the capacity of an economy to invest in new capital goods and to achieve continued improvement in living standards. Although household saving is low, saving by business firms has been significant. Moreover, business saving has been increasing over the past few decades: As Figure 21.4 shows, business saving slowly increased from around 11 percent of GDP in the early 1960s to around 13 to 15 percent in the 2010s. Overall, the decline in the U.S. national saving rate shown in Figure 21.3 has been less dramatic than the decline in the household saving rate shown in Figure 21.1. Although U.S. national saving is somewhat low compared to that of other industrialized countries, it has been sufficient to allow the United States to become one of the world's most productive economies.[3]

From a microeconomic perspective, however, the low household saving rate does signal a problem, which is the large and growing inequality in wealth among U.S. households. Saving patterns tend to increase this inequality since the economically better-off households tend not only to save more but, as business owners or shareholders, are also the ultimate beneficiaries of the saving done by businesses. Thus the wealth of these households, including both personal assets and the value of the businesses, is great. In contrast, lower-income families, many of whom save very little and do not own a business or shares in a corporation, have very little wealth—in many cases, their life savings are less than $5,000, or even *negative* (with debts and other liabilities that are greater than their assets). These households have little protection against setbacks such as chronic illness or job loss and must rely almost entirely on government support programs such as Social Security to fund their retirement. For this group, the low household saving rate is definitely a concern.

> **RECAP ↑**
>
> **NATIONAL SAVING AND ITS COMPONENTS**
>
> *National saving,* the saving of the nation as a whole, is defined by $S = Y - C - G$, where Y is GDP, C is consumption spending, and G is government purchases of goods and services. National saving is the sum of public saving and private saving: $S = S_{private} + S_{public}$.

[3]In addition to its domestic saving, the U.S. attracts savings from abroad, as we discuss in Chapter 23, *Financial Markets and International Capital Flows.*

Private saving, the saving of the private sector, is defined by $S_{private} = Y - T - C$, where T is net tax payments. Private saving can be broken down further into household saving and business saving.

Public saving, the saving of the government, is defined by $S_{public} = T - G$. Public saving equals the government budget surplus, $T - G$. When the government budget is in surplus, government saving is positive; when the government budget is in deficit, public saving is negative.

INVESTMENT AND CAPITAL FORMATION

From the point of view of the economy as a whole, the importance of national saving is that it provides the funds needed for investment. Investment—the creation of new capital goods and housing—is critical to increasing average labor productivity and improving standards of living.

What factors determine whether and how much firms choose to invest? Firms acquire new capital goods for the same reason they hire new workers: they expect that doing so will be profitable. We saw in Chapter 20, *The Labor Market: Workers, Wages, and Unemployment,* that the profitability of employing an extra worker depends primarily on two factors: the cost of employing the worker and the value of the worker's marginal product. In the same way, firms' willingness to acquire new factories and machines depends on the expected *cost* of using them and the expected *benefit,* equal to the value of the marginal product that they will provide.

Cost-Benefit

EXAMPLE 21.5   Investing in a Capital Good (Part 1)

Should Lauren buy a riding lawn mower?

Lauren is thinking of going into the lawn care business. She can buy a $4,000 riding mower by taking out a loan at 6 percent annual interest. With this mower and her own labor, Lauren can net $6,000 per summer, after deduction of costs such as gasoline and maintenance. Of the $6,000 net revenues, 20 percent must be paid to the government in taxes. Assume that Lauren could earn $4,400 after taxes by working in an alternative job. Assume also that the lawn mower can always be resold for its original purchase price of $4,000. Should Lauren buy the lawn mower?

To decide whether to invest in the capital good (the lawn mower), Lauren should compare the financial benefits and costs. With the mower she can earn revenue of $6,000, net of gasoline and maintenance costs. However, 20 percent of that, or $1,200, must be paid in taxes, leaving Lauren with $4,800. Lauren could earn $4,400 after taxes by working at an alternative job, so the financial benefit to Lauren of buying the mower is the difference between $4,800 and $4,400, or $400; $400 is the value of the marginal product of the lawn mower.

Since the mower does not lose value over time and since gasoline and maintenance costs have already been deducted, the only remaining cost Lauren should take into account is the interest on the loan for the mower. Lauren must pay 6 percent interest on $4,000, or $240 per year. Since this financial cost is less than the financial benefit of $400, the value of the mower's marginal product, Lauren should buy the mower.

Lauren's decision might change if the costs and benefits of her investment in the mower change, as Example 21.6 shows.

EXAMPLE 21.6   Investing in a Capital Good (Part 2)

How do changes in the costs and benefits affect Lauren's decision?

With all other assumptions the same as in Example 21.5, decide whether Lauren should buy the mower:

a. If the interest rate is 12 percent rather than 6 percent.

b. If the purchase price of the mower is $7,000 rather than $4,000.

c. If the tax rate on Lauren's net revenues is 25 percent rather than 20 percent.

d. If the mower is less efficient than Lauren originally thought so that her net revenues will be $5,500 rather than $6,000.

In each case, Lauren must compare the financial costs and benefits of buying the mower.

a. If the interest rate is 12 percent, then the interest cost will be 12 percent of $4,000, or $480, which exceeds the value of the mower's marginal product ($400). Lauren should not buy the mower.

b. If the cost of the mower is $7,000, then Lauren must borrow $7,000 instead of $4,000. At 6 percent interest, her interest cost will be $420—too high to justify the purchase, since the value of the mower's marginal product is $400.

c. If the tax rate on net revenues is 25 percent, then Lauren must pay 25 percent of her $6,000 net revenues, or $1,500, in taxes. After taxes, her revenues from mowing will be $4,500, which is only $100 more than she could make working at an alternative job. Furthermore, the $100 will not cover the $240 in interest that Lauren would have to pay. So again, Lauren should not buy the mower.

d. If the mower is less efficient than originally expected so that Lauren can earn net revenues of only $5,500, Lauren will be left with only $4,400 after taxes—the same amount she could earn by working at another job. So in this case, the value of the mower's marginal product is zero. At any interest rate greater than zero, Lauren should not buy the mower.

 SELF-TEST 21.5

Repeat Example 21.5, but assume that, over the course of the year, wear and tear reduces the resale value of the lawn mower from $4,000 to $3,800. Should Lauren buy the mower?

The examples involving Lauren and the lawn mower illustrate the main factors firms must consider when deciding whether to invest in new capital goods. On the cost side, two important factors are the *price of capital goods* and the *real interest rate*. Clearly, the more expensive new capital goods are, the more reluctant firms will be to invest in them. Buying the mower was profitable for Lauren when its price was $4,000, but not when its price was $7,000.

Why is the real interest rate an important factor in investment decisions? The most straightforward case is when a firm has to borrow (as Lauren did) to purchase its new capital. The real interest rate then determines the real cost to the firm of paying back its debt. Since financing costs are a major part of the total cost of owning and operating a piece of capital, much as mortgage payments are a major part of the cost of owning a home, increases in the real interest rate make the purchase of capital goods less attractive to firms, all else being equal.

Even if a firm does not need to borrow to buy new capital—say, because it has accumulated enough profits to buy the capital outright—the real interest rate remains an important determinant of the desirability of an investment. If a firm does not use its profits to acquire new capital, most likely it will use those profits to acquire financial assets such as bonds, which will earn the firm the real rate of interest. If the firm uses its profits to buy capital rather than to purchase a bond, it forgoes the opportunity to earn the real rate of interest on its funds. Thus the real rate of interest measures the *opportunity cost* of a capital investment. Since an increase in the real interest rate raises the opportunity cost of investing in new capital, it lowers the willingness of firms to invest, even if they do not literally need to borrow to finance new machines or equipment.

On the benefit side, the key factor in determining business investment is the *value of the marginal product* of the new capital, which should be calculated net of both operating and maintenance expenses and taxes paid on the revenues the capital generates. The value of the marginal product is affected by several factors. For example, a technological advance that allows a piece of capital to produce more goods and services would increase the value of its marginal product, as would lower taxes on the revenues produced by the new capital. An increase in the relative price of the good or service that the capital is used to produce will also increase the value of the marginal product and, hence, the desirability of the investment. For example, if the going price for lawn-mowing services were to rise, then all else being equal, investing in the mower would become more profitable for Lauren.

RECAP

FACTORS THAT AFFECT INVESTMENT

Any of the following factors will increase the willingness of firms to invest in new capital:

1. A decline in the price of new capital goods.
2. A decline in the real interest rate.
3. Technological improvement that raises the marginal product of capital.
4. Lower taxes on the revenues generated by capital.
5. A higher relative price for the firm's output.

SAVING, INVESTMENT, AND FINANCIAL MARKETS

Saving and investment are determined by different forces. Ultimately, though, in an economy without international borrowing and lending, national saving must equal investment. The supply of savings (by households, firms, and the government) and the demand for savings (by firms that want to purchase or construct new capital) are equalized through the workings of *financial markets*. Figure 21.5 illustrates this process. Quantities of national saving and investment are measured on the horizontal axis; the real interest rate is shown on the vertical axis. As we will see, in the market for saving, the real interest rate functions as the "price."

In Figure 21.5, the supply of savings is shown by the upward-sloping curve marked *S*. This curve shows the quantity of national saving that households, firms, and the government are willing to supply at each value of the real interest rate. The saving curve is upward-sloping because empirical evidence suggests that increases in the real interest rate stimulate saving. The demand for saving is given by the downward-sloping curve marked *I*. This curve shows the quantity of investment in new capital that firms would choose and hence the amount they would need to borrow in financial markets, at each value of the real interest rate. Because higher real interest rates raise the cost of borrowing and reduce firms' willingness to invest, the demand for saving curve is downward-sloping.

Putting aside the possibility of borrowing from foreigners (discussed in Chapter 23, *Financial Markets and International Capital Flows*), a country can invest only those resources that its savers make available. In equilibrium, then, desired investment (the demand for savings)

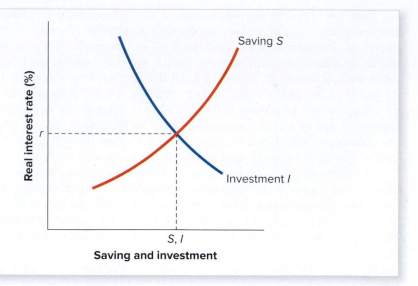

FIGURE 21.5

The Supply of and Demand for Savings.

Savings are supplied by households, firms, and the government and demanded by borrowers wishing to invest in new capital goods. The supply of saving (S) increases with the real interest rate, and the demand for saving by investors (I) decreases with the real interest rate. In financial market equilibrium, the real interest rate takes the value that equates the quantity of saving supplied and demanded.

and desired national saving (the supply of savings) must be equal. As Figure 21.5 suggests, desired saving is equated with desired investment through adjustments in the real interest rate, which functions as the "price" of saving. The movements of the real interest rate clear the market for saving in much the same way that the price of apples clears the market for apples. In Figure 21.5, the real interest rate that clears the market for saving is *r,* the real interest rate that corresponds to the intersection of the supply and demand curves.

The forces that push the real interest rate toward its equilibrium level are similar to the forces that lead to equilibrium in any other supply and demand situation. Suppose, for example, that the real interest rate exceeded *r.* At a higher real interest rate, savers would provide more funds than firms would want to invest. As lenders (savers) competed among themselves to attract borrowers (investors), the real interest rate would be bid down. The real interest rate would fall until it equaled *r,* the only interest rate at which both borrowers and lenders are satisfied, and no opportunities are left unexploited in the financial market. The Equilibrium Principle thus holds for this market. What would happen if the real interest rate were *lower* than *r?*

Equilibrium

Changes in factors *other than the real interest rate* that affect the supply of or demand for saving will shift the curves, leading to a new equilibrium in the financial market. Changes in the real interest rate cannot shift the supply or demand curves, just as a change in the price of apples cannot shift the supply or demand for apples, because the effects of the real interest rate on savings are already incorporated in the slopes of the curves. A few examples will illustrate the use of the supply and demand model of financial markets.

EXAMPLE 21.7

The Effects of New Technology

How does the introduction of new technologies affect saving, investment, and the real interest rate?

The late 1990s saw the introduction and application of exciting new technologies, ranging from the Internet to new applications of genetics. A number of these technologies appeared at the time to have great commercial potential. How does the introduction of new technologies affect saving, investment, and the real interest rate?

The introduction of any new technology with the potential for commercial application creates profit opportunities for those who can bring the fruits of the technology to the public. In economists' language, the technical breakthrough

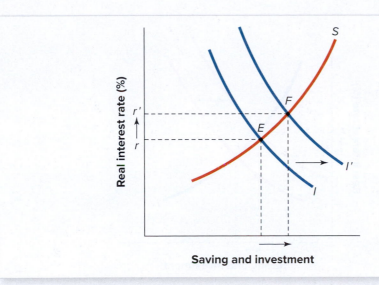

raises the marginal product of new capital. Figure 21.6 shows the effects of a technological breakthrough, with a resulting increase in the marginal product of capital. At any given real interest rate, an increase in the marginal product of capital makes firms more eager to invest. Thus, the advent of the new technology causes the demand for saving to shift upward and to the right, from *I* to *I'*.

At the new equilibrium point *F*, investment and national saving are higher than before, as is the real interest rate, which rises from *r* to *r'*. The rise in the real interest rate reflects the increased demand for funds by investors as they race to apply the new technologies. Because of the incentive of higher real returns, saving increases as well. Indeed, the real interest rate in the United States was relatively high in the late 1990s (see Figure 18.2), as was the rate of investment, reflecting the opportunities created by new technologies.

Example 21.8 examines the effect of changing fiscal policies on the market for saving.

EXAMPLE 21.8   The Effects of Changing Fiscal Policies

How does an increase in the government budget deficit affect saving, investment, and the real interest rate?

Suppose the government increases its spending without raising taxes, thereby increasing its budget deficit (or reducing its budget surplus). How will this decision affect national saving, investment, and the real interest rate?

National saving includes both private saving (saving by households and businesses) and public saving, which is equivalent to the government budget surplus. An increase in the government budget deficit (or a decline in the surplus) reduces public saving. Assuming that private saving does not change, the reduction in public saving will reduce national saving as well.

Figure 21.7 shows the effect of the increased government budget deficit on the market for saving and investment. At any real interest rate, a larger deficit reduces national saving, causing the saving curve to shift to the left, from *S* to *S'*. At the new equilibrium point *F*, the real interest rate is higher at *r'*, and both national saving and investment are lower. In economic terms, the government has dipped further into the pool of private savings to borrow the funds to finance its budget deficit. The government's extra borrowing forces investors to compete for

FIGURE 21.7

The Effects of an Increase in the Government Budget Deficit on National Saving and Investment.

An increase in the government budget deficit reduces the supply of saving, raising the real interest rate and lowering investment. The tendency of increased government deficits to reduce investment in new capital is called *crowding out*.

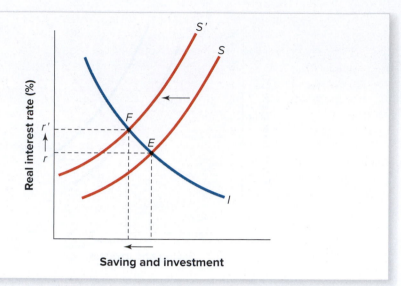

a smaller quantity of available saving, driving up the real interest rate. The higher real interest rate makes investment less attractive, ensuring that investment will decrease along with national saving.

crowding out the tendency of increased government deficits to reduce investment spending

The tendency of government budget deficits to reduce investment spending is called **crowding out.** Reduced investment spending implies slower capital formation, and thus lower economic growth. This adverse effect of budget deficits on economic growth is probably the most important cost of deficits, and a major reason why economists advise governments to minimize their deficits.

✓ SELF-TEST 21.6

Suppose the general public becomes more "grasshopper-like" and less "ant-like" in their saving decisions, becoming less concerned about saving for the future. How will the change in public attitudes affect the country's rate of capital formation and economic growth?

At the national level, high saving rates lead to greater investment in new capital goods and thus higher standards of living. At the individual or family level, a high saving rate promotes the accumulation of wealth and the achievement of economic security. In this chapter we have studied some of the factors that underlie saving and investment decisions. The next chapter will look more closely at how savers hold their wealth and at how the financial system allocates the pool of available savings to the most productive investment projects.

The Economic Naturalist 21.4

Why have real interest rates declined globally in recent decades?

Real interest rates around the world have declined appreciably in the past few decades. In the U.S., the real interest rate on 10-year Treasury bonds—funds borrowed by the federal government for a term of 10 years—declined from around 7–8 percent in the early 1980s to around 0–2 percent in the 2010s. (Figure 18.2 in Chapter 18, *Measuring the Price Level and Inflation*, showed a similar trend in the real interest rate on three-month Treasury bills.) Such trends are found in all advanced economies. What can explain them?

In general, changes in the real interest rate can be caused by shifts in the supply of saving, shifts in the demand for new capital investment, or both. Because the decades-long decline in interest rates has been a global phenomenon, potential explanations have to consider shifts in *global* supply and demand. Indeed, both supply and demand have played an important role.

For simplicity, let's think of the world as a single market.[4] On the supply side, global saving has risen as global incomes have risen (recall our discussion of the rise in global incomes in Chapter 19, *Economic Growth, Productivity, and Living Standards*). Demographic factors, including aging populations and rising life spans, have also been important. Due to aging populations, more people are in the ages in which the need to save for retirement is greatest. And due to rising life spans, people expect to be retired for more years, causing them to save more.

On the demand side, slower global population growth has led to slower workforce growth, in turn reducing the need and thus the demand for new capital (recall our discussion in Chapter 20, *The Labor Market: Workers, Wages, and Unemployment*). In addition, many new industries, like social media companies, require less physical capital than traditional manufacturing industries, further reducing demand.

The combination of higher global saving and lower global investment helps explain the downward trend in real interest rates.[5]

RECAP ↑

SAVING, INVESTMENT, AND FINANCIAL MARKETS

- Financial markets bring together the suppliers of savings (households, firms, and the government) and demanders for savings (firms that want to purchase or construct new capital).
- Putting aside the possibility of borrowing from foreigners (discussed in Chapter 23, *Financial Markets and International Capital Flows*), a country can invest only those resources that its savers make available. In equilibrium, then, desired investment (the demand for savings) must equal desired national saving (the supply of savings).
- In equilibrium, supply and demand are equated through adjustments in the real interest rate, which functions as the "price" of saving.
- Changes in factors other than the real interest rate that affect the supply of or demand for saving will shift the supply and demand curves, leading to a new equilibrium in the financial market.
- For example, any of the following factors will increase the willingness of firms to invest in new capital, and will therefore shift the demand curve outward:

  1. A decline in the price of new capital goods.
  2. Technological improvement that raises the marginal product of capital.
  3. Lower taxes on the revenues generated by capital.
  4. A higher relative price for the firm's output.

---

[4]In this chapter, we focused on *domestic* financial markets, putting aside the possibility of borrowing from foreigners and the possibility of investing abroad. These will be discussed in Chapter 23, *Financial Markets and International Capital Flows*. Here we simply treat the entire world as a single country.

[5]The increase in global saving relative to global investment has been called *the global saving glut*. See "The Global Saving Glut and the U.S. Current Account Deficit," remarks by Governor Ben S. Bernanke at the Sandridge Lecture, Richmond, Virginia Association of Economists, Richmond, Virginia, March 10, 2005, www.federalreserve.gov/boarddocs/speeches/2005/200503102/. Slower growth and lower demand for capital are aspects of *the secular stagnation hypothesis*. See "U.S. Economic Prospects: Secular Stagnation, Hysteresis, and the Zero Lower Bound," keynote address by Lawrence H. Summers at the NABE Policy Conference, February 24, 2014, *Business Economics* 49, pp. 65–73.

SUMMARY

- In general, *saving* equals current income minus spending on current needs; the *saving rate* is the percentage of income that is saved. *Wealth,* or net worth, equals the market value of assets (real or financial items of value) minus liabilities (debts). Saving is a *flow,* being measured in dollars per unit of time; wealth is a *stock,* measured in dollars at a point in time. As the amount of water in a bathtub changes according to the rate at which water flows in, the stock of wealth increases at the saving rate. Wealth also increases if the value of existing assets rises (*capital gains*) and decreases if the value of existing assets falls (*capital losses*). *(LO1)*

- Individuals and households save for a variety of reasons, including *life-cycle* objectives, such as saving for retirement or a new home; the need to be prepared for an emergency (*precautionary saving*); and the desire to leave an inheritance (*bequest saving*). The amount people save is also affected by the real interest rate, which is the "reward" for saving. Evidence suggests that higher real interest rates lead to modest increases in saving. Saving can also be affected by psychological factors, such as the degree of self-control and the desire to consume at the level of one's neighbors (demonstration effects). *(LO2)*

- The saving of an entire country is *national saving S.* National saving is defined by $S = Y - C - G,$ where Y represents total output or income, C equals consumption spending, and G equals government purchases of goods and services. National saving can be broken up into private saving, or $Y - T - C,$ and public saving, or $T - G,$ where T stands for taxes paid to the government less transfer payments and interest paid by the government to the private sector. Private saving can be further broken down into household saving and business saving. In the United States, the bulk of private saving is done by businesses. *(LO3)*

- Public saving is equivalent to the government budget surplus, $T - G;$ if the government runs a budget deficit, then public saving is negative. The U.S. national saving rate is low relative to other industrialized countries, but it is higher than U.S. household saving, and it declined less over the past few decades. *(LO3)*

- Investment is the purchase or construction of new capital goods, including housing. Firms will invest in new capital goods if the benefits of doing so outweigh the costs. Two factors that determine the cost of investment are the price of new capital goods and the real interest rate. The higher the real interest rate, the more expensive it is to borrow, and the less likely firms are to invest. The benefit of investment is the value of the marginal product of new capital, which depends on factors such as the productivity of new capital goods, the taxes levied on the revenues they generate, and the relative price of the firm's output. *(LO4)*

- In the absence of international borrowing or lending, the supply of and demand for national saving must be equal. The supply of national saving depends on the saving decisions of households and businesses and the fiscal policies of the government (which determine public saving). The demand for saving is the amount business firms want to invest in new capital. The real interest rate, which is the "price" of borrowed funds, changes to equate the supply of and demand for national saving. Factors that affect the supply of or demand for saving will change saving, investment, and the equilibrium real interest rate. For example, an increase in the government budget deficit will reduce national saving and investment and raise the equilibrium real interest rate. The tendency of government budget deficits to reduce investment is called *crowding out. (LO5)*

KEY TERMS

assets	government budget deficit	private saving
balance sheet	government budget surplus	public saving
bequest saving	liabilities	saving
capital gains	life-cycle saving	saving rate
capital losses	national saving	stock
crowding out	net worth	transfer payments
flow	precautionary saving	wealth

REVIEW QUESTIONS

1. Explain the relationship between saving and wealth, using the concepts of flows and stocks. Is saving the only means by which wealth can increase? Explain. *(LO1)*

2. Give three basic motivations for saving. Illustrate each with an example. What other factors would psychologists cite as being possibly important for saving? *(LO2)*

3. Define national saving, relating your definition to the general concept of saving. Why does the standard U.S. definition of national saving potentially understate the true amount of saving being done in the economy? *(LO3)*

4. Household saving rates in the U.S. are very low. Is this fact a problem for the U.S. economy? Why or why not? *(LO3)*

5. Why do increases in real interest rates reduce the quantity of saving demanded? (*Hint:* Who are the "demanders" of saving?) *(LO4, LO5)*

6. Name one factor that could increase the supply of saving and one that could increase the demand for saving. Show the effects of each on saving, investment, and the real interest rate. *(LO5)*

PROBLEMS

Mc Graw Hill **connect**

1. Corey has a mountain bike worth $300, credit card debt of $150, $200 in cash, a Sandy Koufax baseball card worth $400, $1,200 in a checking account, and an electric bill due for $250. *(LO1)*
   a. Construct Corey's balance sheet and calculate his net worth. For each remaining part, explain how the event affects Corey's assets, liabilities, and wealth.
   b. Corey goes to a baseball card convention and finds out that his baseball card is a worthless forgery.
   c. Corey uses $150 from his paycheck to pay off his credit card balance. The remainder of his earnings is spent.
   d. Corey writes a $150 check on his checking account to pay off his credit card balance.

   Of the events in parts b–d, which, if any, correspond(s) to saving on Corey's part?

2. State whether each of the following is a stock or a flow, and explain. *(LO1)*
   a. The gross domestic product.
   b. National saving.
   c. The value of the U.S. housing stock on January 1, 2020.
   d. The amount of U.S. currency in circulation as of this morning.
   e. The government budget deficit.
   f. The quantity of outstanding government debt on January 1, 2020.

3. Ellie and Vince are a married couple, both with college degrees and jobs. How would you expect each of the following events to affect the amount they save each month? Explain your answers in terms of the basic motivations for saving. *(LO2)*
   a. Ellie learns she is pregnant.
   b. Vince reads in the paper about possible layoffs in his industry.

   c. Vince had hoped that his parents would lend financial assistance toward the couple's planned purchase of a house, but he learns that they can't afford it.
   d. Ellie announces that she would like to go to law school in the next few years.
   e. A boom in the stock market greatly increases the value of the couple's retirement funds.
   f. Vince and Ellie agree that they would like to leave a substantial amount to local charities in their wills.

4. Individual retirement accounts, or IRAs, were established by the U.S. government to encourage saving. An individual who deposits part of current earnings in an IRA does not have to pay income taxes on the earnings deposited, nor are any income taxes charged on the interest earned by the funds in the IRA. However, when the funds are withdrawn from the IRA, the full amount withdrawn is treated as income and is taxed at the individual's current income tax rate. In contrast, an individual depositing in a non-IRA account has to pay income taxes on the funds deposited and on interest earned in each year but does not have to pay taxes on withdrawals from the account. Another feature of IRAs that is different from a standard saving account is that funds deposited in an IRA cannot be withdrawn prior to retirement, except upon payment of a substantial penalty. *(LO2)*
   a. Sarah, who is five years from retirement, receives a $10,000 bonus at work. She is trying to decide whether to save this extra income in an IRA account or in a regular savings account. Both accounts earn 5 percent nominal interest, and Sarah is in the 30 percent tax bracket in every year (including her retirement year). Compare the amounts that Sarah will have in five years under each of the two saving strategies, net of all taxes. Is the IRA a good deal for Sarah?
   b. Would you expect the availability of IRAs to increase the amount that households save? Discuss in light of (1) the response of saving to changes in the real interest rate and (2) psychological theories of saving.

5. In each part that follows, use the economic data given to find national saving, private saving, public saving, and the national saving rate. *(LO3)*
   a. Household saving = 200   Business saving = 400
      Government purchases of goods and services = 260
      Government transfers and interest payments = 135
      Tax collections = 245   GDP = 3,000
   b. GDP = 6,400   Tax collections = 1,925
      Government transfers and interest payments = 400
      Consumption expenditures = 4,570
      Government budget surplus = 100
   c. Consumption expenditures = 4,800
      Investment = 1,000
      Government purchases = 1,000   Net exports = 16
      Tax collections = 1,700
      Government transfers and interest payments = 500

6. Ellie and Vince are trying to decide whether to purchase a new home. The house they want is priced at $200,000. Annual expenses such as maintenance, taxes, and insurance equal 4 percent of the home's value. If properly maintained, the house's real value is not expected to change. The real interest rate in the economy is 6 percent, and Ellie and Vince can qualify to borrow the full amount of the purchase price (for simplicity, assume no down payment) at that rate. Ignore the fact that mortgage interest payments are tax-deductible in the United States. *(LO4)*
   a. Ellie and Vince would be willing to pay $1,500 monthly rent to live in a house of the same quality as the one they are thinking about purchasing. Should they buy the house?
   b. Does the answer to part a change if they are willing to pay $2,000 monthly rent?
   c. Does the answer to part a change if the real interest rate is 4 percent instead of 6 percent?
   d. Does the answer to part a change if the developer offers to sell Ellie and Vince the house for $150,000?
   e. Why do home-building companies dislike high interest rates?

7. The builder of a new movie theater complex is trying to decide how many screens she wants. Below are her estimates of the number of patrons the complex will attract each year, depending on the number of screens available. *(LO4)*

Number of screens	Total number of patrons
1	40,000
2	75,000
3	105,000
4	130,000
5	150,000

After paying the movie distributors and meeting all other noninterest expenses, the owner expects to net $2.00 per ticket sold. Construction costs are $1,000,000 per screen.
   a. Make a table showing the value of marginal product for each screen from the first through the fifth. What property is illustrated by the behavior of marginal products?

   How many screens will be built if the real interest rate is:
   b. 5.5 percent?
   c. 7.5 percent?
   d. 10 percent?
   e. If the real interest rate is 5.5 percent, how far would construction costs have to fall before the builder would be willing to build a five-screen complex?

8. For each of the following scenarios, use supply and demand analysis to predict the resulting changes in the real interest rate, national saving, and investment. Show all your diagrams. *(LO5)*
   a. The legislature passes a 10 percent investment tax credit. Under this program, for every $100 that a firm spends on new capital equipment, it receives an extra $10 in tax refunds from the government.
   b. A reduction in military spending moves the government's budget from deficit into surplus.
   c. A new generation of computer-controlled machines becomes available. These machines produce manufactured goods much more quickly and with fewer defects.
   d. The government raises its tax on corporate profits. Other tax changes are also made, such that the government's deficit remains unchanged.
   e. Concerns about job security raise precautionary saving.
   f. New environmental regulations increase firms' costs of operating capital.

ANSWERS TO SELF-TESTS

21.1 If Consuelo's student loan were for $6,500 instead of $3,000, her liabilities would be $6,750 (the student loan plus the credit card balance) instead of $3,250. The value of her assets, $6,280, is unchanged. In this case Consuelo's wealth is negative, since assets of $6,280 less liabilities of $6,750 equals −$470. Negative wealth or net worth means one owes more than one owns. *(LO1)*

21.2 If water is being drained from the tub, the flow is negative, equal to −3 gallons per minute. There are 37 gallons in the tub at 7:16 p.m. and 34 gallons at 7:17 p.m. The rate of change of the stock is −3 gallons per minute, which is the same as the flow. *(LO1)*

21.3 a. Consuelo has set aside her usual $20, but she has also incurred a new liability of $50. So her net saving for the week is *minus* $30. Since her assets (her checking account) have increased by $20 but her liabilities (her credit card balance) have increased by $50, her wealth has also declined by $30. *(LO1)*

b. In paying off her credit card bill, Consuelo reduces her assets by $300 by drawing down her checking account and reduces her liabilities by the same amount by reducing her credit card balance to zero. Thus there is no change in her wealth. There is also no change in her saving (note that Consuelo's income and spending on current needs have not changed).

c. The increase in the value of Consuelo's car raises her assets by $500. So her wealth also rises by $500. Changes in the value of existing assets are not treated as part of saving, however, so her saving is unchanged.

d. The decline in the value of Consuelo's furniture is a capital loss of $300. Her assets and wealth fall by $300. Her saving is unchanged.

21.4 The federal government had expenditures greater than receipts, so it ran a deficit. The federal deficit equaled expenditures of 4,507.4 minus revenues of 3,497.7, or $1,009.7 billion. Equivalently, the federal budget surplus was *minus* $1,009.7 billion. State and local governments had a deficit equal to expenditures of 2,862.1 minus receipts of 2,623.0, or $239.1 billion. The entire government sector ran a deficit of 1,009.7 + 239.1 = $1,248.8 billion. (You can also find this answer by adding federal to state and local expenditures and comparing this number to the sum of federal and state–local receipts.) The government sector's contribution to national saving in 2018 was negative, equal to −$1,248.8 billion. *(LO3)*

21.5 The loss of value of $200 over the year is another financial cost of owning the mower, which Lauren should take into account in making her decision. Her total cost is now $240 in interest costs plus $200 in anticipated loss of value of the mower (known as depreciation), or $440. This exceeds the value of marginal product, $400, and so now Lauren should not buy the mower. *(LO4)*

21.6 Household saving is part of national saving. A decline in household saving, and hence national saving, at any given real interest rate shifts the saving supply curve to the left. The results are as in Figure 21.7. The real interest rate rises and the equilibrium values of national saving and investment fall. Lower investment is the same as a lower rate of capital formation, which would be expected to slow economic growth. *(LO5)*

CHAPTER 22

Money, Prices, and the Federal Reserve

Mykola Sosiukin/Getty Images

What role does money play in the economy?

You have probably heard expressions such as "on the money," "smart money," "time is money," "money talks," and "put your money where your mouth is." When people use the word *money,* they often mean something different than what economists mean when they use the word. For an economist, when you get a paycheck, you are receiving income, and any amount that you do not spend on current consumption is saving. Or think about someone who has done well in the stock market: Most people would say that they "made money" in the market. No, an economist would answer, their wealth increased. These terms don't make for a catchy expression, but a good economic naturalist must use words like *income, saving, wealth,* and *money* carefully because each plays a different role in the financial system.

In this chapter, we discuss the role of money in modern economies: why it is important, how it is measured, and how it is created. Money plays a major role in everyday economic transactions but, as we will see, it is also quite important at the macro level. For example, as we mentioned in Chapter 16, *Macroeconomics: The Bird's-Eye View of the Economy,* one of the three main types of macroeconomic policy, monetary policy, relates primarily to decisions about how much money should be allowed to circulate in the economy. In the United States, monetary policy is made by the Federal Reserve, the nation's central bank. Because the Federal Reserve, or the Fed, determines the nation's money supply, this chapter also introduces the Fed and discusses some of the policy tools at its disposal. Finally, the chapter discusses the important relationship between the amount of money in circulation and the rate of inflation in an economy.

MONEY AND ITS USES

money any asset that can be used in making purchases

What exactly is money? To the economist, **money** is any asset that can be used in making purchases. Common examples of money in the modern world are currency and coin. A checking account balance represents another asset that can be used in making payments (as when you write a check or use a debit card to pay for your weekly groceries) and so is also counted as money. In contrast, shares of stock, for example, cannot be used directly in most transactions. Stock must first be sold—that is, converted into cash or a checking account deposit—before further transactions, such as buying your groceries, can be made.

Historically, a wide variety of objects have been used as money, including cacao beans (used by the Aztec people, who dominated central Mexico until the coming of the Spanish in the sixteenth century), gold and silver coins, shells, beads, feathers, and, on the island of Yap, large, immovable boulders. Prior to the use of metallic coins, by far the most common form of money was the cowrie, a type of shell found in the South Pacific. Cowries were used as money in some parts of Africa until recently, being officially accepted for payment of taxes in Uganda until the beginning of the twentieth century. Today, money can be virtually intangible, as in the case of your checking account.

Why do people use money? Money has three principal uses: a *medium of exchange,* a *unit of account,* and a *store of value.*

medium of exchange an asset used in purchasing goods and services

Money serves as a **medium of exchange** when it is used to purchase goods and services, as when you pay cash for a newspaper or write a check to cover your utilities bill. This is perhaps money's most crucial function. Think about how complicated daily life would become if there were no money. Without money, all economic transactions would have to be in the form of **barter,** which is the direct trade of goods or services for other goods or services.

barter the direct trade of goods or services for other goods or services

Barter is highly inefficient because it requires that each party to a trade has something that the other party wants, a so-called double coincidence of wants. For example, under a barter system, a musician could get her dinner only by finding someone willing to trade food for a musical performance. Finding such a match of needs, where each party happens to want exactly what the other person has to offer, would be difficult to do on a regular basis. In a world with money, the musician's problem is considerably simpler. First, she must find someone who is willing to pay money for her musical performance. Then, with the money received, she can purchase the food and other goods and services that she needs. In a society that uses money, it is not necessary that the person who wants to hear music and the person willing to provide food to the musician be one and the same. In other words, there need not be a double coincidence of wants for trades of goods and services to take place.

In a world without money, she could eat only by finding someone willing to trade food for a musical performance.

By eliminating the problem of having to find a double coincidence of wants in order to trade, the use of money in a society permits individuals to specialize in producing particular goods or services, as opposed to having every family or village produce most of what it needs. Specialization greatly increases economic efficiency and material standards of living, as discussed in Chapter 2, *Comparative Advantage,* when we developed the Principle of Comparative Advantage. This usefulness of money in making transactions explains why savers hold money, even though money generally pays a low rate of return. Cash, for example, pays no interest at all, and the balances in checking accounts usually pay a lower rate of interest than could be obtained in alternative financial investments.

Comparative Advantage

unit of account a basic measure of economic value

Money's second function is as a *unit of account.* As a **unit of account,** money is the basic yardstick for measuring economic value. In the United States, virtually all prices— including the price of labor (wages) and the prices of financial assets, such as shares of General Motors stock—are expressed in dollars. Expressing economic values in a common unit of account allows for easy comparisons. For example, grain can be measured in bushels and coal in tons, but to judge whether 20 bushels of grain is economically more or less valuable than a ton of coal, we express both values in dollar terms. The use of money as a unit of account is closely related to its use as a medium of exchange; because money is used to buy and sell things, it makes sense to express prices of all kinds in money terms.

As a **store of value,** its third function, money is a way of holding wealth. For example, the miser who stuffs cash in his mattress or buries gold coins under the old oak tree at midnight is holding wealth in money form. Likewise, if you regularly keep a balance in your checking account, you are holding part of your wealth in the form of money. Although money is usually the primary medium of exchange or unit of account in an economy, it is not the only store of value. There are numerous other ways of holding wealth, such as owning stocks, bonds, or real estate.

For most people, money is not a particularly good way to hold wealth, apart from its usefulness as a medium of exchange. Unlike government bonds and other types of financial assets, most forms of money pay no interest, and there is always the risk of cash being lost or stolen. However, cash has the advantage of being anonymous and difficult to trace, making it an attractive store of value for smugglers, drug dealers, and others who want their assets to stay out of the view of the Internal Revenue Service.

store of value an asset that serves as a means of holding wealth

The Economic Naturalist 22.1

From Ithaca Hours to Bitcoin: What is private money, communally created money, and open-source money?

Since money is such a useful tool, why is money usually issued only by governments? Are there examples of privately issued, or communally created, money?

Money is usually issued by the government, not private individuals, but in part, this reflects legal restrictions on private money issuance. Where the law allows, private moneys do sometimes emerge.[1] For example, privately issued currencies circulate in several U.S. communities. In Ithaca, New York, a private currency famously known as "Ithaca Hours" has circulated since 1991. Instituted by town resident Paul Glover, each Ithaca Hour was originally equivalent to $10, the average hourly wage of workers in the county. The bills, printed with specially developed inks to prevent counterfeiting, honor local people and the environment. Many hundreds of individuals and businesses are estimated to have earned and spent Hours. The idea behind launching local currencies such as Ithaca Hours, which can't be spent elsewhere, is that they may induce people to do more of their shopping in the local economy.

A more recent development in private money was the emergence of the virtual currency known as "Bitcoin" in 2009. This is a peer-to-peer, open-source online payment system without a central administrator, where payments are recorded in a public ledger using Bitcoin as the unit of account. New bitcoins are created as a reward for payment-processing work, known as mining, in which users offer their computing power to verify and record payments into the public ledger. Already circulating bitcoins can be obtained in exchange for other currencies, products, and services. Users can send and receive bitcoins electronically using special wallet software on a personal computer, mobile device, or web application. As of mid June, 2020, the value of one bitcoin was around US$9,300, with more than 18 million bitcoins in circulation.

Despite its promise as a decentralized digital currency, Bitcoin has not been very successful as a money so far, and it is not widely accepted for most transactions. The relatively small commercial use of Bitcoin compared to its use by speculators has contributed to significant price volatility. In a famous episode, in November 2013 one bitcoin traded for more than $1,100—more than 10 times

▶ Visit your instructor's Connect course and access your eBook to view this video.

Are all currencies issued by governments?

bitcoin

---

[1]Barbara A. Good, "Private Money: Everything Old Is New Again," Federal Reserve Bank of Cleveland, *Economic Commentary,* April 1, 1998.

its price in dollars a few months earlier—before sharply declining and trading for less than $300 during much of 2015. More recently, during 2017, the digital currency's price climbed from below $1,000 on January 1 to above $20,000 on December 17. The currency subsequently lost around 85 percent of its value within a single year, and its price dipped below $3,200 on December 15, 2018. This volatility limits Bitcoin's ability to act as a stable store of value and as a reliable unit of account in which prices could be quoted—two of the three principal uses of money described earlier in this chapter.

What do Ithaca Hours and Bitcoin have in common? By functioning as a medium of exchange, each facilitates trade within a community.

MEASURING MONEY

How much money, defined as financial assets usable for making purchases, is there in the U.S. economy at any given time? This question is not simple to answer because, in practice, it is not easy to draw a clear distinction between those assets that should be counted as money and those that should not. Dollar bills are certainly a form of money, and a van Gogh painting certainly is not. However, brokerage firms now offer accounts that allow their owners to combine financial investments in stocks and bonds with check-writing and credit card privileges. Should the balances in these accounts, or some part of them, be counted as money? It is difficult to tell.

Economists skirt the problem of deciding what is and isn't money by using several alternative definitions of money, which vary in how broadly the concept of money is defined. A relatively "narrow" definition of the amount of money in the U.S. economy is called **M1;** it is the sum of currency outstanding and balances held in checking accounts. A broader measure of money, called **M2,** includes all the assets in M1 plus some additional assets that are usable in making payments, but at greater cost or inconvenience than currency or checks. Table 22.1 lists the components of M1 and M2 and also gives the amount of each type of asset outstanding as of January 2020. For most purposes, however, it is sufficient to think of money as the sum of currency outstanding and balances in checking accounts, or M1.

M1 the sum of currency outstanding and balances held in checking accounts

M2 all the assets in M1 plus some additional assets that are usable in making payments but at greater cost or inconvenience than currency or checks

TABLE 22.1
Components of M1 and M2, January 2020

M1		**3,951.3**
Currency	1,717.7	
Demand deposits	1,564.2	
Other checkable deposits	669.4	
M2		**15,432.2**
M1	3,951.3	
Savings deposits	9,908.7	
Small-denomination time deposits	582.1	
Money market mutual funds	990.1	

Notes: Billions of dollars, adjusted for seasonal variations. In M1, currency refers to cash and coin. Demand deposits are non-interest-bearing checking accounts, and "other checkable deposits" includes checking accounts that bear interest. M2 includes all the components of M1, balances in savings accounts, "small-denomination" (under $100,000) deposits held at banks for a fixed term, and money market mutual funds (MMMFs). MMMFs are organizations that sell shares, use the proceeds to buy safe assets (like government bonds), and often allow their shareholders some check-writing privileges.

Source: Federal Reserve release H.6, www.federalreserve.gov/releases/h6/20200116.

Note that credit card balances are not included in either M1 or M2 even though people increasingly use credit cards to pay for many of their purchases, including food, clothing, and even college tuition. The main reason credit card balances are not included in the money supply is that they do not represent part of people's wealth. Indeed, a credit card charge of $1,000 represents an obligation to pay someone else $1,000.

> ### RECAP
>
> **MONEY AND ITS USES**
>
> - *Money* is any asset that can be used in making purchases, such as currency or a checking account. Money serves as a *medium of exchange* when it is used to purchase goods and services. The use of money as a medium of exchange eliminates the need for *barter* and the difficulties of finding a "double coincidence of wants." Money also serves as a *unit of account* and a *store of value*.
> - In practice, two basic measures of money are M1 and M2. M1, a narrower measure, is made up primarily of currency and balances held in checking accounts. The broader measure, M2, includes all the assets in M1 plus some additional assets usable in making payments.
> - Credit card balances are never counted as or considered money because credit card balances are merely obligations to pay others.

COMMERCIAL BANKS AND THE CREATION OF MONEY

What determines the amount of money in the economy? If the economy's supply of money consisted entirely of currency, the answer would be simple: The supply of money would just be equal to the value of the currency created and circulated by the government. However, as we have seen, in modern economies the money supply consists not only of currency but also of deposit balances held by the public in commercial, that is, private, banks. The determination of the money supply in a modern economy thus depends in part on the behavior of commercial banks and their depositors.

To see how the existence of commercial banks affects the money supply, we will use the example of a fictional country, the Republic of Gorgonzola. Initially, we assume, Gorgonzola has no commercial banking system. To make trading easier and eliminate the need for barter, the government directs the central bank of Gorgonzola to put into circulation a million identical paper notes, called guilders. The central bank prints the guilders and distributes them to the populace. At this point, the Gorgonzolan money supply is a million guilders.

However, the citizens of Gorgonzola are unhappy with a money supply made up entirely of paper guilders since the notes may be lost or stolen. In response to the demand for safekeeping of money, some Gorgonzolan entrepreneurs set up a system of commercial banks. At first, these banks are only storage vaults where people can deposit their guilders. When people need to make a payment they can either physically withdraw their guilders or, more conveniently, write a check on their account.

Checks give the banks permission to transfer guilders from the account of the person paying by check to the account of the person to whom the check is made out. With a system of payments based on checks the paper guilders need never leave the banking system, although they flow from one bank to another as a depositor of one bank makes a payment to a depositor in another bank. Deposits do not pay interest in this economy; indeed, the banks can make a profit only by charging depositors fees in exchange for safeguarding their cash.

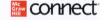

▶ Visit your instructor's Connect course and access your eBook to view this video.

Why can it be more expensive to transfer funds between banks electronically than it is to send a check through the mail?

Let's suppose for now that people prefer bank deposits to cash and so deposit all of their guilders with the commercial banks. With all guilders in the vaults of banks, the balance sheet of all of Gorgonzola's commercial banks taken together is as shown in Table 22.2.

TABLE 22.2

Consolidated Balance Sheet of Gorgonzolan Commercial Banks (Initial)

Assets		Liabilities	
Currency	1,000,000 guilders	Deposits	1,000,000 guilders

The *assets* of the commercial banking system in Gorgonzola are the paper guilders sitting in the vaults of all the individual banks. The banking system's *liabilities* are the deposits of the banks' customers, since checking account balances represent money owed by the banks to the depositors.

bank reserves cash or similar assets held by commercial banks for the purpose of meeting depositor withdrawals and payments

Cash or similar assets held by banks are called **bank reserves.** In this example, bank reserves, for all the banks taken together, equal 1,000,000 guilders—the currency listed on the asset side of the consolidated balance sheet. Banks hold reserves to meet depositors' demands for cash withdrawals or to pay checks drawn on their depositors' accounts. In this example, the bank reserves of 1,000,000 guilders equal 100 percent of banks' deposits, which are also 1,000,000 guilders. A situation in which bank reserves equal 100 percent of bank deposits is called **100 percent reserve banking.**

100 percent reserve banking a situation in which banks' reserves equal 100 percent of their deposits

Bank reserves are held by banks in their vaults, rather than circulated among the public, and thus are *not* counted as part of the money supply. However, bank deposit balances, which can be used in making transactions, *are* counted as money. So, after the introduction of "safekeeper" banks in Gorgonzola, the money supply, equal to the value of bank deposits, is 1,000,000 guilders, which is the same as it was prior to the introduction of banks.

To continue the story, after a while the commercial bankers of Gorgonzola begin to realize that keeping 100 percent reserves against deposits is not necessary. True, a few guilders flow in and out of the typical bank as depositors receive payments or write checks, but for the most part the stacks of paper guilders just sit there in the vaults, untouched and unused. It occurs to the bankers that they can meet the random inflow and outflow of guilders to their banks with reserves that are less than 100 percent of their deposits. After some observation, the bankers conclude that keeping reserves equal to only 10 percent of deposits is enough to meet the random ebb and flow of withdrawals and payments from their individual banks. The remaining 90 percent of deposits, the bankers realize, can be lent out to borrowers to earn interest.

So the bankers decide to keep reserves equal to 100,000 guilders, or 10 percent of their deposits. The other 900,000 guilders they lend out at interest to Gorgonzolan cheese producers who want to use the money to make improvements to their farms. After the loans are made, the balance sheet of all of Gorgonzola's commercial banks taken together has changed, as shown in Table 22.3.

TABLE 22.3

Consolidated Balance Sheet of Gorgonzolan Commercial Banks after One Round of Loans

Assets		Liabilities	
Currency (= reserves)	100,000 guilders	Deposits	1,000,000 guilders
Loans to farmers	900,000 guilders		

After the loans are made, the banks' reserves of 100,000 guilders no longer equal 100 percent of the banks' deposits of 1,000,000 guilders. Instead, the **reserve-deposit ratio**, which is bank reserves divided by deposits, is now equal to 100,000/1,000,000, or 10 percent. A banking system in which banks hold fewer reserves than deposits so that the reserve-deposit ratio is less than 100 percent is called a **fractional-reserve banking system.**

Notice that 900,000 guilders have flowed out of the banking system (as loans to farmers) and are now in the hands of the public. But we have assumed that private citizens prefer bank deposits to cash for making transactions. So ultimately people will redeposit the 900,000 guilders in the banking system. After these deposits are made, the consolidated balance sheet of the commercial banks is as in Table 22.4.

> **reserve-deposit ratio** bank reserves divided by deposits
>
> **fractional-reserve banking system** a banking system in which bank reserves are less than deposits so that the reserve-deposit ratio is less than 100 percent

TABLE 22.4

Consolidated Balance Sheet of Gorgonzolan Commercial Banks after Guilders Are Redeposited

Assets		Liabilities	
Currency (= reserves)	1,000,000 guilders	Deposits	1,900,000 guilders
Loans to farmers	900,000 guilders		

Note that bank deposits, and hence the economy's money supply, now equal 1,900,000 guilders. In effect, the existence of the commercial banking system has permitted the creation of new money. These deposits, which are liabilities of the banks, are balanced by assets of 1,000,000 guilders in reserves and 900,000 guilders in loans owed to the banks. The fractional-reserve commercial banking system has thus led to the creation of additional money over and above the initial 1,000,000 guilders in currency.

However, the story does not end here. On examining their balance sheets, the bankers are surprised to see that they once again have "too many" reserves. With deposits of 1,900,000 guilders and a 10 percent reserve-deposit ratio, they need only 190,000 guilders in reserves. But they have 1,000,000 guilders in reserves—810,000 too many. Since lending out their excess guilders is always more profitable than leaving them in the vault, the bankers proceed to make another 810,000 guilders in loans. Eventually these loaned-out guilders are redeposited in the banking system, after which the consolidated balance sheet of the banks is as shown in Table 22.5.

TABLE 22.5

Consolidated Balance Sheet of Gorgonzolan Commercial Banks after Two Rounds of Loans and Redeposits

Assets		Liabilities	
Currency (= reserves)	1,000,000 guilders	Deposits	2,710,000 guilders
Loans to farmers	1,710,000 guilders		

Now the money supply has increased to 2,710,000 guilders, equal to the value of bank deposits. Despite the expansion of loans and deposits, however, the bankers find that their reserves of 1,000,000 guilders *still* exceed the desired level of 10 percent of deposits, which are 2,710,000 guilders. And so yet another round of lending will take place.

 SELF-TEST 22.1

Determine what the balance sheet of the banking system of Gorgonzola will look like after a third round of lending to farmers and redeposits of guilders into the commercial banking system. What is the money supply at that point?

The process of expansion of loans and deposits will end only when reserves equal 10 percent of bank deposits, because as long as reserves exceed 10 percent of deposits the banks will find it profitable to lend out the extra reserves. Since reserves at the end of every round equal 1,000,000 guilders, for the reserve-deposit ratio to equal 10 percent, total deposits must equal 10,000,000 guilders. Further, since the balance sheet must balance, with assets equal to liabilities, we know as well that at the end of the process loans to cheese producers must equal 9,000,000 guilders. If loans equal 9,000,000 guilders, then bank assets, the sum of loans and reserves (1,000,000 guilders), will equal 10,000,000 guilders, which is the same as bank liabilities (bank deposits). The final consolidated balance sheet is as shown in Table 22.6.

TABLE 22.6
Final Consolidated Balance Sheet of Gorgonzolan Commercial Banks

Assets		Liabilities	
Currency (= reserves)	1,000,000 guilders	Deposits	10,000,000 guilders
Loans to farmers	9,000,000 guilders		

The money supply, which is equal to total deposits, is 10,000,000 guilders at the end of the process. We see that the existence of a fractional-reserve banking system has multiplied the money supply by a factor of 10, relative to the economy with no banks or the economy with 100 percent reserve banking. Put another way, with a 10 percent reserve-deposit ratio, each guilder deposited in the banking system can "support" 10 guilders worth of deposits.

To find the money supply in this example more directly, we observe that deposits will expand through additional rounds of lending as long as the ratio of bank reserves to bank deposits exceeds the reserve-deposit ratio desired by banks. When the actual ratio of bank reserves to deposits equals the desired reserve-deposit ratio, the expansion stops. So ultimately, deposits in the banking system satisfy the following relationship:

$$\frac{\text{Bank reserves}}{\text{Bank deposits}} = \text{Desired reserve-deposit ratio.}$$

This equation can be rewritten to solve for bank deposits:

$$\text{Bank deposits} = \frac{\text{Bank reserves}}{\text{Desired reserve-deposit ratio.}} \tag{22.1}$$

In Gorgonzola, since all the currency in the economy flows into the banking system, bank reserves equal 1,000,000 guilders. The reserve-deposit ratio desired by banks is 0.10. Therefore, using Equation 22.1, we find that bank deposits equal (1,000,000 guilders)/0.10, or 10 million guilders, the same answer we found in the consolidated balance sheet of the banks, Table 22.6.

 SELF-TEST 22.2

Find deposits and the money supply in Gorgonzola if the banks' desired reserve-deposit ratio is 5 percent rather than 10 percent. What if the total amount of currency circulated by the central bank is 2,000,000 guilders and the desired reserve-deposit ratio remains at 10 percent?

THE MONEY SUPPLY WITH BOTH CURRENCY AND DEPOSITS

In the example of Gorgonzola, we assumed that all money is held in the form of deposits in banks. In reality, of course, people keep only part of their money holdings in the form of bank accounts and hold the rest in the form of currency. Fortunately, allowing for the fact that people hold both currency and bank deposits does not greatly complicate the determination of the money supply, as Example 22.1 shows.

EXAMPLE 22.1 | The Money Supply with Both Currency and Deposits

What is the money supply in Gorgonzola when there are both currency and bank deposits?

Suppose that the citizens of Gorgonzola choose to hold a total of 500,000 guilders in the form of currency and to deposit the rest of their money in banks. Banks keep reserves equal to 10 percent of deposits. What is the money supply in Gorgonzola?

The money supply is the sum of currency in the hands of the public and bank deposits. Currency in the hands of the public is given as 500,000 guilders. What is the quantity of bank deposits? Since 500,000 of the 1,000,000 guilders issued by the central bank are being used by the public in the form of currency, only the remaining 500,000 guilders are available to serve as bank reserves. We know that deposits equal bank reserves divided by the reserve-deposit ratio, so deposits are 500,000 guilders/0.10 = 5,000,000 guilders. The total money supply is the sum of currency in the hands of the public (500,000 guilders) and bank deposits (5,000,000 guilders), or 5,500,000 guilders.

We can write a general relationship that captures the reasoning of this example. First, let's write out the fact that the money supply equals currency plus bank deposits:

$$\text{Money supply} = \text{Currency held by the public} + \text{Bank deposits}.$$

We also know that bank deposits equal bank reserves divided by the reserve-deposit ratio that is desired by commercial banks (Equation 22.1). Using that relationship to substitute for bank deposits in the expression for the money supply, we get:

$$\text{Money supply} = \text{Currency held by public} + \frac{\text{Bank reserves}}{\text{Desired reserve-deposit ratio}}. \quad (22.2)$$

We can use Equation 22.2 to confirm our answer to Example 22.1. In that example, currency held by the public is 500,000 guilders, bank reserves are 500,000 guilders, and the desired reserve-deposit ratio is 0.10. Plugging these values into Equation 22.2, we get that the money supply equals 500,000 + 500,000/0.10 = 5,500,000, the same answer we found before.

EXAMPLE 22.2 | The Money Supply at Christmas

How does Christmas shopping affect the money supply?

During the Christmas season people choose to hold unusually large amounts of currency for shopping. With no action by the central bank, how would this change in currency holding affect the national money supply?

To illustrate with a numerical example, suppose that initially bank reserves are 500, the amount of currency held by the public is 500, and the desired reserve-deposit ratio in the banking system is 0.2. Inserting these values into Equation 22.2, we find that the money supply equals 500 + 500/0.2 = 3,000.

Now suppose that because of Christmas shopping needs, the public increases its currency holdings to 600 by withdrawing 100 from commercial banks. These withdrawals reduce bank reserves to 400. Using Equation 22.2 we find now that the money supply is 600 + 400/0.2 = 2,600. So the public's increased holdings of currency have caused the money supply to drop, from 3,000 to 2,600. The reason for the drop is that with a reserve-deposit ratio of 20 percent, every dollar in the vaults of banks can "support" $5 of deposits and hence $5 of money supply. However, the same dollar in the hands of the public becomes $1 of currency, contributing only $1 to the total money supply. So when the public withdraws cash from the banks, the overall money supply declines. (We will see in the next section, however, that in practice the central bank has means to offset the impact of the public's actions on the money supply.)

Later in this book, we discuss situations where an increase in bank reserves does not increase the money supply. Equation 22.2 shows that this will be the case when the reserve-deposit ratio desired by commercial banks increases together with bank reserves. For now, it is important to remember that whether an increase in bank reserves increases the money supply depends on what commercial banks do with their newly acquired reserves.

> **RECAP**
>
> **COMMERCIAL BANKS AND THE CREATION OF MONEY**
>
> - Part of the money supply consists of deposits in private commercial banks. Hence the behavior of commercial banks and their depositors helps to determine the money supply.
> - Cash or similar assets held by banks are called *bank reserves*. In modern economies, banks' reserves are less than their deposits, a situation called *fractional-reserve banking*. The ratio of bank reserves to deposits is called the *reserve-deposit ratio;* in a fractional-reserve banking system, this ratio is less than 1.
> - The portion of deposits not held as reserves can be lent out by the banks to earn interest. Banks will continue to make loans and accept deposits as long as the reserve-deposit ratio exceeds its desired level. This process stops only when the actual and desired reserve-deposit ratios are equal. At that point, total bank deposits equal bank reserves divided by the desired reserve-deposit ratio, and the money supply equals the currency held by the public plus bank deposits.

THE FEDERAL RESERVE SYSTEM

Federal Reserve System (or **the Fed**) the central bank of the United States

monetary policy determination of the nation's money supply

For participants in financial markets and the average citizen as well, one of the most important branches of the government is the **Federal Reserve System**, often called **the Fed.** The Fed is the *central bank* of the United States. Like central banks in other countries, the Fed has two main responsibilities.

First, it is responsible for **monetary policy,** which means that the Fed determines how much money circulates in the economy. As we will see in later chapters, changes in the supply of money can affect many important macroeconomic variables, including interest rates, inflation, unemployment, and exchange rates. Because of its ability to affect key variables, particularly financial variables such as interest rates, financial market participants pay close attention to Fed actions and announcements. As a necessary first step in understanding how Fed policies have the effects that they do, in this chapter we will focus on the basic question of how the Fed affects the supply of money, leaving for later the explanation of why changes in the money supply affect the economy.

Second, along with other government agencies, the Federal Reserve bears important responsibility for the oversight and regulation of financial markets. The Fed also plays a major role during periods of crisis in financial markets. To lay the groundwork for discussing how the Fed carries out its responsibilities, we first briefly review the history and structure of the Federal Reserve System.

THE HISTORY AND STRUCTURE OF THE FEDERAL RESERVE SYSTEM

The Federal Reserve System was created by the Federal Reserve Act, passed by Congress in 1913, and began operations in 1914. Like all central banks, the Fed is a government agency. Unlike commercial banks, which are private businesses whose principal objective is making a profit, central banks like the Fed focus on promoting public goals such as economic growth, low inflation, and the smooth operation of financial markets.

The Federal Reserve Act established a system of 12 regional Federal Reserve banks, each associated with a geographical area called a Federal Reserve district. Congress hoped that the establishment of Federal Reserve banks around the country would ensure that different regions were represented in the national policymaking process. In fact, the regional Feds regularly assess economic conditions in their districts and report this information to policymakers in Washington. Regional Federal Reserve banks also provide various services, such as check-clearing services, to the commercial banks in their district.

At the national level, the leadership of the Federal Reserve System is provided by its **Board of Governors.** The Board of Governors, together with a large professional staff, is located in Washington, D.C. The Board consists of seven governors, who are appointed by the president of the United States to 14-year terms. The terms are staggered so that one governor comes up for reappointment every other year. The president also appoints one of these Board members to serve as chair of the Board of Governors for a term of four years. The Fed chair, along with the secretary of the Treasury, is probably one of the two most powerful economic policymakers in the United States government, after the president. Recent Fed chairs include Paul Volcker (1979–1987), Alan Greenspan (1987–2006), Ben Bernanke (2006–2014), Janet Yellen (2014–2018), and Jerome Powell (2018–present).

Decisions about monetary policy are made by a 12-member committee called the **Federal Open Market Committee (FOMC).** The FOMC consists of the seven Fed governors, the president of the Federal Reserve Bank of New York, and four of the presidents of the other regional Federal Reserve banks, who serve on a rotating basis. The FOMC meets approximately eight times a year to review the state of the economy and to determine monetary policy.

CONTROLLING THE MONEY SUPPLY: OPEN-MARKET OPERATIONS

The Fed's primary responsibility is making monetary policy, which involves decisions about the appropriate size of the nation's money supply. As we saw in the previous section, central banks in general, and the Fed in particular, do not control the money supply directly. However, they can control the money supply indirectly by changing the supply of reserves held by commercial banks.

The Fed has several ways of affecting the supply of bank reserves. Historically, the most important of these is *open-market operations*. Suppose that the Fed wants to increase bank reserves, with the ultimate goal of increasing bank deposits and the money supply. To accomplish this, the Fed buys financial assets, usually government bonds, from the public. The people who sell the bonds to the Fed will deposit the proceeds they receive as payment for their bonds in commercial banks. Thus, the reserves of the commercial banking system will increase by an amount equal to the value of the bonds purchased by the Fed. The increase in bank reserves will lead in turn, through the process of lending and redeposit of funds described in the previous section, to an expansion of bank deposits and the money supply, as summarized by Equation 22.2. The Fed's purchase of government bonds from the public, with the result that bank reserves and the money supply are increased, is called an **open-market purchase.**

Board of Governors the leadership of the Fed, consisting of seven governors appointed by the president to staggered 14-year terms

Federal Open Market Committee (FOMC) the committee that makes decisions concerning monetary policy

open-market purchase the purchase of government bonds from the public by the Fed for the purpose of increasing the supply of bank reserves and the money supply

To reduce bank reserves and hence the money supply, the Fed reverses the procedure. It sells some of the government bonds that it holds (acquired in previous open-market purchases) to the public. Assume that the public pays for the bonds by writing checks on their accounts in commercial banks. Then, when the Fed presents the checks to the commercial banks for payment, reserves equal in value to the government bonds sold by the Fed are transferred from the commercial banks to the Fed. The Fed retires these reserves from circulation, lowering the supply of bank reserves and, hence, the overall money supply. The sale of government bonds by the Fed to the public for the purpose of reducing bank reserves and hence the money supply is called an **open-market sale.** Open-market purchases and sales together are called **open-market operations.**

Open-market operations are the most convenient and flexible tool that the Federal Reserve has for affecting the money supply if we assume, as we have in this chapter, that banks always act to maintain a desired reserve-deposit ratio that never changes. In such a state of affairs, banks always attempt to avoid holding "too many" or "too few" reserves relative to that (never-changing) desired ratio. Changes in reserves caused by open-market operations are therefore immediately translated by banks into changes in lending conditions and the supply of money. Until the 2007–2008 financial crisis, things worked roughly this way, and open-market operations were employed on a regular basis for controlling the money supply. The details and purpose of open-market operations changed following the crisis, as we will discuss in later chapters. In that discussion, we will also introduce additional means by which the Fed can affect the money supply.

open-market sale the sale by the Fed of government bonds to the public for the purpose of reducing bank reserves and the money supply

open-market operations open-market purchases and open-market sales

---

EXAMPLE 22.3 | **Increasing the Money Supply by Open-Market Operations**

How do open-market operations affect the money supply?

In a particular economy, currency held by the public is 1,000 shekels, bank reserves are 200 shekels, and the desired reserve-deposit ratio is 0.2. What is the money supply? How is the money supply affected if the central bank prints 100 shekels and uses this new currency to buy government bonds from the public? Assume that the public does not wish to change the amount of currency it holds.

As bank reserves are 200 shekels and the reserve-deposit ratio is 0.2, bank deposits must equal 200 shekels/0.2, or 1,000 shekels. The money supply, equal to the sum of currency held by the public and bank deposits, is therefore 2,000 shekels, a result you can confirm using Equation 22.2.

The open-market purchase puts 100 more shekels into the hands of the public. We assume that the public continues to want to hold 1,000 shekels in currency, so they will deposit the additional 100 shekels in the commercial banking system, raising bank reserves from 200 to 300 shekels. As the desired reserve-deposit ratio is 0.2, multiple rounds of lending and redeposit will eventually raise the level of bank deposits to 300 shekels/0.2, or 1,500 shekels. The money supply, equal to 1,000 shekels held by the public plus bank deposits of 1,500 shekels, equals 2,500 shekels. So the open-market purchase of 100 shekels, by raising bank reserves by 100 shekels, has increased the money supply by 500 shekels. Again, you can confirm this result using Equation 22.2.

 SELF-TEST 22.3

Continuing Example 22.3, suppose that instead of an open-market purchase of 100 shekels the central bank conducts an open-market sale of 50 shekels' worth of government bonds. What happens to bank reserves, bank deposits, and the money supply?

THE FED'S ROLE IN STABILIZING FINANCIAL MARKETS: BANKING PANICS

Besides controlling the money supply, the Fed also has the responsibility (together with other government agencies) of ensuring that financial markets operate smoothly. Indeed, the creation of the Fed in 1913 was prompted by a series of financial market crises that disrupted both the markets themselves and the U.S. economy as a whole. The hope of the Congress was that the Fed would be able to eliminate or at least control such crises.

Historically, in the United States, *banking panics* were perhaps the most disruptive type of recurrent financial crisis. In a **banking panic,** news or rumors of the imminent bankruptcy of one or more banks leads bank depositors to rush to withdraw their funds. Next, we will discuss banking panics and the Fed's attempts to control them.

Why do banking panics occur? An important factor that helps make banking panics possible is the existence of fractional-reserve banking. In a fractional-reserve banking system, like that of the United States and all other industrialized countries, bank reserves are less than deposits, which means that banks do not keep enough cash on hand to pay off their depositors if they were all to decide to withdraw their deposits. Normally this is not a problem, as only a small percentage of depositors attempt to withdraw their funds on any given day. But if a rumor circulates that one or more banks are in financial trouble and may go bankrupt, depositors may panic, lining up to demand their money. Since bank reserves are less than deposits, a sufficiently severe panic could lead even financially healthy banks to run out of cash, forcing them into bankruptcy and closure.

The Federal Reserve was established in response to a particularly severe banking panic that occurred in 1907. The Fed was equipped with two principal tools to try to prevent or moderate banking panics. First, the Fed was given the power to supervise and regulate banks. It was hoped that the public would have greater confidence in banks, and thus be less prone to panic, if people knew that the Fed was keeping a close watch on bankers' activities. Second, the Fed was allowed to make direct loans to banks through a new facility called the *discount window,* which we will discuss in a later chapter. The idea was that, during a panic, banks could borrow cash from the Fed with which to pay off depositors, avoiding the need to close.

No banking panics occurred between 1914, when the Fed was established, and 1930. However, between 1930 and 1933 the United States experienced the worst and most protracted series of banking panics in its history. Economic historians agree that much of the blame for this panic should be placed on the Fed, which neither appreciated the severity of the problem nor acted aggressively enough to contain it.

> **banking panic** a situation in which news or rumors of the imminent bankruptcy of one or more banks leads bank depositors to rush to withdraw their funds

---

The Economic Naturalist 22.2

Why did the banking panics of 1930–1933 reduce the national money supply?

The worst banking panics ever experienced in the United States occurred during the early stages of the Great Depression, between 1930 and 1933. During this period, approximately one-third of the banks in the United States were forced to close. This near-collapse of the banking system was probably an important reason that the Depression was so severe. With many fewer banks in operation, it was very difficult for small businesses and consumers during the early 1930s to obtain credit. Another important effect of the banking panics was to greatly reduce the nation's money supply. Why should banking panics reduce the national money supply?

During a banking panic, people are afraid to keep deposits in a bank because of the risk that the bank will go bankrupt and their money will be lost (this was prior to the introduction of federal deposit insurance, discussed below). During the 1930–1933 period, many bank depositors withdrew their money from banks, holding currency instead. These withdrawals reduced bank reserves. Each extra dollar of currency held by the public adds $1 to the money supply; but each extra dollar of bank reserves translates into several dollars of money supply because in a fractional-reserve banking system, each dollar of reserves can "support" several dollars in bank deposits. Thus the public's withdrawals from banks, which increased currency holdings by the public but reduced bank reserves by an equal amount, led to a net decrease in the total money supply (currency plus deposits).

In addition, fearing banking panics and the associated withdrawals by depositors, banks increased their reserve-deposit ratios, which reduced the quantity of deposits that could be supported by any given level of bank reserves. This change in reserve-deposit ratios also tended to reduce the money supply.

Data on currency holdings by the public, the reserve-deposit ratio, bank reserves, and the money supply for selected dates are shown in Table 22.7. Notice the increase over the period in the amount of currency held by the public and in the reserve-deposit ratio, as well as the decline in bank reserves after 1930. The last column shows that the U.S. money supply dropped by about one-third between December 1929 and December 1933.

TABLE 22.7
Key U.S. Monetary Statistics, 1929–1933

	Currency held by public	Reserve-deposit ratio	Bank reserves	Money supply
December 1929	3.85	0.075	3.15	45.9
December 1930	3.79	0.082	3.31	44.1
December 1931	4.59	0.095	3.11	37.3
December 1932	4.82	0.109	3.18	34.0
December 1933	4.85	0.133	3.45	30.8

Note: Data on currency, the monetary base, and the money supply are in billions of dollars.

Source: Milton Friedman and Anna J. Schwartz, *A Monetary History of the United States, 1863–1960* (Princeton, NJ: Princeton University Press, 1963), Table A-1.

Using Equation 22.2, we can see that increases in currency holdings by the public and increases in the reserve-deposit ratio both tend to reduce the money supply. These effects were so powerful in 1930–1933 that the nation's money supply, shown in the fourth column of Table 22.7, dropped precipitously, even though currency holdings and bank reserves, taken separately, actually rose during the period.

 SELF-TEST 22.4

Using the data from Table 22.7, confirm that the relationship between the money supply and its determinants is consistent with Equation 22.2. Would the money supply have fallen in 1931–1933 if the public had stopped withdrawing deposits after December 1930 so that currency held by the public had remained at its December 1930 level?

✅ **SELF-TEST 22.5**

According to Table 22.7, the U.S. money supply fell from $44.1 billion to $37.3 billion over the course of 1931. The Fed did use open-market purchases during 1931 to replenish bank reserves in the face of depositor withdrawals. Find (a) the quantity of reserves that the Fed injected into the economy in 1931 and (b) the quantity of reserves the Fed would have had to add to the economy to keep the money supply unchanged from 1930, assuming that public currency holdings and reserve-deposit ratios for each year remained as reported in the table. Why has the Fed been criticized for being too timid in 1931?

When the Fed failed to stop the banking panics of the 1930s, policymakers decided to look at other strategies for controlling panics. In 1934 Congress instituted a system of deposit insurance. Under a system of **deposit insurance,** the government guarantees depositors—specifically, under current rules, those with deposits of less than $250,000—that they will get their money back even if the bank goes bankrupt. Deposit insurance eliminates the incentive for people to withdraw their deposits when rumors circulate that the bank is in financial trouble, which nips panics in the bud. Indeed, since deposit insurance was instituted, the United States has had no significant banking panics.

Unfortunately, deposit insurance is not a perfect solution to the problem of banking panics. An important drawback is that when deposit insurance is in force, depositors know they are protected no matter what happens to their bank, and they become completely unconcerned about whether their bank is making prudent loans. This situation can lead to reckless behavior by banks or other insured intermediaries. For example, during the 1980s many savings and loan associations in the United States went bankrupt, in part because of reckless lending and financial investments. Like banks, savings and loans have deposit insurance, so the U.S. government had to pay savings and loan depositors the full value of their deposits. This action ultimately cost U.S. taxpayers hundreds of billions of dollars.

The Fed's role in stabilizing financial markets took center stage in more recent episodes of financial panic. During the global financial crisis of 2008 and, more recently, the financial disruptions related to the global COVID-19 pandemic of 2020, the Fed acted as a "lender of last resort." In this role, the Fed provided urgently needed credit lines to stressed financial institutions. To be able to lend to a set of institutions broader than commercial banks—to which the Fed can typically lend—the Fed revived a rarely used provision found in Section 13(3) of the Federal Reserve Act. The section, which was added in 1932 during the banking panics, allows the Fed to lend to nonbank institutions under certain "unusual and exigent" circumstances. Using this section for the first time since the 1930s, the Fed set up in 2008 special lending facilities for nonbank institutions. It further provided special assistance to specific firms that it considered "too big to fail." The Fed revived Section 13(3) lending in 2020, when it again found itself under unusual market conditions. We discuss monetary policy during the 2008 and 2020 episodes in later chapters.

deposit insurance a system under which the government guarantees that depositors will not lose any money even if their bank goes bankrupt

---

RECAP ↑

THE FEDERAL RESERVE SYSTEM

- The Fed is the central bank of the United States. Like central banks in other countries, it has two main responsibilities. First, it is in charge of monetary policy—that is, it determines how much money circulates in the economy. Second, it bears important responsibility for the oversight and regulation of financial markets. The Fed also plays a major role during periods of crisis in financial markets.

- An open-market purchase is the purchase of government bonds from the public by the Fed for the purpose of increasing the supply of bank reserves and the money supply. An open-market sale is the sale by the

> Fed of government bonds to the public for the purpose of reducing bank reserves and the money supply.
> - Historically, such open-market operations are the most important among several ways that the Fed has of affecting the supply of bank reserves and the money supply.

MONEY AND PRICES

From a macroeconomic perspective, a major reason that control of the supply of money is important is that, *in the long run, the amount of money circulating in an economy and the general level of prices are closely linked.* Indeed, it is virtually unheard of for a country to experience high, sustained inflation without a comparably rapid growth in the amount of money held by its citizens. The late economist Milton Friedman summarized the inflation–money relationship by saying, "Inflation is always and everywhere a monetary phenomenon." We will see in a later chapter that, over short periods, inflation can arise from sources other than an increase in the supply of money. But over a longer period, and particularly for more severe inflations, Friedman's dictum is certainly correct: The rate of inflation and the rate of growth of the money supply are closely related.

The existence of a close link between money supply and prices should make intuitive sense. Imagine a situation in which the available supply of goods and services is approximately fixed. Then the more cash (say, dollars) that people hold, the more they will be able to bid up the prices of the fixed supply of goods and services. Thus, a large money supply relative to the supply of goods and services (too much money chasing too few goods) tends to result in high prices. Likewise, a rapidly *growing* supply of money will lead to quickly *rising* prices—that is, inflation.

VELOCITY

velocity a measure of the speed at which money circulates, that is, the speed at which money changes hands in transactions involving final goods and services, or, equivalently, nominal GDP divided by the stock of money. Numerically, $V = (P \times Y)/M$, where V is velocity, $P \times Y$ is nominal GDP, and M is the money supply whose velocity is being measured

To explore the relationship of money growth and inflation in a bit more detail, it is useful to introduce the concept of *velocity.* In economics, **velocity** is a measure of the speed at which money circulates, that is, the speed at which money changes hands in transactions involving final goods and services. For example, a given dollar bill might pass from your hand to the grocer's when you buy a quart of milk. The same dollar may then pass from the grocer to a new car dealer when your grocer buys a car, and then from the car dealer to her doctor in exchange for medical services. The more quickly money circulates from one person to the next, the higher its velocity. More formally, velocity is defined as the value of transactions completed in a period of time divided by the stock of money required to make those transactions. The higher this ratio, the faster the "typical" dollar is circulating.

As a practical matter, we usually do not have precise measures of the total value of transactions taking place in an economy; so, as an approximation, economists often measure the total value of transactions in a given period by nominal GDP for that period. A numerical value of velocity can be obtained from the following formula:

$$\text{Velocity} = \frac{\text{Value of transactions}}{\text{Money stock}}$$

$$= \frac{\text{Nominal GDP}}{\text{Money stock}}.$$

Let V stand for velocity and let M stand for the particular money stock being considered (for example, M1 or M2). Nominal GDP (a measure of the total value of transactions) equals the price level P times real GDP (Y). Using this notation, we can write the definition of velocity as

$$V = \frac{P \times Y}{M}. \tag{22.3}$$

The higher the V, the faster money is circulating.

EXAMPLE 22.4	The Velocity of Money in the U.S. Economy

What is the velocity of the U.S. money supply?

In 2018, M1 was \$3,677.2 billion, M2 was \$14,103.5 billion, and nominal GDP was \$20,580.2 billion. We can use these data along with Equation 22.3 to find velocity for both definitions of the money supply. For M1, we have

$$V = \frac{\$20{,}580.2 \text{ billion}}{\$3{,}677.2 \text{ billion}} = 5.60.$$

Similarly, velocity for M2 was

$$V = \frac{\$20{,}580.2 \text{ billion}}{\$14{,}103.5 \text{ billion}} = 1.46.$$

You can see that the velocity of M1 is higher than that of M2. This makes sense: Because the components of M1, such as cash and checking accounts, are used more frequently for transactions, each dollar of M1 "turns over" more often than the average dollar of M2.

A variety of factors determine velocity. A leading example is advances in payment technologies such as the introduction of credit cards and debit cards or the creation of networks of automated teller machines (ATMs). These technologies and payment methods have allowed people to carry out their daily business while holding less cash, and thus have tended to increase velocity over time. Other examples include economic conditions and monetary policy, which could increase or decrease velocity more quickly. As we will discuss in Chapter 26, *Stabilizing the Economy: The Role of the Fed,* velocity for M1 increased from less than 4 in 1960 to more than 10 in 2007, before declining again to less than 6 more recently.

MONEY AND INFLATION IN THE LONG RUN

We can use the definition of velocity to see how money and prices are related in the long run. First, rewrite the definition of velocity, Equation 22.3, by multiplying both sides of the equation by the money stock M. This yields

$$M \times V = P \times Y. \qquad (22.4)$$

Equation 22.4 is called the *quantity equation*. The **quantity equation** states that money times velocity equals nominal GDP. Because the quantity equation is simply a rewriting of the definition of velocity, Equation 22.3, it always holds exactly.

The quantity equation is historically important because late nineteenth- and early twentieth-century monetary economists, such as Yale's Irving Fisher, used this relationship to theorize about the relationship between money and prices. We can do the same thing here. To keep things simple, imagine that velocity V is determined by current payment technologies and thus is approximately constant over the period we are considering. Likewise, suppose that real output Y is approximately constant. If we use a bar over a variable to indicate that the variable is constant, we can rewrite the quantity equation as

$$M \times \overline{V} = P \times \overline{Y}, \qquad (22.5)$$

where we are treating $\overline{V}$ and $\overline{Y}$ as fixed numbers.

Now look at Equation 22.5 and imagine that for some reason the Federal Reserve increases the money supply M by 10 percent. Because $\overline{V}$ and $\overline{Y}$ are assumed to be fixed, Equation 22.5 can continue to hold only if the price level P also rises by 10 percent. That is, according to the quantity equation, a 10 percent increase in the money supply M should cause a 10 percent increase in the price level P, that is, an inflation of 10 percent.

quantity equation money times velocity equals nominal GDP: $M \times V = P \times Y$

The intuition behind this conclusion is the one we mentioned at the beginning of this section. If the quantity of goods and services Y is approximately constant (and assuming that velocity V also is constant), an increase in the supply of money will lead people to bid up the prices of the available goods and services. Thus, high rates of money growth will tend to be associated with high rates of inflation. Figure 22.1 shows this relationship for 10 countries in Latin America during the period 1995–2001. You can see that countries with higher rates of money growth tend also to have higher rates of inflation. The relationship between money growth and inflation is not exact, in part because—as we mentioned earlier, and contrary to the simplifying assumption we made here—velocity and output are not constant but vary over time.

FIGURE 22.1

Inflation and Money Growth in Latin America, 1995–2001.

Latin American countries with higher rates of growth in their money supplies also tended to have higher rates of inflation between 1995 and 2001. (The data for Argentina and Uruguay end on 2000 and the data for Ecuador end in 1997. In 1997 Ecuador abandoned its currency, the sucre, and began using dollars instead.)

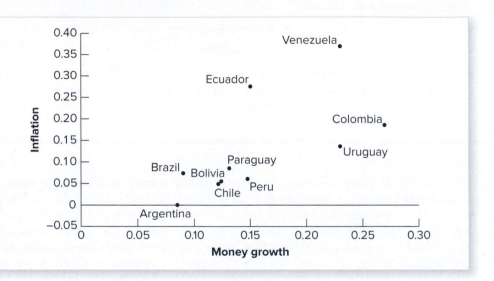

If high rates of money growth lead to inflation, why do countries allow their money supplies to rise quickly? Usually, rapid rates of money growth are the result of large government budget deficits. Particularly in developing countries or countries suffering from war or political instability, governments sometimes find that they cannot raise sufficient taxes or borrow enough from the public to cover their expenditures. In this situation, the government's only recourse may be to print new money and use this money to pay its bills. If the resulting increase in the amount of money in circulation is large enough, the result will be inflation.

A very large budget deficit that is financed by printing money can lead to *hyperinflation,* which we discussed in Chapter 18, *Measuring the Price Level and Inflation.* The Confederate States of America during the Civil War, Germany after World War I, and, more recently, Zimbabwe and Venezuela, found themselves in exactly this situation: They could not raise sufficient taxes to cover government spending, so they printed large quantities of paper money to pay for government expenditures. As Equation 22.5 predicts, the initial large increase in M led to a large increase in P. But this made the deficit still larger in nominal terms, leading in turn to a larger increase in M in order to finance that larger nominal deficit. This in turn led to an even larger increase in P, and so on, with both M and P growing at an accelerating rate.

Equation 22.5 also provides a way to stop hyperinflations: reduce the growth rate of the money supply. This is, of course, easier said than done. To accomplish this, the government must somehow cut spending and/or raise taxes so that the budget deficit is smaller and can be financed through borrowing rather than money issue. The German government, for example, enacted reforms in late 1923 that made it difficult for the government to print money to cover its budget deficits. Inflation slowed dramatically in the months after the reform. The Confederacy, on the other hand, was unable to stop its hyperinflation. After the battles of Gettysburg and Vicksburg in 1863, it was clear that the Confederacy would ultimately lose the war. It could only sell bonds at exorbitant interest rates and could not collect taxes since the individual states controlled tax collections. Hyperinflation ended only with the Confederacy's defeat in April 1865.

As we have mentioned, episodes of hyperinflation rarely last for long. It is not rare for them to end with a fall of the government.

RECAP

THE MONEY SUPPLY AND PRICES

- A high rate of money growth generally leads to inflation. The larger the amount of money in circulation, the higher the public will bid up the prices of available goods and services.
- *Velocity* measures the speed at which money circulates, that is, the speed at which money changes hands in transactions involving final goods and services; equivalently it is equal to nominal GDP divided by the stock of money. A numerical value for velocity can be obtained from the equation $V = (P \times Y)/M$, where V is velocity, $P \times Y$ is nominal GDP, and M is the money supply.
- The *quantity equation* states that money times velocity equals nominal GDP, or, in symbols, $M \times V = P \times Y$. The quantity equation is a restatement of the definition of velocity and thus always holds. If velocity and output are approximately constant, the quantity equation implies that a given percentage increase in the money supply leads to the same percentage increase in the price level. In other words, the rate of growth of the money supply equals the rate of inflation.

SUMMARY

- *Money* is any asset that can be used in making purchases, such as currency and checking account balances. Money has three main functions: It is a *medium of exchange,* which means that it can be used in transactions. It is a *unit of account,* in that economic values are typically measured in units of money (for example, dollars). And it is a *store of value,* a means by which people can hold wealth. In practice, it is difficult to measure the money supply since many assets have some moneylike features. A relatively narrow measure of money is M1, which includes currency and checking accounts. A broader measure of money, M2, includes all the assets in M1 plus additional assets that are somewhat less convenient to use in transactions than those included in M1. *(LO1)*

- Because bank deposits are part of the money supply, the behavior of commercial banks and of bank depositors affects the amount of money in the economy. A key factor is the *reserve-deposit ratio* chosen by banks. *Bank reserves* are cash or similar assets held by commercial banks, for the purpose of meeting depositor withdrawals and payments. The reserve-deposit ratio is bank reserves divided by deposits in banks. A banking system in which all deposits are held as reserves practices *100 percent reserve banking.* Modern banking systems have reserve-deposit ratios less than 100 percent and are called *fractional-reserve banking systems. (LO2)*

- Commercial banks create money through multiple rounds of lending and accepting deposits. This process of lending and increasing deposits comes to an end when banks' reserve-deposit ratios equal their desired levels. At that point, bank deposits equal bank reserves divided by the desired reserve-deposit ratio. The money supply equals currency held by the public plus deposits in the banking system. *(LO2)*

- The central bank of the United States is called the *Federal Reserve System,* or the Fed for short. The Fed's two main responsibilities are making monetary policy, which means determining how much money will circulate in the economy, and overseeing and regulating financial markets, especially banks. Created in 1914, the Fed is headed by a *Board of Governors* made up of seven governors appointed by the president. One of these seven governors is appointed chair. The *Federal Open Market Committee,* which meets about eight times a year to determine monetary policy, is made up of the seven governors, the president of the Federal Reserve Bank of New York, and four of the presidents of the regional Federal Reserve banks. *(LO3)*

- One of the original purposes of the Federal Reserve was to help eliminate or control banking panics. A *banking panic* is an episode in which depositors, spurred by news or rumors of the imminent bankruptcy of one or more banks, rush to withdraw their deposits from the banking system. Because banks do not keep enough reserves on hand to pay off all depositors, even a financially healthy bank can run out of cash during a panic and be forced to close. The Federal Reserve failed to contain banking panics during the Great Depression, which led to sharp declines in the money supply. The adoption of a system of *deposit insurance* in the United States eliminated banking panics. A disadvantage of deposit insurance is that if banks or other insured intermediaries make bad loans or financial investments, the taxpayers may be responsible for covering the losses. *(LO3)*

- In the long run, the rate of growth of the money supply and the rate of inflation are closely linked because a larger amount of money in circulation allows people to bid up the prices of existing goods and services. *Velocity* measures the speed at which money circulates; equivalently, it is the value of transactions completed in a period of time, divided by the stock of money required to make those transactions. Velocity is defined by the equation $V = (P \times Y)/M$, where V is velocity, $P \times Y$ is nominal GDP (a measure of the total value of transactions), and M is the money supply. The definition of velocity can be rewritten as the *quantity equation*, $M \times V = P \times Y$. The quantity equation shows that, if velocity and output are constant, a given percentage increase in the money supply will lead to the same percentage increase in the price level. *(LO4)*

KEY TERMS

bank reserves	fractional-reserve banking	open-market purchase
banking panic	system	open-market sale
barter	M1	quantity equation
Board of Governors	M2	reserve-deposit ratio
deposit insurance	medium of exchange	store of value
Federal Open Market Committee	money	unit of account
(FOMC)	monetary policy	velocity
Federal Reserve System	100 percent reserve banking	
(or the Fed)	open-market operations	

REVIEW QUESTIONS

1. What is *money?* Why do people hold money even though it pays a lower return than other financial assets? *(LO1)*

2. Suppose that the public switches from doing most of its shopping with currency to using checks instead. If the Fed takes no action, what will happen to the national money supply? Explain. *(LO2, LO3)*

3. The Fed wants to reduce the U.S. money supply using open-market operations. Describe what it would do and explain how this action would accomplish the Fed's objective. *(LO3)*

4. What is a *banking panic?* Prior to the introduction of deposit insurance, why might even a bank that had made sound loans have reason to fear a panic? *(LO3)*

5. Define *velocity.* How has the introduction of new payment technologies affected velocity? Explain. *(LO4)*

6. Use the quantity equation to explain why money growth and inflation tend to be closely linked. *(LO4)*

PROBLEMS

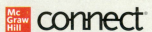

1. During World War II, an Allied soldier named Robert Radford spent several years in a large German prisoner-of-war camp. At times, more than 50,000 prisoners were held in the camp, with some freedom to move about within the compound. Radford later wrote an account of his experiences. He described how an economy developed in the camp, in which prisoners traded food, clothing, and other items. Services, such as barbering, were also exchanged. Lacking paper money, the prisoners began to use cigarettes (provided monthly by the Red Cross) as money. Prices were quoted, and payments made, using cigarettes. *(LO1)*

a. In Radford's POW camp, how did cigarettes fulfill the three functions of money?

b. Why do you think the prisoners used cigarettes as money, as opposed to other items of value such as squares of chocolate or pairs of boots?

c. Do you think a nonsmoking prisoner would have been willing to accept cigarettes in exchange for a good or service in Radford's camp? Why or why not?

2. Redo the example of Gorgonzola in the text (see Tables 22.2 to 22.6), assuming that (1) initially, the Gorgonzolan central bank puts 5,000,000 guilders into circulation, and (2) commercial banks desire to hold reserves of 20 percent of deposits. As in the text, assume that the public holds no currency. Show the consolidated

balance sheets of Gorgonzolan commercial banks for each of the following instances. *(LO2)*

a. After the initial deposits (compare to Table 22.2).

b. After one round of loans (compare to Table 22.3).

c. After the first redeposit of guilders (compare to Table 22.4).

d. After two rounds of loans and redeposits (Table 22.5).

e. What are the final values of bank reserves, loans, deposits, and the money supply (compare to Table 22.6)?

3. Answer each of the following questions: *(LO2)*

a. Bank reserves are 100, the public holds 200 in currency, and the desired reserve-deposit ratio is 0.25. Find deposits and the money supply.

b. The money supply is 500, and currency held by the public equals bank reserves. The desired reserve-deposit ratio is 0.25. Find currency held by the public and bank reserves.

c. The money supply is 1,250, of which 250 is currency held by the public. Bank reserves are 100. Find the desired reserve-deposit ratio.

4. When a central bank increases bank reserves by $1, the money supply rises by more than $1. The amount of extra money created when the central bank increases bank reserves by $1 is called the *money multiplier. (LO2)*

a. Explain why the money multiplier is generally greater than 1. In what special case would it equal 1?

b. The initial money supply is $1,000, of which $500 is currency held by the public. The desired reserve-deposit ratio is 0.2. Find the increase in money supply associated with increases in bank reserves of $1, $5, and $10. What is the money multiplier in this economy?

c. Find a general rule for calculating the money multiplier.

5. Refer to Table 22.7. Suppose that the Fed had decided to set the U.S. money supply in December 1932 and in December 1933 at the same value as in December 1930. Assuming that the values of currency held by the public and the reserve-deposit ratio had remained as given in the table, by how much more should the Fed have increased bank reserves at each of those dates to accomplish that objective? *(LO3)*

6. The Federal Reserve System was created by the Federal Reserve Act, passed by Congress in 1913, and began operations in 1914. Like all central banks, the Fed is a government agency. Which of the following statements about the Fed is false? *(LO3)*

a. The Fed has the power to supervise and regulate banks.

b. The Fed's goals are to promote economic growth, maintain low inflation, and watch over a smooth operation of financial markets.

c. The Fed is the "lender of last resort."

d. The Fed is allowed to make a profit like commercial banks.

7. Consider a country in which real GDP is $9 trillion, nominal GDP is $12 trillion, M1 is $2.5 trillion, and M2 is $5.5 trillion. *(LO4)*

a. Find velocity for M1 and for M2.

b. Show that the quantity equation holds for both M1 and M2.

8. Consider the following hypothetical data for 2019 and 2020: *(LO4)*

	2019	2020
Money supply	1,000	1,050
Velocity	8	8
Real GDP	12,000	12,000

a. Find the price level for 2019 and 2020. What is the rate of inflation between the two years?

b. What is the rate of inflation between 2019 and 2020 if the money supply in 2020 is 1,100 instead of 1,050?

c. What is the rate of inflation between 2019 and 2020 if the money supply in 2020 is 1,100 and output in 2020 is 12,600?

ANSWERS TO SELF-TESTS

22.1 Table 22.5 shows the balance sheet of banks after two rounds of lending and redeposits. At that point, deposits are 2,710,000 guilders and reserves are 1,000,000 guilders. Since banks have a desired reserve-deposit ratio of 10 percent, they will keep 271,000 guilders (10 percent of deposits) as reserves and lend out the remaining 729,000 guilders. Loans to farmers are now 2,439,000 guilders. Eventually the 729,000 guilders lent to the farmers will be redeposited into the banks, giving the banks deposits of 3,439,000 guilders and reserves of 1,000,000 guilders. The balance sheet is as shown in the accompanying table:

Assets	
Currency (= reserves)	1,000,000 guilders
Loans to farmers	2,439,000 guilders
Liabilities	
Deposits	3,439,000 guilders

Notice that assets equal liabilities. The money supply equals deposits, or 3,439,000 guilders. Currency held in the banks as reserves does not count in the money supply. *(LO2)*

22.2 Because the public holds no currency, the money supply equals bank deposits, which in turn equal bank reserves divided by the reserve-deposit ratio (Equation 22.1). If bank reserves are 1,000,000 and the reserve-deposit ratio is 0.05, then deposits equal 1,000,000/0.05 = 20,000,000 guilders, which is also the money supply. If bank reserves are 2,000,000 guilders and the reserve-deposit ratio is 0.10, then the money supply and deposits are again equal to 20,000,000 guilders, or 2,000,000/0.10. *(LO2)*

22.3 If the central bank sells 50 shekels of government bonds in exchange for currency, the immediate effect is to reduce the amount of currency in the hands of the public by 50 shekels. To restore their currency holding to the desired level of 1,000 shekels, the public will withdraw 50 shekels from commercial banks, reducing bank reserves from 200 shekels to 150 shekels. The desired reserve-deposit ratio is 0.2, so ultimately deposits must equal 150 shekels in reserves divided by 0.2, or 750 shekels. (*Note:* To contract deposits, the commercial banks will have to "call in" loans, reducing their loans outstanding.) The money supply equals 1,000 shekels in currency held by the public plus 750 shekels in deposits, or 1,750 shekels. Thus the open-market purchase has reduced the money supply from 2,000 to 1,750 shekels. *(LO3)*

22.4 Verify directly for each date in Table 22.7 that:

Money supply =

$$\text{Currency} + \frac{\text{Bank reserves}}{\text{Desired reserve-deposit ratio}}.$$

For example, for December 1929 we can check that 45.9 = 3.85 + 3.15/0.075.

Suppose that the currency held by the public in December 1933 had been 3.79, as in December 1930, rather than 4.85, and that the difference (4.85 − 3.79 = 1.06) had been left in the banks. Then bank reserves in December 1933 would have been 3.45 + 1.06 = 4.51, and the money supply would have been 3.79 + 4.51/0.133 = 37.7. So the money supply would still have fallen between 1930 and 1933 if people had not increased their holdings of currency, but only by about half as much. *(LO3)*

22.5 Over the course of 1931, currency holdings by the public rose by $0.80 billion but bank reserves fell overall by only $0.20 billion. Thus the Fed must have replaced $0.60 billion of lost reserves during the year through open-market purchases or discount window lending.

Currency holdings at the end of 1931 were $4.59 billion. To have kept the money supply at the December 1930 value of $44.1 billion, the Fed would have had to ensure that bank deposits equaled $44.1 billion − $4.59 billion, or $39.51 billion. As the reserve-deposit ratio in 1931 was 0.095, this would have required bank reserves of 0.095 × $39.51 billion, or $3.75 billion, compared to the actual value in December 1931 of $3.11 billion. Thus, to keep the money supply from falling, the Fed would have had to increase bank reserves by $0.64 billion more than it did. The Fed has been criticized for increasing bank reserves by only about half what was needed to keep the money supply from falling. *(LO3)*

Financial Markets and International Capital Flows

How does the financial system work in a modern economy?

Danil Melekhin/Getty Images

LEARNING OBJECTIVES

After reading this chapter, you should be able to:

LO1 Describe the role of financial intermediaries, such as commercial banks in the financial system, and differentiate between bonds and stocks.

LO2 Show how the financial market improves the allocation of saving to productive uses.

LO3 Analyze the factors that determine international capital flows to understand how domestic saving, the trade balance, and net capital flows are related.

A n old television ad for an online trading company aired around the turn of the millennium and showed an office worker, call him Ed, sitting in front of his computer. Instead of working, Ed is checking the prices of stocks he bought online. Suddenly his eyes widen, as on the computer screen a graph shows the price of his stock shooting up like a rocket. With a whoop Ed heads down to his boss's office, delivers a few well-chosen insults, and quits his job. Unfortunately, when Ed returns to his desk to pack up his belongings, the computer screen shows that the price of his stock has fallen as quickly as it rose. The last we hear of Ed are his futile attempts to convince his boss that he was only kidding.

Ed's story is not a bad metaphor for the behavior of U.S. financial markets—back then, as well as more recently. The 1990s were a boom period in the United States, with strong economic growth, record low unemployment rates, and almost nonexistent inflation. This prosperity was mirrored in the spectacular performance of the stock market. In 1999, the Dow Jones index, a popular measure of stock prices, broke 10,000 and then 11,000 for the first time—almost triple the value of the index five years earlier. Stock prices of start-up companies, particularly high-technology and Internet companies, rose to stunning levels, making billionaires of some entrepreneurs still in their twenties. And the benefits of rising stock prices were not confined to the very rich or the very nerdy. Stock ownership among the general population—including both direct ownership of stocks and indirect ownership through mutual funds and pension plans—reached record levels. The stock market boom, however, was not sustained. High-tech companies did not produce the profits that their investors had hoped for, and stock prices began to drop. Many start-up companies saw their stock become nearly worthless, and the values of even established companies fell by one-third or more.

The bust of the early 2000s, in turn, did not last forever either. By late 2006, the Dow Jones index recovered all the ground it had lost since 2000 and broke 12,000 for the first time. In 2007, it broke 13,000 and then 14,000—before again collapsing, this time to less than 7,000, losing more than half its value, and returning by 2009 to its level more than a decade earlier. Since then, stocks have experienced a new boom, and in early January 2020, the Dow broke 29,000 for the first time—before dropping by more than a third in the following two months, and again recovering all lost ground by September.

During boom periods, people often begin to think of the stock market as a place to gamble and, maybe, to strike it rich. Some people do get rich playing the market, and some people, like Ed and many real-life investors in stocks in recent decades, lose everything. But the stock market, as well as other financial markets, plays a crucial role in the economy that is not shared by the gambling establishments in Las Vegas or Atlantic City. That role is to ensure that national saving is devoted to the most productive uses.

In Chapter 21, *Saving and Capital Formation*, we discussed the importance of national saving. Under most circumstances, a high rate of national saving permits a high rate of capital formation, which both economic logic and experience predict will tend to increase labor productivity and living standards. However, creating new capital does not *guarantee* a richer and more productive economy. History is full of examples of "white elephants"—capital projects in which millions, and even billions, of dollars were invested with little economic benefit: nuclear power plants that were never opened; massive dams whose main effect was to divert water supplies and disrupt the local agriculture; new technologies that just didn't work as planned.

A healthy economy not only saves adequately, but also invests those savings in a productive way. In market economies, like that of the United States, channeling society's savings into the best possible capital investments is the role of the financial system: banks, stock markets, bond markets, and other financial markets and institutions. For this reason, many economists have argued that the development of well-functioning financial markets is a crucial precursor to sustained economic growth. In the first part of this chapter, we discuss some major financial markets and institutions and their role in directing saving to productive uses.

Many of the people who purchase stock in U.S. companies are foreigners, looking to the United States for investment opportunities. More broadly, in the modern world, saving often flows across national boundaries; savers purchase financial assets in countries other than their own and borrowers look abroad for sources of financing. Flows of funds between lenders and borrowers located in different countries are referred to as *international capital flows*. We discuss the international dimension of saving and capital formation in the second part of the chapter. As we will see, for many countries, including the United States, foreign savings provide an important supplement to domestic savings as a means of financing the formation of new capital.

THE FINANCIAL SYSTEM AND THE ALLOCATION OF SAVING TO PRODUCTIVE USES

In Chapter 21, *Saving and Capital Formation*, we emphasized the importance of high rates of saving and capital formation for economic growth and increased productivity. High rates of saving and investment by themselves are not sufficient, however. A successful economy not only saves, but also uses its savings wisely by applying these limited funds to the investment projects that seem likely to be the most productive. In a market economy like that of the United States, savings are allocated by means of a decentralized, market-oriented financial system. The U.S. financial system consists of both financial institutions, like banks, and financial markets, such as bond markets and stock markets.

The financial system improves the allocation of savings in at least two distinct ways. First, the financial system provides *information* to savers about which of the many possible uses of their funds are likely to prove most productive and hence pay the highest return. By evaluating the potential productivity of alternative capital investments, the financial system helps direct savings to its best uses. Second, financial markets help savers *share the risks* of individual investment projects. Sharing of risks protects individual savers from bearing excessive risk, while at the same time making it possible to direct savings to projects, such as the development of new technologies, which are risky but potentially very productive as well.

In this section, we briefly discuss three key components of the U.S. financial system: the banking system, the bond market, and the stock market. In doing so, we elaborate on the role of the financial system as a whole in providing information about investment projects and in helping savers share the risks of lending. In the next section, we add a global dimension and discuss international flows of financial assets through which savers in one country can invest in another country.

THE BANKING SYSTEM

The banking system consists of commercial banks, of which there are thousands in the United States. Commercial banks, whose role in the creation of money was discussed in Chapter 22, *Money, Prices, and the Federal Reserve,* are privately owned firms that accept deposits from individuals and businesses and use those deposits to make loans. Banks are the most important example of a class of institutions called **financial intermediaries,** firms that extend credit to borrowers using funds raised from savers. Other examples of financial intermediaries are savings and loan associations and credit unions.

Why are financial intermediaries such as banks, which "stand between" savers and investors, necessary? Why don't individual savers just lend directly to borrowers who want to invest in new capital projects? The main reason is that, through specialization, banks and other intermediaries develop a comparative advantage in evaluating the quality of borrowers—the information-gathering function that we referred to a moment ago. Most savers, particularly small savers, do not have the time or the knowledge to determine for themselves which borrowers are likely to use the funds they receive most productively. In contrast, banks and other intermediaries have gained expertise in performing the information-gathering activities necessary for profitable lending, including checking out the borrower's background, determining whether the borrower's business plans make sense, and monitoring the borrower's activities during the life of the loan. Because banks specialize in evaluating potential borrowers, they can perform this function at a much lower cost, and with better results, than individual savers could on their own. Banks also reduce the costs of gathering information about potential borrowers by pooling the savings of many individuals to make large loans. Each large loan needs to be evaluated only once, by the bank, rather than separately by each of the hundreds of individuals whose savings may be pooled to make the loan.

Banks help savers by eliminating their need to gather information about potential borrowers and by directing their savings toward higher-return, more productive investments. Banks help borrowers as well, by providing access to credit that might otherwise not be available. Unlike a *Fortune* 500 corporation, which typically has many ways to raise funds, a small business that wants to buy equipment or remodel its offices will have few options other than going to a bank. Because the bank's lending officer has developed expertise in evaluating small-business loans, and may even have an ongoing business relationship with the small-business owner, the bank will be able to gather the information it needs to make the loan at a reasonable cost. Likewise, consumers who want to borrow to finish a basement or add a room to a house will find few good alternatives to a bank. In sum, banks' expertise at gathering information about alternative lending opportunities

financial intermediaries
firms that extend credit to borrowers using funds raised from savers

Comparative Advantage

allows them to bring together small savers, looking for good uses for their funds, and small borrowers with worthwhile investment projects.

In addition to being able to earn a return on their savings, a second reason that people hold bank deposits is to make it easier to make payments. Most bank deposits allow the holder to write a check against them or draw on them using a debit card or ATM card. For many transactions, paying by check or debit card is more convenient than using cash. For example, it is safer to send a check through the mail than to send cash, and paying by check gives you a record of the transaction, whereas a cash payment does not; and it is faster (and often more convenient) to make an electronic transfer from your bank account to that of someone else. Moreover, for transactions such as online purchases from a laptop or a mobile device, cash is simply not an option.

The Economic Naturalist 23.1

What happens to national economies during banking crises?

The economists Carmen Reinhart and Kenneth Rogoff studied the relation between banking crises and several important economic outcomes, including real GDP growth, government finances, and housing prices.[1] They looked at dozens of historical banking crisis episodes, spanning many decades, in both emerging and advanced economies. They found that across countries and across time, bank failures are associated with negative outcomes that include deep and prolonged recessions, dramatic increases in government debt, and drops in real estate values.

As Reinhart and Rogoff note, establishing causality from historical data is difficult. But even though most banking crises are not the sole causes of recessions, they certainly amplify them. When a country's economic growth slows—for example, due to a productivity slowdown—banks suffer because borrowers are less able to pay back their loans. The value of the banks' assets then deteriorates, confidence in the banks decreases, withdrawals of money increase, and, sometimes, banking panics and bank failures follow. Bank failures, in turn, make it difficult for households and businesses to borrow, further bringing down economic activity. This leads to further deterioration of banks' balance sheets, withdrawals, loss of confidence, shrinkage of credit, and so on, in a vicious cycle.

When a bank closes down, the expertise it developed as financial intermediary is lost. As discussed in this chapter, the lost expertise includes, for example, personalized knowledge regarding the bank's small-business customers—knowledge that the bank acquired during years of doing business together. It is therefore not easy for other banks, even if they are still in healthy financial condition, to step in and provide credit to the previous customers of banks that closed. Fixing a banking system that suffered bank failures can therefore be a slow and costly process. In addition to slower economic growth, during this process, many economies have also suffered asset value declines (due to the shortage of access to credit and financing options) and increased levels of government borrowing.

BONDS AND STOCKS

Large and well-established corporations that wish to obtain funds for investment will sometimes go to banks. Unlike the typical small borrower, however, a larger firm usually has alternative ways of raising funds, notably through the corporate bond market and the

[1]C. Reinhart and K. Rogoff, *This Time Is Different: Eight Centuries of Financial Folly* (Princeton, NJ: Princeton University Press, 2009).

stock market. We first discuss some of the mechanics of bonds and stocks, and then return to the role of bond and stock markets in allocating saving.

Bonds

A **bond** is a legal promise to repay a debt, usually including both the **principal amount,** which is the amount originally lent, and regular interest payments. The promised interest rate when a bond is issued is called the **coupon rate.** The regular interest payments made to the bondholder are called coupon payments. The **coupon payment** of a bond that pays interest annually equals the coupon rate times the principal amount of the bond. For example, if the principal amount of a bond is $1,000,000 and its coupon rate is 5 percent, then the annual coupon payment made to the holder of the bond is (0.05)($1,000,000), or $50,000.

Corporations and governments frequently raise funds by issuing bonds and selling them to savers. The coupon rate that a newly issued bond has to promise in order to be attractive to savers depends on a number of factors, including the bond's term, its credit risk, and its tax treatment. The *term* of a bond is the length of time before the debt it represents is fully repaid, a period that can range from 30 days to 30 years or more. Generally, lenders will demand a higher interest rate to lend for a longer term. *Credit risk* is the risk that the borrower will go bankrupt and thus not repay the loan. A borrower that is viewed as risky will have to pay a higher interest rate to compensate lenders for taking the chance of losing all or part of their financial investment. For example, so-called high-yield bonds, less formally known as "junk bonds," are bonds issued by firms judged to be risky by credit-rating agencies; these bonds pay higher interest rates than bonds issued by companies thought to be less risky.

Bonds also differ in their *tax treatment*. For example, interest paid on bonds issued by local governments, called *municipal bonds,* is exempt from federal taxes, whereas interest on other types of bonds is treated as taxable income. Because of this tax advantage, lenders are willing to accept a lower interest rate on municipal bonds.

Bondholders are not required to hold bonds until *maturity,* the time at which they are supposed to be repaid by the issuer, but are always free to sell their bonds in the *bond market,* an organized market run by professional bond traders. The market value of a particular bond at any given point in time is called the *price* of the bond. As it turns out, there is a close relationship between the price of a bond at a given point of time and the interest rate prevailing in financial markets at that time, illustrated by the following example.

> **bond** a legal promise to repay a debt, usually including both the principal amount and regular interest, or coupon, payments
>
> **principal amount** the amount originally lent
>
> **coupon rate** the interest rate promised when a bond is issued; the annual coupon payments are equal to the coupon rate times the principal amount of the bond
>
> **coupon payments** regular interest payments made to the bondholder

---

EXAMPLE 23.1   Bond Prices and Interest Rates

What is the relationship between bond prices and interest rates?

On January 1, 2020, Tanya purchases a newly issued, two-year government bond with a principal amount of $1,000. The coupon rate on the bond is 5 percent, paid annually. Hence Tanya, or whoever owns the bond at the time, will receive a coupon payment of $50 (5 percent of $1,000) on January 1, 2021, and $1,050 (a $50 coupon payment plus repayment of the original $1,000 lent) on January 1, 2022.

On January 1, 2021, after receiving her first year's coupon payment, Tanya decides to sell her bond to raise the funds to take a vacation. She offers her bond for sale in the bond market. How much can she expect to get for her "used" bond if the prevailing interest rate in the bond market is 6 percent? If the prevailing interest rate is 4 percent?

As we mentioned, the price of a "used" bond at any point in time depends on the prevailing interest rate. Suppose first that, on January 1, 2021, when Tanya takes her bond to the bond market, the prevailing interest rate on newly issued one-year bonds is 6 percent. Would another saver be willing to pay Tanya the full $1,000 principal amount of her bond? No, because the purchaser of Tanya's bond will receive $1,050 in one year, when the bond matures; whereas if he uses his $1,000 to buy a new one-year bond paying 6 percent interest, he will receive $1,060 ($1,000 principal repayment plus $60 interest) in one year. So Tanya's bond is not worth $1,000 to another saver.

How much would another saver be willing to pay for Tanya's bond? Since newly issued one-year bonds pay a 6 percent return, he will buy Tanya's bond only at a price that allows him to earn at least that return. As the holder of Tanya's bond will receive $1,050 ($1,000 principal plus $50 interest) in one year, the price for her bond that allows the purchaser to earn a 6 percent return must satisfy the equation

$$\text{Bond price} \times 1.06 = \$1,050.$$

Solving the equation for the bond price, we find that Tanya's bond will sell for $1,050/1.06, or just under $991. To check this result, note that in one year the purchaser of the bond will receive $1,050, or $59 more than he paid. His rate of return is $59/$991, or 6 percent, as expected.

What if the prevailing interest rate had been 4 percent rather than 6 percent? Then the price of Tanya's bond would satisfy the relationship bond price × 1.04 = $1,050, implying that the price of her bond would be $1,050/1.04, or almost $1,010.

What happens if the interest rate when Tanya wants to sell is 5 percent, the same as it was when she originally bought the bond? You should show that in this case the bond would sell at its face value of $1,000.

This example illustrates a general principle, that *bond prices and interest rates are inversely related*. When the interest rate being paid on newly issued bonds rises, the price financial investors are willing to pay for existing bonds falls, and vice versa.

 SELF-TEST 23.1

Three-year government bonds are issued at a face value (principal amount) of 100 and a coupon rate of 7 percent, interest payable at the end of each year. One year prior to the maturation of these bonds, a headline reads, "Bad Economic News Causes Prices of Bonds to Plunge," and the story reveals that these three-year bonds have fallen in price to 96. What has happened to interest rates? What is the one-year interest rate at the time of the story?

Issuing bonds is one means by which a corporation or a government can obtain funds from savers. Another important way of raising funds, but one restricted to corporations, is by issuing stock to the public.

Stocks

stock (or **equity**) a claim to partial ownership of a firm

A share of **stock** (or **equity**) is a claim to partial ownership of a firm. For example, if a corporation has 1 million shares of stock outstanding, ownership of 1 share is equivalent to ownership of one-millionth of the company. Stockholders receive returns on their financial investment in two forms. First, stockholders receive a regular payment called a **dividend** for each share of stock they own. Dividends are determined by the firm's management and usually depend on the firm's recent profits. Second, stockholders receive returns in the form of *capital gains* when the price of their stock increases (we discussed capital gains and losses in Chapter 21, *Saving and Capital Formation*).

dividend a regular payment received by stockholders for each share that they own

Prices of stocks are determined through trading on a stock exchange, such as the New York Stock Exchange. A stock's price rises and falls as the demand for the stock changes. Demand for stocks in turn depends on factors such as news about the prospects of the company. For example, the stock price of a pharmaceutical company that announces the discovery of an important new drug is likely to rise on the announcement, even if actual production and marketing of the drug is some time away, because financial investors expect the company to become more profitable in the future. Example 23.2 illustrates numerically some key factors that affect stock prices.

EXAMPLE 23.2	Buying Shares in a New Company

How much should you pay for a share of FortuneCookie.com?

You have the opportunity to buy shares in a new company called FortuneCookie .com, which plans to sell gourmet fortune cookies over the Internet. Your stock-broker estimates that the company will pay $1.00 per share in dividends a year from now and that in a year, the market price of the company will be $80.00 per share. Assuming that you accept your broker's estimates as accurate, what is the most that you should be willing to pay today per share of FortuneCookie.com? How does your answer change if you expect a $5.00 dividend? If you expect a $1.00 dividend but an $84.00 stock price in one year?

Based on your broker's estimates, you conclude that in one year, each share of FortuneCookie.com you own will be worth $81.00 in your pocket—the $1.00 dividend plus the $80.00 you could get by reselling the stock. Thus, finding the maximum price you would pay for the stock today boils down to asking how much would you invest today to have $81.00 a year from today. In turn, answering this question requires one more piece of information, which is the expected rate of return that you require in order to be willing to buy stock in this company.

How would you determine your required rate of return to hold stock in FortuneCookie.com? For the moment, let's imagine that you are not too worried about the potential riskiness of the stock, either because you think that it is a "sure thing" or because you are a devil-may-care type who is not bothered by risk. In that case, you can apply the Cost-Benefit Principle. Your required rate of return to hold FortuneCookie.com should be about the same as you can get on other financial investments, such as government bonds. The available return on other financial investments gives the *opportunity cost* of your funds. So, for example, if the interest rate currently being offered by government bonds is 6 percent, you should be willing to accept a 6 percent return to hold FortuneCookie.com as well. In that case, the maximum price you would pay today for a share of Fortune-Cookie satisfies the equation

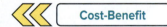
Cost-Benefit

$$\text{Stock price} \times 1.06 = \$81.00.$$

This equation defines the stock price you should be willing to pay if you are willing to accept a 6 percent return over the next year. Solving this equation yields stock price = $81.00/1.06 = $76.42. If you buy FortuneCookie.com for $76.42, then your return over the year will be ($81.00 − $76.42)/$76.42 = $4.58/$71.42 = 6 percent, which is the rate of return you required to buy the stock.

If, instead, the dividend is expected to be $5.00, then the total benefit of holding the stock in one year, equal to the expected dividend plus the expected price, is $5.00 + $80.00, or $85.00. Assuming again that you are willing to accept a 6 percent return to hold FortuneCookie.com, the price you are willing to pay for the stock today satisfies the relationship Stock price × 1.06 = $85.00. Solving this equation for the stock price yields Stock price = $85.00/1.06 = $80.19. Comparing with the previous case, we see that a higher expected dividend in the future increases the value of the stock today. That's why good news about the future prospects of a company—such as the announcement by a pharmaceutical com-pany that it has discovered a useful new drug—affects its stock price immediately.

If the expected future price of the stock is $84.00, with the dividend at $1.00, then the value of holding the stock in one year is once again $85.00, and the calculation is the same as the previous one. Again, the price you should be willing to pay for the stock is $80.19.

These examples show that an increase in the future dividend or in the future expected stock price raises the stock price today, whereas an increase in the return a saver requires to hold the stock lowers today's stock price. Since we expect required returns in the stock market to be closely tied to market interest rates, this last result implies that increases in interest rates tend to depress stock prices as well as bond prices.

Our examples also took the future stock price as given. But what determines the future stock price? Just as today's stock price depends on the dividend shareholders expect to receive this year and the stock price a year from now, the stock price a year from now depends on the dividend expected for next year and the stock price two years from now, and so on.

Ultimately, then, today's stock price is affected not only by the dividend expected this year but future dividends as well. A company's ability to pay dividends depends on its earnings. Thus, as we noted in the example of the pharmaceutical company that announces the discovery of a new drug, news about future earnings—even earnings quite far in the future—is likely to affect a company's stock price immediately.

 SELF-TEST 23.2

As in Example 23.2, you expect a share of FortuneCookie.com to be worth $80.00 per share in one year and also to pay a dividend of $1.00 in one year. What should you be willing to pay for the stock today if the prevailing interest rate, equal to your required rate of return, is 4 percent? What if the interest rate is 8 percent? In general, how would you expect stock prices to react if economic news arrives that implies that interest rates will rise in the very near future?

In the examples we have studied, we assumed that you were willing to accept a return of 6 percent to hold FortuneCookie.com, the same return that you could get on a government bond. However, financial investments in the stock market are quite risky in that returns to holding stocks can be highly variable and unpredictable. For example, although you expect a share of FortuneCookie.com to be worth $80.00 in one year, you also realize that there is a chance it might sell as low as $50.00 or as high as $110.00 per share. Most financial investors dislike risk and unpredictability and thus have a higher required rate of return for holding risky assets like stocks than for holding relatively safe assets like government bonds. The difference between the required rate of return to hold risky assets and the rate of return on safe assets, like government bonds, is called the **risk premium.** The following example illustrates the effect of financial investors' dislike of risk on stock prices.

risk premium the rate of return that financial investors require to hold risky assets minus the rate of return on safe assets

EXAMPLE 23.3 **Riskiness and Stock Prices**

What is the relationship between risk and stock prices?

Continuing Example 23.2, suppose that FortuneCookie.com is expected to pay a $1.00 dividend and have a market price of $80.00 per share in one year. The interest rate on government bonds is 6 percent per year. However, to be willing to hold a risky asset like a share of FortuneCookie.com, you require an expected return four percentage points higher than the rate paid by safe assets like government bonds (a risk premium of 4 percent). Hence you require a 10 percent expected return to hold FortuneCookie.com. What is the most you would be willing to pay for the stock now? What do you conclude about the relationship between perceived riskiness and stock prices?

As a share of FortuneCookie.com is expected to pay $81.00 in one year and the required return is 10 percent, we have Stock price × 1.10 = $81.00. Solving for the stock price, we find the price to be $81.00/1.10 = $73.64, less than the price of $76.42 we found when there was no risk premium and the required rate of return was 6 percent. We conclude that financial investors' dislike of risk, and the resulting risk premium, lowers the prices of risky assets like stocks.

RECAP ↑

THE FINANCIAL SYSTEM AND THE ALLOCATION OF SAVING

- The role of the financial system is allocating saving to productive uses. Three key components of the financial system are the banking system, the bond market, and the stock market.
- Commercial banks are financial intermediaries: they extend credit to borrowers using funds raised from savers.
- Bonds are legal promises to repay a debt. The prices of existing bonds decline when interest rates rise.
- Stocks (or equity) are claims to partial ownership of a firm. Factors affecting stock prices:

  1. An increase in expected future dividends or in the expected future market price of a stock raises the current price of the stock.
  2. An increase in interest rates, implying an increase in the required rate of return to hold stocks, lowers the current price of stocks.
  3. An increase in perceived riskiness, as reflected in an increase in the risk premium, lowers the current price of stocks.

BOND MARKETS, STOCK MARKETS, AND THE ALLOCATION OF SAVINGS

Like banks, bond markets and stock markets provide a means of channeling funds from savers to borrowers with productive investment opportunities. For example, a corporation that is planning a capital investment but does not want to borrow from a bank has two other options: it can issue new bonds, to be sold to savers in the bond market, or it can issue new shares in itself, which are then sold in the stock market. The proceeds from the sales of new bonds or stocks are then available to the firm to finance its capital investment.

How do stock and bond markets help ensure that available savings are devoted to the most productive uses? As we mentioned earlier, two important functions served by these markets are gathering information about prospective borrowers and helping savers share the risks of lending.

THE INFORMATIONAL ROLE OF BOND AND STOCK MARKETS

Savers and their financial advisors know that to get the highest possible returns on their financial investments, they must find the potential borrowers with the most profitable opportunities. This knowledge provides a powerful incentive to scrutinize potential borrowers carefully.

For example, companies considering a new issue of stocks or bonds know that their recent performance and plans for the future will be carefully studied by professional analysts on Wall Street and other financial investors. If the analysts and other potential purchasers have doubts about the future profitability of the firm, they will offer a relatively low price for the newly issued shares, or they will demand a high interest rate on newly issued bonds. Knowing this, a company will be reluctant to go to the bond or stock market for financing unless its management is confident that it can convince financial investors that the firm's planned use of the funds will be profitable. *Thus the ongoing search by savers and their financial advisors for high returns leads the bond and stock markets to direct funds to the uses that appear most likely to be productive.*

RISK SHARING AND DIVERSIFICATION

Many highly promising investment projects are also quite risky. For example, the successful development of a new drug to lower cholesterol could create billions of dollars in profits for a drug company, but if the drug turns out to be less effective than some others on the market, none of the development costs will be recouped. An individual who lent his or her life savings to help finance the development of the anti-cholesterol drug might enjoy a handsome return but also takes the chance of losing everything. Savers are generally reluctant to take large risks, so without some means of reducing the risk faced by each saver, it might be very hard for the company to find the funds to develop the new drug.

diversification the practice of spreading one's wealth over a variety of different financial investments to reduce overall risk

Bond and stock markets help reduce risk by giving savers a means to *diversify* their financial investments. **Diversification** is the practice of spreading one's wealth over a variety of different financial investments to reduce overall risk. The idea of diversification follows from the adage that "you shouldn't put all your eggs in one basket." Rather than putting all of his or her savings in one very risky project, a financial investor will find it much safer to allocate a small amount of savings to each of a large number of stocks and bonds. That way, if some financial assets fall in value, there is a good chance that others will rise in value, with gains offsetting losses. The following example illustrates the benefits of diversification.

EXAMPLE 23.4   **The Benefits of Diversification**

What are the benefits of diversification?

Vikram has $1,000 to invest and is considering two stocks, the Smith Umbrella Company and the Jones Suntan Lotion Company. The price of Smith Umbrella stock will rise by 10 percent if it rains but will remain unchanged if the weather is sunny. The price of Jones Suntan stock is expected to rise by 10 percent if it is sunny but will remain unchanged if there is rain. The chance of rain is 50 percent, and the chance of sunshine is 50 percent. How should Vikram invest his $1,000?

If Vikram were to invest all his $1,000 in Smith Umbrella, he has a 50 percent chance of earning a 10 percent return, in the event that it rains, and a 50 percent chance of earning zero, if the weather is sunny. His average return is 50 percent times 10 percent plus 50 percent times zero, or 5 percent. Similarly, an investment in Jones Suntan yields 10 percent return half the time, when it's sunny, and 0 percent return the other half the time, when it rains, for an average return of 5 percent.

Although Vikram can earn an *average* return of 5 percent in either stock, investing in only one stock or the other is quite risky since the actual return he receives varies widely depending on whether there is rain or shine. Can Vikram *guarantee* himself a 5 percent return, avoiding the uncertainty and risk? Yes, all he has to do is put $500 into each of the two stocks. If it rains, he will earn $50 on his Smith Umbrella stock and nothing on his Jones Suntan. If it's sunny, he will earn nothing on Smith Umbrella but $50 on Jones Suntan. Rain or shine, he is guaranteed to earn $50—a 5 percent return—without risk.

The existence of bond markets and stock markets makes it easy for savers to diversify by putting a small amount of their savings into each of a wide variety of different financial assets, each of which represents a share of a particular company or investment project. From society's point of view, diversification makes it possible for risky but worthwhile projects to obtain funding, without individual savers having to bear too much risk.

For the typical person, a particularly convenient way to diversify is to buy bonds and stocks indirectly through *mutual funds*. A **mutual fund** is a financial intermediary that sells shares in itself to the public and then uses the funds raised to buy a wide variety of financial assets. Holding shares in a mutual fund thus amounts to owning a little bit of many different financial assets, which helps achieve diversification. The advantage of mutual funds is that it is usually less costly and time-consuming to buy shares in one or two mutual funds than to buy many different stocks and bonds directly. Over the past few decades mutual funds have become increasingly popular in the United States.

mutual fund a financial intermediary that sells shares in itself to the public and then uses the funds raised to buy a wide variety of financial assets

The Economic Naturalist 23.2

Why did the U.S. stock market rise sharply and fall sharply in the 1990s and again in the 2000s?

Stock prices soared during the 1990s in the United States. The Standard & Poor's (S&P) 500 index, which summarizes the stock price performance of 500 major companies, rose 60 percent between 1990 and 1995 and then more than doubled between 1995 and 2000. However, in the first two years of the new millennium, this index lost nearly half its value. Why did the U.S. stock market boom in the 1990s and then bust?

The prices of stocks depend on their purchasers' expectations about future dividends and stock prices and on the rate of return required by potential stockholders. The required rate of return in turn equals the interest rate on safe assets plus the risk premium. In principle, a rise in stock prices could be the result of increased optimism about future dividends, a fall in the required return, or some combination.

Probably both factors contributed to the boom in stock prices in the 1990s. Dividends grew rapidly in the 1990s, reflecting the strong overall performance of the U.S. economy. Encouraged by the promise of new technologies, many financial investors expected future dividends to be even higher.

There is also evidence that the risk premium that people required to hold stocks fell during the 1990s, thereby lowering the total required return and raising stock prices. One possible explanation for a decline in the risk premium in the 1990s is increased diversification. During that decade, the number and variety of mutual funds available increased markedly. Millions of Americans invested in these funds, including many who had never owned stock before or had owned stock in only a few companies. This increase in diversification for the typical stock market investor may have lowered the perceived risk of holding stocks, which in turn reduced the risk premium and raised stock prices.

After 2000, both of these favorable factors reversed. The growth in dividends was disappointing to stockholders, in large part because many high-tech firms did not prove as profitable as had been hoped. An additional blow was a series of corporate accounting scandals in 2002, in which it became known that some large firms had taken illegal or unethical actions to make their profits seem larger than in fact they were. A number of factors, including a recession, a major terrorist attack, and the accounting scandals, also increased stockholders' concerns about the riskiness of stocks, so that the risk premium they required to hold stocks rose from its 1990s lows. The combination of lower expected dividends and a higher premium for risk sent stock prices sharply downward.

As you already know, the stock boom and bust that ended around 2002 was by no means the last dramatic roller coaster in U.S. stock values. During the following five years, the S&P 500 almost doubled again, reaching all-time record levels in 2007 before collapsing again in the next 18 months to levels not seen since the 1990s. That latter collapse, of 2007–2008, arose in the context of a financial crisis and a deep recession, which both lowered expected dividends and increased the perceived riskiness of holding stocks. (The financial crisis and recession will be further discussed in later chapters.)

Since 2009, stocks have more than fully recovered, and on January 16, 2020, the S&P 500 pushed past the 3,300 milestone for the first time—more than double the previous records of 2000 and 2007. This recent rally reflects historically low interest rates on safe assets and considerable changes in recent years to stock-holders' expectations and risk perceptions. Indeed, as these expectations and risk preferences suddenly reversed during February and March 2020—when the U.S. was hit by the COVID-19 pandemic—the S&P 500 declined sharply. As investors quickly updated downward their dividend expectations, and as they sought safer assets, the S&P dipped below 2,400 in late March—before again recovering and hitting an all-time record, 3,500, by August, as expectations recovered.

> **RECAP** ↑
>
> **BOND MARKETS, STOCK MARKETS, AND THE ALLOCATION OF SAVINGS**
>
> Two important functions served by bond and stock markets are gathering information about prospective borrowers and helping savers share the risks of lending through diversification. A convenient way to diversify is to buy bonds and stocks through mutual funds.

INTERNATIONAL CAPITAL FLOWS

Our discussion thus far has focused on financial markets operating within a given country, such as the United States. However, economic opportunities are not necessarily restricted by national boundaries. The most productive use of a U.S. citizen's savings might be located far from U.S. soil, such as helping build a factory in Thailand or starting a small business in Poland. Likewise, the best way for a Brazilian saver to diversify her assets and reduce her risks could be to hold bonds and stocks from a number of different countries. Over time, extensive financial markets have developed to permit cross-border borrowing and lending. Financial markets in which borrowers and lenders are residents of different countries are called **international financial markets.**

International financial markets differ from domestic financial markets in at least one important respect: Unlike a domestic financial transaction, an international financial transaction is subject to the laws and regulations of at least two countries, the country that is home to the lender and the country that is home to the borrower. Thus the size and vitality of international financial markets depend on the degree of political and economic cooperation among countries. For example, during the relatively peaceful decades of the late nineteenth and early twentieth centuries, international financial markets were remarkably highly developed. Great Britain, at the time the world's dominant economic power, was a major international lender, dispatching its savings for use around the globe. However, during the turbulent years 1914–1945, two world wars and the Great Depression substantially reduced both international finance and international trade in goods and services. The extent of international finance and trade returned to the levels achieved in the late nineteenth century only in the 1980s.

In thinking about international financial markets, it is useful to understand that lending is economically equivalent to acquiring a real or financial asset, and borrowing is economically equivalent to selling a real or financial asset. For example, savers lend to companies by purchasing stocks or bonds, which are financial assets for the lender and financial liabilities for the borrowing firms. Similarly, lending to a government is accomplished in practice

international financial markets financial markets in which borrowers and lenders are residents of different countries

by acquiring a government bond—a financial asset for the lender, and a financial liability for the borrower, in this case the government. Savers can also provide funds by acquiring real assets such as land; if I purchase a parcel of land from you, though I am not making a loan in the usual sense, I am providing you with funds that you can use for consuming or investing. In lieu of interest or dividends from a bond or a stock, I receive the rental value of the land that I purchased.

Purchases or sales of real and financial assets across international borders (which are economically equivalent to lending and borrowing across international borders) are known as **international capital flows.** From the perspective of a particular country, say the United States, purchases of domestic (U.S.) assets by foreigners are called **capital inflows;** purchases of foreign assets by domestic (U.S.) households and firms are called **capital outflows.** To remember these terms, it may help to keep in mind that capital inflows represent funds "flowing in" to the country (foreign savers buying domestic assets), while capital outflows are funds "flowing out" of the country (domestic savers buying foreign assets). The difference between the two flows is expressed as *net capital inflows*—capital inflows minus capital outflows—or *net capital outflows*—capital outflows minus capital inflows. Note that capital inflows and outflows are *not* counted as exports or imports because they refer to the purchase of existing real and financial assets rather than currently produced goods and services. In the U.S., the Bureau of Economic Analysis (BEA)—which was mentioned earlier in the text as the government agency in charge of measuring exports, imports, and the other components of GDP—is also in charge of measuring capital inflows and outflows. Every quarter, the BEA publishes its most recent estimates of capital flows in the "Financial Account" section of its *International Transactions Accounts.*

From a macroeconomic perspective, international capital flows play two important roles. First, they allow countries whose productive investment opportunities are greater than domestic savings to fill in the gap by borrowing from abroad. Second, they allow countries to run trade imbalances—situations in which the country's exports of goods and services do not equal its imports of goods and services. The rest of this chapter discusses these key roles. We begin by analyzing the important link between international capital flows and trade imbalances.

international capital flows purchases or sales of real and financial assets across international borders

capital inflows purchases of domestic assets by foreign households and firms

capital outflows purchases of foreign assets by domestic households and firms

CAPITAL FLOWS AND THE BALANCE OF TRADE

In Chapter 17, *Measuring Economic Activity: GDP and Unemployment,* we introduced the term **net exports** *(NX),* the value of a country's exports less the value of its imports. An equivalent term for the value of a country's exports less the value of its imports is the **trade balance.** Because exports need not equal imports in each quarter or year, the trade balance (or net exports) need not always equal zero. If the trade balance is positive in a particular period so that the value of exports exceeds the value of imports, a country is said to have a **trade surplus** for that period equal to the value of its exports minus the value of its imports. If the trade balance is negative, with imports greater than exports, the country is said to have a **trade deficit** equal to the value of its imports minus the value of its exports.

Figure 23.1 shows the components of the U.S. trade balance since 1960 (see Figure 16.5 for data extending back to 1929). The blue line represents U.S. exports as a percentage of GDP; the red line, U.S. imports as a percentage of GDP. When exports exceed imports, the vertical distance between the two lines gives the U.S. trade surplus as a percentage of GDP. When imports exceed exports, the vertical distance between the two lines represents the U.S. trade deficit. Figure 23.1 shows first that international trade has become an increasingly important part of the U.S. economy in the past several decades. In 1960, only 5 percent of U.S. GDP was exported, and the value of imports equaled 4.2 percent of U.S. GDP. In 2019, by comparison, 11.7 percent of U.S. production was sold abroad, and imports amounted to 14.6 percent of U.S. GDP. Second, the figure shows that since the late 1970s the United States has consistently run trade deficits, frequently equal to 2 percent or more of GDP. For a few years in the mid-2000s, these trade deficits ballooned to more than 5 percent of GDP. Why has the U.S. trade balance been in deficit for so long? We will answer that question later in this section.

trade balance (or **net exports**) the value of a country's exports less the value of its imports in a particular period (quarter or year)

trade surplus when exports exceed imports, the difference between the value of a country's exports and the value of its imports in a given period

trade deficit when imports exceed exports, the difference between the value of a country's imports and the value of its exports in a given period

FIGURE 23.1

The U.S. Trade Balance, 1960–2019.

This figure shows U.S. exports and imports as a percentage of GDP. Since the late 1970s, the United States has run a trade deficit, with imports exceeding exports.

Source: Bureau of Economic Analysis, www.bea.gov.

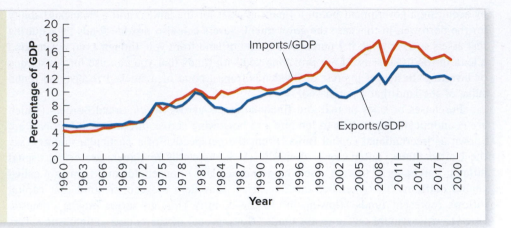

The trade balance represents the difference between the value of goods and services exported by a country and the value of goods and services imported by the country. Net capital inflows represent the difference between purchases of domestic assets by foreigners and purchases of foreign assets by domestic residents. There is a precise and very important link between these two imbalances, which is that in any given period, *the trade balance and net capital inflows sum to zero*. For future reference, let's write this relationship as an equation:

$$NX + KI = 0, \tag{23.1}$$

where NX is the trade balance (the same as net exports) and we use KI to stand for net capital inflows. The relationship given by Equation 23.1 is an identity, meaning that it is true by definition.[2]

To see why Equation 23.1 holds, consider what happens when (for example) a U.S. resident purchases an imported good—say, a Japanese automobile priced at $20,000. Suppose the U.S. buyer pays by check so that the Japanese car manufacturer now holds $20,000 in an account in a U.S. bank. What will the Japanese manufacturer do with this $20,000? Basically, there are two possibilities.

First, the Japanese company may use the $20,000 to buy U.S.-produced goods and services, such as U.S.-manufactured car parts or Hawaiian vacations for its executives. In this case, the United States has $20,000 in exports to balance the $20,000 automobile import. Because exports equal imports, the U.S. trade balance is unaffected by these transactions (for these transactions, $NX = 0$). And because no assets are bought or sold, there are no capital inflows or outflows ($KI = 0$). So under this scenario, the condition that the trade balance plus net capital inflows equals zero, as stated in Equation 23.1, is satisfied.

Alternatively, the Japanese car producer might use the $20,000 to acquire U.S. assets, such as a U.S. Treasury bond or some land adjacent to its plant in Tennessee. In this case, the United States compiles a trade deficit of $20,000, because the $20,000 car import is not offset by an export ($NX = -\$20,000$). But there is a corresponding capital inflow of $20,000, reflecting the purchase of a U.S. asset by the Japanese ($KI = \$20,000$). So once again the trade balance and net capital inflows sum to zero, and Equation 23.1 is satisfied.[3]

---

[2]For simplicity, we do not discuss in this book the *current account balance* (*CA*), a measure that consists of the trade balance (*NX*) plus two additional components. The two components are net *primary income* (consisting mostly of investment income—that is, the net inflow of income on U.S.-owned assets abroad) and net *secondary income* (unilateral current transfers—that is, nonmarket transfers from foreigners to U.S. residents, such as foreign government grants and personal remittances). Technically, Equation 23.1 is not quite correct, and the precise relationship is $CA + KI = 0$. However, for the U.S., net primary plus secondary income is a relatively small share of the current account balance. Since it makes the discussion easier, we use net exports, rather than the current account balance, in Equation 23.1.

[3]If the Japanese company simply left the $20,000 in the U.S. bank, it would still count as a capital inflow, since the deposit would still be a U.S. asset acquired by foreigners.

In fact, there is a third possibility, which is that the Japanese car company might swap its dollars to some other party outside the United States. For example, the company might trade its dollars to another Japanese firm or individual in exchange for Japanese yen. However, the acquirer of the dollars would then have the same two options as the car company—to buy U.S. goods and services or acquire U.S. assets—so that the equality of net capital inflows and the trade deficit would continue to hold.

 SELF-TEST 23.3

A U.S. saver purchases a $20,000 Japanese government bond. Explain why Equation 23.1 is satisfied no matter what the Japanese government does with the $20,000 it receives for its bond.

THE DETERMINANTS OF INTERNATIONAL CAPITAL FLOWS

Capital inflows, recall, are purchases of domestic assets by foreigners, while capital outflows are purchases of foreign assets by domestic residents. For example, capital inflows into the United States include foreign purchases of items such as the stocks and bonds of U.S. companies, U.S. government bonds, and real assets such as land or buildings owned by U.S. residents. Why would foreigners want to acquire U.S. assets, and, conversely, why would Americans want to acquire assets abroad?

The basic factors that determine the attractiveness of any asset, either domestic or foreign, are *return* and *risk*. Financial investors seek high real returns; thus, with other factors (such as the degree of risk and the returns available abroad) held constant, a higher real interest rate in the home country promotes capital inflows by making domestic assets more attractive to foreigners. By the same token, a higher real interest rate in the home country reduces capital outflows by inducing domestic residents to invest their savings at home. Thus, all else being equal, a higher real interest rate at home leads to net capital inflows. Conversely, a low real interest rate at home tends to create net capital outflows, as financial investors look abroad for better opportunities.

Figure 23.2 shows the relationship between a country's net capital inflows and the real rate of interest prevailing in that country. When the domestic real interest rate is high, net capital inflows are positive (foreign purchases of domestic assets exceed domestic purchases of foreign assets). But when the real interest rate is low, net capital inflows are negative (that is, the country experiences net capital outflows).

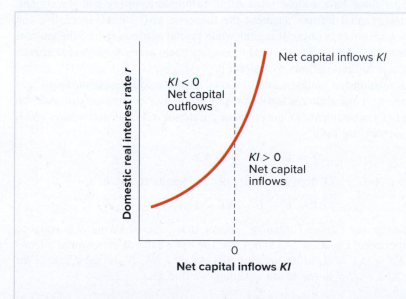

FIGURE 23.2

Net Capital Inflows and the Real Interest Rate.

Holding constant the degree of risk and the real returns available abroad, a high real interest rate in the home country will induce foreigners to buy domestic assets, increasing capital inflows. A high real rate in the home country also reduces the incentive for domestic savers to buy foreign assets, reducing capital outflows. Thus, all else being equal, the higher the domestic real interest rate *r*, the higher will be net capital inflows *KI*.

The effect of risk on capital flows is the opposite of the effect of the real interest rate. For a given real interest rate, an increase in the riskiness of domestic assets reduces net capital inflows, as foreigners become less willing to buy the home country's assets, and domestic savers become more inclined to buy foreign assets. For example, political instability, which increases the risk of investing in a country, tends to reduce net capital inflows. Figure 23.3 shows the effect of an increase in risk on capital flows: at each value of the domestic real interest rate, an increase in risk reduces net capital inflows, shifting the capital inflows curve to the left.

FIGURE 23.3

An Increase in Risk Reduces Net Capital Inflows.

An increase in the riskiness of domestic assets, arising, for example, from an increase in political instability, reduces the willingness of foreign and domestic savers to hold domestic assets. The supply of capital inflows declines at each value of the domestic real interest rate, shifting the *KI* curve to the left.

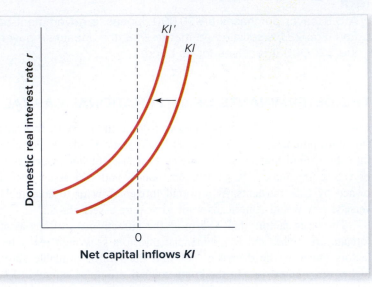

✔ **SELF-TEST 23.4**

For a given real interest rate and riskiness in the home country, how would you expect net capital inflows to be affected by an increase in real interest rates abroad? Show your answer graphically.

SAVING, INVESTMENT, AND CAPITAL INFLOWS

International capital flows have a close relationship to domestic saving and investment. As we will see next, capital inflows augment the domestic saving pool, increasing the funds available for investment in physical capital, while capital outflows reduce the amount of saving available for investment. Thus capital inflows can help promote economic growth within a country, and capital outflows to restrain it.

To derive the relationship among capital inflows, saving, and investment, recall that total output or income Y must always equal the sum of the four components of expenditure: consumption (C), investment (I), government purchases (G), and net exports (NX). Writing out this identity, we have

$$Y = C + I + G + NX.$$

Next, we subtract $C + G + NX$ from both sides of the identity to obtain

$$Y - C - G - NX = I.$$

In Chapter 21, *Saving and Capital Formation,* we saw that national saving S is equal to $Y - C - G$. Furthermore, Equation 23.1 states that the trade balance plus capital inflows equals zero, or $NX + KI = 0$, which implies that $KI = -NX$. If we substitute S for $Y - C - G$ and KI for $-NX$ in the above equation, we find that

$$S + KI = I. \tag{23.2}$$

Equation 23.2, a key result, says that the sum of national saving S and capital inflows from abroad KI must equal domestic investment in new capital goods, I. In other words, in an open economy, the pool of saving available for domestic investment includes not only national saving (the saving of the domestic private and public sectors) but funds from savers abroad as well.

Chapter 21, *Saving and Capital Formation*, introduced the saving–investment diagram, which shows that in a closed economy, the supply of saving must equal the demand for saving. A similar diagram applies to an open economy, except that the supply of saving in an open economy includes net capital inflows as well as domestic saving. Figure 23.4 shows the open-economy version of the saving–investment diagram. The domestic real interest rate is shown on the vertical axis and saving and investment flows on the horizontal axis. As in a closed economy, the downward-sloping curve I shows the demand for funds by firms that want to make capital investments. The solid upward-sloping curve, marked $S + KI$, shows the total supply of saving, including *both* domestic saving S and net capital inflows from abroad KI. Also shown, for comparison, is the supply of domestic saving, marked S. You can see that for higher values of the domestic real interest rate, net capital inflows are positive, so the $S + KI$ curve falls to the right of the curve S showing domestic saving only. But at low enough values of the real interest rate r, the economy sustains net capital outflows, as savers look abroad for higher returns on their financial investments. Thus, at low values of the domestic real interest rate, the net supply of savings is lower than it would be in a closed economy, and the $S + KI$ curve falls to the left of the domestic supply of saving curve S. As Figure 23.4 shows, the equilibrium real interest rate in an open economy, r^*, is the level that sets the total amount of saving supplied (including capital inflows from abroad) equal to the amount of saving demanded for purposes of domestic capital investment.

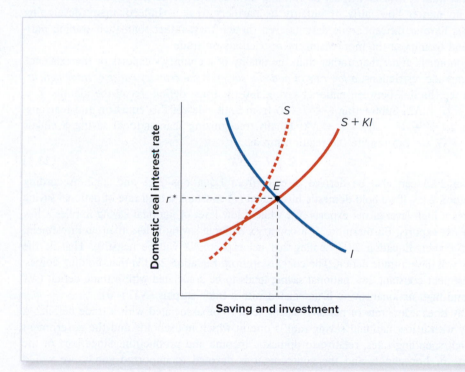

Saving and investment

Domestic real interest rate (vertical axis)

FIGURE 23.4

The Saving–Investment Diagram for an Open Economy. The total supply of savings in an open economy is the sum of national saving S and net capital inflows KI. The supply of domestic saving S is shown for comparison. Because a low real interest rate prompts capital outflows ($KI < 0$), at low values of the domestic interest rate the total supply of saving $S + KI$ is smaller than national saving S. The domestic demand for saving for purposes of capital investment is shown by the curve labeled I. The equilibrium real interest rate r^* sets the total supply of saving, including capital inflows, equal to the domestic demand for saving.

Figure 23.4 also indicates how net capital inflows can benefit an economy. A country that attracts significant amounts of foreign capital flows will have a larger pool of total saving and hence both a lower real interest rate and a higher rate of investment in new capital than it otherwise would. The United States and Canada both benefited from large inflows of capital in the early stages of their economic development, as do many developing countries today. Because capital inflows tend to react very sensitively to risk, an implication is that countries that are politically stable and safeguard the rights of foreign investors will attract more foreign capital and thus grow more quickly than countries without those characteristics.

Although capital inflows are generally beneficial to the countries that receive them, they are not costless. Countries that finance domestic capital formation primarily by capital inflows face the prospect of paying interest and dividends to the foreign financial investors from whom they have borrowed. A number of developing countries have experienced *debt crises,* arising because the domestic investments they made with foreign funds turned out poorly, leaving them insufficient income to pay what they owed their foreign creditors. An advantage to financing domestic capital formation primarily with domestic saving is that the returns from the country's capital investments accrue to domestic savers rather than flowing abroad.

THE SAVING RATE AND THE TRADE DEFICIT

We have seen that a country's exports and imports do not necessarily balance in each period. Indeed, the United States has run a trade deficit, with its imports exceeding exports, for many years. What causes trade deficits? People sometimes think that trade deficits occur because a country produces inferior goods that no one wants to buy or because other countries impose unfair trade restrictions on imports. Despite the popularity of these explanations, however, there is little support for them in either economic theory or evidence. Economists acknowledge, of course, that trade restrictions can affect the overall levels of exports and imports—and that trade agreements can therefore increase gross trade flows. It is also true that trade barriers and agreements can affect a country's mix of imports, exports, and trading partners. So, for example, trade frictions between the United States and China, which, starting in 2018, included both countries imposing steep tariffs on imports from each other, reduced flows of trade in certain goods between the two countries. But as long as a country spends more than it produces—or, equivalently, saves less than it invests—it must be running an overall trade deficit with the rest of the world, no matter how fairly or unfairly its partners treat it. Indeed, many developing countries have significant trade deficits even though they, rather than their trading partners, tend to impose the more stringent restrictions on trade.

Economists argue that, rather than the quality of a country's exports or the existence of unfair trade restrictions, *a low rate of national saving is the primary cause of trade deficits.*

To see the link between national saving and the trade deficit, recall the identity $Y = C + I + G + NX$. Subtracting $C + I + G$ from both sides of this equation and rearranging, we get $Y - C - G - I = NX$. Finally, recognizing that national saving S equals $Y - C - G$, we can rewrite the relationship as:

$$S - I = NX. \qquad (23.3)$$

Equation 23.3 can also be derived directly from Equations 23.1 and 23.2. According to Equation 23.3, if we hold domestic investment (I) constant, a high rate of national saving S implies a high level of net exports NX, while a low level of national saving implies a low level of net exports. Furthermore, if a country's national saving is less than its investment, or $S < I$, then Equation 23.3 implies that net exports NX will be negative. That is, the country will have a trade deficit. The conclusion from Equation 23.3 is that, holding domestic investment constant, low national saving tends to be associated with a trade deficit ($NX < 0$), and high national saving is associated with a trade surplus ($NX > 0$).

Why does a low rate of national saving tend to be associated with a trade deficit? A country with a low national saving rate is one in which households and the government have high spending rates, relative to domestic income and production. Since part of the spending of households and the government is devoted to imported goods, we would expect a low-saving, high-spending economy to have a high volume of imports. Furthermore, a low-saving economy consumes a large proportion of its domestic production, reducing the quantity of goods and services available for export. With high imports and low exports, a low-saving economy will experience a trade deficit.

A country with a trade deficit must also be receiving capital inflows, as we have seen. (Equation 23.1 tells us that if a trade deficit exists so that $NX < 0$, then it must be true that $KI > 0$—net capital inflows are positive.) Is a low national saving rate also consistent with the existence of net capital inflows? The answer is yes. A country with a low national saving rate will not have sufficient savings of its own to finance domestic investment. Thus there likely will be many good investment opportunities in the country available to foreign savers, leading to capital inflows. Equivalently, a shortage of domestic saving will tend to drive up the domestic real interest rate, which attracts capital flows from abroad.

We conclude that a low rate of national saving tends to create a trade deficit, as well as to promote the capital inflows that must accompany a trade deficit. The Economic Naturalist 23.3 illustrates this effect for the case of the United States.

The Economic Naturalist 23.3

Why is the U.S. trade deficit so large?

As shown by Figure 23.1, U.S. trade was more or less in balance until the mid-1970s. Since the late 1970s, however, the United States has run large trade deficits, particularly in the mid-1980s and even more so since the latter part of the 1990s. Indeed, from 2004 to 2007, the trade deficit was 5 percent or more of U.S. GDP. Why is the U.S. trade deficit so large?

Figure 23.5 shows national saving, investment, and the trade balance for the United States from 1960 to 2019 (all measured relative to GDP). Note that the trade balance has been negative since the late 1970s, indicating a trade deficit. Note also that trade deficits correspond to periods in which investment exceeds national saving, as required by Equation 23.3.[4]

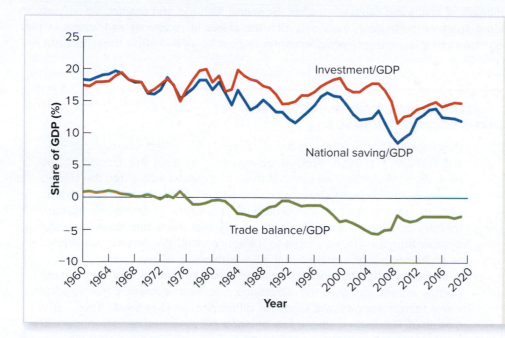

FIGURE 23.5

National Saving, Investment, and the Trade Balance in the United States, 1960–2019.

Since the 1970s, U.S. national saving has fallen below domestic investment, implying a significant trade deficit.

Source: Bureau of Economic Analysis, www.bea.gov.

U.S. national saving and investment were roughly in balance in the 1960s and early 1970s, and hence the U.S. trade balance was close to zero during that period. However, U.S. national saving fell during the late 1970s and 1980s. One factor that contributed to the decline in national saving was the large government deficits of the era. Because investment did not decline as much as saving, the U.S. trade deficit ballooned in the 1980s, coming under control only when investment fell during the recession of 1990–1991. Saving and investment both recovered during the 1990s, but in the latter part of the 1990s, national saving dropped again. This time the federal government was not at fault since its budget showed a healthy surplus. Rather, the fall in national saving reflected a decline in private

---

[4]If you look at Figure 23.5 very carefully, you may notice that in some years the gap between national saving and investment is slightly different from the trade balance. That difference, referred to as *statistical discrepancy,* results from imperfections in the measurement of these macroeconomic indicators. While typically much smaller, the statistical discrepancy in some years can reach around 2 percent of GDP.

saving, the result of a powerful upsurge in consumption spending. Much of the increase in consumption spending was for imported goods and services, which pushed the trade deficit to record levels.

Following the 2001 recession, large government deficits returned, and as household saving kept declining, by the mid-2000s the trade deficit broke the record again, reaching levels above 5 percent of GDP. The trade deficit changed course following the 2007–2009 recession, shrinking to about 3 percent of GDP, where it remained as of 2019. While saving declined dramatically during the recession as a result of large government deficits, and took years to recover, investment declined even faster, and has been recovering more slowly.

Is the U.S. trade deficit a problem? The trade deficit implies that the United States is relying heavily on foreign savings to finance its domestic capital formation (net capital inflows). These foreign loans must ultimately be repaid with interest. If the foreign savings are well invested and the U.S. economy grows, repayment will not pose a problem. However, if economic growth in the United States slackens, repaying the foreign lenders will impose an economic burden in the future.

To this point in the book we have discussed a variety of issues relating to the long-run performance of the economy, including economic growth, the sources of increasing productivity and improved living standards, the determination of real wages, and the determinants of saving and capital formation. Beginning with the next chapter, we will take a more short-run perspective, examining first the causes of recessions and booms in the economy and then turning to policy measures that can be used to affect these fluctuations.

> **RECAP**
>
> **INTERNATIONAL CAPITAL FLOWS AND THE BALANCE OF TRADE**
>
> - Purchases or sales of assets across borders are called international capital flows. If a person, firm, or government in (say) the United States borrows from abroad, we say that there is a capital inflow into the United States. In this case, foreign savers are acquiring U.S. assets. If a person, firm, or government in the United States lends to someone abroad, thereby acquiring a foreign asset, we say that there has been a capital outflow from the United States to the foreign country. Net capital inflows to a given country equal capital inflows minus outflows.
> - If a country imports more goods and services than it exports, it must borrow abroad to cover the difference. Likewise, a country that exports more than it imports will lend the difference to foreigners. Thus, as a matter of accounting, the trade balance NX and net capital inflows KI must sum to zero in every period.
> - The funds available for domestic investment in new capital goods equal the sum of domestic saving and net capital inflows from abroad. The higher the return and the lower the risk of investing in the domestic country, the greater will be the capital inflows from abroad. Capital inflows benefit an economy by providing more funds for capital investment, but they can become a burden if the returns from investing in new capital goods are insufficient to pay back the foreign lenders.
> - An important cause of a trade deficit is a low national saving rate. A country that saves little and spends a lot will tend to import a greater quantity of goods and services than it is able to export. At the same time, the country's low saving rate implies a need for more foreign borrowing to finance domestic investment spending.

SUMMARY

- Corporations that do not wish to borrow from banks can obtain finance by issuing bonds or stocks. A *bond* is a legal promise to repay a debt, including both the *principal amount* and regular interest payments. The prices of existing bonds decline when interest rates rise. A share of *stock* is a claim to partial ownership of a firm. The price of a stock depends positively on the *dividend* the stock is expected to pay and on the expected future price of the stock and negatively on the rate of return required by financial investors to hold the stock. The required rate of return in turn is the sum of the return on safe assets and the additional return required to compensate financial investors for the riskiness of stocks, called the *risk premium*. *(LO1)*

- Besides balancing saving and investment in the aggregate, financial markets and institutions play the important role of allocating saving to the most productive investment projects. The financial system improves the allocation of saving in two ways: First, it provides information to savers about which of the many possible uses of their funds are likely to prove must productive, and hence pay the highest return. For example, *financial intermediaries* such as banks develop expertise in evaluating prospective borrowers, making it unnecessary for small savers to do that on their own. Similarly, stock and bond analysts evaluate the business prospects of a company issuing shares of stock or bonds, which determines the price the stock will sell for or the interest rate the company will have to offer on its bond. Second, financial markets help savers share the risks of lending by permitting them to *diversify* their financial investments. Individual savers often hold stocks through *mutual funds,* a type of financial intermediary that reduces risk by holding many different financial assets. By reducing the risk faced by any one saver, financial markets allow risky but potentially very productive projects to be funded. *(LO1, LO2)*

- The *trade balance,* or net exports, is the value of a country's exports less the value of its imports in a particular period. Exports need not equal imports in each period. If exports exceed imports, the difference is called a *trade surplus,* and if imports exceed exports, the difference is called a *trade deficit*. Trade takes place in assets as well as goods and services. Purchases of domestic assets (real or financial) by foreigners are called *capital inflows,* and purchases of foreign assets by domestic savers are called *capital outflows*. Because imports that are not financed by sales of exports must be financed by sales of assets, the trade balance and net capital inflows sum to zero. *(LO3)*

- The higher the real interest rate in a country, and the lower the risk of investing there, the higher its capital inflows. The availability of capital inflows expands a country's pool of saving, allowing for more domestic investment and increased growth. A drawback to using capital inflows to finance domestic capital formation is that the returns to capital (interest and dividends) accrue to foreign financial investors rather than domestic residents. *(LO3)*

- A low rate of national saving is the primary cause of trade deficits. A low-saving, high-spending country is likely to import more than a high-saving country. It also consumes more of its domestic production, leaving less for export. Finally, a low-saving country is likely to have a high real interest rate, which attracts net capital inflows. Because the sum of the trade balance and capital inflows is zero, a high level of net capital inflows is consistent with a large trade deficit. *(LO3)*

KEY TERMS

bond
capital inflows
capital outflows
coupon payments
coupon rate
diversification

dividend
financial intermediaries
international capital flows
international financial markets
mutual fund
principal amount

risk premium
stock (or equity)
trade balance
  (or net exports)
trade deficit
trade surplus

REVIEW QUESTIONS

1. Arjay plans to sell a bond that matures in one year and has a principal value of $1,000. Can he expect to receive $1,000 in the bond market for the bond? Explain. *(LO1)*

2. Give two ways that the financial system helps improve the allocation of savings. Illustrate with examples. *(LO2)*

3. Suppose you are much less concerned about risk than the typical person. Are stocks a good financial investment for you? Why or why not? *(LO1, LO2)*

4. How are capital inflows or outflows related to domestic investment in new capital goods? *(LO3)*

5. Explain with examples why, in any period, a country's net capital inflows equal its trade deficit. *(LO3)*

6. How would increased political instability in a country likely affect capital inflows, the domestic real interest rate, and investment in new capital goods? Show graphically. *(LO3)*

PROBLEMS

McGraw Hill **connect**

1. Simon purchases a bond, newly issued by the Amalgamated Corporation, for $1,000. The bond pays $60 to its holder at the end of the first and second years and pays $1,060 upon its maturity at the end of the third year. *(LO1)*
   a. What are the principal amount, the term, the coupon rate, and the coupon payment for Simon's bond?
   b. After receiving the second coupon payment (at the end of the second year), Simon decides to sell his bond in the bond market. What price can he expect for his bond if the one-year interest rate at that time is 3 percent? 8 percent? 10 percent?
   c. Can you think of a reason that the price of Simon's bond after two years might fall below $1,000, even though the market interest rate equals the coupon rate?

2. Shares in Brothers Grimm Inc., manufacturers of gingerbread houses, are expected to pay a dividend of $5.50 in one year and to sell for $99.00 per share at that time. How much should you be willing to pay today per share of Grimm: *(LO1)*
   a. If the safe rate of interest is 5.1 percent and you believe that investing in Grimm carries no risk?
   b. If the safe rate of interest is 10.1 percent and you believe that investing in Grimm carries no risk?
   c. If the safe rate of interest is 5.1 percent but your risk premium is 2 percent?
   d. Repeat parts a–c, assuming that Grimm is not expected to pay a dividend but the expected price is unchanged.

3. Your financial investments consist of U.S. government bonds maturing in 10 years and shares in a start-up company doing research in pharmaceuticals. How would you expect each of the following news items to affect the value of your assets? Explain. *(LO1)*
   a. Interest rates on newly issued government bonds rise?
   b. Inflation is forecasted to be much lower than previously expected? (*Hint:* Recall the Fisher effect from Chapter 18, *Measuring the Price Level and Inflation.*) Assume for simplicity that this information does not affect your forecast of the dollar value of the pharmaceutical company's future dividends and stock price.
   c. Large swings in the stock market increase financial investors' concerns about market risk. (Assume that interest rates on newly issued government bonds remain unchanged.)

4. You have $1,000 to invest and are considering buying some combination of the shares of two companies, DonkeyInc and ElephantInc. Shares of DonkeyInc will pay a 10 percent return if the Democrats are elected, an event you believe to have a 40 percent probability; otherwise, the shares pay a zero return. Shares of ElephantInc will pay 8 percent if the Republicans are elected (a 60 percent probability), zero otherwise. Either the Democrats or the Republicans will be elected. *(LO1, LO2)*
   a. If your only concern is maximizing your average expected return, with no regard for risk, how should you invest your $1,000?
   b. What is your expected return if you invest $500 in each stock? (*Hint:* Consider what your return will be if the Democrats win and if the Republicans win; then weight each outcome by the probability that event occurs.)
   c. The strategy of investing $500 in each stock does *not* give the highest possible average expected return. Why might you choose it anyway?
   d. Devise an investment strategy that guarantees at least a 4.4 percent return, no matter which party wins.
   e. Devise an investment strategy that is riskless—that is, one in which the return on your $1,000 does not depend at all on which party wins.

5. How do each of the following transactions affect (1) the trade surplus or deficit and (2) capital inflows or outflows for the United States? Show that in each case, the identity that the trade balance plus net capital inflows equals zero applies. *(LO3)*
   a. A U.S. exporter sells software to Israel. She uses the Israeli shekels received to buy stock in an Israeli company.
   b. A Mexican firm uses proceeds from its sale of oil to the United States to buy U.S. government debt.
   c. A Mexican firm uses proceeds from its sale of oil to the United States to buy oil drilling equipment from a U.S. firm.

6. Use a diagram like Figure 23.4 (solid lines only) to show the effects of each of the following on the real interest rate and capital investment of a country that is a net borrower from abroad. *(LO3)*
   a. Investment opportunities in the country improve owing to new technologies.
   b. The government budget deficit rises.
   c. Domestic citizens decide to save more.
   d. Foreign investors believe that the riskiness of lending to the country has increased.

7. A country's domestic supply of saving, domestic demand for saving for purposes of capital formation, and supply of net capital inflows are given by the following equations: *(LO3)*

$$S = 1,800 + 2,000r$$
$$I = 2,000 - 4,000r$$
$$KI = -100 + 6,000r$$

   a. Assuming that the market for saving and investment is in equilibrium, find national saving, capital inflows, domestic investment, and the real interest rate.

   b. Repeat part a, assuming that desired national saving declines by 120 at each value of the real interest rate. What effect does a reduction in domestic saving have on capital inflows?

   c. Concern about the economy's macroeconomic policies causes capital inflows to fall sharply so that now $KI = -700 + 6,000r$. Repeat part a. What does a reduction in capital inflows do to domestic investment and the real interest rate?

ANSWERS TO SELF-TESTS

23.1 Since bond prices fell, interest rates must have risen. To find the interest rate, note that bond investors are willing to pay only 96 today for a bond that will pay back 107 (a coupon payment of 7 plus the principal amount of 100) in one year. To find the one-year return, divide 107 by 96 to get 1.115. Thus, the interest rate must have risen to 11.5 percent. *(LO1)*

23.2 The share of stock will be worth $81.00 in one year—the sum of its expected future price and the expected dividend. At an interest rate of 4 percent, its value today is $81.00/1.04 = $77.88. At an interest rate of 8 percent, the stock's current value is $81.00/1.08 = $75.00. Recall from Example 23.2 that when the interest rate is 6 percent, the value of a share of FortuneCookie.com is $76.42. Since higher interest rates imply lower stock values, news that interest rates are about to rise should cause the stock market to fall. *(LO1)*

23.3 The purchase of the Japanese bond is a capital outflow for the United States, or $KI = -\$20,000$. The Japanese government now holds $20,000. What will it do with these funds? There are basically three possibilities. First, it might use the funds to purchase U.S. goods and services (military equipment, for example). In that case, the U.S. trade balance equals +$20,000,

and the sum of the trade balance and capital inflows is zero. Second, the Japanese government might acquire U.S. assets—for example, deposits in U.S. banks. In that case, a capital inflow to the United States of $20,000 offsets the original capital outflow. Both the trade balance and net capital outflows individually are zero, and so their sum is zero.

Finally, the Japanese government might use the $20,000 to purchase non-U.S. goods, services, or assets—oil from Saudi Arabia, for example. But then the non-U.S. recipient of the $20,000 is holding the funds, and it has the same options that the Japanese government did. Eventually, the funds will be used to purchase U.S. goods, services, or assets, satisfying Equation 23.1. Indeed, even if the recipient holds onto the funds (in cash, or as a U.S. bank deposit), they would still count as a capital inflow to the United States, as U.S. dollars or accounts in a U.S. bank are U.S. assets acquired by foreigners. *(LO3)*

23.4 An increase in the real interest rate abroad increases the relative attractiveness of foreign financial investments to both foreign and domestic savers. Net capital inflows to the home country will fall at each level of the domestic real interest rate. The supply curve of net capital inflows shifts left, as in Figure 23.3. *(LO3)*

CHAPTER 24

Short-Term Economic Fluctuations: An Introduction

Unemployment among construction workers rises substantially during recessions.

"Home Sales and Prices Continue to Plummet"

"As Jobs Vanish, Motel Rooms Become Home"

"Global Stock Markets Plummet"

"Steep Slide in Economy as Unsold Goods Pile Up"

"Fed Plans to Inject Another $1 Trillion to Aid the Economy"

"World Bank Says Global Economy Will Shrink in '09"

These headlines from *The New York Times* tell the story: From late 2007 to mid-2009, the U.S. economy passed through its worst economic downturn since the Great Depression of the 1930s. Average incomes fell; millions of Americans lost their jobs, many lost their health insurance, and even their homes; and governments at all levels struggled to deal with falling tax collections colliding with increased demands for public services like unemployment benefits and health care.

Other economic downturns between the Great Depression of the 1930s and the *Great Recession*—as the 2007–2009 downturn has come to be called—were generally milder. But they too inflicted great economic cost, most importantly lost jobs. And in some cases they had important political consequences.

LEARNING OBJECTIVES

After reading this chapter, you should be able to:

LO1 List the four phases of the business cycle and explain the primary characteristics of recessions and expansions.

LO2 Use potential output and the output gap to analyze an economy's position in the business cycle.

LO3 Define the natural rate of unemployment and show how it is related to cyclical unemployment.

LO4 Apply Okun's law to analyze the relationship between the output gap and cyclical unemployment.

LO5 Discuss the basic differences between how the economy operates in the short run versus the long run.

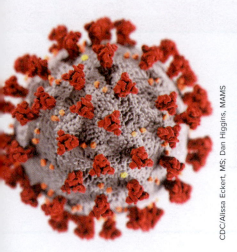

The Great Recession of 2007–2009 was followed by almost 11 years without a downturn—the longest such period on record. Then, in early 2020, the U.S. was hit by the COVID-19 pandemic. The reaction to the pandemic caused sudden collapse in global and domestic travel, closure of many businesses, and sharp increase in unemployment (see The Economic Naturalist 20.2 in Chapter 20, *The Labor Market: Workers, Wages, and Unemployment*). How deep and long this most recent recession is remains to be seen.

In preceding chapters, we discussed the factors that determine long-run economic growth. Over the broad sweep of history, those factors determine the economic success of a society. Indeed, over a span of 30, 50, or 100 years, relatively small differences in the rate of economic growth can have an enormous effect on the average person's standard of living. But even though the economic "climate" (long-run economic conditions) is the ultimate determinant of living standards, changes in the economic "weather" (short-run fluctuations in economic conditions) are also important. A good long-run growth record is not much consolation to a worker who has lost her job due to a recession. The bearing that short-term macroeconomic performance has on election results is one indicator of the importance the average person attaches to it (see The Economic Naturalist 24.1).

In this chapter, we begin our study of short-term fluctuations in economic activity. Commonly known as *business cycles,* these fluctuations consist of *expansions* and *recessions*. We will start with some background on the history and characteristics of these economic ups and downs. We next develop concepts that allow us to measure the severity of business cycles. These concepts allow us to analyze short-run economic activity from different perspectives and to link fluctuations in output to changes in unemployment. Finally, we introduce a verbal description of a basic model of expansions and recessions. Throughout this chapter, we will connect the theory to real-world examples, focusing on the two most recent recessions, the Great Recession of 2007–2009 and the coronavirus recession of 2020.

The Economic Naturalist 24.1

Do economic fluctuations affect presidential elections?

In early 1991, following the defeat of Iraq in the Gulf War by the United States and its allies, one poll showed that 89 percent of the American public approved of the job George H. W. Bush was doing as president. Prior to Bush, the last U.S. president to enjoy such a high approval rating was Harry Truman in 1945, shortly after World War II ended with the U.S. a victorious global superpower. The Gulf War victory followed a number of other popular developments in the foreign policy sphere, including the ouster of the corrupt leader General Manuel Noriega from Panama in December 1989, improved relations with China, apparent progress in Middle East peace talks, and the end of apartheid in South Africa. The collapse of the Soviet Union in December 1991—a stunning event that signaled the end of the Cold War—also occurred during Bush's term. Yet despite these political pluses, in the months following the Gulf War, Bush's sky-high approval rating declined sharply. According to the same poll, by the time of the Republican National Convention in the summer of 1992, only 29 percent of the public approved of Bush's performance. Although the president's ratings improved during the campaign, Bush and his running mate, Dan Quayle, lost the 1992 general election to Bill Clinton and Al Gore, receiving only 39 million of the 104 million votes cast. A third-party candidate, Ross Perot, received nearly 20 million votes. What caused this turnaround in (the first) President Bush's political fortunes?

Despite his high marks from voters in foreign policy, the president's domestic economic policies were widely viewed as ineffective. Bush received much criticism for breaking his campaign pledge not to raise taxes. More important, the economy weakened significantly in 1990–1991 and then recovered only slowly. Although inflation was low, by mid-1992, unemployment had reached 7.8 percent of the labor force—2.5 percentage points higher than in the first year of Bush's term and the highest level since 1984. A sign in Democratic candidate Bill Clinton's campaign headquarters summarized Clinton's strategy for winning the White House: "It's the economy, stupid." Clinton realized the importance of the nation's economic problems and pounded away at the Republican administration's inability to pull the country out of the doldrums. Clinton's focus on the economy was the key to his election.

Clinton's ability to parlay criticism of economic conditions into electoral success is not unusual in U.S. political history. Weakness in the economy played a decisive role in helping Franklin D. Roosevelt beat Herbert Hoover in 1932, John F. Kennedy to best Richard Nixon in 1960, and Ronald Reagan to defeat Jimmy Carter in 1980. And in an echo of his father's experience, President George W. Bush found the political popularity he enjoyed after the 9/11 attacks in 2001—a record 90 percent approval rating—eroded by an economic downturn and a slow subsequent recovery. His approval rating as president hit a record low of 25 percent in October 2008, at the height of the financial crisis. A few weeks later, Barack Obama was elected president, defeating the Republican candidate (and war hero) John McCain.

On the other hand, strong economic conditions have often helped incumbent presidents (or the incumbent's party) retain office, including Nixon in 1972, Reagan in 1984, and Clinton in 1996. Indeed, a number of empirical studies have suggested that economic performance in the year preceding the election is among the most important determinants of whether an incumbent president is likely to win reelection.

Finally, it is important to remember that the economic conditions as measured by macroeconomic indicators (such as the rate of unemployment) do not necessarily reflect the economic conditions as perceived by all voters. For example, recall from Chapter 16, *Macroeconomics: The Bird's-Eye View of the Economy,* that the construction of macroeconomic indicators involves aggregation and averaging. These indicators can therefore hide economic differences and inequalities across regions, economic sectors, and demographic groups. Indeed, in spite of low and decreasing unemployment rate under Obama, frustration among populations that felt left behind economically was a frequent theme raised by Republican candidate Donald Trump in the 2016 elections and may help explain, among other reasons, why the Democrats lost the presidency.

RECESSIONS AND EXPANSIONS

As background to the study of short-term economic fluctuations, let's review the historical record of the fluctuations in the U.S. economy. Figure 24.1 shows the path of real GDP in the United States since 1929. As you can see, the growth path of real

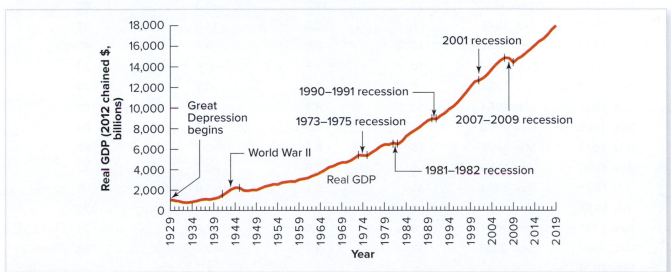

FIGURE 24.1

Fluctuations in U.S. Real GDP, 1929–2019.

Real GDP does not grow smoothly but has speedups (expansions or booms) and slowdowns (recessions or depressions).

Source: Federal Reserve of St. Louis Economic Data (FRED), https://fred.stlouisfed.org/series/GDPCA.

GDP is not always smooth; the bumps and wiggles correspond to short periods of faster or slower growth.

recession (or **contraction**) a period in which the economy is growing at a rate significantly below normal

depression a particularly severe or protracted recession

A period in which the economy is growing at a rate significantly below normal is called a **recession** or a **contraction**. An extremely severe or protracted recession is called a **depression**. You should be able to pick out the Great Depression in Figure 24.1, particularly the sharp initial decline between 1929 and 1933. But you can also see that the U.S. economy was volatile in the mid-1970s and the early 1980s, with serious recessions in 1973–1975 and 1981–1982. A moderate recession (but not moderate enough for the first President Bush) occurred in 1990–1991. The next recession began in March 2001, exactly 10 years after the end of the 1990–1991 recession, which was declared over as of March 1991. This 10-year period without a recession was at that time the longest such period in U.S. history, and the 2001 recession that ended it was again short and relatively mild, lasting eight months. In contrast, the Great Recession was long and severe. Its beginning in 2007 and its end in 2009 are clearly visible in Figure 24.1. The Great Recession was followed by almost 11 years without a recession—a new U.S. record. That boom period ended in 2020 with the arrival of COVID-19, which triggered the most recent recession.

A more informal definition of a recession, often cited by reporters, is a period during which real GDP falls for at least two consecutive quarters. This definition is not a bad rule of thumb because real GDP usually does fall during recessions. However, many economists would argue that periods in which real GDP growth is well below normal, though not actually negative, should be counted as recessions. Indeed, real GDP fell in only one quarter during the 2001 recession. Another problem with relying on GDP figures for dating recessions is that GDP data can be substantially revised, sometimes years after the fact. In practice, when trying to determine whether a recession is in progress, economists look at a variety of economic data, not just GDP.

Table 24.1 lists the beginning and ending dates of U.S. recessions since 1929, as well as the *duration* (length, in months) of each. The table also gives the highest unemployment rate

TABLE 24.1
U.S. Recessions since 1929

Peak date (beginning)	Trough date (end)	Duration (months)	Highest unemployment rate (%)	Change in real GDP (%)	Duration of subsequent expansion (months)
Aug. 1929	Mar. 1933	43	24.9	−26.3	50
May 1937	June 1938	13	19.0	−3.3	80
Feb. 1945	Oct. 1945	8	3.9	−11.6	37
Nov. 1948	Oct. 1949	11	5.9	−0.5	45
July 1953	May 1954	10	5.5	−0.6	39
Aug. 1957	Apr. 1958	8	6.8	−0.7	24
Apr. 1960	Feb. 1961	10	6.7	2.6	106
Dec. 1969	Nov. 1970	11	5.9	0.2	36
Nov. 1973	Mar. 1975	16	8.5	−0.7	58
Jan. 1980	July 1980	6	7.6	−0.2	12
July 1981	Nov. 1982	16	9.7	−1.9	92
July 1990	Mar. 1991	8	7.5	−0.1	120
Mar. 2001	Nov. 2001	8	6.0	1.0	73
Dec. 2007	June 2009	18	9.6	−3.1	128
Feb. 2020					

Notes: Unemployment rate is the annual rate for the trough year or the subsequent year, whichever is higher. Change in annual real GDP (chained 2009 dollars) is measured from the peak year to the trough year, except that the entry for the 1945 recession is the 1945–1946 change in real GDP, the entry for the 1980 recession is the 1979–1980 change, and the entry for 2001 is the 2000–2001 change.

Sources: Peak and trough dates: National Bureau of Economic Research; Unemployment: Bureau of Labor Statistics; Real GDP: Bureau of Economic Analysis.

recorded during each recession and the percentage change in real GDP. (Ignore the last column of the table for now.) The beginning of a recession is called the **peak,** because it represents the high point of economic activity prior to a downturn. The end of a recession, which marks the low point of economic activity prior to a recovery, is called the **trough.** The dates of peaks and troughs reported in Table 24.1 were determined by the National Bureau of Economic Research (NBER), a nonprofit organization of economists that has been a major source of research on short-term economic fluctuations since its founding in 1920 (see The Economic Naturalist 24.2). The NBER is not a government agency, but it is usually treated by the news media and the government as the "official" arbiter of the dates of peaks and troughs.

Table 24.1 shows that since 1929, by far the longest and most severe recession in the United States was the 43-month economic collapse that began in August 1929 and lasted until March 1933, initiating what became known as the Great Depression. Between 1933 and 1937, the economy grew fairly rapidly, so technically the period was not a recession, although unemployment remained very high at close to 20 percent of the workforce. In 1937–1938, the nation was hit by another significant recession. Full economic recovery from the Depression did not come until U.S. entry into World War II at the end of 1941. The economy boomed from 1941 to 1945 (see Figure 24.1), reflecting the enormous wartime production of military equipment and supplies.

In sharp contrast to the 1930s, U.S. recessions since World War II have generally been short—between 6 and 18 months, from peak to trough. As Table 24.1 shows, the two most severe postwar recessions prior to 2007, 1973–1975 and 1981–1982, lasted just 16 months. And, though unemployment rates during those two recessions were quite high by today's standards, they were low compared to the Great Depression. During the quarter century (25 years) from 1982 to 2007, the U.S. economy has experienced only two relatively mild recessions, in 1990–1991 and in 2001. The decline in macroeconomic volatility during those years was dubbed the Great Moderation, and some economists and other observers wondered whether we were witnessing "the end of the business cycle." But then came the 2007–2009 recession, the longest and deepest since the end of World War II, lasting 18 months with annual real GDP falling 3.1 percent from peak year to trough year and the annual unemployment rate reaching 9.6 percent. And we are yet to see how long and deep the recession that started in 2020 will be. Such events warn us to guard against overconfidence. Prosperity and economic stability can never be guaranteed.

The opposite of a recession is an **expansion**—a period in which the economy is growing at a rate that is significantly *above* normal. A particularly strong and protracted expansion is called a **boom.** In the United States, strong expansions occurred during 1933–1937, 1961–1969, 1982–1990, and 1991–2001, with exceptionally strong growth during 1995–2000 (see Figure 24.1). On average, expansions have been much longer than recessions. The final column of Table 24.1 shows the duration, in months, of U.S. expansions since 1929. As you can see in the table, the 1961–1969 expansion lasted 106 months; the 1982–1990 expansion, 92 months. The longest expansion before the most recent one began in March 1991, at the trough of the 1990–1991 recession. That expansion lasted 120 months, a full 10 years, until a new recession began in March 2001. And the longest expansion of all began in June 2009 and lasted 128 months, ending with the coronavirus recession that began in February 2020.

peak the beginning of a recession, the high point of economic activity prior to a downturn

trough the end of a recession, the low point of economic activity prior to a recovery

expansion a period in which the economy is growing at a rate significantly above normal

boom a particularly strong and protracted expansion

The Economic Naturalist 24.2

How was the 2020 recession called?

The Business Cycle Dating Committee of the National Bureau of Economic Research determined that a recession began in February 2020. What led the committee to choose that date?

The eight economists who form the Business Cycle Dating Committee met by conference call, and announced on Monday, June 8, 2020, that a recession had begun in February.

The determination of whether and when a recession has begun involves intensive statistical analysis, mixed in with a significant amount of human judgment.

Indeed, it took four months' worth of economic data before the committee called the recession. The Business Cycle Dating Committee typically relies heavily on a small set of statistical indicators that measure the overall strength of the economy. The committee prefers indicators that are available monthly because they are available quickly and may provide relatively precise information about the timing of peaks and troughs. Three of the most important indicators used by the committee in its June 2020 meeting were:

- Nonfarm employment (the number of people at work outside of agriculture), measured in two different ways: one based on a survey of employers, the other based on the BLS's survey of households.

- Real after-tax income received by households, excluding transfers like Social Security payments.

- Real personal consumption expenditures.

Each of these indicators measures a different aspect of the economy. Because their movements tend to coincide with the overall movements in the economy, they are called *coincident indicators*.

In its long and detailed statement calling the recession (available at www.nber .org/cycles/june2020.pdf), the committee included the following text:

> Because a recession is a broad contraction of the economy, not confined to one sector, the committee emphasizes economy-wide indicators of economic activity. The committee believes that domestic production and employment are the primary conceptual measures of economic activity.
>
> . . . The committee normally views the payroll employment measure, which is based on a large survey of employers, as the most reliable comprehensive estimate of employment. This series reached a clear peak in February.

The committee determined that the other monthly indicators listed above also supported a clear peak in February 2020. In its deliberations, the committee also looked at quarterly domestic production measures (including GDP), which, as the committee determined, provided consistent evidence with its announcement that a new recession began.

 SELF-TEST 24.1

Using the National Bureau of Economic Research website (www.nber.org/ cycles.html), is the U.S. economy currently in recession or expansion? How much time has elapsed since the last peak or trough? Explore the NBER website to find additional useful information about current conditions in the U.S. economy.

SOME FACTS ABOUT SHORT-TERM ECONOMIC FLUCTUATIONS

Although Figure 24.1 and Table 24.1 show data starting only in 1929, periods of expansion and recession have been a feature of industrial economies since at least the late eighteenth century. Karl Marx and Friedrich Engels referred to these fluctuations, which they called "commercial crises," in their *Communist Manifesto* of 1848. In the United States, economists have been studying short-term fluctuations for at least a century. The traditional term for these fluctuations is **business cycles,** and they are still often referred to as **cyclical fluctuations.** Neither term is accurate though; as Figure 24.1 shows, economic fluctuations are not "cyclical" at all in the sense that they recur at predictable intervals, but instead are *irregular in their length and severity*. This irregularity makes the dates of peaks and

business cycles (or **cyclical fluctuations**) short-term fluctuations in GDP and other indicators of economic activity

troughs extremely hard to predict, despite the fact that professional forecasters have devoted a great deal of effort and brainpower to the task.

Expansions and recessions usually are not limited to a few industries or regions but, as noted in The Economic Naturalist 24.2, are *felt throughout the economy*. Indeed, the largest fluctuations may have a *global impact*. For instance, the Great Depression of the 1930s affected nearly all the world's economies, and the 1973–1975 and 1981–1982 recessions were also widely felt outside the United States. When East Asia suffered a major slowdown in the late 1990s, the effects of that slowdown spilled over into many other regions (although not so much the United States). As you already know, the 2007–2009 recession quickly became worldwide in scope, and some of its effects are still being felt around the world today. And the recession that started in 2020 was a global phenomenon, hitting much of the world at the same time.

Recessions are very difficult to forecast.

But even a relatively moderate recession, like the one that occurred in 2001, can have global effects. Figure 24.2, which shows annual growth rates of real GDP over the period 1999–2014 for China, Germany, Japan, the United Kingdom, and the United States, illustrates this point. (The figure's shaded areas show U.S. recession dates, taken from Table 24.1.) You can see that all five economies—the world's largest by GDP—slowed significantly in 2008 and, except for China, they all contracted rather significantly in 2009. All five economies also started recovering together, but after a promising 2010, they all slowed again in 2011 and have, in general, been growing more slowly in recent years than in the years just before the crisis. Figure 24.2 also shows that all five economies slowed at least somewhat from 2000 to 2001.

Unemployment is a key indicator of short-term economic fluctuations. The unemployment rate typically rises sharply during recessions and recovers (although more slowly) during expansions. Figure 16.3 showed the U.S. unemployment rate since 1929, and Figure 17.4 showed the rate since 1965. You should be able to identify, most recently, the recessions that began in 1969, 1973, 1981, 1990, 2001, and 2007 by noting the sharp peaks in the unemployment rate in those or the following years. Recall that the part of unemployment that is associated with recessions is called *cyclical unemployment*. Beyond this increase in unemployment, labor market conditions generally worsen during recessions. For example, during recessions real wages grow more slowly, workers are less likely to receive promotions or bonuses, and new entrants to the labor force (such as college graduates) have a much tougher time finding attractive jobs.

Generally, industries that produce **durable goods,** such as cars, houses, and capital equipment, are more affected than others by recessions and booms. In contrast, industries that provide *services* and **nondurable goods** like food are much less sensitive to short-term fluctuations. Thus an automobile worker or a construction worker is far more likely to lose his or her job in a recession than is a barber or a baker.

durable goods goods that yield utility over time and are made to last for three years or more

nondurable goods goods that can be quickly consumed or immediately used, having a life span of less than three years

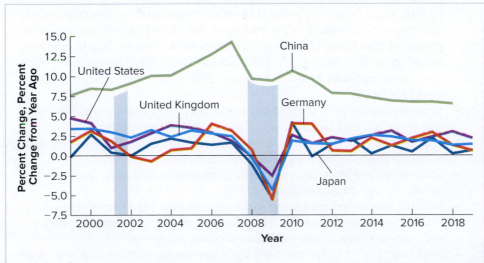

FIGURE 24.2

Real GDP Growth in Five Major Countries, 1999–2019.

Annual growth rates (measured as the change in real GDP over the past four quarters) for the world's five largest economies show that all the countries slowed somewhat in 2001—the year of a relatively mild recession—and slowed significantly in 2008 and 2009—during the much more severe Great Recession.

Source: Federal Reserve of St. Louis Economic Data (FRED), https://fred.stlouisfed.org.

FIGURE 24.3

U.S. Inflation, 1960–2019.

U.S. inflation since 1960 is measured by the change in the CPI, and periods of recession are indicated by the shaded vertical bars. Note that inflation declined during or following each of those recessions and rose prior to many of those recessions.

Source: U.S. Bureau of Labor Statistics, www.bls.gov.

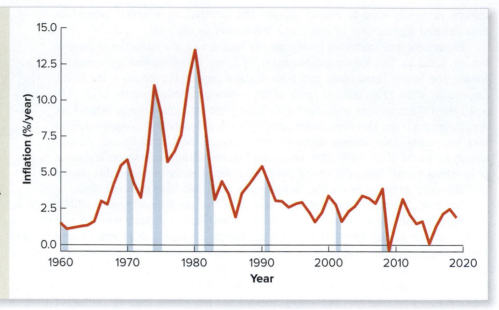

Like unemployment, *inflation* follows a typical pattern in recessions and expansions, though it is not so sharply defined. Figure 16.4 showed the U.S. inflation rate since 1929, and Figure 24.3 shows the rate since 1960 (periods of recession are again indicated by shaded vertical bars). As you can see, recessions tend to be followed soon after by a decline in the rate of inflation. For example, the recession of 1981–1982 was followed by a sharp reduction in inflation, and the recession of 2007–2009 ended with slightly negative inflation. Furthermore, many—though not all—postwar recessions have been preceded by increases in inflation, as Figure 24.3 shows. The behavior of inflation during expansions and recessions will be discussed more fully in the next two chapters.

RECAP↑

RECESSIONS, EXPANSIONS, AND SHORT-TERM ECONOMIC FLUCTUATIONS

- A recession is a period in which output is growing more slowly than normal. An expansion, or boom, is a period in which output is growing more quickly than normal.
- The beginning of a recession is called the peak, and its end (which corresponds to the beginning of the subsequent expansion) is called the trough.
- The sharpest recession in the history of the United States was the initial phase of the Great Depression in 1929–1933. Severe recessions also occurred in 1973–1975, 1981–1982, and 2007–2009. Two relatively mild recessions occurred in 1990–1991 and 2001. The most recent recession started in 2020.
- Short-term economic fluctuations (recessions and expansions) are irregular in length and severity, and thus are difficult to predict.
- Expansions and recessions have widespread (and sometimes global) impacts, affecting most regions and industries.
- Unemployment rises sharply during a recession and falls, usually more slowly, during an expansion.
- Durable goods industries are more affected by expansions and recessions than other industries. Services and nondurable goods industries are less sensitive to ups and downs in the economy.
- Recessions tend to be followed by a decline in inflation and are often preceded by an increase in inflation.

OUTPUT GAPS AND CYCLICAL UNEMPLOYMENT

How can we tell whether a particular recession or expansion is "big" or "small"? The answer to this question is important to both economists who study business cycles and policymakers who must formulate responses to economic fluctuations. Intuitively, a "big" recession or expansion is one in which output and the unemployment rate deviate significantly from their normal or trend levels. In this section, we will attempt to be more precise about this idea by introducing the concept of the *output gap,* which measures how far output is from its normal level at a particular time. We will also revisit the idea of *cyclical unemployment,* or the deviation of unemployment from its normal level. Finally, we will examine how these two concepts are related.

POTENTIAL OUTPUT

The concept of potential output is a useful starting point for thinking about the measurement of expansions and recessions. **Potential output,** also called **potential GDP** or **full-employment output,** is the amount of output (real GDP) that an economy can produce when using its resources, such as capital and labor, at normal rates. The term *potential output* is slightly misleading, in that *potential* output is not the same as *maximum* output. Because capital and labor can be utilized at greater-than-normal rates, at least for a time, a country's actual output can exceed its potential output. These greater-than-normal utilization rates, however, cannot be sustained indefinitely, partly because workers cannot work overtime every week and machinery must occasionally be shut down for maintenance and repairs.

Potential output is not a fixed number but grows over time, reflecting increases in both the amounts of available capital and labor and their productivity. We discussed the sources of growth in potential output (the economy's productive capacity) in Chapter 19, *Economic Growth, Productivity, and Living Standards.* We will use the symbol Y^* to signify the economy's potential output at a given point in time. Figure 24.4 presents estimated potential output for the United States from 1949 to 2019. Compare this graph with the data on actual real GDP shown in Figure 24.1. Notice that the estimate for potential output, Y^*, is much smoother than actual output, Y. This reflects the fact that increases in the economy's productive capacity are due to factors (such as human capital) that grow relatively smoothly over time. Potential output is therefore predicted to grow relatively smoothly as well.

potential output, Y^* (or **potential GDP** or **full-employment output**) the amount of output (real GDP) that an economy can produce when using its resources, such as capital and labor, at normal rates

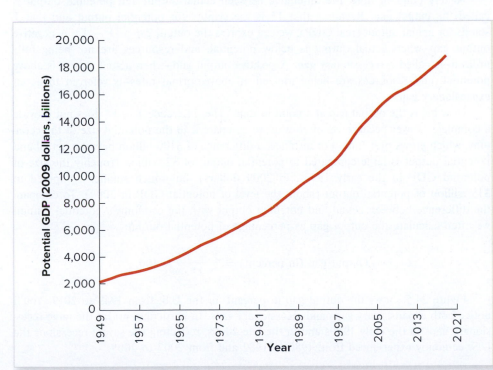

FIGURE 24.4

U.S. Potential Output, 1949–2019.

Estimated potential output Y^* grows more smoothly than actual output Y. Compare these data with Figure 24.1.

Source: U.S. Congressional Budget Office, Real Potential Gross Domestic Product [GDPPOT], retrieved from FRED, Federal Reserve Bank of St. Louis; https://fred.stlouisfed.org/series/GDPPOT.

Why does a nation's output sometimes grow quickly and sometimes slowly, as shown for the United States in Figure 24.1? Logically, there are two possibilities: First, changes in the rate of output growth may reflect *changes in the rate at which the country's potential output is increasing*. For example, unfavorable weather conditions, such as a severe drought, would reduce the rate of potential output growth in an agricultural economy, and a decline in the rate of technological innovation might reduce the rate of potential output growth in an industrial economy. Under the assumption that the country is using its resources at normal rates, so that actual output equals potential output, a significant slowdown in potential output growth would tend to result in recession. Similarly, new technologies, increased capital investment, or a surge in immigration that swells the labor force could produce unusually brisk growth in potential output, and hence an economic boom.

Undoubtedly, changes in the rate of growth of potential output are part of the explanation for expansions and recessions. In the United States, for example, the economic boom of the second half of the 1990s was propelled in part by new information technologies, such as the Internet. And the slow recovery in the first half of the 2010s from the financial crisis seems to reflect, at least in part, a slowdown in potential output caused by demographic changes and slow productivity growth. When changes in the rate of GDP growth reflect changes in the growth rate of potential output, the appropriate policy responses are those discussed in Chapter 19, *Economic Growth, Productivity, and Living Standards*. In particular, when a recession results from slowing growth in potential output, the government's best response is to try to promote saving, investment, technological innovation, human capital formation, and other activities that support growth.

THE OUTPUT GAP

A second possible explanation for short-term economic fluctuations is that *actual output does not always equal potential output*. For example, potential output may be growing normally, but for some reason the economy's capital and labor resources may not be fully utilized, so that actual output is significantly below the level of potential output. This low level of output, resulting from underutilization of economic resources, would generally be interpreted as a recession. Alternatively, capital and labor may be working much harder than normal—firms may put workers on overtime, for example—so that actual output expands beyond potential output, creating a boom.

output gap the difference between the economy's actual output and its potential output at a point in time $(Y - Y^*)$

recessionary gap a negative output gap, which occurs when potential output exceeds actual output $(Y^* > Y)$

expansionary gap a positive output gap, which occurs when actual output is higher than potential output $(Y > Y^*)$

At any point in time, the difference between actual output and potential output is called the **output gap.** Recalling that Y^* is the symbol for potential output and that Y stands for actual output (real GDP), we can express the output gap as $Y - Y^*$. A negative output gap—when actual output is below potential, and resources are not being fully utilized—is called a **recessionary gap**. A positive output gap—when actual output is above potential, and resources are being utilized at above-normal rates—is referred to as an **expansionary gap.**

How big is the output gap at a point in time? The difference $Y - Y^*$ does not provide a complete answer because we often want to compare it to the potential size of the economy, which grows over time. For instance, a difference of $100 billion between actual and potential output is large compared to potential output of $2 trillion (roughly the size of potential GDP in the early 1950s, in 2009 dollars), but much smaller compared to $15 trillion of potential output (about the level of potential GDP in 2009). To compare the difference between actual and potential output with the economy's potential output, we often calculate the output gap as percentage of potential output:

$$\text{Output gap (in percent)} = \frac{Y - Y^*}{Y^*} \times 100.$$

Figure 24.5 shows the output gap in percent for the U.S. from 1949 to 2019. You'll notice both expansionary gaps and recessionary gaps. In particular, notice the large recessionary gaps in the early 1980s and in the late 2000s, reflecting the severe recessions the U.S. economy experienced from 1980 to 1982 and from 2007 to 2009.

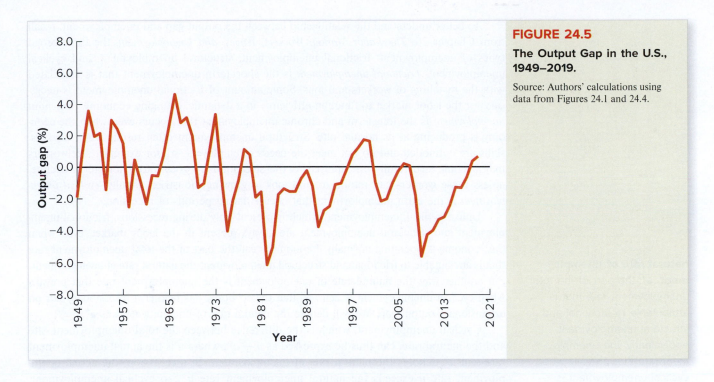

FIGURE 24.5

The Output Gap in the U.S., 1949–2019.

Source: Authors' calculations using data from Figures 24.1 and 24.4.

Policymakers generally view both recessionary gaps and expansionary gaps as problems. It is not difficult to see why a recessionary gap is bad news for the economy: When there is a recessionary gap, capital and labor resources are not being fully utilized, and output and employment are below normal levels (that is, they are below maximum sustainable levels). This is the sort of situation that poses problems for politicians' reelection prospects, as discussed in The Economic Naturalist 24.1. An expansionary gap is considered a problem by policymakers for a more subtle reason: What's wrong, after all, with having higher output and employment than normal? A prolonged expansionary gap is problematic because, when faced with a demand for their products that significantly exceeds their normal capacity, firms tend to raise prices. Thus an expansionary gap typically results in increased inflation, which reduces the efficiency of the economy in the longer run.

So, whenever an output gap exists, whether it is recessionary or expansionary, policymakers have an incentive to try to eliminate the gap by returning actual output to potential. In this and the next chapters we will discuss both how output gaps arise and the tools that policymakers have for *stabilizing* the economy—that is, bringing actual output into line with potential output.

THE NATURAL RATE OF UNEMPLOYMENT AND CYCLICAL UNEMPLOYMENT

Whether recessions arise because of slower growth in potential output or because actual output falls below potential, they bring bad times. In either case, output falls (or at least grows more slowly), implying reduced living standards. Recessionary output gaps are particularly frustrating for policymakers, however, because they imply that the economy has the *capacity* to produce more, but for some reason available resources are not being fully utilized. Recessionary gaps violate the Efficiency Principle in that they unnecessarily reduce the total economic pie, making the typical person worse off.

Efficiency

An important indicator of the low utilization of resources during recessions is the unemployment rate. In general, a *high* unemployment rate means that labor resources are not being fully utilized so that output has fallen below potential (a recessionary gap). By the same logic, an unusually *low* unemployment rate suggests that labor is being utilized at a rate greater than normal so that actual output exceeds potential output (an expansionary gap).

To better understand the relationship between the output gap and unemployment, recall from Chapter 20, *The Labor Market: Workers, Wages, and Unemployment,* the three broad types of unemployment: frictional unemployment, structural unemployment, and cyclical unemployment. *Frictional unemployment* is the short-term unemployment that is associated with the matching of workers and jobs. Some amount of frictional unemployment is necessary for the labor market to function efficiently in a dynamic, changing economy. *Structural unemployment* is the long-term and chronic unemployment that occurs even when the economy is producing at its normal rate. Structural unemployment often results when workers' skills are outmoded and do not meet the needs of employers—so, for example, steelworkers may become structurally unemployed as the steel industry goes into a long-term decline, unless those workers can retrain to find jobs in growing industries. Finally, *cyclical unemployment* is the extra unemployment that occurs during periods of recession.

Unlike cyclical unemployment, which is present only during recessions, frictional unemployment and structural unemployment are always present in the labor market, even when the economy is operating normally. Economists call the part of the total unemployment rate that is attributable to frictional and structural unemployment the **natural rate of unemployment.** Put another way, the natural rate of unemployment is the unemployment rate that prevails when cyclical unemployment is zero, so that the economy has neither a recessionary nor an expansionary output gap. We will denote the natural rate of unemployment as u^*.

Cyclical unemployment, which is the difference between the total unemployment rate and the natural rate, can thus be expressed as $u - u^*$, where u is the actual unemployment rate and u^* denotes the natural rate of unemployment. In a recession, the actual unemployment rate u exceeds the natural unemployment rate u^*, so cyclical unemployment, $u - u^*$, is positive. When the economy experiences an expansionary gap, in contrast, the actual unemployment rate is lower than the natural rate, so that cyclical unemployment is negative. Negative cyclical unemployment corresponds to a situation in which labor is being used more intensively than normal, so that actual unemployment has dipped below its usual frictional and structural levels.

natural rate of unemployment, u^* the part of the total unemployment rate that is attributable to frictional and structural unemployment; equivalently, the unemployment rate that prevails when cyclical unemployment is zero, so that the economy has neither a recessionary nor an expansionary output gap

The Economic Naturalist 24.3

Why has the natural rate of unemployment in the United States declined?

According to the Congressional Budget Office, which regularly estimates the natural rate of unemployment in the United States, the long-term natural rate has been falling almost steadily since 1978, when it was 6.2 percent (this long-term trend reversed only briefly following the 2008 global financial crisis).[1] By 2020, it was estimated at 4.4 percent, and the CBO predicts that it will keep declining in the next 10 years. Why is the U.S. natural rate of unemployment apparently so much lower nowadays than it was in the late 1970s?

The natural rate of unemployment may have fallen because of reduced frictional unemployment, reduced structural unemployment, or both. A variety of ideas have been advanced to explain declines in both types of unemployment. One promising suggestion is based on the changing age structure of the U.S. labor force.[2] The average age of U.S. workers is rising, reflecting the aging of the baby boom generation. Indeed, over the past four decades, the share of the labor force aged 16–24 has fallen from about 25 percent to below 14 percent and is projected by the BLS to keep falling to about 12 percent by 2026. Since young workers are more prone to unemployment than older workers, the aging of the labor force may help explain the overall decline in unemployment.

[1]U.S. Congressional Budget Office, *Natural Rate of Unemployment (Long-Term)* [NROU], FRED, Federal Reserve Bank of St. Louis, https://fred.stlouisfed.org/series/NROU (accessed June 15, 2020).
[2]See Robert Shimer, "Why Is the U.S. Unemployment Rate So Much Lower?," in *NBER Macroeconomics Annual 1998,* B. Bernanke and J. Rotemberg, eds. (Cambridge, MA: MIT Press, 1999).

Why are young workers more likely to be unemployed? Compared to teenagers and workers in their twenties, older workers are much more likely to hold long-term, stable jobs. In contrast, younger workers tend to hold short-term jobs, perhaps because they are not ready to commit to a particular career or because their time in the labor market is interrupted by schooling or military service. Because they change jobs more often, younger workers are more prone than others to frictional unemployment. They also have fewer skills, on average, than older workers, so they may experience more structural unemployment. As workers age and gain experience, however, their risk of unemployment declines.

Another possible explanation for the declining natural rate of unemployment is that labor markets have become more efficient at matching workers with jobs, thereby reducing both frictional and structural unemployment. For example, agencies that arrange temporary help have become much more commonplace in the United States in recent years. Although the placements these agencies make are intended to be temporary, they often become permanent when an employer and worker discover that a particularly good match has been made. Online job services, which allow workers to search for jobs nationally and even internationally, have also become increasingly important. By reducing the time people must spend in unemployment and by creating more lasting matches between workers and jobs, temporary help agencies, online job services, job-search apps, and similar innovations may have reduced the natural rate of unemployment.[3]

Technological change can also promote temporary job matches. For example, ride-sharing apps allow drivers to work on their own schedule, perhaps to supplement income from another job. Ride-sharing and other types of irregular work are known as the *gig economy*. Participants in the gig economy are officially counted as employed, even if they work only a few hours a week.

RECAP ↑

OUTPUT GAPS AND CYCLICAL UNEMPLOYMENT

- Potential output is the amount of output (real GDP) that an economy can produce when using its resources, such as capital and labor, at normal rates. The output gap, $Y - Y^*$, is the difference between actual output Y and potential output Y^*. The output gap in percent is:

$$\frac{Y - Y^*}{Y^*} \times 100.$$

- When actual output is below potential, the resulting output gap is called a recessionary gap. When actual output is above potential, the difference is called an expansionary gap.
- A recessionary gap reflects a waste of resources, while an expansionary gap threatens to ignite inflation; hence policymakers have an incentive to try to eliminate both types of output gaps.
- The natural rate of unemployment u^* is the sum of the frictional and structural unemployment rates. It is the rate of unemployment that is observed when the economy is operating at a normal level, with no output gap.
- Cyclical unemployment, $u - u^*$, is the difference between the actual unemployment rate u and the natural rate of unemployment u^*. Cyclical unemployment is positive when there is a recessionary gap, negative when there is an expansionary gap, and zero when there is no output gap.

---

[3]For a detailed analysis of factors affecting the natural rate, see Lawrence Katz and Alan Krueger, "The High-Pressure U.S. Labor Market of the 1990s," *Brookings Papers on Economic Activity* 1 (1999), pp. 1–88.

OKUN'S LAW

What is the relationship between an output gap and the amount of cyclical unemployment in the economy? We have already observed that by definition, cyclical unemployment is positive when the economy has a recessionary gap, negative when there is an expansionary gap, and zero when there is no output gap. A more quantitative relationship between cyclical unemployment and the output gap is given by a rule of thumb called *Okun's law*, after Arthur Okun, one of President Kennedy's chief economic advisors. According to **Okun's law,** each 1 percent increase in cyclical unemployment is associated with about a 2 percent widening of a negative output gap, measured in relation to potential output.[4] So, for example, if cyclical unemployment increases from 1 percent to 2 percent of the labor force, the recessionary gap will increase from −2 percent to −4 percent of potential GDP.

We can also express Okun's law as an equation. Using our expression for the output gap, we have:

$$\frac{Y - Y^*}{Y^*} \times 100 = -2 \times (u - u^*).$$

The following example further illustrates Okun's law.

Okun's law each extra percentage point of cyclical unemployment is associated with about a 2 percentage point increase in the output gap, measured in relation to potential output

| EXAMPLE 24.1 | Okun's Law and the Output Gap in the U.S. Economy |

How is Okun's law applied to real-world data?

The table below presents data on the actual unemployment rate, the natural unemployment rate, and potential GDP (in billions of 2009 dollars) for the U.S. economy in five selected years.

Year	u	u*	Y*
1995	5.6%	5.4%	10,630.3
2000	4.0	5.2	13,131.0
2005	5.1	5.0	14,912.5
2010	9.6	5.0	15,598.8
2015	5.3	4.7	17,403.8

In 1995, cyclical unemployment, $u - u^*$, was 0.2 percent of the labor force (5.6% − 5.4%). Applying Okun's law, the output gap for 1995 was −2 times that percentage, or −0.4 percent of potential output. Potential output was estimated to be $10,630.3 billion, so the value of the negative output gap for that year was $42.5 billion.

2000 was near the end of an expansion and the actual unemployment rate was below the natural rate. Specifically, cyclical unemployment was −1.2 percent; using Okun's law, this means that the output gap was 2.4 percent and the U.S. economy's output was $315.1 billion more than it typically would have been in 2000.

The data for 2010 give a sense of the depth of the most recent recession. Although the 2007–2009 recession had already ended, cyclical unemployment was still very high, at 4.6 percent, implying an output gap of −9.2 percent. Thus, according to Okun's law, the U.S. economy was producing about $1,435.1 (0.092 × 15,598.8) billion *less* than it would produce had all resources been fully employed. There were about 309 million people in the United States in 2010, so Okun's law implies that average incomes (i.e., per capita GDP) could have been around

---

[4]This relationship between unemployment and output has weakened over time. When Arthur Okun first formulated his law in the 1960s, he suggested that each extra percentage point of unemployment was associated with about a 3 percentage point widening in the (negative) output gap. At the same time, the weakened relationship has held up surprisingly well over time. For a recent discussion, see Mary C. Daly, John Fernald, Òscar Jordà, and Fernanda Nechio, "Interpreting Deviations from Okun's Law," *FRBSF Economic Letter 2014-12,* April 21, 2014, www.frbsf. org/economic-research/publications/economic-letter/2014/april/okun-law-deviation-unemployment-recession/.

$4,600 higher in 2010—about $18,400 for a family of four—had the economy not been operating below potential. Thus output gaps and cyclical unemployment have significant costs, a conclusion that justifies the concern that the public and policymakers have about recessions.

Of course, Okun's law is only a rule of thumb. The Congressional Budget Office's estimates of the output gap for the years shown in the table above are somewhat different from the numbers we have just calculated. However, those estimates, which use better—and significantly more complicated—techniques to more accurately estimate the output gap, are in the same order of magnitude as the numbers we calculated above.

 SELF-TEST 24.2

According to the table in Example 24.1, in 2015 the U.S. unemployment rate was 5.3 percent. The Congressional Budget Office estimated that in 2015 the natural rate of unemployment was 4.7 percent. Applying Okun's law, by what percentage did actual GDP differ from potential GDP in 2015?

The Economic Naturalist 24.4

Why did the Federal Reserve act to slow down the economy in 1999 and 2000?

As we have noted in earlier chapters, monetary policy decisions of the Federal Reserve—actions that change the level of the nation's money supply—affect the performance of the U.S. economy. Why did the Federal Reserve take measures to slow down the economy in 1999 and 2000?

Throughout the 1990s, cyclical unemployment in the United States fell dramatically, becoming negative sometime in 1997, according to Congressional Budget Office estimates. Okun's law indicates that growing negative cyclical unemployment rates signal an increasing expansionary gap and, with it, an increased risk of future inflation.

In 1997 and 1998, the Federal Reserve argued that the inflationary pressures typically caused by rapidly expanding output and falling unemployment rates were being offset by productivity gains and international competition, leaving inflation rates lower than expected. Because inflation remained low during this period—despite a small but growing expansionary gap—the Federal Reserve did little to eliminate the gap.

However, as the actual unemployment rate continued to fall throughout 1999 and early 2000, the expansionary gap continued to widen, causing the Federal Reserve to grow increasingly concerned about the growing imbalance between actual and potential GDP and the threat of increasing inflation. In response, the Federal Reserve took actions in 1999 and 2000 to slow the growth of output and bring actual and potential output closer into alignment (we will give more details in Chapter 26, *Stabilizing the Economy: The Role of the Fed,* and Chapter 27, *Aggregate Demand, Aggregate Supply, and Inflation,* about how the Fed can do this). The Fed's actions helped "promote overall balance in the economy"[5] and restrain inflation throughout 2000. By early 2001, however, the U.S. economy stalled and fell into recession, leading the Federal Reserve to reverse course and take policy measures aimed at eliminating the growing *recessionary* gap.

---

[5]Testimony of Chairman Alan Greenspan, *The Federal Reserve's Semiannual Report on the Economy and Monetary Policy,* Committee on Banking and Financial Services, U.S. House of Representatives, February 17, 2000. Available online at www.federalreserve.gov/boarddocs/hh/2000/February/Testimony.htm.

WHY DO SHORT-TERM FLUCTUATIONS OCCUR? A PREVIEW AND A TALE

What causes periods of recession and expansion? In the preceding sections, we discussed two possible reasons for slowdowns and speedups in real GDP growth. First, growth in potential output itself may slow down or speed up, reflecting changes in the growth rates of available capital and labor and in the pace of technological progress. Second, even if potential output is growing normally, actual output may be higher or lower than potential output—that is, expansionary or recessionary output gaps may develop. Earlier in this book, we discussed some of the reasons that growth in potential output can vary, and the options that policymakers have for stimulating growth in potential output. But we have not yet addressed the question of how output gaps can arise or what policymakers should do in response. The causes and cures of output gaps will be a major topic of the next three chapters. Here is a brief preview of the main conclusions of these chapters:

1. In a world in which prices adjusted immediately to balance the quantities supplied and demanded for all goods and services, output gaps would not exist. However, for many goods and services, the assumption that prices will adjust immediately is not realistic. Instead, many firms adjust the prices of their output only periodically. In particular, rather than changing prices with every variation in demand, firms tend to adjust to changes in demand in the short run by varying the quantity of output they produce and sell. This type of behavior is known as "meeting the demand" at a preset price.

2. Because, in the short run, firms tend to meet the demand for their output at preset prices, changes in the amount that customers decide to spend will affect output. When total spending is low for some reason, output may fall below potential output; conversely, when spending is high, output may rise above potential output. In other words, *changes in economywide spending are the primary cause of output gaps*. Thus government policies can help eliminate output gaps by influencing total spending. For example, the government can affect total spending directly simply by changing its own level of purchases.

3. Although firms tend to meet demand in the short run, they will not be willing to do so indefinitely. If customer demand continues to differ from potential output, firms will eventually adjust their prices to eliminate output gaps. If demand exceeds potential output (an expansionary gap), firms will raise their prices aggressively, spurring inflation. If demand falls below potential output (a recessionary gap), firms will raise their prices less aggressively or even cut prices, reducing inflation.

4. Over the longer run, price changes by firms eliminate any output gap and bring production back into line with the economy's potential output. Thus the economy is "self-correcting" in the sense that it operates to eliminate output gaps over time. Because of this self-correcting tendency, in the long run actual output equals potential output, so that output is determined by the economy's productive capacity rather than by the rate of spending. In the long run, total spending influences only the rate of inflation.

These ideas will become clearer as we proceed through the next chapters. Before plunging into the details of the analysis, though, let's consider an example that illustrates the links between spending and output in the short and long run.

ALICE'S ICE CREAM STORE: A TALE ABOUT SHORT-RUN FLUCTUATIONS

Alice's ice cream store produces gourmet ice cream on the premises and sells it directly to the public. What determines the amount of ice cream that she produces on a daily basis? The productive capacity, or potential output, of the shop is one important factor. Specifically, Alice's potential output of ice cream depends on the amount of capital (number of ice cream makers) and labor (number of workers) that she employs and on the productivity of that capital and labor. Although Alice's potential output usually changes rather slowly, on occasion it can fluctuate significantly—for example, if an ice cream maker breaks down or Alice contracts the flu.

The main source of day-to-day variations in Alice's ice cream production, however, is not changes in potential output but fluctuations in the demand for ice cream by the public. Some of these fluctuations in spending occur predictably over the course of the day (more demand in the afternoon than in the morning, for example), the week (more demand on weekends), or the year (more demand in the summer). Other changes in demand are less regular—more demand on a hot day than a cool one, or when a parade is passing by the store. Some changes in demand are hard for Alice to interpret: For example, a surge in demand for rocky road ice cream on one particular Tuesday could reflect a permanent change in consumer tastes, or it might just be a random, one-time event.

How should Alice react to these ebbs and flows in the demand for ice cream? The basic supply and demand model that we introduced in Chapter 3, *Supply and Demand,* if applied to the market for ice cream, would predict that the price of ice cream should change with every change in the demand for ice cream. For example, prices should rise just after the movie theater next door to Alice's shop lets out on Friday night, and they should fall on unusually cold, blustery days, when most people would prefer a hot cider to an ice cream cone. Indeed, taken literally, the supply and demand model predicts that ice cream prices should change almost moment to moment. Imagine Alice standing in front of her shop like an auctioneer, calling out prices in an effort to determine how many people are willing to buy at each price!

Of course, we do not expect to see this behavior by an ice cream store owner. Price setting by auction does in fact occur in some markets, such as the market for grain or the stock market, but it is not the normal procedure in most retail markets, such as the market for ice cream. Why this difference? The basic reason is that sometimes the economic benefits of setting up an auction (including hiring an auctioneer, or implementing an automatic auction platform and having customers use it) exceed the costs of doing so, and sometimes they do not. In the market for grain, for example, many buyers and sellers gather together in the same place at the same time to trade large volumes of standardized goods (bushels of grain). In that kind of situation, an auction is an efficient way to determine prices and balance the quantities supplied and demanded. In an ice cream store, by contrast, customers come in by twos and threes at random times throughout the day. Some want shakes, some cones, and some sodas. With small numbers of customers and a low sales volume at any given time, the costs involved in selling ice cream by auction are much greater than the benefits of allowing prices to vary with demand.

So how does Alice the ice cream store manager deal with changes in the demand for ice cream? Observation suggests that she begins by setting prices based on the best information she has about the demand for her product and the costs of production. Perhaps she prints up a menu or makes a sign announcing the prices. Then, over a period of time, she will keep her prices fixed and serve as many customers as want to buy (up to the point where she runs out of ice cream or room in the store at these prices). This behavior is what we call "meeting the demand" at preset prices, and it implies that *in the short run,* the amount of ice cream Alice produces and sells is determined by the demand for her products.

However, *in the long run,* the situation is quite different. Suppose, for example, that Alice's ice cream earns a citywide reputation for its freshness and flavor. Day after day Alice observes long lines in her store. Her ice cream maker is overtaxed, as are her employees and her table space. There can no longer be any doubt that at current prices, the quantity of ice cream the public wants to consume exceeds what Alice is able and willing to supply on a normal basis (her potential output). Expanding the store is an attractive possibility, but not one (we assume) that is immediately feasible. What will Alice do?

Certainly one thing Alice can do is raise her prices. At higher prices, Alice will earn higher profits. Moreover, raising ice cream prices will bring the quantity of ice cream demanded closer to Alice's normal production capacity—her potential output. Indeed, when the price of Alice's ice cream finally rises to its equilibrium level, the shop's actual output will equal its potential output. Thus, over the long run, ice cream prices adjust to their equilibrium level, and the amount that is sold is determined by potential output.

This example illustrates, in a simple way, the links between spending and output—except, of course, that we must think of this story as applying to the whole economy, not to a single business. The key point is that there is an important difference between the short run and the long run. In the short run, producers often choose not to change their prices, but rather to meet the demand at preset prices. Because output is determined by demand, in the short run total spending plays a central role in determining the level of economic activity. Thus Alice's ice cream store enjoys a boom on an unusually hot day, when the demand for ice cream is strong, while an unseasonably cold day brings an ice cream recession. But in the long run, prices adjust to their market-clearing levels, and output equals potential output. Thus the quantities of inputs and the productivity with which they are used are the primary determinants of economic activity in the long run, as we saw in Chapter 19, *Economic Growth, Productivity, and Living Standards.* Although total spending affects output in the short run, in the long run its main effects are on prices.

SUMMARY

- Real GDP does not grow smoothly. Periods in which the economy is growing at a rate significantly below normal are called *recessions;* periods in which the economy is growing at a rate significantly above normal are called *expansions.* A severe or protracted recession, like the long decline that occurred between 1929 and 1933, is called a *depression,* while a particularly strong expansion is called a *boom. (LO1)*

- The beginning of a recession is called the *peak* because it represents the high point of economic activity prior to a downturn. The end of a recession, which marks the low point of economic activity prior to a recovery, is called the *trough.* Since World War II, U.S. recessions have been much shorter on average than booms, lasting between 6 and 18 months. The two longest boom periods in U.S. history are pretty recent. The first began with the end of the 1990–1991 recession in March 1991, ending exactly 10 years later in March 2001 when a new recession began. The second began with the end of the 2007–2009 recession and lasted almost 11 years. *(LO1)*

- Short-term economic fluctuations are irregular in length and severity, and are thus hard to forecast. Expansions and recessions are typically felt throughout the economy and may even be global in scope. Unemployment rises sharply during recessions, while inflation tends to fall during or shortly after

a recession. *Durable goods* industries tend to be particularly sensitive to recessions and booms, whereas services and *nondurable goods* industries are less sensitive. *(LO1)*

- *Potential output,* also called potential GDP or full-employment output, is the maximum sustainable amount of output (real GDP) that an economy can produce. The difference between the economy's actual output and its potential output is called the *output gap.* When output is below potential, the gap is called a *recessionary gap;* when output is above potential, the difference is called an *expansionary gap.* Recessions can occur either because potential output is growing unusually slowly or because actual output is below potential. Because recessionary gaps represent wasted resources and expansionary gaps threaten to create inflation, policymakers have an incentive to try to eliminate both types of gap. *(LO2)*

- The *natural rate of unemployment* is the part of the total unemployment rate that is attributable to frictional and structural unemployment. Equivalently, the natural rate of unemployment is the rate of unemployment that exists when the output gap is zero. Cyclical unemployment, the part of unemployment that is associated with recessions and expansions, equals the total unemployment rate less the natural unemployment rate. *(LO3)*

- Cyclical unemployment is related to the output gap by *Okun's law,* which states that each extra percentage point of cyclical unemployment is associated with about a 2 percent widening of a negative output gap, measured in relation to potential output. *(LO4)*

- Our further study of recessions and expansions will focus on the role of economywide spending. If firms adjust prices only periodically, and in the meantime produce enough output to meet demand, then fluctuations in spending will lead to fluctuations in output over the short run. During that short-run period, government policies that influence aggregate spending may help eliminate output gaps. In the long run, however, firms' price changes will eliminate output gaps—that is, the economy will "self-correct"—and total spending will influence only the rate of inflation. *(LO5)*

KEY TERMS

boom
business cycles (or cyclical fluctuations)
depression
durable goods
expansion
expansionary gap

natural rate of
  unemployment, u^*
nondurable goods
Okun's law
output gap
peak

potential output, Y^* (or potential
  GDP or full-employment
  output)
recession (or contraction)
recessionary gap
trough

REVIEW QUESTIONS

1. Define recession and expansion. What are the beginning and ending points of a recession called? In the postwar United States, which have been longer on average: recessions or expansions? *(LO1)*

2. Which firm is likely to see its profits reduced the most in a recession: an automobile producer, a manufacturer of boots and shoes, or a janitorial service? Which is likely to see its profits reduced the least? Explain. *(LO1)*

3. Define potential output. Is it possible for an economy to produce an amount greater than potential output? Explain. *(LO2)*

4. How is each of the following likely to be affected by a recession: the natural unemployment rate, the cyclical unemployment rate, the inflation rate, the poll ratings of the president? *(LO1, LO3)*

5. True or false: When output equals potential output, the unemployment rate is zero. Explain. *(LO4)*

6. If the natural rate of unemployment is 5 percent, what is the total rate of unemployment according to Okun's law if output is 2 percent below potential output? What if output is 2 percent above potential output? *(LO4)*

PROBLEMS

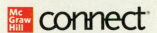

1. Using Table 24.1, find the average duration, the minimum duration, and the maximum duration of expansions in the United States since 1929. Are expansions getting longer or shorter on average over time? Is there any tendency for long expansions to be followed by long recessions? *(LO1)*

2. From the home page of the Bureau of Economic Analysis (www.bea.gov), obtain quarterly data for U.S. real GDP from these recessions: 1981–1982, 1990–1991, 2001, and 2007–2009. *(LO1)*

a. How many quarters of negative real GDP growth occurred in each recession?

b. Which, if any, of the recessions satisfied the informal criterion that a recession must have two consecutive quarters of negative GDP growth?

3. Given below are data on real GDP and potential GDP for the United States for the years 2005–2016, in billions of 2009 dollars. For each year, calculate the output gap as a percentage of potential GDP and state whether the gap is a recessionary gap or an expansionary gap. Also calculate the year-to-year growth rates of

real GDP. Identify the recessions that occurred during this period. *(LO2)*

Year	Real GDP	Potential GDP
2005	14,234.2	14,272.6
2006	14,613.8	14,578.7
2007	14,873.7	14,843.6
2008	14,830.4	15,098.3
2009	14,418.7	15,310.3
2010	14,783.8	15,457.0
2011	15,020.6	15,615.8
2012	15,354.6	15,815.5
2013	15,612.2	16,049.4
2014	16,013.3	16,305.7
2015	16,471.5	16,573.4
2016	16,716.2	16,832.8

Sources: Potential GDP, Federal Reserve Bank of St. Louis; real GDP, www.bea.gov.

4. From the home page of the Bureau of Labor Statistics (www.bls.gov), obtain the most recent available data on the unemployment rate for workers aged 16–19 and workers aged 20 or over. How do they differ? What are some of the reasons for the difference? How does this difference relate to the decline in the overall natural rate of unemployment since 1980? *(LO3)*

5. Using Okun's law, fill in the four pieces of missing data in the table below. The data are hypothetical. *(LO4)*

Year	Real GDP ($ billions)	Potential GDP ($ billions)	Natural unem-ployment rate (%)	Actual unem-ployment rate (%)
2015	13,536	14,400	5	(a)
2016	14,500	(b)	5	5
2017	(c)	14,800	5	4.5
2018	15,444	14,850	(d)	4

6. Of the following, identify the incorrect statement. *(LO5)*
   a. Output gaps are caused by inflationary pressures generated by the unintended side effects of government policy.
   b. Low aggregate spending can make output fall below potential output.
   c. When spending is high, output may rise above potential output.
   d. Government policies can help eliminate output gaps.

ANSWERS TO SELF-TESTS

24.1 Answers will vary, depending on when the data are obtained. As of mid-2020, the last recession started in February 2020. *(LO1)*

24.2 The actual unemployment rate in 2015 exceeded the natural rate by 0.6 percent. Applying Okun's law, actual output fell below potential output by 1.2 percent. *(LO4)*

CHAPTER 25

Spending and Output in the Short Run

How are consumer spending and GDP related?

LEARNING OBJECTIVES

After reading this chapter, you should be able to:

LO1 Identify the key assumption of the basic Keynesian model and explain how it affects the production decisions made by firms and the consumption decisions made by households.

LO2 Discuss the determinants of planned investment and aggregate consumption spending and how these concepts are used to develop a model of planned aggregate expenditure.

LO3 Analyze, using graphs and numbers, how an economy reaches short-run equilibrium in the basic Keynesian model.

LO4 Show how a change in planned aggregate expenditure can cause a change in short-run equilibrium output and how this is related to the income-expenditure multiplier.

LO5 Explain why the basic Keynesian model suggests that fiscal policy is useful as a stabilization policy.

LO6 Discuss the qualifications that arise in applying fiscal policy in real-world situations.

When one of the authors of this book was a small boy, he used to spend some time every summer with his grandparents, who lived a few hours from his home. A favorite activity of his during these visits was to spend a summer evening on the front porch with his grandmother, listening to her stories.

Grandma had spent the early years of her marriage in New England, during the worst part of the Great Depression. In one of her reminiscences, she remarked that, at that time, in the mid-1930s, it had been a satisfaction to her to be able to buy her children a new pair of shoes every year. In the small town where she and her family lived, many children had to wear their shoes until they fell apart, and a few unlucky boys and girls went to school barefoot. Her grandson thought this was scandalous: "Why didn't their parents just buy them new shoes?" he demanded.

"They couldn't," said Grandma. "They didn't have the money. Most of the fathers had lost their jobs because of the Depression."

"What kind of jobs did they have?"

"They worked in the shoe factories, which had to close down."

"Why did the factories close down?"

"Because," Grandma explained, "nobody had any money to buy shoes."

The grandson was only six or seven years old at the time, but even he could see that there was something badly wrong with Grandma's logic. On the one side were boarded-up shoe factories and shoe workers with no jobs; on the other, children without shoes. Why couldn't the shoe factories just open and produce the shoes the children so badly needed? He made his point quite firmly, but Grandma just shrugged and said it didn't work that way.

The story of the closed-down shoe factories illustrates in a microcosm the cost to society of a recessionary gap. In an economy with a recessionary gap, available resources, which in principle could be used to produce valuable goods and services, are instead allowed to lie fallow. This waste of resources lowers the economy's output and economic welfare, compared to its potential.

Grandma's account also suggests how such an unfortunate situation might come about. Suppose factory owners and other producers, being reluctant to accumulate unsold goods on their shelves, produce just enough output to satisfy the demand for their products. And suppose that, for some reason, the public's willingness or ability to spend declines. If spending declines, factories will respond by cutting their production (because they don't want to produce goods they can't sell) and by laying off workers who are no longer needed. And because the workers who are laid off will lose most of their income—a particularly serious loss in the 1930s, in the days before government-sponsored unemployment insurance was common—they must reduce their own spending. As their spending declines, factories will reduce their production again, laying off more workers, who in turn reduce their spending—and so on, in a vicious circle. In this scenario, the problem is not a lack of productive capacity—the factories have not lost their ability to produce—but rather *insufficient spending* to support the normal level of production.

The idea that a decline in aggregate spending may cause output to fall below potential output was one of the key insights of John Maynard Keynes (pronounced "canes"), perhaps the most influential economist of the twentieth century.[1] He lived from 1883 to 1946 and was a remarkable individual who combined a brilliant career as an economic theorist with an active life in diplomacy, finance, journalism, and the arts. In the period between World War I and II, among his many other activities, Keynes was a Cambridge professor, developing an imposing intellectual reputation, editing Great Britain's leading scholarly journal in economics, writing articles for newspapers and magazines, advising the government, and playing a major role in the political and economic debates of the day.

Like other economists of the time, Keynes struggled to understand the Great Depression that gripped the world in the 1930s. His work on the problem led to the publication in 1936 of *The General Theory of Employment, Interest, and Money*. In *The General Theory*, Keynes tried to explain how economies can remain at low levels of output and employment for protracted periods. He stressed a number of factors, most notably that aggregate spending may be too low to permit full employment during such periods. Keynes recommended increases in government spending as the most effective way to increase aggregate spending and restore full employment.

The General Theory is a difficult book, reflecting Keynes's own struggle to understand the complex causes of the Depression. In retrospect, some of *The General Theory*'s arguments seem unclear or even inconsistent. Yet the book is full of fertile ideas, many of which had a worldwide impact and eventually led to what has been called the *Keynesian revolution*. Over the years, many economists have added to or modified Keynes's conception, to the point that Keynes himself, were he alive today, probably would not recognize much of what is now called Keynesian economics. But the ideas that insufficient aggregate spending can lead to recession and that government policies can help restore full employment are still critical to Keynesian theory.

The goal of this chapter is to present a theory, or model, of how recessions and expansions may arise from fluctuations in aggregate spending, along the lines first suggested by Keynes. This model, which we call the *basic Keynesian model,* is also known as the *Keynesian cross,* after the diagram that is used to illustrate the theory. In the body of the chapter, we will emphasize a numerical and graphical approach to

[1] A brief biography of Keynes is available at www.bbc.co.uk/history/historic_figures/keynes_john_maynard.shtml.

the basic Keynesian model. Appendix A to this chapter provides a more general algebraic analysis.

We begin with a brief discussion of the key assumptions of the basic Keynesian model. We then turn to the important concept of total, or aggregate, *planned spending* in the economy. We show how, in the short run, the rate of aggregate spending helps determine the level of output, which can be greater than or less than potential output. In other words, depending on the level of spending, the economy may develop an output gap. "Too little" spending leads to a recessionary output gap, while "too much" creates an expansionary output gap.

An implication of the basic Keynesian model is that government policies that affect the level of spending can be used to reduce or eliminate output gaps. Policies used in this way are called *stabilization policies*. Keynes himself argued for the active use of fiscal policy—policy relating to government spending and taxes—to eliminate output gaps and stabilize the economy. In the latter part of this chapter, we'll show why Keynes thought fiscal policy could help stabilize the economy and discuss the usefulness of fiscal policy as a stabilization tool.

The basic Keynesian model is not a complete or entirely realistic model of the economy since it applies only to the relatively short period during which firms do not adjust their prices but, instead, meet the demand forthcoming at preset prices. Furthermore, by treating prices as fixed, the basic Keynesian model presented in this chapter does not address the determination of inflation. Nevertheless, this model is an essential building block of leading current theories of short-run economic fluctuations and stabilization policies. In subsequent chapters, we will extend the basic Keynesian model to incorporate monetary policy, inflation, and other important features of the economy.

THE KEYNESIAN MODEL'S CRUCIAL ASSUMPTION: FIRMS MEET DEMAND AT PRESET PRICES

The basic Keynesian model is built on a key assumption: *In the short run, firms meet the demand for their products at preset prices.* Firms do not respond to every change in the demand for their products by changing their prices. Instead, they typically set a price for some period and then meet the demand at that price. By "meeting the demand," we mean that firms produce just enough to satisfy their customers at the prices that have been set.[2] As we will see, the assumption that firms vary their production in order to meet demand at preset prices implies that fluctuations in spending will have powerful effects on the nation's real GDP.

The assumption that, over short periods of time, firms meet the demand for their products at preset prices is generally realistic. Think of the stores where you shop. The price of a pair of jeans does not fluctuate from moment to moment according to the number of customers who enter the store or the latest news about the price of denim. Instead, the store posts a price and sells jeans to any customer who wants to buy at that price, at least until the store runs out of stock. Similarly, the corner pizza restaurant may leave the price of its large pie unchanged for months or longer, allowing its pizza production to be determined by the number of customers who want to buy at the preset price.

Firms do not normally change their prices frequently because doing so would be costly. Economists refer to the costs of changing prices as **menu costs.** In the case of the pizza restaurant, the menu cost is literally just that—the cost of printing up a new menu when prices change. Similarly, the clothing store faces the cost of remarking all its merchandise if the manager changes prices. But menu costs also may include other kinds of costs—for example, the cost of doing a market survey to determine what price to charge and the cost of informing customers about price changes. The Economic Naturalist 25.1 discusses how technology may affect menu costs in the future.

menu costs the costs of changing prices

---

[2]Obviously, firms can meet the forthcoming demand only up to the point where they reach the limit of their capacity to produce. For that reason, the Keynesian analysis of this chapter is relevant only when producers have unused capacity.

Menu costs will not prevent firms from changing their prices indefinitely. As we saw in the case of Alice's ice cream store (in Chapter 24, *Short-Term Economic Fluctuations: An Introduction*), too great an imbalance between demand and supply, as reflected by a difference between sales and potential output, will eventually lead firms to change their prices. If no one is buying jeans, for example, at some point the clothing store will mark down its jeans prices. Or if the pizza restaurant becomes the local hot spot, with a line of customers stretching out the door, eventually the manager will raise the price of a large pie.

Like many other economic decisions, the decision to change prices reflects a cost-benefit comparison: Prices should be changed if the benefit of doing so—the fact that sales will be brought more nearly in line with the firm's normal production capacity—outweighs the menu costs associated with making the change. As we have stressed, the basic Keynesian model developed in this chapter ignores the fact that prices will eventually adjust and, therefore, should be interpreted as applying to the short run.

Cost-Benefit ⟫

The Economic Naturalist 25.1

Will new technologies eliminate menu costs?

▶ Visit your instructor's Connect course and access your eBook to view this video.

Will new technologies eliminate menu costs?

Thanks to new technologies, changing prices and informing customers about price changes is becoming increasingly less costly. Will technology eliminate menu costs as a factor in price setting?

Keynesian theory is based on the assumption that costs of changing prices, which economists refer to as *menu costs,* are sufficiently large to prevent firms from adjusting prices immediately in response to changing market conditions. However, in many industries, new technologies have eliminated or greatly reduced the direct costs of changing prices. For example, the use of bar codes to identify individual products, together with scanner technologies, allows a grocery store manager to change prices with just a few keystrokes, without having to change the price label on each can of soup or loaf of bread. Airlines use sophisticated computer software to implement complex pricing strategies, under which two travelers on the same flight to Milwaukee may pay very different fares, depending on whether they are business or vacation travelers and on how far in advance their flights were booked. Online retailers have the ability to vary their prices by type of customer and even by individual customer, while other Internet-based companies, such as eBay, allow for negotiation over the price of each individual purchase. Ride-sharing apps evaluate, in real time, customers' demand for rides and drivers' supply of rides; their pricing systems estimate the market-clearing price, and when supply does not meet demand, they send a notification of instant price increases that customers view on their phones and have to accept before they are connected to a driver.

Will these reductions in the direct costs of changing prices make the Keynesian theory, which assumes that firms meet demand at preset prices, less relevant to the real world? This is certainly a possibility that macroeconomists must take into account. However, it is unlikely that new technologies will completely eliminate the costs of changing prices any time soon. In many sectors of the economy, gathering the information about market conditions needed to set the profit-maximizing price—including the prices charged by competitors, the costs of producing the good or service, and the likely demand for the product—will remain costly for firms. Another cost of changing prices is the use of valuable managerial time and attention needed to make informed pricing decisions. A more subtle cost of changing prices—particularly raising prices—is that doing so may lead regular customers to rethink their choice of suppliers and decide to search for a better deal elsewhere. Even when they do not switch suppliers, a price increase that is perceived by customers as unfair may cause antagonism toward the price-setting supplier.

PLANNED AGGREGATE EXPENDITURE

In the simple Keynesian model, output at each point in time is determined by the amount that people throughout the economy want to spend—what we will refer to as *planned aggregate expenditure*. Specifically, **planned aggregate expenditure (*PAE*)** is total planned spending on final goods and services.

The four components of spending on final goods and services were introduced in Chapter 17, *Measuring Economic Activity: GDP and Unemployment*:

1. *Consumption expenditure,* or simply *consumption* (*C*), is spending by households on final goods and services. Examples of consumption expenditure are spending on food, clothes, and entertainment and on consumer durable goods like automobiles and furniture.

2. *Investment* (*I*) is spending by domestic firms on new capital goods, such as office buildings, factories, and equipment. Spending on new houses and apartment buildings (residential investment) and increases in inventories (inventory investment) also are included in investment.[3]

3. *Government purchases* (*G*) are purchases by federal, state, and local governments of final goods and services. Examples of government purchases include new schools and hospitals; military hardware; equipment for the space program; and the services of government employees such as soldiers, police, and government office workers. Recall from Chapter 17, *Measuring Economic Activity: GDP and Unemployment,* that *transfer payments* such as Social Security benefits and unemployment insurance and interest on the government debt are *not* included in government purchases. Transfer payments and interest contribute to aggregate expenditure only at the point when they are spent by their recipients (for example, when a recipient of a Social Security check uses the funds to buy food, clothing, or other consumption goods).

4. *Net exports* (*NX*) equal exports minus imports. Exports are sales of domestically produced goods and services to foreigners. Imports are purchases by domestic residents of goods and services produced abroad that have been included in *C, I,* and *G* but must now be subtracted because they do not represent domestic production. Net exports therefore represent the net demand for domestic goods and services by foreigners.

Together, these four types of spending—by households, firms, the government, and the rest of the world—sum to total, or aggregate, spending.

PLANNED SPENDING VERSUS ACTUAL SPENDING

In the Keynesian model, output is determined by planned aggregate expenditure, or planned spending, for short. Could *planned* spending ever differ from *actual* spending? The answer is yes. The most important case is that of a firm that sells either less or more of its product than expected. Note that additions to the stocks of goods sitting in a firm's warehouse are treated in official government statistics as inventory investment by the firm. In effect, government statisticians assume that the firm buys its unsold output from itself; they then count those purchases as part of the firm's investment spending.[4]

Suppose, then, that a firm's actual sales are less than expected, so that part of what it had planned to sell remains in the warehouse. In this case, the firm's actual investment, including the unexpected increases in its inventory, is greater than its planned investment, which did not include the added inventory. Suppose we agree to let I^p equal the firm's planned investment, including planned inventory investment. A firm that sells less of its output than planned, and therefore adds more to its inventory than planned, will find that

planned aggregate expenditure (*PAE*) total planned spending on final goods and services

---

[3]As we discussed earlier, we use "investment" here to mean spending on new capital goods such as factories, housing, and equipment, which is not the same as financial investment. This distinction is important to keep in mind.

[4]For the purposes of measuring GDP, treating unsold output as being purchased by its producer has the advantage of ensuring that actual production and actual expenditure are equal.

its actual investment (including unplanned inventory investment) exceeds its planned investment, so that $I > I^p$.

What about a firm that sells more of its output than expected? In that case, the firm will add less to its inventory than it planned, so actual investment will be less than planned investment, that is, $I < I^p$. The following example gives a numerical illustration.

EXAMPLE 25.1 — Planned versus Actual Investment

What is the difference between planned investment and actual investment?

Fly-by-Night Kite Co. produces $5,000,000 worth of kites during the year. It expects sales of $4,800,000 for the year, leaving $200,000 worth of kites to be stored in the warehouse for future sale. During the year, Fly-by-Night adds $1,000,000 in new production equipment as part of an expansion plan. Find Fly-by-Night's actual investment, I, and its planned investment, I^p, if actual kite sales turn out to be $4,600,000. What if sales are $4,800,000? What if they are $5,000,000?

Fly-by-Night's planned investment, I^p, equals its purchases of new production equipment ($1,000,000) plus its planned additions to inventory ($200,000), for a total of $1,200,000 in planned investment. The company's planned investment does not depend on how much it actually sells.

If Fly-by-Night sells only $4,600,000 worth of kites, it will add $400,000 in kites to its inventory instead of the $200,000 worth originally planned. In this case, actual investment equals the $1,000,000 in new equipment plus the $400,000 in inventory investment, so $I = \$1,400,000$. We see that, when the firm sells less output than planned, actual investment exceeds planned investment ($I > I^p$).

If Fly-by-Night has $4,800,000 in sales, then it will add $200,000 in kites to inventory, just as planned. In this case, actual and planned investment are the same:

$$I = I^p = \$1,200,000.$$

Finally, if Fly-by-Night sells $5,000,000 worth of kites, it will have no output to add to inventory. Its inventory investment will be zero, and its total actual investment (including the new equipment) will equal $1,000,000, which is less than its planned investment of $1,200,000 ($I < I^p$).

Because firms that are meeting the demand for their product or service at preset prices cannot control how much they sell, their actual investment (including inventory investment) may well differ from their planned investment. However, for households, the government, and foreign purchasers, we may reasonably assume that actual spending and planned spending are the same. Thus, from now on we will assume that, for consumption, government purchases, and net exports, actual spending equals planned spending.

With these assumptions, we can define planned aggregate expenditure by the following equation:

$$PAE = C + I^p + G + NX. \tag{25.1}$$

Equation 25.1 says that planned aggregate expenditure is the sum of planned spending by households, firms, governments, and foreigners. We use a superscript p to distinguish planned investment spending by firms, I^p, from actual investment spending, I. However, because planned spending equals actual spending for households, the government, and foreigners, we do not need to use superscripts for consumption, government purchases, or net exports.

CONSUMER SPENDING AND THE ECONOMY

In the U.S. economy, the largest component of planned aggregate expenditure is consumption spending, *C*. As already mentioned, consumer spending includes household purchases of goods such as groceries and clothing; services such as health care, concerts, and college tuition; and consumer durables such as cars, furniture, and computers. Thus, consumers' willingness to spend affects sales and profitability in a wide range of industries. (Households' purchases of new homes are classified as investment, rather than consumption, but home purchases represent another channel through which household decisions affect total spending.)

What factors determine how much people plan to spend on consumer goods and services in a given period? While many factors are relevant, a particularly important determinant of the amount people plan to consume is their after-tax, or *disposable,* income. All else being equal, households and individuals with higher **disposable incomes** will consume more than those with lower disposable incomes. Keynes himself stressed the importance of disposable income in determining household consumption decisions, claiming a "psychological law" that people would tie their spending closely to their incomes.

Figure 25.1 shows the relationship between aggregate real consumption expenditures and real disposable income in the United States for the period 1960–2019. Each point on the graph corresponds to a year between 1960 and 2019 (selected years are indicated in the figure). The position of each point is determined by the combination of consumption (on the vertical axis) and disposable income (on the horizontal axis) associated with that

disposable income the after-tax amount of income that people are able to spend

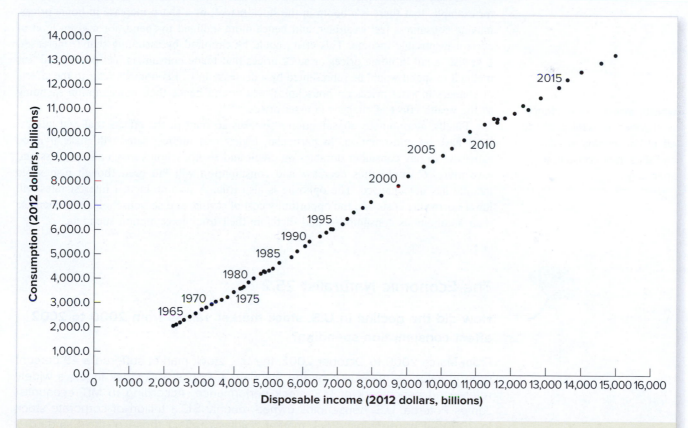

FIGURE 25.1

The U.S. Consumption Function, 1960–2019.

Each point on this figure represents a combination of aggregate real consumption and aggregate real disposable income for a specific year between 1960 and 2019. Note the strong positive relationship between consumption and disposable income.

Source: U.S. Bureau of Economic Analysis, Real Disposable Personal Income [DSPIC96] and Real Personal Consumption Expenditures [PCECCA], retrieved from FRED, Federal Reserve Bank of St. Louis; https://fred.stlouisfed.org/series/DSPIC96.

year. As you can see, there is indeed a close relationship between aggregate consumption and disposable income: Higher disposable income is associated with higher consumption.

Recall from Chapter 21, *Saving and Capital Formation,* that the disposable income of the private sector is the total production of the economy, *Y,* less net taxes (taxes minus transfers), or *T.* So we will assume that consumption spending (*C*) increases as disposable income (*Y − T*) increases. As already mentioned, other factors may also affect consumption, such as the real interest rate. We return to some of these other factors shortly.

We can write this relationship between consumption and disposable income as a linear equation[5]

$$C = \overline{C} + (mpc)(Y - T). \tag{25.2}$$

consumption function the relationship between consumption spending and its determinants, in particular, disposable income

This equation, which we will dissect in a moment, is known as the *consumption function.* The **consumption function** relates consumption spending (*C*) to its determinants, in particular, disposable (after-tax) income (*Y − T*).

Let's look at the consumption function, Equation 25.2, more carefully. The right side of the equation contains two terms, $\overline{C}$ and (*mpc*)(*Y − T*). The amount of consumption represented by $\overline{C}$ is called **autonomous consumption** since it is consumption that is not related to (i.e., autonomous from) changes in disposable income. For example, suppose consumers became more optimistic about the future, so that they wanted to consume more and save less at any given level of their current disposable income. In this case, $\overline{C}$ will increase and consumption will increase even though disposable income has not changed.

autonomous consumption consumption spending that is not related to the level of disposable income

We can imagine other factors that could affect autonomous consumption. Suppose, for example, that there is a boom in the stock market or a sharp increase in home prices, making consumers feel wealthier, and hence more inclined to spend, for a given level of current disposable income. This effect could be captured by assuming that $\overline{C}$ increases. Likewise, a fall in home prices or stock prices that made consumers feel poorer and less inclined to spend would be represented by a decrease in $\overline{C}$. Economists refer to the effects of changes in asset prices on households' wealth and hence their consumption spending as the **wealth effect** of changes in asset prices.

wealth effect the tendency of changes in asset prices to affect households' wealth and thus their consumption spending

Finally, autonomous consumption also takes account of the effects that real interest rates have on consumption. In particular, higher real interest rates will make it more expensive to buy consumer durables on credit and so households may consume less and save more. $\overline{C}$ would thus decrease and consumption will fall even though disposable income has not changed. The opposite is also true: A decline in real interest rates will lower borrowing costs and the opportunity cost of saving, and so households may increase their autonomous consumption and therefore their total consumption spending.

The Economic Naturalist 25.2

How did the decline in U.S. stock market values from 2000 to 2002 affect consumption spending?

From March 2000 to October 2002, the U.S. stock market suffered a 49 percent drop in value as measured by the Standard & Poor's 500 stock index, a widely referenced benchmark of U.S. stock performance. According to MIT economist James Poterba, U.S. households owned roughly $13.3 trillion of corporate stock in 2000.[6] If households' stock market holdings reflect those of the Standard & Poor's stock index, the 49 percent drop in the value of the stock market wiped out approximately $6.5 trillion of household wealth in two years. According to economic models based on historical experience, a dollar's decrease in household

---

[5]You should review the material in the appendix to Chapter 1, *Thinking Like an Economist,* if you don't regularly work with linear equations.

[6]See Table 1 in James M. Poterba, "Stock Market Wealth and Consumption," *Journal of Economic Perspectives* 14 (Spring 2000), pp. 99–118.

wealth reduces consumer spending by 3 to 7 cents per year, so the reduction in stock market wealth had the potential to reduce overall consumer spending by $195 billion to $455 billion, a drop of approximately 3 to 7 percent. Yet, real consumption spending continued to rise from 2000 through 2002. Why did this happen?

Despite the start of a recession in March 2001, overall consumption spending remained strong during 2000–2002 for a variety of reasons. First, consumers' real after-tax income continued to grow into the fall of 2001, helping maintain strong consumer spending despite the drop in the stock market. Furthermore, throughout 2001 and into early 2002, the Federal Reserve significantly reduced interest rates; we'll discuss how the Federal Reserve does this in another chapter. As we discussed, a reduction in interest rates helps promote consumer spending, especially on durable goods such as automobiles, by reducing consumers' borrowing costs. Finally, housing prices rose dramatically during this period, increasing consumers' housing wealth and partially offsetting their decline in stock-related wealth. Data on repeat house sales that measure the price of individual houses that are sold and resold over time indicate that housing prices rose by 20.1 percent between the first quarter of 2000 and the third quarter of 2002.[7] The total market value of household real estate was about $12 trillion in 2000, so house price appreciation added about $2.4 trillion to household wealth, offsetting about 37 percent of the decline in stock market wealth during this period.[8]

Overall, while the drop in stock market values clearly had a negative effect on consumer wealth, other offsetting factors helped keep the 2000–2002 stock market decline from dampening consumption spending during this period.

The second term on the right side of Equation 25.2, $(mpc)(Y - T)$, measures the effect of disposable income, $Y - T$, on consumption. The **marginal propensity to consume** (***mpc***), a fixed number, is the amount by which consumption rises when current disposable income rises by one dollar. The intuition behind the marginal propensity to consume is straightforward: If people receive an extra dollar of income, they will consume part of the dollar and save the rest. That is, their consumption will increase, but by less than the full dollar of extra income. It is therefore realistic to assume that the marginal propensity to consume is greater than 0 (an increase in income leads to an increase in consumption) but less than 1 (the increase in consumption will be less than the full increase in income). Mathematically, we can summarize these assumptions as $0 < mpc < 1$.

Figure 25.2 shows a hypothetical consumption function, with consumption spending (C) on the vertical axis and disposable income ($Y - T$) on the horizontal axis. The intercept of the consumption function on the vertical axis equals autonomous consumption ($\overline{C}$), and the slope of the consumption function equals the marginal propensity to consume (mpc).

> **marginal propensity to consume (*mpc*)** the amount by which consumption rises when disposable income rises by $1; we assume that $0 < mpc < 1$

PLANNED AGGREGATE EXPENDITURE AND OUTPUT

Thinking back to Grandma's reminiscences, recall that an important element of her story involved the links among production, income, and spending. As the shoe factories in Grandma's town reduced production, the incomes of both factory workers and factory owners fell. Workers' incomes fell as the number of hours of work per week were reduced (a common practice during the Depression), as workers were laid off, or as wages were cut. Factory owners' income fell as profits declined. Reduced incomes, in turn, forced both workers and factory owners to curtail their spending—which led to still lower production and further reductions in income. This vicious circle led the economy further and further into recession.

---

[7]U.S. Federal Housing Finance Agency, "All-Transactions House Price Index for the United States [USSTHPI]," retrieved from FRED, Federal Reserve Bank of St. Louis; https://fred.stlouisfed.org/series/USSTHPI, November 2, 2017. House prices continued to rise, peaking in 2007.
[8]Federal Reserve Board, "Flow of Funds Accounts of the United States," www.federalreserve.gov.

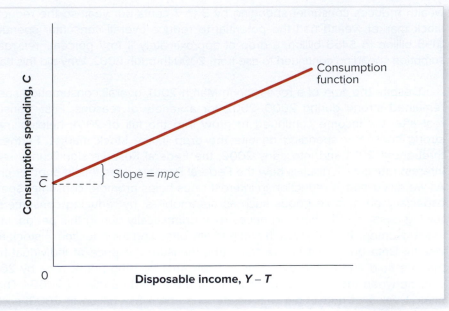

FIGURE 25.2

A Consumption Function.

The consumption function relates consumption spending (C) to disposable income, (Y − T). The vertical intercept of the consumption function is autonomous consumption ($\overline{C}$), and the slope of the line equals the marginal propensity to consume (mpc).

The logic of Grandma's story has two key elements: (1) declines in production (which imply declines in the income received by producers) lead to reduced spending and (2) reductions in spending lead to declines in production and income. In this section, we look at the first part of the story, the effects of production and income on spending. We return later in this chapter to the effects of spending on production and income.

Why do changes in production and income affect planned aggregate spending? The consumption function, which relates consumption to disposable income, is the basic source of this relationship. Because consumption spending C is a large part of planned aggregate spending, and because consumption depends on output Y, aggregate spending as a whole depends on output.

Let's examine the link between planned aggregate expenditure and output in two ways. We will begin by working with a specific numerical example so that you can see the relationship clearly. Next, we will plot the relationship on a graph so that you can see its general shape and start working with these concepts using graphs.

EXAMPLE 25.2   **Linking Planned Aggregate Expenditure to Output**

What is the relationship between planned aggregate expenditure and output?

In a particular economy, the consumption function is

$$C = 620 + 0.8(Y - T),$$

so that the intercept term in the consumption function $\overline{C}$ equals 620 and the marginal propensity to consume mpc equals 0.8. Also, suppose that we are given that planned investment spending $I^P = 220$, government purchases $G = 300$, net exports $NX = 20$, and taxes $T = 250$.

Write a numerical equation linking planned aggregate expenditure PAE to output Y. How does planned spending change when output and hence income change?

Recall the definition of planned aggregate expenditure, Equation 25.1

$$PAE = C + I^P + G + NX.$$

To find a numerical equation for planned aggregate expenditure, we need to find numerical expressions for each of its four components. The first component of spending, consumption, is defined by the consumption function, $C = 620 + 0.8(Y - T)$. Since taxes $T = 250$, we can substitute for T to write the consumption function as $C = 620 + 0.8(Y - 250)$. Now plug this expression for C into the definition of planned aggregate expenditure above to get:

$$PAE = [620 + 0.8(Y - 250)] + I^P + G + NX,$$

where we have just replaced C by its value as determined by the consumption function. Similarly, we can substitute the given numerical values of planned investment I^P, government purchases G, and net exports NX into the definition of planned aggregate expenditure to get:

$$PAE = [620 + 0.8(Y - 250)] + 220 + 300 + 20.$$

To simplify this equation, first note that $0.8(Y - 250) = 0.8Y - 200$, and then add together all the terms that don't depend on output Y. The result is:

$$PAE = (620 - 200 + 220 + 300 + 20) + 0.8Y$$
$$= 960 + 0.8Y.$$

The final expression shows the relationship between planned aggregate expenditure and output in this numerical example. Note that, according to this equation, a \$1 increase in Y leads to an increase in PAE of $(0.8)(\$1)$, or 80 cents. The reason for this is that the marginal propensity to consume, *mpc,* in this example is 0.8. Hence, a \$1 increase in income raises consumption spending by 80 cents. Since consumption is a component of total planned spending, total spending rises by 80 cents as well.

The solution to Example 25.2 illustrates a general point: Planned aggregate expenditure can be divided into two parts, a part that depends on output (Y) and a part that is independent of output. The portion of planned aggregate expenditure that is independent of output is called **autonomous expenditure.** In the equation above, autonomous expenditure is the constant term and is equal to 960. This portion of planned spending, being a fixed number, does not vary when output varies. By contrast, the portion of planned aggregate expenditure that depends on output (Y) is called **induced expenditure.** In the equation above, induced expenditure equals $0.8Y$, the second term in the expression for planned aggregate expenditure. Note that the numerical value of induced expenditure depends, by definition, on the numerical value taken by output. Autonomous expenditure and induced expenditure together equal planned aggregate expenditure.

Figure 25.3 is a graph of the equation $PAE = 960 + 0.8Y$, which is a straight line with a vertical intercept of 960 and a slope of 0.8. This line, which shows the relationship between planned aggregate expenditure and output graphically, is called the **expenditure line.**

There are three properties of the expenditure line that are important to note. First, the slope of this line is equal to the marginal propensity to consume for our specific numerical example. This point holds in general: The slope of the expenditure line is equal to the marginal propensity to consume. Second, the vertical intercept is equal to autonomous expenditure for our example. This point also holds more generally: The vertical intercept of the expenditure line equals the level of autonomous expenditure. Third, changes in autonomous expenditure will shift the expenditure line: Increases in autonomous expenditure will shift the expenditure line up while decreases will shift the line down. We will apply all three of these properties in the rest of the chapter.

autonomous expenditure the portion of planned aggregate expenditure that is independent of output

induced expenditure the portion of planned aggregate expenditure that depends on output Y

expenditure line a line showing the relationship between planned aggregate expenditure and output

FIGURE 25.3

The Expenditure Line.

The line $PAE = 960 + 0.8Y$, referred to as the expenditure line, shows the relationship of planned aggregate expenditure to output.

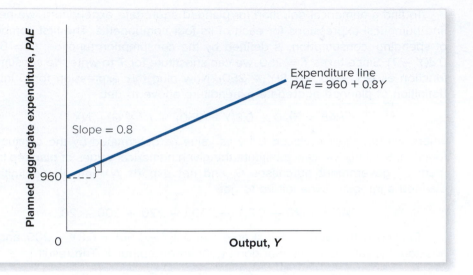

RECAP

PLANNED AGGREGATE EXPENDITURE

- Planned aggregate expenditure (*PAE*) is total planned spending on final goods and services. The four components of planned spending are consumer expenditure (*C*), planned investment (I^P), government purchases (*G*), and net exports (*NX*). Planned investment differs from actual investment when firms' sales are different from what they expected, so that additions to inventory (a component of investment) are different from what firms anticipated.

- In the U.S. economy, the largest component of aggregate expenditure is consumer expenditure, or simply consumption. Consumption depends on disposable, or after-tax, income, according to a relationship known as the consumption function, stated algebraically as $C = \overline{C} + (mpc)(Y - T)$.

- The constant term in the consumption function, $\overline{C}$, captures factors other than disposable income that affect consumer spending. For example, an increase in housing or stock prices that makes households wealthier and thus more willing to spend—an effect called the wealth effect—could be captured by an increase in $\overline{C}$. The slope of the consumption function equals the marginal propensity to consume, *mpc*, where $0 < mpc < 1$. This is the amount by which consumption rises when disposable income rises by one dollar.

- Increases in output *Y*, which imply equal increases in income, cause consumption to rise. As consumption is part of planned aggregate expenditure, planned spending depends on output as well. The portion of planned aggregate expenditure that depends on output is called induced expenditure. The portion of planned aggregate expenditure that is independent of output is autonomous expenditure.

SHORT-RUN EQUILIBRIUM OUTPUT

Now that we have defined planned aggregate expenditure and seen how it is related to output, the next task is to see how output itself is determined. Recall the assumption of the basic Keynesian model: In the short run, producers leave prices at preset levels and simply meet the demand that is forthcoming at those prices. In other words, during the short-run period in which prices are preset, firms produce an amount that is equal to planned aggregate expenditure. Accordingly, we define **short-run equilibrium output** as the level of output at which output Y equals planned aggregate expenditure PAE

$$Y = PAE. \tag{25.3}$$

Short-run equilibrium output is the level of output that prevails during the period in which prices are predetermined.

We can find the short-run equilibrium output for the economy described in Example 25.2. There are two approaches to doing this, and we will demonstrate both. First, we can take a numerical approach, and find where $Y = PAE$ either by using a table or by solving the equations directly. (We will again demonstrate both methods, as each method illustrates an important point about the basic Keynesian model.) Second, we can add a line to our graph of the expenditure line to find short-run equilibrium output. The resulting graph is called the Keynesian cross since it involves two lines intersecting. This approach will help us in generalizing the ideas we develop using the numerical approach.

FINDING SHORT-RUN EQUILIBRIUM OUTPUT: NUMERICAL APPROACH

Recall that in Example 25.2, planned spending is determined by the equation

$$PAE = 960 + 0.8Y.$$

Thus, for instance, when $Y = 4{,}000$, $PAE = 960 + 0.8(4{,}000) = 4{,}160$. Table 25.1 shows the results of similar calculations for different levels of output; column 1 shows various levels of output (Y), and column 2 lists the levels of planned aggregate expenditure (PAE) for the different levels of output given in column 1.

In Table 25.1, notice that since consumption rises with output, total planned spending (which includes consumption) rises also. But if you compare columns 1 and 2, you will see that every time output rises by 200, planned spending rises by only 160. That is because the marginal propensity to consume in this economy is 0.8 so that each dollar in added income raises consumption and planned spending by 80 cents.

Again, short-run equilibrium output is the level of output at which $Y = PAE$, or, equivalently, $Y - PAE = 0$. At this level of output, actual investment will equal planned investment, and there will be no tendency for output to change. Looking at Table 25.1, we can see there is only one level of output that satisfies that condition, $Y = 4{,}800$. At that level, output and planned aggregate expenditure are precisely equal, so that producers are just meeting the demand for their goods and services.

In this economy, what would happen if output differed from its equilibrium value of 4,800? Suppose, for example, that output were 4,000. Looking at the second column of Table 25.1, you can see that, when output is 4,000, planned aggregate expenditure equals

short-run equilibrium output the level of output at which output Y equals planned aggregate expenditure PAE; the level of output that prevails during the period in which prices are predetermined

TABLE 25.1
Numerical Determination of Short-Run Equilibrium Output

(1) Output Y	(2) Planned aggregate expenditure $PAE = 960 + 0.8Y$	(3) $Y - PAE$	(4) $Y = PAE$?
4,000	4,160	−160	No
4,200	4,320	−120	No
4,400	4,480	−80	No
4,600	4,640	−40	No
4,800	4,800	0	Yes
5,000	4,960	40	No
5,200	5,120	80	No

$960 + 0.8(4,000)$, or 4,160. Thus, if output is 4,000, firms are not producing enough to meet the demand. They will find that, as sales exceed the amounts they are producing, their inventories of finished goods are being depleted by 160 per year, and that actual investment (including inventory investment) is less than planned investment. Under the assumption that firms are committed to meeting their customers' demand, firms will respond by expanding their production.

Would expanding production to 4,160, the level of planned spending firms faced when output was 4,000, be enough? The answer is no because of induced expenditure. That is, as firms expand their output, aggregate income (wages and profits) rises with it, which in turn leads to higher levels of consumption. Indeed, if output expands to 4,160, planned spending will increase as well, to $960 + 0.8(4,160)$, or 4,288. So an output level of 4,160 will still be insufficient to meet demand. As Table 25.1 shows, output will not be sufficient to meet planned aggregate expenditure until it expands to its short-run equilibrium value of 4,800.

What if output were initially greater than its equilibrium value—say, 5,000? From Table 25.1, we can see that when output equals 5,000, planned spending equals only 4,960—less than what firms are producing. So at an output level of 5,000, firms will not sell all they produce, and they will find that their merchandise is piling up on store shelves and in warehouses (actual investment, including inventory investment, is greater than planned investment). In response, firms will cut their production runs. As Table 25.1 shows, they will have to reduce production to its equilibrium value of 4,800 before output just matches planned spending.

We can also find short-run equilibrium output directly by using the equation for planned aggregate expenditure

$$PAE = 960 + 0.8Y.$$

By definition, an economy is in short-run equilibrium when

$$Y = PAE.$$

So, using our equation for planned aggregate expenditure, we have

$$Y = 960 + 0.8Y.$$

Solving for Y, we have $Y = 4,800$, the same result we obtained using Table 25.1.

 SELF-TEST 25.1

Construct a table like Table 25.1 for an economy like the one we have been working with, assuming that the consumption function is $C = 820 + 0.7(Y - T)$ and that $I^P = 600$, $G = 600$, $NX = 200$, and $T = 600$.

What is short-run equilibrium output in this economy? (*Hint:* Try using values for output above 5,000.) Check your answer by finding short-run equilibrium output directly using the equation for planned aggregate expenditure.

FINDING SHORT-RUN EQUILIBRIUM OUTPUT: GRAPHICAL APPROACH

Figure 25.4 shows the graphical determination of short-run equilibrium output for the economy we analyzed numerically above. Output (Y) is plotted on the horizontal axis and planned aggregate expenditure (PAE) on the vertical axis.

The figure contains two lines. The blue line is the expenditure line, which we discussed earlier. It shows how planned spending depends on output. The red dashed line is a 45° line extending from the origin. In general, a 45° line from the origin includes the points at which the variable on the vertical axis equals the variable on the horizontal axis. Hence, in this case, the 45° line shows all of the points at which PAE equals Y. Since an economy is in short-run equilibrium when $Y = PAE$, the short-run equilibrium for our example must be somewhere along this line.

At which particular point on the $Y = PAE$ line will the economy be in short-run equilibrium? Only one point in the figure is on both the $Y = PAE$ line and the expenditure

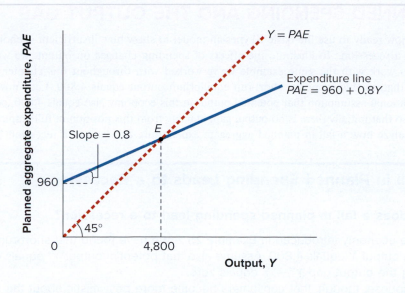

FIGURE 25.4

Determination of Short-Run Equilibrium Output (Keynesian Cross).

The 45° line represents the short-run equilibrium condition $Y = PAE$. The line $PAE = 960 + 0.8Y$, referred to as the expenditure line, shows the relationship of planned aggregate expenditure to output. Short-run equilibrium output (4,800) is determined at point E, the intersection of the expenditure line and the equilibrium condition ($Y = PAE$). This type of diagram is known as a Keynesian cross.

line: point E, where the two lines intersect. At point E, short-run equilibrium output equals 4,800, which is the same value that we obtained with the numerical approach either by using Table 25.1 or by solving the equation directly.

What if the economy is above or below point E? At levels of output higher than 4,800, output exceeds planned aggregate expenditure. Hence, firms will be producing more than they can sell, which will lead them to reduce their rate of production. They will continue to reduce their production until output reaches 4,800, where output equals planned aggregate expenditure. By contrast, at levels of output below 4,800, planned aggregate expenditure exceeds output. In that region, firms will not be producing enough to meet demand, and they will tend to increase their production. Only at point E, where output equals 4,800, will firms be producing enough to just satisfy planned spending on goods and services.

The diagram in Figure 25.4 is called the *Keynesian cross* due to the fact that it is a crosslike, graphical model of Keynes's basic ideas. The Keynesian cross shows graphically how short-run equilibrium output is determined in a world in which producers meet demand at predetermined prices.

 SELF-TEST 25.2

Use a Keynesian-cross diagram to show graphically the determination of short-run equilibrium output for the economy described in Self-Test 25.1. What are the intercept and the slope of the expenditure line?

RECAP

SHORT-RUN EQUILIBRIUM OUTPUT

- Short-run equilibrium output is the level of output at which output equals planned aggregate expenditure, or, in symbols, $Y = PAE$. For an example economy, short-run equilibrium output can be solved for numerically or graphically.
- The graphical solution is based on a diagram called the Keynesian cross. The Keynesian-cross diagram includes two lines: a 45° line that represents the condition $Y = PAE$, and the expenditure line, which shows the relationship of planned aggregate expenditure to output. Short-run equilibrium output is determined at the intersection of the two lines.

PLANNED SPENDING AND THE OUTPUT GAP

We're now ready to use the basic Keynesian model to show how insufficient spending can lead to a recession. To illustrate the effects of spending changes on output, we will continue to work with the same example we've worked with throughout this chapter. We've shown that, in this economy, short-run equilibrium output equals 4,800. Let's now make the additional assumption that potential output in this economy also equals 4,800, or $Y^* = 4,800$, so that initially there is no output gap. Starting from this position of full employment, let's analyze how a fall in planned aggregate expenditure can lead to a recession.

EXAMPLE 25.3   **A Fall in Planned Spending Leads to a Recession**

Why does a fall in planned spending lead to a recession?

For the economy introduced in Example 25.2, we have found that short-run equilibrium output Y equals 4,800. Assume also that potential output Y^* equals 4,800, so that the output gap $Y^* - Y$ equals zero.

Suppose, though, that consumers become more pessimistic about the future, so that they begin to spend less at every level of current disposable income. We can capture this change by assuming that $\overline{C}$, the constant term in the consumption function, falls to a lower level. To be specific, suppose that $\overline{C}$ falls by 10 units, which in turn implies a decline in autonomous expenditure of 10 units. What is the effect of this reduction in planned spending on the economy?

We can see the effects of the decline in consumer spending on the economy using the Keynesian-cross diagram. Figure 25.5 shows the original short-run equilibrium point of the model (E), at the intersection of the 45° line, along which $Y = PAE$, and the original expenditure line, representing the equation $PAE = 960 + 0.8Y$. As before, the initial value of short-run equilibrium output is 4,800, which we have now assumed also corresponds to potential output Y^*. But what happens if $\overline{C}$ declines by 10 units, reducing autonomous expenditure by 10 units as well?

FIGURE 25.5

A Decline in Planned Spending Leads to a Recession.

(1) A decline in consumers' willingness to spend at any current level of disposable income reduces planned autonomous expenditure and shifts the expenditure line down; (2) the short-run equilibrium point moves from E to F; (3) equilibrium output falls from 4,800 to 4,750; a recessionary gap of 50 is created.

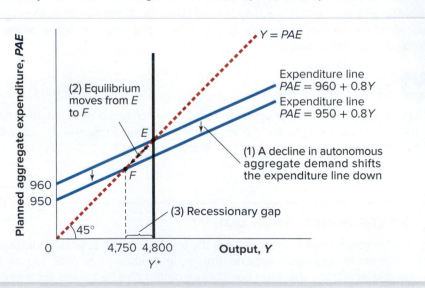

Originally, autonomous expenditure in this economy was 960, so a decline of 10 units causes it to fall to 950. Instead of the economy's planned spending being described by the equation $PAE = 960 + 0.8Y$, as initially, it is now given by $PAE = 950 + 0.8Y$. What does this change imply for the graph in Figure 25.5? Since the intercept of the expenditure line (equal to autonomous expenditure) has decreased from 960 to 950, the effect of the decline in consumer spending will be to shift the expenditure line down in parallel fashion, by 10 units. Figure 25.5 indicates this downward shift in the expenditure line. The new short-run equilibrium point is at point *F*, where the new, lower expenditure line intersects the 45° line (or the *Y* = *PAE* line).

Point *F* is to the left of the original equilibrium point *E*, so we can see that output and spending have fallen from their initial levels. Since output at point *F* is lower than potential output, 4,800, we see that the fall in consumer spending has resulted in a recessionary gap in the economy. More generally, starting from a situation of full employment (where output equals potential output), any decline in autonomous expenditure leads to a recession.

Numerically, how large is the recessionary gap in Figure 25.5? To answer this question, we can use Table 25.2, which is in the same form as Table 25.1. The key difference is that in Table 25.2 planned aggregate expenditure is given by $PAE = 950 + 0.8Y$, rather than by $PAE = 960 + 0.8Y$, as in Table 25.1.

TABLE 25.2

Determination of Short-Run Equilibrium Output after a Fall in Spending

(1)	(2)	(3)	(4)
Output	Planned aggregate expenditure		
Y	PAE = 950 + 0.8Y	Y − PAE	Y = PAE?
4,600	4,630	−30	No
4,650	4,670	−20	No
4,700	4,710	−10	No
4,750	4,750	0	**Yes**
4,800	4,790	10	No
4,850	4,830	20	No
4,900	4,870	30	No
4,950	4,910	40	No
5,000	4,950	50	No

As in Table 25.1, column 1 of the table shows alternative possible values of output *Y*, and column 2 shows the levels of planned aggregate expenditure *PAE* implied by each value of output in column 1. Notice that 4,800, the value of short-run equilibrium output found in Table 25.1, is no longer an equilibrium; when output is 4,800, planned spending is 4,790, so output and planned spending are not equal. As the table shows, following the decline in planned aggregate expenditure, short-run equilibrium output is 4,750, the only value of output for which $Y = PAE$. (We can also find this short-run equilibrium output directly by solving the equation $Y = 950 + 0.8Y$.) Thus, a drop of 10 units in autonomous expenditure has led to a 50-unit decline in short-run equilibrium output. If full-employment output is 4,800, then the recessionary gap shown in Figure 25.5 is 4,800 − 4,750 = 50 units.

 SELF-TEST 25.3

In the economy described in Example 25.3, we found a recessionary gap of 50, relative to potential output of 4,800. Suppose that, in this economy, the natural rate of unemployment u^* is 5 percent. What will the actual unemployment rate be after the recessionary gap appears? (*Hint:* Recall Okun's law from Chapter 24, *Short-Term Economic Fluctuations: An Introduction*.)

The example that we just worked through showed that a decline in autonomous expenditure, arising from a decreased willingness of consumers to spend, causes short-run equilibrium output to fall and opens up a recessionary gap. The same conclusion applies to declines in autonomous expenditure arising from other sources. Suppose, for instance, that firms become disillusioned with new technologies and cut back their planned investment in new equipment. In terms of the model, this reluctance of firms to invest can be interpreted as a decline in planned investment spending I^p. Under our assumption that planned investment spending is given and does not depend on output, planned investment is part of autonomous expenditure. So a decline in planned investment spending depresses autonomous expenditure and output, in precisely the same way that a decline in the autonomous part of consumption spending does. Similar conclusions apply to declines in other components of autonomous expenditure, such as government purchases and net exports, as we will see in later applications.

 SELF-TEST 25.4

Repeat the analysis of Example 25.3, except assume that consumers become *more* rather than less confident about the future. As a result, $\overline{C}$ rises by 10 units, which in turn raises autonomous expenditure by 10 units. Show graphically that this increase in consumers' willingness to spend leads to an expansionary output gap. Find the numerical value of the expansionary output gap.

 ## The Economic Naturalist 25.3

What caused the 2007–2009 recession in the United States?

The house price bubble that burst in summer 2006 is a primary cause of the 2007–2009 recession. The average price of American homes rose at a spectacular rate from the late 1990s until the summer of 2006; this phenomenon attracted both borrowers and lenders who wished to profit from the record real estate boom.

Figure 21.1 in Chapter 21, *Saving and Capital Formation* (see The Economic Naturalist 21.1), showed real house prices between 1975 and 2019. The highest average annual rate of increase in house prices previously was the spike of 1976 to 1979, when house prices rose 4.7 percent per year. By contrast, from 2001 to 2006, average house prices rose by an average of 8.2 percent per year. This number masks the fact that over the period the rate of increase *itself* rose, starting at 4 percent in 2001 and peaking at an annual rate of 12 percent in 2004–2005.

We can use the rule of 72, discussed in Chapter 19, *Economic Growth, Productivity, and Living Standards,* to put these numbers in context. At the growth rates experienced in the 1970s and 1980s, the average price of a house doubles in 15 to 19 years. By contrast, at the growth rates experienced in the house price boom in the 2000s, *the average price of a house doubles in about 10 years,* that is, between 50 percent and 100 percent faster than ever before.

The average home price peaked in July 2006. Prices at first fell gradually, declining by about 6 percent from July 2006 through May 2007. The decline accelerated, however, and between May 2007 and February 2009 the average home price dropped by more than 20 percent.

The bursting of the housing bubble and the financial market crisis it induced caused both businesses and households to cut back on their spending in two ways. First, the financial market disruptions made it difficult for businesses to borrow funds for investment spending and for consumers to borrow funds for purchasing housing and automobiles. Second, the financial crisis reduced household

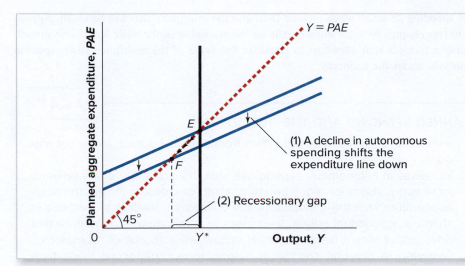

FIGURE 25.6

The End of the House Price Bubble.

wealth and increased the level of uncertainty about the future, which led to a reduction in autonomous spending, or spending independent of output.

Analytically, this situation can be represented as a downward shift in the planned aggregate expenditure (*PAE*) line as shown in Figure 25.6. At point *E*, planned spending and output are both equal to potential output *Y**. After the expenditure line shifts down, planned spending is less than actual output; the natural response of businesses is to reduce production until their output again meets demand (seen as the movement from point *E* to point *F* in Figure 25.6). At *F*, the economy is in a recession, with output below potential. Further, since output is below potential, Okun's law tells us that unemployment has now risen above the natural rate.

THE MULTIPLIER

In Example 25.3 and Table 25.2, we analyzed a case in which the initial decline in consumer spending (as measured by the fall in $\overline{C}$), and hence in autonomous expenditure, was only 10 units, and yet short-run equilibrium output fell by 50 units. Why did a relatively modest initial decline in consumer spending lead to a much larger fall in output?

The reason the impact on output was greater than the initial change in spending is the "vicious circle" effect suggested by Grandma's reminiscences about the Great Depression. Specifically, a fall in consumer spending not only reduces the sales of consumer goods directly; it also reduces the incomes of workers and owners in the industries that produce consumer goods. As their incomes fall, these workers and capital owners reduce their spending, which reduces the output and incomes of *other* producers in the economy. And these reductions in income lead to still further cuts in spending. Ultimately, these successive rounds of declines in spending and income may lead to a decrease in planned aggregate expenditure and output that is significantly greater than the change in spending that started the process.

The effect on short-run equilibrium output of a 1-unit increase in autonomous expenditure is called the **income-expenditure multiplier,** or the **multiplier** for short. In our example economy, the multiplier is 5. That is, each 1-unit change in autonomous expenditure leads to a 5-unit change in short-run equilibrium output in the same direction. The idea that a change in spending may lead to a significantly larger change in short-run equilibrium output is a key feature of the basic Keynesian model.

What determines how large the multiplier will be? An important factor is the marginal propensity to consume (*mpc*) out of disposable income. If the *mpc* is large, then falls in income will cause people to reduce their spending sharply, and the multiplier effect will then also be large. If the marginal propensity to consume is small, then people will not

income-expenditure multiplier (or **multiplier**) the effect of a one-unit increase in autonomous expenditure on short-run equilibrium output

reduce spending so much when income falls, and the multiplier also will be small. Appendix B to this chapter provides more details on the multiplier in the basic Keynesian model, including a formula that allows us to calculate the value of the multiplier under specific assumptions about the economy.

RECAP ↑

PLANNED SPENDING AND THE OUTPUT GAP

- If short-run equilibrium output differs from potential output, an output gap exists.
- Increases in autonomous expenditure shift the expenditure line upward, increasing short-run equilibrium output; decreases in autonomous expenditure shift the expenditure line downward, leading to declines in short-run equilibrium output. Decreases in autonomous expenditure that drive actual output below potential output are a source of recessions.
- Generally, a one-unit change in autonomous expenditure leads to a larger change in short-run equilibrium output, reflecting the working of the income-expenditure multiplier. The multiplier arises because a given initial increase in spending raises the incomes of producers, which leads them to spend more, raising the incomes and spending of other producers, and so on.

STABILIZING PLANNED SPENDING: THE ROLE OF FISCAL POLICY

According to the basic Keynesian model, inadequate spending is an important cause of recessions. To fight recessions—at least, those caused by insufficient demand rather than slow growth of potential output—policymakers must find ways to stimulate planned spending. Policies that are used to affect planned aggregate expenditure, with the objective of eliminating output gaps, are called **stabilization policies.** Policy actions intended to increase planned spending and output are called **expansionary policies;** expansionary policy actions are normally taken when the economy is in recession. It is also possible, as we have seen, for the economy to be "overheated," with output greater than potential output (an expansionary gap). The risk of an expansionary gap, as we will see in more detail later, is that it may lead to an increase in inflation. To offset an expansionary gap, policymakers will try to reduce spending and output. **Contractionary policies** are policy actions intended to reduce planned spending and output.

The two major tools of stabilization policy are *monetary policy* and *fiscal policy.* Recall that monetary policy refers to decisions about the size of the money supply, whereas fiscal policy refers to decisions about the government's budget—how much the government spends and how much tax revenue it collects. In the remainder of this chapter we will focus on how fiscal policy can be used to influence spending in the basic Keynesian model, as well as on some practical issues that arise in the use of fiscal policy in the real world. Monetary policy will be discussed in upcoming chapters.

GOVERNMENT PURCHASES AND PLANNED SPENDING

Decisions about government spending represent one of the two main components of fiscal policy, the other being decisions about taxes and transfer payments. Keynes himself felt that changes in government purchases were probably the most effective tool for reducing or eliminating output gaps. His basic argument was straightforward: Government purchases of goods and services, being a component of planned aggregate expenditure, directly affect total spending. If output gaps are caused by too much or too little total spending, then the government can help guide the economy toward full employment by changing its own level of spending. Keynes's views seemed to be vindicated by the events

---

stabilization policies
government policies that are used to affect planned aggregate expenditure, with the objective of eliminating output gaps

expansionary policies
government policy actions intended to increase planned spending and output

contractionary policies
government policy actions designed to reduce planned spending and output

of the 1930s, notably the fact that the Depression did not end until governments greatly increased their military spending in the latter part of the decade.

Example 25.4 shows how increased government purchases of goods and services can help eliminate a recessionary gap. (The effects of government spending on transfer programs, such as unemployment benefits, are a bit different. We will return to that case shortly.)

EXAMPLE 25.4	Recessionary Gap

How can the government eliminate an output gap by changing its purchases of goods and services?

In our example economy, we found that a drop of 10 units in consumer spending creates a recessionary gap of 50 units. How can the government eliminate the output gap and restore full employment by changing its purchases of goods and services G?

Planned aggregate expenditure was given by the equation $PAE = 960 + 0.8Y$, so that autonomous expenditure equaled 960. The 10-unit drop in $\overline{C}$ implied a 10-unit drop in autonomous expenditure, to 950. Because the multiplier in that sample economy equaled 5, this 10-unit decline in autonomous expenditure resulted in turn in a 50-unit decline in short-run equilibrium output.

To offset the effects of the consumption decline, the government would have to restore autonomous expenditure to its original value, 960. Under our assumption that government purchases are simply given and do not depend on output, government purchases are part of autonomous expenditure, and changes in government purchases change autonomous expenditure one-for-one. Thus, to increase autonomous expenditure from 950 to 960, the government should simply increase its purchases by 10 units (for example, by increasing spending on military defense or road construction). According to the basic Keynesian model, this increase in government purchases should return autonomous expenditure and, hence, output to their original levels.

The effect of the increase in government purchases is shown graphically in Figure 25.7. After the 10-unit decline in the autonomous component of consumption spending $\overline{C}$, the economy is at point F, with a 50-unit recessionary gap.

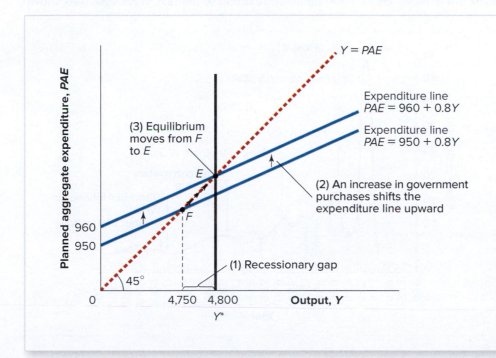

FIGURE 25.7

An Increase in Government Purchases Eliminates a Recessionary Gap.

After a 10-unit decline in the autonomous part of consumer spending $\overline{C}$, (1) the economy is initially at point F, with a recessionary gap of 50 (see Figure 25.5); (2) a 10-unit increase in government purchases raises autonomous expenditure by 10 units, shifting the expenditure line back to its original position and raising the equilibrium point from F to E; (3) the new equilibrium is at point E, where output equals potential output ($Y - Y^* = 4,800$), the output gap has been eliminated.

A 10-unit increase in government purchases raises autonomous expenditure by 10 units, raising the intercept of the expenditure line by 10 units and causing the expenditure line to shift upward in parallel fashion. The economy returns to point *E*, where short-run equilibrium output equals potential output ($Y = Y^* = 4,800$) and the output gap has been eliminated.

 SELF-TEST 25.5

In Self-Test 25.4, you considered the case in which consumers become more rather than less confident, leading to an expansionary output gap. Discuss how a change in government purchases could be used to eliminate an expansionary gap. Show your analysis graphically.

To this point we have been considering the effect of fiscal policy on a hypothetical economy. The Economic Naturalist 25.4 illustrates the application of fiscal policy in a real economy.

The Economic Naturalist 25.4

Does military spending stimulate the economy?

An antiwar poster from the 1960s bore the message "War is good business," referring to the uncomfortable fact that there are sectors in the economy that can do quite well during wars. War itself poses too many economic and human costs to be good business, but military spending could be a different matter. According to the basic Keynesian model, increases in aggregate expenditure resulting from stepped-up government purchases may help bring an economy out of a recession or depression. Does military spending stimulate aggregate demand?

Figure 25.8 shows U.S. military spending as a share of GDP from 1929 to 2019. The shaded areas in the figure correspond to periods of recession as shown

FIGURE 25.8

U.S. Military Expenditures as a Share of GDP, 1929–2019.

Military expenditures as a share of GDP rose during World War II, the Korean War, the Vietnam War, the Reagan military buildup of the early 1980s, and during the wars in Afghanistan and Iraq. Increased military spending is often associated with an expanding economy and declining unemployment. The shaded areas indicate periods of recession.

Source: Bureau of Economic Analysis, NIPA Table 1.1.5, www.bea.gov.

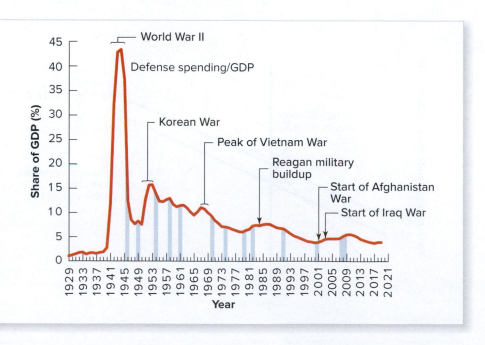

earlier in Table 24.1. Note the spike that occurred during World War II (1941–1945), when military spending exceeded 43 percent of U.S. GDP, as well as the surge during the Korean War (1950–1953). Smaller increases in military spending relative to GDP occurred at the peak of the Vietnam War in 1967–1969, during the Reagan military buildup of the 1980s, and during the wars in Afghanistan and Iraq (which started in 2001 and 2003, respectively).

Figure 25.8 provides some support for the idea that expanded military spending tends to promote growth in aggregate demand. The clearest case is the World War II era, during which massive military spending helped the U.S. economy recover from the Great Depression. The U.S. unemployment rate fell from 17.2 percent of the workforce in 1939 (when defense spending was less than 2 percent of GDP) to 1.2 percent in 1944 (when defense spending was greater than 43 percent of GDP). Two brief recessions, in 1945 and 1948–1949, followed the end of the war and the sharp decline in military spending. At the time, though, many people feared that the war's end would bring a resumption of the Great Depression, so the relative mildness of the two postwar recessions was something of a relief.

Increases in defense spending during the post–World War II period were also associated with economic expansions. The Korean War of 1950–1953 occurred simultaneously with a strong expansion, during which the unemployment rate dropped from 5.9 percent in 1949 to 2.9 percent in 1953. A recession began in 1954, the year after the armistice was signed, though military spending had not yet declined much. Economic expansions also occurred during the Vietnam-era military buildup in the 1960s and the Reagan buildup of the 1980s. Finally, on a smaller scale, increased government spending for military purposes and homeland security probably contributed to the relative mildness of the U.S. recession that began in 2001. These episodes support the idea that increases in government purchases—in this case, of weapons, other military supplies, and the services of military personnel—can help stimulate the economy.

TAXES, TRANSFERS, AND AGGREGATE SPENDING

Besides making decisions about government purchases of goods and services, fiscal policymakers also determine the level and types of taxes to be collected and transfer payments to be made. (Transfer payments, recall, are payments made by the government to the public, for which no current goods or services are received. Examples of transfer payments are unemployment insurance benefits, Social Security benefits, and income support payments to farmers. Once again, transfer payments are *not* included in government purchases of goods and services.) The basic Keynesian model implies that, like changes in government purchases, changes in the level of taxes or transfers can be used to affect planned aggregate expenditure and thus eliminate output gaps.

Unlike changes in government purchases, however, changes in taxes or transfers do not affect planned spending directly. Instead they work indirectly, by changing disposable income in the private sector. For example, either a tax cut or an increase in government transfer payments increases disposable income, equal to $Y - T$. According to the consumption function, when disposable income rises, households should spend more. Specifically, households should initially increase their expenditures by *mpc* times the increase in disposable income (Equation 25.2). Thus a tax cut or increase in transfers should increase planned aggregate expenditure. Likewise, an increase in taxes or a cut in transfers, by lowering households' disposable income, will tend to lower planned spending. The following example illustrates the effects of a tax cut on spending and output.

EXAMPLE 25.5

Using a Tax Cut to Close a Recessionary Gap

How can the government eliminate an output gap by cutting taxes?

In our hypothetical economy, an initial drop in consumer spending of 10 units creates a recessionary gap of 50 units. We showed that this recessionary gap could be eliminated by a 10-unit increase in government purchases. Suppose that, instead of increasing government purchases, fiscal policymakers decided to stimulate consumer spending by changing the level of tax collections. By how much should they change taxes to eliminate the output gap?

A common first guess to the answer to this problem is that policymakers should cut taxes by 10, but that guess is not correct. Let's see why.

The source of the recessionary gap in Example 25.3 is the reduction that households made in their consumption spending by 10 units at each level of output Y—that is, the constant term $\overline{C}$ in the consumption function is assumed to have fallen 10 units. To eliminate this recessionary gap, the change in taxes must induce households to increase their consumption spending by 10 units at each output level. However, if taxes T are cut by 10 units, raising disposable income $Y - T$ by 10 units, consumption at each level of output Y will increase by only 8 units.

Why? The reason is that the marginal propensity to consume in our example is 0.8, so that consumption spending increases by only 0.8 times the amount of the tax cut. (The rest of the tax cut is saved.) An increase in autonomous expenditure of 8 units is not enough to return output to its full-employment level, in this example.

To raise consumption spending by 10 units at each level of output, fiscal policymakers must instead cut taxes by 12.5 units. This will raise the level of disposable income, $Y - T$, by 12.5 units at each level of output Y. Consequently, consumption will increase by the marginal propensity to consume times the increase in disposable income, or by $0.8(12.5) = 10$. Thus, a tax cut of 12.5 will spur households to increase their consumption by 10 units at each level of output.

These changes are illustrated in Table 25.3. Following the initial 10-unit drop in consumer spending, the equilibrium level of output fell to 4,750. When net taxes are equal to their initial level of 250, column 3 illustrates that disposable income equals $4{,}750 - 250 = 4{,}500$. After the drop in consumer spending, the consumption function becomes $C = 610 + 0.8(Y - T)$. Thus, when $Y = 4{,}750$ and $T = 250$, consumption will equal $610 + 0.8(4{,}750 - 250) = 610 + 0.8(4{,}500) = 4{,}210$, as shown in column 4. If taxes are cut by 12.5 to 237.5, disposable income at that level of output will rise by 12.5 to $4{,}750 - 237.5 = 4{,}512.5$. Consumption at that level of output will rise by $0.8(12.5) = 10$ so that $C = 610 + 0.8(4{,}750 - 237.5) = 4{,}220$. This increase will just offset the initial 10-unit decrease in $\overline{C}$ and will bring the economy back to full employment.

TABLE 25.3

Initial Effect of a Reduction in Taxes of 12.5

(1) Output Y	(2) Net taxes T	(3) Disposable income $Y - T$	(4) Consumption $610 + 0.8(Y - T)$
4,750	250	4,500	4,210
4,750	237.5	4,512.5	4,220

Note that, since *T* refers to net taxes, or taxes less transfers, the same result could be obtained by increasing transfer payments by 12.5 units. Because households spend 0.8 times any increase in transfer payments they receive, this policy also would raise consumption spending by 10 units at any level of output.

Graphically, the effect of the tax cut is identical to the effect of the increase in government purchases, shown in Figure 25.8. Because it leads to a 10-unit increase in consumption at any level of output, the tax cut shifts the expenditure line up by 10 units. Equilibrium is attained at point *E* in Figure 25.8, where output again equals potential output.

SELF-TEST 25.6

In a particular economy, a 20-unit increase in planned investment moved the economy from an initial situation with no output gap to a situation with an expansionary gap. Describe two ways in which fiscal policy could be used to offset this expansionary gap. Assume the marginal propensity to consume equals 0.5.

The Economic Naturalist 25.5

Why did the federal government temporarily cut taxes in 2001, 2009, and 2020?

On May 25, 2001, Congress passed the Economic Growth and Tax Relief Reconciliation Act (EGTRRA) of 2001, which President George W. Bush signed on June 7. The EGTRRA made significant cuts in income tax rates and also provided for one-time tax rebate checks of up to $300 for individual taxpayers and up to $600 for married taxpayers filing a joint return. Millions of families received these checks in August and September of 2001, with payments totaling about $38 billion.

Almost eight years later, in February 2009, Congress passed the American Recovery and Reinvestment Act (ARRA) of 2009, which President Barack Obama signed on February 17, 2009. Among its provisions, the ARRA included $288 billion of tax relief, including a new payroll tax credit of $400 for individuals and $800 for couples in 2009 and 2010.

Most recently, in March 2020, Congress passed the Coronavirus Aid, Relief, and Economic Security (CARES) Act, which President Donald Trump signed into law on March 27, 2020. It was the largest economic relief bill in U.S. history, totaling around $2.2 trillion. It included hundreds of billions of dollars in tax-relief provisions, among them one-time checks of up to $1,200 for individuals and up to $2,400 for couples, with an additional $500 per child, as well as payroll tax credit for employers of up to $5,000 per employee.

Why did the federal government make these tax cuts?

Although the 2001 recession was not officially "declared" until November 2001 (when the National Bureau of Economic Research announced that the recession had begun in March), there was clear evidence by the spring of 2001 that the economy was slowing. Congress and the president hoped that by sending tax rebate checks to households, they could stimulate spending and perhaps avoid recession. In retrospect, the timing of the tax rebate was quite good since the economy and consumer confidence were further buffeted by the terrorist attacks on New York City and Washington on September 11, 2001.

Did the 2001 tax rebates have their intended effect of stimulating consumer spending? It is difficult to know with any certainty, since we do not know how much households would have spent if they had not received these extra funds. In a study published in 2006, economists found that households spent about two-thirds of their rebates within six months of receiving them.[9] This suggests that the rebate had a substantial effect on consumer spending, which held up remarkably well during the last quarter of 2001 and into 2002, assisting the economy's recovery substantially. Most economists would agree that fiscal policy generally—including not only the tax rebates, but also significantly increased spending for the military and for domestic security following September 11—was an important reason that the 2001 recession was relatively short and mild.

In contrast with the 2001 recession, the 2007–2009 recession was at the time the most severe recession since the end of World War II. By the time the ARRA was passed, not only had the beginning of the recession already been officially declared, but the recession's effects were already widely felt. For example, unemployment had already increased by around 3 percent since December 2007. Congress and the president hoped that a large tax cut, in addition to about half a trillion dollars of direct government spending and increased transfer payments, would stimulate the economy and help it recover from the recession.

Finally, at the time the CARES was passed, in late March 2020, the economic implications of the COVID-19 pandemic were only beginning to be felt in the U.S. However, it was already feared that the fast-spreading pandemic could trigger a global recession of historic proportions. Congress and the president hoped that by acting promptly and on an unprecedented scale, they could provide urgently needed stimulus to the economy.

Empty streets and frozen economic activity. Times Square, March 2020.

Kena Betancur/Getty Images

> **RECAP**
>
> **FISCAL POLICY AND PLANNED SPENDING**
>
> - Fiscal policy consists of two tools for affecting total spending and eliminating output gaps: (1) changes in government purchases and (2) changes in taxes or transfer payments.
> - An increase in government purchases increases autonomous expenditure by an equal amount. A reduction in taxes or an increase in transfer payments increases autonomous expenditure by an amount equal to the marginal propensity to consume times the reduction in taxes or increase in transfers.
> - The ultimate effect of a fiscal policy change on short-run equilibrium output equals the change in autonomous expenditure times the multiplier. Accordingly, if the economy is in recession, an increase in government purchases, a cut in taxes, or an increase in transfers can be used to stimulate spending and eliminate the recessionary gap.

FISCAL POLICY AS A STABILIZATION TOOL: THREE QUALIFICATIONS

The basic Keynesian model might lead you to think that precise use of fiscal policy can eliminate output gaps. But as is often the case, the real world is more complicated than economic models suggest. We close the chapter with three qualifications about the use of fiscal policy as a stabilization tool.

[9]David S. Johnson, Jonathan A. Parker, and Nicholas S. Souleles, "Household Expenditure and the Income Tax Rebates of 2001," *American Economic Review,* December 2006, pp. 1589–1610.

FISCAL POLICY AND THE SUPPLY SIDE

We have focused so far on the use of fiscal policy to affect planned aggregate expenditure. However, most economists would agree that *fiscal policy may affect potential output as well as planned aggregate expenditure*. On the spending side, for example, investments in public capital, such as roads, airports, and schools, can play a major role in the growth of potential output, as we discussed in Chapter 19, *Economic Growth, Productivity, and Living Standards*. On the other side of the ledger, tax and transfer programs may well affect the incentives, and thus the economic behavior, of households and firms. For example, a high tax rate on interest income may reduce the willingness of people to save for the future, while a tax break on new investment may encourage firms to increase their rate of capital formation. Such changes in saving or investment will in turn affect potential output. Many other examples could be given of how taxes and transfers affect economic behavior and thus possibly affect potential output as well.

Some critics of the Keynesian theory have gone so far as to argue that the *only* effects of fiscal policy that matter are effects on potential output. This was essentially the view of the so-called *supply-siders,* a group of economists and journalists whose influence reached a high point during the first Reagan term (1981–1985). Supply-siders focused on the need for tax cuts, arguing that lower tax rates would lead people to work harder (because they would be allowed to keep a larger share of their earnings), to save more, and to be more willing to innovate and take risks. Through their arguments that lower taxes would substantially increase potential output, with no significant effect on spending, the supply-siders provided crucial support for the large tax cuts that took place under the Reagan administration. Supply-sider ideas also were used to support the long-term income tax cut passed under President George W. Bush in 2001.

A more balanced view is that fiscal policy affects *both* spending *and* potential output. Thus, in making fiscal policy, government officials should take into account not only the need to stabilize aggregate expenditure but also the likely effects of government spending, taxes, and transfers on the economy's productive capacity.

THE PROBLEM OF DEFICITS

A second consideration for fiscal policymakers thinking about stabilization policies is *the need to avoid large and persistent budget deficits*. Recall from Chapter 21, *Saving and Capital Formation,* that the government's budget deficit is the excess of government spending over tax collections. Sustained government deficits can be harmful because they reduce national saving, which in turn reduces investment in new capital goods—an important source of long-run economic growth. The need to keep deficits under control may make increasing spending or cutting taxes to fight a slowdown a less attractive option, both economically and politically.

Moreover, international lenders would not let a country run large and persistent deficits for too long even if at home deficits appeared politically attractive. As an extreme example, for many years Greece's government was running large budget deficits—estimated at more than 7 percent of GDP, on average, from 1995 to 2015. These large deficits eventually led to a government-debt crisis. As international lenders questioned the Greek government's ability to pay back any future loans, Greece's government became very limited in its ability to run further deficits to stimulate the economy and fight recessions. Indeed, in 2016, the Greek government was forced to run a small budget surplus in spite of no real GDP growth and a very high unemployment rate (more than 23 percent!). It kept running small surpluses in the following years. (By late 2019—before the COVID-19 pandemic—unemployment in Greece was still above 16 percent.)

THE RELATIVE INFLEXIBILITY OF FISCAL POLICY

The third qualification about the use of fiscal policy is that *fiscal policy is not always flexible enough to be useful for stabilization*. Our examples have implicitly assumed that the government can change spending or taxes relatively quickly in order to eliminate output gaps. In reality, changes in government spending or taxes must usually go through a lengthy legislative process, which reduces the ability of fiscal policy to respond in a timely way to economic conditions. For example, budget and tax changes proposed by the president must typically be submitted to Congress 18 months or more before they go into effect. Another factor that limits the flexibility of fiscal policy is that fiscal policymakers have many other objectives besides stabilizing aggregate spending, from ensuring an adequate national defense to providing income support to the poor. What happens if, say, the need to strengthen the national defense requires an increase in government spending, but the need to contain aggregate expenditure requires a decrease in government spending? Such conflicts can be difficult to resolve through the political process.

This lack of flexibility means that fiscal policy is less useful for stabilizing spending than the basic Keynesian model suggests. Nevertheless, most economists view fiscal policy as an important stabilizing force, for two reasons. The first is the presence of **automatic stabilizers,** provisions in the law that imply *automatic* increases in government spending or decreases in taxes when real output declines. For example, some government spending is earmarked as "recession aid"; it flows to communities automatically when the unemployment rate reaches a certain level. Taxes and transfer payments also respond automatically to output gaps: When GDP declines, income tax collections fall (because households' taxable incomes fall) while unemployment insurance payments and welfare benefits rise—all without any explicit action by Congress. These automatic changes in government spending and tax collections help increase planned spending during recessions and reduce it during expansions, without the delays inherent in the legislative process.

The second reason that fiscal policy is an important stabilizing force is that although fiscal policy may be difficult to change quickly, it may still be useful for dealing with prolonged episodes of recession, when other economic policies including monetary policy may prove insufficient. The Great Depression of the 1930s, the Japanese slump of the 1990s, the global recession of 2007–2009, and the COVID-19 recession that started in 2020 are four cases in point. However, because of the relative lack of flexibility of fiscal policy, in the absence of an unusual economic shock, in modern economies aggregate spending is more usually stabilized through monetary policy. The stabilizing role of monetary policy is the subject of the next chapter.

automatic stabilizers
provisions in the law that imply *automatic* increases in government spending or decreases in taxes when real output declines

---

RECAP ↑

FISCAL POLICY AS A STABILIZATION TOOL: THREE QUALIFICATIONS

- Changes in taxes and transfer programs may affect the incentives and economic behavior of households and firms.
- Governments must weigh the short-run effects of fiscal policy against the possibility of large and persistent budget deficits.
- Changes in spending and taxation take time and thus fiscal policy can be relatively slow and inflexible.

SUMMARY

- The basic Keynesian model shows how fluctuations in planned aggregate expenditure, or total planned spending, can cause actual output to differ from potential output. Too little spending leads to a recessionary output gap; too much spending creates an expansionary output gap. This model relies on the crucial assumption that firms do not respond to every change in demand by changing prices. Instead, they typically set a price for some period and then meet the demand forthcoming at that price. Firms do not change prices continually because changing prices entails costs, called *menu costs*. *(LO1)*

- *Planned aggregate expenditure* is total planned spending on final goods and services. The four components of total spending are consumption, investment, government purchases, and net exports. Planned and actual consumption, government purchases, and net exports are generally assumed to be the same. Actual investment may differ from planned investment because firms may sell a greater or lesser amount of their production than they expected. If firms sell less than they expected, for example, they are forced to add more goods to inventory than anticipated. And because additions to inventory are counted as part of investment, in this case actual investment (including inventory investment) is greater than planned investment. *(LO2)*

- Consumption is related to disposable, or after-tax, income by a relationship called the *consumption function*. The amount by which consumption rises when disposable income rises by one dollar is called the marginal propensity to consume (*mpc*). The marginal propensity to consume is always greater than zero but less than one (that is, $0 < mpc < 1$). *(LO2)*

- An increase in real output raises planned aggregate expenditure since higher output (and, equivalently, higher income) encourages households to consume more. Planned aggregate expenditure can be broken down into two components: autonomous expenditure and induced expenditure. *Autonomous expenditure* is the portion of planned spending that is independent of output; *induced expenditure* is the portion of spending that depends on output. *(LO2)*

- In the period in which prices are fixed, *short-run equilibrium output* is the level of output that just equals planned aggregate expenditure. Short-run equilibrium can be determined numerically by a table that compares alternative values of output and the planned spending implied by each level of output, or by directly manipulating the relevant equations. Short-run equilibrium output also can be determined graphically in a Keynesian-cross diagram. *(LO3)*

- Changes in autonomous expenditure will lead to changes in short-run equilibrium output. In particular, if the economy is initially at full employment, a fall in autonomous expenditure will create a recessionary gap and a rise in autonomous expenditure will create an expansionary gap. The amount by which a one-unit increase in autonomous expenditure raises short-run equilibrium output is called the *multiplier*. An increase in autonomous expenditure not only raises spending directly; it also raises the incomes of producers, who in turn increase their spending, and so on. Hence the multiplier is greater than one; that is, a one-dollar increase in autonomous expenditure tends to raise short-run equilibrium output by more than one dollar. *(LO4)*

- To eliminate output gaps and restore full employment, the government employs *stabilization policies*. The two major types of stabilization policy are monetary policy and fiscal policy. Stabilization policies work by changing planned aggregate expenditure and hence short-run equilibrium output. For example, an increase in government purchases raises autonomous expenditure directly, so it can be used to reduce or eliminate a recessionary gap. Similarly, a cut in taxes or an increase in transfer payments increases the public's disposable income, raising consumption spending at each level of output by an amount equal to the marginal propensity to consume times the cut in taxes or increase in transfers. Higher consumer spending, in turn, raises short-run equilibrium output. *(LO5)*

- Three qualifications must be made to the use of fiscal policy as a stabilization tool. First, fiscal policy may affect potential output as well as aggregate spending. Second, large and persistent government budget deficits reduce national saving and growth; the need to keep deficits under control may limit the use of expansionary fiscal policies. Finally, because changes in fiscal policy must go through a lengthy legislative process, fiscal policy is not always flexible enough to be useful for short-run stabilization. However, *automatic stabilizers*—provisions in the law that imply automatic increases in government spending or reductions in taxes when output declines—can overcome the problem of legislative delays to some extent and contribute to economic stability. *(LO6)*

KEY TERMS

automatic stabilizers
autonomous consumption
autonomous expenditure
consumption function
contractionary policies
disposable income

expansionary policies
expenditure line
income-expenditure multiplier
 (or multiplier)
induced expenditure
marginal propensity to consume (*mpc*)

menu costs
planned aggregate
 expenditure (*PAE*)
short-run equilibrium output
stabilization policies
wealth effect

REVIEW QUESTIONS

1. What is the key assumption of the basic Keynesian model? Explain why this assumption is needed if one is to accept the view that aggregate spending is a driving force behind short-term economic fluctuations. *(LO1)*

2. Give an example of a good or service whose price changes very frequently and one whose price changes relatively infrequently. What accounts for the difference? *(LO1)*

3. Define planned aggregate expenditure and list its components. Why does planned spending change when output changes? *(LO2)*

4. Explain how planned spending and actual spending can differ. Illustrate with an example. *(LO2)*

5. Sketch a graph of the consumption function, labeling the axes of the graph. Discuss the economic meaning of (a) a movement from left to right along the graph of the consumption function and (b) a parallel upward shift of the consumption function. Give an example of a factor that could lead to a parallel upward shift of the consumption function. *(LO2)*

6. Sketch the Keynesian-cross diagram. Explain in words the economic significance of the two lines graphed in the diagram. Given only this diagram, how could you determine autonomous expenditure, induced expenditure, the marginal propensity to consume, and short-run equilibrium output? *(LO3)*

7. Define the multiplier. In economic terms, why is the multiplier greater than one? *(LO4)*

8. The government is considering two alternative policies, one involving increased government purchases of 50 units, the other involving a tax cut of 50 units. Which policy will stimulate planned aggregate expenditure by more? Why? *(LO5)*

9. Discuss three reasons why the use of fiscal policy to stabilize the economy is more complicated than suggested by the basic Keynesian model. *(LO6)*

PROBLEMS

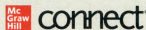

1. Acme Manufacturing is producing $4,000,000 worth of goods this year and expects to sell its entire production. It also is planning to purchase $1,500,000 in new equipment during the year. At the beginning of the year, the company has $500,000 in inventory in its warehouse. Find actual investment and planned investment if Acme actually sells
   a. $3,850,000 worth of goods.
   b. $4,000,000 worth of goods.
   c. $4,200,00 worth of goods.
   Assuming that Acme's situation is similar to that of other firms, in which of these three cases is output equal to short-run equilibrium output? *(LO2, LO3)*

2. Data on before-tax income, taxes paid, and consumption spending for the Simpson family in various years are given below: *(LO2)*

Before-tax income ($)	Taxes paid ($)	Consumption spending ($)
25,000	3,000	20,000
27,000	3,500	21,350
28,000	3,700	22,070
30,000	4,000	23,600

   a. Graph the Simpsons' consumption function and find their household's marginal propensity to consume.

   b. How much would you expect the Simpsons to consume if their income was $32,000 and they paid taxes of $5,000?

   c. Homer Simpson wins a lottery prize. As a result, the Simpson family increases its consumption by $1,000 at each level of after-tax income. ("Income" does not include the prize money.) How does this change affect the graph of their consumption function? How does it affect their marginal propensity to consume?

3. An economy is described by the following equations: *(LO2)*

$$C = 1,800 + 0.6(Y - T)$$
$$I^p = 900$$
$$G = 1,500$$
$$NX = 100$$
$$T = 1,500$$
$$Y^* = 9,000$$

   a. Find a numerical equation linking planned aggregate expenditure to output.
   b. Find autonomous expenditure and induced expenditure in this economy.

4. For the economy described in Problem 3: *(LO3)*
   a. Construct a table like Table 25.1 to find short-run equilibrium output. Consider possible values for short-run equilibrium output ranging from 8,200 to 9,000.
   b. Show the determination of short-run equilibrium output for this economy using the Keynesian-cross diagram.
   c. What is the output gap for this economy? If the natural rate of unemployment is 4 percent, what is the

actual unemployment rate for this economy? (*Hint:* Use Okun's law.)

5. For the economy described in Problem 3, take as given that the multiplier for this economy is 2.5. Find the effect on short-run equilibrium output of: *(LO4)*
   a. An increase in government purchases from 1,500 to 1,600.
   b. A decrease in tax collections from 1,500 to 1,400 (leaving government purchases at their original value).
   c. A decrease in planned investment spending from 900 to 800.

6. An economy is initially at full employment, but a decrease in planned investment spending (a component of autonomous expenditure) pushes the economy into recession. Assume that the *mpc* of this economy is 0.75 and that the multiplier is 4. *(LO4, LO5)*
   a. How large is the recessionary gap after the fall in planned investment?
   b. By how much would the government have to change its purchases to restore the economy to full employment?
   c. Alternatively, by how much would the government have to change taxes?
   d.* Suppose that the government's budget is initially in balance, with government spending equal to taxes collected. A balanced-budget law forbids the government from running a deficit. Is there anything that fiscal policymakers could do to restore full employment in this economy, assuming they do not want to violate the balanced-budget law?

7. An economy is described by the following equations:

$$C = 40 + 0.8(Y - T)$$
$$I^p = 70$$
$$G = 120$$
$$NX = 10$$
$$T = 150$$
$$Y^* = 580$$

The multiplier in this economy is 5. *(LO4, LO5)*
   a. Find a numerical equation relating planned aggregate expenditure to output.
   b. Construct a table to find the value of short-run equilibrium output. (*Hint:* The economy is fairly close to full employment.)

c. By how much would government purchases have to change in order to eliminate any output gap? By how much would taxes have to change? Show the effects of these fiscal policy changes in a Keynesian-cross diagram.
   d. Repeat part c assuming that $Y^* = 630$.
   e. Show your results for parts b through d on a Keynesian-cross diagram.

8.* An economy is described by the following equations: *(LO3, LO4, LO5)*

$$C = 2,500 + 0.8(Y - T)$$
$$I^p = 2,500$$
$$G = 3,500$$
$$NX = 300$$
$$T = 3,000$$
$$Y^* = 31,400$$

a. For this economy, find the following: autonomous expenditure, the multiplier, short-run equilibrium output, and the output gap.
   b. Illustrate this economy's short-run equilibrium on a Keynesian-cross diagram.
   c. Calculate the amount by which autonomous expenditure would have to change to eliminate the output gap.
   d. Suppose that the government decided to close the output gap by reducing taxes. By how much must taxes be reduced in order to do this?

9.* An economy has zero net exports. Otherwise, it is identical to the economy described in Problem 7. *(LO3, LO4, LO5)*
   a. Find short-run equilibrium output.
   b. Economic recovery abroad increases the demand for the country's exports; as a result, NX rises to 100. What happens to short-run equilibrium output?
   c. Repeat part b, but this time assume that foreign economies are slowing, reducing the demand for the country's exports, so that $NX = -100$. (A negative value of net exports means that exports are less than imports.)
   d. How do your results help explain the tendency of recessions and expansions to spread across countries?

*Denotes more difficult problem.

ANSWERS TO SELF-TESTS

25.1 First we need to find an equation that relates planned aggregate expenditure *PAE* to output *Y.* We start with the definition of planned aggregate expenditure and then substitute the numerical values given in the problem:

$$PAE = C + I^p + G + NX$$
$$= [820 + 0.7(Y - 600)] + 600 + 600 + 200$$
$$= 1,800 + 0.7Y.$$

Using this relationship, we construct a table analogous to Table 25.1. Some trial and error is necessary to find an appropriate range of guesses for output (column 1).

Determination of Short-Run Equilibrium Output

(1) Output Y	(2) Planned aggregate expenditure PAE = 1,800 + 0.7Y	(3) Y = PAE	(4) Y = PAE?
5,000	5,300	−300	No
5,200	5,440	−240	No
5,400	5,580	−180	No
5,600	5,720	−120	No
5,800	5,860	−60	No
6,000	6,000	0	**Yes**
6,200	6,140	60	No
6,400	6,280	120	No
6,600	6,420	180	No

Short-run equilibrium output equals 6,000, as that is the only level of output that satisfies the condition $Y = PAE$. Using the equation for planned aggregate expenditure, in equilibrium we have $Y = 1,800 + 0.7Y$. Solving for Y, we find that $Y = 6,000$, just as we found using the table. *(LO3)*

25.2 The graph shows the determination of short-run equilibrium output, $Y = 6,000$. The intercept of the expenditure line is 1,800 and its slope is 0.7. Notice that the intercept equals autonomous expenditure and the slope equals the marginal propensity to consume. *(LO3)*

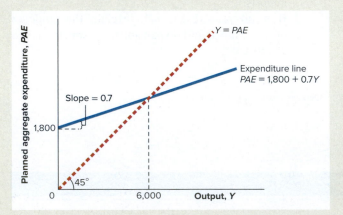

25.3 This problem is an application of Okun's law, introduced in Chapter 24, *Short-Term Economic Fluctuations: An Introduction*. The recessionary gap in this example is −50/4,800, or about −1.04 percent, of potential output. By Okun's law, cyclical unemployment is one-half the percentage size of the output gap, or 0.52 percent. As the natural rate of unemployment is 5 percent, the total unemployment rate after the recessionary gap appears will be approximately 5.52 percent. *(LO4)*

25.4 This self-test is just the reverse of the analysis in the text. An increase in $\overline{C}$ of 10 units raises autonomous expenditure and hence the intercept of the expenditure line by 10 units. The expenditure line shifts up, in parallel fashion, by 10 units, leading to an increase in output and an expansionary output gap. As output falls by 50 units in the text in Example 25.3, it rises by 50 units, to 4,850, in the case analyzed here. To verify that short-run equilibrium output equals 4,850, note that an increase of 10 units in autonomous expenditure implies that *PAE* rises from $960 + 0.8Y$ to $970 + 0.8Y$. When $Y = 4,850$, then $PAE = 970 + 0.8(4,850) = 4,850$, so that we have $Y = PAE$. *(LO4)*

25.5 In Self-Test 25.4, we saw that a 10-unit increase in $\overline{C}$ increases autonomous expenditure and hence the intercept of the expenditure line by 10 units. The expenditure line shifts upward, in parallel fashion, by 10 units, leading to an expansionary output gap. To offset this gap, the government should reduce its purchases by 10 units, returning autonomous expenditure to its original level. The expenditure line shifts back down to its original position, restoring output to its initial full-employment level. The graph is just the reverse of Figure 25.8, with the expenditure line being shifted up by the increase in consumption and down (back to point E) by the offsetting reduction in government purchases. *(LO5)*

25.6 The 20-unit increase in planned investment is a 20-unit increase in autonomous expenditure, which will lead to an even greater increase in short-run equilibrium output. To offset the 20-unit increase in autonomous expenditure by means of fiscal policy, the government can reduce its purchases by 20 units. Alternatively, it could raise taxes (or cut transfers) to reduce consumption spending. Since the *mpc* = 0.5, to reduce consumption spending by 20 units at each level of output, the government will need to increase taxes (or reduce transfers) by 40 units. At each level of output, a 40-unit tax increase will reduce disposable income by 40 units and cause consumers to reduce their spending by $0.5 \times 40 = 20$ units, as needed to eliminate the expansionary output gap. *(LO5)*

An Algebraic Solution of the Basic Keynesian Model

This chapter has shown how to solve the basic Keynesian model numerically and graphically, using the Keynesian-cross diagram. In this appendix, we will show how to find a more general algebraic solution for short-run equilibrium output in the basic Keynesian model. This solution has the advantage of showing clearly the links between short-run equilibrium output, the multiplier, and autonomous expenditure. The general method can also be applied when we make changes to the basic Keynesian model, as we will see in following chapters.

The model we will work with is the same one presented in the main part of the chapter. Start with the definition of planned aggregate expenditure, Equation 25.1:

$$PAE = C + I^p + G + NX. \tag{25.1}$$

Equation 25.1 says that planned aggregate expenditure is the sum of the four types of planned spending: consumption spending by households, C; planned investment spending by firms, I^p; government purchases, G; and net exports purchased by foreigners, NX.

The first component of planned aggregate expenditure, consumption spending, is determined by the consumption function, Equation 25.2. It is copied below, with one change: While in the body of this and the following chapters we use *mpc* for the *marginal propensity to consume,* in the appendices we will use just one letter, *c.* This will simplify the notation in our algebraic treatment.

$$C = \overline{C} + c(Y - T). \tag{25.2}$$

The consumption function says that consumption spending increases when disposable (after-tax) income $Y - T$ increases. Each dollar increase in disposable income raises consumption spending by c dollars, where c, the marginal propensity to consume, is a number between 0 and 1. Other factors affecting consumption spending are captured by the term $\overline{C}$. For example, a boom in the stock market that leads consumers to spend more at each level of disposable income (a *wealth effect*) would be represented as an increase in $\overline{C}$.

As in the body of the chapter, we assume that planned investment, government purchases, net exports, and net tax collections are simply given numbers. A variable whose value is fixed and given from outside the model is called an exogenous variable; so, in other words, we are assuming that planned investment, government purchases, net exports, and net tax collections are exogenous variables. Using an overbar to denote the given value of an exogenous variable, we can write this assumption as:

$$I^p = \overline{I} \qquad \text{Planned investment,}$$
$$G = \overline{G} \qquad \text{Government purchases,}$$
$$NX = \overline{NX} \qquad \text{Net exports,}$$
$$T = \overline{T} \qquad \text{Net taxes (taxes less transfers).}$$

So, for example, $\overline{I}$ is the given value of planned investment spending, as determined outside the model. In our examples we will set $\overline{I}$ and the other exogenous variables equal to some particular number.

Our goal is to solve algebraically for *short-run equilibrium output*, the level of output that prevails during the period in which prices are predetermined. The first step is to relate planned aggregate expenditure *PAE* to output *Y*. Starting with the definition of planned aggregate expenditure (Equation 25.1), use the consumption function (Equation 25.2) to substitute for consumption spending *C* and replace I^p, *G*, *NX*, and *T* with their exogenous values. With these substitutions, planned aggregate expenditure can be written as

$$PAE = [\overline{C} + c(Y - \overline{T})] + \overline{I} + \overline{G} + \overline{NX}.$$

Rearranging this equation to separate the terms that do and do not depend on output *Y*, we get

$$PAE = [\overline{C} + c\overline{T} + \overline{I} + \overline{G} + \overline{NX}] + cY. \tag{25A.1}$$

Equation 25A.1 is an important equation because it shows the relationship between planned aggregate expenditure *PAE* and output *Y*. The bracketed term on the right side of the equation represents *autonomous expenditure,* the part of planned spending that does not depend on output. The term *cY* represents *induced expenditure,* the part of planned spending that does depend on output. Equation 25A.1 is also the equation that describes the expenditure line in the Keynesian-cross diagram; it shows that the intercept of the expenditure line equals autonomous expenditure and the slope of the expenditure line equals the marginal propensity to consume.

We can illustrate how Equation 25A.1 works numerically by using Example 25.2 in the text. That example assumed the following numerical values: $\overline{C} = 620$, $\overline{I} = 220$, $\overline{G} = 300$, $\overline{NX} = 20$, $\overline{T} = 250$, and $c = 0.8$. Plugging these values into Equation 25A.1 and simplifying, we get

$$PAE = 960 + 0.8Y,$$

which is the same answer we found in Example 25.2. Autonomous expenditure in this example equals 960, and induced expenditure equals $0.8Y$.

The second step in solving for short-run equilibrium output begins with the definition of short-run equilibrium output (Equation 25.3)

$$Y = PAE.$$

Remember that short-run equilibrium output is the value of output at which output equals planned aggregate expenditure. Using Equation 25A.1 to substitute for *PAE* in the definition of short-run equilibrium output, we get

$$Y = [\overline{C} - c\overline{T} + \overline{I} + \overline{G} + \overline{NX}] + cY.$$

The value of *Y* that solves this equation is the value of short-run equilibrium output. To solve for *Y*, group all terms involving *Y* on the left side of the equation

$$Y - cY = [\overline{C} - c\overline{T} + \overline{I} + \overline{G} + \overline{NX}]$$

or

$$Y(1 - c) = [\overline{C} - c\overline{T} + \overline{I} + \overline{G} + \overline{NX}].$$

Dividing both sides of the equation by $(1 - c)$ gives

$$Y = \left(\frac{1}{1 - c}\right)[\overline{C} - c\overline{T} + \overline{I} + \overline{G} + \overline{NX}]. \tag{25A.2}$$

Equation 25A.2 gives short-run equilibrium output for our model economy in terms of the exogenous values $\overline{C}$, $\overline{I}$, $\overline{G}$, $\overline{NX}$, and $\overline{T}$ and the marginal propensity to consume, *c*. We can use this formula to solve for short-run equilibrium output in specific numerical examples.

For example, suppose that we once again plug in the numerical values assumed in Example 25.2: $\overline{C} = 620$, $\overline{I} = 220$, $\overline{G} = 300$, $\overline{NX} = 20$, $\overline{T} = 250$, and $c = 0.8$. We get

$$Y = \left(\frac{1}{1 - 0.8}\right)[620 - 0.8(250) + 220 + 300 + 20] = \frac{1}{0.2}(960) = 5(960) = 4,800,$$

which is the same answer we found more laboriously using Table 25.1.

 SELF-TEST 25A.1

Use Equation 25A.2 to find short-run equilibrium output for the economy described in Self-Test 25.1 in the text. What are the intercept and the slope of the expenditure line?

Equation 25A.2 shows clearly the relationship between autonomous expenditure and short-run equilibrium output. Autonomous expenditure is the first term on the right side of Equation 26A.1, equal to $\overline{C} - c\overline{T} + \overline{I} + \overline{G} + \overline{NX}$. The equation shows that a one-unit increase in autonomous expenditure increases short-run equilibrium output by $1/(1 - c)$ units. In other words, we can see from Equation 25A.2 that the *multiplier* for this model equals $1/(1 - c)$. Further discussion of the multiplier is given in Appendix B to this chapter.

ANSWER TO APPENDIX SELF-TEST

25A.1 The equation describing short-run equilibrium output is:

$$Y = \left(\frac{1}{1 - c}\right)(\overline{C} - c\overline{T} + \overline{I} + \overline{G} + \overline{NX}). \quad (25A.2)$$

Using data from Self-Test 25.1, set $\overline{C} = 820$, $c = 0.7$, $\overline{I} = 600$, $\overline{G} = 600$, $\overline{NX} = 200$, and $\overline{T} = 600$. Plugging these values into Equation (25A.2) we get:

$$Y = \left(\frac{1}{1 - 0.7}\right)[820 - 0.7(600 + 600 + 600 + 200)]$$

$$= 3.33 \times 1,800 = 6,000,$$

which is the same result obtained in Self-Test 25.1.

The Multiplier in the Basic Keynesian Model

This appendix builds on the example economy used throughout the chapter to give a more complete explanation of the *income-expenditure multiplier* in the basic Keynesian model. In the chapter, we saw that a drop in autonomous expenditure of 10 units caused a decline in short-run equilibrium output of 50 units, five times as great as the initial change in spending. Hence, the multiplier in this example is 5.

To see why this multiplier effect occurs, note that the initial decrease of 10 in consumer spending (more precisely, in the constant term of the consumption function, $\overline{C}$) has two effects. First, the fall in consumer spending directly reduces planned aggregate expenditure by 10 units. Second, the fall in spending also reduces by 10 units the incomes of producers (workers and firm owners) of consumer goods. Since the marginal propensity to consume is 0.8, the producers of consumer goods will therefore reduce *their* consumption spending by 8, or 0.8 times their income loss of 10. This reduction in spending cuts the income of *other* producers by 8 units, leading them to reduce their spending by 6.4, or 0.8 times their income loss of 8. These income reductions of 6.4 lead still other producers to cut their spending by 5.12, or 0.8 times 6.4, and so on. In principle, this process continues indefinitely, although after many rounds of spending and income reductions, the effects become quite small.

When all these "rounds" of income and spending reductions are added, the *total* effect on planned spending of the initial reduction of 10 in consumer spending is

$$10 + 8 + 6.4 + 5.12 + \cdots.$$

The three dots indicate that the series of reductions continues indefinitely. The total effect of the initial decrease in consumption also can be written as

$$10[1 + 0.8 + (0.8)^2 + (0.8)^3 + \cdots].$$

This expression highlights the fact that the spending that takes place in each round is 0.8 times the spending in the previous round (0.8) because that is the marginal propensity to consume out of the income generated by the previous round of spending.

A useful algebraic relationship, which applies to any number x greater than 0 but less than 1, is

$$1 + x + x^2 + x^3 + \cdots = \frac{1}{1 - x}.$$

If we set $x = 0.8$, this formula implies that the total effect of the decline in consumption spending on aggregate demand and output is

$$10\left(\frac{1}{1 - 0.8}\right) = 10\left(\frac{1}{0.2}\right) = 10 \times 5 = 50.$$

This answer is consistent with our earlier calculation, which showed that short-run equilibrium output fell by 50 units, from 4,800 to 4,750.

By a similar analysis, we also can find a general algebraic expression for the multiplier in the basic Keynesian model. Recalling that in the appendices, we use c for the marginal propensity to consume out of disposable income (in the body of the chapters we use *mpc*), we know that a one-unit increase in autonomous expenditure raises spending and income by one unit in the first round; by $c \times 1 = c$ units in the second round; by $c \times c = c^2$ units in the third round; by $c \times c^2 = c^3$ units in the fourth round; and so on. Thus, the total effect on short-run equilibrium output of a one-unit increase in autonomous expenditure is given by

$$1 + c + c^2 + c^3 + \cdots.$$

Applying the algebraic formula given above, and recalling that $0 < c < 1$, we can rewrite this expression as $1/(1 - c)$. Thus, in a basic Keynesian model with a marginal propensity to consume of c, the multiplier equals $1/(1 - c)$. Note that if $c = 0.8$ then $1/(1 - c) = 1/(1 - 0.8) = 5$, which is the same value of the multiplier we found numerically above.

CHAPTER 26

Stabilizing the Economy: The Role of the Fed

Jonathan Larsen/iStock/Getty Images

How does the Federal Reserve affect spending and output in the short run?

LEARNING OBJECTIVES

After reading this chapter, you should be able to:

LO1 Show how the demand for money and the supply of money interact to determine the equilibrium nominal interest rate.

LO2 Explain how the Fed uses its ability to affect the money supply to influence nominal and real interest rates.

LO3 Discuss how the Fed uses its ability to affect bank reserves and the reserve-deposit ratio to affect the money supply.

LO4 Describe the additional monetary policy tools that the Fed can use when interest rates hit the zero lower bound.

LO5 Explain how changes in real interest rates affect aggregate expenditure and how the Fed uses changes in the real interest rate to fight a recession or inflation.

LO6 Discuss the extent to which monetary policy-making is an art or science.

Financial market participants and commentators go to remarkable lengths to try to predict the actions of the Federal Reserve. At the end of 2015, investors had been listening to every word uttered by Chair Janet Yellen to learn whether the Fed intended to raise interest rates for the first time in almost a decade. Then, in the summer of 2019, all eyes were on Chair Jerome Powell to learn whether—for the first time in *more* than a decade—interest rates were going to be *cut*. The close attention being paid to Fed chairs is not a new occurrence. For a while, the CNBC financial news program *Squawk Box* reported regularly on what the commentators called the Greenspan Briefcase Indicator. The idea was to spot Alan Greenspan, one of Yellen's and Powell's predecessors as Fed chair, on his way to meet with the Federal Open Market Committee (FOMC), the group that determines U.S. monetary policy. If Greenspan's briefcase was packed full, presumably with macroeconomic data and analyses, the guess was that the Fed planned to change interest rates. A slim briefcase meant no change in rates was likely.

"It was right 17 out of the first 20 times," the program's anchor Mark Haines noted, "but it has a built-in self-destruct mechanism, because Greenspan packs his [own] briefcase. He can make it wrong or right. He has never publicly acknowledged the indicator, but we have reason to believe that he knows about it. We have to consider the fact that he wants us to stop doing it because the last two times the briefcase has been wrong, and that's disturbing."[1]

[1] Robert H. Frank, "Safety in Numbers," *New York Times Magazine,* November 28, 1999, p. 35.

The Briefcase Indicator is but one example of the close public scrutiny that the chair of the Federal Reserve and other monetary policymakers face. Every speech, every congressional testimony, every interview from a member of the Board of Governors is closely analyzed for clues about the future course of monetary policy. The reason for the intense public interest in the Federal Reserve's decisions about monetary policy—and especially the level of interest rates—is that those decisions have important implications both for financial markets and for the economy in general.

In this chapter, we examine the workings of monetary policy, one of the two major types of *stabilization policy*. (The other type, fiscal policy, was discussed in the previous chapter.) As we have seen, stabilization policies are government policies that are meant to influence aggregate expenditure, with the goal of eliminating output gaps. Both types of stabilization policy, monetary and fiscal, are important and have been useful at various times. However, monetary policy, which can be changed quickly by a decision of the Federal Reserve's FOMC, is more flexible and responsive than fiscal policy, which can be changed only by legislative action by Congress. Under normal circumstances, therefore, monetary policy is used more actively than fiscal policy to help stabilize the economy.

We will begin this chapter by discussing how the Fed uses its ability to control the money supply to influence the level of interest rates. We then turn to the economic effects of changes in interest rates. Building on our analysis of the basic Keynesian model in Chapter 25, *Spending and Output in the Short Run,* we will see that, in the short run, monetary policy works by affecting planned spending and thus short-run equilibrium output. We will defer discussion of the other major effect of monetary policy actions, changes in the rate of inflation. The effects of monetary policy on inflation are addressed in the next chapter.

THE FEDERAL RESERVE AND INTEREST RATES: THE BASIC MODEL

When we introduced the Federal Reserve System in Chapter 22, *Money, Prices, and the Federal Reserve,* we focused on the Fed's tools for controlling the *money supply*—that is, the quantity of currency and checking accounts held by the public. Determining the nation's money supply is the primary task of monetary policymakers. But if you follow the economic news regularly, you may find the idea that the Fed's job is to control the money supply a bit foreign because the news media nearly always focus on the Fed's decisions about *interest rates*. Indeed, the announcement the Fed makes after each meeting of the FOMC nearly always includes its plan for a particular short-term interest rate, called the *federal funds rate* (more on the federal funds rate later).

Actually, there is no contradiction between the two ways of looking at monetary policy—as control of the money supply or as the setting of interest rates. As we will see in this section, controlling the money supply and controlling the nominal interest rate are two sides of the same coin: any value of the money supply chosen by the Fed implies a specific setting for the nominal interest rate, and vice versa. The reason for this close connection is that the nominal interest rate is effectively the "price" of holding money (or, more accurately, its opportunity cost). So, by controlling the quantity of money supplied to the economy, the Fed also controls the "price" of holding money (the nominal interest rate).

In this section, we focus on the basic model of the market for money. To keep the discussion easy to follow, we will keep making two simplifying assumptions that we have made throughout the book. First, when discussing the money supply, we will keep assuming, as we did in Chapter 22, that the Fed can fully control the amount of money by controlling the amount of bank reserves. Second, when discussing interest rates, we will keep assuming that they all move more or less together. To better understand how the Fed determines interest rates, we will look first at the demand side of that market. We will see that given the demand for money by the public, the Fed can control interest rates by changing the amount of money it supplies. Having discussed the basics—that is, how the market for money works when our two simplifying assumptions hold—in the next section, we will discuss the market for money in more detail and highlight the changes that occurred in this market since 2008. In the last section of this chapter, we will show how the Fed uses control of interest rates to influence spending and the state of the economy.

THE DEMAND FOR MONEY

Recall that *money* refers to the set of assets, such as cash and checking accounts, that are usable in transactions. Money is also a store of value, like stocks, bonds, or real estate—in other words, a type of financial asset. As a financial asset, money is a way of holding wealth.

Anyone who has some wealth must determine the *form* in which he or she wishes to hold that wealth. For example, if Louis has wealth of $10,000, he could—if he wished—hold all $10,000 in cash. Or he could hold $5,000 of his wealth in the form of cash and $5,000 in government bonds. Or he could hold $1,000 in cash, $2,000 in a checking account, $2,000 in government bonds, and $5,000 in rare stamps. Indeed, there are thousands of different real and financial assets to choose from, all of which can be held in different amounts and combinations, so Louis's choices are virtually infinite. The decision about the forms in which to hold one's wealth is called the **portfolio allocation decision.**

What determines the particular mix of assets that Louis or another wealth holder will choose? All else being equal, people generally prefer to hold assets that they expect to pay a high *return* and do not carry too much *risk*. They may also try to reduce the overall risk they face through *diversification*—that is, by owning a variety of different assets.[2] Many people own some real assets, such as a car or a home, because they provide services (transportation or shelter) and often a financial return (an increase in value, as when the price of a home rises in a strong real estate market).

Here we do not need to analyze the entire portfolio allocation decision, but only one part of it—namely, the decision about how much of one's wealth to hold in the form of *money* (cash and checking accounts). The amount of wealth an individual chooses to hold in the form of money is that individual's **demand for money.** So if Louis decided to hold his entire $10,000 in the form of cash, his demand for money would be $10,000. But if he were to hold $1,000 in cash, $2,000 in a checking account, $2,000 in government bonds, and $5,000 in rare stamps, his demand for money would be only $3,000—that is, $1,000 in cash plus the $2,000 in his checking account.

portfolio allocation decision the decision about the forms in which to hold one's wealth

demand for money the amount of wealth an individual or firm chooses to hold in the form of money

---

EXAMPLE 26.1   Consuelo's Demand for Money

What is Consuelo's demand for money, and how could she increase or reduce her money holdings?

Consuelo's balance sheet is shown in Table 26.1. What is Consuelo's demand for money? If she wanted to increase her money holdings by $100, how could she do so? What if she wanted to reduce her money holdings by $100?

Looking at Table 26.1, we see that Consuelo's balance sheet shows five different asset types: cash, a checking account, shares of stock, a car, and furniture. Of these assets, the first two (the cash and the checking account) are forms of money. Consuelo's money holdings consist of $80 in cash and $1,200 in her checking account. Thus Consuelo's demand for money—the amount of wealth she chooses to hold in the form of money—is $1,280.

---

[2]We examined risk, return, and diversification in Chapter 23, *Financial Markets and International Capital Flows.*

TABLE 26.1

Consuelo's Balance Sheet

Assets		Liabilities	
Cash	$ 80	Student loan	$3,000
Checking account	1,200	Credit card balance	250
Shares of stock	1,000		
Car (market value)	3,500		
Furniture (market value)	500		
Total	**$6,280**		**$3,250**
		Net worth	**$3,030**

There are many different ways in which Consuelo could increase her money holdings, or demand for money, by $100. She could sell $100 worth of stock and deposit the proceeds in the bank. That action would leave the total value of her assets and her wealth unchanged (because the decrease in her stockholdings would be offset by the increase in her checking account) but would increase her money holdings by $100. Another possibility would be to take a $100 cash advance on her credit card. That action would increase both her money holdings and her assets by $100 but would also increase her liabilities—specifically, her credit card balance—by $100. Once again, her total wealth would not change, though her money holdings would increase.

To reduce her money holdings, Consuelo need only use some of her cash or checking account balance to acquire a nonmoney asset or pay down a liability.

For example, if she were to buy an additional $100 of stock by writing a check against her bank account, her money holdings would decline by $100. Similarly, writing a check to reduce her credit card balance by $100 would reduce her money holdings by $100. You can confirm that though her money holdings decline, in neither case does Consuelo's total wealth change.

Cost-Benefit

How much money should an individual (or household) choose to hold? Application of the *Cost-Benefit Principle* tells us that an individual should increase his or her money holdings only so long as the benefit of doing so exceeds the cost. As we saw in Chapter 22, *Money, Prices, and the Federal Reserve,* the principal *benefit* of holding money is its usefulness in carrying out transactions. Consuelo's shares of stock, her car, and her furniture are all valuable assets, but she cannot use them to buy groceries or pay her rent. She can make routine payments using cash or her checking account, however. Because of its usefulness in daily transactions, Consuelo will almost certainly want to hold some of her wealth in the form of money. Furthermore, if Consuelo is a high-income individual, she will probably choose to hold more money than someone with a lower income would, because she is likely to spend more and carry out more transactions than the low-income person.

Consuelo's benefit from holding money is also affected by the technological and financial sophistication of the society she lives in. For example, in the United States, developments such as credit cards, debit cards, ATMs, online and mobile payments, and electronic money transfers have generally reduced the amount of money people need to carry out routine transactions, decreasing the public's demand for money at given levels of income. In the United States in 1960, for example, money holdings in the form of cash and checking account balances (the monetary aggregate M1) were about 26 percent of GDP. By 2007, that ratio had fallen to less than 10 percent of GDP.

Although money is an extremely useful asset, there is also a cost to holding money—more precisely, an opportunity cost—that arises from the fact that most forms of money pay little or no interest. Cash pays zero interest, and most checking accounts pay either no interest or very low rates. For the sake of simplicity, we will just assume that *the nominal interest rate on money is zero*. In contrast, most alternative assets, such as bonds or stocks, pay a positive nominal return. A bond, for example, pays a fixed amount of interest each period to the holder, while stocks pay dividends and may also increase in value (capital gains).

The cost of holding money arises because, in order to hold an extra dollar of wealth in the form of money, a person must reduce by one dollar the amount of wealth held in the form of higher-yielding assets, such as bonds or stocks. The *opportunity cost* of holding money is measured by the interest rate that could have been earned if the person had chosen to hold interest-bearing assets instead of money. All else being equal, the higher the nominal interest rate, the higher the opportunity cost of holding money, and hence the less money people will choose to hold. Indeed, as the nominal interest rate fell dramatically during 2007–2008 and remained below 1 percent until mid-2017, M1 steadily increased from less than 10 percent of GDP in 2007 to more than 18 percent of GDP in 2017.

Cost-Benefit

We have been talking about the demand for money by individuals, but businesses also hold money to carry out transactions with customers and to pay workers and suppliers. The same general factors that determine individuals' money demand also affect the demand for money by businesses. That is, in choosing how much money to hold, a business, like an individual, will compare the benefits of holding money for use in transactions with the opportunity cost of holding a non-interest-bearing asset. Although we will not differentiate between the money held by individuals and the money held by businesses in discussing money demand, you should be aware that in the U.S. economy, businesses hold a significant portion of the total money stock. Example 26.2 illustrates the determination of money demand by a business owner.

EXAMPLE 26.2   A Business's Demand for Money

How much money should Kim's restaurants hold?

Kim owns several successful restaurants. Her accountant informs her that on a typical day, her restaurants are holding a total of $50,000 in cash on the premises. The accountant points out that if Kim's restaurants reduced their cash holdings, Kim could use the extra cash to purchase interest-bearing government bonds.

The accountant proposes two methods of reducing the amount of cash Kim's restaurants hold. First, she could increase the frequency of cash pickups by her armored car service. The extra service would cost $500 annually but would allow Kim's restaurants to reduce their average cash holding to $40,000. Second, in addition to the extra pickups, Kim could employ a computerized cash management service to help her keep closer tabs on the inflows and outflows of cash at her restaurants. The service costs $700 a year, but the accountant estimates that, together with more frequent pickups, the more efficient cash management provided by the service could help Kim reduce average cash holdings at her restaurants to $30,000.

The interest rate on government bonds is 6 percent. How much money should Kim's restaurants hold? What if the interest rate on government bonds is 8 percent?

Kim's restaurants need to hold cash to carry out their normal business, but holding cash also has an opportunity cost, which is the interest those funds could be earning if they were held in the form of government bonds instead of zero-interest cash. Because the interest rate on government bonds is 6 percent, each $10,000 by which Kim can reduce her restaurants' money holdings yields an annual benefit of $600 (6 percent of $10,000).

If Kim increases the frequency of pickups by her armored car service, reducing the restaurants' average money holdings from $50,000 to $40,000, the benefit will be the additional $600 in interest income that Kim will earn. The cost is the $500 charged by the armored car company. Since the benefit exceeds the cost, Kim should purchase the extra service and reduce the average cash holdings at her restaurants to $40,000.

Should Kim go a step further and employ the cash management service as well? Doing so would reduce average cash holdings at the restaurants from $40,000 to $30,000, which has a benefit in terms of extra interest income of $600 per year. However, this benefit is less than the cost of the cash management service, which is $700 per year. So Kim should *not* employ the cash management service and instead should maintain average cash holdings in her restaurants of $40,000.

If the interest rate on government bonds rises to 8 percent, then the benefit of each $10,000 reduction in average money holdings is $800 per year (8 percent of $10,000) in extra interest income. In this case, the benefit of employing the cash management service, $800, exceeds the cost of doing so, which is $700. So Kim should employ the service, reducing the average cash holdings of her business to $30,000. The example shows that a higher nominal interest rate on alternative assets reduces the quantity of money demanded.

 SELF-TEST 26.1

The interest rate on government bonds falls from 6 percent to 4 percent. How much cash should Kim's restaurants hold now?

MACROECONOMIC FACTORS THAT AFFECT THE DEMAND FOR MONEY

In any household or business, the demand for money will depend on a variety of individual circumstances. For example, a high-volume retail business that serves thousands of customers each day will probably choose to have more money on hand than a legal firm that bills clients and pays employees monthly. But while individuals and businesses vary considerably in the amount of money they choose to hold, three macroeconomic factors affect the demand for money quite broadly: the nominal interest rate, real output, and the price level. As we see next, the nominal interest rate affects the cost of holding money throughout the economy, while real output and the price level affect the benefits of money.

• *The nominal interest rate (i).* We have seen that the interest rate paid on alternatives to money, such as government bonds, determines the opportunity cost of holding money. The higher the prevailing nominal interest rate, the greater the opportunity cost of holding money, and hence the less money individuals and businesses will demand.

What do we mean by *the* nominal interest rate? As we have discussed, there are thousands of different assets, each with its own interest rate (rate of return). So can we really talk about *the* nominal interest rate? The answer is that, while there are many different assets, each with its own corresponding interest rate, the rates on those assets tend to rise and fall together. This is to be expected, because if the interest rates on some assets were to rise sharply while the rates on other assets declined, financial investors would flock to the assets paying high rates and refuse to buy the assets paying low rates. So, although there are many different interest rates in practice, speaking of the general level of interest rates usually does make sense. In this book, when we talk about *the* nominal interest rate, what we have in mind is some average measure of interest rates. This simplification is one more application of the macroeconomic concept of *aggregation,* introduced in Chapter 16, *Macroeconomics: The Bird's-Eye View of the Economy.* (We will discuss post-2008 deviations from this simplifying assumption in the next section.)

The nominal interest rate is a macroeconomic factor that affects the cost of holding money. A macroeconomic factor that affects the *benefit* of holding money is:

- *Real income or output (Y).* An increase in aggregate real income or output—as measured, for example, by real GDP—raises the quantity of goods and services that people and businesses want to buy and sell. When the economy enters a boom, for example, people do more shopping and stores have more customers. To accommodate the increase in transactions, both individuals and businesses need to hold more money. Thus higher real output raises the demand for money.

A second macroeconomic factor affecting the benefit of holding money is:

- *The price level (P).* The higher the prices of goods and services, the more dollars (or yen, or euros) are needed to make a given set of transactions. Thus a higher price level is associated with a higher demand for money.

Today, when a couple of teenagers go out for a movie and snacks on Saturday night, they need about twice as much cash as their parents did 30 years ago. Because the prices of movie tickets and popcorn have risen steeply over 30 years, more money (that is, more dollars) is needed to pay for a Saturday night date than in the past. By the way, the fact that prices are higher today does *not* imply that people are worse off today than in the past, because nominal wages and salaries have also risen substantially. In general, however, higher prices do imply that people need to keep a greater number of dollars available, in cash or in a checking account.

THE MONEY DEMAND CURVE

For the purposes of monetary policymaking, economists are most interested in the aggregate, or economywide, demand for money. The interaction of the aggregate demand for money, determined by the public, and the supply of money, which is set by the Fed, determines the nominal interest rate that prevails in the economy.

The economywide demand for money can be represented graphically by the *money demand curve* (see Figure 26.1). The **money demand curve** relates the aggregate quantity of money demanded M to the nominal interest rate i. The quantity of money demanded M is a nominal quantity, measured in dollars (or yen, or euros, depending on the country). Because an increase in the nominal interest rate increases the opportunity cost of holding money, which reduces the quantity of money demanded, the money demand curve slopes down.

money demand curve a curve that shows the relationship between the aggregate quantity of money demanded M and the nominal interest rate i

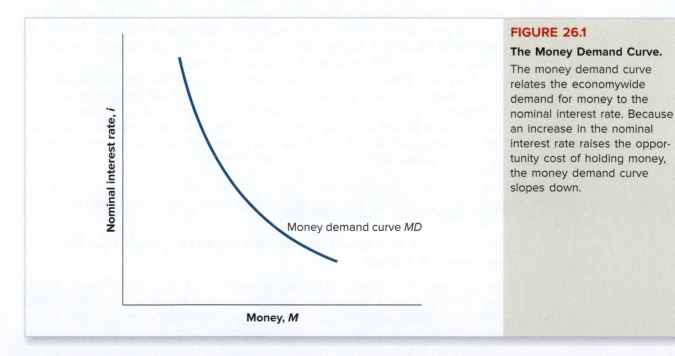

FIGURE 26.1

The Money Demand Curve.

The money demand curve relates the economywide demand for money to the nominal interest rate. Because an increase in the nominal interest rate raises the opportunity cost of holding money, the money demand curve slopes down.

FIGURE 26.2

A Shift in the Money Demand Curve.

At a given nominal interest rate, any change that makes people want to hold more money—such as an increase in the general price level or in real GDP—will shift the money demand curve to the right.

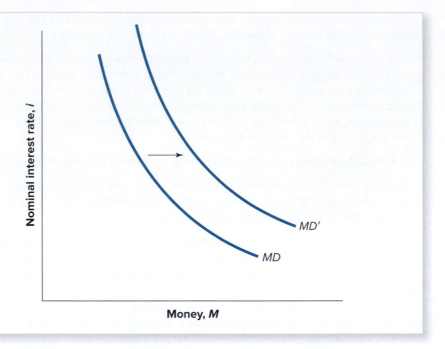

If we think of the nominal interest rate as the "price" (more precisely, the opportunity cost) of money and the amount of money people want to hold as the "quantity," the money demand curve is analogous to the demand curve for a good or service. As with a standard demand curve, the fact that a higher price of money leads people to demand less of it is captured in the downward slope of the demand curve. Furthermore, as in a standard demand curve, changes in factors other than the price of money (the nominal interest rate) can cause the demand curve for money to shift.

For a given nominal interest rate, any change that makes people want to hold more money will shift the money demand curve to the right, and any change that makes people want to hold less money will shift the money demand curve to the left. Thus, as in a standard demand curve, changes in factors other than the price of money (the nominal interest rate) cause the demand curve for money to shift. We have already identified two macroeconomic factors other than the nominal interest rate that affect the economywide demand for money: real output and the price level. Because an increase in either of these variables increases the demand for money, it shifts the money demand curve rightward, as shown in Figure 26.2. Similarly, a fall in real output or the general price level reduces money demand, shifting the money demand curve leftward.

The money demand curve may also shift in response to other changes that affect the cost or benefit of holding money, such as the technological and financial advances we mentioned earlier. For example, the introduction of ATMs reduced the amount of money people choose to hold and thus shifted the economywide money demand curve to the left. The Economic Naturalist 26.1 describes another potential source of shifts in the demand for money, holdings of U.S. dollars by foreigners.

The Economic Naturalist 26.1

Why does the average Argentine hold more U.S. dollars than the average U.S. citizen?

Estimates are that the value of U.S. dollars circulating in Argentina exceeds $1,000 per person, which is higher than the per capita dollar holdings in the United States. A number of other countries, including those that once belonged to the former Soviet Union, also hold large quantities of dollars. In all, as much as $600 billion in U.S. currency—about one-third of the total amount issued—may be circulating outside the borders of the United States. Why do Argentines and other non-U.S. residents hold so many dollars?

U.S. residents and businesses hold dollars primarily for transactions purposes, rather than as a store of value. As a store of value, interest-bearing bonds and dividend-paying stocks are a better choice for Americans than zero-interest money. But this is not necessarily the case for the citizens of other countries, particularly nations that are economically or politically unstable. Argentina, for example, endured many years of high and erratic inflation in the 1970s and 1980s, which sharply eroded the value of financial investments denominated in Argentine pesos. Lacking better alternatives, many Argentines began saving in the form of U.S. currency—dollar bills hidden in the mattress or plastered into the wall—which they correctly believed to be more stable in value than peso-denominated assets.

▶ Visit your instructor's Connect course and access your eBook to view this video.

Why does the average Argentine citizen hold more U.S. dollars than the average U.S. citizen?

Argentina's use of dollars became officially recognized in 1990. In that year, the country instituted a new monetary system, called a currency board, under which U.S. dollars and Argentine pesos by law traded freely one for one. Under the currency board system, Argentines became accustomed to carrying U.S. dollars in their wallets for transactions purposes, along with pesos. However, in 2001 Argentina's monetary problems returned with a vengeance as the currency board system broke down, the peso plummeted in value relative to the dollar, and inflation returned. In the past few years, inflation in Argentina has been estimated to be between 25 and 55 percent. (For a while, the government's official inflation figures were not considered reliable.) The Argentine demand for dollars is thus likely only to increase in the next few years.

The African nation of Zimbabwe provides another example. After years of hyperinflation and price speculation, the Zimbabwean dollar was effectively abandoned as an official currency on April 12, 2009. This followed a year when the growth in the money supply rose from 81,143 percent to 658 billion percent from January to December, and an egg was reportedly selling for Z$50 billion. On January 29, 2014, the Zimbabwe central bank announced that the U.S. dollar would be one of several foreign currencies that would be accepted as legal currency within that country. (The central bank introduced a new Zimbabwean dollar in 2019.)

Feije Riemersma/Alamy Stock Photo

Some countries, including a number of those formed as a result of the breakup of the Soviet Union, have endured not only high inflation, but political instability and uncertainty as well. In a politically volatile environment, citizens face the risk that their savings, including their bank deposits, will be confiscated or heavily taxed by the government. Often they conclude that a hidden cache of U.S. dollars—an estimated $1 million in 100-dollar bills can be stored in a suitcase—is the safest way to hold wealth. Indeed, such wealth in a relatively small container is one reason international criminals, most notably drug dealers, allegedly hold so many $100 bills. Now that the European currency, the euro (€), which is worth more than $1, can be held in the form of a €500 banknote, it has been suggested that drug dealers and other cash-hoarders have been switching to holding €500 bills in even smaller suitcases. Concerned by this possibility, the European Central Bank announced in 2016 that it would phase out the €500 note and, since April 2019, the note has no longer been issued. This may further increase the demand for dollars.

In practice, changes in the foreign demand for U.S. dollars are an important source of fluctuation in the U.S. money demand curve. During periods of war, instability, or financial stress, foreign holdings of dollars tend to go up. Such increases in the demand for dollars shifts the U.S. money demand curve substantially to the right, as in Figure 26.2. Because policymakers at the Federal Reserve are concerned primarily with the number of dollars circulating in the U.S. economy, rather than in the world as a whole, they pay close attention to these international flows of greenbacks.

THE SUPPLY OF MONEY AND MONEY MARKET EQUILIBRIUM

Where there is demand, can supply be far behind? As we have discussed, for now we assume that the *supply* of money is determined by the supply of reserves, and hence is fully controlled by the central bank—in the United States, the Federal Reserve, or Fed. Historically, the Fed's primary tool for controlling the money supply is *open-market operations*. For example, to increase the money supply, the Fed can use newly created money to buy government bonds from the public (an open-market purchase), which puts the new money into circulation.

Figure 26.3 shows the demand for and the supply of money in a single diagram. The nominal interest rate is on the vertical axis, and the nominal quantity of money (in dollars) is on the horizontal axis. As we have seen, because a higher nominal interest rate increases the opportunity cost of holding money, the money demand curve slopes downward. And because the Fed fixes the supply of money, we have drawn the *money supply curve* as a vertical line that intercepts the horizontal axis at the quantity of money chosen by the Fed, denoted *M*.

As in standard supply and demand analysis, equilibrium in the market for money occurs at the intersection of the supply and demand curves, shown as point *E* in Figure 26.3. The equilibrium amount of money in circulation, *M,* is simply the amount of money the Fed chooses to supply. The equilibrium nominal interest rate *i* is the interest rate at which the quantity of money demanded by the public, as determined by the money demand curve, equals the fixed supply of money made available by the Fed.

To understand how the market for money reaches equilibrium, it may be helpful to recall the relationship between interest rates and the market price of bonds that was introduced in Chapter 23, *Financial Markets and International Capital Flows*. As we saw in the earlier chapter, the prices of existing bonds are *inversely related* to the current interest rate. Higher interest rates imply lower bond prices, and lower interest rates imply higher bond prices. With this relationship between interest rates and bond prices in mind, let's ask what happens if, say, the nominal interest rate is initially below the equilibrium level in the market for money—for example, at a value such as *i′* in Figure 26.3. At that interest rate the public's demand for money is *M′*, which is greater than the actual amount of money in circulation, equal to *M*. How will the public—households and firms—react if the amount of money they hold is less than they would like? To increase their holdings of money, people will try to sell some of the interest-bearing assets they hold, such as bonds. But if everyone is trying to sell bonds and there are no willing buyers, then all the

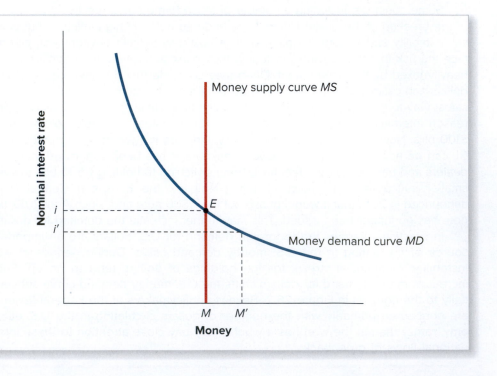

FIGURE 26.3

Equilibrium in the Market for Money.

Equilibrium in the market for money occurs at point *E*, where the demand for money by the public equals the amount of money supplied by the Federal Reserve. The equilibrium nominal interest rate, which equates the supply of and demand for money, is *i*.

attempt to reduce bond holdings will achieve is to drive down the price of bonds, in the same way that a glut of apples will drive down the price of apples.

A fall in the price of bonds, however, is equivalent to an increase in interest rates. Thus the public's collective attempt to increase its money holdings by selling bonds and other interest-bearing assets, which has the effect of lowering bond prices, also implies higher market interest rates. As interest rates rise, the quantity of money demanded by the public will decline (represented by a right-to-left movement along the money demand curve), as will the desire to sell bonds. Only when the interest rate reaches its equilibrium value, i in Figure 26.3, will people be content to hold the quantities of money and other assets that are actually available in the economy.

 SELF-TEST 26.2

Describe the adjustment process in the market for money if the nominal interest rate is initially above rather than below its equilibrium value. What happens to the price of bonds as the money market adjusts toward equilibrium?

RECAP

MONEY DEMAND AND SUPPLY

- For the economy as a whole, the demand for money is the amount of wealth that individuals, households, and businesses choose to hold in the form of money. The opportunity cost of holding money is measured by the nominal interest rate i, which is the return that could be earned on alternative assets such as bonds. The benefit of holding money is its usefulness in transactions.

- Increases in real GDP (Y) or the price level (P) raise the nominal volume of transactions and thus the economywide demand for money. The demand for money is also affected by technological and financial innovations, such as the introduction of ATMs, that affect the costs or benefits of holding money.

- The money demand curve relates the economywide demand for money to the nominal interest rate. Because an increase in the nominal interest rate raises the opportunity cost of holding money, the money demand curve slopes downward.

- Changes in factors other than the nominal interest rate that affect the demand for money can shift the money demand curve. For example, increases in real GDP or the price level raise the demand for money, shifting the money demand curve to the right, whereas decreases shift the money demand curve to the left.

- In the market for money, the money demand curve slopes downward, reflecting the fact that a higher nominal interest rate increases the opportunity cost of holding money and thus reduces the amount of money people want to hold. The money supply curve is vertical at the quantity of money that the Fed chooses to supply. The equilibrium nominal interest rate i is the interest rate at which the quantity of money demanded by the public equals the fixed supply of money made available by the Fed.

HOW THE FED CONTROLS THE NOMINAL INTEREST RATE

We began this chapter by noting that the public and the press usually talk about Fed policy in terms of decisions about the nominal interest rate rather than the money supply. Indeed, Fed policymakers themselves usually describe their plans in terms of a target value

FIGURE 26.4

The Fed Lowers the Nominal Interest Rate.

The Fed can lower the equilibrium nominal interest rate by increasing the supply of money. For the given money demand curve, an increase in the money supply from *M* to *M'* shifts the equilibrium point in the money market from *E* to *F*, lowering the equilibrium nominal interest rate from *i* to *i'*.

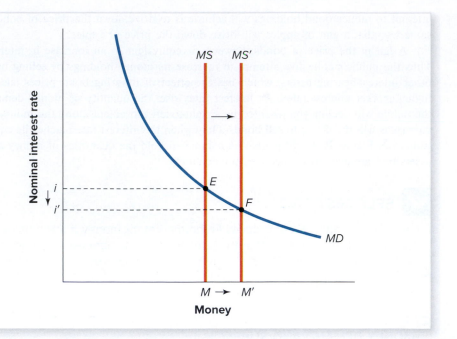

(or a narrow target range) for the interest rate. We now have the necessary background to understand how the Fed translates the ability to determine the economy's money supply into control of the nominal interest rate.

Figure 26.3 showed that the nominal interest rate is determined by equilibrium in the market for money. Let's suppose that for some reason the Fed decides to lower the interest rate. As we will see, to lower the interest rate the Fed must increase the supply of money, which can be accomplished by using newly created money to purchase government bonds from the public (an open-market purchase).

Figure 26.4 shows the effects of such an increase in the money supply by the Fed. If the initial money supply is *M*, then equilibrium in the money market occurs at point *E* in the figure, and the equilibrium nominal interest rate is *i*. Now suppose the Fed, by means of open-market purchases of bonds, increases the money supply to *M'*. This increase in the money supply shifts the vertical money supply curve to the right, which shifts the equilibrium in the money market from point *E* to point *F* (see Figure 26.4). Note that at point *F* the equilibrium nominal interest rate has declined, from *i* to *i'*. The nominal interest rate must decline if the public is to be persuaded to hold the extra money that has been injected into the economy.

To understand what happens in financial markets when the Fed expands the money supply, recall once again the inverse relationship between interest rates and the price of bonds. To increase the money supply, the Fed must buy government bonds from the public. However, if households and firms are initially satisfied with their asset holdings, they will be willing to sell bonds only at a price that is higher than the initial price. That is, the Fed's bond purchases will drive up the price of bonds in the open market. But we know that higher bond prices imply lower interest rates. Thus the Fed's bond purchases lower the prevailing nominal interest rate.

A similar scenario unfolds if the Fed decides to raise interest rates. To raise interest rates, the Fed must *reduce* the money supply. Reduction of the money supply is accomplished by an open-market sale—the sale of government bonds to the public in exchange for money.[3] (The Fed keeps a large inventory of government bonds, acquired through

---

[3]The sale of existing government bonds by the Federal Reserve in an open-market sale should not be confused with the sale of newly issued government bonds by the Treasury when it finances government budget deficits. Whereas open-market sales reduce the money supply, Treasury sales of new bonds do not affect the money supply. The difference arises because the Federal Reserve does not put the money it receives in an open-market sale back into circulation, leaving less money for the public to hold. In contrast, the Treasury puts the money it receives from selling newly issued bonds back into circulation as it purchases goods and services.

previous open-market purchases, for use in open-market operations.) But in the attempt to sell bonds on the open market, the Fed will drive down the price of bonds. Given the inverse relationship between the price of bonds and the interest rate, the fall in bond prices is equivalent to a rise in the interest rate. In terms of money demand and money supply, the higher interest rate is necessary to persuade the public to hold less money.

As Figures 26.3 and 26.4 illustrate, control of the interest rate is not separate from control of the money supply. If Fed officials choose to set the nominal interest rate at a particular level, they can do so only by setting the money supply at a level consistent with the target interest rate. The Fed *cannot* set the interest rate and the money supply independently, since for any given money demand curve, a particular interest rate implies a particular size of the money supply, and vice versa.

Since monetary policy actions can be expressed in terms of either the interest rate or the money supply, why does the Fed (and almost every other central bank) choose to communicate its policy decisions to the public in terms of a target nominal interest rate rather than a target money supply? One reason, as we will see shortly, is that the main effects of monetary policy on both the economy and financial markets are exerted through interest rates. Consequently, the interest rate is often the best summary of the overall impact of the Fed's actions. Another reason for focusing on interest rates is that they are more familiar to the public than the money supply. Finally, interest rates can be monitored continuously in the financial markets, which makes the effects of Fed policies on interest rates easy to observe. By contrast, measuring the amount of money in the economy requires collecting data on bank deposits, with the consequence that several weeks may pass before policymakers and the public know precisely how Fed actions have affected the money supply.

THE ROLE OF THE FEDERAL FUNDS RATE IN MONETARY POLICY

Although thousands of interest rates are used throughout the economy and are easily available, the interest rate that is perhaps most closely watched by the public, politicians, the media, and the financial markets is the *federal funds rate*.

The **federal funds rate** is the interest rate commercial banks charge each other for very short-term (usually overnight) loans. For example, a bank that has insufficient reserves to meet its legal reserve requirements might borrow reserves for a few days from a bank that has extra reserves (we return to the topic of reserve requirements in the next section). Despite its name, the federal funds rate is not an official government interest rate and is not connected to the federal government.

federal funds rate the interest rate that commercial banks charge each other for very short-term (usually overnight) loans

Because the market for loans between commercial banks is tiny compared to some other financial markets, such as the market for government bonds, one might expect the federal funds rate to be of little interest to anyone other than the managers of commercial banks. But enormous attention is paid to this interest rate, because over most of the past half-century, the Fed has expressed its policies in terms of a target value for it (since December 2008, the target is actually a narrow range of values). Indeed, at the close of every meeting of the Federal Open Market Committee, the Fed announces whether the federal funds rate will be increased, decreased, or left unchanged. The Fed may also indicate the likely direction of future changes in the federal funds rate. Thus more than any other financial variable, changes in the federal funds rate indicate the Fed's plans for monetary policy.[4]

Why does the Fed choose to focus on this particular nominal interest rate over all others? As we saw in Chapter 22, *Money, Prices, and the Federal Reserve,* historically, the Fed affected the money supply through its control of bank reserves, which made the Fed's control over the federal funds rate particularly tight. Today, after decades of using this particular interest rate as the Fed's main policy tool, the public has gotten used to it, which is one reason to keep using it. However, if Fed officials chose to do so, they could probably signal their intended policies just as effectively in terms of another short-term nominal interest rate, such as the rate on short-term government debt.

---

[4]The Federal Open Market Committee's announcements are available on the Federal Reserve's website, www. federalreserve.gov.

FIGURE 26.5

The Federal Funds Rate, 1970–2020.

The federal funds rate is the interest rate commercial banks charge each other for short-term loans. It is closely watched because the Fed expresses its policies in terms of a target for the federal funds rate. The Fed has allowed the federal funds rate to vary considerably in response to economic conditions.

Source: Federal Reserve Bank of St. Louis, https://fred.stlouisfed.org/series/FEDFUNDS.

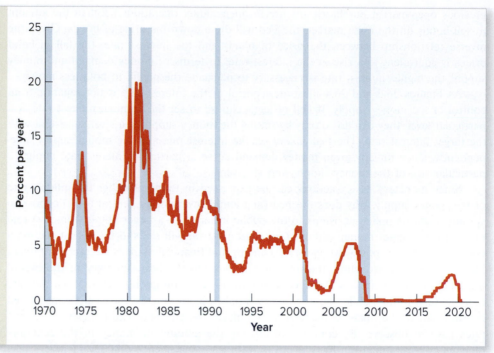

Figure 26.5 shows the behavior of the federal funds rate since 1970 (as usual, shaded areas correspond to recessions). As you can see, the Fed has allowed this interest rate to vary considerably in response to economic conditions. Note, however, how the federal funds rate has remained close to zero since the end of 2008—in fact, it has been effectively *at* zero in most years since. That is, it has remained both considerably lower and more stable than in the preceding four decades shown here. Later in the chapter we will consider two specific episodes in which the Fed changed the federal funds rate in response to an economic slowdown, and we will also discuss the situation since 2008.

CAN THE FED CONTROL THE REAL INTEREST RATE?

Through its control of the money supply the Fed can control the economy's *nominal* interest rate. But many important economic decisions, such as the decisions to save and invest, depend on the *real* interest rate. To affect those decisions, the Fed must exert some control over the real interest rate.

Most economists believe that the Fed can control the real interest rate, at least for some period. To see why, recall the definition of the real interest rate from Chapter 18, *Measuring the Price Level and Inflation*

$$r = i - \pi.$$

The real interest rate r equals the nominal interest rate i minus the rate of inflation π. As we have seen, the Fed can control the nominal interest rate quite precisely through its ability to determine the money supply. Furthermore, inflation appears to change relatively slowly in response to changes in policy or economic conditions, for reasons we will discuss in the next chapter. Because inflation tends to adjust slowly, actions by the Fed to change the nominal interest rate generally lead the real interest rate to change by about the same amount.

The idea that the Fed can set the real interest rate appears to contradict the analysis in Chapter 21, *Saving and Capital Formation*, which concluded that the real interest rate is determined by the condition that national saving must equal investment in new capital goods. This apparent contradiction is rooted in a difference in the time frame being considered. Because inflation does not adjust quickly, the Fed can control the real interest rate over the short run. In the long run, however—that is, over periods of several years or more—the inflation rate and other economic variables will adjust, and the balance of saving and investment will determine the real interest rate. Thus the Fed's ability to influence consumption and investment spending through its control of the real interest rate is strongest in the short run.

In discussing the Fed's control over interest rates, we should also return to a point mentioned earlier in this chapter: In reality, not just one but many thousands of interest rates are seen in the economy. Because interest rates tend to move together (allowing us to speak of *the* interest rate), an action by the Fed to change the federal funds rate generally causes other interest rates to change in the same direction. However, the tendency of other interest rates (such as the long-term government bond rate or the rate on bonds issued by corporations) to move in the same direction as the federal funds rate is only a tendency, not an exact relationship. In practice, then, the Fed's control of other interest rates may be somewhat less precise than its control of the federal funds rate—a fact that complicates the Fed's policymaking. In the next section we will discuss what the Fed has been doing since 2008 to lower those other interest rates through channels other than the traditional channel of lowering the federal funds rate.

> **RECAP**
>
> **THE FEDERAL RESERVE AND INTEREST RATES**
>
> - The Federal Reserve controls the nominal interest rate by changing the supply of money. An open-market purchase of government bonds increases the money supply and lowers the equilibrium nominal interest rate. Conversely, an open-market sale of bonds reduces the money supply and increases the nominal interest rate. The Fed can prevent changes in the demand for money from affecting the nominal interest rate by adjusting the quantity of money supplied appropriately. The Fed typically expresses its policy intentions in terms of a target for a specific nominal interest rate, the federal funds rate.
> - Because inflation is slow to adjust, in the short run the Fed can control the real interest rate (equal to the nominal interest rate minus the inflation rate) as well as the nominal interest rate. In the long run, however, the real interest rate is determined by the balance of saving and investment.

THE FEDERAL RESERVE AND INTEREST RATES: A CLOSER LOOK

To this point in the book, we have discussed the basic market for money and how it works. We have seen how, by controlling the supply of money, the Fed controls the nominal interest rate (the nominal price of money) and hence, in the short run, the real interest rate (the real price of money). To keep the discussion simple, we assumed that the Fed has full control over the money supply, and we assumed that the different interest rates in the economy move more or less together, allowing us to talk about *the* interest rate. In this section we take a closer look at the market for money, and see how it works in times when these assumptions hold less well. As an important example of such times, we discuss the Fed's monetary policy since the 2008 peak of the financial crisis.

CAN THE FED FULLY CONTROL THE MONEY SUPPLY?

We have seen that central banks in general, and the Fed in particular, do not control the money supply directly. But we assumed that central banks can control the money supply *indirectly* by changing the supply of reserves that commercial banks hold. We will now look at this assumption more closely. In Chapter 22, *Money, Prices, and the Federal Reserve,* we introduced Equation 22.2, copied below:

$$\text{Money supply} = \text{Currency held by public} + \frac{\text{Bank reserves}}{\text{Desired reserve-deposit ratio}} \qquad (26.1)$$

The equation shows that given a certain amount of currency that the public wants to hold, and given a certain reserve-deposit ratio that the banks desire to maintain, the central bank can control the money supply by controlling the amount of bank reserves. Let's assume for now that the amount of currency that the public wants to hold and the reserve-deposit ratio that the banks desire to maintain are fixed at their present levels. Then, to increase the money supply, the central bank has to increase bank reserves; to decrease the money supply, the central bank has to decrease bank reserves. Moreover, the equation suggests a simple relationship between any change in reserves and the resulting change in the money supply: for every $1 of change (increase or decrease) in reserves, the money supply would change by $1/(Desired reserve-deposit ratio). For example, if the desired reserve-deposit ratio is 5 percent (that is, 0.05), then an increase in reserves by $1 (initiated by the central bank) would increase the money supply by $1/0.05 = $20.

The Fed can increase and decrease reserves using different methods, as we will now discuss. We will also see that the Fed can directly affect the desired reserve-deposit ratio.

Affecting Bank Reserves through Open-Market Operations

How can the Fed increase and decrease bank reserves? So far we have emphasized its main tool, open-market operations. In an open-market purchase, the Fed buys securities and, effectively, sells reserves. In an open-market sale, the Fed sells securities and, effectively, buys back reserves. Hence, as we have seen, the Fed can change the quantity of reserves in the banking system through open-market operations.

Affecting Bank Reserves through Discount Window Lending

Another tool by which the Fed can affect bank reserves is called *discount window lending.* Recall that the cash or assets held by a commercial bank for the purpose of meeting depositor withdrawals are called its reserves. Its desired amount of reserves is equal to its deposits multiplied by the desired reserve-ratio (as implied by Equation 22.1 in Chapter 22). When individual commercial banks are short of reserves, they may choose to borrow reserves from the Fed. For historical reasons, lending of reserves by the Federal Reserve to commercial banks is called **discount window lending.** The interest rate that the Fed charges commercial banks that borrow reserves is called the **discount rate.** The Fed offers three discount window programs (called primary credit, secondary credit, and seasonal credit), each with its own interest rate; different depository institutions qualify for different programs. Loans of reserves by the Fed directly increase the quantity of reserves in the banking system.[5]

discount window lending the lending of reserves by the Federal Reserve to commercial banks

discount rate the interest rate that the Fed charges commercial banks to borrow reserves

Setting and Changing Reserve Requirements

As we have shown, the economy's money supply depends on three factors: the amount of currency the public chooses to hold, the supply of bank reserves, and the reserve-deposit ratio maintained by commercial banks. The reserve-deposit ratio is equal to total bank reserves divided by total deposits. If banks kept all of their deposits as reserves, the reserve-deposit ratio would be 100 percent (that is, 1.00), and banks would not make any loans. As banks lend out more of their deposits, the reserve-deposit ratio falls.

For given quantities of currency held by the public and of reserves held by the banks, an increase in the reserve-deposit ratio reduces the money supply. A higher reserve-deposit ratio implies that banks lend out a smaller share of their deposits in each of the rounds of lending and redeposit, limiting the overall expansion of loans and deposits.

[5]Be careful not to confuse the discount rate and the federal funds rate. The discount rate is the interest rate commercial banks pay to the Fed; the federal funds rate is the interest rate commercial banks charge each other for short-term loans.

Within a certain range, commercial banks are free to set the reserve-deposit ratio they want to maintain. However, Congress granted the Fed the power to set minimum values of the reserve-deposit ratio for commercial banks. The legally required values of the reserve-deposit ratio set by the Fed are called **reserve requirements.**

Changes in reserve requirements can be used to affect the money supply, although the Fed does not usually use them in this way. For example, suppose that commercial banks are maintaining the legally mandated minimum of 3 percent reserve-deposit ratio, and the Fed wants to contract the money supply. By raising required reserves to, say, 5 percent of deposits, the Fed could force commercial banks to raise their reserve-deposit ratio, at least until it reached 5 percent. As you can verify by looking at Equation 26.1, an increase in the reserve-deposit ratio lowers deposits and the money supply. Similarly, a reduction in required reserves by the Fed might allow at least some banks to lower their ratio of reserves to deposits. A decline in the economywide reserve-deposit ratio would in turn cause the money supply to rise.

Excess Reserves: The Norm since 2008

We have seen that the Fed can effectively control bank reserves through tools that include open-market operations and discount window lending. We have also seen that the Fed can set reserve requirements. This, however, gives the Fed only partial control over the desired reserve-deposit ratio, leaving some control in the hands of commercial banks. Specifically, while reserve requirements prevent banks from maintaining reserve-deposit ratios *below* a minimum level, reserve requirements do not prevent banks from maintaining reserve-deposit ratios that are well *above* that minimum level. By letting their reserve-deposit ratios increase when the Fed increases the quantity of reserves, commercial banks can "absorb" at least part of the increases in reserves without increasing bank deposits. Indeed, commercial banks could, in principle, absorb the entire increase in reserves initiated by the Fed, fully offsetting the effects of increases in reserves on the noncurrency component of the money supply.[6]

Up to this point, we assumed that banks would always translate an addition in reserves initiated by the Fed into an addition in their deposits (rather than into an increase in their reserve-deposit ratios). This is a reasonable assumption; banks generally do behave this way. But there are situations when banks prefer to let their reserve-deposit ratios (and excess reserves) increase in response to an increase in reserves. For example, to protect themselves from bank runs in times of economic or financial uncertainty, banks may prefer to respond to an increase in reserves by letting their reserve-deposit ratios increase to levels significantly above the minimum level mandated by official reserve requirements. Another reason for banks to let increases in reserves increase their reserve-deposit ratio rather than increasing deposits in times of uncertainty is that in such times banks may find only limited lending opportunities that seem sufficiently safe.

Bank reserves that exceed the reserve requirements set by the central bank are called **excess reserves.** Excess reserves are thus reserves that the central bank makes available to commercial banks, but that do not add to the money supply because commercial banks do not use them for making additional loans. Because excess reserves do not add to the money supply, they allow for the possibility that the money supply will not change in spite of the central bank increasing or decreasing the supply of reserves.

During the 20 years that ended in August 2008, excess reserves in the U.S. banking system averaged less than $2 billion on most months—a negligible amount, considering the size of the U.S. banking system. The only notable exception was a short period in 2001, immediately following the events of 9/11, during which excess reserves increased temporarily

reserve requirements set by the Fed, the minimum values of the ratio of bank reserves to bank deposits that commercial banks are allowed to maintain

excess reserves bank reserves in excess of the reserve requirements set by the central bank

[6]You can verify this by looking again at the second term of Equation 26.1. This second term represents the noncurrency component of the money supply. While the Fed controls its numerator (bank reserves), it only partially controls its denominator (desired reserve-deposit ratio) because the Fed can set only a legally binding *minimum,* but not a maximum, on the denominator. Indeed, banks can choose to let the denominator increase when the Fed increases the numerator, breaking the simple link from increased reserves to increased money supply. Banks could in principle even let the denominator increase at the same pace as the numerator, keeping the second term of Equation 26.1 constant, and thus preventing the increase in reserves from having any effect on the money supply.

as the financial industry was reeling from the effects of the terrorist attack on New York City. Since August 2008, however, things have changed dramatically. As the Fed injected unprecedented amounts of reserves into the system in its attempt to bring interest rates down, excess reserves grew to around $800 billion by the end of the year, and kept growing in the following years until they peaked in 2014 at more than $2.5 trillion, or almost 15 percent of GDP (for comparison, in 2014 the monetary aggregate M1 was about 16 percent of GDP). Excess reserves decreased in subsequent years, reaching around $1.3 trillion by late 2019–still a hefty sum. In early 2020, excess reserves shot up again, as the Fed injected large amounts of reserves into the system in its fight against the COVID-19 economic fallout.

The Fed's actions in 2008 and subsequent years were successful in reducing the price of money and increasing its supply, helping prevent another Great Depression (The Economic Naturalist 22.2 discussed the shrinking of the money supply during the Great Depression). As you can verify from Equation 26.1, for the money supply to increase as a result of the Fed-initiated increase in the quantity of reserves, the reserve-deposit ratio had to increase more slowly than the increase in the quantity of reserves. Indeed, while since 2008 banks absorbed much of the increase in reserves initiated by the Fed, they did not absorb it all, and some of it led to increases in the money supply.

We have seen, then, that the Fed does not always fully control the money supply. But even in times of great uncertainty, the Fed can still strongly *affect* the money supply through the Fed's control of the supply of reserves. The basic money-market model's assumption–that the Fed controls the money supply–should therefore be viewed as a useful simplifying assumption even in times when it does not hold exactly.

We now take a closer look at the other simplifying assumption made in the basic money-market model: that interest rates move together.

RECAP ↑

CAN THE FED FULLY CONTROL THE MONEY SUPPLY?

- The Fed can effectively control the amount of bank reserves through tools that include open-market operations and discount window lending. The Fed can also set reserve requirements (a legally binding minimum on banks' reserve-deposit ratio). This however gives the Fed only partial control over the money supply. In particular, a Fed-initiated increase in bank reserves will not lead to an increase in the money supply if banks absorbed the increase in reserves by letting their reserve-deposit ratios increase at the same pace.
- In certain times banks may choose to let their reserve-deposit ratio increase substantially above the reserve requirements set by the Fed. Indeed, since 2008, banks have accumulated unprecedented amounts of excess reserves, that is, of reserves in excess of reserve requirements. While this broke the simple link between an increase in reserves and an increase in the money supply, the Fed was still successful in increasing the money supply.
- We conclude that the basic money-market model's assumption—that the Fed controls the money supply—should be viewed as a useful simplifying assumption even in times when it does not hold exactly.

DO INTEREST RATES ALWAYS MOVE TOGETHER?

To this point in the discussion, we have assumed that the many different nominal interest rates in the economy move more or less together, allowing us to speak of *the* interest rate. Like the assumption that banks do not hold significant amounts of excess reserves, the assumption that interest rates move more or less together is a reasonably accurate description of the market for money during most times, but not always. In particular, this assumption has held less well since 2008.

The Zero Lower Bound and the Need for "Unconventional" Monetary Policy

Earlier in this chapter, we presented Figure 26.5, which shows the federal funds rate from 1970 to 2020. Until December 2008, the Fed's main tool for conducting monetary policy was open-market operations aimed at increasing and decreasing the federal funds rate in accordance with the Fed's target rate. Other interest rates in the economy, which are typically higher than the federal funds rate due to a combination of higher risk and longer maturity, were expected to move up and down more or less together with the federal funds rate. But in December 2008 the Fed reduced its target for the federal funds rate to the range 0 to $\frac{1}{4}$ percent, effectively hitting what is called the **zero lower bound.** Attempting to stimulate the economy by reducing the federal funds rate further was no longer a viable option, because interest rates cannot in general be much below zero. (A negative nominal interest rate would mean that lending institutions pay borrowing institutions to hold their money—something lending institutions would not normally do.)

zero lower bound a level, close to zero, below which the Fed cannot further reduce short-term interest rates

The federal funds rate remained effectively zero in the years following December 2008 (Figure 26.5). But other interest rates in the economy remained significantly above zero during that period. For example, the nominal interest rate on 10-year debt issued by the U.S. government was in the range 1.5 to 4 percent between 2009 and 2015. After December 2008, the Fed could no longer effectively reduce the different interest rates in the economy that were still above zero by reducing the federal funds rate (which was already at its zero lower bound) and "pulling" other rates down with it. To keep stimulating the economy by making money cheaper, the Fed had to turn to less conventional methods: targeting such higher interest rates more directly. We now discuss some of these new methods the Fed used.

Quantitative Easing

You are already familiar with one way for making money more cheaply available: open-market operations. Following the financial crisis, the Fed engaged in a specific type of such operations, referred to as *large-scale asset purchase programs* (LSAPs). These programs, aimed to help in bringing down longer-term interest rates once the federal funds rate was already at (or close to) its zero lower bound, are examples of what is known as *quantitative easing*. **Quantitative easing (QE)** refers to a central bank buying specified amounts of financial assets from commercial banks and other private financial institutions, thereby lowering the yield or return of those assets while increasing the money supply. Quantitative easing basically includes the same steps as regular open-market purchases, but is distinguished from these regular purchases in the type and term of the financial assets purchased as well as in the overall goal of the policy. While conventional expansionary policy usually involves the purchase of short-term government bonds in order to keep interest rates at a specified target value, quantitative easing is used by central banks to stimulate the economy by purchasing assets of longer maturity, thereby lowering longer-term interest rates.

quantitative easing (QE) an expansionary monetary policy in which a central bank buys long-term financial assets, thereby lowering the yield or return of those assets while increasing the money supply

Since the peak of the financial crisis in 2008, the Federal Reserve has expanded its balance sheet dramatically, adding trillions of dollars' worth of longer-term treasury notes and mortgage-backed securities (MBS) through several rounds of quantitative easing. Under special emergency conditions, when credit markets are not working properly, the Fed's purchases have also included private debt and securities, as was the case when the Fed announced programs to lend to businesses during the coronavirus crisis of 2020.

In short, by purchasing *longer-term* assets (including bonds and other debt) the Fed increased the amount of bank reserves while exerting downward pressure on longer-term interest rates (recall that bond prices and interest rates are inversely related). And by purchasing specific *types* of assets—such as debt related to mortgages—the Fed could help decrease interest rates in specific markets—such as mortgage and housing markets that were hit particularly hard during the financial crisis.

Forward Guidance

Quantitative easing helps lower long-term interest rates in the economy through open-market purchases. Another means for lowering long-term rates is known as **forward guidance.** The idea behind it is simple: by guiding markets regarding the central bank's future intentions,

forward guidance information that a central bank provides to the financial markets regarding its expected future monetary-policy path

the central bank can influence long-term interest rates because these rates are affected by what market participants believe the central bank will do in the future. To illustrate this, imagine that financial markets believe that short-term interest rates, currently at around zero, will remain close to zero for several more years. Then the market price of a three-year bond, for example, will be such that the implied interest rate (or yield, or return) on the bond is close to zero. But if financial markets believed that short-term interest rates, while currently at zero, were about to increase dramatically in the next few months and stay elevated for several years, then a three-year bond's current price would reflect these beliefs, and hence the implied interest rate on the bond would be much higher.

In its September 2015 meeting, for example, the Federal Open Market Committee (FOMC) decided to keep the federal funds rate at its 0 to $\frac{1}{4}$ percent target range—that is, effectively at its zero lower bound. The FOMC's statement following the meeting included sentences such as this: "The Committee currently anticipates that, . . . economic conditions may, for some time, warrant keeping the target federal funds rate below levels the Committee views as normal in the longer run." On the Fed's website, it was further explained how such forward guidance is expected to support economic recovery:[7]

> Through "forward guidance," the Federal Open Market Committee provides an indication to households, businesses, and investors about the stance of monetary policy expected to prevail in the future. By providing information about how long the Committee expects to keep the target for the federal funds rate exceptionally low, the forward guidance language can put downward pressure on longer-term interest rates and thereby lower the cost of credit for households and businesses and also help improve broader financial conditions.

The Fed returned to forward guidance in 2020, as part of its response to the COVID-19 pandemic. In its March 15, 2020 meeting statement, the FOMC announced that the federal funds rate was again cut to a 0-to-¼ percent target range. The statement then read: "The Committee expects to maintain this target range until it is confident that the economy has weathered recent events and is on-track to achieve its maximum employment and price stability goals." Six months later, in its September 16, 2020 statement, the FOMC extended its forward guidance still further into the future, citing more stringent conditions before it would raise its target range: "The Committee decided to keep the target range for the federal funds rate at 0-to-¼ percent and expects it will be appropriate to maintain this target range until labor market conditions have reach levels consistent with the Committee's assessments of maximum employment and inflation has risen to 2 percent and is on track to moderately exceed 2 percent for some time."

Interest on Reserves and the New Tools of Monetary Policy

We have seen that starting in 2008 and continuing in the following years, the Fed took unprecedented steps to support the economy and help it recover from a historically deep global recession. The close-to-zero federal funds rate, the several rounds of quantitative easing (or large-scale asset purchases) and the resulting massive amounts of excess reserves, and other policies such as forward guidance were an unusual combination, designed for unusual times. At the time, these policies were viewed as temporary, unconventional methods for addressing temporary, unusual problems. As time passed, however, the reality of low interest rates and large amounts of assets held by the Fed has been increasingly recognized as "a new normal"—a situation that is here to stay. Accordingly, many economists have changed their view of these methods, thinking of them less as "unconventional" and more simply as new tools of monetary policy.

In late 2015—after more than seven years with the federal funds rate at the zero lower bound (see Figure 26.5), and with around four times the amount of assets that the Fed held seven years earlier—the Fed concluded that it was time to start raising interest rates again, slowly and cautiously, as the recovery from the Great Recession was well under way.

[7]"How Does Forward Guidance about the Federal Reserve's Target for the Federal Funds Rate Support the Economic Recovery?," updated September 17, 2015, www.federalreserve.gov/monetarypolicy/fomcminutes 20150917.htm.

To raise the federal funds rate without first engaging in a large-scale asset sale, the Fed's main channel has been to increase the interest rate it pays banks on the reserves they hold with the Fed. These include banks' required reserves (reserves held with the Fed in order to meet the required reserve-deposit ratios) and banks' excess reserves. The Fed paid an interest rate of $\frac{1}{4}$ percent on required and excess reserve balances between 2008 and 2015. When the Fed started raising this interest rate in December 2015, the federal funds rate started rising with it, because banks have little incentive to lend their excess reserves to other banks at rates below the rate they get on these reserves from the Fed.[8]

Figure 26.5 shows that after several years of slow increases, the federal funds rate reached rates just above 2.25 percent in 2019. Then, in light of increasing uncertainties in the global economy during 2019, the Fed reversed its trend, and by year-end it had reduced the rate to below 1.75 percent. When COVID-19 hit the U.S. economy in early 2020, the Fed quickly cut the rate to close to zero. With the federal funds rate at its zero lower bound again, the Fed's new tools of monetary policy were again taking center stage—at an unprecedented scale and pace. As discussed above, in March 2020 the Fed announced new quantitative easing rounds and several new lending programs that were expected to increase its balance sheet by several trillion dollars. It also emphasized forward guidance.

As we discussed in the previous section, such movements in nominal interest rates translate, in the short run, to movements in real interest rates. We now turn to discuss how movements in real interest rates affect the economy. As in the rest of the book, we return to our simplifying assumption that the different interest rates in the economy move more or less together, as the basic money-market model assumes.

RECAP ↑

DO INTEREST RATES ALWAYS MOVE TOGETHER?

- The zero lower bound is a level, close to zero, below which the Fed cannot further reduce short-term interest rates. After December 2008, the Fed could no longer reduce the different interest rates in the economy that were still above zero by reducing the federal funds rate, because the federal funds rate had reached its zero lower bound.

- To keep stimulating the economy after December 2008, the Fed had to turn to less conventional methods that are aimed at lowering higher interest rates more directly. These included quantitative easing (formally, large-scale asset purchase programs) and forward guidance.

- The federal funds rate remained effectively zero from 2008 to 2015. When the Fed concluded, in late 2015, that the time to start tightening monetary policy has come, the Fed started increasing the interest rate it pays banks on the reserves they hold with the Fed. These include banks' required reserves (reserves held with the Fed in order to meet the required reserve-deposit ratios) and banks' excess reserves. That is, the Fed's main policy tool from late 2015 to early 2020 was again moving the federal funds rate, a short-term interest rate.

- As the COVID-19 pandemic hit the U.S. economy, the Fed reacted promptly and decisively. In March 2020 the Fed quickly reduced both short-term interest rates (to the zero lower bound) and long-term interest rates (using its new tools such as quantitative easing and forward guidance). It also greatly expanded its lending facilities, and provided credit easing in several markets.

---

[8]The federal funds rate can be somewhat below the interest rate that the Fed pays on reserves because some nonbank financial institutions are not eligible to earn interest on the balances they keep with the Fed and, therefore, have incentives to lend reserves at rates below the Fed's interest rate on reserves. However, as banks can profit by borrowing from such institutions and then receiving interest from the Fed on the borrowed reserves, the price of these reserves—the federal funds rate—is bid up until it is closely below the Fed's interest rate on reserves. In addition, the Fed can offer to borrow directly from such institutions (through an arrangement called a reverse repurchase agreement), reducing their incentives to lend out reserves at rates below the rates offered by the Fed.

THE EFFECTS OF FEDERAL RESERVE ACTIONS ON THE ECONOMY

Now that we have seen how the Fed can influence interest rates (both nominal and real), we can consider how monetary policy can be used to eliminate output gaps and stabilize the economy. The basic idea is relatively straightforward. As we will see in this section, planned aggregate expenditure is affected by the level of real interest rate prevailing in the economy. Specifically, a lower real interest rate encourages higher planned spending by households and firms, while a higher real interest rate reduces spending. By adjusting the real interest rate, the Fed can move planned spending in the desired direction. Under the assumption of the basic Keynesian model that firms produce just enough goods and services to meet the demand for their output, the Fed's stabilization of planned spending leads to stabilization of aggregate output and employment as well. In this section we will first explain how planned aggregate expenditure is related to the real interest rate. Then we will show how the Fed can use changes in the real interest rate to fight a recession or inflation.

PLANNED AGGREGATE EXPENDITURE AND THE REAL INTEREST RATE

In Chapter 25, *Spending and Output in the Short Run,* we saw how planned spending is affected by changes in real output Y. Changes in output affect the private sector's disposable income $(Y - T)$, which in turn influences consumption spending—a relationship captured by the consumption function.

A second variable that has potentially important effects on aggregate expenditure is the real interest rate r. In Chapter 23, *Financial Markets and International Capital Flows,* in our discussion of saving and investment, we saw that the real interest rate influences the behavior of both households and firms.

For households, the effect of a higher real interest rate is to increase the reward for saving, which leads households to save more.[9] At a given level of income, households can save more only if they consume less. Thus, saying that a higher real interest rate *increases* saving is the same as saying that a higher real interest rate *reduces* consumption spending at each level of income. The idea that higher real interest rates reduce household spending makes intuitive sense. Think, for example, about people's willingness to buy consumer durables, such as automobiles or furniture. Purchases of consumer durables, which are part of consumption spending, are often financed by borrowing from a bank, credit union, or finance company. When the real interest rate rises, the monthly finance charges associated with the purchase of a car or a piano are higher, and people become less willing or able to make the purchase. Thus a higher real interest rate reduces people's willingness to spend on consumer goods, holding constant disposable income and other factors that affect consumption.

When the real interest rate rises, financing a new car becomes more expensive and fewer cars are purchased.

Besides reducing consumption spending, a higher real interest rate also discourages firms from making capital investments. As in the case of a consumer thinking of buying a car or a piano, when a rise in the real interest rate increases financing costs, firms may reconsider their plans to invest. For example, upgrading a computer system may be profitable for a manufacturing firm when the cost of the system can be financed by borrowing at a real interest rate of 3 percent. However, if the real interest rate rises to 6 percent, doubling the cost of funds to the firm, the same upgrade may not be profitable and the firm may choose not to invest. We should also remember that residential investment—the building of houses and apartment buildings—is also part of investment spending. Higher interest rates, in the form of higher mortgage rates, certainly discourage this kind of investment spending as well.

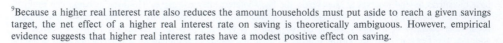

[9]Because a higher real interest rate also reduces the amount households must put aside to reach a given savings target, the net effect of a higher real interest rate on saving is theoretically ambiguous. However, empirical evidence suggests that higher real interest rates have a modest positive effect on saving.

The conclusion is that, at any given level of output, *both consumption spending and planned investment spending decline when the real interest rate increases.* Conversely, a fall in the real interest rate tends to stimulate consumption and investment spending by reducing financing costs. Example 26.3 is a numerical illustration of how planned aggregate expenditure can be related to the real interest rate and output.

EXAMPLE 26.3　Planned Aggregate Expenditure and the Real Interest Rate

How does the interest rate affect planned aggregate expenditure?

In a certain economy, the components of planned spending are given by

$$C = 640 + 0.8(Y - T) - 400r,$$
$$I^P = 250 - 600r,$$
$$G = 300,$$
$$NX = 20,$$
$$T = 250.$$

Find the relationship of planned aggregate expenditure to the real interest rate r and output Y in this economy. Find autonomous expenditure and induced expenditure.

This example is similar to Example 25.2, except that now the real interest rate r is allowed to affect both consumption and planned investment. For example, the final term in the equation describing consumption, $-400r$, implies that a 1 percent (0.01) increase in the real interest rate, from 4 percent to 5 percent, for example, reduces consumption spending by $400(0.01) = 4$ units. Similarly, the final term in the equation for planned investment tells us that in this example, a 1 percent increase in the real interest rate lowers planned investment by $600(0.01) = 6$ units. Thus the overall effect of a 1 percent increase in the real interest rate is to lower planned aggregate expenditure by 10 units, the sum of the effects on consumption and investment. As in the earlier examples, disposable income $(Y - T)$ is assumed to affect consumption spending through a marginal propensity to consume of 0.8 (see the first equation), and government purchases G, net exports NX, and taxes T are assumed to be fixed numbers.

To find a numerical equation that describes the relationship of planned aggregate expenditure (*PAE*) to output, we can begin as in Chapter 25, *Spending and Output in the Short Run,* with the general definition of planned aggregate expenditure

$$PAE = C + I^P + G + NX.$$

Substituting for the four components of expenditure, using the equations describing each type of spending, we get

$$PAE = [640 + 0.8(Y - 250) - 400r] + [250 - 600r] + 300 + 20.$$

The first term in brackets on the right side of this equation is the expression for consumption, using the fact that taxes $T = 250$; the second bracketed term is planned investment; and the last two terms correspond to the given numerical values of government purchases and net exports. If we simplify this equation and group together the terms that do not depend on output Y and the terms that do depend on output, we get

$$PAE = [(640 - 0.8 \times 250 - 400r) + (250 - 600r) + 300 + 20] + 0.8Y,$$

or, simplifying further,

$$PAE = [1{,}010 - 1{,}000r] + 0.8Y. \qquad (26.2)$$

In Equation 26.1, the term in brackets is *autonomous expenditure,* the portion of planned aggregate expenditure that does not depend on output. *Notice that in this example autonomous expenditure depends on the real interest rate r.* Induced expenditure, the portion of planned aggregate expenditure that does depend on output, equals $0.8Y$ in this example.

EXAMPLE 26.4   The Real Interest Rate and Short-Run Equilibrium Output

How does the interest rate affect short-run equilibrium output?

In the economy described in Example 26.3, the real interest rate r is set by the Fed to equal 0.05 (5 percent). Find short-run equilibrium output.

We found in Example 26.3 that, in this economy, planned aggregate expenditure is given by Equation 26.2. We are given that the Fed sets the real interest rate at 5 percent. Setting $r = 0.05$ in Equation 26.2 gives

$$PAE = [1{,}010 - 1{,}000 \times (0.05)] + 0.8Y.$$

Simplifying, we get

$$PAE = 960 + 0.8Y.$$

So, when the real interest rate is 5 percent, autonomous expenditure is 960 and induced expenditure is $0.8Y$. Short-run equilibrium output is the level of output that equals planned aggregate spending. To find short-run equilibrium output, we could now apply the tabular method used in Chapter 25, *Spending and Output in the Short Run,* comparing alternative values of output with the planned aggregate expenditure at that level of output. Short-run equilibrium output would be determined as the value of output such that output just equals spending, or

$$Y = PAE.$$

However, conveniently, when we compare this example with Example 25.2 in the previous chapter, we see that the equation for planned aggregate expenditure, $PAE + 960 + 0.8Y$, is identical to what we found there. Thus Table 25.1, which we used to solve Example 25.2, applies to this example as well, and we get the same answer for short-run equilibrium output, which is $Y = 4{,}800$.

Short-run equilibrium output can also be found graphically, using the Keynesian cross diagram from Chapter 25. Again, since the equation for planned aggregate output is the same as in Example 25.2, Figure 25.3 applies equally well here.

 SELF-TEST 26.3

For the economy described in Example 26.4, suppose the Fed sets the real interest rate at 3 percent rather than at 5 percent. Find short-run equilibrium output. (*Hint:* Consider values between 4,500 and 5,500.)

THE FED FIGHTS A RECESSION

We have seen that the Fed can control the real interest rate, and that the real interest rate in turn affects planned spending and short-run equilibrium output.

$$\downarrow r \Rightarrow \uparrow \text{ planned } C \text{ and planned } I \Rightarrow \uparrow PAE \Rightarrow \text{(via the multiplier) } \uparrow Y.$$

A decrease in the real interest rate causes increases in both planned consumption and planned investment, which lead to an increase in planned spending. The increase in planned spending leads, through the multiplier, to an increase in short-run equilibrium output. Similarly,

$$\uparrow r \Rightarrow \downarrow \text{ planned } C \text{ and planned } I \Rightarrow \downarrow PAE \Rightarrow \text{(via the multiplier) } \downarrow Y.$$

That is, an increase in the real interest rate causes decreases in both planned consumption and planned investment, which lead to a decrease in planned spending. The decrease in planned spending leads, through the multiplier, to a decrease in short-run equilibrium output.

These two relationships are the key to understanding how monetary policy affects short-run economic activity. Let's first analyze how monetary policy can be used to fight a recession; then we will turn to how the Fed can fight inflation.

Suppose the economy faces a recessionary gap—a situation in which real output is below potential output, and spending is "too low." To fight a recessionary gap, the Fed should reduce the real interest rate, stimulating consumption and investment spending. According to the theory we have developed, this increase in planned spending will cause output to rise, restoring the economy to full employment. Example 26.5 illustrates this point by extending Example 26.4.

EXAMPLE 26.5   The Fed Fights a Recession

How can monetary policy eliminate a recessionary gap?

For the economy described in Example 26.4, suppose potential output Y^* equals 5,000. As before, the Fed has set the real interest rate equal to 5 percent. At that real interest rate, what is the output gap? What should the Fed do to eliminate the output gap and restore full employment? You are given that the multiplier in this economy is 5.

In Example 26.4, we showed that with the real interest rate at 5 percent, short-run equilibrium output for this economy is 4,800. We are now given that potential output is 5,000, so the output gap $(Y - Y^*)$ equals $5,000 - 4,800 = 200$. Because actual output is below potential, this economy faces a recessionary gap.

To fight the recession, the Fed should lower the real interest rate, raising aggregate expenditure until output reaches 5,000, the full-employment level. That is, the Fed's objective is to increase short-run equilibrium spending and output by 200. Because the multiplier equals 5, to increase output by 200 the Fed must increase autonomous expenditure by $200/5 = 40$ units. By how much should the Fed reduce the real interest rate to increase autonomous expenditure by 40 units? Autonomous expenditure in this economy is $[1,010 - 1,000r]$, as you can see from Equation 26.2, so that each percentage point reduction in r increases autonomous expenditure by $1,000 \times (0.01) = 10$ units. To increase autonomous expenditure by 40, then, the Fed should lower the real interest rate by 4 percentage points, from 5 percent to 1 percent.

In summary, to eliminate the recessionary gap of 200, the Fed should lower the real interest rate from 5 percent to 1 percent. Notice that the Fed's decrease in the real interest rate increases short-run equilibrium output, as economic logic suggests.

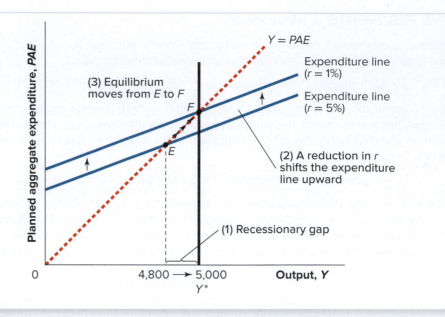

FIGURE 26.6

The Fed Fights a Recession.

(1) The economy is initially at point E, with a recessionary gap of 200; (2) the Fed reduces the real interest rate from 5 percent to 1 percent, shifting the expenditure line up; (3) the new equilibrium is at point F, where output equals potential output. The output gap has been eliminated.

The Fed's recession-fighting policy is shown graphically in Figure 26.6. The reduction in the real interest rate raises planned spending at each level of output, shifting the expenditure line upward. When the real interest rate equals 1 percent, the expenditure line intersects the $Y = PAE$ line at $Y = 5,000$, so that output and potential output are equal. A reduction in interest rates by the Fed, made with the intention of reducing a recessionary gap in this way, is an example of an *expansionary* monetary policy—or, less formally, a *monetary easing*.

 SELF-TEST 26.4

Suppose that in Example 26.5, potential output is 4,850 rather than 5,000. By how much should the Fed cut the real interest rate to restore full employment? You may take as given that the multiplier is 5.

The Economic Naturalist 26.2

How did the Fed respond to recession and the terrorist attacks in 2001?

The U.S. economy began slowing in the fall of 2000, with investment in high-tech equipment falling particularly sharply. According to the National Bureau of Economic Research, a recession began in March 2001. To make matters worse, on September 11, 2001, terrorist attacks on New York City and Washington shocked the nation and led to serious problems in the travel and financial industries, among others. How did the Federal Reserve react to these events?

The Fed first began to respond to growing evidence of an economic slowdown at the end of the year 2000. At the time, the federal funds rate stood at about 6.5 percent (see Figure 26.5). The Fed's most dramatic move was a surprise cut of 0.5 percentage point in the funds rate in January 2001, between regularly scheduled meetings of the Federal Open Market Committee. Further rate cuts followed, and by July the funds rate was below 4 percent. By summer's end, however, there was still considerable uncertainty about the likely severity of the economic slowdown.

The picture changed suddenly on September 11, 2001, when the terrorist attacks on the World Trade Center and the Pentagon killed more than 3,000 people.

The terrorist attacks imposed great economic as well as human costs. The physical damage in lower Manhattan was in the billions of dollars, and many offices and businesses in the area had to close. The Fed, in its role as supervisor of the financial system, worked hard to assist in the restoration of normal operations in the financial district of New York City. (The Federal Reserve Bank of New York, which actually conducts open-market operations, is only a block from the site of the World Trade Center.) The Fed also tried to ease financial conditions by temporarily lowering the federal funds rate to as low as 1.25 percent in the week following the attack.

In the weeks and months following September 11, the Fed turned its attention from the direct impact of the attack to the possible indirect effects on the U.S. economy. The Fed was worried that consumers, nervous about the future, would severely cut back their spending; together with the ongoing weakness in investment, a fall in consumption spending could sharply worsen the recession. To stimulate spending, the Fed continued to cut the federal funds rate. By January 2002, the funds rate was at 1.75 percent, nearly 5 percentage points lower than a year earlier. The Fed kept the interest rate at that low level until November 2002, when it lowered the federal funds rate another 0.5 percentage point, to 1.25 percent. Although the recession officially ended in late 2001, the recovery remained quite weak. Unemployment kept increasing, until it peaked at 6.3 percent in June 2003. That month, the Fed further lowered the federal funds rate to 1 percent, keeping it at that record low until June 2004.

A variety of factors helped the economy recover from the 2001 recession, including expansionary fiscal policy (see The Economic Naturalist 25.5). Most economists agree that expansionary actions by the Fed also played a constructive role in reducing the economic impact of the recession and the September 11 attacks.

THE FED FIGHTS INFLATION

To this point, we have focused on the problem of stabilizing output, without considering inflation. In the next chapter, we will see how ongoing inflation can be incorporated into our analysis. For now, we will simply note that one important cause of inflation is an expansionary output gap—a situation in which spending, and hence actual output, exceeds potential output. When an expansionary gap exists, firms find that the demand for their output exceeds their normal rate of production. Although firms may be content to meet this excess demand at previously determined prices for some time, if the high demand persists, they will ultimately raise their prices, spurring inflation.

Because an expansionary gap tends to lead to inflation, the Fed moves to eliminate expansionary gaps as well as recessionary gaps. The procedure for getting rid of an expansionary gap—a situation in which output is "too high" relative to potential output—is the reverse of that for fighting a recessionary gap, a situation in which output is "too low." As we have seen, the cure for a recessionary gap is to reduce the real interest rate, an action that stimulates spending and increases output. The cure for an expansionary gap is to *raise* the real interest rate, which reduces consumption and investment by raising the cost of borrowing. The resulting fall in spending leads in turn to a decline in output and to a reduction in inflationary pressures.

EXAMPLE 26.6	**The Fed Fights Inflation**

How can monetary policy eliminate an expansionary gap?

For the economy studied in Examples 26.4 and 26.5, assume that potential output is 4,600 rather than 5,000. At the initial real interest rate of 5 percent, short-run equilibrium output is 4,800, so this economy has an expansionary gap of 200. How should the Fed change the real interest rate to eliminate this gap?

In Example 26.5, we were told that multiplier in this economy is 5. Hence, to reduce total output by 200, the Fed needs to reduce autonomous expenditure by 200/5 = 40 units. From Equation 26.2, we know that autonomous expenditure in this economy is [1,010 − 1,000r], so that each percentage point (0.01) increase in the real interest rate lowers autonomous expenditure by 10 units (1,000 × 0.01). We conclude that to eliminate the inflationary gap, the Fed should raise the real interest rate by 4 percentage points (0.04), from 5 percent to 9 percent. The higher real interest rate will reduce planned aggregate expenditure and output to the level of potential output, 4,600, eliminating inflationary pressures.

The effects of the Fed's inflation fighting policy are shown in Figure 26.7. With the real interest rate at 5 percent, the expenditure line intersects the Y = PAE line at point E in the figure, where output equals 4,800. To reduce planned spending and output, the Fed raises the real interest rate to 9 percent. The higher real interest rate slows consumption and investment spending, moving the expenditure line downward. At the new equilibrium point G, actual output equals potential output at 4,600. The Fed's raising the real interest rate—a contractionary policy action—has thus eliminated the expansionary output gap, and with it, the threat of inflation.

FIGURE 26.7

The Fed Fights Inflation.

(1) The economy is initially at point E, with an expansionary gap of 200; (2) the Fed increases the real interest rate from 5 percent to 9 percent, shifting the expenditure line down; (3) the new equilibrium is at point G, where output equals potential output. The output gap has been eliminated.

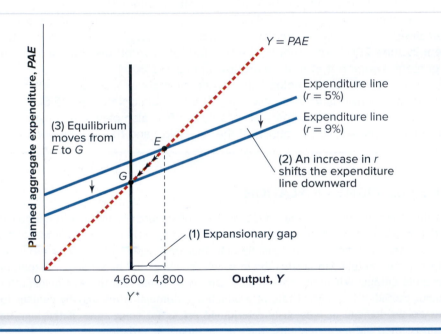

The Economic Naturalist 26.3

Why did the Fed raise interest rates 17 times in a row between 2004 and 2006?

The Fed began tightening monetary policy in June 2004 when it increased the federal funds rate from 1.0 to 1.25 percent. (See Figure 26.5.) It continued to tighten by raising the federal funds rate by one-quarter percent at each successive meeting of the Federal Open Market Committee. By the end of June 2006, after more than two years of tightening, the federal funds rate was 5.25 percent. Why did the Fed begin increasing the funds rate in 2004?

Because the recovery that began in November 2001 was slower than normal and marked by weak job growth, the Fed kept reducing the funds rate until it reached 1.0 percent in June 2003. Once the recovery took hold, however, this very low rate was no longer necessary. While employment had not risen as much during the recovery as it had in previous recoveries, real GDP grew at a rate of nearly 6 percent during the second half of 2003 and nearly 4 percent in 2004. Furthermore, by June 2004, the unemployment rate had fallen to 5.6 percent, not far above most estimates of the natural rate of unemployment at the time. Although inflation began to rise in 2004, most of the increase was due to the sharp run-up in oil prices, and the rate of inflation excluding energy remained low. Nevertheless, the Fed began to raise the federal funds rate in order to prevent the emergence of an expansionary gap, which would result in higher inflation. Thus, the Fed's rate increases could be viewed as a preemptive strike against future inflation. Had the Fed waited until an expansionary gap appeared, a significant inflation problem could have emerged, and the Fed might have had to raise the federal funds rate by even more than it did.

The Fed's interest rate policies affect the economy as a whole, but they have a particularly important effect on financial markets. The introduction to this chapter noted the tremendous lengths financial market participants will go to in an attempt to anticipate Federal Reserve policy changes. The Economic Naturalist 26.4 illustrates the type of information financial investors look for, and why it is so important to them.

The Economic Naturalist 26.4

Why does news of inflation hurt the stock market?

Financial market participants watch data on inflation extremely closely. A report that inflation is increasing or is higher than expected often causes stock prices to fall sharply. Why does bad news about inflation hurt the stock market?

Investors in the financial markets worry about inflation because of its likely impact on Federal Reserve policy. Financial investors understand that the Fed, when faced with signs of an expansionary gap, is likely to raise interest rates in an attempt to reduce planned spending and "cool down" the economy. This type of contractionary policy action hurts stock prices in two ways. First, it slows down economic activity, reducing the expected sales and profits of companies whose shares are traded in the stock market. Lower profits, in turn, reduce the dividends those firms are likely to pay their shareholders.

Second, higher real interest rates reduce the value of stocks by increasing the required return for holding stocks. We saw in Chapter 23, *Financial Markets and International Capital Flows,* that an increase in the return financial investors require in order to hold stocks lowers current stock prices. Intuitively, if interest rates rise, interest-bearing alternatives to stocks such as newly issued government bonds will become more attractive to investors, reducing the demand for, and hence the price of, stocks.

The Economic Naturalist 26.5

Should the Federal Reserve respond to changes in asset prices?

Many credit the Federal Reserve and its chair, Alan Greenspan, for effective monetary policymaking that set the stage for sustained economic growth and rising asset prices throughout the 1990s—in particular, in the second half of the decade. Between January 1995 and March 2000, the S&P 500 stock market index rose from a value of 459 to 1,527, a phenomenal 233 percent increase in just over five years, as the U.S. economy enjoyed a record-long business cycle expansion. Indeed, the stock market's strong, sustained rise helped fuel additional consumer spending, which in turn promoted further economic expansion.

However, as stock prices fell sharply in the two years after their March 2000 peak, some people questioned whether the Federal Reserve should have pre-emptively raised interest rates to constrain investors' "irrational exuberance."[10] Overly optimistic investor sentiment led to a speculative run-up in stock prices that eventually burst in 2000 as investors began to realize that firms' earnings could not support the stock prices that were being paid. Earlier intervention by the Federal Reserve, critics argued, would have slowed down the dramatic increase in stock prices and therefore could have prevented the resulting stock market "crash" and the resulting loss of consumer wealth.

Similar criticism was raised toward the Fed after the collapse of the housing bubble and the ensuing financial crisis of 2007–2008. Like stock prices, housing prices rose dramatically in the late 1990s, and they continued to rise into the early 2000s even as stock prices fell. Housing prices accelerated further during 2004–2005, increasing more than 15 percent a year. However, prices slowed in 2006, and fell sharply in the following years. In light of the severity of the financial crisis and the deep global recession that followed, some people again questioned whether the accommodative monetary policy of the Fed in the early 2000s (see The Economic Naturalist 26.2) contributed to the housing bubble.

Most recently, the Great Recession of 2007–2009 was followed by the longest economic expansion in U.S. history. The expansion was again accompanied by dramatic increases in stock and housing prices, interrupted only in early 2020 by the COVID-19 pandemic. If these asset prices again collapse, some observers are sure to criticize the Fed for inflating them by keeping interest rates "too low" from 2008 onward.

As this chapter makes clear, the Federal Reserve's primary focus is on reducing output gaps and keeping inflation low. Should the Fed also respond to changing asset prices when it makes decisions about monetary policy?

At a symposium in August 2002, Alan Greenspan defended the Fed's monetary policymaking performance in the late 1990s, pointing out that it is very difficult to identify asset bubbles—surges in prices of assets to unsustainable levels—"until after the fact—that is, when its bursting confirm(s) its existence."[11] Even if such a speculative bubble could be identified, Greenspan noted, the Federal Reserve could have done little—short of "inducing a substantial contraction in economic activity"—to prevent investors' speculation from driving up stock prices. Indeed, Greenspan claimed, "the notion that a well-timed incremental tightening could have been calibrated to prevent the late 1990s bubble is almost surely an illusion." Rather, the Federal Reserve was focusing as early as 1999 on policies that would "mitigate the fallout when it occurs and, hopefully, ease the transition to the next expansion."[12]

Seven years later, at the annual meeting of the American Economic Association in January 2010, then Fed chair Ben Bernanke delivered a speech defending the Fed's monetary policy during the early 2000s.[13] The evidence reviewed in his speech suggested that the links between the Fed's monetary policy and the rapid rise in housing prices that occurred at roughly the same time were, at best, weak. Rather,

---

[10]Fed chair Alan Greenspan mentioned the possibility of "irrational exuberance" driving investor behavior in a December 5, 1996, speech, which is available online at www.federalreserve.gov/boarddocs/speeches/1996/19961205.htm.

[11]The text of Greenspan's speech is available online at www.federalreserve.gov/boarddocs/speeches/2002/20020830/default.htm.

[12]*The Federal Reserve's Semiannual Report on Monetary Policy,* testimony of Chair Alan Greenspan before the Committee on Banking and Financial Services, U.S. House of Representatives, July 22, 1999. Available online at www.federalreserve.gov/boarddocs/hh/1999/July/Testimony.htm.

[13]The text of the speech is available online at www.federalreserve.gov/newsevents/speech/bernanke20100103a.htm.

the evidence pointed to increased use of "exotic" types of mortgages with very low down payment—in which both lenders and borrowers knew that the only way borrowers could afford making future payments would be a continued rise in home values—as a more likely cause of the housing bubble. This in turn suggested that the best response to the housing bubble would have been better regulation, such as tougher limits on risky mortgage lending, rather than tighter monetary policy.

Asset price bubbles can cause severe damage. The question of how we can improve our institutions and policymaking framework to reduce the risk of their occurrence is sure to remain an important topic for macroeconomists to study. While monetary policy cannot be ruled out as part of the answer, in general, regulation that is focused directly on the causes of bubbles is likely to be a more effective first line of defense.

THE FED'S POLICY REACTION FUNCTION

The Fed attempts to stabilize the economy by manipulating the real interest rate. When the economy faces a recessionary gap, the Fed reduces the real interest rate in order to stimulate spending. When an expansionary gap exists, so that inflation threatens to become a problem, the Fed restrains spending by raising the real interest rate. Economists sometimes find it convenient to summarize the behavior of the Fed in terms of a *policy reaction function*. In general, a **policy reaction function** describes how the action a policymaker takes depends on the state of the economy. Here, the policymaker's action is the Fed's choice of the real interest rate, and the state of the economy is given by factors such as the output gap or the inflation rate. The Economic Naturalist 26.6 describes one attempt to quantify the Fed's policy reaction function.

policy reaction function describes how the action a policymaker takes depends on the state of the economy

The Economic Naturalist 26.6

What is the Taylor rule?

In 1993, economist John Taylor proposed a "rule," now known as the Taylor rule, to describe the behavior of the Fed.[14] What is the Taylor rule? Does the Fed always follow it?

The rule Taylor proposed is not a rule in any legal sense but is, instead, an attempt to describe the Fed's behavior in terms of a quantitative policy reaction function. Taylor's "rule" can be written as

$$r = 0.01 + 0.5 \left(\frac{Y - Y^*}{Y^*} \right) + 0.5\pi,$$

where r is the real interest rate set by the Fed, expressed as a decimal (for example, 5% = 0.05); $Y - Y^*$ is the current output gap (the difference between actual output and potential output); $(Y - Y^*)/Y^*$ is the output gap relative to potential output; and π is the inflation rate, expressed as a decimal (for example, a 2 percent inflation rate is expressed as 0.02). According to the Taylor rule, the Fed responds to both output gaps and the rate of inflation. For example, the formula implies that if a recessionary gap equal to a fraction 0.01 of potential output develops, the Fed will reduce the real interest rate by 0.5 percentage point (that is, 0.005). Similarly, if inflation rises by 1 percentage point (0.01), according to the Taylor rule the Fed will increase the real interest rate by 0.5 percentage point (0.005). In his 1993

[14]John Taylor, "Discretion versus Policy Rules in Practice," *Carnegie-Rochester Conference Series on Public Policy,* 1993, pp. 195–227.

paper, Taylor showed that his rule did in fact describe the behavior of the Fed under Chair Alan Greenspan reasonably accurately between 1987 and 1992. Thus the Taylor rule is a real-world example of a policy reaction function.

Although the Taylor rule worked well as a description of the Fed's behavior in the five years preceding the publication of Taylor's 1993 paper, the rule has worked less well in describing the Fed's behavior in the years following its publication. Modified variants of the Taylor rule, in which the Fed reacts more strongly to output gaps than the original rule suggested, or in which the Fed reacts to inflation *forecasts* rather than to current inflation, appear to provide better descriptions of the Fed's behavior in the following decades. While different economists prefer different versions of the Taylor rule, we reiterate that it is not a rule in any legal sense. The Fed is perfectly free to deviate from it and does so when circumstances warrant. Still, variants of the Taylor rule provide a useful benchmark for assessing, and predicting, the Fed's actions.

 SELF-TEST 26.5

This exercise asks you to apply the Taylor rule. Suppose inflation is 3 percent and the output gap is zero. According to the Taylor rule, at what value should the Fed set the real interest rate? The nominal interest rate? Suppose the Fed were to receive new information showing that there is a 1 percent recessionary gap (inflation is still 3 percent). According to the Taylor rule, how should the Fed change the real interest rate, if at all?

Notice that according to the Taylor rule, the Fed responds to two variables—the output gap and inflation. In principle, any number of economic variables, from stock prices to the value of the dollar in terms of the Japanese yen, could affect Fed policy and thus appear in the policy reaction function. For the sake of simplicity, in applying the policy reaction function idea in the next chapter, we will assume that the Fed's choice of the real interest rate depends on only one variable—the rate of inflation. This simplification will not change our main results in any significant way. Furthermore, as we will see, having the Fed react only to inflation captures the most important aspect of Fed behavior—namely, its tendency to raise the real interest rate when the economy is "overheating" (experiencing an expansionary gap) and to reduce it when the economy is sluggish (experiencing a recessionary gap).

Table 26.2 describes an example of a policy reaction function according to which the Fed reacts only to inflation. According to the policy reaction function given in the table,

TABLE 26.2
A Policy Reaction Function for the Fed

Rate of inflation, π	Real interest rate set by Fed, r
0.00 (= 0%)	0.02 (= 2%)
0.01	0.03
0.02	0.04
0.03	0.05
0.04	0.06

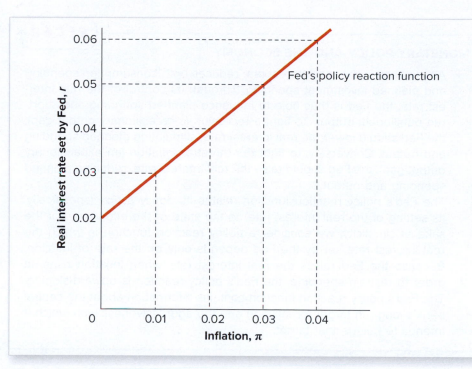

FIGURE 26.8

An Example of a Fed Policy Reaction Function.

This hypothetical example of a policy reaction function for the Fed shows the real interest rate the Fed sets in response to any given value of the inflation rate. The upward slope captures the idea that the Fed raises the real interest rate when inflation rises. The numerical values in the figure are from Table 26.2.

the higher the rate of inflation, the higher the real interest rate set by the Fed. This relationship is consistent with the idea that the Fed responds to an expansionary gap (which threatens to lead to increased inflation) by raising the real interest rate. Figure 26.8 is a graph of this policy reaction function. The vertical axis of the graph shows the real interest rate chosen by the Fed; the horizontal axis shows the rate of inflation. The upward slope of the policy reaction function captures the idea that the Fed reacts to increases in inflation by raising the real interest rate.

How does the Fed determine its policy reaction function? In practice, the process is a complex one, involving a combination of statistical analysis of the economy and human judgment. However, two useful insights into the process can be drawn even from the simplified policy reaction function shown in Table 26.2 and Figure 26.8. First, as we mentioned earlier in the chapter, though the Fed controls the real interest rate in the short run, in the long run the real interest rate is determined by the balance of saving and investment. To illustrate the implication of this fact for the Fed's choice of policy reaction function, suppose that the Fed estimates the long-run value of the real interest rate (as determined by the supply and demand for saving) to be 4 percent, or 0.04. By examining Table 26.2, we can see that the Fed's policy reaction function implies a long-run value of the real interest rate of 4 percent only if the inflation rate in the long run is 2 percent. Thus the Fed's choice of this policy reaction function makes sense only if the Fed's long-run target rate of inflation is 2 percent. We conclude that one important determinant of the Fed's policy reaction function is the policymakers' objective for inflation.

Second, the Fed's policy reaction function contains information not only about the central bank's long-run inflation target but also about how aggressively the Fed plans to pursue that target. To illustrate, suppose the Fed's policy reaction function was very flat, implying that the Fed changes the real interest rate rather modestly in response to increases or decreases in inflation. In this case we would conclude that the Fed does not intend to be very aggressive in its attempts to offset movements in inflation away from the target level. In contrast, if the reaction function slopes steeply upward, so that a given change in inflation elicits a large adjustment of the real interest rate by the Fed, we would say that the Fed plans to be quite aggressive in responding to changes in inflation.

RECAP ↑

> **MONETARY POLICY AND THE ECONOMY**
>
> - An increase in the real interest rate reduces both consumption spending and planned investment spending. Through its control of the real interest rate, the Fed is thus able to influence planned spending and short-run equilibrium output. To fight a recession (a recessionary output gap), the Fed should lower the real interest rate, stimulating planned spending and output. Conversely, to fight the threat of inflation (an expansionary output gap), the Fed should raise the real interest rate, reducing planned spending and output.
> - The Fed's policy reaction function relates its policy action (specifically, its setting of the real interest rate) to the state of the economy. For the sake of simplicity, we consider a policy reaction function in which the real interest rate set by the Fed depends only on the rate of inflation. Because the Fed raises the real interest rate when inflation rises, in order to restrain spending, the Fed's policy reaction is upward-sloping. The Fed's policy reaction function contains information about the central bank's long-run target for inflation and the aggressiveness with which it intends to pursue that target.

MONETARY POLICYMAKING: ART OR SCIENCE?

In this chapter, we analyzed the basic economics underlying real-world monetary policy. As part of the analysis, we worked through some examples showing the calculation of the real interest rate that is needed to restore output to its full-employment level. While those examples are useful in understanding how monetary policy works—as with our analysis of fiscal policy in Chapter 25, *Spending and Output in the Short Run*—they overstate the precision of monetary policymaking. The real-world economy is highly complex, and our knowledge of its workings is imperfect. For example, though we assumed in our analysis that the Fed knows the exact value of potential output, in reality potential output can be estimated only approximately. As a result, at any given time the Fed has only a rough idea of the size of the output gap. Similarly, Fed policymakers have only an approximate idea of the effect of a given change in the real interest rate on planned spending, or the length of time before that effect will occur. Because of these uncertainties, the Fed tends to proceed cautiously. Fed policymakers avoid large changes in interest rates and rarely raise or lower the federal funds rate more than one-half of a percentage point (from 5.50 percent to 5.00 percent, for example) at any one time. Indeed, the typical change in the interest rate is one-quarter of a percentage point.

Is monetary policymaking an art or a science, then? In practice it appears to be both. Scientific analyses, such as the development of detailed statistical models of the economy, have proved useful in making monetary policy. But human judgment based on long experience—what has been called the "art" of monetary policy—plays a crucial role in successful policymaking and is likely to continue to do so.

SUMMARY

- Monetary policy is one of two types of stabilization policy, the other being fiscal policy. Although in the basic model of the market for money, the Federal Reserve operates by controlling the money supply, the media's attention nearly always focuses on the Fed's decisions about interest rates, not the money supply. There is no contradiction between these two ways of looking at monetary policy, however, as the Fed's ability to control the money supply is the source of its ability to control interest rates. *(LO1)*

- The nominal interest rate is determined in the market for money, which has both a demand side and a supply side. For the economy as a whole, the *demand for money* is the amount of wealth households and businesses choose to hold in the form of money (such as cash or checking accounts). The demand for money is determined by a comparison of cost and benefits. The opportunity cost of holding money, which pays either zero interest or very low interest, is the interest that could have been earned by holding interest-bearing assets instead of money. Because the nominal interest rate measures the opportunity cost of holding a dollar in the form of money, an increase in the nominal interest rate reduces the quantity of money demanded. The benefit of money is its usefulness in carrying out transactions. All else being equal, an increase in the volume of transactions increases the demand for money. At the macroeconomic level, an increase in the price level or in real GDP increases the dollar volume of transactions, and thus the demand for money. *(LO1)*

- The *money demand curve* relates the aggregate quantity of money demanded to the nominal interest rate. Because an increase in the nominal interest rate increases the opportunity cost of holding money, which reduces the quantity of money demanded, the money demand curve slopes down. Factors other than the nominal interest rate that affect the demand for money will shift the demand curve to the right or left. For example, an increase in the price level or real GDP increases the demand for money, shifting the money demand curve to the right. *(LO1)*

- In the basic model of the market for money, the Federal Reserve determines the supply of money through the use of open-market operations. The supply curve for money is vertical at the value of the money supply set by the Fed. Money market equilibrium occurs at the nominal interest rate at which money demand equals the money supply. The Fed can reduce the nominal interest rate by increasing the money supply (shifting the money supply curve to the right) or increase the nominal interest rate by reducing the money supply (shifting the money supply curve to the left). The nominal interest rate that the Fed targets most closely is the *federal funds rate,* which is the rate commercial banks charge each other for very short-term loans. *(LO2)*

- In the short run, the Fed can control the real interest rate as well as the nominal interest rate. Recall that the real interest rate equals the nominal interest rate minus the inflation rate. Because the inflation rate adjusts relatively slowly, the Fed can change the real interest rate by changing the nominal interest rate. In the long run, the real interest rate is determined by the balance of saving and investment. *(LO2)*

- The Fed can effectively control the amount of bank reserves through tools that include open-market operations and *discount window lending*. The Fed can also set *reserve requirements* (a legally binding minimum on banks' reserve-deposit ratio). This, however, gives the Fed only partial control over the money supply—something that the basic model of the market for money does not consider. In particular, a Fed-initiated increase in bank reserves will not lead to an increase in the money supply if banks absorb the increase in reserves by letting their reserve-deposit ratios increase at the same pace. *(LO3)*

- In December 2008 the federal funds rate effectively reached its *zero lower bound*. In the years that followed, the Fed used what started as unconventional methods to stimulate the economy. Such methods, including *quantitative easing* and *forward guidance,* go beyond the basic model of the market for money, which assumes that all the interest rates in the economy move together and that the Fed fully controls the money supply. These new methods used by the Fed directly aimed at lowering interest rates in the economy that were higher than the federal funds rate. Although the above two basic assumptions did not hold well after December 2008 (which explains why the Fed had to resort to the new methods to keep stimulating the economy), they still provide useful approximations. This in turn provides some justification for continuing to make these simplifying assumptions, in particular when speaking of the Fed's control of the interest rate. *(LO4)*

- The Federal Reserve's actions affect the economy because changes in the real interest rate affect spending. For example, an increase in the real interest rate raises the cost of borrowing, reducing consumption and investment. Thus, by increasing the real interest rate, the Fed can reduce spending and short-run equilibrium output. Conversely, by reducing the real interest rate, the Fed can stimulate aggregate expenditure and thereby raise short-run equilibrium output. The Fed's ultimate objective is to eliminate output gaps. To eliminate a recessionary output gap, the Fed will lower the real interest rate. To eliminate an expansionary output gap, the Fed will raise the real interest rate. *(LO5)*

- A *policy reaction function* describes how the action a policymaker takes depends on the state of the economy. For example, a policy reaction function for the Fed could specify the real interest rate set by the Fed for each value of inflation. *(LO5)*

- In practice, the Fed's information about the level of potential output and the size and speed of the effects of its actions is imprecise. Thus monetary policymaking is as much an art as a science. *(LO6)*

KEY TERMS

demand for money	federal funds rate	portfolio allocation decision
discount rate	forward guidance	quantitative easing (QE)
discount window lending	money demand curve	reserve requirements
excess reserves	policy reaction function	zero lower bound

REVIEW QUESTIONS

1. What is the *demand for money?* How does the demand for money depend on the nominal interest rate? On the price level? On income? Explain in terms of the costs and benefits of holding money. *(LO1)*

2. Show graphically how the Fed controls the nominal interest rate. Can the Fed control the real interest rate? *(LO2)*

3. What effect does an open-market purchase of bonds by the Fed have on nominal interest rates? Discuss in terms of (a) the effect of the purchase on bond prices and (b) the effect of the purchase on the supply of money. *(LO2)*

4. What other methods does the Fed have for affecting short-run interest rates besides open-market operations? Discuss whether these methods can be used for only lowering short-run interest rates, for only increasing them, or for both lowering and increasing them. *(LO3)*

5. In a situation where short-run interest rates have hit their zero lower bound, can the Fed still lower other, higher, longer-term interest rates? Discuss specific actions that the Fed can take and how they would work. *(LO4)*

6. Why does the real interest rate affect planned aggregate expenditure? Give examples. *(LO5)*

7. The Fed faces a recessionary gap. How would you expect it to respond? Explain step by step how its policy change is likely to affect the economy. *(LO5)*

8. The Fed decides to take a *contractionary* policy action. What would you expect to happen to the nominal interest rate, the real interest rate, and the money supply? Under what circumstances would this type of policy action most likely be appropriate? *(LO5)*

9. Discuss why the analysis of this chapter overstates the precision with which monetary policy can be used to eliminate output gaps. *(LO6)*

PROBLEMS

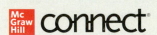

1. During the heavy Christmas shopping season, sales of retail stores, online sales firms, and other merchants rise significantly. *(LO1)*
   a. What would you expect to happen to the money demand curve during the Christmas season? Show graphically.
   b. If the Fed took no action, what would happen to nominal interest rates around Christmas?
   c. In fact, nominal interest rates do not change significantly in the fourth quarter of the year, due to deliberate Fed policy. Explain and show graphically how the Fed can ensure that nominal interest rates remain stable around Christmas.

2. The following table shows Uma's estimated annual benefits of holding different amounts of money: *(LO1)*

Average money holdings ($)	Total benefit ($)
500	35
600	47
700	57
800	65
900	71
1,000	75
1,100	77
1,200	77

a. How much money will Uma hold on average if the nominal interest rate is 9 percent? 5 percent? 3 percent? Assume that she wants her money holding to be a multiple of $100. (*Hint:* Make a table comparing the extra benefit of each additional $100 in money holdings with the opportunity cost, in terms of forgone interest, of additional money holdings.)

b. Graph Uma's money demand curve for interest rates between 1 percent and 12 percent.

3. How would you expect each of the following to affect the economywide demand for U.S. money? Explain. *(LO1)*

a. Competition among brokers forces down the commission charge for selling holdings of bonds or stocks.

b. Grocery stores begin to accept credit cards in payment.

c. Financial investors become concerned about increasing riskiness of stocks.

4. Suppose the economywide demand for money is given by $P(0.3Y - 25,000i)$. The price level P equals 3.0, and real output Y equals 10,000. At what value should the Fed set the nominal money supply if: *(LO1, LO2)*

a. It wants to set the nominal interest rate at 4 percent.

b. It wants to set the nominal interest rate at 6 percent.

5. Using a supply and demand graph of the market for money, show the effects on the nominal interest rate if the Fed takes the following monetary policy actions: *(LO2, LO3)*

a. The Fed lowers the discount rate and increases discount lending.

b. The Fed increases the reserve requirements for commercial banks.

c. The Fed conducts open-market sales of government bonds to the public.

d. The Fed decreases the reserve requirements for commercial banks.

6. Assume that the central bank of a nation decides to lower the reserve requirements for commercial banks. What changes can one predict regarding the amount of: required reserves, excess reserves, the amount of loans generated by commercial banks, the economywide money supply, and finally interest rates in that nation? *(LO3)*

7. In August 2015, the Chinese central bank decided to reduce China's required reserve-deposit ratio from 18.5 percent to 18 percent. Assuming no change in the amount of cash held by the Chinese public, that commercial banks lend all their excess reserves, and that bank reserves was a constant 4,329 billion yuan both before and after the change, compute the maximum change in Chinese banks deposits as a consequence of the change in the reserve-deposit. *(LO3)*

8. Which of the following is not an example of an "unconventional" monetary policy tool available to the Fed when the federal funds rate is already at or close to zero: forward guidance, quantitative easing, or discount lending? *(LO4)*

9. Explain why an increase in interest that banks receive from the Fed on the required and excess reserves that banks hold with the Fed, would also increase the interest rates that commercial banks charge their borrowers. *(LO4)*

10. An economy is described by the following information:

$$C = 2,600 + 0.8(Y - T) - 10,000r,$$
$$I^P = 2,000 - 10,000r,$$
$$G = 1,800,$$
$$NX = 0,$$
$$T = 3,000.$$

The real interest rate, expressed as a decimal, is 0.10 (that is, 10 percent). *(LO5)*

a. Find a numerical equation relating planned aggregate expenditure to output.

b. Using a table (or algebra), solve for short-run equilibrium output.

c. Show your result graphically using the Keynesian-cross diagram.

11. For the economy described in Problem 10, suppose that potential output Y^* equals 12,000. *(LO5)*

a. What real interest rate should the Fed set to bring the economy to full employment? You may take as a given that the multiplier for this economy is 5.

b. Repeat part a for the case in which potential output Y^* equals 9,000.

c. Show that the real interest rate you found in part a sets national saving at potential output, defined as $Y^* - C - G$, equal to planned investment, I^P. This result shows that the real interest rate must be consistent with equilibrium in the market for saving when the economy is at full employment. *(Hint: Review the material on national saving in Chapter 21, Saving and Capital Formation.)*

12.* Here is another set of equations describing an economy: *(LO5)*

$$C = 14,400 + 0.5(Y - T) - 40,000r,$$
$$I^P = 8,000 - 20,000r,$$
$$G = 7,800,$$
$$NX = 1,800,$$
$$T = 8,000,$$
$$Y^* = 40,000.$$

a. Find a numerical equation relating planned aggregate expenditure to output and to the real interest rate.

b. At what value should the Fed set the real interest rate to eliminate any output gap? *(Hint: Set output Y equal to the value of potential output given above in the equation you found in part a. Then solve for the real interest rate that also sets planned aggregate expenditure equal to potential output.)*

13. What are some of the uncertainties that Fed policymakers face, and how do these uncertainties affect monetary policymaking? *(LO6)*

*Denotes more difficult problem.

ANSWERS TO SELF-TESTS

26.1 At 4 percent interest, the benefit of each $10,000 reduction in cash holdings is $400 per year (4% × $10,000). In this case, the cost of the extra armored car service, $500 a year, exceeds the benefit of reducing cash holdings by $10,000. Kim's restaurants should therefore continue to hold $50,000 in cash. Comparing this result with Example 26.2, you can see that the demand for money by Kim's restaurants is lower, the higher the nominal interest rate. *(LO1)*

26.2 If the nominal interest rate is above its equilibrium value, then people are holding more money than they would like. To bring their money holdings down, they will use some of their money to buy interest-bearing assets such as bonds.

If everyone is trying to buy bonds, however, the price of bonds will be bid up. An increase in bond prices is equivalent to a fall in market interest rates. As interest rates fall, people will be willing to hold more money. Eventually interest rates will fall enough that people are content to hold the amount of money supplied by the Fed, and the money market will be in equilibrium. *(LO1)*

26.3 If $r = 0.03$, then consumption is $C = 640 + 0.8(Y - 250) - 400(0.03) + 428 + 0.8Y$, and planned investment is $I^P = 250 - 600(0.03) = 232$. Planned aggregate expenditure is given by = 4,900. Notice that the lower interest of

$$PAE = C + I^P + G + NX$$
$$= (428 + 0.8Y) + 232 + 300 + 20$$
$$= 980 + 0.8Y.$$

To find short-run equilibrium output, we can construct a table analogous to Table 26.2. As usual, some trial and error is necessary to find an appropriate range of guesses for output (column 1).

(1)	(2)	(3)	(4)
	Planned aggregate expenditure		
Output Y	PAE = 980 + 08Y	Y − PAE	Y = PAE?
4,500	4,580	−80	No
4,600	4,660	−60	No
4,700	4,740	−40	No
4,800	4,820	−20	No
4,900	4,900	0	Yes
5,000	4,980	20	No
5,100	5,060	40	No
5,200	5,140	60	No
5,300	5,220	80	No
5,400	5,300	100	No
5,500	5,380	120	No

Short-run equilibrium output equals 4,900, as that is the only level of output that satisfies the condition $Y = PAE$.

The answer can be obtained more quickly by simply setting $Y = PAE$ and solving for short-run equilibrium output Y. Remembering that $PAE = 980 + 0.8Y$ and substitution for *PAE,* we get

$$Y = 980 + 0.8Y$$
$$Y(1 - 0.8) = 980$$
$$Y = 5 \times 980 = 4,900.$$

So lowering the real interest rate from 5 percent to 3 percent increases short-run equilibrium output from 4,800 (as found in Example 26.4) to 4,900.

If you have read Appendix B in Chapter 25, *Spending and Output in the Short Run,* on the multiplier, there is yet another way to find the answer. Using that appendix, we can determine that the multiplier in this model is 5, since $1/(1 - c) = 1/(1 - 0.8) = 5$. Each percentage point reduction in the real interest rate increases consumption by 4 units and planned investment by 6 units, for a total impact on planned spending of 10 units per percentage point reduction. Reducing the real interest rate by 2 percentage points, from 5 percent to 3 percent, thus increases autonomous expenditure by 20 units. Because the multiplier is 5, an increase of 20 in autonomous expenditure raises short-run equilibrium output by $20 \times 5 = 100$ units, from the value of 4,800 we found in Example 26.4 to the new value of 4,900. *(LO5)*

26.4 When the real interest rate is 5 percent, output is 4,800. Each percentage point reduction in the real interest rate increases autonomous expenditure by 10 units. Since the multiplier in this model is 5, to raise output by 50 units, the real interest rate should be cut by 1 percentage point, from 5 percent to 4 percent. Increasing output by 50 units, to 4,850, eliminates the output gap. *(LO5)*

26.5 If $\pi = 0.03$ and the output gap is zero, we can plug these values into the Taylor rule to obtain

$$r = 0.01 - 0.5(0) + 0.5(0.03) = 0.025 = 2.5\%.$$

So the real interest rate implied by the Taylor rule when inflation is 3 percent and the output gap is zero is 2.5 percent. The nominal interest rate equals the real rate plus the inflation rate, or 2.5% + 3% = 5.5%.

If there is a recessionary gap of 1 percent of potential output, the Taylor rule formula becomes

$$r = 0.01 - 0.5(0.01) + 0.5(0.03) = 0.02 = 2\%.$$

The nominal interest rate implied by the Taylor rule in this case is the 2 percent real rate plus the 3 percent inflation rate, or 5 percent. So the Taylor rule has the Fed lowering the interest rate when the economy goes into recession, which is both sensible and realistic. *(LO5)*

Monetary Policy in the Basic Keynesian Model

This appendix extends the algebraic analysis of the basic Keynesian model that was presented in Appendix A to Chapter 25, *Spending and Output in the Short Run,* to include the role of monetary policy. The main difference from that appendix is that in this analysis, the real interest rate is allowed to affect planned spending. We will not describe the supply and demand for money algebraically but will simply assume that the Fed can set the real interest rate r at any level it chooses.

The real interest rate affects consumption and planned investment. To capture these effects, we will modify the equations for those two components of spending as follows

$$C = \overline{C} + c(Y - T) - ar,$$
$$I^P = \overline{I} - br.$$

The first equation is the consumption function (recall that in the appendices, we use c for the *marginal propensity to consume*) with an additional term, equal to $-ar$. Think of a as a fixed number, greater than zero, that measures the strength of the interest rate effect on consumption. Thus the term $-ar$ captures the idea that when the real interest rate r rises, consumption declines by a times the increase in the interest rate. Likewise, the second equation adds the term $-br$ to the equation for planned investment spending. The parameter b is a fixed positive number that measures how strongly changes in the real interest rate affect planned investment; for example, if the real interest rate r rises, planned investment is assumed to decline by b times the increase in the real interest rate. We continue to assume that government purchases, taxes, and net exports are exogenous variables, so that $G = \overline{G}$, $T = \overline{T}$, and $NX = \overline{NX}$.

To solve for short-run equilibrium output, we start as usual by finding the relationship of planned aggregate expenditure to output. The definition of planned aggregate expenditure is

$$PAE = C + I^P + G + NX.$$

Substituting the modified equations for consumption and planned investment into this definition, along with the exogenous values of government spending, net exports, and taxes, we get

$$PAE = [\overline{C} + c(Y - \overline{T}) - ar] + [\overline{I} - br] + \overline{G} + \overline{NX}.$$

The first term in brackets on the right side describes the behavior of consumption, and the second bracketed term describes planned investment. Rearranging this equation in order to group together terms that depend on the real interest rate and terms that depend on output, we find

$$PAE = [\overline{C} - c\overline{T} + \overline{I} + \overline{G} + \overline{NX}] - (a + b)r + cY.$$

This equation is similar to Equation 25A.1, as shown in Appendix A to Chapter 25, except that it has an extra term, $-(a + b)r$, on the right side. This extra term captures the idea that an increase in the real interest rate reduces consumption and planned investment, lowering planned spending. Notice that the term $-(a + b)r$ is part of autonomous expenditure, since it does not depend on output. Since autonomous expenditure determines the intercept of the expenditure line in the Keynesian cross diagram, changes in the real interest rate will shift the expenditure line up (if the real interest rate decreases) or down (if the real interest rate increases).

To find short-run equilibrium output, we uses the definition of short-run equilibrium output to set $Y = PAE$ and solve for Y

$$Y = PAE$$
$$= [\overline{C} - c\overline{T} + \overline{I} + \overline{G} + \overline{NX}] - (a + b)r + cY$$
$$Y(1 - c) = [\overline{C} - c\overline{T} + \overline{I} + \overline{G} + \overline{NX}] - (a + b)r$$
$$Y = \left(\frac{1}{1 - c}\right)[(\overline{C} - c\overline{T} + \overline{I} + \overline{G} + \overline{NX}) - (a + b)r]. \qquad (26A.1)$$

Equation 26A.1 shows that short-run equilibrium output once again equals the multiplier, $1/(1 - c)$, times autonomous expenditure, $\overline{C} - c\overline{T} + \overline{I} + \overline{G} + \overline{NX}) - (a + b)r$. Autonomous expenditure in turn depends on the real interest rate r. The equation also shows that the impact of a change in the real interest rate on short-run equilibrium output depends on two factors: (1) the effect of a change in the real interest rate on consumption and planned investment, which depends on the magnitude of $(a + b)$, and (2) the size of the multiplier, $1/(1 - c)$, which relates changes in autonomous expenditure to changes in short-run equilibrium output. The larger the effect of the real interest rate on planned spending, and the larger the multiplier, the more powerful will be the effect of a given change in the real interest rate on short-run equilibrium output.

To check Equation 26A.1, we can use it to resolve Example 26.4. In that example, we are given $\overline{C} = 640$, $\overline{I} = 250$, $\overline{G} = 300$, $\overline{NX} = 20$, $\overline{T} = 250$, $c = 0.8$, $a = 400$, and $b = 600$. The real interest rate set by the Fed is 5 percent, or 0.05. Substituting these values into Equation 26A.1 and solving, we obtain

$$Y = \left(\frac{1}{1 - 0.8}\right)[640 - 0.8 \times 250 + 250 + 300 + 20 - (400 + 600) \times 0.05]$$
$$= 5 \times 960 = 4,800$$

This is the same result we found in Example 26.4.

CHAPTER 27

Aggregate Demand, Aggregate Supply, and Inflation

What impact do rising prices have on the economy?

Dave and Les Jacobs/Blend Images/Getty Images

O n October 6, 1979, the Federal Open Market Committee, the policymaking committee of the Federal Reserve, held a highly unusual—and unusually secretive—Saturday meeting. Fed chair Paul Volcker may have called the Saturday meeting because he knew the financial markets would be closed and thus would not be able to respond to any "leaks" to the press about the discussions. Or perhaps he hoped that the visit of Pope John Paul II to Washington on the same day would distract the news media from goings-on at the Fed. However unnoticed this meeting may have been at the time, in retrospect it marked a turning point in postwar U.S. economic history.

When Volcker called the October 6 meeting, he had been Fed chair for only six weeks. Six feet eight inches tall with a booming bass voice, and a chain-smoker of cheap cigars, Volcker had a reputation for financial conservatism and personal toughness. Partly for those qualities, President Carter had appointed Volcker to head the Federal Reserve in August 1979. Carter needed a tough Fed chair to restore confidence in both the economy and the government's economic policies. The U.S. economy faced many problems, including a doubling of oil prices following the overthrow of the Shah of Iran and a worrisome slowdown in productivity growth. But in the minds of the public, the biggest economic worry was an inflation rate that seemed to be out of control. In the second half of 1979, the annual rate of increase in consumer prices had reached 13 percent; by the spring of 1980, the inflation rate had risen to nearly 16 percent. Volcker's assignment: to bring inflation under control and stabilize the U.S. economy.

Volcker knew that getting rid of inflation would not be easy, and he warned his colleagues that a "shock treatment" might be necessary. His plan was couched in technical details, but in essence he proposed to reduce the rate of growth of the money supply sharply. Everyone in the room knew that slowing the growth of the money supply would cause interest rates to rise and aggregate spending to fall. Inflation might be brought down, but at what cost in terms of recession, lost output, and lost jobs? And how would the financial markets, which were already shaky, react to the new approach?

Officials in the room stirred nervously as Volcker spoke about the necessity of the move. Finally a vote was called. Every hand went up.

What happened next? We'll return to this story before the chapter ends, but first we need to introduce the basic framework for understanding inflation and the policies used to control it. In the previous two chapters, we made the assumption that firms are willing to meet the demand for their products at preset prices. When firms simply produce what is demanded, the level of planned aggregate expenditure determines the nation's real GDP. If the resulting level of short-run equilibrium output is lower than potential output, a recessionary output gap develops, and if the resulting level of output exceeds potential output, the economy experiences an expansionary gap. As we saw in the previous two chapters, policymakers can attempt to eliminate output gaps by taking actions that affect the level of autonomous expenditure, such as changing the level of government spending or taxes (fiscal policy) or using the Fed's control of the money supply to change the real interest rate (monetary policy).

The basic Keynesian model is useful for understanding the role of spending in the short-run determination of output, but it is too simplified to provide a fully realistic description of the economy. The main shortcoming of the basic Keynesian model is that it does not explain the behavior of *inflation*. Although firms may meet demand at preset prices for a time, as assumed in the basic Keynesian model, prices do *not* remain fixed indefinitely. Indeed, sometimes they may rise quite rapidly—the phenomenon of high inflation—imposing significant costs on the economy in the process. In this chapter, we will extend the basic Keynesian model to allow for ongoing inflation. As we will show, the extended model can be conveniently represented by a new diagram, called the *aggregate demand–aggregate supply diagram*. Using this extended analysis, we will be able to show how macroeconomic policies affect inflation as well as output, illustrating in the process the difficult trade-offs policymakers sometimes face. We will emphasize numerical and graphical analysis of output and inflation in the body of the chapter. The appendix at the end of the chapter presents an algebraic treatment.

Dennis Brack/Newscom

Paul Volcker faced a tough assignment.

aggregate demand (*AD*) curve a curve that shows the relationship between short-run equilibrium output *Y* and the rate of inflation π; it thus shows the amount of output consumers, firms, government, and foreign entities want to purchase at each inflation rate, holding all other factors constant

INFLATION, SPENDING, AND OUTPUT: THE AGGREGATE DEMAND CURVE

To begin incorporating inflation into the model, our first step is to introduce a new relationship, called the *aggregate demand curve,* which is shown graphically in Figure 27.1. The **aggregate demand (*AD*) curve** shows the relationship between short-run equilibrium output *Y* and the rate of inflation, denoted π. The name of the curve reflects the fact that, as we have seen, short-run equilibrium output is determined by total planned spending, or demand, in the economy. Indeed, by definition, short-run equilibrium output *equals* planned aggregate expenditure, so that we could just as well say that the *AD* curve shows the relationship between inflation and spending.[1]

---

[1]It is important to distinguish the aggregate demand curve from the expenditure line, introduced as part of the Keynesian-cross diagram in Chapter 25, *Spending and Output in the Short Run.* The upward-sloping expenditure line shows the relationship between planned aggregate expenditure and output. Again, the aggregate demand (*AD*) curve shows the relationship between short-run equilibrium output (which equals planned spending) and inflation.

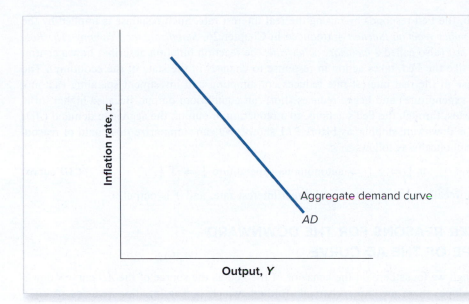

FIGURE 27.1

The Aggregate Demand (*AD*) Curve.

The *AD* curve shows the relationship between short-run equilibrium output *Y* and the rate of inflation π. Because short-run equilibrium output equals planned spending, the *AD* curve also shows the relationship between inflation and planned spending. The downward slope of the *AD* curve implies that an increase in inflation reduces short-run equilibrium output.

We will see shortly that, all else being equal, *an increase in the rate of inflation tends to reduce short-run equilibrium output.* Therefore, in a diagram showing inflation π on the vertical axis and output *Y* on the horizontal axis (Figure 27.1), the aggregate demand curve is downward-sloping.[2] Note that we refer to the *AD* "curve," even though the relationship is drawn as a straight line in Figure 27.1. In general, the *AD* curve can be either straight or curving.

Why does higher inflation lead to a lower level of planned spending and short-run equilibrium output? As we will see next, one important reason is the Fed's response to increases in inflation.

INFLATION, THE FED, AND WHY THE *AD* CURVE SLOPES DOWNWARD

One of the primary responsibilities of the Fed, or any central bank, is to maintain a low and stable rate of inflation. For example, in recent years the Fed has tried to keep inflation in the United States at 2 percent over the long run. By keeping inflation low, the central bank tries to avoid the costs high inflation imposes on the economy.

What can the Fed do to keep inflation low and stable? As we have already mentioned, one situation that is likely to lead to increased inflation is an expansionary output gap, in which short-run equilibrium output exceeds potential output. When output is above potential output, firms must produce at above-normal capacity to meet the demands of their customers. Like Alice's ice cream store, described in Chapter 24, *Short-Term Economic Fluctuations: An Introduction,* firms may be willing to do this for a time. But eventually they will adjust to the high level of demand by raising prices, contributing to inflation. To control inflation, then, the Fed needs to dampen planned spending and output when they threaten to exceed potential output.

How can the Fed avoid a situation of economic "overheating," in which spending and output exceed potential output? As we saw in the previous chapter, the Fed can act to reduce autonomous expenditure, and hence short-run equilibrium output, by raising the real interest rate. This behavior by the Fed is a key factor that underlies the link between inflation and output that is summarized by the aggregate demand curve. When inflation

[2]Economists sometimes define the aggregate demand curve as the relationship between aggregate demand and the *price level,* rather than inflation, which is the *rate of change* of the price level. The definition used here both simplifies the analysis and yields results more consistent with real-world data. For a comparison of the two approaches, see David Romer, "Keynesian Macroeconomics without the LM Curve," *Journal of Economic Perspectives,* Spring 2000, pp. 149–170. The graphical analysis used in this chapter follows closely the approach recommended by Romer.

is high, the Fed responds by raising the real interest rate. Such response is implied by the Fed's *policy reaction function,* introduced in Chapter 26, *Stabilizing the Economy: The Role of the Fed* (also called a *monetary policy rule,* the reaction function describes how a central bank, like the Fed, takes action in response to changes in the state of the economy). The increase in the real interest rate reduces consumption and investment spending (autonomous expenditure) and hence reduces short-run equilibrium output. Because higher inflation leads, through the Fed's actions, to a reduction in output, the aggregate demand (*AD*) curve is downward-sloping, as Figure 27.1 shows. We can summarize this chain of reasoning symbolically as follows

$$\pi \uparrow \Rightarrow r \uparrow \Rightarrow \text{autonomous expenditure} \downarrow \Rightarrow Y \downarrow, \qquad (AD \text{ curve})$$

where, recall, π is inflation, r is the real interest rate, and Y is output.

OTHER REASONS FOR THE DOWNWARD SLOPE OF THE *AD* CURVE

Although we focus here on the behavior of the Fed as the source of the *AD* curve's downward slope, there are other channels through which higher inflation reduces planned spending and thus short-run equilibrium output. Hence the downward slope of the *AD* curve does not depend on the Fed behaving in the particular way just described.

One additional reason for the downward slope of the *AD* curve is the effect of inflation on the *real value of money* held by households and businesses. At high levels of inflation, the purchasing power of money held by the public declines rapidly. This reduction in the public's real wealth may cause households to restrain consumption spending, reducing short-run equilibrium output.

A second channel by which inflation may affect planned spending is through **distributional effects.** Studies have found that people who are less well off are often hurt more by inflation than wealthier people are. For example, retirees on fixed incomes and workers receiving the minimum wage (which is set in dollar terms) lose buying power when prices are rising rapidly. Less affluent people are also likely to be relatively unsophisticated in making financial investments and hence less able than wealthier citizens to protect their savings against inflation.

People at the lower end of the income distribution tend to spend a greater percentage of their disposable income than do wealthier individuals. Thus, if a burst of inflation redistributes resources from relatively high-spending, less affluent households toward relatively high-saving, more affluent households, overall spending may decline.

A third connection between inflation and aggregate demand arises because higher rates of inflation generate *uncertainty* for households and businesses. When inflation is high, people become less certain about what things will cost in the future, and uncertainty makes planning more difficult. In an uncertain economic environment, both households and firms may become more cautious, reducing their spending as a result.

A final link between inflation and total spending operates through the *prices of domestic goods and services sold abroad.* As we will see in the next chapter, the foreign price of domestic goods depends in part on the rate at which the domestic currency, such as the dollar, exchanges for foreign currencies, such as the British pound. However, for constant rates of exchange between currencies, a rise in domestic inflation causes the prices of domestic goods in foreign markets to rise more quickly. As domestic goods become relatively more expensive to prospective foreign purchasers, export sales decline. Net exports are part of aggregate expenditure, and so once more we find that increased inflation is likely to reduce spending. All these factors contribute to the downward slope of the *AD* curve, together with the behavior of the Fed.

FACTORS THAT SHIFT THE AGGREGATE DEMAND CURVE

The downward slope of the aggregate demand, or *AD*, curve shown in Figure 27.1 reflects the fact that *all other factors held constant,* a higher level of inflation will lead to lower

distributional effects changes in the distribution of income or wealth in the economy

planned spending and thus lower short-run equilibrium output. Again, a principal reason higher inflation reduces planned spending and output is that the Fed tends to react to increases in inflation by raising the real interest rate, which in turn reduces consumption and planned investment, two important components of planned aggregate expenditure.

However, even if inflation is held constant, various factors can affect planned spending and short-run equilibrium output. Graphically, as we will see in this section, these factors will cause a **change in aggregate demand,** which causes the *AD* curve to shift. Specifically, for a given level of inflation, if there is a change in the economy that *increases* short-run equilibrium output, the *AD* curve will shift to the *right* (we provide an example in Figure 27.2). If, on the other hand, the change *reduces* short-run equilibrium output at each level of inflation, the *AD* curve will shift to the *left* [Figure 27.3(b) provides an example]. We will focus on two sorts of changes in the economy that shift the aggregate demand curve: (1) changes in spending caused by factors other than output or interest rates, which we will refer to as *exogenous* changes in spending, and (2) changes in the Fed's monetary policy, as reflected in a shift in the Fed's policy reaction function.

change in aggregate demand a shift of the *AD* curve

Changes in Spending

We have seen that planned aggregate expenditure depends both on output (through the consumption function) and on the real interest rate (which affects both consumption and planned investment). However, many factors other than output or the real interest rate can affect planned spending. For example, at given levels of output and the real interest rate, fiscal policy affects the level of government purchases, and changes in consumer confidence can affect consumption spending. Likewise, new technological opportunities may lead firms to increase their planned investment, and an increased willingness of foreigners to purchases domestic goods will raise net exports. We will refer to changes in planned spending unrelated to changes in output or the real interest rate as *exogenous* changes in spending.

For a given inflation rate (and thus for a given real interest rate set by the Fed), an exogenous increase in spending raises short-run equilibrium output, for the reasons we have discussed in the past two chapters. Because it increases output at each level of inflation, *an exogenous increase in spending shifts the AD curve to the right*. This result is illustrated graphically in Figure 27.2. Imagine, for example, that a rise in the stock market makes consumers more willing to spend (the wealth effect). Then, for each level of inflation, aggregate spending and short-run equilibrium output will be higher, a change which is shown as a shift of the *AD* curve to the right, from *AD* to *AD′*.

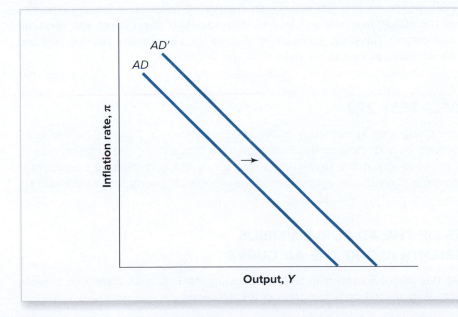

FIGURE 27.2

Effect of an Increase in Exogenous Spending.

The *AD* curve is seen both *before* (*AD*) and *after* (*AD′*) an increase in exogenous spending—specifically, an increase in consumption spending resulting from a rise in the stock market. If the inflation rate and the real interest rate set by the Fed are held constant, an increase in exogenous spending raises short-run equilibrium output. As a result, the *AD* curve will shift to the right, from *AD* to *AD′*.

Similarly, at a given inflation rate, an exogenous decline in spending—for example, a fall in government purchases resulting from a more restrictive fiscal policy—causes short-run equilibrium output to fall. We conclude that *an exogenous decrease in spending shifts the AD curve to the left.*

SELF-TEST 27.1

Determine how the following events will affect the AD curve:

a. Due to widespread concerns about future weakness in the economy, businesses reduce their spending on new capital.

b. The federal government reduces income taxes.

Changes in the Fed's Policy Reaction Function

Recall that the Fed's policy reaction function describes how the Fed sets the real interest rate at each level of inflation. This relationship is built into the *AD* curve—indeed, it accounts in part for the curve's downward slope. As long as the Fed sets the real interest rate according to an unchanged reaction function, its adjustments in the real rate will not cause the *AD* curve to shift. Under normal circumstances, the Fed generally follows a stable policy reaction function.

However, on occasion the Fed may choose to be significantly "tighter" or "easier" than normal for a given rate of inflation. For example, if inflation is high and has stubbornly refused to decrease, the Fed might choose a tighter monetary policy, setting the real interest rate higher than normal at each given rate of inflation. This change of policy can be interpreted as an upward shift in the Fed's policy reaction function, as shown in Figure 27.3(a), where the real interest rate on the vertical axis is depicted as a function of inflation on the horizontal axis. A decision by the Fed to become more "hawkish" about inflation—that is, to set the real interest rate at a higher level for each given rate of inflation—reduces planned expenditure and thus short-run equilibrium output at each rate of inflation. Thus an upward shift of the Fed's policy reaction function leads the *AD* curve to shift to the left [Figure 27.3(b)]. Later in the chapter, we will interpret Chair Volcker's attack on inflation in 1979 as precisely such a policy shift.

Similarly, if the nation is experiencing an unusually severe and protracted recession, the Fed may choose to change its policies and set the real interest rate lower than normal, given the rate of inflation. This change in policy can be interpreted as a downward shift of the Fed's policy reaction function. Given the rate of inflation, a lower-than-normal setting of the real interest rate will lead to higher levels of expenditure and short-run equilibrium output. Therefore, a downward shift of the Fed's policy reaction function causes the *AD* curve to shift to the right.

SELF-TEST 27.2

Explain why a shift in monetary policy like that shown in Figure 27.3 can be interpreted as a decline in the Fed's long-run "target" for the inflation rate. (*Hint:* In the long run, the real interest rate set by the Fed must be consistent with the real interest rate determined in the market for saving and investment.)

SHIFTS OF THE *AD* CURVE VERSUS MOVEMENTS ALONG THE *AD* CURVE

Let's end this section by reviewing and summarizing the important distinction between *movements along* the *AD* curve and *shifts* of the *AD* curve.

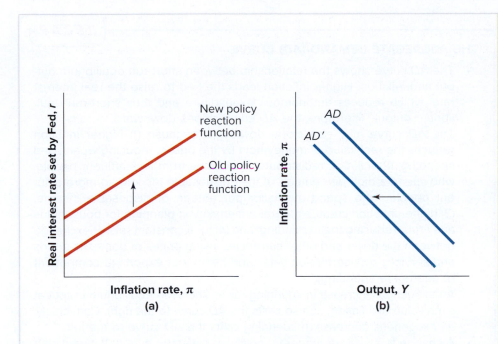

FIGURE 27.3

A Shift in the Fed's Policy Reaction Function.

If inflation has remained too high for an extended period, the Fed may choose a "tighter" monetary policy by setting the real interest rate at a higher level than usual for each given rate of inflation. Graphically, this change corresponds to an upward movement in the Fed's policy reaction function (a). This change to a tighter monetary policy shifts the *AD* curve to the left (b). If a protracted recession led the Fed to decide to set a lower real interest rate at each level of inflation, the Fed's policy reaction function would shift downward, and the *AD* curve would shift to the right.

The downward slope of the *AD* curve captures the inverse relationship between inflation, on the one hand, and short-run equilibrium output, on the other. As we have seen, a rise in the inflation rate leads the Fed to raise the real interest rate, according to its policy reaction function. The higher real interest rate, in turn, depresses planned spending and hence lowers short-run equilibrium output. The downward slope of the *AD* curve embodies this relationship among inflation, spending, and output. Hence changes in the inflation rate, and the resulting changes in the real interest rate and short-run equilibrium output, are represented by *movements along* the *AD* curve. In particular, as long as the Fed sets the real interest rate in accordance with a fixed policy reaction function, changes in the real interest rate will *not* shift the *AD* curve.

However, any factor that changes the short-run equilibrium level of output *at a given level of inflation* will *shift* the *AD* curve—to the right if short-run equilibrium output increases or to the left if short-run equilibrium output decreases. We have identified two factors that can shift the *AD* curve: exogenous changes in spending (that is, changes in spending unrelated to output or the real interest rate) and changes in the Fed's policy reaction function. An exogenous increase in spending or a downward shift of the Fed's policy reaction function increases short-run equilibrium output at every level of inflation, hence shifting the *AD* curve to the right. An exogenous decline in spending or an upward shift in the Fed's policy reaction function decreases short-run equilibrium output at every level of inflation, shifting the *AD* curve to the left.

 SELF-TEST 27.3

What is the difference, if any, between the following?

a. An upward shift in the Fed's policy reaction function.

b. A response by the Fed to higher inflation, for a given policy reaction function.

How does each scenario affect the *AD* curve?

> **RECAP** ↑
>
> ### THE AGGREGATE DEMAND (*AD*) CURVE
>
> - The *AD* curve shows the relationship between short-run equilibrium output and inflation. Higher inflation leads the Fed to raise the real interest rate, which reduces autonomous expenditure and thus short-run equilibrium output. Therefore, the *AD* curve slopes downward.
> - The *AD* curve may also slope downward because (1) higher inflation reduces the real value of money held by the public, reducing wealth and spending; (2) inflation redistributes resources from less affluent people, who spend a high percentage of their disposable income, to more affluent people, who spend a smaller percentage of disposable income; (3) higher inflation creates greater uncertainty in planning for households and firms, reducing their spending; and (4) for a constant rate of exchange between the dollar and other currencies, rising prices of domestic goods and services reduce foreign sales and hence net exports (a component of aggregate spending).
> - An exogenous increase in spending raises short-run equilibrium output at each value of inflation, and so shifts the *AD* curve to the right. Conversely, an exogenous decrease in spending shifts the *AD* curve to the left.
> - A change to an easier monetary policy, as reflected by a downward shift in the Fed's policy reaction function, shifts the *AD* curve to the right. A change to a tighter, more anti-inflationary monetary policy, as reflected by an upward shift in the Fed's policy reaction function, shifts the *AD* curve to the left.
> - Assuming no change in the Fed's reaction function, changes in inflation correspond to movements *along* the *AD* curve; they do not *shift* the *AD* curve.

INFLATION AND AGGREGATE SUPPLY

Thus far in this chapter, we have focused on how changes in inflation affect spending and short-run equilibrium output, a relationship captured by the *AD* curve. But we have not yet discussed how inflation itself is determined. In the rest of the chapter, we will examine the main factors that determine the inflation rate in modern industrial economies, as well as the options that policymakers have to control inflation. In doing so, we will introduce a useful diagram for analyzing the behavior of output and inflation, called the *aggregate demand–aggregate supply diagram*.

Physicists have noted that a body will tend to keep moving at a constant speed and direction unless it is acted upon by some outside force—a tendency they refer to as *inertia*. Applying this concept to economics, many observers have noted that inflation seems to be inertial, in the sense that it tends to remain roughly constant as long as the economy is at full employment and there are no external shocks to the price level. In the first part of this section, we will discuss why inflation behaves in this way.

However, just as a physical object will change speed if it is acted on by outside forces, so various economic forces can change the rate of inflation. Later in this chapter, we will discuss three factors that can cause the inflation rate to change. The first, which we will discuss in this section, is the presence of an *output gap*: Inflation tends to rise when there is an expansionary output gap and to fall when there is a recessionary output gap. The second factor that can affect the inflation rate is a shock that directly affects prices, which we will refer to as an *inflation shock*. A large increase in the price of imported oil, for example, raises the price of gasoline, heating oil, and other fuels, as well as of goods made with oil or services using oil, such as transportation. Finally, the third factor that directly affects the inflation rate is a *shock to potential output,* or a sharp change in the level of potential output—a natural disaster that destroyed a significant portion of a country's factories and businesses is one extreme example. Together, inflationary shocks and shocks to potential output are known as *aggregate supply shocks;* we postpone discussing them until the next section.

INFLATION INERTIA

In low-inflation industrial economies like that of the United States today, inflation tends to change relatively slowly from year to year, a phenomenon that is sometimes referred to as *inflation inertia.* If the rate of inflation in one year is 2 percent, it may be 3 percent or even 4 percent in the next year. But unless the nation experiences very unusual economic conditions, inflation is unlikely to rise to 6 percent or 8 percent or fall to −2 percent in the following year. This relatively sluggish behavior contrasts sharply with the behavior of economic variables such as stock or commodity prices, which can change rapidly from day to day. For example, oil prices might well rise by 20 percent over the course of a year and then fall 20 percent over the next year. Over the past 30 years or so, however, the U.S. inflation rate has generally remained in the range of 2–3 percent per year, with only small and short-lived deviations.

Why does inflation tend to adjust relatively slowly in modern industrial economies? To answer this question, we must consider two closely related factors that play an important role in determining the inflation rate: the behavior of the public's *inflation expectations* and the existence of *long-term wage and price contracts.*

Inflation Expectations

First, consider the public's expectations about inflation. In negotiating future wages and prices, both buyers and sellers take into account the rate of inflation they expect to prevail in the next few years. As a result, today's *expectations* of future inflation may help determine the future inflation rate. Suppose, for example, that office worker Fred and his boss Colleen agree that Fred's performance this past year justifies an increase of 2 percent in his real wage for next year. What *nominal,* or dollar, wage increase should they agree on? If Fred believes that inflation is likely to be 3 percent over the next year, he will ask for a 5 percent increase in his nominal wage to obtain a 2 percent increase in his real wage. If Colleen agrees that inflation is likely to be 3 percent, she should be willing to go along with a 5 percent nominal increase, knowing that it implies only a 2 percent increase in Fred's real wage. Thus the rate at which Fred and Colleen *expect* prices to rise affects the rate at which at least one price—Fred's nominal wage— *actually* rises.

A similar dynamic affects the contracts for production inputs other than labor. For example, if Colleen is negotiating with her office supply company, the prices she will agree to pay for next year's deliveries of copy paper and staples will depend on what she expects the inflation rate to be. If Colleen anticipates that the price of office supplies will not change relative to the prices of other goods and services, and that the general inflation rate will be 3 percent, then she should be willing to agree to a 3 percent increase in the price of office supplies. On the other hand, if she expects the general inflation rate to be 6 percent, then she will agree to pay 6 percent more for copy paper and staples next year, knowing that a nominal increase of 6 percent implies no change in the price of office supplies relative to other goods and services.

Economywide, then, the higher the expected rate of inflation, the more nominal wages and the cost of other inputs will tend to rise. But if wages and other costs of production grow rapidly in response to expected inflation, firms will have to raise their prices rapidly as well in order to cover their costs. Thus a high rate of expected inflation tends to lead to a high rate of actual inflation. Similarly, if expected inflation is low, leading wages and other costs to rise relatively slowly, actual inflation should be low as well.

> ✅ **SELF-TEST 27.4**
>
> Assume that employers and workers agree that real wages should rise by 2 percent next year.
>
> a.   If inflation is expected to be 2 percent next year, what will happen to nominal wages next year?
>
> b.   If inflation is expected to be 4 percent next year, rather than 2 percent, what will happen to nominal wages next year?
>
> c.   Use your answers from parts a and b to explain how an increase in expected inflation will tend to affect the following year's actual rate of inflation.

The conclusion that actual inflation is partially determined by expected inflation raises the question of what determines inflation expectations. To a great extent, people's expectations are influenced by their recent experience. If inflation has been low and stable for some time, people are likely to expect it to continue to be low. But if inflation has recently been high, people will expect it to continue to be high. If inflation has been unpredictable, alternating between low and high levels, the public's expectations will likewise tend to be volatile, rising or falling with news or rumors about economic conditions or economic policy.

Figure 27.4 illustrates schematically how low and stable inflation may tend to be self-perpetuating. As the figure shows, if inflation has been low for some time, people will continue to expect low inflation. Increases in nominal wages and other production costs will thus tend to be small. If firms raise prices only by enough to cover costs, then actual inflation will be low, as expected. This low actual rate will in turn promote low expected inflation, perpetuating the "virtuous circle." The same logic applies in reverse in an economy with high inflation: A persistently high inflation rate leads the public to expect high inflation, resulting in higher increases in nominal wages and other production costs. This in turn contributes to a high rate of actual inflation, and so on in a vicious circle. This role of inflation expectations in the determination of wage and price increases helps explain why inflation often seems to adjust slowly.

Long-Term Wage and Price Contracts

The role of inflation expectations in the slow adjustment of inflation is strengthened by a second key element, the existence of *long-term wage and price contracts*. Union wage contracts, for example, often extend for three years into the future. Likewise, contracts that set

---

FIGURE 27.4

A Virtuous Circle of Low Inflation and Low Expected Inflation.

Low inflation leads people to expect low inflation in the future. As a result, they agree to accept small increases in wages and in the prices of the goods and services they supply, which keeps inflation—and expected inflation—low. In a similar way, high inflation leads people to expect high inflation, which in turn tends to produce high inflation.

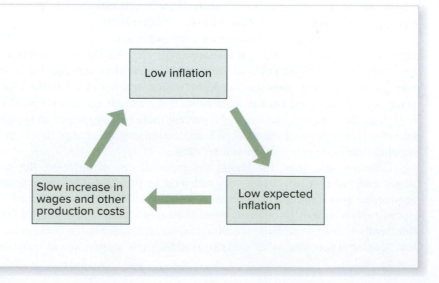

the prices manufacturing firms pay for parts and raw materials often cover several years. Long-term contracts serve to "build in" wage and price increases that depend on inflation expectations at the time the contracts were signed. For example, a union negotiating in a high-inflation environment is much more likely to demand a rapid increase in nominal wages over the life of the contract than would a union in an economy in which prices are stable.

To summarize, in the absence of external shocks, inflation tends to remain relatively stable over time—at least in low-inflation industrial economies like that of the United States. In other words, inflation is *inertial* (or as some people put it, "sticky"). Inflation tends to be inertial for two main reasons. The first is the behavior of people's expectations of inflation. A low inflation rate leads people to expect low inflation in the future, which results in reduced pressure for wage and price increases. Similarly, a high inflation rate leads people to expect high inflation in the future, resulting in more rapid increases in wages and prices. Second, the effects of expectations are reinforced by the existence of long-term wage and price contracts, which is the second reason inflation tends to be stable over time. Long-term contracts tend to build in the effects of people's inflation expectations.

Although the rate of inflation tends to be inertial, it does of course change over time. We next discuss a key factor causing the inflation rate to change.

 SELF-TEST 27.5

Based on Figure 27.4, discuss why the Federal Reserve has a strong incentive to maintain a low inflation rate in the economy.

THE OUTPUT GAP AND INFLATION

An important factor influencing the rate of inflation is the output gap, or the difference between actual output and potential output $(Y - Y^*)$. We have seen that, in the short run, firms will meet the demand for their output at previously determined prices. For example, Alice's ice cream shop will serve ice cream to any customer who comes into the shop at the prices posted behind the counter. The level of output that is determined by the demand at preset prices is called short-run equilibrium output.

At a particular time the level of short-run equilibrium output may happen to equal the economy's long-run productive capacity, or potential output. But that is not necessarily the case. Output may exceed potential output, giving rise to an expansionary gap, or it may fall short of potential output, producing a recessionary gap. Let's consider what happens to inflation in each of these three possible cases: no output gap, an expansionary gap, and a recessionary gap. The resulting outcomes are summarized in Table 27.1.

TABLE 27.1
The Output Gap and Inflation

The table shows three possible situations. With no output gap, the rate of inflation will tend to remain the same. With expansionary gap, the rate of inflation will tend to increase. With recessionary gap, the rate of inflation will tend to decrease.

Relationship of output to potential output		Behavior of inflation
1. No output gap	$\rightarrow$	Inflation remains unchanged
$\quad Y = Y^*$		
2. Expansionary gap	$\rightarrow$	Inflation rises
$\quad Y > Y^*$		$\pi \uparrow$
3. Recessionary gap	$\rightarrow$	Inflation falls
$\quad Y < Y^*$		$\pi \downarrow$

No Output Gap: $Y = Y^*$

If actual output equals potential output, then by definition, there is no output gap. When the output gap is zero, firms are satisfied in the sense that their sales equal their normal production rates. As a result, firms have no incentive either to reduce or increase their prices *relative* to the prices of other goods and services. However, the fact that firms are satisfied with their sales does *not* imply that inflation–the rate of change in the overall price level–is zero.

To see why, let's go back to the idea of inflation inertia. Suppose that inflation has recently been steady at 3 percent per year, so that the public has come to expect an inflation rate of 3 percent per year. If the public's inflation expectations are reflected in the wage and price increases agreed to in long-term contracts, then firms will find their labor and materials costs are rising at 3 percent per year. To cover their costs, firms will need to raise their prices by 3 percent per year. Note that if all firms are raising their prices by 3 percent per year, the *relative* prices of various goods and services in the economy–say, the price of ice cream relative to the price of a taxi ride–will not change. Nevertheless, the economywide rate of inflation equals 3 percent, the same as in previous years. We conclude that, *if the output gap is zero, the rate of inflation will tend to remain the same.*

Expansionary Gap: $Y > Y^*$

Suppose instead that an expansionary gap exists so that most firms' sales exceed their normal production rates. As we might expect in situations in which the quantity demanded exceeds the quantity firms desire to supply, firms will ultimately respond by trying to increase their relative prices. To do so, they will increase their prices by *more* than the increase in their costs. If all firms behave this way, then the general price level will begin to rise more rapidly than before. Thus, *when an expansionary gap exists, the rate of inflation will tend to increase.*

Recessionary Gap: $Y < Y^*$

Finally, if a recessionary gap exists, firms will be selling an amount less than their capacity to produce, and they will have an incentive to cut their relative prices so they can sell more. In this case, firms will raise their prices less than needed to cover fully their increases in costs, as determined by the existing inflation rate. As a result, *when a recessionary gap exists, the rate of inflation will tend to decrease.*

EXAMPLE 27.1 **Spending Changes and Inflation**

How will a fall in consumer confidence affect the rate of inflation?

In Chapter 25, *Spending and Output in the Short Run,* and Chapter 26, *Stabilizing the Economy: The Role of the Fed,* we saw that changes in spending can create expansionary or recessionary gaps. Therefore, based on the discussion above, we can conclude that changes in spending also lead to changes in the rate of inflation. If the economy is currently operating at potential output, what effect will a fall in consumer confidence that makes consumers less willing to spend at each level of disposable income have on the rate of inflation in the economy?

An exogenous decrease in consumption spending, *C,* for a given level of inflation, output, and real interest rates, reduces aggregate expenditures and short-run equilibrium output. If the economy was originally operating at potential output, the reduction in consumption will cause a recessionary gap since actual output, *Y,* will now be less than potential output, *Y*.* As indicated above, when $Y < Y^*$, the rate of inflation will tend to fall because firms' sales fall short of normal production rates, leading them to slow down the rate at which they increase their prices.

✓ **SELF-TEST 27.6**

Suppose that firms become optimistic about the future and decide to increase their investment in new capital. What effect will this have on the rate of inflation, assuming that the economy is currently operating at potential output?

THE AGGREGATE DEMAND–AGGREGATE SUPPLY DIAGRAM

The adjustment of inflation in response to an output gap can be shown conveniently in a diagram. Figure 27.5, drawn with inflation π on the vertical axis and real output Y on the horizontal axis, is an example of an *aggregate demand–aggregate supply diagram,* or *AD-AS diagram* for short. The diagram has three elements, one of which is the downward-sloping *AD* curve, introduced earlier in the chapter. Recall that the *AD* curve shows how planned aggregate spending, and hence short-run equilibrium output, depends on the inflation rate. The second element is a vertical line marking the economy's potential output Y^*. Because potential output represents the economy's long-run productive capacity, we will refer to this vertical line as the **long-run aggregate supply (*LRAS*) line.** The third element in Figure 27.5, and a new one, is the *short-run aggregate supply line,* labeled *SRAS* in the diagram. The **short-run aggregate supply (*SRAS*) line** is a horizontal line that shows the current rate of inflation in the economy, which in the figure is labeled π. We can think of the current rate of inflation as having been determined by past expectations of inflation and past pricing decisions. The short-run aggregate supply line is horizontal because, in the short run, producers supply whatever output is demanded at preset prices.

The *AD-AS* diagram can be used to determine the level of output prevailing at any particular time. As we have seen, the inflation rate at any moment is given directly by the position of the *SRAS* line—for example, current inflation equals π in Figure 27.5. To find the current level of output, recall that the *AD* curve shows the level of short-run equilibrium output at any given rate of inflation. Since the inflation rate in this economy is π, we can infer from Figure 27.5 that short-run equilibrium output must equal Y, which corresponds to the intersection of the *AD* curve and the *SRAS* line (point *A* in the figure). Notice that in Figure 27.5, short-run equilibrium output Y is smaller than potential output Y^*, so there is a recessionary gap in this economy.

long-run aggregate supply (*LRAS*) line a vertical line showing the economy's potential output Y^*

short-run aggregate supply (*SRAS*) line a horizontal line showing the current rate of inflation, as determined by past expectations and pricing decisions

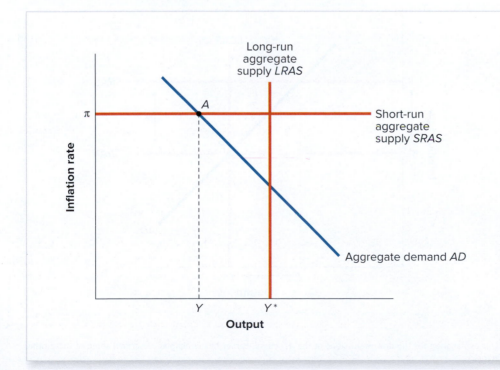

FIGURE 27.5

The Aggregate Demand–Aggregate Supply (*AD-AS*) Diagram.

This diagram has three elements: the *AD* curve, which shows how short-run equilibrium output depends on inflation; the long-run aggregate supply (*LRAS*) line, which marks the economy's potential output Y^*; and the short-run aggregate supply (*SRAS*) line, which shows the current value of inflation π. Short-run equilibrium output, which is equal to Y here, is determined by the intersection of the *AD* curve and the *SRAS* line (point *A*). Because actual output Y is less than potential output Y^*, this economy has a recessionary gap.

short-run equilibrium a situation in which inflation equals the value determined by past expectations and pricing decisions and output equals the level of short-run equilibrium output that is consistent with that inflation rate; graphically, short-run equilibrium occurs at the intersection of the *AD* curve and the *SRAS* line

The intersection of the *AD* curve and the *SRAS* line (point *A* in Figure 27.5) is referred to as the point of *short-run equilibrium* in this economy. When the economy is in **short-run equilibrium,** inflation equals the value determined by past expectations and past pricing decisions, and output equals the level of short-run equilibrium output that is consistent with that inflation rate.

Although the economy may be in short-run equilibrium at point *A* in Figure 27.5, it will not remain there. The reason is that at point *A,* the economy is experiencing a recessionary gap (output is less than potential output, as indicated by the *LRAS* line). As we have just seen, when a recessionary gap exists, firms are not selling as much as they would like to and so they slow down the rate at which they increase their prices. Eventually, the low level of aggregate demand that is associated with a recessionary gap causes the inflation rate to fall.

The adjustment of inflation in response to a recessionary gap is shown graphically in Figure 27.6. As inflation declines, the *SRAS* line moves downward, from *SRAS* to *SRAS'*. Because of inflation inertia (caused by the slow adjustment of the public's inflation expectations and the existence of long-term contracts), inflation adjusts downward only gradually. However, as long as a recessionary gap exists, inflation will continue to fall, and the *SRAS* line will move downward until it intersects the *AD* curve at point *B* in the figure. At that point, actual output equals potential output and the recessionary gap has been eliminated. Because there is no further pressure on inflation at point *B,* the inflation rate stabilizes at the lower level. A situation like that represented by point *B* in Figure 27.6, in which the inflation rate is stable and actual output equals potential output, is referred to as **long-run equilibrium** of the economy. Long-run equilibrium occurs when the *AD* curve, the *SRAS* line, and the *LRAS* line all intersect at a single point.

long-run equilibrium a situation in which actual output equals potential output and the inflation rate is stable; graphically, long-run equilibrium occurs when the *AD* curve, the *SRAS* line, and the *LRAS* line all intersect at a single point

Figure 27.6 illustrates the important point that when a recessionary gap exists, inflation will tend to fall. It also shows that as inflation declines, short-run equilibrium output rises, increasing gradually from *Y* to *Y** as the short-run equilibrium point moves down the *AD* curve. The source of this increase in output is the behavior of the Federal Reserve, which lowers the real interest rate as inflation falls, stimulating aggregate demand. Falling inflation stimulates spending and output in other ways, such as by reducing uncertainty.[3] As output rises cyclical unemployment, which by

FIGURE 27.6

The Adjustment of Inflation When a Recessionary Gap Exists.

At the initial short-run equilibrium point *A,* a recessionary gap exists, which puts downward pressure on inflation. As inflation gradually falls, the *SRAS* line moves downward until it reaches *SRAS',* and actual output equals potential output (point *B*). Once the recessionary gap has been eliminated, inflation stabilizes at π^*, and the economy settles into long-run equilibrium at the intersection of *AD, LRAS,* and *SRAS'* (point *B*).

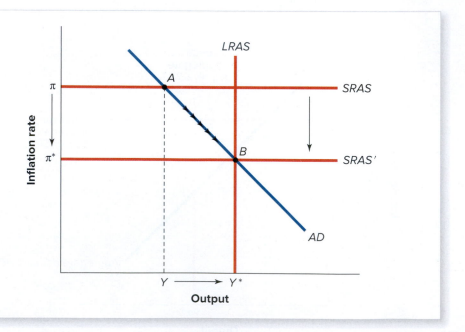

[3]Our explanation for the downward slope of the *AD* curve, earlier in the chapter, described some of these other factors.

Okun's law is proportional to the output gap, also declines. This process of falling inflation, falling real interest rates, rising output, and falling unemployment continues until the economy reaches full employment at point *B* in Figure 27.6, the economy's long-run equilibrium point.

What happens if instead of a recessionary gap, the economy has an expansionary gap, with output greater than potential output? An expansionary gap would cause the rate of inflation to *rise,* as firms respond to high demand by raising their prices more rapidly than their costs are rising. In graphical terms, an expansionary gap would cause the *SRAS* line to move upward over time. Inflation and the *SRAS* line would continue to rise until the economy reached long-run equilibrium, with actual output equal to potential output. This process is illustrated in Figure 27.7. Initially, the economy is in short-run equilibrium at point *A,* where $Y > Y^*$ (an expansionary gap). The expansionary gap causes inflation to rise over time; graphically, the short-run aggregate supply line moves upward, from *SRAS* to *SRAS'.* As the *SRAS* line rises, short-run equilibrium output falls—the result of the Fed's tendency to increase the real interest rate when inflation rises. Eventually the *SRAS* line intersects the *AD* curve *LRAS* and line at point *B,* where the economy reaches long-run equilibrium, with no output gap and stable inflation.

THE SELF-CORRECTING ECONOMY

Our analysis of Figures 27.6 and 27.7 makes an important general point: The economy tends to be *self-correcting* in the long run. In other words, given enough time, output gaps tend to disappear without changes in monetary or fiscal policy (other than the change in the real interest rate embodied in the Fed's policy reaction function). Expansionary output gaps are eliminated by rising inflation, while recessionary output gaps are eliminated by falling inflation. This result contrasts sharply with the basic Keynesian model, which does not include a self-correcting mechanism. The difference in results is explained by the fact that the basic Keynesian model concentrates on the short-run period, during which prices do not adjust, and does not take into account the changes in prices and inflation that occur over a longer period.

Does the economy's tendency to self-correct imply that aggressive monetary and fiscal policies are not needed to stabilize output? The answer to this question depends crucially on the *speed* with which the self-correction process takes place. If self-correction

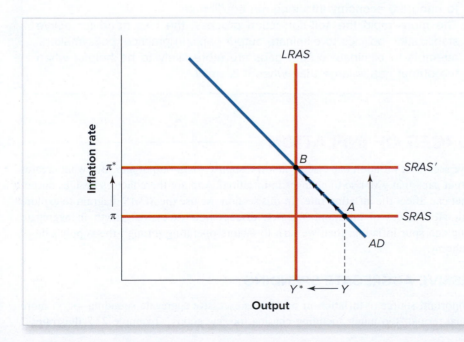

FIGURE 27.7

The Adjustment of Inflation When an Expansionary Gap Exists.

At the initial short-run equilibrium point *A*, an expansionary gap exists. Inflation rises gradually (the *SRAS* line moves upward) and output falls. The process continues until the economy reaches long-run equilibrium at point *B*, where inflation stabilizes and the output gap is eliminated.

takes place very slowly, so that actual output differs from potential for protracted periods, then active use of monetary and fiscal policy can help stabilize output. But if self-correction is rapid, then active stabilization policies are probably not justified in most cases, given the lags and uncertainties that are involved in policymaking in practice. Indeed, if the economy returns to full employment quickly, then attempts by policymakers to stabilize spending and output may end up doing more harm than good, for example, by causing actual output to "overshoot" potential output.

The speed with which a particular economy corrects itself depends on a variety of factors, including the prevalence of long-term contracts and the efficiency and flexibility of product and labor markets. (For a case study, see the discussion of U.S. and European labor markets in Chapter 20, *The Labor Market: Workers, Wages, and Unemployment*.) However, a reasonable conclusion is that the greater the initial output gap, the longer the economy's process of self-correction will take. This observation suggests that stabilization policies should not be used actively to try to eliminate relatively small output gaps, but that they may be quite useful in remedying large gaps—for example, when the unemployment rate is exceptionally high.

> **RECAP**
>
> **INFLATION, *AD-AS*, AND THE SELF-CORRECTING ECONOMY**
>
> - The economy is in short-run equilibrium when inflation equals the value determined by past expectations and pricing decisions, and output equals the level of short-run equilibrium output that is consistent with that inflation rate. Graphically, short-run equilibrium occurs at the intersection of the *AD* curve and the *SRAS* line. We refer to the fact that inflation is determined by past inflation (which affects past expectations and pricing decisions) as inflation inertia.
> - The economy is in long-run equilibrium when actual output equals potential output (there is no output gap) and the inflation rate is stable. Graphically, long-run equilibrium occurs when the *AD* curve, the *SRAS* line, and the *LRAS* line intersect at a common point.
> - Inflation adjusts gradually to bring the economy into long-run equilibrium (a phenomenon called the economy's self-correcting tendency). Inflation rises to eliminate an expansionary gap and falls to eliminate a recessionary gap. Graphically, the *SRAS* line moves up or down as needed to bring the economy into long-run equilibrium.
> - The more rapid the self-correction process, the less need for active stabilization policies to eliminate output gaps. In practice, policymakers' attempts to eliminate output gaps are more likely to be helpful when the output gap is large than when it is small.

SOURCES OF INFLATION

We have seen that inflation can rise or fall in response to an output gap. But what creates the output gaps that give rise to changes in inflation? And are there factors besides output gaps that can affect the inflation rate? In this section, we use the *AD-AS* diagram to explore the ultimate sources of inflation. We first discuss how excessive growth in aggregate spending can spur inflation; then we turn to factors operating through the supply side of the economy.

EXCESSIVE AGGREGATE SPENDING

One important source of inflation in practice is excessive aggregate spending—or, in more colloquial terms, "too much spending chasing too few goods." Example 27.2 illustrates.

EXAMPLE 27.2   Military Buildups and Inflation

Can the Fed do anything to prevent inflation caused by wars or military buildups?

Wars and military buildups are sometimes associated with increased inflation. Explain why, using the *AD-AS* diagram. Can the Fed do anything to prevent the increase in inflation caused by a military buildup?

Wars and military buildups are potentially inflationary because increased spending on military hardware raises total demand relative to the economy's productive capacity. In the face of rising sales, firms increase their prices more quickly, raising the inflation rate.

The two panels of Figure 27.8 illustrate this process. Looking first at Figure 27.8(a), suppose that the economy is initially in long-run equilibrium at point *A,* where the aggregate demand curve *AD* intersects both the short-run and long-run aggregate supply lines, *SRAS* and *LRAS,* respectively. Point *A* is a long-run equilibrium point, with output equal to potential output and stable inflation. Now suppose that the government decides to spend more on armaments. Increased military spending is an increase in government purchases *G,* an exogenous increase in spending. We saw earlier that, for a given level of inflation, an exogenous increase in spending raises short-run equilibrium output, shifting the *AD* curve to the right. Figure 27.8(a) shows the aggregate demand curve shifting rightward, from *AD* to *AD',* as the result of increased military expenditure. The economy moves to a new, short-run equilibrium at point *B,* where *AD'* intersects *SRAS.* Note that at point *B* actual output has risen above potential, to $Y > Y^*$, creating an expansionary gap. Because inflation is inertial and does not change in the short run, the immediate effect of the increase in government purchases is only to increase output, just as we saw in the Keynesian cross analysis in Chapter 25, *Spending and Output in the Short Run.*

The process doesn't stop there, however, because inflation will not remain the same indefinitely. At point *B,* an expansionary gap exists, so inflation will gradually begin to increase. Figure 27.8(b) shows this increase in inflation as a shift of the *SRAS* line from its initial position to a higher level, *SRAS'.* When inflation

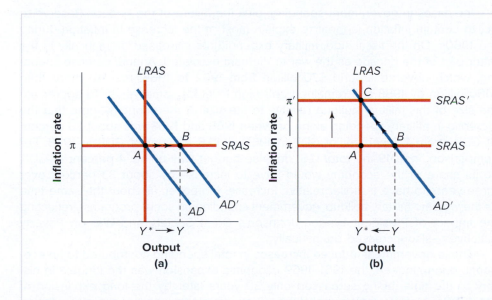

FIGURE 27.8

War and Military Buildup as a Source of Inflation.

(a) An increase in military spending shifts the *AD* curve to the right, from *AD* to *AD'.* At the new short-run equilibrium point *B,* actual output has risen above potential output Y^*, creating an expansionary gap. (b) This gap leads to rising inflation, shown as an upward movement of the *SRAS* line, from *SRAS* to *SRAS'.* At the new long-run equilibrium point *C,* actual output has fallen back to the level of potential output, but at π' inflation is higher than it was originally.

has risen to π', enough to eliminate the output gap (point C), the economy is back in long-run equilibrium. We see now that the increase in output created by the military buildup was only temporary. In the long run, actual output has returned to the level of potential output, but at a higher rate of inflation.

Does the Fed have the power to prevent the increased inflation that is induced by a rise in military spending? The answer is yes. We saw earlier that a decision by the Fed to set a higher real interest rate at any given level of inflation—an upward shift in the policy reaction function—will shift the AD curve to the left. So if the Fed aggressively tightens monetary policy (shifts its reaction function) as the military buildup proceeds, it can reverse the rightward shift of the AD curve caused by increased government spending. Offsetting the rightward shift of the AD curve in turn avoids the development of an expansionary gap, with its inflationary consequences. The Fed's policy works because the higher real interest rate it sets at each level of inflation acts to reduce consumption and investment spending. The reduction in private spending offsets the increase in demand by the government, eliminating—or at least moderating—the inflationary impact of the military purchases.

We should not conclude, by the way, that avoiding the inflationary consequences of a military buildup makes the buildup costless to society. As we have just noted, inflation can be avoided only if consumption and investment are reduced by a policy of higher real interest rates. Effectively, the private sector must give up some resources so that more of the nation's output can be devoted to military purposes. This reduction in resources reduces both current living standards (by reducing consumption) and future living standards (by reducing investment).

The Economic Naturalist 27.1

How did inflation get started in the United States in the 1960s?

In the United States from 1959 through 1963, inflation hovered around 1 percent per year. Beginning in 1964, however, inflation began to rise, reaching nearly 6 percent in 1970. Why did inflation become a problem in the United States in the 1960s?

Increases in government spending, plus the failure of the Federal Reserve to act to contain inflation, appear to explain most of the increase in inflation during the 1960s. On the fiscal side, military expenditures increased dramatically in the latter part of the decade as the war in Vietnam escalated. Annual defense spending, which hovered around $70 billion from 1962 to 1965, rose to more than $100 billion by 1968 and remained at a high level for some years. To appreciate the size of this military buildup relative to the size of the economy, note that the *increase* in military spending alone between 1965 and 1968 was about 1.3 percent of GDP—from 9.5 percent of GDP in 1965 to 10.8 percent of GDP in 1968. For comparison, in 2019 the *total* U.S. defense budget was below 4 percent of GDP, so its share of the economy would have to increase by about 33 percent over three years to have a similar relative increase. Moreover, at about the same time as the wartime military buildup, government spending on social programs—reflecting the impact of President Lyndon Johnson's Great Society and War on Poverty initiatives—also increased dramatically.

These government-induced increases in total spending contributed to an economic boom. Indeed, the 1961–1969 economic expansion was the longest in history at the time, being surpassed only 30 years later by the long expansion of the 1990s. However, an expansionary gap developed and eventually inflation began to rise, as would have been predicted by the analysis in Example 27.2.

An interesting contrast exists between these effects of the 1960s military buildup and those of the 1980s buildup under President Reagan, which did not lead to an increase in inflation. One important difference between the two eras was the behavior of the Federal Reserve. As we saw in Example 27.2, the Fed can offset the inflationary impact of increased government spending by fighting inflation more aggressively (shifting its policy reaction function upward). Except for a brief attempt in 1966, the Federal Reserve generally did not try actively to offset inflationary pressures during the 1960s. That failure may have been simply a miscalculation, or it may have reflected a reluctance to take the politically unpopular step of slowing the economy during a period of great political turmoil. But in the early 1980s, under Paul Volcker, the Federal Reserve acted vigorously to contain inflation. As a result, inflation actually declined in the 1980s, despite the military buildup.

 SELF-TEST 27.7

In Example 27.1, we found that a decline in consumer spending tends to reduce the rate of inflation. Using the *AD-AS* diagram, illustrate the short-run and long-run effects of a fall in consumer spending on inflation. How does the decline in spending affect output in the short run and in the long run?

Whereas output gaps cause gradual changes in inflation, on occasion an economic shock can cause a relatively rapid increase or decrease in inflation. Such jolts to prices, which we call *inflation shocks,* are the subject of the next section.

INFLATION SHOCKS

In late 1973, at the time of the Yom Kippur War between Israel and a coalition of Arab nations, the Organization of the Petroleum Exporting Countries (OPEC) dramatically cut its supplies of crude oil to the industrialized nations, quadrupling world oil prices. The sharp increase in oil prices was quickly transferred to the price of gasoline, heating oil, and goods and services that were heavily dependent on oil, such as air travel. The effects of the oil price increase, together with agricultural shortages that increased the price of food, contributed to a significant rise in the overall U.S. inflation rate in 1974.[4]

The increase in inflation in 1974 is an example of what is referred to as an *inflation shock*. An **inflation shock** is a sudden change in the normal behavior of inflation, unrelated to the nation's output gap. An inflation shock that causes an increase in inflation, like the large rise in oil prices in 1973, is called an *adverse* inflation shock. An inflation shock that reduces inflation is called a *favorable* inflation shock.

In contrast with the experience of the 1970s, when sharp increases in oil prices led to higher inflation, since the mid-1980s the effects of oil price changes on inflation have been much smaller. The Economic Naturalist 27.2 gives more details on the economic effects of inflation shocks, and discusses explanations for the smaller effects of oil price changes on inflation in more recent years.

Everett Collection Historical/Alamy Stock Photo

OPEC's 1974 cutback in oil production created long lines, rising prices, and frayed tempers at the gas pump.

inflation shock a sudden change in the normal behavior of inflation, unrelated to the nation's output gap

---

[4]In Chapter 18, *Measuring the Price Level and Inflation,* we distinguished between relative price changes (changes in the prices of individual goods) and inflation (changes in the overall price level). In the 1973–1974 episode, changes in the prices of individual categories of goods, such as energy and food, were sufficiently large and pervasive that the overall price level was significantly affected. Thus these relative price changes carried an inflationary impact as well.

The Economic Naturalist 27.2

Why did oil price increases cause U.S. inflation to escalate in the 1970s but not in the 2000s and 2010s?

Having risen in the second half of the 1960s, inflation continued to rise in the 1970s. Already at 6.2 percent in 1973, inflation jumped to 11.0 percent in 1974. After subsiding from 1974 to 1978, it began to rise again in 1979, to 11.4 percent, and reached 13.5 percent in 1980. Why did inflation increase so much in the 1970s?

We have already described the quadrupling of oil prices in late 1973 and the sharp increases in agricultural prices at about the same time, which together constituted an adverse inflation shock. A second inflation shock occurred in 1979, when the turmoil of the Iranian Revolution restricted the flow of oil from the Middle East and doubled oil prices yet again.

Figure 27.9 shows the effects of an adverse inflation shock on a hypothetical economy. Before the inflation shock occurs, the economy is in long-run equilibrium at point A, at the intersection of AD, LRAS, and SRAS. At point A, actual output is equal to potential output Y*, and the inflation rate is stable at π. However, an adverse inflation shock directly increases inflation so that the SRAS line shifts rapidly upward to SRAS'. A new short-run equilibrium is established at point B, where SRAS' intersects the aggregate demand curve AD. In the wake of the inflation shock, inflation rises to π' and output falls, from Y* to Y'. Thus an inflation shock creates the worst possible scenario: higher inflation coupled with a recessionary gap. The combination of inflation and recession has been referred to as *stagflation,* or stagnation plus inflation. The U.S. economy experienced a stagflation in 1973–1975, after the first oil shock, and again in 1980, after the second oil shock.

An adverse inflation shock poses a difficult dilemma for macroeconomic policymakers. To see why, suppose monetary and fiscal policies were left unchanged

FIGURE 27.9

The Effects of an Adverse Inflation Shock.

Starting from long-run equilibrium at point A, an adverse inflation shock directly raises current inflation, causing the SRAS line to shift upward to SRAS'. At the new short-run equilibrium, point B, inflation has risen to π' and output has fallen to Y', creating a recessionary gap. If the Fed does nothing, eventually the economy will return to point A, restoring the original inflation rate but suffering a long recession in the process. The Fed could ease monetary policy by shifting down its policy reaction function, shifting the AD curve to AD', and restoring full employment more quickly at point C. The cost of this strategy is that inflation remains at its higher level.

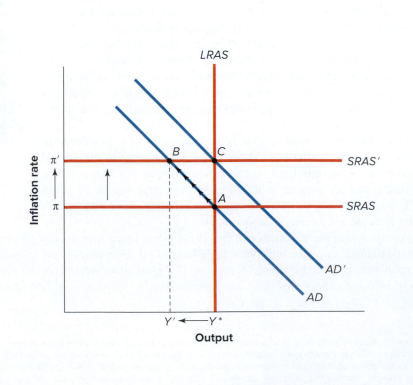

following an inflationary shock. In that case, inflation would eventually abate and return to its original level. Graphically, the economy would reach its short-run equilibrium at point *B* in Figure 27.9 soon after the inflation shock. However, because of the recessionary gap that exists at point *B,* eventually inflation would begin to drift downward, until finally the recessionary gap is eliminated. Graphically, this decline in inflation would be represented by a downward movement of the *SRAS* line, from *SRAS'* back to *SRAS.* Inflation would stop declining only when long-run equilibrium is restored, at point *A* in the figure, where inflation is at its original level of π and output equals potential output.

However, although a "do-nothing" policy approach would ultimately eliminate both the output gap and the surge in inflation, it would also put the economy through a deep and protracted recession, as actual output remains below potential output until the inflation adjustment process is completed. To avoid such an economically and politically costly outcome, policymakers might opt to eliminate the recessionary gap more quickly. By aggressively easing monetary policy (more precisely, by shifting down its policy reaction function), for example, the Fed could shift the *AD* curve to the right, from *AD* to *AD',* taking the economy to a new long-run equilibrium, point *C* in Figure 27.9. This expansionary policy would help restore output to the full-employment level more quickly, but as the figure shows, it would also allow inflation to stabilize at the new, higher level.

In sum, inflation shocks pose a true dilemma for policymakers. If they leave their policies unchanged, inflation will eventually subside, but the nation may experience a lengthy and severe recession. If, instead, they act aggressively to expand aggregate spending, the recession will end more quickly, but inflation will stabilize at a higher level. In the 1970s, though U.S. policymakers tried to strike a balance between stabilizing output and containing inflation, the combination of recession and increased inflation hobbled the economy.

The 1970s were not the last time, however, that oil prices sharply increased. Since the late 1990s, oil prices have swung even more wildly than in the 1970s, yet inflation remained relatively stable. Why did the oil price increases of the 2000s and 2010s not lead to the effects analyzed in Figure 27.9?

Economists proposed different answers to this important question, and it appears that for a full explanation, several factors should be combined. For example, the economists Olivier Blanchard and Jordi Galí, who studied this question, focused on the following three explanations, and concluded that all three are likely to have played an important role.[5] First, labor markets have become more flexible, and wages less sticky, since the 1970s. If wages and prices adjust more quickly, the economy in Figure 27.9 would return to point *A* more quickly, even with a do-nothing policy by the Fed. Second, the share of oil in the economy has declined since the 1970s. With oil less important in both production and consumption, the effects of oil price changes on the economy are expected to be smaller.

Third, and most closely related to the discussion in this chapter, the public's expectations regarding the Fed's reaction to oil price increases were dramatically different in the 2000s and 2010s compared with those in the 1970s. Specifically, in the 1970s, people did not believe that the Fed would return inflation to a low level following an oil price increase. As a result, firms responded by increasing their prices more quickly, and workers demanded wage increases to reflect higher costs of living. But in the 2000s and 2010s, after Fed chairs Paul Volcker and his successor Alan Greenspan had brought inflation down and showed that the Fed was committed to keeping it low, expectations of inflation were much more stable and, as a result, the oil price shocks did not lead to extended periods of increases in wages and other prices.

---

[5]Olivier J. Blanchard and Jordi Galí, "The Macroeconomic Effects of Oil Price Shocks: Why Are the 2000s So Different from the 1970s?," in *International Dimensions of Monetary Policy* (Chicago: University of Chicago Press, 2010).

The Economic Naturalist 27.2 ended by returning to the idea that a central bank's credibility and perceived commitment to maintaining low inflation can by themselves help in achieving the goal of low inflation. This idea has already appeared on several occasions earlier in the chapter—for example, when we discussed Volcker's reputation of conservatism and toughness (in the introduction) and when we illustrated the virtuous cycle of low expected inflation and low inflation (in Figure 27.4). We will revisit this idea again later in the chapter, when mentioning some central banks' commitment to an explicit inflation target.

In Chapter 22, *Money, Prices, and the Federal Reserve,* we discussed the long-run relationship between inflation and money growth. The example of an inflation shock shows that inflation does not always originate from excessive money growth; it can arise from a variety of factors. However, our analysis also shows that, in the absence of monetary easing, inflation that arises from factors such as inflation shocks will eventually die away. By contrast, *sustained* inflation requires that monetary policy remain easy, that is, policymakers allow the money supply to rise rapidly. In this respect, our analysis of this chapter is constant with the earlier long-run analysis, which concluded that sustained inflation is possible only if monetary policy is sufficiently expansionary.

 SELF-TEST 27.8

Inflation shocks can also be beneficial for the economy, such as when oil prices declined by 50 percent in late 2014. What effect would a decrease in oil prices have on output and inflation, if the public did not believe that the Fed would immediately act to keep inflation stable?

SHOCKS TO POTENTIAL OUTPUT

In analyzing the effects of increased oil prices on the U.S. economy in the 1970s, we assumed that potential output was unchanged in the wake of the shock. However, the sharp rise in oil prices during that period probably affected the economy's potential output as well. As oil prices rose, for example, many companies retired less energy-efficient equipment or scrapped older "gas-guzzling" vehicles. A smaller capital stock implies lower potential output.

If the increases in oil prices did reduce potential output, their inflationary impact would have been compounded. Figure 27.10 illustrates the effects on the economy of a sudden decline in potential output. For the sake of simplicity, the figure includes only the effects of the reduction in potential output, and not the direct effect of the inflation shock. (Problem 7 at the end of the chapter asks you to combine the two effects.)

Suppose once again that the economy is in long-run equilibrium at point *A*. Then potential output falls unexpectedly, from Y^* to $Y^{*\prime}$, shifting the long-run aggregate supply line leftward from *LRAS* to *LRAS'*. After this decline in potential output, is the economy still in long-run equilibrium at point *A*? The answer is no, because output now exceeds potential output at that point. In other words, an expansionary gap has developed. This gap reflects the fact that although planned spending has not changed, the capacity of firms to supply goods and services has been reduced.

As we have seen, an expansionary gap leads to rising inflation. In Figure 27.10, increasing inflation is represented by an upward movement of the *SRAS* line. Eventually the short-run aggregate supply line reaches *SRAS'*, and the economy reaches a new long-run equilibrium at point *B*. (Why is point *B* a long-run, and not just a short-run, equilibrium?) At that point, output has fallen to the new, lower level of potential output, $Y^{*\prime}$, and inflation has risen to π'.

aggregate supply shock
either an inflation shock or a shock to potential output; adverse aggregate supply shocks of both types reduce output and increase inflation

Sharp changes in potential output and inflation shocks are both referred to as **aggregate supply shocks.** As we have seen, an adverse aggregate supply shock of either type leads to lower output and higher inflation and, therefore, poses a difficult challenge for policymakers. A difference between the two types of aggregate supply shocks is that the output losses associated with an adverse inflation shock are temporary (because the

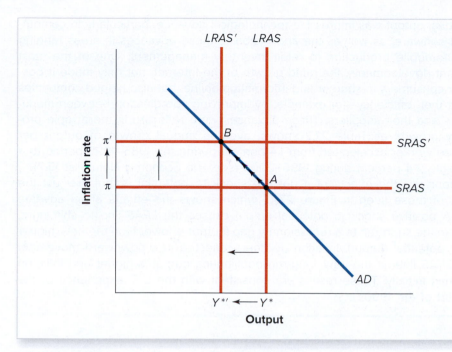

FIGURE 27.10

The Effects of a Shock to Potential Output.

The economy is in long-run equilibrium at point *A* when a decline in potential output, from Y^* to $Y^{*\prime}$, creates an expansionary gap. Inflation rises, and the short-run aggregate supply line shifts upward from *SRAS* to *SRAS'*. A new long-run equilibrium is reached at point *B*, where actual output equals the new, lower level of potential output, $Y^{*\prime}$, and inflation has risen to π'. Because it is the result of a fall in potential output, the decline in output is permanent.

economy self-corrects and will ultimately return to its initial level of potential output), but those associated with a fall in potential output are permanent (output remains lower even after the economy has reached a new long-run equilibrium).

The Economic Naturalist 27.3

Why was the United States able to experience rapid growth and low inflation in the latter part of the 1990s?

The second half of the 1990s was a boom period in the U.S. economy. As Table 27.2 shows, real GDP growth during the 1995–2000 period was 4.3 percent per year, significantly higher than the average growth rate over the previous decade; and unemployment averaged only 4.6 percent, also significantly better than the prior decade. Despite this rapid economic growth, inflation during 1995–2000 was contained, averaging only 2.5 percent per year. Why was the United States able to enjoy both rapid growth and low inflation in the latter 1990s?

During the latter part of the 1990s, the U.S. economy benefited from a positive shock to potential output. An important source of the faster-than-usual expansion

TABLE 27.2

U.S. Macroeconomic Data, Annual Averages, 1985–2000

Years	% Growth in real GDP	Unemployment rate (%)	Inflation rate (%)	Productivity growth (%)
1985–1995	3.0	6.3	3.5	1.4
1995–2000	4.3	4.6	2.5	2.4

Sources: Bureau of Economic Analysis; Bureau of Labor Statistics. Real GDP is measured in 2012 dollars. The unemployment rate is the average civilian unemployment rate for the period. Inflation is measured by the CPI. Productivity is measured by real GDP per employed worker.

of potential output was impressive technological advance, particularly in computers and software, as well as the application of these advances in areas ranging from automobile production to retail inventory management. One of the most prominent developments, the rapid growth of the Internet, not only made it possible for consumers to shop or find information online, but also helped companies improve their efficiency—for example, by improving coordination between manufacturers and their suppliers. These advances were reflected in more rapid productivity growth; as Table 27.2 shows, average annual growth of output per employed worker accelerated from 1.4 percent during the 1985–1995 period to a remarkable 2.4 percent during 1995–2000 (see The Economic Naturalist 19.2).

Graphically, the effects of a positive shock to potential output are just the reverse of those seen in Figure 27.10, which shows the effects of an adverse shock. A positive shock to potential output causes the *LRAS* line to shift right, leading in the short run to a recessionary gap (output is lower than the new, higher level of potential output). Inflation declines, reflected in a downward movement of the *SRAS* line. In the new, long-run equilibrium, output is higher and inflation lower than initially. These results are consistent with the U.S. experience of the latter part of the 1990s.

SELF-TEST 27.9

What if productivity hadn't increased in the late 1990s? How would the economy have been different in 2000?

RECAP

SOURCES OF INFLATION

- Inflation may result from excessive spending, which creates an expansionary output gap and puts upward pressure on inflation. An example is a military buildup, which raises government purchases. Monetary policy or fiscal policy can be used to offset excessive spending, preventing higher inflation from emerging.
- Inflation may also arise from an aggregate supply shock, either an inflation shock or a shock to potential output. An inflation shock is a sudden change in the normal behavior of inflation, unrelated to the nation's output gap. An example of an inflation shock is a run-up in energy and food prices large enough to raise the overall price level. In the absence of public beliefs that the central bank is committed to maintaining low inflation, an inflation shock would lead to stagflation, a combination of recession and higher inflation.
- Stagflation poses a difficult dilemma for policymakers. If they take no action, eventually inflation will subside and output will recover, but in the interim the economy may suffer a protracted period of recession. If they use monetary or fiscal policy to increase aggregate demand, they will shorten the recession but will also lock in the higher level of inflation.
- A shock to potential output is a sharp change in potential output. Like an adverse inflation shock, an adverse shock to potential output results in both higher inflation and lower output. Because lower potential output implies that productive capacity has fallen, however, output does not recover following a shock to potential output, as it eventually does following an inflation shock.

CONTROLLING INFLATION

High or even moderate rates of inflation can impose significant costs to the economy. Indeed, over the past several decades a consensus has developed among economists and policymakers that low and stable inflation is important and perhaps necessary for sustained economic growth. What, then, should policymakers do if the inflation rate is too high? As Example 27.3 will show, inflation can be slowed by policies that shift the aggregate demand curve leftward. Unfortunately, although they produce long-term gains in productivity and economic growth, such policies are likely to impose significant short-run costs in the form of lost output and increased unemployment.

EXAMPLE 27.3   The Effects of Anti-Inflationary Monetary Policy

How will output, unemployment, and inflation react to a monetary-policy tightening?

Suppose that, although the economy is at full employment, the inflation rate is 10 percent—too high to be consistent with economic efficiency and long-term economic growth. The Fed decides to tighten monetary policy to reduce the inflation rate to 3 percent. What will happen to output, unemployment, and inflation in the short run? Over the long run?

The economic effects of a monetary tightening are very different in the short and long run. Figure 27.11(a) shows the short-run effect. Initially, the economy is in long-run equilibrium at point *A*, where actual output equals potential output.

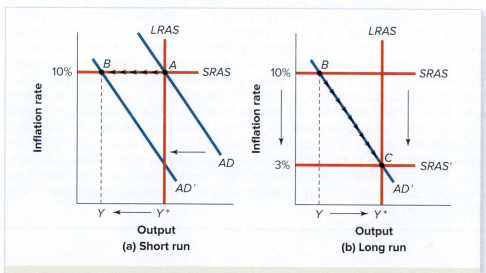

FIGURE 27.11

Short-Run and Long-Run Effects of an Anti-inflationary Monetary Policy.

(a) Initially the economy is in long-run equilibrium at point *A*, with actual output equal to potential and the inflation rate at 10 percent. If an anti-inflationary policy shift by the Fed shifts the *AD* curve to the left, from *AD* to *AD′*, the economy will reach a new short-run equilibrium at point *B*, at the intersection of *AD′* and *SRAS*. As short-run equilibrium output falls to *Y*, a recessionary gap opens up. The inflation rate does not change in the short run. (b) Following the tightening of monetary policy, a recessionary gap exists at point *B*, which eventually causes inflation to decline. The short-run aggregate supply line moves downward, from *SRAS* to *SRAS′*. Long-run equilibrium is restored at point *C*. In the long run, real output returns to potential and inflation stabilizes at a lower level (3 percent in this figure).

But at point *A*, the inflation rate (10 percent) is high, as indicated by the aggregate supply line, *SRAS*.

To bring inflation down to 3 percent, what can policymakers do? To get "tough" on inflation, the Fed must set the real interest rate at a level higher than normal, given the rate of inflation. In other words, the Fed must shift its policy reaction function upward, as in Figure 27.11(a). At a constant rate of inflation, an increase in the real interest rate set by the Fed will reduce consumption and investment spending, lowering aggregate demand at every inflation rate. As we saw earlier in the chapter, this monetary tightening by the Fed causes the *AD* curve to shift leftward, from *AD* to *AD'* in Figure 27.11(a).

After the Fed's action, the *AD'* curve and the *SRAS* line intersect at point *B* in Figure 27.11(a), the new short-run equilibrium point. At point *B* actual output has fallen to *Y*, which is less than potential output *Y**. In other words, the Fed's action has allowed a recessionary gap to develop, one result of which will be that unemployment will exceed the natural rate. At point *B*, however, the inflation rate has not changed, remaining at 10 percent. We conclude that in the short run, a monetary tightening pushes the economy into recession but has little or no effect on the inflation rate, because of inflation inertia.

The short-run effects of the anti-inflationary shift in monetary policy—lower output, higher unemployment, and little or no reduction of inflation—are to say the least not very encouraging, and they explain why such policy shifts are often highly unpopular in their early stages. Fortunately, however, we have not reached the end of the story—because the economy will not remain at point *B* indefinitely. The reason is that the existence of a recessionary gap at that point eventually causes inflation to decline, as firms become more reluctant to raise their prices in the face of weak demand.

Graphically, the eventual decline in inflation that results from a recessionary gap is represented by the downward movement of the short-run aggregate supply line, from *SRAS* to *SRAS'* in Figure 27.11(b). Inflation will continue to fall until the economy returns to long-run equilibrium at point *C*. At that point, actual output has returned to potential, and the inflation rate has stabilized at 3 percent. So we see that a tight monetary policy inflicts short-term pain (a decline in output, high unemployment, and a high real interest rate) to achieve a long-term gain (a permanent reduction in inflation). Incidentally, the result that an upward shift in the monetary policy reaction function leads to a permanently lower rate of inflation suggests a useful alternative way to think about such shifts: An upward shift in the Fed's reaction function is equivalent to a decline in its long-term target for inflation (see Self-Test 27.2). Similarly, a downward shift in the Fed's reaction function could be interpreted as an increase in the Fed's long-term inflation target.

The Economic Naturalist 27.4 discusses the real-life episode of Fed tightening with which we began this chapter.

 SELF-TEST 27.10

Show the typical time paths of output, inflation, and the real interest rate when the Fed employs an anti-inflationary monetary policy. Draw a separate graph for each variable, showing time on the horizontal axis. Be sure to distinguish the short run from the long run. Specific numerical values are not necessary.

The Economic Naturalist 27.4

How was inflation conquered in the 1980s?

After reaching double-digit levels in the late 1970s, inflation in the United States declined sharply in the 1980s. After peaking at 13.5 percent in 1980, the inflation rate fell all the way to 3.2 percent in 1983, and it remained in the 2–5 percent range for the rest of the decade. In the 1990s inflation fell even lower, in the 2–3 percent range in most years. How was inflation conquered in the 1980s?

The person who was most directly responsible for the conquest of inflation in the 1980s was the Federal Reserve's chair, Paul Volcker. Following the secret Saturday meeting he called on October 6, 1979 (described in the introduction to this chapter), the Federal Open Market Committee agreed to adopt a strongly anti-inflationary monetary policy. The results of this policy change on the U.S. economy are shown in Table 27.3, which includes selected macroeconomic data for the period 1978–1985.

The data in Table 27.3 fit our analysis of anti-inflationary monetary policy quite well. First, as our model predicts, in the short run the Fed's sharp tightening of monetary policy led to a recession. In fact, two recessions followed the Fed's action in 1979, a short one in 1980 and a deeper one in 1981–1982. Note that growth in real GDP was negative in 1980 and 1982, and the unemployment rate rose significantly, peaking at 9.7 percent in 1982. Nominal and real interest rates also rose, a direct effect of the shift in monetary policy. Inflation, however, did not respond much during the period 1979–1981. All these results are consistent with the short-run analysis in Figure 27.11.

TABLE 27.3
U.S. Macroeconomic Data, 1978–1985

Year	Growth in real GDP (%)	Unemployment rate (%)	Inflation rate (%)	Nominal interest rate (%)	Real interest rate (%)
1978	5.5	6.1	7.6	8.3	0.7
1979	3.2	5.8	11.3	9.7	−1.6
1980	−0.3	7.1	13.5	11.6	−1.9
1981	2.5	7.6	10.4	14.4	4.0
1982	−1.8	9.7	6.2	12.9	6.7
1983	4.6	9.6	3.2	10.5	7.3
1984	7.2	7.5	4.4	11.9	7.5
1985	4.2	7.2	3.5	9.6	6.1

Sources: Bureau of Economic Analysis; Bureau of Labor Statistics; Federal Reserve Bank of St. Louis. Real GDP is measured in 2012 dollars. Inflation is measured by the CPI. The nominal interest rate is the average annual value of the three-year Treasury bill rate. The real interest rate equals the nominal interest rate minus the inflation rate.

By 1983, however, the situation had changed markedly. The economy had recovered, with strong growth in real GDP in 1983–1985 (see Table 27.3). In 1984, the unemployment rate, which tends to lag the recovery, began to decline. Interest rates remained relatively high, perhaps reflecting other factors besides monetary policy. Most significantly, inflation fell in 1982–1983 and stabilized at a much lower level. Inflation has remained low in the United States ever since.

disinflation a substantial reduction in the rate of inflation

A substantial reduction in the rate of inflation, like the one the Fed engineered in the 1980s, is called a **disinflation.** But again, disinflation comes at the cost of a large recessionary gap and high unemployment like that experienced by the United States in the early 1980s. Is this cost worth bearing? This question is not an easy one to answer, because the costs of inflation are difficult to measure. Policymakers around the world appear to agree on the necessity of containing inflation, however, as many countries fought to bring their own inflation rates down to 2 percent or less in the 1980s and 1990s. Canada and Great Britain are among the many industrial countries that have borne the costs of sharp reductions in inflation.

Can the costs of disinflation be reduced? Unfortunately, no one has found a pain-free method of lowering the inflation rate. Accordingly, in recent decades central banks around the world have striven to keep inflation at manageable levels, to avoid the costs of disinflation. In the United States, under Alan Greenspan (Paul Volcker's immediate successor, who was chair of the Fed from 1987 to 2006), the Federal Reserve followed a strategy of *preemptive strikes,* raising interest rates at the first sign that inflation might soon begin to creep upward. This strategy appears to have been successful in keeping inflation low and avoiding the need for costly disinflation. Other countries—Canada, Great Britain, Sweden, Mexico, Brazil, Chile, Israel, and many others—have announced explicit numerical *targets* for the long-run inflation rate, usually in the range of 1–3 percent per year. More recently, the Fed announced that it views a 2 percent inflation rate as "most consistent over the longer run with the Federal Reserve's statutory mandate."[6] In its statement, the Fed added: "Communicating this inflation goal clearly to the public helps keep longer-term inflation expectations firmly anchored." The philosophy behind inflation targets is the same as that behind the preemptive approach to inflation: If inflation can be kept low, the economy can enjoy the resulting long-term benefits without having to incur the short-term costs of disinflationary policies like the ones followed by Chair Volcker.

The Economic Naturalist 27.5

Can inflation be too low?

Can inflation be too low?

As the last section points out, the Federal Reserve is normally focused on keeping inflation from rising too fast, but by late 2002, some Fed policymakers began to worry that inflation might actually be too low. Why?

Minutes of the Federal Reserve's September 24, 2002, Federal Open Market Committee meeting, where Federal Reserve policymakers determine future monetary policy actions, indicate that committee members were concerned that continuing weakness in the U.S. economy was likely to lead to "quite low and perhaps declining inflation" well into 2003.[7] With prices of consumer goods rising only about 1.5 percent from September 2001 to September 2002, members noted that "further sizable disinflation that resulted in a nominal inflation rate near zero could create problems for the implementation of monetary policy through conventional means in the event of an adverse shock to the economy."

The potential for future monetary policymaking problems was raised by the combination of low inflation rates, low interest rates, and the possibility of further economic weakness. During 2001 and 2002, the Federal Reserve reduced its target for the federal funds rate to 1.75 percent, the lowest level in four decades, in an attempt to provide economic stimulus to an economy slowly emerging from recession. With an inflation rate of 1.5 percent, the resulting real rate of interest—the difference between the nominal interest rate and the inflation rate—was nearly zero percent by September 2002.

---

[6]"FOMC Statement of Longer-Run Goals and Policy Strategy," January 25, 2012, www.federalreserve.gov/newsevents/press/monetary/20120125c.htm.

[7]Minutes from the Federal Reserve's September 2002 FOMC meeting, www.federalreserve.gov/fomc/minutes/20020924.htm.

Why did this create a potential problem for the Federal Reserve? With inflation rates already low and possibly falling, if the Fed was forced in the future to further stimulate aggregate spending in response to a negative economywide spending shock—a real possibility given the concerns about a U.S. military confrontation with Iraq—it might need to reduce the real rate of interest below zero percent. As pointed out in Chapter 26, *Stabilizing the Economy: The Role of the Fed,* business and consumer spending respond to real interest rates, not nominal interest rates. However, in a period of declining inflation, the Federal Reserve needs to reduce nominal interest rates by more than the fall in inflation to reduce the real rate of interest. With the federal funds rate already at historic lows, Fed officials were worried that they would not be able to lower nominal interest rates enough to reduce real interest rates further. In particular, if the inflation rate fell to zero percent, the Fed would not be able to generate a negative real federal funds rate even if it pushed the (nominal) federal funds rate to its zero lower bound, thereby limiting the Fed's ability to conduct conventional expansionary monetary policy to offset a recessionary gap. Indeed, partly as a preemptive measure to prevent further economic weakening and declines in inflation, the Fed acted at its next meeting, in November 2002, to cut the federal funds rate to 1.25 percent.

However, Fed officials at the time also noted that, even if the federal funds rate were to be reduced all the way to zero percent, the Fed would still have a variety of options available to stimulate aggregate spending in the U.S. economy. For example, the Federal Reserve could buy long-term U.S. Treasury bonds (a form of quantitative easing), reducing long-term interest rates, in an effort to spur investment spending. As pointed out in the previous chapter, the Fed's monetary actions typically focus on the federal funds rate, a very short-term interest rate that may or may not move in concert with long-term interest rates that particularly influence mortgage lending. In addition, the Federal Reserve could increase its discount window lending to banks to promote increased consumer and business lending, intervene in foreign exchange markets to reduce the value of the dollar in an attempt to stimulate net exports, or finance a federal government tax cut by buying additional bonds, expanding the money supply in the process.

All of these nontraditional Fed policy actions have the effect of injecting more money into the economy, leading to increased aggregate spending and higher inflation rates over time. By using these monetary policy tools the Fed could, if necessary, generate negative real interest rates by inducing higher inflation, even if the federal funds rate is at zero percent. Thus, while low inflation rates, coupled with low interest rates, make monetary policymaking more complicated, interest rates can't ever really be "too low" to eliminate the Fed's ability to stimulate the economy. Indeed, as discussed in the previous chapter, six years after these late-2002 FOMC meetings the Fed would embark on a massive campaign of unconventional expansionary monetary policy to offset the recessionary gap of the 2007–2009 recession. Having successfully implemented some of these new tools of monetary policy during and following the 2007–2009 recession, the Fed and the public gained familiarity with them. In early 2020, when the COVID-19 pandemic struck, the Fed was therefore ready to move swiftly with new quantitative easing and other emergency lending programs on an unprecedented scale. These measures were aimed to help preemptively offset an expected large recessionary gap.

Too-low inflation has again been a recurring concern since 2015 not only in the U.S., but also in other major economies, including those of Europe and Japan, where inflation persists below central banks' targets. To try to get inflation up to target, both the European Central Bank (ECB) and the Bank of Japan (BOJ), following the example of the Fed from a few years earlier, introduced new tools such as quantitative easing programs.

RECAP ↑

CONTROLLING INFLATION

Inflation can be controlled by policies that shift the aggregate demand curve leftward, such as a move to a "tighter" monetary policy (an upward shift in the monetary policy reaction function). In the short run, the effects of an anti-inflationary monetary policy are felt largely on output, so that a disinflation (a substantial reduction in inflation) may create a significant recessionary gap. According to the theory, in the long run output should return to potential and inflation should decline. These predictions appear to have been borne out during the Volcker disinflation of the early 1980s.

SUMMARY

- This chapter extended the basic Keynesian model to include inflation. First, we showed how planned spending and short-run equilibrium output are related to inflation, a relationship that is summarized by the aggregate demand curve. Second, we discussed how inflation itself is determined. In the short run, inflation is determined by past expectations and pricing decisions, but in the longer run inflation adjusts as needed to eliminate output gaps. *(LO1)*

- The *aggregate demand (AD) curve* shows the relationship between short-run equilibrium output and inflation. Because short-run equilibrium output is equal to planned spending, the aggregate demand curve also relates spending to inflation. Increases in inflation reduce planned spending and short-run equilibrium output, so the aggregate demand curve is downward-sloping. *(LO1)*

- The inverse relationship of inflation and short-run equilibrium output is the result, in large part, of the behavior of the Federal Reserve. To keep inflation low and stable, the Fed reacts to rising inflation by increasing the real interest rate. A higher real interest rate reduces consumption and planned investment, lowering planned aggregate expenditure and hence short-run equilibrium output. Other reasons that the aggregate demand curve slopes downward include the effects of inflation on the real value of money, *distributional effects* (inflation redistributes wealth from the poor, who save relatively little, to the more affluent, who save more), uncertainty created by inflation, and the impact of inflation on foreign sales of domestic goods. *(LO1)*

- For any given value of inflation, an exogenous increase in spending (that is, an increase in spending at given levels of output and the real interest rate) raises short-run equilibrium output, shifting the aggregate demand (*AD*) curve to the right. Likewise, an exogenous decline in spending shifts the *AD* curve to the left. The *AD* curve can also be shifted by a change in the Fed's policy reaction function. If the Fed gets "tougher," shifting up its reaction function and thus choosing a higher real interest rate at each level of inflation, the aggregate demand curve will shift to the left. If the Fed gets "easier," shifting down its reaction function and thus setting a lower real interest rate at each level of inflation, the *AD* curve will shift to the right. *(LO1)*

- In low-inflation industrial economies like the United States today, inflation tends to be inertial, or slow to adjust to changes in the economy. This inertial behavior reflects the fact that inflation depends in part on people's expectations of future inflation, which in turn depend on their recent experience with inflation. Long-term wage and price contracts tend to "build in" the effects of people's expectations for multiyear periods. In the aggregate demand–aggregate supply diagram, the *short-run aggregate supply (SRAS) line* is a horizontal line that shows the current rate of inflation, as determined by past expectations and pricing decisions. *(LO2)*

- Although inflation is inertial, it does change over time in response to output gaps. An expansionary gap tends to raise the inflation rate because firms raise their prices more quickly when they are facing demand that exceeds their normal productive capacity. A recessionary gap tends to reduce the inflation rate as firms become more reluctant to raise their prices. *(LO2)*

- The economy is in *short-run equilibrium* when the inflation rate equals the value determined by past expectations and pricing decisions and output equals the level of short-run equilibrium output that is consistent with that inflation rate. Graphically, short-run equilibrium occurs at the intersection of the *AD* curve and the *SRAS* line. If an output gap exists, however, the inflation rate will adjust to eliminate the gap. Graphically, the *SRAS* line moves upward or downward as needed to restore output to its full-employment level. When the inflation rate is stable and actual output equals potential output, the economy is in *long-run equilibrium*. Graphically, long-run equilibrium corresponds to the common intersection point of the *AD* curve, the *SRAS* line, and the *long-run aggregate supply* (*LRAS*) *line,* a vertical line that marks the economy's potential output. *(LO2)*

• Because the economy tends to move toward long-run equilibrium on its own through the adjustment of the inflation rate, it is said to be self-correcting. The more rapid the self-correction process, the smaller the need for active stabilization policies to eliminate output gaps. In practice, the larger the output gap, the more useful such policies are. *(LO2)*

• One source of inflation is excessive spending, which leads to expansionary output gaps. Aggregate supply shocks are another source of inflation. *Aggregate supply shocks* include both *inflation shocks*—sudden changes in the nor-

mal behavior of inflation, created, for example, by a rise in the price of imported oil—and shocks to potential output. Adverse supply shocks both lower output and—in the absence of public beliefs that the central bank is committed to maintaining low inflation—increase inflation, creating a difficult dilemma for policymakers. *(LO3)*

• To reduce inflation, policymakers must shift the aggregate demand curve to the left, usually through a shift in monetary policy toward greater "tightness." In the short run, the main effects of an anti-inflationary policy may be reduced output and higher unemployment as the economy experiences a recessionary gap. These short-run costs of *disinflation* must be balanced against the long-run benefits of a lower rate of inflation. Over time, output and employment will return to normal levels and inflation declines. The disinflation engineered by the Fed under Chair Paul Volcker in the early 1980s followed this pattern. *(LO4)*

KEY TERMS

aggregate demand (*AD*) curve
aggregate supply shock
change in aggregate demand
disinflation

distributional effects
inflation shock
long-run aggregate supply
 (*LRAS*) line

long-run equilibrium
short-run aggregate supply
 (*SRAS*) line
short-run equilibrium

REVIEW QUESTIONS

1. What two variables are related by the aggregate demand (*AD*) curve? Explain how the behavior of the Fed helps determine the slope of this curve. List and discuss two other factors that lead the curve to have the slope that it does. *(LO1)*

2. State how each of the following affects the *AD* curve and explain: *(LO1)*

   a. An increase in government purchases.
   b. A cut in taxes.
   c. A decline in planned investment spending by firms.
   d. A decision by the Fed to lower the real interest rate at each level of inflation.

3. Why does the overall rate of inflation tend to adjust more slowly than prices of commodities, such as oil or grain? *(LO2)*

4. Discuss the relationship between output gaps and inflation. How is this relationship captured in the aggregate demand–aggregate supply diagram? *(LO2)*

5. Sketch an aggregate demand–aggregate supply diagram depicting an economy away from long-run equilibrium.

Indicate the economy's short-run equilibrium point. Discuss how the economy reaches long-run equilibrium over a period of time. Illustrate the process in your diagram. *(LO2)*

6. True or false: The economy's self-correcting tendency makes active use of stabilization policy unnecessary. Explain. *(LO2)*

7. What factors led to increased inflation in the United States in the 1960s and 1970s? *(LO3)*

8. Why, in the absence of public beliefs that the central bank is committed to maintaining low inflation, does an adverse inflation shock pose a particularly difficult dilemma for policymakers? *(LO3)*

9. How does a tight monetary policy, like that conducted by the Volcker Fed in the early 1980s, affect output, inflation, and the real interest rate in the short run? In the long run? *(LO4)*

10. Most central banks place great value on keeping inflation low and stable. Why do they view this objective as so important? *(LO4)*

PROBLEMS

Mc
Graw
Hill **connect**

1. We have seen that short-run equilibrium output falls when the Fed raises the real interest rate. Suppose the relationship between short-run equilibrium output Y and the real interest rate r set by the Fed is given by

$$Y = 1{,}000 - 1{,}000r.$$

Suppose also that the Fed's reaction function is the one shown in the following table. For whole-number inflation rates between 0 and 4 percent, find the real interest rate set by the Fed and the resulting short-run equilibrium output. Graph the aggregate demand curve numerically. *(LO1)*

Rate of inflation, π	Real interest rate, r
0.0	0.02
0.01	0.03
0.02	0.04
0.03	0.05
0.04	0.06

2. For the economy in Problem 1, suppose that potential output $Y^* = 960$. From the policy reaction function in the table in Problem 1, what can you infer about the Fed's objective for the inflation rate in the long term? *(LO1)*

3. An economy's relationship between short-run equilibrium output and inflation (its aggregate demand curve) is described by the equation

$$Y = 13{,}000 - 20{,}000\pi.$$

Initially, the inflation rate is 4 percent, or $\pi = 0.04$. Potential output Y^* equals 12,000. *(LO2)*
   a. Find the output in short-run equilibrium.
   b. Find the inflation rate in long-run equilibrium. Show your work.

4. This problem asks you to trace out the adjustment of inflation when the economy starts with an output gap. Suppose that the economy's aggregate demand curve is

$$Y = 1{,}000 - 1{,}000\pi,$$

where Y is short-run equilibrium output and π is the inflation rate, measured as a decimal. Potential output Y^* equals 950, and the initial inflation rate is 10 percent ($\pi = 0.10$). *(LO2)*
   a. Find output for this economy in short-run equilibrium and inflation in long-run equilibrium.

b. Suppose that, each quarter, inflation adjusts according to the following rule:

$$\text{This quarter's inflation} = \text{Last quarter's inflation} - 0.0004(Y^* - Y).$$

Starting from the initial value of 10 percent for inflation, find the value of inflation for each of the next five quarters. Remember, Y will continuously change as the current inflation rate change according to the given relationship $Y = 1{,}000 - 1{,}000\pi$. Does inflation come close to its long-run value?

5. For each of the following, use an *AD-AS* diagram to show the short-run and long-run effects on output and inflation. Assume the economy starts in long-run equilibrium. *(LO1, LO2, LO3)*
   a. An increase in consumer confidence that leads to higher consumption spending.
   b. A reduction in taxes.
   c. An easing of monetary policy by the Fed (a downward shift in the policy reaction function).
   d. A sharp drop in oil prices.
   e. A war that raises government purchases.

6. Suppose that the government cuts taxes in response to a recessionary gap, but because of legislative delays, the tax cut is not put in place for 18 months. Using an *AD-AS* diagram and assuming that the government's objective is to stabilize output and inflation, show how this policy action might actually prove to be counterproductive. *(LO2)*

7. Suppose that a permanent increase in oil prices both creates an inflationary shock and reduces potential output. Use an *AD-AS* diagram to show the effects of the oil price increase on output and inflation in the short run and the long run, assuming that there is no policy response. What happens if the Fed responds to the oil price increase by tightening monetary policy? *(LO3)*

8. An economy is initially in recession. Using the *AD-AS* diagram, show the process of adjustment: *(LO2, LO4)*
   a. If the Fed responds by easing monetary policy (moving its reaction function down).
   b. If the Fed takes no action.
   What are the costs and benefits of each approach, in terms of output loss and inflation?

9.* Planned aggregate expenditure in Lotusland depends on real GDP and the real interest rate according to the following equation

$$PAE = 3{,}000 + 0.8Y - 2{,}000r.$$

*Denotes more difficult problem.

The Bank of Lotusland, the central bank, has announced that it will set the real interest rate according to the following policy reaction function:

Rate of inflation, π	Real interest rate, r
0.0	0.02
0.01	0.03
0.02	0.04
0.03	0.05
0.04	0.06

For the rates of inflation given, find autonomous expenditure and short-run equilibrium output in Lotusland. Graph the *AD* curve. *(LO1)*

10.* An economy is described by the following equations:

$$C = 1,600 + 0.6(Y - T) - 2,000r,$$
$$I^p = 2,500 - 1,000r,$$
$$G = \overline{G} = 2,000,$$
$$NX = \overline{NX} = 50,$$
$$T = \overline{T} = 2,000.$$

Suppose also that the central bank's policy reaction function is the same as in Problem 9. *(LO1)*

a. Find an equation relating planned spending to output and the real interest rate.

b. Construct a table showing the relationship between short-run equilibrium output and inflation, for inflation

rates between 0 and 4 percent. Using this table, graph the *AD* curve for the economy.

c. Repeat parts a and b, assuming that government purchases have increased to 2,100. How does an increase in government purchases affect the *AD* curve?

11.* For the economy described in Problem 10, suppose that the central bank's policy reaction function is as follows: *(LO1)*

Rate of inflation, π	Real interest rate, r
0.0	0.04
0.01	0.045
0.02	0.05
0.03	0.055
0.04	0.06

a. Construct a table showing the relationship between short-run equilibrium output and the inflation rate for values of inflation between 0 and 4 percent. Graph the aggregate demand curve of the economy.

b. Suppose that the central bank decides to lower the real interest rate by 0.5 percentage point at each value of inflation. Repeat part a. How does this change in monetary policy affect the aggregate demand curve?

*Denotes more difficult problem.

ANSWERS TO SELF-TESTS

27.1 a. At the current level of inflation, output, and real interest rate, an exogenous reduction in business spending on new capital will reduce investment, causing a decline in overall aggregate expenditures (*AE*) and a reduction in short-run equilibrium output. Because output has fallen for a given level of inflation, the decrease in business spending leads to a leftward shift in the *AD* curve. *(LO1)*

b. At the current level of inflation, output, and real interest rate, a reduction in federal income taxes increases consumers' disposable income (*Y* − *T*), which leads to an exogenous increase in consumption at all income levels. The upward shift in the consumption function increases overall aggregate expenditures (*AE*) and leads to an increase in short-run equilibrium output. Because output has increased for a given level of inflation, the reduction in income taxes leads to a rightward shift in the *AD* curve. *(LO1)*

27.2 In the long run, the real interest rate set by the Fed must be consistent with the real interest rate determined in the market for saving and investment. To find the Fed's long-run inflation target, take as given the real interest rate determined in the long run by

the market for saving and investment and read off the corresponding inflation rate from the Fed's policy reaction function. As the accompanying figure illustrates, a tightening of Fed policy (an upward shift of the policy reaction function) implies that, for any given long-run real interest rate, the Fed's inflation target must be lower. *(LO1)*

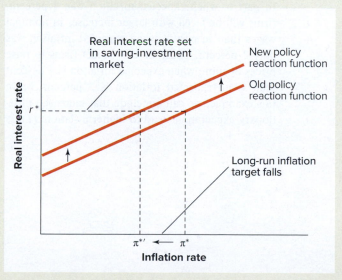

27.3 a. An upward shift in the Fed's policy reaction function means that the Federal Reserve is raising the real interest rate associated with a given level of inflation. An increase in the real interest rate causes both consumption and investment spending to fall, reducing overall aggregate expenditures and short-run equilibrium output. Thus, a shift in the Fed's policy reaction function causes the output level to fall for a given level of inflation, resulting in a leftward shift in the *AD* curve. *(LO1)*

b. The Federal Reserve's policy reaction function illustrates that the Federal Reserve responds to rising inflation rates by raising the real interest rate (a move *along* the policy reaction function), which causes a reduction in overall aggregate expenditures and short-run equilibrium output. However, in this case the Fed's response to higher inflation causes a *move along* a given *AD* curve.

Note that while the two actions appear to be similar, there is a key difference. In the first case the Fed is changing its policy rule for a *given inflation rate,* while in the second case the Fed is responding to a *changing inflation rate.* Changes in aggregate spending for a given inflation rate shift the *AD* curve, while changes in aggregate spending resulting from Fed policy responses to a rise or fall in inflation lead to moves along a given *AD* curve. *(LO1)*

27.4 a. If inflation is expected to be 2 percent next year and workers are expecting a 2 percent increase in their real wages, then they will expect, and ask for, a 4 percent increase in their nominal wages. *(LO2)*

b. If inflation is expected to be 4 percent next year, rather than 2 percent, workers will expect, and ask for, a 6 percent increase in their nominal wages. *(LO2)*

c. If wage costs rise, firms will need to increase the prices of their goods and services to cover their increased costs, leading to an increase in inflation. In part b, when expected inflation was 4 percent, firms will be faced with larger increases in nominal wages than in part a, when expected inflation was only 2 percent. Thus, we can expect firms to raise prices by more when expected inflation is 4 percent than when expected inflation is 2 percent. From this example, we can conclude that increased inflationary expectations lead to higher inflation. *(LO2)*

27.5 If the inflation rate is high, the economy will tend to stay in this high-inflation state due to expectations of high inflation and the existence of long-term wage and price contracts, while if the inflation rate is low, the economy will likewise tend to stay in this low-inflation state for similar reasons. However, since high inflation rates impose economic costs on society, the Federal Reserve has an incentive to avoid the high-inflation state by keeping inflation low, which helps maintain people's expectations of low inflation and leads to lower future inflation rates—perpetuating the "virtuous circle" illustrated in Figure 27.4. *(LO2)*

27.6 An increase in spending on new capital by firms for a given level of inflation, output, and real interest rate increases aggregate expenditures and short-run equilibrium output. Since the economy was originally operating at potential output, the increase in investment spending will lead to an expansionary gap; actual output, *Y,* will now be greater than potential output, *Y**. When $Y > Y^*$, the rate of inflation will tend to rise. *(LO2)*

27.7 The effects will be the opposite of those illustrated in Figure 27.8. Beginning in a long-run equilibrium with output equal to potential output and stable inflation [that is, where the aggregate demand (*AD*) curve intersects both the short-run and long-run aggregate supply lines (*SRAS* and *LRAS,* respectively)], the fall in consumption spending will initially lead to a leftward shift in the *AD* curve and the economy moves to a new, lower, short-run equilibrium output level at the same inflation rate. The shift in *AD* creates a recessionary gap, since *Y* is now less than *Y**. The immediate effect of the decrease in consumption spending is only to reduce output. However, over time inflation will fall because of the recessionary gap. As inflation falls the *SRAS* line will shift downward. The Federal Reserve responds to the fall in inflation by reducing real interest rates, leading to an increase in aggregate expenditure and output, a move down along the new *AD* curve. When inflation has fallen enough (and real interest rates have fallen enough) to eliminate the output gap the economy will be back in long-run equilibrium where output equals potential output but the inflation rate will be lower than before the fall in consumption spending. *(LO3)*

27.8 A decrease in oil prices is an example of a "beneficial" inflation shock and the economic effects of such a shock are the reverse of those illustrated in Figure 27.9. In this case, starting from a long-run equilibrium where output equals potential output, a beneficial inflation shock reduces current inflation, causing the *SRAS* line to shift downward. The downward shift in the *SRAS* curve leads to a short-run equilibrium with lower inflation and higher output, creating an expansionary gap. If the Fed does nothing, eventually the *SRAS* will begin to shift upward and the economy will return to its original inflation and output levels. However, the Fed may instead choose to tighten its monetary policy by shifting up its policy reaction function, raising the current real interest rate, shifting the *AD* curve to the left and restoring equilibrium at potential GDP, but at the new, lower inflation rate. *(LO3)*

27.9 If productivity growth hadn't increased in the last half of the 1990s the *LRAS* would not have shifted as far to the right as it actually did. As a consequence, the average inflation rate would not have fallen as much as illustrated in Table 27.2 and average real GDP growth would have been smaller. Similarly, if productivity growth slows in the future from its actual 1995–2000 rate, we can expect higher inflation and lower GDP growth than we otherwise would have experienced. *(LO3)*

27.10 See graphs below. *(LO4)*

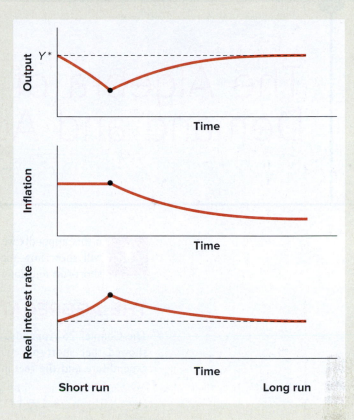

The Algebra of Aggregate Demand and Aggregate Supply

I n this appendix we will derive the aggregate demand curve algebraically. Then we will show how together aggregate demand and aggregate supply determine the short-run and long-run equilibrium points of the economy.

THE AGGREGATE DEMAND CURVE

The Chapter 26 Appendix, *Monetary Policy in the Basic Keynesian Model,* Equation 26A.1 showed that short-run equilibrium output depends on both exogenous components of expenditure and the real interest rate, shown here

$$Y = \left(\frac{1}{1-c}\right)[\overline{C} - c\overline{T} + \overline{I} + \overline{G} + \overline{NX} - (a+b)r], \qquad (26A.1)$$

where $1/(1-c)$ is the multiplier, $\overline{C} - c\overline{T} + \overline{I} + \overline{G} + \overline{NX}$ is the exogenous component of planned spending, the term in brackets is autonomous expenditure, and a and b are positive numbers that measure the effect of changes in the real interest rate on consumption and planned investment, respectively.

The aggregate demand curve incorporates the behavior of the Fed, as described by its policy reaction function. According to its policy reaction function, when inflation rises, the Fed raises the real interest rate. Thus the Fed's policy reaction function can be written as an equation relating the real interest rate r to inflation π

$$r = \bar{r} + g\pi, \qquad (27A.1)$$

where $\bar{r}$ and g are positive constants chosen by Fed officials. This equation states that when inflation π rises by 1 percentage point—say from 2 to 3 percent per year—the Fed responds by raising the real interest rate by g percentage points. So, for example, if $g = 0.5$, an increase in inflation from 2 to 3 percent would lead the Fed to raise the real interest rate by 0.5 percent. The intercept term $\bar{r}$ tells us at what level the Fed would set the real interest rate if inflation happened to be zero (so that the term $g\pi$ dropped out of the equation).

Equations 26A.1 and 27A.1 together allow us to derive the aggregate demand curve. We can think of the curve as being derived in two steps: First, for any given value of inflation π, use the policy reaction function, Equation 27A.1, to find the real interest rate by the Fed. Second, for that real interest rate, use Equation 26A.1 to find short-run equilibrium output Y. The relationship between inflation and short-run equilibrium output derived in these two steps is the aggregate demand curve.

Alternatively, we can combine the equation for short-run equilibrium output with the equation for the policy reaction function by substituting the right-hand side of Equation 27A.1 for the real interest rate r in Equation 26A.1

$$Y = \left(\frac{1}{1-c}\right)[\overline{C} - c\overline{T} + \overline{I} + \overline{G} + \overline{NX} - (a+b)(\bar{r} + g\pi)]. \qquad (27A.2)$$

This equation, which is the general algebraic expression for the *AD* curve, summarizes the link between inflation and short-run equilibrium output, as shown graphically in Figure 27.1. Note that Equation 27A.2 implies that an increase in inflation π reduces short-run equilibrium output *Y,* so that the *AD* curve is downward-sloping.

For a numerical illustration, we can use the parameter values from Example 26.3. For the economy studied in Example 26.3, we assumed that $\overline{C} = 640, \overline{T} = 250, \overline{I} = 250, \overline{G} = 300, \overline{NX} = 20, c = 0.8, a = 400,$ and $b = 600.$ To derive the aggregate demand curve, we also need values for the Fed's policy reaction function; for illustration, we use the policy reaction function shown in Table 26.1, reproduced here as Table 27A.1 for convenience.

TABLE 27A.1
A Policy Reaction Function for the Fed

Rate of inflation, π	Real interest rate set by Fed, r
0.00 (= 0%)	0.02 (= 2%)
0.01	0.03
0.02	0.04
0.03	0.05
0.04	0.06

Table 27A.1 relates the Fed's choice of the real interest rate to the inflation rate. To derive the aggregate demand curve, it will be useful to express the policy reaction function in the form of an equation like Equation 27A.1. To do this, note that when inflation π equals zero, the real interest rate r equals 2 percent. Therefore, the constant term in the Fed's policy reaction function $\bar{r}$ equals 2 percent, or 0.02. Second, Table 27A.1 shows that the real interest rate rises one point for each point that inflation rises; therefore the slope g of the reaction function equals 1.0. So the Fed's policy reaction function can be expressed as

$$r = 0.02 + \pi,$$

which is Equation 27A.1 with $\bar{r} = 0.02$ and $g = 1.$

Substituting these numerical values into Equation 27A.2 and simplifying, we get the following numerical equation for the *AD* curve:

$$Y = 5[640 - 0.8(250) + 250 + 300 + 20 - (400 + 600)(0.02 + \pi)], \quad (27A.3)$$

$$Y = 4,950 - 5,000\pi. \quad (27A.4)$$

Note that in this equation, higher values of inflation imply lower values of short-run equilibrium output, so the aggregate demand curve is downward-sloping. To check this equation, suppose that inflation is 3 percent, so that the Fed sets the real interest rate at 5 percent (see Table 27A.1). Setting $\pi = 0.03$ in Equation 27A.4 yields $Y = 4,800.$ This is consistent with the answer we found in Example 26.4, where we showed for the same economy that when $r = 0.05$ (the value of the real interest rate set by the Fed when $\pi = 0.03$), then short-run equilibrium output $Y = 4,800.$

SHIFTS OF THE AGGREGATE DEMAND CURVE

Recall that exogenous changes in spending or in the Fed's policy reaction function will shift the *AD* curve. These results follow from Equation 27A.2. First, the equation shows that for a given rate of inflation π, an increase in exogenous spending, $\overline{C} - c\overline{T} + \overline{I} + \overline{G} + \overline{NX},$ will raise short-run equilibrium output *Y.* Thus an increase in exogenous spending shifts the *AD* curve to the right; conversely, a decrease in exogenous spending shifts the *AD* curve to the left.

A shift in the Fed's policy reaction can be captured by a change in the intercept term $\bar{r}$ in Equation 27A.1. For example, suppose the Fed tightens monetary policy by setting the real interest rate 1 percent higher than before at every level of inflation. Such a change is equivalent to raising the intercept term $\bar{r}$ in the policy reaction function by 0.01. If you look at Equation 27A.2, you will see that with the level of inflation held constant, an increase in $\bar{r}$ reduces short-run equilibrium output. Thus a tightening of monetary policy (an upward movement in the monetary policy reaction function) shifts the *AD* curve to the left. Conversely, an easing of monetary policy (represented by a decline in $\bar{r}$ or a downward shift in the policy reaction function) shifts the *AD* curve to the right.

> ✔ **SELF-TEST 27A.1**
>
> a. For the economy described above, find an algebraic equation for the *AD* curve after an exogenous increase in spending (say, in planned investment) of 10 units.
>
> b. For the economy described above, find an algebraic equation for the *AD* curve after a tightening of monetary policy that involves setting the real interest rate 1 percent higher at each level of inflation.

SHORT-RUN EQUILIBRIUM

Recall that in short-run equilibrium, inflation is equal to its previously determined value and the *SRAS* line is horizontal at that value. At that level of inflation, the level of output in short-run equilibrium is given by the aggregate demand curve, Equation 27A.2. For instance, in the economy described, suppose the current value of inflation is 5 percent. The value of short-run equilibrium output is therefore

$$Y = 4{,}950 - 5{,}000\pi = 4{,}950 - 5{,}000(0.05)$$
$$= 4{,}700.$$

LONG-RUN EQUILIBRIUM

In long-run equilibrium, actual output Y equals potential output Y^*. Thus, in long-run equilibrium, the inflation rate can be obtained from the equation for the *AD* curve by substituting Y^* for Y. To illustrate, let's write the equation for the *AD* curve in this sample economy, Equation 27A.4, once again

$$Y = 4{,}950 - 5{,}000\pi.$$

Suppose, in addition, that potential output $Y^* = 4{,}900$. Substituting this value for Y in the aggregate demand equation yields

$$4{,}900 = 4{,}950 - 5{,}000\pi.$$

Solving for the inflation rate π we get

$$\pi = 0.01 = 1\%.$$

When this economy is in long-run equilibrium, then, the inflation rate will be 1 percent. If we start from the value of inflation in short-run equilibrium, 5 percent, we can see that the short-run aggregate supply line must shift downward until inflation reaches 1 percent before long-run equilibrium can be achieved.

ANSWER TO APPENDIX SELF-TEST

27A.1 The algebraic solutions for the *AD* curves in each case, obtained by substituting the numerical values into the formula, are given as follows:

a. $Y = 5{,}000 - 5{,}000\pi$.
b. $Y = 4{,}900 - 5{,}000\pi$.

CHAPTER 28

Exchange Rates and the Open Economy

What determines exchange rates in the short and long run?

Maria Toutoudaki/Getty Images

Two Americans discussing their foreign travels were commiserating over their problems understanding foreign currency. "Euro, yuan, yen, pounds, rubles, rupees, it's driving me crazy," said the first American. "They all look different and have different values. When I visit a foreign country, I can never figure out how much to pay the taxi driver."

The second American was more upbeat. "Actually," he said, "since I adopted my new system, I haven't had any problems at all."

The first American looked interested. "What's your new system?"

"Well," replied the second, "now, whenever I take a taxi abroad, I just give the driver all the local money I have. And would you believe it, I have got the fare exactly right every time!"

Dealing with unfamiliar currencies—and translating the value of foreign money into dollars—is a problem every international traveler faces. The traveler's problem is complicated by the fact that *exchange rates*—the rates at which one country's money trades for another—may change unpredictably. Thus the number of British pounds, Russian rubles, Japanese yen, or Australian dollars that a U.S. dollar can buy may vary over time, sometimes quite a lot.

The economic consequences of variable exchange rates are much broader than their impact on travel and tourism, however. For example, the competitiveness of U.S. exports depends in

part on the prices of U.S. goods in terms of foreign currencies, which in turn depend on the exchange rate between the U.S. dollar and those currencies. Likewise, the prices Americans pay for imported goods depend in part on the value of the dollar relative to the currencies of the countries that produce those goods. Exchange rates also affect the value of financial investments made across national borders. For countries that are heavily dependent on trade and international capital flows—the majority of the world's nations—fluctuations in the exchange rate may have a significant economic impact.

Moreover, such impact has been increasing over time. One of the defining economic trends of recent decades is the "globalization" of national economies. From the mid-1980s to 2008, the value of international trade has increased at nearly twice the rate of world GDP, and the volume of international financial transactions has expanded at many times that rate.[1] From a long-run perspective, the rapidly increasing integration of national economies we see today is not unprecedented: Before World War I, Great Britain was the center of an international economic system that was in many ways nearly as "globalized" as our own, with extensive international trade and lending. But even the most far-seeing nineteenth-century merchant or banker would be astonished by the sense of *immediacy* that recent revolutionary changes in communications and transportation have imparted to international economic relations. For example, ubiquitous cell phone–based videoconferencing now permits people on opposite sides of the globe to conduct "face-to-face" business negotiations and transactions.

This chapter discusses exchange rates and the role they play in open economies. We will start by distinguishing between the *nominal exchange rate*—the rate at which one national currency trades for another—and the *real exchange rate*—the rate at which one country's goods trade for another's. We will show how exchange rates affect the prices of exports and imports, and thus the pattern of trade.

Next we will turn to the question of how exchange rates are determined. Exchange rates may be divided into two broad categories, flexible and fixed. The value of a *flexible* exchange rate is determined freely in the market for national currencies, known as the *foreign exchange market*. Flexible exchange rates vary continually with changes in the supply of and demand for national currencies. In contrast, the value of a *fixed* exchange rate is set by the government at a constant level. Because most large industrial countries, including the United States, have a flexible exchange rate, we will focus on that case first. We will see that a country's monetary policy plays a particularly important role in determining the exchange rate. Furthermore, in an open economy with a flexible exchange rate, the exchange rate becomes a tool of monetary policy, in much the same way as the real interest rate.

Although most large industrial countries have a flexible exchange rate, many small and developing economies fix their exchange rates at least to some extent, so we will consider the case of fixed exchange rates as well. We will explain first how a country's government (usually, its central bank) goes about maintaining a fixed exchange rate at the officially determined level. Though fixing the exchange rate generally reduces day-to-day fluctuations in the value of a nation's currency, we will see that, at times, a fixed exchange rate can become severely unstable, with potentially serious economic consequences. We will close the chapter by discussing the relative merits of fixed and flexible exchange rates.

While this chapter focuses on the two extreme exchange rate approaches—fixed versus flexible—in today's world, most countries' exchange rates lie somewhere between the two extremes, with arrangements that combine the two approaches. Moreover, many countries constantly move between more flexible and more fixed exchange rate regimes. For example, for years China used to fix its currency, the renminbi (whose unit of account is the yuan),

---

[1]Since the global financial crisis of 2008, trade has been growing at roughly the same rate as world GDP. The volume of international financial transactions declined dramatically during the financial crisis, but it is still several times higher today than in the mid-1980s.

to the U.S. dollar. Since 2005, however, China has been switching between different exchange rate arrangements. In one recent arrangement, the People's Bank of China—China's central bank—let the renminbi float but only within a fixed band that shifts gradually over time or that is set by the central bank.

EXCHANGE RATES

The economic benefits of trade between nations in goods, services, and assets are similar to the benefits of trade within a nation. In both cases, trade in goods and services permits greater specialization and efficiency, whereas trade in assets allows financial investors to earn higher or less volatile returns while providing funds for worthwhile capital projects. However, there is a difference between the two cases, which is that trade in goods, services, and assets *within* a nation normally involves a single currency—dollars, yen, pesos, or whatever the country's official form of money happens to be—whereas trade *between* nations usually involves dealing in different currencies. So, for example, if an American resident wants to purchase an automobile manufactured in South Korea, she (or more likely, the automobile dealer) must first trade dollars for the Korean currency, called the won. The Korean car manufacturer is then paid in won. Similarly, an Argentine who wants to purchase shares in a U.S. company (a U.S. financial asset) must first trade his Argentine pesos for dollars and then use the dollars to purchase the shares.

NOMINAL EXCHANGE RATES

Because international transactions generally require that one currency be traded for another, the relative values of different currencies are an important factor in international economic relations. The rate at which two currencies can be traded for each other is called the **nominal exchange rate,** or more simply the *exchange rate,* between the two currencies. For example, if one U.S. dollar can be exchanged for 110 Japanese yen, the nominal exchange rate between the U.S. and Japanese currencies is 110 yen per dollar. Each country has many nominal exchange rates, one corresponding to each currency against which its own currency is traded. Thus the dollar's value can be quoted in terms of English pounds, Swedish kroner, Israeli shekels, Russian rubles, or dozens of other currencies. Table 28.1 gives exchange rates between the dollar and seven other important currencies as of the close of business in New York City on March 6, 2020.

nominal exchange rate the rate at which two currencies can be traded for each other

TABLE 28.1
Nominal Exchange Rates for the U.S. Dollar

Country	Foreign currency/dollar	Dollar/foreign currency
Canada (Canadian dollar)	1.3413	0.7455
China (yuan)	6.9320	0.1443
Mexico (peso)	20.1091	0.0497
Japan (yen)	105.29	0.00950
Euro area (euro)	0.8861	1.1286
South Korea (won)	1188.80	0.0008412
United Kingdom (pound)	0.7665	1.3047

Source: *The Wall Street Journal,* March 8, 2020, www.wsj.com/market-data/currencies/exchangerates.

As Table 28.1 shows, exchange rates can be expressed either as the amount of foreign currency needed to purchase one dollar (middle column) or as the number of dollars needed to purchase one unit of the foreign currency (right column). These two ways of expressing the exchange rate are equivalent: Each is the reciprocal of the other. For example, on March 6, 2020, the U.S.-Canadian exchange rate could have been expressed either as 1.3413 Canadian dollars per U.S. dollar or as 0.7455 U.S. dollars per Canadian dollar, where 0.7455 = 1/1.3413.

EXAMPLE 28.1   Nominal Exchange Rates

What is the exchange rate between the British pound and Canadian dollar?

Based on Table 28.1, find the exchange rate between the British and Canadian currencies. Express the exchange rate in both Canadian dollars per pound and pounds per Canadian dollar.

From Table 28.1, we see that 0.7665 British pounds will buy a U.S. dollar, and that 1.3413 Canadian dollars will buy a U.S. dollar. Therefore, 0.7665 British pounds and 1.3413 Canadian dollars are equal in value

$$0.7665 \text{ pounds} = 1.3413 \text{ Canadian dollars.}$$

Dividing both sides of this equation by 1.3413 we get

$$0.5715 \text{ pounds} = 1 \text{ Canadian dollar.}$$

In other words, the British–Canadian exchange rate can be expressed as 0.5715 pounds per Canadian dollar. Alternatively, the exchange rate can be expressed as 1/0.5715 = 1.7498 Canadian dollars per pound.

 SELF-TEST 28.1

From the business section of the newspaper or an online source (try *The Wall Street Journal*, www.wsj.com), find recent quotations of the value of the U.S. dollar against the British pound, the Canadian dollar, and the Japanese yen. Based on these data, find the exchange rate (a) between the pound and the Canadian dollar and (b) between the Canadian dollar and the yen. Express the exchange rates you derive in two ways (for example, both as pounds per Canadian dollar and as Canadian dollars per pound).

Figure 28.1 shows the nominal exchange rate for the U.S. dollar for 1973 to 2020. Rather than showing the value of the dollar relative to that of an individual foreign currency, such as the Japanese yen or the British pound, the figure expresses the value of the dollar as an average of its values against other major currencies. This average value of the dollar is measured relative to a base value of 100 in 2006. So, for example, a value of 120 for the dollar in a particular year implies that the dollar was 20 percent more valuable in that year, relative to other major currencies, than it was in 2006.

You can see from Figure 28.1 that the dollar's value has fluctuated over time, sometimes increasing (as in the periods 1980–1985 and 1995–2001) and sometimes decreasing (as in 1985–1987 and 2002–2004). An increase in the value of a currency relative to other currencies is known as an **appreciation;** a decline in the value of a currency relative to other currencies is called a **depreciation.** So we can say that the dollar appreciated in 1980–1985 and depreciated in 1985–1987. We will discuss the reasons a currency may appreciate or depreciate later in this chapter.

In this chapter, we will use the symbol e to stand for a country's nominal exchange rate. Although the exchange rate can be expressed either as foreign currency units per unit of domestic currency or vice versa, as we saw in Table 28.1, let's agree to define e as *the number of units of the foreign currency that the domestic currency will buy*. For

appreciation an increase in the value of a currency relative to other currencies

depreciation a decrease in the value of a currency relative to other currencies

FIGURE 28.1

The U.S. Nominal Exchange Rate, 1973–2020.

This figure expresses the value of the dollar from 1973 to 2020 as an average of its values against other major currencies, relative to a base value of 100 in January 2006.

Source: Federal Reserve Bank of St. Louis, FRED database, https://research.stlouisfed.org/fred2/series/TWEXMMTH (until January 2006) and https://fred.stlouisfed.org/series/TWEXAFEGSMTH (from January 2006).

example, if we treat the United States as the "home" or "domestic" country and Japan as the "foreign" country, *e* will be defined as the number of Japanese yen that one dollar will buy. Defining the nominal exchange rate this way implies that an *increase* in *e* corresponds to an *appreciation,* or a strengthening, of the home currency, while a *decrease* in *e* implies a *depreciation,* or weakening, of the home currency.

FLEXIBLE VERSUS FIXED EXCHANGE RATES

As we saw in Figure 28.1, the exchange rate between the U.S. dollar and other currencies isn't constant but varies continually. Indeed, changes in the value of the dollar occur daily, hourly, minute by minute, and even within split seconds. Such fluctuations in the value of a currency are normal for countries like the United States, which have a *flexible* or *floating exchange rate*. The value of a **flexible exchange rate** is not officially fixed but varies according to the supply and demand for the currency in the **foreign exchange market**—the market on which currencies of various nations are traded for one another. We will discuss the factors that determine the supply and demand for currencies shortly.

Some countries do not allow their currency values to vary with market conditions but instead maintain a *fixed exchange rate*. The value of a **fixed exchange rate** is set by official government policy. (A government that establishes a fixed exchange rate typically determines the exchange rate's value independently, but sometimes exchange rates are set according to an agreement among a number of governments.) Some countries fix their exchange rates in terms of the U.S. dollar (Hong Kong, for example), but there are other possibilities. Some French-speaking African countries have traditionally fixed the value of their currencies in terms of the French franc and then in terms of the euro since it was introduced as a new currency on January 1, 1999. Under the gold standard, which many countries used until its collapse during the Great Depression, currency values were fixed in terms of ounces of gold. In the next part of the chapter we will focus on flexible exchange rates, but we will return later to the case of fixed rates. We will also discuss the costs and benefits of each type of exchange rate.

THE REAL EXCHANGE RATE

The nominal exchange rate tells us the price of the domestic currency in terms of a foreign currency. As we will see in this section, the *real exchange rate* tells us the price of the average domestic *good or service* in terms of the average foreign *good or service*. We will also see that a country's real exchange rate has important implications for its ability to sell its exports abroad.

To provide background for discussing the real exchange rate, imagine you are in charge of purchasing for a U.S. corporation that is planning to acquire a large number of new computers. The company's computer specialist has identified two models, one

flexible exchange rate an exchange rate whose value is not officially fixed but varies according to the supply and demand for the currency in the foreign exchange market

foreign exchange market the market on which currencies of various nations are traded for one another

fixed exchange rate an exchange rate whose value is set by official government policy

Japanese-made and one U.S.-made, that meet the necessary specifications. Since the two models are essentially equivalent, the company will buy the one with the lower price. However, since the computers are priced in the currencies of the countries of manufacture, the price comparison is not so straightforward. Your mission—should you decide to accept it—is to determine which of the two models is cheaper.

To complete your assignment you will need two pieces of information: the nominal exchange rate between the dollar and the yen and the prices of the two models in terms of the currencies of their countries of manufacture. Example 28.2 shows how you can use this information to determine which model is cheaper.

EXAMPLE 28.2 — Purchasing a Domestic versus Imported Good

Which computer is the better buy, the import or the domestic computer?

A U.S.-made computer costs $2,400, and a similar Japanese-made computer costs 242,000 yen. If the nominal exchange rate is 110 yen per dollar, which computer is the better buy?

To make this price comparison, we must measure the prices of both computers in terms of the same currency. To make the comparison in dollars, we first convert the Japanese computer's price into dollars. The price in terms of Japanese yen is ¥242,000 (the symbol ¥ means "yen"), and we are told that ¥110 = $1. To find the dollar price of the computer, then, we observe that for any good or service,

Price in yen = Price in dollars × Value of dollar in terms of yen.

Note that the value of a dollar in terms of yen is just the yen–dollar exchange rate. Making this substitution and solving, we get

$$\text{Price in dollars} = \frac{\text{Price in yen}}{\text{Yen–dollar exchange rate}}$$

$$= \frac{¥242,000}{¥110/\$1} = \$2,200.$$

Notice that the yen symbol appears in both the numerator and the denominator of the ratio, so it cancels out. Our conclusion is that the Japanese computer is cheaper than the U.S. computer at $2,200, or $200 less than the price of the U.S. computer, $2,400. The Japanese computer is the better deal.

 SELF-TEST 28.2

Continuing Example 28.2, compare the prices of the Japanese and American computers by expressing both prices in terms of yen.

In Example 28.2, the fact that the Japanese computer was cheaper implied that your firm would choose it over the U.S.-made computer. In general, a country's ability to compete in international markets depends in part on the prices of its goods and services *relative* to the prices of foreign goods and services, when the prices are measured in a common currency. In the hypothetical example of the Japanese and U.S. computers, the price of the domestic (U.S.) good relative to the price of the foreign (Japanese) good is $2,400/$2,200, or 1.09. So the U.S. computer is 9 percent more expensive than the Japanese computer, putting the U.S. product at a competitive disadvantage.

More generally, economists ask whether *on average* the goods and services produced by a particular country are expensive relative to the goods and services produced by other countries. This question can be answered by the country's *real exchange rate*. Specifically, a country's **real exchange rate** is the price of the average domestic good or service *relative* to the price of the average foreign good or service, when prices are expressed in terms of a common currency.

real exchange rate the price of the average domestic good or service *relative* to the price of the average foreign good or service, when prices are expressed in terms of a common currency

To obtain a formula for the real exchange rate, recall that e equals the nominal exchange rate (the number of units of foreign currency per dollar) and that P equals the domestic price level, as measured, for example, by the consumer price index. We will use P as a measure of the price of the "average" domestic good or service. Similarly, let P^f equal the foreign price level. We will use P^f as the measure of the price of the "average" foreign good or service.

The real exchange rate equals the price of the average domestic good or service relative to the price of the average foreign good or service. It would not be correct, however, to define the real exchange rate as the ratio P/P^f because the two price levels are expressed in different currencies. As we saw in Example 28.2, to convert foreign prices into dollars, we must divide the foreign price by the exchange rate. By this rule, the price in dollars of the average foreign good or service equals P^f/e. Now we can write the real exchange rate as

$$\text{Real exchange rate} = \frac{\text{Price of domestic good}}{\text{Price of foreign good, in dollars}}$$

$$= \frac{P}{P^f/e}.$$

To simplify this expression, multiply the numerator and denominator by e to get

$$\text{Real exchange rate} = \frac{eP}{P^f}, \tag{28.1}$$

which is the formula for the real exchange rate.

To check this formula, let's use it to re-solve the computer example, Example 28.2. (For this exercise, we imagine that computers are the only good produced by the United States and Japan, so the real exchange rate becomes just the price of U.S. computers relative to Japanese computers.) In that example, the nominal exchange rate e was ¥110/\$1, the domestic price P (of a computer) was \$2,400, and the foreign price P^f was ¥242,000. Applying Equation 28.1, we get

$$\text{Real exchange rate (for computers)} = \frac{(¥110/\$1) \times \$2,400}{¥242,000}$$

$$= \frac{¥264,000}{¥242,000}$$

$$= 1.09,$$

which is the same answer we got earlier.

The real exchange rate, an overall measure of the cost of domestic goods relative to foreign goods, is an important economic variable. As Example 28.2 suggests, when the real exchange rate is high, domestic goods are—on average—more expensive than foreign goods (when priced in the same currency). A high real exchange rate implies that domestic producers will have difficulty exporting to other countries (domestic goods will be "overpriced"), while foreign goods will sell well in the home country (because imported goods are cheap relative to goods produced at home). Since a high real exchange rate tends to reduce exports and increase imports, we conclude that *net exports will tend to be low when the real exchange rate is high*. Conversely, if the real exchange rate is low, then the home country will find it easier to export (because its goods are priced below those of foreign competitors), while domestic residents will buy fewer imports (because imports are expensive relative to domestic goods). *Thus net exports will tend to be high when the real exchange rate is low.*

Equation 28.1 also shows that the real exchange rate tends to move in the same direction as the nominal exchange rate e (since e appears in the numerator of the formula for the real exchange rate). To the extent that real and nominal exchange rates move in the same direction, we can conclude that net exports will be hurt by a high nominal exchange rate and helped by a low nominal exchange rate.

The Economic Naturalist 28.1

Does a strong currency imply a strong economy?

Does a strong currency imply a strong economy?

Politicians and the public sometimes take pride in the fact that their national currency is "strong," meaning that its value in terms of other currencies is high or rising. Likewise, policymakers sometimes view a depreciating ("weak") currency as a sign of economic failure. Does a strong currency necessarily imply a strong economy?

Contrary to popular impression, there is no simple connection between the strength of a country's currency and the strength of its economy. For example, Figure 28.1 shows that the value of the U.S. dollar relative to other major currencies was greater in the year 1973 than in the 1990s, though U.S. economic performance was considerably better in the 1990s than in 1973, a period of deep recession and rising inflation. Indeed, the one period shown in Figure 28.1 during which the dollar rose the most in value, 1980–1985, was a time of recession and high unemployment in the United States.

One reason a strong currency does not necessarily imply a strong economy is that an appreciating currency (an increase in e) tends to raise the real exchange rate (equal to eP/P^f), which may hurt a country's net exports. For example, if the dollar strengthens against the yen (that is, if a dollar buys more yen than before), Japanese goods will become cheaper in terms of dollars. The result may be that Americans prefer to buy Japanese goods rather than goods produced at home. Likewise, a stronger dollar implies that each yen buys fewer dollars, so exported U.S. goods become more expensive to Japanese consumers. As U.S. goods become more expensive in terms of yen, the willingness of Japanese consumers to buy U.S. exports declines. A strong dollar may therefore imply lower sales and profits for U.S. industries that export, as well as for U.S. industries (like automobile manufacturers) that compete with foreign firms for the domestic U.S. market.

RECAP ↑

EXCHANGE RATES

- The nominal exchange rate between two currencies is the rate at which the currencies can be traded for each other. More precisely, the nominal exchange rate e for any given country is the number of units of foreign currency that can be bought for one unit of the domestic currency.
- An appreciation is an increase in the value of a currency relative to other currencies (a rise in e); a depreciation is a decline in a currency's value (a fall in e).
- An exchange rate can be flexible—meaning that it varies freely according to supply and demand for the currency in the foreign exchange market—or fixed—meaning that its value is established by official government policy. (While not our focus in this chapter, an exchange rate can also combine the two approaches.)
- The real exchange rate is the price of the average domestic good or service relative to the price of the average foreign good or service, when prices are expressed in terms of a common currency. A useful formula for the real exchange rate is eP/P^f, where e is the nominal exchange rate, P is the domestic price level, and P^f is the foreign price level.
- An increase in the real exchange rate implies that domestic goods are becoming more expensive relative to foreign goods, which tends to reduce exports and stimulate imports. Conversely, a decline in the real exchange rate tends to increase net exports.

THE DETERMINATION OF THE EXCHANGE RATE IN THE LONG RUN

Countries that have flexible exchange rates, such as the United States, see the international values of their currencies change continually. What determines the value of the nominal exchange rate at any point in time? In this section we will try to answer this basic economic question. Again, our focus for the moment is on flexible exchange rates, whose values are determined by the foreign exchange market. Later in the chapter we discuss the case of fixed exchange rates.

A SIMPLE THEORY OF EXCHANGE RATES: PURCHASING POWER PARITY (PPP)

The most basic theory of how nominal exchange rates are determined is called *purchasing power parity,* or PPP. To understand this theory, we must first discuss a fundamental economic concept, called *the law of one price*. The **law of one price** states that if transportation costs are relatively small, the price of an internationally traded commodity must be the same in all locations. For example, if transportation costs are not too large, the price of a bushel of wheat ought to be the same in Mumbai, India, and Sydney, Australia. Suppose that were not the case—that the price of wheat in Sydney were only half the price in Mumbai. In that case, grain merchants would have a strong incentive to buy wheat in Sydney and ship it to Mumbai, where it could be sold at double the price of purchase. As wheat left Sydney, reducing the local supply, the price of wheat in Sydney would rise, while the inflow of wheat into Mumbai would reduce the price in Mumbai.

According to the Equilibrium Principle, the international market for wheat would return to equilibrium only when unexploited opportunities to profit had been eliminated—specifically, only when the prices of wheat in Sydney and in Mumbai became equal or nearly equal (with the difference being less than the cost of transporting wheat from Australia to India).

If the law of one price were to hold for all goods and services (which is not a realistic assumption, as we will see shortly), then the value of the nominal exchange rate would be determined as Example 28.3 illustrates.

law of one price if transportation costs are relatively small, the price of an internationally traded commodity must be the same in all locations

 Equilibrium

---

EXAMPLE 28.3   **The Law of One Price**

How many Indian rupees equal 1 Australian dollar?

Suppose that a bushel of grain costs 5 Australian dollars in Sydney and 150 rupees in Mumbai. If the law of one price holds for grain, what is the nominal exchange rate between Australia and India?

Because the market value of a bushel of grain must be the same in both locations, we know that the Australian price of wheat must equal the Indian price of wheat, so that

5 Australian dollars = 150 Indian rupees.

Dividing by 5, we get

1 Australian dollar = 30 Indian rupees.

Thus the nominal exchange rate between Australia and India should be 30 rupees per Australian dollar.

SELF-TEST 28.3

The price of gold is $900 per ounce in New York and 7,500 kronor per ounce in Stockholm, Sweden. If the law of one price holds for gold, what is the nominal exchange rate between the U.S. dollar and the Swedish krona?

purchasing power parity (PPP) the theory that nominal exchange rates are determined as necessary for the law of one price to hold

Example 28.3 and Self-Test 28.3 illustrate the application of the purchasing power parity theory. According to the **purchasing power parity (PPP)** theory, nominal exchange rates are determined as necessary for the law of one price to hold.

A particularly useful prediction of the PPP theory is that in the long run, the *currencies of countries that experience significant inflation will tend to depreciate*. To see why, we will extend the analysis in Example 28.3.

EXAMPLE 28.4   **Purchasing Power Parity**

How does inflation affect the nominal exchange rate?

Suppose India experiences significant inflation so that the price of a bushel of grain in Mumbai rises from 150 to 300 rupees. Australia has no inflation, so the price of grain in Sydney remains unchanged at 5 Australian dollars. If the law of one price holds for grain, what will happen to the nominal exchange rate between Australia and India?

As in Example 28.3, we know that the market value of a bushel of grain must be the same in both locations. Therefore,

$$5 \text{ Australian dollars} = 300 \text{ rupees.}$$

Equivalently,

$$1 \text{ Australian dollar} = 60 \text{ rupees.}$$

The nominal exchange rate is now 60 rupees per Australian dollar. Before India's inflation, the nominal exchange rate was 30 rupees per Australian dollar (Example 28.3). So in this example, inflation has caused the rupee to depreciate against the Australian dollar. Conversely, Australia, with no inflation, has seen its currency appreciate against the rupee.

This link between inflation and depreciation makes economic sense. Inflation implies that a nation's currency is losing purchasing power in the domestic market. Analogously, exchange rate depreciation implies that the nation's currency is losing purchasing power in international markets.

Figure 28.2 shows annual rates of inflation and nominal exchange rate depreciation for the 10 largest South American countries from 1995 to 2004.[2] Inflation is measured as the annual rate of change in the country's consumer price index; depreciation is measured relative to the U.S. dollar. As you can see, inflation varied greatly among South American countries during the period. For example, Chile's inflation rate was within two percentage points of the inflation rate of the United States, while Venezuela's inflation was 33 percent per year.

---

[2]Since Ecuador adopted the U.S. dollar as its currency in 2000, the data for Ecuador refer to the period 1995–2000.

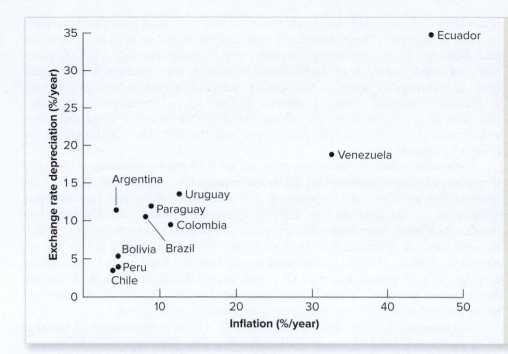

FIGURE 28.2

Inflation and Currency Depreciation in South America, 1995–2004.

The annual rates of inflation and nominal exchange rate depreciation (relative to the U.S. dollar) in the 10 largest South American countries varied considerably during 1995–2004. High inflation was associated with rapid depreciation of the nominal exchange rate. (Data for Ecuador refer to the period 1995–2000.)

Sources: International Monetary Fund, *International Financial Statistics;* authors' calculations.

Figure 28.2 shows that, as the PPP theory implies, countries with higher inflation during the 1995–2004 period tended to experience the most rapid depreciation of their currencies.

SHORTCOMINGS OF THE PPP THEORY

Empirical studies have found that the PPP theory is useful for predicting changes in nominal exchange rates over the relatively long run. In particular, this theory helps explain the tendency of countries with high inflation to experience depreciation of their exchange rates, as shown in Figure 28.2. However, the theory is less successful in predicting short-run movements in exchange rates.

A particularly dramatic failure of the PPP theory occurred in the United States in the early 1980s. As Figure 28.1 indicates, between 1980 and 1985, the value of the U.S. dollar rose nearly 50 percent relative to the currencies of U.S. trading partners. This strong appreciation was followed by an even more rapid depreciation during 1986 and 1987. PPP theory could explain this roller-coaster behavior only if inflation were far lower in the United States than in U.S. trading partners from 1980 to 1985 and far higher from 1986 to 1987. In fact, inflation was similar in the United States and its trading partners throughout both periods.

Why does the PPP theory work less well in the short run than the long run? Recall that this theory relies on the law of one price, which says that the price of an internationally traded commodity must be the same in all locations. The law of one price works well for goods such as grain or gold, which are standardized commodities that are traded widely. However, *not all goods and services are traded internationally,* and *not all goods are standardized commodities.*

Many goods and services are not traded internationally because the assumption underlying the law of one price—that transportation costs are relatively small—does not hold for them. For example, for Indians to export haircuts to Australia, they would need to transport an Indian barber to Australia every time a Sydney resident desired a trim. Because transportation costs prevent haircuts from being traded internationally, the law of one price does not apply to them. Thus, even if the price of haircuts in Australia were double the price of haircuts in India, market forces would not necessarily force prices toward equality in the short run. (Over the long run, some Indian barbers might emigrate to Australia.) Other examples of nontraded goods and services are agricultural land, buildings, heavy construction materials (whose value is low relative to their transportation costs), and highly perishable foods. In addition, some products use nontraded goods and services as inputs: A McDonald's hamburger served in Moscow has both a tradable component (frozen hamburger patties) and a nontradable component (the labor of counter workers). In general, the greater the share of nontraded goods and services in a nation's output, the less precisely the PPP theory will apply to the country's exchange rate.[3]

The second reason the law of one price and the PPP theory sometimes fail to apply is that not all internationally traded goods and services are perfectly standardized commodities, like grain or gold. For example, U.S.-made automobiles and Japanese-made automobiles are not identical; they differ in styling, horsepower, reliability, and other features. As a result, some people strongly prefer one nation's cars to the other's. Thus if Japanese cars cost 10 percent more than American cars, U.S. automobile exports will not necessarily flood the Japanese market, since many Japanese will still prefer Japanese-made cars even at a 10 percent premium. Of course, there are limits to how far prices can diverge before people will switch to the cheaper product. But the law of one price, and hence the PPP theory, will not apply exactly to nonstandardized goods.

To summarize, the PPP theory works reasonably well as an explanation of exchange rate behavior over the long run, but not in the short run. Because transportation costs limit international trade in many goods and services, and because not all goods that are traded are standardized commodities, the law of one price (on which the PPP theory is based) works only imperfectly in the short run. To understand the short-run movements of exchange rates we need to incorporate some additional factors. In the next section, we will study a supply and demand framework for the determination of exchange rates.

> **RECAP**
>
> **DETERMINING THE EXCHANGE RATE IN THE LONG RUN**
>
> - The most basic theory of nominal exchange rate determination, purchasing power parity (PPP), is based on the law of one price. The law of one price states that if transportation costs (and other costs and barriers to trade) are relatively small, the price of an internationally traded commodity must be the same in all locations. According to the PPP theory, the nominal exchange rate between two currencies can be found by setting the price of a traded commodity in one currency equal to the price of the same commodity expressed in the second currency.
> - A useful prediction of the PPP theory is that the currencies of countries that experience significant inflation will tend to depreciate over the long run. However, the PPP theory does not work well in the short run. The fact that many goods and services are nontraded, and that not all traded goods are standardized, reduces the applicability of the law of one price, and hence of the PPP theory.

THE DETERMINATION OF THE EXCHANGE RATE IN THE SHORT RUN

Although the PPP theory helps explain the long-run behavior of the exchange rate, supply and demand analysis is more useful for studying its short-run behavior. As we will see, dollars are demanded in the foreign exchange market by foreigners who seek to

---

[3]Trade barriers, such as tariffs and quotas, also increase the costs associated with shipping goods from one country to another. Thus trade barriers reduce the applicability of the law of one price in much the same way that physical transportation costs do.

purchase U.S. goods and assets and are supplied by U.S. residents who need foreign currencies to buy foreign goods and assets. The equilibrium exchange rate is the value of the dollar that equates the number of dollars supplied and demanded in the foreign exchange market.

THE FOREIGN EXCHANGE MARKET: A SUPPLY AND DEMAND ANALYSIS

In this section, we will discuss the factors that affect the supply and demand for dollars in the foreign exchange market, and thus the U.S. exchange rate.

One note before we proceed: In Chapter 26, *Stabilizing the Economy: The Role of the Fed,* we described how the supply of money by the Fed and the demand for money by the public help determine the nominal interest rate. However, the supply and demand for money in the domestic economy, as presented in that chapter, are *not* equivalent to the supply and demand for dollars in the foreign exchange market. As mentioned, the foreign exchange market is the market in which the currencies of various nations are traded for one another. The supply of dollars to the foreign exchange market is *not* the same as the money supply set by the Fed; rather, it is the number of dollars U.S. households and firms offer to trade for other currencies. Likewise, the demand for dollars in the foreign exchange market is *not* the same as the domestic demand for money, but the number of dollars holders of foreign currencies seek to buy. To understand the distinction, it may help to keep in mind that while the Fed determines the total supply of dollars in the U.S. economy, a dollar does not "count" as having been supplied to the foreign exchange market until some holder of dollars, such as a household or firm, tries to trade it for a foreign currency.

The Supply of Dollars

Anyone who holds dollars, from an international bank to a Russian citizen whose dollars are buried in the backyard, is a potential supplier of dollars to the foreign exchange market. In practice, however, the principal suppliers of dollars to the foreign exchange market are U.S. households and firms. Why would a U.S. household or firm want to supply dollars in exchange for foreign currency? There are two major reasons. First, a U.S. household or firm may need foreign currency *to purchase foreign goods or services.* For example, a U.S. automobile importer may need euros to purchase German cars, or an American tourist may need euros to make purchases in Paris, Rome, or Barcelona.[4] Second, a U.S. household or firm may need foreign currency *to purchase foreign assets.* For example, an American mutual fund may wish to acquire stocks issued by Dutch companies, or an individual U.S. saver may want to purchase Irish government bonds. Because these assets are priced in euros, the U.S. household or firm will need to trade dollars for euros to acquire these assets.

The supply of dollars to the foreign exchange market is illustrated in Figure 28.3. We will focus on the market in which dollars are traded for euros, but bear in mind that similar markets exist for every other pair of traded currencies. The vertical axis of the figure shows the U.S.–European exchange rate as measured by the number of euros that can be purchased with each dollar. The horizontal axis shows the number of dollars being traded in the euro–dollar market.

Note that the supply curve for dollars is upward-sloping. In other words, the more euros each dollar can buy, the more dollars people are willing to supply to the foreign exchange market. Why? At given prices for European goods, services, and assets, the more euros a dollar can buy, the cheaper those goods, services, and assets will be in dollar terms. For example, if a washing machine costs 200 euros in Germany and a dollar can buy 1 euro, the dollar price of the washing machine will be $200. However,

---

[4]The following 19 countries use euros as their local currency: Austria, Belgium, Cyprus, Estonia, Finland, France, Germany, Greece, Ireland, Italy, Latvia, Lithuania, Luxembourg, Malta, the Netherlands, Portugal, Slovakia, Slovenia, and Spain. See The Economic Naturalist 28.7 later in the chapter.

FIGURE 28.3

The Supply and Demand for Dollars in the Euro–Dollar Market.

The supply of dollars to the foreign exchange market is upward-sloping because an increase in the number of euros offered for each dollar makes European goods, services, and assets more attractive to U.S. buyers. Similarly, the demand for dollars is downward-sloping because holders of euros will be less willing to buy dollars the more expensive they are in terms of euros. The equilibrium exchange rate e*, also called the *fundamental value of the exchange rate*, equates the quantities of dollars supplied and demanded.

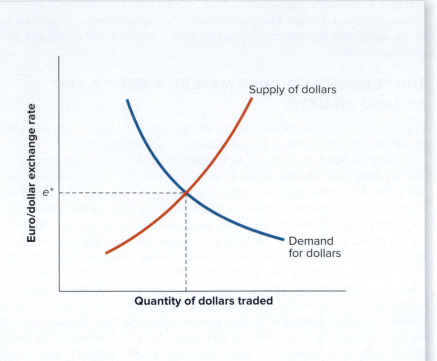

if a dollar can buy 2 euros, then the dollar price of the same washing machine will be $100. Assuming that lower dollar prices will induce Americans to increase their expenditures on European goods, services, and assets, a higher euro–dollar exchange rate will increase the supply of dollars to the foreign exchange market. Thus the supply curve for dollars is upward-sloping.

The Demand for Dollars

In the euro–dollar foreign exchange market, demanders of dollars are those who wish to acquire dollars in exchange for euros. Most demanders of dollars in the euro–dollar market are European households and firms, although anyone who happens to hold euros is free to trade them for dollars. Why demand dollars? The reasons for acquiring dollars are analogous to those for acquiring euros. First, households and firms that hold euros will demand dollars *so that they can purchase U.S. goods and services*. For example, a Portuguese firm that wants to license U.S.-produced software needs dollars to pay the required fees, and a Portuguese student studying in an American university must pay tuition in dollars. The firm or the student can acquire the necessary dollars only by offering euros in exchange. Second, households and firms demand dollars *in order to purchase U.S. assets*. The purchase of Hawaiian real estate by a Finnish company or the acquisition of Google stock by an Austrian pension fund are two examples.

The demand for dollars is represented by the downward-sloping curve in Figure 28.3. The curve slopes downward because the more euros a European person must pay to acquire a dollar, the less attractive U.S. goods, services, and assets will be. Hence the demand for dollars will be low when dollars are expensive in terms of euros and high when dollars are cheap in terms of euros.

The Equilibrium Value of the Dollar

As mentioned earlier, the United States maintains a flexible, or floating, exchange rate, which means that the value of the dollar is determined by the forces of supply and demand in the foreign exchange market. In Figure 28.3 the equilibrium value of the dollar is e*, the euro–dollar exchange rate at which the quantity of dollars supplied equals the quantity of dollars demanded. The **equilibrium exchange rate** is also called the **fundamental value of the exchange rate.** In general, the equilibrium value of the dollar is not constant but changes with shifts in the supply of and demand for dollars in the foreign exchange market.

CHANGES IN THE SUPPLY OF DOLLARS

Recall that people supply dollars to the euro–dollar foreign exchange market in order to purchase European goods, services, and assets. Factors that affect the desire of U.S. households and firms to acquire European goods, services, and assets will therefore affect the supply of dollars to the foreign exchange market. Some factors that will *increase* the supply of dollars, shifting the supply curve for dollars to the right, include:

- An increased preference for European goods. For example, suppose that European firms produce some popular new consumer electronics. To acquire the euros needed to buy these goods, American importers will increase their supply of dollars to the foreign exchange market.

- An increase in U.S. real incomes. An increase in the incomes of Americans will allow Americans to consume more goods and services (recall the consumption function, introduced in Chapter 25, *Spending and Output in the Short Run*). Some part of this increase in consumption will take the form of goods imported from Europe. To buy more European goods, Americans will supply more dollars to acquire the necessary euros.

- An increase in the real interest rate on European assets. Recall that U.S. households and firms acquire euros in order to purchase European assets as well as goods and services. Other factors, such as risk, held constant, the higher the real interest rate paid by European assets, the more European assets Americans will choose to hold. To purchase additional European assets, U.S. households and firms will supply more dollars to the foreign exchange market.

Conversely, reduced demand for European goods, lower real U.S. incomes, or a lower real interest rate on European assets will *reduce* the number of euros Americans need, in turn reducing their supply of dollars to the foreign exchange market and shifting the supply curve for dollars to the left. Of course, any shift in the supply curve for dollars will affect the equilibrium exchange rate, as Example 28.5 shows.

fundamental value of the exchange rate (or **equilibrium exchange rate**) the exchange rate that equates the quantities of the currency supplied and demanded in the foreign exchange market

---

EXAMPLE 28.5	**Washing Machines and the Exchange Rate**

How would increased demand for German washing machines affect the euro–dollar exchange rate?

Suppose German firms come to dominate the washing machine market, with washing machines that are more efficient and reliable than those produced in the United States. All else being equal, how will this change affect the relative value of the euro and the dollar?

The increased quality of German washing machines will increase the demand for the washing machines in the United States. To acquire the euros necessary to buy more German washing machines, U.S. importers will supply more dollars to the foreign exchange market. As Figure 28.4 shows, the increased supply of dollars will reduce the value of the dollar. In other words, a dollar will buy fewer euros than it did before. At the same time, the euro will increase in value: A given number of euros will buy more dollars than it did before.

An Increase in the Supply of Dollars Lowers the Value of the Dollar.

Increased U.S. demand for German washing machines forces Americans to supply more dollars to the foreign exchange market to acquire the euros they need to buy the machines. The supply curve for dollars shifts from S to S', lowering the value of the dollar in terms of euros. The fundamental value of the exchange rate falls from e^* to $e^{*'}$.

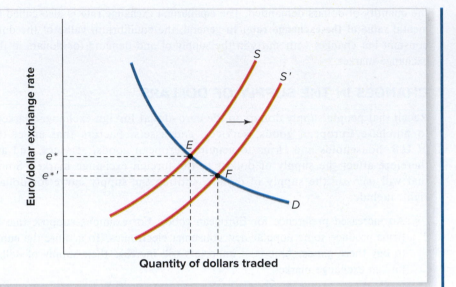

 SELF-TEST 28.4

The U.S. goes into a recession, and real GDP falls. All else equal, how is this economic weakness likely to affect the value of the dollar?

CHANGES IN THE DEMAND FOR DOLLARS

The factors that can cause a change in the demand for dollars in the foreign exchange market, and thus a shift of the dollar demand curve, are analogous to the factors that affect the supply of dollars. Factors that will *increase* the demand for dollars include:

- An increased preference for U.S. goods. For example, European airlines might find that U.S.-built aircraft are superior to others and decide to expand the number of American-made planes in their fleets. To buy the American planes, European airlines would demand more dollars on the foreign exchange market.

- An increase in real incomes abroad and thus more demand for imports from the United States.

- An increase in the real interest rate on U.S. assets, which would make those assets more attractive to foreign savers. To acquire U.S. assets, European savers would demand more dollars.

 ## The Economic Naturalist 28.2

What is a safe haven currency?

Certain currencies, such as the U.S. dollar, the Swiss franc, and the Japanese yen, are in high demand during times of global uncertainty. The tendency of individuals to "pull their wealth out" of other currencies (i.e., to sell assets denominated in other currencies) and "park their wealth in" certain currencies (e.g., by buying and holding cash or bonds denominated in dollar, Swiss franc, or yen) earned these currencies the name *safe haven currencies*.

What makes a currency a safe haven? In times of uncertainty, individuals seek safe and liquid assets. An asset such as cash or bond is considered safe when its issuing government has a good history of issuing assets that turned out to be safe—and is therefore considered financially reliable and stable. Governments that did not in the past default on their debt or suffer from high inflation make good candidates. A currency is considered liquid when it is widely recognized and used, and is therefore widely accepted and can be easily exchanged in global markets. Naturally, these features of currencies—safety and liquidity—help in making the countries that issue them global financial hubs, which, in turn, helps in making these currencies safer and even more liquid.

As a safe haven currency, the U.S. dollar's exchange rate spiked around the global financial crisis and again around the global coronavirus crisis. As Figure 28.1 shows, the dollar gained around 20 percent within a few months in late 2008. It also gained around 8 percent within two weeks in March 2020.

The Economic Naturalist 26.1 (in Chapter 26, *Stabilizing the Economy: The Role of the Fed*) discussed how the demand for the safety and liquidity of the dollar is an important source of demand for dollars in specific *countries,* such as Argentina, that have a history of financial instability. Similarly, the safety and liquidity of U.S. assets are a source of global demand for dollars in specific *times* of global uncertainty.

RECAP

DETERMINING THE EXCHANGE RATE IN THE SHORT RUN

- Supply and demand analysis is a useful tool for studying the short-run determination of the exchange rate. U.S. households and firms supply dollars to the foreign exchange market to acquire foreign currencies, which they need to purchase foreign goods, services, and assets. Foreigners demand dollars in the foreign exchange market to purchase U.S. goods, services, and assets. The equilibrium exchange rate, also called the fundamental value of the exchange rate, equates the quantities of dollars supplied and demanded in the foreign exchange market.

- An increased preference for foreign goods, an increase in U.S. real incomes, or an increase in the real interest rate on foreign assets will increase the supply of dollars on the foreign exchange market, lowering the value of the dollar. An increased preference for U.S. goods by foreigners, an increase in real incomes abroad, or an increase in the real interest rate on U.S. assets will increase the demand for dollars, raising the value of the dollar.

- Safe haven currencies, including the dollar, tend to appreciate in periods of uncertainty when investors look to hold safe and liquid assets.

MONETARY POLICY AND THE EXCHANGE RATE

Of the many factors that could influence a country's exchange rate, among the most important is the monetary policy of the country's central bank. As we will see, monetary policy affects the exchange rate primarily through its effect on the real interest rate.

Suppose the Fed is concerned about inflation and tightens U.S. monetary policy in response. The effects of this policy change on the value of the dollar are shown in Figure 28.5. Before the policy change, the equilibrium value of the exchange rate is e^*, at the intersection of supply curve S and the demand curve D (point E in the figure). The tightening of monetary policy raises the domestic U.S. real interest rate r, making U.S. assets more attractive to foreign financial investors. The increased willingness of foreign investors to buy U.S. assets increases the demand for dollars, shifting the demand curve rightward from D to D' and the equilibrium point from E to F. As a result of this increase in demand, the equilibrium value of the dollar rises from e^* to $e^{*'}$.

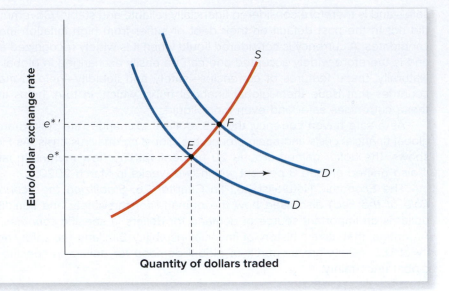

FIGURE 28.5

A Tightening of Monetary Policy Strengthens the Dollar.

Tighter monetary policy in the United States raises the domestic real interest rate, increasing the demand for U.S. assets by foreign savers. An increased demand for U.S. assets in turn increases the demand for dollars. The demand curve shifts from D to D', leading the exchange rate to appreciate from e^* to $e^{*'}$.

In short, a tightening of monetary policy by the Fed raises the demand for dollars, causing the dollar to appreciate. By similar logic, an easing of monetary policy, which reduces the real interest rate, would weaken the demand for the dollar, causing it to depreciate.

The Economic Naturalist 28.3

Why did the dollar appreciate nearly 50 percent in the first half of the 1980s and nearly 40 percent in the second half of the 1990s?

Figure 28.1 showed the strong appreciation of the U.S. dollar in 1980–1985, followed by a sharp depreciation in 1986–1987. It also showed a strong appreciation in 1995–2001, followed by depreciation in 2002–2004. We saw earlier that the PPP theory cannot explain this roller-coaster behavior. What *can* explain it?

Tight monetary policy, and the associated high real interest rate, were important causes of the dollar's remarkable appreciation during 1980–1985. U.S. inflation peaked at 13.5 percent in 1980. Under the leadership of Chair Paul Volcker, the Fed responded to the surge in inflation by raising the real interest rate sharply in hopes of reducing aggregate demand and inflationary pressures. As a result, the real interest rate in the United States rose from negative values in 1979 and 1980 to more than 7 percent in 1983 and 1984. Attracted by these high real returns, foreign savers rushed to buy U.S. assets, driving the value of the dollar up significantly.

The Fed's attempt to bring down inflation was successful. By the middle of the 1980s the Fed was able to ease U.S. monetary policy. The resulting decline in the real interest rate reduced the demand for U.S. assets, and thus for dollars, at which point the dollar fell back almost to its 1980 level.

One reason for the dollar's appreciation in the late 1990s was the U.S. stock market boom and the generally strong pace of growth. These raised expected returns on U.S. assets, leading foreigners to want to buy these assets, increasing the demand for and thus appreciating the dollar. The relatively tight monetary policy during these years also played a role.

Stock markets peaked in the early 2000s before reversing course, and the U.S. economy was in recession during much of 2001, accompanied by a significant expansion in monetary policy starting early in 2001. While the dollar did not reverse its general upward trend until early 2002, when it eventually did, it started a long period of depreciation. By early 2004, with the federal funds rate at a historic low, the dollar fell back to its 1995 level.

THE EXCHANGE RATE AS A TOOL OF MONETARY POLICY

In a closed economy, monetary policy affects aggregate demand solely through the real interest rate. For example, by raising the real interest rate, a tight monetary policy reduces consumption and investment spending. We will see next that in an open economy with a flexible exchange rate, the exchange rate serves as another channel for monetary policy, one that reinforces the effects of the real interest rate.

To illustrate, suppose that policymakers are concerned about inflation and decide to restrain aggregate demand. To do so, they increase the real interest rate, reducing consumption and investment spending. But, as Figure 28.5 shows, the higher real interest rate also increases the demand for dollars, causing the dollar to appreciate. The stronger dollar, in turn, further reduces aggregate demand. Why? As we saw in discussing the real exchange rate, a stronger dollar reduces the cost of imported goods, increasing imports. It also makes U.S. exports more costly to foreign buyers, which tends to reduce exports. Recall that net exports—or exports minus imports—is one of the four components of aggregate demand. Thus, by reducing exports and increasing imports, a stronger dollar (more precisely, a higher real exchange rate) reduces aggregate demand.[5]

In sum, when the exchange rate is flexible, a tighter monetary policy reduces net exports (through a stronger dollar) as well as consumption and investment spending (through a higher real interest rate). Conversely, an easier monetary policy weakens the dollar and stimulates net exports, reinforcing the effect of the lower real interest rate on consumption and investment spending. Thus, relative to the case of a closed economy we studied earlier, *monetary policy is more effective in an open economy with a flexible exchange rate.*

The tightening of monetary policy under Fed chair Volcker in the early 1980s illustrates the effect of monetary policy on net exports (the trade balance). As we saw in The Economic Naturalist 28.3, Volcker's tight-money policies were a major reason for the 50 percent appreciation of the dollar during 1980–1985. In 1980 and 1981, imports into the United States were only slightly above exports from the U.S., and the trade deficit did not exceed 0.5 percent of GDP. Largely in response to a stronger dollar, the U.S. trade deficit increased substantially after 1981. By the end of 1985 the U.S. trade deficit was about 3 percent of GDP, a substantial shift in less than half a decade.

> **RECAP**
>
> ### MONETARY POLICY AND THE EXCHANGE RATE
>
> A tight monetary policy raises the real interest rate, increasing the demand for dollars and strengthening the dollar. A stronger dollar reinforces the effects of tight monetary policy on aggregate spending by reducing net exports, a component of aggregate demand. Conversely, an easy monetary policy lowers the real interest rate, weakening the dollar.

FIXED EXCHANGE RATES

So far we have focused on the case of flexible exchange rates, the relevant case for most large industrial countries like the United States. However, the alternative approach, fixing the exchange rate, has been quite important historically and is still used in many countries, especially small or developing nations. Furthermore, as mentioned earlier, even China—currently the world's second-largest economy—lets its currency float only within a fixed narrow band that shifts gradually over time or that is set by the central bank. (China kept its exchange rate fixed to the dollar throughout much of the 1990s and 2000s but has recently attempted to make its exchange rate somewhat more flexible.)

In this section, we will see how our conclusions change when the nominal exchange rate is fixed rather than flexible. One important difference is that when a country maintains a fixed exchange rate, its ability to use monetary policy as a stabilization tool is greatly reduced.

---

[5] We are temporarily assuming that the prices of U.S. goods in dollars and the prices of foreign goods in foreign currencies are not changing.

HOW TO FIX AN EXCHANGE RATE

In contrast to a flexible exchange rate, whose value is determined solely by supply and demand in the foreign exchange market, the value of a fixed exchange rate is determined by the government (in practice, usually the finance ministry or treasury department, with the cooperation of the central bank). Today, the value of a fixed exchange rate is usually set in terms of a major currency (for instance, Hong Kong pegs its currency to the U.S. dollar at an exchange rate of HK$7.8 to US$1), or relative to a "basket" of currencies, typically those of the country's trading partners. Historically, currency values were often fixed in terms of gold or other precious metals, but in recent years, precious metals have rarely if ever been used for that purpose.

Once an exchange rate has been fixed, the government usually attempts to keep it unchanged for some time.[6] However, sometimes economic circumstances force the government to change the value of the exchange rate. A reduction in the official value of a currency is called a **devaluation;** an increase in the official value is called a **revaluation.** The devaluation of a fixed exchange rate is analogous to the depreciation of a flexible exchange rate; both involve a reduction in the currency's value. Conversely, a revaluation is analogous to an appreciation.

The supply and demand diagram we used to study flexible exchange rates can be adapted to analyze fixed exchange rates. Let's consider the case of a country called Latinia, whose currency is called the peso. Figure 28.6 shows the supply and demand for the Latinian peso in the foreign exchange market. Pesos are *supplied* to the foreign exchange market by Latinian households and firms that want to acquire foreign currencies to purchase foreign goods and assets. Pesos are *demanded* by holders of foreign currencies who need pesos to purchase Latinian goods and assets. Figure 28.6 shows that the quantities of pesos supplied and demanded in the foreign exchange market are equal when a peso equals 0.1 dollar (10 pesos to the dollar). Hence 0.1 dollar per peso is the *fundamental value* of the peso. If Latinia had a flexible exchange rate system, the peso would trade at 10 pesos to the dollar in the foreign exchange market.

devaluation a reduction in the official value of a currency (in a fixed exchange rate system)

revaluation an increase in the official value of a currency (in a fixed exchange rate system)

FIGURE 28.6

An Overvalued Exchange Rate.
The peso's official value (0.125 dollars) is shown as greater than its fundamental value (0.10 dollars), as determined by supply and demand in the foreign exchange market. Thus the peso is overvalued. To maintain the fixed value, the government must purchase pesos in the quantity *AB* each period.

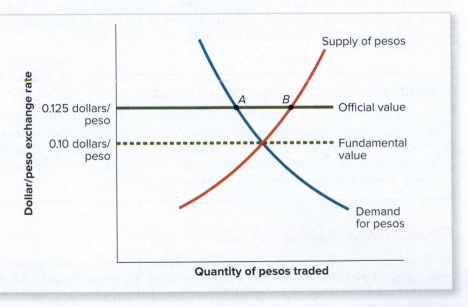

But let's suppose that Latinia has a fixed exchange rate and that the government has decreed the value of the Latinian peso to be 8 pesos to the dollar, or 0.125 dollars per peso. This official value of the peso, 0.125 dollars, is indicated by the solid horizontal line in Figure 28.6. Notice that it is greater than the fundamental value, corresponding

[6]There are exceptions to this statement. Some countries employ a *crawling peg* system, under which the exchange rate is fixed at a value that changes in a preannounced way over time. For example, the government may announce that the value of the fixed exchange rate will fall 2 percent each year. Other countries use a *target zone* system, in which the exchange rate is allowed to deviate by a small amount from its fixed value. To focus on the key issues, we will assume that the exchange rate is fixed at a single value for a protracted period.

to the intersection of the supply and demand curves. When the officially fixed value of an exchange rate is greater than its fundamental value, the exchange rate is said to be **overvalued.** The official value of an exchange rate can also be lower than its fundamental value, in which case the exchange rate is said to be **undervalued.**

In this example, Latinia's commitment to hold the peso at 8 to the dollar is inconsistent with the fundamental value of 10 to the dollar, as determined by supply and demand in the foreign exchange market (the Latinian peso is overvalued). How could the Latinian government deal with this inconsistency? There are several possibilities. First, Latinia could simply devalue its currency, from 0.125 dollars per peso to 0.10 dollars per peso, which would bring the peso's official value into line with its fundamental value. As we will see, devaluation is often the ultimate result of an overvaluation of a currency. However, a country with a fixed exchange rate will be reluctant to change the official value of its exchange rate every time the fundamental value changes. If a country must continuously adjust its exchange rate to market conditions, it might as well switch to a flexible exchange rate.

As a second alternative, Latinia could try to maintain its overvalued exchange rate by restricting international transactions. Imposing quotas on imports and prohibiting domestic households and firms from acquiring foreign assets would effectively reduce the supply of pesos to the foreign exchange market, raising the fundamental value of the currency. An even more extreme action would be to prohibit Latinians from exchanging the peso for other currencies without government approval, a policy that would effectively allow the government to determine directly the supply of pesos to the foreign exchange market. Such measures might help maintain the official value of the peso. However, restrictions on trade and capital flows are extremely costly to the economy, because they reduce the gains from specialization and trade and deny domestic households and firms access to foreign capital markets. Thus, a policy of restricting international transactions to maintain a fixed exchange rate is likely to do more harm than good.

The third and most widely used approach to maintaining an overvalued exchange rate is for the government to become a demander of its own currency in the foreign exchange market. Figure 28.6 shows that at the official exchange rate of 0.125 dollars per peso, the private-sector supply of pesos (point B) exceeds the private-sector demand for pesos (point A). To keep the peso from falling below its official value, in each period the Latinian government could purchase a quantity of pesos in the foreign exchange market equal to the length of the line segment AB in Figure 28.6. If the government followed this strategy, then at the official exchange rate of 0.125 dollars per peso, the total demand for pesos (private demand at point A plus government demand AB) would equal the private supply of pesos (point B). This situation is analogous to government attempts to keep the price of a commodity, like grain or milk, above its market level. To maintain an official price of grain that is above the market-clearing price, the government must stand ready to purchase the excess supply of grain forthcoming at the official price. In the same way, to keep the "price" of its currency above the market-clearing level, the government must buy the excess pesos supplied at the official price.

To be able to purchase its own currency and maintain an overvalued exchange rate, the government (usually the central bank) must hold foreign currency assets, called **international reserves,** or simply *reserves*. For example, the Latinian central bank may hold dollar deposits in U.S. banks or U.S. government debt, which it can trade for pesos in the foreign exchange market as needed. In the situation shown in Figure 28.6, to keep the peso at its official value, in each period the Latinian central bank will have to spend an amount of international reserves equal to the length of the line segment AB.

Because a country with an overvalued exchange rate must use part of its reserves to support the value of its currency in each period, over time its available reserves will decline. The net decline in a country's stock of international reserves over a year is called its **balance-of-payments deficit.** Conversely, if a country experiences a net increase in its international reserves over the year, the increase is called its **balance-of-payments surplus.**

overvalued exchange rate
an exchange rate that has an officially fixed value greater than its fundamental value

undervalued exchange rate
an exchange rate that has an officially fixed value less than its fundamental value

international reserves
foreign currency assets held by a government for the purpose of purchasing the domestic currency in the foreign exchange market

balance-of-payments deficit
the net decline in a country's stock of international reserves over a year

balance-of-payments surplus the net increase in a country's stock of international reserves over a year

EXAMPLE 28.6   Latinia's Balance-of-Payments Deficit

What is the balance-of-payments cost of keeping a currency overvalued?

The demand for and supply of Latinian pesos in the foreign exchange market are

$$Demand = 25{,}000 - 50{,}000e,$$
$$Supply = 17{,}600 + 24{,}000e,$$

where the Latinian exchange rate e is measured in dollars per peso. Officially, the value of the peso is 0.125 dollars. Find the fundamental value of the peso and the Latinian balance-of-payments deficit, measured in both pesos and dollars.

To find the fundamental value of the peso, equate the demand and supply for pesos

$$25{,}000 - 50{,}000e = 17{,}600 + 24{,}000e.$$

Solving for e, we get

$$7{,}400 = 74{,}000e$$
$$e = 0.10.$$

So the fundamental value of the exchange rate is 0.10 dollars per peso, as in Figure 28.6.

At the official exchange rate, 0.125 dollars per peso, the demand for pesos is $25{,}000 - 50{,}000(0.125) = 18{,}750$, and the supply of pesos is $17{,}600 + 24{,}000$ $(0.125) = 20{,}600$. Thus the quantity of pesos supplied to the foreign exchange market exceeds the quantity of pesos demanded by $20{,}600 - 18{,}750 = 1{,}850$ pesos. To maintain the fixed rate, the Latinian government must purchase 1,850 pesos per period, which is the Latinian balance-of-payments deficit. Since pesos are purchased at the official rate of 8 pesos to the dollar, the balance-of-payments deficit in dollars is $(1{,}850 \text{ pesos}) \times (0.125 \text{ dollars/peso}) = \$(1{,}850/8) = \$231.25$.

 SELF-TEST 28.5

Repeat Example 28.6 under the assumption that the fixed value of the peso is 0.15 dollars per peso. What do you conclude about the relationship between the degree of currency overvaluation and the resulting balance-of-payments deficit?

Although a government can maintain an overvalued exchange rate for a time by offering to buy back its own currency at the official price, there is a limit to this strategy, since no government's stock of international reserves is infinite. Eventually the government will run out of reserves, and the fixed exchange rate will collapse. As we will see next, the collapse of a fixed exchange rate can be quite sudden and dramatic.

 SELF-TEST 28.6

Diagram a case in which a fixed exchange rate is *undervalued* rather than overvalued. Show that to maintain the fixed exchange rate, the central bank must use domestic currency to purchase foreign currency in the foreign exchange market. With an undervalued exchange rate, is the country's central bank in danger of running out of international reserves? (*Hint:* Keep in mind that a central bank is always free to print more of its own currency.)

SPECULATIVE ATTACKS

A government's attempt to maintain an overvalued exchange rate can be ended quickly and unexpectedly by the onset of a *speculative attack*. A **speculative attack** involves massive selling of domestic currency assets by both domestic and foreign financial investors. For example, in a speculative attack on the Latinian peso, financial investors would attempt to get rid of any financial assets—stocks, bonds, deposits in banks—denominated in pesos. A speculative attack is most likely to occur when financial investors fear that an overvalued currency will soon be devalued since, in a devaluation, financial assets denominated in the domestic currency suddenly become worth much less in terms of other currencies. Ironically, speculative attacks, which are usually prompted by *fear* of devaluation, may turn out to be the *cause* of devaluation. Thus a speculative attack may actually be a self-fulfilling prophecy.

The effects of a speculative attack on the market for pesos are shown in Figure 28.7. At first, the situation is the same as in Figure 28.6: The supply and demand for Latinian pesos are indicated by the curves marked *S* and *D*, implying a fundamental value of the peso of 0.10 dollars per peso. As before, the official value of the peso is 0.125 dollars per peso—greater than the fundamental value—so the peso is overvalued. To maintain the fixed value of the peso, each period the Latinian central bank must use its international reserves to buy back pesos, in the amount corresponding to the line segment *AB* in the figure.

speculative attack a massive selling of domestic currency assets by financial investors

FIGURE 28.7

A Speculative Attack on the Peso.

Initially, the peso is overvalued at 0.125 dollars per peso. To maintain the official rate, the central bank must buy pesos in the amount *AB* each period. Fearful of possible devaluation, financial investors launch a speculative attack, selling peso-denominated assets and supplying pesos to the foreign exchange market. As a result, the supply of pesos shifts from *S* to *S'*, lowering the fundamental value of the currency still further and forcing the central bank to buy pesos in the amount *AC* to maintain the official exchange rate. This more rapid loss of reserves may lead the central bank to devalue the peso, confirming financial investors' fears.

Suppose, though, that financial investors fear that Latinia may soon devalue its currency, perhaps because the central bank's reserves are getting low. If the peso were to be devalued from its official value of 8 pesos to the dollar to its fundamental value of 10 pesos per dollar, then a 1 million peso investment, worth $125,000 at the fixed exchange rate, would suddenly be worth only $100,000. To try to avoid these losses, financial investors will sell their peso-denominated assets and offer pesos on the foreign exchange market. The resulting flood of pesos into the market will shift the supply curve of pesos to the right, from *S* to *S'* in Figure 28.7.

This speculative attack creates a serious problem for the Latinian central bank. Prior to the attack, maintaining the value of the peso required the central bank to spend each period an amount of international reserves corresponding to the line segment *AB*. Now suddenly the central bank must spend a larger quantity of reserves, equal to the distance *AC* in Figure 28.7, to maintain the fixed exchange rate. These extra reserves are needed to purchase the pesos being sold by panicky financial investors. In practice, such speculative attacks often force a devaluation by reducing the central bank's reserves to the point where further defense of the fixed exchange rate is considered hopeless. Thus a speculative attack ignited by fears of devaluation may actually end up producing the very devaluation that was feared.

MONETARY POLICY AND THE FIXED EXCHANGE RATE

We have seen that there is no truly satisfactory way of maintaining a fixed exchange rate above its fundamental value for an extended period. A central bank can maintain an overvalued exchange rate for a time by using international reserves to buy up the excess supply of its currency in the foreign exchange market. But a country's international reserves are limited and may eventually be exhausted by the attempt to keep the exchange rate artificially high. Moreover, speculative attacks often hasten the collapse of an overvalued exchange rate.

An alternative to trying to maintain an overvalued exchange rate is to take actions that increase the fundamental value of the exchange rate. If the exchange rate's fundamental value can be raised enough to equal its official value, then the overvaluation problem will be eliminated. The most effective way to change the exchange rate's fundamental value is through monetary policy. As we saw earlier in the chapter, a tight monetary policy that raises the real interest rate will increase the demand for the domestic currency, as domestic assets become more attractive to foreign financial investors. Increased demand for the currency will in turn raise its fundamental value.

The use of monetary policy to support a fixed exchange rate is shown in Figure 28.8. At first, the demand and supply of the Latinian peso in the foreign exchange market are given by the curves D and S, so the fundamental value of the peso equals 0.10 dollars per peso—less than the official value of 0.125 dollars per peso. Just as before, the peso is overvalued. This time, however, the Latinian central bank uses monetary policy to eliminate the overvaluation problem. To do so, the central bank increases the domestic real interest rate, making Latinian assets more attractive to foreign financial investors and raising the demand for pesos from D to D'. After this increase in the demand for pesos, the fundamental value of the peso equals the officially fixed value, as can be seen in Figure 28.8. Because the peso is no longer overvalued, it can be maintained at its fixed value without loss of international reserves or fear of speculative attack. Conversely, an

FIGURE 28.8

A Tightening of Monetary Policy Eliminates an Overvaluation.

With the demand for the peso given by D and the supply given by S, equilibrium occurs at point E and the fundamental value of the peso equals 0.10 dollars per peso—below the official value of 0.125 dollars per peso. The overvaluation of the peso can be eliminated by tighter monetary policy, which raises the domestic real interest rate, making domestic assets more attractive to foreign financial investors. The resulting increase in demand for the peso, from D to D', raises the peso's fundamental value to 0.125 dollars per peso, the official value. The peso is no longer overvalued.

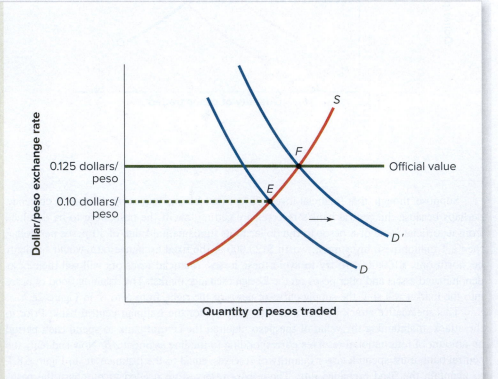

easing of monetary policy (a lower real interest rate) could be used to remedy an under-valuation, in which the official exchange rate is below the fundamental value.

Although monetary policy can be used to keep the fundamental value of the exchange rate equal to the official value, using monetary policy in this way has some drawbacks. In particular, *if monetary policy is used to set the fundamental value of the exchange rate equal to the official value, it is no longer available for stabilizing the domestic economy.* Suppose, for example, that the Latinian economy were suffering a recession due to insufficient aggregate demand at the same time that its exchange rate is overvalued. The Latinian central bank could lower the real interest rate to increase spending and output, or it could raise the real interest rate to eliminate overvaluation of the exchange rate, *but it cannot do both.* Hence, if Latinian officials decide to maintain the fixed exchange rate, they must give up any hope of fighting the recession using monetary policy. The fact that a fixed exchange rate limits or eliminates the use of monetary policy for the purpose of stabilizing aggregate demand is one of the most important features of a fixed exchange rate system.

The conflict monetary policymakers face, between stabilizing the exchange rate and stabilizing the domestic economy, is most severe when the exchange rate is under a speculative attack. A speculative attack lowers the fundamental value of the exchange rate still further, by increasing the supply of the currency in the foreign exchange market (see Figure 28.7). To stop a speculative attack, the central bank must raise the fundamental value of the currency a great deal, which requires a large increase in the real interest rate. (In a famous episode in 1992, the Swedish central bank responded to an attack on its currency by raising the short-term interest rate to 500 percent!) However, because the increase in the real interest rate that is necessary to stop a speculative attack reduces aggregate demand, it can cause a severe economic slowdown. The Economic Naturalist 28.4 describes a real-world example of this phenomenon.

The Economic Naturalist 28.4

What were the causes and consequences of the East Asian crisis of 1997–1998?

During the last three decades of the twentieth century, the countries of East Asia enjoyed impressive economic growth and stability. But the "East Asian miracle" seemed to end in 1997, when a wave of speculative attacks hit the region's currencies. Thailand, which had kept a constant value for its currency in terms of the U.S. dollar for more than a decade, was the first to come under attack, but the crisis spread to other countries, including South Korea, Indonesia, and Malaysia. Each of these countries was ultimately forced to devalue its currency. What caused this crisis, and what were its consequences?

Because of the impressive economic record of the East Asian countries, the speculative attacks on their currencies were unexpected by most policymakers, economists, and financial investors. With the benefit of hindsight, however, we can identify some problems in the East Asian economies that contributed to the crisis. Perhaps the most serious problems concerned their banking systems. In the decade prior to the crisis, East Asian banks received large inflows of capital from foreign financial investors hoping to profit from the East Asian miracle. Those inflows would have been a boon if they had been well invested, but unfortunately, many bankers used the funds to make loans to family members, friends, or the politically well-connected—a phenomenon that became known as *crony capitalism*. The results were poor returns on investment and defaults by many borrowers. Ultimately, foreign investors realized that the returns to investing in East Asia would be much lower than expected. When they began to sell off their assets, the process snowballed into a full-fledged speculative attack on the East Asian currencies.

Despite assistance by international lenders such as the International Monetary Fund (see The Economic Naturalist 28.5), the effects of the speculative attacks on the East Asian economies were severe. The prices of assets such as stocks and land plummeted, and there were banking panics in several nations. (See Chapter 22, *Money, Prices, and the Federal Reserve* for a discussion of banking panics.) In an attempt to raise the fundamental values of their exchange rates and stave off additional devaluation, several of the countries increased their real interest rates sharply. However, the rise in real interest rates depressed aggregate demand, contributing to sharp declines in output and rising unemployment.

Fortunately, by 1999 most East Asian economies had begun to recover. Still, the crisis impressed the potential dangers of fixed exchange rates quite sharply in the minds of policymakers in developing countries. Another lesson from the crisis is that banking regulations need to be structured so as to promote economically sound lending rather than crony capitalism.

The Economic Naturalist 28.5

What is the IMF, and how has its mission evolved over the years?

The International Monetary Fund (IMF) was established after World War II. An international agency, the IMF is controlled by a 24-member executive board. Eight executive board members represent individual countries (China, France, Germany, Japan, Russia, Saudi Arabia, the United Kingdom, and the United States); the other 16 members each represent a group of countries.[7] A managing director oversees the IMF's operations and its approximately 2,700 staff (half of whom are economists).

The original purpose of the IMF was to help manage the system of fixed exchange rates, called the Bretton Woods system, put in place after the war. Under Bretton Woods, the IMF's principal role was to lend international reserves to member countries that needed them so that those countries could maintain their exchange rates at the official values. However, by 1973 the United States, the United Kingdom, Germany, and most other industrial nations had abandoned fixed exchange rates for flexible rates, leaving the IMF to find a new mission. Since 1973, the IMF has been involved primarily in lending to developing countries. For example, during the currency crises of the 1990s, it lent to Mexico, Russia, Brazil, and several East Asian countries. During the 2008 crisis, it again made loans to countries that saw their currencies under pressure. During the 2010s, the IMF joined European countries in making loans to Greece—a developed country—with the Europeans providing two-thirds of the money Greece needs to pay its government debts, and the IMF providing one-third. And in early 2020, the IMF made available $50 billion for low-income and emerging-market economies seeking loans related to addressing the global coronavirus epidemic.

The Economic Naturalist 28.6

How did policy mistakes contribute to the Great Depression?

We introduced the study of macroeconomics with the claim that policy mistakes played a major role in causing the Great Depression. Now that we are close to completing our study of macroeconomics, we can be more specific about that claim. How did policy mistakes contribute to the Great Depression?

Many policy mistakes (as well as a great deal of bad luck) contributed to the severity of the Depression. For example, U.S. policymakers, in an attempt to

[7]The Russian representative also represents Syria.

protect domestic industries, imposed the infamous Hawley-Smoot tariff in 1930. Other countries quickly retaliated with their own tariffs, leading to the virtual collapse of international trade.

However, the most serious mistakes by far were in the realm of monetary policy.[8] As we saw in Chapter 22, *Money, Prices, and the Federal Reserve,* the U.S. money supply contracted by one-third between 1929 and 1933. Associated with this unprecedented decline in the money supply were sharply falling output and prices and surging unemployment.

At least three separate policy errors were responsible for the collapse of the U.S. money supply between 1929 and 1933. First, the Federal Reserve tightened monetary policy significantly in 1928 and 1929, despite the absence of inflation. Fed officials took this action primarily in an attempt to "rein in" the booming stock market, which they feared was rising too quickly. Their "success" in dampening stock market speculation was more than they bargained for, however, as rising interest rates and a slowing economy contributed to a crash in stock prices that began in October 1929.

The second critical policy error was allowing thousands of U.S. banks to fail during the banking panics of 1930 to 1933. Apparently officials believed that the failures would eliminate only the weakest banks, strengthening the banking system overall. However, the banking panics sharply reduced bank deposits and the overall money supply, for reasons discussed in The Economic Naturalist 22.2.

The third policy error, related to the subject of this chapter, arose from the U.S. government's exchange rate policies. When the Depression began, the United States, like most other major countries, was on the gold standard, with the value of the dollar officially set in terms of gold.[9] By establishing a fixed value for the dollar, the United States effectively created a fixed exchange rate between the dollar and other currencies whose values were set in terms of gold. As the Depression worsened, Fed officials were urged by Congress to ease monetary policy to stop the fall in output and prices. However, as we saw earlier, under a fixed exchange rate, monetary policy cannot be used to stabilize the domestic economy. Specifically, policymakers of the early 1930s feared that if they eased monetary policy, foreign financial investors might perceive the dollar to be overvalued and launch a speculative attack, forcing a devaluation of the dollar or even the abandonment of the gold standard altogether. The Fed therefore made no serious attempt to arrest the collapse of the money supply.

With hindsight, we can see that the Fed's decision to put a higher priority on remaining on the gold standard than on stimulating the economy was a major error. Indeed, countries that abandoned the gold standard in favor of a floating exchange rate, such as Great Britain and Sweden, or that had never been on the gold standard (Spain and China) were able to increase their money supplies and to recover much more quickly from the Depression than the United States did. The Fed evidently believed, erroneously as it turned out, that stability of the exchange rate would somehow translate into overall economic stability.

Upon taking office in March 1933, Franklin D. Roosevelt reversed several of these policy errors. He took active measures to restore the health of the banking system, and he suspended the gold standard. The money supply stopped falling and began to grow rapidly. Output, prices, and stock prices recovered rapidly during 1933 to 1937, although unemployment remained high. However, ultimate recovery from the Depression was interrupted by another recession in 1937–1938.

---

[8]A classic 1963 book by Milton Friedman and Anna Schwartz, *A Monetary History of the United States: 1867–1960* (Princeton, NJ: Princeton University Press), was the first to provide detailed support for the view that poor monetary policy helped cause the Depression.

[9]The value of the dollar in 1929 was such that the price of 1 ounce of gold was fixed at $20.67.

RECAP↑

FIXED EXCHANGE RATES

- The value of a fixed exchange rate is set by the government. The official value of a fixed exchange rate may differ from its fundamental value, as determined by supply and demand in the foreign exchange market. An exchange rate whose officially fixed value exceeds its fundamental value is overvalued; an exchange rate whose officially fixed value is below its fundamental value is undervalued.

- For an overvalued exchange rate, the quantity of the currency supplied to the foreign exchange market at the official exchange rate exceeds the quantity demanded. The government can maintain an overvalued exchange rate for a time by using its international reserves (foreign currency assets) to purchase the excess supply of its currency. The net decline in a country's stock of international reserves during the year is its balance-of-payments deficit.

- Because a country's international reserves are limited, it cannot maintain an overvalued exchange rate indefinitely. Moreover, if financial investors fear an impending devaluation of the exchange rate, they may launch a speculative attack, selling domestic currency assets and supplying large amounts of the country's currency to the foreign exchange market—an action that exhausts the country's reserves even more quickly. Because rapid loss of reserves may force a devaluation, financial investors' fear of devaluation may prove a self-fulfilling prophecy.

- A tight monetary policy, which increases the real interest rate, raises the demand for the currency and hence its fundamental value. By raising a currency's fundamental value to its official value, tight monetary policies can eliminate the problem of overvaluation and stabilize the exchange rate. However, if monetary policy is used to set the fundamental value of the exchange rate, it is no longer available for stabilizing the domestic economy.

SHOULD EXCHANGE RATES BE FIXED OR FLEXIBLE?

Should countries adopt fixed or flexible exchange rates? In briefly comparing the two systems, we will focus on two major issues: (1) the effects of the exchange rate system on monetary policy and (2) the effects of the exchange rate system on trade and economic integration.

On the issue of monetary policy, we have seen that the type of exchange rate a country has strongly affects the central bank's ability to use monetary policy to stabilize the economy. A flexible exchange rate actually strengthens the impact of monetary policy on aggregate demand. But a fixed exchange rate prevents policymakers from using monetary policy to stabilize the economy because they must instead use it to keep the exchange rate's fundamental value at its official value (or else risk speculative attack).

In large economies like that of the United States, giving up the power to stabilize the domestic economy via monetary policy makes little sense. Thus large economies should nearly always employ a flexible exchange rate. However, in small economies, giving up this power may have some benefits. An interesting case is that of Argentina, which for the period 1991–2001 maintained a one-to-one exchange rate between its peso and the U.S. dollar. Although prior to 1991 Argentina had suffered periods of hyperinflation, while the peso was pegged to the dollar, Argentina's inflation rate essentially equaled that of the United States. By tying its currency to the dollar and giving up the freedom to set its monetary policy, Argentina attempted to commit itself to avoiding the inflationary policies of the past, and instead placed itself under the "umbrella" of the Federal Reserve. Unfortunately, early in 2002 investors' fears that Argentina would not be able to repay its international debts led to a speculative attack on the Argentine peso. The fixed exchange rate collapsed, the peso depreciated, and Argentina experienced an economic crisis. The lesson is that a fixed exchange rate alone cannot stop inflation in a small economy, if other policies are not sound as well. Large fiscal deficits, which were financed by foreign borrowing, ultimately pushed Argentina into crisis.

The second important issue is the effect of the exchange rate on trade and economic integration. Proponents of fixed exchange rates argue that fixed rates promote international trade and cross-border economic cooperation by reducing uncertainty about future exchange rates. For example, a firm that is considering building up its export business knows that its potential profits will depend on the future value of its own country's currency relative to the currencies of the countries to which it exports. Under a flexible exchange rate regime, the value of the home currency fluctuates with changes in supply and demand and is therefore difficult to predict far in advance. Such uncertainty may make the firm reluctant to expand its export business. Supporters of fixed exchange rates argue that if the exchange rate is officially fixed, uncertainty about the future exchange rate is reduced or eliminated.

One problem with this argument, which has been underscored by episodes like the East Asian crisis, the Argentine crisis, and, recently, the Greek crisis (see The Economic Naturalist 28.7), is that fixed exchange rates are not guaranteed to remain fixed forever. Although they do not fluctuate from day to day as flexible rates do, a speculative attack on a fixed exchange rate, or even a change in elected politicians' economic views, may lead suddenly and unpredictably to a large devaluation. Thus a firm that is trying to forecast the exchange rate 10 years into the future may face as much uncertainty if the exchange rate is fixed as if it is flexible.

The potential instability of fixed exchange rates caused by speculative attacks has led some countries to try a more radical solution to the problem of uncertainty about exchange rates: the adoption of a common currency. The Economic Naturalist 28.7 describes an important instance of this strategy.

The Economic Naturalist 28.7

Why have 19 European countries adopted a common currency?

Effective January 1, 1999, eleven western European nations, including France, Germany, and Italy, adopted a common currency, called the euro. In several stages, the euro replaced the French franc, the German mark, the Italian lira, and other national currencies. The process was completed in early 2002 when the old currencies were completely eliminated and replaced by euros. Since then, more European nations, including eastern European ones, have joined the common currency. As of 2020, the last nation to join was Lithuania, which on January 1, 2015, became the 19th member of the *euro area* (or *eurozone*). Why have these nations adopted a common currency?

Since the end of World War II the nations of western Europe have worked to increase economic cooperation and trade among themselves. European leaders recognized that a unified and integrated European economy would be more productive and perhaps more competitive with the U.S. economy than a fragmented one. As part of this effort, these countries established fixed exchange rates under the auspices of a system called the European Monetary System (EMS). Unfortunately, the EMS did not prove stable. Numerous devaluations of the various currencies occurred, and in 1992, severe speculative attacks forced several nations, including Great Britain, to abandon the fixed exchange rate system.

In December 1991, in Maastricht in the Netherlands, the member countries of the European Community (EC) adopted a treaty popularly known as the Maastricht Treaty. One of the major provisions of the treaty, which took effect in November 1993, was that member countries would strive to adopt a common currency. This common currency, known as the euro, was formally adopted on January 1, 1999. The advent of the euro means that Europeans from eurozone countries no longer have to change currencies when trading with other eurozone countries, much as Americans from different states can trade with each other without worrying that a "New York dollar" will change in value relative to a "California dollar." The euro has helped promote European trade and cooperation while eliminating the problem of speculative attacks on the currencies of individual countries.

Because 19 European nations now have a single currency, they also must have a common monetary policy. The EC members agreed that European monetary policy would be put under the control of a new European Central Bank (ECB), a multinational institution located in Frankfurt, Germany. The ECB has in effect become "Europe's Fed." One potential problem with having a single monetary policy for so many different countries is that different countries may face different economic conditions, so a single monetary policy cannot respond to all of them. Indeed, in recent years countries in southern Europe like Spain and Italy have been in serious recessions (which requires an easing of monetary policy), while Germany has been close to full employment. With such a wide variation in economic conditions, the requirement of a single monetary policy has been creating conflicts of interest among the member nations of the European Community.

SUMMARY

- The *nominal exchange rate* between two currencies is the rate at which the currencies can be traded for each other. A rise in the value of a currency relative to other currencies is called an *appreciation;* a decline in the value of a currency is called a *depreciation. (LO1)*

- Exchange rates can be flexible or fixed. (Approaches that combine the two are not our focus in this chapter.) The value of a *flexible exchange rate* is determined by the supply and demand for the currency in the *foreign exchange market,* the market on which currencies of various nations are traded for one another. The government sets the value of a *fixed exchange rate. (LO1)*

- The *real exchange rate* is the price of the average domestic good or service *relative* to the price of the average foreign good or service, when prices are expressed in terms of a common currency. An increase in the real exchange rate implies that domestic goods and services are becoming more expensive relative to foreign goods and services, which tends to reduce exports and increase imports. Conversely, a decline in the real exchange rate tends to increase net exports. *(LO1)*

- A basic theory of nominal exchange rate determination, the *purchasing power parity* (PPP) theory, is based on the

law of one price. The *law of one price* states that if transportation costs are relatively small, the price of an internationally traded commodity must be the same in all locations. According to the PPP theory, we can find the nominal exchange rate between two currencies by setting the price of a commodity in one of the currencies equal to the price of the commodity in the second currency. The PPP theory correctly predicts that the currencies of countries that experience significant inflation will tend to depreciate in the long run. However, the fact that many goods and services are not traded internationally, and that not all traded goods are standardized, makes the PPP theory less useful for explaining short-run changes in exchange rates. *(LO2)*

- Supply and demand analysis is a useful tool for studying the determination of exchange rates in the short run. The equilibrium exchange rate, also called the *fundamental value of the exchange rate,* equates the quantities of the currency supplied and demanded in the foreign exchange market. A currency is supplied by domestic residents who wish to acquire foreign currencies to purchase foreign goods, services, and assets. An increased preference for foreign goods, an increase in the domestic incomes, or an increase in the real interest rate on foreign assets will all increase the supply of a currency on the foreign exchange market and thus lower its value. A currency is demanded by foreigners who wish to purchase domestic goods, services, and assets. An increased preference for domestic goods by foreigners, an increase in real incomes abroad, or an increase in the domestic real interest rate will all increase the demand for the currency on the foreign exchange market and thus increase its value. *(LO3)*

- If the exchange rate is flexible, a tight monetary policy (by raising the real interest rate) increases the demand for the currency and causes it to appreciate. The stronger currency reinforces the effects of the tight monetary policy on aggregate demand by reducing net exports. Conversely, easy monetary policy lowers the real interest rate and weakens the currency, which in turn stimulates net exports. *(LO4)*

- The value of a fixed exchange rate is officially established by the government. A fixed exchange rate whose official value exceeds its fundamental value in the foreign exchange market is said to be *overvalued*. An exchange rate whose official value is below its fundamental value is *undervalued*. A reduction in the official value of a fixed exchange rate is called a *devaluation;* an increase in its official value is called a *revaluation*. *(LO5)*

- For an overvalued exchange rate, the quantity of the currency supplied at the official exchange rate exceeds the quantity demanded. To maintain the official rate, the country's central bank must use its *international reserves*

(foreign currency assets) to purchase the excess supply of its currency in the foreign exchange market. Because a country's international reserves are limited, it cannot maintain an overvalued exchange rate indefinitely. Moreover, if financial investors fear an impending devaluation of the exchange rate, they may launch a *speculative attack,* selling their domestic currency assets and supplying large quantities of the currency to the foreign exchange market. Because speculative attacks cause a country's central bank to spend its international reserves even more quickly, they often force a devaluation. *(LO5)*

- A tight monetary policy, by raising the fundamental value of the exchange rate, can eliminate the problem of overvaluation. However, if monetary policy is used to set the fundamental value of the exchange rate equal to the official value, it is no longer available for stabilizing the domestic economy. Thus under fixed exchange rates, monetary policy has little or no power to affect domestic output and employment. *(LO5)*

- Because a fixed exchange rate implies that monetary policy can no longer be used for domestic stabilization, most large countries employ a flexible exchange rate. A fixed exchange rate may benefit a small country by forcing its central bank to follow the monetary policies of the country to which it has tied its rate. Advocates of fixed exchange rates argue that they increase trade and economic integration by making the exchange rate more predictable. However, the threat of speculative attacks greatly reduces the long-term predictability of a fixed exchange rate. *(LO6)*

KEY TERMS

appreciation
balance-of-payments deficit
balance-of-payments surplus
depreciation
devaluation
fixed exchange rate
flexible exchange rate

foreign exchange market
fundamental value of the exchange rate (or equilibrium exchange rate)
international reserves
law of one price
nominal exchange rate
overvalued exchange rate

purchasing power parity (PPP)
real exchange rate
revaluation
speculative attack
undervalued exchange rate

REVIEW QUESTIONS

1. Japanese yen trade at 110 yen per dollar and Mexico pesos trade at 10 pesos per dollar. What is the nominal exchange rate between the yen and the peso? Express in two ways. *(LO1)*

2. Define nominal exchange rate and real exchange rate. How are the two concepts related? Which type of exchange rate most directly affects a country's ability to export its goods and services? *(LO1)*

3. Would you expect the law of one price to apply to crude oil? To fresh milk? To taxi rides? To music produced in different countries by local recording artists? Explain your answer in each case. *(LO2)*

4. Why do U.S. households and firms supply dollars to the foreign exchange market? Why do foreigners demand dollars in the foreign exchange market? *(LO3)*

5. Under a flexible exchange rate, how does an easing of monetary policy (a lower real interest rate) affect the value of the exchange rate? Does this change in the exchange rate tend to weaken or strengthen the effect of the monetary ease on output and employment? Explain. *(LO4)*

6. Define overvalued exchange rate. Discuss four ways in which government policymakers can respond to an overvaluation. What are the drawbacks of each approach? *(LO5)*

7. Use a supply and demand diagram to illustrate the effects of a speculative attack on an overvalued exchange rate. Why do speculative attacks often result in a devaluation? *(LO5)*

8. Contrast fixed and flexible exchange rates in terms of how they affect (a) the ability of monetary policy to stabilize domestic output and (b) the predictability of future exchange rates. *(LO6)*

PROBLEMS

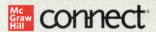

1. Using the data in Table 28.1, find the nominal exchange rate between the Mexican peso and the Japanese yen. Express in two ways. How do your answers change if the peso appreciates by 10 percent against the dollar while the value of the yen against the dollar remains unchanged? *(LO1)*

2. A British-made automobile is priced at £20,000 (20,000 British pounds). A comparable U.S.-made car costs $26,000. One pound trades for $1.50 in the foreign exchange market. Find the real exchange rate for automobiles from the perspective of the United States and from the perspective of Great Britain. Which country's cars are more competitively priced? *(LO1)*

3. Between last year and this year, the CPI in Blueland rose from 100 to 120 and the CPI in Redland rose from 100 to 115. Blueland's currency unit, the blue, was worth 80 cents (U.S.) last year and is worth 60 cents (U.S.) this year. Redland's currency unit, the red, was worth 20 cents (U.S.) last year and is worth 15 cents (U.S.) this year.

    Find the percentage change from last year to this year in Blueland's *nominal* exchange rate with Redland and in Blueland's *real* exchange rate with Redland. (Treat Blueland as the home country.) Relative to Redland, do you expect Blueland's exports to be helped or hurt by these changes in exchange rates? *(LO1)*

4. The demand for U.S.-made cars in Japan is given by

    Japanese demand = 10,000 − 0.001(Price of U.S. cars in yen).

    Similarly, the demand for Japanese-made cars in the United States is

    U.S. demand = 30,000 − 0.2(Price of Japanese cars in dollars).

The domestic price of a U.S.-made car is $20,000, and the domestic price of a Japanese-made car is ¥2,500,000. From the perspective of the United States, find the real exchange rate in terms of cars and net exports of cars to Japan, if: *(LO1)*

a. The nominal exchange rate is 100 yen per dollar.

b. The nominal exchange rate is 125 yen per dollar.

How does an appreciation of the dollar affect U.S. net exports of automobiles (considering only the Japanese market)?

5. a. Gold is $350 per ounce in the United States and 2,800 pesos per ounce in Mexico. What nominal exchange rate between U.S. dollars and Mexican pesos is implied by the PPP theory? *(LO2)*

   b. Mexico experiences inflation so that the price of gold rises to 4,200 pesos per ounce. Gold remains $350 per ounce in the United States. According to the PPP theory, what happens to the exchange rate? What general principle does this example illustrate? *(LO2)*

   c. Gold is $350 per ounce in the United States and 4,200 pesos per ounce in Mexico. Crude oil (excluding taxes and transportation costs) is $30 per barrel in the United States. According to the PPP theory, what should a barrel of crude oil cost in Mexico? *(LO2)*

   d. Gold is $350 per ounce in the United States. The exchange rate between the United States and Canada is 0.70 U.S. dollars per Canadian dollar. How much does an ounce of gold cost in Canada? *(LO2)*

6. How would each of the following be likely to affect the value of the dollar, all else being equal? Explain. *(LO3)*

   a. U.S. stocks are perceived as having become much riskier financial investments.

   b. European computer firms switch from U.S.-produced software to software produced in India, Israel, and other nations.

c. As East Asian economies recover, international financial investors become aware of many new, high-return investment opportunities in the region.

7. Suppose a French bottle of champagne costs 20.5 euros. *(LO3)*
   a. If the euro–dollar exchange rate is 0.8 euros per dollar, so that a dollar can buy 0.8 euros, how much will the champagne cost in the United States?
   b. If the euro–dollar exchange rate rises to 1.05 euro per dollar, how much will the champagne cost in the United States?
   c. If an increase in the euro–dollar exchange rate leads to an increase in Americans' dollar expenditures on French champagne, what will happen to the amount of dollars supplied to the foreign exchange market as the euro–dollar exchange rate rises?

8. Consider an Apple iPod that costs $240. *(LO3)*
   a. If the euro–dollar exchange rate is 1 euro per dollar, so that it costs a European 1 euro to buy a dollar, how much will the iPod cost in France?
   b. If the euro–dollar exchange rate falls to 0.8 euros per dollar, how much will the iPod cost in France?
   c. Consequently, what will happen to French purchases of iPods and the amount of dollars demanded in the foreign exchange market as the euro–dollar exchange rate falls?

9. If the government follows an easy monetary policy and the exchange rate is flexible, which of the following will likely be the result? *(LO4)*
   a. A falling real interest rate but higher net exports.
   b. A higher real interest rate but lower net exports.
   c. A strong currency that helps stimulate exports.
   d. Increases in the demand for the currency and decreases in the supply of the currency.

10. The demand for and supply of shekels in the foreign exchange market are

$$\text{Demand} = 30{,}000 - 8{,}000e,$$
$$\text{Supply} = 25{,}000 + 12{,}000e,$$

where the nominal exchange rate is expressed as U.S. dollars per shekel. *(LO3, LO5)*
   a. What is the fundamental value of the shekel?
   b. The shekel is fixed at 0.30 U.S. dollars. Is the shekel overvalued, undervalued, or neither? Find the balance-of-payments deficit or surplus in both shekels and dollars. What happens to the country's international reserves over time?
   c. Repeat part b for the case in which the shekel is fixed at 0.20 U.S. dollars.

11. The annual demand for and supply of shekels in the foreign exchange market is as given in Problem 10. The shekel is fixed at 0.30 dollars per shekel. The country's international reserves are $600. Foreign financial investors hold checking accounts in the country in the amount of 5,000 shekels. *(LO3, LO5)*
   a. Suppose that foreign financial investors do not fear a devaluation of the shekel and, thus, do not convert their shekel checking accounts into dollars. Can the shekel be maintained at its fixed value of 0.30 U.S. dollars for the next year?
   b. Now suppose that foreign financial investors come to expect a possible devaluation of the shekel to 0.25 U.S. dollars. Why should this possibility worry them?
   c. In response to their concern about devaluation, foreign financial investors withdraw all funds from their checking accounts and attempt to convert those shekels into dollars. What happens?
   d. Discuss why the foreign investors' forecast of devaluation can be considered a "self-fulfilling prophecy."

ANSWERS TO SELF-TESTS

28.1 Answers will vary, depending on when the data are obtained. *(LO1)*

28.2 The dollar price of the U.S. computer is $2,400, and each dollar is equal to 110 yen. Therefore the yen price of the U.S. computer is (110 yen/dollar) × ($2,400), or 264,000 yen. The price of the Japanese computer is 242,000 yen. Thus the conclusion that the Japanese model is cheaper does not depend on the currency in which the comparison is made. *(LO1)*

28.3 Since the law of one price holds for gold, its price per ounce must be the same in New York and Stockholm:

$$\$900 = 7{,}500 \text{ kronor.}$$

Dividing both sides by 900, we get:

$$\$1 = 8.33 \text{ kronor.}$$

So the exchange rate is 8.33 kronor per dollar. *(LO2)*

28.4 A decline in U.S. GDP reduces consumer incomes and hence imports. As Americans are purchasing fewer imports, they supply fewer dollars to the foreign exchange market, so the supply curve for dollars shifts to the left. Reduced supply raises the equilibrium value of the dollar. *(LO3)*

28.5 At a fixed value for the peso of 0.15 dollars, the demand for the peso equals $25{,}000 - 50{,}000(0.15) = 17{,}500$. The supply of the peso equals $17{,}600 + 24{,}000(0.15) =$

21,200. The quantity supplied at the official rate exceeds the quantity demanded by 3,700. Latinia will have to purchase 3,700 pesos each period, so its balance-of-payments deficit will equal 3,700 pesos, or $3,700 \times 0.15 = 555$ dollars. This balance-of-payments deficit is larger than we found in Example 28.6. We conclude that the greater the degree of overvaluation, the larger the country's balance-of-payments deficit is likely to be. *(LO5)*

28.6 The figure shows a situation in which the official value of the currency is *below* the fundamental value, as determined by the supply of and demand for the currency in the foreign exchange market, so the currency is undervalued. At the official value of the exchange rate, the quantity demanded of the domestic currency (point *B*) exceeds the quantity supplied (point *A*). To maintain the official value, the central bank must supply domestic currency to the foreign exchange market each period in the amount *AB*. In contrast to the case of an overvalued exchange rate, here the central bank is providing its own currency to the foreign exchange market and receiving foreign currencies in return.

The central bank can print as much of its own currency as it likes, and so with an undervalued currency there is no danger of running out of international reserves. Indeed, the central bank's stock of international reserves increases in the amount *AB* each period as it receives foreign currencies in exchange for the domestic currency it supplies. *(LO5)*

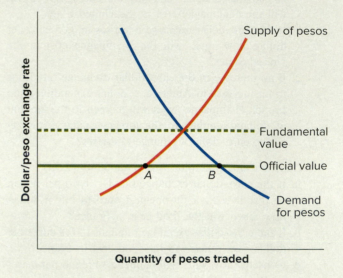

An Algebraic Approach to Trade Analysis

 hus far, we have used a graphical approach to show how international trade and various restrictions on trade affect economic welfare. In this appendix, we illustrate how the same issues can be approached in an algebraic framework.

EXAMPLE 15A.1   A Tariff on Imported Computers

What are the effects of a tariff on trade?

Suppose the demand for computers by Costa Rican consumers is given by

$$Q^D = 3{,}000 - 0.5P_C,$$

where Q^D is the annual quantity of computers demanded and P_C is the price per computer in dollars. The supply of computers by domestic Costa Rican producers is

$$Q^S = 1{,}000 + 0.5P_C,$$

where Q^S is the annual quantity of computers supplied.

a. Assuming that the Costa Rican economy is closed to trade, find the equilibrium price and quantity in the Costa Rican computer market.

b. Assume the economy opens to trade. If the world price of computers is $1,500, find annual Costa Rican consumption, production, and imports of computers.

c. At the request of domestic producers, the Costa Rican government imposes a tariff of $300 per imported computer. Find Costa Rican consumption, production, and imports of computers after the imposition of the tariff. How much revenue does the tariff raise for the government?

a. To find the closed-economy price and quantity, we set supply equal to demand:

$$1{,}000 + 0.5P_C = 3{,}000 - 0.5P_C.$$

Solving for P_C gives the equilibrium price, equal to $2,000 per computer. Substituting this equilibrium price into either the supply equation or the demand equation, we find the equilibrium quantity of computers in the Costa Rican market, equal to 2,000 computers per year. This equilibrium price and quantity correspond to a point like point E in Figure 15A.1.

b. If the economy opens to trade, the domestic price of computers must equal the world price, which is $1,500. At this price, the domestic quantity demanded for computers is $3{,}000 - 0.5(1{,}500) = 2{,}250$ computers per year; the domestic quantity supplied is $1{,}000 + 0.5(1{,}500) = 1{,}750$ computers per year. These

FIGURE 15A.1

The Market for Computers in Costa Rica.

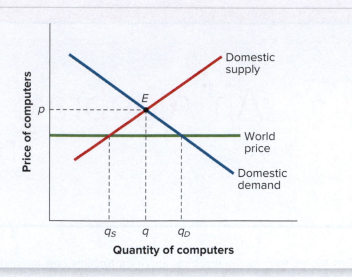

quantities correspond to q_D and q_S, respectively, in Figure 15A.1. Imports equal the difference between domestic quantities demanded and supplied, or 2,250 − 1,750 = 500 computers per year.

c. The imposition of a tariff of $300 per computer raises the price from $1,500 (the world price without the tariff) to $1,800. To find Costa Rican consumption and production at this price, we set the price equal to $1,800 in the demand and supply equations. Thus the domestic quantity demanded is 3,000 − 0.5(1,800) = 2,100 computers per year; the domestic quantity supplied is 1,000 + 0.5(1,800) = 1,900 computers per year. Imports, the difference between the quantity demanded by Costa Ricans and the quantity supplied by domestic firms, is 2,100 − 1,900 = 200 computers per year. Thus the tariff has raised the price of computers by $300 and reduced imports by 300 computers per year. The tariff revenue collected by the government is $300/imported computer × 200 computers/year = $60,000 per year.

 SELF-TEST 15A.1

Repeat parts (b) and (c) of Example 15A.1 under the assumption that the world price of computers is $1,200 (the tariff is still $400). What happens if the world price is $1,800?

EXAMPLE 15A.2   **Effects of an Import Quota**

What are the effects of an import quota on trade?

Suppose the supply of and demand for computers in Costa Rica is as given in Example 15A.1, and the government imposes an import quota of 200 computers. Find the equilibrium price in the domestic computer market, as well as the quantities produced by domestic firms and purchased by domestic consumers.

The quantity of computers supplied by domestic Costa Rican producers was stated in Example 15A.1 to be $1,000 + 0.5P_C$. The quota allows 200 computers per year to be imported. Thus the total quantity of computers supplied, including both domestic production and imports, is $1,000 + 0.5P_C + 200$, or $1,200 + 0.5P_C$. Setting the quantity supplied equal to the quantity demanded, we get

$$1,200 + 0.5P_C = 3,000 - 0.5P_C.$$

Solving for P_C, we find that the price of computers in the domestic Costa Rican market is $1,800. Domestic production of computers is $1,000 + 0.5(1,800) = 1,900$ computers per year, while quantity demanded domestically is $3,000 - 0.5(1,800) = 2,100$ computers per year. The difference between domestic quantity demanded and domestic production, 200 computers per year, is made up by imports.

Note that the domestic price, domestic production, and domestic demand are the same in Examples 15A.1 and 15A.2. Thus the tariff and the quota have the same effects on the domestic market for computers. The only difference between the two policies is that with a quota, the government does not get the tariff revenue it got in Example 15A.1. That revenue goes instead to the holders of import licenses, who can buy computers on the world market at $1,500 and sell them in the domestic market at $1,800.

PROBLEMS

1. The demand for automobiles in a certain country is given by

$$D = 12,000 - 200P,$$

where P is the price of a car. Supply by domestic automobile producers is

$$S = 7,000 + 50P.$$

(LO2, LO3, LO4)

a. Assuming that the economy is closed, find the equilibrium price and production of automobiles.
b. The economy opens to trade. The world price of automobiles is 18. Find the domestic quantities demanded and supplied and the quantity of imports or exports. Who will favor the opening of the automobile market to trade, and who will oppose it?
c. The government imposes a tariff of 1 unit per car. Find the effects on domestic quantities demanded and supplied and on the quantity of imports or exports. Also find the revenue raised by the tariff.

Who will favor the imposition of the tariff, and who will oppose it?
d. Can the government obtain the same results as you found in part c by imposing a quota on automobile imports? Explain.

2. Suppose the domestic demand and supply for automobiles is given by Problem 1. The world price of automobiles is 16. Foreign car firms have a production cost of 15 per automobile, so they earn a profit of 1 per car. *(LO3, LO4)*
a. How many cars will be imported, assuming this country trades freely?
b. Now suppose foreign car producers are asked "voluntarily" to limit their exports to the home country to half of free trade levels. What will be the equilibrium price of cars in the domestic market if foreign producers comply? Find domestic quantities of cars supplied and demanded.
c. How will the "voluntary" export restriction affect the profits of foreign car producers?

ANSWER TO APPENDIX SELF-TEST

15A.1 If the world price of computers is $1,200, domestic demand for computers is $3,000 - 0.5(1,200) = 2,400$ computers. Domestic supply is $1,000 + 0.5(1,200) = 1,600$ computers. The difference between the quantity demanded and the quantity supplied, 800 computers, is imported. A tariff of $400 raises the domestic price of computers to $1,600. Now domestic demand is 2,200 and domestic supply is 1,800. The difference, 400 computers, equals imports. Revenue for the

government is ($400/computer)(400 imported computers) = $160,000. If the world price of computers is $1,800 and there is no tariff, domestic demand is 2,100; domestic supply is 1,900; and imports are 200. A tariff of $400 raises the world price to $2,200, which is greater than the domestic price when there is no trade ($2,000). No computers are imported in this case and no tariff revenue is raised. *(LO3)*

GLOSSARY

A

absolute advantage one person has an absolute advantage over another if he or she takes fewer hours to perform a task than the other person

accounting profit the difference between a firm's total revenue and its explicit costs

adaptive rationality standard a variant of the rational choice model that permits additional preferences to be added if they can be shown not to handicap resource acquisition in competitive environments

adverse selection the pattern in which insurance tends to be purchased disproportionately by those who are most costly for companies to insure

aggregate demand (*AD*) curve a curve that shows the relationship between short-run equilibrium output *Y* and the rate of inflation π; it thus shows the amount of output consumers, firms, government, and entities abroad want to purchase at each inflation rate, holding all other factors constant

aggregate expenditure the sum of consumer expenditures, firms' investment, government purchases, and net exports

aggregate supply shock either an inflation shock or a shock to potential output; adverse aggregate supply shocks of both types reduce output and increase inflation

aggregation the adding up of individual economic variables to obtain economywide totals

allocative function of price changes in prices direct resources away from overcrowded markets and toward markets that are underserved

anchoring and adjustment an estimation technique that begins with an initial approximation (the anchor), which is then modified in accordance with additional available information (the adjustment)

appreciation an increase in the value of a currency relative to other currencies

assets anything of value that one *owns*

asymmetric information situations in which buyers and sellers are not equally well informed about the characteristics of goods and services for sale in the marketplace

attainable point any combination of goods that can be produced using currently available resources

autarky a situation in which a country is economically self-sufficient

automatic stabilizers provisions in the law that imply *automatic* increases in government spending or decreases in taxes when real output declines

autonomous consumption consumption spending that is not related to the level of disposable income

autonomous expenditure the portion of planned aggregate expenditure that is independent of output

availability heuristic a rule of thumb that estimates the frequency of an event by the ease with which it is possible to summon examples from memory

average benefit the total benefit of undertaking *n* units of an activity divided by *n*

average cost the total cost of undertaking *n* units of an activity divided by *n*

average labor productivity output per employed worker

average total cost (*ATC*) total cost divided by total output

average variable cost (*AVC*) variable cost divided by total output

B

balance sheet a list of an economic unit's assets and liabilities on a specific date

balance-of-payments deficit the net decline in a country's stock of international reserves over a year

balance-of-payments surplus the net increase in a country's stock of international reserves over a year

bank reserves cash or similar assets held by commercial banks for the purpose of meeting depositor withdrawals and payments

banking panic a situation in which news or rumors of the imminent bankruptcy of one or more banks leads bank depositors to rush to withdraw their funds

barrier to entry any force that prevents firms from entering a new market

barter the direct trade of goods or services for other goods or services

basic elements of a game the players, the strategies available to each player, and the payoffs each player receives for each possible combination of strategies

bequest saving saving done for the purpose of leaving an inheritance

better-than-fair gamble a gamble whose expected value is positive

Board of Governors the leadership of the Fed, consisting of seven governors appointed by the president to staggered 14-year terms

bond a legal promise to repay a debt, usually including both the principal amount and regular interest, or coupon, payments

boom a particularly strong and protracted expansion

business cycles (or **cyclical fluctuations**) short-term fluctuations in GDP and other indicators of economic activity

buyer's reservation price the largest dollar amount the buyer would be willing to pay for a good

buyer's surplus the difference between the buyer's reservation price and the price he or she actually pays

C

capital gains increases in the value of existing assets

capital good a long-lived good that is used in the production of other goods and services

capital inflows purchases of domestic assets by foreign households and firms

capital losses decreases in the value of existing assets

capital outflows purchases of foreign assets by domestic households and firms

cartel a coalition of firms that agree to restrict output for the purpose of earning an economic profit

cash on the table an economic metaphor for unexploited gains from exchange

change in aggregate demand a shift of the entire *AD* curve

change in demand a shift of the entire demand curve

change in supply a shift of the entire supply curve

change in the quantity demanded a movement along the demand curve that occurs in response to a change in price

change in the quantity supplied a movement along the supply curve that occurs in response to a change in price

closed economy an economy that does not trade with the rest of the world

Coase theorem if, at no cost, people can negotiate the purchase and sale of the right to perform activities that cause externalities, they can always arrive at efficient solutions to the problems caused by externalities

collective good a good or service that, to at least some degree, is nonrival but excludable

commitment device a way of changing incentives so as to make otherwise empty threats or promises credible

commitment problem a situation in which people cannot achieve their goals because of an inability to make credible threats or promises

comparative advantage one person has a comparative advantage over another if his or her opportunity cost of performing a task is lower than the other person's opportunity cost

compensating wage differential a difference in the wage rate—negative or positive—that reflects the attractiveness of a job's working conditions

complements two goods are complements in consumption if an increase in the price of one causes a leftward shift in the demand curve for the other (or if a decrease causes a rightward shift)

compound interest the payment of interest not only on the original deposit, but on all previously accumulated interest

constant (or parameter) a quantity that is fixed in value

constant returns to scale a production process is said to have constant returns to scale if, when all inputs are changed by a given proportion, output changes by the same proportion

consumer price index (CPI) for any period, a measure of the cost in that period of a standard basket of goods and services relative to the cost of the same basket of goods and services in a fixed year, called the *base year*

consumer surplus the difference between a buyer's reservation price for a product and the price actually paid

consumption *See* **consumption expenditure**

consumption expenditure (or consumption) spending by households on goods and services such as food, clothing, and entertainment

consumption function the relationship between consumption spending and its determinants, in particular, disposable (after-tax) income

consumption possibilities the combinations of goods and services that a country's citizens might feasibly consume

contraction *See* **recession**

contractionary policies government policy actions designed to reduce planned spending and output

cost-plus regulation a method of regulation under which the regulated firm is permitted to charge prices that cover explicit costs of production plus a markup to cover the opportunity cost of resources provided by the firm's owners

costly-to-fake principle to communicate information credibly to a potential rival, a signal must be costly or difficult to fake

coupon payments regular interest payments made to the bondholder

coupon rate the interest rate promised when a bond is issued; the annual coupon payments are equal to the coupon rate times the principal amount of the bond

credible promise a promise to take an action that is in the promiser's interest to keep

credible threat a threat to take an action that is in the threatener's interest to carry out

cross-price elasticity of demand the percentage by which the quantity demanded of the first good changes in response to a 1 percent change in the price of the second

crowding out the tendency of increased government deficits to reduce investment spending

customer discrimination the willingness of consumers to pay more for a product produced by members of a favored group, even if the quality of the product is unaffected

cyclical fluctuations *See* **business cycles**

cyclical unemployment the extra unemployment that occurs during periods of recession

D

deadweight loss the loss of consumer and producer surplus caused by disparity between price and marginal cost

decision tree (or game tree) a diagram that describes the possible moves in a game in sequence and lists the payoffs that correspond to each possible combination of moves

deflating (a nominal quantity) the process of dividing a nominal quantity by a price index (such as the CPI) to express the quantity in real terms

deflation a situation in which the prices of most goods and services are falling over time so that inflation is negative

demand curve a schedule or graph showing the quantity of a good that buyers wish to buy at each price

demand for money the amount of wealth an individual or firm chooses to hold in the form of money

dependent variable a variable in an equation whose value is determined by the value taken by another variable in the equation

deposit insurance a system under which the government guarantees that depositors will not lose any money even if their bank goes bankrupt

depreciation a decrease in the value of a currency relative to other currencies

depression a particularly severe or protracted recession

descriptive economic principle *See* **positive economic principle**

devaluation a reduction in the official value of a currency (in a fixed exchange rate system)

diminishing returns to capital if the amount of labor and other inputs employed is held constant, then the greater the amount of capital already in use, the less an additional unit of capital adds to production

diminishing returns to labor if the amount of capital and other inputs in use is held constant, then the greater the quantity of labor already employed, the less each additional worker adds to production

disappearing political discourse the theory that people who support a position may remain silent because speaking out would create a risk of being misunderstood

discount rate the interest rate that the Fed charges commercial banks to borrow reserves

discount window lending the lending of reserves by the Federal Reserve to commercial banks

discouraged workers people who say they would like to have a job but have not made an effort to find one in the past four weeks

disinflation a substantial reduction in the rate of inflation

disposable income the after-tax amount of income that people are able to spend

distributional effects changes in the distribution of income or wealth in the economy

diversification the practice of spreading one's wealth over a variety of different financial investments to reduce overall risk

dividend a regular payment received by stockholders for each share that they own

dominant strategy one that yields a higher payoff no matter what the other players in a game choose

dominated strategy any other strategy available to a player who has a dominant strategy

durable goods goods that yield utility over time and are made to last for three years or more

duration the length of an unemployment spell

E

earned-income tax credit (EITC) a policy under which low-income workers receive credits on their federal income tax

economic efficiency See **efficiency**

economic loss an economic profit that is less than zero

economic profit (or excess profit) the difference between a firm's total revenue and the sum of its explicit and implicit costs

economic rent that part of the payment for a factor of production that exceeds the owner's reservation price, the price below which the owner would not supply the factor

economic surplus the benefit of taking an action minus its cost

economics the study of how people make choices under conditions of scarcity and of the results of those choices for society

economies of scale See **increasing returns to scale**

efficiency (or economic efficiency) a condition that occurs when all goods and services are produced and consumed at their respective socially optimal levels

efficient (or Pareto efficient) a situation is efficient if no change is possible that will help some people without harming others

efficient point any combination of goods for which currently available resources do not allow an increase in the production of one good without a reduction in the production of the other

elastic the demand for a good is elastic with respect to price if its price elasticity of demand is greater than 1

employer discrimination an arbitrary preference by an employer for one group of workers over another

entrepreneurs people who create new economic enterprises

equation a mathematical expression that describes the relationship between two or more variables

equilibrium a balanced or unchanging situation in which all forces at work within a system are canceled by others

equilibrium exchange rate See **fundamental value of the exchange rate**

equilibrium price and equilibrium quantity the price and quantity at the intersection of the supply and demand curves for the good

equity See **stock**

excess demand (or shortage) the amount by which quantity demanded exceeds quantity supplied when the price of a good lies below the equilibrium price

excess profit See **economic profit**

excess reserves bank reserves in excess of the reserve requirements set by the central bank

excess supply (or surplus) the amount by which quantity supplied exceeds quantity demanded when the price of the good exceeds the equilibrium price

expansion a period in which the economy is growing at a rate significantly above normal

expansionary gap a positive output gap, which occurs when actual output is higher than potential output ($Y > Y^*$)

expansionary policies government policy actions intended to increase planned spending and output

expected value of a gamble the sum of the possible outcomes of the gamble multiplied by their respective probabilities

expenditure line a line showing the relationship between planned aggregate expenditure and output

explicit costs the actual payments a firm makes to its factors of production and other suppliers

external benefit (or positive externality) a benefit of an activity received by people other than those who pursue the activity

external cost (or negative externality) a cost of an activity that falls on people other than those who pursue the activity

externality an external cost or benefit of an activity

F

factor of production an input used in the production of a good or service

fair gamble a gamble whose expected value is zero

federal funds rate the interest rate that commercial banks charge each other for very short-term (usually overnight) loans

Federal Open Market Committee (FOMC) the committee that makes decisions concerning monetary policy

Federal Reserve System (or the Fed) the central bank of the United States

final goods or services goods or services consumed by the ultimate user; because they are the end products of the production process, they are counted as part of GDP

financial intermediaries firms that extend credit to borrowers using funds raised from savers

first-dollar insurance coverage insurance that pays all expenses generated by the insured activity

fiscal policy decisions that determine the government's budget, including the amount and composition of government expenditures and government revenues

Fisher effect the tendency for nominal interest rates to be high when inflation is high and low when inflation is low

fixed cost the sum of all payments made to the firm's fixed factors of production

fixed exchange rate an exchange rate whose value is set by official government policy

fixed factor of production an input whose quantity cannot be altered in the short run

flexible exchange rate an exchange rate whose value is not officially fixed but varies according to the supply and demand for the currency in the foreign exchange market

flow a measure that is defined *per unit of time*

foreign exchange market the market on which currencies of various nations are traded for one another

forward guidance information that a central bank provides to the financial markets regarding its expected future monetary-policy path

fractional-reserve banking system a banking system in which bank reserves are less than deposits so that the reserve-deposit ratio is less than 100 percent

free-rider problem an incentive problem in which too little of a good or service is produced because nonpayers cannot be excluded from using it

frictional unemployment the short-term unemployment associated with the process of matching workers with jobs

full-employment output *See* **potential output,** Y^*

fundamental value of the exchange rate (or equilibrium exchange rate) the exchange rate that equates the quantities of the currency supplied and demanded in the foreign exchange market

fungibility the property of an entity whose individual units are interchangeable, as money in separate accounts

G

game tree *See* **decision tree**

government budget deficit the excess of government spending over tax collections $(G - T)$

government budget surplus the excess of government tax collections over government spending $(T - G)$; the government budget surplus equals public saving

government purchases purchases by federal, state, and local governments of final goods and services; government purchases do *not* include transfer payments, which are payments made by the government in return for which no current goods or services are received, nor do they include interest paid on the government debt

gross domestic product (GDP) the market value of the final goods and services produced in a country during a given period

H

head tax a tax that collects the same amount from every taxpayer

health maintenance organization (HMO) a group of physicians that provides health services to individuals and families for a fixed annual fee

homo economicus the narrowly self-interested, well-informed, highly disciplined, and cognitively formidable actor often assumed in traditional economic models

human capital an amalgam of factors such as education, training, experience, intelligence, energy, work habits, trustworthiness, and initiative that affects the value of a worker's marginal product

human capital theory a theory of pay determination that says a worker's wage will be proportional to his or her stock of human capital

hurdle method of price discrimination the practice by which a seller offers a discount to all buyers who overcome some obstacle

hyperinflation a situation in which the inflation rate is extremely high

I

imperfectly competitive firm (or price setter) a firm that has at least some control over the market price of its product

implicit costs the opportunity costs of the resources supplied by the firm's owners

in-kind transfer a payment made not in the form of cash, but in the form of a good or service

income effect the change in the quantity demanded of a good that results because a change in the price of a good changes the buyer's purchasing power

income elasticity of demand the percentage by which a good's quantity demanded changes in response to a 1 percent change in income

income-expenditure multiplier (or multiplier) the effect of a one-unit increase in autonomous expenditure on short-run equilibrium output

increasing returns to scale (or economies of scale) a production process is said to have increasing returns to scale if, when all inputs are changed by a given proportion, output changes by more than that proportion

independent variable a variable in an equation whose value determines the value taken by another variable in the equation

indexing the practice of increasing a nominal quantity each period by an amount equal to the percentage increase in a specified price index; indexing prevents the purchasing power of the nominal quantity from being eroded by inflation

induced expenditure the portion of planned aggregate expenditure that depends on output Y

inefficient point any combination of goods for which currently available resources enable an increase in the production of one good without a reduction in the production of the other

inelastic the demand for a good is inelastic with respect to price if its price elasticity of demand is less than 1

inferior good a good whose demand curve shifts leftward when the incomes of buyers increase and rightward when the incomes of buyers decrease

inflation shock a sudden change in the normal behavior of inflation, unrelated to the nation's output gap

inflation-protected bonds bonds that pay a nominal interest rate each year equal to a fixed real rate plus the actual rate of inflation during that year

intermediate goods or services goods or services used up in the production of final goods and services and therefore not counted as part of GDP

international capital flows purchases or sales of real and financial assets across international borders

international financial markets financial markets in which borrowers and lenders are residents of different countries

international reserves foreign currency assets held by a government for the purpose of purchasing the domestic currency in the foreign exchange market

investment spending by firms on final goods and services, primarily capital goods

invisible hand theory Adam Smith's theory that the actions of independent, self-interested buyers and sellers will often result in the most efficient allocation of resources

involuntary part-time workers people who say they would like to work full-time but are able to find only part-time work

J

judgmental and decision heuristics rules of thumb that reduce computation costs

L

labor force the total number of employed and unemployed people in the economy

labor union a group of workers who bargain collectively with employers for better wages and working conditions

law of demand people do less of what they want to do as the cost of doing it rises

law of diminishing marginal utility the tendency for the additional utility gained from consuming an additional unit of a good to diminish as consumption increases beyond some point

law of diminishing returns a property of the relationship between the amount of a good or service produced and the amount of a variable factor required to produce it; the law says that when some factors of production are fixed, increased production of the good eventually requires ever-larger increases in the variable factor

law of one price if transportation costs are relatively small, the price of an internationally traded commodity must be the same in all locations

lemons model George Akerlof's explanation of how asymmetric information tends to reduce the average quality of goods offered for sale

liabilities the debts one *owes*

life-cycle saving saving to meet long-term objectives such as retirement, college attendance, or the purchase of a home

logrolling the practice whereby legislators support one another's legislative proposals

long run a period of time of sufficient length that all the firm's factors of production are variable

long-run aggregate supply (*LRAS*) line a vertical line showing the economy's potential output Y^*

long-run equilibrium a situation in which actual output equals potential output and the inflation rate is stable; graphically, long-run equilibrium occurs when the AD curve, the $SRAS$ line, and the $LRAS$ line all intersect at a single point

loss aversion the tendency to experience losses as more painful than the pleasures that result from gains of the same magnitude

M

M1 the sum of currency outstanding and balances held in checking accounts

M2 all the assets in M1 plus some additional assets that are usable in making payments but at greater cost or inconvenience than currency or checks

macroeconomic policies government actions designed to affect the performance of the economy as a whole

macroeconomics the study of the performance of national economies and the policies that governments use to try to improve that performance

marginal benefit the increase in total benefit that results from carrying out one additional unit of an activity

marginal cost the increase in total cost that results from carrying out one additional unit of an activity

marginal product of labor (*MPL*) the additional output a firm gets by employing one additional unit of labor

marginal propensity to consume (*mpc*) the amount by which consumption rises when disposable income rises by $1; we assume that $0 < mpc < 1$

marginal revenue the change in a firm's total revenue that results from a one-unit change in output

marginal utility the additional utility gained from consuming an additional unit of a good

market the market for any good consists of all buyers or sellers of that good

market equilibrium occurs in a market when all buyers and sellers are satisfied with their respective quantities at the market price

market interest rate *See* **nominal interest rate**

market power a firm's ability to raise the price of a good without losing all its sales

market value the selling prices of goods and services in the open market

means-tested a benefit program whose benefit level declines as the recipient earns additional income

medium of exchange an asset used in purchasing goods and services

menu costs the costs of changing prices

microeconomics the study of individual choice under scarcity and its implications for the behavior of prices and quantities in individual markets

monetary policy determination of the nation's money supply

money any asset that can be used in making purchases

money demand curve a curve that shows the relationship between the aggregate quantity of money demanded M and the nominal interest rate i

monopolistic competition an industry structure in which a large number of firms produce slightly differentiated products that are reasonably close substitutes for one another

moral hazard the tendency of people to expend less effort protecting those goods that are insured against theft or damage

multiplier *See* **income-expenditure multiplier**

mutual fund a financial intermediary that sells shares in itself to the public and then uses the funds raised to buy a wide variety of financial assets

N

Nash equilibrium any combination of strategy choices in which each player's choice is his or her best choice, given the other players' choices

national saving the saving of the entire economy, equal to GDP less consumption expenditures and government purchases of goods and services, or $Y - C - G$

natural monopoly a monopoly that results from economies of scale (increasing returns to scale)

natural rate of unemployment, *u** the part of the total unemployment rate that is attributable to frictional and structural unemployment; equivalently, the unemployment rate that prevails when cyclical unemployment is zero, so that the economy has neither a recessionary nor an expansionary output gap

negative externality *See* **external cost**

negative income tax (NIT) a system under which the government would grant every citizen a cash payment each year, financed by an additional tax on earned income

net exports *See* **trade balance**

net worth an economic unit's wealth determined by subtracting liabilities from assets

nominal exchange rate the rate at which two currencies can be traded for each other

nominal GDP a measure of GDP in which the quantities produced are valued at current-year prices; nominal GDP measures the *current dollar value* of production

nominal interest rate (or **market interest rate**) the annual percentage increase in the nominal value of a financial asset

nominal price the absolute price of a good in dollar terms

nominal quantity a quantity that is measured in terms of its current dollar value

nondurable goods goods that can be quickly consumed or immediately used, having a life span of less than three years

nonexcludable good a good that is difficult, or costly, to exclude nonpayers from consuming

nonpositional good a good whose value does not depend heavily on how it compares with other goods in the same category

nonrival good a good whose consumption by one person does not diminish its availability for others

normal good a good whose demand curve shifts rightward when the incomes of buyers increase and leftward when the incomes of buyers decrease

normal profit the opportunity cost of the resources supplied by the firm's owners, equal to accounting profit minus economic profit

normative analysis addresses the question of whether a policy *should* be used; normative analysis inevitably involves the values of the person doing the analysis

normative economic principle one that says how people should behave

O

Okun's law each extra percentage point of cyclical unemployment is associated with about a 2 percentage point increase in the output gap, measured in relation to potential output

oligopoly an industry structure in which a small number of large firms produce products that are either close or perfect substitutes

100 percent reserve banking a situation in which banks' reserves equal 100 percent of their deposits

open economy an economy that trades with other countries

open-market operations open-market purchases and open-market sales

open-market purchase the purchase of government bonds from the public by the Fed for the purpose of increasing the supply of bank reserves and the money supply

open-market sale the sale by the Fed of government bonds to the public for the purpose of reducing bank reserves and the money supply

opportunity cost (OC) the value of what must be forgone to undertake an activity

optimal combination of goods the affordable combination that yields the highest total utility

output gap, $Y - Y^*$ the difference between the economy's actual output and its potential output at a point in time

outsourcing a term increasingly used to connote having services performed by low-wage workers overseas

overvalued exchange rate an exchange rate that has an officially fixed value greater than its fundamental value

P

parameter *See* constant

Pareto efficient *See* efficient

participation rate the percentage of the working-age population in the labor force (that is, the percentage that is either employed or looking for work)

payoff matrix a table that describes the payoffs in a game for each possible combination of strategies

peak the beginning of a recession; the high point of economic activity prior to a downturn

perfect hurdle a threshold that completely segregates buyers whose reservation prices lie above it from others whose reservation prices lie below it, imposing no cost on those who jump the hurdle

perfectly competitive market a market in which no individual supplier has significant influence on the market price of the product

perfectly discriminating monopolist a firm that charges each buyer exactly his or her reservation price

perfectly elastic demand demand is perfectly elastic with respect to price if price elasticity of demand is infinite

perfectly elastic supply supply is perfectly elastic with respect to price if elasticity of supply is infinite

perfectly inelastic demand demand is perfectly inelastic with respect to price if price elasticity of demand is zero

perfectly inelastic supply supply is perfectly inelastic with respect to price if elasticity is zero

Personal Responsibility and Work Opportunity Reconciliation Act the 1996 federal law that transferred responsibility for welfare programs from the federal level to the state level and placed a five-year lifetime limit on payment of AFDC benefits to any given recipient

physical capital equipment and tools (such as machines and factories) needed to complete one's work

planned aggregate expenditure (*PAE*) total planned spending on final goods and services

policy reaction function describes how the action a policy-maker takes depends on the state of the economy

pork barrel spending a public expenditure that is larger than the total benefit it creates but that is favored by a legislator because his or her constituents benefit from the expenditure by more than their share of the resulting extra taxes

portfolio allocation decision the decision about the forms in which to hold one's wealth

positional arms control agreement an agreement in which contestants attempt to limit mutually offsetting investments in performance enhancement

positional arms race a series of mutually offsetting investments in performance enhancement that is stimulated by a positional externality

positional externality this occurs when an increase in one person's performance reduces the expected reward of another's in situations in which reward depends on relative performance

positional good a good whose value depends relatively heavily on how it compares with other goods in the same category

positive (or **descriptive**) **economic principle** one that predicts how people will behave

positive analysis addresses the economic consequences of a particular event or policy, not whether those consequences are desirable

positive externality *See* external benefit

potential GDP *See* potential output, Y^*

potential output, Y^* (or **potential GDP** or **full-employment output**) the amount of output (real GDP) that an economy can produce when using its resources, such as capital and labor, at normal rates

poverty threshold the level of income below which the federal government classifies a family as poor

precautionary saving saving for protection against unexpected setbacks such as the loss of a job or a medical emergency

present-aim standard of rationality a variant of the rational choice model that permits greater flexibility in assumptions about preferences

price ceiling a maximum allowable price, specified by law

price discrimination the practice of charging different buyers different prices for essentially the same good or service

price elasticity of demand the percentage change in the quantity demanded of a good or service that results from a 1 percent change in its price

price elasticity of supply the percentage change in quantity supplied that occurs in response to a 1 percent change in price

price index a measure of the average price of a given class of goods or services relative to the price of the same goods or services in a base year

price level a measure of the overall level of prices at a particular point in time as measured by a price index such as the CPI

price setter *See* **imperfectly competitive firm**

price taker a firm that has no influence over the price at which it sells its product

principal amount the amount originally lent

prisoner's dilemma a game in which each player has a dominant strategy, and when each plays it, the resulting payoffs are smaller than if each had played a dominated strategy

private saving the saving of the private sector of the economy is equal to the after-tax income of the private sector minus consumption expenditures ($Y - T - C$); private saving can be further broken down into household saving and business saving

producer surplus the amount by which price exceeds the seller's reservation price

production possibilities curve (PPC) a graph that describes the maximum amount of one good that can be produced for every possible level of production of the other good

profit the total revenue a firm receives from the sale of its product minus all costs—explicit and implicit—incurred in producing it

profit-maximizing firm a firm whose primary goal is to maximize the difference between its total revenues and total costs

profitable firm a firm whose total revenue exceeds its total cost

progressive tax one in which the proportion of income paid in taxes rises as income rises

proportional income tax one under which all taxpayers pay the same proportion of their incomes in taxes

protectionism the view that free trade is injurious and should be restricted

public good a good or service that, to at least some degree, is both nonrival and nonexcludable

public saving the saving of the government sector is equal to net tax payments minus government purchases ($T - G$)

purchasing power parity (PPP) the theory that nominal exchange rates are determined as necessary for the law of one price to hold

pure commons good one for which nonpayers cannot easily be excluded and for which each unit consumed by one person means one less unit available for others

pure monopoly the only supplier of a unique product with no close substitutes

pure private good one for which nonpayers can easily be excluded and for which each unit consumed by one person means one less unit available for others

pure public good a good or service that, to a high degree, is both nonrival and nonexcludable

Q

quantitative easing (QE) an expansionary monetary policy in which a central bank buys long-term financial assets, thereby lowering the yield or return of those assets while increasing the money supply

quantity equation money times velocity equals nominal GDP: $M \times V = P \times Y$

quota a legal limit on the quantity of a good that may be imported

R

rate of inflation the annual percentage rate of change in the price level, as measured, for example, by the CPI

rational person someone with well-defined goals who tries to fulfill those goals as best he or she can

rational spending rule spending should be allocated across goods so that the marginal utility per dollar is the same for each good

rationing function of price changes in prices distribute scarce goods to those consumers who value them most highly

real exchange rate the price of the average domestic good or service *relative* to the price of the average foreign good or service, when prices are expressed in terms of a common currency

real GDP a measure of GDP in which the quantities produced are valued at the prices in a base year rather than at current prices; real GDP measures the actual *physical volume* of production

real interest rate the annual percentage increase in the purchasing power of a financial asset; the real interest rate on any asset equals the nominal interest rate on that asset minus the inflation rate

real price the dollar price of a good relative to the average dollar price of all other goods

real quantity a quantity that is measured in physical terms—for example, in terms of quantities of goods and services

real wage the wage paid to workers measured in terms of purchasing power; the real wage for any given period is calculated by dividing the nominal (dollar) wage by the CPI for that period

recession (or contraction) a period in which the economy is growing at a rate significantly below normal

recessionary gap a negative output gap, which occurs when potential output exceeds actual output ($Y^* > Y$)

regression to the mean the phenomenon that unusual events are likely to be followed by more nearly normal ones

regressive tax a tax under which the proportion of income paid in taxes declines as income rises

relative price the price of a specific good or service *in comparison to* the prices of other goods and services

rent-seeking the socially unproductive efforts of people or firms to win a prize

repeated prisoner's dilemma a standard prisoner's dilemma that confronts the same players repeatedly

representativeness heuristic a rule of thumb according to which the likelihood of something belonging to a given category increases with the extent to which it shares characteristics with stereotypical members of that category

reserve requirements set by the Fed, the minimum values of the ratio of bank reserves to bank deposits that commercial banks are allowed to maintain

reserve-deposit ratio bank reserves divided by deposits

revaluation an increase in the official value of a currency (in a fixed exchange rate system)

rise *See* **slope**

risk premium the rate of return that financial investors require to hold risky assets minus the rate of return on safe assets

risk-averse person someone who would refuse any fair gamble

risk-neutral person someone who would accept any gamble that is fair or better

run *See* **slope**

S

satisficing a decision-making strategy that aims for adequate results because optimal results may necessitate excessive expenditure of resources

saving current income minus spending on current needs

saving rate saving divided by income

seller's reservation price the smallest dollar amount for which a seller would be willing to sell an additional unit, generally equal to marginal cost

seller's surplus the difference between the price received by the seller and his or her reservation price

short run a period of time sufficiently short that at least some of the firm's factors of production are fixed

short-run aggregate supply (SRAS) line a horizontal line showing the current rate of inflation, as determined by past expectations and pricing decisions

short-run equilibrium a situation in which inflation equals the value determined by past expectations and pricing decisions and output equals the level of short-run equilibrium output that is consistent with that inflation rate; graphically, short-run equilibrium occurs at the intersection of the *AD* curve and the *SRAS* line

short-run equilibrium output the level of output at which output *Y* equals planned aggregate expenditure *PAE*; the level of output that prevails during the period in which prices are predetermined

shortage *See* **excess demand**

skill-biased technological change technological change that affects the marginal products of higher-skilled workers differently from those of lower-skilled workers

slope in a straight line, the ratio of the vertical distance the straight line travels between any two points *(rise)* to the corresponding horizontal distance *(run)*

socially optimal quantity the quantity of a good that results in the maximum possible economic surplus from producing and consuming the good

speculative attack a massive selling of domestic currency assets by financial investors

stabilization policies government policies that are used to affect planned aggregate expenditure, with the objective of eliminating output gaps

standard of living the degree to which people have access to goods and services that make their lives easier, healthier, safer, and more enjoyable

statistical discrimination the practice of making judgments about the quality of people, goods, or services based on the characteristics of the groups to which they belong

status quo bias the general resistance to change, often stemming from *loss aversion*

stock a measure that is defined *at a point in time*

stock (or **equity**) a claim to partial ownership of a firm

store of value an asset that serves as a means of holding wealth

structural policy government policies aimed at changing the underlying structure, or institutions, of the nation's economy

structural unemployment the long-term and chronic unemployment that exists even when the economy is producing at a normal rate

substitutes two goods are substitutes in consumption if an increase in the price of one causes a rightward shift in the demand curve for the other (or if a decrease causes a leftward shift)

substitution effect the change in the quantity demanded of a good that results because buyers switch to or from substitutes when the price of the good changes

sunk cost a cost that is beyond recovery at the moment a decision must be made

supply curve a graph or schedule showing the quantity of a good that sellers wish to sell at each price

surplus *See* **excess supply**

T

tariff a tax imposed on an imported good

the Fed *See* **Federal Reserve System**

tit-for-tat a strategy for the repeated prisoner's dilemma in which players cooperate on the first move and then mimic their partner's last move on each successive move

total cost the sum of all payments made to the firm's fixed and variable factors of production

total expenditure (or **total revenue**) the dollar amount that consumers spend on a product ($P \times Q$) is equal to the dollar amount that sellers receive

total revenue *See* **total expenditure**

total surplus the difference between the buyer's reservation price and the seller's reservation price

trade balance (or **net exports**) the value of a country's exports less the value of its imports in a particular period (quarter or year)

trade deficit when imports exceed exports, the difference between the value of a country's imports and the value of its exports in a given period

trade surplus when exports exceed imports, the difference between the value of a country's exports and the value of its imports in a given period

tragedy of the commons the tendency for a resource that has no price to be used until its marginal benefit falls to zero

transfer payments payments the government makes to the public for which it receives no current goods or services in return

trough the end of a recession; the low point of economic activity prior to a recovery

U

ultimatum bargaining game a game in which the first player has the power to confront the second player with a take-it-or-leave-it offer

unattainable point any combination of goods that cannot be produced using currently available resources

undervalued exchange rate an exchange rate that has an officially fixed value less than its fundamental value

unemployment rate the number of unemployed people divided by the labor force

unemployment spell a period during which an individual is continuously unemployed

unit elastic the demand for a good is unit elastic with respect to price if its price elasticity of demand equals 1

unit of account a basic measure of economic value

V

value added for any firm, the market value of its product or service minus the cost of inputs purchased from other firms

value of marginal product of labor (*VMPL*) the dollar value of the additional output a firm gets by employing one additional unit of labor

variable a quantity that is free to take a range of different values

variable cost the sum of all payments made to the firm's variable factors of production

variable factor of production an input whose quantity can be altered in the short run

velocity a measure of the speed at which money circulates, that is, the speed at which money changes hands in transactions involving final goods and services, or, equivalently, nominal GDP divided by the stock of money. Numerically, $V = (P \times Y)/M$, where V is velocity, $P \times Y$ is nominal GDP, and M is the money supply whose velocity is being measured

vertical intercept in a straight line, the value taken by the dependent variable when the independent variable equals zero

W

wealth the value of assets minus liabilities

wealth effect the tendency of changes in asset prices to affect households' wealth and thus their consumption spending

Weber-Fechner law the relationship according to which the perceived change in any stimulus varies according to the size of the change measured as a proportion of the original stimulus

winner-take-all labor market one in which small differences in human capital translate into large differences in pay

worker mobility the movement of workers between jobs, firms, and industries

workers' compensation a government insurance system that provides benefits to workers who are injured on the job

world price the price at which a good or service is traded on international markets

Z

zero lower bound a level, close to zero, below which the Fed cannot further reduce short-term interest rates

INDEX

Page numbers followed by n refer to notes.